DAO Object Variable Tags

Tag	Object Type	Tag	Object Type
cnt	Container	prms	
cnts	Containers	pdbe	PrivDBEngine
db	Database	prp	Property
dbs	Databases	prps	Properties
dbe	DBEngine	qry (or qdf)	QueryDef
doc	Document	qrys (or qdfs)	QueryDefs
docs	Documents	rst	Recordset
err	Error	rsts	Recordsets
errs	Errors	rel	Relation
fld	Field	rels	Relations
flds	Fields	tbl (or tdf)	TableDef
grp	Group	tbls (or tdfs)	TableDefs
grps	Groups	usr	User
idx	Index	usrs	Users
idxs	Indexes	wrk	Workspace
prm	Parameter	wrks	Workspaces

General Access Database Explorer Object Tags

Tag	Object Type	Tag	Object Type
tbl	Table	rpt	Report
qry	Query	mcr	Macro
frm	Form	bas	Module

Specific Access Database Explorer Object Tags*

Tag	Suffix	Object Type	Tag	Suffix	Object Type
tlkp	Lookup	Table (lookup)	qtot	Totals	Query (totals)
qsel	(none)	Query (select)	quni	Union	Query (union)
qapp	Append	Query (append)	qupd	Update	Query (update)
qxtb	XTab	Query (crosstab)	fdlg	Dlg	Form (dialog)
qddl	DDL	Query (DDL)	fmnu	Mnu	Form (menu)
qdel	Delete	Query (delete)	fmsg	Msg	Form (message)
qflt	Filter	Query (filter)	fsfr	Subform	Form (subform)
qlkp	Lookup	Query (lookup)	rsrp	SubReport	Form (subreport)
qmak	MakeTable	Query (make table)	mmnu	Mnu	Macro (menu)
qspt	PassThru	Query (SQL pass-through)			

*Use either the general tag from the previous table plus the suffix from this table or the specific tag from this table with no suffix.

Microsoft® Access® 95
Developer's Handbook™

Second Edition

Paul Litwin
Ken Getz
With Mike Gilbert
and Greg Reddick

SYBEX®

San Francisco • Paris • Düsseldorf • Soest

Acquisitions Manager: Kristine Plachy
Developmental Editor: Melanie Spiller
Editor: Dusty Bernard
Project Editor: Lee Ann Pickrell
Technical Editor: Mike Gunderloy
Book Series Design: Suzanne Albertson
Desktop Publisher: Dina F Quan
Production Coordinator: Nathan Johanson
Indexer: Ted Laux
Cover Designer: Design Site
Cover Photograph: Furnished by FPG International

Library of Congress Card Number: 95-71247
ISBN: 0-7821-1765-1

Manufactured in the United States of America
10 9 8 7 6 5 4 3 2

To my wife Alicia and son Geoffrey: thank you for being infinitely understanding and supportive while I was working on the book.
—*P.L.*

To Peter Mason, for his continuing support, patience, and, of course, legal advice; and to Joe Clark, for continuing to speak to me after my three nonstop months of SCSI hell.
—*K.G.*

To my wife Karen and her never-ceasing encouragement and support.
—*M.G.*

To Abbie Jacobsen, Bob Reddick, Gene Reddick, Pat Reddick, Djaerik Rudolph-Peck, and Gery Rudolph. Thanks for support while I was working on this book.
—*G.R.*

ACKNOWLEDGMENTS

This book wouldn't have been possible without the concerted effort of many individuals in addition to the authors. First of all, we'd like to thank Mike Gunderloy, our technical editor for the book. Mike's contributions cannot be overstated—because of his technical editing prowess, this is a much better book. In addition, Mike was responsible for Chapter 14, "Developing Client-Server Applications," and made contributions to several other chapters. Mike is a Microsoft Certified Engineer, Solution Developer, and Certified Trainer. He's currently working on a few books of his own, including two for SYBEX. He's also a partner at Brooklyn, New York–based Pyramid Computers and a contributing editor to *Smart Access*.

Michael Kaplan wrote two of the appendixes for this book: Appendix B, "Migrating Applications to Access 95," and Appendix C, "Using the Access Developer's Toolkit." He also provided technical editing support for several chapters.

Thanks also go out to the several individuals who helped write chapters for the first edition of this book: Scott Alexander, Brian Randell, and Dan Haught.

We'd also like to thank the following people who provided ideas or technical editing support for one or more chapters and thus improved the text considerably: Mary Chipman, Sue Hogemeier, Joe Maki, and Jim Newman.

Special thanks go to Chris Bell and John Viescas. Chris helped in deciphering the filter properties and events. (He actually wrote the first draft of that section in Chapter 8.) John suggested a new technique, which we adopted, for carrying values forward to the next row (see Chapter 7).

Thanks to all the current and former members of the Access and Jet teams at Microsoft. In particular, the following individuals gave us early access to information, answered technical questions, or reviewed chapters: Steve Alboucq, MariEsther Burnham, Kevin Collins, Dan Frumin, Jim Hance, Roger Harui, Debbie Johnson, David Lazar, Michael Mee, Andrew Miller, Tad Orman, Chris Payne, Tony Poll, David Risher, Joe Robison, Monte Slichter, Sterling Smith, George Snelling, and James Sturms.

We'd also like to thank Pinnacle Publishing for making it possible to reprint material from *Smart Access* and for being understanding when newsletter deadlines were sometimes missed because of book deadlines. In addition, we'd like to thank Erik Ruthruff at Application Developers Training Company for cutting us some slack on his expectations during the first half of 1995, allowing us to spend time writing rather than training.

Thanks also to all the individuals and companies who contributed content to the companion CD.

Of course, without the hard work and support of the staff at SYBEX, this book would be nothing more than a dream. We are especially appreciative of the super-human efforts of Dusty Bernard, Lee Ann Pickrell, and Melanie Spiller. Thanks for keeping everything running smoothly and inspiring us when we didn't feel very inspired.

Finally, we'd like to thank our friends, significant others, and family members who put up with us during yet another long and trying book-writing season.

CONTENTS AT A GLANCE

TABLE OF CONTENTS

PART IV **Multiuser Issues** **747**

12 Developing Multiuser Applications   749

APPENDIXES

FOREWORD

Microsoft Access has fundamentally changed the desktop database world. In the distant past of the 1980s, databases resided strictly in the domain of the professional developer. However, Microsoft Access introduced the power of a relational database to a much wider audience, and for the first time, entry-level end users and high-end developers alike could be comfortable using the same tools. At one end of the spectrum, users can perform ad hoc queries to make sense of their data; at the other end, professional developers can create sophisticated multiuser and client-server systems that drive businesses. This "single solution" aspect of the product has made Microsoft Access the world's most popular database for Microsoft Windows.

Microsoft Access 95 extends this power and reach to an even broader audience, and this book—*Microsoft Access 95 Developer's Handbook*—helps developers get the most out of our product. As members of the Microsoft Access "insider community" that helps us define our product, Paul Litwin, Ken Getz, Mike Gilbert, and Greg Reddick have all had the opportunity to work closely with the people who developed the product and have come to know it intimately. Each has spent years in the database world, and they have come to understand everything from the fundamentals of database design to the subtleties of the Microsoft Windows API. With that knowledge, they've written a book that reaches far beyond the basics of creating forms and reports, delving into such areas as the power of Visual Basic for Applications, the in's and out's of OLE, and the intricacies of replication—areas that are best explored with an experienced guide. As a professional developer you'll learn much from their experience, just as we at Microsoft have.

Microsoft Access 95 is a major revision of our product, and this book is an equally major upgrade from the previous version. The authors have spent considerable time and energy revising their book to account for both their new learning and the new features in the product. I guarantee that even the most experienced Microsoft Access developer will find much of value between these pages. I congratulate Paul, Ken, Mike, and Greg for continuing to expose the power of Microsoft Access to the developer community.

Now: read, learn, and enjoy developing with Microsoft Access 95!

David Risher
Microsoft Access Product Unit Manager

ABOUT THE AUTHORS

Paul Litwin

Paul Litwin is an independent developer and a writer, editor, trainer, and speaker. He's a Microsoft Certified Solution Developer and the owner of Seattle-based Litwin Consulting. Paul is the editor of *Smart Access,* a monthly newsletter from Pinnacle Publishing for Access developers, and has written articles and reviews for various publications, including *Smart Access, Visual Basic Programmer's Journal, Visual Basic Developer,* and *PC World.* He also wrote the Jet Engine White Paper for Microsoft. Paul trains developers for the Application Developers Training Company and is a regular speaker at conferences, including Tech*Ed, Windows Solutions, Windows Solutions Tokyo, DevDays, Access Teach, and VB Teach. In what little spare time he has, Paul enjoys spending time with his family, running, and coaching his nine-year-old son's grade school soccer team. You can reach Paul on CompuServe at 76447,417 or on the Internet at 76447.417@compuserve.com or PaulLitwin@msn.com.

Ken Getz

Ken Getz is an independent consultant who focuses on the Microsoft suite of products. He has received Microsoft's MVP award for each of the past three years and has written two books on developing applications using Microsoft Access. Ken is also a contributing editor to *Smart Access.* He and co-author Paul Litwin also collaborated on *Microsoft Access 95 How-To* (Waite Group Press, 1996). Currently, Ken spends a great deal of time traveling around the country for Application Developer's Training Company, presenting training classes aimed at Access developers. He also speaks at many conferences and shows throughout the world. When taking a break from the computer, he turns the chair around and handles the other keyboard: the grand piano that fills the other half of his office. You can reach Ken on CompuServe at 76137,3650 or on the Internet at 76137.3650@compuserve.com or kengetz@msn.com.

Mike Gilbert

Mike Gilbert is an independent consultant and trainer specializing in application development using Microsoft Access, Visual Basic, SQL Server, and Office. He has worked with Microsoft on numerous ventures, including the Workgroup Templates, Office Developer's Kit, and DevCast. He writes for several periodicals and is a contributing editor to *Smart Access*. He is a trainer with Application Developer's Training Company and a regular speaker at conferences such as Tech*ED, Advisor Access Developers Conference, and VB Teach. He was named a Microsoft MVP in 1995 for his support of Microsoft Schedule+ on CompuServe. He spends what spare time he has enjoying life with his wife Karen and their two cats, Chicago and Cairo. You can reach Mike on CompuServe at 73427,1053 or on the Internet at 73427.1053@compuserve.com or pzone@msn.com.

Greg Reddick

Greg Reddick is the President of Gregory Reddick & Associates, a consulting firm based in Redmond, Washington, that specializes in developing Windows programs in Microsoft Access, Visual Basic, and C/C++. Greg has done database development for the last 12 years. He worked as a software design engineer at Microsoft and spent 4 years on the development team for Microsoft Access 1.0. After leaving Microsoft, he wrote *Access to Word*, the first commercial Access add-on. He writes for *Smart Access* and is the author of the industry standard naming conventions for Access (which appear in Appendix A). Greg also travels internationally to perform training for Application Developer's Training Company. You can reach Greg on CompuServe at 71501,2564 or on the Internet at 71501.2564@compuserve.com.

INTRODUCTION

When it was released in late 1992, Microsoft Access took the database world by storm because of its aggressive $99 price. But when the dust settled after the first million were sold, many users and developers were pleasantly surprised to find a *real database* hidden beneath that ridiculously cheap price tag. Access 1.0 and the soon-to-follow modest upgrade, version 1.1, were certainly far from perfect, but users found an instantly usable product that broke down the walls of database accessibility. At the same time, almost overnight, a large and healthy developer community (that included the authors of this book) was born and began to develop professional applications that ran businesses of all sizes throughout the world.

Since its introduction, Microsoft has released two major updates: version 2.0, which hit the streets in May of 1994, and Access for Windows 95 (aka Access 95 and Access 7.0), which appeared in November of 1995. These updates fixed most of the limitations and annoyances of version 1.x and made numerous improvements in the areas of usability, programmability, and extendibility.

Access 95 is a wonderfully powerful development platform, but like any powerful product, it takes considerable time to master. Fortunately for you, the four of us (plus a few others) spent many months and countless hours tearing apart Access 95, exposing its undocumented secrets, and making it do things that few have imagined were possible—all for your benefit.

About the Book

This book is not a substitute for the Microsoft documentation, nor is it meant as a comprehensive reference manual. Instead, we strove to address the major issues we feel will face most developers. When we had to choose whether to cover a given topic or feature—one has to stop somewhere—we tended to favor the undocumented or poorly documented over the well documented.

In addition to the text, this book includes the usual assortment of figures, examples, and tables. It also includes lots of notes, tips, and warnings to call special attention to certain features or "gotchas."

About This Edition

This edition of the book is a significant rewrite of the best-selling *Microsoft Access 2 Developer's Handbook.* Almost every page has changed in some way, but some chapters have changed more than others. You'll notice the most changes in the areas of Access that have changed the most. Thus, for example, we didn't change too much in the database design and SQL chapters, but we made major revisions to our coverage of OLE, add-ins, multiuser development, and many other topics. We've added several new chapters ("The Access Event Model," "Mastering Replication," and "Controlling Access as an OLE Server") and have condensed or combined others.

One thing you can be sure of: this is *not* an Access 2 book with an Access 95 cover. It is very much an Access 95 book—from cover to cover.

Is This Book for You?

This book is for the Access developer or someone who would like to become one. It doesn't matter whether you develop Access applications full time, as only one component of your job, or in your spare time during the evenings and weekends. What matters is that you take the product seriously and want your applications to be the very best.

If you only care to get your toes wet with Access and are happy to throw together quick-and-dirty applications that are automated with nothing more than a few macros, you probably don't need this book. However, if you're ready to dive into the thick of Access and get down to the business of developing industrial-strength applications that utilize Access to its fullest, you've picked the right book.

If you already own a copy of *Microsoft Access 2 Developer's Handbook,* should you buy this book, too? Yes—if you're planning to develop applications with Access 95 and you liked the Access 2 edition, we're sure you'll get a lot out of this edition, as well. So much in Access has changed for the developer, and we cover it all—okay, not all, but almost all.

What You Need to Know

For you to benefit most from an advanced book such as this, we've had to dispense with the fundamentals and make several assumptions about you. We assume you already have a basic level of familiarity with the product. At a minimum, you should be comfortable creating tables and simple queries, forms, and reports and have at least a rudimentary understanding of macros and Access Basic or Visual Basic for Applications. If you aren't up to speed, you may wish to put down this book for the moment and spend some time with Access and the manuals (including the *Building Applications* guide), the Help system, or an introductory text such as *Mastering Microsoft Access for Windows 95* by Alan Simpson and Elizabeth Olson (SYBEX, 1995).

Conventions Used in This Book

It goes without saying that the professional developer must consistently follow *some* standard. We followed several standard conventions in this book to make it easier for you to follow along.

We have used the Reddick VBA (RVBA) naming conventions for the naming of Access objects, which has become the de facto naming standard in the Access development community. (One of the authors of this book, Greg Reddick, developed the standard, which bears his name.) Even if you don't subscribe to the RVBA standard, however, you'll likely appreciate the fact that it has been consistently used throughout the book. These conventions, which were first published in *Smart Access,* are included in their entirety in Appendix A (on the CD) and excerpted in the inside front cover of this book.

In addition to following the RVBA standard, we have prefaced all functions, subroutines, and user-defined types that you may wish to use from your own code with the "glr" prefix (which stands for the three original authors of this book: Getz, Litwin, and Reddick), aliased all Windows API declarations using a "glr_api" prefix, and prefixed all global constants with "glrc". These conventions should avoid naming conflicts with any existing code in your applications. If, however, you import multiple modules from various chapters' sample databases into a single database, you may find naming conflicts as a result of our using consistent naming throughout the chapters. In that case you'll need to comment out any conflicting API declarations or user-defined types.

Chapter Walk-Through

This book consists of seven parts and four appendixes. In every chapter you'll find lots of examples, with all but the most trivial included in sample databases you can find on the CD that accompanies this book.

Part I: Overview of Access

Part I begins with Chapter 1, which includes a brief history of Access and an overview of what's new in Access 95. In Chapter 2 you'll find a discussion of Access' event model and the sequence of events in Access.

Part II: Manipulating Data

When you design your database, you need to follow the principles of relational database design theory, which are detailed in Chapter 3. You'll also find a discussion of primary and foreign keys, relationships, the normal forms, and integrity constraints.

Chapter 4 discusses advanced query design, with lots of examples, including coverage of joins and of aggregate, action, and parameter queries. This chapter also includes an overview of the Jet engine, including how Jet processes and optimizes queries. In addition, this chapter details the improvements to the Jet engine in Access 95.

You can use Chapter 5 as the Access SQL reference that Microsoft never provided. This chapter provides the syntax of every Access SQL statement and clause, with numerous examples, and a discussion of how Access SQL differs from the ANSI SQL standards.

In Chapter 6 you'll find a discussion of data access objects (DAO), the programmatic interface to the Jet engine. Here you'll learn how to programmatically create TableDefs, QueryDefs, Relationships, and other objects; how to set and retrieve object properties; how to manipulate recordsets; and—using the Containers and Documents collections—how to build your own replacement database container.

Part III: Presenting Data

Chapter 7 presents a comprehensive discussion of controls and their properties and methods, along with numerous examples. In this chapter you learn about list-filling functions, creating paired multi-select list boxes, using the Tag property, and creating forms and controls programmatically.

After you've mastered controls, you'll be ready to think about the forms themselves, which is the topic of Chapter 8. In this chapter you'll find a thorough discussion of the different types of forms and how best to use them. You'll also find numerous examples and reusable generic routines—some quite extensive, such as the example that shows you how to make any form resolution independent.

In Chapter 9 you'll learn how to master sorting and grouping, as well as the myriad of report properties and events. Again, you'll find lots of useful examples you can use in your applications.

Chapter 10 explains how to programmatically retrieve information about your printer, change print destinations, and perform many other printing wonders by using the prtDevMode, prtDevNames, and prtMip report properties.

Part III concludes with Chapter 11. In this chapter you'll learn when you have to use macros, how to set and retrieve global application and database options, and how to use and manipulate Access menus and toolbars.

Part IV: Multiuser Issues

In the chapters contained in Part IV, you'll learn how to *think* multiuser. Chapter 12 covers using Access in a shared file-server environment. You'll find discussions of page-locking options, development strategies, transaction processing, linked table management, forcing record locking, determining who has a database open, and multiuser error handling.

Chapter 13 focuses on replication. In this chapter you'll learn when to use replication and how to use it. You'll also find discussions on various replication options and strategies, synchronization and conflict management, using Replication Manager, and how to programmatically manipulate replication, synchronization, and conflict resolution.

Chapter 14 provides an introduction to Access client-server development. This chapter begins by detailing the difference between client-server and file-server development and discusses when to use one versus the other. It provides a comparison of the various data access methods, including the use of normal Access queries, SQL pass-through queries, and remote data objects (RDO). The chapter also discusses various client-server design strategies, potential problems, application optimization, and the Microsoft Upsizing Wizard.

Part V: Building Applications

Chapter 15 provides a thorough discussion of user interface issues. You'll learn how to design consistent, user-aware applications that coexist with Windows 95. This chapter includes an example that shows you how to use the TabStrip control that is part of the Windows 95 Common Control OLE custom control (which ships with the Access ADT) to create your own property dialogs.

In Chapter 16 you'll find a discussion of application debugging strategies and how to recover gracefully from and handle application errors. This chapter includes a generic set of routines for logging errors.

In Chapter 17 you'll learn how to optimize the various Access components, including queries, forms, reports, and VBA code. After you read this chapter, you should be able to make any sluggish application run more quickly.

Part VI: Interoperability

Part VI concentrates on interacting with the outside world from Access. Chapter 18 explains how to use the Windows API and other Dynamic Link Libraries (DLLs) to do things that are otherwise impossible using Access itself. This chapter includes a discussion of the Windows Registry and how to manipulate it using the Windows API, as well as a discussion of 16-bit to 32-bit DLL conversion issues.

In Chapter 19 you'll discover how you can use the undocumented library MSAU7032.DLL that comes with every copy of Access to perform all sorts of neat tricks, like the ones Access does in its Wizards. While much of this functionality is also available through the Windows API, this chapter demonstrates how to save yourself a lot of trouble by using the higher-level functions found in MSAU7032 instead.

Dynamic Data Exchange (DDE) is the subject of Chapter 20. It explains how to use regular DDE to communicate with applications running on your machine and how to use NetDDE to communicate with applications running on other machines across the network.

In Chapter 21 you'll learn how to manipulate other applications using the more robust alternative to DDE, OLE automation. This chapter includes examples that demonstrate how to use OLE automation to control Microsoft Schedule+, Word, and Excel. The chapter also covers how to use OLE custom controls.

Chapter 22 presents the flip side of Chapter 21. Here you'll learn how to manipulate Access from Visual Basic, Excel, and other OLE automation controllers. The chapter includes an example Access reporting system that is controlled from Excel.

Part VII: Finishing Touches

Chapter 23 shows you, with examples, how to build and install Access Wizards, builders, libraries, and other add-ins you can use to enhance your Access applications.

Finally, Chapter 24 discusses the *right* way to secure your Access databases. In this chapter you'll find a complete discussion of the Access security model, the Access Security Wizard, accounts, permissions, and ownership. You'll also learn how to manipulate security programmatically.

Appendixes

This book contains four appendixes on disk. Due to space limitations, we have provided these appendixes in electronic format only. Each appendix exists in its own .RTF file. You should be able to read the appendixes with any standard word processor. (For example, Word, WordPerfect, WordPro, and Windows 95 WordPad will all work.)

Appendix A provides a description of the RVBA naming conventions used throughout this book. You'll find this useful both when reading this book and if you wish to use the same naming conventions in your own development work. The file APPA.RTF contains the text for this appendix.

Appendix B discusses the issues you need to consider when migrating applications from prior versions of Access to Access 95. If you plan to migrate any existing applications, you won't want to miss this appendix. The file APPB.RTF contains the text for this appendix.

Appendix C takes a look at the Access 95 Developer's Toolkit (ADT 95). You'll find an overview of the ADT 95 and a discussion of run-time application development issues, as well as an explanation of how to use the Setup Wizard to create distribution disks for your application. You'll also find a work-around for a bug that disables shortcut menus in run-time applications. The file APPC.RTF contains the text for this appendix.

Appendix D details the changes made to the programming language in Access. Access Basic has been replaced, in Access 95, with Visual Basic for Applications (VBA). In this appendix you'll learn what's different between Access Basic and VBA. Appendix D discusses many of the differences and shows most of the new features VBA adds to Access 95. This is the place to look if you want more information about any specific language element that's new. The file APPD.RTF contains the text for this appendix.

About the CD

The CD that comes with this book (attached to the inside back cover) is a valuable companion to the book. It includes all the chapter databases discussed in the book, as well as several extra goodies that should make your Access development work more efficient.

What's on the CD?

On the CD we've included the appendixes and the chapter databases. We've also included white papers, freeware and shareware utilities, and demo versions of several commercial products. Most of these files have some restrictions on their use; please read the provided supporting documentation and respect the rights of the vendors who were kind enough to provide these files. For shareware programs, please register the program with the vendor if you find it useful.

The CD files are described here:

- **Appendixes A–D:** (\Appendix) We've included in this folder the text of the four appendixes to this book. The text of each appendix is included in a rich text format (.RTF) file that you should be able to read with most word processors or with the Windows 95 WordPad program.

- **Chapter Databases:** (\Chapter) Here's where you'll find the chapter databases containing all the examples from the text. Each chapter database includes the tables, queries, forms, reports, macros, and modules discussed in the book so you can try out the examples yourself. These databases also include lots of reusable code and other objects you can copy and paste into your own applications. We've also included several Access add-ins, a DLL, and a few other supporting files in the Chapter folder.

- **WinHelp Inspector:** (\Other\Bluesky\Inspctr) From Blue Sky Software. WinHelp Inspector allows you to investigate the contents of existing Windows 95 Help files. This is a "spelunking" tool to help you find out what's actually in those Help files. To install this freeware utility, run SETUP.EXE from the directory on the CD.

- **What's New in Windows 95 Help:** (\Other\Bluesky\Whatsnew) Also from Blue Sky Software. Blue Sky has provided a Help file explaining what's new in the Windows 95 Help system. If you're creating Help files (and you will be if you're distributing Access applications using the run-time version), you'll want to investigate this Help file before you get started. To install this Help file, run SETUP.EXE from the directory on the CD.

- **Complexity Meter:** (\Other\Fms\Dcomplex and \Other\Fms\Dcomplx2) From FMS, Inc. FMS has provided the free Complexity Meter Add-In in both Access 95 (Dcomplex) and Access 2 (Dcomplx2) versions. The add-ins aren't terribly useful on their own, but now you'll be able to compare the complexity of your application with others. To install the add-ins, start Access 95 or

Access 2 and run Add-In Manager. (See DCOMPLEX.WRI and DCOMPLX2.WRI for more details.)

- **Jet Statistics Meter:** (\Other\Fms\Jetmeter) Also from FMS, Inc. This free add-in makes use of the undocumented ISAMStats method of the DBEngine object. You can use it to help optimize your queries. To install the add-in, start Access 95 and run Add-In Manager, installing JETMETER.MDA. See JETMETER.WRI for more details.

- **Query Statistics:** (\Other\Qrystats) From Trigeminal Software. Like FMS' Jet Statistics Meter Add-In, this free Access 95 add-in from Michael Kaplan of Trigeminal Software makes use of the undocumented ISAMStats method of the DBEngine object. Michael's add-in works quite a bit differently than FMS' add-in, so we decided to include both and let you decide which one works best for you (or perhaps you'll use both). To install the add-in, start Access 95 and run Add-In Manager, installing QRYSTATS.MDA. For more information, see QRYSTATS.TXT.

- **Tab Custom Control:** (\Other\Tabocx) From Andrew Miller. You can use this free OLE custom control from Microsoft's Andrew Miller to create tabbed dialogs. This is an update of Andrew's Access 2 custom control. Although Andrew works at Microsoft, this is *not* a Microsoft product and is provided as-is. To install the control, copy OC30.DLL, TAB32.OCX, and TAB.LIC to your \Windows\System directory. Then, run the following in an MSDOS box under Windows 95 or Windows NT:

```
REGSVR32.EXE C:\WINDOWS\SYSTEM\OC30.DLL

REGSVR32.EXE C:\WINDOWS\SYSTEM\TAB32.OCX
```

See the TAB.HLP Help file for details on how to use this control in your applications.

- **Access 2 Certification Test Demo:** (\Other\Transcnd\Access2) From Transcender Corporation. This is a demo version of Transcender's preparation program for the Microsoft Access 2 certification exam. Use the setup program (SETUP.EXE) to install the demo. Information is also provided on ordering the full product.

- **VB 3 Certification Test Demo:** (\Other\Transcnd\Vb3) Also from Transcender Corporation. This is a demo version of Transcender's preparation program for the Microsoft Visual Basic 3 certification exam. Use the setup program (SETUP.EXE) to install the demo. Information is also provided on ordering the full product.

- **WOSSA-I Certification Test Demo:** (\Other\Transcnd\Wossa-1) Also from Transcender Corporation. This is a demo version of Transcender's preparation program for the Microsoft WOSSA-I certification exam. Use the setup program (SETUP.EXE) to install the demo. Information is also provided on ordering the full product.

- **Process Custom Control:** (\Other\Wright\Process) From Wright Futures. You can use this shareware OLE custom control to manage external processes from within Access. Run the provided setup program (SETUP.EXE) to install this control. For information on using the control, see WPROC.HLP.

- **Registry custom control:** (\Other\Wright\Registry) Also from Wright Futures. This book discusses several different methods for reading and writing to the Registry. Less Wright has made it even easier, however, with this shareware custom control. Run the provided setup program (SETUP.EXE) to install this control. For information on using the control, see WREG.HLP.

- **Replication White Paper:** (\Other\Msft\Repwp) From Microsoft. This is a useful white paper from Microsoft that discusses Jet replication. It includes a few details that are not discussed in Chapter 13. Copy REPLICAT.DOC to your hard disk and open it with Word for Windows or Windows 95 WordPad.

- **Jet Locking White Paper and DLL:** (\Other\Msft\Jetlock) From Microsoft. This folder includes a white paper, a dynamic link library, a utility program, a sample Access 95 database, and a sample Visual Basic 4 application. You'll find this white paper and supporting files very useful for understanding how Jet locks records, for viewing locking information, and for determining which users have a database open. To use it, copy the MSLDBUSR.DLL file to your Windows\System folder and the remaining files to a new folder on your hard disk. Open JETLOCK.DOC with Word for Windows or Windows 95 WordPad for more details. An example of calling MSLDBUSR.DLL is included in Chapter 12.

- **Unsecured Wizard code:** (\Other\Msft\Wizards) From Microsoft. The Wizards that ship with Access 95 are secured, so you cannot open them. This is unfortunate because the Wizard code provides lots of examples of undocumented calls and techniques advanced developers can learn from. Fortunately, Microsoft has graciously provided these unsecured copies of the Access 95 Wizards. To use them, back up the secured copies of the Wizards and copy the unsecured Wizards to your Access folder. From then on, you're on your own; Microsoft provides no support for the unsecured Wizards. It's best if you use these Wizards only on test machines because the unsecured version of the Wizards will be slower. See WIZREAD.TXT for more details.

- **Win32 API text file:** (\Other\Msft\Win32api) From Microsoft. This is a free text file that contains all the declarations for the Win32 API. To use it, copy this text file to a new folder on your hard disk and open it with any text editor.

- **WinZip 6.0a:** (\Other\Winzip) From Nico Mak Computing, Inc. This is a shareware evaluation version of WinZip 6.0a (32-bit). WinZip is a Windows 95/NT utility for zipping and unzipping files. It includes its own zipping and unzipping routines, but it also can be configured to call PKZip, LHA, and other archiving programs. Run the provided setup program (SETUP.EXE) to install WinZip. See the online help for more information on using WinZip and registering the product.

- **DDE Share:** (\Other\Ddeshr) From Software Assist Corporation. This freeware utility is useful for creating DDE shares under Windows 3.x and Windows 95. (You must create DDE shares before you can use NetDDE.) To install DDE Share, copy all the files in this folder to a new folder on your hard disk. See README.WRI for more information on installing and using DDE Share.

- **SPEED Ferret Demo:** (\Other\Ferret) From Black Moshannon Systems. This is a working but limited version of the full product. SPEED Ferret is a global search-and-replace add-in for Access 95. (An Access 2 version is also available.) This utility will propagate object name changes throughout your database. Run the provided setup program (SETUP.EXE) to install this program. See the online help for more information on using the SPEED Ferret Demo and ordering the full product.

- **ClickBook Surf 'n' Print:** (\Other\Clikbook) From Bookmaker Corporation. ClickBook is a Windows printing utility that makes it easy to print double-sided booklets, brochures, and other double-sided printouts. ClickBook Surf 'n' Print is a full working version of ClickBook that limits itself to a single layout. Run the provided setup program (SETUP.EXE) to install this program. See the online help for more information on using ClickBook Surf 'n' Print and ordering the full Clickbook product.

Using the Files from the CD

The CD that accompanies this book is organized into several folders (subdirectories) that contain the chapter databases and other files. See the README.TXT file in the root folder of the CD for any late-breaking details on the CD files.

Installing the Chapter Samples

The sample chapter databases are located in the \Chapter folder. To install and use the files, follow these instructions:

- Most chapters contain only one database, named CH*xx*.MDB. To use this database, simply copy the file to a new folder on your hard disk and open the database with Access 95.

- For some chapters we've included multiple database files, all of which begin with the name CH*xx*. In this case, copy all these files to a new folder on your hard disk and open the database with Access 95. See the description of these files in the text of the chapter for more details.

- A few chapters have other non-database supporting files. These include Access add-ins (*xxx*.MDA) and Dynamic Link Libraries (*xxx*.DLL). See the description of these files in the text of the chapter for more details.

Installing the Appendixes

To read an appendix file, copy the APPx.RTF file from the \Appendix folder of the CD to a new folder on your hard disk. Open the file using any word processor or the Windows 95 WordPad program.

Installing the Other Files

All other (non-chapter) files are located in subfolders of the \Other folder. See the section "What's On the Disk?" earlier in this introduction for a description of the files and installation details.

WARNING Most of the files cannot be run directly off the CD. Copy them to a folder on your hard disk before using them, or—when it's provided—run the Setup program, which will copy and prepare the files for you.

How to Use This Book

While you may find it easiest to read the chapters in the order in which they appear in the book, it's not essential. One of our goals as we wrote the book was to make it possible for you to pick up and read any individual chapter without having to read through several other chapters first. Thus, the book is *not* a linear progression that starts with Chapter 1 and ends with Chapter 24. Instead, we have logically grouped together similar chapters, but otherwise (with a few exceptions) the chapters do not particularly build upon each other. To make it easy for you to jump from one chapter to another, we have included cross-references throughout the book.

While we've done a lot of the work for you, you'll get the most benefit from this book by putting the material to real use. Take the examples and generic routines found in the book and expand on them. Add and subtract from them as you incorporate them into your applications. Experiment and enjoy!

PART I

Overview of Access

CHAPTER

ONE

Access 95, the Desktop Database of Choice

- Why Access is the desktop database platform of choice

- What's new in Access 95

Chances are, if you're reading this book, you've already decided that Microsoft Access for Windows 95 (we'll refer to it as *Access 95*) is a worthy platform for your development endeavors. Chances are, you're right. Microsoft has created a serious, full-featured, and powerful development environment for creating database applications on single-user and networked personal computers.

Where Access Fits in the Desktop Database Market

Certainly, Access is not without competition. Several other Windows-based database development environments are available from which to choose. Borland's Paradox for Windows and Visual dBASE for Windows, as well as Powersoft's Power-Builder, are also capable desktop database development packages. There's even competition within the ranks at Microsoft: both Visual FoxPro and Visual Basic compete with Access. We feel quite strongly, however, that if you want to manage databases on Windows-based PCs, Access is far and away the best tool for the job. Here are just some of the reasons we have come to this conclusion:

- Access 95 is a true 32-bit database management system with a multi-threaded, 32-bit database engine (the Jet 3.0 engine).

- Access has the strongest support for the relational model. Its support for the dynaset, integrated data dictionary, referential integrity (including support for cascading updates and deletes), and SQL all bear witness to this fact.

- Access is primarily a nonprocedural environment, although it contains a powerful procedural language—Visual Basic for Applications (VBA)—when you need it.

- VBA is a standard language implemented across a wide variety of Microsoft products, including Visual Basic, Microsoft Excel, and Microsoft Project.

- Access has an excellent object model for the manipulation of data using VBA code: Data Access Objects (DAO).

- Access exposes a rich event model and supports the manipulation of almost every property at run time.

- Access supports OLE 2 both as an OLE automation client and as a server.

- Access is very extensible, including support for 32-bit OLE custom controls, the Windows 32 API, and VBA add-ins.

- Access supports multiuser database sharing in both file-server and client-server environments. This means you can scale your applications from single-user to file-server to client-server with the same front-end tool.

- The Jet engine, the database engine behind Access, is a mature, well-architected relational database engine based on 1990s technology. The Jet engine is shared across Microsoft products, most notably Visual Basic and Visual C++.

- The Jet engine includes Rushmore optimization technology borrowed from FoxPro.

- Access has built-in support for replication without the need for a high-end database server.

- Access has a companion run-time package, included in the Access Developer's Toolkit, you can use to distribute Access applications without paying royalties.

Access has the best combination of power, ease of use, extensibility, and long-term market viability.

Opportunity Knocks

Microsoft tells us that the vast majority of Access sales go to end users (as opposed to developers) either in the stand-alone package or as part of Microsoft Office Professional. This might tempt you to say, "Well, then, it's an end-user package, so I'm going to use Paradox for Windows instead." But you'd be closing the door on opportunity. It's just this popularity among end users that makes Access a perfect development platform. Of course, power users might be able to get things set up just fine in Access, but once they get past a certain point (and that point has moved a little higher again with the introduction of Access 95), they're going to need some help. When they see what Access is capable of, they'll want more, and their wants will usually exceed their grasp. That's where you, the Access developer, fit in. Most users can't be bothered with reading manuals or figuring out the complexities of programming. You will, after going through the material in this book, be prepared to handle many of the situations with which end users will confront you.

There's another side to this issue, too: you can deliver solutions onto users' desktops that they can tweak and extend themselves. In other words, you're empowering your users. Can you do this with Paradox, FoxPro, dBASE, or PowerBuilder? Probably not. If you're an in-house developer in a large corporation or government agency, empowering your users can be a big advantage. Even independent developers will have the occasional client who wants to be able to "play with things." This means you don't have to spend all your time perfecting the formatting of that report. Let your sophisticated power users do it instead.

A Brief Access History

Access 1.0 really opened the eyes of many database developers. It was one of the first relational database products available for the Windows 3 platform, and it was certainly the first to fill the needs of many developers, both corporate and independent. Besides its ease of use in getting started, Access 1.0 made it very easy to create simple applications. It did have some limitations when developers got past a certain point in their applications, and it had a severe limitation in that databases couldn't be larger than 128 megabytes. Access 1.1 fixed that limitation, expanding the maximum database size to 1 gigabyte, and fixed some other limitations, as well. Still, many professional features were lacking. Programmers used to Visual Basic's nearly complete flexibility were stymied by Access' inability to change control and form properties at run time, for example. On the other hand, there was no simpler way to get data in and out of forms than Access, so developers worked around Access 1.1's limitations.

Access 2.0 offered great gains for developers. Although it also provided numerous improvements for end users, the greatest leap from 1.1 came in the improvements for the developer community. For the professional programmer, Access 2.0 added features in almost every area of the product, including:

- A vastly extended object and event model
- Run-time access to most form and report properties
- Event procedures (Code-Behind-Forms)
- Cascading updates and deletes for referential integrity
- Engine-level enforcement of rules

- New query types: union, data definition, and pass-through queries and support for subqueries
- Rushmore query optimization
- Data Access Objects (DAO), a consistent object model for the manipulation of Jet engine data
- OLE automation client support
- Programmable security
- Support for 16-bit OLE custom controls

What's New in Access 95

Things only get better with Access 95. In the next few sections we detail the most important new features for Access developers.

Access 95 Forms

The improvements to forms in Access 95 are not as radical as the upgrade from version 1.1 to 2.0. Nonetheless, there are some significant changes, including:

- **Multi-instance forms:** You can easily create and manage multiple instances of the same form.
- **Simplified properties:** If you thought DefaultEditing and AllowEditing were confusing, you'll be happy to know they've been replaced with AllowEdits, AllowDeletions, AllowAdditions, and DataEntry. Also, AllowUpdating has been replaced with RecordsetType.
- **KeyPreview property:** This property allows you to intercept keystrokes at the form level before any controls see them.
- **NewRecord property:** This property allows you to detect whether you are on the new record.
- **Cycle property (All Records, Current Record, Current Page):** Inclusion of this property means you can dispense with the tab sentries work-around that was needed in prior versions to prevent users from inadvertently tabbing to the next record.

- **List box controls:** These controls now have a MultiSelect property, which can be None, Simple, or Extended, like Visual Basic's list box. (When you set this property to Simple or Extended, the list box can no longer be bound to a field.)

- **Combo box performance:** Performance is much improved. The version 2 penalty for using a numeric bound field as the row source is pretty much eliminated.

- **DropDown method for combo boxes:** This method makes it easy to force a combo box to drop down.

- **Lightweight image control:** Image control uses less overhead than an unbound object frame for bitmap images.

- **ControlTip property for controls:** With this property, creating tool tips (for any type of control) is a snap.

- **SpecialEffect property:** This property has expanded from Normal, Raised, and Sunken to Flat, Raised, Sunken, Etched, Shadowed, and Chiseled.

- **ControlType property for controls:** This property allows you to detect and alter the type of control.

- **Picture property:** With this property, you can create form watermarks.

- **RecordDividers property:** You can use this property to eliminate the line between form sections.

- **Filter by Form:** Access forms support a new built-in query-by-form feature called Filter by Form (along with the lesser Filter by Selection). You can control whether this is available through the AllowFilters property, and you can manipulate filters and sorts using the Filter, FilterOn, OrderBy, and OrderByOn properties.

- **Form modules:** Form modules now support public functions and Let, Get, and Set property procedures. You can use these new features to create user-defined methods and properties for forms. This means you can create forms that hide their internals, exposing only public methods and properties to the outside world.

- **Built-in and custom form style sheets:** You can apply these style sheets to existing forms to standardize their look.

These changes are discussed in detail in Chapters 7 and 8.

Access 95 Reports

Microsoft made some useful changes to reports that bring report programmability to a new level, including the following:

- With the NoData event, you can now choose to not print a report if there are no records.

- The Page event occurs after all the Format events for the report and after all the Print events for the page, but before the page is actually printed. You can use the Line, Circle, or PSet method in an event procedure attached to this event to create a graphic or page border.

- Like forms, reports now have Filter, FilterOn, OrderBy, and OrderByOn properties. You can set these properties at run time to equal the same properties of a filtered form to print only the user-filtered records.

- You can use the RepeatSection property to repeat a group header at the top of continuation pages.

- You can keep groups from splitting across columns using the report's GrpKeepTogether property.

- Report print preview now supports an unlimited (or at least much less limited) zoom capability and multipage preview.

Chapter 9 discusses the changes to reports in detail.

Access 95 Tables and Queries

Although Microsoft added a number of user-oriented changes to tables and queries, not a lot has changed in this area for the developer. The limited changes include the following:

- AutoNumber fields replace counter fields. These fields have two new properties: FieldSize (LongInteger or ReplicationID) and NewValues (Increment or Random).

- Fields in tables now have a new set of lookup properties you can use to create a default control type for a field. This default control type—which you can set to be a text box, combo box, list box, or check box (the choices will differ based on the datatype of the control)—will then be used anytime you use that field on datasheets, queries, or forms. This means you have to specify only once, for example, that CustomerId should always be a combo box with a row source that comes from tblCustomer.

Chapters 3 and 4 discuss these changes.

Access 95 Programming Language: VBA

Access Basic has been replaced with the Visual Basic for Applications (VBA) programming language that first appeared in Microsoft Excel 5.0. This language is part of Excel, Project, Visual Basic 4.0, and now Access. This fact makes your code that much more portable across these applications. In addition, VBA comes with many new features, including the following:

- The With…End With construct helps you reduce your object references.
- The For Each…Next construct lets you iterate through a collection or an array without worrying about the collection or array's boundaries.
- You can now make Option Explicit the default with the Require Variable Declaration option found in the Modules tab of the Tools ➤ Options dialog.
- You can use a space followed by an underscore as a line-continuation character, to indicate that a line is continued on the next line.
- VBA offers support for conditional compilation, which can be useful when you debug or need to include operating system–specific code for applications that will run under both Windows 95 and Windows NT.
- VBA includes support for named parameters, optional parameters, and parameter arrays.
- VBA offers support for new Date, Boolean, and Byte datatypes.
- Improvements to the editor and debugger include Watch variables, color-coded syntax, and the ability to jump from one procedure to another and return to where you came from.
- With on-demand VBA library loading, you no longer have to exit Access to finish the installation of an add-in.

These changes and others are discussed in detail in Chapter 2 and throughout many other chapters.

Access 95 Database Engine: Jet 3.0

Access 95 provides several significant changes to the Jet engine and its access language, DAO. The changes include the following:

- Replication support allows you to keep multiple copies of a database in sync with one other. Replication is programmable through extensions made to DAO.

- There is no row-level locking yet, but pessimistic locking has been refined so that users are much less likely to be locked out of inserting new records.

- Several other changes (fewer read locks, deferred page reuse, more compact indexes, more contiguous page allocation, faster delete operations) should improve single- and multiuser performance.

- The Jet Errors collection makes it easy to parse out and handle local, server, and ODBC errors when connecting to server back ends.

- Jet now offers database passwords as an alternative to workgroup-based security. (For those needing the more robust workgroup-based security model, it's still there.)

- The AllPermissions property of document objects now gives you access to both explicit and implicit permissions without requiring iteration of user's groups.

These changes are discussed in more detail in many of the chapters in this book, including Chapters 4, 6, 12, 13, 14, and 24.

Access 95 OLE Support

The big story here is more complete OLE support. Improvements include the following:

- With OLE automation server support, you can now control Access from Visual Basic and other applications. Printing an Access report from VB, for example, is now trivial.

- Access includes an integrated object browser and better OLE automation client support and support for type libraries. These features make it easy for you to browse and use another application's objects, properties, and methods.

- Access 95 includes support for 32-bit OLE custom controls, including simple data bound controls (controls that bind to fields—but not recordsets).

- Custom control properties are now merged into the Access Control property sheet.

These changes are covered in greater detail in Chapters 21 and 22.

Other Access 95 Improvements

Additional changes have been made to the product that don't fit into any of the above categories, including the following:

- The performance analyzer helps you find and fix performance bottlenecks in your application.

- The improved Explorer-like database container, now called the Database Explorer, lets you toggle among several levels of detail to reveal an object description, as well as created and last-modified dates and times.

- You now have support for user-defined database properties.

- Startup properties let you disable access to the Database Explorer and change the application's title bar and icon.

- In the Database Explorer Object property sheet, you can make objects hidden, create an object description, and specify whether that object should be replicated.

- Integrated support for the Microsoft Office spelling and auto-correction engine brings spell-checking and auto-correction support to Access.

- The smarter AutoForm Wizard makes for better quick-and-dirty forms.

Many of these miscellaneous changes are discussed throughout the book.

Summary

Access is by far the best-selling desktop database program on the market today. It has the right mix of features for both users and developers. It's easy to learn and use, but it's also built on a sound, modern relational database architecture and has the power and extendibility to take you well into the 21st century.

CHAPTER

TWO

2

The Access
Event Model

- Working with objects and events

- Reacting to form and control events

- Handling data events

- Determining the sequence of events

As with many applications that shield you from the details of working with Windows, one of the largest hurdles facing beginning Access developers is finding out how to make something happen. To create an application in Access, you must create and manipulate objects in response to events. An *object* in Access is one of the things you can see in the Database Explorer (also known as the Database Container or Database Window), plus the things these objects contain. Thus tables, queries, and forms are all objects, but so are fields, indexes, and controls. An *event* is a change in state that occurs when a user, a program, or the computer does something. For example, an event occurs when you move the mouse, click a button with the mouse, or press a key. An event also occurs when another application attempts to open a form using OLE automation or when the time-counting mechanism built in to your computer gets to the next increment in time.

The Access programming model uses an event-driven programming paradigm. In *event-driven programming,* the programming language operates in response to events that occur, usually in response to some user action. A relatively simple action by the user—moving the mouse over the form and clicking several controls, for example—causes Access to trigger many events, including MouseMove, Mouse-Down, MouseUp, GotFocus, LostFocus, Enter, Exit, and Click events. At any of these events, you can step in and perform some action. The code that is activated when an event occurs is called an *event handler.*

NOTE If you look in the property sheet listing the event properties for an object, you'll see names such as On Mouse Move and On Click. These names (with the spaces removed) are the names of the event properties. The events themselves, however, are named without the *On*. We'll refer to the MouseMove event (which corresponds to the OnMouseMove event property) or the Click event (which corresponds to the OnClick event property).

So Many Events, So Little Time

The more events Access generates when something happens, the finer the control you have, because you can take control at any point where an event is generated.

On the other hand, it takes more work to react to lower-level events than to higher-level events. For example, when you type characters into a text box and press the Tab key, the KeyDown, KeyUp, KeyPress, Change, BeforeUpdate, AfterUpdate, Exit, and LostFocus events all occur. How do you know which event to react to, for any specific action you want to take? If you wanted to be able to open a popup form when the user pressed and released the Ctrl key twice, you would need to make use of the KeyDown and KeyUp events. If all you cared about was running a validation procedure when the user entered a new value into the text box, however, you'd be wasting your time working at this low keystroke-by-keystroke level. Instead, you'd likely want to use the BeforeUpdate event, which validates the entire value once the user is done entering it, instead of worrying about each key as it's typed.

Hooking In

Events happen continuously in Access, but they're not terribly interesting unless you can react to them. Access provides several ways for you to hook into events and react to them. You hook into an event in Access by placing a reference to an event handler in the property sheet of an object. In Table 2.1 you'll find the four kinds of event handlers, an example of calling each of them, and a description of when you should use them.

The last three event handlers in Table 2.1 use the Access VBA language. While macros are useful for quickly prototyping applications, we don't recommend their use in professional applications, because macros:

- Can't recover from errors
- Can't be used to call DLLs
- Can't easily be used for looping
- Can't be used to step through recordsets
- Can't be used in transaction processing
- Can't pass parameters
- Are difficult to debug
- Can be halted by users with Ctrl+Break (and this can never be turned off)

TABLE 2.1: Event Handlers

Event Handler	Example	When to Use It
Macro	mcrRunMe	In simple prototypes or single-user applications that don't need to be bulletproofed
Event procedure	[Event Procedure]	When you wish to have code encapsulated in the form or report or when you need parameters that are passed only to event procedures
Global module function	=GenericFunction()	When you want to call generic code or when you want the ability to copy a control to another form or report and want its event handler reference to go with it. You can call only functions (not subroutines) directly from the property sheet
Form module function	=LocalModuleFunction()	When you need to call the same event handler from multiple events or objects and you wish the code to be encapsulated within the form. Again, you can call only functions from here

The bottom line is that you should program using VBA code for all your Access application development, except when you only need to create a quick-and-dirty prototype or you wish to create a simple application that only you will use. (See Chapter 11 for more information on using macros in applications and for situations in which you don't have any choice about using them.)

In prior versions of Access, the programming language was called Access Basic (or Embedded Basic). With the introduction of Access 95, Access Basic has been replaced with Visual Basic for Applications (VBA). We detail the differences between Access Basic and VBA in Appendix D on the companion disk.

Which type of VBA event handler you use depends on your coding style. Many developers use all three or use some combination of them. For example, if you wish to call a generic function from a control's AfterUpdate event, you might use an event procedure that calls a function stored in a global module.

NOTE Report events are not discussed in this chapter. You can find a detailed discussion of these in Chapter 9.

Form Events

Three types of events can occur for a form:

- Form events
- Section events
- Control events

Form events are those events associated with the form itself. Some form events oc-cur for all forms (for example, Open and Close); others (GotFocus, LostFocus) occur only if the form contains no controls; while still others come into play only in cer-tain situations. (For example, the Timer event occurs only when the TimerInterval property is set to a nonzero value; the KeyDown, KeyUp, and KeyPress events oc-cur only when the KeyPreview property is set to True.) Table 2.2 provides a descrip-tion of each of the form events. (For more information on using Form, Section, and Control events, see Chapters 7 and 8.)

TABLE 2.2: Form Events

Event	Occurs	Can Be Canceled?
Current	When you move to a different record	No
BeforeInsert	When a new record is first dirtied	Yes
AfterInsert	After the new record is saved	No
BeforeUpdate	Just before edits to a record are saved	Yes
AfterUpdate	Just after edits to a record are saved	No
Delete	Just before each record is deleted. For multirecord deletes, occurs once per record	Yes
BeforeDelConfirm	After all records are deleted, but before the confirmation dialog	Yes

TABLE 2.2: Form Events (continued)

Event	Occurs	Can Be Canceled?
AfterDelConfirm	After the record is deleted or the deletion is canceled	No
Open	As the form is opened, but before data or controls are loaded	Yes
Load	After the form is loaded and the recordsource is opened	No
Resize	As the form is resized. Also occurs during form opening	Yes
Unload	When the form close is initiated, but before the form is actually closed	Yes
Close	When the form is closed, at the moment the form vanishes	No
Activate	When the form receives focus	No
Deactivate	When the form loses focus	No
GotFocus	After the form gets focus. Occurs only when the form contains no controls that can receive the focus	No
LostFocus	Before the form loses focus. Occurs only when the form contains no controls that can receive the focus	No
Click	When you click on the form's record selector or dead space* on a form	No
DblClick	When you double-click on the form's record selector or dead space* on a form	Yes**
MouseDown	When you click either mouse button on the form's record selector or dead space* on a form, but before the Click event fires	No
MouseMove	When you move the mouse over the form's record selector or dead space* on a form, but before the Click event fires	No
MouseUp	When you release either mouse button on the form's record selector or dead space* on a form, but before the Click event fires	No
KeyDown	If KeyPreview is True, whenever you depress a key anywhere on the form (If KeyPreview is False, KeyDown occurs only when you depress a key while the record selector is selected.)	Yes***

TABLE 2.2: Form Events (continued)

Event	Occurs	Can Be Canceled?
KeyUp	If KeyPreview is True, whenever you release a key (If KeyPreview is False, KeyUp occurs only when you release a key while the record selector is selected.)	No
KeyPress	If KeyPreview is True, whenever you depress and release an ANSI key (If KeyPreview is False, KeyPress occurs only when you depress and release a key while the record selector is selected.)	Yes****
Error	Occurs when the form causes a run-time data error. This includes validation and datatype errors, as well as most locking errors	No*****
Filter	When you choose to edit a filter, using either Records ➤ Filter ➤ Filter By Form or Records ➤ Filter ➤ Advanced Filter/Sort	Yes
ApplyFilter	When you apply a filter	Yes
Timer	When the timer interval has elapsed. You set the interval using the TimerInterval property	No

*Space that occurs when the form is sized larger than the height of its combined sections.

**Canceling this event cancels the second Click event.

***Keystroke (and KeyPress, Change, and KeyUp events) can be canceled by setting KeyCode to 0.

****Keystroke (and Change event) can be canceled by setting KeyAscii to 0.

*****Although you can't cancel Error, you can suppress the display of Access' error message.

Each section on a form also has events, which are described in Table 2.3. It's unlikely that section events will play a major role in your applications, since these events are rather limited, essentially revolving around mouse movement and clicking on the background of sections.

Although many events are common to most controls, each type of control has its own specific set of events, as well (and not all controls react to events at all). Table 2.4 shows which controls react to which events. Table 2.5 describes the control events.

TABLE 2.3: Section Events

Event	Occurs	Can Be Canceled?
Click	When you click on the background of a section	No
DblClick	When you double-click on the background of a section	Yes*
MouseDown	When you click either mouse button on the background of a section, but before the Click event fires	No
MouseMove	When you move the mouse over the background of a section	No
MouseUp	When you release either mouse button on the background of a section, but before the Click event fires	No

* Canceling this event cancels the second Click event

TABLE 2.4: Controls* and Events

Event	Label**, Image, or Box	Text Box	Option Group	Toggle Button, Option Button, or Check Box	Combo Box	List Box	Command Button	Object Frame	Subform
BeforeUpdate		✓	✓	I***	✓	✓		B****	
AfterUpdate		✓	✓	I	✓	✓		B	
Updated								✓	
Change		✓			✓				
NotInList					✓				
Enter		✓	✓	I	✓	✓	✓	✓	✓
Exit		✓	✓	I	✓	✓	✓	✓	✓
GotFocus		✓		✓	✓	✓	✓		
LostFocus		✓		✓	✓	✓	✓		
Click	✓	✓	✓	I	✓	✓	✓	✓	
DblClick	✓	✓	✓	I	✓	✓	✓	✓	
MouseDown	✓	✓	✓	I	✓	✓	✓	✓	
MouseMove	✓	✓	✓	I	✓	✓	✓	✓	
MouseUp	✓	✓	✓	I	✓	✓	✓	✓	
KeyDown		✓		✓	✓	✓		B	

TABLE 2.4: Controls* and Events (continued)

Event	Label**, Image, or Box	Text Box	Option Group	Toggle Button, Option Button, or Check Box	Combo Box	List Box	Command Button	Object Frame	Subform
KeyUp		✓		✓	✓	✓		B	
KeyPress		✓		✓	✓	✓		B	

*The following controls do not have any events: line and page break.

**Listed events are for free-standing labels. Labels attached to other controls have no events.

***I = only independent (when not a member of an option group) toggle button, option button, and check box controls have this event.

****B = occurs only for bound object frames.

TABLE 2.5: Control Events

Event	Occurs	Can Be Canceled?
BeforeUpdate	When you commit changes to a control by moving to another control or saving a record	Yes
AfterUpdate	After changes have been saved to a control	No
Updated	When you insert or update a source OLE object. May fire multiple times	No
Change	When data in control changes. May occur because a character was typed or a value was selected from the list	No
NotInList	When you enter a value in a combo box that is not in the list. Fires only when LimitToList is set to Yes	No*
Enter	When you have moved to a control that can receive the focus, but just prior to the control receiving the focus	No
Exit	When you have moved away from a control, but just prior to the control losing focus	Yes
GotFocus	After a control gets focus	No
LostFocus	Before a control loses focus	No
Click	When you click a control	No
DblClick	When you double-click a control	Yes**

TABLE 2.5: Control Events (continued)

Event	Occurs	Can Be Canceled?
MouseDown	When you depress either mouse button on a control, but before the Click event fires	No
MouseMove	When you move the mouse over a control	No
MouseUp	When you release either mouse button on a control, but before the Click event fires	No
KeyDown	When you depress a key while a control has focus	Yes***
KeyUp	When you release a key while a control has focus	No
KeyPress	When you depress and release an ANSI key while a control has focus	Yes****

*While you can't cancel NotInList, you can suppress the display of Access' error message.

**Canceling this event cancels the second Click event.

***Keystroke (and KeyPress, Change, and KeyUp events) can be canceled by setting KeyCode to 0.

****Keystroke (and Change event) can be canceled by setting KeyAscii to 0.

The Sequence of Events

Because there are so many events on Access forms, it can be difficult to determine which event is the one to which you really want to react. In addition, determining the exact sequence of events for a particular scenario—for example, the opening of a form—can be a chore. In the sections that follow, we describe which events occur for various scenarios. While this is not meant to be comprehensive, we have tried to include the most commonly encountered situations.

The easiest way to determine which events occur and in what order is to create a mechanism that will log events as they occur. In the CH02.MDB database you will find an event-debugging facility made up of two forms: frmLog and frmEventTest. These forms allow you to test various scenarios and see the resulting event sequence (see Figure 2.1). To use this facility, load frmLog and adjust the level of event detail by checking and unchecking the ShowEvents check boxes. Then, load frmEventTest and try different actions, noting the resulting events in frmLog.

FIGURE 2.1:

Each and every event that occurs while frmEventTest is active gets logged to frmLog.

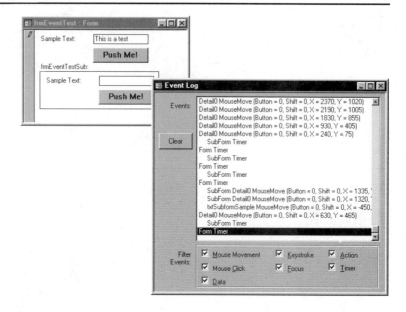

Figure 2.2 shows frmEventTest in Design view. We've created this facility by adding event procedures for each event on frmLog. The event procedures call the Log-Event subroutine found in the basEvents module that then logs the information to the list box on frmLog.

General Form Actions

The following sections describe the sequence of events that occurs when you open and close a form or perform other general form actions.

Opening a Form

When you open a form, the following events occur:

```
Open → Load → Resize → Activate → Current →
1st Control (in tab order) Enter →
1st Control (in tab order) GotFocus
```

You can cancel the opening of the form from the Open event.

FIGURE 2.2:

Event procedures are attached to every event on frmEventTest.

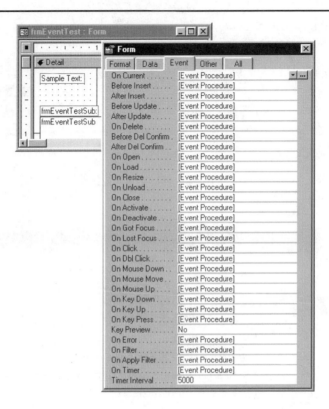

If the form contains a subform, the following events for the subform occur *prior* to the main form's Open event:

```
Open → Load → Resize → Current →
1st Control Enter → 1st Control GotFocus
```

During the Open event you don't normally have access to the values in the form's controls. If you need the control values, you should use the Load event instead. However, you can also force the Load event to occur within an event procedure attached to the Open event by using the following statement in the Open event procedure:

```
Me.SetFocus
```

Closing a Form

When you close a form, the following events occur:

```
Active Control Exit → Active Control LostFocus →
Unload → Deactivate → Close
```

This sequence assumes that any data on the form has already been saved. See the section "Data-Related Actions" later in this chapter for more details.

If the form contains a subform and one of the main form's controls has the focus, the following subform events occur *after* the main form's Close event:

```
Unload → Close
```

If the form contains a subform and one of the subform's controls has the focus, the following events occur (notice the addition of the main form's Exit event) instead:

```
Active Subform Control Exit → Active Subform Control LostFocus →
Form Exit → Form Unload → Form Deactivate → Form Close →
Subform Unload → Subform Close
```

Form Resizing Actions

When you minimize a form, the following events occur:

```
Resize → Active Control LostFocus → Deactivate
```

When you restore a minimized form, the following events occur:

```
Activate → Last Active Control GotFocus → Resize
```

When you maximize a form or restore a maximized form, the following form event occurs:

```
Resize
```

When you resize a form, one or more Resize events will fire. The number will be affected by the speed and area of the resize. If the change in area is large or the resize occurs slowly, more resize events will occur than if the change in area is small or the resize occurs quickly.

Changing the Visibility of a Form

When you hide a form, the following events occur:

```
Active Control LostFocus → Deactivate
```

When you unhide a form, the following events occur:

```
Activate → Last Active Control GotFocus
```

Shifting Focus to Another Form

When you shift the focus from one form to another, by clicking the title bar of the second form, the following events occur:

```
Active Control on 1st Form LostFocus → 1st Form Deactivate →
2nd Form Activate → Active Control on 2nd Form GotFocus
```

Keyboard Actions

When you type a character into a control that accepts keystrokes (see Table 2.4), the following events occur:

```
KeyDown → KeyPress → Change → KeyUp
```

When you press a keystroke that causes the focus to move to another control (for example, Tab, BackTab, or Enter), some of the keyboard events will be received by one control and others will be received by the second control:

```
1st Control KeyDown → 1st Control Exit →
1st Control LostFocus → 2nd Control Enter → 2nd Control GotFocus →
2nd Control KeyPress → 2nd Control KeyUp
```

If the first control were updated prior to the navigation keystroke, the first control's BeforeUpdate and AfterUpdate events would also fire between the KeyDown and Exit events.

Using the KeyPreview Property

The form object doesn't normally receive keystrokes unless you have set the KeyPreview property of the form to Yes. When this is set, the form receives all keystrokes typed into controls on the form prior to the controls' receiving those same keystrokes.

Canceling Keystrokes

If you set the KeyCode parameter passed to your KeyDown event procedure to 0, Access cancels the remaining events, and the keystroke will never appear on the screen.

If you set the KeyAscii parameter passed to your KeyPress event procedure to 0, Access cancels the Change event, and the keystroke will never appear on the screen.

If KeyPreview has been set to Yes and you set KeyCode for the form to 0 in an event procedure attached to the form's KeyDown event, the control's KeyDown event will receive a KeyCode of 0, and all other keyboard events will be canceled. Similarly, if KeyPreview has been set to Yes and you set KeyAscii for the form to 0 in an event procedure attached to the form's KeyPress event, the control's KeyPress event will receive a KeyAscii of 0, and the control's Change event will be canceled.

Using the KeyCode, KeyAscii, and Shift Parameters

You can use the KeyDown and KeyUp events to trap all keystrokes, including special non-ANSI keys, such as the function keys and the Ctrl, Shift, and Alt keys. You can determine which keys were pressed by investigating the KeyCode and Shift parameters that Access passes to your KeyDown and KeyUp event procedures. Microsoft has defined KeyCode constants you can use when checking for various keys. There are constants for alphanumeric keys (for example, vbKeyA and vbKey1) and special keys (for example, vbKeyBack, vbKeySpace, vbNumPad0, and vbKeyF10). You can find these constants and others listed in the Access for Windows 95 type library using the Object Browser (View ➤ Object Browser) or in the Help file by searching on constants, Microsoft Access Constants and then taking the See Also jump to Keycode Constants.

If you wish to check whether the Shift, Alt, or Ctrl key has been pressed in combination with another key, use the Shift parameter, applying the appropriate bit mask (acShiftMask, acCtrlMask, or acAltMask) to the passed parameter. For example, the following code sets three Boolean variables to match the state of the three corresponding Shift keys:

```
fShift = (Shift AND acShiftMask) <> 0
fCtrl = (Shift AND acCtrlMask) <> 0
fAlt = (Shift AND acAltMask) <> 0
```

KeyDown and KeyUp versus KeyPress

Unless you need to trap special (non-ANSI) keystrokes, you'll find it easier to react to the KeyPress and Change events in your applications. Access passes the

KeyPress event procedure the ANSI code of the key that triggered the event in the KeyAscii parameter. This parameter is similar to the KeyDown and KeyUp event procedures' KeyCode parameter, except that the KeyPress event never gets triggered for non-ANSI keys. In addition, KeyPress gets distinct codes for lower- and uppercase alphabetic characters. (KeyDown and KeyUp always get the hardware code of the key itself, not of the character that key represents; you must check whether the keystroke is lower- or uppercase by checking the Shift parameter.) Since the KeyPress event receives only ANSI keys, you can use the Chr() and Asc() functions to convert back and forth between the KeyAscii parameter and the equivalent ANSI character. For example:

```
strKey = Chr(KeyAscii)
KeyAscii = Asc(strKey)
```

Repeating Keyboard Events

If you press and hold down a key, the KeyDown event occurs repeatedly until you release the key, at which point the KeyUp event occurs. If the key is an ANSI key, the KeyPress and Change events also repeat.

Mouse Actions

When you move the mouse cursor over a section, control, or other part of a form, the MouseMove event for that object is triggered. More MouseMove events are triggered the further and more slowly the mouse is moved.

Mouse Click Actions

When you single-click the default (usually defined as the left) mouse button on a control, or the background of a section, or the record selector or dead space area of a form (the space that occurs when the form is sized larger than the height of its combined sections), the following events occur:

```
MouseDown  →  MouseUp  →  Click
```

Often you don't care about capturing the individual MouseDown and MouseUp events. In these cases you'll want to attach code to the Click event.

If one control has the focus and you click a second control, the following events occur instead:

```
1st Control Exit → 1st Control LostFocus →
2nd Control Enter → 2nd Control GotFocus →
2nd Control MouseDown → 2nd Control MouseUp → 2nd Control
Click
```

If the first control were updated prior to the mouse click, the first control's Before-Update and AfterUpdate events would also fire before the Exit event.

Keystrokes That Cause Command Button Click Events

For command buttons, the Click event occurs (in addition to several keyboard events) in the following situations:

- If the command button has the focus and the spacebar is depressed and released

- If the Default property of the command button is set to Yes and the Enter key is depressed and released

- If the Cancel property of the command button is set to Yes and the Esc key is depressed and released

- If you've included an ampersand (&) character in the Caption property of the control to define a command button accelerator key and you depress and release the accelerator key along with the Alt key

Mouse Double-Click Actions

If you double-click the default mouse button on a control other than a command button, the following events occur:

```
MouseDown → MouseUp → Click → DblClick → MouseUp
```

If you double-click a command button, an additional Click event occurs after the second MouseUp event. This makes it virtually impossible for you to assign different actions to the Click and DblClick events of a button: both events occur when you double-click the button. There's no easy way to *not* have that first Click event's procedure execute, somehow knowing that there's a DblClick event to follow.

Data-Related Actions

When you change the data on forms, Access generates several additional events at various levels. In this section we describe those events.

Access' Data Buffers

When you edit data on a bound form, Access maintains the following two buffers to support two levels of undo:

- Current record buffer
- Current control buffer

These buffers are depicted in Figure 2.3. When you move to a record, Access loads the values from the current record of the form's record source into the current record buffer. Then, as you move from field to field, Access loads the data from the current record buffer into the current control buffer.

When you change the value of a field and tab to another field, the control's Before-Update and AfterUpdate events occur. Between these two events, Access takes the value from the control buffer and uses it to replace the value in the record buffer. Similarly, when you save the current record—by explicitly saving the record, navigating to another record, or closing the form—Access replaces the data in the underlying record with the values in the current record buffer.

If, during the editing of data in a control, you press Esc or select Edit ➤ Undo, Access discards the contents of the current control buffer, refreshing it with the value from the current record buffer. If you press Esc a second time or select Edit ➤ Undo Record, Access discards the contents of the current record buffer, refreshing it with the values from the underlying record.

When using bound forms, you always edit the data in the control buffer; you never directly edit data in the underlying tables.

Changing Data in a Text Box

When you change the data in a text box control and tab to another control, Access triggers the following events (ignoring keyboard events):

```
1st Control Change (one for each typed character) →
1st Control BeforeUpdate → 1st Control AfterUpdate →
```

FIGURE 2.3:

Access maintains a two-level undo buffer for bound forms.

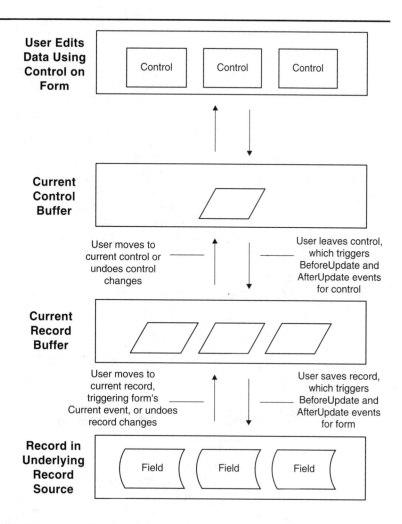

```
1st Control Exit → 1st Control Lost Focus →
2nd Control Enter → 2nd Control GotFocus
```

Combo Box Actions

When you select a value from a combo box control that already has the focus, the following events occur (ignoring keyboard, MouseDown, and MouseUp events):

```
BeforeUpdate → AfterUpdate → Click → Change
```

The Click event occurs even when you select the value using the keyboard.

When you type an entry in a combo box and tab to another control, the following events occur:

```
1st Control Change (one for each typed character) →
1st Control BeforeUpdate → 1st Control AfterUpdate →
1st Control Click → 1st Control Exit → 1st Control Lost Focus →
2nd Control Enter → 2nd Control GotFocus
```

When the LimitToList property has been set to Yes and you enter a value that is not in the list, the following events occur:

```
Change (one for each typed character) → NotInList → Form Error
```

You may wish to create an event procedure for the NotInList event that adds a new row to the underlying list in this circumstance. You can prevent the form's Error event from occurring by setting the Response parameter of the NotInList event procedure. (See Chapter 7 for more information.)

List Box Actions

When you select a value from a list box control that already has the focus, the following events occur (ignoring keyboard, MouseDown, and MouseUp events):

```
BeforeUpdate → AfterUpdate → Click
```

The Click event occurs even when you select the value using the keyboard.

BeforeUpdate versus AfterUpdate for a Control

In many situations you can use BeforeUpdate and AfterUpdate interchangeably, attaching code to either event. Sometimes, however, it *does* matter which event you react to.

You should use a control's BeforeUpdate event when you need to:

- Validate the value entered into a control. You can cancel the committed changes by setting the Cancel parameter to True in the control's Before-Update event procedure.

- Compare the changed value with the previous value (which is available by using the OldValue property of the control).

You should use a control's AfterUpdate event when you need to:

- Change the value the user entered
- React to a change in value

The BeforeUpdate and AfterUpdate events are not triggered when you change the value of a control programmatically.

BeforeUpdate versus AfterUpdate for a Form

You should use a form's BeforeUpdate event when you need to:

- Validate the data entered for the current record. You can cancel the changes by setting the Cancel parameter to True in the form's BeforeUpdate event procedure.
- Make changes to the data in the current record before the record is saved. For example, you might want to save the current date and time in an event procedure attached to the BeforeUpdate event. (If you made these changes in an event procedure attached to the AfterUpdate event, you could get into an infinite loop because your changes would continue to dirty the record and cause it to trigger the AfterUpdate event repeatedly.)

You should use a form's AfterUpdate event when you need to react to the saving of the record.

OLE Control Actions

When you insert an object into an empty bound object frame, the following event occurs:

```
Updated
```

When you change the source object of a bound object frame by double-clicking the control, editing the source, and returning to the form, the following events occur:

```
OLE Control Click → OLE Control DblClick →
OLE Control Updated (may occur multiple times)
```

The Updated event may occur multiple times if the source document changes are extensive.

The following additional events occur when you commit the changes by moving to another control:

```
OLE Control BeforeUpdate → OLE Control AfterUpdate →
OLE Control Click → OLE Control Exit →
OLE Control LostFocus → Other Control Enter →
Other Control GotFocus → OLE Control Updated (three times)
```

Additional events that occur for OLE custom controls are discussed in Chapter 21.

Saving and Navigating between Records

When you save the current record by either pressing Shift+Enter or selecting Records ➤ Save Record, the following events occur:

```
Control BeforeUpdate → Control AfterUpdate →
Form BeforeUpdate → Form AfterUpdate
```

If the current record is dirty (contains unsaved changes) and you move to another record, the following events occur:

```
Control BeforeUpdate → Control AfterUpdate →
Form BeforeUpdate → Form AfterUpdate → Control Exit →
Control LostFocus → Form Current → Control Enter →
Control GotFocus
```

When you navigate to another record without changing data in the current record, the following events occur:

```
Control Exit → Control LostFocus → Form Current →
Control Enter → Control GotFocus
```

Inserting a Record

The following events occur when you move to the new record:

```
Control Exit → Control LostFocus → Form Current →
Control Enter → Control GotFocus
```

When you then dirty the new record, the following event occurs (ignoring keyboard, MouseDown, and MouseUp events) prior to other events that would occur when changing data in a control:

```
Form BeforeInsert
```

Finally, when you save the new record, the following events occur:

```
Control BeforeUpdate → Control AfterUpdate →
Form BeforeUpdate → Form AfterUpdate → Form AfterInsert
```

Deleting a Record

When you delete the current record, the following events occur before the deletion confirmation dialog appears:

```
Control Exit → Control LostFocus → Form Delete →
Form Current → Control Enter → Control GotFocus →
Form BeforeDelConfirm → Form Error
```

For multirecord deletions, the Delete event occurs once per deleted record.

If the deletion is canceled, the following events occur:

```
Control Exit → Control LostFocus → Form AfterDelConfirm
```

If you have set the ConfirmRecordChanges option in the Edit/Find tab of the Tools ➤ Options dialog to False (or have used the SetOption method of the Application object to set the equivalent using VBA code), the BeforeDelConfirm and AfterDel-Confirm events are skipped. If you have set off warnings by using the SetWarnings method of the DoCmd object, BeforeDelConfirm and AfterDelConfirm events still occur, but the confirming dialog is skipped.

When the Delete event occurs, Access removes the record and stores it in a temporary buffer. You can cancel the Delete event (and restore the deleted record) by setting its Cancel parameter to True in an event procedure attached to this event. This will serve to cancel the delete operation and all subsequent deletion events.

You can also cancel the BeforeDelConfirm by setting its Cancel event to True. This also cancels the deletion, but the AfterDelConfirm will still occur. If you want to create your own custom deletion message, you should display it from an event procedure attached to the BeforeDelConfirm event. If you wish to continue the delete operation but suppress the built-in deletion message, set the Response parameter to the acDataErrContinue constant.

You can't cancel the deletion from the AfterDelConfirm event. The records have already been deleted (or the deletion has already been canceled). This is a good time, however, to react to the deletion. You can use the Status parameter that is passed to event procedures attached to this event to determine what happened. The value of Status can be

Constant	Meaning
acDeleteOk	The deletion occurred
acDeleteCancel	The deletion was canceled by your VBA code
acDeleteUserCancel	The deletion was canceled by the user

The Error Event

If you attach an event procedure to the form's Error event, your procedure will be called whenever a trappable error occurs while the form is running. You can use the DataErr parameter passed to your event procedure to determine which error has occurred and react accordingly. For example, you might use the MsgBox statement to provide a custom error message to the user. By setting the response parameter to the acDateErrContinue constant, you can tell Access to skip the display of the built-in error message. (See Chapters 8, 12, and 16 for more information on the Error event.)

The Indispensable Timer Event

The form's Timer event occurs only when you have set the TimerInterval property to a value greater than 0. This property—measured in milliseconds—determines how often the Timer interval fires.

The Timer event is useful for performing some action at regular intervals of time. For example, you could create a Timer event procedure that waited ten seconds and then closed the form. You could also use the Timer event to check on a regular basis to see whether some state was true and do something when this was the case. For example, you could create an automated import procedure that checked every ten minutes to see whether mainframe data had been downloaded to a certain file.

You can also use the Timer event to simulate user-defined events. The possibilities are endless. For example, you could create a user-defined "Locked" event by attaching code to the Timer event that checked once a second to see whether the current record had been locked by another user. Similarly, you could use the Timer event to simulate a "Dirty" event that occurred whenever a record was changed.

(You can find examples of using the Timer event to simulate Dirty and Locked events in Chapters 8 and 12, respectively.)

You can stop Access from triggering a form's Timer event by setting the TimerInterval property back to 0.

Actions That Can't Be Trapped

The following events cannot be trapped in Access:

- Selecting a menu command
- Scrolling
- Discarding changes using the Edit ➤ Undo command
- Clicking the right or middle mouse button
- Dirtying a record
- Another user's locking the current record
- Dragging and dropping an object
- Doing anything with toolbars

As mentioned in the preceding section, you can simulate some of these events by making use of the Timer event.

Summary

In this chapter we introduced you to the Access event model. We discussed

- The Access 95 event model
- Event handlers
- The different types of events that occur on forms
- The sequence of form events
- Access' data buffers
- Which actions in Access can't be trapped

PART II

Manipulating Data

CHAPTER

THREE

Database Design

- Database design and normalization theory

- Designing your databases: a practical, 20-step approach

- Normalizing a poorly designed database

Database design theory is a topic many people avoid learning; either they lack the time or they give up because of the dry, academic treatment the topic is usually given. Unfortunately, this is a recipe for disaster, because building databases without a solid understanding of relational database design theory is like building houses that lack solid foundations.

This chapter begins with an introduction to relational database design theory, including a discussion of keys, relationships, integrity rules, and the often-dreaded normal forms. The chapter then presents a practical step-by-step approach to good database design and furnishes an example that demonstrates how to normalize an existing, poorly designed database.

The Relational Model

The relational database model was conceived in 1969 by E.F. Codd, then a researcher at IBM. The model is based on branches of mathematics called set theory and predicate logic. The basic idea behind the relational model is that a database consists of a series of unordered tables (or relations) that can be manipulated using nonprocedural operations that return tables. This model was in vast contrast to the more traditional database theories of the time, which were more complicated and less flexible and were dependent on the physical methods used to store the data.

NOTE

It is commonly thought that the word *relational* in the relational model comes from the fact that you *relate* tables to each other in a relational database. Although this is a convenient way to think of the term, it's not accurate. Instead, the word *relational* has its roots in the terminology Codd used to define the relational model. The table in Codd's writings was actually referred to as a relation (a related set of information). In fact, Codd (and other relational database theorists) use the terms *relations, attributes,* and *tuples* where most of us use the more common terms *tables, columns,* and *rows,* respectively (or the more physically oriented—and thus less preferable for discussions of database design theory—*files, fields,* and *records*).

The relational model can be applied to both databases and database management programs themselves. The *relational fidelity* of database programs can be compared using Codd's 12 rules (since Codd's seminal paper on the relational model, the number of rules has been expanded to more than 300) for determining how DBMS products conform to the relational model. When compared with other database management programs, Access fares quite well in terms of relational fidelity. Still, it has a way to go before it meets all 12 rules completely.

Fortunately, you don't have to wait until Access is fully relational before you can benefit from the relational model. The relational model can also be applied to the design of databases, which is the subject of the remainder of this chapter.

Relational Database Design

When designing a database, you have to make decisions regarding how best to take some system in the real world and model it in a database. This process consists of deciding which tables to create and which columns they will contain, as well as the relationships between the tables. While it would be nice if this process were totally intuitive and obvious or, even better, automated, this is simply not the case. A well-designed database takes time and effort to conceive, refine, and build.

The benefits of a database that has been designed according to the relational model are numerous. Here are some of them:

- Data entry, updates, and deletions are efficient.

- Data retrieval, summarization, and reporting are efficient.

- Since the database follows a well-formulated model, it behaves predictably.

- Since much of the information is stored in the database rather than in the application, the database is somewhat self documenting.

- Changes to the database schema are easy to make.

The goal of this chapter is to explain the basic principles behind relational database design and demonstrate how to apply these principles when designing a database using Access. This chapter is by no means comprehensive and is certainly not definitive. Many books have been written on database design theory; in fact, many careers have been devoted to its study. Instead, this chapter is meant as an informal introduction to database design theory for the Access developer.

NOTE
For a more detailed discussion of database design, we suggest *An Introduction to Database Systems, Volume I,* **by C.J. Date (Addison-Wesley);** *SQL and Relational Basics* **by Fabian Pascal (M&T Books); or** *Database Processing: Fundamentals, Design, and Implementation* **by David M. Kroenke (Macmillan).**

Tables, Uniqueness, and Keys

Tables in the relational model are used to represent "things" in the real world. Each table should represent only one type of thing. These things (or *entities*) can be real-world objects or events. For example, a real-world object might be a customer, an inventory item, or an invoice. Examples of events include patient visits, orders, and telephone calls.

Tables are made up of rows and columns. The relational model dictates that each row in a table be unique. If you allow duplicate rows in a table, there's no way to uniquely address a given row programmatically. This creates all sorts of ambiguities and problems.

You guarantee uniqueness for a table by designating a *primary key*—a column or set of columns that contains unique values for a table. Each table can have only one primary key, even though several columns or combinations of columns may contain unique values. All columns (or combinations of columns) in a table with unique values are referred to as *candidate keys,* from which the primary key must be drawn. All other candidate key columns are referred to as *alternate keys.* Keys can be simple or composite. A *simple key* is a key made up of one column, whereas a *composite key* is made up of two or more columns.

The decision as to which candidate key is the primary one rests in your hands; there's no absolute rule as to which candidate key is best. Fabian Pascal, in his book *SQL and Relational Basics,* notes that the decision should be based on the principles of minimality (choose the fewest columns necessary), stability (choose a key that seldom changes), and simplicity/familiarity (choose a key that is both simple and familiar to users). For example, let's say a company has a table of customers called tblCustomer that looks like the table shown in Figure 3.1.

The best choice for primary key for tblCustomer would be CustomerId.

CustomerId	LastName	FirstName	Address	City	State	ZipCode	Phone
1	Litwin	Elizabeth	1313 Mockingbird Lane	New York	NY	11358	2068886902
2	Wirkus	Mark	45-39 173rd St	Redmond	WA	98119	2069809099
3	Hinton	Mike	2345 16th NE	Kent	WA	98109	2067837890
4	Litwin	Geoff	1313 Mockingbird Lane	New York	NY	11358	2068886902

tblCustomer : Table

Record: 1 of 4

Candidate keys for tblCustomer might include CustomerId, (LastName + First-Name), Phone, (Address, City, State), and (Address + ZipCode). Following Pascal's guidelines, you would rule out the last three candidates because addresses and phone numbers can change fairly frequently. The choice between CustomerId and the name composite key is less obvious and would involve trade-offs. How likely is it that a customer's name will change (for example, because of marriage)? Will misspelling of names be common? How likely is it that two customers will have the same first and last names? How familiar will CustomerId be to users? There's no right answer, but most developers favor numeric primary keys because names do sometimes change and because searches and sorts of numeric columns are more efficient than searches and sorts of text columns in Access (and most other databases) *AutoNumber* columns (referred to as counter columns in prior versions of Access) make good primary keys, especially when you're having trouble coming up with good candidate keys and no existing arbitrary identification number is already in place. Don't use an Autonumber column if you'll sometimes need to renumber the values or if you must have an automatically incrementing number with no gaps in the sequence of values.

Foreign Keys and Domains

Although primary keys are a function of individual tables, if you created databases that consisted only of independent and unrelated tables, you'd have little need for

Determining Which Type of AutoNumber Column to Use

The Counter field type has been renamed AutoNumber in Access 95. In addition, Microsoft has added two new field properties to the AutoNumber properties collection: FieldSize and NewValues.

You can set FieldSize to either Long Integer or Replication ID, with the default being Long Integer. Unless you're using the replication facilities of Access 95, you should leave this set to the default. (See Chapter 13 for more details on replication.)

You can set the NewValues property to Increment or Random. Prior versions of Access supported Increment only. Increment is a good choice when you want an AutoNumber column that increases by 1 for each new record and you want the number to approximate the number of records in the table. We use the term *approximate* here because an incrementing AutoNumber column will invariably contain gaps of records that were undone or deleted. You can't reuse the numbers that fall into these gaps.

A NewValues property setting of Random might be a better choice when you want to have data entered at multiple sites and then want to merge the separate databases at some later time (whether or not you are using Acess replication). In this situation an incrementing AutoNumber column won't work, because each copy of the database would be assigning the same numbers. If you used a random AutoNumber column, however, there's only a slight chance that each copy of the database would use the same number.

them. Primary keys become essential, however, when you start to create relationships that join multiple tables in a database. A *foreign key* is a column in one table that references the primary key of another table.

Continuing the example presented earlier, let's say you choose CustomerId as the primary key for tblCustomer. Now define a second table, tblOrder, that looks like the one shown in Figure 3.2.

FIGURE 3.2:

CustomerId is a foreign key in
tblOrder you can use to reference a
customer stored in tblCustomer.

OrderId	CustomerId	OrderDate
1	1	5/1/94
2	3	5/9/94
3	1	7/4/94
4	2	8/1/94
5	1	8/2/94
6	2	8/2/94

tblOrder : Table

Record: 1 of 6

CustomerId is considered a foreign key in tblOrder, since you can use it to refer to
a row in the tblCustomer table.

It is important that both foreign keys and the primary keys they reference share a common meaning and draw their values from the same domain. *Domains* are simply pools of values from which columns are drawn. For example, CustomerId is of the domain of valid customer ID numbers, which might in this case be Long Integers ranging between 1 and 50,000. Similarly, a column named Sex might be based on a one-letter domain made up of the letters *M* and *F*. You can think of domains as user-defined column types, the definition of which implies certain rules the columns must follow and certain operations you can perform on those columns.

Access supports domains only partially. For example, Access will not let you create a relationship between two tables using columns that do not share the same datatype (for example, text, number, date/time, and so on). On the other hand, Access will not prevent you from joining the Integer column EmployeeAge from one table to the Integer column YearsWorked from a second table, even though these two columns are obviously from different domains.

Relationships

You define foreign keys in a database to model relationships in the real world. Relationships between real-world entities can be quite complex, involving numerous entities, all having multiple relationships with each other. For example, a family has multiple relationships among multiple people—all at the same time. In a relational database such as Access, however, you only consider relationships between two tables at a time. These pairs of tables can be related in one of three different ways: one-to-one, one-to-many, or many-to-many.

In Access, you specify relationships using the Tools ➤ Relationships command. In addition, you can create ad hoc relationships at any point, using queries.

One-to-One Relationships

Two tables are related in a *one-to-one* (1→1) relationship if, for each row in the first table, there is at most one row in the second table. True one-to-one relationships seldom occur in the real world. This type of relationship is often created to get around some limitation of the database management software rather than to model a real-world situation.

In Access, 1→1 relationships may be necessary in a database when you have to split a table into two or more tables because of security or performance concerns or because of the limit of 255 columns per table. For example, in a medical research database you might keep most patient information in tblPatient but put especially sensitive information (for example, patient name, social security number, and address) in tblPtConfidential (see Figure 3.3). Access to the information in tblPtConfidential could be more restricted than for tblPatient. Tables in a 1→1 relationship should always have the same primary key, which serves as the join column.

FIGURE 3.3:

The tables tblPatient and tblConfidential have a one-to-one relationship. The primary key of both tables is PatientId.

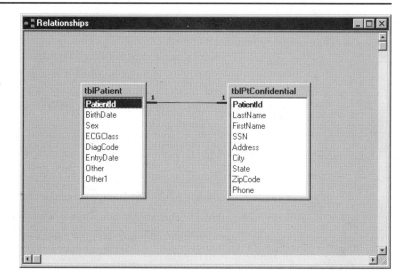

One-to-Many Relationships

Two tables are related in a *one-to-many* (1→M) relationship if, for each row in the first table, there can be zero, one, or many rows in the second table, but for each row in the second table, there is exactly one row in the first table. For example, each order for a pizza delivery business can have multiple items. Therefore, tblOrder is related to tblOrderDetail in a 1→M relationship (see Figure 3.4).

FIGURE 3.4:

There can be many detail lines for each order in the pizza delivery business, but each detail line applies to only one order. tblOrder and tblOrderDetail are therefore related in a one-to-many relationship.

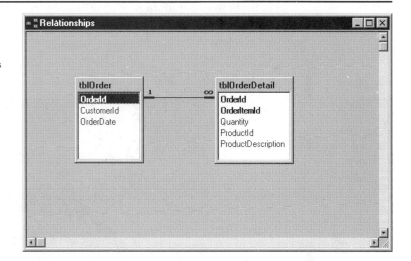

The 1→M relationship is also referred to as a *parent-child* or *master-detail* relationship. 1→M relationships are the most commonly modeled type of relationship. They are also used to link base tables to information stored in *lookup tables*. For example, tblPatient has short one-letter DischargeDiagnosis codes that can be linked to a lookup table, tblDiagCode, to get more complete diagnosis descriptions (stored in DiagnosisName). In this case tblDiagCode is related to tblPatient in a 1→M relationship. (That is, one row in the lookup table can be used in zero or more rows in the patient table.)

Many-to-Many Relationships

Two tables have a *many-to-many* (M→M) relationship when, for each row in the first table, there can be many rows in the second table, *and* for each row in the second table, there can be many rows in the first table. M→M relationships can't be directly modeled in relational database programs, including Access. These types of relationships must be broken into multiple 1→M relationships. For example, a patient may be covered by multiple insurance plans, and an insurance company covers multiple patients. Thus, the tblPatient table in a medical database would be related to the tblInsurer table using a M→M relationship. To model the relationship between these two tables, you would create a third table, a *linking table,* perhaps called tblPtInsurancePgm, that would contain a row for each insurance program under which a patient was covered (see Figure 3.5). Then the M→M relationship between tblPatient and tblInsurer could be broken into two 1→M relationships. (tblPatient would be related to tblPtInsurancePgm, and tblInsurer would be related to tblPtInsurancePgm, in 1→M relationships.)

FIGURE 3.5:

A linking table, tblPtInsurancePgm, is used to model the many-to-many relationship between tblPatient and tblInsurer.

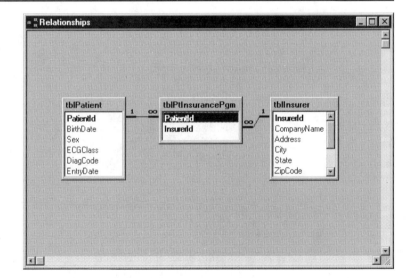

Normalizing a Set of Tables

As mentioned at the beginning of this chapter, when designing databases you are faced with a series of choices. How many tables will there be and what will they represent? Which columns will go in which tables? What will be the relationships between the tables? The answer to each of these questions lies in something called *normalization,* the process of simplifying the design of a database so it achieves the optimum structure.

Normalization theory gives us the concept of normal forms to assist in achieving the optimum structure. The *normal forms* are a linear progression of rules you apply to your database, with each higher normal form achieving a better, more efficient design. The normal forms are

- First Normal Form
- Second Normal Form
- Third Normal Form
- Boyce Codd Normal Form
- Fourth Normal Form
- Fifth Normal Form

In this chapter we discuss normalization through Third Normal Form.

Before First Normal Form: Relations

The normal forms are based on *relations,* special types of tables that have the following attributes:

- They describe one entity.
- They have no duplicate rows; hence there is always a primary key.
- The columns are unordered.
- The rows are unordered.

Access doesn't require you to define a primary key for each and every table, but it strongly recommends you do so. Needless to say, the relational model makes this an absolute requirement. In addition, tables in Access generally meet the third and fourth attributes listed above. That is, with a few exceptions, the manipulation of tables in Access doesn't depend on a specific ordering of columns or rows. (One notable exception is that encountered when you specify the data source for a combo or list box.)

> **NOTE**
>
> For all practical purposes, the terms *table* and *relation* are inter-changeable, and we use the term *table* in the remainder of this chapter. However, when we use the term *table,* we actually mean a table that also meets the definition of a relation.

First Normal Form

First Normal Form (1NF) says that all column values must be atomic. The word *atom* comes from the Latin *atomis,* meaning "indivisible" (or, literally, "not to cut"). 1NF dictates that for every row-by-column position, there exists only one value, not an array or list of values. The benefits from this rule should be fairly obvious. If lists of values are stored in a single column, there is no simple way to manipulate those values. Retrieval of data becomes much more laborious and less generalizable. For example, the table in Figure 3.6, tblOrder1, used to store order records for a hard-ware store, would violate 1NF.

You'd have a difficult time retrieving information from this table because too much information is stored in the Items column. Think how difficult it would be to create a report that summarized purchases by item.

1NF also prohibits the presence of *repeating groups* of information, even if they are stored in multiple columns. For example, you might improve upon the same table by replacing the single Items column with six columns: Quant1, Item1, Quant2, Item2, Quant3, Item3 (see Figure 3.7).

FIGURE 3.6:

tblOrder1 violates First Normal Form because the data stored in the Items column is not atomic.

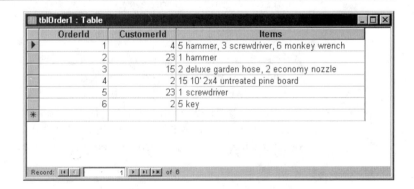

OrderId	CustomerId	Items
1	4	5 hammer, 3 screwdriver, 6 monkey wrench
2	23	1 hammer
3	15	2 deluxe garden hose, 2 economy nozzle
4	2	15 10' 2x4 untreated pine board
5	23	1 screwdriver
6	2	5 key

FIGURE 3.7:

A better, but still flawed, version of the Orders table, tblOrder2. The repeating groups of information violate First Normal Form.

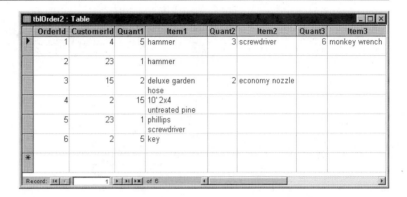

	OrderId	CustomerId	Quant1	Item1	Quant2	Item2	Quant3	Item3
▶	1	4	5	hammer	3	screwdriver	6	monkey wrench
	2	23	1	hammer				
	3	15	2	deluxe garden hose	2	economy nozzle		
	4	2	15	10' 2x4 untreated pine				
	5	23	1	phillips screwdriver				
	6	2	5	key				

Record: ◄◄ ◄ [1] ► ►► ►* of 6

While this design has divided the information into several columns, it's still problematic. For example, how would you go about determining the quantity of hammers ordered by all customers during a particular month? Any query would have to search all three Item columns to determine whether a hammer was purchased and then sum over the three Quantity columns. Even worse, what if a customer ordered more than three items in a single order? You could always add more columns, but where would you stop—10 items, 20 items? Say you decided a customer would never order more than 25 items in any one order and designed the table accordingly. That means you would be using 50 columns to store the item and quantity information for each record, even for orders that involved only one or two items. Clearly, this is a waste of space. And someday, someone would want to order more than 25 items.

Tables in 1NF do not have the problems of tables containing repeating groups. The table in Figure 3.8, tblOrder3, is in 1NF, since each column contains one value and there are no repeating groups of columns. To attain 1NF, we have added a column, OrderItemId. The primary key of this table is a composite key made up of OrderId and OrderItemId.

You could now easily construct a query to calculate the number of hammers ordered. Figure 3.9 shows an example of such a query.

FIGURE 3.8:

The tblOrder3 table is in First Normal Form, since all column values are atomic.

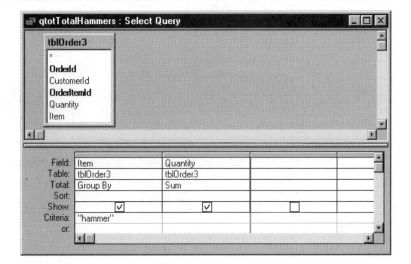

OrderId	OrderItemId	CustomerId	Quantity	Item
1	1	4	5	hammer
1	2	4	3	screwdriver
1	3	4	6	monkey wrench
2	1	23	1	hammer
3	1	15	2	deluxe garden hose
3	2	15	2	ecomomy nozzle
4	1	2	15	10' 2x4 untreated pine board
5	1	23	1	screwdriver
6	1	2	5	key

FIGURE 3.9:

Since tblOrder3 is in First Normal Form, you can easily construct a totals query to determine the total number of hammers ordered by customers.

Second Normal Form

A table is said to be in Second Normal Form (2NF) if it is in 1NF and every non-key column is fully dependent on the (entire) primary key. Put another way, tables should store data relating to only one "thing" (or entity), and that entity should be fully described by its primary key.

The table shown in Figure 3.10, tblOrder4, is a slightly modified version of tblOrder3. Like tblOrder3, tblOrder4 is in First Normal Form. Each column is atomic, and there are no repeating groups.

FIGURE 3.10:

The tblOrder4 table is in First Normal Form. Its primary key is a composite of OrderId and OrderItemId.

	OrderId	OrderItemId	CustomerId	OrderDate	Quantity	ProductId	ProductDescription
▶	1	1	4	5/1/94	5	32	hammer
	1	2	4	5/1/94	3	2	screwdriver
	1	3	4	5/1/94	6	40	monkey wrench
	2	1	23	5/9/94	1	32	hammer
	3	1	15	7/4/94	2	113	deluxe garden hose
	3	2	15	7/4/94	2	121	ecomomy nozzle
	4	1	2	8/1/94	15	1024	10' 2x4 untreated pine boards
	5	1	23	8/2/94	1	2	screwdriver
	6	1	2	8/2/94	5	52	key

tblOrder4 : Table — Record: 1 of 9

To determine whether tblOrder4 meets 2NF, you must first note its primary key. The primary key is a composite of OrderId and OrderItemId. Thus, in order to be 2NF, each non-key column (that is, every column other than OrderId and OrderItemId) must be fully dependent on the primary key. In other words, does the value of OrderId and OrderItemId for a given record imply the value of every other column for that record? The answer is no. Given the OrderId, you know the customer and date of the order, *without* having to know the OrderItemId. Thus, these two columns are not dependent on the *entire* primary key, which is composed of both OrderId and OrderItemId. For this reason tblOrder4 is not 2NF.

You can achieve Second Normal Form by breaking tblOrder4 into two tables. The process of breaking a non-normalized table into its normalized parts is called *decomposition*. Since tblOrder4 has a composite primary key, decomposition is simple: put everything that applies to each order in one table and everything that applies to each order item in a second table. The two decomposed tables, tblOrder and tblOrderDetail, are shown in Figure 3.11.

Two points are worth noting here:

- When normalizing, you don't throw away information. In fact, this form of decomposition is termed *non-loss* decomposition because no information is sacrificed to the normalization process.

- You decompose the tables in such a way as to allow them to be put back together using queries. Thus, it's important to make sure tblOrderDetail contains a foreign key to tblOrder. The foreign key in this case is OrderId, which appears in both tables.

The tblOrder table (top) and tblOrderDetail table (bottom) satisfy Second Normal Form. OrderId is a foreign key in tblOrderDetail that you can use to rejoin the tables.

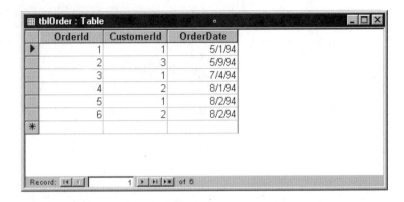

tblOrder : Table

OrderId	CustomerId	OrderDate
1	1	5/1/94
2	3	5/9/94
3	1	7/4/94
4	2	8/1/94
5	1	8/2/94
6	2	8/2/94

Record: 1 of 6

tblOrderDetail : Table

OrderId	OrderItemId	Quantity	ProductId	ProductDescription
1	1	5	32	hammer
1	2	3	2	screwdriver
1	3	6	40	monkey wrench
2	1	1	32	hammer
3	1	2	113	deluxe garden hose
3	2	2	121	ecomomy nozzle
4	1	15	1024	10' 2x4 untreated pine boards
5	1	1	2	screwdriver
6	1	5	52	key

Record: 1 of 9

Third Normal Form

A table is said to be in Third Normal Form (3NF) if it is in 2NF and if all non-key columns are mutually independent. One example of a dependency is a calculated column. For example, if a table contains the columns Quantity and PerItemCost, you could opt to calculate and store in that same table a TotalCost column (which would be equal to Quantity * PerItemCost), but this table wouldn't be in 3NF. It's better to leave this column out of the table and make the calculation in a query or on a form or report instead. This saves room in the database and keeps you from having to update TotalCost every time Quantity or PerItemCost changes.

Dependencies that aren't the result of calculations can also exist in a table. The tblOrderDetail table in Figure 3.11, for example, is in 2NF because all its non-key columns (Quantity, ProductId, and ProductDescription) are fully dependent on the primary key. (That is, given an OrderID and an OrderItemId, you know the values of Quantity, ProductId, and ProductDescription.) Unfortunately, tblOrderDetail also contains a dependency between two of its non-key columns, ProductId and ProductDescription.

Dependencies cause problems when you add, update, or delete records. For example, say you need to add 100 detail records, each of which involves the purchase of screwdrivers. This means you will have to input a ProductId code of 2 *and* a ProductDescription of "screwdriver" for each of these 100 records. Clearly, this is redundant. Similarly, if you decide to change the description of the item to "No. 2 Phillips-head screwdriver" at some later time, you will have to update all 100 records. As a further example, let's say you wish to delete all the 1994 screwdriver purchase records at the end of the year. Once all the records are deleted, you will no longer know what a ProductId of 2 is, since you've deleted from the database both the history of purchases and the fact that ProductId 2 means "No. 2 Phillips-head screwdriver." You can remedy each of these anomalies by further normalizing the database to achieve Third Normal Form.

> **NOTE**
>
> An *anomaly* is an error or inconsistency in the database. A poorly designed database runs the risk of introducing numerous anomalies. There are three types of anomalies: insert, delete, and update. These anomalies occur during the insertion, deletion, and updating of rows, respectively. For example, an insert anomaly would occur if the insertion of a new row caused a calculated total field stored in another table to report the wrong total. If the deletion of a row in the database deleted more information than you intended, this would be a delete anomaly. Finally, if updating a description column for a single part in an inventory database required you to make a change to thousands of rows, this would be classified as an update anomaly.

You can further decompose the tblOrderDetail table to achieve 3NF by breaking out the ProductId-ProductDescription dependency into a lookup table, as shown in Figure 3.12. This gives you a new detail table, tblOrderDetail1, and a lookup table, tblProduct. When decomposing tblOrderDetail, take care to put a copy of the linking column, in this case ProductId, in both tables. ProductId becomes the primary

FIGURE 3.12:

The tblOrderDetail1 table (top) and tblProduct table (bottom) are in Third Normal Form. The ProductId column in tblOrderDetail1 is a foreign key referencing tblProduct.

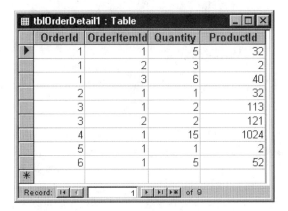

	OrderId	OrderItemId	Quantity	ProductId
▶	1	1	5	32
	1	2	3	2
	1	3	6	40
	2	1	1	32
	3	1	2	113
	3	2	2	121
	4	1	15	1024
	5	1	1	2
	6	1	5	52

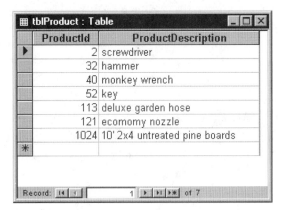

	ProductId	ProductDescription
▶	2	screwdriver
	32	hammer
	40	monkey wrench
	52	key
	113	deluxe garden hose
	121	ecomomy nozzle
	1024	10' 2x4 untreated pine boards

key of the new table, tblProduct, and becomes a foreign key column in tblOrderDetail1. This allows you to rejoin the two tables later using a query.

Higher Normal Forms

After Codd defined the original set of normal forms, it was discovered that Third Normal Form, as originally defined, had certain inadequacies. This led to several higher normal forms, including the Boyce/Codd, Fourth, and Fifth Normal Forms. This book does not discuss these higher normal forms because the discussion would require the introduction of additional terminology and concepts and, more important, because all that extra effort would give you very little added value over

3NF. Instead we direct you to the books listed in the section "Relational Database Design" earlier in this chapter. Still, several points are worth noting here:

- Every higher normal form is a superset of all lower forms. Thus, if your design is in Third Normal Form, by definition it is also in 1NF and 2NF.

- If you've normalized your database to 3NF, you've likely also achieved Boyce/Codd Normal Form (and maybe even 4NF or 5NF).

- To quote C.J. Date, the principles of database design are "nothing more than *formalized common sense.*"

- Database design is more art than science.

This last item needs to be emphasized. While it's relatively easy to work through the examples in this chapter, the process gets more difficult when you are presented with a business problem (or another scenario) that needs to be computerized (or downsized). We outline one approach later in this chapter, but first we must introduce the subject of integrity rules.

Integrity Rules

The relational model defines several integrity rules that, while not part of the definition of the normal forms, are nonetheless a necessary part of any relational database. There are two types of integrity rules: general and database specific.

General Integrity Rules

The relational model specifies two general integrity rules: entity integrity and referential integrity. They are referred to as general rules because they apply to all databases.

The *entity integrity rule* is very simple. It says that primary keys cannot contain null (missing) data. The reason for this rule should be obvious. You can't uniquely identify or reference a row in a table if the primary key of that table can be null. It's important to note that this rule applies to both simple and composite keys. For composite keys, none of the individual columns can be null. Fortunately, Access automatically enforces the entity integrity rule for you; no component of a primary key in Access can be null.

The *referential integrity rule* says that the database must not contain any unmatched foreign key values. This implies that

- A row may not be added to a table with a foreign key unless the referenced value exists in the referenced table
- If the value in a table that's referenced by a foreign key is changed (or the entire row is deleted), the rows in the table with the foreign key must not be "orphaned"

As defined by the relational model, three options are available when a referenced primary key value changes or a row is deleted:

- **Disallow:** The change is completely disallowed.
- **Cascade:** For updates, the change is cascaded to all dependent tables. For deletions, the rows in all dependent tables are deleted.
- **Nullify:** For deletions, the dependent foreign key values are set to null.

Access allows you to disallow or cascade referential integrity updates and deletions using the Tools ➤ Relationships command (see Figure 3.13). There is no Nullify option. In the example shown in Figure 3.13, any updates of CustomerId in tblCustomer will be cascaded to tblOrder. Since the Cascade Delete check box hasn't been checked, deletions of rows in tblCustomer will be disallowed if rows in tblOrder would be orphaned.

Database-Specific Integrity Rules

All integrity constraints that do not fall under entity integrity or referential integrity are termed *database-specific rules*, or *business rules*. This type of rule is specific to each database and comes from the rules of the business being modeled by the database. Nonetheless, the enforcement of business rules is just as important as the enforcement of the general integrity rules discussed in the previous section.

FIGURE 3.13:

FIGURE 3.13:

Specifying a relationship with referential integrity between the tblCustomer and tblOrder tables using the Tools ➤ Relationships command

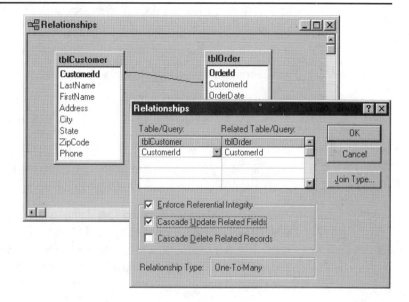

Starting with version 2.0, rules in Access are enforced at the engine level, which means that forms, action queries, and table imports can no longer ignore your rules as they could in version 1.x. Because of this change, however, column rules can no longer reference other columns or use domain, aggregate, or user-defined functions. Access supports the specification of a table rule you can use to check columns against each other.

Without the specification and enforcement of business rules, bad data will get into the database. The old adage "garbage in, garbage out" applies aptly to the application (or lack of application) of business rules. For example, a pizza delivery business might have the following rules that would need to be modeled in the database:

- The order date must always be greater than or equal to the date the business started and less than or equal to the current date.

- The order time and delivery time can occur only during business hours.

- The delivery date and time must be greater than or equal to the order date and time.

- New orders cannot be created for discontinued menu items.

- Customer zip codes must be within a certain range (the delivery area).

- The quantity ordered can never be fewer than 1 or greater than 50.

- Non-null discounts can never be smaller than 1 percent or greater than 30 percent.

Access supports the specification of validation rules for each column in a table. For example, the first business rule from the preceding list has been specified in Figure 3.14.

Access 2.0 added support for the specification of a global rule that applies to the entire table. This is useful for creating rules that cross-reference columns, as the example in Figure 3.15 demonstrates. Unfortunately, you can create only one global rule for each table, which can make for some awful validation error messages (for example, "You have violated one of the following rules: 1. Delivery Date >= Order Date. 2. Delivery Time > Order Time…").

FIGURE 3.14:
A column validation rule has been created to limit all order dates to sometime between the first operating day of the business (5/3/93) and the current date.

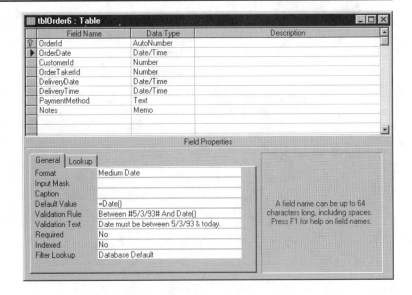

FIGURE 3.15:

A table validation rule has been created to require that deliveries be made on or after the date the pizza was ordered.

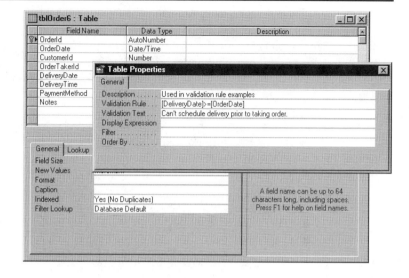

Although Access business rule support is better than most other desktop DBMS programs, it is still limited, so you will typically build additional business rule logic into applications, usually in the data entry forms. This logic should be layered on top of any table-based rules and can be built into the application using combo boxes, list boxes, and option groups that limit available choices; form-level and field-level validation rules; and event procedures.

TIP

Use application-based rules only when the table-based rules cannot do the job. The more you can build in business rules at the table level, the better, because these rules will always be enforced and will require less maintenance.

A Practical Approach to Database Design

As mentioned earlier in the chapter, database design is more art than science. While it's true that a properly designed database should follow the normal forms and the relational model, you still have to come up with a design that reflects the business you are trying to model. Relational database design theory can usually tell you what *not* to do, but it won't tell you where to start or how to manage your business. This is where it helps to understand the business (or other scenario) you are trying to model. A well-designed database requires business insight, time, and experience. Above all, it shouldn't be rushed.

To assist you in the creation of databases, we've outlined the following 20-step approach to sound database design:

1. Take some time to learn the business (or other system) you are trying to model. This usually means meeting with the people who will be using the system and asking them lots of questions.

2. On paper, write out a basic mission statement for the system. For example, you might write something like "This system will be used to take orders from customers and track orders for accounting and inventory purposes." In addition, list the requirements of the system. These requirements will guide you in creating the database schema (the definition of the tables) and business rules. Create a list that includes entries such as "Must be able to track customer addresses for subsequent direct mail."

3. Start to rough out (on paper) the data entry forms. (If rules come to mind as you lay out the tables, add them to the list of requirements described in step 2.) The specific approach you take will be guided by the state of any existing system:

   - If this system was never before computerized, take the existing paper-based system and rough out the table design based on these forms. It's very likely that these forms will be non-normalized.

   - If the database will be converted from an existing computerized system, use its tables as a starting point. Remember, however, that the existing schema will probably be non-normalized. It's much easier to normalize the database *now* than later. Print out the existing schema, table by table, and the existing data entry forms to use in the design process.

   - If you are starting from scratch (for example, for a brand-new business), rough out on paper the forms you envision using.

4. Based on the forms you created in step 3, rough out your tables on paper. If normalization doesn't come naturally (or from experience), you can start by creating one huge, non-normalized table for each form that you will later normalize. If you're comfortable with normalization theory, try to keep it in mind as you create your tables, remembering that each table should describe a single entity.

5. Look at your existing paper or computerized reports. (If you're starting from scratch, rough out the types of reports you'd like to see on paper.) For existing systems that aren't currently meeting user needs, it's likely that key reports are missing. Create them now on paper.

6. Take the roughed-out reports from step 5 and make sure the tables from step 4 include this data. If information is not being collected, add it to the existing tables or create new ones.

7. On paper, add several rows to each roughed-out table. Use real data if at all possible.

8. Start the normalization process. First, identify candidate keys for every table and, using the candidates, choose the primary key. Remember to choose a primary key that is minimal, stable, simple, and familiar. (See the section "Tables, Uniqueness, and Keys" earlier in this chapter.) Every table must have a primary key! Make sure the primary key will guard against all present *and* future duplicate entries.

9. Note foreign keys also, adding them if necessary to related tables. Draw relationships between the tables, noting whether they are 1→1 or 1→M. If they are M→M, create linking tables. (See the section "Relationships" earlier in this chapter.)

10. Determine whether the tables are in First Normal Form. Are all fields atomic? Are there any repeating groups? Decompose if necessary to meet 1NF.

11. Determine whether the tables are in Second Normal Form. Does each table describe a single entity? Are all non-key columns fully dependent on the primary key? Put another way, does the primary key imply all other columns in each table? Decompose to meet 2NF. If the table has a composite primary key, you should, in general, decompose the table by breaking apart the key.

12. Determine whether the tables are in Third Normal Form. Are there any computed columns? Are there any mutually dependent non-key columns? Remove computed columns. Eliminate mutually dependent columns by breaking out lookup tables.

13. Using the normalized tables from step 12, refine the relationships between the tables.

14. Create the tables using Access. Create the relationships between the tables using the Tools ➤ Relationships command. Add sample data to the tables.

15. Create prototype queries, forms, and reports. While you are creating these objects, design deficiencies should become obvious. Refine the design as needed.

16. Bring the users back in. Have them evaluate your forms and reports. Are their needs met? If not, refine the design. Remember to renormalize if necessary (steps 8–12).

17. Go back to the Table Design screen and add business rules.

18. Create the final forms, reports, and queries. Develop the application. Refine the design as necessary.

19. Have the users test the system. Refine the design as needed.

20. Deliver the final system.

This list doesn't cover every facet of the design process, but you may find it useful as a framework from which you can start.

Normalizing a Database with Existing Data

From time to time you may be faced with having to normalize a poorly designed database. You can usually accomplish this without loss of data by using a series of action queries. For example, you could normalize the version of the orders table (tblOrder4) shown earlier in Figure 3.10, taking it from 1NF to 3NF, using the following steps.

NOTE

Access 95 ships with a new Wizard, the Table Analyzer. You start the Table Analyzer by choosing the Tools ➤ Analyze ➤ Table command. If you run the Table Analyzer against tblOrder4 in automatic mode ("Yes, let the wizard decide."), you can see how it fares: not so well. The Wizard only knows how to remove lookup tables (taking you from 2NF to 3NF). If you use the Wizard in manual mode ("No, I want to decide.") against tblOrder4, you'll find you can use it to break out the product information, but you can't decompose tblOrder4 further into order and order detail components. Perhaps the next version of this Wizard will be a bit smarter.

1. Make a copy of your table and work on the copy. For example, we have made a copy of tblOrder4 and named it tblOrder5. At this time it's also a good idea to make a backup copy of the database. Store it safely in case you make a mistake.

2. Break out the item-related columns that are dependent on both OrderId and OrderItemId from tblOrder5 using a make-table query. This query, qmakOrderDetail5, will create tblOrderDetail5 and is shown in Design view in Figure 3.16. Don't delete any columns from tblOrder5 yet.

FIGURE 3.16:

The qmakOrderDetail5 make-table query copies item-related data to a new table as part of the normalization process.

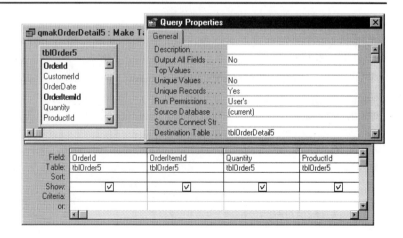

3. Move the product description information into a third table. Create this lookup table using a query based on tblOrderDetail5 with the UniqueValues property set to Yes. You use this type of query because you want only one record created for each instance of the ProductId code. This query, qmakProduct5, is shown in Design view in Figure 3.17. It creates the tblProduct5 lookup table. Don't delete any columns from tblOrderDetail5 yet.

4. Open the tblOrder5 table in Datasheet view and make certain it contains the required information. It's important that things look okay before you delete any columns from the tables. Repeat this step for tblOrderDetail5 and tblProduct5.(You should still see duplicate rows in tblOrder5 and tblOrderDetail5, which you will fix in the next two steps.) At this point you may find it helpful to create a select query that rejoins the three tables to help you make certain all is well.

5. Create a third make-table query based on tblOrder5 to create the final orders table, tblOrder5a. This query, qmakOrder5a, is shown in Design view in Figure 3.18. In this query include only columns that will be in the final orders table (OrderId, CustomerId, and OrderDate). Since tblOrder5 contains duplicate rows, you must set the UniqueValues property of the query to Yes.

6. Create one more make-table query to create the final normalized version of the order details table, tblOrderDetail5a. This query, based on tblOrderDetail5, is shown in Design view in Figure 3.19. In this query include only columns that should remain in the final order details table (OrderId, OrderItemId, Quantity, and ProductId).

FIGURE 3.17:

The qmakProduct5 make-table query copies product-related data to a new lookup table as part of the normalization process.

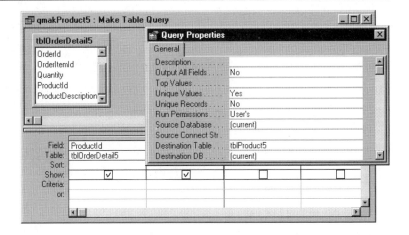

71

FIGURE 3.18:

The qmakOrder5a make table query creates the normalized version of the orders table.

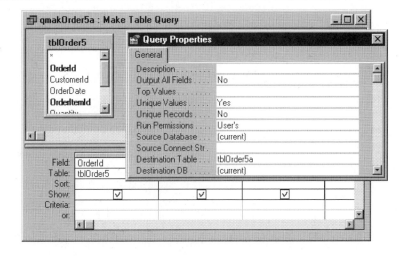

FIGURE 3.19:

The qmakOrderDetail5a make-table query creates the normalized version of the order details table.

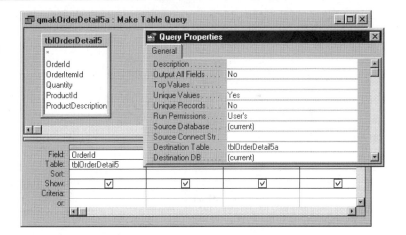

7. Open tblOrder5a, tblOrderDetail5, and tblProduct5, in turn, in Design view and define the primary key columns for each (OrderId, OrderId+Order-ItemId, and ProductId, respectively).

8. Create another select query that joins the three tables. If the datasheet looks okay, delete the original tables and rename the three new tables to their final names.

9. Create relationships between the tables using the Tools ➤ Relationships command. The screen in Figure 3.20 shows the relationships prior to renaming the tables.

FIGURE 3.20:

Relationships for the normalized tables, which are now in Third Normal Form

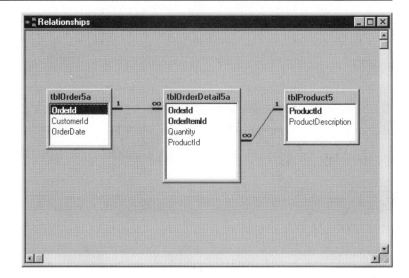

Breaking the Rules: When to Denormalize

Sometimes it's necessary to break the rules of normalization and create a database that is deliberately less normal than Third Normal Form. You'll usually do this for performance reasons or because the users of the database demand it. While this won't get you any points with database design purists, ultimately you have to deliver a solution that satisfies your users. If you do decide to break the rules and denormalize your database, it's important that you follow these guidelines:

- Break the rules deliberately; have a good reason for denormalizing.
- Be fully aware of the trade-offs this decision entails.
- Thoroughly document your decision.
- Create the necessary application adjustments to avoid anomalies.

When to Break the Rules

Here are two scenarios where you might choose to break the rules of normalization:

You decide to store an indexed computed column, Soundex, in tblCustomer to improve query performance, in violation of 3NF (because Soundex is dependent on LastName). The Soundex column contains the sound-alike code for the LastName column. It's an indexed column (with duplicates allowed), and it's calculated using a user-defined function. If you wish to perform searches on Soundex code with any but the smallest tables, you'll find a significant performance advantage in storing the Soundex column in the table and indexing this computed column. You'd likely use an event procedure attached to a form to perform the Soundex calculation and store the result in the Soundex column. To avoid update anomalies, you'll want to ensure that the user cannot update this column and that it is updated every time LastName changes.

To improve report performance, you decide to create a column named TotalOrderCost that contains a sum of the cost of each order item in tblOrder. This violates 2NF because TotalOrderCost is not dependent on the primary key of the table. TotalOrderCost is calculated on a form by summing the column TotalCost for each item. Since you often create reports that need to include the total order cost but not the cost of individual items, you break 2NF to avoid having to join these two tables every time this report needs to be generated. As in the preceding example, you have to be careful to avoid update anomalies. Whenever a record in tblOrderDetail is inserted, updated, or deleted, you will need to update tblOrder, or the information stored there will be erroneous.

This last point is worthy of elaboration. In most cases when you denormalize, you will be required to create additional application code to avoid insert, update, and deletion anomalies that a more normalized design would avoid. For example, if you decide to store a calculation in a table, you'll need to create extra event procedure code and attach it to the appropriate event properties of forms that are used to update the data on which the calculation is based.

If you're considering denormalizing for performance reasons, don't always assume the denormalized approach is the best. Instead, we suggest you first fully normalize the database (to Third Normal Form or higher) and then denormalize only if it becomes necessary for performance reasons.

If you're considering denormalizing because your users think they need it, investigate the reason. Often they will be concerned about simplifying data entry, which you can usually accomplish by basing forms on queries while keeping your base tables fully normalized.

Summary

This chapter has covered the basics of database design in the context of Microsoft Access. Here are the main concepts we covered:

- The relational database model, created by E.F. Codd in 1969, is founded on set theory and predicate logic. A database designed according to the relational model will be efficient, predictable, self documenting, and easy to modify.

- Every table must have a primary key that uniquely identifies each row.

- Foreign keys are columns used to reference a primary key in another table.

- You can establish three kinds of relationships between tables in a relational database: one-to-one, one-to-many, or many-to-many. Many-to-many relationships require a linking table.

- Normalization is the process of simplifying the design of a database so it achieves the optimum structure.

- A well-designed database follows the Normal Forms: First Normal Form requires all column values to be atomic; Second Normal Form requires every non-key column to be fully dependent on the table's primary key; Third Normal Form requires all non-key columns to be mutually independent.

- The entity integrity rule forbids nulls in primary key columns.

- The referential integrity rule says the database must not contain any unmatched foreign key values.

- A well-designed database implements business rules (domain integrity) and requires business insight, time, and experience.

- You can normalize a poorly designed database using a series of action queries.

- Sometimes you may need to denormalize a database. Always have a good reason, and fully normalize to Third Normal Form before denormalizing.

CHAPTER

FOUR

Queries and the Jet Engine

- Joining tables using inner, outer, and self joins

- Constructing totals and crosstab queries

- Using the different types of action queries

- Creating queries with run-time parameters

- Understanding how the Jet engine processes and optimizes queries

- Taking advantage of Rushmore query optimizations

Queries are one of the components of Access that set it apart from most other desktop databases and client-server front ends. While there are many similarities between an Access query and a "View" in SQL, Access queries are actually considerably more powerful. The result of an Access query is a *dynaset,* a two-way updatable *virtual table*—even when the query is based on multiple tables. In addition, Access queries can be built on top of other Access queries, up to 50 levels deep.

> **NOTE**
>
> In relational database terminology, a *View* refers to an abstract representation of one or more tables in a database. In standard SQL you create a view using the CREATE VIEW statement. In Access a *query* is equivalent to the relational View, but instead of the CREATE VIEW statement, Access uses a SQL SELECT statement for the query definition (or *querydef*). The term *dynaset* refers to the dynamic, updatable set of data (or view) returned by a query. The terms *View*, *query*, and *dynaset* are often used interchangeably. In this book we use the terms *query* and *querydef* to refer to the query's definition and *dynaset* (and the more general *recordset*) to refer to the results of a query.

When working in Access, be aware that queries take a much more prominent role in application design than in most other database programs. In most situations where a table is called for (for example, in a lookup table specification for a combo box control on a form or for the source of a report), you can use a query instead.

In this chapter we'll cover most of the different kinds of Access queries, including select, totals, crosstab, and action queries. In Chapter 5 we'll discuss the SQL-specific queries. This chapter does *not* attempt to cover query basics, however. If you're not already familiar with the creation of basic queries, we suggest you work through the Access manuals or consider buying an introductory text such as Alan Simpson's *Mastering Microsoft Access for Windows 95* (SYBEX, ISBN 1764-3).

You can find all the examples discussed in this chapter in the CH04.MDB sample database.

QBE versus SQL

You can create queries in Access using the visual query by example (QBE) designer—also known as Design view—or by directly entering structured query language (SQL) commands using the command-oriented SQL view (not to be confused with a SQL View). You can make edits to the query definition in either of the design views, switching between them as often as you like. Regardless of which view you use to create the query, Access maps the query definition internally to a SQL statement.

If you make changes to the SQL statement that Access can't map to the QBE grid—if you use the UNION clause, for example—Access disables Query Design view, and you can make further changes only by using SQL view. This doesn't necessarily mean the query is syntactically incorrect. Union queries, subqueries, SQL pass-through queries, and data definition queries all have no counterpart in Access QBE.

If you prefer, you can ignore QBE entirely and directly enter SQL statements from scratch into an empty SQL view window. Developers well versed in SQL may prefer this method for creating queries. However, Access SQL is a unique dialect that differs substantially from the ANSI standard. So if you have previous experience with SQL, you may want to read Chapter 5 prior to this chapter for a discussion of the differences between Access and ANSI SQL.

If you are new to either SQL or QBE (or find Access' departures from the standards confusing), you'll likely find SQL view invaluable. If, for example, you are comfortable with QBE but wish to learn more about SQL, just enter a query using QBE and then switch to SQL view to see how the SQL equivalent looks. On the other hand, if you have a long history of using SQL but you need to learn QBE, you can do just the opposite.

Choosing the Right Type of Join

By default, Access joins tables using an inner join. In an *inner join*, records are included in the dynaset only if a record in the first table matches a record in the second table. In addition to inner joins, Access supports two types of *outer joins:* left and right. In a *left outer join*, all records from the first (or left) table are included in the dynaset, even if some of the records from the first table do not match any records in the second table. In a left outer join, the "left" table is sometimes referred to as the *preserved* table. As you might guess, the opposite is true for the right outer join. In a *right outer join,* the second (or right) table is preserved. That is, all records from the "right" table are preserved in the dynaset, even if some of its records do not match any records in the first table. Another type of join, the *full outer join,* would include all matching records, plus all records that do not match from each of the two tables. Access does *not* support this type of outer join.

> **TIP**
>
> Although Access does not directly support full outer joins, you can create a left outer join query and a right outer join query and then splice the two queries together using a union query. See the section "Union Queries" in Chapter 5 for more details.

Unless you specify otherwise, all joins in Access are inner joins. To create an outer join in Access, you double-click the join line connecting two tables. The Join Properties dialog is displayed (see Figure 4.1) for a join between the tables tblOrder1993 and tblCustomer. In this dialog, the options are as follows:

- The inner join (the default) is option 1. (Only include rows where the joined fields from both tables are equal.)

FIGURE 4.1:

The Join Properties dialog box for the join of tblOrder1993 and tblCustomer is shown here for qryOrder1993_LJ_Customer. A left outer join has been selected for this query.

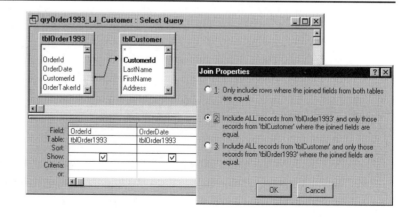

- The left outer join option is option 2. (Include ALL records from tblOrder-1993 and only those records from tblCustomer where the joined fields are equal.)

- The right outer join option is presented as option 3. (Include ALL records from tblCustomer and only those records from tblOrder1993 where the joined fields are equal.)

TIP Which table is considered the "left" table for outer joins in the Join Properties dialog has nothing to do with the physical ordering of tables in the table pane of query design. For preexisting relationships, Access always designates the primary table (as defined using the Tools ➤ Relationships command) as the left table. For ad hoc joins, Access considers the table containing the field you dragged the join line *from* to be the left table. For both types of joins, the actual physical order of the tables in the table pane is immaterial. For the sake of simplicity, however, it's a good practice always to put the primary table on the left side of any join lines. Following this scheme guarantees that option 2 of the Join Properties dialog is always the left outer join, no matter how you define *left.*

The three types of Access joins are best explained using an example based on the tables shown in Figure 4.1. The first table, tblOrder1993, consists of a set of 5 archived order records from 1993, and tblCustomer contains 12 customer records. Because tblOrder1993 contains archived records, it references several customer IDs that are no longer in tblCustomer. In addition, there are several new customers in tblCustomer who have no corresponding records in tblOrder1993. (If we had used tblOrder in this example instead of tblOrder1993, we couldn't have had any orders with nonexistent customer records, because there is a referential integrity–enforced relationship between these two tables.) These two tables and their records are shown in Figure 4.2. The dynasets returned by an inner join of the two tables (qryOrder1993_IJ_Customer), a left outer join (qryOrder1993_LJ_Customer), and a right outer join (qryOrder1993_RJ_Customer) are shown in Figure 4.3.

FIGURE 4.2:

The records in tblOrder1993 (top) and tblCustomer (bottom)

tblOrder1993 : Table

	OrderId	OrderDate	CustomerId	OrderTakerId	DeliveryDate
▶	1	10/15/93	1	2	10/15/93
	2	10/15/93	2	2	10/15/93
	5	11/1/93	13	3	11/2/93
	6	11/6/93	14	7	11/6/93
	7	1/15/93	5	4	1/17/93
*	(AutoNumber)				

Record: ◄◄ ◄ 1 ► ►► ►* of 5

tblCustomer : Table

	CustomerId	LastName	FirstName	Address	City
▶	1	Johnson	Alicia	1313 Mockingbird Lan	Seattle
	2	Reddick	Greg	45-39 173rd St	Redmond
	3	Stevens	Ken	2345 16th NE	Kent
	4	Jones	Jerry	2525 12th Ave W	Seattle
	5	Smith	Myrna	201 3rd Ave, #2109	Seattle
	6	Jenning	Roger	1312 45th Ave NE	Seattle
	7	Fallon	Jane	3434 34th Ave, #B-4	Redmond
	8	Phoner	Phil	2 Elm Street	Bellevue
	9	Jones	Bert	3456 NW 92nd	Seattle
	10	Babitt	Lucy	1919 24th NW	Seattle
	11	Litwin	Paul	2529 12th Ave West	Seattle
	12	Ayala	Steve	1919 South Plum	Woodinvil
*					

Record: ◄◄ ◄ 1 ► ►► ►* of 12

For the inner join query, qryOrder1993_IJ_Customer, only matching records from both tables are included in the dynaset. You might use this query to list old orders of current customers.

The left outer join query, qryOrder1993_LJ_Customer, might be used to create a list of *all* archived order records, even if the customer has no matching record in tblCustomer. Finally, the right outer join query, qryOrder1993_RJ_Customer, might be used to create a list of *all* customers and their archived orders, if they have any.

FIGURE 4.3:

A set of queries joining the tblOrder1993 and tblCustomer tables. The inner, or natural, join, qryOrder1993_IJ_Customer, returns only matching records from both tables (shown at the top of the figure). In the middle of the figure is the left outer join query, qryOrder1993_LJ_Customer. The bottom is the right outer join, qryOrder1993_RJ_Customer.

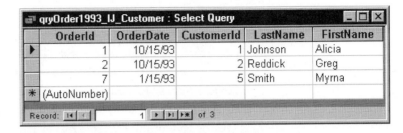

qryOrder1993_IJ_Customer : Select Query

	OrderId	OrderDate	CustomerId	LastName	FirstName
▶	1	10/15/93	1	Johnson	Alicia
	2	10/15/93	2	Reddick	Greg
	7	1/15/93	5	Smith	Myrna
*	(AutoNumber)				

Record: 1 of 3

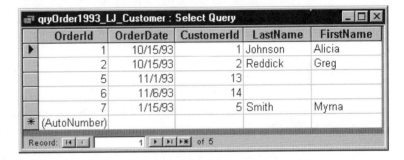

qryOrder1993_LJ_Customer : Select Query

	OrderId	OrderDate	CustomerId	LastName	FirstName
▶	1	10/15/93	1	Johnson	Alicia
	2	10/15/93	2	Reddick	Greg
	5	11/1/93	13		
	6	11/6/93	14		
	7	1/15/93	5	Smith	Myrna
*	(AutoNumber)				

Record: 1 of 5

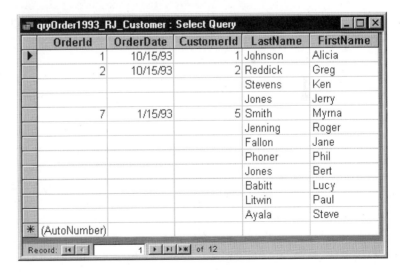

qryOrder1993_RJ_Customer : Select Query

	OrderId	OrderDate	CustomerId	LastName	FirstName
▶	1	10/15/93	1	Johnson	Alicia
	2	10/15/93	2	Reddick	Greg
				Stevens	Ken
				Jones	Jerry
	7	1/15/93	5	Smith	Myrna
				Jenning	Roger
				Fallon	Jane
				Phoner	Phil
				Jones	Bert
				Babitt	Lucy
				Litwin	Paul
				Ayala	Steve
*	(AutoNumber)				

Record: 1 of 12

TIP

When you've selected an outer join, Access displays a line with an arrowhead at one end. For left outer joins, Access displays a right-pointing arrow at the right side of the join line (see Figure 4.1). Conversely, Access displays a left-pointing arrowhead at the left side of the join line for right outer joins. Confusing, isn't it? Not really, if you think of the arrow as always pointing away from the table that includes all records and toward the table that includes only matching records.

Inner joins are, by far, the most common type of join. That's why they are also sometimes called natural joins.

NOTE

If you create queries with at least three tables and one or more outer joins, you may encounter the dreaded "Query contains ambiguous outer joins" error message. This misnamed error message occurs because there are restrictions on how you may combine multiple outer joins in a query. These restrictions are detailed in the section "Multiple Joins" in Chapter 5.

Self Joins: Joining a Table to Itself

Sometimes it is necessary to join a table to itself in order to answer a question. Although *self joins* are not as common as inter-table joins, they are nonetheless useful—for example, for answering certain types of queries where you have recursive relationships or where you wish to pull together and "flatten" multiple rows from a table. For instance, in a database in which you stored multiple addresses of a customer in separate rows of an address table, you could use a self join to pull together into a single record both home and work addresses. The trick to creating self joins in QBE is to alias the second copy of a table so it is treated as though it were a separate table.

TIP

When you drop multiple copies of a table into a query, Access creates an alias so that each copy is uniquely named. For example, the second copy of tblEmployee would be named tblEmployee_1, the third copy would be named tblEmployee_2, and so on. You can change the alias of a table by altering the Alias property of the table's field list properties. (See the section "Using Properties to Customize the Behavior of Queries" later in this chapter.) You'll probably find it easier to remember which copy of the table is which when you've aliased the second copy as tblSupervisor instead of the more confusing tblEmployee_1.

For example, EmployeeId is the primary key for the table tblEmployee in CH4.MDB. This table also contains a column, SupervisorId, for recording the EmployeeId of each employee's supervisor. Thus, the table contains a recursive relationship between SupervisorId and EmployeeId. (It's important that these two columns come from the same domain—that is, SupervisorId must be based on the same domain as EmployeeId. See Chapter 3 for a discussion of domains.) Say you wished to view the names of all employees and the names of their direct superiors, even if an employee lacked a superior. This last requirement means you need to use an outer self join to create the query. Self joins can use inner joins or left or right outer joins just like other (non–self-join) queries.

The Query Design view for such a query is shown in Figure 4.4. Its datasheet is shown in Figure 4.5.

TIP

You can define recursive relationships, such as the one between SupervisorId and EmployeeId, using the Tools ➤ Relationships command. You can even have Access enforce referential integrity for recursive relationships so that, for example, users are prevented from entering the supervisor number of an employee that doesn't exist.

FIGURE 4.4:

The qryEmployees&Supervisors query in Design view. This query joins tblEmployee to itself using a left outer join to produce a list of all employees and their supervisors, even if they don't have a supervisor.

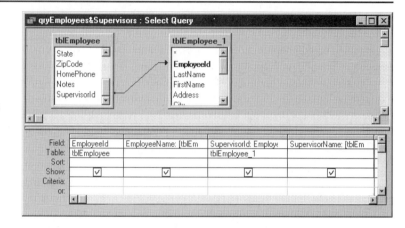

FIGURE 4.5:

The qryEmployees&Supervisors datasheet displays all employees and their supervisors.

EmployeeId	EmployeeName	SupervisorId	SupervisorName
1	Mary Jones		
2	Steve Alabaster	1	Mary Jones
5	Beth Peters	1	Mary Jones
6	Phil Carey	1	Mary Jones
3	Rita Lovely	5	Beth Peters
4	Alan Ronald	5	Beth Peters
7	Joe Peters	5	Beth Peters

Record: |◄| ◄ | 1 | ► |►|►*| of 7

Aggregate Queries: Totals and Crosstab

You use *aggregate queries* to summarize and analyze data. You can use them to spot trends in your data, to generate summary statistics, and as the source for summary reports and graphs.

Aggregate queries are very different from ordinary select queries because you can use them to condense data contained in hundreds, thousands, or even millions of rows into a few screens of useful information. When you run aggregate queries, you'll notice that none of the fields in the query's datasheet are updatable. This occurs because the data has been aggregated or summarized and therefore each output row no longer points back to a single row from the original table.

If you need to analyze the data you collect in your Access databases, you'll find aggregate queries indispensable. The two types of aggregate queries in Access are totals and crosstab queries. The next two sections discuss the details of these queries.

Totals Queries

You change a regular select query to a totals query by choosing View ➤ Totals or clicking the Sigma icon on the Query Design toolbar. The first thing you will notice when you turn on Totals is that a new row, Total, appears in the query grid just above the Sort row.

A totals query is commonly used to summarize the data across multiple records and produce summary statistics. For example, suppose you wanted to count the number of orders by the method the customer used to pay for the order (for example, check, cash, or credit card). You could create a query such as qtotPaymentMethod, shown in Design view in Figure 4.6 and in Datasheet view in Figure 4.7.

FIGURE 4.6:

The qtotPaymentMethod query in Design view. This query counts the number of orders placed using each payment method.

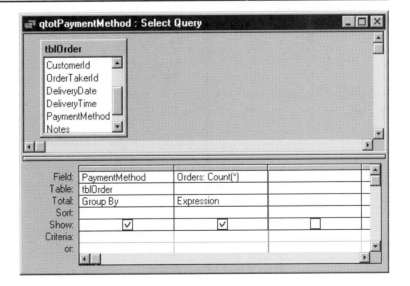

FIGURE 4.7:
The qtotPaymentMethod datasheet. This totals query displays a frequency distribution of payment method.

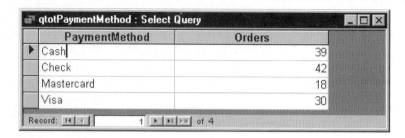

Here are the basic steps for creating a totals query:

1. Create a new select query and add any necessary tables.

2. Drag to the query grid any fields that will be used to define the groups.

3. Change the type of query to a totals query. Any columns you added to the query grid should have Group By selected for the Total cell.

4. Decide what you wish to appear in each cell of the query's datasheet. If you wish to use an aggregate function, choose a column to aggregate on and select the appropriate aggregate function for the Total cell. You can also use a custom expression, in which case you would enter the expression in the Field cell and select Expression for the Total cell.

5. Set any criteria desired and run the query.

Totals Options

In totals queries, every field in the query grid (table fields and calculated fields) must have a Total row option selected. By default, Access assigns table fields the Group By option and calculated fields the Expression option. The three types of totals options are

- Group By, for defining grouping levels

- Aggregate functions (Count, Sum, Min, Max, First, Last, Avg, StDev, Var, and Expression), for computing summary statistics for each group

- Where, for specifying criteria on fields for which you do not wish to define groups

Table 4.1 outlines the use of these options.

TABLE 4.1: The Totals Query Options and When to Use Them

Totals Option	When to Use It
Group By	To define the groups for which you wish to calculate totals. If you choose only one Group By field, Access creates a group (a row in the recordset) for each unique value of that field. If you choose multiple Group By fields, a group will be created for each unique combination of values of the grouping fields
Count	To calculate the number of records with non-null values for a group
Sum	To calculate the sum of the values for a field in each group. Null values are not counted
Min	To calculate the smallest value for a field in each group. Null values are not counted
Max	To calculate the largest value for a field in each group. Null values are not counted
First	To calculate the first value (in whatever order the records are output) for a field in each group. Note how this differs from Min. Null values are not counted
Last	To calculate the last value (in whatever order the records are output) for a field in each group. Note how this differs from Max. Null values are not counted
Avg	To calculate the average of the values for a field in each group. The average is a statistical estimate of the center (or the mean) of the distribution of values in a group. Null values are not counted
StDev	To calculate the standard deviation for a field in each group. The standard deviation is a statistical estimate of the dispersion of the distribution of values in a group. Larger values indicate a group with a great variation in values. Null values are not counted
Var	To calculate the variance for a field in each group. The variance is the square of the standard deviation. Null values are not counted
Expression	To calculate a custom aggregate expression. One special case of a custom expression is Count(*), which counts the total number of rows in a group, including rows with null values in one or more fields
Where	To specify criteria that limit the records in the recordset without using the fields to define groups. When you use this option, you must also clear the check box in the Show row

TIP The Jet database engine (see the section "Query Execution and the Jet Engine" later in this chapter) has built-in optimizations for aggregate counts of the form Count(*), which counts all rows in the table meeting any optional criteria. Because of these optimizations, queries using this form of Count are significantly faster than those using Count([*column*]). (These two forms of Count yield the same results if there are no nulls in *column*.)

Sorting Totals Queries

When you use multiple Group By fields without any Sort fields, Access sorts and groups the data in the order in which the fields appear on the query grid (from left to right). If you're using aggregate queries to spot trends in the data, you may wish to try different orderings of the Group By fields. For example, if you wanted to summarize the sales for each employee by month, you could choose to group by month and then by employee (see Figure 4.8, qtotSalesByMonth&Employee) or by employee and month (see Figure 4.9, qtotSalesByEmployee&Month). The first

qtotSalesByMonth&Employee : Select Query

Month	Employee	Sales
1	Alabaster, Steve	$360.41
1	Jones, Mary	$117.40
1	Lovely, Rita	$89.16
1	Peters, Beth	$19.22
1	Peters, Joe	$10.38
1	Ronald, Alan	$200.92
2	Alabaster, Steve	$398.45
2	Jones, Mary	$91.55
2	Lovely, Rita	$164.82
2	Peters, Beth	$474.93
2	Peters, Joe	$157.19
2	Ronald, Alan	$310.92
3	Alabaster, Steve	$48.77
3	Carey, Phil	$163.76
3	Jones, Mary	$69.92
4	Alabaster, Steve	$59.40
4	Jones, Mary	$51.40

Record: 1 of 51

FIGURE 4.8: Because qtotSalesByMonth-&Employee groups the data by month first and then by employee, you can use it to easily compare different employees' sales for any given month.

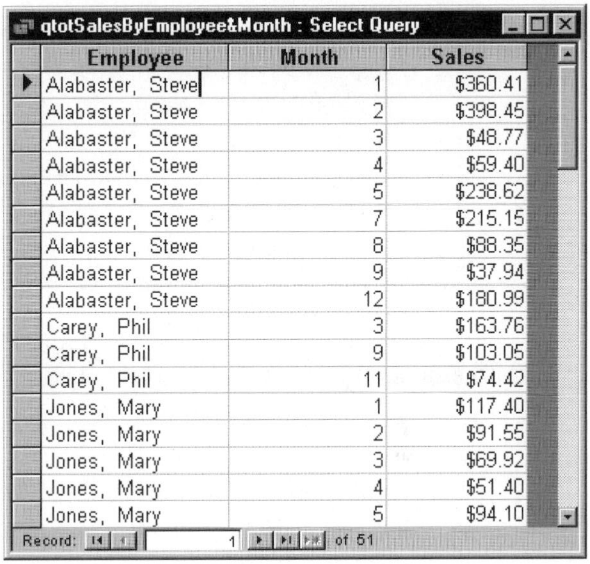

qtotSalesByEmployee&Month : Select Query

Employee	Month	Sales
Alabaster, Steve	1	$360.41
Alabaster, Steve	2	$398.45
Alabaster, Steve	3	$48.77
Alabaster, Steve	4	$59.40
Alabaster, Steve	5	$238.62
Alabaster, Steve	7	$215.15
Alabaster, Steve	8	$88.35
Alabaster, Steve	9	$37.94
Alabaster, Steve	12	$180.99
Carey, Phil	3	$163.76
Carey, Phil	9	$103.05
Carey, Phil	11	$74.42
Jones, Mary	1	$117.40
Jones, Mary	2	$91.55
Jones, Mary	3	$69.92
Jones, Mary	4	$51.40
Jones, Mary	5	$94.10

Record: 1 of 51

FIGURE 4.9:
Because qtotSalesByEmployee&Month groups the data by employee first and then by month, you can use it to show month-to-month sales growth for any given employee.

option would make it easy to make employee-to-employee sales comparisons for a given month, and the second option would make it easy to track monthly sales growth for each employee. A third option would be to use a crosstab query, as discussed later in this chapter.

Access follows these rules when determining how to sort the recordsets for totals queries:

- If you don't specify any sorting, Access sorts Group By fields in ascending order, using a left-to-right precedence when there are multiple Group By fields.
- If you specify sorting on *all* Group By fields, Access sorts them in the chosen order (ascending or descending), again using a left-to-right precedence when there are multiple Group By fields.
- If you specify sorting on *some* but not all Group By fields, on aggregate fields only, or on some combination of Group By fields and aggregate fields, Access sorts only those fields with specified sorts.

TIP You may find it useful to sort by the results of a totals query—one of the aggregate fields—instead of by the Group By fields. For example, if you calculated sales totals, TotalSales, grouped by EmployeeName, you might want to sort by TotalSales in descending order rather than by EmployeeName. This would list employees in order of sales performance rather than alphabetically (which would be the default if no sorting were specified).

Controlling Criteria Timing

In an aggregate query, by changing the placement of your criteria you can control when those criteria are applied. Any criteria placed on fields with the Group By or Where option are applied *prior* to any grouping, whereas criteria placed on aggregate functions (Count, Sum, Min, Max, First, Last, Avg, StDev, Var, and Expression) are applied *after* the aggregation of data.

For example, say you wished to count the total number of pizza orders by employee and type of pizza, but only if an employee sold a given type of pizza more than once. Such a query might be constructed like qtotPizzaSalesByEmployee, which is shown in both Design and Datasheet views in Figure 4.10. The >1 in the aggregate Total Sold column implies that you want Access to group by employee and pizza type and then count the number of pizzas sold, including a group only if the total number of pizzas sold exceeds 1. Criteria placed on aggregate fields are equivalent to using the SQL HAVING clause.

There will also be times when you wish criteria to be applied prior to the aggregation of data. In this case you must place the criteria on Group By or Where fields. For example, suppose you created the same query as above but you wished to count individual orders only if more than one pizza was sold *for that order*. A query that does just this, qtotMultPizzaSalesByEmployee, is shown in both Design and Datasheet views in Figure 4.11. This is accomplished by removing the ">1" criterion from under Total Sold and placing it under a nonaggregated copy of Quantity using the Where option. Fields with the Where option selected are used only for applying criteria and will not show up in the query's output. In SQL, Where option fields are equivalent to placing the criteria in the WHERE clause.

FIGURE 4.10:

The qtotPizzaSalesByEmployee query totals the orders for each combination of pizza and employee. A group is included only if the total quantity sold for the entire group is greater than one pizza.

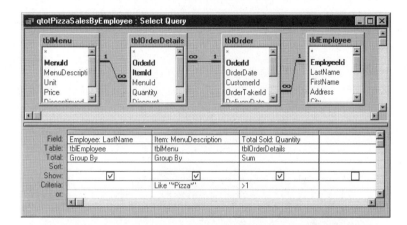

> **NOTE**   Criteria placed on grouping fields—even though these types of criteria are applied *before* the groups are created—show up in SQL in the HAVING clause.

FIGURE 4.11:

The qtotMultPizzaSalesByEmployee query totals the orders for each combination of pizza and employee. An individual order is included for a group only if more than one pizza was sold for that order.

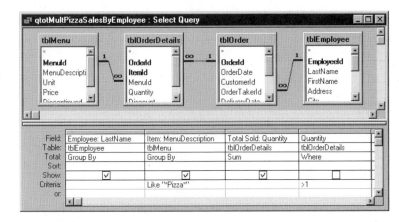

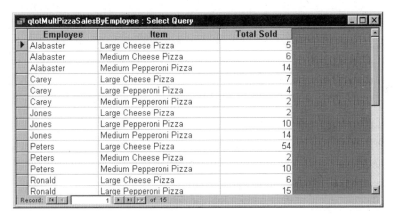

Crosstab Queries

Crosstab queries are closely related to totals queries. Like totals queries, crosstab queries summarize data across records. In fact, you can redefine many crosstab queries as totals queries, and vice versa. Crosstab queries differ from totals queries, however, in how the results are displayed. While totals queries present results in a tabular grid with the groups as rows and the fields as columns, crosstab queries change the grid so that one field's values are the rows and a second field's values are the columns. Recall the pair of nested totals queries presented earlier in this chapter, qtotSalesByEmployee&Month and qtotSalesByMonth&Employee, and the fact that, depending on how you wanted to analyze the data, you needed to choose one query over the other. This situation is a good candidate for a crosstab query because with a single crosstab query, you can analyze the data by both month and employee at the same time. Figure 4.12 shows this crosstab query, qxtbSalesByEmployee&Month, in both Design and Datasheet views.

Here are the basic steps you use to create a crosstab query:

1. Create a new select query and add any necessary tables.

2. Drag to the query grid the two fields that will define the groups. (In the preceding example, we used expressions rather than table fields for the two Group By fields. You can use either.)

3. Change the type of query to a crosstab query. The two columns you added to the query grid should have Group By selected for the Total cell.

FIGURE 4.12:

The qxtbSalesByEmployee&Month crosstab query makes it easy to analyze either monthly trends by employee or employee trends by month.

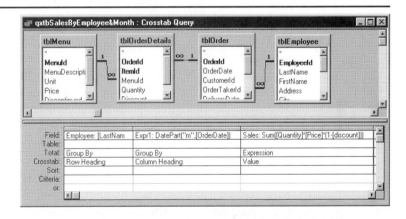

4. Decide which field you want for the rows and which field you want for the columns. For the field you will use for the rows, select Row Heading in the Crosstab cell. Likewise, for the field you will use for the columns, select Column Heading.

5. Decide what you want to appear in each cell of the cross-table. If you want the cell value to be a count of records, create an additional column with the expression *fieldname*:Count(*) in the Field cell, select Expression for the Total cell, and select Value for the Crosstab cell. If you wish to use an aggregate function instead, drag an additional field to the query grid, and select the appropriate aggregate function for the Total cell and Value for the Crosstab cell. You can also use a custom expression like that used in the preceding example.

6. Set any criteria desired and run the query.

> **TIP**
>
> If you find the creation of crosstab queries confusing, you may wish to use the Access Crosstab Query Wizard to create the crosstab query for you.

In Access SQL, you create crosstab queries using the TRANSFORM and PIVOT statements. See Chapter 5 for more details.

Crosstab Options

Crosstab queries have both a Total row (like totals queries) and a Crosstab row. The options for the Total row are the same as for totals queries: Group By for defining grouping levels; aggregate functions (Count, Sum, Min, Max, First, Last, Avg, StDev, Var, and Expression) for computing summary statistics for each group; and Where for specifying criteria on fields for which you do not wish to define groups. The crosstab options are Row Heading, Column Heading, Value, and "(not shown)".

The total and crosstab options are closely related. Table 4.2 details the relationship of the two options.

You may select only one value and one column heading for a crosstab query. You may select multiple row headings, however, just as in totals queries. For example,

TABLE 4.2: Relationship between Crosstab and Totals Options in Crosstab Queries

Totals Option	Row Heading	Column Heading	Value	(not shown)
Group By	Yes	Yes	No	No
Aggregate Function	No	No	Yes	No
Where	No	No	No	Yes

if you wished to expand qxtbSalesByEmployee&Month so it also grouped on menu item (in addition to employee and month), you'd have to choose one of the fields as the column heading of the crosstab and the other two as the row headings. Multiple row headings are nested from left to right, just as for multiple GroupBy fields in a totals query.

Creating Row Totals

You can create an extra row heading for crosstab queries that totals the values for an entire row. You create this special row heading by adding a Row Heading column to the query grid with the same attributes as the Value entry, except you replace Value with Row Heading and create an alias for the entry, such as Total Orders. (It's simple if you just cut-and-paste the Value column, change the Crosstab cell to Row Heading, and alias the field name.) For example, you could add a totals column to the qxtbSalesByEmployee&Month presented earlier in this chapter. Figure 4.13 shows this new query, qxtbSalesByEmployee&Month&Totals, in both Design and Datasheet views.

Access always positions this special totals row heading in the datasheet to the left of the column headings.

Crosstab Limitations

Crosstab queries and totals queries have many similarities. For example, you can use both of them to analyze data, and both produce read-only recordsets (snapshots). However, even though crosstab snapshots appear similar to and behave similarly to totals query snapshots, you need to be aware of some important differences.

FIGURE 4.13:

The qxtbSalesByEmployee&Month-&Totals query displays both monthly and total year-to-date (YTD) sales.

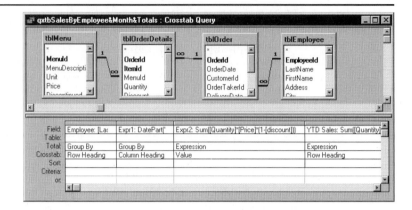

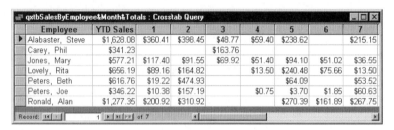

First, you must recall that the columns in crosstab snapshots are derived from the *values* of the crosstab Column field. This means the column names will often contain characters that, while perfectly legal as parts of values, are no longer legal in column names. Access provides some relief here: for floating-point numbers containing decimal places, Access replaces decimal points with underscore characters. However, text columns can still produce illegal or reserved names. For example, if you had a two-character text column for State/Province, it might contain the value ON for Ontario, but On is a reserved Access constant. This won't affect your ability to run the crosstab query, but you will encounter difficulties when trying to use the crosstab as a source for a report, a graph, or another query. Usually you can work around this problem by enclosing the illegal column name reference in brackets— for example, [on].

Second, unlike totals queries, in a crosstab query you cannot define criteria on the Value field. Thus, you can't create a crosstab query that is equivalent to the earlier totals query example that grouped by employee and type of pizza and included a group only if the total pizzas sold were greater than 1 (see Figure 4.10). That is, you can't do it in one step. You can work around this limitation by first creating a totals query with the desired criteria and then basing a crosstab query on the results of the totals query.

For example, recall the qtotPizzaSalesByEmployee query shown earlier. You wouldn't be able to create the equivalent crosstab query in one step because that query includes criteria on the Value field. If you attempt to run the query, you'll get the alert dialog "Value field can't specify a Criteria clause." The solution is to create a query, qxtbPizzaSalesByEmployee, that uses qtotPizzaSalesByEmployee as its source. The only tricky part is deciding which aggregate function to use for the value column—in this case, the TotalSold column. Since the data has already been aggregated once, you don't want (or need) to further aggregate it, but Access requires you to choose *some* aggregate function. You can choose any aggregate function that will return that value when applied to just one value. Most aggregate functions, including Sum, Avg, Min, Max, First, and Last, will do the trick; we have chosen Sum for qxtbPizzaSalesByEmployee, which is shown in both Design and Datasheet views in Figure 4.14.

FIGURE 4.14:
The qxtbPizzaSalesByEmployee crosstab query is based on the results of a totals query, qtotPizzaSalesByEmployee.

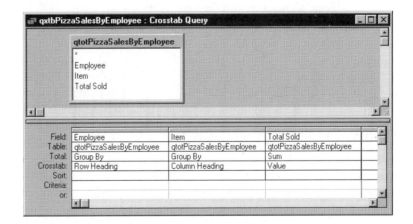

Finally, crosstab queries, in contrast to totals queries, cannot contain implicit parameters. An *implicit parameter* is a parameter that has *not* been explicitly defined using the Query ➤ Parameters dialog. The work-around is to explicitly define each parameter used in a crosstab query.

Fixed Column Headings

Crosstab queries have a unique property called *ColumnHeadings* that you can use for several purposes:

- To place the columns in a certain order. If you don't use the ColumnHeadings property, text columns will be ordered alphabetically, numeric columns will be sorted numerically, and date columns will be sorted chronologically.

- To include a certain column, even if it has no values.

- To exclude a column, even if it *does* have values.

Using Fixed Column Headings for Dates

By default, Access arranges column headings in ascending order. Although you can easily change the sort order to descending, sometimes it is more appropriate to order the columns differently. In these cases you can use the ColumnHeadings property to stabilize the headings and gain added control over the layout of the columns. For example, in the qxtbSalesByEmployee&Month crosstab query presented earlier, you'd probably prefer to list months as Jan and Feb instead of 1 and 2. You can change this easily by using Format([OrderDate], "mmm") instead of DatePart("m",[OrderDate]) for the Column field. Unfortunately, since the Format() function returns a variant text string, Access orders the Month column alphabetically instead of chronologically. The solution is to use the ColumnHeadings property. For this query, qxtbSalesByEmployee&Month1, you would enter the following in the ColumnHeadings property:

```
"Jan", "Feb", "Mar"
```

Figure 4.15 shows the revised query in both Design and Datasheet views.

FIGURE 4.15:

This crosstab query shows employee sales by month (as a three-character string). The query was constructed using the Format() function and the ColumnHeadings property.

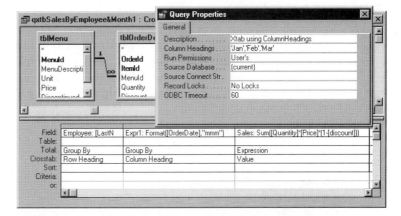

Fixed column headings must match the data values *exactly*. When you use the ColumnHeadings property, you can inadvertently hide data that does not match the specified headings. For example, let's say you were looking at 1995 sales by country. If the data values for the Country field were "USA", "Canada", "France", and so on, and you choose fixed headings of United States, Canada, France, and so on, the USA records would not appear in the crosstab and you might wrongly conclude that there were no United States sales in 1995.

Action Queries

Although the phrase *action query* is something of an oxymoron, action queries are nonetheless a very important aspect of Access. They allow you to efficiently make bulk changes to your tables and move data among them. Although you can do anything an action query can do by defining and stepping through recordsets one row at a time using VBA code, you'll find using action queries almost always a simpler and more efficient (faster) way to perform bulk updates to your data.

TIP You can "try before you buy" an action query (see the rows that will be affected—updated, deleted, or copied to another table—by the action query) by choosing View ➤ Datasheet or clicking the Datasheet icon.

The four types of action queries are

- Update
- Delete
- Make-table
- Append

TIP Action queries, like select queries, can contain parameters.

NOTE There may be times when you are forced to use procedural code because either you cannot express the operation using an action query or you need more control in a multiuser environment. See Chapters 6 and 12 for more information on using data access objects (DAO) and multiuser development.

Update Queries

You use update queries to make bulk updates to data in a table. This is usually a far more efficient process than either making the changes through the user interface (using the search-and-replace dialog) or opening a recordset and "walking the table," updating data one row at a time.

For example, say you wished to change the discount for all items ordered after a certain date to a new formula that was based on quantity sold. The following expression:

```
IIf([Quantity]>5,IIf([Quantity]<50,[Quantity]/1000,.5),0)
```

changes the discount to:

- 0, if 5 or fewer were ordered
- (Quantity/1000), if 6–49 were ordered (for example, 0.20, or a 20-percent discount for a quantity of 20)
- 0.50, or a 50-percent discount rate if 50 or more were ordered

You could accomplish this using an update query such as qupdDiscount, shown in Design view in Figure 4.16.

FIGURE 4.16:

The update query qupdDiscount changes the discount rate, stored in the field Discount, to a formula based on quantity.

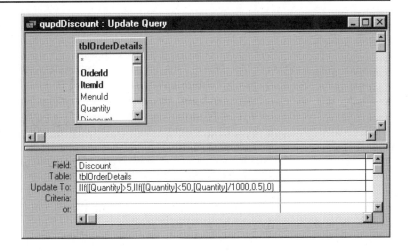

You enter the new value in the Update To row. This value can be a constant, the value of another column, or an expression such as the one shown in Figure 4.16. For complex scenarios the expression can even reference a user-defined function.

You'll find update queries are useful for taking data you've imported into Access from another source and massaging it into a usable format. Other good uses for update queries include making global changes to tax rates, cascading changes from one table to another, and updating calculated fields in tables.

WARNING   Records updated using an update query may cause records in other tables to be updated if you've created relationships and have checked Cascade Update Related Fields.

Updating Data across Tables

At times you'll need to update the records in one table based on data from a second table—for instance, when you receive records from another office with changes to customer phone numbers. Once the new table is attached or imported, you'll need to find some way to copy the changes from this new table to the regular customer table. Although you might be tempted to accomplish this task using DAO, walking the records of the first table and then making changes to the second table, you'll probably find an update query to be more efficient.

For example, say you have just imported a table named tblCustomerMods that contains the same records as your regular customer table, tblCustomer, except for changes to phone numbers in five of the records. You could update the phone numbers in tblCustomer using an update query that joined the two tables by CustomerId and include one field, Phone from tblCustomer, on the query grid. You would enter the following in the Update cell of this field to change the value of Phone in tblCustomer to the value found in tblCustomerMods:

```
[tblCustomerMods].[Phone]
```

and the following in the Criteria cell for Phone:

```
<>[tblCustomerMods].[Phone]
```

These criteria would ensure that you updated only records that needed to be changed. The update query, qupdCustomerPhone, is shown in Figure 4.17.

FIGURE 4.17:

This update query updates the phone number in tblCustomer with the value in tblCustomerMods when the two values are different.

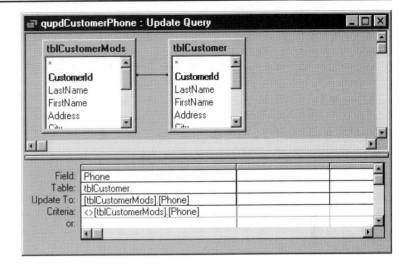

Delete Queries

You use delete queries to delete batches of records from tables. As is the case for update queries, this is almost always more efficient than either deleting records via the user interface or walking the table and deleting records one row at a time.

For example, say you wished to delete all the discontinued menu items from tblMenu. You could accomplish this by using the qdelDiscontinuedItems delete query shown in Figure 4.18.

As with other queries, you can refer to multiple tables in a delete query. You indicate which table to delete records from by dragging the * (asterisk) field from that table to the query grid and choosing From in the Delete row. (You can skip this step when you've included only one table in the delete query.) You can also add other fields to the query grid to restrict which records get deleted. For these fields, select Where in the Delete row.

If two tables are related in a *one-to-one relationship*, you may delete both tables with a single delete query by dragging both asterisk fields to the query grid.

For two tables related in a *one-to-many relationship*, however, you need to run two queries to delete records from both tables. The next section describes how to do this.

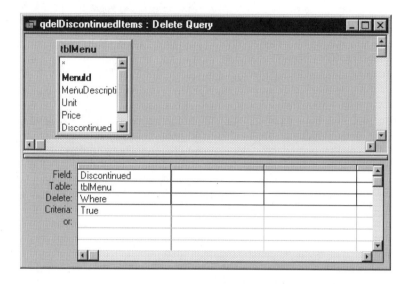

FIGURE 4.18:

The delete query qdelDiscontinued-Items removes all discontinued menu items from tblMenu.

> **WARNING** Records deleted using a delete query may cause records in other tables to be deleted when you have created relationships and have turned on the cascading deletes option. Of course, this may be exactly what you want.

Deleting Data from Related Records in Multiple Tables

If you wish to delete records from both sides of a one-to-many relationship and you've enabled referential integrity and turned on the cascading deletes option, you only need to construct a query that deletes records from the "one" side of the relationship.

If you need to delete records from both sides of a one-to-many relationship, however, and you haven't enabled cascading deletes, you'll have to create at least two queries and do some careful planning, because the order of the delete queries matters. The order in which you delete the tables is dictated by the criteria you use to select records to be deleted. The various scenarios are summarized here:

Criteria Based on	Query Order
Linking column (primary key of "one" table) only	Order doesn't matter
Field(s) from "one" table	Delete "many" table first
Field(s) from "many" table	Delete "one" table first
Field(s) from both tables	You'll need to *project* the primary keys to a temporary table using a make-table query and then link that temporary table back to each of the other tables to perform the deletes (in any order)

For example, say you wished to delete an entire order (both tblOrder records and tblOrderDetails records) if either the order date was prior to 2/1/94 *or* the order included the purchase of lasagna. Since you wish to delete records from two tables related in a one-to-many relationship with fields from both tables, you'll need to create a temporary *projection table* (a table that has been projected from another table) that contains the OrderId for any orders meeting these criteria. Figure 4.19 shows such a query, qmakDeleteProjection, which creates the temp table tblDeleteProjection. (Make-table queries are discussed further in the next section.)

FIGURE 4.19:

The qmakDeleteProjection make-table query creates a temporary delete projection table you can then use to delete records from both sides of the one-to-many relationship.

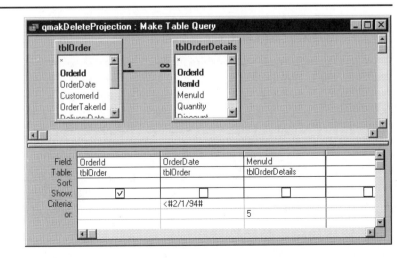

Once you've created the temporary table, you can create the two delete queries that will delete the records from the two tables. To delete the appropriate records from the orders table, create a delete query that joins tblDeleteProjection to tblOrder by OrderId and drag the asterisk field from tblOrder to the query grid. Similarly, to delete the appropriate records from the order details table, create a delete query that joins tblDeleteProjection to tblOrderDetails by OrderId and drag the asterisk field from tblOrderDetails to the query grid. An example of this query, qdel1toMOrderDetails, is shown in Figure 4.20.

FIGURE 4.20:

This delete query deletes detail records from tblOrderDetails when the order date was prior to 2/1/94 *or* the order included lasagna, using a temporary table, tblDeleteProjection.

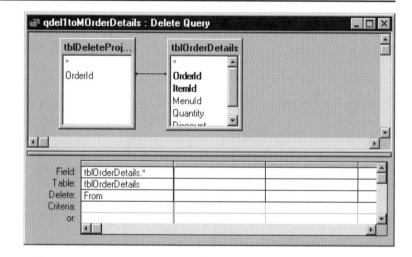

Make-Table Queries

You use make-table queries to create tables from other tables or queries. Make-table queries are useful for creating permanent, temporary, and archive tables. As with append queries (discussed in the next section), you'll find make-table queries very handy for massaging imported data into the proper format. Fields in the new (destination) table can come from existing tables or queries, can be created using an expression, or can be constants.

For example, say you wished to back up all records from tblOrder that occurred during 1994 to a new backup table, tblOrder1994. You could accomplish this using the qmakOrder1994 make-table query shown in Figure 4.21.

FIGURE 4.21:

The make-table query qmakOrder1994 backs up 1994 orders to the tblOrder1994 table.

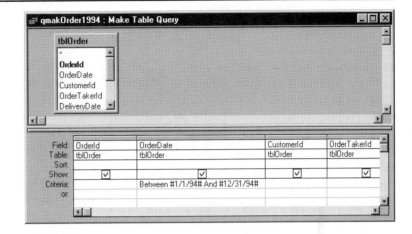

The qmakOrder1994 query will not, of course, delete the records from tblOrder, but you could accomplish this easily by changing qmakOrder1994 into a delete query and then executing that query without making any other changes to the design.

When using make-table queries, Access creates a field in the target table for each field on the query grid with its Show check box checked. Access uses the name of the field in the source table for each table-based field or the name you give to any calculated expressions. (It's not a good idea to let Access use default names unless you find Exp1, Exp2, and so forth, to your liking.) You can also change the name of any table-based fields by aliasing them. Simply add an alias name, in the format

AliasName: *FieldName*

to the field name in the query grid.

One convenient feature of make-table queries is that you can create the new table in another database (Access, non-native ISAM, or ODBC). This is especially useful for archiving or transferring data to another database without having to export it. For more information, see the section "Using Properties to Customize the Behavior of Queries" later in this chapter.

> **TIP**
>
> A totals query can also be an action query. Thus, you can easily make permanent tables to hold the results of a totals query in one step. Just create your totals query as usual and then convert it to a make-table or an append query before running it.

Append Queries

Append queries are similar to make-table queries. The difference is that you use an append query to add records to an existing table, whereas make-table queries always create a new table, wiping out any existing table with the same name.

Append queries will fail if the target table does not exist. Other than this difference, append and make-table queries behave very much the same. Append queries are useful for moving data between tables. They often are used (along with an initial make-table query) to populate a table from either multiple sources or the same source at different times.

For example, you might want to run an append query each month that archived orders more than one month old to the tblOrderArchive table. Such a query, qappOrderArchive, is shown in Figure 4.22.

FIGURE 4.22:

The append query qappOrderArchive archives orders with order dates older than one month to the tblOrderArchive table.

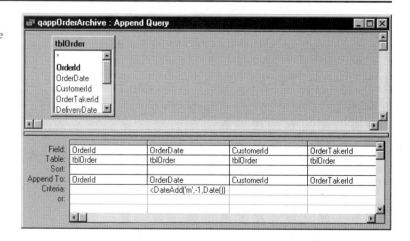

Like a make-table query, an append query does not delete the records from the original table. Also like make-table queries, append queries can be used to copy data to tables in other databases.

The fields for an append query don't have to exactly match the fields in the target table. By default, Access copies data to fields with the same name, but you can override this behavior simply by adjusting the name of the target field in the Append To cell. You can also use a field to set criteria without sending its data to the target table by blanking out the name of the field in the Append To cell. (This is equivalent to unchecking the Show check box for select queries.)

An Example: Removing Duplicates

Have you ever tried to create a primary key for a column with existing duplicate values? This is a common occurrence when you import records from another database program that doesn't support primary keys. Access refuses to create a primary key when duplicate values are present. But how do you quickly and easily locate and eliminate the duplicate records?

We offer two solutions. Both solutions use aggregate action queries. The first—the *hand-pruning method*—involves the use of an aggregate make-table query and a second select query to create an updatable dynaset of duplicate records that you can then use to browse and prune out the duplicates by hand. The second—the *bulk-project method,* from Access developer Michael Corning—uses an aggregate append query to project one copy of the duplicate rows to a second table. (A third method that employs subqueries is presented in Chapter 5.)

The chapter database includes a table called tblImport, which contains some duplicate order records that prevent you from designating OrderId as the primary key for the table. If you attempt to create a primary key on OrderId, Access complains with the dialog shown in Figure 4.23.

Here are the steps for removing the duplicates using the hand-pruning technique from tblImport:

1. Create a totals query that includes the column (or columns) you wish to become the primary key (the candidate key). Set this column's Total cell to

FIGURE 4.23:

Access does not allow you to create
a primary key on a column with
duplicate values.

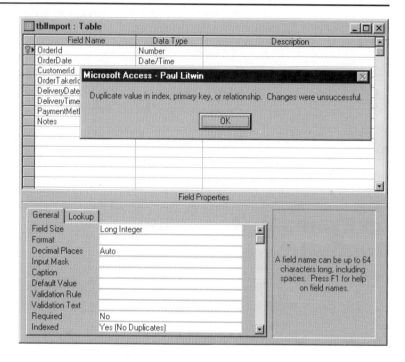

Group By. Also, add an expression column to count the number of rows for
each group. Add criteria for this column to select only groups in which there
are duplicates (Count > 1). For tblImport, create a totals query on tblImport,
placing OrderId on the QBE grid and choosing Group By for the Total cell.
Create the following new column:

```
RecCount: Count(*)
```

In the Total cell for this column, select Expression. In the Criteria cell for this
column, enter the following:

```
>1
```

This restricts the query to return only records where the count of OrderId is
greater than 1 (that is, those with duplicate entries).

2. After previewing the query to make sure it returns the correct records, convert it into a make-table query. (By using a make-table rather than a select
query, you ensure that the dynaset created in step 3 will be updatable.) For
the tblImport example, the name of the table created by the make-table

query will be tblImportDups. This query, qmakImportDups, is shown in Design view in Figure 4.24.

3. Create a select query joining the original table to the new table made in step 2. Join the two tables on the candidate key column. Include all columns from the original table and none from the new table in the query. For the tblImport example, create a select query that joins the new table, tblImportDups, with the original table, tblImport, on the column OrderId. Include all the columns from tblImport in the query grid. Don't include any columns from tblImport-Dups; you're including this table only to filter the records from tblImport. Sort by OrderId so all duplicate records will be displayed together. Execute the query.

4. You will now have a dynaset that contains all the records with duplicate orders. Since this dynaset is updatable, you can browse through it and prune out the true duplicates (see Figure 4.25).

Here are the steps for removing the duplicate records from tblImport using the bulk-project method:

1. Use a make-table query (or the Copy and Paste commands) to make a copy of the structure of the table. For the tblImport example, call the make-table query qmakImportNew and the new table tblImportNew.

FIGURE 4.24:

The qmakImportDups query lists all duplicate IDs.

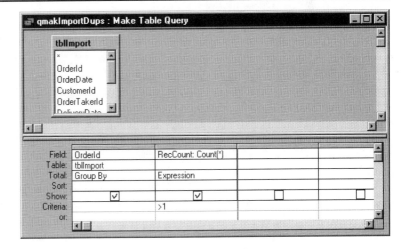

FIGURE 4.25:

The qryHandPruneDups query joins tblImportDups to tblImport in a one-to-many relationship. You can use it to interactively browse and prune records with duplicate order numbers.

OrderId	OrderDate	CustomerId	OrderTakerId	DeliveryDate	DeliveryTime
6	2/11/94	10	5	2/11/94	2:35:00 PM
6	1/26/94	2	1	1/28/94	
13	2/16/94	11	7	2/16/94	4:40:58 PM
13	2/16/94	5	7	2/18/94	1:20:59 AM
13	2/14/94	1	2		
13	2/14/94	1	2		
35	2/17/94	5	3	2/18/94	3:44:09 AM
35	2/17/94	6	4	2/18/94	9:42:58 AM
41	2/17/94	2	2	2/18/94	9:50:30 AM
41	2/17/94	11	7	2/17/94	4:40:58 PM

2. Create a totals query that groups by the candidate key column and uses an aggregate function such as First or Last for each remaining column in the table. For the tblImport example, create a totals query based on tblImport. Place all the columns from tblImport on the query grid. For OrderId, choose Group By in the Total cell. For the remaining columns, choose First. (You might also wish to use Last, Min, or Max.)

3. After you have run this query to make sure it returns the correct records, convert it to an append query. For the tblImport example, choose tblImportNew as the target table. Match up the columns for the two tables. Name this query qappBulkProject and execute it. This should populate tblImportNew with only one copy of each order. qappBulkProject is shown in Figure 4.26 in Design view.

NOTE If you tried to combine the first three steps into one make-table totals query, you'd find that Access renames all the fields in the new table to something like FirstofFirstName and so forth. This is why we suggest going to the trouble of copying the structure of the table and appending records to the copy instead.

4. Delete the original table and rename the copy, which should now contain the desired records. For the tblImport example, delete the original table, tblImport, and rename tblImportNew as tblImport.

The qappBulkProject query projects only one row per OrderId to tblImportNew, eliminating any duplicates.

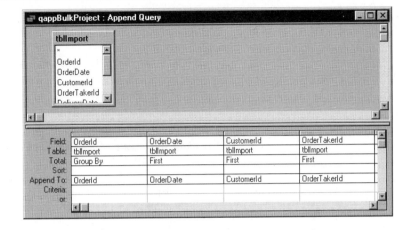

One of these two techniques should work in most situations in which you are faced with duplicate records that must be eliminated prior to creating a primary key. The bulk-project method doesn't require any hand pruning of records, which is both its strong point and its downfall. Use this technique if you don't care which duplicate record is deleted or if you always wish to keep the first (or last) copy of a duplicate set of records. Use the hand-pruning method instead if the occurrence of duplicates is less predictable and requires a case-by-case analysis.

Using Properties to Customize the Behavior of Queries

You can modify three sets of properties in queries: query, field list, and field properties. For many queries, you'll never need to adjust the properties. In fact, make-table and append queries prompt you for the DestinationTable and DestinationDB properties so you can set these properties without having to open the query's property sheet. In addition to query properties that apply to the entire query, each source table has a set of field list properties, and each field on the query grid has a set of field properties. All three types of query properties are summarized in Table 4.3.

TABLE 4.3: Properties Available for Queries

Property Set	Property	Description	SQL	Default Value
Query Properties	Description	Documents purpose of the query	*None*	*None*
	Output All Fields	Places all fields from all tables/queries in the dynaset. Equivalent to using * for each table list. Use of this option may adversely affect the updatability of the dynaset. Not available for crosstab, update, or delete queries	*	No
	Top Values	Returns only the top *n* or top *n* percent of rows. If *n* is entered as a percent value (for example, 75%), Access returns the top percentage. Otherwise, it returns the top number of rows. Not available for crosstab, update, or delete queries	TOP *n* or TOP *n* PERCENT	Returns all rows per specified criteria
	Unique Values	When set to Yes, Access will return only unique rows based on a comparison of all outputted fields. This option significantly slows down queries. Not available for crosstab, update, or delete queries	DISTINCT	No
	Unique Records	For certain types of queries, setting this property to Yes ensures that the dynaset is updatable (For most queries, however, this setting doesn't matter. See the section "The ALL, DISTINCTROW, and DISTINCT Predicates" in Chapter 5 for more details.) Not available for crosstab queries	DISTINCTROW	Yes
	Run-Permissions	Determines whether the query is run with the owner's (the person who created the query) set of permissions or the user's (the person running the query). Note that version 1.x defaulted to using the owner's permissions (See Chapter 24 for further details.)	WITH OWNERACCESS OPTION	User's

TABLE 4.3: Properties Available for Queries (continued)

Property Set	Property	Description	SQL	Default Value
	Source-Database	Name of the database that contains the source tables.[1] Use the Source property of each source table's field list properties to include tables from more than one database	FROM	(current)
	Source-ConnectStr	Type of database or ODBC connect string for external source tables[2]	FROM	None
	Destination-Table	Name of the table that will hold the results of the make-table or append query (not available for other types of queries)	INTO for make-table queries; INSERT INTO for append queries	None
	Destination-Database	The name of the database that will hold the results of the make-table or append query (not available for other types of queries)[1]	INTO for make-table queries; INSERT INTO for append queries	(current)
	Destination-ConnectStr	Type of database or ODBC connect string for the database that will hold the results of the make-table or append query (not available for other types of queries)[2]	INTO for make-table queries; INSERT INTO for append queries	None
	RecordLocks	Type of multiuser record locking to use for the dynaset (No Locks, All Records, or Edited Record) (See Chapter 12 for more details.)	None	No Locks
	ODBC-Timeout	Time in seconds to cancel query if ODBC server doesn't respond. Not applicable for non-ODBC tables	None	60
	Filter	Run-time criteria applied on top of the query's criteria. Normally applied by the user in Datasheet view using the Filter By Form, Filter By Selection, or Advanced Filter/Sort command on the Records menu. Stored in the form of a SQL WHERE clause without "WHERE". Not available for crosstab or action queries	None	None

TABLE 4.3: Properties Available for Queries (continued)

Property Set	Property	Description	SQL	Default Value
	OrderBy	Run-time sorting applied on top of the query's sorting. Normally applied by the user in Datasheet view using the Sort or Advanced Filter/Sort command on the Records menu. Stored in the form of a SQL ORDER BY clause without "ORDER BY". Not available for crosstab or action queries	*None*	*None*
	Column-Headings	Specifies a fixed set of column headings in a crosstab query. Not available for other types of queries (See the section "Fixed Column Headings" earlier in this chapter.)	PIVOT *fieldname* IN (*heading1, heading2, …*)	*None*
Field List Properties	Alias	Alternate temporary name given to a table. You must use it when creating self joins	AS	*Table/query name*
	Source	Similar to the SourceDatabase and SourceConnectStr query properties. Use Source instead of the query properties if you will be using multiple unattached external tables from different sources. Enter in the format *database-path "database-type;"* for non-ODBC databases. For ODBC databases, you must enter a product-specific connection string	FROM	*None*
Field Properties—General	Description	Description of field for documentation purposes only	*None*	*None*
	Format	The display format for the field—for example, General, Date, Currency	*None*	For table fields, the field's Format property from the table. For calculated fields, *None*

TABLE 4.3: Properties Available for Queries (continued)

Property Set	Property	Description	SQL	Default Value
	Decimal-Places	For number fields, the number of decimal places to display	*None*	For table fields, the field's DecimalPlaces property from the table. For calculated fields, *None*
	InputMask	Template for masking user input—for example, 999-99-9999 for social security numbers	*None*	For table fields, the field's InputMask property from the table. For calculated fields, *None*
	Caption	Caption or title for the field that will be displayed in the query's datasheet or the default label on a form	*None*	For table fields, the field's Caption property from the table. For calculated fields, *None*
Field Properties—Lookup	Display Control	Type of control for displaying this field on datasheets and forms. Can be Text Box, Check Box, List Box, or Combo Box. Available only for numeric, yes/no, and text fields. If List Box or Combo Box is selected, several additional properties become available, including RowSourceType, RowSource, BoundColumn, and so on	*None*	Text Box (number, yes/no, and text fields only)

[1]For the current database (or any attached tables in the current database), enter (current); for a different Access database, enter the path and name of the database—for example, C:\ACCESS\DATA\CLIENTS.MDB; for non-native ISAM databases, enter the subdirectory in which the database is located—for example, D:\DATA; for ODBC databases, leave blank. Note that when using non-native tables, it's usually more efficient to work with attached tables than to use this property.

[2]For the current database or another Access database (or any attached tables in the current database), leave blank; for non-native ISAM databases, enter a string to identify the type and version of the product followed by a semicolon—dBASE III;, dBASE IV;, FoxPro 2.0;, FoxPro 2.5;, FoxPro 2.6;, FoxPro 3.0;, Paradox 3.x;, Paradox 4.x;, Paradox 5.x;, Excel 3.0;, Excel 4.0;, Excel 5.0;, Text;, or Btrieve;; for ODBC databases you must enter a product-specific connection string—for example, "ODBC;DSN=custdsn;UID=userid;PWD=password;DATABASE=customer;". Note that when using non-native tables, it's usually more efficient to work with attached tables than to use this property.

Query Properties

Query properties are the most general and apply to the entire query. You can use query properties, for example, to change settings for multiuser locking, to create "top n" queries, and to output only unique records.

Field List Properties

Field list properties apply to the source table/query's field lists. You would use these properties to create an alias for a table or to specify use of an external file as the source of a table. (You can also use a similar query property for this purpose—see the section "Using Properties to Indicate External Data Sources" later in this chapter.)

Field Properties

Field properties apply to individual output fields and affect the appearance of the fields. There are two types of field properties: general and lookup.

Lookup properties are new to Access 95. These properties allow you to specify the type of control Access will use when displaying the field on a datasheet and the default type of control Access will use when you create a form based on the query. For number and text fields, you can choose text box (the default), list box, or combo box. For yes/no fields, you can choose text box (the default), check box, or combo box. For all other types of fields, this property does not apply; text boxes are used. If you choose either list box or combo box, several other properties become visible that you can use to specify the source for the list box or combo box's values.

General properties include all other field properties, such as Description, Format, Caption, and so on.

Normally, field properties are inherited from the underlying field's property set. This inheritance link is a *hot* one-way link, so if you later change a table's property, the query will reflect the change also—that is, unless you change the property on the *query*. Once you change a property—for example, change the Format property for a General number to Currency—the link from the underlying table will be broken for that property only.

Using Properties to Indicate External Data Sources

There is some overlap of field list properties and query properties regarding external data sources. Use the SourceDatabase and SourceConnectStr *query* properties when all the query's field lists (tables) are coming from a single source database (or subdirectory, in the case of non-ODBC sources). If the query is using data from different data sources, however, you should use the Source *field list* property instead (which combines SourceDatabase and SourceConnectStr into one string).

When using attached tables of any type, *don't* use these properties. Instead, treat attached tables as though they were local Access tables. In fact, it is preferable and usually more efficient to use attached tables.

Using Top Value Queries

You can create a *top value* query by entering either a whole number (n) or a percent (n%) in the TopValues property of the query's property sheet. This type of query returns the top (or bottom) n rows or top (or bottom) n percent of rows from a recordset. Top value queries are useful when you wish to return only a select proportion of records meeting the query criteria.

TIP — Instead of using the query's property sheet, you can use the top value drop-down list on the Form toolbar to quickly create a top values query.

Normally, you use top value queries only when you've also chosen sort fields; otherwise you'll be getting a more or less random assortment of records. (It's worth noting, however, that this won't be a *true* random sample; instead it will be whatever proportion of records happens to come up first.)

If you use an ascending sort, Access returns the bottom-most records. If you use a descending sort instead, Access returns the top-most records. Nulls are treated as the smallest numeric value, earliest date, or first alphabetically ordered string. Thus, when you know that the "top" column may contain nulls, you may wish to explicitly exclude them using criteria.

For example, to display the top 20 percent of customers as ordered by the amount of money they spent, you could create a query such as the one shown in Figure 4.27 in both Design and Datasheet views.

Access processes the TopValues property after all criteria, joins, sorts, and groupings have been applied. When processing percent top values, Access chooses the closest number of records *greater than or equal to* the requested percentage. In the preceding example, Access returned 3 out of 11 rows, or 27 percent of the rows—20 percent had been requested.

Ties are treated like any other row, except when multiple rows qualify as the last selected row. When there is a tie on the last selected row, Access returns *all* rows with the last value. For example, if you constructed a top 3 query that ordered people by age in descending order, with ages of 79, 75, 72, 72, 72, 68, 68, and 65, Access would return the first five rows.

With no sorts defined, Access uses all the query's output columns to decide on ties. Otherwise, Access uses only the sort columns to determine both the ordering of the rows and the resolution of ties.

FIGURE 4.27:

The qtotCustomerTop20pct query returns the top 20 percent of customers by the total dollars they spent.

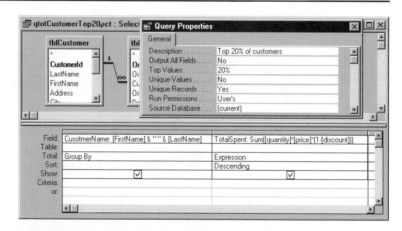

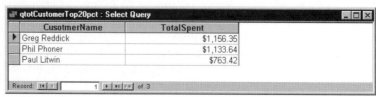

Using Parameters to Specify Criteria at Run Time

You can create queries that allow the specification of criteria at run time in Access using parameters. *Parameters* are simply references in criteria or expressions that have not been previously defined. Most often, you will use parameters in query criteria to dynamically change the criteria based on user input.

To create a parameter query, you need to:

- Add a reference to a parameter in the query's criteria. Enclose the parameter reference—which may include spaces and special characters—in square brackets.

- Use the Query ➤ Parameters command to declare the parameter and set its datatype. (The brackets are optional here.)

For example, say you wished to list descriptive information for customers with last names that begin with a particular letter of the alphabet to be determined at run time. You could accomplish this with a simple parameter query such as qryCustomerPrm, which is shown in Design view in Figure 4.28. The criteria for the Last-Name field are

Like [*Enter one or more chars of last name*] & "*"

FIGURE 4.28:

The qryCustomerPrm parameter query. A parameter has been defined using the Query Parameters dialog box.

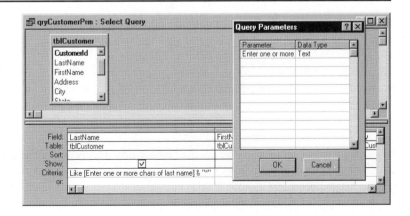

NOTE   In prior versions of Access, you could often get away without having to declare your parameters using the Query ➤ Parameters command. This is no longer true. You need to declare all parameter references.

Using Form-Based Parameters

When you create parameter queries, Access, by default, prompts the user for unresolved parameters with one or more Enter Parameter Value dialogs. You don't, however, have to use these default dialogs. You may prefer instead to create a form to prompt the user for the parameters and have the query parameters point to these form controls. This works because Access will not prompt the user for parameters that have already been satisfied. When using form references, Access encloses each component of the reference in brackets. (For this reason, don't place additional brackets around the entire reference.)

For example, the parameter query qrySalesHistoryPrm uses a form, fdlgSalesHistoryPrm (the "fdlg" tag denotes that this is a dialog form), to feed it two parameters. This form is used to print a report, rptSalesHistory, which has as its record source the qrySalesHistory parameter query. This report lists the sales history for a particular time period. The parameters, which are entered onto the fdlgSalesHistoryPrm form, control the time period for which the report is based. The criteria for the field OrderDate are

> Between [Forms]![fdlgSalesHistoryPrm]![txtDate1]
>
> And [Forms]![fdlgSalesHistoryPrm]![txtDate2]

When you click the OK button, Access executes the following event procedure:

```
Private Sub cmdOK_Click()
    DoCmd.OpenReport "rptSalesHistory", acPreview
End Sub
```

The fdlgSalesHistoryPrm form is shown in Figure 4.29.

Note that you needn't create any additional code to make the report work with the parameter query. When you open the report, Access runs the query, which checks

FIGURE 4.29:

The fdlgSalesHistoryPrm form collects two parameters needed to run the rptSalesHistory report.

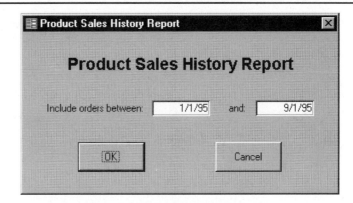

to see whether it has any parameters. If the parameters are already satisfied—by an opened form, in this case—Access doesn't bother to prompt for the parameters. Once the parameters are taken care of, the report executes with no problem.

Referencing Parameters from Reports

If you create a report based on a parameter query, it's likely you'll want to make reference to the run-time values of the parameters on the report itself. We have done this in the rptSalesHistory report using a text box that directly references the parameters from the form. The txtParameters text box in the page header of the report has a ControlSource of:

```
="Time Period: " & [Forms]![fdlgSalesHistoryPrm]![txtDate1]
& " through " & [Forms]![fdlgSalesHistoryPrm]![txtDate2]
```

You can see this txtParameters text box in the page header of the rptSalesHistory report in Print Preview view in Figure 4.30.

You can also reference the parameters on a report, even if you don't use a form to collect the parameters, by treating the parameters as though they were hidden controls on the report. For example, if the above parameters were simple parameters with the names [Enter beginning date] and [Enter ending date], the txtParameters text box would be

```
="Time Period: " & [Enter beginning date] & " through "
& [Enter ending date]
```

FIGURE 4.30:
The beginning and ending date parameters from rptSalesHistory's underlying query are displayed in the report's page header.

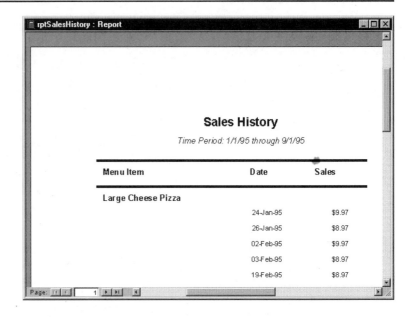

Setting Parameters from VBA

When you open a form, a report, or another query from the user interface that is based on a parameter query, Access knows how to make sure the parameters are satisfied (by either prompting the user or grabbing the parameters from an opened form). However, when you create a recordset from code, VBA doesn't know how to "fix up" the same parameter references, even when the parameters are already satisfied by an open form. Instead, it complains with the "*n* parameters were expected, but only 0 were supplied" error message.

You can get around this problem, however, by following these steps:

1. Create a querydef based on the parameter query.
2. "Plug" each of the query's parameters.
3. Create the recordset from the opened querydef.

For example, the following subroutine, which can be found in basPrmQryRecordset, will create a recordset based on qrySalesHistoryPrm and print the number of records returned by the query to the Debug window:

```
Sub CreatePrmQryRecordset()

    ' Example of creating a recordset based on a
    ' parameter query from code.
    ' The form fdlgSalesHistoryPrm must be open
    ' prior to running this subroutine.

    Dim db As database
    Dim qdf As querydef
    Dim rst As Recordset

    Set db = CurrentDb()

    ' Open querydef
    Set qdf = db.QueryDefs("qrySalesHistoryPrm")

    ' Plug query's parameters
    qdf.Parameters("Forms!fdlgSalesHistoryPrm!txtDate1") = _
     Forms!fdlgSalesHistoryPrm!txtDate1
    qdf.Parameters("Forms!fdlgSalesHistoryPrm!txtDate2") = _
     Forms!fdlgSalesHistoryPrm!txtDate2

    ' Create recordset based on querydef
    Set rst = qdf.OpenRecordset()

    ' Move to end of recordset to get count
    ' Skip for an empty recordset
    If Not rst.EOF Then rst.MoveLast

    Debug.Print "There are " & rst.RecordCount & _
     " sales records between " & _
     Forms!fdlgSalesHistoryPrm!txtDate1 & " and " & _
     Forms!fdlgSalesHistoryPrm!txtDate2 & "."

    rst.Close
    qdf.Close

End Sub
```

Parameter queries and their collections of parameters are discussed in more detail in Chapter 6. In that chapter you will also find a more generic method for plugging the parameters of parameter queries when creating a recordset.

Dynasets: Updatable Recordsets

Select queries in Access that don't involve the aggregation of data produce dynasets. Dynasets and snapshots are both types of recordsets. *Snapshots* are the read-only recordsets produced by totals, crosstabs, and certain nonupdatable select queries. Using VBA code, you can also force a normally updatable select query to produce a snapshot by using the type argument of the OpenRecordset method. Chapter 6 discusses this subject.

Version 1 of Access introduced the concept of the updatable dynaset. As mentioned at the beginning of this chapter, the Access dynaset is a revolutionary concept in desktop databases. Still, although the concept of dynasets is both exciting and powerful, figuring out when a 1.x Access dynaset was updatable was often confusing. Fortunately, Microsoft reworked this area considerably for version 2.0, and the end result is nothing short of startling: with a few exceptions (see the next section), almost every field in an Access dynaset is updatable!

Determining When a Dynaset Is Updatable

Access follows a few rules to determine the *updatability* of a dynaset.

The following queries are *never* updatable:

- Action queries
- Crosstab queries
- Totals queries
- SQL pass-through queries
- Union queries
- Queries containing fields from linked (external) tables that do not have a unique index
- Multitable queries joined on non–primary key fields (or fields that don't have unique indexes)

- Multitable queries with no joined fields (This type of query is often referred to as a Cartesian product query.)
- Queries with the UniqueValues query property set to Yes (SELECT DISTINCT queries)

If a query doesn't fall into one of the preceding categories, the Access query processor determines dynaset behavior using the following rules:

- Calculated fields are never updatable.
- The fields in single-table queries are fully updatable. Records can be deleted. Records can be added as long as the primary key of the table is included in the dynaset.
- Multitable queries with output fields from only one table behave like single-table queries that have been filtered using the second table's records. The fields are updatable, and records can be deleted and added. All changes affect the table with output fields only.
- The fields in two-table queries with one-to-one relationships are updatable. Record deletions affect both tables. You can add records as long as the primary key of one of the tables is included in the dynaset. Added records affect both tables.
- The fields in two-table queries with one-to-many relationships are updatable. Record deletions affect the "many-sided" table only. You can add records, and they will affect both tables as long as the primary key of each is included in the dynaset. If a table's primary key is not included in the dynaset, any record additions will not affect that table. If neither table's primary key is included, record additions are disallowed.
- The fields in three-table many-to-many queries (two one-to-many relationships) are updatable. Record deletions affect the *linking* (middle) table. You can add records, and they will affect each table as long as that table's primary key is included in the dynaset.
- In other multitable queries with three or more tables, use the two-table rules as guidelines. With a few exceptions (noted above), most fields are updatable. Usually one table will be the "most many" of the tables. When fields from more than one table are included in the query, record deletions affect the "most many" table.

- In one-to-many queries with fields from both tables, changes to the foreign key column of the "many-sided" table cause Access to perform a row fix-up operation, requerying the "one" table for data matching the new foreign key value. If the lookup fails because no matching key exists in the "one" table, however, Access disallows the key change.

- In one-to-many queries with fields from both tables, changes to the primary key column of the "one-sided" table are disallowed.

Using Dynasets in Applications

Because the rules for dynaset updatability were more complicated in Access version 1, you had to be very careful about their use in applications. This situation is much simpler now. Most dynaset fields are now updatable, and inserts and deletes are more predictable. All this extra power, however, comes at a price, because sometimes you don't want users updating certain fields or adding or deleting records.

The solution, however, is quite simple: never give users of applications direct access to a query's datasheet. Instead, present your dynasets to users through forms and reports. Reports, by their nature, are read-only, so they don't present a problem. For forms, you can control the user's ability to edit by adjusting several form properties (AllowEdits, AllowDeletions, AllowUpdates, and RecordsetType) and control properties (Enabled and Locked). In addition, you may wish to attach subprocedures or functions to various events of the form and its controls (for example, OnDelete, BeforeUpdate, BeforeInsert, and so on) to control editing behavior even further. Chapters 7 and 8 discuss controls and forms in more detail.

Troubleshooting Dynasets

If you create a dynaset whose updatability differs from what you expected, look for one of the following possible causes:

- **Joins on non–primary key fields:** In order for a multitable dynaset to be updatable, tables must be joined on primary key or unique indexed fields.

- **Joins to the results of a query with totals:** This situation also renders the dynaset read-only. One work-around you may wish to consider is this: make the totals query into a make-table query, create a primary key on the resulting table, and use that table in the second query instead.

- **Including fields from a table that aren't absolutely needed:** Don't include all the fields from every table just because you might need one of its fields. In some cases you may need to include a table to join two other tables, but you don't need to include any of its fields in the dynaset.

- **Setting a query's UniqueValues property to Yes:** Don't use the Unique-Values property (equivalent to SELECT DISTINCT) unless you really need distinct rows.

- **Including the wrong copy of a primary/foreign key field that appears in two tables related in a one-to-many relationship:** If you wish to edit fields from the "one" side of the relationship, include its copy of the field. If you wish to edit fields from the "many" side of the relationship (and use the row fix-up feature mentioned earlier), include its copy of the linking field (the foreign key copy) instead.

Query Execution and the Jet Engine

You can easily create queries in Access that are quite complex or that use one or more tables with a large number of recordsets. In these situations it's important to create the most efficient queries you possibly can to minimize query execution time. But in order to create fast-performing queries, you need to understand a part of Access called the *Jet engine*.

NOTE   Access 95 ships with version 3.0 of the Jet engine.

While you may think of Access as a single program, it's really made up of a number of separate but well-integrated components (see Figure 4.31). One of the most important components is the Jet database engine (or simply Jet), which handles all the database processing for Access (and Visual Basic). In the next few sections we will describe the architecture of Jet, with an emphasis on Jet's query optimizer.

FIGURE 4.31:

Access and Jet

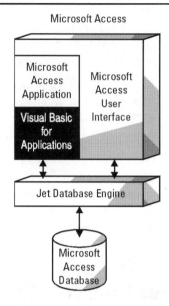

The Jet engine is composed of a series of Dynamic Link Libraries (DLLs). These DLLs can be thought of as distinct but interconnected programs, all working together under the "hood" of the Jet engine. They are the

- Jet engine
- Data Access Objects DLL
- Expression evaluator
- Replication services
- External ISAM DLLs
- ODBC Driver Manager DLL

Figure 4.32 shows how these components interrelate.

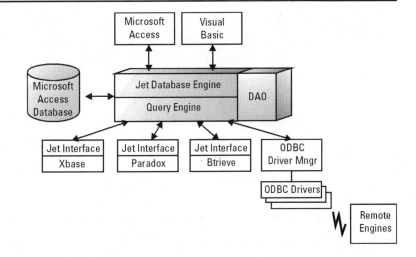

FIGURE 4.32:

Microsoft Jet database engine
architecture

The Jet DLL

The Jet DLL (MSJT3032.DLL) is the main Jet engine program; it evaluates and executes requests for data. If the request is for native Jet data—data stored in the Access Database (.MDB) format—the Jet DLL also handles reading and writing the data. If the request involves non-native data, the Jet DLL makes calls to either the ODBC Driver Manager DLL or one of the external ISAM DLLs.

The Data Access Objects DLL

The Data Access Objects DLL is the Jet component that provides the programmer interface to the Jet engine. Data access objects (DAO) are the part of VBA you use to programmatically manipulate Jet data from Access, Visual Basic, Visual Basic for Applications, and any other product that can act as an OLE Automation client. Chapter 6 discusses DAO in detail.

External ISAM DLLs

Jet provides access to several external Indexed Sequential Access Method (ISAM) format files using a series of installable .DLL files. The Jet engine supports five external ISAM formats: Xbase, Paradox, Btrieve, Excel, and text.

NOTE

Indexed Sequential Access Method (ISAM) is a physical method for storing data in a database. The term is also commonly used to refer to nonserver databases.

Expression Evaluator

Jet has its own expression evaluator (VBAJET32.DLL) to evaluate the functions and expressions in SQL statements. This expression evaluator is different from the expression evaluator built into Access.

The Jet Expression Evaluator

Jet has its own expression evaluator (VBAJET32.DLL), separate from the expression evaluator used by Access' VBA language, that is used to evaluate expressions such as "(intValue1 + 2) > intValue2". Having two different expression evaluators in Access has subtle repercussions because they work slightly differently. The Jet expression evaluator is used in WHERE clauses (criteria) in queries and validation rules. The VBA expression evaluator is used in all VBA code, including user-defined functions called from a query's WHERE clause.

One difference between the two expression evaluators is that the VBA expression evaluator treats logical operators, such as And, on a bit level, whereas the Jet expression evaluator operates on an integer level. Thus "1 And 2" evaluates to False in VBA (since the binary representations of 1 and 2 have no bits in common) but to True in Jet (since they're both True expressions, as far as Jet is concerned; remember, any nonzero quantity is treated as True). For example, suppose you have a query like the following, which is attempting to return only rows in which the value in intColumn1 is odd. (Odd numbers all have their least-significant bit set.)

```
SELECT tblTable1.intColumn1
FROM tblTable1
WHERE (tblTable1.intColumn1 And 1);
```

The result will not be what you might expect. Jet's expression evaluator operates on integers instead of bits; the 1 is treated as the value True. Since any value Anded with True returns the truth value of the original value, the "And 1" becomes superfluous in this case. The WHERE clause always evaluates to True unless intColumn1 contains 0. Thus, the query returns the records in which intColumn1 contains nonzero numbers.

In contrast, suppose you rewrote the query so it looked like this:

```
SELECT tblTable1.intColumn1
FROM tblTable1
WHERE PerformAnd(tblTable1.intColumn1, 1);
```

using the function PerformAnd(), which looked like this:

```
Function PerformAnd(intValue1 As Integer, _
 intValue2 As Integer) As Integer
    PerformAnd = intValue1 And intValue2
End Function
```

Since VBA performs logical operations on a bit level, the function returns True only if the low-order bit is 1. Only odd numbers have the low-order bit set to 1, so the query returns the rows in which intColumn1 contains odd numbers. Therefore, this version of the query will satisfy your original goal of showing rows in which intColumn1 contains odd values.

These differences do not show up often, but you nonetheless should be aware of them.

Replication Services

Replication Services are handled by several DLLs, the main one being MSWNG300.DLL. These DLLs take care of moving data among replicas and reconciliation.

The ODBC Driver Manager DLL

The Open Database Connectivity (ODBC) standard is a Microsoft-sponsored industry standard for accessing client-server data. When Jet needs to access data stored in an ODBC-supported data source, such as Microsoft SQL Server, Sybase SQL Server, or Oracle, it calls the ODBC Driver Manager (ODBC.DLL). The Driver Manager—which technically is not part of Jet—then calls the host database program using the appropriate ODBC driver.

You can also gain access to Jet (Access) databases from other programs using the *Access* ODBC driver. This allows users to get at Jet data from Microsoft Word for Windows, Excel, and other ODBC-compliant clients. Chapter 14 discusses ODBC in detail.

> **NOTE** We've presented a somewhat simplified view of the Jet engine in this section. In actuality, there are additional DLLs and other supporting files, but these have been left out of the discussion for the sake of simplicity.

The Jet Query Engine

The Jet query engine is responsible for the interpretation and execution of queries. Jet processes queries in four steps:

1. Definition
2. Compilation
3. Optimization
4. Execution

This process is shown in Figure 4.33.

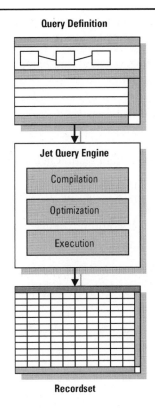

FIGURE 4.33:
The Jet query engine compiles, optimizes, and executes a query definition to produce a recordset.

Query Definition

You can define queries using one of several mechanisms: QBE, SQL, or DAO. Whichever method you use to create the query definition, the query eventually gets converted to SQL, and it is passed to the Jet query optimizer, which then compiles and optimizes the query.

Query Compilation

Before Jet can optimize a query, it must parse the SQL statement that defines the query and bind the names referenced in the query to columns in the underlying tables. The Jet query engine compiles the SQL string into an internal query object definition format, replacing common parts of the query string with tokens. The internal format can be likened to an inverted tree: the query's result set sits at the top of the tree (the tree's root) and the base tables are at the bottom (the leaves). The query compilation step is depicted in Figure 4.34.

Query definitions are parsed into distinct elements when compiled. These elements include the

- Base tables
- Output columns (the columns that will appear in the query's result set)
- Restrictions (in QBE, the criteria; in SQL, WHERE clause elements)
- Join columns (in QBE, the lines connecting two tables; in SQL, the columns in the JOIN clause)
- Sort columns (in QBE, sort columns; in SQL, the columns in the ORDER BY clause)

Each of these elements comes into play as the query optimizer considers different execution strategies, as described in the next few sections.

FIGURE 4.34:
During query compilation, Jet parses SQL and compiles it into a query tree.

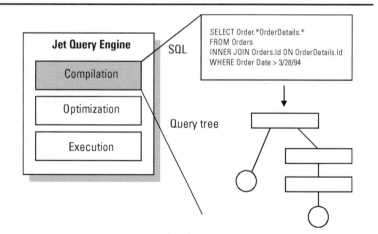

Query Optimization

The query optimizer is the most complex component of Jet. It's responsible for choosing the optimum query execution plan for the compiled query tree. The Jet query engine uses a cost-based algorithm, costing and comparing each potential execution strategy and choosing the one that's fastest. Jet calculates the cost for two major operations in the execution of queries: base table accesses and joins.

Base Table Access Plans

For each table in the query, the Jet query optimizer must choose a base table access plan. The three ways of accessing the rows in a table are

- **Table scan:** Scanning a table record by record without use of an index. This may be necessary if a restriction column is not indexed or if the restriction is not very selective (a large percentage of the base table rows are being requested). Each data page is read only once for a table scan.

- **Index range:** Reading records in a table using an index over one of the single-table restrictions (query criteria). A data page may be read more than once for an index range.

- **Rushmore restriction:** A Rushmore restriction is used when there are restrictions on multiple indexed columns. By using multiple indexes, Jet is able to reduce considerably the number of data pages it needs to read. In many cases Jet can execute Rushmore queries without reading any data pages. (Of course, Jet still has to read index pages, but reading only index pages is almost always more efficient.)

Rushmore Query Optimizations

Jet 3.0 (the version of Jet included with Access 95) includes support for Rushmore query optimizations. In Jet 1.x, Jet could use only one index for a base table access. Using techniques borrowed from FoxPro, Jet 3.0 (as well as Jet 2.0 and 2.5) can make use of more than one index to restrict records. Rushmore-based query optimization is used on queries involving restrictions on multiple indexed columns of the following types:

- **Index Intersection:** The two indexes are intersected with And. Used on restrictions of the form

    WHERE Company = 'Ford' And CarType = 'Sedan'

- **Index Union:** The two indexes are unioned with Or. Used on restrictions of the form

    WHERE CarType = 'Wagon' Or Year = '1994'

- **Index Counts:** Queries that return record counts only. In these cases Jet can execute the query by reading only index pages. Used for queries of the form

    SELECT Count(*) FROM Autos WHERE Company = 'Dodge' And

    CarType='Truck';

You can execute many queries much more quickly using the Rushmore query optimizer. Rushmore can't work, however, if you don't build multiple indexes for each table. It also doesn't come into play for those queries that don't contain index intersections, index unions, or index counts.

Join Strategies

For queries involving more than one table, the optimizer must consider the cost of joins, choosing from the following five types of joins:

- Nested iteration join

- Index join

- Lookup join

- Merge join

- Index-merge join

The Jet query optimizer uses statistics about the tables in the query (discussed in the next section) to determine which join strategy to use. Each possible join combination is considered to determine which will yield the least costly query execution plan. The five join strategies are contrasted in Table 4.4.

TABLE 4.4: Contrasting Jet Join Strategies

Join Strategy	Description	When Used
Nested iteration join	"Brute-force" iteration through the rows in both tables	Only as a last-ditch effort. May be used when there are few records or no indexes
Index join	Scans rows in the first table and looks up matching rows in the second table using an index	When the rows in the second table are small (or no data needs to be retrieved from this table) or when the rows in the first table are small or highly restrictive

TABLE 4.4: Contrasting Jet Join Strategies (continued)

Join Strategy	Description	When Used
Lookup join	Similar to the index join except that a projection and sort on the second table are done prior to the join	When rows in the second table are small but not indexed by the join columns
Merge join	Sorts rows in the two tables by the join columns and combines the two tables by scanning down both tables simultaneously	When the two tables are large and the result set needs to be ordered on the join columns
Index-merge join	Similar to a merge join, except that indexes are used to order the two tables	Instead of a merge join when each input is a table in native Jet database format. Each input must have an index over its join columns, and at least one of the indexes must not allow nulls if there is more than one join column

Query Statistics

When evaluating various base table access plans and join strategies, the Jet query optimizer looks at the following statistics for each base table:

- Number of records in the base table.

- Number of data pages occupied by the base table. The greater the number of data pages that need to be read, the more costly the query.

- Location of the table. Is the table in a local ISAM format or is it from an ODBC database?

- Indexes on the table. When looking at indexes, the optimizer is concerned with

   Selectivity: How "unique" is the index? Does the index allow for duplicates? A unique index is the most highly selective index available, since every value is distinct. The more selective the index, the better.

   Number of index pages: As with data pages, the greater the number of index pages, the more costly the query.

   Whether nulls are allowed in the index: Nulls in an index may rule out the usage of an index-merge join.

Putting It All Together

In determining the optimum query execution plan, the Jet query optimizer iterates through the various combinations of base table access plans and join strategies. Before choosing a join strategy, the optimizer selects a base table access plan. The optimizer then stores the estimated number of records returned and a cost indicating how expensive it would be to read the table. Next, the optimizer generates all combinations of pairs of tables and costs each join strategy. Finally, the optimizer adds tables to the joins and continues to calculate statistics until it finds the cheapest overall execution plan.

The query optimizer also considers the type of result set when costing various join strategies. When returning a dynaset, Jet often favors join strategies that are efficient at returning the first page of records quickly, even if the chosen execution strategy is slower at returning the complete result set. For dynasets, this tends to rule out joins that require sorting, such as lookup joins and merge joins.

For queries based on many tables, the time spent estimating the cost of all potential join combinations could easily exceed the time spent executing any given execution strategy. Because of this, the query optimizer reduces the potential number of joins it needs to consider by using the following rule: Consider joining only the results of a join to a base table. The query optimizer will never consider joining the results of one join to the results of another. This considerably reduces the potential number of joins Jet needs to look at. The optimization steps are depicted in Figure 4.35.

After the Jet query optimizer has compiled and optimized the query, two additional steps are taken prior to the execution of the query.

For queries involving ODBC data sources, the remote post-processor determines how much of a query can be sent to the back end for processing by the database server application. The goal here is to send as much of the query as possible to the server, taking advantage of the server's abilities in executing queries involving server tables. This reduces the number of records that need be sent across the network wire to Jet. The remote post processor identifies those parts of the query tree that can be satisfied by server queries and generates the server SQL strings for each remote query. (Chapter 14 discusses this partitioning of ODBC queries in more detail.)

Finally, the post processor takes the compiled query tree and moves it to a new, cleaner, and smaller execution segment. This is the final step prior to query execution.

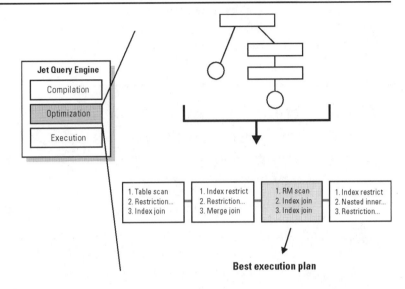

FIGURE 4.35:
The query optimizer determines the cost of various execution plans and chooses the best (the least costly plan as measured by estimated execution time).

Jet Query Engine
Compilation
Optimization
Execution

1. Table scan	1. Index restrict	1. RM scan	1. Index restrict
2. Restriction...	2. Restriction...	2. Index join	2. Nested inner...
3. Index join	3. Merge join	3. Index join	3. Restriction...

Best execution plan

Query Execution

Once the optimizer has determined the optimum query execution plan, the query engine runs through the final query tree and executes each step to return the recordset.

You can direct Jet to create dynasets or snapshots. When Jet runs a dynaset-based query, it creates a set of unique key values called a *keyset* in memory that points back to the rows in the underlying tables. This keyset-driven cursor model is very efficient, since Jet needs to read only these key values and store them in memory (overflowing to disk if necessary). The values of the other columns in the dynaset aren't read until needed (such as when a user scrolls the datasheet to that screen of dynaset rows), minimizing the time needed to execute the query.

For snapshot-based queries, Jet must run the query to completion and extract all the query's columns into the snapshot. When the query contains many rows, it's likely that Jet won't be able to fit the entire snapshot into memory, requiring Jet to overflow the result set to disk, substantially slowing the query. Since Jet reads only the key values of dynasets into memory, the same dynaset-based query might fit entirely in memory, resulting in a significant performance boost. On the other hand, queries with a small number of columns and rows will likely execute more quickly as snapshots. (Of course, snapshots can be used only when you don't need to update data.)

Jet 3.0 Performance Enhancements

Microsoft's only stated goal for Jet version 3.0 was to improve performance. To accomplish this, they decided not to add any new features to Jet. They did, however, make the following performance enhancements:

- **32-bit architecture**: Jet 3.0 is now a 32-bit engine.

- **Multi-threading**: Jet 3.0 uses multiple threads to increase performance. Threads are generated internally for background processes, such as the reading ahead of pages of data, and cache maintenance. By default, Jet uses up to three threads. You can increase the maximum number of threads by adding (or modifying) a THREADS value of the HKEY_LOCAL_MACHINE\SOFTWARE\MICROSOFT\JET\3.0\ENGINES\JET system registry key. This value has a datatype of DWORD.

- **Deferred page reuse:** Jet 3.0 will *not* reclaim index pages that are no longer needed. This greatly reduces the number of read locks Jet places on index pages, increasing concurrency and reducing network traffic.

- **Fast deletion of rows**: Deleting all records in a table without criteria (DELETE FROM *tablename*) is now much faster.

- **Simplified index structure and compact indexes**: Jet 3.0's indexing structures have been simplified. Whereas Jet 2.x uses three different index structures, Jet 3.0 uses only one. In addition, Jet 3.0 supports leading key compression in indexes. This means that repeated key values are stored only once in the index, which makes for much smaller indexes. (Unfortunately, you probably won't notice this because other parts of Access—principally VBA module storage—take up more space in Access 95.)

- **Internal transactions**: Jet 3.0 detects DAO update code that could benefit from a transaction and automatically wraps the sequence of statements in a transaction. These internal transactions are transparent.

- **Concurrent inserts**: Jet 2.x locks the table header page and last data page when a user is adding a new row to a table. In a multiuser situation, this means only one user can add a new record to a table at a time. Jet 3.0 no longer locks these pages, so it is much less likely to lock *any* users out of adding new rows.

- **Database compacts in primary key order**: During a compact operation, Jet 3.0 orders rows of data in primary key order rather than physical order. This means that Jet 3.0 indexes (after compaction) behave like clustered indexes. (Jet 3.0, however, does not maintain indexes in clustered order.)

- **Faster lock detection**: Jet 3.0 is now faster at detecting when another user has locked a page of records.

- **Improved memo/OLE data storage**: Jet 2.x stores all memo and OLE datatype fields in a hidden system table. This means an update to a memo/OLE field in one table can affect an update to memo/OLE data in another table. Jet 3.0 minimizes potential conflicts by storing each memo/OLE field in a different set of pages.

- **Least-recently-used page replacement**: Jet 2.0 uses a first-in, first-out buffer replacement system, which means that a page of data might be flushed from its buffers even if it was used often. Jet 3.0 uses a least-used, first-out system instead.

These changes to Jet 3.0 should result in faster data access.

When executing a query using DAO, you can also create forward-only snapshots (using the dbFowardOnly option of the OpenRecordset method). This special kind of snapshot is faster than the normal (backward- and forward-scrolling) snapshot, since Jet doesn't have to maintain back-scroll cursors. (On the downside, you can move forward only through a forward-only snapshot.)

Forcing Jet to Recompile and Optimize a Query

Queries are compiled and optimized the first time you run a query. They are not re-compiled until you resave and rerun the query. Make sure you run all queries at least once before delivering an application to users. This will eliminate subsequent compilations. Save the query in Design view and then run it without saving it again. You shouldn't save the query *after* running it, or it may be saved in an un-compiled state.

Since Jet makes optimization decisions based on the size of source tables when you compiled the query, it's a good idea to force Jet to recompile a query after you've altered indexes or significantly changed the schema or number of rows in the tables. You can force recompilation by opening the query in Design view, saving it, and then reexecuting it.

Taking Advantage of Rushmore

There is no way to turn Rushmore on or off. Jet takes advantage of Rushmore op-timizations anytime you have criteria that reference multiple indexed columns from the same table. If you have queries that *don't* include multiple restrictions or that contain restrictions on columns for which you haven't created indexes, Rush-more won't be used. Thus, it's important to create indexes on all columns that are used in query restrictions.

Rushmore works for both native and attached Access tables, as well as for attached FoxPro and dBASE tables. Queries involving ODBC, Btrieve, Excel, text, or Paradox tables do not benefit from Rushmore.

Keeping Statistics Accurate

The costing algorithms the query optimizer uses are dependent on the accuracy of the statistics provided by the underlying engine. Statistics for non-native tables will, in general, be less accurate than for native Access tables. For ODBC queries in which the whole query is sent to the server for processing, however, this is irrele-vant, since the server will be optimizing and executing the entire query.

For native Access tables, statistics may be inaccurate if many transactions are rolled back. Statistics can also be wrong if Jet (or the database application calling Jet) terminates abnormally without being able to update statistics to disk.

TIP
To force Jet to update the statistics in a Jet database, you should regularly compact the database. Compacting the database may also speed up queries because it writes all the data in a table to contiguous pages. This makes scanning sequential pages much faster than when the database is fragmented. Before compacting a database, it's a good idea to also run a disk defrag utility so Jet can store the newly compacted database in contiguous space on disk.

See Chapter 17 for additional tips on query optimization.

Summary

Select queries and the updatable dynasets they produce play a central role in most Access applications. They are the building blocks on which you construct the rest of your application. In this chapter, you learned

- The differences between inner, outer, and self joins
- About the different types of query properties
- How to construct top value queries
- How to use parameter queries to allow the specification of criteria at run
- How to construct totals and crosstab queries
- How to create update, delete, make-table, and append queries
- When dynasets are updatable

Finally, you learned about the database engine under Access called Jet. This information included

- The parts of the Jet database engine and how they relate to each other
- The steps Jet takes in processing a query: definition, compilation, optimization, and execution
- How queries are optimized
- How and when Rushmore works
- How to force Jet to recompile a query
- How to keep Jet's statistics accurate
- Changes made to Jet 3.0

Chapter 5 builds on this chapter, discussing the construction of queries using Access SQL.

CHAPTER

FIVE

Access SQL

- Understanding Access SQL

- Learning the differences between Access SQL and ANSI SQL

- Using subqueries and union queries

- Creating SQL pass-through queries

Structured Query Language (or SQL, pronounced both as "ess-cue-ell" and "see-quel"; we prefer the latter pronunciation) is by far the most popular nonprocedural data access language today on computers of all sizes. Access includes support for this pervasive standard, but its implementation is incomplete and diverges from the standard in many places. Just pinning down Access' level of conformance is a chore; while Access SQL supports only a subset of SQL-89, at the same time it supports some elements of the newer SQL-92 standard. Thus, if you're already familiar with SQL, you may find Access' uneven support for the standard confusing. And if you're new to SQL and want to learn Access SQL in detail, you'll find a dearth of documentation on Microsoft's dialect of the standard query language. This chapter hopes to make up for this documentation deficiency.

A Brief History of SQL

Like many database standards, including the relational model itself and query by example, SQL was invented at an IBM research laboratory in the early 1970s. SQL was first described in a research paper presented at an Association for Computing Machinery (ACM) meeting in 1974. Created to implement E.F. Codd's relational model (originally described in an ACM paper in 1970), it began life as SEQUEL (for Structured English Query Language), briefly becoming SEQUEL/2 and then simply SQL.

Today there are hundreds of databases on platforms ranging from billion-dollar supercomputers down to thousand-dollar personal computers supporting SQL. This makes it the de facto data access language standard, but at the same time it's also an official standard. There are three American National Standards Institute (ANSI) SQL standards: SQL-86 (the most commonly implemented SQL today), SQL-89 (a minor revision), and the recently published SQL-92 (a major revision).

When most people speak of SQL, they are talking about the SQL-86 or SQL-89 standard, often extended by vendors to make it a more complete language. Only very recently have vendors begun to implement parts of the much more comprehensive SQL-92 standard. It will take years for many vendors (including Microsoft) to fully implement SQL-92.

Access SQL really shines in one crucial area: most of Access SQL directly maps to Access query by example (QBE)—in both directions. This means you can learn Access SQL by constructing queries using QBE and switching to SQL view to see the equivalent SQL. Conversely, the SQL-savvy developer can skip QBE entirely and directly enter queries using SQL view. In fact, such developers can use their SQL knowledge to learn Access QBE.

This chapter covers Access SQL in its entirety. It should prove useful to both the SQL-fluent developer coming to Access from other SQL implementations *and* the SQL-naive developer looking to make sense of this strange new language.

Where Can You Use Access SQL?

Unlike most other products that support SQL, Access has no SQL command line or similar facility into which you can directly enter SQL statements and press the ↵ key or click a button to view the results. The closest thing to this in Access is the VBA Debug window, but it doesn't allow you to directly enter SQL statements. Instead, you must enter SQL statements into the SQL view of the Access query facility and switch to Datasheet view to display the results.

Most of the time you'll find Access' way of doing things preferable to a SQL command-line interface because Access formats the data in a fully forward- and backward-scrollable window. What's more, you can instantly switch between SQL view, where you enter the SQL statements; Query view, where you compose and view the equivalent query specification using QBE; and Datasheet view, where the results of the query are displayed.

If you find yourself still missing a SQL command-line type facility, you can always create your own using a simple form, such as the one shown in Figure 5.1. The main advantage of this type of SQL scratchpad facility is that you can view the SQL statement and its output simultaneously.

We created this scratchpad form using a text box, where the SQL statement is entered, and a list box control, where the results are displayed. A list-filling function (see Chapter 7) is used to fill the list box with the results of the query. We have

FIGURE 5.1:

Simple SQL scratchpad form for testing SQL statements

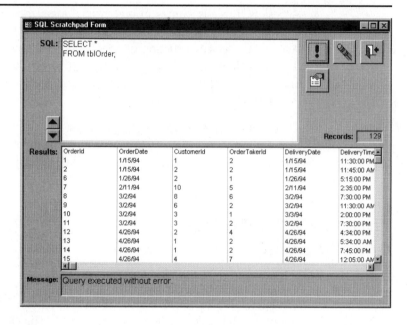

included two additional text boxes to display the total number of returned records and any error messages encountered when running the query.

The form, frmSQLScratchpad, is included in the CH05.MDB database. Since we have implemented this form using Code-Behind-Forms, it will work without any changes if you import it into any other database. Many of the examples in this chapter are shown using this simple SQL scratchpad form.

NOTE The SQL scratchpad form and all the tables and queries used in the examples in this chapter are included in the CH05.MDB database on the companion disk. In addition, we have created an add-in version of this form, SQLSRAT.MDA, which you can also find on the CD included with this book. Once you install this add-in, you can call up the SQL Scratchpad form from any database using the Tools ➤ Add-ins command.

In addition to SQL view, there are several other places in Access where you can use SQL statements. You can use SQL as the record source for a form or report or the row source for a combo box, list box, or embedded graph control. In addition, you can use SQL to create and modify query definitions that are manipulated with Access' data access objects (DAO) language (see Chapter 6).

Learning Access SQL

Although SQL may seem at first daunting in complexity, when it comes right down to it, it's a fairly straightforward language to learn and use. Except for a few additions, Access SQL is pretty much a subset of ANSI SQL-89. The remainder of this chapter describes Access SQL in detail.

The SELECT Statement

The *SELECT statement* is the bread and butter of Access SQL, or any SQL, for that matter. If you learn the SELECT statement and all its clauses, you'll know most of what's to know about SQL. Select queries *select* rows of data and return them as a dynaset recordset.

The basic syntax of the SELECT statement is

SELECT *column-list*

FROM *table-list*

[WHERE *where-clause*]

[ORDER BY *order-by-clause*];

SELECT statements *must* include SELECT and FROM clauses. The WHERE and ORDER BY clauses are optional.

SQL Syntax Conventions

This chapter uses the following conventions for the specification of SQL syntax:

Items in all UPPERCASE indicate keywords you must enter literally. Items in *italicized* lowercase indicate placeholders for specific values you enter.

If the placeholder includes the word *list* or *clause,* this indicates a simplification of a more detailed syntax that will be discussed later in the chapter. For example, "WHERE *where-clause*" is the syntax for a simplified WHERE clause.

Square brackets ([item]) in the syntax diagrams in this chapter denote optional items. For example, "CONSTRAINT [UNIQUE] *index*" indicates that CONSTRAINT is required, that the keyword UNIQUE is optional, and that you must enter the name of an index in place of *index*.

Curly braces combined with vertical bars ({OPTION1 | OPTION2}) denote a choice. In this case you can choose only OPTION1 *or* OPTION2.

An ellipsis (...) combined with the square brackets notation indicates a repeating sequence. For example, "*column1* [,*column2* [, ...]]" indicates that you may include one or more columns.

You customarily start each clause of a SQL statement on a new line, but this is done only for the sake of clarity, since you may break the lines wherever you please. Another custom is to enter keywords in all caps, but this is not required. We follow these customs throughout this chapter. You should terminate SQL statements with a semicolon, although Access (but not many other SQL implementations) will still process SQL statements that lack semicolon terminators.

The SELECT Clause

You use the *SELECT clause* to specify which columns to include in the resulting recordset. The column names are analogous to fields dropped onto the QBE grid with the Show box checked. Just as in QBE, you can use an asterisk (*) to indicate all fields from a table. The syntax of the SELECT clause is

> SELECT {* | *expression1* [AS *alias1*] [, *expression2* [AS *alias2*] [, ...]]]}

The expressions can be simple column names, computed columns, or SQL aggregate functions. For example, you can select all the columns in a table like this:

```
SELECT *
```

You indicate a single column—for example, LastName—like this:

```
SELECT LastName
```

You choose multiple columns—for example, Customer#, FirstName, and Last-Name—like this:

```
SELECT [Customer#], LastName, FirstName
```

In the preceding example, the Customer# column is enclosed in square brackets because its name contains a *nonalphanumeric* character. You need to use square brackets to delimit all column names that include these characters or spaces. (Don't confuse these *required* brackets with the square brackets used in the syntax diagrams to indicate optional parameters.) At your discretion you may also use brackets to enclose names that don't require brackets. For example, you could enter the preceding statement as

```
SELECT [Customer#], [LastName], [FirstName]
```

You can change the name of output columns and create computed columns using SQL, just as you can in QBE. To create a computed column, enter an expression instead of a table-based column. To rename a column, add "AS *aliasname*" after the column or expression.

For example, to return Customer#, renamed as "ID", and the concatenation of first and last names, renamed as "Customer Name", you could enter the following:

```
SELECT [Customer#] AS ID, [FirstName] & " " & [LastName] AS
[Customer Name]
```

If you include multiple tables (or queries) in the SELECT statement (see the section "Joining Tables" later in this chapter), you will likely need to refer to a particular column that has the same name in more than one table included in the query. In this case you must use the fully qualified version of the column name using this syntax:

> *table-or-query.column*

For example, you could select the column OrderId from table tblOrderDetails using the following:

```
SELECT tblOrderDetails.OrderId
```

The FROM Clause

You use the *FROM clause* to specify the names of the tables or queries from which to select records. If you use more than one table, you must specify here how the tables are to be joined. See the section "Joining Tables" later in this chapter for more details on multitable queries. For now, here's the simplified single-table syntax:

FROM *table-or-query* [AS *alias*]

For example, you would enter the following SELECT statement to return all columns and all rows from table tblOrder. (This query was shown earlier in Figure 5.1.)

```
SELECT *
FROM tblOrder;
```

If you wished to return only the OrderId and OrderDate columns, you could enter the following SELECT statement:

```
SELECT OrderId, OrderDate
FROM tblOrder;
```

As with the SELECT clause, where you can alias (temporarily rename) columns, you can alias table names in the FROM clause. Include the alias, sometimes called a *correlation name,* immediately after the table name, along with the AS keyword. To expand on the last example, you could have renamed tblOrder as Orders Table using the following SELECT statement:

```
SELECT OrderId, OrderDate
FROM tblOrder AS [Orders Table];
```

Correlation names are often used for convenience—correlation names such as T1 and T2 (where T1 stands for *table 1*) are often used to reduce typing—but *sometimes* they are required. You must use them for the specification of self joins (see the section "Self Joins" later in this chapter) and certain correlated subqueries (see the section "Subqueries" later in this chapter).

The WHERE Clause

You use the optional *WHERE clause* to restrict or filter the rows returned by a query. The WHERE clause corresponds to the Criteria and Or lines of QBE. Columns referenced in the WHERE clause needn't be included in the SELECT clause column list. (You can accomplish the same end in QBE by unchecking the Show box under a column used to set criteria.) A WHERE clause in Access SQL may contain up to 40 columns or expressions linked by the logical operator AND or OR. You may also use parentheses to group logical conditions.

The syntax of the WHERE clause is

WHERE *expression1* [{And | Or} *expression2* [, ...]]

For example, you could restrict the rows returned by the SQL statement presented earlier to only those orders in which OrderTakerId = 2 with the following SELECT statement:

```
SELECT OrderId, OrderDate
FROM tblOrder
WHERE OrderTakerId = 2;
```

Figure 5.2 shows the result of this query.

WHERE clause expressions take the same format as expressions in QBE. You may reference columns, built-in and user-defined functions, constants, and operators in each expression. Here are several examples of valid WHERE clauses:

```
WHERE CustomerId = 4
WHERE Sex = "Female" AND Age BETWEEN 21 AND 29
WHERE LastName IS NOT NULL OR (LastName IS NULL AND
FirstName = "Joe")
WHERE OrderDate > DateAdd("yyyy", -1, Date())
```

FIGURE 5.2:

Simple select query that displays OrderId and OrderDate for all orders taken by order takers with an OrderTakerId of 2

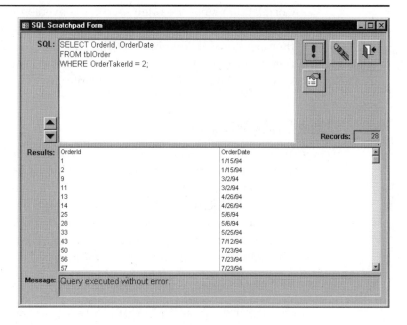

Access SQL is less forgiving than Access QBE about the specification of criteria, so you need to keep the following rules in mind when entering expressions:

- Always enclose text strings in WHERE clauses in quotes; either single or double quotes are fine. For example:

  ```
  WHERE LastName = "Jones"
  ```

- Enclose dates with the pound sign (#). For example:

  ```
  WHERE OrderDate > #4/15/95#
  ```

- Always use the keyword LIKE with wildcard characters when you wish to use inexact pattern-matching criteria. For example:

  ```
  WHERE FirstName LIKE "P*"
  ```

NOTE ANSI SQL uses double quotes the same way Access uses square brackets. In ANSI SQL you can use only single quotes for text strings.

The ORDER BY Clause

You use the optional *ORDER BY clause* to sort the rows returned by the query by one or more columns. You use the ASC or DESC keyword to specify ascending or descending order. Ascending is the default. The ORDER BY clause corresponds to the Sort line in QBE. As with QBE, precedence in sorting is left to right.

NOTE The sort order Access uses is specified at the time you create the database using the Tools ➤ Options ➤ New Database Sort Order setting. By default, Access uses the "General" (U.S.) sort order, which you can change to some other sort order. Once a database is created, a change in sort order has no effect until you compact the database.

Just as with the WHERE clause, columns referenced in the ORDER BY clause needn't be included in the SELECT clause column list. You can sort text, numeric, and date/time columns, which will be sorted alphabetically, numerically, and chronologically, respectively, just as you'd expect. Don't include memo or OLE-object type fields in an ORDER BY clause; you cannot sort on these column types. The ORDER BY syntax is as follows:

ORDER BY *column1* [{ASC | DESC}] [, *column2* [{ASC | DESC}] [, …]]

For example, if you wanted to list your customers alphabetically by last and then first name, you could use the following SQL statement:

```
SELECT *
FROM tblCustomer
ORDER BY LastName, FirstName;
```

Joining Tables

If you've properly normalized your database (see Chapter 3), you'll undoubtedly need to create queries that draw data from more than one table. When you access multiple tables in SQL, just as in Access QBE, you must *join* the tables on one or more columns to produce meaningful results. If you don't join the tables, you'll produce a Cartesian product query, which is usually undesired. (A *Cartesian product* is the arithmetic product of two or more input tables. For example, two 25-row tables joined this way result in a 625-row recordset.)

There are two ways to join tables in Access SQL (actually, three, if you include subselects, which are covered in the section "Subqueries" later in this chapter): in the FROM clause and in the WHERE clause. Joins in the WHERE clause have always been a part of SQL; joins in the FROM clause are a feature that was added to the ANSI standard in SQL-92.

Using the older SQL-89–compliant syntax, you join tables like this:

> SELECT *column-list*
>
> FROM *table1*, *table2*
>
> WHERE *table1.column1 = table2.column2*;

Note that this syntax makes no provision for outer joins (see Chapter 4 for more information on outer joins), although some vendors have suggested extensions to the standard.

In contrast, the SQL-92–compliant syntax looks like this:

> SELECT *column-list*
>
> FROM *table1* {INNER | LEFT [OUTER] | RIGHT [OUTER]} JOIN *table2*
>
> ON *table1.column1 = table2.column2*;

The keyword OUTER is optional.

The next example contrasts the two join methods. For example, say you wished to select OrderId, OrderDate, and CustomerName for all orders occurring on or after January 1, 1995. Using the older SQL-89–compliant join syntax, you would enter the SQL statement shown in Figure 5.3. Using the newer syntax, you would enter the equivalent statement shown in Figure 5.4.

Although it's useful to be familiar with the SQL-89–style join syntax (especially if you will be using other products that are SQL-89 compliant), we recommend using the SQL-92–compliant syntax for joining tables. It's more powerful, and it's consistent with the SQL generated by Access QBE. More important, recordsets produced using the SQL-89 syntax are not updatable.

FIGURE 5.3:

SELECT statement that joins the tables tblOrder and tblCustomer using SQL-89–compliant join syntax. The results of this query will be read-only.

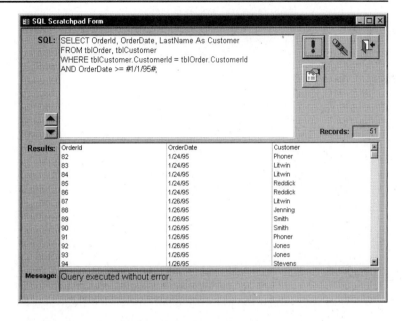

FIGURE 5.4:

SELECT statement that joins the tables tblOrder and tblCustomer using SQL-92–compliant join syntax. The results of this query will be fully updatable.

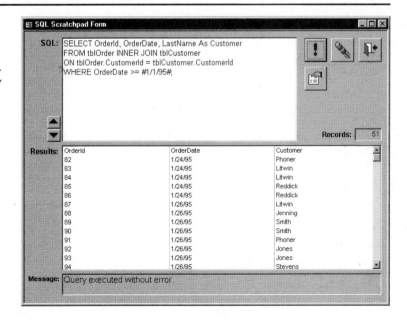

Multiple Joins

As when using Access QBE, you can create SELECT statements that join more than two tables. A simplified syntax for specifying joins of multiple tables in the FROM clause is

FROM (… (*table1* JOIN *table2* ON *conditionA*) JOIN *table3* ON *conditionB*) JOIN …)

> **NOTE**
>
> To simplify the preceding syntax diagram, we've used the word *JOIN* to indicate *any* type of join. You would, of course, use one of the following instead: INNER JOIN, LEFT OUTER JOIN, or RIGHT OUTER JOIN.

You may find this nested-style syntax a little confusing. It implies a set order in which the joins are performed—for example, "first join table1 to table2 and then join that result to table3 and then…." But the order of joins doesn't really matter in Access. No matter how you specify the order in the FROM clause, the Jet query processor decides on the optimum ordering of joins for the sake of efficiency. This is the way it *should* be in the relational model.

So it would seem that this syntax is counter intuitive. Alas, this type of syntax *is* necessary for the specification of outer joins in the ANSI SQL standard because order *does* matter with outer joins. But there's yet another twist: even though ANSI SQL supports the use of parentheses to allow you to arbitrarily combine outer and inner joins in any order, Access does not. This arises from the fact that the Jet query processor ignores the placement of parentheses when processing queries. Because of this, Access SQL has very specific rules on how outer joins can be combined with inner joins or other outer joins.

The Jet engine enforces the following rules when combining joins in a single query:

- The nonpreserved table in an outer join *cannot* participate in an inner join.

- The nonpreserved table in an outer join *cannot* be the nonpreserved table of another outer join.

In a left outer join, the unmatched rows in the table on the left side of the join are *preserved*. In a right outer join, the unmatched rows in the table on the right side of the join are preserved. As Access executes an outer join, it first looks at each row in the preserved table. If a row in the other (nonpreserved) table matches a row in the preserved table, Access creates a result row from the two. Otherwise Access creates a result row from the columns in the preserved table and fills the columns from the other (nonpreserved) table with nulls. An outer join will always have as many rows as or more rows than the equivalent inner join.

These rules can also be expressed using QBE: a table with an arrow pointing toward it *can't* also be connected to either a line with no arrow or another arrow pointing toward it.

So even though you must use the parentheses, for all practical purposes they are ignored as the Jet query engine processes your query. Instead, you must follow the preceding rules when combining outer joins. If you fail to, you will receive the "Query contains ambiguous outer joins" or "Join expression not supported" error message.

If you need to create a query that does not follow these rules, you can usually break it up into multiple stacked queries that Jet *can* handle. For example, say you wished to list all customers and the items they ordered but include customers who made no orders. To solve this problem, you might create a four-table, three-join query that looks like this:

```
SELECT LastName, OrderDate,
Quantity, MenuDescription
FROM ((tblOrder INNER JOIN tblOrderDetails
ON tblOrder.OrderId = tblOrderDetails.OrderId)
INNER JOIN tblMenu ON tblOrderDetails.MenuId = tblMenu.MenuId)
RIGHT JOIN tblCustomer ON tblOrder.CustomerId =
tblCustomer.CustomerId
ORDER BY LastName, OrderDate;
```

Unfortunately, the preceding query will not work. If you attempt to execute it, you get the "Join expression not supported" error message. This is because the non-preserved side of the outer join (in this case, a right outer join) is combined with several inner joins.

The solution to this dilemma is to create the query in two steps:

1. Create a query that joins the tables tblOrder, tblOrderDetails, and tblMenu using inner joins. Save the query, for example, as qryItems.

2. Create a second query that combines the result of qryItems with tblCustomer using an outer join.

The first query's SELECT statement (qryItems) would look like this:

```
SELECT CustomerId, OrderDate,
Quantity, MenuDescription
FROM (tblOrder INNER JOIN tblOrderDetails
ON tblOrder.OrderId = tblOrderDetails.OrderId)
INNER JOIN tblMenu
ON tblOrderDetails.MenuId = tblMenu.MenuId;
```

The second query would then look like this:

```
SELECT LastName, OrderDate,
Quantity, MenuDescription
FROM tblCustomer LEFT JOIN qryItems ON
tblCustomer.CustomerId = qryItems.CustomerId
ORDER BY LastName, OrderDate;
```

You can use these two *stacked* queries, the datasheet for which is shown in Figure 5.5, to produce the correct answer.

Self Joins

Self joins are useful for answering certain types of queries when you have recursive relationships or when you wish to pull together and "flatten" multiple rows from a table. For example, if you stored the ID number of supervisors in an employees table, you could join the employees table to itself to display employees and their supervisors on a single row of a report. And in a database in which you stored multiple addresses of a customer in separate rows of an address table, you could also use a self join to pull together into a single record both home and work addresses.

FIGURE 5.5:

Customers and their orders, including rows where no orders were made. (Note the first row.) This query, because it requires combining outer and inner joins with inner joins on the nonpreserved side of the outer join, must be created using two stacked queries.

LastName	OrderDate	Quantity	MenuDescription
Ayala			
Babitt	11-Feb-94	45	Large Cheese Pizza
Babitt	13-Sep-94	6	Small Diet Coke
Babitt	13-Sep-94	1	Small Sprite
Babitt	13-Sep-94	1	Large Sprite
Babitt	13-Sep-94	5	Small Sprite
Babitt	13-Sep-94	1	Salad
Babitt	13-Sep-94	6	Lasagna
Fallon	23-Jul-94	8	Small Diet Coke
Fallon	01-Aug-94	3	Lasagna
Fallon	01-Aug-94	9	Large Sprite
Fallon	01-Aug-94	3	Salad
Fallon	01-Aug-94	4	Large Pepsi
Fallon	01-Aug-94	1	Medium Pepperoni Pizza
Fallon	14-Nov-94	5	Large Diet Pepsi
Fallon	14-Nov-94	10	Small Diet Coke
Fallon	14-Nov-94	8	Small Sprite
Fallon	14-Nov-94	1	Large Coke
Jenning	02-Mar-94	1	Medium Cheese Pizza
Jenning	02-Mar-94	2	Medium Pepperoni Pizza
Jenning	25-May-94	10	Lasagna

Record: ◄ ◄ | 1 | ► ►I ►* | of 344

The trick to creating self joins in QBE is to alias the second copy of a table so it is treated as though it were a separate table. You use this same trick to create self joins using SQL. For example, tblEmployee contains a column, SupervisorId, that is used to reference the EmployeeId of the employee's supervisor (see Figure 5.6). Say you wished to view the names of all employees and their supervisors' names and include employees who lacked a supervisor. (This last requirement means you need to use an outer join to create the desired query.) The SELECT statement that accomplishes this is shown in Figure 5.7.

FIGURE 5.6:

The tblEmployee table was designed with a recursive relationship between EmployeeId and SupervisorId. This design allows you to store information about both employees and their supervisors in a single table.

EmployeeId	LastName	FirstName	Address	City	State	ZipCode	HomePhone	SupervisorId
1	Jones	Mary	34 15th Ave Wes	Fall City	WA	98789	2067897890	
2	Alabaster	Steve	3409 Red Street	Federal Way	WA	98009		1
3	Lovely	Rita	3 Maple NE	Kent	WA	98019	2066786787	5
4	Ronald	Alan	624 NW 79th St	Seattle	WA	98117	2067836901	5
5	Peters	Beth	89 NE 64th St	Seattle	WA	98109	2067869098	1
6	Carey	Phil	37 West Governn	Mountlake T	WA	98789	2065649089	1
7	Peters	Joe	2529 13th Ave E	NYC	WA	98909		5

Record: ◄ ◄ | 1 | ► ►I ►* | of 7

FIGURE 5.7:

This self-join query produces a list of all employees and their supervisors. By using an outer join, you can include the CEO, Mary Jones, even though she has no supervisor.

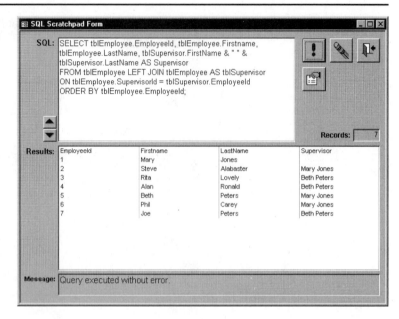

Non–Equi-Joins

All the joins discussed in this chapter so far have been *equi-joins*—joins based on one field being equal to another. You can also create *non–equi-joins* in Access using the operators >, >=, <, <=, <>, and Between. You'll likely use non–equi-joins far less frequently than the standard equi-join, but sometimes a non–equi-join is exactly what you need.

The CH05.MDB database includes a table called tblEvents that lists special sales events and the beginning and ending dates for each event (see Figure 5.8). Say you'd like to create a query that lists information on each order (from tblOrder) linked to the special events table and limited to Visa sales on or after June of 1995. Since the events from tblEvents are listed as a range of dates, you can't use an equi-join to link this table to tblOrder. You can, however, join the two tables using the BETWEEN operator like this:

```
ON (tblOrder.OrderDate BETWEEN tblEvents.BeginningDate AND
tblEvents.EndingDate)
```

The complete query is shown in Figure 5.9. We used a left outer join to include all orders, not just those occurring during special events.

FIGURE 5.8:

The tblEvents table tracks special events for a restaurant.

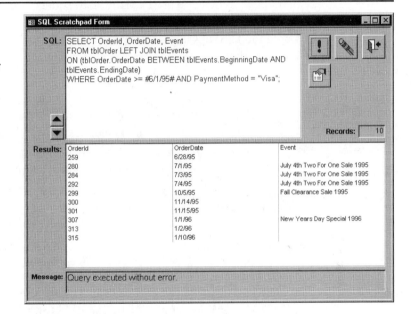

FIGURE 5.9:

This query joins the tblOrder and tblEvents tables using the BETWEEN operator and a left outer join.

The ALL, DISTINCTROW, and DISTINCT Predicates

You can precede the SELECT clause column-name list with one of the mutually exclusive quantifier predicates: ALL, DISTINCTROW, or DISTINCT. (The DISTINCTROW predicate is unique to Access SQL.) These quantifiers control how duplicate values and duplicate records are handled. Here's the basic syntax of the SELECT clause predicates:

SELECT [{ ALL | DISTINCT | DISTINCTROW }] *column-list*

If you use no keyword, ALL is assumed. ALL returns all rows that meet the specified criteria. No special processing of the rows is performed to ensure uniqueness. This is equivalent in QBE to setting *both* the UniqueValues and UniqueRecords properties to No.

If you use the keyword DISTINCT, Access eliminates any duplicate rows in the result set *based on the columns contained in the SELECT clause.* If more than one column is specified in the SELECT clause, Access discards duplicates based on the values of them all. When you use DISTINCT, the query's recordset is never updatable, and performance may be adversely affected. Thus, use DISTINCT only when necessary. Using the DISTINCT predicate in a SELECT statement is equivalent to setting the UniqueValues property to Yes in QBE.

NOTE When you've included the primary key for a single-table query or each of the primary keys for a multitable query, including the DISTINCT predicate has no effect (other than slowing down execution of the query and making the results read-only) because the presence of the primary keys already guarantees uniqueness of the rows.

If you use the keyword DISTINCTROW, Access eliminates any duplicate rows in the result set *based on all columns in the source tables.* DISTINCTROW has *no* effect when the query references only one table or returns at least one column from all included tables. In these cases, which include the vast majority of queries, using DISTINCTROW is equivalent to using ALL (or no predicate) and doesn't affect the performance of the query. The DISTINCTROW predicate corresponds to the UniqueRecords property in QBE (which is the QBE default). The DISTINCTROW predicate is unique to Access SQL.

It's worth noting that for most types of queries for which DISTINCTROW is applicable—queries with multiple tables *and* where at least one table is included in the FROM clause without a corresponding column in the SELECT clause (that is, a table is included without any output columns)—it produces the same result as the DISTINCT predicate, with one significant difference: the query's recordset is updatable.

For example, you might use the following query to list the descriptions of all menu items that have been ordered at least once since January of 1995:

```
SELECT ALL MenuDescription
FROM (tblMenu INNER JOIN tblOrderDetails ON tblMenu.MenuId =
tblOrderDetails.MenuId)
INNER JOIN tblOrder ON tblOrderDetails.OrderId =
tblOrder.OrderId
WHERE tblOrder.OrderDate > #1/1/95#
ORDER BY MenuDescription;
```

With the ALL predicate, this query returns 248 rows—one row for each Order Detail item since 1/1/95. Replacing ALL with DISTINCT returns 17 rows in a read-only recordset—one row for each distinct menu item ordered at least once since 1/1/95. Replacing DISTINCT with DISTINCTROW returns the same 17 rows, but this time the query is updatable. The datasheets returned by the three queries, each using a different predicate, are contrasted in Figure 5.10.

The TOP Predicate

You use the TOP predicate to return the top *n* rows or top *n* percent of rows from a recordset. This is useful when you wish to return only a select proportion of records meeting the query criteria. The TOP predicate is unique to Access SQL and is equivalent to using the TopValues property in QBE.

We recommend using the TOP predicate only *along with* an ORDER BY clause; otherwise you get a more or less random assortment of records. (It's worth noting, however, that this *won't* be a true random sample; instead it will be whatever proportion of records happens to come up first based on the query optimization path the Jet engine chooses.)

If you use an ORDER BY clause with the ASC keyword (or no keyword), TOP returns the bottom-most records. If you use an ORDER BY clause with the DESC keyword, TOP returns the top-most records.

NOTE The TOP predicate treats nulls as the smallest numeric value, earliest date, or first alphabetical text string. Thus, when you know in advance that the Top column may contain nulls, you may wish to explicitly exclude nulls in the WHERE clause.

FIGURE 5.10:

Three queries of menu items sold within the last year. The first query (top) uses the ALL predicate, which returns 140 rows, including duplicates. The second query (middle) uses DISTINCT and returns 17 rows, but the recordset is read-only. The third query (bottom) uses DISTINCTROW and also returns 17 rows, but the recordset is updatable. (Note the new-row asterisk at the bottom of the datasheet.)

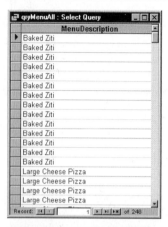

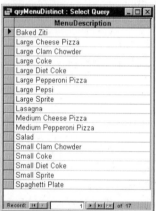

There are two forms of TOP: alone and with PERCENT. You can combine either form of TOP with the ALL, DISTINCT, or DISTINCTROW predicate. The syntax is as follows:

SELECT [{ ALL | DISTINCT | DISTINCTROW }] [TOP *n* [PERCENT]] *column-list*

For example, to return the top seven most costly items ever ordered, where cost equals Quantity∗Price∗(1–Discount), you could use the SELECT statement shown in Figure 5.11.

Access processes the TOP predicate after all criteria, joins, sorts, grouping, and other predicates have been applied. Ties are treated like any other row, except when multiple rows qualify as the last selected row—for example, the seventh row for a Top 7 specification (see Figure 5.11). When there is a tie on the last selected row, Access returns *all* rows with equivalent values. With no ORDER BY clause, Access uses all the columns from the SELECT clause to decide on ties. Otherwise Access uses only the columns contained in the ORDER BY clause to determine both the ordering of rows and the resolution of ties, even if some or all of the ORDER BY columns don't appear in the SELECT clause.

FIGURE 5.11:

This query returns the top seven largest item sales by using the TOP predicate and a descending ORDER BY clause. Note that more than seven rows are returned because of a tie for seventh place.

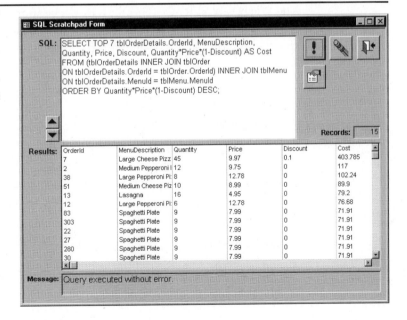

The WITH OWNERACCESS OPTION Declaration

You use the WITH OWNERACCESS OPTION declaration to allow users of a query you have created to inherit *your* security rights while running the query. This gives the users of a query you've created the ability to run the query, even if they don't have the necessary security permissions to one or more of the underlying tables. When you omit this declaration, the user without proper security clearance to the source tables does not inherit your security and thus cannot run the query. Using the declaration is equivalent to setting the RunPermissions property in QBE to "Owner's". Omitting the declaration is equivalent to setting it to "User's". The syntax for using the WITH OWNERACCESS OPTION declaration is as follows:

> SELECT *column-list*
>
> FROM *table-list*
>
> [WHERE *where-clause*]
>
> [ORDER BY *order-by-clause*]
>
> [WITH OWNERACCESS OPTION];

The WITH OWNERACCESS OPTION declaration works only with saved queries; if you use it in a SQL statement that has not been saved as a query (for example, by directly entering a SQL statement in a form's RecordSource property), it has no effect.

Aggregating Data

Aggregate queries are useful for summarizing data, calculating statistics, spotting bad data, and looking for trends. These types of queries, which produce read-only recordsets, were discussed in detail in Chapter 4 in the context of Access QBE. In this section we outline how they are specified using Access SQL.

You can construct three types of aggregate queries using Access SQL:

- Simple aggregate queries based on a SELECT statement *without* a GROUP BY clause

- GROUP BY queries using a SELECT statement *with* a GROUP BY clause
- Crosstab queries that use the TRANSFORM statement

All these queries have one thing in common: they use at least one aggregate function in the SELECT clause. The valid aggregate functions are detailed in Table 5.1.

TABLE 5.1: The SQL Aggregate Functions and Their Usage

Aggregate Function	Purpose
Avg([column[1]])	Mean or average of non-null values for the column
Count([column])	Count of the number of non-null values for a column
Count(*)	Count of the total number of rows in the result set, including rows with null values
Sum([column])	Sum of the non-null values for the column
Min([column])	Smallest non-null value for the column
Max([column])	Largest non-null value for the column
First([column])	Value of the column in the first row of the result set, which can be null[2]
Last([column])	Value of the column in the last row of the result set, which can be null[3]
StDev([column])	Sample standard deviation for the column. Null values are not included. This is a measure of the dispersion of values[4]
StDevP([column])	Population standard deviation for the column. Null values are not included. This is a measure of the dispersion of values[4]
Var([column])	Sample variance for the column. Null values are not included. The square of the sample standard deviation[4]
VarP([column])	Population standard deviation for the column. Null values are not included. The square of the population standard deviation[4]

[1]Although [column] is used throughout the table, you can also use expressions instead of columns in each of the aggregate functions.

[2]This may be null and is not the same as Min() unless the query also sorts by the same column in ascending order and there are no null values.

[3]This is not the same as Max() unless the query also sorts by the same column in ascending order and there are no null values.

[4]The sample standard deviation and variance use a denominator of $(n-1)$, whereas the population aggregate functions use a denominator of (n), where n = the number of records in the result set. For most statistical analyses, the sample aggregate functions are preferable.

You can create expressions made up of a combination of aggregate functions combined mathematically. Aggregate functions can also reference expressions. For example, these aggregate expressions are all valid:

Aggregate Expression	Use
Sum(Abs(Discontinued))	Calculates the sum of the absolute value of the yes/no column Discontinued, which counts the *number of Yes values*
Sum(Abs(Discontinued+1))	Calculates the sum of the absolute value of the yes/no column Discontinued plus 1, which counts the *number of No values* (since Access stores Yes as −1 and No as 0)
Avg(DeliveryDate)–Avg(OrderDate)	Calculates the difference in the average delivery and order dates
Avg(Price*Quantity*(1–Discount))	Calculates the average cost of items

Aggregate Queries without a GROUP BY Clause

You can use an aggregate SELECT statement without a GROUP BY clause to calculate summary statistics on all rows meeting the WHERE clause criteria. This is useful for calculating grand totals for an entire table or a subset of a table. To create this type of aggregate SELECT, you must include aggregate functions and nothing *but* aggregate functions in the SELECT clause of a SELECT statement. (If you try to mix aggregate and nonaggregate expressions without a GROUP BY clause, you will get an error message.)

For example, say you wished to count the total number of orders in the tblOrder table and the earliest and latest times an order was taken. You could construct an aggregate query like the one shown in Figure 5.12.

FIGURE 5.12:

This simple aggregate query calculates the total number of orders and the earliest and latest delivery times.

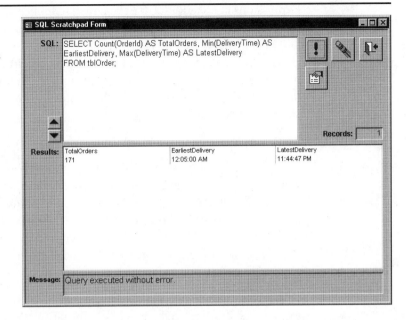

Using a GROUP BY Clause

You use a *GROUP BY clause* to define groups of rows for which you wish to calculate some aggregate function. Here's how the GROUP BY clause (and HAVING clause) fit into the overall SELECT statement syntax:

SELECT *column-list*

FROM *table-list*

[WHERE *where-clause*]

[GROUP BY *group-by-clause*]

[HAVING *having-clause*]

[ORDER BY *order-by-clause*];

The syntax of the GROUP BY clause is

GROUP BY *group-by-expression1* [*,group-by-expression2* [, …]]

Expressions in the GROUP BY clause can reference table columns, calculated fields, or constants. Calculations cannot include references to aggregate functions. The GROUP BY fields define the groups in the recordset. When you use a GROUP BY clause, all fields in the SELECT clause must be either arguments to an aggregate function or present in the GROUP BY clause. In other words, each column included in the resulting recordset must either define a group or compute some summary statistic for one of the groups.

For example, the SQL statement in Figure 5.13 computes the number of orders by customer.

When you use multiple GROUP BY fields, the groups are defined from left to right, just as in an ORDER BY clause. The GROUP BY clause automatically orders values in ascending order without need of an ORDER BY clause (see Figure 5.13). If you wish, however, for the groups to be sorted in descending order, you can reference the same fields in an ORDER BY clause with the keyword DESC.

For example, say you wished to count the number of orders by menu item and date, with menu items sorted alphabetically and dates sorted in descending order so as to show the most recent orders first. This GROUP BY SELECT statement is shown in Figure 5.14.

FIGURE 5.13:

This GROUP BY SELECT statement counts the number of orders each customer made.

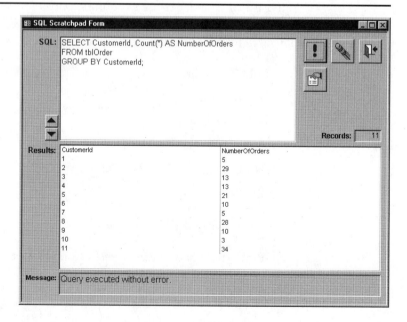

FIGURE 5.14:

This SELECT statement groups alphabetically by MenuDescription and then in reverse date order to show the total number of orders taken each day for a particular menu item.

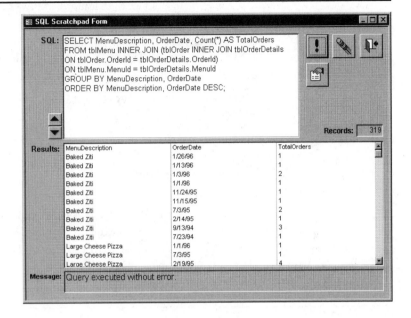

You may also find it useful to sort by one of the aggregate columns. For example, if you calculated total sales grouped by employee, you could sort by total sales in descending order rather than by employee. This would allow you to list the top-performing employees first.

You can specify up to ten GROUP BY fields, but be careful about adding unnecessary fields to the GROUP BY clause, since each additional field causes the query to execute more slowly.

Using the HAVING Clause

Aggregate select queries may contain a WHERE clause, a *HAVING clause,* or both. Any criteria contained in a WHERE clause is applied *before* the grouping of rows. Thus, you can use WHERE clause criteria to exclude rows you don't want grouped. In contrast, any criteria contained in a HAVING clause is applied *after* grouping. This allows you to filter records based on the summary statistics calculated for each group. The syntax for the HAVING clause is similar to that for the WHERE clause:

HAVING *expression1* [{AND | OR} *expression2* [, ...]]

For example, say you wished to calculate the average quantity ordered for each menu item but exclude any individual order from the calculation if a quantity of 5 or fewer were ordered. Since this requires the rows with a quantity of 5 or fewer to be excluded prior to grouping, you would use a WHERE clause. The SELECT statement would be constructed as follows:

```
SELECT MenuDescription, Avg(Quantity)
AS AvgOrdered
FROM tblMenu INNER JOIN tblOrderDetails ON tblMenu.MenuId =
tblOrderDetails.MenuId
WHERE Quantity > 5
GROUP BY MenuDescription;
```

On the other hand, you might want to calculate the same query but eliminate a menu item from the recordset if, *on average,* fewer than six of the item were sold for each order. This type of query requires the criteria to be applied *after* the average quantity has been calculated for each group, so you would use a HAVING clause instead. The SQL statement and result of this query are shown in Figure 5.15.

FIGURE 5.15:

The criteria for this query need to be applied after the grouping of data, so you use a HAVING clause.

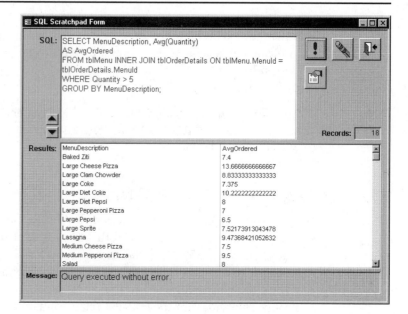

TIP You can also use a HAVING clause without a GROUP By. (See the earlier section "Aggregate Queries without a GROUP By Clause.") The whole table is treated as a single group for the sake of the HAVING clause.

Creating Crosstab Queries with the TRANSFORM Statement

Microsoft added the *TRANSFORM statement* to Access SQL to support the creation of crosstab queries. Crosstab queries, which were discussed in detail in Chapter 4, are useful for summarizing data in a condensed, tabular format.

The basic syntax of the TRANSFORM statement is shown here:

TRANSFORM *aggregate-function*

select-statement

PIVOT *column-headings-field* [IN (*value1*, [*value2*, [, ...]])];

The *aggregate-function* must be one of the SQL aggregate functions discussed earlier in this chapter. This aggregate function is used for the values of each cell of the crosstab table. The *select-statement* is a slightly modified GROUP BY SELECT statement. The *column-headings-field* is the field that is pivoted to become the column headings. The values in the optional IN clause specify fixed column headings.

Transforming a Group By Query into a Crosstab Query

The TRANSFORM statement is tricky to construct, especially since it is non-standard SQL. An easy way to create a TRANSFORM statement is to *transform* (maybe that's why they call it that) an existing GROUP BY SELECT statement into a TRANSFORM statement.

Before you can hope to do this, however, you must have a suitable SELECT statement. It must have at least two GROUP BY fields and no HAVING clause. The TRANSFORM statement doesn't support the use of HAVING clauses. (You can work around this limitation by basing a crosstab query on the results of a totals query that has already applied the needed HAVING clause. There's an example in Chapter 4 that does just this, in the "Crosstab Limitations" section.) In addition, you'll want to make sure the column headings field won't have more than 254 values. (While this is the theoretical limit, in practice you'll find that crosstab queries are probably inappropriate where the column headings field contains more than 20 or so values.) As long as your SELECT statement meets these criteria, you can convert it into a TRANSFORM statement.

An example should help make this clearer. Say you wished to look at the total dinner sales for each dinner menu item by employee. You might start by constructing a GROUP BY query that joined the tables tblMenu, tblEmployee, tblOrder, and tblOrderDetails. The GROUP BY columns would be tblEmployee.LastName and tblMenu.MenuDescription. The query would look like this:

```
SELECT LastName AS Employee,
MenuDescription, Sum(Quantity*Price*(1-Discount))
AS Sales
FROM tblMenu INNER JOIN (tblEmployee INNER JOIN
(tblOrder INNER JOIN tblOrderDetails ON tblOrder.OrderId =
tblOrderDetails.OrderId) ON tblEmployee.EmployeeId =
tblOrder.OrderTakerId) ON tblMenu.MenuId =
tblOrderDetails.MenuId
WHERE Unit = "Dinner"
GROUP BY LastName, MenuDescription;
```

The datasheet for this query is shown in Figure 5.16.

Continuing with this example, say you wanted the result of this query displayed as a crosstab table instead. You could convert the SELECT statement into a TRANSFORM statement using the following steps:

1. Take the existing GROUP BY SELECT statement and plug it into the skeleton of a TRANSFORM statement. That is, insert a line with the word *TRANSFORM* before the SELECT statement and a line with the word *PIVOT* after it. This would give you the following:

```
TRANSFORM
SELECT LastName AS Employee,
MenuDescription, Sum(Quantity*Price*(1-Discount))
AS Sales
FROM tblMenu INNER JOIN (tblEmployee INNER JOIN
(tblOrder INNER JOIN tblOrderDetails ON tblOrder.OrderId =
tblOrderDetails.OrderId) ON tblEmployee.EmployeeId =
```

Employee	MenuDescription	Sales
Alabaster	Baked Ziti	70.5
Alabaster	Lasagna	391.05
Alabaster	Spaghetti Plate	631.21
Carey	Baked Ziti	51.7
Carey	Lasagna	49.5
Carey	Spaghetti Plate	95.88
Jones	Baked Ziti	89.3
Jones	Lasagna	94.05
Jones	Spaghetti Plate	63.92
Lovely	Baked Ziti	4.7
Lovely	Lasagna	29.7
Lovely	Spaghetti Plate	535.33
Peters	Baked Ziti	18.8
Peters	Lasagna	138.6
Peters	Spaghetti Plate	209.338
Ronald	Baked Ziti	65.8
Ronald	Lasagna	297
Ronald	Spaghetti Plate	287.64

Record: 1 of 18

```
tblOrder.OrderTakerId) ON tblMenu.MenuId =
tblOrderDetails.MenuId
WHERE Unit = "Dinner"
GROUP BY LastName, MenuDescription;
PIVOT;
```

2. Move the aggregate function that will define the value of each crosstab cell into the TRANSFORM clause. In this example you would move the expression that calculates sales. Thus, the SQL becomes

```
TRANSFORM Sum(Quantity*Price*(1-Discount)) AS Sales
SELECT LastName AS Employee, MenuDescription
FROM tblMenu INNER JOIN (tblEmployee INNER JOIN
(tblOrder INNER JOIN tblOrderDetails ON tblOrder.OrderId =
tblOrderDetails.OrderId) ON tblEmployee.EmployeeId =
tblOrder.OrderTakerId) ON tblMenu.MenuId =
tblOrderDetails.MenuId
WHERE Unit = "Dinner"
GROUP BY LastName, MenuDescription;
PIVOT;
```

3. Move the field from the GROUP BY clause that will become the column headings to the PIVOT clause. Also, delete the reference to this field from the SELECT clause. Thus, you have

```
TRANSFORM Sum(Quantity*Price*(1-Discount)) AS Sales
SELECT LastName AS Employee
FROM tblMenu INNER JOIN (tblEmployee INNER JOIN
(tblOrder INNER JOIN tblOrderDetails ON tblOrder.OrderId =
tblOrderDetails.OrderId) ON tblEmployee.EmployeeId =
tblOrder.OrderTakerId) ON tblMenu.MenuId =
tblOrderDetails.MenuId
WHERE Unit = "Dinner"
GROUP BY LastName
PIVOT tblMenu.MenuDescription;
```

That's it! The crosstab datasheet produced by the preceding TRANSFORM statement is shown in Figure 5.17.

FIGURE 5.17:

This crosstab query is equivalent to the totals query shown in Figure 5.16. Note that the crosstab statement produces a more compact, readable summarization of the data.

Employee	Baked Ziti	Lasagna	Spaghetti Plate
Alabaster	70.5	391.05	631.21
Carey	51.7	49.5	95.88
Jones	89.3	94.05	63.92
Lovely	4.7	29.7	535.33
Peters	18.8	138.6	209.338
Ronald	65.8	297	287.64

qxtbEmployeeDinnerSales : Crosstab Query — Record: 1 of 6

NOTE The datasheets shown in Figure 5.16 and 5.17 lack any field formatting. We could have used the field property sheet in QBE to format the cell values as currency. Unfortunately, you can't alter field properties from SQL view.

To recap the conversion process in more general terms, here are the steps for converting a SELECT statement into a TRANSFORM statement.

1. Ensure that the SELECT statement contains at least two GROUP BY fields, no HAVING clause, and a field suitable to become the column headings.

Enclose the existing SELECT statement in a Transform "shell" like this:

TRANSFORM

select-statement

PIVOT;

2. Move the aggregate function that will be used for the Crosstab cell values into the TRANSFORM clause. The SQL should now look like this:

TRANSFORM *aggregate-function*

select-statement

PIVOT;

3. Move one of the GROUP BY fields—the one that is to become the column headings—to the PIVOT clause. Delete the reference to this same field from the SELECT clause. The resulting TRANSFORM statement should now produce a crosstab query:

TRANSFORM *aggregate-function*

select-statement

PIVOT *column-heading-field*;

Multiple Row Headings

TRANSFORM statements can include multiple row headings. You create the additional row headings by adding another GROUP BY field to the embedded SELECT statement. For example, you might wish to break down sales additionally by PaymentMethod. The SQL statement that creates this additional row heading and its output are shown in Figure 5.18. Note that the only difference between the earlier SQL statement and this one is the addition of PaymentMethod to the SELECT and GROUP BY clauses of the embedded SELECT statement.

Creating a Totals Column

You can create an additional column to calculate row totals in a crosstab query by adding an additional aggregate field to the SELECT clause of the TRANSFORM statement. Don't include the additional aggregate function anywhere else in the TRANSFORM statement. Any aggregate functions you add to the TRANSFORM statement's SELECT clause will be added to the crosstab between the row headings

FIGURE 5.18:
This TRANSFORM statement produces a crosstab table that contains two row headings, Employee and PaymentMethod.

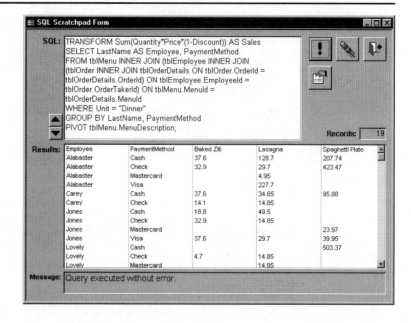

field(s) and the column headings field. For example, the TRANSFORM statement shown in Figure 5.19 was created by adding the Sum() aggregate function to the SELECT clause.

This additional aggregate function isn't limited to totaling the row values; you can use any valid SQL aggregate function here. For example, you could calculate the average sales per order. You could also include multiple aggregate functions in the SELECT clause; each would be displayed between the row headings and column headings fields.

Using the IN Clause to Create Fixed Columns

You can create fixed column headings by using the *IN clause*. Place the optional IN clause immediately after the PIVOT clause in the TRANSFORM statement. The syntax is

PIVOT *column-headings-field* [IN (*value1*, [*value2*, [, …]])]

FIGURE 5.19:

By adding an aggregate function to the SELECT clause, you can create a column that totals the values for each row.

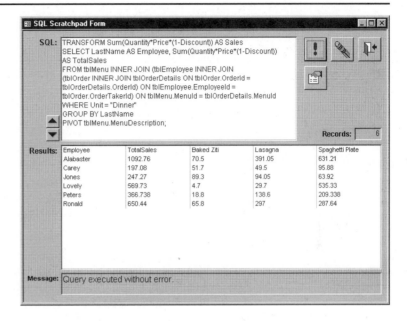

You can use the IN clause to order the values other than alphabetically (this is especially useful for alphanumeric date strings), exclude columns you don't wish to appear in the crosstab result, or include columns that may not exist in the recordset. For example, to create a crosstab table that excluded sales of "Spaghetti Plate" but included columns for "Baked Ziti", "Lasagna", and "Dinner Salad", even if there weren't any sales of these items, you would use the following PIVOT and IN clauses:

```
PIVOT MenuDescription IN ("Baked Ziti", "Lasagna","Dinner Salad").
```

Union Queries

Union queries are supported in Access only using SQL; there is no equivalent QBE method for creating a union query. UNION is not a SQL statement or even a clause. Instead it is an operator you can use to horizontally splice together two or more compatible queries. The basic syntax is as follows:

select-statement1

UNION [ALL]

select-statement2

[UNION [ALL]

select-statement3]

[...]

Union queries produce *read-only* recordsets. Access then matches columns from each SELECT statement by their position in the SELECT statement, *not* by their names.

For example, say you wished to create a query that combined the names and addresses of both employees and customers for a mailing you wished to do. You might create a union query like that shown in Figure 5.20.

FIGURE 5.20:

This union query combines the names and addresses from the tblEmployee and tblCustomer tables.

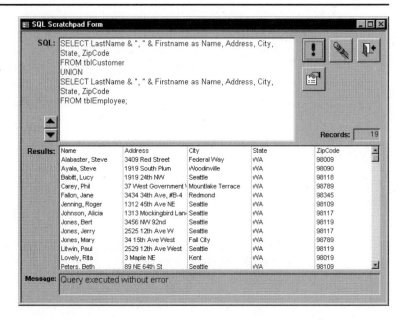

WARNING Although the Design view button is disabled when you create a SQL-specific (union, data definition, or SQL pass-through) query, you can always change the type of the query to a select or action query using the Query menu. Be careful, however, because when you change the query type of a SQL-specific query, your existing SQL statement is erased without so much as a confirming dialog.

Using the TABLE Option

You can use a shortcut syntax when you wish to include all the columns from a table or another query. This syntax employs the TABLE option and allows you to replace any of the SELECT statements with:

TABLE *table-or-query*

which is equivalent to the following SELECT statement:

SELECT * FROM *table-or-query*

For example, the following two union queries are equivalent:

```
SELECT * FROM tblOrder
UNION
SELECT * FROM tblBackOrder;
```

and

```
TABLE tblOrder
UNION
TABLE tblBackOrder;
```

The ALL Option

By default, Access eliminates duplicate records for union queries. You can force Access to include duplicates, however, by using the *ALL option* after the UNION operator. Using the ALL option speeds up the execution of union queries even if they don't have any duplicate records because Access can skip the extra comparison step, which can be significant with large recordsets.

Sorting the Results

You can use an ORDER BY clause in the *last* SELECT statement of a union query to order the resulting recordset. If some of the column names differ, you need to reference the name assigned to the column by the *first* SELECT statement. For example, the following union query is valid:

```
SELECT LastName FROM tblNames
UNION
SELECT EmployeeName FROM tblEmployees
ORDER BY LastName;
```

While each SELECT statement in a union query *can* have an ORDER BY clause, all but the last one are ignored.

Compatible Queries

You can string together as many select queries as you like in a union query; you're limited only by the fact that as for all queries, the entire compiled query definition must fit into memory. The queries need to be *compatible,* however, which means they must have the same number of columns. Typically, the column names and datatypes of the two unioned queries would be the same, but this isn't required. If they aren't the same, Access uses the following rules to combine them:

- For columns with *different names,* Access uses the column name from the first query.

- For columns with *different datatypes,* Access converts the columns to a single datatype that is compatible with all the columns' datatypes. For example, Access uses the Long Integer type when you combine an integer column with a long integer column. Similarly, text combined with a number produces a text column, date data combined with a yes/no column produces a text type, and so on.

- You can't use memo- or OLE-type fields in a union query.

For example, the query shown in Figure 5.21 is valid syntactically, although it makes little sense.

FIGURE 5.21:

This nonsensical but syntactically correct union query combines LastName from tblCustomer with OrderId and CustomerId from tblCustomer. The datatype of the output column will be text.

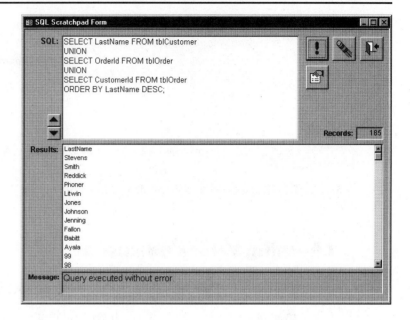

Subqueries

Subqueries are a useful part of SQL that allow you to embed SELECT statements within other SELECT statements (or action SQL statements, which are covered later in this chapter in the section "Updating Data with SQL"). Typically you use subqueries (which are also known as subselects) in the WHERE clause of a SQL statement to filter the query based on the values in another query (the subquery). There are three forms of syntax for subqueries:

- *expression* [NOT] IN (*select-statement*)

- *comparison* [{ANY | SOME | ALL}] (*select-statement*)

- [NOT] EXISTS (*select-statement*)

You may nest subqueries several levels deep; the actual limits on subquery nesting are undocumented.

We discuss the use of each of the three types of subqueries in the next sections.

Most of the time you can use either a subquery or a join to create equivalent queries. You'll find a subquery is often easier to conceptualize than the same query that employs joins, but it's really a matter of personal preference.

You can also use subqueries in Access QBE. Their use in QBE is analogous to their use in Access SQL. In QBE you can use subqueries in the Criteria or Field cell of a query.

Checking Values against a Lookup Table

Often you'd like to be able to check the value of a column against some list of values in another table or query. For these situations you would use the IN form of a subquery. For example, say you wished to view the number, name, and price of all menu items that have ever been sold in quantities of ten or more. You could do this with the subquery shown in Figure 5.22. (Alternatively, this query could have been expressed using a join instead of a subquery. The equivalent join query is shown in Figure 5.23.)

This form of subquery can return only a single column. If it returns more than one column, Access complains with an error message.

Using the NOT operator, you can also use this form of a subquery to look for values that are not contained in the list.

Comparing Values against Other Values

Subqueries also come in handy when you wish to compare a value against rows in another query. You can do this using the second form of the subquery syntax. This form of subquery also is limited to returning a single column. For example, you could use the subquery in Figure 5.24 to list all menu items that are more expensive than "Baked Ziti" (which sells for $4.70).

FIGURE 5.22:

This select query employs a subquery to find all menu items that have sold in quantities of ten or more.

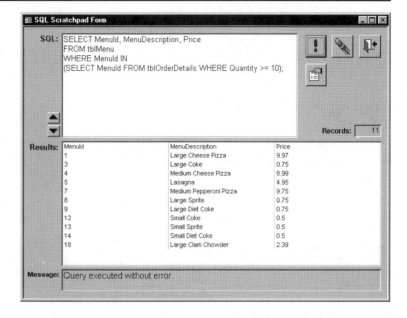

FIGURE 5.23:

This select query uses a join to find all menu items that have sold in quantities of ten or more. This query produces the same result as the query in Figure 5.22.

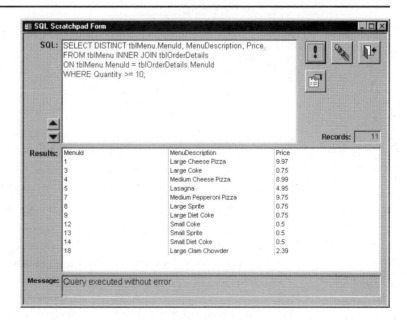

FIGURE 5.24:

This query lists all menu items for which the price is higher than the price of baked ziti ($4.70).

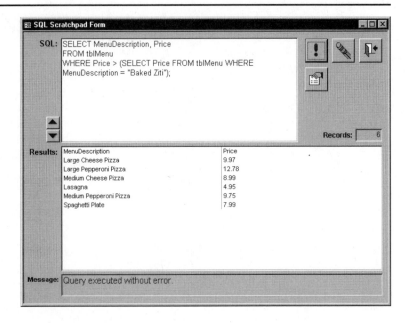

Note that the subquery in the query in Figure 5.24 returns one value, so you don't need to use a special predicate. If it had returned more than one row, it would have produced an error. When the output of a subquery is multiple rows, you must use one of the following predicates:

Predicate	Meaning
None	Makes a comparison with a single value
ANY or SOME	Is true if the comparison is true for any row returned by the subquery—in other words, if the comparison is true against the first row *or* the second row *or* the third row, and so on
ALL	Is true if the comparison is true for all rows returned by the subquery—in other words, if the comparison is true against the first row *and* the second row *and* the third row, and so on

If you don't use the ALL, SOME, or ANY predicate, you must guarantee that at most one value is returned. You can accomplish this by placing criteria on the subquery that select a row by its primary key value. Alternately, you could use a SQL aggregate function or a Top 1 predicate in the subquery. For example, the following three comparisons might all be used to ensure that Age is less than the age of the oldest student (assuming, of course, you knew in advance that student number 35 was the oldest):

```
WHERE Age < (SELECT Age FROM tblStudent WHERE StudentId = 35)
WHERE Age < (SELECT MAX(Age) FROM tblStudent)
WHERE Age < (SELECT Top 1 Age FROM tblStudent ORDER BY Age DESC)
```

You can use the ANY or SOME predicate (the two are equivalent) to make a comparison against any of the rows returned or use the ALL predicate to make a comparison against all the rows returned by the subquery. For example, the following comparison would select rows in which Age was less than the age of *any* of the students—in other words, where age was *less than the oldest student:*

```
WHERE Age < ANY (SELECT Age FROM tblStudent)
```

On the other hand, you could use the following comparison to select rows in which Age was less than the age of *all* of the students—in other words, where Age was *less than the youngest student:*

```
WHERE Age < ALL (SELECT Age FROM tblStudent)
```

NOTE The ANY, SOME, and ALL predicates will include rows with null values. This differs from the equivalent statements using the Min( ) and Max( ) aggregate functions, which exclude nulls.

Checking for Existence

The last form of a subquery comparison uses the EXISTS predicate to compare values against the existence of one or more rows in the subquery. If the subquery returns any rows, the comparison is True; if it returns no rows, the comparison is False. You can also use NOT EXISTS to get the opposite effect. Since you're checking only for the existence of rows, this form of subquery has no restriction on the number of columns returned.

So far, all the subqueries presented in this chapter have been independent of the *outer* query (the query that contains the subquery). You can also create subqueries that are linked to the outer query. This type of subquery is termed a *correlated subquery* because it references the other query using its correlation name (discussed in the section "The FROM Clause" earlier in this chapter). The correlation name can be the same as the table name or it can be a table's alias.

Each of the three types of subqueries can be correlated, but subqueries that use the EXISTS predicate are almost always correlated. (Otherwise they wouldn't be very useful.)

For example, you might want to find menu items that have never been ordered. You could accomplish this using the NOT EXISTS subquery shown in Figure 5.25. Running this query shows you that large anchovy pizzas have never been ordered.

The subquery in Figure 5.25 is termed a correlated subquery because it references the data in the outer query—the data in tblMenu—in the WHERE clause of the subquery.

FIGURE 5.25:

Using a NOT EXISTS correlated subquery, you can determine that no one has ever ordered a large anchovy pizza.

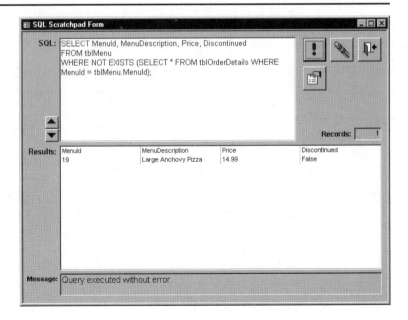

Using Subqueries in the SELECT Clause

Typically you use subqueries in the WHERE clause of a query, but you may also find occasion to use a subquery that returns a single value in the SELECT clause. For example, say you wished to create a query similar to the one in Figure 5.25, but instead of listing only menu items that have never been ordered, you'd prefer to list all menu items with an additional field that indicates whether they've ever been ordered. You could accomplish this with the query shown in Figure 5.26. This query moves the subquery into the SELECT clause, gives it an alias, "Ever Ordered?", and formats it using the IIf() function.

You might also use a subquery in a SELECT clause to list a calculated constant that was used in selecting the rows. For example, you might want to list all menu items with prices higher than the average price, along with the average price as an output column. You could accomplish this with the following subquery:

```
SELECT MenuId, MenuDescription, Price,
(SELECT Avg(Price) FROM tblMenu)
AS AveragePrice
FROM tblMenu
WHERE Price > (SELECT Avg(Price) FROM tblMenu);
```

Example: Using a Subquery to Find Duplicates

In the section "An Example: Removing Duplicates" in Chapter 4, we showed several alternate ways to find and eliminate duplicate rows using action queries. In that chapter we presented the hand-pruning and bulk-project methods. Using a subquery, you can create an updatable dynaset of duplicate rows similar to the one produced by the hand-pruning method but with only a single query and no temporary tables.

Recounting the example from Chapter 4, say you have a table called tblImport that contains duplicate orders that prevent you from designating OrderId as the primary key for the table. You can eliminate the duplicates using the following correlated subquery:

```
SELECT *
FROM tblImport
```

FIGURE 5.26:

This query lists each menu item and whether or not it has ever been ordered. It accomplishes this using a correlated subquery in the SELECT clause of a query.

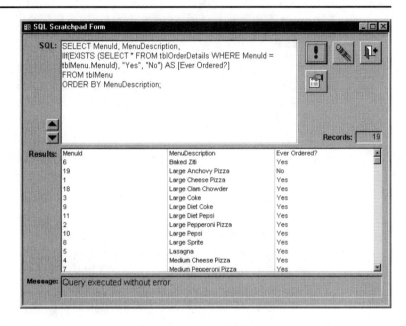

```
WHERE OrderId In (SELECT OrderId FROM tblImport
GROUP BY OrderId HAVING Count(*)>1) ORDER BY OrderId;
```

This subquery produces a dynaset with all the columns from tblImport but only the duplicate records. You can use this dynaset to visually scan through each of the duplicate rows and prune out the true duplicates. This method is how the Find Duplicates Query Wizard works.

Subqueries have many more uses than the ones this chapter has presented. As mentioned previously, you can solve most queries as either subqueries or joined queries. Choose the method that makes the most sense for you.

Parameterized SQL

Just as in Access QBE, you can specify *parameters* to be resolved at run time using SQL. To do this, you use the PARAMETERS declaration. The syntax for its usage is

PARAMETERS *parameter1 datatype1* [, *parameter2 datatype2* [, …]];

sql-statement;

For example, if you wanted to list the date and employee number of all items for a particular order but have the user select the order when the query was run, you could construct a SELECT statement with a PARAMETERS declaration like this:

```
PARAMETERS [Enter Customer Number] Long;
SELECT OrderDate, OrderTakerId
FROM tblOrder
WHERE CustomerId=[Enter Customer Number]
ORDER BY OrderDate;
```

You can find a list of acceptable SQL datatypes later in this chapter, in Table 5.2.

Using External Data Sources

There are three ways to refer to data sources physically located outside an Access database in a SQL statement:

- Use linked tables.
- Use the IN clause.
- Use direct references to the external tables.

Using Linked Tables

By far the easiest and most efficient way to reference external tables is to use linked tables. (Prior to Access 95, these were known as attached tables.) Once a table is linked to an Access database, you refer to it in SQL statements exactly the same as you would if it were a native Access table. Chapter 12 discusses linked tables in more detail.

Although it is less efficient, you can also refer to nonlinked tables from a query using either the IN clause or the direct reference technique. These techniques are discussed in the next two sections.

Using the IN Clause

For nonlinked tables, you can use either the IN clause or the direct reference technique. To refer to one or more nonlinked tables located in the same Access database, the same ODBC database, or the same subdirectory for a given type of non-native

ISAM database, it's easiest to use the IN clause. The syntax you use depends on the type of table you are querying. Access is not very forgiving; if you misplace a semi-colon, a quote, or even, in some cases, a space, the SQL statement will fail.

Access Databases

For Access databases, you use the following syntax:

> FROM *tablelist* IN *"path-and-database"*

The following SQL statement selects fields from the tblOrder and tblCustomer tables located in another Access database:

```
SELECT OrderId, OrderDate, LastName AS Customer
FROM tblOrder INNER JOIN tblCustomer
ON tblOrder.CustomerId = tblCustomer.CustomerId
IN "c:\bksybex2\paul\ch04\ch04.mdb";
```

External ISAM Databases

For external ISAM databases you use either the following syntax:

> FROM *tablelist* IN *"path" "product;"*

or this syntax:

> FROM *tablelist* IN "" [*product*; DATABASE=*path*;]

NOTE Unlike prior syntax statements in this chapter, the brackets in the preceding statement represent literal bracket characters.

Product must be one of the following:

dBASE III	Paradox 3.x
dBASE IV	Paradox 4.x
dBASE 5	Paradox 5.x

FoxPro 2.0	Btrieve
FoxPro 2.5	Excel 3.0
FoxPro 2.6	Excel 4.0
FoxPro 3.0	Excel 5.0

When specifying the path for Excel files, you need to include the name of the spreadsheet and its extension. For Btrieve files, you need to include the name of the data definition file (DDF) and its extension. For all other products, include only the path to the subdirectory containing the table.

The following SQL statement selects fields from the FoxPro 3.0 Order and Customer tables (files) using the first version of the syntax:

```
SELECT OrderId, OrderDate, LastName AS Customer
FROM Order INNER JOIN Customer
ON Order.CustomerId = Customer.CustomerId
IN "c:\bksybex2\paul\ch05" "FoxPro 3.0;";
```

The next SQL statement uses the alternate syntax to return the same data:

```
SELECT OrderId, OrderDate, LastName AS Customer
FROM Order INNER JOIN Customer
ON Order.CustomerId = Customer.CustomerId
IN "" [FoxPro 3.0;DATABASE=c:\bksybex2\paul\ch05;];
```

Take care not to mix the two forms of the syntax. You must use one or the other; a hybrid will not work.

ODBC Databases

For ODBC data sources, you must use yet another syntax:

FROM *tablelist* IN "" [ODBC;*connect-string*;]

NOTE The brackets in the preceding statement represent literal bracket characters.

The exact connect string is dependent on the ODBC driver you use. Microsoft SQL Server uses a connect string like this:

DSN=*data-source*;UID=*user-id*;PWD=*password*;DATABASE=*database*

The *data-source* (DSN) is the name of the data source you have prespecified using the ODBC driver manager program. A DSN can refer to either a single database or multiple databases; if it refers to a single database, you don't need to use the DATABASE parameter. The UID and PWD parameters are optional. In a secured environment, however, you probably *won't* want to embed the password in the connect string. If you leave out these or any other parameters, you will be prompted for the missing parameters at run time.

The following SELECT statement selects data from two SQL Server tables that are part of the SQLPizza data source. This SELECT statement is analogous to those presented earlier in this chapter that used Access and FoxPro data sources.

```
SELECT OrderId, OrderDate, LastName AS Customer
FROM tblOrder INNER JOIN tblCustomer
ON tblOrder.CustomerId = tblCustomer.CustomerId
IN ""[ODBC;DSN=SQLPizza;UID=Bob;];
```

Anyone who executes this SQL statement will be prompted for Bob's password.

TIP It is more efficient to use linked tables than the IN clause or direct external table references, although for ISAM data sources the difference in speed may not be noticeable. This is not true for ODBC data sources, however, where the IN clause or direct external table references are very inefficient. You should normally use linked tables for ODBC data sources because Jet can then manage the connections more efficiently.

Using Direct Table References

Sometimes you need to refer to multiple external data sources that are located either in different subdirectories/databases or in heterogeneous data sources. For example, you might want to join a table that's stored in dBASE format with a Paradox table. In these cases the IN clause technique will not work, but Access provides another way to refer to these tables: the *direct reference* method. The syntax for each different data source type is detailed in the following table:

Data Source Type	Direct Reference Syntax
Access	[*path-and-database*].*tablename*
External ISAM	[*product*;DATABASE=*path*;].*tablename*
ODBC	[ODBC;*connect-string*;].*tablename*

NOTE   **The brackets in the preceding statements represent literal bracket characters.**

For example, the query shown in Figure 5.27 joins two native Access tables, tblEmployee and tblOrderDetails, to an external FoxPro table, tblCustomer; a non-native Access table, tblOrder; and a SQL Server table, tblMenu; all in a single SELECT statement. Of course, this is an extreme example of what you *could* do, and a very

FIGURE 5.27:

This SELECT statement performs a heterogeneous join of two native Access tables, tblEmployee and tblOrderDetails; a FoxPro table, tblCustomer; a non-native Access-table, tblOrder; and a SQL Server table, tblMenu.

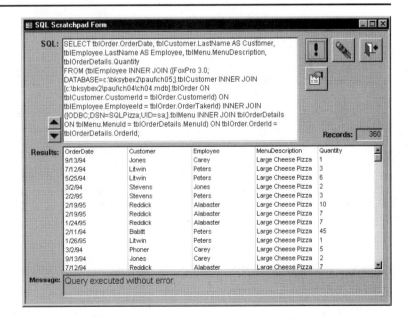

inefficient example at that. In general, it's best to design your database and queries so that you minimize the number of heterogeneous joins (joins across tables from different data sources). This is of special importance when one of the data sources comes from a client-server database. Since this will almost always force Access to perform the join locally, it should be avoided. Also, it's worth repeating that you could improve efficiency by using linked tables. (See Chapters 14 and 17 for more information on creating efficient queries.)

Updating Data with SQL

In addition to querying data, you can use SQL to make changes to data. You can use Access SQL to update records, delete records, or copy records to another table. Access SQL has four commands for updating data, all of which have analogous counterparts in Access QBE:

SQL Statement	QBE Query
UPDATE	Update
DELETE	Delete
INSERT INTO	Append
SELECT INTO	Make-table

All but the last one, SELECT INTO, are part of the ANSI SQL standard. (The ANSI standard uses SELECT INTO in a very different way to move a single row of data into a list of variables. The two usages are not equivalent.)

Once you have learned the SELECT statement and all its predicates, declarations, and clauses, you'll find learning the action SQL statements relatively easy. This is because each of these statements is similar syntactically to SELECT. Thus, even though each one includes WHERE clauses, for example, we will not repeat the discussion of WHERE clauses here. We will note, however, where there are differences between clauses in action SQL statements and the SELECT statement.

The UPDATE Statement

You use the *UPDATE statement* to change values in one or more columns in a table. The syntax is

UPDATE *table-or-query*

SET *column1 = expression1* [, *column2 = expression2*] [, ...]

[WHERE *criteria*];

You can update the values in either a table or a query, but if you use a query it must be updatable. The expressions in the SET clause can be a constant or the result of a calculation. For example, to increase the price of all non-pizza menu items by 10 percent, you could use the following update query:

```
UPDATE tblMenu
SET tblMenu.Price = [Price]*1.1
WHERE MenuDescription Not Like "*Pizza*";
```

The ANSI standard supports the use of subqueries in the SET clause, while Access SQL does not. Fortunately, Access SQL supports the use of joins in the UPDATE clause (this is nonstandard SQL), which gives you almost equivalent functionality. The syntax used for joins in the UPDATE clause is the same as the join syntax used for SELECT statements in the FROM clause. For example, to change the phone numbers in the tblCustomer table to new phone numbers stored in another table, tblCustomerMods—which you might have imported from another copy of the database on another machine—you could use the following UPDATE statement:

```
UPDATE tblCustomerMods INNER JOIN tblCustomer ON
tblCustomerMods.CustomerId = tblCustomer.CustomerId
SET tblCustomer.Phone = tblCustomerMods.Phone
WHERE tblCustomer.Phone<>tblCustomerMods.Phone;
```

This UPDATE statement uses a WHERE clause to limit the updates only to records that need to be modified—those in which the phone numbers are different.

The DELETE Statement

You use the *DELETE statement* to delete rows from tables. Its syntax is

DELETE [*table.**]

FROM *from-clause*

[WHERE *criteria*];

The use of *table*.* is optional for delete queries that refer to only a single table.

> **NOTE** Access also allows you to refer to a single column in the DELETE clause—for example, "DELETE tblOrder.OrderDate". In fact, Access QBE often generates DELETE statements in this misleading style, but don't let this confuse you; the entire record is deleted, not just the values in the column.

For single-table queries, the syntax can be simplified:

DELETE

FROM *table*

[WHERE *criteria*];

For example, to delete all discontinued items from tblMenu, you could use the following DELETE statement:

```
DELETE
FROM tblMenu
WHERE Discontinued = True;
```

You can create DELETE statements that reference multiple tables, but you must follow these rules:

- You can use the data in one table to decide which rows to delete from another related table. You can accomplish this by using a join in the FROM clause or by using a subquery in the WHERE clause. Tables can be related in either a one-to-one or a one-to-many relationship. (Note that you may be prevented from deleting rows from a table if referential integrity is turned on without cascaded updates.)

- You can delete rows from multiple tables in a single delete query if the tables are related in a one-to-one relationship.

- You can delete rows from multiple tables related in a one-to-many relationship with a series of DELETE queries. See the examples presented in Chapter 4 for details.

You can use a single DELETE statement to delete the records in two tables related in a one-to-many relationship if you've defined a relationship between the two tables and have turned on the cascading deletes option. In this case, if you delete a row from the "one" side of a relationship, Access automatically deletes the related rows in the "many-sided" table.

For example, to delete all customers from tblCustomer who have not placed an order during the past year, you would create and execute the following DELETE statement, which uses a subquery to find the proper rows:

```
DELETE
FROM tblCustomer
WHERE tblCustomer.CustomerId NOT IN
(SELECT CustomerId FROM tblOrder WHERE OrderDate >
DateAdd('yyyy',-1,Date()));
```

Access SQL departs from the ANSI standard through its support for named tables in the DELETE clause and joins in the FROM clause.

If you wish to delete the value in one or more columns but not the entire record, use the UPDATE statement instead of DELETE and set the values to null. For example, you could use the following UPDATE statement to set the LastName and FirstName columns in tblCustomer to null for a particular customer:

```
UPDATE tblCustomer
SET LastName = NULL, FirstName = NULL
WHERE CustomerId = 4;
```

The INSERT INTO Statement

You use the *INSERT INTO statement* to copy rows from one table (or query) into another table. You can also use it to add a single row of data to a table using a list of values. The syntax of the first form of the INSERT INTO statement is

INSERT INTO *target-table*

select-statement;

In its simplest form, you can use this form of the INSERT INTO statement to copy the contents of one table to another. For example, to copy all the rows from tblCustomerNew to tblCustomer, you could use the following INSERT INTO statement:

```
INSERT INTO tblCustomer
SELECT * FROM tblCustomerNew;
```

You can use any valid SELECT statement that produces recordsets, including SELECT statements with GROUP BY clauses, joins, UNION operators, and subqueries. This embedded SELECT statement can also include references to one or more queries. For example, to append records from the SELECT GROUP BY statement presented earlier in the chapter in the section "Creating Crosstab Queries with the TRANSFORM Statement" to a table named tblEmployeeDinnerSales, you could use the following INSERT INTO statement:

```
INSERT INTO tblEmployeeDinnerSales
SELECT tblEmployee.LastName, tblMenu.MenuDescription,
Sum(Quantity*Price*(1-Discount)) AS Sales
FROM tblMenu INNER JOIN (tblEmployee INNER JOIN
(tblOrder INNER JOIN tblOrderDetails ON tblOrder.OrderId =
tblOrderDetails.OrderId) ON tblEmployee.EmployeeId =
tblOrder.OrderTakerId) ON
tblMenu.MenuId = tblOrderDetails.MenuId
WHERE ((tblMenu.Unit="Dinner"))
GROUP BY tblEmployee.LastName, tblMenu.MenuDescription;
```

You use the second form of the INSERT INTO statement to add a single row to a table and populate it with values. Its syntax is

INSERT INTO *target-table* [(*column1* [, *column2* [, ...]])]

VALUES (*value1* [, *value2* [, ...]]);

If you omit the column references in the INSERT INTO clause, you must include a value for each column in the target table in the exact order in which the columns appear in the table definition. If you include the column references, you may omit columns (other than the primary key and other required columns) or change the order in which they appear in the table definition. For example, you could add a new row to tblMenu using the following INSERT INTO statement:

```
INSERT INTO tblMenu (MenuId, Price, MenuDescription)
VALUES (50, 29.99, "Family Platter");
```

The SELECT INTO Statement

You use the *SELECT INTO statement*, unique to Access SQL, to create a new table from the rows in another table or query. Its syntax is

SELECT *column1* [, *column2* [, ...]] INTO *new-table*

FROM *table-list*

[WHERE *where-clause*]

[ORDER BY *order-by clause*];

For example, you could use the following SELECT INTO statement to copy all purchases made by CustomerId = 9 (Bert Jones) from tblOrder to a new table called tblJonesOrders:

```
SELECT OrderId, OrderDate, CustomerId, OrderTakerId,
DeliveryDate, DeliveryTime, PaymentMethod, Notes
INTO tblJonesOrders
FROM tblOrder
WHERE CustomerId=9;
```

Like the INSERT INTO statement, the SELECT INTO statement can include any valid SELECT statement that produces recordsets, including SELECT statements with GROUP BY clauses, joins, UNION operators, and subqueries.

NOTE Tables created by SELECT INTO statements will not contain primary keys, indexes, or any column or table properties other than the defaults assigned to any new table.

Data Definition with SQL

You can use two methods to programmatically create and manipulate table schemas in Access: data access objects (DAO) and Data Definition Language (DDL) queries. In this section we discuss the use of DDL queries. Chapter 6 covers using DAO to create and modify schemas.

It's important to note that DDL queries offer only a subset of the schema definition capabilities that either the Access user interface or DAO provides. For example, you can't define validation rules, define default values for fields, create foreign key relationships with cascading updates or deletes, or create a nonunique index for a table using a DDL query. But DDL queries still have their place: they help bridge the gap between the SQL standard and Access SQL. Furthermore, it's likely that the support for DDL queries will only get better in future versions of Access. In the meantime, there's at least one good reason for using DDL rather than either of the alternatives: it's based on a standard language that has widespread support—SQL. If you already have a fair amount of experience with SQL, using DDL queries will likely seem more natural than the other language-based alternative, DAO. Still, be aware that Access DDL support is incomplete and you may be required to go elsewhere in Access to get the job finished.

As with union queries, you must enter DDL queries using SQL view; there's no QBE counterpart. You can also execute a DDL query by defining and executing a QueryDef created using VBA.

Access SQL supports four DDL statements:

DDL Statement	Purpose
CREATE TABLE	Creates a new table schema
ALTER TABLE	Modifies an existing table schema
CREATE INDEX	Creates a new index
DROP	Deletes a table schema or an index

In addition, you can use the CONSTRAINT clause in either a CREATE TABLE or ALTER TABLE statement to create constraints. (In Access' simplified support of CONSTRAINT, this means the creation of indexes.) The next few sections discuss each of these statements and the CONSTRAINT clause.

The CREATE TABLE Statement

You use the *CREATE TABLE statement* to create a new table. Its syntax is

CREATE TABLE *table*

(*column1 type1* [(*size1*)] [CONSTRAINT *column-constraint1*]

[, *column2 type2* [(*size2*)] [CONSTRAINT *column-constraint2*]

[, ...]]

[CONSTRAINT *table-constraint1* [, *table-constraint2* [, ...]]]);

You specify the datatype of a column using one of the Jet engine SQL datatype identifiers or its synonyms. They are summarized in Table 5.2.

TABLE 5.2: SQL Datatypes and Their Counterparts in Table Design View

SQL Datatype and Synonyms	Table Design Field Type
BIT, BOOLEAN, LOGICAL, LOGICAL1, YESNO	Yes/No
BYTE, INTEGER1	Number, FieldSize = Byte
COUNTER, AUTOINCREMENT	Autonumber, FieldSize = Long Integer
CURRENCY, MONEY	Currency
DATETIME, DATE, TIME	Date/Time
SHORT, INTEGER2, SMALLINT	Number, FieldSize = Integer
LONG, INT, INTEGER, INTEGER4	Number, FieldSize = Long
SINGLE, FLOAT4, IEEESINGLE, REAL	Number, FieldSize = Single
DOUBLE, FLOAT, FLOAT8, IEEEDOUBLE, NUMBER, NUMERIC	Number, FieldSize = Double
TEXT, ALPHANUMERIC, CHAR, CHARACTER, STRING, VARCHAR	Text
LONGTEXT, LONGCHAR, MEMO, NOTE	Memo
LONGBINARY, GENERAL, OLEOBJECT	OLE Object
GUID	Autonumber, FieldSize = Replication ID

WARNING The Jet engine SQL datatypes and their synonyms, which are derived from ANSI SQL datatypes, differ from the Access datatypes in several subtle ways. Use care when selecting the correct datatype keyword. Most notably, using the SQL datatype INTEGER produces a number column with Size = *Long* because INTEGER in ANSI SQL is a 4-byte integer value (which in Access is a Long Integer).

You can use the optional *size* parameter to specify the length of a text column. If *size* is left blank, text columns are assigned a size of 255. Note that this differs from the default column size of 50 assigned when new tables are created with the user interface. Other datatypes do not use this option.

You can create two types of constraints using a CREATE TABLE statement: single-column indexes and multicolumn (or table) indexes. You specify both of these indexes using the CONSTRAINT clause, which is discussed in the next section.

For example, to create a table tblNewMenu to mimic the schema of the tblMenu table found in the CH05.MDB sample database, you could use the following CREATE TABLE statement:

```
CREATE TABLE tblNewMenu
(MenuId LONG, MenuDescription TEXT (50), Unit TEXT (50),
Price CURRENCY, Discontinued BIT);
```

The CONSTRAINT Clause

In the SQL-92 standard, *constraints* are used to restrict the values that can be added to a table. You can use constraints in SQL-92 to create primary and foreign keys, constrain columns to be UNIQUE or NOT NULL, and to create validation rules (the CHECK constraint). Access SQL supports each of these uses except for the NOT NULL and CHECK constraints. Since the only constraints Access currently supports are ones requiring the definition of indexes, you might find it convenient to think of the Access CONSTRAINT clause as being used to create indexes. (Be aware, however, that support for the NOT NULL and CHECK constraints may be added at a later date.)

You use the CONSTRAINT clause in CREATE TABLE and ALTER TABLE statements. The CONSTRAINT syntax takes two forms. You use the first form for single-column constraints:

CONSTRAINT *name* {PRIMARY KEY | UNIQUE |

REFERENCES *foreign-table* [(*foreign-column*)]}

The multiple-column version of the CONSTRAINT clause is

CONSTRAINT *name* {PRIMARY KEY (*column1*, [*column2* [, ...]]) |

UNIQUE | REFERENCES *foreign-table* [(*foreign-column1*

[, *foreign-column2* [, ...]])]}

For example, you could use the following CREATE TABLE statement to create the tblNewMenu table and a unique index on the column MenuDescription:

```
CREATE TABLE tblNewMenu
(MenuId LONG, MenuDescription TEXT CONSTRAINT MenuDescription
UNIQUE, Unit TEXT, Price CURRENCY, Discontinued BIT);
```

TIP

Anytime you create an index in Access, even a single-column index, you must assign it a name. Since the Access UI assigns primary key indexes the name PrimaryKey and single-column indexes the same name as the column and there's no good reason to do otherwise, we recommend using these same naming conventions in DDL queries. Less clear is what to name foreign key indexes; we have chosen here to use the naming convention "*referenced-tablename*FK". For example, a foreign key to tblCustomer would be tblCustomerFK. (The Access UI gives less descriptive names of the form *Reference, Reference1,* and so forth.)

As a second example, say you wished to create two tables, tblNewOrders and tblNewItems, and relate them in a one-to-many relationship. You need tblNew-Orders to have the following columns: OrderId (the primary key), OrderDate, and

CustomerId. Table tblNewItems should contain OrderId, ItemId, and ItemDescription. For tblNewItems, OrderId and ItemId will make up the primary key and OrderId will be a foreign key reference to the same-named column in tblNewOrders. You could use the following two CREATE TABLE statements, executed one after the other (you can't place multiple SQL statements in a DDL query), to create the two tables:

```
CREATE TABLE tblNewOrders
(OrderId LONG CONSTRAINT PrimaryKey PRIMARY KEY,
OrderDate DATETIME, CustomerId LONG );

CREATE TABLE tblNewItems
(OrderId LONG CONSTRAINT tblNewOrdersFK REFERENCES
tblNewOrders, ItemId LONG, ItemDescription TEXT (30),
CONSTRAINT PrimaryKey PRIMARY KEY (OrderId, ItemId) );
```

TIP

For foreign key references you can omit the name of the foreign key column if it is the primary key in the referenced table.

Both forms of CONSTRAINT lack any way to create nonunique indexes within a CREATE TABLE or ALTER TABLE statement. This *is* consistent with the SQL-92 standard. Fortunately, you can use the CREATE INDEX statement, described in the next section, to create this type of index. Another shortcoming of Access' CONSTRAINT clause is that there's no support for the specification of foreign key relationships with either cascading deletes or updates. (ANSI SQL supports this feature.)

The CREATE INDEX Statement

In addition to the CONSTRAINT clause of the CREATE TABLE and ALTER TABLE commands, you can use the *CREATE INDEX statement* to create an index on an existing table. (CREATE INDEX is not a part of the ANSI standard, but many vendors include it.) The syntax of the CREATE INDEX statement is

CREATE [UNIQUE] INDEX *index*

ON *table* (*column1* [, *column2* [, ...]])

[WITH {PRIMARY | DISALLOW NULL | IGNORE NULL}];

If you include the UNIQUE keyword, the index disallows duplicate values. You must give a name to each index, even if it's a single-column index. See the preceding section for suggested index-naming conventions.

You can create a primary key index by using the PRIMARY option in the WITH clause. All primary key indexes are automatically unique indexes, so you needn't (but you can if you insist) use the UNIQUE keyword when you use the PRIMARY option.

You use the IGNORE NULL option to prevent Jet from creating index entries for null values. If the indexed column will contain nulls and there may be many nulls, you can improve the performance of searches on non-null values by using this option. This is equivalent to using the IgnoreNulls property of the index in Table Design view.

You can use the DISALLOW NULL option to have the Jet engine prevent the user from entering null values in the column. This is similar to setting the Required property of a column in Table Design view to Yes. Choosing this option has the same effect, but this "hidden" feature is maintained by the index, not the column, and has no analogous property in the UI. If you use this option, you won't be able to turn it off through the user interface—the Required property of the underlying column will act independently—unless you delete the index.

You can create a multicolumn index by including more than one column name in the ON clause.

You can create only one index at a time with the CREATE INDEX statement. Also, there's no facility for creating descending-ordered indexes using the CREATE INDEX statement; you must use the UI or DAO to alter the sort order of any indexes created using DDL queries.

You could use the following CREATE INDEX statement to add a unique index that ignored nulls to the column Price in tblNewMenu:

```
CREATE UNIQUE INDEX Price
ON tblNewMenu (Price)
WITH IGNORE NULL;
```

The ALTER TABLE Statement

You can use the *ALTER TABLE statement* to alter the schema of an existing table. With it you can add a new column or constraint or delete a column or constraint. (You can't modify the definition of either.) You can operate on only one field or index with a single ALTER TABLE statement. The ALTER TABLE statement has four forms.

You use the first form to *add a column* to a table:

> ALTER TABLE *table* ADD [COLUMN] *column datatype* [(*size*)]
>
> [CONSTRAINT *single-column-constraint*];

The keyword COLUMN is optional. As in the CREATE TABLE statement, you specify the datatype of the new column by using one of the Jet engine SQL datatype identifiers or its synonyms (see Table 5.2 earlier in this chapter). You can use the optional SIZE parameter to specify the length of a text column. If *size* is left blank, text columns are assigned a size of 255. You can also specify an optional index for the column using the CONSTRAINT clause. (See the section "The CONSTRAINT Clause" earlier in this chapter.)

For example, you could use the following ALTER TABLE statement to add the integer column Quantity to the tblNewItems table:

```
ALTER TABLE tblNewItems ADD Quantity SHORT;
```

NOTE　One annoying "feature" of ALTER TABLE is that all added columns are inserted at the beginning of the table. Thus, in the preceding example, Quantity becomes the first column in tblNewItems.

You can use the second form of ALTER TABLE to *add constraints* to a table:

> ALTER TABLE *table* ADD CONSTRAINT *constraint*;

For example, you could use the following ALTER TABLE statement to add an index to the new column:

```
ALTER TABLE tblNewItems ADD CONSTRAINT Quantity UNIQUE (Quantity);
```

As with the CREATE TABLE statement, you are limited to creating indexes that are unique or serve as primary or foreign keys.

You use the third form of ALTER TABLE to *remove a column* from a table:

ALTER TABLE *table* DROP [COLUMN] *column;*

Again, the keyword COLUMN is optional. For example, you could use the following ALTER TABLE statement to remove the ItemDescription column from tblNewItems:

```
ALTER TABLE tblNewItems DROP COLUMN ItemDescription;
```

NOTE You can't remove an indexed column from a table without first removing its index.

You use the final form of ALTER TABLE to *remove an index* from a table:

ALTER TABLE *table* DROP CONSTRAINT *index;*

You refer to an index by its name. For example, to remove the primary key from tblNewOrders, you would use the following ALTER TABLE statement:

```
ALTER TABLE tblNewOrders DROP CONSTRAINT PrimaryKey;
```

NOTE You can't delete an index that is involved in a relationship without first deleting all the relationships in which it participates.

The DROP Statement

You can use the *DROP statement* to remove tables or indexes. It has two forms.

You use the first to *remove a table* from a database:

DROP TABLE *table;*

For example, you could use the following DROP statement to remove the tblNewItems table from the current database:

```
DROP TABLE tblNewItems;
```

You use the second form of DROP to *remove an index* from a table:

DROP INDEX *index* ON *table*;

For example, to delete the index named Price from tblNewMenu, you could use the following DROP statement:

```
DROP INDEX Price ON tblNewMenu;
```

> **NOTE** To drop an index from a table, you can use either the ALTER TABLE statement or the DROP statement. You must use caution when using DROP because there is no confirming dialog when it is executed.

Creating SQL Pass-Through Queries

You can use SQL pass-through queries to send uninterpreted SQL statements to a server database. Pass-through queries can be used only with ODBC data sources. Access performs no syntax checking, interpretation, or translation of the SQL in a pass-through query. It's entirely up to you to compose your query using the proper syntax of the server's dialect of SQL.

You create a SQL pass-through query by creating a new blank query and then choosing Query ➤ SQL Specific ➤ Pass-Through. It's important that you choose this command rather than just switch to SQL view because if you don't, Access will think you are creating a normal (non–pass-through) query.

> **TIP** You can convert a non–pass-through query entered into SQL view by choosing Query ➤ SQL Specific ➤ Pass-Through from within SQL view.

When you create a pass-through query, Access adds several new properties to the query's property sheet. These new properties are summarized in Table 5.3 and shown in Figure 5.28.

SQL pass-through queries are useful for:

- Using server-specific SQL that's not supported by ODBC
- Running SQL DDL (Data Definition Language) commands to create and modify the schema of server databases
- Executing stored procedures on the server
- Joining more than one database on the server (If run as a normal query, Jet would have to join the databases locally.)
- Forcing a query to be fully executed on the server

SQL pass-through queries have the following disadvantages:

- Any records returned in an SPT query are read-only.
- Jet will not check the syntax of SPT queries.
- You can't use Access' built-in or user-defined functions (although the server may have similar functions).

Most client-server applications will incorporate a combination of normal queries using linked tables and SQL pass-through queries. (See Chapter 14 for more information on creating client-server applications.)

TABLE 5.3: Query Properties Unique to SQL Pass-Through Queries

Property	Description	Default Value
ODBCConnectStr	The ODBC connection string to be used when executing the pass-through query	ODBC;
ReturnsRecords	Specifies whether or not the query returns any records	Yes
LogMessages	Specifies whether Access logs warning and informational messages from the server to a local table. Messages are logged to a table the name of which is derived from the user name (for example, Mary-00, Mary-01, Mary-02, and so on). This does not include error messages	No

FIGURE 5.28:

The qsptCreatetblRemoteOrders pass-through query creates a table on the SQLPizza data source.

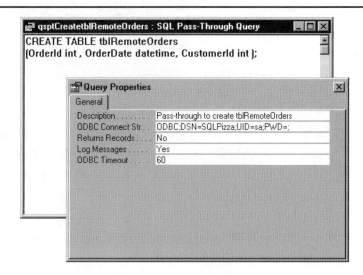

There are two types of pass-through queries: those that return records and those that don't. Pass-through select queries and some stored procedures return records. DDL queries and server action queries, as well as many stored procedures, do not return records.

For example, a pass-through query that creates a three-column table, tblRemote-Orders, on a Microsoft SQL Server 4.2 database is shown in Figure 5.28. Since this is a DDL query, its ReturnsRecords property is set to No. On the other hand, the pass-through query shown in Figure 5.29 returns a snapshot of records, so we have set its ReturnsRecords property to Yes.

The pass-through query shown in Figure 5.30 executes a SQL Server 4.2 system stored procedure, sp_primarykey, to mark the OrderId column in tblRemoteOrders as the primary key.

Differences between Access SQL and SQL-92

Access SQL is a hybrid SQL. It differs considerably from each of the SQL standards and doesn't *completely* support *any* of the ANSI SQL standards. It lacks large chunks

FIGURE 5.29:

The qsptRemoteOrders pass-through query executes a simple SELECT statement on the tblRemoteOrders table, returning a snapshot recordset to Access.

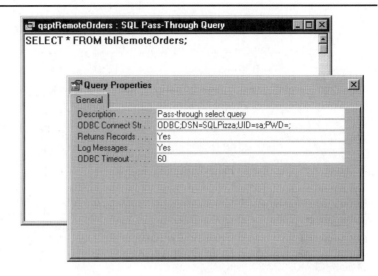

FIGURE 5.30:

This pass-through query executes a stored procedure, sp_primarykey, to mark the OrderId column in the tblRemoteOrders table as the primary key.

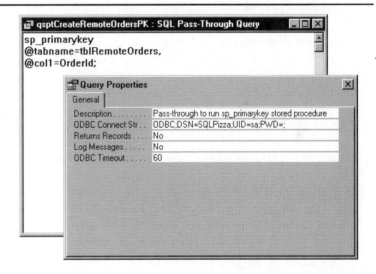

of the standards, particularly in the areas of security and cursors. Sometimes it supports the same functionality found in one of the standards, but with a different syntax. For example, the syntax of the UPDATE statement is nonstandard but essentially equivalent to the functionality of the SQL-92 UPDATE statement. In other cases, similar functionality is provided elsewhere in Access. For example, you handle security in Access using either the UI or DAO. Finally, Access SQL has some useful extensions that are not present in any of the standards. A few of the extensions are dynaset updatability, support for crosstab queries, and the SELECT INTO command.

The ANSI SQL standards are so varied that it's difficult to pin down all the differences between Access and the various flavors of SQL. Many of these differences have been noted throughout the chapter. Nonetheless, we have attempted to summarize the major differences between Access SQL and SQL-92 in Table 5.4. (Note that this table is not comprehensive; it covers only the major differences.)

TABLE 5.4: Major Differences between Access SQL and ANSI SQL-92

Feature	Supported by SQL-92	Supported by Access SQL	Comments
Security (GRANT, REVOKE, and so on)	Yes	No	Access' security system serves the same purpose
Transaction support (COMMIT, ROLLBACK, and so on)	Yes	No	Access offers a similar facility in DAO
Views (CREATE VIEW statement)	Yes	No	A saved query is equivalent to a view except that it is also updatable
Temporary tables (in the SQL-92 sense)	Yes	No	All tables are persistent
Joins in FROM clause	Yes	Yes	Access doesn't support all the variations on the syntax
Joins in UPDATE and DELETE statements	No	Yes	Unique to Access SQL
Support for FULL OUTER JOIN and UNION JOIN	Yes	No	A union join is different from the UNION operator
Full support for mixing heterogeneous joins	Yes	No	Access has limited support for mixing heterogeneous joins
Support for subqueries in the SET clause of UPDATE statements	Yes	No	Access offers support for joins instead
Support for multiple tables in DELETE statements	No	Yes	Unique to Access SQL
SELECT DISTINCTROW	No	Yes	Unique to Access SQL
SELECT TOP N	No	Yes	Unique to Access SQL

TABLE 5.4: Major Differences between Access SQL and ANSI SQL-92 (continued)

Feature	Supported by SQL-92	Supported by Access SQL	Comments
Cursors (DECLARE CURSOR, FETCH, and so on)	Yes	No	DAO supports the equiva-lent use of table cursors
Domain support (CREATE DO-MAIN, ALTER DOMAIN, and so on)	Yes	No	Access doesn't support domains
Complete support for constraints	Yes	No	Access supports only a subset of constraint functionality
Assertions (CREATE ASSERTION, DROP ASSERTION, and so on)	Yes	No	Access doesn't support system-wide rules
Row value constructors	Yes	No	Access doesn't support this feature
Case expressions	Yes	No	Similar functionality is found using the IIf() function
Full referential integrity support in CREATE TABLE statement	Yes	No	Access only partially supports this feature in SQL. Cascade support is also provided using the Access UI
Standardized system tables and error codes	Yes	No	Access uses its own system for naming system tables and error codes
Standard datatypes	Yes	Yes	Access supports most but not all the SQL datatypes
Standard string operators	Yes	No	Access provides several alternative string-manipulation functions
Standard wildcard characters	Yes	No	Access uses ? and * instead of the SQL _ and %
Support for VBA functions	No	Yes	You can use most VBA functions in Access SQL
Additional aggregate functions	No	Yes	StDev, Var, StDevP, and VarP are unique to Access SQL
TRANSFORM statement	No	Yes	For creating crosstab queries
Parameters	No	Yes	For defining parameters to be determined at run time
SELECT INTO statement	No	Yes	Unique to Access SQL

Summary

In this chapter we have covered all the components of Access SQL, including

- The SELECT statement and all its clauses, predicates, and variations
- The various types of joins: inner, outer, self, and non–equi-joins
- The ALL, DISTINCT, and DISTINCTROW predicates
- The TOP predicate
- The WITH OWNERACCESS OPTION declaration
- Aggregate queries, including GROUP BY and TRANSFORM (crosstab) queries
- Union queries
- Subqueries and all their variations
- Parameterized SQL
- Using external data sources
- Action SQL: UPDATE, DELETE, INSERT INTO, and SELECT INTO
- Data Definition Language (DDL) SQL: CREATE TABLE, CONSTRAINT, CREATE INDEX, ALTER TABLE, and DROP
- SQL pass-through queries
- The differences between ANSI SQL and Access SQL

CHAPTER

SIX

Using Data Access Objects

- Handling Access objects programmatically

- Creating, deleting, and modifying database objects from VBA

- Working with recordsets

- Creating a simple Database Explorer replacement

No matter which program you're using as an interface to your data, at times you'll need programmatic access to your database's structure and to its data. You might want to retrieve the schema of a table, create a new index, or walk through the data returned by a query, one row at a time. Perhaps you need to manipulate your application's security or find a particular row on a form. You can accomplish any of these tasks thanks to Access' use of data access objects (DAO), a feature of the Jet engine that is not only part of Access but is also exposed through OLE automation. In this chapter we'll cover the basics of DAO and present some useful examples along the way.

Although Microsoft introduced the Jet engine in Access 1.0, it's since been substantially upgraded. As of this writing, any application that supports OLE automation can use the Jet engine to work with database objects. Due to this shared use of the technology, the Jet engine must be application independent. The services it supplies must work with any application that needs those services. Therefore, you'll see throughout this chapter references to *engine-defined properties* and *application-defined properties*. Those things the engine must support need to be generic enough that all the applications that call the engine requesting data services can use it.

Dueling Object Hierarchies

Although it can be confusing, before investigating DAO you must realize that Access supports its own object hierarchy, in addition to that supplied by DAO. That is, Access provides a mechanism whereby you can gather information about any open form or report, write to the Debug object, or retrieve information from the Screen object, for example. This application hierarchy is completely separate from the Jet engine hierarchy (see Figure 6.1).

The application hierarchy consists of the UI objects that Access itself maintains. These objects consist of all the open forms and reports; the controls, sections, and modules associated with those objects; and the Application, DoCmd, Screen, Err, and Debug objects. These objects will play only a peripheral part in this chapter, since the focus is the Jet engine hierarchy—the objects the database engine supports. These objects are outlined in Figure 6.2.

FIGURE 6.1:

The two object hierarchies in Access

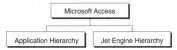

FIGURE 6.2:

The Jet engine hierarchy

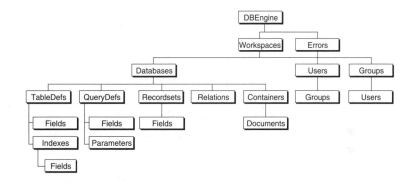

NOTE
If you're converting from Access 2, you may be confused by the change in the DoCmd statement: it used to be a statement, and now it's an object. Why this transformation? To enable OLE automation, DoCmd must be an object. That way you can perform macro actions from outside Access. In the same vein, the Application object has more properties and methods in each succeeding version of Access.

Nuts and Bolts: Syntax Explained

To use DAO, you'll need to be able to refer to objects and use the correct syntax when building expressions. The next few sections discuss issues surrounding the various methods of using and referring to objects.

Properties and Methods

Objects have both properties and methods. *Properties* are attributes of objects that can normally be retrieved and (sometimes) set. For example, most objects expose the Name property, which returns the name of the object. You could use the following statement to retrieve the name of a TableDef object referred to by the variable tdf:

```
strName = tdf.Name
```

You can think of properties as the adjectives that describe objects.

Methods are actions that can be applied to objects. For example, Recordset objects provide the MoveNext method, which moves the current record pointer to the next record. You could use the following statement to move to the next record of the recordset referred to by the variable rst:

```
rst.MoveNext
```

You can think of methods as the verbs that act upon objects.

Using Object Variables

Through the course of this book, we make many assumptions about your knowledge of Access and VBA. We use standard variable types without explanation, assuming you'll understand statements like the following:

```
Dim intX as Integer
```

On the other hand, *object variables,* the basis of all your program code surrounding Data Access Objects, require a little explanation.

When you create a normal variable, you're asking Access to reserve enough space to hold the information for which you've specified a datatype. If you don't specify a datatype, Access assumes the most space the variable might need and uses a Variant-type variable. When you create an object variable (a variable that will refer to either a user-interface object or a data access object), Access creates only a "pointer." That is, the variable it creates only *refers* to a real object; it's not a real object itself.

For example, when you write code like this:

```
Dim db As Database
Dim rst As Recordset
```

```
Dim frm As Form
Dim ctl As Control
```

none of those variables actually hold any data, nor do they refer to any real objects at this point. To make an object variable actually refer to a real object, you must use the Set keyword. In every case you use Set to "point" the variable either at a real object (which must already exist) or at an instance of the object created with the New keyword. (See the section "Displaying Multiple Instances of Forms" in Chapter 8 for more information.) For example, using the variables in the previous example, you might see code like this:

```
Set db = CurrentDb()
Set rst = db.OpenRecordset("tblCustomers")
Set frm = Forms!frmCustomers
Set ctl = frm.Controls!txtCompanyName
```

In each case you've made the object variable refer to an actual object. Without this step, the object variables are just placeholders, waiting to actually refer to something.

If in the course of your code you point a data access object variable (such as a tabledef or recordset) at an actual object, Access will destroy the reference when the variable goes out of scope. If you have qualms about Access releasing the memory your object references use, you can explicitly delete the linkage by setting the variable equal to the predefined value Nothing:

```
Set rst = Nothing
```

In addition, if you created an object as part of your assignment and want to be completely overt about your intentions, you should also use the Close method of the object to close it:

```
Set db = CurrentDb()
Set rst = db.OpenRecordset("tblCustomers")
.
.
.
rst.Close
Set rst = Nothing
```

Although these steps aren't required, and we, too, tend to count on Access for these housekeeping details, you may want to consider these options. As you'll see in the section "CurrentDb() versus DBEngine(0)(0)" later in this chapter, however, you should close only objects you've created as part of your code. CurrentDb(), for example, returns a reference to the current user database. Although you can write

```
Set db = CurrentDb( )
    .
    .
    .
db.Close
```

in your code, there's no reason to do so. Since you didn't open CurrentDb() in your code, you can't close it. On the other hand, if being symmetrical is important, db.Close will fail silently, without triggering an error. (If you really want to close the current database, however, you can use the CloseCurrentDatabase method of the Application object.)

DBEngine and the Workspaces Collection

The DBEngine object represents the Jet database engine and is the top-level object in any DAO reference. To refer to any object in the Jet hierarchy, you'll always start by referring to the DBEngine object. As you can see in Figure 6.2, the DBEngine object contains two collections: the collection of open workspaces and the Errors collection.

If you're using DAO from outside Access, you have no choice: the DBEngine object is the only way to get to any object. From within Access, you can and should use the CurrentDb() function to obtain a reference to the current database. (See the section "CurrentDb() versus DBEngine(0)(0)" later in this chapter for more information.) To reference objects that aren't part of the current database, however, you'll need to start with DBEngine even within Access.

> **NOTE**
>
> We could list, in this chapter, all the properties and methods of each object. However, this information is neatly encapsulated in Access' online help. For each object type, search through online help and choose the object summary page for a complete list of the properties and methods each object exposes.

A workspace object represents a user's session. It contains all the open databases and provides for transaction processing and a secure workgroup. The Workspaces collection (of the DBEngine object) is the collection of all active workspaces. Unless you need to open an additional workspace, you'll rarely have any interaction with any workspace besides the default workspace Access opens for you.

As you can see in Figure 6.2, each workspace object contains three collections: Databases, Users, and Groups. The Databases collection contains all the opened databases, and the Users and Groups collections contain information about (you guessed it) all the users and groups in the current workgroup.

Referring to Objects

You refer to data access objects by following the hierarchy presented in the preceding section. Start with the DBEngine object and work your way down. The general format for referring to objects is

DBEngine.*ParentCollectionItem*.*ChildCollection*("*ChildObject*")

where it may take several iterations through parent collections before you get to the child collection you're interested in.

Access provides a special way to refer to the current user database: the CurrentDb() function. (See the next section, "CurrentDb() versus DBEngine(0)(0)," for more information.) From code, we'll almost always refer to the user's database with the CurrentDb() function, because this is the preferred method. In addition, you can use the CurrentDb() function in place of DBEngine.Workspaces(0).Databases(0) when retrieving properties, like this (the parentheses following CurrentDb() are optional in this syntax):

```
Debug.Print CurrentDb.TableDefs(0).Name
```

To refer to any member of any collection, you can use one of four syntactical constructs. Table 6.1 lists the four available methods. (In each example you're attempting to refer to the database named Sales that you'd previously opened as the only database in workspace 0.)

TABLE 6.1: Methods for Referring to Objects

Syntax	Details	Example
collection("name")		DBEngine.Workspaces(0).Databases ("Sales")
collection(*var*)	Where *var* is a string or variant variable	strDatabase="Sales" DBEngine.Workspaces(0). Databases(strDatabase)
collection(*ordinal position*)	Where *ordinal position* is the object's position within its collection	DBEngine.Workspaces(0). Databases(0)
collection!*name* collection![*name*]	Brackets are necessary if *name* contains a nonstandard character, such as a space	DBEngine.Workspaces(0). Databases!Sales

WARNING Access numbers all built-in collections with ordinal values, beginning with 0. Microsoft Excel and Graph both number their collections starting with 1, and user-defined collections within Access are also numbered starting with 1, so this is a point about which you'll want to be very careful.

All objects except DBEngine have an associated collection that contains all the objects of the given type. For example, the TableDefs collection contains a TableDef object for each table saved in the database. Collections make it easy to "visit" all the objects of a specific type, looping through all the items in the collection. Since you can refer to all the items in a collection either by name or by position, you have the best of both worlds. If you know the specific object's name, you can find it by name, as in the following code fragment:

```
Debug.Print CurrentDb.TableDefs("tblCompanies").RecordCount
```

If you want to refer to an object by number, you can do that, too:

```
Debug.Print CurrentDb.TableDefs(0).Name
```

By the way, in Access 2, a subtle problem made it impossible to chain together references below the current database in the DAO hierarchy until you had already referred to the current database itself at least once. Therefore, all Access 2 code had to declare a database variable, set it equal to a database, and then create references from there:

```
Dim db As Database
Dim tdf As Tabledef
Set db = DBEngine.Workspaces(0).Databases(0)
Set tdf = db.TableDefs(0)
Debug.Print tdf.Name
```

This problem has been fixed in Access 95, and you can now create references in one long string, if you wish. Either of the following statements will work:

```
Debug.Print DBEngine.Workspaces(0).Databases(0). _
 Tabledefs(0).Name
```

or

```
Debug.Print CurrentDb.TableDefs(0).Name
```

TIP

The "strung-out" reference using CurrentDb() is useful only for retrieving properties; you cannot use it reliably to retrieve object references. In some situations it will work, but you're best off creating a variable that refers to the database and then using that variable for retrieving other references, just as you did in Access 2. You can use DBEngine.Workspaces(0).Databases(0) to retrieve references directly, in one statement, but it's simpler to subscribe to the old technique: get an object variable that refers to the current database, and work from there.

CurrentDb() versus DBEngine(0)(0)

To retrieve a reference to the current user's database, the DAO solution is to start with the DBEngine object, work your way through the Workspaces collection (Access creates Workspaces(0) for you when you log in to Access) and through the Databases collection (Access places the user database into Databases(0) for you), all the way to:

```
DBEngine.Workspaces(0).Databases(0)
```

which you can shorten to:

```
DBEngine(0)(0)
```

if you count on default collections. (See the section "Using Default Collections" later in this chapter.)

Why, then, does Access *also* provide the CurrentDb() function, which returns a reference to the current user's database? And why, when Microsoft stated quite clearly in Access 2 that CurrentDb() was to be faded out and that the DAO reference was the preferred method for referencing the user's database, have they turned around and stated that CurrentDb() is again the preferred method?

It all boils down to this: Jet and Access are two separate products. Jet provides the database services that Access requires, but Access provides its own layer on top of Jet, which you're using if you're designing applications inside Access. Access provides CurrentDb() as a reference to the current database, and Jet provides DBEngine.Workspaces(0).Databases(0) (which can be condensed to DBEngine(0)(0)).

Certainly, the DBEngine(0)(0) syntax is required if you're working outside of Access. That is, if you're using OLE automation to control DAO, this is the only way to get a reference to the user's database in Access. On the other hand, Access provides the CurrentDb() function, which will always refer to the current database from within Access.

Access presents some rather subtle problems having to do with the currency of the reference to the user's database. CurrentDb() and DBEngine(0)(0) are not the same object internally, although they do both refer to the same database. Every time you retrieve a reference using CurrentDb(), you're asking Access to create a new internal object that refers to the current database. On the other hand, Jet maintains only a single reference, DBEngine(0)(0). This explains why you can't create references using CurrentDb() in a single long string: As VBA executes the line of code, Access creates a new database reference and gives you an object reference in that database. It's as though you've executed an explicit OpenDatabase() on the current database. As soon as the line of code has finished executing, Access closes the database reference it just opened. For certain types of objects (recordsets, in particular), Access attempts to keep the reference to the recordset viable. For other types of objects, however, Access does not maintain the open reference, and further attempts at using the object will fail.

For example, attempting to run this procedure:

```
Sub ThisDoesntWork()
    Dim doc As Document
    Set doc = CurrentDb.Containers!Tables.Documents(0)
    Debug.Print doc.Name
End Sub
```

will fail with an error when the code attempts to print doc.Name. The database object that was used to reference that particular document is long gone, and "doc" becomes an invalid reference. Note, however, that if you were to replace CurrentDb with DBEngine(0)(0), this procedure would work fine. If you change the code to use a database variable instead of a single long reference, it will also work fine:

```
Sub ThisDoesWork()
    Dim db As Database
    Dim doc As Document

    Set db = CurrentDb()
    Set doc = db.Containers!Tables.Documents(0)
    Debug.Print doc.Name
End Sub
```

How do you choose between CurrentDb() and DBEngine(0)(0) in your applications? If you're working with Access using OLE automation, your answer is simple: you can use DBEngine(0)(0) only to refer to the current database. If you're working in Access, however, you can use either CurrentDb() or DBEngine(0)(0) to refer to the current database. Certainly, using CurrentDb() is simpler, and it is easier to understand as you peruse code. On the other hand, it's slower. (Experimentation has shown that retrieving a reference using CurrentDb() can be an order of magnitude slower than using DBEngine(0)(0). See Chapter 17 for details on testing this out.) There's one big difference between the two that may make your decision for you: the database referred to by CurrentDb() is always up to date with the user interface. You must call the Refresh method before you use any collection retrieved using a reference through DBEngine(0)(0). The Refresh method is quite expensive (slow, that is) and will immediately obviate any speed gains you made by choosing DBEngine(0)(0) over CurrentDb(). Almost every example in this book that refers to the current database uses CurrentDb().

TIP

Although Microsoft has made no such promises, it's quite possible that a future version of Access will support multiple databases open on the Access desktop. If so, at that point there will be another difference between CurrentDb( ) and DBEngine(0)(0): CurrentDb( ) will always refer to the database containing the code that is currently executing, but DBEngine(0)(0) might refer to another database, the one that was added to the databases collection first—that is, the one that was opened first. Therefore, using CurrentDb( ) adds a tiny amount of "forward-thinking" to your code, although we can only speculate at this point as to whether it will ever make a difference.

Bang (!) versus Dot (.)

The bang (!) and dot (.) identifier operators help describe the relationships among collections, objects, and properties in an expression. They indicate that one part of an expression belongs to another.

In general, you follow the bang with the name of something you created: a form, report, or control. The bang also indicates that the item to follow is an element of a collection. You'll usually follow the dot with a property, collection, or method name.

You can also think of the uses of these operators this way: a bang separates an object from the collection it's in (a field in a table, a form in the Forms collection, a control on a form), while a dot separates an object from a property, method, or collection of that object.

Ordinal Positions

As you've seen, you can refer to an object using the ordinal position within its collection. The Jet engine assigns and maintains these ordinal positions, and they always start with position number 0. For the Workspaces and Databases objects, ordinal position 0 always refers to the current workspace and the current database (the one that's open in the user interface). For example, when you start Microsoft Access, it opens a Jet engine session, creates a workspace, and assigns it to the first ordinal position in the Workspaces collection. When you open a database through the user interface (using the File ➤ Open Database menu item), Access assigns the database to the first ordinal position in the Databases collection.

For objects other than workspaces and databases, an object's ordinal position is dependent on the order in which it was added to its collection. The first table you create will have a lower ordinal position than tables you create later. As you create and delete objects, an object's ordinal position changes within its collection. Additionally, Access creates objects (such as the system tables) that may preclude your objects from starting at ordinal position 0. For this reason it is not a good idea to refer to a specific object using its ordinal position. You should use the ordinal position of objects only as loop indexes, for iterating through all the objects in a collection.

Using Default Collections

You can see from previous examples that a simple object reference can result in a long line of code. Fortunately, DAO provides default collections for most object types: if you don't specify a collection, Access assumes you're referring to the default collection for the parent object. You can use the default collection behavior of objects to make your code more compact (but somewhat less readable). Table 6.2 lists the default collection within each object type.

Using default collections, you can shorten this expression:

```
DBEngine.Workspaces(0).Databases(0).TableDefs(0)
```

to

```
DBEngine(0)(0)(0)
```

This expression means, "Refer to the first tabledef within the first database within the first workspace," because the default collection for DBEngine is the Workspaces collection, the default collection for a workspace object is the Databases collection, and the default collection for a database object is the TableDefs collection.

You can use similar contractions to simplify your code. Be aware, though, that using default collections to reduce your code also makes it less readable: whoever is reading the code will have to understand the meaning of the expression without any visual clues. On the other hand, leaving out the default collection names makes your code run a tiny bit more quickly. (See Chapter 17 for more information.)

TABLE 6.2: Default Collections for DAO Objects

Object	Default Collection
Container	Documents
Database	TableDefs
DBEngine	Workspaces
Group	Users
Index	Fields
QueryDef	Parameters
Recordset	Fields
Relation	Fields
TableDef	Fields
User	Groups
Workspace	Databases

Enumerating through Collections

Because you can access any object in any of the data access object collections by its position in the collection, you can loop through the elements of any collection to look at or modify any object in the collection. Use the Count property of a collection to determine the size of the collection. Remember that the ordinal position of objects within a DAO collection starts at 0; if a collection contains three elements, they'll be numbered 0 through 2.

For example, you could use code like this to print out the names of all the tables in your database:

```
Dim db As Database
Dim intI As Integer
Dim tdf As Tabledef

Set db = CurrentDb()
For intI = 0 To db.TableDefs.Count - 1
    Set tdf = db.TableDefs(intI)
    Debug.Print tdf.Name
Next intI
```

The simplest way to loop through any collection, however, is to use the For Each…Next syntax. This syntax requires you to create a variable that can refer to the object type in the collection you're looping through and then use code like this to do the work:

```
Dim db As Database
Dim tdf As TableDef

Set db = CurrentDb()
For Each tdf In db.TableDefs
    Debug.Print tdf.Name
Next intI
```

In this case, For Each…Next does the "Set" operation for you.

Working with Properties

If you have worked with forms, reports, and controls, you are already familiar with referencing properties. (See Chapters 7 through 9 for more information on user-interface objects.) However, data access objects and the interaction between the Jet engine and Microsoft Access introduce new subtleties when you are working with properties.

Properties for data access objects behave somewhat differently from Microsoft Access properties. As you saw earlier in this chapter, every object has a collection of properties. For Access objects (forms and reports, for example), every property in the Properties collection that will ever exist for the object exists when you create the object. This is not necessarily the case for data access objects. Properties may not exist in the collection until you set them to a value, depending on the specific object. Therefore, it's important that you understand the differences among the different types of properties used in DAO.

Types of Properties

DAO properties can be either built in or user defined.

Built-in properties always exist for an object. They define the basic characteristics of an object and are available to any application that uses the Jet engine. For example, for Field objects, Name and Type are built-in properties. They define the basic characteristics of a field.

User-defined properties are added to the Properties collection of an object. These properties may be added either by Microsoft Access as a client of the Jet engine or by you as an application developer. If Microsoft Access added the property to the object, it's treated as a special case of a user-defined property. The properties Access adds are properties it needs in order to do its job. The Jet engine can't provide them, because they're specific to Access.

User-defined properties do not exist until they are added to the object's Properties collection. While this may seem obvious, it does cause some unexpected behavior. For example, a field's description is not a built-in property. Even though you can enter a field's description while defining the table, the Jet engine doesn't know about it until you've actually typed it into the property list for the field. If you try to retrieve the Description property of an object that has not yet had this property set, you will get a trappable run-time error.

TIP

Online help includes a list of the DAO run-time error codes. Finding that list is, unfortunately, not a trivial task. There are several ways to get there (and there may be a direct method, but we've not found it): from the Help Index, choose *DAO Collections, Errors*. From the popup menu, choose *Error Object, Errors Collection Summary*. On that page, choose the *Number* jump topic, and finally, on the Number property page, choose the *Trappable Data Access Errors* jump topic. Online help will reward your efforts with a list of the trappable DAO errors.

Referring to Data Access Object Properties

As in referencing any other property, you can use the standard

object.property

syntax for referring to a built-in property of an object. On the other hand, to refer to a user-defined property (whether the "user" is you, your application, or Access as a client of the Jet engine), you must refer to the property through the Properties collection of the object (and this syntax always works, even for built-in properties):

> *object.Properties("property")*

or

> *object.Properties!property*

For example, to retrieve the Description property for the tblClients table, you could use code like the following. (Note that this code will fail with a run-time error if the Description property hasn't already been set.)

```
Dim db As Database
Dim tdf As TableDef
Dim strDescription As String

Set db = CurrentDb()
Set tdf = db.TableDefs!tblClient
strDescription = tdf.Properties!Description
```

(For more information on adding user-defined properties, see the section "Creating Your Own Properties" later in this chapter.)

Enumerating the Properties

Listing 6.1 shows code you could use to print out all the properties of any table:

Listing 6.1

```
Function ListProperties(strTable As String)
    Dim db As Database
    Dim tdf As TableDef
    Dim prp As Property

    Set db = CurrentDb()
    ' You could use the following expression:
    ' Set tdf = db.TableDefs(strTable)
    ' but the TableDefs collection is the default collection
    ' for a database object. So its use is unnecessary
    ' in the expression.
    Set tdf = db(strTable)
```

```
    For Each prp In tdf.Properties
        Debug.Print prp.Name, prp.Value
    Next prp
End Function
```

You'll find ListProperties() in basTestProperties (in CH06.MDB).

The output from the preceding code might look something like this:

Name	tblCustomers
Updatable	True
DateCreated	5/29/95 3:04:24 PM
LastUpdated	5/30/95 12:54:48 PM
Connect	
Attributes	0
SourceTableName	
RecordCount	91
ValidationRule	
ValidationText	
ConflictTable	
OrderOn	False

Setting and Retrieving Properties

To make it simpler to set and get properties of objects, we've provided the glrGet-Prop() and glrSetProp() functions in basHandleProps (in CH06.MDB). The glr-SetProp() function takes as its parameters an object reference, a property name, and a value. It attempts to set the property, and if it fails, it attempts to create the property and then set its value. Of course, this feature can work only for objects that allow you to create user-defined properties (tables, indexes, relations, documents, and fields). For example:

```
Set db = CurrentDb()
varRetval = glrSetProp(db.TableDefs("tblCustomer"), _
  "Description", "This is the customer table")
```

```
If Not IsError(varRetval) Then
    MsgBox "Description set successfully!"
End If
```

will set the Description property. If that property hadn't existed before the function call, glrSetProp() would have created it and then set it. (See basHandleProps for the details.)

The glrGetProp() function is simpler: it just attempts to retrieve the requested property, and it returns the value if the property exists or an error value otherwise. For example:

```
Set db = CurrentDb()
varRetval = glrGetProp( _
 db.TableDefs("tblCustomers").Fields("CustomerID"), _
 "Description")
If Not IsError(varRetval) Then
    MsgBox "The Description property was: " & varRetval
End If
```

will return either the Description property for the CustomerID field in tblCustomers or an error value if that property doesn't exist.

Data Definition Using DAO

The previous sections have been using data access objects to refer to existing objects and properties. A large portion of DAO's power, though, lies in its ability to programmatically create and manipulate objects. Using the Create... and Append methods, you can create and modify virtually any data access object.

Creating Objects

To create a new object, follow these three steps:

1. Use one of the Create... methods to create the object (CreateTable, CreateIndex, and so on).

2. Define the new object's characteristics by setting its properties. Some properties (such as its name) are essential to its existence and must be specified when you create the object. Others may be specified later. (In most cases this

step can be rolled up into the previous one. All the Create… methods accept optional parameters letting you specify essential properties of the new object.)

3. Append the object to its collection to make it a permanent part of your database.

In cases where the new object contains other objects (a table contains fields, for instance), you must create the main object, then create the subordinate objects, append them to the appropriate collection, and then append the main object to its collection. You can use this same technique when creating a new table, index, or relation programmatically. Each operation is unique in one way or another, so consult the online help for more information on the CreateTable, CreateField, CreateIndex, and CreateRelation methods. The following sections demonstrate how to create these complex objects.

Creating a New Table

The following example creates a new table called tblOrders and adds two fields to it. You'll find the complete function in Listing 6.2 a little later in this section (and in basCreateTable in CH06.MDB):

```
Function CreateOrdersTable()
    Dim db As Database
    Dim tdfOrders As TableDef
    Dim fld1 As Field
    Dim fld2 As Field

    Set db = CurrentDb()
    Set tdfOrders = db.CreateTableDef()
    tdfOrders.Name = "tblOrders"

    Set fld1 = tdfOrders.CreateField("OrderID", dbLong)
    Set fld2 = tdfOrders.CreateField("CustomerName", _
      dbText, 30)
```

At this point the new table and its two fields exist only in memory. To make the new objects a permanent part of the database, you must use the Append method. If you do not append a new object to a collection, it will not be saved as an object in the database.

Creating objects and giving them properties is not enough. You must take the step of appending them to the correct collection, or Access will never know of their existence. If your program exits before you've used the Append method to add them to a collection, they will be discarded.

The next lines save the new objects to the database:

```
With tdfOrders.Fields
    .Append fld1
    .Append fld2
End With
```

```
db.TableDefs.Append tdfOrders
```

Finally, you can refresh the TableDefs collection to ensure that the new objects are included in it. In a multiuser environment, the new table may not be immediately available to other users unless you refresh the collection. The following line refreshes the TableDefs collection:

```
db.TableDefs.Refresh
```

Even using the Refresh method, Access won't update the database window itself until it must. It will only show the new table you've created once you move to a different collection and then back to the list of tables.

This simple example does not include error handling and will therefore fail if you attempt to run it more than once. If you want to try it again, first delete the table the example created from the Database Explorer.

Listing 6.2

```
Function CreateOrdersTable()
    Dim db As Database
    Dim tdfOrders As TableDef
    Dim fld1 As Field
    Dim fld2 As Field
```

```
    Set db = CurrentDb()
    Set tdfOrders = db.CreateTableDef()
    tdfOrders.Name = "tblOrders"

    Set fld1 = tdfOrders.CreateField("OrderID", dbLong)
    Set fld2 = tdfOrders.CreateField("CustomerName", dbText, 30)

    With tdfOrders.Fields
        .Append fld1
        .Append fld2
    End With

    With db.TableDefs
        .Append tdfOrders
        .Refresh
    End With
End Function
```

TIP

The With Object...End With syntax can make it simpler to modify multiple properties or use multiple methods of an object. The previous example used the syntax only for the purpose of introducing it, but it can both simplify your code and make its intent clearer. You'll want to use it whenever possible.

You can also use the

Dim objectVar As New *Object*

syntax to create the objects. When you do this, Access instantiates the objects automatically. Rather than having to call CreateTable explicitly, Access creates the tabledef for you when you write

```
Dim tdf As New TableDef
```

This syntax creates, at the same time, both the object variable and the object to which it points. Once you've created an object this way (by running the procedure that includes the declaration), you still need to assign the values of the properties of the object, and you need to append it to the appropriate collection.

For example, you could rewrite the preceding function as shown here:

```
Function CreateOrdersTable2()
    Dim db As Database

    ' Create the objects RIGHT NOW, as opposed
    ' to creating variables to point to objects that
    ' you'll create later.
    Dim tdfOrders As New TableDef
    Dim fld1 As New Field
    Dim fld2 As New Field

    Set db = CurrentDb()
    ' The tabledef's already created, so
    ' just assign the properties.
    tdfOrders.Name = "tblOrders"

    ' The fields are already created, so just
    ' assign the properties.
    With fld1
        .Type = dbLong
        .Name = "OrderID"
    End With

    With fld2
        .Type = dbText
        .Size = 30
        .Name = "CustomerName"
    End With

    With tdfOrders.Fields
        .Append fld1
        .Append fld2
    End With

    With db.TableDefs
        .Append tdfOrders
        .Refresh
    End With
End Function
```

We can't recommend a real preference for either method, except that calling the Create… methods directly makes your code more *explicit:* on viewing the code, it's easier to see exactly what it's doing.

The Create... Methods

For each data access object that you can create programmatically, there's an associated *Create* method. Table 6.3 summarizes the methods and their syntax.

TABLE 6.3: Object Creation Methods

Object	Method	Arguments	Datatype	Description
Table	CreateTableDef	Name	String	Name of the new table
		Attributes	Integer	Settings for attached, system, and hidden tables
		Source	String	An attached table's base table type information
		Connect	String	An attached table's base table path and file name
Field	CreateField	Name	String	Name of the new field
		Type	Integer	Datatype of the new field
		Size	Integer	Size of the field if it is a text field
Index	CreateIndex	Name	String	Name of the new index
Query	CreateQueryDef	Name	String	Name of the new query
		SQL	String	Valid SQL string that defines the new query
Relation	CreateRelation	Name	String	Name of the new relation
		Table	String	Name of the relation's primary table
		ForeignTable	String	Name of the relation's foreign table
		Attributes	Integer	Settings for relationship type, enforced referential integrity, and cascaded updates and deletes
Workspace	CreateWorkspace	Name	String	Name of the new workspace
		User	String	Name of an existing user. This user will become the owner of the new workspace object. For code that references the new workspace object, *User* will, in effect, be the user executing the code
		Password	String	Password for the new workspace object. Can contain any characters except ASCII null (Chr$(0))

TABLE 6.3: Object Creation Methods (continued)

Object	Method	Arguments	Datatype	Description
Database	CreateDatabase	DatabaseName	String	Name of the file that contains the database
		Locale	String	Collating order of the database
		Options	Integer	Options for the new database. You can specify whether or not the database is to be encrypted and which version (2.0 or 3.0) of the file format to use when saving the database
Group	CreateGroup	Name	String	Name of the new group
		PID	String	Personal identifier for the new group
User	CreateUser	Name	String	Name of the new user
		PID	String	Personal identifier for the new user

Creating an Index

As part of your applications, you may need to create an index programmatically. Follow these steps to create a new index:

1. Use the CreateIndex method of a TableDef object to create the index object, and set its Name property (either in the function call itself or by assigning a value to the Name property sometime before you append the index to the Indexes collection).

2. Assign values to the new index's properties, as appropriate. All the properties are read/write for an index object that hasn't yet been appended to the Indexes collection but are read-only once that has occurred. The ones you'll most likely be interested in are the Name, Primary, Unique, and Required properties.

3. Use the CreateField method to create a field object for each field that makes up part of the index, and append each to the index's Fields collection. This collection of fields indicates to the index the fields for which it must maintain values in order to keep itself current.

4. Use the Append method of the original TableDef object to append the index object to its Indexes collection.

NOTE

Since all the properties of an index object are read-only once the object has been appended to its collection, if you need to modify a property of an index once it's been created, you must delete the object and then create a new one.

TIP

In Access, using DAO, you can name your indexes any way you wish. If you have code you're using, however, that counts on your primary key being named PrimaryKey (and almost anyplace you're using the Seek method in your code, you will), you must ensure that your primary keys are named the standard value, PrimaryKey. Otherwise, existing code might break.

The CreatePrimaryKey() function in Listing 6.3 creates the primary key for any specified table. You pass to this function the name of the table, the name of the primary key, and a variant that may contain an array of field names or just a single field name to use as part of the primary key. Along the way, CreatePrimaryKey() calls the FindPrimaryKey() function, which returns the name of the primary key if it exists or Null if it doesn't. If a primary key already exists, CreatePrimaryKey() deletes the primary key so it can create a new one. We've also included a test procedure, TestCreatePK, to test the functionality. You'll find all these examples in the module basPK in CH06.MDB.

Listing 6.3

```
Function glrCreatePrimaryKey(strTableName As String, _
 strKeyName As String, varFields As Variant) As Boolean
    Dim db As Database
    Dim idx As Index
    Dim tdf As TableDef
    Dim fld As Field
    Dim varPK As Variant
    Dim varIdx As Variant
    Dim idxs As Indexes

    On Error GoTo CreatePrimaryKey_Err
```

```
    Set db = CurrentDb()
    Set tdf = db.TableDefs(strTableName)
    Set idxs = tdf.Indexes

    ' Find out if the table currently has a primary key.
    ' If so, delete it now.
    varPK = FindPrimaryKey(tdf)
    If Not IsNull(varPK) Then
        idxs.Delete varPK
    End If
    ' Create the new index object.
    Set idx = tdf.CreateIndex(strKeyName)

    ' Set up the new index as the primary key.
    ' This will also set:
    '    IgnoreNulls property to False,
    '    Required property to True,
    '    Unique property to True.
    idx.Primary = True

    ' Now create the fields that make up the index,
    ' and append each to the collection of fields.

    ' Loop through all the elements in the varFields array,
    ' if it's an array. If it's not, just add the single
    ' item it contains.
    If IsArray(varFields) Then
        For Each varIdx In varFields
            AddField idx, varIdx
        Next varIdx
    Else
        AddField idx, varFields
    End If
    ' Now append the index to the TableDef's
    ' index collection
    idxs.Append idx
    glrCreatePrimaryKey = True

CreatePrimaryKey_Exit:
    Exit Function

CreatePrimaryKey_Err:
    MsgBox "Error: " & Error & " (" & Err & ")"
    glrCreatePrimaryKey = False
```

```
        Resume CreatePrimaryKey_Exit
End Function

Private Function FindPrimaryKey(tdf As TableDef) As Variant

    ' Given a particular tabledef, find the primary
    ' key name, if it exists.

    ' Return the name of the primary key's index, if
    ' it exists, or Null if there wasn't a primary key.

    Dim idx As Index

    For Each idx In tdf.Indexes
        If idx.Primary Then
            FindPrimaryKey = idx.Name
            Exit Function
        End If
    Next idx
    FindPrimaryKey = Null
End Function

Private Function AddField(idx As Index, varIdx As Variant) As _
Boolean
    ' Given an index object, and a field name, add
    ' the field to the index.
    ' Return True on success, False otherwise.

    Dim fld As Field

    On Error GoTo AddIndex_Err
    If Len(varIdx & "") > 0 Then
        Set fld = idx.CreateField(varIdx)
        idx.Fields.Append fld
    End If
    AddField = True

AddIndex_Exit:
    Exit Function

AddIndex_Err:
    AddField = False
    Resume AddIndex_Exit
End Function
```

```
Sub TestCreatePK()
    Debug.Print glrCreatePrimaryKey("tblCustomerItems", _
    "PrimaryKey", Array("CustomerID", "ItemID"))
End Sub
```

Creating Relationships

To create a relationship, use the CreateRelation method of a database object. Follow these steps to create a new relation:

1. Open the database that will be the basis for your relation.

2. Verify that the referenced table (the primary table in the relation) has a primary key in place.

3. Use the CreateRelation method of the database to create the relation object. Either set the relation's properties when you create it or set them one by one after the fact. These properties include the Table, ForeignTable, and Attributes properties.

4. Create a field object for each primary key field from the primary table involved in the relationship. For each field object, supply the ForeignName property, which corresponds to the name of the matching key field in the secondary table. Append each new field object to the relationship's Fields collection.

5. Use the Append method to append the new relation object to the database's Relations collection.

The following table lists all the possible values for the Attributes property of a relation object:

Constant	Description
dbRelationUnique	Relationship is one-to-one
dbRelationDontEnforce	Relationship isn't enforced (no referential integrity)
dbRelationInherited	Relationship exists in the database that contains the two attached tables
dbRelationLeft	Relationship is a left outer join
dbRelationRight	Relationship is a right outer join

Constant	Description
dbRelationUpdateCascade	Updates will cascade
dbRelationDeleteCascade	Deletions will cascade

Set the property to be the sum of any of these constants. (Most programmers use the Or operator to combine these sorts of flags, just to make it clear they're working with flag values, not doing some sort of arithmetic.) If you set no value for the Attributes property, Access attempts to create a one-to-many inner-joined relationship with referential integrity enabled.

Listing 6.4 demonstrates, in the simplest case, the steps involved in creating a relationship. This function (from basRelations in CH06.MDB) creates a left outer join between tblCustomers and tblCustomerItems and enables cascading updates. Just to make sure the function succeeds, if it finds that the relation already exists, it deletes that relation and re-creates it.

Listing 6.4

```
Const glrcErrObjectExists = 3012

Function CreateRelationship() As Boolean

    ' Create a relationship between tblCustomers and
    ' tblCustomerItems.
    ' The relation will be a left outer join,
    ' with cascading deletes enabled.

    Dim db As Database
    Dim rel As Relation
    Dim fld As Field

    On Error GoTo CreateRelationship_Err

    Set db = CurrentDb()

    ' Create the new relation object.
    Set rel = db.CreateRelation()

    ' Set the relation's properties.
    With rel
        .Name = "Relation1"
        .Table = "tblCustomers"
```

```
            .ForeignTable = "tblCustomerItems"

            ' Create a left outer join containing
            ' tblCustomers and tblItems, with cascading
            ' updates enabled.
            .Attributes = dbRelationLeft Or _
            dbRelationDeleteCascade
        End With
        ' Or you could set all the properties when you create
        ' the object:
        ' Set rel = db.CreateRelation("Relation1", _
        '   "tblCustomers", "tblCustomerItems", _
        '   dbRelationLeft Or dbRelationDeleteCascade)

        ' Set the relation's field collection.
        Set fld = rel.CreateField("CustomerID")
        ' What field does this map to in the OTHER table?
        fld.ForeignName = "CustomerID"
        rel.Fields.Append fld
        ' You could append more fields, if you needed to.

        ' Append the relation to the database's
        ' relations collection.
        db.Relations.Append rel
        CreateRelationship = True

CreateRelationship_Exit:
    Exit Function

CreateRelationship_Err:
    Select Case Err.Number
        Case glrcErrObjectExists
            ' If the relationship already exists,
            ' just delete it, and then try to
            ' append it again.
            db.Relations.Delete rel.Name
            Resume
        Case Else
            MsgBox "Error: " & Err.Description & _
            " (" & Err.Number & ")"
            CreateRelationship = False
            Resume CreateRelationship_Exit
    End Select
End Function
```

Creating Your Own Properties

Access' support for DAO makes it possible for you to create your own properties and append them to the Properties collection for an object. For example, you might like to add a LastUpdated property to a table to keep track of the last time a user touched the table. Just as for adding an object of any other type, you take three steps:

1. Use the CreateProperty method to create the new property.

2. Define the new property's characteristics by setting its properties. (You may have done this in step 1.)

3. Append the object to the Properties collection to make it a permanent part of your database.

The code in Listing 6.5 creates the LastChanged and LastUser properties and appends them to the tblCustomers table. (You can find the function in basTestProperties in CH06.MDB.) The following paragraphs examine the function in detail.

The function's caller has passed in the name of the table on which to operate, so the first step is to set up a reference to the correct TableDef object:

```
Dim db As Database
Dim tdf As TableDef
Dim prpLastChanged As Property
Dim prpLastUser As Property
Dim prp As Property

Set tdf = db.TableDefs(strName)
```

Then you need to create the new property objects. When you call CreateProperty, you may supply the property's name, type, and initial value. You may also set those properties later, before you append the property to the table's Properties collection. In this case it's simpler just to do it all in the call to CreateProperty(). You set the LastChanged property to contain the current time and the LastUser property to contain the current user ("Admin", unless you've logged in as someone else). (This step corresponds to steps 1 and 2 in the previous list of steps necessary to create new properties.)

```
Set prpLastChanged = tdf.CreateProperty("LastChanged", _
  dbDate, Now)
```

```
Set prpLastUser = tdf.CreateProperty("LastUser", _
  dbText, CurrentUser())
```

Use the Append method to add the properties to the table so they become persistent. Since the Append method triggers a run-time error if you've already appended the properties, you can avoid the problem by turning off error checking while appending:

```
On Error Resume Next
With tdf.Properties
    .Append prpLastChanged
    .Append prpLastUser
End With
On Error GoTo 0
```

To list the properties, you can loop through the Properties collection:

```
Dim prp As Property
For Each prp In tdf.Properties
    Debug.Print prp.Name, prp.Value
Next prp
```

To modify the LastChanged property, use one of the two possible syntax variations:

```
tdf.Properties!LastChanged = Now
```

or

```
tdf.Properties("LastChanged") = Now
```

Listing 6.5

```
Function TestAddProps(strName As String)
    Dim db As Database
    Dim tdf As TableDef
    Dim prpLastChanged As Property
    Dim prpLastUser As Property
    Dim prp As Property

    Set tdf = db.TableDefs(strName)

    ' Create the two new properties.
    Set prpLastChanged = tdf.CreateProperty("LastChanged", _
      dbDate, Now)
    Set prpLastUser = tdf.CreateProperty("LastUser", _
      dbText, CurrentUser())
```

```
' This code will fail if the properties have already
' been added, so just let the errors occur,
' and keep on going.
On Error Resume Next
With tdf.Properties
    .Append prpLastChanged
    .Append prpLastUser
End With
On Error GoTo 0

' Now list out all the properties.
For Each prp In tdf.Properties
    Debug.Print prp.Name, prp.Value
Next prp

' Reset the LastChanged property, just to show how:
tdf.Properties!LastChanged = Now
' or:
' tdf.Properties("LastChanged") = Now
End Sub
```

Modifying Objects

You can modify an existing object using DAO methods and properties without having to open the object in Design view. There are, however, other restrictions to keep
in mind when setting properties of data access objects. Some properties can be set
only when the object is created and cannot be changed after the object has been appended to its collection. The Attributes property of Tabledefs objects is an example
of this restriction. You cannot change the Attributes property of an existing
TableDef object but must set this value when you first create the object. If you must
alter the Attributes property for a given tabledef, you need to create a new one,
copy in all the information from the existing one, and set the Attributes property
before you use the Append method to add the tabledef to your database. Also, you
need to be aware that some properties do not exist for a data access object until they
have been set to a value. (See the section "Types of Properties" earlier in this chapter
for a reminder about this limitation.)

Connecting and Reconnecting Attached Tables

The Connect property of TableDef objects gives you control over attached tables. Using this property in conjunction with the SourceTableName property and the RefreshLink method, you can alter the location of the table feeding data to Access.

The Connect Property

Every TableDef object has a Connect property—a string that identifies the type of attached table and its location in the system's file structure. It does not specify the particular table (or file name, in the case of many of the external datatypes). The SourceTableName property contains the actual file name. Table 6.4 lists all the possible connection types, the necessary Connect string, and an example. (For local native Access tables, the Connect property is a zero-length string [""].)

TABLE 6.4: Connection Strings for Various Connection Types

Connection Type	Connect String	Example
Microsoft Access Database	;DATABASE=*drive:\path\filename*	;DATABASE=C:\DATA\MYDB.MDB
dBASE III	dBASE III;DATABASE=*drive:\path*	dBASE III;DATABASE=C:\DBASE
dBASE IV	dBASE IV;DATABASE=*drive:\path*	dBASE IV;DATABASE=C:\DBASE
dBASE 5	dBASE 5;DATABASE=*drive:\path*	dBASE 5;DATABASE=C:\DBASE
Paradox 3.x	Paradox 3.x;DATABASE=*drive:\path*	Paradox 3.x;DATABASE=C:\PDOXDATA
Paradox 4.x	Paradox 4.x;DATABASE=*drive:\path*	Paradox 4.x;DATABASE=C:\PDOXDATA
Paradox 5.x	Paradox 5.x;DATABASE=*drive:\path*	Paradox 5.x;DATABASE=C:\PDOXDATA
FoxPro 2.0	FoxPro 2.0;*drive:\path*	FoxPro 2.0;DATABASE=C:\FOXDATA
FoxPro 2.5	FoxPro 2.5;*drive:\path*	FoxPro 2.5;DATABASE=C:\FOXDATA
FoxPro 2.6	FoxPro 2.6;*drive:\path*	FoxPro 2.6;DATABASE=C:\FOXDATA
Excel 3.0	Excel 3.0;*drive:\path\filename.xls*	Excel 3.0;DATABASE=C:\XLDATA\DATA.XLS
Excel 4.0	Excel 4.0;*drive:\path\filename.xls*	Excel 4.0;DATABASE=C:\XLDATA\DATA.XLS

TABLE 6.4: Connection Strings for Various Connection Types (continued)

Connection Type	Connect String	Example
Excel 5.0	Excel 5.0;*drive:\path\filename.xls*	Excel 5.0;DATABASE=C:\XLDATA\DATA.XLS
Excel 7.0	Excel 7.0;*drive:\path\filename.xls*	Excel 7.0;DATABASE=C:\XLDATA\DATA.XLS
ODBC	ODBC;DATABASE=defaultdatabase; UID=*username*;PWD=*password*;DSN= *datasourcename*	ODBC;DATABASE=mycust;UID=dan;PWD= Secret; DSN=CustTable

In general, the Connect string names the database that contains the table to which you want to connect. Notice in Table 6.4 that for native Access tables, the database is the actual .MDB file. For many other datatypes, use the directory that contains the table as the database. This makes sense here because other DBMS programs, such as Paradox and FoxPro, use the DOS directory structure as the database; there is no single central file as with Access.

Creating an Attached Access Table

The function in Listing 6.6 creates an attached table in the current database, pulling in data from a different .MDB file. To use it, you might try this:

```
fSuccess = CreateAttached("AttachedTable", _
 "C:\AppPath\MDBFile.MDB", "tblContacts")
```

To create a new attached table, you must follow the same steps that have been covered already: create the object, set its properties, and then append it to the parent collection. CreateAttached() first creates the new TableDef object:

```
Dim db As Database
Dim tdf As TableDef
Dim strConnect As String
Dim fRetval As Boolean

On Error GoTo CreateAttachedError

Set db = CurrentDb()
Set tdf = db.CreateTableDef(strTable)
```

Then the function must set the appropriate properties. For an attached table, you need to set the Connect and SourceTableName properties. Because you're attaching a native Access table, the Connect string doesn't specify a data source; it just describes the path to the .MDB file:

```
With tdf
    .Connect = ";DATABASE=" & strPath
    .SourceTableName = strBaseTable
End With
```

Finally, the code must append the new TableDef object to the TableDefs collection:

```
db.TableDefs.Append tdf
```

In addition, the function adds some error handling. For example, you might already have created a TableDef object with a particular name, or you might try to attach data from an .MDB file that doesn't exist. In either case the error handler pops up a message box and causes the function to return a False value (instead of the True value it returns if it succeeds in creating the new TableDef object). You'll find CreateAttached() in the module basAttach in CH06.MDB.

Listing 6.6

```
Function CreateAttached(strTable As String, strPath As String, _
  strBaseTable As String) As Boolean

    Dim db As Database
    Dim tdf As TableDef
    Dim strConnect As String
    Dim fRetval As Boolean

    On Error GoTo CreateAttachedError

    Set db = CurrentDb()
    Set tdf = db.CreateTableDef(strTable)

    With tdf
        ' Set up the tabledef's properties.
        ' Set the path to the MDB file.
        .Connect = ";DATABASE=" & strPath
        ' Set the source table name.
        .SourceTableName = strBaseTable
    End With
```

```
    ' Append the new tabledef to the Tabledefs collection.
    db.TableDefs.Append tdf
    fRetval = True

CreateAttachedExit:
    CreateAttached = fRetval
    Exit Function

CreateAttachedError:
    MsgBox "Error: " & Error & " (" & Err & ")"
    fRetval = False
    Resume CreateAttachedExit
End Function
```

Modifying an Existing Attached Table

As users work with your application, sooner or later its attached tables will need to be moved to a new location in the system's file structure. Your application will trigger a run-time error when it later tries to access the moved table. To take care of this problem, you can write a function that checks attached tables and then reconnects them if necessary. The function CheckAttachedTable(), in Listing 6.7, tests an attached table and makes sure it's still where Access thinks it is. ReattachTable(), also in Listing 6.7, reattaches the table if necessary. Its code is very similar to that in CreateAttached() (in Listing 6.6). You'll find both functions in basAttach in CH06.MDB. (For a more complete discussion on handling the problems that can come up in applications that use attached tables, see Chapter 12. That chapter discusses a generalized solution for reattaching tables.)

After setting up the requisite database and tabledef object variables, the code in ReAttachTable() checks the Connect property for the particular tabledef. If it's a zero-length string, the table is a native table, and there's nothing to be done. Otherwise it builds up the new connection string and assigns it to the Connect property of the TableDef object:

```
If Len(tdf.Connect) > 0 Then
    tdf.Connect = ";DATABASE=" & strNewPath
    '
    '
End If
```

The code's next step is to attempt to refresh the link between the local Access database and the foreign data. The function uses the tabledef's RefreshLink method to do this. If the link isn't valid, this RefreshLink fails and the error-handling code posts a message and returns a False value from the function. If it succeeds, the function returns a True value, indicating its success:

```
On Error Resume Next
tdf.RefreshLink
ReAttachTable = (Err = 0)
```

Armed with a function to reattach tables if necessary, you can attack the problem of checking to make sure your tables are correctly attached, reattaching them if necessary. CheckAttachedTable() does this work for you.

The majority of the code in CheckAttachedTable() can be summarized in a few steps:

1. Turn on inline error handling (On Error Resume Next).
2. Attempt to retrieve the Name property of the first field in the requested table.
3. If the attempt fails, call ReattachTable() to attempt to reattach it. If that fails, post a failure message and return False.
4. If the recordset creation succeeded, just close the recordset and return a True value from the function.

Listing 6.7

```
Function CheckAttachedTable(strTable As String, _
strNewPath As String) As Boolean

    ' Checks the named table and attempts to reattach it if
    ' it's not attached properly.
    '
    Dim db As Database
    Dim strName As String

    ' Assume success
    CheckAttachedTable = True

    On Error Resume Next
    ' Attempt to retrieve the name of the first field. This
    ' will fail if the attachment isn't valid.
```

```
    Set db = CurrentDb()                        •
    strName = db.TableDefs(strTable).Fields(0).Name

    If Err.Number <> 0 Then
        If Not ReattachTable(strTable, strNewPath) Then
            MsgBox "Could not reattach table '" & strTable & "'"
            CheckAttachedTable = False
        End If
    End If
    On Error GoTo 0
End Function

Private Function ReattachTable(strTable As String, _
strNewPath As String) As Boolean

    Dim db As Database
    Dim tdf As TableDef

    ' Assume success.
    ReattachTable = True

    Set db = CurrentDb()
    Set tdf = db.TableDefs(strTable)

    ' If Connect is blank, it's not an attached table
    If Len(tdf.Connect) > 0 Then
        tdf.Connect = ";DATABASE=" & strNewPath

        ' The RefreshLink might fail if the new path
        ' isn't OK. So trap errors inline.
        On Error Resume Next
        tdf.RefreshLink
        ReattachTable = (Err = 0)
        On Error GoTo 0
    End If
End Function
```

Working with Non-Native Attached Tables

The previous examples all deal with Access tables. You can also create attached tables based on other data sources. When dealing with external data sources, you use the Connect property to specify the directory in which the file exists (its "database") and the SourceTableName property to specify the actual table. The example in Listing 6.8 creates an attached Paradox table in the current database. (Look in basAttach in CH06.MDB for CreatePDX3Attached().)

Two features that distinguish this function from the previous examples that created attached tables are centered around the Connect string itself. First of all, the information you need to attach a foreign table is different than with a native table. For Access tables you need to supply the new table name, the path and file name of the foreign MDB file, and the table within that database you'd like to attach. For other data sources you'll need to supply the new table name, the DOS path or database name that contains the external data, and the name of the table containing the data you'd like to attach. Second, as you can see in the following code fragment, the Connect property itself must indicate the data source for all but Access native tables:

```
With tdf
    .Connect = "Paradox 3.x;DATABASE=" & strPath
    .SourceTableName = strBaseTable
End With
```

WARNING Although the code in Listing 6.8 does successfully attach the table if all goes well, in real-world use you *must* include error-handling code with any procedures that access any data, especially those that deal with file manipulations. Although we've left out the error handling here for the sake of clarity, understand that this is not code you can use for applications. Without robust error handling in code that's used to handle attachments, you're just begging for trouble. Too many things can go wrong at run time.

Listing 6.8

```
Function CreatePDX3Attached(strTable As String, _
  strPath As String, strBaseTable As String)
    Dim db As Database
    Dim tdf As TableDef

    Set db = CurrentDb()
    Set tdf = db.CreateTableDef(strTable)
```

```
With tdf
    ' Set the tabledef's properties and append it
    ' to the TableDefs collection.
    .Connect = "Paradox 3.x;DATABASE=" & strPath
    .SourceTableName = strBaseTable
End With
db.TableDefs.Append tdf
CreatePDX3Attached = True
End Function
```

Knowing Your Limitations

Access cannot allow you to change the data source type of an existing attached table; nor can you change the name of the base table. For example, you cannot change an attached Paradox table into an attached dBASE III table, and you cannot change an attachment based on MYCUST.DBF into one based on MYCUST2.DBF. You can change only the path of an existing attached table.

If you need to change the type or base table name of an existing attached table, you must first delete the attached table and then re-create it. Note that deleting an attached table does not delete the underlying table, only the Access link to that table.

Determining the Type of an Attached Table

When you examine an attached table, you may want to know its type. The function in Listing 6.9 (from basAttach in CH06.MDB) returns the type of an attached table as a string representing the portion of the Connect string that indicates the attachment type.

The logic behind the function is simple. It takes four steps to determine the attachment type, attempting to be as "smart" about it as possible. It first compares the Attributes property of the table in question against the intrinsic constant, dbAttachedODBC. If this comparison returns a nonzero value, you're assured that the table is an ODBC table, and the function returns "ODBC".

The rest of the tests count on the tabledef's Connect property. If the string is zero-length, the table must be native (nonattached). If the first character is a semicolon, the table must be an attached Access table. Otherwise the function returns the portion of the Connect property that falls before the first semicolon in the string.

Listing 6.9

```
Function glrGetTableType(strTableName As String) As String

    ' Return the type of table, given the name:
    '     "Unknown" (table doesn't exist?)
    '     "ODBC"
    '     "Access Native"
    '     "Access Attached"
    '     or the specific attachment type

    Dim db As Database
    Dim strTableType As String
    Dim strConnect As String
    Dim tdf As TableDef
    Dim lngAttributes As Long
    Dim strConnectType As String
    Dim intPos As Integer

    On Error GoTo glrGetTableType_Err
    Set tdf = db.TableDefs(strTableName)
    lngAttributes = tdf.Attributes

    If (lngAttributes And dbAttachedODBC) Then
        strTableType = "ODBC"
    Else
        strConnect = tdf.Connect
        If Len(strConnect) = 0 Then
            strTableType = "Access Native"
        ElseIf Left$(strConnect, 1) = ";" Then
            strTableType = "Access Attached"
        Else
            intPos = InStr(strConnect, ";")
            If intPos > 0 Then
                strTableType = Left$(strConnect, intPos - 1)
            Else
                strTableType = "Unknown"
            End If
        End If
    End If

glrGetTableType_Exit:
    glrGetTableType = strTableType
```

```
glrGetTableType_Err:
    glrGetTableType = "UNKNOWN"
    Resume glrGetTableType_Exit
End Function
```

Working with Recordsets

In almost any Access application, sooner or later you'll need to manipulate data from VBA. Access provides a rich set of data access objects to allow you to view, edit, add, and delete fields, rows, and tables. In its attempt to be as flexible as possible, Access provides three separate means of working with data: tables, dynasets, and snapshots. Each has its own uses and capabilities. The following sections discuss these issues.

Meet the Recordsets

Although Access provides three types of recordset objects, the one you use in any given situation depends on the source of the data being referenced and the methods you need to use to access the data. Table 6.5 lists each recordset type, along with its benefits and drawbacks.

Creating a Recordset

You use an expression such as one of the following to create a recordset:

Dim rst As Recordset

Set rst = db.OpenRecordset(*Source* [, *Type* [, *Options*]])

or

Set rst = *object*.OpenRecordset([*Type* [, *Options*]])

(Parameters enclosed in square brackets are optional.)

TABLE 6.5: Recordset Types and Their Benefits/Drawbacks

Recordset Type	Description	Benefits	Drawbacks
Table	Set of records in a table in a database	Can use indexes for quick searches. Data can be edited	Works only works for local Access tables, not attached tables
Dynaset	Set of pointers (bookmarks) referring to data in tables or queries in a database	Can include data from multiple tables, either local or attached. Can be based on a SQL string. Data can be edited in most cases	Some dynasets may not be editable. Cannot perform indexed searches using the faster Seek method
Snapshot	Copy of a set of records as it exists at the time the snapshot is created	Can optionally be set to scroll forward only, allowing faster operations	Data cannot be edited. All records in RecordSet's data source are read before control is returned to the program. Doesn't reflect changes to data made in a multiuser environment. A snapshot is a picture of the data at the time the snapshot is created, and no updates will be reflected in its set of rows. Cannot perform indexed searches using the faster Seek method

In the first example you're creating a new recordset based on something in the database referred to by the database variable db. The *Source* parameter indicates where the data will come from and must be one of the following:

- An existing table
- An existing query that returns rows
- A SQL statement that returns rows

In the second example, *object* can be any previously opened database object, such as a table, a query, or even another recordset variable. Since you've already specified the source of the data, you needn't specify it again when creating a recordset based on an existing object.

In both cases the *Type* parameter specifies the type of the recordset. It should be one of the following built-in constant values:

- dbOpenTable, to open a table recordset
- dbOpenDynaset, to open a dynaset recordset

- dbOpenSnapshot, to open a snapshot recordset

If you don't specify a type, Access automatically chooses the type it will open for the given *Source*. For example, if you create a recordset based on a table in the current database and don't specify *Type*, Access automatically opens a table recordset. Likewise, if *Source* is an attached table, a query, or a SQL string and you've not specified the *Type* parameter, Access automatically opens a dynaset recordset. In addition, you cannot specify dbOpenTable if the *Source* parameter is a SQL expression or a tabledef that refers to an attached table. If you do, Access triggers trappable error 3011, "Couldn't find object...," for SQL expressions or 3219, "Invalid operation," for attached tables.

The *Options* parameter controls the multiuser access and update behavior of the recordset. It can be one of the values listed in Table 6.6.

TABLE 6.6: Options for Recordsets

Constant	Description
dbDenyWrite	Other users can't modify or add records. This effectively write-locks the recordset's underlying data source(s). Note that when you lock a dynaset recordset, you are locking all the underlying tables
dbDenyRead	Other users can't view records. This option applies only to table recordsets. By setting this option you are completely locking other users out of viewing the table
dbReadOnly	You can only view records; other users can modify them. This is a useful safeguard that can keep your code from inadvertently modifying data
dbAppendOnly	You can only append new records. This option applies only to dynaset recordsets
dbInconsistent	Inconsistent updates are allowed. This option is for dynaset recordsets only
dbConsistent	Only consistent updates are allowed. This option is for dynaset recordsets only
dbForwardOnly	The recordset is a forward-scrolling snapshot. Use this type of recordset when you are making only one pass through the records. Since a forward-only snapshot does not copy data into a scrollable buffer, it can run much more quickly.
dbSQLPassThrough	Causes the SQL to be passed through directly to the back-end server for processing
dbSeeChanges	Jet triggers a run-time error if another user changes data you're currently editing

Consistent versus Inconsistent Updates

When you create a recordset object based on more than one table, Access by default allows you to make changes only to the "many" side of a join. This is known as a *consistent update*. At times you may want to update both sides of join. To do this, set the dbInconsistent option. This allows you to update fields in both sides of the join. Note that this may violate the relationships between tables that your application needs. It is up to you to provide the necessary code to ensure that any "implied" referential integrity is maintained.

If you've turned on referential integrity for a relationship and enabled cascading updates, the dbInconsistent and dbConsistent options will cause identical behavior. In this case the referential integrity takes control, and the cascading updates will update the "many" side of the relationship when you update the "one" side.

Creating Recordset Objects

The following examples show a number of ways you can create recordset objects. This list isn't exhaustive, but it does show some representative cases.

- **To create a recordset based on a table or a saved query:**

```
Dim db As Database
Dim rstCustomers As Recordset
Dim rstSales As Recordset

Set db = CurrentDb()

' This will create a table-type Recordset.
Set rstCustomers = db.OpenRecordset("tblCustomers", _
  dbOpenTable)

' This will create a dynaset-type Recordset.
Set rstSales = db.OpenRecordset("qryCustSales", dbOpenDynaset)
```

- **To create a dynaset-type recordset based on a SQL string:**

```
Dim db As Database
Dim rstCustomers As Recordset
```

```
Dim strSQL As String

strSQL = "SELECT [Contact Name] As Name From Customers " & _
  "ORDER BY [Contact Name]"
Set db = CurrentDb()
Set rstCustomers = db.OpenRecordset(strSQL, dbOpenDynaset)
```

- **To create a table-type recordset that locks other users out of the source's records:**

```
Dim db As Database
Dim rstCustomers As Recordset

Set db = CurrentDb()
Set rstCustomers = db.OpenRecordset( _
  "tblCustomers", dbOpenTable, dbDenyRead)
```

- **To create a snapshot-type recordset based on a table:**

```
Dim db As Database
Dim rstCustomers As Recordset

Set db = CurrentDb()
Set rstCustomers = db.OpenRecordset("tblCustomers", _
  dbOpenSnapshot)
```

Moving through a Recordset

Once you've created a recordset, Access provides a variety of methods for navigating through the rows: MoveFirst, MoveLast, MovePrevious, and MoveNext. Each of these works in the manner you would expect, based on the name. In addition, Access provides the Move method, which can move a specified number of rows forward or backward, either from the current row or from a stored bookmark. If the object is a table-type recordset, the movement follows the order of the active index, which you can set using the Index property of the recordset. If you have not specified the index for table-type recordsets, the row order is undefined. Recordsets also support the AbsolutePosition and PercentPosition properties, which allow you to read and write the current position within the recordset, based on the data in the current set of rows. (Table-type recordsets do not support the AbsolutePosition property, but the other types do.)

Using the Move Method

Although the actions of the other Move... methods are obvious, based on their names, the Move method is a bit more ambiguous. The Move method of a recordset accepts one or two parameters:

rst.Move *rows*[, *start*]

The *rows* parameter indicates the number of rows to move (greater than 0 for forward, less than 0 for negative), and the optional *start* parameter can contain a saved bookmark. If you supply the value for the bookmark, Access starts there and moves the appropriate number of rows from that spot. If you don't specify the start location, Access assumes you want to start moving from the current row. See the section "Adding New Records to a Recordset" later in this chapter for an example of using the Move method.

Using the AbsolutePosition and PercentPosition Properties

You can set the value of either the AbsolutePosition property or the PercentPosition property to move to a specific row in the recordset. If you wanted to move to the row approximately 50 percent of the way through your rows, you could use code like this:

```
rst.PercentPosition = 50
```

To move to the 35th row in the rows currently in the recordset, given the current filtering and sorting, you could try this:

```
rst.AbsolutePosition = 35
```

You can also use these two properties to tell where you are in the recordset.

TIP
Table-type recordsets do not support the AbsolutePosition property. That's just one more reason not to use table-type recordsets for anything but lookups.

WARNING   The AbsolutePosition property is *not* a record number and should not be thought of as such. It just returns the current row's position within the current set of rows, and it will change as you modify the filter or the sort order of the rows. To be able to find a row, no matter how you've modified the sorting or filtering, you'll need to use a bookmark (see "Using Bookmarks" later in this chapter) or store the primary key for later retrieval.

Finding the Number of Rows in a Recordset

In spite of any implication made by its name, the RecordCount property of recordsets may not return the actual number of rows in a given recordset. It actually returns the number of rows *accessed so far* in the recordset if the recordset is not a table-type recordset. This common misconception leads to a lot of confusion. To find the actual number of rows in a recordset, you must first use the MoveLast method (and then move somewhere else, if you like) before checking the value of the RecordCount property. If you don't move to the last row, the RecordCount property returns either 0 (if there are no rows) or 1 (if one or more rows exist) when you first create the recordset. (Table-type recordsets maintain their RecordCount property without moving to the last row, and certain types of recordsets in which Access cannot determine the number of rows always return −1 for their RecordCount.)

In a single-user environment, the RecordCount property always correctly returns the number of rows in the recordset, once you've let Access calculate how many there are by moving to the last row. If you delete a row, either interactively or programmatically, the RecordCount property stays in sync. In a multiuser environment things are a bit more complex. If you're sharing data with another user and you both have a recordset open that's based on the same data, deletions made on the other machine won't immediately show up on your machine. Access won't update the RecordCount value until the code actually accesses the deleted row. Then Access decrements the RecordCount. Therefore, in a multiuser environment, if you must know exactly how many rows are currently in the recordset, you should take the following steps:

1. Use the Requery method on the recordset object.
2. Use the MoveLast method to move to the end of the recordset.
3. Check RecordCount for the current value.

You could use the GetRecordCount() function in Listing 6.10 as a simple example. (You'll find GetRecordCount() in basRecordset in CH06.MDB.) It uses the Restartable property of the recordset to make sure it can requery the recordset and just returns −1 if it can't. In that case the caller would know that the GetRecordCount() function wasn't able to requery the recordset and that it needs to find a less generic means of solving the problem. Once GetRecordCount() knows it can requery the recordset, it follows the steps outlined above, preserving and resetting the position in the recordset using the recordset's Bookmark property. (See the section "Using Bookmarks" later in this chapter for more information.) This function is actually useful only for dynaset-type recordsets, since table-type recordsets can't be requeried and snapshot-type recordsets don't need to be requeried. Since a snapshot-type recordset won't reflect any changes made by other users, its RecordCount property won't change once it's created.

Listing 6.10

```
Function GetRecordCount(rst As Recordset) As Long

    ' Return the current record count for a Recordset.
    ' If the Recordset isn't Restartable (and table-type
    ' Recordsets aren't) then just return -1, indicating
    ' that the caller needs to reopen the Recordset in order
    ' to pick up any foreign changes.

    Dim strBM As String

    With rst
        If .Restartable Then
            .Requery
            If .Bookmarkable Then
                strBM = .Bookmark
            End If
            .MoveLast
            GetRecordCount = .RecordCount
```

```
            If .Bookmarkable Then
                   .Bookmark = strBM
              End If
         Else
             GetRecordCount = -1
         End If
     End With
End Function
```

Testing for Boundaries

Every recordset supports two properties, BOF and EOF, that indicate whether the current row is currently at the end of the recordset (EOF) or at the beginning of the recordset (BOF):

- If you use MovePrevious while the first row is current, BOF becomes True and there is no current row.

- If you use MovePrevious again, BOF stays True but a run-time error occurs.

- If you use MoveNext while the last row is current, EOF becomes True and there is no current row.

- If you use MoveNext again, EOF stays True but a run-time error occurs.

Testing for an Empty Recordset

Often when you create a recordset you want to know immediately whether that recordset actually contains any rows. It's quite possible to create a recordset that doesn't return any rows, and you might need to take different steps based on whether the result contained any rows.

You can test for an empty recordset in a number of ways, but the two methods that follow ought to serve your needs. The following expression:

```
Set rst = db.OpenRecordset("qryCust")
If Not rst.BOF And Not rst.EOF Then
    '   You'll only be in here if there are some rows.
End If
```

checks to see whether both the BOF and the EOF properties for the recordset are True. If so, there must *not* be any rows, since that's the only way the current position could be both at the beginning and the end of the recordset. In addition, you often will want to loop through the rows of your recordset. In that case you needn't check; just write the loop so that it won't even start if there are no rows:

```
Set rst = db.OpenRecordset("qryCust")
Do Until rst.EOF
    ' Process rows in here
Loop
```

Looping through All the Rows

Although you're likely to have less reason than you'd think to loop through all the rows of a recordset (that's what action queries are for), the syntax is quite simple. The code in Listing 6.11 walks through a recordset backwards, from the end to the beginning, and if there are any records to be had, it prints out one of the fields in the underlying data. (Look for ListNames() in basRecordset.)

Listing 6.11

```
Function ListNames()
    Dim db as Database
    Dim rst As Recordset

    Set db = CurrentDb()
    Set rst = db.OpenRecordset("tblCustomers")
    ' Check first to see if there are any rows.
    With rst
        If Not .BOF And Not .EOF Then
            ' Move to the end.
            .MoveLast
            ' Loop back towards the beginning.
            Do Until .BOF
                Debug.Print ![ContactName]
                .MovePrevious
            Loop
        End If
        .Close
    End With
End Function
```

Using Arrays to Hold Recordset Data

You can use the GetRows() method of any recordset to copy its data into a variant variable. Access will create a two-dimensional array with enough space to hold the data:

```
varData = rst.GetRows(intRowsToGrab)
```

You don't have to dimension or size the array; Access will do that for you. Because arrays give you random access to any row or column within the array, you may find it more convenient to work with arrays than with the recordset itself. For example, if you want the fastest access to data that you don't need to write to, you might want to use a forward-only snapshot. But using this type of snapshot limits your movement in the data. If you create a forward-only snapshot and copy its data to an array, you've got the best of both worlds: fast access *and* random access.

If you ask for more rows than exist, Access returns as many as there are. Use the UBound() function to find out how many rows were actually returned:

```
intRows = UBound(varData, 2) + 1
```

The ", 2" tells UBound to find the number of rows (the second dimension of the array); then you must add 1 to the result, since the array is zero-based.

> **TIP**
> Be careful when creating your recordset before calling the GetRows method. Since Access will copy all the columns, including memos and long binary fields, you may want to exclude large fields from the recordset before you create the array, since they can consume large amounts of memory and be slow to load.

For example, the following code (from basRecordset in CH06.MDB) fills an array with data and then prints it out backwards:

```
Function TryGetRows()
    ' Use an array to process data in a recordset.

    Dim db As Database
    Dim rst As Recordset
    Dim varData As Variant
```

```
        Dim intCount As Integer
        Dim intI As Integer

        Set db = CurrentDb()
        Set rst = db.OpenRecordset("tblCustomers", _
         dbOpenSnapshot, dbForwardOnly)
        ' Pick some arbitrary large number of rows to retrieve.
        varData = rst.GetRows(1000)

        ' How many rows did it actually send back?
        intCount = UBound(varData, 2) + 1
        ' Loop through all the rows, printing out the
        ' data from the second column.
        For intI = intCount - 1 To 0 Step -1
            Debug.Print varData(1, intI)
        Next intI
End Function
```

Creating a Recordset Based on a Querydef

If you need to create a recordset based on any select query (about which you might know nothing at all until your program is running), you must supply the recordset with all the parameters the querydef requires. Without DAO, doing so requires knowing in advance what the parameters are and supplying their values in your code. Using DAO, you can loop through all the parameters of your querydef and evaluate the necessary parameters.

A problem occurs because Access cannot fill in the parameters' values when you're creating a recordset based on a querydef. It's up to you to supply those values for the querydef before you attempt to create the recordset.

TIP
Your query won't be able to run at all unless all the necessary parameters are available. If your query uses form objects as parameters, for example, you need to make sure the appropriate form is open and running, with appropriate values filled in, before you attempt to run a query based on those parameters.

The following code works with any QueryDef object that represents a select query:

```
Dim db As Database
Dim qdf As QueryDef
Dim prm As Parameter
Dim rst As Recordset

Set db = CurrentDb()
Set qdf = db.QueryDefs("qrySomeQuery")
For Each prm In qdf.Parameters
    prm.Value = Eval(prm.Name)
Next prm
Set rst = qdf.OpenRecordset(dbOpenDynaset)
```

It loops through all the parameters of the object (and there may be none, in which case the loop won't ever execute), pointing a parameter variable at each of the parameters for the querydef, one at a time. For each parameter, the code evaluates the Name property using the Eval() function and assigns the return value to the Value property of the parameter. This retrieves the value of each parameter, without your having to know in advance where the parameter is getting its value.

For example, if your query has a single parameter, on the City field:

```
Forms!frmInfo!CityField
```

the QueryDef container contains a single parameter object, for which the Name property is Forms!frmInfo!CityField. Through the use of the Eval() function, the code in the previous example retrieves the value stored in that field and assigns it to the *Value* property of the specific parameter object. This satisfies the needs of the QueryDef object, and you'll be able to create the recordset you need, based on that querydef. The Incremental Search example in Chapter 7 uses this mechanism to allow the underlying code to create a recordset on almost any select query, whether or not it requires parameter values.

Finding Specific Records

You handle the task of finding specific data in a recordset in different ways, depending on the type of the recordset. Table-type recordsets can use an indexed search to find data, but dynaset- and snapshot-type recordsets often cannot.

Finding Data in Table-Type Recordsets

If you've created a table-type recordset object, you can use the fast Seek method to locate specific rows. (Attempting to use the Seek method with any recordset other than a table-type recordset results in run-time error 3219, "Invalid Operation.") You must take two specific steps to use the Seek method to find data:

1. Set the recordset's Index property. This tells Access which index you'd like it to search through. If you want to use the primary key for searching, you must know the name of the primary key. (It's usually PrimaryKey, unless your application has changed it.)

2. Use the Seek method to find the value you want, given a search operator and one or more values to search for. The search operator must be <, <=, =, >=, or >, indicating how you want Access to search. If the operator is =, >=, or >, Access searches from the beginning of the recordset. Otherwise it starts at the end and works its way backward. To indicate to Access what it needs to search for, you supply one or more values, corresponding to the keys in the index you selected. If you based your index on one value, you need to supply only one value here. If your index includes multiple columns, you must supply all the values unless your search operator is something other than =.

For example, if your database contained an index named OrderIndex consisting of three columns—OrderNumber, OrderItem, and OrderDate—and you wanted to find the first item for order number 3, order item 17, for any date, the following fragment could get you to the correct row:

```
rst.Index = "OrderIndex"
rst.Seek ">=", 3, 17
```

The values you send to the Seek method must match the datatypes of the values in the index. In this case the values were numeric. Had they been strings or dates, you would have needed to use matching datatypes in the call to the Seek method.

Once you've used the Seek method to find a row, you must, *without fail*, use the recordset's NoMatch property to check that you actually found a row. The following code expands on the previous fragment, handling the success or failure of the seek:

```
rst.Index = "OrderIndex"
rst.Seek ">=", 3, 17
```

```
If rst.NoMatch Then
    MsgBox "Unable to find a match!"
Else
    MsgBox "The item name is: " & rst!ItemName
End If
```

TIP
The Seek method always starts at the beginning (or end) of the recordset when it searches. Therefore, using Seek inside a loop, searching for subsequent rows that match the criteria, is generally fruitless. Unless you modify the value once you find it so that further searches no longer find a match on that row, your loop will continually find the same row.

Finding Data in Dynaset- and Snapshot-Type Recordsets

Unlike table-type recordsets, dynaset- and snapshot-type recordsets cannot use the Seek method for finding data. Because these recordsets might well be based on ordered subsets of the original data, Access can't always use an index to speed up the search. Therefore, a search involving dynasets or snapshots might be a linear search, visiting every row in the recordset until it finds a match. Access will use an index if it can.

On a bright note, however, Access provides much greater flexibility in dynaset/snapshot searches. The four different methods (FindFirst, FindNext, FindPrevious, and FindLast) allow you to optimize the search so it has to look through the smallest number of rows to find the data it needs. Since you can use FindNext with these searches, you won't need to start back at the beginning of the recordset to find subsequent matches. In addition, you can use loops to walk your way through the records, since you can restart the search without going back to the first row.

You use the same syntax for each of these methods:

Recordset.{FindFirst | FindPrevious | FindNext | FindLast} *criteria*

where *Recordset* is an open dynaset- or snapshot-type recordset variable and *criteria* is a WHERE clause formatted as though in a SQL expression, without the word

WHERE. For example, the following fragment searches for a last name of "Smith".

```
rst.FindFirst "[LastName] = 'Smith'"
```

Just as with the Seek method, you must follow every call to a Find method with a check of the recordset's NoMatch property. If that property is True, there is no current row, and the search fails. Often, when performing some operation that requires looping through all the rows that match some criteria, you can use code like this:

```
strCriteria = "[LastName] = 'Smith'"
With rst
    .FindFirst strCriteria
    Do While Not .NoMatch
        ' Since you know you found a match,
        ' do something with the current row.
        Debug.Print ![FirstName]
        .FindNext strCriteria
    Loop
End With
' When you get here, you know that rst.NoMatch is True.
```

Of course, many such loops can be replaced with action queries, which are almost always a better solution to the given programming problem.

Using Quotes in Strings

In building criteria for Find methods and in several other places in VBA (when calling domain functions and when creating SQL strings, for example), you often need to embed variable values into a string. Because the Jet engine has no way of finding the value of VBA variables, you need to supply their values before you ask it to do any work for you. This can cause trouble because Access requires delimiters (quotes for strings, # for dates) around those values, but they aren't part of the variables themselves. This causes many Access developers, experienced and neophyte alike, a great deal of anguish.

For example, imagine you have a variable named strName that contains the name you'd like to match in your call to the FindFirst method (for the sake of simplicity here, "Smith"). You need to build a string that represents the required WHERE clause:

```
[LastName] = 'Smith'
```

As a first attempt, you might try this:

```
strCriteria = "[LastName] = strName"
```

But when you attempt to run the search, Access complains with a run-time error, "Can't Bind Name 'strName'." The problem is that the expression in strCriteria was this:

```
[LastName] = strName
```

Most likely, no one in your table has that particular last name.

As a second attempt, you might try a new approach:

```
strCriteria = "[LastName] = " & strName
```

When you attempt to run the search this time, Access again complains with a run-time error, "Can't Bind Name 'Smith'." In this case it was using the value

```
[LastName] = Smith
```

which won't work because Access expects string values to be enclosed in quotes.

It should be clear by now that you need to get the quotes into that string. Access provides no fewer than three solutions to this problem.

All the solutions need to arrive at a value for strCriteria that looks like this:

```
[LastName] = "Smith"
```

or like this:

```
[LastName] = 'Smith'
```

Following are several solutions to this particular problem. These exercises are actually easier to envision if you do the work in reverse order.

The first solution is based on the fact that Access treats two quote characters side by side inside a string as representing one quote character. Remembering that every string expression must be enclosed in a pair of quotes, the first step in the first solution involves enclosing the final expression in those quotes. When enclosed in quotes, each internal quote needs to be replaced with two. The expression then becomes

```
"[LastName] = ""Smith"""
```

With the name separated out, the expression becomes

```
"[LastName] = """ & "Smith" & """"
```

Finally, with the constant replaced with the variable, the expression becomes

```
"[LastName] = """ & strName & """"
```

This last expression is the one you'd use with the FindFirst method.

You could also replace each quote with its ANSI representation, Chr$(34). If you go to the Immediate window and ask Access to print out the value

```
? Chr$(34)
```

it responds by printing a double-quote symbol. Therefore, again working backward:

```
[LastName] = "Smith"
```

becomes

```
"[LastName] = " & Chr$(34) & "Smith" & Chr$(34)
```

which becomes

```
"[LastName] = " & Chr$(34) & strName & Chr$(34)
```

If you create a string variable (perhaps named strQuote) and assign to it the value Chr$(34), you can use this expression:

```
"[LastName] = " & strQuote & strName & strQuote
```

You can also create a constant and assign to it a value that will resolve to be the string that is just a quotation mark. You can't use the Chr$() function when creating a constant, so this is the only way to create a constant value that does what you need:

```
Const QUOTE = """"
```

This might be the most straightforward solution to the problem.

The third solution involves replacing each internal quote with an apostrophe. That is, following the same backward steps:

```
[LastName] = "Smith"
```

becomes

```
[LastName] = 'Smith'
```

which becomes

```
"[LastName] = 'Smith'"
```

which becomes

```
"[LastName] = '" & "Smith" & "'"
```

which becomes (finally)

```
"[LastName] = '" & strName & "'"
```

The main problem with this solution (which many developers use) is that the value stored in strName cannot contain a single-quote symbol. If it did, you'd end up with an apostrophe embedded within a string that's enclosed in apostrophes. That's not allowed in Access' syntax. Therefore, you can use this method only when strName contains a value that could never contain an apostrophe. (And of course, the previous two solutions will fail if the string in question contains a double quote. But that's far less likely to happen than to have a string contain an apostrophe.)

To summarize, when building a string expression in Access that needs to contain a variable that represents a string, you must ensure that the final expression includes the quotes that enclose that string variable. The three suggested solutions are

```
Const QUOTE = """"
strCriteria = "[LastName] = """ & strName & """"
strCriteria = "[LastName] = " & QUOTE & strName & QUOTE
strCriteria = "[LastName] = '" & strName & "'"
```

To complicate issues, date variables need to be delimited with #, not quotes, in an expression. Following the steps presented above, the solution for the date problem would be

```
"[DateField] = #" & varDate & "#"
```

That's a lot simpler than the string case.

Finally, numeric values require no delimiters at all, and you can simply represent a string variable using an expression like this:

```
"[NumericField] = " & intNumber
```

In each case the important issue is that you place the *value* of the variable into the string being sent off to FindFirst rather than the *name* of the variable. The Jet engine (which ultimately receives the request to find a row) has no clue as to what to do with an Access variable. It's up to your code to supply the value before requesting help from the Jet engine.

If you want to completely generalize this problem, what about the case in which you have both apostrophes and quotes inside the text you're trying to embed in a string? This can't work:

```
strName = Forms!txtStoreName
strCriteria = "StoreName = " & QUOTE & strName & QUOTE
```

if the text box on the form happens to contain the string

Joe's "Pizza" Store

since the string contains a quote. This won't work, either:

```
strCriteria = "StoreName = '" & strName & "'"
```

because the string contains an apostrophe, too.

Since you'll be able to use neither quotes nor apostrophes as delimiters, what's the solution? In this case, and if you wish to be as general as possible in your solution, the answer is always to modify the delimited value by doubling any occurrences of whatever delimiter you choose. To do this you'll need a function that accepts a string value and the delimiter character as parameters and returns the string with any occurrences of the delimiter inside it "doubled up." You'll find that function, glrHandleQuotes(), in basHandleQuotes in CH06.MDB. It can solve the previous problem:

```
strCriteria = "StoreName = " & _
    QUOTE & glrHandleQuotes(strName, QUOTE) & QUOTE
```

or

```
strCriteria = "StoreName = '" & _
    glrHandleQuotes(strName, "'") & "'"
```

The glrHandleQuotes() function looks for all the delimiter characters inside strName, doubles them, and returns the string. Since Access allows double quotes inside a quoted string, all will be well, no matter what the delimiter and the string. If you're interested in seeing how glrHandleQuotes() works, look in basHandleQuotes; the code uses brute-force string manipulations. If you want to use this technique in your own applications, just import the basHandleQuotes module and call glrHandleQuotes() yourself.

Using Bookmarks

One of the primary functions needed in any database product is the ability to move quickly to a specified row. Access provides a number of ways to move about in recordsets, as seen in the section "Moving through a Recordset" earlier in this chapter. In addition to the methods presented there, Access provides the Bookmark property.

What Is a Bookmark?

Every active recordset maintains a single current row. To retrieve a reference to that row, you can store the bookmark for that row. The bookmark itself is a string, the exact value of which is of no particular importance to you. Access uses the value, but under no circumstances can you use the value in any sort of calculation. You can perform two basic operations with bookmarks:

- Retrieve the value of the bookmark, in order to store it for later retrieval
- Set the value of the bookmark to a previously stored value, effectively setting the current row to be the row where you were when you originally saved the bookmark

You can retrieve and store as many bookmarks for a given recordset as you wish to maintain. Manipulating bookmarks in Access is the fastest way to maneuver through rows. For example, if you need to move from the current row and then move back to it, you can use one of two methods:

- **Store the primary key value:** Move from the row, and use the Seek or Find-First method to move back to the original row, using the saved primary key value to find the row.
- **Store the bookmark:** Move from the row, and then use the bookmark to move back to the original row.

The second method, using the bookmark, is much faster than the first. (For proof of this, see Chapter 17.) The code to do this might look something like the following example:

```
Dim strBM as String

strBM = rst.Bookmark
```

```
' Move to the first row.
rst.MoveFirst
'
' Now do whatever you moved from the current row to do.
'
' Then move back to the original row.
rst.Bookmark = strBM
```

Bookmarks and Record Numbers

If you're moving to Access from an Xbase environment, you might be tempted to think of bookmarks as a replacement for record numbers. In reality, that's not the case. Because Access is set based, row numbers really have no validity here. Access neither stores nor maintains a record number in its data, and you can't count on a bookmark to act as a permanent locator for any given row. Once you close a recordset, the bookmark value is no longer valid. In addition, you cannot use bookmarks as locators across different recordsets, even though the recordsets might be based on the same data and might contain the same rows in the same order. On the other hand, as stated in the preceding section, bookmarks provide an excellent means of moving about in an open recordset.

To Bookmark or Not to Bookmark

Not all recordsets in Access support the Bookmark property. Some data sources make it impossible for Access to maintain bookmarks, so it is your responsibility as a developer to check the Bookmarkable property of a recordset before attempting to use bookmarks with that recordset. Any recordset based on native Access data always supports bookmarks, but external data may not. If the recordset does not support bookmarks, attempting to use the Bookmark property results in trappable error 3159, "Not a valid bookmark."

Also be aware that there is no valid bookmark when you've positioned the current row to be the "new" row in a recordset. That is, the following code will trigger run-time error 3021, "No Current Record":

```
rst.MoveLast
' Move to the "new" row.
rst.MoveNext
strBM = rst.Bookmark
```

> **TIP**
>
> In previous versions of Access, one of the few ways to know that you were currently working with the "new" row on a form was to count on the fact that retrieving a bookmark for the new row would fail. Access forms now provide the NewRecord property, making this technique unnecessary.

The Clone Method

Every recordset maintains a single "current" row. For bookmarkable recordsets, you can use the Bookmark property to set and retrieve a marker for this row. If you need to refer to the same recordset in two different ways, with two different current rows, you can use the Clone method to create a clone of a recordset. With a clone of the original recordset, you can effectively maintain two separate "current" rows. This way you can compare the values in two of the rows in the recordset, for example.

You might be tempted to ask, "Why use the Clone method instead of just creating a new recordset based on the same source?" The answer is clear: creating a recordset clone is faster, in most cases, than creating a new recordset object. When the source of the data is a querydef, the difference can be enormous. Rather than re-executing the entire query to produce the new recordset, the Clone method just points a separate object variable at the original set of rows. This effectively gives you two current rows and two bookmarks, based on the same data. You can also assign the bookmark from one recordset to its clone, since they really are the same recordset.

Be aware of these two issues:

- A recordset created with the Clone method does not have a current row. To set a specific row as the current row, use any of the Find or Move methods (FindFirst, MoveFirst, and so on) or set the recordset's Bookmark property with a value retrieved from the original recordset. Remember that bookmark assignments work only when applied to identical recordsets (as are the original and its clone).

- Using the Close method on either the original recordset or its clone doesn't affect the other recordset.

As an example of using the Clone method, imagine the following situation: you'd like to create a function to compare certain columns in the current row to see whether they have the same value as the same columns in the previous row. You could use the Clone method to handle this problem, as you'll see in Listing 6.12. In this case you just check the value in the Country field. This example also uses the form's RecordsetClone property to retrieve the underlying recordset, which is covered in the next section. The sample form, frmLookup in CH06.MDB, uses this function in the Current event of the form to display or hide a label if the current Country field has the same value as the field in the previous row. Figure 6.3 shows this form in action.

FIGURE 6.3:

frmLookup displays or hides a label, based on the comparison of the current and previous values in the Country field.

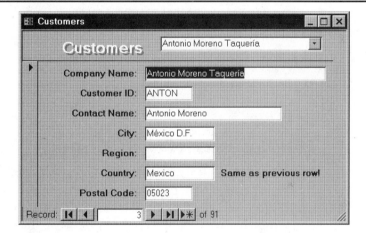

Listing 6.12

```
Function CheckPreviousRow(frm As Form, strFieldName As String) _
  As Boolean

    Dim rst As Recordset
    Dim rstClone As Recordset

    ' Set rst to refer to the form's Recordset,
    ' and set its bookmark to match the form's.
    Set rst = frm.RecordSetClone
    rst.Bookmark = frm.Bookmark
```

```
' Now create the Recordset clone, and make it
' refer to the same row as rst, which is on the same
' row as the form.
Set rstClone = rst.Clone()
rstClone.Bookmark = rst.Bookmark

' Move the clone Recordset to the previous row.
' If this puts us at the BOF, then the result has to be
' False, and leave the function.
rstClone.MovePrevious
If rstClone.BOF Then
    CheckPreviousRow = False
Else
    ' If you're not at BOF, then retrieve
    ' the necessary info.
    CheckPreviousRow = _
    (rst(strFieldName) = rstClone(strFieldName))
End If

rstClone.Close
End Function
```

The RecordsetClone Property

You use the RecordsetClone property to retrieve a reference to a form's recordset. Any bound form maintains its own recordset, the set of rows onto which the form provides a window. You'll often need to manipulate that set of rows without showing your work on the visible form. To do this you create a recordset based on the form's recordset and do your manipulations there. For example, the code in Listing 6.13, called from the AfterUpdate event of a combo box, searches for a specific company name on a form and sets the form to show the correct row once it finds a match. To see this form in action, try out frmLookup in CH06.MDB. Figure 6.4 shows this form in use.

Listing 6.13

```
Const QUOTE = """"
Sub cboCompany_AfterUpdate()
    Dim rst As Recordset

    Set rst = Me.RecordSetClone
    rst.FindFirst "[Company Name] = " & QUOTE & _
```

FIGURE 6.4:

Choosing a name from the combo box forces the code in Listing 6.13 to locate the correct row.

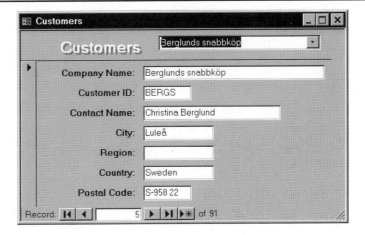

```
        glrHandleQuotes(Me!cboCompany, QUOTE) & QUOTE
    If rst.NoMatch Then
        MsgBox "No match was found. Something is REALLY wrong!"
    Else
        Me.Bookmark = rst.Bookmark
    End If
    rst.Close
End Sub
```

NOTE   Assigning a recordset variable using the RecordsetClone property is the only time you set a recordset object without using the standard syntax, starting with a database object. Because you're retrieving a special kind of recordset, Access treats this case a bit differently. The results are almost the same, though: you end up with a recordset object variable referring to the set of rows filling the form. The recordset you're pointing to, however, doesn't support all the same properties as a real recordset. You can't set a form recordset's Filter or Sort property, for example. (For more information on using a form's RecordsetClone property, see Chapter 8.) Because you're not creating a new recordset, but obtaining a reference to an existing one, the current row is undefined once you return the reference.

Sorting Recordsets

When using recordsets as part of your applications, you'll often need to present the rows in a specific order. Again, Access treats table-type recordsets differently from dynaset- and snapshot-type recordsets. For all objects, however, remember that if you want a particular sort order, you must specify it yourself.

Sorting Table-Type Recordsets

For table-type recordsets, you can specify the ordering by setting the Index property. (Access does not allow you to set the Index property of any other type of recordset. Attempting to do so will only get you a run-time error 3219, "Invalid Operation.") As soon as you set that property, the rows appear in their new ordering. After applying an index, Access appears to set the first row as the current row. This behavior is not documented, however, and you would be wise to explicitly set the current row after setting the Index property.

Listing 6.14 shows a function that lists the fields in the index, in index order, for each index in a specified table. ListIndexFields() does its work by looping through the TableDef object's collection of indexes. For each index in the collection, it gathers up the index name and the field names and uses them to set the index and to print out the value of each field for each row in the recordset. To test ListIndexFields() you might want to create a table with just a few rows and create an index for a few of the columns. Then, in the Immediate window, enter

> ? ListIndexFields("*YourTableName*")

replacing *YourTableName* with the name of your table. This should show all the indexes in your table, with the first indexed field in indexed order. (Look for ListIndexFields() in basRecordset in CH06.MDB.)

Listing 6.14

```
Function ListIndexFields(strTable As String)
    Dim rst As Recordset
    Dim db As Database
    Dim tdf As TableDef
    Dim idx As Index
    Dim fld As Field
```

```
Dim strField As String

Set db = CurrentDb()
Set tdf = db.TableDefs(strTable)
Set rst = db.OpenRecordset(strTable, dbOpenTable)

' List values for each index in the collection.
For Each idx In tdf.Indexes
    ' Set the index to use in the recordset
    rst.Index = idx.Name
    ' The index object contains a collection of fields,
    ' one for each field the index contains.
    Debug.Print
    Debug.Print "Index: " & rst.Index
    Debug.Print "==========================="
    ' Move through the whole recordset, in index order,
    ' printing out the index fields, separated with tabs.
    rst.MoveFirst
    Do While Not rst.EOF
        For Each fld In idx.Fields
            strField = strField & vbTab & rst(fld.Name)
        Next fld
        If Len(strField) > 0 Then
            strField = Mid(strField, 2)
        End If
        Debug.Print strField
        strField = ""
        rst.MoveNext
    Loop
Next idx
rst.Close
End Function
```

Sorting Dynaset- and Snapshot-Type Recordsets

Just as with table-type recordsets, unless you specify a sorting order for dynaset- and snapshot-type recordsets, the rows will show up in an indeterminate order. The natural order for these derived recordsets is a bit more complex, because it might depend on more than one table. In any case, if you need a specific ordering, you must set up that ordering yourself.

To create sorted dynaset- or snapshot-type recordsets, you have two choices, outlined in the next two sections.

Using a SQL ORDER BY Clause

You can create a recordset object using a SQL statement including an ORDER BY clause. To do so, specify the SQL expression as the row source for the OpenRecordset method. For example, this fragment:

```
Set db = CurrentDb()
Set rstSorted = db.OpenRecordset( _
 "SELECT * FROM tblCustomers ORDER BY [LastName];")
```

creates a recordset based on tblCustomers, including all the columns, sorted by the LastName column. You can base a recordset on a SQL string only when creating recordsets based on a database object (as opposed to other uses of OpenRecordset(), which can be based on tables, queries, or other recordsets). Attempting to do so will get you run-time error 3001, "Invalid Argument." Creating a recordset using a SQL expression creates a dynaset-type recordset (unless you request a snapshot-type recordset).

Using the Sort Property

You can set the Sort property of any non–table-based recordset to change its sort order. The Sort property must be a string, in the same style as the ORDER BY clause of a SQL expression. You must specify the column on which to sort and, optionally, the ordering. The next time you create a recordset based on this recordset, the new sort order will take effect. (This is different from the way table-type recordset sorting works; there, the sorting takes effect immediately.) The following fragments show how to set the Sort property:

```
rst.Sort = "[LastName]"          ' Defaults to ascending
rst.Sort = "[LastName] Asc"      ' Ascending sort
rst.Sort = "[LastName] Desc"     ' Descending sort
```

Here are some items to remember when using the Sort property:

- The new sort order doesn't take effect until you create a new recordset, based on the old one.

- The Sort property doesn't apply to table-type recordsets. Use the Index property for them.

- It might be faster to open a new recordset based on a SQL expression than to use the Sort property.

The following code shows two methods for creating a sorted dynaset-type recordset:

```
Dim db As Database
Dim rst As Recordset
Dim rstSorted1 As Recordset
Dim rstSorted2 As Recordset

Set db = CurrentDb()
' Create a sorted Recordset using SQL.
Set rstSorted1 = db.OpenRecordset( _
 "SELECT * FROM tblCustomers ORDER BY [LastName];")
' Create a sorted Recordset based on an existing Recordset.
Set rst = db.OpenRecordset("tblCustomers", dbOpenDynaset)
rst.Sort = "[LastName]"
Set rstSorted2 = rst.OpenRecordset()
'
' Do whatever you need to do here with the sorted recordsets
'
rst.Close
rstSorted1.Close
rstSorted2.Close
```

Filtering Non-Table Recordsets

Just as with sorting a recordset, you have two choices if you want to create a filtered subset of rows. These choices are outlined in the next two sections. You'll need to decide which method to use based on the circumstances of your application.

Using a SQL WHERE Clause

You can create a recordset by using a SQL statement including a WHERE clause. To do so, specify the SQL expression as the row source for the OpenRecordset method.

For example, this fragment:

```
Set db = CurrentDb()
Set rstSorted = db.OpenRecordset( _
 "SELECT * FROM tblCustomers WHERE [ZipCode] = '90210';")
```

creates a recordset based on all the columns in tblCustomers, including only the rows where the ZipCode field is "90210". You can use this method only when creating recordsets based on a database object (as opposed to other uses of OpenRecordset(), which can be based on tables, queries, or other recordsets). Attempting to do otherwise will get you run-time error 3001, "Invalid Argument."

Using the Filter Property

You can also set the Filter property of any dynaset- or snapshot-type recordset to change the set of rows it contains. The Filter property must be a string, in the same style as the WHERE clause of a SQL expression. The next time you create a recordset based on this recordset, the new filtering will take effect. For example, you generally use the Filter property like this:

```
' rst is an existing recordset.
rst.Filter = "[Age] > 35"
Set rstFiltered = rst.OpenRecordset()
' Now rstFiltered contains all the rows from rst that
' have an [Age] field greater than 35.
```

Here are some items to remember when using the Filter property:

- The new filtering doesn't take effect until you create a new recordset based on the old one.

- The Filter property doesn't apply to table-type recordsets.

- It might be faster to open a new recordset based on a SQL expression than to use the Filter property.

- The new filtering will never retrieve additional rows from the original source tables. It will filter only rows that are in the base recordset you are filtering.

The following code shows two methods for creating a filtered dynaset-type recordset:

```
Dim db As Database
Dim rst As Recordset
```

```
Dim rstSQL as Recordset
Dim rstFiltered As Recordset

Set db = CurrentDb()
Set rstSQL = db.OpenRecordset( _
  "SELECT * FROM tblCustomers WHERE [ZipCode] = '90210';")
Set rst = db.OpenRecordset("tblCustomers", dbOpenDynaset)
rst.Filter= "[ZipCode] = '90210'"
Set rstFiltered = rst.OpenRecordset()
```

Editing Data in a Recordset Object

Of course, any database application needs to be able to add, update, and delete data. Access provides methods for accomplishing each of these tasks. The next few sections discuss the various data-manipulation methods that Access supports.

When Is a Recordset Modifiable?

You can modify data, of course, only if you have permission to do so. When you open a recordset, you may be able to retrieve the data for viewing only. If so, your attempts to modify the data will result in a run-time trappable error. You can always edit table-type recordsets unless someone else has placed a lock on that table (opened it exclusively or created a recordset based on it with an option that precludes others from changing its data). You can edit dynaset-type recordsets unless locks have been placed by other users, just as with table-type recordsets. In addition, join rules may prevent editing of certain fields. (For more information on join-based editing rules, see Chapter 4.) Snapshot-type recordsets are never modifiable, since they're read-only by definition.

Changing Data in a Recordset

To programmatically change the data in any recordset (assuming the recordset is updatable), take the following steps:

1. Move to the desired row.

2. Use the Edit method to put the current row in edit mode.

3. Make changes.

4. Use the Update method to save the edits.

Skipping any of these steps will lead to undesirable results. The most important step, however, is the final one. If you make changes to the row but forget to use the Update method to commit those changes, Access treats the row as though you'd never made any changes at all. (If you want to explicitly discard a change, you can do so with the recordset's CancelUpdate method, new in Access 95.)

The following code finds the first row in the recordset in which the LastName field contains "Smith" and changes it to "Smythe":

```
With rst
    .FindFirst "[LastName] = 'Smith'"
    If .NoMatch Then
        MsgBox "No Match was Found!"
    Else
        .Edit
            ![LastName] = "Smythe"
        .Update
    End If
End With
```

Adding New Records to a Recordset

To programmatically add new rows to a recordset (assuming neither updatability nor security keeps you from doing so), follow these steps:

1. Use the AddNew method to add a new row. (All fields will be set to their default values.)

2. Fill in fields as needed.

3. Use the Update method to save the new row.

As in the preceding section, if you neglect to call the Update method before you leave the current row, Access discards any changes you've made and does not add the new row.

When you use the AddNew method, the current row remains the row that was current before you added the new row. If you want the new row to be the current row, employ the Move method, using as its parameter the bookmark returned from the LastModified property of the recordset.

The following example adds a new row to the recordset and fills in a few of the fields. Once it's done, it makes the new row the current row:

```
With rst
    .AddNew
        ![LastName] = "Smith"
        ![FirstName] = "Tommy"
    .Update

    .Move O, .LastModified
End With
```

Dynaset-type recordsets treat new rows a bit differently than do table-type recordsets. For a dynaset-type recordset object, Access always places the new row at the end of the recordset. For table-type recordsets, if you've set the Index property, Access places the row at its correct spot in the index. For dynaset-type recordsets, Access adds the new row to the end of the underlying table. If you're working with a table-type recordset, though, new rows added to the table won't be seen by users who've based a recordset on that table until they refresh their rows.

In previous versions of Access (and the Jet database engine), adding new rows could result in page-lock collisions. With pessimistic locking, the final page of a table might have been locked, and your attempts to add a row would have failed. In Access 95 (and Jet 3.0), these sorts of collisions should be a thing of the past. (See Chapter 12 for more information on inserting new rows and page locking.)

Deleting Data from a Recordset

To delete a row from a recordset, follow these steps:

1. Move to the desired row.

2. Use the Delete method to delete it.

TIP

You don't need to use the Update methods when deleting a row, unlike the other methods of modifying rows. Once you delete it, it's gone—unless, of course, you wrapped the entire thing in a transaction. In that case you can roll back the transaction to retrieve the deleted row.

TIP

After you delete a record, it is still the current record. The previous row is still the previous row, and the next row is still the next row. Use MoveNext to move to the next row, if that's where you'd like to be.

The code in Listing 6.15 deletes all the rows from a table, although it is not necessarily the best way to solve the problem. In reality, you'd use a delete query to do the work. To try this function out, check in basRecordset in CH06.MDB.

Listing 6.15

```
Function ZapTable(strTable As String)
    Dim db As Database
    Dim rst As Recordset
    Dim wrk As Workspace

    Set wrk = DBEngine.Workspaces(0)
    Set db = CurrentDb()
    Set rst = db.OpenRecordset(strTable)
    With rst
        If Not .BOF And Not .EOF Then
            wrk.BeginTrans
            .MoveFirst
            Do
                .Delete
                ' Without this MoveNext, Access would
                ' continually try to delete the same row,
                ' the first one.
                .MoveNext
            Loop Until .EOF
            wrk.CommitTrans
        End If
        .Close
    End With
End Function
```

Using Transactions to Speed Recordset Operations

Any recordset operations that change data can benefit dramatically from using *transactions*. Transactions are primarily intended for allowing rollbacks and committals of bulk data changes (see Chapter 12 for more details on transactions), but since transactions buffer data reads and writes, you may be able to use them to speed up update, edit, and delete operations. Begin a transaction after opening the recordset but before you make any changes. Commit the transaction after you've made the last change but before you close the recordset.

To speed its operations, the current version of Jet applies its own internal transactions when you work with a recordset. You'll find that explicitly adding transactions to your code may or may not speed the operation. Experiment with your application to see whether or not adding your own transaction processing helps.

Listing 6.15 uses this technique to attempt to speed the row deletions. It starts a transaction before the first row change and commits it after the final change.

TIP

Adding your own transactions in an attempt to speed bulk operations may, in fact, backfire. Because Access must buffer the entire transaction in memory (whether real or virtual), a very large transaction may cause spooling to disk. In that case you're better off *not* using transactions at all. This was why, in Access 2, using action queries for bulk updates with small numbers of rows was faster than using Access Basic code to do the work, but for large operations, writing code was sometimes faster. Because Jet wrapped all action queries in its own internal transaction, large operations could cause spooling. If you handled the transactions yourself, you could commit them periodically, before Jet had to start spooling. With Access 95 and Jet 3.0, all bets are off. Because of its use of multi-threading and intelligent caching, you'll have to experiment to see when adding your own explicit transactions makes sense. (See Chapter 17 for a technique you can use to time optimizations.)

Using Containers to Handle Saved Documents

A *container* object contains information about saved database objects. Its main purpose is to provide the Jet engine with some mechanism for knowing about all the Access UI objects. Since Jet provides security for Access, it must maintain information about ownership and permissions, and it does so in these containers. Some of the containers are provided by the Jet engine and some by the application. Table 6.7 lists the useful containers, the parent for each container, and what each contains.

TABLE 6.7: Containers and Their Parents

Container	Parent	Contains Information about
Databases	Jet database engine	Containing database, database properties
Tables	Jet database engine	Saved tables and queries
Relationships	Jet database engine	Saved relationships
SysRel	Jet database engine	Saved relationship layout information
Forms	Microsoft Access	Saved forms
Reports	Microsoft Access	Saved reports
Scripts	Microsoft Access	Saved macros
Modules	Microsoft Access	Saved modules

Each container object contains a collection of Document objects, each of which is a saved object in the database. The Document objects contain information about the saved objects, but not about the data they contain. For example, the Tables container includes a Document object for each table and query in the database. Each document stores information about the permissions, creation date, and owner of the stored object. But documents in the Tables container don't store the actual data. The same goes for documents in the Forms container: each document object contains information about the form object but provides no information about the structure or content of the form itself. The Containers collection, and each container's collection of Documents, makes it possible to retrieve information about the documents in the database; this is how you can find out what exactly is *in* the database, when it was last modified, and so on.

Each container object is a collection that contains non-engine objects. The Jet engine can get very limited information about them, such as their creator and creation time, through DAO. This allows the engine to know, in a limited sense, about the objects that are application specific. The main significance of containers is that they

- Give you information about the live Access objects; that is, they give you a mechanism you can use to walk through collections of non-DAO objects

- Provide the only method for retrieving information about your saved macros, modules, reports, and forms

- Let you treat non-engine objects as though they were data access objects instead of application-provided objects; that is, they let you use the set of DAO rules and tools with non-DAO objects

Since security is provided at the engine level, Jet has to know about non-DAO objects so it can handle their security. (For more information on this topic, see Chapter 24.)

To refer to a particular container, use the syntax

Containers("*name*")

or

Containers!Name

where *name* is one of the items in the first column from Table 6.7.

NOTE The Forms and Reports containers are very different from the Forms and Reports collections. Using the containers, you can work with any forms or reports in the database but can only retrieve information such as the owner, permissions, and date of creation. Using the collections, you can refer only to currently opened forms and reports, but you can retrieve information about the controls on the form, their layout, and so on.

To examine the various containers and their contents, run the function ListContainers() in basContainers in CH06.MDB. This function can display, in the Debug window, a list of containers and the documents within them and, if you like, all the properties and their values for each document. To make the function a bit more useful, you can pass it parameters that limit the output. (See the header comments for more information.) Listing 6.16 shows the function, and Figure 6.5 shows sample output.

Listing 6.16

```
Function ListContainers(Optional fListProps As Variant, _
  Optional varContainer As Variant)

    ' List contents of containers, all or selected.
    ' Get lists of properties, too, if requested.

    ' In:
    '   fListProps: (optional, default is False)
    '       If True, list properties for all objects
```

ListContainers() can display lists of all the containers and their properties.

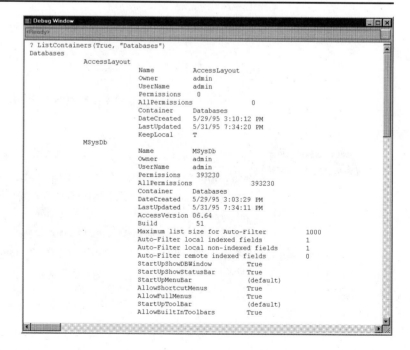

```
'    varContainer: (optional, default is "ALL")
'        Leave blank for "ALL", or one of
'            "Databases", "Forms", "Modules", "Relationships"
'            "Reports", "Scripts", "SysRel", "Tables"

Dim db As Database
Dim con As Container
Dim doc As Document
Dim db As Database
Dim tdf As TableDef
Dim prp As Property

If IsMissing(fListProps) Then fListProps = False
If IsMissing(varContainer) Then varContainer = "ALL"

Set db = CurrentDb()
For Each con In db.Containers
    If varContainer = "ALL" Or (varContainer = con.Name) Then
        Debug.Print con.Name
        For Each doc In con.Documents
            Debug.Print , doc.Name
            If fListProps Then
                For Each prp In doc.Properties
                    Debug.Print , , prp.Name, prp.Value
                Next prp
            End If
        Next doc
    End If
Next con
End Function
```

Database Properties

Access allows you to set database properties with the File ➤ Database Properties menu. Those properties are stored as properties of the SummaryInfo document in the Databases container. If you set up user-defined properties for your database (choose the Custom tab on the File ➤ Database Properties dialog box to set these properties), they're stored as properties of the UserDefined document within the Databases container.

You may need to supply an interface for setting and retrieving your database's summary information from within your application. To get you started, we've supplied a simple form, frmSummaryInfo in CH06.MDB, that does the work for you and looks very similar to the built-in dialog box (see Figure 6.6).

To use this form within your own applications, import it (frmSummaryInfo) and the module containing the property-handling functions, basHandleProps, from CH06.MDB. You may find it interesting to study the code in frmSummaryInfo's module. It makes several calls to the glrGetProp() and glrSetProp() functions, to handle the various database summary information properties.

FIGURE 6.6:

frmSummaryInfo allows you to set and retrieve database summary info from your applications.

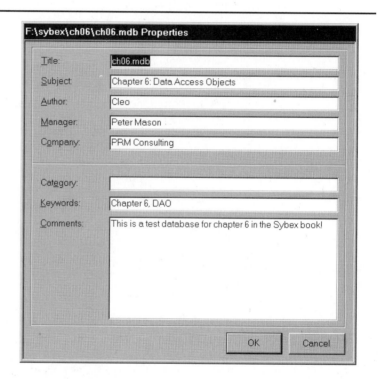

A Case Study: Using DAO

As an example of using DAO as part of an application, we've provided a simple replacement for the Database Explorer (see Figure 6.7) that you can import into any application. You can use it directly as is, or you can modify it to add new functionality. You might want to remove some of the objects for your own applications. For example, you might like to provide users with a list of only certain tables and queries. Perhaps you don't want to show your users a list of macros or modules. Given frmDBC as a starting place, you can make as many changes as you wish to fit your own needs. The point of the sample is to demonstrate the use of DAO when working with table and query objects and the Access-specific code to handle the other database objects: forms, reports, macros, and modules. In the interest of simplicity, we've modeled this form on the Access 2 database container. If your users are familiar with that interface, they'll be happy with this look. If not, you can certainly use one of the many custom controls available for Access to display this information in a different format. (For a different approach to this problem, see Chapter 19.)

FIGURE 6.7:

The sample database container is simpler than the one you'll find in Access, but it provides many of the same features.

Designing frmDBC

The design considerations for frmDBC were to

- Provide a list of all the tables, queries, forms, reports, macros, and modules in the current database

- Keep the interface as simple as possible

- Allow resizing of the list to match the size of the form

- Allow for customization

The following sections discuss the form itself and how it does its work.

Choosing an Object Type and an Action

The buttons on the left side of frmDBC are part of an option group (grpObjects). When you click one of the buttons, the code attached to the option group's AfterUpdate event refills the list box (lstObjects) that displays the list of objects. The particular list that lstObjects displays depends, of course, on the value of grpObjects.

TIP

> To make the code as simple as possible, we've used the intrinsic constants acTable, acQuery, acForm, acReport, acMacro, and acModule wherever possible. These constants provide the values for the buttons in the option group and make up the choices available in all the Select Case statements within the code. Whenever possible, use the Access-defined constants in your code.

Once you've chosen an object type (and forced the list box to refill itself) and selected an object from the list, you can select one of the action buttons at the top of the form (New, Open, or Design). Depending on the circumstances, one or more of those buttons might have a different caption and might be disabled.

Visual Effects and Speed (or Lack Thereof)

We attempted to make the faux-database window as useful as possible to give you a recognizable starting point. Although it would be possible to emulate the "tabbed" look of the Access Database Explorer, we decided time would be better spent on the workings of the form than on the look of the buttons.

On the other hand, the list box does resize to fit the form, no matter what size you choose for the form itself. This trick is possible because of the modifiability of control characteristics at run time. Every time the form fires off its Resize event, the code figures out the current form size and resizes the list box inside the form accordingly. (For more information on modifying controls and their sizes based on the size of the parent form, see Chapter 8.)

NOTE Every time you resize a list box, Access forces it to requery its record source. In this case you'll find this requery totally unnecessary, and it occurs several times for each resize. Therefore, we've played a little trick. Before the code actually performs the resize, it stores the list box's RowSourceType property. (The list box is filled from a list-filling function, so the information is stored in the RowSourceType property.) After it's done resizing the control, the code resets the RowSourceType property. Of course, this forces one requery, but at least it's only one, not three or more. You may want to try this mechanism yourself whenever you need to modify the properties of a list or combo box and find it's taking longer than you'd like.

Displaying the Object List

For this example we use a list-filling callback function to fill the list of objects. For more information on the mechanics of writing and using these functions, see Chapter 7. For now, the important issue is filling an array with a list of all the objects of a particular type. Access calls the function ListObjects(), in frmDBC's module, when it needs to fill the list. The most important piece of ListObjects() is the call to GetObjectList(), which fills a dynamic array (astrObjects()) with a list of all the objects of the type specified by grpObjects (the option group on the form):

```
Set db = CurrentDb()
intCount = GetObjectList(db, grpObjects, astrObjects(), False, _
  QRY_ANYTYPE, False)
```

The function GetObjectList() takes six parameters, described in the following table, and returns the number of objects it finds. Once ListObjects() gets the list it needs from GetObjectList(), it can display it in the list box.

Parameter	Datatype	Description
db	Database	A reference to the current database
intType	Integer	One of acTable, acQuery, and so on
astrList()	String array (dynamic)	Array to hold the returned list
fIncSysObjs	Boolean	Include the system objects in the list?
lngFlags	Long	Special flags indicating what to show in the list. Show all queries, for example?
fIncThisForm	Boolean	Include the current form in the list?

Filling the Object List

The function GetObjectList() is the heart of this entire form. Given a reference to the current database and a value indicating the object type on which it should check, it fills the array it's been passed with a list of all the items of the requested type. Listing 6.17 shows the entire function, and the following paragraphs go through the code, one bit at time.

Listing 6.17

```
Private Function GetObjectList(db As Database, _
  ByVal intType As Integer, astrList() As String, _
  fIncSysObjs As Boolean, lngFlags As Long, _
  fIncThisForm As Boolean)
```

```
' Fill an array with a list of objects of a given type.
' Parameters:
'    db -- a database reference, so you COULD
'          show objects from a different database
'    intType -- one of acTable, acQuery, acForm,
'               acReport, acMacro or acModule
'    astrList() -- the dynamic string array to be filled in
'    fIncSysObjs -- Include System objects (Yes/No)
'    lngFlags -- special flags about the list (for example,
'                you could specify the query type here)
'  fIncThisForm -- Show the current form name? (Yes/No)
'
' Fills in astrList() with the list of object names.
' Returns the number of objects added to the list.

Dim intCount As Integer
Dim intNumObjs As Integer
Dim intI As Integer
Dim fSystemObj As Boolean
Dim ctr As Container
Dim strName As String

Const glrcObjHidden = &H1

intCount = 0

On Error GoTo GetObjectListError
DoCmd.Hourglass True
Select Case intType
    Case acTable
        db.TableDefs.Refresh
        ' Get the number of tables and
        ' make the array that size.
        intNumObjs = db.TableDefs.Count
        ReDim astrList(0 To intNumObjs)

        Dim tdf As TableDef
        For Each tdf In db.TableDefs
            ' Check and see if this is a system object.
            fSystemObj = isSystemObject(acTable, _
            tdf.Name, tdf.Attributes)
            ' Unless this is a system object and you're
            ' not showing system objects, or this table
            ' has its hidden bit set, add it to the list.
            If (fSystemObj Imp fIncSysObjs) And _
```

```
                            ((tdf.Attributes And glrcObjHidden) = 0) Then
                            astrList(intCount) = tdf.Name
                            intCount = intCount + 1
                    End If
            Next tdf
        Case acQuery
            db.QueryDefs.Refresh
            ' Get the number of queries and
            ' make the array that size.
            intNumObjs = db.QueryDefs.Count
            ReDim astrList(0 To intNumObjs)

            Dim qry As QueryDef
            For Each qry In db.QueryDefs
                ' Check and see if this is a system object.
                fSystemObj = isSystemObject( _
                 acQuery, qry.Name, 0)
                ' Unless this is a system object and you're
                ' not showing system objects, or it's the
                ' wrong query type, add it to the list.
                If (fSystemObj Imp fIncSysObjs) Then
                    If ((qry.Type = lngFlags) Or _
                     (lngFlags = QRY_ANYTYPE)) Then
                        astrList(intCount) = qry.Name
                        intCount = intCount + 1
                    End If
                End If
            Next qry
        Case acForm
            Set ctr = db.Containers("Forms")
        Case acReport
            Set ctr = db.Containers("Reports")
        Case acMacro
            Set ctr = db.Containers("Scripts")
        Case acModule
            Set ctr = db.Containers("Modules")
End Select
Select Case intType
    Case acForm, acReport, acMacro, acModule
        ctr.Documents.Refresh
        intNumObjs = ctr.Documents.Count

        ReDim astrList(0 To intNumObjs)
        Dim doc As Document
        For Each doc In ctr.Documents
```

```
        strName = doc.Name
        fSystemObj = isSystemObject(intType, strName, 0)
        ' Unless this is a system object and you're
        ' not showing system objects, add it to the
        ' list.
        If (fSystemObj Imp fIncSysObjs) Then
              ' If it's not true that you're to skip
              ' this form and you've hit this form in
              ' the container, add the item to the list.
              If Not (Not fIncThisForm And _
                (intType = acForm) And _
                (strName = Me.Name)) And _
                Not isDeleted(strName) Then
                    astrList(intCount) = strName
                    intCount = intCount + 1
              End If
        End If
    Next doc
  End Select

GetObjectListExit:
    DoCmd.Hourglass False
    GetObjectList = intCount
    Exit Function

GetObjectListError:
    HandleErrors Err, "GetObjectList"
    ' If there was an error, better reset
    ' the count of objects back to 0.
    intCount = 0
    Resume GetObjectListExit
End Function
```

The main body of GetObjectList(), once it's initialized local variables and set up the environment by turning on the hourglass cursor, consists of a Select Case statement with one case for each of the possible object types. For tables and queries, the code uses DAO methods to compile the list. For forms, reports, macros, and modules, the code uses Access' version of DAO—its containers—to iterate through the different objects. (For a completely different solution to this same problem, see Chapter 19, which uses a special library to retrieve lists of objects.)

Creating a List of Tables

The first step in compiling the list of tables is to refresh the TableDefs collection. This ensures that the collection is completely current and that it contains the entire list. Then you can retrieve the count of objects in the collection and resize the passed-in dynamic array so it's large enough to hold the entire list of items:

```
db.TableDefs.Refresh
intNumObjs = db.TableDefs.Count
ReDim astrList(0 To intNumObjs)
```

Once you know the number of tables in the collection, you can loop through each of the tabledefs, assigning the variable tdf to refer to each, in turn:

```
Dim tdf As TableDef
For Each tdf In db.TableDefs
'
'
Next tdf
```

Deciding Whether to Add a Table

For each particular tabledef, you may or may not want to add it to the output array. If you have not requested that the function include system tables and the current table is a system table, you'll want to skip it and not add it to the output array. In any case, skip tables that have their hidden attribute set.

```
fSystemObj = isSystemObject(acTable, tdf.Name, tdf.Attributes)
' Unless this is a system object and you're not showing system
' objects, or this table has its hidden bit set,
' add it to the list.
If (fSystemObj Imp fIncSysObjs) And _
 Not (tdf.Attributes And glrcObjHidden) Then
    astrList(intCount) = tdf.Name
    intCount = intCount + 1
End If
```

Checking for System Objects

The first step in the preceding code was to determine whether or not the current table is a system object. To determine this you can call the function isSystemObject():

```
Private Function isSystemObject(intType As Integer, _
 ByVal strName As String, ByVal lngAttribs As Long)
```

```
        If (Left$(strName, 4) = "USys") Then
            isSystemObject = True
        Else
            isSystemObject = ((intType = acTable) And _
            ((lngAttribs And dbSystemObject) <> 0))
        End If
End Function
```

In two instances the current object could be treated as a system object:

- If the name of the object is Usys followed by any text. This naming convention allows the user to create objects that Access will display, in the database container, only when the Show System Objects option is set to Yes.

- The object is a table, and its Attribute field has its dbSystemObject bit set.

Checking for Inclusion

You'll want to include the table in your list unless one of the following situations exists:

- Its attribute includes the bit that indicates the table is to be hidden.

- You've asked to not include system tables, and this table is a system table.

Using Bitwise Operators to Check Attributes

Checking to see whether a particular attribute has been set for an object requires you to use the bitwise And operator. The And operator returns a non-zero value if the value you're checking and the appropriate intrinsic constant (dbSystemObject, in this case) have at least one bit set in the same position. Therefore, to check whether a particular object is a system table, you can use the following expression:

```
isSystemObject = ((intType = acTable) And _
  ((lngAttribs And dbSystemObject) <> 0))
```

This expression returns a True value if both parts of the expression are True; that is, if the type is acTable and the bitwise comparison of the object's attribute and dbSystemObject isn't 0.

To check whether the table's attribute includes the hidden bit, you need to check the return value from Anding it with glrcObjHidden(1). If

```
tdf.Attributes AND glrcObjHidden
```

returns a nonzero value, the matching bit is set in both values.

You also need to check whether to include a table, based on whether you've requested to include system tables and whether this particular table is a system table. Based on these two conditions, you have four possible outcomes, as shown in Table 6.8.

TABLE 6.8: Decision Table for System Table Inclusion

System Table?	Include System Tables?	Include This Table?
Yes	Yes	Yes
Yes	No	No
No	Yes	Yes
No	No	Yes

As you can see in Table 6.8, you'll want to include the current table in the output array unless the current table is a system table and you've elected not to include system tables. You could build a complex logical expression to indicate this information to Access, but Access makes this a bit simpler by providing a single logical operator that works exactly as you need.

The IMP (implication) operator takes two values and returns a True value *unless* the first operand is True and the second is False. This exactly matches the truth table shown in Table 6.8. Given that the variable fSystemObj indicates whether or not the current table is a system object and the variable fIncSysObjs indicates whether or not you want to include system objects, you can use the expression

```
fSystemObj IMP fIncSysObjs
```

to know whether to exclude the table based on whether or not it's a system table. Therefore, to check both criteria for inclusion, you can use the following expression:

```
If (fSystemObj Imp fIncSysObjs) And _
 Not (tdf.Attributes And glrcObjHidden) Then
```

This expression returns a True value if both parts return a True value.

Adding the Table

Once you've decided that a particular table is to be added to the list of tables, you'll want to place the Name property of the current tabledef in the output array and then increment the count of objects:

```
astrList(intCount) = tdf.Name
intCount = intCount + 1
```

When the loop is done, the output array, astrList(), will contain one item for each acceptable table in the database.

Creating a List of Queries

To create a list of queries, the steps are almost completely parallel to the steps necessary to create a list of tables. The following sections discuss the few differences.

Using Different Datatypes

To manipulate queries rather than tables, you need to use querydef variables instead of tabledef variables. Therefore, the initialization code, when you are building the query list, looks like this:

```
db.QueryDefs.Refresh
' Get the number of queries and
' make the array that size.
intNumObjs = db.QueryDefs.Count
ReDim astrList(0 To intNumObjs)

Dim qry As QueryDef
For Each qdf In db.QueryDefs
'
'
Next intI
```

Aside from the changes from tabledef to querydef references, the code is identical to the code that handles tables.

Checking for System Objects

Since queries can't be system objects in the normal sense, the only way isSystemObject() will return True is if the query has a name that starts with *Usys*. Therefore, in the call to isSystemObject(), there's no point in passing in the object's attribute, since you aren't really interested in checking the attribute to see whether the query is a system object. The function call is

```
fSystemObj = isSystemObject(acQuery, qry.Name, 0)
```

The third parameter, the object's attributes value, could actually be anything, since isSystemObject() looks at the attribute only if the object happens to be a table.

Checking the Query Type

The fifth parameter to GetObjectList(), lngFlags, allows you to indicate exactly which type of queries you'd like to find in the output array. If you pass a specific query type, the code returns only queries of that type. If you pass in the constant QRY_ANYTYPE, the function returns queries of any type. The following code shows these steps:

```
' Unless this is a system object and you're not showing system
' objects, or it's the wrong query type, add it to the list.
If (fSystemObj Imp fIncSysObjs) Then
    If ((qry.Type = lngFlags) Or (lngFlags = QRY_ANYTYPE)) Then
```

In summary, aside from the differences noted, gathering a list of queries is just like gathering a list of tables. Both use DAO to enumerate the collections, and both use Jet engine–provided properties to know whether or not to include the object in the output array.

Gathering Lists of Access Objects

Although the lists of objects in your Access database, aside from tables and queries, aren't handled by the Jet engine and aren't technically part of data access objects, we discuss them here just to complete the description of the replacement database container. From the users' point of view, there's no difference between Jet objects and Access objects, but from the developer's point of view, they're really separate entities.

Finding a Container

If you've asked GetObjectList() to retrieve a list of the available forms, reports, macros, or modules, you won't be enumerating through a Jet collection. Instead, you'll be looping through one of four different Access containers. Since one container can be treated like any other, your first step is to create a variable of type Container to refer to the correct Access container. Following is the code from GetObjectList() that performs this task:

```
Case acForm
    Set ctr = db.Containers("Forms")
Case acReport
    Set ctr = db.Containers("Reports")
Case acMacro
    Set ctr = db.Containers("Scripts")
Case acModule
    Set ctr = db.Containers("Modules")
```

Looping through the Containers

Once you've pointed the variable ctr at a particular container, the code to loop through all the elements of the container should look very familiar. Once you've determined that the current object matches the caller's interest in system objects, you have two new problems to handle:

- If this object is a form, should you list the current form?
- Is this object deleted? Access doesn't immediately remove deleted objects from the containers, and you won't want to display these objects in the list.

One of the parameters you passed to GetObjectList(), fIncThisForm, indicates whether or not you want to include the current form in the list. Therefore, the following line of code excludes the current form name from the list, as well as any deleted objects:

```
If Not (Not fIncThisForm And (intType = acForm) And _
 (strName = Me.Name)) And Not isDeleted(strName) Then
```

The isDeleted() function takes a very low-tech approach to checking for deleted objects:

```
Private Function isDeleted (ByVal strName As String) As Boolean
    isDeleted = (Left(strName, 4) = "~TMPCLP")
End Function
```

It just looks for object names that start with ~TMPCLP, which is how Access renames deleted objects.

Finishing It Up

Finally, once you've filled in the array of items, GetObjectList() returns the count of items in the array it's filled in. The calling function, ListObjects(), uses that count to know how many items to display.

Using frmDBC in Your Own Applications

To use frmDBC in your own applications, just import it. Since all the code it requires to run is encapsulated in its module, you need nothing else. However, you might want to consider making various alterations to it. For example, you might want to add some columns or remove some of the toggle buttons that appear along the left side of the form. In any case, we left the sample form simple so you can modify it for your own needs. Probably the only serious complication you'll run across is the resizing of the list box. You'll need to decide for yourself how resizing the form will affect the resizing of individual columns.

TIP

Although Jet does not expose a method for finding out whether any specific object is hidden (that is, you've set its Hidden property to True from the object's properties dialog), you can retrieve the information from a system table. This information is undocumented, and retrieving it for any specific object is slow, as well, because it requires a table access for each object. FrmDBC includes code to follow the setting of the Show Hidden Objects global option, but it's commented out and not included in the discussion here. If you want more information, look into basHidden in CH06.MDB. If you want to use this feature, you'll also need to distribute basHidden with frmDBC. See the comments in frmDBC for information on checking for hidden objects (using the glrcTrackHidden constant).

Summary

This chapter has presented a broad overview of Access' object model. Although we've made attempts to bring our own personal perspectives into this chapter, a full understanding of this material requires far more depth than we can cover here. Because of the similarities between the object models in Access, Visual Basic, and Excel, you would be well served to spend as much time as possible "digging in" to this material, since this is clearly the way future Microsoft products will be going.

This chapter has covered these major topics:

- Access' support for DAO
- Objects that Access provides
- Referring to objects
- Iterating through collections
- Using properties
- Data definition using DAO
- Working with Access' recordsets
- Using Access' application-supplied containers

There's much, much more to know. As a start, Chapter 24, focusing on Access Security, covers (among other things) programmatic control over security features using DAO.

PART III

Presenting Data

CHAPTER

SEVEN

Controlling Controls

- Using form and report controls

- Understanding control events and properties

- Using the Tag property in a standardized way

- Combining controls to work together

- Creating forms and controls programmatically

In this chapter you'll learn about each of the different Access controls, and you'll find some hints on deciding which control is best for a given datatype or situation, along with examples of many of the control types. (For examples using OLE custom controls, see Chapters 15 and 21.) In addition, you'll find a number of reusable solutions to common challenges you'll confront when designing your user interfaces.

Controls and Their Uses

Controls are the workhorses of Access applications. You can use them for inputting and outputting data, as well as for displaying static information. In addition, you can use controls as global variables, to calculate intermediate values, or to add aesthetic interest to your forms. Forms and reports share the same controls. (You can put a button on a report, for example, but it doesn't really make much sense to do so.) The focus of this chapter is on controls for forms.

You can think of controls in Access as being windows, just as all the other elements of a Windows application are windows. As with any window, a control can receive information from the user only when it has input focus. To allow a user to be able to enter text into a text box or to check an item in a check box, that control must first have been selected, either by the user or under your program's control.

Controls have *values,* supplied by you at design time, by the data from which the control is being fed, or by the user at run time. The value of the control is the value you see displayed in that control. For a text box, the value is obviously the text displayed inside the box. For a list box, the value of the control is the chosen item (or Null, if no item is chosen). For an OLE object, the value of the control is the object (whether it be a *Paint* bitmap, an *Excel* spreadsheet, or a *Word* document).

Controls also have *properties* that your application can set and change. This chapter touches on the useful, pertinent, and difficult properties throughout its discussion of the various controls. If you're upgrading to Access 95 from an earlier version, you'll find many new properties, and some new control types, as well.

Code-Behind-Forms

In Access, every form and report carries its own module with it. The code in this module is normally referred to as *Code-Behind-Forms,* or *CBF,* and it's in this module that you'll usually attach code to any event property for any control. Chapter 8 discusses this feature in greater depth, but be aware that when this chapter refers to attaching code to a given control or to a property of a control, it is talking about creating event procedure functions and subroutines that are stored with the form itself. You can gain access to the Code-Behind-Forms by clicking the "…" button next to the specific event on the property sheet and choosing Code Builder from the Choose Builder dialog box. Note that you can also reverse the order. If you choose [Event Procedure] from the row's drop-down list, you can then click the Build (…) button, and Access will take you directly to the CBF. You can also choose the Code button on the toolbar to access this code. The property sheet (with a builder button) is shown here:

Figure 7.1 shows the dialog box.

FIGURE 7.1:
Choose the Code Builder item to edit code attached to the chosen event.

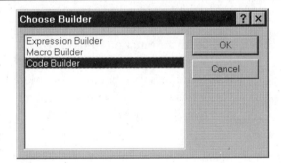

Some Standard Control Properties

Before we launch into a discussion of all the different controls and their various properties and events, this seems like a good time to discuss some of the standard properties and events that most controls share. Later in the chapter we'll discuss individual controls with their unique properties and events.

Using the Tag Property to Create Your Own Properties

Access provides the general-purpose Tag property, which allows you to specify and store up to 2048 characters of information attached to any control. Access never uses what's stored in this property, so it makes a perfect place to store information about a control that is pertinent to your application. You might find it tempting to place arbitrary values in this unused slot, but it's a good idea to avoid this urge. If you adopt a standard method of storing values in the Tag property, you can actually create your own user-defined properties for controls. In the previous edition of this book, we proposed a standard that has gained acceptance within the Access development community for formatting this information.

DOS stores values within its environment using a very structured format:

Name1=Value1;Name2=Value2;Name3=Value3;

We suggest just such a format for using the Tag property to contain user-defined information. This format guarantees that various pieces of your application won't overwrite information stored in the Tag property of a given control. If all access to the Tag property goes through a set of functions that set and get the specific values by their names, you have a very ordered and safe way to store and retrieve values. Using this method allows you to store multiple bits of information about a control and retrieve those bits when necessary.

To implement this functionality we've provided a set of functions you can include in any of your applications. (To use the functions, import the module basParse from CH07.MDB.) We'll use the function in basParse throughout this book, not only to work with the Tag property, but any place we need to store more than one item in a single string. The set of functions includes glrCtlTagPutItem(), which puts a tag name and its value into the Tag property for a specific control, and glrCtlTag-GetItem(), which retrieves a specific tag value from the Tag property of a specific control. These two functions, described below, should provide the flexibility you need to use the Tag property to its fullest advantage. Figure 7.2 shows the glrCtlTag-PutItem() and glrCtlTagGetItem() functions setting and retrieving the tag value, TimeModified.

FIGURE 7.2:
Use the glrCtlTagPutItem() and glrCtlTagGetItem() functions to place and retrieve values from the Tag property of a control.

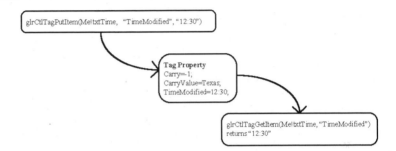

In addition, to make this interface as simple as possible, we've made the rules for the structure of the Tag property string a bit more stringent than those controlling the DOS environment. In particular, the syntax for the Tag property is as follows:

TagName1=TagValue1;TagName2=TagValue2;...;TagNameN=TagValueN;

To use glrCtlTagGetItem() and glrCtlTagPutItem(), follow these rules:

- Separate each item name and value pair with an equal sign (=).
- Follow each pair with a semicolon (;), although you can change this particular separator by modifying the glrcSeparator constant in the code.
- Do not include the separator character (;) in the tag value.

If you use the provided functions to place values into the Tag property, these rules won't be a concern, since the code will follow them. The only problem occurs when you place values into the Tag property at design time. In that case, be careful to follow the rules exactly, since the provided functions may not work otherwise. The functions are declared as follows:

```
Function glrCtlTagGetItem(ctl As Control, _
 ByVal varItemName As Variant) As Variant
Function glrCtlTagPutItem(ctl As Control, _
 ByVal varItemName As Variant, _
 ByVal varItemValue As Variant) As Integer
```

The following list describes the parameters for each of the functions:

Argument	Description
ctl	Control containing the Tag property you want to manipulate
varItemName	String expression resulting in the name you want associated with the piece of data stored in the tag property
varItemValue	Variant expression resulting in the value you want to have stored in the Tag property of the specified control

TIP

To include the functionality described here in your own applications, include the basParse module from CH07.MDB.

NOTE

Access never records any property changes your running application makes while a form is in Form view. Just as with any other property, changes made to the Tag property with glrCtlTagPutItem( ) will not appear in the property sheet. If you want to make persistent changes to any property, you need to make them when your form is in Design view.

TIP

The basParse module includes a second set of useful functions that work with any string, not just a control's Tag property. You'll find these functions to be more general-purpose, and we'll use them when necessary throughout the book. Take a look at the public functions in basParse for more information now, if you wish.

The ControlType Property

In previous versions of Microsoft Access, you needed to use ugly and arcane syntax to find out the control type for a given control:

> If TypeOf *control* Is *controlType* Then
>
> ' Do something
>
> End If

Now, you can query the ControlType property of a control directly and get an integer that indicates the control type. Table 7.1 lists the different control types, along with their ControlType values and the Access constants that represent them.

TABLE 7.1: ControlType Property Values

Control	Integer	Constant
Label	100	acLabel
Rectangle	101	acRectangle
Line	102	acLine
Image frame	103	acImageFrame
Command button	104	acCommandButton
Option button	105	acOptionButton
Check box	106	acCheckBox
Option group	107	acOptionGroup
Bound object frame	108	acBoundObjectFrame
Text box	109	acTextBox
List box	110	acListBox
Combo box	111	acComboBox
Subform/subreport	112	acSubform
Unbound object frame	114	acObjectFrame
Page break	118	acPageBreak
Custom control	119	acCustomControl
Toggle button	122	acToggleButton

In addition, the ControlType property is read/write in Design view. (You can't change a control's type while a form is running in Form view.) This makes it possible to write tools that directly manipulate the control's type (and this is just how the Format ➤ Change To menu item works).

The ControlTipText and ShortCutMenuBar Properties

Access 95 allows you to create your own *control tips* (those little boxes describing controls you see when you leave your mouse over a control for a short period of time) and *context-sensitive menus* (the menus you get when you right-click an object) for any control. The ControlTipText property can contain up to 255 characters of text, and you can modify this property at run time if you need to. Although you won't, in general, supply control tips for controls other than command buttons, they can be handy in other circumstances, as well. For example, frmFillTest, shown in Figure 7.3, allows you to fill a list with different items. (You'll see how frmFillTest fills its lists in the section "Changing the RowSource Property" later in this chapter.) Depending on which items you're displaying, you may want a different control tip for the list box. The fragment of the code that does the work, from the SetListBox-Contents procedure in the form's module, just sets the ControlTipText property of the selected list box when you choose one of the command buttons:

```
Set ctl = Me!lstShowList
Select Case intFlag
    Case glrcShowProducts
        strField = "Products"
        strTable = "tblProducts"
        ctl.ControlTipText = "Choose a product"
    Case glrcShowLocations
        strField = "Locations"
        strTable = "tblLocations"
        ctl.ControlTipText = "Choose a location"
    Case Else
        Exit Function
End Select
```

To supply a context-sensitive menu for a control, create a normal menu bar (see Chapter 11 for more information on creating menus) and choose that menu name for the ShortCutMenuBar property of the control. The sample form, frmFillTest,

FIGURE 7.3:
Attach tool tips to controls with the
ControlTipText property.

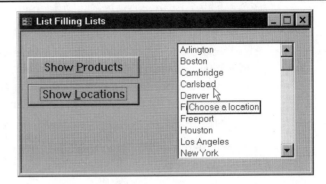

uses this technique on the list box, as shown in Figure 7.4. The menu macro, ChooseList, adds two menu items: one to fill the list with products, the other with locations. In either case, the menus end up calling the public SetListBoxContents() function in the form's module.

FIGURE 7.4:
Attach a context-sensitive menu to a
control using the ShortCutMenuBar
property.

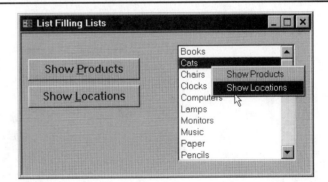

Using the TabStop and TabIndex Properties

The TabIndex property allows you to control the order in which users will arrive at controls as they use the Tab or ↵ key to move from control to control on your form. The TabIndex property lets you assign an ordinal value (zero-based) to each control on your form, specifying how you want the user to move between controls. Access maintains the list, ensuring that no value is used twice and that no value is skipped.

333

You can also use the View ➤ Tab Order menu item to edit the TabStop properties in a more visual environment.

The TabStop property (Yes/No) can remove a control from the form's tab list. Normally, if you press the Tab key to move from control to control on a form, the focus moves in tab order through the controls. If you set a control's TabStop property to No, Access skips that particular control. Controls that have their TabStop property set to No will still appear in the View ➤ Tab Order dialog box, however.

You can use the TabStop and TabIndex properties to gain complete control over the flow of your application's forms. You could, for example, change the tab order of fields based on a choice the user made. The example form, frmTabOrder (in CH07.MDB), changes the tab order from row-first to column-first, based on a choice the user made (see Figure 7.5).

FIGURE 7.5:

You can control the tab order programmatically, allowing users to choose the order in which they'd like to fill out a form.

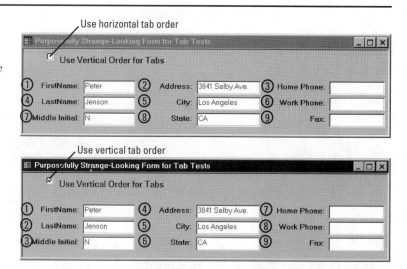

The code required to change the tab order at run time is simple. The following example was attached to the AfterUpdate event of the chkTabOrder control. All it needs to do is check the state of the check box and set the tab order accordingly.

```
Private Sub chkTabOrder_AfterUpdate()
    With Me
        If chkTabOrder Then
            ' Use a column-wise ordering
```

```
            !txtFirstName.TabIndex = 1
            !txtLastName.TabIndex = 2
            !txtMiddleInitial.TabIndex = 3
            .
            .
            .
            !txtFax.TabIndex = 9
        Else
            ' Use the AutoOrder ordering.
            !txtFirstName.TabIndex = 1
            !txtAddress.TabIndex = 2
            !txtHomePhone.TabIndex = 3
            .
            .
            .
            !txtFax.TabIndex = 9
        End If
    End With
End Sub
```

Using the DisplayWhen Property

On forms, you can influence when Access will display a control with the Display-When property. (Report controls don't include the DisplayWhen property but must use the Visible setting instead.) If you want the control to appear only when you print the form, set the DisplayWhen property to Print Only (1). To make the control appear at all times, select Always (0), and to make it display only on screen and not at print time, choose Screen Only (2). You set the DisplayWhen property to Screen Only for all the controls you want displayed only when you're looking at the form on screen.

Using Labels

Labels are the simplest of all nongraphic Access controls. A label presents *static* text on a form or report. That is, the text doesn't change as you move from record to record. Labels can never receive input focus and thus can never be used to input data. The form's tab order skips over them. Labels, then, are best for displaying information on forms you never want your users to be able to change, such as data-gathering instructions or your company's name. Generally, you also use labels to display the field names for bound controls. Unless told otherwise, Access creates a label control to accompany any bound control you create, including the field name and a colon.

> **TIP**
>
> If you want to change the way Access creates labels for your bound fields, edit the default text box properties (and those of other controls you use). If you select the text box button in the toolbox, the property sheet heading should be "Default Textbox." Modify the AutoLabel and AddColon properties to match your preferences. In addition, you can set the LabelX and LabelY properties to control the offset of the label from the text box to which it's attached.

> **NOTE**
>
> You cannot create a label without text. That sounds obvious, but it's very disconcerting when you accidentally try to do it. If you size a label just right but then click some other control before entering a caption value, Access just removes the label as though you had never created it. You can delete the text once you've created it, however, but a label without text isn't very useful.

You can change the color, font name, font size, and text alignment for text in a label. You can also change the Color and SpecialEffect properties of the label itself. It's best to standardize the appearance of the field labels in your application, and you'll find that the control default properties can help you out. (See the section "Using Default Control Properties to Your Advantage" later in this chapter for more information.)

Once you've changed the font (name or size) for a particular label, you may find the text no longer fits inside the label. Double-clicking any of the control *handles* (the little black boxes that surround the control frame) causes Access to resize the control for best fit—that is, Access resizes the control so it's just big enough for your text. This can be useful if you're trying out different font sizes. It's equivalent to choosing the Format ➤ Size ➤ To Fit menu item. Figure 7.6 shows this autosizing in action. You can emulate this in your code using the SizeToFit method, as well.

You may be tempted to create labels with lots of different styles and attributes. If so, remember that end users generally appreciate and benefit from consistency in appearance and functionality. The following sections outline some ideas for standardizing your use of labels. (Although all the concepts here apply equally to other controls, labels are prime candidates for artistic misuse.) See Chapter 15 for a more thorough discussion of user-interface design issues.

FIGURE 7.6:
Double-clicking a sizing handle chooses the best-fit size for your labels.

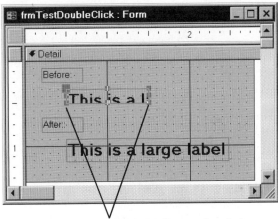

Double-click any of the handles to set best-fit size

The Parent Property

Although you won't find it on the property sheet, labels expose a Parent property, which returns to you the control that is the parent for the label. Other control types return the logical value for their Parent property: items in option groups return the option group as their parent, and all other controls return the form as their parent. (For more information on option groups, see the section "Using Option Groups—Controls inside Controls" later in this chapter.)

For example, imagine you have a label named Label2 that's attached to an option button, Option1, which resides inside the option group Frame0 on Form1. The Debug window session shown in Figure 7.7 demonstrates the relationships between controls and their parents.

FIGURE 7.7:

The Parent property allows you to walk up the hierarchy of controls on a form.

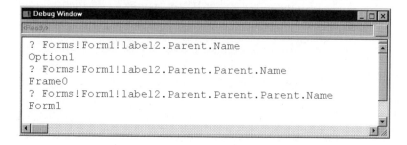

> **NOTE**
>
> Although each label provides a property that indicates the control to which it's attached, other controls provide no corresponding property to tell you which label is attached to them. This makes it impossible to write tools that would require you to know this information. Certainly, Access knows this information, but you, as a developer, cannot. Let's hope Access exposes this crucial piece of information in a future version.

Using Text Boxes

Although labels are the simplest of all Access controls, text boxes are the most ubiquitous. You can use text boxes to display data, as well as to capture it. They can contain single or multiple lines. They can display scroll bars if you wish. Text boxes can contain any amount of textual information, up to approximately 32,000 characters (although in reality this will probably be less, depending on your particular circumstances).

You can think of a text box as a mini-notepad, allowing you to enter free-form text. If you think your data entry will require more than one line or if you are using a text box to display information from a memo field, your best bet is to enable scroll bars. (Set the ScrollBars property to Vertical rather than None.)

As is the Windows standard, the ↵ key causes Access not to insert a carriage return/line feed in your text box but rather to move to the next control. To move to a new line, you must press Shift+↵. To make the ↵ key insert a carriage return/line feed, set the EnterKeyBehavior property of the text box to New Line in Field. This makes the text box work more like what you might expect but less like the rest of Windows.

If you are using text boxes for data entry on a form (and chances are good you are), you should strongly consider displaying a label control for each text box you use, making clear the purpose of that particular text box. That's the default behavior in Access, and you probably are better off sticking with it unless you have a specific reason not to.

Just as with label controls, your applications will be more coherent if you adopt a standard format for your data input and form display. If you use the Forms Wizards to create your forms, you know that one "look" for a form can be very attractive. Once you've set a standard for your forms, stick with it. You may find that adhering to the concept, "If it's raised I can click it; if it's sunken I can type into it" helps your design process. You might also consider color schemes to indicate fields the user cannot change as opposed to those that need user input. A darker background for read-only fields (the BackColor property) might be useful, and the etched border style helps, too.

At this point Access text boxes can support only a single font and a single text attribute (bold, italic, or underline). Unless you care to embed an OLE object (either the RTF text OLE control available with Visual Basic and the Access Developer's Toolkit, or a WordPad or Word for Windows document), you will need to forego multiple fonts and formatting within text boxes.

Carrying Values Forward into New Records

In some instances your application may require the ability to carry forward values into the new row when your user adds a new row using a form. Access does not provide this ability on its own, but it's not difficult to implement it in Basic. This functionality requires modifying the DefaultValue property of your controls, storing away field values as Access writes the current record to the underlying table. Then, when you add a new row, those default values will be placed into the controls for you.

This is a perfect case for using the Tag property, as described in the section "Using the Tag Property to Create Your Own Properties" earlier in this chapter. To control which fields get carried over into the new record, you must place a tag value in the Tag property (Carry=−1, in this example). If the code finds this tag value in the Tag property, it knows to carry forward the value in that particular field. Figure 7.8 shows the form frmCarryTest (from CH07.MDB), which demonstrates these ideas. The module basCarry contains all the code.

The glrSweep supporting routine requires special mention here. This subroutine accepts two parameters, the name of the form on which to operate, and a command to execute for each control on that form that has the Carry tag value in its Tag property. This subroutine loops through each control on the form, and for each one that passes its test, it calls the built-in Eval() function to execute the function whose name is passed as a parameter, passing it information about the current control. We

FIGURE 7.8:

City and State values are carried over from record to record as you add new records.

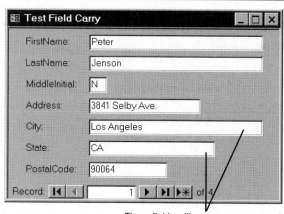

These fields will carry to a new record

used this mechanism here to show how you can write one procedure that can loop through all the controls on a form (or through all the objects in any collection), acting on each one. Rather than write the looping and checking code multiple times, you can localize the code to one location and call the appropriate function from within the loop. There are, of course, other ways to accomplish the same end result: you could pass in a constant indicating which function to call, for example. This seemed like a good opportunity to show off the powerful Eval() function, which is often forgotten in application development.

For the carrying code to work, your form must contain code attached to several form events. In the form's Load event you need code that places the Carry tag value into the Tag property for the fields you're interested in carrying over. You could also place the value

```
Carry=-1;
```

into the Tag properties for the selected controls at design time and not worry about doing it when the form loads. If you have a large number of fields to carry over, this method may result in better performance, since there's less code to run at form-load time. A sample Form_Load event procedure might look like this:

```
Sub Form_Load()
    ' Replace these two lines with calls to glrCtlTagPutItem()
    ' for each field on your form for which you want to
    ' carry values.
    glrCtlTagPutItem Me!City, "Carry", True
    glrCtlTagPutItem Me!State, "Carry", True
End Sub
```

After you enter data into the new record, you'll want to store it away to be used in creating the next new record. To do this, attach code to the AfterUpdate event of the form to walk through all the controls on the form and copy the values for "tagged" fields into the DefaultValue property of the appropriate controls:

```
Sub Form_AfterUpdate()
    glrSweep Me, "glrStoreValues"
End Sub
```

When you move to the new record, Access will use the DefaultValue property to fill in the values for the new row.

The function that does the real work, glrStoreValues(), receives the name of the form, and the name of the specific control, from the glrSweep() function. It stores the current value of the control, as a string, into the control's DefaultValue property, so that the next time you move to the new row, Access will fill in the current value for you:

```
Set ctl = Forms(strForm)(strControl)
If Err = 0 Then
    ctl.DefaultValue = glrcQuote & ctl.Value & glrcQuote
End If
```

One interesting item to note about this function is its rather odd syntax:

```
Set ctl = Forms(strForm)(strControl)
```

In this case strForm and strControl are both string variables. If you knew the names of these two objects, you could use the standard syntax

Set ctl = *Forms!YourForm!YourControl*

Because you know neither of these values until run time, you can use the variable syntax instead. This syntax can save you a few lines of code each time you use it. That is, the alternative is to use something like this:

```
Dim frm As Form
Set frm = Forms(strForm)
Set ctl = frm(strControl)
```

To use basCarry in your own applications, follow these steps:

1. Import the basCarry module from CH07.MDB.

2. Import the basParse module from CH07.MDB.

3. Attach code, as mentioned above, to your form's Open and AfterUpdate events.

Using the Eval() Function

You can use the Eval() function in Access to evaluate an expression and return its value. It provides a mechanism for emulating other languages' (such as C/C++) support for function pointers. This powerful concept is one of the bases of object-oriented languages.

VBA cannot do all that C/C++ can, nor does it attempt to. But the Eval() function can give you some very powerful capabilities. As described in the online help, the Eval() function "Evaluates an expression and returns its value." What Help doesn't state is that the expression can be just about anything!

To use Eval() to execute functions, you just need to build a string expression that, when evaluated, creates the function call you want. Since the Eval() function must retrieve a value and return it, the expression you build must either return a value itself or call a function that returns a value. (Subroutines are not allowed.) In addition, any functions you call must be global in scope. (You won't be able to call any functions that are private.)

You may work with Access for a long time before you find a situation for which Eval() is uniquely suited. When you do, however, its availability will make your code much tighter and easier to maintain.

The ControlSource Property and Calculated Controls

Access developers often use text boxes to display calculated values. Figure 7.9 shows a form with a DueDate field, drawing its data from a table, and two text boxes displaying the number of days overdue for this payment. To create a calculated control, you have two choices:

- Use an expression.
- Use a user-defined function.

The second and third text boxes on the sample form use one of the preceding methods for calculating the number of days late.

In either case you must precede the value in the property sheet with an equal sign (=), which indicates to Access that it must include what follows.

To create an expression that will be evaluated when the control gets recalculated—for example, to calculate the past due amount—use the expression

```
=Date() - CVDate([txtDueDate])
```

This simple expression calculates the number of days since the due date and displays it. Figure 7.9 shows this example in action.

Your other option is to create a function that places a value in the text box.

NOTE

In general, if you want a specific event to place a value into a control on a form, it is not enough to specify a function call in the property sheet. Your function must explicitly place its value into the control. In most properties, Access completely disregards the return value from the function. Combined with the fact that Access can call only functions (which must return values), not subroutines (which do not return values), from the property sheet, it's easy to get confused. On top of that, Access is inconsistent as to how it treats function calls from the property sheet. The DefaultValue and ControlSource properties, for example, pass the return value from a function call on to the text box. All event properties disregard the return value.

TIP

Access provides five object properties of the Screen object: Active-Control, PreviousControl, ActiveForm, ActiveDatasheet, and Active-Report. Screen.ActiveControl returns the currently active control, Screen.PreviousControl the last active control, Screen.Active-Form the currently active form, Screen.ActiveDatasheet the currently active datasheet, and Screen.ActiveReport the currently active report. You might be tempted to count on these properties to allow you to write generic functions to be called from forms. In several cases these are helpful, but for the most part you're better off passing the Form property (from the property sheet) or the Me object (from CBF) down to functions called in global modules. The main problem is that often in the Access environment there is actually no current form or control. Attempting to access one of these properties at those times causes a run-time error. This makes it particularly difficult to debug code that contains these objects.

Using the same example as above, you could create a function:

```
Function CalcHowLate()
    CalcHowLate = Date() - CVDate(Me!txtDueDate)
End Function
```

FIGURE 7.9:

Using calculated controls on a form. Note that both methods (using an expression and using a function) return the same value.

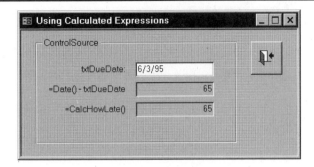

To use a function to supply the ControlSource value, precede its name with an equal (=) sign. That is, use =CalcHowLate() in this example. Figure 7.9 shows this form in action.

> **NOTE**
>
> The expression in the previous example uses the CVDate( ) function to convert the value in the text box into a date. Because all control values are stored internally as variants but this calculation requires a date value, the CVDate( ) function ensures that Access understands what it is the expression needs to do.

Using Two-State Controls (the Yes/No Crowd)

All the controls described in the following sections (toggle button, option button, and check box) can represent data that has two states when used outside an option group on a form. (When grouped in an option group, they can represent more information.) Therefore, they all represent reasonable ways to present the user with yes/no data for acceptance. Each represents its two states differently, and you can use these differences to your advantage.

If you also need to represent a third state in which you don't yet know the value for the control, Access provides the TripleState property for toggle buttons, option buttons, and check boxes, as long as they're not embedded in an option group.

The Toggle Button

In an option group, the toggle button has two states: up and down. Its "up" state represents the False/No condition (unselected), and its "down" state represents the True/Yes condition (selected). It can display either text or a picture (but, unfortunately, not both). Access creates a dithered version of the picture on the button for its depressed state, relieving you from having to supply two separate bitmaps, one for the "up" state and one for the "down" state. Outside an option group, you can set the TripleState property to allow the button to also show a null value.

TIP If you require a button that includes both text and a picture, you can create a bitmap in Paint that includes both and use that bitmap as the image for your button. From the user's perspective, it will look right, even though it's just a bitmap. You can even include a hot key: in your bitmap, underline the character you'd like to have activate the button, and include, in the button's Caption property, a string with that specific character preceded with "&" ("&A", for example, to make Alt+A trigger your button).

Using toggle buttons to represent yes/no information to the user can make your forms more visually appealing than using simple check boxes, but they make sense in only a limited number of situations. If your user is inputting information that answers a simple yes/no question, toggle buttons aren't as clear as check boxes. On the other hand, if you are gathering other two-state information (alive or deceased, U.S. citizen or not), toggle buttons often are quite useful. Here's the real test: if you're tempted to use a toggle button alone on a form with a text description, use a check box instead. If you need a group of check boxes or if you can use a picture instead of text, consider using toggle buttons.

The Option Button

Option buttons do represent two states, but common usage suggests you use them most often in option groups to allow selection of a single item from the group. In that situation the two states can be thought of as "selected" and "not selected."

For that reason, programmers often refer to option buttons as *radio buttons*, harkening back to the automobile radios of yesteryear with mechanical buttons that you could depress only one at a time to select a station and pressing one "un-pressed" the rest.

When representing yes/no data, the option button displays a filled circle when it's in the True/Yes state. When representing the False/No state, it displays just an empty ring.

Although you can use option buttons alone on a form and can use the TripleState property in that situation, avoid using single option buttons on forms. You should limit their usage to the radio button image in option groups. If you need a single option button, use a check box instead.

The Check Box

The check box is the standard two-state control. When in the Yes (True) state, the control displays a check mark inside a box. When in the No (False) state, it displays just an empty box. Check boxes commonly stand alone or are used in groups to select multiple options. You can use check boxes in option groups, but common usage suggests you avoid this situation. Using check boxes in an option group allows you to choose only a single value, and this spoils the imagery of check boxes—allowing multiple choices. If you want to make a group of check boxes *look* like an option group, you can enclose them within a rectangle. Figure 7.10 shows all the combinations of subcontrols.

FIGURE 7.10:

All the two-state controls (in rectangles, not option groups, so they can be null)

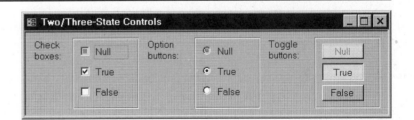

Using Option Groups—
Controls inside Controls

The option group is a one-of-a-kind control in Access. It allows you to group multiple controls (toggle buttons, option buttons, or check boxes) for the purpose of choosing a single value. Each subcontrol has its own value (set in its OptionValue property), and when it's chosen it assigns that value to the option group. Usually an option group consists of multiples of a single type of control. Figure 7.11 shows three different option groups, one for each type of subcontrol. In addition, this figure includes an option group composed of various subcontrols. Although there's no reason not to create an option group combining different subcontrols, it's a good idea to avoid doing so, since it's confusing and serves no real purpose.

FIGURE 7.11:

Four option group examples. We don't recommend creating option groups composed of different subcontrols.

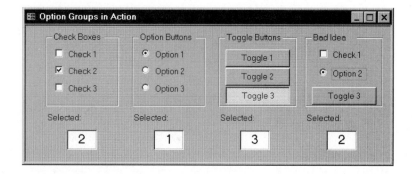

There's nothing keeping you from assigning the same OptionValue property to multiple subcontrols. As a matter of fact, if you copy a control within an option group, Access assigns the new control the same option value as the original control. This can be confusing, because choosing one subcontrol will simultaneously select all subcontrols with the same OptionValue property. On the other hand, there's nothing keeping you from skipping option values. They need not be contiguous. The only limitation is that they must be Integer or Long Integer values (whole numbers).

TIP

In the interest of preserving screen real-estate and simplifying your input forms, consider using a combo box if you find your option group includes more than five items. Option groups take up a great deal of space on the screen, and with more than five subcontrols in the group, it becomes difficult to choose the correct item.

The value of an option group can be only a single whole number, no matter how much you'd like an option group to return a string or any other datatype. This means the option value of each internal subcontrol is also limited to being a whole number. If you must use text values, for example, you can create an array of strings in your application and use the value returned from the option group as an index into your array. (See the section "Returning 'Real' Information from Option Groups" later in this chapter for information on returning string values.)

TIP

Since option groups can return only a single value, you are limited to making only one choice from the group of subcontrols inside it. This design indicates you would be better off using only toggle buttons or option buttons in an option group, because each of those is suited for making a single choice. If you need an option group that contains check boxes, allowing you to choose several items, consider creating a "faux" option group. To do this, enclose your check boxes within a rectangle (rather than within an option group). This way they'll look as though they are part of an option group but will allow multiple selections. Note, though, that you will have to examine each check box separately to find which ones you have selected. If you have controls inside an option group, you don't need to examine each separately, because all you care about is the single control you've selected, and Access assigns that value to the option group.

Access treats the option group, once it's populated with subcontrols, as a single control; when you select the container and move it, all the internal controls move, too. When you delete the container, Access deletes all the internal controls. Unless you're aware that this will happen, it can cause havoc in your development. Make sure you really intend to delete all the internal controls before you delete an option group!

Moving Controls to a New Neighborhood

You'll find that moving a currently existing control into an option group does not work. Although the subcontrol will appear to be inside the option group, the two will not function together. To add items to an option group, use either of the following two methods:

- **Create a new control:** Select the option group and then choose your subcontrol from the toolbar and place it in the option group. Note that when you move the cursor to drop a subcontrol, the option group becomes highlighted as you pass the cursor over it. This visual prompt indicates that the option group is ready to receive a subcontrol.

- **Cut-and-paste an existing control:** Once you've used the Edit ➤ Cut menu item to cut the control, select the option group. With the option group selected, choose Edit ➤ Paste. Access places the control inside the option group as a real, active subcontrol.

NOTE   Controls in an option group lose their properties that deal with the underlying data, such as the ControlSource, TripleState, and ValidationRule properties, since they are no longer independent representations of data from the underlying record source. On the other hand, they gain the OptionValue property, since you must assign each a unique value. This is the value the control will return to the option group once you've made a choice. Therefore, you'll note that the property sheet for an independent control is a bit different from the property sheet for an identical control in an option group.

Assigning and Retrieving Values

Because the option group's value is the value of the chosen subcontrol, you can assign a value to the option group by making an assignment to the option group name. For example, the following code assigns the value 3 to the option group grpTestGroup:

```
Me!grpTestGroup = 3
```

Access would select the subcontrol in grpTestGroup that had the OptionValue of 3.

Likewise, you can retrieve the value of the option group just by referencing its name. The expression

```
varNewValue = Me!grpTestGroup
```

assigns the value chosen in grpTestGroup to the variant variable varNewValue.

To be completely clear, the reason the previous assignment works is that you're actually assigning the Value property of grpTestGroup to varNewValue. Since the Value property of a control is its default property, Access knows that's what you meant when you specified no property at all.

NOTE   The option group's value is Null when there are no items chosen. Therefore, just as with any other form control, consider retrieving its value into a variant-type variable that can handle the possible null return value.

Returning "Real" Information from Option Groups

Although option groups can return only integral values, you can work around this problem if you want an option group to gather and show information from a text field that has only a limited number of possible values. It may be that you're sharing data with other applications or that you just aren't able to change the field format to meet Access' requirements. In that case you'll need a few tricks to use option groups to represent textual information.

TIP

If at all possible, try to reorganize your tables in such a way that limited-option fields can be stored as whole numbers. Not only does this make it simple to use an option group to show the data, it cuts down on memory usage. Imagine you have 1000 records, with one of the following in the Delivery field: "Overnight", "2nd Day Air", or "Ground". Not only is this field prone to data entry problems, it's using a lot more disk/memory space than necessary. If you were to create a small table with those three values and an integer attached to each, you could just store the integers in your main table. Data entry would be simpler, you'd be using less memory, and everyone involved would be happier.

To bind the option group to text values rather than integer values, create an extra text box on your form. Normally you would make this text box invisible (set its Visible property to No), but for this example it will stay visible. Figure 7.12 shows the finished form (frmDelivery in CH07.MDB). For the purposes of this example, the option group's name is grpDelivery and the text box's name is txtDelivery. The text box is bound to the field containing the text, and the option group is unbound; the text box is the control that will send and receive data to and from the underlying table, and the option group will be used just to collect and display that data.

FIGURE 7.12:

Binding an option group to a text value. Note the bound text box, which normally would be invisible.

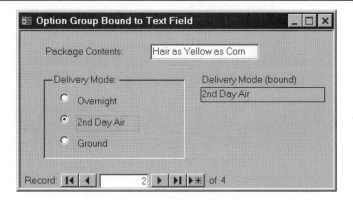

Once you have the bound text box on the form, you need to solve two problems:

- As you move from record to record, how do you get the right option in the option group to be chosen?

- As you make a choice in the option group, how do you get its value written out to the underlying data, if it's not bound?

To answer the first question you need to attach code to the form's Current event. Access fires off this event each time it makes a record current and allows you to set the value of the option group for each record. For this simple case you can use the Switch() function, which returns the value corresponding to the first True statement it finds in its parameters:

```
Me!grpDelivery = Switch(Me!txtDelivery = "Overnight", 1, _
 Me!txtDelivery = "2nd Day Air", 2, _
 Me!txtDelivery = "Ground", 3, True, Null)
```

Using the Switch( ) Function

You can use Switch( ) to take the place of nested If...Then...Else...End If statements. Its general syntax is

retval = Switch(*expr1*, *var1* [, *expr2*, *var2*...[, *expr7*, *var7*]])

where *expr1* through *expr7* are expressions that return either True (–1) or False (0) and *var1* through *var7* are the values to be returned if the corresponding expression is True. Switch() returns the value corresponding to the first expression it finds in its list that returns True.

For example, the Switch() function call in the previous example:

```
Me!grpDelivery = Switch(Me!txtDelivery = "Overnight", 1, _
 Me!txtDelivery = "2nd Day Air", 2, _
 Me!txtDelivery = "Ground", 3, True, Null)
```

could have been written as

```
If Me!txtDelivery = "Overnight" Then
    Me!grpDelivery = 1
ElseIf Me!txtDelivery = "2nd Day Air" Then
    Me!grpDelivery = 2
ElseIf Me!txtDelivery = "Ground" Then
    Me!grpDelivery = 3
```

```
Else
    Me!grpDelivery = Null
End If
```

Be aware of a few issues that arise when you use Switch():

- You can include up to seven expression/value pairs. To check more than seven different expressions, you need to use some other control structure—most likely a Select Case structure.

- Switch( ) returns Null if either none of the expressions return a True value or if the value associated with the first True expression is Null.

- Although only one of the expressions may be True, Access will evaluate every one of the expressions. This can lead to undesirable side effects. For example, if you try this:

```
varValue = Switch(x = 0 Or y = 0, 0, x >= y, x/y, x < y, y/x)
```

you will inevitably end up with an Overflow error since, if either x or y is 0, you end up dividing by 0 even though it appears that you've checked for that in the first expression.

To answer the second question, you need to attach code to the AfterUpdate event of the option group. This code will place the correct value into the bound txtDelivery text box, which will, in turn, send it to the underlying data source. For this example, you should use code like this:

```
Me!txtDelivery = Choose(Me!grpDelivery, "Overnight", _
 "2nd Day Air", "Ground")
```

Using the Choose( ) Function

Like the Switch( ) function, the Choose( ) function is yet another replacement for nested If…Then…Else…End If statements. It takes an integer between 1 and 13 as its first parameter and then a list of up to 13 parameters from which to choose. Access returns the value corresponding, in position, to the index you passed as the first parameter. Its general syntax is

Choose(intIndex, *expr1* [, *expr2*]…)

Be aware of the following issues that arise when you use Choose():

- You can include only 13 possible return values. To include more you need to use some other control structure—most likely a Select Case structure.

- The index value can only be a value between 1 and 13, inclusive. If you pass a floating-point value, Access converts it to an integer following the same rules it does for the Fix() function.

- Although Choose() returns only one of the values, it evaluates them all. Beware of possible side effects. If you call a function in one or more expressions, each of those functions will be called. For example, if each of your expressions called the InputBox() function, each and every one of the expressions would get evaluated, causing the InputBox() dialog box to pop up multiple times as Access evaluated the list of expressions.

Using List and Combo Boxes

List boxes and combo boxes (otherwise known as drop-down list boxes) share many similar properties and uses. Combo boxes combine a text box and a list box in one control. Both list and combo boxes present a list of values, allowing you to choose a single item. They can present multiple columns of data, and you can use them as full data structures, with hidden columns that can contain data.

Differences between List and Combo Boxes

Although list and combo boxes share many of the same properties, events, and uses, several of their specific details are unique to their particular control type. Table 7.2 lists those idiosyncrasies.

Important Properties of List and Combo Boxes

Access' Control Wizards can perform most of the work of creating list and combo boxes on your forms. At times, though, you might want to create the combo or list box from scratch, if you find you don't get the flexibility you need when using the

TABLE 7.2: Differences between List and Combo Boxes

Item	List Box	Combo Box
Item choices	Allows you to choose only from the items already in the list	Allows you either to choose from the values in the list or to add new ones. This actually depends on the LimitToList property and also on which column is bound to the underlying field (For more information, see the section "The LimitToList Problem" later in this chapter.)
Screen real estate	Takes up as much space as you assign it. Works best when as many items as possible are immediately visible	Takes up the space of a single text box when it doesn't have the input focus and as many lines as you specify (in the ListRows property) when it has the focus
Keyboard handling	Matches only the first character of items in its list against letters you press. Pressing an M matches the first item that starts with M. Pressing it again finds the next, and so on. Pressing a different letter finds the first item that starts with that letter	Performs an incremental search as you type. That is, if you press M, it scrolls to find the first item that begins with M. If you then press i, it finds the first item that begins with Mi and scrolls to that item. Pressing Backspace returns the selection to the previous item you chose. In addition, if you've set the AutoExpand property to Yes, as you type, Access automatically finds and displays the first underlying data element that matches the number of characters you've typed so far. This auto-fill feature, similar to that found in several popular financial packages, is extremely useful, especially when combined with the LimitToList property. On the other hand, it does slow down data entry
Selected Items	List boxes can be configured to allow multiple selections. Once you set the MultiSelect property appropriately, you can choose one or more contiguous or noncontiguous items	Combo boxes can never select more than a single item

Wizard. List and combo boxes provide great flexibility in how they allow you, as a programmer, to display information to the user while controlling the input. Unfortunately, with this degree of flexibility, the plethora of options can be daunting. Many of the properties are interrelated and collectively affect how the control operates. The following sections detail some of the properties you need to understand to get the full benefit of these controls.

The Name Property

The Name property specifies the internal reference name for the control. The actual value of this property has no real significance, except as a convenience for the programmer.

Many beginning Access programmers confuse the Name property with the ControlSource property. The control name specifies only the name by which you, the programmer, will refer to the control. It has nothing to do with the underlying data, while the control source is actually linked with the data.

The ControlSource Property

The ControlSource property links the control with the underlying data. Specifying a field name tells Access where to retrieve the value of the control and where to place the value returned from the control once you select an item. The control returns the value from the column set in the BoundColumn property. With other controls, you can enter an expression preceded by an equal (=) sign for the ControlSource property. With list and combo boxes, this option succeeds only in making the control read-only.

The RowSourceType Property

The RowSourceType property specifies where to retrieve the rows of data the control displays. The options are

- **Table/Query:** The data comes from a table or query or from a SQL expression. In any case, the RowSource property specifies the table/query name or the SQL expression that will retrieve the dataset.

- **Value List:** The data comes from a list you specify explicitly in the RowSource property.

- **Field List:** The data will consist of a list of fields from the table or query specified in the RowSource property.

- **(User-Defined):** If you specify a function name with no equal sign and no trailing parentheses, Access calls it to fill the list or combo box. (See the section "Filling a List or Combo Box Programmatically" later in this chapter for more information.)

The RowSource Property

The RowSource property specifies which data to retrieve for presentation in the list or combo box. Its syntax depends on the RowSourceType property. Figure 7.13 (frmLists from CH07.MDB) demonstrates some of the methods of filling a list box via the property sheet. The following sections detail the information you need to supply for the RowSource property, based on your choice in the RowSourceType property.

Table/Query   Enter the name of a table, query, or SQL expression that will retrieve the data you wish to display. Here are some examples:

- **tblNames:** Retrieves as many columns from the table named tblNames as the ColumnCount property specifies.

- **SELECT Name, Address, Age FROM tblNames ORDER BY Age:** Retrieves a maximum of three columns from tblNames, ordered by age. If the number in the ColumnCount property is less than the requested number of columns in the RowSource, the ColumnCount property controls the number of columns Access displays.

FIGURE 7.13:

One form showing some of the various methods of filling a list or combo box via the property sheet

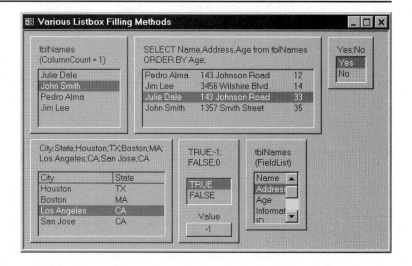

WARNING   If you use a table name as the RowSource, you must be aware of changes to the table. For example, making a database replicable will add new columns to the front of every table and will therefore break such combo boxes. (See Chapter 13 for more information on replication.)

Value List   Enter a list of values, separated by semicolons, one row at a time (up to 2048 characters). If the ColumnHeads property is Yes, the first row of data will go into the column headings in the control. If you set the ColumnCount property incorrectly, the data will not go into the columns and rows as you had planned. Here are some examples:

- **Yes;No:** Displays just the two values Yes and No. Note that the display is also tied to the ColumnCount property. If the ColumnCount is 1, Yes and No each appears in its own row. If the ColumnCount is 2 or higher, Yes and No both appear on the first row of the control.

- **City;State;Houston;TX;Boston;MA;Los Angeles;CA;San Jose;CA:** Displays a two-column list with four rows of data, assuming these properties:

    ColumnCount = 2

    ColumnHeads = Yes

- **True;-1;False;0:** Displays just the two values True and False and stores a yes/no value back to the underlying field, given these properties:

    ColumnCount = 2

    ColumnWidths = ;0

    BoundColumn = 2

    ControlSource = a Yes/No field from the underlying data source

Figure 7.13 shows these examples, and more, in action.

Field List   Enter the name of a table or query from the form's RecordSource. The fields will be listed in their physical order in the table or in the order in which they were placed into the query. There is no way to alphabetize the list.

The ColumnCount Property

The ColumnCount property controls the number of columns of data Access will store in the control's data area. The actual number of displayed columns can be no more than the number specified in this property, but it might be less, depending on the contents of the ColumnWidths property. Even if you render some of the data invisible (by using a ColumnWidth setting of 0), it's still loaded into the control, and you can retrieve it by using the Column property.

Set the ColumnCount property with a number or a numeric value. Access rounds nonintegral values to the nearest whole number.

The ColumnWidths Property

The ColumnWidths property sets the widths of the columns in the control and should be filled with a semicolon-delimited list of numbers, one per column. The default width is approximately 1 inch or 3 centimeters, depending on the unit of measurement. Leaving a value out of the list accepts the default width. A setting of 0 hides a column. If the physical area dedicated to the control is not wide enough to display all the columns, Access truncates the right-most column, and the control displays horizontal scroll bars. Note that a single-column control will never have horizontal scroll bars, no matter how wide that single column is.

For each of the examples, the control contains four columns and is 5 inches wide. All measurements are in inches:

- **2;2;2;2:** Each column is 2 inches wide. Since this is 3 inches wider than the control, Access provides horizontal scroll bars.

- **2:** The first column is 2 inches wide, and the rest assume the default width (1 inch).

- **2;0;3;0:** The first and third columns are displayed. The second and fourth are hidden.

- **(Blank):** All four columns are evenly spaced over the width of the control, since the control is wider than the sum of the default widths. If it were narrower than the total widths, the first three columns would each be 1 inch wide (the default width) and the last column would use the rest of the space (2 inches).

Figure 7.14 shows these example list boxes (frmListWidths from CH07.MDB).

FIGURE 7.14:

Various ColumnWidths settings

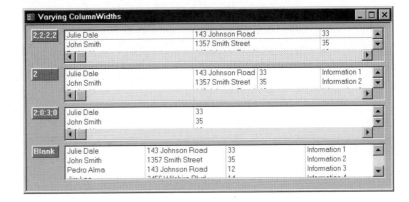

The ColumnHeads Property

The ColumnHeads property indicates whether or not Access should display a single row of column headings at the top of the control. (For combo boxes, Access displays this heading row only when you've asked it to expose the drop-down list.) When the RowSourceType property is ValueList, the first row of data goes into the header. If the RowSourceType is FieldList, the first field in the list goes into the header row. You should therefore not use the FieldList row source type when displaying column headers. If you do, Access displays field names in the header row.

The BoundColumn Property

The BoundColumn property indicates which of the columns in the control will actually be returned when you've made a selection from the list. This means the control returns the value from this column when you assign its value to a variable, for example.

Normal Operation   You must set the BoundColumn property as an integer between 0 and the number stored in the ColumnCount property. To retrieve the value from the control, use an expression like this:

```
varMyVariable = Me!cboTestCombo
```

The variable varMyVariable receives the value from the chosen row in cboTest-Combo, from the column specified in its BoundColumn property.

To set the value of the control, use an expression like this:

```
Me!cboTestCombo = varMyVariable
```

This code selects the first row in cboTestCombo in which the value in the column specified in the BoundColumn property matches the value stored in varMyVariable. If Access can't find a match, the control value will be Null.

The Special Case   If you set the BoundColumn property to 0, Access returns the selected row number in the control; the value of the control will be the row number of the selected row. Although this isn't very useful for bound controls—the chosen row number won't mean much when stored in a database—it can be very useful if you need to select a particular row in the control.

Suppose, for example, you want to make sure you've selected the first row of an unbound list box for each record, before the user even gets a chance to make a choice. Normally, to specify the row of the control you want selected, you would just assign a value to the control.

Unfortunately, in some cases (for example, when the RowSource of the control is a SQL query), you don't know the value of the bound field in the first row. To get around this problem, you can set the BoundColumn property to 0. Once you've done this, you can just assign the control the value 0, which will select the first row. (The row values are zero based.) To retrieve values from a control with the Bound-Column set to 0, use the Column property, discussed in the next section. For an example of setting the BoundColumn property to 0, see the section "Making Multiple Selections in a List Box" later in this chapter.

There are alternatives, of course. The ItemData method of a list or combo box returns the data from the bound column in any row you want. For example, rather than set the BoundColumn property to 0 in order to initialize a list box to the first row, you can set the default value to this expression instead:

```
=cboExample.ItemData(0)
```

The Column Property

The Column property of list and combo boxes is not available at design time but figures prominently at run time. It allows you access to data in any of the columns of any row of the control. The general syntax looks like this:

$$value = FormReference!ListOrCombo.\text{Column}(column[, row])$$

In a fit of nonstandardization, Access uses zero-based numbers for the column and row numbers: when you set the BoundColumn property to 1, you use Column(0) to retrieve the value stored there.

For example, to retrieve the data stored in the second column of the chosen row of cboTestCombo, use

```
varTestVariable = Me!cboTestCombo.Column(1)
```

To retrieve the value in the third column of the fourth row of cboTestCombo, use

```
varTestVariable = Me!cboTestCombo(2, 3)
```

Present a Name, Store an ID

Given these facts:

- A list/combo box can contain more than one column (ColumnCount > 0).
- The first visible column is the one Access displays in the text box portion of the combo box.
- Any column in the list/combo box can be bound to the underlying data (BoundColumn).
- You can set the width of any column to 0, rendering it invisible (Column Widths).
- List/combo boxes have their own separate source of data (RowSource).

it's easy to create a list or combo box that displays user-friendly information (such as a name) but stores information the user doesn't normally care to see (such as a counter value). Figure 7.15 shows such a combo box in action. In this example you're filling in a shipping form and want to choose the delivery method from a combo box. The delivery method is stored as an integer, but you can't expect users to remember the integer associated with each carrier. Therefore, you can use a query (qryDeliveryMethod) to feed the data for the combo's RowSource property. The second column in the combo has been made invisible (ColumnWidths set to ";0"), and the combo box will store the chosen value in its second column, the ID, to the underlying data (BoundColumn = 2, ControlSource = *DeliveryMethod*). You should be able to apply this same method to any situation in which you want to present the user with one piece of information but store a different, related piece of information.

FIGURE 7.15:

Display text, but store an ID to the underlying data.

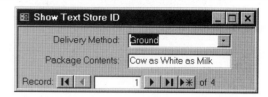

> **TIP**
>
> When your combo is bound to a numeric field (as it is in the previous example), you need to set the TextAlign property yourself. Because Access thinks you're really displaying a numeric value, it aligns the text to the right (which is how it treats numeric values). Set the TextAlign property manually to display the text the way you want it aligned.

Multi-Select List Boxes

One of the most oft-heard complaints about Access list boxes has always been that you could select only a single item. Access 95 finally adds a MultiSelect property for list boxes, allowing you to choose from three options, shown in the following table:

Setting	Description	Value
None	Single selection only (default)	0
Extended	Shift + click or Shift + arrow key extends the selection from the previously selected item to the current item. Ctrl + click selects or deselects an item	1
Simple	The user selects or deselects multiple items by choosing them with the mouse or pressing the spacebar	2

By choosing Extended or Simple, you can choose one or more items from the list box.

The MultiSelect property is read-only at run time. You won't be able to switch selection types while your form is in use; you can do so only at design time.

How can you tell which items are selected? There are two methods, and they're both read/write. That is, you can both retrieve the selected list and set it. Figure 7.16 shows a list box with its MultiSelect property set to Extended. As you select each item, code attached to the list box's AfterUpdate event updates the text box to its right.

FIGURE 7.16:

Multi-select list boxes allow you to Shift + click and Ctrl + click on multiple items.

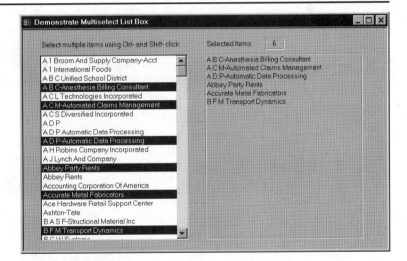

The Selected Property

The Selected property of a list box returns an array of Boolean values, one for each row of data in the list box. If there are 100 items in the list box, the Selected property will return an array of 100 True or False values. Each value in the array indicates whether or not the corresponding item in the list is selected. You can check to see whether the first item is selected:

```
If Me!lstCompanies.Selected(0) Then
    MsgBox "You've selected the first item!"
End If
```

or you can set the first four items as selected (as long as you've set the MultiSelect property to something other than None):

```
With Me!lstCompanies
    For intI = 0 To 3
        .Selected(intI) = True
    Next intI
End With
```

At the time of this writing, you cannot use the Selected array with a single-select list box during the list box's AfterUpdate event, because it hasn't yet been updated at that point. After that event it's current, but it will always have only one item that's True; the rest will always be False, since you can select only one item in the list box. This limits its usefulness for single-select list boxes.

The ItemsSelected Property

If you want to do something with every selected item in a multi-select list box, you could use the Selected property to return an array of items and walk the array looking for rows in which the Selected array holds a True value. That is, you could use code such as this to list out the selected items:

```
Dim intI As Integer
With Me!lstCompanies
    For intI = 0 To .ListCount - 1
        If .Selected(intI) Then
            Debug.Print .ItemData(intI)
        End If
    Next intI
End With
```

This requires Access to loop through every single row of the Selected array, which is a lot of effort. To make this simpler, Access supplies the ItemsSelected property, which returns a collection of selected row numbers. To do something with each selected item, just walk this collection, working with each item in the collection, as in this fragment from frmMultiSelect (Figure 7.16):

```
' Show the list of selected companies.
With Me!lstCompanies
    For Each varItem In .ItemsSelected
        strList = strList & .Column(0, varItem) & vbCrLf
    Next varItem
    Me!txtSelected = strList
End If
```

This example also uses the ability of the Column property of a list box to return data from any column of any row. In this case you want the data from the first column (column number 0) in the row specified by varItem.

Like any other collection, the ItemsSelected collection provides a Count property that tells you how many items are currently selected. In frmMultiSelect, the text box showing the number of selected items has this expression as its ControlSource:

```
=lstCompanies.ItemsSelected.Count
```

The LimitToList Problem

The LimitToList property indicates to Access whether or not it should allow you to enter new values into a combo box. Setting this property to No allows you to disregard the current list of values and enter a new one, and setting it to Yes forces you to choose a value from the current list. If you set your combo box's BoundColumn property to any column aside from the first visible column, Access will (and must) set the LimitToList property to Yes.

You may not, at first thought, agree with this design decision. Imagine, though, for a moment, what's really going on here. Access displays and lets you enter values for the first visible column in the combo box. Therefore, if the control's Bound-Column property is set to 1, Access can take whatever it is you type and store it in the underlying data, even if it's not currently in the list. On the other hand, if the BoundColumn property is greater than 1 and you enter a value that's not already part of the list, Access needs to be able to store a value it doesn't have. Therefore, Access has no choice but to disallow new entries into combo boxes where the first column isn't displaying the bound field. Figure 7.17 shows, in pictorial form, why Access must make this limitation.

Combo boxes don't always do exactly what you might expect in terms of string matching. For example, if the LimitToList property is set to Yes, you might think that typing enough characters to find a match at all would be sufficient for Access to accept the selected value. That is not the case. You must type enough characters to indicate a *unique* match before Access will accept your value and let you leave the field. This can be frustrating for users who will type some characters, see the match in the combo box, and attempt to accept that value by pressing ↵. Unless the characters they've typed so far constitute a unique match,

FIGURE 7.17:

LimitToList must be set to Yes if you've bound your combo box to a column other than the first column.

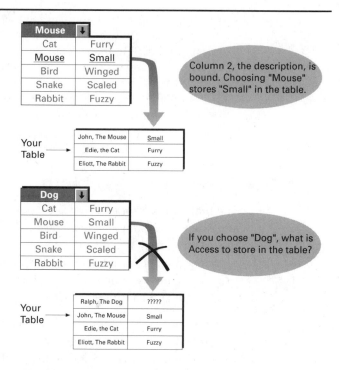

they'll need to keep typing. Combining the LimitToList property with the AutoExpand property, though, will make many users happy. If you set both Limit-ToList and AutoExpand to Yes, your users can leave the combo box as soon as Access has found any matching value in the list. This will, however, add some serious processing overhead. Although combo box performance in Access 95 has been greatly improved, if you find the performance still doesn't meet your needs, turn off the AutoExpand property.

In addition, null values are always a problem. If the LimitToList property is Yes and you type a value into a combo box and then delete it by backspacing over all the characters, the value now will not match any value in your list (unless you happen to have an empty value in the list). In previous versions of Access, you were not able to leave the combo box. In Access 95, LimitToList accepts null values, so you can just delete the value and exit. Another easy way out is to press the Esc key, which undoes your change and lets you leave the control.

Taming the NotInList Event

When a user attempts to enter an item into a combo box (whose LimitToList property is set to Yes) that doesn't match one of the existing items in the list, Access triggers the NotInList event. If you have code in the form's module reacting to that event, you can take one of three actions, depending on how you fill in the Response argument that Access passes to the subroutine:

- If you place the value acDataErrDisplay in Response, Access displays its standard error message.

- If you place acDataErrContinue in Response, Access doesn't display its error message, giving you the chance to display your own. If you use this option, make sure you really do display your own error message. Otherwise, users will be confused.

- If you place acDataErrAdded in Response, you must add the item to the underlying record source, and then Access requeries the combo box for you, effectively adding it to the list.

Since the third option is the most interesting, this option is the focus of the following discussion.

Access passes your procedure two parameters: NewData contains the current text in the combo box, and Response allows you to send back the results of your subroutine.

The following simple case, from frmNotInList in CH07.MDB, just asks the user whether or not to add the new item to the list:

```
Private Sub cboNotInList_NotInList(NewData As String, _
 Response As Integer)
    Dim strMsg As String
    Dim rst As Recordset
    Dim db As Database

    strMsg = "'" & NewData & "' is not in the list. "
    strMsg = strMsg & "Would you like to add it?"
    If MsgBox(strMsg, vbYesNo + vbQuestion, "New Company") = _
     vbNo Then
        Response = acDataErrDisplay
    Else
```

```
Set db = CurrentDb()
    Set rst = db.OpenRecordset("tblCompanies")
    rst.AddNew
        rst!Company = NewData
    rst.Update
    Response = acDataErrAdded
    rst.Close
End If
End Sub
```

The code first pops up a message box, asking you whether to add the new value. If you consent, the procedure runs code to add the new value. By passing back acDataErrAdded in the Response parameter, you're telling Access it should requery the combo and then try again to verify that the item exists in the list. If the item still isn't in the list for some reason (the sample code doesn't deal with errors, and it ought to), you'll still see the default error message from Access.

In general, your situations won't be this simple. Most likely, you'll need to gather some information from the user before adding a new row to the table. In that case you'll probably want to pop up a form (using the acDialog WindowMode option), gather the information, add it to the table, and then send the acDataErrAdded back to Access to indicate that you've added the new row.

Auto-Drop Combo Boxes

In many situations you may want to have a combo box drop down automatically when you enter the combo box. Although this was possible in earlier versions of Access, it was difficult to implement reliably. Access 95 provides the DropDown method for combo boxes, which forces a combo box to open.

The simplest solution is to add code to your combo box's GotFocus event:

```
Sub cboOpenSesame_GotFocus()
    Me!cboOpenSesame.DropDown
End Sub
```

That way, anytime you enter this combo box, it'll drop its list.

The BeforeUpdate and AfterUpdate Events

As with the other controls, Access fires off the BeforeUpdate event just before it attempts to update the underlying record set, and the AfterUpdate event occurs just after. You can attach code to either of these events to trap the selection event in either a list or combo box.

Even more interesting is the ability to trap *movement* in a list box. Access triggers both the BeforeUpdate and AfterUpdate events every time you move the selection bar in a list box. Access must do this because, were you to leave the list box with a Tab or Shift+Tab key at any point, the currently selected item would become the value of the control. This doesn't occur in a combo box, though, since Access won't write any value to the recordset until you've made a selection by clicking, pressing ↵, or leaving the combo. Since you can attach code to the Before/AfterUpdate events in a list box, you can make changes to other controls on your form based on the current value in the list box. Thus, you have the choice of using a "push" method for filling unbound controls on your form (that is, you *push* values into them) in addition to the simpler "pull" method, where the controls use expressions to pull in their values from other sources.

Using Combo and List Boxes to Fill In Other Controls

Access provides several methods by which you can choose a value and have the corresponding data from other fields filled in for you on a form. The method you choose depends on whether or not the controls to be filled in are bound and how many controls you want filled in.

Data Filled In for Free: Using Row Fixup

Row Fixup is a very misunderstood and underutilized feature. It comes into play anytime you have a one-to-many join, your form's RecordsetType property is set to Dynaset (or you're working with a raw query datasheet instead of a form), and you make a change to the joining field on the "many" side of the one-to-many relationship. If the field you change on the "many" side is the linking value between the two tables, Access knows only one set of data will match that value and fills in all the new data, based on the changed value. Row Fixup is really of value only when you're looking up some information for part of a larger form, such as information in an address on a shipping form, since the lookup must take place in a one-to-many relationship.

To see Row Fixup in action, open frmRowFixupDemo in CH07.MDB. This form, shown in Figure 7.18, draws its data from qryRowFixup: this query gets its data from the Customers and Orders tables. The important issue is that the combo box on frmRowFixupDemo is bound to the Customer ID field from the Orders table. It's crucial in this situation that you take the linking field from the *many* side of the relationship. When you make a choice in the combo box, Access automatically looks up the values in the "one" side of the relationship, and those values are the ones you see in the etched read-only text boxes on the form.

FIGURE 7.18:
Row Fixup makes it easy to look up values, but only in a one-to-many relationship.

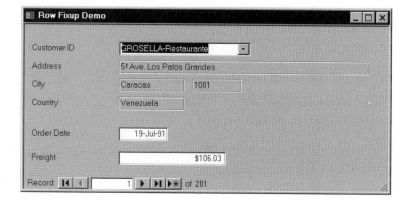

Pulling versus Pushing Data into Controls

Imagine you want to provide a combo box from which you can choose a value. Once a value has been chosen, you want to fill in various other controls on the form with data found in the row that corresponds to the value the user just chose. The methods for doing this differ, depending on whether or not those other fields are bound. If the other controls are bound, you must "push" data into them; otherwise, they can "pull" the new data in themselves. You might think of the pull method as being *passive*, since the data just flows in, and the push method as being *active*, since you must provide code to copy the data from the list or combo box. For examples of each type of mechanism, you can investigate frmPullTest and frmPushTest in CH07.MDB. Figure 7.19 shows frmPullTest in action, and Figure 7.20 shows frmPushTest.

FIGURE 7.19:

frmPullTest uses the Column property in each of its text boxes to retrieve the values from the current row.

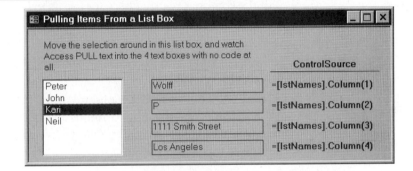

FIGURE 7.20:

frmPushTest uses a small function to copy values from 1stNames to each of the text boxes.

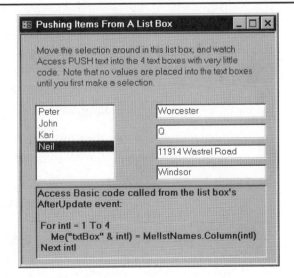

Pulling Data into Unbound Controls

If the controls to be filled in are unbound, their ControlSource property is otherwise empty, and you can use an expression to pull in data from the combo box where the user just made a choice. All references in this example work equally well for list boxes and combo boxes.

To pull in data from the combo box, follow these steps:

1. **Fill the combo:** Create a query (or use an existing table) that contains the data you want to present, plus any other fields you want filled in automatically once the user makes a choice. Later steps will be simpler if you make sure the value to be displayed in the combo is the first field in the table or query, but that isn't imperative.

2. **Prepare the combo:** Set the ColumnWidths property so that the correct column is visible and the other columns are invisible. If the first column is the one you want displayed and you have five columns total, your ColumnWidths setting would be

    ;0;0;0;0

    This tells Access to use the default width for the first column and 0 width (hidden) for the next four columns.

3. **Prepare the other controls:** Set the ControlSource property for each of the controls into which you want data pulled. In each case, set the ControlSource property to

    =*YourCombo*.Column(*n*)

    where *YourCombo* is the ControlName of the combo and *n* is the column number (starting at 0) you want pulled into the control.

Once you've set up the form, Access takes care of the rest. Anytime the combo box changes, the other controls on the form will recalculate and pull the value they need from the combo box. If you're pulling information from a list box, the information will be updated each time you move the selection bar in the list box. This is a convenient way for users to browse items as they move through the list box using the arrow keys. It takes absolutely no programming to accomplish a great deal!

NOTE

Although the method described above is very simple, it exacts a heavy price in performance. Because Access recalculates all dependencies on the form anytime you change a value on the form, you may find that pulling in data from a combo or list box is quite slow if the control contains a large number of rows. If you implement the "pull" method demonstrated here and your form slows down, you'll want to switch to the "push" method described in the next section.

TIP

Since the controls must have a calculated ControlSource for the method described above to work (and are therefore read-only), you might find it useful to also set the Locked property to Yes and the Enabled property to No. This way the control will appear normal, but your user won't be able to make changes.

Pushing Data into Bound Controls

If you need to fill in controls that are bound, their ControlSource property is not empty, and you can't use the "pull" method described in the previous section. In this case you'll need to push data into the controls once you've made a choice from the combo or list box. This is also simple, but it requires a bit of code.

The steps you follow to implement this method are the same as they were for the "pull" method. In this case, though, you need to leave the ControlSource property of the text boxes alone. The assumption is that you're using this method because those controls are bound to data fields. To apply the "push" method, you attach code to the AfterUpdate event of the combo or list box, which will fill the appropriate controls. In the example form, frmPushText, the code just loops through all the columns and sends out data to each of the four conveniently named text boxes:

```
Dim intI As Integer
For intI = 1 To 4
    Me("txtBox" & intI) = Me!lstNames.Column(intI)
Next intI
```

Filling a List or Combo Box Programmatically

Access provides you with many ways to get data into a list box without programming at all. You can supply a table or query name, a list of items, or a SQL string.

There is still at least one case in which you'll need to write code to fill a list box: if you need to fill the list box with values from an array, you must write code to do it. We suggest two such methods, but creative programmers can probably come up with others. You can either manipulate the RowSource property directly, providing a semicolon-delimited list of values, or write a callback function to provide Access with the needed values.

Changing the RowSource Property

Imagine a situation in which you have two buttons on your form. Choosing one of those buttons fills a list box with values from one specific field, and choosing the other fills the list box with values from a different field. Figure 7.21 shows a form like this in action (frmFillTest in CH07.MDB).

FIGURE 7.21:
Click the Show Locations button to see a list of locations or the Show Products button to see a list of products.

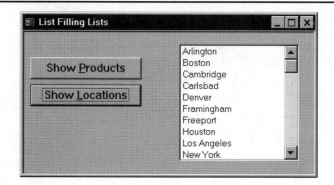

The following method creates a semicolon-delimited list of items for the list box (which must have its RowSourceType property set to ValueList) based on the recordset the user chose.

```
Set rst = db.OpenRecordset("SELECT [" & strField & _
 "] FROM " & strTable & " ORDER BY [" & strField & "]", _
 dbOpenDynaset)
Do Until rst.EOF
    strFill = strFill & rst(strField) & ";"
    rst.MoveNext
Loop
ctl.RowSource = strFill
rst.Close
```

This code creates the Recordset object and walks through that object, building up a string in the format

Item1;Item2;Item3;Item4;…ItemN;

and then places that string in the list box's RowSource property. Since the RowSource property can contain only 2048 characters, however, you're limited to small recordsets when you use this method.

Listing 7.1 shows the entire function. Interestingly, we performed some simple timing tests. Compared to the more obvious method, which is to set the RowSource-Type to Table/Query and the RowSource to a SQL string describing the list, this method performed favorably for small lists. For larger lists, you'll have to try both and convince yourself.

Listing 7.1

```
Public Function SetListBoxContents(intFlag As Integer)
    Dim db As Database
    Dim rst As Recordset
    Dim strField As String
    Dim strTable As String
    Dim strFill As String
    Dim ctl As Control

    Set ctl = Me!lstShowList

    Select Case intFlag
        Case glrcShowProducts
            strField = "Products"
            strTable = "tblProducts"
            ctl.ControlTipText = "Choose a product"
        Case glrcShowLocations
            strField = "Locations"
```

```
            strTable = "tblLocations"
            ctl.ControlTipText = "Choose a location"
        Case Else
            Exit Function
    End Select
    db = CurrentDb()
    Set rst = db.OpenRecordset("SELECT [" & _
     strField & "] FROM " & strTable & " ORDER BY [" & _
     strField & "]", dbOpenDynaset)
    Do Until rst.EOF
        strFill = strFill & rst(strField) & ";"
        rst.MoveNext
    Loop
    ctl.RowSource = strFill
    rst.Close
End Function
```

Using a Callback Function to Fill the List Box

To fill a list or combo box with an array of values or display information from an internal Access data structure, your best alternative is to use a list-filling function. Access allows you to supply a function that tells it all about the list or combo box you want displayed. You tell Access the number of columns, the number of rows, the formatting for individual elements, and the actual data elements. This is the only case in which Access directly calls a user-created function and uses the information it receives back from that function. This is, in effect, what makes your function a *callback* function—you are supplying information Access needs to do its job.

All this flexibility comes at a price, however. For Access to be able to communicate with your function, it needs to have a very specific interface, and it must respond in expected ways when Access requests information from it. Access calls your function at various times as it's filling the list box and indicates to your function exactly which piece of information it requires at that moment by providing an action code as one of the parameters. Metaphorically, every time Access calls this function, it's asking a question. It's up to your function to supply the answer. The question might be, "How many columns are there?" or "What value do you want displayed in row 1, column 2?" In any case, Access supplies all the information you need to retrieve or calculate the necessary answer. The return value from the function returns the question's answer to Access.

To attach your function to the list/combo box on a form, type its name (*without* a leading equal sign and *without* trailing parentheses) in the RowSourceType on the property sheet. This break in the normal syntax for the property sheet tells Access you're specifying a callback function. This is the property sheet set up to use a callback function:

Setting Up Your Callback Function

Any function that will be used as a list-filling callback function must accept exactly five parameters, the first declared As Control and the rest using simple datatypes. The following table lists the various parameters (the names used for them by convention; feel free to choose your own) and their descriptions:

Parameter	Description
ctl	Control-type variable that refers to the list box or combo box being filled
varID	Unique value that identifies the control being filled; you may find it more useful to check ctl.Name if you need to differentiate between controls using this code
lngRow	Row being filled in (zero-based)
lngCol	Column being filled in (zero-based)
intCode	The "question" Access is asking your function; its value indicates what action your function should take

A typical function declaration looks like this:

```
Function FillList(ctl as Control, varID as Variant, _
  lngRow as Long, lngCol as Long, intCode as Integer) _
  As Variant
```

Your function reacts to each of the values in intCode, returning the information Access requests. Table 7.3 lists the possible values for intCode, their constant names as defined by Access, and the information Access is requesting when it sends you each of the constants.

When Access requests values for the list (acLBGetValue), it supplies a row and a column number in the lngRow and lngCol parameters, implying that you need to

TABLE 7.3: The acLB... Constants and Their Uses in Filling a List or Combo Box Programmatically

intCode	Constant	Meaning	Return Value
0	acLBInitialize	Initialize	Nonzero if your function can successfully fill the list; 0 or Null otherwise
1	acLBOpen	Open	Nonzero ID value if the function can successfully fill the list; 0 or Null otherwise. Many functions use the return value from the Timer() function to get a unique value
2	Not used		Not used, although Access does call the function with this value. Its use is not documented
3	acLBGetRowCount	Number of rows	Number of rows in the list (can be 0); −1 if unknown. If you specify −1, Access calls the function to retrieve values (acLBGetValue) until you return a null value
4	acLGGetColumnCount	Number of columns	Number of columns in the list (can't be 0); should match the value in the property sheet. You can, of course, just pass back ctlField.ColumnCount or skip this option altogether
5	acLBGetColumnWidth	Column width	Width of the column specified in the varCol parameter (can be 0), measured in twips ($\frac{1}{1440}$ inch). Specify −1 to use the property sheet values, or just skip this option
6	acLBGetValue	Value	Value to be displayed at row varRow and column varCol
7	acLBGetFormat	Format string	Format string to be used in displaying the value at row varRow and column varCol. Specify −1 to use the default format, or skip this option
8	acLBClose	Not used	Not used, so no return value. Access does call your function with this value, though. Its use is not documented
9	acLBEnd	End	Returns nothing. Used when you close the form or requery the control. Use this portion of your function to release memory or clean up as necessary

have random access to your data. Filling a list box from a recordset, then, is a tricky issue, because you don't really have random access to all Recordset objects in Access. (You can use the AbsolutePosition property to set the position directly for all but table-type recordsets.) You can emulate random access, however, using the Move method for Recordset objects. We present both methods of solving this problem. The first solution here suggests copying data from your recordset into an array, so you actually *can* access specific rows at will, but this method becomes quite slow when your datasets are large. The second solution uses the Move method to get to the exact record you need, based on the most recent record you were on and the new row number you need to get to. This method starts up more quickly since it's not copying data into an array, but it's slower in execution since it must refer to actual data on disk to display its contents.

In general, your callback function will probably look something like the example code in Listing 7.2. It needn't be terribly complex, and once you've written a few of these functions, you should be able to cut-and-paste a new one in seconds.

Listing 7.2

```
Function FillList(ctl As Control, varId As Variant, _
  lngRow As Long, lngCol As Long, intCode As Integer) _
  As Variant

    Dim varRetval as Variant
    Dim intRows as Integer
    Dim intCols as Integer
    Static aData() as Variant

    Select Case intCode
        Case acLBInitialize
            ' Initialization code
            ' Figure out how many rows and columns there are
            ' to be, and ReDim the array to hold them.
            ReDim aData(intRows, intCols)
            ' Code to fill the array would go here.
            varRetval = True

        Case acLBOpen
            ' Return a Unique ID code. The built-in Timer
            ' function works well.
            varRetval = Timer
```

```
        Case acLBGetRowCount
            ' Return number of rows
            varRetval = intRows

        Case acLBGetColumnCount
            ' Return number of columns
            varRetval = intCols

        Case acLBGetColumnWidth
            ' Return the column widths. If you return -1
            ' from this call, Access will use the default
            ' width for the specific column. That way,
            ' you can use the property sheet to supply the
            ' column widths.
            Select Case lngCol
                Case 0
                    ' Handle the first column
                    varRetval = 1440
                Case 1
                    ' Handle the second column
                    ' and so on.
                    varRetval = -1
            End Select

        Case acLBGetValue
            ' Return actual data.
            ' This example returns an element of the
            ' array filled in case acLBInitialize
            varRetval = aData(lngRow, lngCol)

        Case acLBGetFormat
            ' Return the formatting info for a given row
            ' and column.
            Select Case lngCol
                Case 0
                    ' Handle each column, setting the format.
                    varRetval = "ddd"
            End Select

        Case acLBEnd
            ' Clean up
            Erase aData
    End Select
    FillList = varRetval
End Function
```

Using a Callback Function

Displaying a list of table and/or query names is a prime candidate for using a callback function. Since you can get such a list only by enumerating Access objects, the callback function provides the most reasonable way to get the values into a list box. This example makes heavy use of data access objects to do its work. (See Chapter 6 for more information on the object collections.) Figure 7.22 shows the example form (frmListTables from CH07.MDB) in use. Open the form's module to follow the description of the code.

In the acLBInitialize case, your goal is to set up the array to be used for later retrieval in the acLBGetValue case. In this example you need to find out how many tables and queries there are and store that value away. If there are no tables or queries (an unlikely event, since every database has at least the system tables), return a False value, telling Access your function is unable to initialize the list box:

```
Set db = CurrentDb()
' Figure out the greatest number of entries
' there might be.
db.TableDefs.Refresh
db.QueryDefs.Refresh
intItems = db.TableDefs.Count + db.QueryDefs.Count
If intItems = 0 Then
    varRetval = False
Else
    .
    .
    .
```

FIGURE 7.22:

Choose Tables, Queries, or Both to display a list of the selected items.

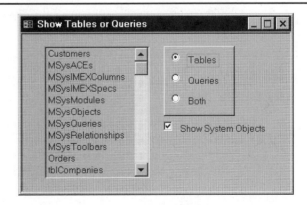

Once you've found there are some tables or queries to display, your next step in the initialization case is to build up the array you will send to Access in the acLB-GetValue case. Based on choices you've made on the form, the function will pull in different items for the list. For example, to get a list of queries, the code looks like this:

```
If ShowQueries() Then
    For Each qdf In db.QueryDefs
        If Not IsTemp(qdf) Then
            sastrNames(sintItems) = qdf.Name
            sintItems = sintItems + 1
        End If
    Next qdf
End If
```

The variable sintItems will indicate the number of elements in the list box once you've finished all the looping, and this is the value you pass back to Access in the acLBGetRowCount case.

The rest of the code closely follows the skeleton example. It uses the default column widths and doesn't even bother dealing with the acLBGetFormat case, because it's just using the default formats. When asked to supply a value (in the acLBGetValue case), it just returns the value for the given row from the array it built in the acLB-Initialize case. Finally, when Access shuts down the list box, the acLBEnd case uses the Erase command to release the memory the array uses.

To include this form in your own application, follow these steps:

1. Import the form frmListTables from CH07.MDB into your application.

2. Modify the AfterUpdate event of the list box lstTables to *do* something with the user's choice. Perhaps you'll want to place it into a global variable for later use.

Using the Move Method to Access Data

The Move method of recordsets provides another choice when filling list and combo boxes programmatically. The syntax of the Move method is this:

Recordset.Move *lngRows*[*, strBookMark*]

where *lngRows* specifies the number of rows to move and *strBookMark* specifies an optional bookmark from which to start. In this example, which fills a list box without using an array (as opposed to the previous example), you keep track of the last row request from Access, as well as the previous bookmark for the recordset. That way, when Access requests that you retrieve the data for a specific row in the list box, you can easily move to the same row in the recordset and retrieve the correct data. Note that this isn't as easy as complete random access, in which you could just move to a specific row in the recordset, but it's awfully close.

The form frmFillMoveList, in CH07.MDB, demonstrates a simple use of this method. The list box, lstCompanies, uses the function FillMoveList() to fill itself. You can find the entire function in the module basFillMoveList in CH07.MDB.

In the acLBInitialize case, the function opens the recordset, storing a reference to it in the static variable, rst. FillMoveList() then stores away, for later use, a bookmark for the current record, varBM. In addition, it initializes the static variable, lngRow, that will keep track of the most recently accessed row:

```
Set rst = db.OpenRecordset("qryCompanies", _
  dbOpenDynaset)
varBM = rst.Bookmark
lngPreviousRow = 0
FillMoveList = True
```

To speed up the form-loading process, you tell Access to figure out for itself how many rows there are in this recordset. By returning a −1 value in the acLBGetRow-Count case, you can avoid the slow process of loading the entire recordset, which is the only way to get to the end of the recordset to find the number of rows:

```
Case acLBGetRowCount
    FillMoveList = -1
```

The only other interesting case, acLBGetValue, does most of the work. It must first calculate the difference between the row for which it's been requested to retrieve data, lngRow, and the last row in the recordset it accessed, lngPreviousRow. This difference tells the Move method the number of rows it will need to move the record pointer. Then it can just use the Move method to move the correct number of rows, store away the new bookmark and row number, and send back the correct data to Access.

To tell Access it's reached the end of the recordset and it should stop trying to re-quest data, you must pass a null value back to Access. When Access has asked your code for data in a row that doesn't exist, your attempt to store the bookmark will fail, since there is no active record. At that point you can check to see whether the value of Err is 0. If it is not, an error has occurred and you can send back Null. Other-wise, just return the data as requested:

```
On Error Resume Next
lngMove = lngRow - lngPreviousRow
rst.Move lngMove, varBM
varBM = rst.Bookmark
If Err = 0 Then
    lngPreviousRow = lngRow
    FillMoveList = rst!Company
Else
    FillMoveList = Null
End If
On Error GoTo 0
```

You'll need to decide for yourself which of these two methods to use when writing a list-filling callback function. If you can pull data from a single record source, you're better off using the Move method, as in the second example. If you're filling the list from an array or are using multiple recordsets, as in the first example, use an array to fill your list.

NOTE   You probably wouldn't use a list-filling callback function in a case as simple as the second example here. If you could specify a single query as your record source, you'd just set the RowSource property for the list box and write no code at all. But there will be times when you need to fill a list or combo box with a callback function, and in those situations you must choose which method is best for you. In some cases using a list-filling function will actually execute more quickly than supplying the recordset name in the RowSource property. You may also find this technique useful in client-server environments where you need more precise control over the timing of record fetches. You'll need to experiment when working with large datasets.

Emulating a Permanently Open Combo Box

Access does not supply a drop-down list box control, and there will be times when you must have the list portion of a combo-like control permanently open. You can emulate this arrangement, however, with the pairing of a list box and a text box. The issue, of course, is performing the incremental search as you type into the text box, finding the matching elements of the list box as you type. Because Access provides the Change event for the text box, you can attach code to this event property that finds the first entry in the list box that matches the text you currently have in the text box. This functionality looks and feels just like the search capability in Windows Help and should fit well into many applications. Figure 7.23 shows a sample form, frmTestIncSrch from CH07.MDB, in action.

FIGURE 7.23:

Typing into the text box will find the first matching value in the list box.

The drawbacks to this pairing, however, are somewhat serious. Because Access must do a lookup in the underlying data source for every change the user makes in the text box, response time can be slow in certain cases. On the other hand, if you can bind the list box to a table (and can guarantee the use of an index for lookups), the speed is quite reasonable even for large lists.

The sequence of steps necessary to accomplish this hybrid control is quite simple. Every time Access fires off the Change event for the text box, it calls the glrIncSrch()

function. This function tries to find the first entry in the list box's underlying record-set that matches the text currently in the text box. If the list box is bound to a table, the function uses the PrimaryKey index (or optionally, any index you specify) with the Seek method to find the first match. This method is quite fast. If the list box is bound to a query (and it must be bound to either a table or a query for this code to work at all), it uses the FindFirst method of the recordset to find the first match. This method can be much slower, depending on Access' ability to use an index for its search.

The function grlIncSrch() uses some interesting techniques. (Look in basIncSearch for a complete listing.) First of all, rather than opening and closing a Recordset object for every lookup, it maintains a global Recordset variable. The first time you try to perform a lookup, the attempt to access the recordset will fail, triggering an error condition. The error handler calls SetUpRst(), which first attempts to open a table-type recordset based on the data source. If it succeeds, and if it manages to set the Index property of the recordset, it's home free.

If SetUpRst can't open a table-type recordset, it'll open a dynaset-type recordset instead. In either case, the global variable mrst ends up pointing to the Recordset object, and the recordset will remain open until you close the form. (The code attached to the form's Close event closes the recordset.) Once everything is opened up, the function resumes back at the top, where it can now successfully do its work. The following code fragment shows the error-handling code in glrIncSrch( ):

```
Set mdb = CurrentDb()
' Set up the recordset.
If IsMissing(varIndex) Then
    varIndex = "PrimaryKey"
End If
If SetUpRst(ctlListBox.RowSource, varIndex) = 0 Then
    Resume LookItUp
Else
    Resume glrDoIncSearchExit
End If
```

Rather than just opening the Recordset object directly, glrIncSrch() calls the SetUpRst() function to do its work. As mentioned above, SetUpRst() first attempts to open a table-type recordset and assign the Index property of the recordset. If both those steps succeed, it's done its work. If that fails, it now knows it will not be able to open a table-type recordset, and it attempts to open a querydef matching the row source it's been passed. To be as flexible as possible, SetUpRst() attempts to resolve any parameters involved with the querydef. By walking through the Parameters collection, it can supply all the values for the query, as long as the values are available.

You should notice that the assignment

```
varValue = ctlTextBox.Text
```

uses the Text property rather than the Value property, which is the default property for text boxes. Since the value in the text box has not yet been committed at the point at which the function needs to access its contents, the Value property has not yet been updated. The Text property is always current while the control is active, but the Value property is not.

Doing the work is really quite simple. If the list box is bound to a table, the function uses the Seek method to find the first value greater than or equal to the value in the text box. If the list box is bound to a query, the function builds a string expression to be used as the criteria for the FindFirst method and uses it to search for the first match. In either case, if the NoMatch property is Yes after the search, there's not much the function can do (especially since the search really can't fail unless something is seriously wrong with the data), and it just displays a message box and quits:

```
If mintType = glrcObjTable Then
    mrst.Seek ">=", varValue
Else
    ' See Chapter 6 for more information on quotes within
    ' quoted strings.
    mrst.FindFirst strField & " >= " & _
        glrcQuote & glrHandleQuotes(varValue, glrcQuote) & _
        glrcQuote
End If
If Not mrst.NoMatch Then
    ctlListBox = mrst(strField)
Else
    ' This shouldn't happen, right?
End If
```

You might also notice that we've included code to fill in the text box with the currently selected value from the list box if you either click it in the list box or leave the text box at any point. This seems like reasonable and helpful behavior, similar to the way the AutoExpand property for combo boxes works.

In summary, the issues surrounding the use of this code are as follows:

- The list box's ControlSource must be either a table or a query.
- If the ControlSource is a table, the field you display must be the primary key, and the primary key must be named PrimaryKey, or you must pass in the name of the index as the final optional parameter.
- Using a query as the ControlSource is far more flexible, but it might be slower than using a table. This issue is far less important on small datasets.
- Because the code uses a global variable to refer to the list box's underlying recordset, you cannot use this code for more than one pair of controls at a time.

To include this functionality in your own application, follow these steps:

1. Import the basIncSrch module from CH07.MDB.
2. Create the text box and the list box.
3. From your text box's Change event, call the glrIncSearch procedure, replacing the control and field names with your own:

   ```
   Call glrIncSearch([txtIncSrch], [lstIncSrch], "Company")
   ```

4. From your text box's Exit event, call the glrUpdateSearch procedure:

   ```
   Call glrUpdateSearch([txtIncSrch], [lstIncSrch])
   ```

5. From your list box's AfterUpdate event, call the glrUpdateSearch procedure:

   ```
   Call glrUpdateSearch([txtIncSrch], [lstIncSrch])
   ```

Making Multiple Selections in a List Box

Access list boxes allow multiple selections, as you saw in the section "Multi-Select List Boxes" earlier in this chapter. The only problem with using multiple-select list boxes is that it's difficult for users to see which items they've selected if the list is too long to fit on the screen. In addition, there's really no way, using a single list box, to change the ordering of the choices.

Fortunately, you can code around these problems by showing the user two list boxes, one representing available items and the other representing selected items. By moving items from one list to the other, your users can select a group of items on which to work. Figure 7.24 shows a sample multi-pick list box (frmMultiPik from CH07.MDB) in action. Both list boxes on frmMultiPik allow multiple selections, so you can select as many items as you wish in either list box and move them all to the other list box. In addition, the buttons to the right of the Selected list box allow users to reorder their chosen items.

FIGURE 7.24:
By clicking the buttons (or double-clicking the list boxes), the user can select a group of items.

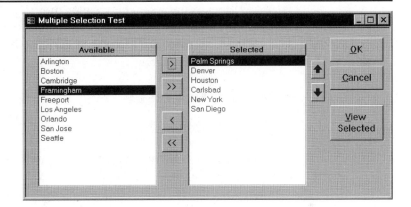

VBA provides several ways to accomplish this goal, and we've chosen a method that allows you some flexibility. By using the code presented here, you'll be able to base your multiple-pick hybrid control on a recordset (either a table or a query) or on two arrays of values, one representing the available list and one representing the selected list. You might want to open frmMultiPik in CH07.MDB and experiment a bit while reading the following sections.

Our implementation of multiple-pick lists uses an array and two collections; the array holds the actual data and the selection status of the items. (For more information on user-defined collections, see Chapter 2.) The two collections keep pointers to the rows in the master array that are available and those that are selected. The array (aFullArray() in the code) is based on this structure:

```
Type typDataRow
    varData As Variant
    fSelected As Integer
End Type
```

The two collections (colAvailable and colSelected) do no more than store the index numbers of the available and selected items. When the code needs to fill in the Available or Selected list, it uses list-filling callback functions. (See the section "Using a Callback Function to Fill the List Box" earlier in this chapter.) In each case the callback function walks through each element of the available or selected collection and fills the appropriate list box with the data from the master array. Given that var-Row represents an index in the Selected list box, the item displayed in the list box will be

```
aFullArray(colSelected.Item(varRow + 1)).varData
```

Like many other examples in this chapter, multiple-pick lists can be easily incorporated into your own applications. Rather than dissecting the full code for multiple-pick lists here, we refer you to basMultiPik in CH07.MDB. There are some points worth discussing here, though.

Filling the Two List Boxes

Unlike most other examples in this book, the two list boxes in this example have their BoundColumn property set to 0. As mentioned in the section "The Special Case" earlier in this chapter, setting the BoundColumn property to 0 effectively binds the list box to the selected row number, starting with 0. If the list box had a ControlSource (which these don't), you'd end up storing the chosen row number in the underlying data. In this case, setting the BoundColumn property to 0 makes it easier to programmatically specify the particular row to select.

In addition, these list boxes contain two columns. The first, visible, column contains the data from the master array. The second, hidden, column contains the master array index from which this particular piece of data came. Therefore, it takes two passes through the callback function to fill both columns. In one call to the function, when varCol is 0, Access retrieves the value for the first column. Access retrieves the value for the second column in a second call to the list-filling function:

```
Case acLBGetValue
    ' Get the data for each of the two columns.
    varValue = colSelected.Item(varRow + 1)
    If varCol = 0 Then
        varRetval = aFullArray(varValue).varData
    Else
        varRetval = varValue
    End If
```

One Callback or Two?

It's true that Access does pass your callback function a unique identifier for each control that calls into that function, and it also passes a handle to the control being filled. Given that information, it would seem that you could write a single function to fill the two list boxes used in this example. Actually, it turns out that combining these two functions, glrFillSelected() and glrFillAvailable(), into one function is more work than it's worth. The problem is, we found, that the two list boxes get filled in bits and pieces, overlapping in time. Although they could physically be combined, the resulting code would be so convoluted and difficult to maintain that it made more sense to separate them.

Retrieving the Selected List

This hybrid control, the pairing of two different list boxes, wouldn't do you much good if you couldn't easily find out which items the user had selected. Therefore, the module basMultiPik includes a function your application can call to retrieve an array containing the list of selected items. The sample form (frmMultiPik) displays the list in a message box when you click the View Selected button. To retrieve the list for your own use, call the function glrGetSelectedItems(), passing in a reference to the active form and a dynamic array the function can fill in with the selected items. For example, in the sample form, the Click event of the View Selected button executes this code:

```
Private Sub cmdChosen_Click()

    Dim aSelected() As Variant
    Dim varItem As Variant
    Dim strShowIt As String

    ' Get an array filled with the selected items.
    Call glrGetSelectedItems(Me, aSelected())

    For Each varItem In aSelected
        strShowIt = strShowIt & varItem & vbCrLf
    Next varItem
    MsgBox strShowIt, , "Multiple Pick Test"
End Sub
```

Issues to Consider

The implementation of multiple-pick lists presented here is not completely generic. You should be aware of several issues before you attempt to use this hybrid control in your own applications:

- The code is non-reentrant—you can't have multiple forms with multiple pick lists on them at the same time. You can have multiple pick lists in your application, but when you move from one to the other, you'll need to reset the code, calling glrRegisterControlNames and glrFillMultiPikField or glrFillMultiPikArray (depending on the data source).

- The data must come from either a table or query or from an array. To use a recordset variable to fill the list, you need to create arrays and fill them with the appropriate data before you call glrFillMultiPikArray.

- Think twice before using this method with large lists (more than 1000 data elements or so). It can take a long time to fill the collections when you have many elements.

- Multiple-pick lists make sense only when the data elements you present to the user are unique. You may need to concatenate multiple fields in a query, creating a list of unique values. Once you have that unique list, you can present it to the user.

To include multiple-pick lists in your own applications, follow these steps:

1. Import the module basMultiPik from CH07.MDB.

2. Create your form, including two list boxes and four data movement buttons. If you want to include the buttons to move selected data up and down, you can add those buttons, as well. You may find it easiest to just copy the eight controls from frmMultiPik in CH07.MDB by first importing frmMultiPik, then copying the appropriate controls, and then deleting frmMultiPik from your database.

3. If you want, set the AutoRepeat properties of all the command buttons to Yes.

4. Set the properties of the two list boxes, as shown here:

Column Count	2
Column Heads	No
Column Widths	;0"
Bound Column	0

You must set the ColumnCount to 2 and the BoundColumn to 0. The other two settings (ColumnHeads and ColumnWidths) presented in the preceding illustration are suggestions only.

5. Add procedure calls to various events, as shown in Table 7.4. The table uses the control names from the examples, but you're welcome to use any names you wish.

    In addition, in the Form_Open event, you'll need to either call glrFill-MultiPikArray, passing to it the current form and the two arrays you want displayed:

```
Call glrFillMultiPikArray(Me, varAvailable, varSelected)
```

   or glrFillMultiPikField, passing to it the form reference, the name of the field to display, and the table from which to retrieve it:

```
Call glrFillMultiPikField(Me, "Locations", "tblLocations")
```

6. In the Declarations section in your copy of basMultiPik, change the values of the constants glrcSelectedList through glrcDeleteAllButton if your control names are different than ours. Again, if you copied the controls from the sample form, there's no need to change the names.

7. If you're filling your list boxes from arrays, you'll need to fill those arrays from your form's Open event, before you call glrFillMultiPikArray. The example form doesn't use this functionality, but if you want to try it out,

TABLE 7.4: Procedure Calls for MultiPik

Event Procedure	Procedure Call
lstAvailable_DblClick	Call glrMultiPikAddOne(Me)
lstSelected_DblClick	Call glrMultiPikDeleteOne(Me)
cmdAddOne_Click	Call glrMultiPikAddOne(Me)
cmdAddAll_Click	Call glrMultiPikAddAll(Me)
cmdDeleteOne_Click	Call glrMultiPikDeleteOne(Me)
cmdDeleteAll_Click	Call glrMultiPikDeleteAll(Me)
cmdUp_Click	Call glrBumpUp(Me)
cmdDown_Click	Call glrBumpDown(Me)
Form_Open	Call glrRegisterCtlNames(glrcSelectedList, glrcAvailableList, glrcAddOneButton, glrcAddAllButton, glrcDeleteOneButton, glrcDeleteAllButton)

change the constant USE_ARRAYS in frmMultiPik's module:

```
#Const USE_ARRAYS = False
```

to True. This causes the sample form to read its data from the arrays instead of from a table.

Other Areas of Interest

If you're interested in studying user-defined collections, MultiPik's source code is a good place to start. It uses all the methods of collections (Add, Remove, Item) and exercises all the mechanisms for working with multi-select list boxes, as well. You'll find the routines that move selected items up and down the list (glrBumpUp and glrBumpDown) of particular interest, since these use many advanced features of collections.

The code that copies data from your table into aFullArray() is interesting, as well. It uses the GetRows method of a recordset to return all the rows you care about in one single statement. Rather than looping through the rows of data one by one, this method returns all the rows you request into a variant array. In our case, since we need the data in an array of user-defined types, we still had to walk the entire set of data. But the loop now is all in memory instead of looping through rows on the disk, one by one. The following code fragment is from glrFillMultiPikField, in basMultiPik:

```
' Get all the data.
rst.MoveFirst
varData = rst.GetRows(intcount)
rst.Close

' Now copy that data into the array of
' total items, avarItemsToFill.
' The array returned by GetRows is 0-based.
Set colSelected = New Collection
Set colAvailable = New Collection
For intLoop = LBound(aFullArray) To UBound(aFullArray)
    ' aFullArray is 1-based, but the array from GetRows
    ' is 0-based. Therefore, the "intLoop - 1" in the
    ' next line.
    aFullArray(intLoop).varData = varData(0, intLoop - 1)
    aFullArray(intLoop).fSelected = False
    Call AddItem(colAvailable, intLoop)
Next intLoop
```

Isn't There a Better Way?

This really seems like a lot of code to do something that ought to be easy. Isn't there a better way? Of course. You can implement this same sort of functionality very easily, with a lot less code. The form frmMultiPikTable implements this technique. It works by using a Yes/No column in your table, Selected, which keeps track of which rows are selected. The code reacts to clicks of the selection buttons by setting the Selected field in the underlying table to either True or False and then refilling the list boxes with the appropriate (selected or not) subset of the data. Experiment with frmMulti-PikTable to get a feel for how this works.

You may find this simple technique satisfies your needs, but you may also find some drawbacks that make it unsuitable:

- Because the code writes directly to the table, you'd have to take extra steps to make this work in a multi-user environment. You could create a new table that works in parallel with the main table, in a one-to-one relationship that's kept locally. This table could keep track of the selected items.

- The code fills the lists directly from the table. If you wanted to control the order of the selected list, you'd need to add another field to keep track of the order in which they were selected. Again, there are multiuser concerns involved.

On the other hand, this technique is quite fast: all it does is write directly to the table, setting the Selected field and then requerying the two list boxes.

How and When to Use Subforms

To display data from more than one table in any but a one-to-one relationship (a single form based on a query will handle the simple one-to-one case), you need to investigate subforms. Although you can use subforms in the one-to-one case, they are not required. A subform is nothing more than a related form displayed within a form; it can be displayed in Datasheet or Form view, and it can, in turn, contain another subform. Access allows nesting subforms two deep so you can display data in a one-to-many-to-many relationship. In addition, subforms have a bit of an identity crisis: from their own point of view, they're forms. From the point of view of their parent form, they're controls, just like any other control.

Why Use a Subform at All?

You may work with Access for quite a while without encountering the need for a subform. To many developers , subforms seem to be a "solution in search of a problem." The next two sections discuss two of the most obvious uses of subforms.

Displaying a One-to-Many Relationship

A subform can be useful for displaying the records that are linked to the current record on the main form. This usage corresponds to the standard one-to-many relationship. Think, for example, of a lawyer on the main form and her project list on the subform or, perhaps, a teacher on the main form and his students on the subform. Since you can display the subform in either Form or Datasheet view (and can switch back and forth at run time unless you set the properties of the subform otherwise at design time), you have maximum flexibility in how you view the data.

Displaying a Consistent Background Form

At some point your application may need to gather a great deal of information from a user (a setup program, for instance) and won't care to gather it all on one single form. One way to handle this situation would be to create a single main form with push buttons indicating the categories of information. (Of course, you can use the TabStrip control that's included in the Access Developer's Toolkit, or one of the commercial Tab OLE controls.) Then, create subforms, one for each category, and place them all on the main form at the same location. Set all their visible properties to False, and in the Click event of each button, set the appropriate subform's Visible property to Yes.

Creating a Subform

You first need to create the form you wish to use as a subform. It needs no special handling and can be any form you happen to have created. Remember that you will need to modify any special form-level properties for the subform on the form itself (not as a subform on some other form). You can make those changes at any point, though. The DefaultView, ViewsAllowed, and ScrollBars properties are important to consider when designing your subforms. If you save the form that will become the subform without scroll bars and in a particular view, that's how Access will display it on the main form.

Drag-and-Drop That Form

The easiest way to create a subform is to select and drag an existing form from the database container to your main form. Access will understand that you intend to create a subform and do the work for you. In addition, if you have created any default relationships between the tables on which you've based the form and subform, Access will fill in the LinkChildFields and LinkMasterFields properties for you. Note that this subform is not a copy of the original form, just a reference to it. That is, if you make changes to the original form that is now a subform, closing and reopening the main form will update all the information stored in the main form, and the subform will reflect any changes you've made.

NOTE   If your main form has its DefaultView property set to Continuous Forms and you place a new subform control on that form, Access displays a dialog box warning you that it will change the form to single-form mode. Access cannot display subforms on continuous forms.

Choosing a Control from the Toolbox

You can create a subform by choosing the Subform control from the toolbox. Once you place your control on the form, you can specify the source object, which tells Access where to retrieve the form at display time. Access provides you with a list of possible objects, which, in this case, will be a list of the currently defined forms in your database. In addition, you can change the SourceObject property while your form is in use. That is, when you change the SourceObject property for the subform control, Access pulls in different forms as you make the change.

TIP   Once your form is neatly embedded in a subform control on the main form, you can edit the form easily: just double-click the control in Design view. Access will bring up the subform control's form for you to work on. When you're done, close the form, and when you run the main form in Form view, your changes should take effect.

Relating the Parent to the Child

The LinkChildFields and LinkMasterFields properties control how the main form and the subform relate and interact. Once you have properly set these properties, record pointer movement in the master form will trigger appropriate movement in the child form. This way, the records displaying in the child form should always match the record displaying in the master form.

Allowable Settings

The LinkChildFields property applies to the subform, and the LinkMasterFields property applies to the main form. In each case, you can enter one of the following:

- A field name from the underlying recordset (a table or query), identified in the RecordSource property
- A list of fields, separated by semicolons

The number of fields you enter must match exactly in both property settings. Although the field names can match, there is no reason why they must. As long as the datatypes match and the data is related, this connection should work.

Setting the Values Automatically

Under either of the following two conditions, Access fills in the LinkChildFields and LinkMasterFields properties automatically:

- Both forms are based on tables, and the Tools ➤ Relationships menu item has been used to create default relationships between the two tables.
- Both forms contain fields of the same name and datatype, and the field on the main form is the primary key of the underlying table.

Always check the validity of the supplied links, since Access might make some incorrect assumptions. Unless one of the preceding conditions is true, Access cannot make a determination of how to link the forms and therefore leaves the properties empty.

Retrieving Calculated Values from Subforms

You may find it useful to employ subforms to display detail records and report on the total of some value displayed there on the main form. This is one of Microsoft Product Support's most popular questions: how do you retrieve values from subforms back to the main form?

The complete syntax is rather complex and not at all obvious:

Forms![*Your Form Name*]![*SubForm Name*].Controls![*Your Control Name*]

The important issue here is that you must use the Controls collection of the subform object to refer to controls on the subform. To explore this syntax, you might take a look at the properties available when you have selected your subform in Design view. You'll notice that none of the actual form properties are available at this point. Therefore, were you to use the syntax

Forms![*Your Form Name*]![*SubForm Name*]

you'd have access only to those properties that you see in the property sheet. For example, you could set the Visible property of the subform:

Forms![*Your Form Name*]![*SubForm Name*].Visible = True

but you couldn't get access to any of the controls on the subform. The Controls collection effectively gives you access to all the controls on the subform itself. You must include the ".Controls" to be able to set or retrieve control properties for controls on the subform. That is, to make a control on the subform invisible, you would use code like this:

Forms![*Your Form Name*]![*SubForm Name*].Controls!

[*Your Control Name*].Visible = False

You can extend this to work with controls on subforms inside subforms, as well:

```
Forms!frmProjects!frmProjectsSub.Controls!frmProjectsSubSub._
  Controls!txtClientName.BackColor = 255
```

> **NOTE**
>
> In previous versions of Access, forms did not have an explicit Controls collection. Instead, they exposed a Form property that functioned the same way but made the syntax even more confusing. Unfortunately, Access' Expression Builder still uses the old syntax.

Going All the Way

Access allows you to nest subforms two deep. That is, you can place a form that it-self contains a subform as a subform on a form. This ability can be quite useful if you want to represent a one-to-many-to-many relationship on a form. For example, your client, a law office, might need to display information about each lawyer, the lawyer's clients, and billing information for each client. By nesting subforms, you could create a form that allowed your client to page through each lawyer and, for each, view each client. For each client, a third form could display the billable events for that client. Figure 7.25 shows a very simple form with two nested subforms.

FIGURE 7.25:

The main form represents a customer, the first subform represents one of the customer's orders, and the second subform represents the order items for that particular order.

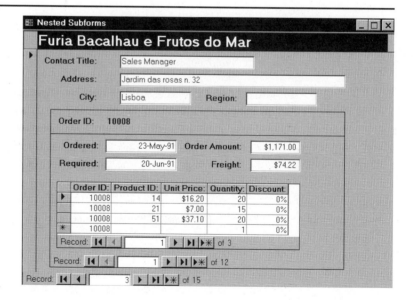

NOTE   Since most of the interesting things you can do with subforms involve their acting as real forms, we cover subforms in detail in Chapter 8.

Graphical Controls

The three graphical controls, line, rectangle, and image, have several properties and no methods. The rectangle can react only to mouse events (Click, DblClick, Mouse-Down, MouseUp, and MouseMove), and the line control has no event properties. Both are provided mostly for aesthetics, although the rectangle and image controls can imitate other controls. For example, a rectangle and a label make a convincing replica of an option group. You can use this fake option group when multiple choices are necessary. You can use the line for separating areas of a form and use the rectangle to group controls on a form and to create borders. An image control uses fewer resources than an unbound object and has some interesting properties (ImageWidth/Height, PictureData) that make it very useful when you need to store images on a form.

The Line Control

The line control has only a few interesting properties. Several of them deal with the sizing box surrounding the line, where the line goes from either the upper-left corner to the lower-right corner or from the lower-left corner to the upper-right corner.

The LineSlant Property

The LineSlant property applies only to the line control. Its value is either a forward slash (/) or a backward slash (\), indicating which way the line slants within its surrounding box.

The Width/Height Properties

The Width and Height properties apply to the box surrounding the line, and their quotient determines the mathematical slope of the line. If you need to ensure that a line control on a form is either horizontal or vertical, you can set its height or width to 0 in the property sheet.

The Rectangle Control

Like the line control, the rectangle has few interesting properties, no methods, and only a few pertinent events. The issues raised here apply to many different controls but have a great impact on rectangles, where you're most likely to use these options.

The Format ➤ Send to Back menu item becomes important as you work with rectangles. For the purposes of form design, it helps if you visualize your forms as layers of transparent plastic, like cartoon cels, with controls painted on them: sending a control to the back is like moving that control's layer of plastic to the back of the stack of cels that make up a form. Unless you send your rectangles to the back of your forms, they will overlay controls you attempt to place within them. You could set the BackStyle property to Clear, but that would only allow you to create rectangles with the same color as the background of the form they're on. If you want rectangles of varying colors to be behind other controls, you need to use the Format ➤ Send to Back menu command.

Because a rectangle can change its look so easily, you can use it to emulate other controls in situations where those other controls won't work as you wish. Changing the SpecialEffect and BackColor properties can make rectangles look like buttons and/or option groups, for example.

NOTE   Buttons, along with OLE custom controls, get special treatment. They always appear on top, no matter how you've changed the layout of controls around them. There is no way to force a text box to overlay a command button, for example. Therefore, although you can emulate buttons with rectangle controls, they will never have the same intrinsic abilities as command buttons.

Rectangles as Buttons

In your application you may want buttons with colored faces on your forms. Normally, command button controls can appear only as gray and raised. For a red button, you can use a rectangle and attach code to its Click event. Although this pairing will not emulate the "pushed-in" button state, it will do in most cases, and you could programmatically create the pushed-in look if you needed it.

Rectangles as Option Groups

Option groups normally allow you to make only a single choice from the available radio buttons, check boxes, or toggle buttons. On some occasions, though, you may need to provide an option group–like container that allows more than one choice. To create this sort of object, you can use a rectangle and a label control. This combination looks exactly like an option group, but that's as far as the similarity goes. Several important characteristics pertinent to option groups are conspicuously absent:

- Option groups return a value, but rectangles cannot. You must examine controls inside a rectangle to determine which you have chosen.

- Controls inside an option group move with the option group when you move it. To move a rectangle and any controls inside it, you need to actively select them all (click the form and drag to surround the entire rectangle) before attempting to move the rectangle.

The Image Control

Access' image control allows you to place almost any graphics image onto a form. Because the image control doesn't allow editing in place, as do OLE containers, its resource usage is far less than for a bound or an unbound OLE container. Choose an image control if you only need to display an image; use an OLE container if you need to *do* something with the image.

Although you can't bind image controls to data, you can set the image either by its Picture property (assigning it the name of a file) or by its PictureData property (assigning it the PictureData property of some other control). That is:

```
Me!Image0.Picture = InputBox("Enter the name of a picture file")
' or
Me!Image0.PictureData = Me!Image1.PictureData
```

The Page Break Control

You can use the page break control on forms differently than you might on a report. On a report, a page break control determines where a user-inserted page break goes. On a form, a page break control determines where Access will position the top of the form when the user presses the PgUp or PgDn key. On a report, modifying the Visible property of the page break control makes common sense: if you want the page break to appear in the output, you make it visible; if you don't, you make it invisible. On a form, though, the Visible property isn't nearly as useful. Making the page break control invisible on a form would alter only which page of the form would become visible when the user pressed one of the paging keys. Modifying this might confuse the user. (See Chapter 8 for a discussion of the use of page break controls and their functionality in multipage forms.)

Using Command Buttons

Command buttons are most often associated with actions. Their most common use is with a macro or Basic code attached to their Click event. They have several interesting and useful properties and events, as described in the following sections.

Macros to Buttons, Automagically

Knowing that many people are likely to create macros and then assign them to command buttons on forms, Access allows you to select a macro name in the Database Explorer and drag it onto a form. Doing this creates a command button for you, with the Caption property set to be the name of the macro. This feature is of limited value if you store more than one macro in a given macro group, but if you store one macro for each group, it's a nice feature. As a developer you're more likely to be writing modules than writing macros, so there's not much point dwelling on this feature.

Command Button Properties

Some of the properties associated with command buttons are different from those for all other controls, so it's worth a moment to go over the unique properties here.

The Picture Property

Unlike any other control, a command button can display either a bitmapped image or a text caption on its surface. (It would be nice if you could mix both on the button, but that option is not currently available. You can, however, use a graphics editor, such as Windows Paint, to create a bitmap image that includes text.) You can specify either a bitmap or an icon file to be placed on the surface of the button. Access displays your chosen picture centered and clipped on the button. In addition, Access attempts to display the *center* of your image in the center of the button; this way, if you shrink the button size so it's smaller than the picture, the center of the picture will still show. To simulate the button being depressed, Access shifts the bitmap to the right and down about 1 or 2 pixels. For this reason, very large bitmaps look rather strange when you click the button. You might consider sticking with icon-sized bitmaps for your buttons.

TIP

Access previously stored only the bitmap image, not a pathname reference to that image, in the button's properties. If you changed your mind about the image or just wanted to find out which file was cur-rently being displayed in the button's picture, you were out of luck. Access 95, however, does store the full path to the image in the Picture property if you use your own image (as opposed to one retrieved from the Command Button Wizard). In addition, the PictureData property can tell you the bit-level image of the picture. You can also use the PictureData property of a button to set the picture on a button. The simplest use for this is to copy a picture from one button to another by assigning a PictureData property from one to the other. See Chapter 19 for more information on using the PictureData property.

The Transparent Property

The command button's Transparent property turns off all display attributes but leaves the button active. This property allows you to overlay a button on another control that might not normally be able to receive focus or fire off events. For example, you could place a transparent command button on top of a line and assign an action to its Click event. To the user it would appear as though the line were reacting to the mouse click! You can also overlay transparent command buttons on bitmaps on forms, allowing various pieces of the bitmap to react to mouse clicks. Imagine a bitmap of the United States, with each state's name printed on the state. With a transparent button overlaid on the state's name, you could allow users to click the image of the state and have Access react to the click.

> **NOTE** Do not confuse the Transparent property with the Visible property. When you set a control's Visible property to No, you completely disable that control. Not only is it invisible; Access removes it from the form's tab order, and it can never receive focus or trigger an event. When the Transparent property is Yes, Access turns off only the display attributes for the button. All the other attributes still apply. You can reach it by tabbing to it or clicking it. All its events are active.

The Default/Cancel Properties

Every form can have exactly one button that acts as the default button (its Click event gets triggered when you press ↵ on the form) and exactly one button that acts as the Cancel button (its Click event gets fired off when you press Esc on the form). A button with its Default property set to Yes acts as the form's default, and a button with its Cancel property set to Yes acts as the form's cancel button. Note that each form can have at most one of each of these, and setting a button's Default or Cancel property to Yes sets any other button's matching property to No.

You might think, as do many developers, that setting a button's Cancel property actually causes something to happen, perhaps closing of the form. This is simply not true. All that happens as a result of a button's Default or Cancel property being set to Yes is that that button receives focus and Access fires off its Click event when you press the correct key.

Give the assignment of Default and Cancel properties some serious thought. For situations in which something destructive might happen at the click of a button, make the Cancel button the default button. To do so, set both the Default and Cancel properties to Yes.

The Visible Property

Unlike the Transparent property, setting the Visible property to No for a button actually disables the button completely. This is the same behavior as with other controls, but it can be confusing for command buttons, which also support the Transparent property.

The DisplayWhen Property

If you are inclined to print single records from your form, you will find the Display-When property indispensable. Since you probably will not wish to print the buttons on the form with the data, set the DisplayWhen property for the buttons to Screen Only. This way, when you print the form, the buttons won't print along with the data.

The Enabled Property

In modern, user-driven applications, it's important to make sure users can't make choices that shouldn't be available. It may have been reasonable at one point for a user to click a button only to be confronted with a dialog box that shouted, "This option is not currently available!" The correct way to handle this situation is for you to disable the button when the option isn't available so the user can't click it in the first place. Set the Enabled property to No when you want the button to be unavailable. Set it to Yes when you want the user to be able to click the button. You may be tempted to make unavailable buttons invisible, but many people find this distracting, since they tend to think, "I saw that option a minute ago; where did it go?"

The AutoRepeat Property

The AutoRepeat property determines whether Access will repeat the code attached to the Click event for a button while you hold down the button. Access fixes the initial repeat to be 0.5 second after the first repetition. Subsequent repeats occur each 0.25 second or at the duration of the macro, whichever is longer.

NOTE   The AutoRepeat property has no effect if the code attached to the button causes record movement on the form. Moving from row to row cancels any automatic repetitions.

One use for the AutoRepeat property is to simulate a spin-button control. In this sort of arrangement you create a text box and two little buttons, usually one with an up arrow and one with a down arrow. As you press the up arrow button, some value in the text box increases, and as you press the down arrow button, the value decreases. One issue to consider when doing this, though, is that Access performs the repeat without consideration for Windows' screen-painting needs. Therefore, your code will probably get far ahead of Windows' ability to repaint the text box. Anytime you cause screen activity using an auto-repeat button, you need to use Do-Events to allow Windows time to catch up.

Why bother creating your own spin buttons when there are OLE custom controls that perform this same function? First of all, most of the spin-button controls we've seen are unattractive. If you create your own, you control how they look. Also, OLE controls exact a somewhat hefty overhead in terms of resources, speed, and application size. Since spin buttons are so easy to create using Access built-in controls, it seems like overkill to use an OLE control for this. In addition, because you're writing the code here, you can control the behavior. For example, the spin buttons we'll create here allow you to limit the range and, possibly, cycle back to the beginning or end once you reach an endpoint.

Example: Simulating Spin-Button Controls

Spin buttons provide one way to both control the values your users input and make it simpler for them to change numeric and date values. The basic concept should be familiar—two buttons, one pointing up and the other pointing down, "attached" to a text box. Pressing the up button increments the value in the text box, and pressing the down button decrements the value. Although you could theoretically use this mechanism for text values, it's not often used that way. For the most part, spin buttons are restricted to date and integer entry.

In basSpin you'll find code that allows you to use spin-button controls in your own projects. We've provided two versions of the code—one for the simple case in which you just want to allow the spin buttons to cause the text box to go up or down in value, and one for the case in which you want to provide minimum and maximum values. This advanced version also allows for value wrapping at either end of the range or at both ends and also works with dates. Figure 7.26 shows the two spin buttons in action, along with text boxes displaying the function calls necessary to make them work. The sample form is frmSpinTest in CH07.MDB.

FIGURE 7.26:

Examples of spin buttons. Note that the advanced example can spin through dates, as well as through numeric values.

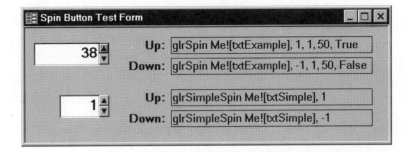

The simple case, in which the code doesn't limit the range your user can spin through, just pulls the current value from the attached text box, increments or decrements it, and then assigns it back to the text box. This code is in the function glrSimpleSpin() in the module basSpin. (You'll find it useful to open this module as you read this discussion.) Of course, this action can cause an error, since the user could have entered a non-numeric value into the text box. The code disregards errors (using On Error Resume Next), so the buttons do nothing if they find an invalid value in the text box. If no error has occurred, the code uses DoEvents to allow Windows to repaint the screen as necessary to keep up with the changing values.

To use the glrSimpleSpin() function, call it from the Click event of the buttons you want to use to control the text box. That is, use something like this:

Call glrSimpleSpin(Me![*txtYourTextBox*], *increment*)

where [*txtYourTextBox*] is the name of the text box containing the value your buttons are going to alter and *increment* is the amount to add to the value in the text box each time the button is pressed. (Generally, use +1 to go up and –1 to go down.) Figure 7.26 shows this function call in use.

The function glrSpin() contains the more complex case, in which you can control the minimum and maximum values allowed in the text box. This function allows you to specify the control to manipulate, the increment (either positive or negative), the minimum and maximum values, and a True/False value indicating whether or not to allow wrapping. If you allow wrapping, the value will go from the maximum value back to the minimum value when moving up and from the minimum to the maximum when moving down. If you don't allow wrapping, no further movement will be allowed once the user reaches an endpoint (either the maximum or the minimum value). Since you call this function from the Click event of both spin buttons,

411

there's nothing stopping you from putting in different parameters for the up button than for the down button. In some cases this makes sense. For example, if you want the user to be able to wrap back to the lowest value after reaching the highest value when moving up but not to be able to wrap after reaching the lowest value when moving down, you can do that.

To use the glrSpin() function, attach a call to it from the Click event of your spin buttons:

Call glrSpin(Me![*txtYourTextBox*], *increment, min, max, allow wrap?*)

where [*txtYourTextBox*] is the name of the text box containing the value your buttons are going to alter and *increment* is the amount to add to the value in the text box each time the button is clicked. (Generally, use +1 to go up and −1 to go down.) The value *min* specifies the minimum value, and *max* specifies the maximum value. If you don't wish to specify a minimum or maximum value, send Null instead of an integer. In addition, if you specify both a minimum and a maximum value, you can enable wrapping by sending True as the final parameter. If you don't send both a minimum and a maximum value or if you send False for the final parameter, the function will not wrap as you move up or down with the spin buttons.

Once you have the correct procedure called from the Click event of the button, you must make sure the AutoRepeat property is set to Yes. This ensures that the action will repeat as you hold down the button.

How the glrSpin() Function Works

The glrSpin() function is much more complicated than the glrSimpleSpin() function since it's attempting to do a great deal more work. The steps it goes through are outlined in the next few paragraphs.

First, check the datatype of the value that's currently in the text box control. If it's anything except a number or a date, just leave the function now. This will keep the function from attempting to modify text values. This check calls the function Get-Type(), which just calls the internal isNull, isDate(), and isNumeric() functions:

```
intDataType = GetType(ctl)
If intDataType <> glrcTypeNumber And _
 intDataType <> glrcTypeDate Then
    Exit Function
End If
```

Next, find the specified boundaries for the up and down motions. First, assume that no boundaries are specified. Check the existence and types of the *min* and *max* parameters. If either of them is both non-null and of the same datatype as the text box's contents, store that information away for later.

This code maintains a single variable, intBoundaries, to keep track of the existence of the boundary settings. If neither boundary value is set, the value of intBoundaries will be glrcBoundNone. If you provide only a minimum setting, its value will be glrcBoundMin. If you provide only a maximum setting, its value will be glrcBound-Max. If you provide both, its value will be glrcBoundBoth.

The following code fragment shows the code from glrSpin() that calculates the value of intBoundaries:

```
intBoundaries = glrcBoundNone
If Not IsNull(varMin) And GetType(varMin) = intDataType Then
    intBoundaries = intBoundaries + glrcBoundMin
End If
If Not IsNull(varMax) And GetType(varMax) = intDataType Then
    intBoundaries = intBoundaries + glrcBoundMax
End If
```

Next, calculate the new value, based on the datatype of the current value and the *increment* parameter. This expression calls the user-defined SetType() function (as opposed to just adding the value to ctl directly) specifically to deal with date datatypes:

```
varNewValue = SetType(ctl, intDataType) + intInterval
```

If you've specified a lower boundary and the newly calculated value for the control is less than the minimum value, set the value to be either the minimum value (if wrapping is not allowed) or the maximum value (if wrapping is allowed). The same logic applies to the upper boundary:

```
If intBoundaries And glrcBoundMin Then
    If varNewValue < varMin Then
        varNewValue = IIf(fAllowWrap, varMax, varMin)
    End If
End If
If intBoundaries And glrcBoundMax Then
    If varNewValue > varMax Then
        varNewValue = IIf(fAllowWrap, varMin, varMax)
    End If
End If
```

Finally, set the text box's value to be the newly calculated value and give Windows some time to catch up. (If you're not sure why the DoEvents is necessary here, try the example without it. You'll see that the numbers don't get repainted for every change.)

```
ctl = varNewValue
DoEvents
```

There's one more area of concern here: when you change the value of a control programmatically, Access does not fire off that control's Before or AfterUpdate event. To get around this problem, both glrSimpleSpin() and glrSpin() call the subroutine HandleProperties once they're done. This subroutine attempts to call the code that the Before/AfterUpdate events would have called. To do so, HandleProperties gathers up the string found in the control's property settings and sends that string to the DoProperty subroutine:

```
Private Sub DoProperty (varProperty As Variant)
    Dim varTemp As Variant

    On Error GoTo DoPropertyErr
    If Not IsNull(varProperty) Then
        If varProperty = "[Event Procedure]" Then
            ' Do nothing, because, in general, you cannot.
        ElseIf Left$(varProperty, 1) = "=" Then
            varTemp = Eval(Mid$(varProperty, 2))
        Else
            DoCmd RunMacro varProperty
        End If
    End If
DoPropertyErr:
    Exit Sub
End Sub
```

DoProperty looks at the property string and, depending on what it finds there, either calls the Eval() function to execute code or runs the attached macro. Unfortunately, if you've attached code directly to the event (using code in the form's module), there's no way this function can execute that code. (Since event procedures are generally private, Eval() can't find them, and since they're subroutines, not functions, Eval() can't call them.) Therefore, if you want some action to occur in the Before/AfterUpdate event for the text box you're using as part of your spin-button trio, you need to place that action in either a macro or a module, not in CBF.

Command Button Events

Command buttons provide the same events as other controls, but you're likely to use just two of them, Click and DblClick. Access fires off the Click event when you click a button and the DblClick event when you click twice within the double-click time interval (as defined through the Windows Control Panel). You can assign any macro or function to either of these events.

TIP

You might be tempted to assign different actions to the Click and DblClick events. Don't bother. Access can't possibly differentiate between the two events and will always attempt to fire off the Click event before the DblClick event. This functionality can be useful to you at times, though. When you want the DblClick event to add to the Click event, it works to your advantage. In general, if you want to attach code to both events, make sure the code attached to the DblClick event extends the action done in the Click event. In actuality, you won't want to use the DblClick event for buttons very often.

Using Default Control Properties to Your Advantage

Access stores default settings for each type of control with each form. To describe the settings for individual controls on the form, Access stores just the settings that *differ* from the default settings. Therefore, if a control has the same settings as the form defaults, Access won't need to store settings for that control. This affects only the stored image of the form; the comparison to the default values is only a save/load issue. All settings for all controls are available once Access loads the form (so there's no actual run-time memory savings).

You can change the default settings for a specific control in two ways. The first involves setting the properties before you actually create the control. The second lets you create the control, specify all its settings, and then tell Access to make those settings the default settings for that type of control.

Either way, when you specify the default settings, other controls of that type you create will inherit the default settings. Previously created controls won't be affected by changes to the default settings.

To set the default settings for a specific type of control before creating one, click that control in the toolbox. Notice that the title for the property sheet has changed to indicate that you're now setting properties for the *default* version of the control. Make whatever changes you want.

To set the default settings based on a specific control you've already created, create your control and set the properties you want. Once you're satisfied, choose the Format ➤ Set Control Defaults menu option. This stores the settings used in the selected control in the form's default settings for that type of control.

Either way you do it, once you've set the default properties, any controls of that type that you create from then on, on the current form, will inherit those properties. When you save the form, Access will save only the properties for each control that differ from the default values. Judicious use of default properties can speed up your development time, as well as make forms smaller and therefore speed their load time.

Creating Controls Programmatically

Access provides functions to create forms and reports, and the controls on these objects, programmatically. This is, of course, how the Access Form and Report Wizards work. They gather information from you about how you want the form or report to look, and then they go through their code and create the requested form or report. Chapter 23 covers in detail how you can create your own Wizards, but there are other uses for those functions. Specifically, if you want to create a form or report with many similar controls that can be easily described programmatically, you may be able to use one or more of these functions.

Functions That Create Forms and Controls

CreateForm( ) and CreateReport( ) create a form or report and return that object as the return value of the function:

CreateForm([*database* [, *formtemplate*]])

CreateReport([*database* [, *reporttemplate*]])

The following table describes the parameters for these two functions:

Argument	Description
database	String expression representing the database in which to look for the template form. To look in the current database, omit this argument
template	String expression representing the form or report template to use in creating the new form or report. Use the word *Normal* to use the standard template. To use the template specified in the Tools ➤ Options menu, omit this argument

The following fragment will create a new form, with the caption "My New Form":

```
Dim frm As Form
Set frm = CreateForm("", "")
frm.Caption = "My New Form"
```

Use CreateControl() and CreateReportControl() to create new controls on forms and reports, respectively. The following fragment details the parameters you use when calling CreateControl() and CreateReportControl():

```
CreateControl(formname As String, controltype As Integer _
 [, sectionnumber As Integer [, parent As String _
 [, fieldname As String [, left As Integer [, top As Integer _
 [, width As Integer [, height As Integer]]]]]]] )
CreateReportControl(reportname As String, _
 controltype As Integer[, section as Integer _
 [, parent As String[, columnname As String _
 [, left As Integer[, top As Integer _
 [, width As Integer[, height As Integer]]]]]]])
```

Table 7.5 lists the parameters for the two functions, along with the possible values for those parameters.

TABLE 7.5: Parameters for CreateControl() and CreateReportControl()

Argument	Description
formname, reportname	String expression identifying the name of the open form or report on which you want to create the control. If you've just created a form using CreateForm() and have assigned the return value of that function to a variable (frmNewForm, for example), you can reference that form's FormName property here (frmNewForm.FormName)
controltype	Constant identifying the type of control you want to create:

Constant	Control Type
acLabel	Label
acRectangle	Rectangle
acLine	Line
acImage	Image
acCommandButton	Command button
acOptionButton	Option button
acCheckBox	Check box
acOptionGroup	Option group
acBoundObjectFrame	Bound object frame
acTextBox	Text box
acListBox	List box
acComboBox	Combo box
acSubform	Subform/subreport
acObjectFrame	Unbound object frame
acPageBreak	Page break
acCustomControl	Custom Control
acToggleButton	Toggle button

section	Constant identifying the section that will contain the new control:

Constant	Section
acDetail	(Default) Detail section
acHeader	Form or report header section

TABLE 7.5: Parameters for CreateControl() and CreateReportControl() (continued)

Argument	Description	
	acFooter	Form or report footer section
	acPageHeader	Form or report page header section
	Constant	**Section**
	acPageFooter	Form or report page footer section
	acGroupLevel1Header	Group-level 1 header section (reports only)
	acGroupLevel1Footer	Group-level 1 footer section (reports only)
	acGroupLevel2Header	Group level 2 header section (reports only)
	acGroupLevel2Footer	Group level 2 footer section (reports only)
	If a report has additional group level sections, the header/footer pairs are numbered consecutively beginning with 9	
parent	String expression identifying the name of the parent control. If you don't wish to specify the parent control, use ""	
bound FieldName	String expression identifying the name of the field to which the new control should be bound. If you specify the boundFieldName, not only does it fill in the ControlSource property, it inherits the table properties, such as the Format and ValidationRule properties	
left	Top, Integer expressions indicating the coordinates for the upper-left corner of the control, in twips	
width	Height, Integer expressions indicating the width and height of the control, in twips	

An Example Using CreateForm() and CreateControl()

As part of a project, you need to create a form with 42 similar command buttons, numbered 1 through 42, in 6 rows of 7 buttons each. You could do this by hand, spending a while getting all the controls just right. You could also do this with the CreateForm() and CreateControl() functions. Listing 7.3 contains the entire function you can use to create the form, as shown in Figure 7.27.

CreateCalendar() creates the form by calling the CreateForm() function. Since it specifies a zero-length string for both the database and the template, it will use the template specified in the Tools ➤ Options settings:

```
Set frm = CreateForm("", "")
frm.Caption = "Calendar"
```

The Calendar form in Design view, after the CreateCalendar( ) function has created all the buttons

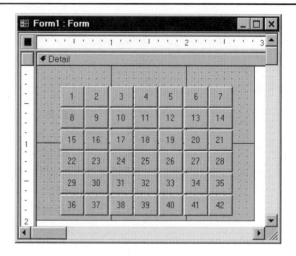

All measurements specified for CreateControl() must be in twips ($\frac{1}{1440}$ of an inch), so you need to convert all your values into twips before calling the function. These controls are to be 0.25 inch in height and 0.30 inch in width, with a 0.03-inch gap between them:

```
intHeight = .25 * glrcTwipsPerInch
intWidth = .30 * glrcTwipsPerInch
intGap = .03 * glrcTwipsPerInch
```

CreateCalendar() loops through six rows of seven command buttons, creating each control with a call to CreateControl(). It uses the width and height values to figure where to place the buttons and then sets the Width, Height, and Caption properties of the button it has just created. Note that this call to CreateControl() uses the FormName property of the newly created form to reference the form, creates a control of type acCommandButton in the Detail section, and specifies no parent or bound field name.

Listing 7.3

```
Function CreateCalendar()

    ' From the immediate window, type
    ' ? CreateCalendar()
    ' to run this function.
    Const glrcTwipsPerInch=1440
```

```
        Dim frm As Form
        Dim ctl As Control

        Dim intI As Integer
        Dim intJ As Integer

        Dim intHeight As Integer
        Dim intWidth As Integer
        Dim intGap As Integer

        Dim intCols As Integer
        Dim intRows As Integer

        intCols = 7
        intRows = 6

        Set frm = CreateForm("", "")
        frm.Caption = "Calendar"

        ' Measurement properties are specified in TWIPS.
        ' So we need to convert all values from
        ' inches to twips, by multiplying by 1440.
        intHeight = 0.25 * glrcTwipsPerInch
        intWidth = 0.3 * glrcTwipsPerInch
        intGap = 0.03 * glrcTwipsPerInch

        For intI = 1 To intRows
            For intJ = 1 To intCols
                With CreateControl(frm.FormName, acCommandButton, _
                  acDetail, "", "", intJ * (intWidth + intGap), _
                  intI * (intHeight + intGap))
                    .Width = intWidth
                    .Height = intHeight
                    .Caption = 7 * (intI - 1) + intJ
                End With
            Next intJ
        Next intI
End Function
```

What Are These Controls, Anyway?

Those readers moving to Access from Visual Basic may be surprised to find out that the controls you see on forms, in Access, are not actual windows. (That is, they don't have window handles and don't respond to Windows messages.) The Access controls are just "paint on the screen," at least until each becomes the active control. Access uses this technique to conserve resources: because you may have 200, 300, or more controls on a single form, it's important that you not run out of window handles, graphics resources, and so on. (Yes, it's still possible to run out of resources under Windows 95. It's difficult, but possible. No one has managed to do this with Windows NT, as far as we know.)

But Visual Basic programmers are used to being able to manipulate controls as windows. You want to be able to use the SendMessage() API function to control your controls. The fact is, this just isn't possible, in general, in Access. There are two important reasons why this won't work:

- The control becomes active at different times, depending on whether you enter it with the mouse or from the keyboard. Because you can't count on either the Enter or GotFocus event to magically transform a painted control into a real window, it's nearly impossible to find an event that will, in general, serve your purposes.

- The controls are subclassed versions of the Windows standard controls. They just don't react to many of the normal Windows messages, if any. Even if you manage to find a control when it's active, it will most likely ignore any message you send to it with SendMessage.

Using SendMessage to Limit Input Characters

You can't count on using SendMessage to manipulate any Access controls. On the other hand, it just so happens that by mistake, chance, or fate, Access text boxes do respond to at least one message: EM_SETLIMITTEXT. You can use the SendMessage()Windows API function to limit the number of characters users can type into a text box. This can be useful if your text box is bound to a memo field and you want to allow users to enter, for example, no more than 1000 characters.

The sample form, frmLimitChars in CH07.MDB, allows you to specify the character limit and then calls the SendMessage() API function to tell the text box the maximum number of characters it should accept. Figure 7.28 shows the form in use. Listing 7.4 shows all the code the form uses to limit the characters in the text box.

FIGURE 7.28:

frmLimitChars shows how you can limit the number of characters typed into a text box.

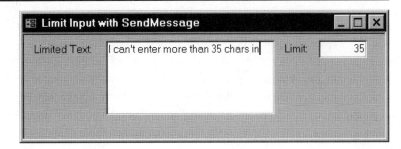

The one limitation on this technique is that you can't count on the control being a real window in either the Enter or GotFocus event, as mentioned above. The only time you're guaranteed that this control is a real window is in its Change event, so that's where we have hooked the code. (You can probably count on the Before-Update event, as well, but we've not tried that.) This means, of course, that the code calls the SendMessage() API every time you type a character. Since this API call incurs so little overhead, compared to the speed at which you can type, the extra work just didn't seem to matter in this case.

The code first gets the window handle for the current window, using the GetFocus() API call:

```
' Get the window handle for the current window.
hWnd = GetFocus()
```

It then plays some tricks to make sure that, if you've set the maximum number of characters to less than the number of characters already in there, it will readjust the allowable number of characters to be the actual number of characters. (Otherwise, the text box wouldn't even let you delete one character at a time. If you have too many characters in a text box, Windows allows you to delete only the entire entry.) Each time you type a character, the code calls SendMessage again, so as you delete characters, the code continually resets the maximum size as necessary:

```
lngNewMax = Len(Me!Text0.Text & "")
lngLimit = Me!txtLimit.Value
```

```
If lngNewMax < lngLimit Then
    lngNewMax = lngLimit
End If
```

Finally, the code calls the SendMessage() API function, which sends a message to the window identified by the supplied window handle:

```
SendMessage hWnd, glrcEM_SETLIMITTEXT, lngNewMax, 0
```

Experimentation has shown that although there are many EM_* messages that normal text boxes understand, Access text boxes respond to very few, if any, of these messages. You may find it interesting to dig through a Windows API reference, trying out various EM_* messages, as we've done here. Be warned: most won't work or will possibly crash Access. The technique we've shown here works not by design, but by chance. Therefore, although it's a useful technique, it may not work in future versions of Access.

Listing 7.4

```
Private Declare Function SendMessage Lib "user32" _
 Alias "SendMessageA" (ByVal hWnd As Long, _
 ByVal wMsg As Long, ByVal wParam As Long, _
 lParam As Any) As Long
Private Declare Function GetFocus Lib "user32" () As Long

Const glrcEM_SETLIMITTEXT = &HC5&

Private Sub Text0_Change()
    ' You actually CAN use SendMessage with
    ' Access controls, but you must remember that
    ' the changes you make are only active
    ' as long as this control has the focus.
    ' Therefore, if you want to limit the text in a text
    ' box, you MUST do it each time you enter the
    ' control. To be safe, the only place you can really
    ' do this is in reaction to the Change, BeforeUpdate
    ' or AfterUpdate event.

    Dim hWnd As Long
    Dim lngResult As Long
    Dim lngNewMax As Long
    Dim lngLimit As Long

    ' Get the window handle for the current window.
    hWnd = GetFocus()
```

```
' Hey, what if there's ALREADY too much text in
' there?  Limiting the text would make it
' impossible to type in there at all. You want
' to set the limit to be the max of the amount
' you want and the amount that's in there!
lngNewMax = Len(Me!Text0.Text & "")
lngLimit = Me!txtLimit.Value
If lngNewMax < lngLimit Then
    lngNewMax = lngLimit
End If

' Send the message to the current text box
' to limit itself to lngNewMax characters.
SendMessage hWnd, glrcEM_SETLIMITTEXT, lngNewMax, 0
End Sub
```

Summary

This chapter has introduced each of the control types (except OLE controls, which are covered in Chapters 15 and 21). We've attempted to cover the nonintuitive properties and events and have suggested solutions to some common Access problems. In general, we covered the following topics:

- Access controls and their properties, events, and methods make up the bulk of your user interface.

- Using VBA and the Tag property, you can emulate the creation of user-defined control properties.

- Using VBA in combination with controls, you can emulate several hybrid controls that are not intrinsic to Access.

- You can use a control's default properties to ease the development burden.

- You can create controls and forms programmatically, leading to a more uniform layout.

- If you're adventurous, you can use the SendMessage API call to control Access controls, but only in a severely limited fashion.

CHAPTER

EIGHT

Topics in Form Design and Usage

- Understanding the appearance and operation of forms

- Retrieving information about forms

- Resizing forms to match screen resolution

- Building form-based encapsulated tools

If your applications are like many of the Access applications in use, a large majority of their functionality is centered around forms. Most likely, from the user's perspective, your application *is* just a set of forms. In this chapter you'll find insights into using and creating forms in ways you might not otherwise have considered, focusing on the new features in Access 95. This chapter doesn't attempt to show you how to create or design forms, but rather how to use the forms you've created in original and interesting ways.

> **NOTE**
>
> Although you won't find a complete discussion of using the Windows API (Application Programmer's Interface) until Chapter 18, some of the examples in this chapter rely heavily on API calls. If you find yourself buried too deeply in the details, you may want to skip ahead to Chapter 18 and peruse the information there concurrently with this chapter.

Introduction to CBF

Access allows you to store program code and a form (or report) in one neat package. Each form and report carries with it its own module and, unless you specify otherwise, every procedure and variable in that module is private. This means that, as in Visual Basic, choosing an event from the property list takes you directly to a subroutine that is tied to that particular event. The event procedures are subroutines named controlName_eventName, and their scope is private to the form. In several cases Access passes parameters to these procedures that provide information about the circumstances of the particular event. For example, mouse events receive information about the mouse location and clicked buttons, and key events receive information about the particular key that was pressed. This encapsulation makes it very easy to create forms that perform a single purpose, which you can reuse in various applications.

NOTE

Controls can contain spaces in their Name properties, but event procedures, being subroutines, cannot have spaces in their names. To solve this problem, Access must do some work on the names of controls that include illegal procedure-name characters before it can name the event procedure. If you need to programmatically retrieve the event procedure name that corresponds to a control, check the EventProcPrefix property of any control on a form or report. This property, which never appears on the property sheet, returns the modified name Access uses in its event procedures. If you're writing an application that creates event procedures, this property is essential.

To get to a form's module, you have several choices:

- From the Database container window, once you see the list of forms, you can click the Code button on the toolbar. (This will open the form in Design view, as well.)

- In Form Design view, click the same toolbar button.

- From the form's property sheet, for any event property, you can click the ... button, which takes you to the particular event procedure for this control.

- In Form Design view, right-click any control and choose the Build Event menu item.

A common misconception about controls and their attached event procedures causes new Access programmers a great deal of trouble. Most beginners assume that copying a control from one form to another also copies the control's event procedures to the new form. But this is not so, unfortunately. Copying a control copies only the control and its properties. You must manually copy its event procedures from one form's module to the other's.

Many of the forms demonstrated in this chapter rely heavily on CBF to maintain their reusability. By keeping all their code in CBF, these forms become encapsulated entities that you can import directly into your own applications. In previous versions of Access, searching through source code using Access' Find/Replace options skipped over code in form or report modules. Happily, Access 95's Find dialog box adds an option to search through all the modules in the database, including form/report modules. Finding procedures hidden away in CBF is no longer an onerous chore.

In addition, you may find that in our attempt to modularize the examples in this chapter, some procedures occur in multiple forms' CBF. If you import more than one of the forms from this chapter into your own applications, you might want to take a few minutes and peruse the imported forms' CBF. You will probably find some general-purpose procedures duplicated. We've attempted to point these out to you along the way. Moving those routines to global modules can save you some memory overhead.

Controlling the Look and Feel of Your Forms

The basic Access form consists of several design elements and built-in functionality, some or all of which you might like to remove or modify for your applications. Figure 8.1 points out many of the built-in elements of forms that Access allows you to control. By changing properties of the form, you can remove or change any of these features.

Using Properties to Control the Look of Your Form

You can use certain properties, in various groups or singularly, to control your form's appearance. Several of these properties are interrelated, and changing one may affect others. For example, if you set the BorderStyle property to None, it doesn't matter what you have set for the MinMaxButton property. In this case those features will be invisible. Or, if you set the ControlBox property to No, Access will remove both the Minimize and Maximize buttons. Table 8.1 shows the form properties you can use to modify the appearance of the form's border.

FIGURE 8.1:

You can change, remove, or include each of the pieces of an Access form at any time.

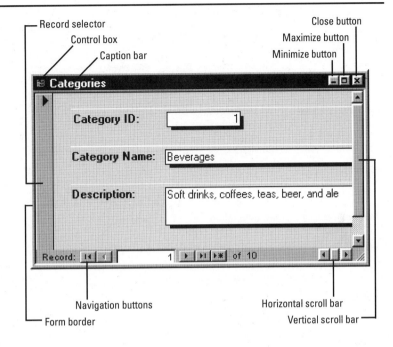

TABLE 8.1: Form Appearance Properties

Property	Determines	Possible Values	Comments
BorderStyle	Type of border and various border elements	None, Thin, Sizable, Dialog	Choosing Dialog disallows Access from displaying the Minimize and Maximize buttons, regardless of the MinMaxButtons property setting
MinMaxButtons	Whether the Minimize and Maximize buttons are enabled/visible	None, Min Enabled, Max Enabled, Both Enabled	Setting this property to None causes Access to display neither button. If you use any other setting, the buttons will both be visible, but one or the other might be disabled. For forms with BorderStyle set to Dialog, Access hides both buttons
CloseButton	Whether to enable the form Close button	Yes, No	Setting this to No also removes the Close option from the Control menu
WhatsThisButton	Whether or not to display the What's This button next to the Close button	Yes, No	This option is available only if the Minimize/Maximize buttons are not displayed. The button appears only if the Close button is also enabled

TABLE 8.1: Form Appearance Properties (continued)

Property	Determines	Possible Values	Comments
ControlBox	Whether the control box (menu) is visible	Yes, No	Under Windows 95, setting this option to No also removes the Minimize/Maximize buttons
NavigationButtons	Whether the record number indicator and navigation buttons are visible	Yes, No	
ScrollBars	Which of the scroll bars are visible	Neither, Horizontal Only, Vertical Only, Both	
RecordSelectors	Whether the record selector bar is visible	Yes, No	
DividingLines	Whether the black line separating rows and sections is visible	Yes, No	Removing dividing lines affects the display of the record selector and other form details, as well
PopUp	Whether your form stays on top of all other forms	Yes, No	Setting this property, along with the Modal property, affects the BorderStyle property
Modal	Whether you can switch to other forms while this form is loaded	Yes, No	Setting this property, along with the Popup property, affects the BorderStyle property

Windows Handles, Classes, Access Forms, and MDI

To make the best use of the different types of forms in Access, you must first have a basic understanding of Windows handles, classes, and parent-child relationships. These concepts will play a large part in your understanding the different form types in Access. You'll also use this information in the section "Using Forms as Toolboxes" later in this chapter to create floating toolbars.

The Windows Handle (or hWnd)

In Windows, almost every object you see on the screen is an object with properties and events, just as in Access. Every button, scroll bar, dialog box, and status bar is a window. To keep all these windows straight, Windows assigns to each a unique window handle—a unique Long Integer—through which it can refer to the specific window. This window handle is generally referred to as the window's *hWnd* (handle to a *wind*ow). Access makes this value available to you, for every form, in that form's hWnd property. (Like many other properties, the hWnd property is available only at run time and therefore can't be found in the form's property sheet.)

Windows Classes

In addition, every window is a member of a window *class*. Window classes share events and code, so windows of the same class can react the same way to outside stimuli. For example, all scroll bars are either part of the class SCROLLBAR or part of a class derived from the SCROLLBAR class. (Actually, not all scroll bars are based on this class, since a programmer can create a scroll bar from scratch. It's just a combination of bitmaps and code. But almost no one does it that way since Windows provides this standard class with little effort on your part.) Every window type in Access has its own class name. You'll find some of these classes listed in Table 8.2, along with the parent for each window type (which will be important in the next section's coverage of the Multiple Document Interface used in Access). Figure 8.2 shows a simple class hierarchy diagram for these Access window classes.

Multiple Document Interface (MDI)

The Multiple Document Interface (MDI) presents a standard way of writing applications for Windows in which one main window can contain many subordinate, or child, windows. Access is such an application, as is Excel, among many others. In MDI applications, the child windows minimize within the bounds of the parent window and show an icon (or tray, in Windows 95) when minimized. You can't size

TABLE 8.2: Sample Access Window Classes and Their Parents

Class Name	Description	Parent
OMain	Main Access window	
MDICLIENT	Access desktop	Main Access window
ODb	Database container	MDIClient window
OForm	Normal form frame	MDIClient window
OFormPopup	Popup form frame	Main Access window
OFormSub	Access form (the area that contains other controls)	Any normal or popup form window

FIGURE 8.2:

Small sample of the Access window class hierarchy

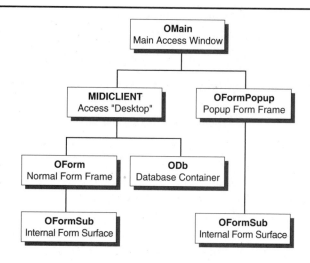

or drag child windows beyond the borders of their parent. The hierarchical organization of every MDI application is basically the same: you have a main window containing a special window—the MDI client—and within that window you have multiple child windows. In Access the MDI client window's class is MDICLIENT and the main Access window's class is OMain. As you'll note in Table 8.2, the MDI client's parent is the main Access window, for which the window class is OMain. It is actually the window that's situated within the Access main window; it contains all the other Access windows, including the design surfaces and running applications. This window normally extends from the bottom of the docked toolbars to the top of the status bar and from the left to the right of the main Access window.

Normal, Popup, and Modal Forms

The Access terms *normal, popup,* and *modal* describe a form's interaction with other forms and with the Access main window. You can control these attributes with the Popup and Modal properties at design time or with the OpenForm action at run time.

A *normal form* allows other forms in Access to both overlay it and take the focus away from it. Unless you specify otherwise, this is the standard behavior for every form you create. Normal forms are children of the MDI client window; therefore, you can't size or drag them outside the Access window's boundaries.

A *popup form* (one that either has its Popup property set to Yes or has been loaded by the OpenForm action with the dialog attribute set) floats above all other Access windows. These forms aren't children of the MDI client window at all; they have the Access main window as their parent. Therefore, they aren't limited to the Access window's area. You can drag them outside the Access window's borders or size them larger than the Access main window. Since they are children of the main Access window, however, if you minimize Access you minimize all its child windows, including popup forms.

A *modal form* (whether or not it's a popup form) retains the focus until you either close or hide it (by setting its Visible property to No). No matter how much you click on other areas of the program, Access ignores those mouse clicks until the modal form lets go of the focus.

NOTE
In Windows 3.x, it was possible to force a form to be modal throughout the entire system, using a Windows API call. Under Windows NT and Windows 95, however, that isn't possible. You can no longer make a window "take over" the entire operating system. This is probably a good thing, even though it appears to be a loss of functionality: you really shouldn't be causing an Access form to monopolize a multitasking operating system.

Before you can decide how you want your form to look, you must decide how you want to use it. In some uses you'll want all the form's features available, but in others you'll want to remove some or all of the trappings. The following sections ask some questions and provide simple answers for the most general cases.

Is Your Form Unbound?

Does your form display rows from a recordset, allowing the user to scroll through them? If so, it's bound, and if not, it's unbound. If it's unbound you don't have any use for the navigation buttons, so you set the NavigationButtons property to No. In addition, you won't need the record selector bar, so you should remove it, also, by setting the RecordSelectors property to No.

Does Your Form Need to Scroll?

Is the viewing surface of your form larger than the window area? If so, you need to use either or both of the scroll bars. If not, you can remove them by setting the ScrollBars property to Horizontal Only, Vertical Only, or Neither. If you have the choice, we recommend that you try to avoid creating forms larger than will fit on your screen and to avoid using scroll bars on forms if possible.

Is Your Form a Custom Dialog?

If your form is a custom dialog box, you won't want your users to resize or maximize it. In this case, disable the Maximize button and perhaps remove the Close button, too. Removing the Close button (setting the CloseButton property to No) also removes the Close menu item on the control menu. If you remove the Close button, though, remember that you must provide a means to close the form. Although you can use the Alt+F4 key to close popup forms and Ctrl+F4 to close other forms, most users don't know that. Removing the control box and not providing some other means of closing the form will confuse users. On the other hand, removing the control menu is not enough to deter users from closing forms when you don't want them to. (See the section "Controlled Closing" below.)

Is Your Form a Popup?

If your form is intended to float on top of all the other Access windows, it's considered a popup form. If that's the case, you'll most likely want to set the Popup property to Yes and the BorderStyle property to Dialog. If you also want your form to grab the focus and retain it until the user is done working with the form, set the Modal property to Yes.

Controlled Closing

You can disable or remove the standard Close button and provide your own Close button in an attempt to control the way users close your forms, but there is still at least one more way to close the form: users can use the Ctrl+F4 key (for normal forms) or the Alt+F4 key (for popup forms) to bypass your own form-closing mechanism. If you want complete control over your forms, you need to plug this one last hole.

You may also want to leave the built-in Close button enabled but, under certain circumstances, disable it. You're not allowed to change the state of the CloseButton property of a form at run time, but you can disable the Close menu item on the control menu at any time; doing so also automatically disables the Close button on your form. In many cases you'll want to combine both methods, disabling the menu item and disallowing the keystrokes to unload the form. The following sections cover both of these techniques.

Disabling the Close Menu Item

Like all the other components of Windows, every menu can be identified by its handle. Once you have that handle you can modify the menu, adding or deleting items or perhaps making items checked or disabled. (For more information on modifying menu components, see Chapter 11.) Windows conveniently provides a mechanism for retrieving the handle for a form's control menu (often called its system menu); you can use the GetSystemMenu() API function to retrieve the menu handle you need. Once you have that handle, you can use the EnableMenuItem() API function to enable or disable items on the control menu.

Because the items you'll find on system menus throughout Windows are relatively standard, the Windows API provides a group of command constants that Windows understands when you tell it to modify a menu item. Listing 8.1 includes the constants from the group that apply to Access as predefined constants. When you tell Windows which item on the menu you want to enable or disable, you specify either a position or a command by "name" (actually, by its value). In this case, since you can't be sure exactly where on the system menu you'll find the Close menu item, you use the glrcSC_CLOSE constant. Listing 8.1 shows the entire set of code you need to disable and reenable the Close item on the system menu.

Listing 8.1

```
' The declarations and constants are from basFormGlobal
' in CH08.MDB.
Declare Function glr_apiGetSystemMenu Lib "User32" _
 Alias "GetSystemMenu" (ByVal hwnd As Long, _
 ByVal bRevert As Long) As Long
Declare Function glr_apiEnableMenuItem Lib "User32" _
 Alias "EnableMenuItem" (ByVal hMenu As Long, _
 ByVal wIDEnableItem As Long, ByVal wEnable As Long) As Long
' Action constants
Public Const glrcMF_BYCOMMAND = &H0
Public Const glrcMF_DISABLED = &H2
Public Const glrcMF_ENABLED = &H0
```

```
Public Const glrcMF_GRAYED = &H1

' Menu item name constants
Public Const glrcSC_SIZE = &HF000
Public Const glrcSC_MOVE = &HF010
Public Const glrcSC_MINIMIZE = &HF020
Public Const glrcSC_MAXIMIZE = &HF030
Public Const glrcSC_NEXTWINDOW = &HF040
Public Const glrcSC_CLOSE = &HF060
Public Const glrcSC_RESTORE = &HF120

' The function itself is in basControlMenu.

Function glrEnableControlMenuItem(frm As Form, _
 lngItem As Long, fEnable As Boolean) As Long

    Dim lngRetval As Long
    Dim lngMenu As Long
    Dim lngAction As Long

    If frm.ControlBox Then
        lngMenu = glr_apiGetSystemMenu(frm.hwnd, False)
    Else
        lngMenu = 0
    End If
    lngRetval = 0

    ' If you got a menu handle, then do the work.
    If lngMenu <> 0 Then
        If fEnable Then
            lngAction = glrcMF_BYCOMMAND Or _
             glrcMF_ENABLED
        Else
            lngAction = glrcMF_BYCOMMAND Or _
             glrcMF_DISABLED Or glrcMF_GRAYED
        End If
        lngRetval = glr_apiEnableMenuItem(lngMenu, _
         lngItem, lngAction)
    End If
    glrEnableControlMenuItem = lngRetval
End Function
```

Disregarding the Alt+F4/Ctrl+F4 Keys

To close the final loophole allowing users to close your forms behind your back, you must restrict the use of the Alt+F4 and Ctrl+F4 keys. Fortunately, you can accomplish this without having to check whether the user pressed either Alt+F4 or Ctrl+F4 to close your form. For this method to work, your form must include some method of allowing the user to close it, usually using a command button. It involves these four simple steps:

1. In your form's CBF, in the Declarations area, define a Boolean variable (fOKToClose, for this example).

2. In your form's Open event, set the value of fOKToClose to False. Either disable the Close button (set the CloseButton property to False) or call glrEnableControlMenuItem(), disabling the Close item on the control menu.

3. In the code attached to the Click event of the button used to close your form, set fOKToClose to True.

4. In your form's Unload event, check the value of fOKToClose. If it's False, set the Cancel variable to True, halting the form's closing.

That's all there is to it. Unless your user clicks your button, there's no way this form is going to close. Listing 8.2 shows the minimal CBF your form might contain to implement this method. You can investigate frmCloseTest in CH08.MDB to see it in action.

Listing 8.2

```
' Variable to control when the form can be closed.
Dim fOKToClose As Boolean

Private Sub cmdClose_Click()
    ' If you click the Close button, set the variable
    ' so the OnUnload event will let you out.
    fOKToClose = True

    ' Now that you've cleared the way, close the form.
    DoCmd.Close
End Sub

Private Sub Form_Open(Cancel As Integer)
```

```
    ' Set the trap, so no one can close the form without
    ' clicking the Close button.
    fOKToClose = False

    ' Disable the Close item on the system menu, just
    ' to be polite, since it wouldn't do anything, anyway.
    glrEnableControlMenuItem Me, glrcSC_CLOSE, False
End Sub

Private Sub Form_Unload(Cancel As Integer)
    Cancel = Not fOKToClose
End Sub
```

If you really care to control when and how your users can close your form, you'll want to incorporate a combination of the suggestions discussed here. You might want to remove the control menu altogether or just disable the Close menu item. In either case you'll probably want to set the Cancel variable in the Unload event so users can't close the form with an unanticipated keystroke.

To disable or enable items on the control menu, you need to import the basControl-Menu and basFormGlobal modules from CH08.MDB. The glrEnableControl-MenuItem() function has the following syntax:

intRetval = glrEnableControlMenuItem (*formObject*,

MenuItem, fEnable)

where *formObject* is a form reference, *MenuItem* is a constant from the list in basControlMenu indicating which menu item to work on, and fEnable is either True (enable) or False (disable).

Removing a Form's Caption Bar

As part of an application you may need to remove a form's caption bar. Although Access allows you to remove the entire border, this may not be what you need for a particular look. Removing the control menu and the Minimize/Maximize buttons and setting the form's caption to a single space will almost work, but it still leaves the thick bar above the form. Figure 8.3 shows a sample form (frmNoCaptionBar from CH08.MDB) with its caption bar removed.

FIGURE 8.3:

Removing a form's caption bar leaves it with a sizable border, but you can't move the form by any means.

Removing the form's caption bar relies on changes to the form's window style. When any application creates a new window, it sets up some information about the style of that window. The Windows API provides functions to retrieve and set the style information, and you can change many of the window styles even after the window has been created. The presence or absence of the caption bar is one of those modifiable styles, and the code in Listing 8.3 (the glrRemoveCaptionBar() function) works by changing the form's window style when called from the form's Open event.

> **TIP**
>
> Even though you've removed the caption bar from the form, astute users will know they can access the items on the form's control menu, using the Alt+– (minus) keystroke. If you want to ensure that users can't move your form by any means, make sure you've set the ControlBox property to No.

Changing the Window Style

To change the window's style, follow these steps:

1. Retrieve the current window style (a Long Integer).

2. Turn off the particular bit in the value that controls whether the window has a caption bar.

3. Set the style for the window with the newly altered style value.

To retrieve and set the style value, you can call the Windows API functions GetWindowLong() (aliased as glr_apiGetWindowLong()) and SetWindowLong() (aliased as glr_apiSetWindowLong()). In each case you tell Windows which particular value you're getting or setting by passing the constant glrcGWL_STYLE.

To tell Windows to turn off the caption bar, you need to change the value returned from the call to GetWindowLong(). Windows treats the 32-bit value as a set of 32 binary flags, each controlling one attribute of the window, where each can have a value of 0 (False) or 1 (True). For example, the window style value contains a bit controlling the display of the caption bar, the Minimize and Maximize buttons, and the control menu. The only one of these Access doesn't give you control over is the display of the caption bar.

To change one of the settings, you use either the And or the Or bitwise operator. The And operator takes any two values and returns 1 in any of the positions that was nonzero in both values and 0 in any of the positions where either or both were 0. The Or operator sets any position to 1 if either of the corresponding positions is 1, and 0 otherwise. Therefore, to force a specific bit to be on, you use the Or operator with a number that has all zeros except in the particular bit you care about, where you have a 1. (This works because any value Ored with 0 isn't changed, but any value Ored with 1 is set to 1.) To force a bit to be off, you use the And operator with 1's in all the bits except the one you care about, where you have a 0. (This works because any value Anded with 1 isn't changed, but any value Anded with 0 is set to 0.) To control whether you're turning bits on or off, you can use the Not logical operator, which flips all the bits of a value from 0 to 1 or from 1 to 0.

Therefore, given that the constant glrcWS_CAPTION contains the correct bit settings to turn on the display of the caption bar, you could Or it with the value returned from GetWindowLong() to force the display on. To turn it off, you And it with NOT glrcWS_CAPTION. This leaves all the bits alone except the one controlling the caption bar display, which is set to 0. When you make this change and call SetWindowLong(), Windows redisplays the window without the caption bar.

The following three lines of code execute the steps necessary to retrieve and set the window style value:

```
lngOldStyle = glr_apiGetWindowLong(hwnd, glrcGWL_STYLE)
lngNewStyle = lngOldStyle And Not glrcWS_CAPTION
lngOldStyle = glr_apiSetWindowLong(hwnd, glrcGWL_STYLE, _
 lngNewStyle)
```

Resizing the Window

Unless you do a little more work, the form will look rather odd at this point. Since you haven't told Windows to redraw the form, Access becomes confused: the caption will still show, but Access won't know it's there. You now must resize the form without the caption bar.

This section of code requires three Windows API functions:

- GetWindowRect() (aliased here as glr_apiGetWindowRect()) fills a user-defined datatype—a variable of type glrTypeRECT—with the current coordinates of the form.

- GetSystemMetrics() (aliased here as glr_apiGetSystemMetrics()) tells you the height of the caption bar that was just removed. When you pass in the glrcSM_CYCAPTION constant, Windows returns to you the height of the caption bar.

- MoveWindow() (aliased here as glr_apiMoveWindow()) moves the window. (Actually, it won't be moved; you'll just call MoveWindow() in order to resize it. Other Windows API functions are available to resize windows, but this one is the easiest to call, given the coordinate information you'll know at this point.)

This code requires some brute-force calculations: figuring out the height of the old caption and subtracting that from the current height of the window. Subtracting the height of the caption bar from the current height of the form should leave you with a form that's the correct height. This technique works on both Windows NT and Windows 95, even though the sizes of various Windows elements differ between the two operating systems, because in each case the GetSystemMetrics() call supplies the correct adjustments. See Listing 8.3 for the details.

Listing 8.3

```
Function glrRemoveCaptionBar(frm As Form)
    ' Remove a form's caption bar
    glrRemoveWindowCaptionBar frm.hwnd
End Function

Sub glrRemoveWindowCaptionBar(ByVal hwnd As Long)

    ' Remove a window's caption bar, given its hWnd.
```

```
Dim lngOldStyle As Long
Dim lngNewStyle As Long
Dim rct As glrTypeRect
Dim intRetval As Integer
Dim intDX As Integer, intDY As Integer

' Get the current window style of the form.
lngOldStyle = glr_apiGetWindowLong(hwnd, glrcGWL_STYLE)

' Turn off the bit that enables the caption.
lngNewStyle = lngOldStyle And Not glrcWS_CAPTION

' Set the new window style.
lngOldStyle = glr_apiSetWindowLong(hwnd, _
 glrcGWL_STYLE, lngNewStyle)

' The caption's been removed, but now resize
' the whole window to match the size of the interior.

' Get the current size, including the caption.
glr_apiGetWindowRect hwnd, rct

' Calculate the new width and height.
intDX = rct.X2 - rct.X1
intDY = rct.Y2 - rct.Y1 - _
 glr_apiGetSystemMetrics(glrcSM_CYCAPTION)

' Move the window to the same left and top,
' but with new width and height.
' This will make the new form appear
' a little lower than the original.
intRetval = glr_apiMoveWindow(hwnd, rct.X1, _
 rct.Y1, intDX, intDY, True)
End Sub
```

Using glrRemoveCaptionBar() in Your Own Applications

To use glrRemoveCaptionBar() in your own applications, follow these steps:

1. Import the modules basCaption and basFormGlobal from CH08.MDB into your own database.

2. Call glrRemoveCaptionBar() from your form's Open event. You'll need either to place a call to it directly from the property sheet:

```
=glrRemoveCaptionBar(Form)
```

or to call it from the code you have currently attached to your Open event:

```
Call glrRemoveCaptionBar(Me)
```

You can also call glrRemoveWindowCaptionBar(), passing the function the window handle for any open window, but this technique is perilous for Office for Windows 95 applications: these applications maintain strict control over their status bars, and attempts to remove the status bar fail in mysterious ways.

Retrieving and Saving Information about Forms

You may find in your applications that you need more information about your forms than Access can give you. You may just want to be able to tell whether or not a specific form is open. You might, for example, need to save and restore your forms' locations from one session to the next. If your users can resize and move forms, this ability is especially important. (See the section "Screen Resolution and Distributing Forms" later in this chapter for more information on scaling forms as they're resized.) You may want to know what the current rows is or whether the user has moved to the new row. You'll find the solutions to these problems in the sections that follow.

Which Form Is This?

If you write Access Basic code attached to controls or sections on a form, you'll often need to pass to that code an object that refers to the current form. Many beginning developers count on the Screen.ActiveForm object to get this information. However, you should avoid this method if at all possible because Screen.ActiveForm often returns a reference to a different form from the one you'd intended.

Access provides a simple solution to this problem. From anywhere on the form's design surface, you can retrieve and pass to Access Basic code any of the form's properties. One of these properties is the form's Form property, which is a reference to the form itself. You can pass this property as a parameter to any function you call from the property sheet so the function can identify the form with which it should be concerned. For example, if your form calls a function named FormOnCurrent() from its Current event, you could place this expression:

```
=FormOnCurrent(Form)
```

in the property sheet to pass a reference to the current form to the function. The function declaration would be something like this:

```
Function FormOnCurrent(frm as Form)
```

On the other hand, if your code exists in the form's CBF (Code Behind Forms) you can use the Me object to refer to the current form. That is, in the external function declared above, you could retrieve the form's caption with this expression:

```
strCaption = frm.Caption
```

but in CBF, you could use this expression:

```
strCaption = Me.Caption
```

without explicitly defining Me. It always contains a reference to the current form. If you need to create global procedures that can be called from multiple forms, you can still call these from CBF. Just pass the Me object to those functions as a parameter from the form's event procedure. For example, to call the previously mentioned FormOnCurrent() function from a form's module, use this:

```
intRetval = FormOnCurrent(Me)
```

At the New Record?

It is sometimes vitally important for your application to be able to sense whether or not your user has moved to the "new" record (the extra record at the end of editable recordsets). Unlike previous versions, Access 95 provides a simple way for you to know whether or not users have positioned themselves on the new record: the NewRecord property. This property returns True if the form is displaying the new row and False otherwise. The sample form frmCategories, in CH08.MDB, includes a single line of code that will make a label visible if you're on the new row. Figure 8.4 shows this form, with the new row current. To set the visibility of the label, the form calls the following line from its Current event:

```
Me!lblNew.Visible = Me.NewRecord
```

FIGURE 8.4:

Use the NewRecord property to sense whether or not you're on the new row.

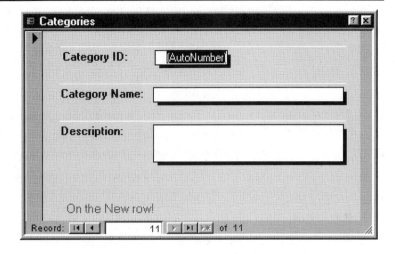

That is, if the NewRecord property returns a True value, it sets the label to be visible and sets it to be invisible otherwise.

What's the Current Row, and How Many Rows Are There, Anyway?

For some applications, you'll want to turn off Access' navigation buttons for your forms. When you do, however, you lose the display of the current row and the total number of rows. Access makes it easy to find out what row you're on, however, by supplying the CurrentRecord property. Every bound form provides this property, allowing you to display the current row number.

The sample form frmNavigate, shown later in this chapter in Figure 8.10, re-creates the current row and total rows display that Access normally provides. The current row is simple. In the form's Current event, the following statement updates that text box:

```
frm!txtCurrRec = frm.CurrentRecord
```

As for determining the total number of rows, you have to work a bit harder; this information isn't available from the form itself, but rather from the recordset that's filling the form. The recordset's RecordCount property ostensibly returns the number of rows that have, as of yet, been loaded. Common knowledge (see Chapter 6) says you must use the MoveLast method to move to the end of the recordset before you can know the number of rows in the recordset. Experience shows that this isn't really necessary for many types of recordsets: if you just wait long enough, Access will actually update the RecordCount value, loading rows in the background until they've all been visited.

> **TIP**
>
> This technique does not appear to work with a form based on a table linked from SQL Server. This behavior is consistent with the Access 2 behavior of not doing background fetches on ODBC recordsets. If you find that the form doesn't update the record count automatically, you will need to perform an explicit MoveLast to fetch the record count.

The sample form counts on this behavior, although it would be simple to change. This is the code that does the work, pulled from code called by the form's Current event:

```
Set rst = frm.RecordsetClone
' Sooner or later, Access will figure out
' how many rows there really are!
frm!txtTotalRecs = rst.RecordCount + _
 IIf(frm.NewRecord, 1, 0)
End If
```

The code displays the current value in the recordset's RecordCount property, assuming that sooner or later, it will be correct. For small recordsets, it's correct immediately. For large recordsets, it may take a few seconds, or longer, to know the total number of rows. Every time you move from row to row and trigger the Current event, the sample form calls this code, which updates the display on the form itself.

If this updating display for large recordsets bothers you, there are a few alternatives:

- In the form's Open event, force the recordset to move to the last row (rst.MoveLast) so it knows immediately how many rows there are. This can be slow, though, for large recordsets.

- In the form's Timer event, call code that uses a static variable to hold the RecordCount from the last time you called the routine. If the current value equals the previous value, you know the value has "settled," and you can change the Visible property of txtTotalRecs from False to True.

No matter how you solve this problem, you'll still want to update the text box during the form's Current event so it always reflects the actual number of rows.

Has the Form's Data Been Changed?

Access always knows if the data on the current form has been changed: if you have the form's RecordSelectors property set to True, you'll see the little pencil icon in the record selector when the data is "dirty." Access also makes this information available to you through the form's Dirty property.

Basically, it's simple: the Dirty property returns True when the little pencil would be visible on the record selector (regardless of whether you're actually displaying the record selector). You can use this property to provide your own indicator when the data has been changed or to cause your code to take action, depending on whether or not the data has been changed.

The sample form, frmCategories from CH08.MDB, makes a label visible if you change the data on the form (see Figure 8.5). Every 250 milliseconds ($\frac{1}{4}$ second), Access calls the Timer event procedure, which checks the state of the Dirty property

FIGURE 8.5:

You can display a message on your forms, indicating that the current row has been changed.

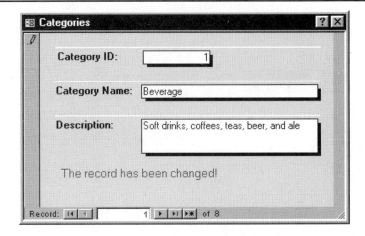

of the form and makes lblDirty visible if the form is dirty:

```
Private Sub Form_Timer()
    ' Turn the label on or off, depending on the state of
    ' the Dirty flag and the current visibility
    ' of the label.

    Dim fDirty As Boolean
    fDirty = Me.Dirty
    With Me!lblDirty
        If Not (fDirty Eqv .Visible) Then .Visible = fDirty
    End With
End Sub
```

In addition, the Dirty property is read/write. You can set the Dirty property to False, and if it's currently True, you'll force Access to save the current row, triggering the BeforeUpdate and AfterUpdate events. To test this, load frmCategories, dirty the form (change a field on it), and then, from the Debug window, type

```
Forms!frmCategories.Dirty = False
```

This writes the data to disk and forces the "dirty" label to become invisible again.

TIP

When writing the code for this example, we were tempted to just set the Visible property of lblDirty to be the same as the Dirty property of the form—that is, if the form was dirty, make the label visible, and vice versa. The problem is that if you set the Visible property of a control every 250 milliseconds, you're tying up a major portion of your application's processing power in this tiny feature. To avoid that problem, the sample code sets the Visible property only if it's not currently equivalent to the form's Dirty flag. If the form is dirty and the label isn't visible, make it visible. If the form isn't dirty but the label is visible (which can happen if you change the data and then undo your change), make the label invisible. This avoids spending any more processing power on this feature than necessary.

NOTE

What Access really needs is an OnDirty event property for forms so you wouldn't have to perform hacks like the ones we've done here. Because there is no such event, you have to resort to adding code to your form's Timer event, watching for changes in the Dirty property or attaching code to check it in the AfterUpdate event of each control on the form. We're not sure why there still isn't a Dirty event (the Dirty property has been around since Access 2, so they've had time to hear the complaints and add it in), but it's not there.

Is a Specific Form Loaded?

Although Access doesn't provide a built-in mechanism to check whether a specific form is open, there's a simple way to detect whether a specific form (or any other object) is loaded into memory. The trick is to use the SysCmd() function, which returns information about any object. If you call SysCmd(), passing to it the constant acSysCmdGetObjectState—along with the name of your object and a constant indicating the object type (acForm, acReport, and so on)—it returns a value indicating the current state of that object. As long as the return value is nonzero, you know the object is open. Both basCalendar and basCalc call this function to check the state of their popup forms. If you pass it just an object name, it assumes you want to know about a form. If you pass it both an object name and an object type, it will look for open objects of the specified type. (For more information on using optional parameters, see Chapter 2.)

Here is the code:

```
Function isOpen(strName As String, _
 Optional varObjectType as Variant)
    ' Returns True if strName is open, False otherwise.
    ' Assume the caller wants to know about a form.
    If IsMissing(varObjectType) Then varObjectType = acForm
    isOpen = (SysCmd(acSysCmdGetObjectState, _
     varObjectType, strName) <> 0)
End Function
```

Which Rows Are Selected?

Access developers have always wanted a way to detect which rows the user has selected on a datasheet, and Access 95 finally makes that possible. Using the new SelLeft, SelTop, SelWidth, and SelHeight properties, you can tell exactly which cells the user has selected.

Take a look at frmSelTest in CH08.MDB. This form, shown in Figure 8.6, allows you to select a region of the datasheet by placing numbers into the text boxes on the right side of the form header, and every 500 milliseconds it updates the text boxes on the left part of the header with the current selected coordinates.

NOTE Access doesn't provide an event when the selection changes, so you'll need to use the Timer event to update those text boxes every now and then. Don't use this technique in an application: to keep the display relatively current, you would need to update the values far too often. That process ties up the computer too much for very little gain. If you run the form, you'll see that this repetitive code causes a great deal of flashing in Access' status bar, as well.

FIGURE 8.6:

Use the SelTop, SelLeft, SelWidth, and SelHeight properties to read or write the selected area in a datasheet.

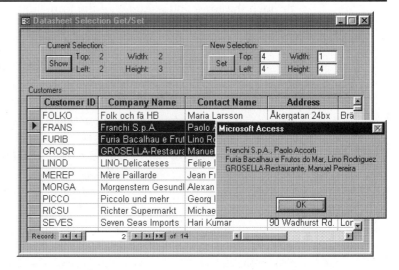

Setting the Selection

Setting the selection is simple. If all the necessary values have been supplied, just set the various properties of the form:

```
Private Sub cmdSet_Click()
    If Not IsNull(Me!txtNewSelLeft + Me!txtNewSelTop _
    + Me!txtNewSelWidth + Me!txtNewSelHeight) Then
        With Me!subCustomers.Form
            .SelLeft = Me!txtNewSelLeft
            .SelTop = Me!txtNewSelTop
            .SelWidth = Me!txtNewSelWidth
            .SelHeight = Me!txtNewSelHeight
        End With
    End If
End Sub
```

This example sets the SelLeft, SelTop, SelWidth, and SelHeight properties of the form embedded in the control named subCustomers.

Retrieving the Selected Values

The sample form, frmSelTest, can also display a message box full of the selected values, as shown in Figure 8.6. The code to do this work, shown in Listing 8.4, walks through the rows and columns of the form's underlying recordset, matching the rows and columns selected on the form.

One small hitch: when you click the Show button, you move the selection from the subform datasheet to the button itself. When you do that, Access "loses" the selection in the datasheet. The code stores away the current values in the text boxes on the main form and immediately resets the selection for you once you click the Show button.

Listing 8.4

```
Private Sub cmdShow_Click()
    ' Demonstrate what you might do with the
    ' Sel... Properties.
    Dim strOut As String
    Dim rst As Recordset
    Dim lngCol As Long
    Dim lngRow As Long
    Dim lngSelLeft As Long
    Dim lngSelTop As Long
    Dim lngSelWidth As Long
    Dim lngSelHeight As Long
    Dim lngLastCol As Long
    Dim lngLastRow As Long

    lngSelLeft = Me!txtSelLeft
    lngSelTop = Me!txtSelTop
    lngSelWidth = Me!txtSelWidth
    lngSelHeight = Me!txtSelHeight

    ' If only part of the cell is selected,
    ' its height and width will be 0. Force them
```

```
' to 1 in that case.
If lngSelWidth = 0 Then lngSelWidth = 1
If lngSelHeight = 0 Then lngSelHeight = 1

' Track where to stop.
lngLastCol = lngSelWidth + lngSelLeft
lngLastRow = lngSelTop + lngSelHeight

With Me!subCustomers.Form
    ' Set the subform's selection again, since you've
    ' just left there.
    .SelLeft = lngSelLeft
    .SelTop = lngSelTop
    .SelWidth = lngSelWidth
    .SelHeight = lngSelHeight
    Set rst = .RecordsetClone
End With

With rst
    ' Only do this if there are some rows!
    If Not (.EOF And .BOF) Then
        lngRow = lngSelTop
        .MoveFirst
        .Move lngRow - 1
        Do While lngRow < lngLastRow
            lngCol = lngSelLeft
            Do While lngCol < lngLastCol
                strOut = strOut & rst(lngCol - 1)
                If lngLastCol - lngCol > 1 Then
                    strOut = strOut & ", "
                End If
                lngCol = lngCol + 1
            Loop
            lngRow = lngRow + 1
            strOut = strOut & vbCrLf
            .MoveNext
        Loop
        MsgBox strOut
    End If
End With
End Sub
```

Saving and Restoring Form Locations

Many Windows applications save information about the size and location of their internal forms (or windows) from one invocation to the next. That way, when the user starts the program, the application is laid out just as it was when it was last used. Although you can explicitly save an Access form's location, you may not want (or be able) to save a form in order to preserve its size and location.

Storing Information in the System Registry

Most applications that save their state do so in the System Registry. VBA provides four procedures that make it possible to read and write values to a specific location in the Registry:

Procedure	Description
SaveSetting	Saves a single item and value to the Registry
GetSetting	Gets the value of a single item in a subkey
GetAllSettings	Gets a list of settings and their respective values from a key in the Registry
DeleteSetting	Deletes a section or setting from the Registry

These procedures are extremely limited. They can work only with subkeys under this particular subkey:

```
HKEY_CURRENT_USER\Software\VB and VBA Programs
```

as shown in Figure 8.7. In addition, you can create new subkeys only to store more values; you cannot create multiple values within a single key. This is a wasteful use of Registry space, and we hope that in future versions Access provides more flexibility. (If you want to dig in, Chapters 18 and 19 cover different ways to work with the Registry: Chapter 18 does its work from scratch, using the Windows API, and Chapter 19 uses MSAU7032.DLL, a library the Wizards use to do their work.) The example shown in the section "Putting It All Together" a little later in this chapter will use the SaveSetting and GetSetting procedures to save and restore the window locations.

FIGURE 8.7:

Use SaveSetting to write form locations to the System Registry.

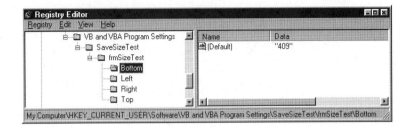

Nuts and Bolts: What Gets Stored Where

Because you can call these Registry functions from Access and since you can call a function when a form loads and when it closes, you can read the information when your form opens and write it back out when the form closes. Each item will be stored in an individual subkey, as shown in Figure 8.7. The goal, then, of the necessary functions is to read the data from the Registry every time you load the form and to move the form to the correct size and location at that point. Then, when closing the form, you call a function to write the coordinates back out to the Registry. (Note that although we've used convenient names for our subkeys, the names are meaningful only to this application. You can use any subkey names you wish, as long as you look for the same subkey names when you save and restore the values.) You can find the necessary functions in the basSaveSize module in CH08.MDB.

NOTE

In previous versions of Windows, the Registry was too difficult to work with to be of use for individual end-user applications, so most applications wrote their state information to text files, usually in the standard .INI format. Because the Registry has now been deemed the correct place to store such information, you might want to get in the habit of using the Registry for saving information about your application, its paths, and so on. On the other hand, there's something to be said for the simpler method of storing information locally, as rows in a settings table. In addition, under Windows 95 you can save and load Registry subtrees, which gives you a way to move configuration information from one computer to another.

Using SaveSetting and GetSetting()

SaveSetting allows you either to write to an existing subkey or to create a new one and write data there. The general syntax is this:

SaveSetting(*appname*, *section*, *key*, *setting*)

Use its parameters as described in the following table:

Parameter	Description	Example
appname	Name of the project or application	SaveSizeTest
section	Name of the item within the project	frmSaveSize
key	Name of the key for which you'd like to set the value	Bottom
setting	Value for the specified key	409

GetSetting works just about the same way. Here is its syntax:

GetSetting(*appname*, *section*, *key*[, *default*])

Use its parameters as described in the following table:

Parameter	Description	Example
appname	Name of the project or application	SaveSizeTest
section	Name of the item within the project	frmSaveSize
key	Name of the key whose value you'd like to retrieve	Bottom
default	Value to use if the key isn't found. If you don't specify a value, Access will use an empty string ("")	0

The Helpful Nz() Function

The GetSetting() function provides a useful way of ensuring that you get back a reasonable value when you try to query the Registry: it allows you to pass a final parameter that is what it will return if it fails in its search.

Similarly, when you're programming, at times it would be useful to have a function that would return one value if a parameter was null and a different value if it was not. In Access 2, almost every programmer wrote a routine like this sooner or later, in order to convert null values to 0:

```
Function NullToZero(varValue As Variant) As Variant
    If IsNull(varValue) Then
        NullToZero = 0
    Else
        NullToZero = varValue
    End If
End Function
```

Access includes such a function, Nz(), but it does much more.

Certainly, you can use Nz() just as you would the NullToZero() function above:

```
varConverted = Nz(varValue)
```

In this case Nz() will return varValue's value if it isn't null and 0 if it is. But Nz() also allows you to pass a second parameter, indicating what you'd like to return in the case where the first parameter is null. This makes it easy to supply a default value for possibly null parameters.

Consider this case (part of the sidebar "Sending Multiple Values in OpenArgs" later in this chapter): you need to call the glrGetItem() function to retrieve a portion of a string, but it's possible your search will fail and return a null value. In that case you'd like to supply a default value. In this example, you're searching for a string formatted like this:

```
Date=5/16/94
```

that starts with the word *Date* within the OpenArgs property of the current form. If it's there, glrGetItem() returns "5/16/94". If not, it returns Null. In that case you'd like to override that value and return today's date instead. Nz() allows you to do all that in one function call:

```
mvarDate = Nz(glrGetItem(Me.OpenArgs, "Date"), Date)
```

If you find yourself writing code that returns one value if a parameter is null and another if it's not, check out the very useful Nz() function instead, and do it all in one line of code.

Putting It All Together

Once you know how to read and write information in the Registry, you still need to know how to retrieve and set the form's size and location. These steps require yet three more Windows API function calls:

```
Declare Function glr_apiGetWindowRect Lib "user32" _
 Alias "GetWindowRect" (ByVal hwnd As Long, _
 lpRect As glrTypeRect) As Long

Declare Function glr_apiMoveWindow Lib "user32" _
 Alias "MoveWindow" (ByVal hwnd As Long, _
 ByVal X As Long, ByVal Y As Long, ByVal nWidth As Long, _
 ByVal nHeight As Long, ByVal bRepaint As Long) As Long

Declare Function glr_apiGetParent Lib "user32" _
 Alias "GetParent" (ByVal hwnd As Long) As Long
```

Retrieving Window Coordinates

The GetWindowRect subroutine fills in a user-defined type with a window's current coordinates relative to the edge of the screen. MoveWindow() moves and sizes a window relative to the window's parent (which in this case is most likely the Access main window). Therefore, when you retrieve a form's coordinates, you must make them relative to its parent's coordinates. To get information about the form's parent, you need the GetParent() function. All three of these functions require a window handle, but this isn't a problem since every form in Access provides its own handle through its hWnd property.

NOTE

Although Access provides the MoveSize macro action, it's not really appropriate in all circumstances. Because it works only with the current form, it requires you to select a form before running the action. For the purposes of this example, this requires setting the focus to the form before changing its position. Even with screen display turned off, the action on screen is quite distracting. In addition, using MoveSize requires you to specify coordinates in twips, not pixels. This requires some extra calculations to convert the retrieved screen location values from twips into pixels. In this example we've decided, for these reasons, to use the MoveWindow API subroutine instead of the Access MoveSize macro action.

Given the GetWindowRect() function, you'll find it easy to retrieve a form's coordinates. This function by itself might be useful to you elsewhere since, although forms provide read-only WindowWidth and WindowHeight properties, they don't provide a Top or Left property. You can use the GetFormSize subroutine (Listing 8.5) in your own applications, filling in a typeRect variable with the coordinates of a form relative to its parent. The parent, by the way, will be either the Access MDI client window (for normal forms) or the Access main window (for modal forms).

Listing 8.5

```
' Store rectangle coordinates.
Type glrTypeRect
    X1 As Long
    Y1 As Long
    X2 As Long
    Y2 As Long
End Type

Private Sub GetFormSize(frm As Form, rct As glrTypeRect)

    ' Fill in rct with the coordinates of the window.

    Dim hWndParent As Long
    Dim rctParent As glrTypeRect

    ' Find the position of the window in question, in
```

```
' relation to its parent window (the Access desktop,
' the MDIClient window).
hWndParent = glr_apiGetParent(frm.hwnd)

' Get the coordinates of the current window and
' its parent.
glr_apiGetWindowRect frm.hwnd, rct

' Catch the case where the form is Popup (that is,
' its parent is NOT the Access main window).  In that
' case, don't subtract off the coordinates of the
' Access MDIClient window.
If hWndParent <> Application.hWndAccessApp Then
    glr_apiGetWindowRect hWndParent, rctParent

    ' Subtract off the left and top parent
    ' coordinates, since you need coordinates
    ' relative to the parent for the glr_apiMoveWindow()
    ' function call.
    With rct
        .X1 = .X1 - rctParent.X1
        .Y1 = .Y1 - rctParent.Y1
        .X2 = .X2 - rctParent.X1
        .Y2 = .Y2 - rctParent.Y1
    End With
End If
End Sub
```

This procedure, given a form object and a rectangle structure to fill in, first finds the parent of the form. It then finds the window coordinates of the two windows (the form and its parent) and calculates the coordinates of the child form as compared to the upper-left coordinates of the parent window. If the parent's hWnd does not equal the Access window handle, you know the current form is a popup form (a popup form's parent is the Windows desktop, not the Access main window), so there's no need to subtract the Access window's coordinates.

Moving Windows

When it comes time to place the form, with a specific size, at a specific location, use the MoveWindow() API function. This function needs the window handle, the upper-left corner's coordinates, the width and height of the window, and information regarding whether or not to repaint the window immediately. The coordinates of the upper-left corner must be relative to the form's parent. Because you previously retrieved this information using the GetFormSize subroutine, this step should be simple.

The SetFormSize subroutine (Listing 8.6) takes a window handle and a rectangle structure filled with the new coordinates of that window, calculates the width and height based on the coordinates in the rectangle structure, and calls MoveWindow() to move the form.

Listing 8.6

```
Private Sub SetFormSize(frm As Form, rct As glrTypeRect)

    Dim intWidth As Integer
    Dim intHeight As Integer
    Dim intSuccess As Integer

    With rct
        intWidth = (.X2 - .X1)
        intHeight = (.Y2 - .Y1)

        ' No sense even trying if either is less than 0.
        If (intWidth > 0) And (intHeight > 0) Then
            ' You would think the MoveSize action
            ' would work here, but that requires actually
            ' SELECTING the window first.  That seemed like
            ' too much work, when this procedure will
            ' move/size ANY window.
            intSuccess = glr_apiMoveWindow(frm.hwnd, _
            .X1, .Y1, intWidth, intHeight, True)
        End If
    End With
End Sub
```

The Final Steps

Once you know how to save and restore the information from the Registry and how to retrieve and set the window size, the only step left is to actually move the information to and from the Registry. When you open the form, you'll call the glrGet-Coords() function, as shown in Listing 8.7. This function calls GetSetting for each of the four coordinates, using a default value of 0 for each coordinate. If the function didn't manage to retrieve nonzero values for the Right and Bottom coordinates, there's not much point in continuing.

Listing 8.7

```
Function glrGetCoords(strApp As String, frm As Form)

    ' This is the entry point for retrieving form info.
    ' Call this from the form's Open event.

    Dim rct As glrTypeRect
    Dim strName As String

    On Error GoTo glrGetCoordsErr

    ' Use the name of the application as the highest
    ' level, and the form's name as the next level.
    ' This way, you could have multiple forms in the same
    ' app use this code.
    strName = frm.Name
    With rct
        .Y1 = GetSetting(strApp, strName, glrcTop, 0)
        .X1 = GetSetting(strApp, strName, glrcLeft, 0)
        .Y2 = GetSetting(strApp, strName, glrcBottom, 0)
        .X2 = GetSetting(strApp, strName, glrcRight, 0)

        If .X2 > 0 And .Y2 > 0 Then
            Call SetFormSize(frm, rct)
        End If
    End With

glrGetCoordsExit:
    Exit Function

glrGetCoordsErr:
    MsgBox "Unable to retrieve all coordinates.", _
      vbInformation, "Get Coords"
    Resume glrGetCoordsExit
End Function
```

When you close your form, you'll need to call the glrSaveCoords() function (Listing 8.8). This function is almost identical, except that it saves the settings rather than retrieving them.

Listing 8.8

```
Function glrSaveCoords(strApp As String, frm As Form)
```

```
' This is the entry point for saving form info.
' Call this from the form's Close event.
Dim rct As glrTypeRect
Dim strName As String

On Error GoTo glrSaveCoordsErr

' Get the form's current size and position.
GetFormSize frm, rct
strName = frm.Name

' Use the name of the application as the highest
' level, and the form's name as the next level.
' This way, you could have multiple forms in the same
' app use this code.
With rct
    SaveSetting strApp, strName, glrcTop, .Y1
    SaveSetting strApp, strName, glrcLeft, .X1
    SaveSetting strApp, strName, glrcBottom, .Y2
    SaveSetting strApp, strName, glrcRight, .X2
End With

glrSaveCoordsExit:
    Exit Function

glrSaveCoordsErr:
    MsgBox "Unable to save all coordinates.", _
      vbInformation, "Save Coords"
    Resume glrSaveCoordsExit
End Function
```

Using glrGetFormInfo() and glrSaveFormInfo() in Your Own Applications

To use the glrGetFormInfo() and glrSaveFormInfo() functionality in your own applications, follow these steps:

1. Import the modules basSaveSize and basFormGlobal from CH08.MDB into your application.

2. Add a call to glrGetFormInfo() to your form's Open event. Either add it to the code you already call or just call it directly. In either case, pass it an

application name and a reference to the current form (the Form property, from the property sheet, or Me, from CBF).

3. Add a call to glrSaveFormInfo() to your form's Close event. Either add it to the code you already call or just call it directly. In either case, pass it the application name and a reference to the current form.

When you open the form, the code attached to the Open event calls the glrGet-FormInfo() function and sizes and positions the form correctly. When you close the form, the Close event code stores away the current size and position information.

Retrieving and Using the Interior Coordinates of a Form

If you allow your users to resize your forms while your application is running, you may at some point need to know the dimensions of the interior portion of your form. (This information will be used extensively in the section "Screen Resolution and Distributing Forms" later in this chapter.) Aside from issues of screen resolution, though, you might want to move or resize controls on your form based on the form's size. The example in this section maintains a single button on a form, half the width and half the height of the form, and centered on the form, no matter how you resize it. Figure 8.8 shows three instances of the same form, sized differently. In each case the code attached to the form's Resize event has calculated the current dimensions of the form and has reset the size and position of the button accordingly.

What was a very difficult operation involving several API calls in Access 2 is now a trivial operation, due to the addition of the InsideWidth and InsideHeight properties of a form. These properties tell you the width and height of the inside area of a form window. (You can't use the Detail section's width to gather this information, because the Detail section's width may be different from the visible window width.) To size a control proportionally, all you need to do now is retrieve the InsideWidth and InsideHeight properties of the form, place the control accordingly, and set the height of the Detail section, as well. Listing 8.9 shows the code attached to the Resize event of the sample form (frmCentered). Note that this example uses integer division ($\backslash$) rather than normal division ($/$) to center the control; this makes the form work more smoothly, because it has no need for the fractional parts of the measurements and can use integer math throughout.

FIGURE 8.8:

The width and height of the form's border control the size and positioning of the button on the form.

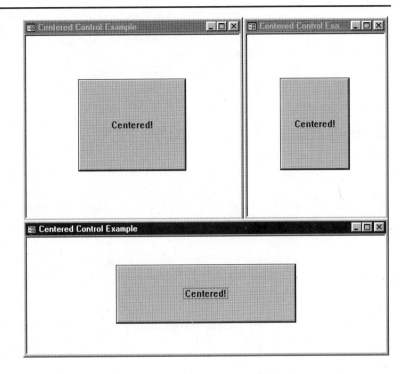

Listing 8.9

```
Private Sub Form_Resize()
    Dim intWidth As Integer
    Dim intHeight As Integer

    ' Get the current coordinates
    intWidth = Me.InsideWidth
    intHeight = Me.InsideHeight

    ' Set the detail section height
    Me.Section(0).Height = intHeight

    ' Set the coordinates of the button so that
    ' it's centered.
    With Me!cmdCentered
        .Width = intWidth \ 2
```

```
        .Height = intHeight \ 2
        .Left = (intWidth - .Width) \ 2
        .Top = (intHeight - .Height) \ 2
    End With
End Sub
```

Using Forms as Toolboxes

As in Access 2, Access 95 gives you very little programmatic control over toolbars. If you want any sort of real control, you'll need to use forms that look and work like toolbars instead of the built-in toolbars. By setting the right combination of properties, you can make a form that you create look and act like a standard toolbox. (Although the terms *toolbar* and *toolbox* are often used interchangeably, we think of a toolbar as a group of buttons fixed to the application window, usually right below the menu bar, and a toolbox as a free-floating collection of buttons.) Generally, most application toolboxes have these characteristics in common:

- They float above all other forms in your application.

- They have a control menu but neither a Minimize nor a Maximize button.

- They have a nonsizable border.

- They consist of buttons with pictures indicating actions, perhaps with a status bar label.

Toolboxes usually provide generic buttons that work with any window your user might have loaded. For example, you might want to provide a record navigation toolbar that would allow your users to move from row to row in a form and would reflect the state of the form the user had most recently chosen. Toolbars are also very useful when working with forms in Design view. Although Access provides a wide range of development tools, you might want to augment these with your own. The simple example you'll find here provides buttons to align groups of controls, as well as to center controls horizontally or vertically. Here is the sample toolbox, frmToolbox from CH08.MDB, in action:

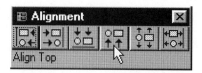

You should be able to take the example you see here and modify it for your own purposes.

Although Access doesn't really help very much, you can find out which Access toolbars the user currently has open. Doing so requires a lot of code and a number of Windows API calls, but it can be done. (For more information, see the section "Determining Which Toolbars Are Open" in Chapter 11.)

Creating Your Toolbox

You'll want your toolbox to float above all the other windows in your Access application. To make this happen you need to set the form's Popup property to Yes. In addition, you need to set other properties to make the form act like a standard popup toolbox. Table 8.3 lists all the properties you'll need to set. Some of these property values are the Access default values, but make sure they're set correctly, in any case.

TABLE 8.3: Toolbox Form Properties

Property	Value
Popup	Yes
BorderStyle	Dialog
ViewsAllowed	Form
ShortcutMenu	No
DefaultView	Single Form
ScrollBars	Neither
RecordSelectors	No
NavigationButtons	No
AutoResize	Yes
AutoCenter	No
MinMaxButtons	Min Enabled

The Popup Property

As mentioned earlier in this chapter, a form that has its Popup property set to Yes has a different parent from a normal window. Normal forms have the Access MDI client window as their parent (and can't be moved outside that window), but popup forms have the Access window itself as their parent. In addition, their Windows class is different, granting them different properties. Therefore, you can move popup windows anywhere on the Windows desktop, and they stay "above" all the other, normal Access forms. Setting the Popup property to Yes, then, is crucial in order to allow your popup toolbox to function correctly; the code that locates the active form will rely on the fact that your toolbox has a different parent from the other forms.

The AutoResize Property

Although setting the AutoResize property to Yes isn't imperative, it certainly makes the design process simpler for you. Normally Access saves the dimensions and location of a form with the form when you save it. In Design view, though, Access always displays the horizontal and vertical scroll bars on a form. Since you're using your toolbox form without scroll bars, you'll want it just the right size to include the controls you've placed on it. Setting the AutoResize property to Yes causes Access to resize the form to the correct size to just contain the internal design surface when it loads the form. (If you want an exercise in design frustration, set this property to No and try to get your form sized correctly.)

Placing Objects on the Form

The sample toolbox form consists of command buttons and a label control. You'll want to choose buttons with pictures that are familiar to your users and actions that are clearly related to the pictures. For the example, we've chosen to use the alignment pictures Access itself uses for the Align Top/Left/Right/Bottom buttons and similar pictures for the Center Horizontal/Vertical buttons. In this case we've also added a simple status bar in the toolbox that updates to describe the current button as you move the mouse over the buttons or as you move from button to button with the keyboard. This provides a different text than the ControlTipText property might, so you can provide two different sets of text, one more verbose than the other, if you wish. There's no reason you can't include other control types in your own toolboxes, but this sample was meant to be simple.

Why Not Use Access' Status Bar?

The sample toolbox includes its own status bar. As you move the mouse over the various buttons, code attached to the MouseMove event of each button keeps the status bar updated. You may be wondering why we chose not to use the standard Access status bar. Yes, you can use the SysCmd() function (with the acSyscmdSetStatus constant) to place text in the Access status bar. However, two problems arise with that method:

- Access itself uses that status bar, and you have no control over when that occurs. If you happen to run a query or any other action that requires Access to show a status meter, it will overwrite your status message without so much as a simple apology.

- Because you have no method for keeping track of exactly what is displayed in the status bar, you never can tell whether you actually need to update the text there. Therefore, all you can do is continually update the status bar. This can cause some unpleasant flashing as Access updates the screen. Using your own status bar on the form itself allows you to avoid this flashing.

- Many end users never notice what's displayed there. Because it's so far (in terms of distance) from the "action," the eye must travel too far to notice the text in the status bar at the bottom of the screen.

Updating the Status Label

If you're creating your own toolbox, this might be a good time to activate the status bar. That is, once you've created the form, including all the buttons and with all the necessary properties set, you can test it out. The toolbox won't actually do anything yet, of course, but you can still add the descriptive text in the status bar label control.

Because you want the text updated every time the mouse enters each button and you also want it updated as each button gets the focus, you need code attached to both the MouseMove and Enter events. To keep from duplicating text in each place, we've used a common procedure, DisplayText, that takes as a parameter an Integer describing the button in question. These constants:

```
Const glrcClearText = -1
Const glrcAlignLeft = 0
Const glrcAlignRight = 1
Const glrcAlignTop = 2
Const glrcAlignBottom = 3
```

```
Const glrcCenterVert = 4
Const glrcCenterHoriz = 5
```

are used throughout the code to indicate which button is current. Then, from both the MouseMove and Enter events, the attached code calls DisplayText, passing the appropriate constant for each button.

The DisplayText procedure in the following listing can react to the parameter, placing the correct text into lblStatus:

```
Private Sub DisplayText(intWhich As Integer)
    Dim strText As String

    Select Case intWhich
        Case glrcAlignTop
            strText = "Align Controls to Top"
        Case glrcAlignBottom
            strText = "Align Controls to Bottom"
        Case glrcAlignLeft
            strText = "Align Controls to Left"
        Case glrcAlignRight
            strText = "Align Controls to Right"
        Case glrcCenterHoriz
            strText = "Center Controls Horizontally"
        Case glrcCenterVert
            strText = "Center Controls Vertically"
        Case Else
            strText = " "
    End Select

    If lblStatus.Caption <> strText Then
        lblStatus.Caption = strText
    End If
End Sub
```

Note that the code updates lblStatus only if the text to be placed there is different from the text that's already there. This reduces the flickering effect you'd see otherwise. Since Access fires off the MouseMove event every time the mouse moves even a tiny amount, this procedure would otherwise be updating the label for each move. This way it updates the label's caption only when there's new text to be placed there. You might find it interesting to try this function without checking the current text, comparing the way the status label looks in either case. You'll probably agree that the extra processing required to check the text first is worth the time it takes, based on the improvement in the screen display.

Beyond the Basics

Once you have your toolbox performing the basic functions (that is, appearing correctly and updating the status bar), you need to perform the following actions for each button:

- Determine the previous active window.
- Return to that window.
- Take the appropriate action.

Finding the Active Window

Once you've created your toolbox form and its buttons and status bar, you need to make it actually *do* something. If your intention is to have it take some action on the form at the point where the user was prior to clicking one of its buttons, it will need some way to figure out what the last active object was. To find this information you need to rely on the fact that Access uses the MDI model for its workspace. Open forms and reports are all children of the same MDI client window, while popup forms are children of the Access window itself. Luckily, the Windows API function GetWindow(), when asked to retrieve information about children of a particular window, finds the top-most child window first. Since the active window is always the top-most window, you can get a handle to the window you want to find.

The module basWindowRelationships includes the functions you need in order to find the most recently active child of Access' MDI client window. To use them you must have a list of the Windows class names for the objects you might need to find from your own toolboxes. Table 8.4 lists several objects and their "official" class names.

TIP   Table 8.4 lists just a few of the many window classes Access creates. If you want to explore on your own, you need a tool that can examine windows and give you information about them. One such tool is SPYXX.EXE, which ships with Microsoft's Visual C++ Compiler. That's the tool we used to gather the class name information you see here. You may also be able to find freeware tools that provide similar functionality.

TABLE 8.4: Sample Access Objects and Their Class Names

Object	Class Name	Comment
Database Container	ODb	There is only one Database container, so finding the first object with this class type is always sufficient
Form	OForm	All forms are of the same class
Report	OReport	All reports are of the same class
Floating Access Toolbar	OTBDock	Container for toolbars. (A docked container can contain more than a single toolbar.) Contains windows of class OToolbar, each of which is an actual toolbar
Access Toolbar	OToolbar	All toolbars are of this class
Macro Design Window	OScript	
Module Design Window	OModule	
Table	OTable	Whether the table is in Design or Datasheet view, the internal display is a window of the class OGrid
Query	OQry	

To find the first occurrence of a particular child class, call glrGetAccessChild() with the appropriate class name. For example,

```
hWnd = glrGetAccessChild("ODb")
```

returns to you the handle of the Database Container window. Calling the function as

```
hWnd = glrGetAccessChild("OForm")
```

returns the handle of the active standard form. It won't find popup forms, since it only looks through the children of the MDI client window.

The more general-purpose function glrFindChildClass() takes two parameters: the handle of a window through which to look for children and the class of the child you're interested in. You could find the Database container's window handle by calling the function like this:

```
hWnd = glrFindChildClass(Application.hWndAccessApp, "ODb")
```

How the Functions Work

The glrGetAccessChild() function starts by using code similar to the previous example to find the handle to the MDI Client window:

```
hwnd = glrFindChildClass(Application.hWndAccessApp, _
 glrcMDIClientClass)
```

Once it finds this handle it can call glrFindChildClass() once more, requesting the necessary child of the MDIClient window:

```
If hwnd <> 0 Then
    ' Going into this function, hWnd is the handle
    ' for the main MDI client window. The return
    ' value is either the handle for the requested child
    ' or 0.
    hwnd = glrFindChildClass(hwnd, strClass)
End If
' It's possible that hWnd will be 0 at this point.
glrGetAccessChild = hwnd
```

glrFindChildClass() uses the Windows API function GetWindow() (aliased as glr_apiGetWindow()), which can iterate through all the children of a window, looking for a specific class type. You can call it once with the glrcGW_CHILD flag, in which case it finds the window's first child. Calling it subsequently, with the handle of that child and the glrcGW_HWNDNEXT flag, finds siblings of that child. If glrFindChildClass() looks through all the children and doesn't find one of the right type, it returns 0 (an invalid window handle), indicating failure. The loop boils down to these lines of code, iterating through all the children of the window for which the handle is hWnd:

```
hWndCurrent = glr_apiGetWindow(hwnd, glrcGW_CHILD)
fFound = False
Do While hWndCurrent <> 0
    intClassLen = glr_apiGetClassName(hWndCurrent, _
     strClassName, glrcMaxLen - 1)
    If Left(strClassName, intClassLen) = _
    strClassNameToMatch Then
        fFound = True
        Exit Do
    End If
    hWndTemp = glr_apiGetWindow(hWndCurrent, _
     glrcGW_HWNDNEXT)
    hWndCurrent = hWndTemp
Loop
```

Armed with glrFindChildClass() and some program such as SPYXX.EXE from Microsoft, you should be able to find a handle to any child window for any application, should the need arise.

Making the Previous Form Current

Once you know the handle of the last-active form, you'll want to make it the current window again. That was the point of all this code. Unfortunately, Access provides no method for activating a window based on its handle. To do that you need one more Windows API function, SetFocus(). Given a window handle, SetFocus() makes the appropriate window active.

For the example toolbox you'll find in CH08.MDB, all the actions are appropriate only if the active form is in Design view. Therefore, the function you call that returns you to the previously active form must also check the mode of the form. It returns a True value if the form is opened in Design view (the CurrentView property is 0) and a False value otherwise. Listing 8.10 shows the GetToForm() function, which the sample toolbox uses to return to the form that was active before you clicked a button on the toolbox. Each button's Click event code checks the return value of GetToForm() before it takes any action. If the function returns a False value, each button does nothing at all.

Listing 8.10

```
' These are the class names used in Access.
Const glrcMDIClientClass = "MDICLIENT"
Const glrcAccessFormClass = "OForm"

Private Function GetToForm() As Boolean

    ' Move back to the first active form.
    Dim hwnd As Long
    Dim varTemp As Variant

    Const acDesignView = 0

    GetToForm = False

    ' Attempt to find the active form.
    hwnd = glrGetAccessChild(glrcAccessFormClass)
```

```
        ' If you found a form, then go to it.
        If hwnd <> 0 Then
            ' Set the focus to the selected form.
            varTemp = glr_apiSetFocus(hwnd)

            ' The form's hWnd had better match the active
            ' form's hWnd!
            Set mfrm = Screen.ActiveForm
            If mfrm.hwnd = hwnd Then
                If mfrm.CurrentView <> acDesignView Then
                    MsgBox "This command is available " & _
                    "only in design view!"
                End If
            Else
                ' If the active form's hWnd doesn't match
                ' the one you just set the focus to, then
                ' something very strange is going on.
                MsgBox "An unknown error has occurred."
            End If
            GetToForm = True
        End If
End Function
```

Taking Action

By checking the return value from GetToForm() in each button's Click event code, you can be assured you won't perform an action that isn't reasonable for the form. If your toolbox is to perform actions that make sense in other contexts, you'll want to modify GetToForm() to check that the object is opened in the appropriate context for your actions. In this case the four buttons that align groups of controls do nothing more than replicate menu items. A sample event code procedure might look like this:

```
Private Sub cmdAlignTop_Click()
    If GetToForm() Then
        On Error Resume Next
        ' Form Design/Format/Align/Top
        DoCmd.DoMenuItem 3, 4, 4, 2, acMenuVer70
    End If
End Sub
```

NOTE To maintain compatibility with older Access applications, the folks at Microsoft devised a clever "hack" to indicate to Access Basic that you're referring to the Access 95 menu tree when you're using DoMenuItem. By adding a fifth parameter, the version number, they made it possible for existing Access Basic code to work correctly as long as no one tries to use any of the new menu items. In this case the Alignment menu items are all counting on the specific locations in the Access 95 menus. Therefore, to make this code work correctly, you must include the version number, using the Access constant acMenu-Ver70. (For more information on DoMenuItem and creating a DoMenuItem builder, see Chapter 19.)

The two buttons that center controls require more code, since there are no built-in menu items to do that job. They both use the InSelection property, checking for inclusion in the selected group of controls. For any control in the selection, the code takes the appropriate action. (The mFrm variable is global to the form, filled in by the GetToForm() function. This saves every event procedure needing to retrieve the form reference.) The following listing shows a function to center controls horizontally:

```
Private Sub cmdCenterHorizontal_Click()
    Dim intI As Integer
    Dim ctl As Control
    Dim intWidth As Integer

    If GetToForm() Then
        intWidth = mfrm.Width

        For Each ctl In mfrm.Controls
            With ctl
                If .InSelection Then
                    .Left = (intWidth - .Width) \ 2
                End If
            End With
        Next ctl
    End If
End Sub
```

TIP The InSelection property is read/write in Access 95. This means that if you want to write tools to be used when designing forms, you can now programmatically add items to the group of selected items on a form. Although this won't appeal to all developers, it's a welcome addition to the product.

Using frmToolbox in Your Own Applications

We've designed frmToolbox so you can just import it from CH08.MDB into your own application database (along with basFormGlobal and basWindowRelationships), open it in Form view, and use it while you're designing forms. You can use it, as is, as a development tool.

More likely, though, you'll want to take the concepts involved in frmToolbox and create your own toolboxes. If you're interested in using the underlying code but not the exact functionality, consider removing some of the code that's stored with the form. If you're going to use frmToolbox as part of your own application or library database, import it into your database. We've included the functions you'll need, along with the necessary declarations, in basWindowRelationships and basFormGlobal in CH08.MDB. To include those functions, just import those particular modules into your application.

Creating Self-Disabling Navigation Buttons

Access provides several methods for your users to move from one row of data on a form to another. You can use the standard form navigation buttons, but they provide absolutely no flexibility to you as a developer. You can also use the Button Wizard to create the navigation buttons on your form. In each case the solutions lack one feature that many clients request: they'd like buttons that don't do anything to be disabled. That is, if users are already at the last row in the recordset, the button that takes them to the last row ought to be disabled. If they're on the new row, the button that takes them there ought not be available. Few things are more frustrating to the end user than clicking a button and having nothing happen or, worse, clicking a button and finding out the action isn't available.

You can create your own buttons that replace the functionality Access provides and additionally give you the functionality described above. As an example, look at frmNavigate in CH08.MDB. This form includes buttons you can copy onto your own forms that handle form navigation for you. Figure 8.9 shows frmNavigate positioned at the last row in the underlying recordset. Note that the buttons that would move you to the next and last rows are currently disabled. (We've left the standard Access navigation buttons enabled for this sample form so you can compare the two sets.) Of course, on a real form, you'd set the NavigationButtons property to No if you were going to use these new controls.

FIGURE 8.9:
Because the current row is the last row in the recordset, the Next and Last buttons are disabled.

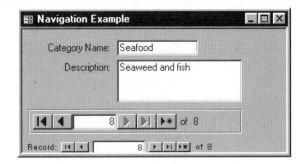

Forms and Their Data

Every bound form acts as a moving "window" for the form's underlying data. At any given time your form can display one or more rows from that dataset, and your Access Basic code can also manipulate that dataset. You can create a Recordset variable and assign to it the value of the form's RecordSetClone property. In this manner Access allows you to view and modify the same set of data that the user sees on the form. Since Access maintains two completely separate record pointers for the form and its underlying recordset, you can move around freely in the recordset, while the form's displayed record doesn't change at all.

In addition, forms maintain a unique bookmark for each row in the underlying data, separate from the bookmark Access maintains for the recordset itself. This allows you to save and retrieve the form's bookmark independently of the form's recordset bookmark. When you first retrieve a copy of the form's recordset (using the RecordSetClone property), your position in the recordset is officially undefined, and you'll need to position yourself on a particular row. You can use any of the Move... (MoveFirst, MoveLast, MoveNext, MovePrevious) methods to position the record pointer, or you can equate the recordset and the form's Bookmark properties. Doing so sets the current row in your recordset to be the same as the row currently shown on the form. Code to do this might look like the following:

```
Dim rst as RecordSet
Set rst = Me.RecordSetClone
rst.Bookmark = Me.Bookmark
```

You may be confused by the use of the Set keyword. The rules for its use are quite simple, though. The only basic concept to remember is that some datatypes are simple (for example: Integer, Double, and Variant) and some are objects (for example: Form, Control, Recordset, and Index). All object variables, when created, are just references. They aren't real objects, but are rather pointers to objects. You must "point" them at a real object before you can use them for anything. You have three ways to connect an object variable with a real object:

- Use the Set keyword to point a variable at an object.
- Use the "Dim x as New obj" syntax.
- Use the Create...() methods, such as CreateReport(), CreateRelation(), Create-Index(), and so on. In this case you first create the variable and then assign it the return value from one of these functions.

In any case, attempting to use an object variable without first attaching it to a real object will get you nothing except an error. (For more information on object variables, see the section "Using Object Variables" in Chapter 6.)

Controlling Row Movement

Two issues are involved in controlling the row movement programmatically:

- Moving from row to row
- Disabling the correct buttons at the correct time

The issues involved in moving from row to row are simple. Each button calls, from its Click event, a distinct procedure in basNavigate. Each of these procedures calls into a common procedure, NavMove, which performs the action. For example, the Last button calls this procedure:

```
Function glrNavLast(frm As Form)
    NavMove frm, acLast
End Function
```

(The constants acLast, acPrevious, acNewRec, acNext, and acLast are all defined by Access.) We could have used the GotoRecord macro action to perform all the work in this example but decided against it. NavMove (Listing 8.11) uses the Move… methods of the form's recordset to move about, because you can control the movement with more precision, trapping errors as necessary, if you move in the form's recordset first and then make the form display the new record once you've found it in the recordset.

Listing 8.11

```
Private Sub NavMove(frm As Form, intWhere As Integer)

    ' Move to the correct row in the form's recordset,
    ' depending on which button was pushed. This code
    ' doesn't really need to check for errors, since the
    ' buttons that would cause errors have been
    ' disabled already.
    '
    Dim rst As Recordset
    Dim fAtNew As Boolean

    Const glrcErrNoCurrentRow = 3021

    If frm.Dirty Then
        ' Put code here that you would have done in the
        ' form's AfterUpdate event. You can't use the
        ' AfterUpdate event if you've got these buttons
        ' in place, since they interfere pretty seriously.
    End If


    On Error GoTo NavMoveError
    ' This only works on the CURRENT form.
    ' You'll need to rethink this if you want
    ' the buttons on one form and the record
    ' movement on another.
    If intWhere = acNewRec Then
        DoCmd.GoToRecord Record:=acNewRec
```

```
    Else
        fAtNew = frm.NewRecord
        Set rst = frm.RecordsetClone
        rst.Bookmark = frm.Bookmark
        Select Case intWhere
            Case acFirst
                rst.MoveFirst
            Case acPrevious
                If fAtNew Then
                    rst.MoveLast
                Else
                    rst.MovePrevious
                End If
            Case acNext
                rst.MoveNext
            Case acLast
                rst.MoveLast
        End Select
        frm.Bookmark = rst.Bookmark
    End If

NavMoveExit:
    Exit Sub

NavMoveError:
    If Err.Number = glrcErrNoCurrentRow And _
      frm.NewRecord Then
        Resume Next
    Else
        MsgBox Err.Description & " (" & Err.Number & ")"
        Resume NavMoveExit
    End If
    Resume NavMoveExit
End Sub
```

In theory, this code should be all you need to move around in your recordset. There are two problems, though. This code won't handle the disabling of unavailable buttons. It also causes an error condition (3021, "No Current Record") when you try to move past the last row or before the first row.

Disabling Buttons

To correctly enable and disable navigation buttons, you need to be able to retrieve the current row location. That is, if you're currently on the first row, you need to know that fact as soon as you get there so the appropriate buttons (Previous and First) can be disabled. If you're on the last row, you'll want the Next and Last buttons to be disabled. If you're on the new row, you'll want the New, Next, and Last buttons disabled.

Checking the Current Location

You can use the form's recordset and the Bookmark property to check the current row's location within its recordset. For example, you could take these steps to check whether the current displayed row in the form was the first row:

1. Retrieve a copy of the form's recordset using the RecordsetClone property.

2. Set the location in the recordset to be the same as that displayed on the form, using the Bookmark property.

3. In the recordset, move to the previous record, using the MovePrevious method. If the recordset's BOF property is now True, you must have been on the first row.

If you want to write a function that just checks to see whether you're on the first row, here's one way to do it:

```
Function AtFirstRow(frm As Form)
    ' Return True if at first row, False otherwise.
    Dim rst as RecordSet
    Set rst = frm.RecordsetClone
    rst.Bookmark = frm.Bookmark
    rst.MovePrevious
    AtFirstRow = rst.BOF
End Function
```

You could apply the same logic to check whether you were at the last row. Armed with the knowledge assembled here, you should now be able to write a single function that checks all these states and disables the correct buttons.

There's one more issue, though. Some forms are not updatable at all. If they're based on nonupdatable queries or tables, if you've set the RecordsetType property for the form to Snapshot, or if you've set the AllowAdditions property for the form to No, you can't add a new row. In this case you also need to disable the New button.

The function you want should execute the following steps to determine which buttons are available as you move from row to row on the form:

1. Check the updatability of the form and its recordset, and set the New button's availability based on that information. Also, if you're on the new row, disable the button, since you can't go there if you're already there.

2. If you're on the new row already, enable the First and Previous buttons if there's any data in the recordset (disable them otherwise), and disable the Next and Last buttons.

3. If you're not on the new row, check for the beginning and end of recordset cases, as discussed above.

You'll find the procedure you need in Listing 8.12. glrEnableButtons() takes a form reference as a parameter and enables and disables the navigation buttons on the form according to your location within the form's recordset. To use it, you must call it from the Current event of your form. Note that the code is dependent on the specific names for buttons (cmdFirst, cmdPrev, cmdNew, cmdNext, cmdLast). Make sure your buttons have the correct Name property before attempting to use this code.

Listing 8.12

```
Function glrEnableButtons(frm As Form)

    Dim rst As Recordset
    Dim fAtNew As Integer
    Dim fUpdatable As Integer

    frm!txtCurrRec = frm.CurrentRecord
    Set rst = frm.RecordsetClone
    ' Sooner or later, Access will figure out
    ' how many rows there really are!
    frm!txtTotalRecs = rst.RecordCount + _
     IIf(frm.NewRecord, 1, 0)

    ' Check to see whether or not you're on the new record.
    fAtNew = frm.NewRecord

    ' If the form isn't updatable, then you sure
    ' can't go to the new record!  If it is, then
    ' the button should be enabled unless you're already
```

```
' on the new record.
fUpdatable = rst.Updatable And frm.AllowAdditions
frm!cmdNew.Enabled = IIf(fUpdatable, Not fAtNew, False)

If fAtNew Then
    frm!cmdNext.Enabled = False
    frm!cmdLast.Enabled = True
    frm!cmdFirst.Enabled = True And _
      (rst.RecordCount > 0)
    frm!cmdPrev.Enabled = True And (rst.RecordCount > 0)
Else
    ' Sync the recordset's bookmark with
    ' the form's bookmark.
    rst.Bookmark = frm.Bookmark

    ' Move backwards to check for BOF.
    rst.MovePrevious
    frm!cmdFirst.Enabled = Not rst.BOF
    frm!cmdPrev.Enabled = Not rst.BOF

    ' Get back to where you started.
    rst.Bookmark = frm.Bookmark

    ' Move forward to check for EOF.
    rst.MoveNext
    frm!cmdNext.Enabled = Not (rst.EOF Or fAtNew)
    frm!cmdLast.Enabled = Not (rst.EOF Or fAtNew)
    End If
End Function
```

Doing Time on the New Row

While you're on the new row, you might enter data, finish the entry, and then want to move immediately to a *new* new row so you can add another record. The problem is that we've disabled cmdNew for as long as you're on the new row. To get around this problem, you can call code to reenable cmdNew as soon as the form becomes dirty. To make that happen, you'd follow these steps:

1. Set the form's KeyPreview property to Yes. This allows the form to react to keystrokes, no matter which control has the focus.

2. Call the glrHandleKeys procedure from the KeyPress event of the form. This procedure checks the enabled status of cmdNew and, if it's not enabled but the form is dirty, sets the button so that it's enabled.

Therefore, you'd need code like this in your KeyPress event:

```
Private Sub Form_KeyPress(KeyAscii As Integer)
    glrHandleKeys Me
End Sub
```

The glrHandleKeys subroutine looks like this:

```
Sub glrHandleKeys(frm As Form)
    ' Users want to be able to move to the new
    ' row from the new row, if they've already filled
    ' in their data. This procedure checks
    ' the Dirty flag for each key and enables the
    ' New button if the row is dirty.

    With frm!cmdNew
        If Not .Enabled And frm.Dirty Then
            .Enabled = True
        End If
    End With
End Sub
```

Specifying a Specific Row Number

Just as with Access' own navigation buttons, these replacement controls allow you to type a row number into the text box, and once you leave that text box, the code will take you to the selected row. This code (glrMoveRow()) does its work by moving to the first row in the recordset and then calling the Move method to move to the requested row:

```
rst.MoveFirst
If lngRow > 0 Then
    rst.Move lngRow - 1
End If
```

The Move method requires as its parameter a zero-based number, so the code must subtract 1 to perform the necessary conversion.

Listing 8.13 shows the entire function, which should be called from the AfterUpdate event of the text box on your form.

Listing 8.13

```
Function glrMoveRow(frm As Form, ByVal lngRow As Long)

    ' Move to a specified row.
    On Error GoTo glrMoveRow_Err
    Dim rst As Recordset

    Set rst = frm.RecordsetClone

    ' Move to the first row, and then
    ' to the selected row.
    rst.MoveFirst
    If lngRow > 0 Then
        rst.Move lngRow - 1
    End If
    ' Sync up the form with its recordset
    frm.Bookmark = rst.Bookmark

glrMoveRow_Exit:
    Exit Function

glrMoveRow_Err:
    Select Case Err
        Case glrcErrNoCurrentRow
            DoCmd.GoToRecord , , acNewRec
            Resume Next
        Case Else
            MsgBox Error & " (" & Err & ")"
            Resume glrMoveRow_Exit
    End Select
End Function
```

Creating Your Own Navigation Buttons

You can easily create your own navigation buttons. To do so, just follow these steps:

1. Import the module basNavigate from CH08.MDB.

2. Create five command buttons, or copy the five buttons from frmNavigate in CH08.MDB. They must be named cmdFirst, cmdPrev, cmdNew, cmdNext, and cmdLast. If you copy the whole set of controls from frmNavigate, you can skip steps 3, 4, and 5.

3. Create the two text boxes (txtCurrRec and txtTotalRecs), or copy the controls from frmNavigate.

4. From each button's Click event, call the appropriate glrNav...() function. For the cmdFirst button, for example, use

```
=glrNavFirst(Form)
' or, from the form's module:
' Call glrNavFirst(Me)
```

The functions to call are glrNavFirst(), glrNavPrev(), glrNavNew(), glrNav-Next(), and glrNavLast().

5. To be able to type a new row number into txtCurrRec, you must handle its AfterUpdate event. To do that, call glrMoveRow(), passing to it the current form reference and the text box from which to retrieve the new row number:

```
=glrMoveRow([Form],[txtCurrRec])
' or, from the form's module:
Call glrMoveRow(Me, Me!txtCurrRec)
```

6. From your form's Current event, call the glrEnableButtons() function. If this is the only item in the form's Current event, you can call it directly from the property sheet, using the expression

```
=glrEnableButtons(Form)
```

If you already have code attached to your Current event, just call the function, passing it the form reference. That is, if you're calling it from CBF, you can use a statement like this:

```
Call glrEnableButtons(Me)
```

7. If you want to reenable cmdNew once you've entered data into the new row, also set the form's KeyPreview property to Yes, and have the KeyPress event call the glrHandleKeys function. From the property sheet, call

```
=glrHandleKeys(Form)
' or, from the form's module:
Call glrHandleKeys(Me)
```

Once you've set up the buttons and the event procedures, you should be able to open the form in Form view and use the navigation buttons to move about in your form's data.

NOTE

Although we normally tend to avoid placing function calls directly in the property sheet, in this case it made sense. You'd like to be able to copy the controls directly from our sample form and use them in your own applications; placing the function calls in the property sheet makes it possible to copy the controls, paste them onto your own forms, and just use them. Access does not copy event procedures when it copies controls, so placing the function calls directly in the property sheet saves you the effort of typing in the event procedures or having to copy them, as well.

NOTE

Even if you set these buttons' AutoRepeat property, they will not move you through rows as long as you keep them pressed. Because moving to a new row moves the focus away from the buttons, Access will not auto-repeat their actions.

We've also included a popup toolbox record navigation tool in CH08.MDB, shown in Figure 8.10. You can use it as part of your own applications, and you might want to take the time to pick it apart, since it uses some interesting design techniques. To use it, follow these steps:

1. Import the form frmRecNavPopup into your application from CH08.MDB.

2. Import the modules basFormGlobal and basWindowRelationships from CH08.MDB.

3. Import the module basRecNavToolbar. (This step is optional if you also skip step 4.)

4. For any form you want to use with frmRecNavPopup, modify the form's Current and Activate events to call the HandleRecNav() function, passing a reference to the current form. (See the forms frmCategories and frmCustomers in CH08.MDB for examples.) Calling HandleRecNav() ensures that the toolbar's display of the current position is correct even if you move from row to row on the form, not the toolbar. (This step is optional.)

FIGURE 8.10:

Use frmRecNavPopup to control record navigation with any bound form.

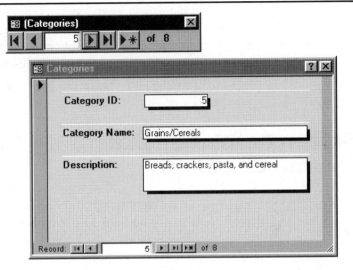

To use the popup toolbox, open a form and then open the toolbox. Clicking the various buttons on the toolbox should navigate through the rows on the form. To fully appreciate the toolbox, though, you should also follow steps 3 and 4 above. If you add the function calls to your form's Current and Activate events, your forms can tell the popup toolbox what they're doing and where they are. This allows frmRecNavPopup to track row changes when the user uses methods other than the toolbox to change rows, and it makes it possible for the toolbox to know exactly which form is the current form. If you're writing applications and want to use frmRecNavPopup, we strongly suggest you set up your forms to call HandleRecNav().

Why Create Your Own Toolbox?

You could create a new toolbar using the tools that Access provides to control record navigation. However, if you create a toolbox from scratch (such as frmRecNavPopup), you can include the features described here:

- You can maintain the current row number for the selected form.

- You can modify the toolbar caption to reflect the current form.

- By creating your own toolbox, you gain complete control over the actions your toolbox takes. Using Access' toolbars, you have no control over the action of each button.

On the other hand, your own toolbox cannot dock itself the way Access' toolbars can. In addition, creating your own toolbox requires a great deal of handwritten code. Using Access' toolbars requires none. (Although it's not documented, built-in Access toolbars can call Access Basic functions directly. For more information, see the section "Calling Expressions from Toolbars" in Chapter 11.)

Screen Resolution and Distributing Forms

When you set up Windows to run on your computer, you must choose a screen driver for use with your hardware. Your choice of screen driver forces your monitor to display a specific screen resolution, usually 640x480 (standard VGA), 800x600 (Super VGA), 1024x768 (Super VGA or 8514/a), or 1280x1024. These numbers refer to the number of picture elements (*pixels*) in the horizontal and vertical directions.

If you create forms that look fine on your screen running at 1024x768, those same forms may be far too large to be displayed by a user who's working at 640x480 (still the most popular screen resolution, since it's the resolution most laptop and portable computers support). Similarly, if you create forms at 640x480, someone working at 1280x1024 will see them as very small forms. (A full-screen form created at 640x480 takes up about a quarter of the screen at 1280x1024—although this is not necessarily something your users will want to change. Many people who use large displays and high-resolution adapters appreciate the fact that they can see not only a full-screen form, but a great many other Access objects at the same time.)

One unattractive solution to this problem is to create multiple versions of your forms, one for each screen resolution you wish to support. This, of course, requires maintaining each of those forms individually if you make changes to the form. The following sections deal directly with the resolution issue. We present code you can use to scale your forms as they load, allowing them to look reasonable at almost any screen resolution. In addition, we include code you can attach to the Resize event of a form, allowing users to resize a form and all its controls at run time.

Understanding Screen Resolutions

Before you can understand the solution to the screen resolution issue, you must understand the problem. Figure 8.11 shows a scale image of the four standard Windows screen resolutions, superimposed. As you can see, a form that appears full screen at 640x480 will take up only a small portion of a 1280x1024 screen, and a full-screen form at 1024x768 will be too large for a screen at 800x600.

The difference in the number of pixels is only one of two issues you need to consider in scaling forms. You must also think about the size of the pixels—the number of pixels per logical inch of screen space. Each screen driver individually controls how large each pixel is in relation to what Windows thinks an "inch" is. Windows provides API calls to gather all this information, which we'll need later in this section. For now, the information of concern is the number of twips per pixel. (A *twip* is equivalent to $\frac{1}{1440}$ inch.) Practical experience shows that screens at 640x480 use 15 twips per pixel, and all other VGA screen resolutions use 12 twips per pixel. (Screens using 800x600 seem to vary; experience has shown that some use 12 twips per pixel and others use 15. You may need to experiment with that particular screen size.) This means that at low-resolution VGA, 100 pixels take up 1500 twips (a little more than one logical inch), while at higher resolutions, 100 pixels take up 1200 twips (a little less than one logical inch). Therefore, to correctly scale your forms for different resolutions, you need to take both ratios into account. You need to compare, for both the screen on which the form was prepared and the screen on which

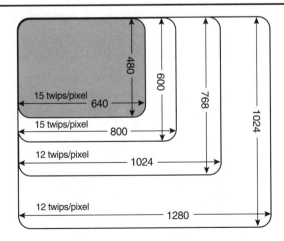

FIGURE 8.11:

All four standard screen resolutions, superimposed

it will be displayed, the pixels used and the twips-per-pixel value. The ratios of these values control how you scale the form.

The module basFormScale includes the code necessary to scale your forms at load time and to allow resizing by users at run time. This code makes extensive use of Windows API calls to retrieve information about the current display and the sizes of forms. (For more information about the Windows API and calling DLLs, see Chapter 18.)

Scaling Forms As They Load

To solve the problem of displaying forms so that they take up the same proportion of the screen real estate on different screen resolutions, it would seem that all you need do is calculate the ratio of the original screen dimensions to the current screen dimensions and scale the form accordingly. Unfortunately, the calculation is further complicated by the twips-per-pixel issue. Since different screen resolutions use a different number of twips for each pixel, you must also take this into account when calculating the new size for the form. The x-axis sizing ratio, when moving from 640x480 to 1024x768, is not just 1024/640. You must multiply that value by the ratio of the twips-per-pixel values, 12/15. (Think of it this way: as far as Windows is concerned, pixels are "bigger" at 640x480, taking 15 twips. At higher resolutions, a pixel takes up only 12 twips.) Therefore, the correct ratio is 1024/640 * 12/15, or 1.28. Figure 8.12 shows a single form, 400x120 pixels, created in 640x480 resolution, as it would display on a screen in 1024x768 resolution. The first example shows it unscaled, and the second example shows it scaled.

Retrieving Display Information

To scale your forms, you must first retrieve information about the current display driver. To do this, you need to use a Windows *device context*, a data structure that provides a link between the Windows API and the device driver. Actually, for this example, you can use an *information context*, which is a lower-powered device context, unable to write information back to the driver. Any calls to the Windows API dealing with the display driver must pass an information context or a device context handle as the first parameter. To get the information context handle, use the following code:

```
lngIC = glr_apiCreateIC("DISPLAY", vbNullString, _
 vbNullString, vbNullString)
```

FIGURE 8.12:

Scaling a form causes it to appear approximately the same on screens with different resolutions.

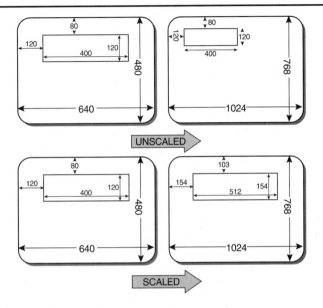

Once you have the information context handle, lngIC, you can obtain the information you need about the current display driver. First of all, you must retrieve the pixel resolutions of the current display driver. You can use the Windows API function GetDeviceCaps() to obtain this information:

```
intScreenX = glr_apiGetDeviceCaps(lngIC, glrcHORZRES)
intScreenY = glr_apiGetDeviceCaps(lngIC, glrcVERTRES)
```

Next, you must find out the number of pixels per logical inch in both the horizontal (X) and vertical (Y) directions. Once you have those values, divide them into the number of twips per inch (glrcTwipsPerInch = 1440) to find the number of twips per pixel. You can again use the Windows API function GetDeviceCaps() to retrieve this information:

```
intTwipsPerPixelX = glrcTwipsPerInch / _
  glr_apiGetDeviceCaps(lngIC, glrcLOGPIXELSX)
intTwipsPerPixelY = glrcTwipsPerInch / _
  glr_apiGetDeviceCaps(lngIC, glrcLOGPIXELSY)
```

Now you can calculate the ratio of the current screen resolution to the resolution that was active when the form was created. The original values will have been passed in to this function in the parameters intX and intY:

```
sglFactorX = intScreenX / intX
sglFactorY = intScreenY / intY
```

But as mentioned before, this isn't accurate enough. You need to take into account the differences in the number of twips per pixel between different display adapters. To do this, scale the scaling factors by the ratio of the twips-per-pixel value for the original display, as compared to the value for the current display:

```
sglFactorX = sglFactorX * (intTwipsPerPixelX / _
 GetTwips(intX, glrcXAxis))
sglFactorY = sglFactorY * (intTwipsPerPixelY / _
 GetTwips(intX, glrcYAxis))
```

(GetTwips() is a local function that attempts to determine the twips-per-pixel value for the original display, given the horizontal resolution of that display.)

Armed with the values for sglFactorX and sglFactorY, you have the information you need to correctly scale the form as you open it in the new display resolution. You should be able to just multiply the form's width, height, and position of the upper-left corner by that scaling factor and end up with the form in a relative position on the screen with the new width and height. Figure 8.12 demonstrates this calculation.

Scaling the Form's Contents

Scaling the form is only part of the problem, however. Just changing the size of the container won't help much if you can't see all the controls inside it. Therefore, you need a way to change the size of all the controls inside the form, as well. The function glrScaleForm(), called from your form's Open event, calls the glrResizeForm() function to resize all the controls. You can also call this subroutine directly from your form's Resize event, allowing you to dynamically resize all the controls on the form every time the user resizes the form. This can be a striking feature, allowing the user to make a form take up less screen real estate but still be available for use. Figure 8.13 shows a form both full size and scaled down to a smaller size.

To accomplish this visual feat, you can attach a call to glrResizeForm() to your form's Resize event. The glrResizeForm() function loops through all the controls on the form, scaling them by the ratio between the previous size of the form and the current size of the form. Note that in this situation you don't care about any screen

FIGURE 8.13:

FIGURE 8.13:

Two copies of the same form, one at full size and one scaled to a smaller size

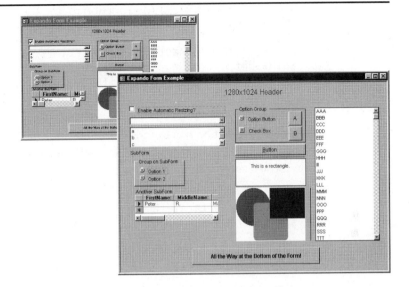

resolution issues; you're just comparing the current size of the form to the previous size of the form to find the sizing ratio.

> **TIP**
>
> If you switch a form from Design view to Form view and the form will shrink at run-time (it was designed at a higher screen resolution than the current resolution), Access will not repaint the screen correctly. You can force a screen repaint in the form's Resize event by uncommenting the lines of code in the sample that use the Application.Echo method. This creates its own problems, however, by causing unnecessary screen repaints. Unless you need to switch back and forth between Design and Form views, we recommend leaving those lines of code commented out.

The function first checks to make sure the user has not sized the form to its minimum size or minimized it, with no space inside the form. In those cases Access acts as though there were no active form, so the code cannot go any farther. The code calls the GetClientRect() API function to find the form's height and just exits if the height is 0 or if it's iconized:

```
glr_apiGetClientRect frm.hwnd, rctNew
intHeight = (rctNew.Y2 - rctNew.Y1)
If intHeight = 0 Or glr_apiIsIconic(frm.hwnd) Then
    Exit Function
End If
```

Once the function has found the dimensions for the current form, it calculates the current width. Then it can calculate and store the scaling factors, based on the previous sizes stored in rctOriginal:

```
intWidth = (rctNew.X2 - rctNew.X1)
sglFactorX = intWidth / (rctOriginal.X2 - rctOriginal.X1)
sglFactorY = intHeight / (rctOriginal.Y2 - rctOriginal.Y1)
```

Finally, it stores away the current form sizes so it will have them available on the next pass-through here:

```
With rctOriginal
    .X1 = rctNew.X1
    .X2 = rctNew.X2
    .Y1 = rctNew.Y1
    .Y2 = rctNew.Y2
End With
```

Once all the preliminary work has been done, if there's resizing to be done, the function now calls the workhorse function, SetFormSize().

Scaling the Controls

In theory, SetFormSize() does nothing more than just loop through all the controls on the form, scaling their locations and sizes by the scaling factors calculated in the calling function. In practice, there are a number of details that aren't, at first, obvious. These are some of the issues:

- The order of events is important. If your form is growing, you must expand the section heights before you allow the controls to expand. Otherwise the expanding controls will push out the boundaries of the sections and make the scaling invalid. The opposite holds true if your form is shrinking. In that case you cannot shrink the section heights until after you've sized all the controls. Otherwise you risk artificially compressing the control locations.

- You must deal carefully with controls that contain other controls. A group can contain toggle buttons, option buttons, and check boxes. A subform can contain any control and possibly yet another subform (nested, at most, two deep). To maintain the correct scaling, you need to walk through all the controls on the form, build an array containing information about all the container controls, scale all the controls on the form, and then scale the containers. In addition, if you run across a subform, you must recursively call the function again, scaling all the controls on that subform. If that subform contains a subform, you must call the function once more to handle that final subform. Once the function has handled all the controls on the form, it loops through the array of containers and scales them correctly.

- Some controls don't need their height or font scaled. For example, you can't really change the height of a check box. (You can try, but it won't look very good.) Several controls don't even own a FontName property. The SetFormSize subroutine calls the ChangeHeight() and ChangeFont() functions to find out whether it should bother trying to change the particular property at all.

- You want to *move* forms only when they're first loaded. After that, moving forms should be up to the user. Therefore, the code that positions the form itself should be called only if the subroutine was called from glrScaleForm().

Steps to Successful Scaling

Due to limitations of the technology, the methodology presented here is far from perfect. Each time Access fires off the Resize event, the function calculates the current control or font size based on the previous size. This iterative calculation inevitably leads to round-off errors. Once your user compresses the form down beyond readability, attempts to expand it will often result in an unreadable mess. One alternative method would have been to store away the original size of each control on the form. Then, at each resize attempt, you could have compared the current size of the form to the original size, scaling each control accordingly. This method might have been more accurate but would have slowed down the process; in the trade-off of speed against accuracy, speed won again.

In any case, there are some rules you must follow to make it possible for this code to work:

- Use TrueType fonts for each control you will scale. This code will scale only the fonts in labels, buttons, and text, combo, and list boxes. Unfortunately, the default font used in all controls is not scalable. You must either modify your form defaults or select all the controls and change the font once you're finished designing. On the other hand, beware of using fonts that won't be available on your users' machines. All copies of Windows 95 and NT ship with Arial and Times Roman fonts; choosing one of these for your buttons, labels, and list, combo, and text boxes guarantees a certain level of success.

- Do not design forms at 1280x1024 and expect them to look good at 640x480. By the time forms get scaled that far down, they're very hard to read. Certainly, using 800x600 or 1024x768 for development should provide forms that look reasonable at all resolutions.

- The current implementation of this code cannot resize subforms shown as datasheets. Although it may be possible to make this work, at this point you should be aware that the contents of datasheets will not scale, although their physical size will.

- Do not attempt to mix the AutoCenter property with a call to glrScaleForm() called from the Open event. The AutoCenter property will attempt to center the form before it's resized and will cause Access to place the form somewhere you don't expect it to be.

- Make labels and text boxes a bit wider than you think you actually need. Windows doesn't always provide the exact font size the code requests, so you're better off erring on the generous side when you size your controls.

To include this functionality in your own applications, follow these steps:

1. Include the modules basFormScale and basFormGlobal from CH08.MDB in your database.

2. Ensure that all the fonts on your form are scalable. (Use TrueType fonts if possible, since they're all scalable.)

3. In the form module for each form you'd like to scale, declare a data structure to hold the size information for the form:

```
' The actual name doesn't matter, of course.
Dim rctOriginal As glrTypeRect
```

4. To scale the form to fit the current resolution when it loads, attach a call to glrScaleForm() to your form's Open event. Pass to the function a reference to your form, the x- and y-resolutions of the screen for which it was designed,

and the structure you created in step 3:

```
Call glrScaleForm(Me, 1024, 768, rctOriginal)
```

5. To allow dynamic resizing of the form's controls, attach a call to glrResize-Form() to your form's Resize event. The first parameter to glrResizeForm() is a reference to your form, the second parameter tells the subroutine whether or not to actually do the resize, and the third is the structure holding the size of the form. If the second parameter's value is True, the subroutine changes all the controls. If it's False, it just resets the storage of the form's current size:

```
Call glrResizeForm(Me, True, rctOriginal)
```

Because your form always calls the function from the Resize event, regardless of whether you're actually resizing all the controls, the function always knows the form's previous size. This way, if you decide to allow resizing in the middle of a session, it will still work correctly. The example forms base this decision on a check box on the form itself.

Changing the Mouse Pointer

Although not documented at the time of this writing, Access' Screen object supports a property that allows you a tiny bit of extra control over the current mouse cursor: the MousePointer property. You can set the mouse pointer using syntax like this:

Screen.MousePointer = *intPointer*

where *intPointer* can be one of the following values:

0: (Default) Shape determined by Access

1: Normal Select (Arrow)

3: Text select (I-Beam)

7: Diagonal Resize (Size NWSE)

9: Horizontal Resize (Size WE)

11: Busy (Hourglass)

The MousePointer property changes the cursor for the entire screen. (That is, Access provides no method for changing the cursor for specific objects.) None of the other integer values work; only the values in the table will work.

You can also retrieve the current setting of the mouse pointer:

```
intCurrentPointer = Screen.MousePointer
```

This way you can retrieve the current mouse pointer, store away its value, set it to a new value, and return it to its original state when you're done with it. As you can imagine, using

```
DoCmd.HourGlass True
```

sets the value of Screen.MousePointer to 11, as it should.

Filtering Data in Access 95

As part of almost any application, you'll be called upon to allow your users to choose a subset of rows and perhaps their own ordering from a table or query. Access 95 provides two new ways to filter data: Filter by Selection and Filter by Form. The next few sections discuss these new features and the form methods and properties that are associated with them. These include the Filter and FilterOn properties and the Filter and ApplyFilter events. Along the way, you'll also need to investigate the FilterLookup property for controls, because this property allows you to fine-tune the performance of your QBF forms.

The Filter Property

Every form and report maintains a Filter property, which contains the current, or last applied, filter for the form. The Filter property takes the form of a SQL WHERE clause, such as

```
[LastName] = "Smith" And [City] Like "S*"
```

A filter can be either active or inactive, depending on the state of the FilterOn Property. (See the section "The FilterOn Property" a little later in this chapter for more information.) Filter By Selection, Filter by Form, Advanced Filter/Sort (that's the mechanism that was available in Access 2), the ApplyFilter method, or direct manipulation via code or macro will update the Filter property. The results of these actions might be different, but they all do their work by modifying the Filter property.

Forms begin life with a null Filter property. Any of the actions listed above will insert a string into the Filter property, and the resulting filter can be either active or inactive, depending on the state of the FilterOn property. Subsequent uses of the actions mentioned above will either replace or add on to the existing Filter property, depending on the specific action and whether or not the filter was active when you took the action.

Filter by Selection

Filter by Selection allows you to create a filter by pointing to the values by which you'd like to filter. For example, selecting the value "Peter" in the FirstName field and then clicking the Filter By Selection toolbar button places

```
[FirstName] = "Peter"
```

in the form's Filter property. Selecting just the P in the Firstname field places

```
[FirstName] Like "P*"
```

in the Filter property, and selecting the t places

```
[FirstName] Like "*t*"
```

in the property.

If there was an existing value in the Filter property before you used Filter by Selection, Access' behavior depends on the setting of the FilterOn property. If the filter was active (the FilterOn property was set to True), using Filter by Selection will be cumulative: Access will place an And operator between the existing Filter property and the new expression generated by your activity in the Filter by Selection mode. Subsequent uses of Filter by Selection will continue to add to your criteria, using the And operator. If the filter was not active when you started your Filter by Selection session, Access replaces the Filter property value with the new criteria rather than adding on to it. When you close your form, Access will save the current Filter property along with the form.

> **WARNING** Access does not check the validity of your criteria. Because of the additive property of filters when you use Filter by Selection, you may end up with completely useless criteria. There's nothing Access can really do about this, so it's just a matter of being aware that it's possible to paint yourself into a corner using Filter by Selection.

Filter by Form

When you start a Filter by Form session, all the existing filter criteria are parsed into the current form's controls. When you leave Filter by Form mode, Access re-creates the filter from the criteria specified in each control. If the form's Filter property references fields that don't exist as controls on the form, then when you leave Filter by Form mode, Access drops the errant criteria from the Filter expression.

In any case, Filter by Form results always replace the current Filter property. Every time you use Filter by Form, Access parses the existing filter, allows you to change it, and then creates a new filter based on your selections in Filter by Form. (See the section "Fine-Tuning Filter by Form" later in the chapter for a few more details on Filter by Form.) When you close the form, Access saves the current Filter property with the form.

Advanced Filter/Sort

The Advanced Filter/Sort mechanism, left over from Access 2, allows you to create any type of filtering/sorting criteria you wish. In all cases, when you change the Filter property using Advanced Filter/Sort, Access completely replaces the value, regardless of whether or not it was active.

The ApplyFilter Method

Access allows you to apply a filter to a form, using the ApplyFilter method of the DoCmd object. You can specify a WHERE clause, a query, or both from which to extract the filter criteria. If you specify either a WHERE clause or a query name, Access places the appropriate criteria in the form's Filter property. That is (assuming the WHERE clause on qrySimple is "ID = 5"), the following two statements will have the same effect: the Filter property of frmSimple will contain the expression "ID = 5".

```
DoCmd.ApplyFilter FilterName:="qrySimple"
' or:
DoCmd.ApplyFilter WhereCondition:="ID = 5"
```

If you use both arguments, Access applies the WHERE clause to the results of the query you specify. In other words, it combines the two WHERE clauses, using the And operator.

Whether you supply one or both parameters to ApplyFilter, Access replaces the existing Filter property for the form with the new criteria specified by your parameters.

What Happens When You Change the Filter Property?

Any of the above actions (Filter by Selection, Filter by Form, Advanced Filter/Sort, or using the ApplyFilter action) will

1. Change the form's Filter property

2. Filter the form accordingly

3. Set the form's FilterOn property to True

4. Requery the underlying recordset

5. Set the "(Filtered)" description next to the form's navigation buttons

6. Put "FLTR" in the Access status bar

Changing the Filter Property Programmatically

When you change the Filter property programmatically (using VBA or macros), the result depends on whether or not the filter was active previously. If filtering is active when you change the Filter property programmatically, the new filter takes effect immediately. If filtering is inactive when you change the Filter property, it remains inactive, but the Filter property accepts the new value. The next time you work with the Filter property (either by setting the FilterOn property to True or by entering Filter by Form mode), Access will use your new filter. If you set the Filter property programmatically, Access will not automatically save the new Filter property when you close the form.

Removing the Filter

Access provides several methods you can use to remove the current filter from a form. If you use the ShowAllRecords method of the DoCmd object or click the Remove Filter toolbar button, Access leaves the current filter intact but sets the FilterOn property to False for you. If you change the form's RecordSource or set the Filter property to Null, you'll actually remove the Filter property's value. The first methods leave the Filter property intact but make it inactive. Using the second set of methods actually removes the Filter property value altogether.

Any change to a form's RecordSource causes Access to remove the Filter property value. For example, even using

```
Me.RecordSource = Me.RecordSource
```

in an event procedure will cause the Filter property to become null.

Saving the Filter Property

If you change the Filter property because of Access user-interface operations (Filter by Form, Filter by Selection, or Advanced Filter/Sort) Access saves the new Filter property when you close the form, regardless of whether you specifically ask for the form to be saved. When you open a form with a Filter property set, Access will not automatically make the filter active; you'll need to set the FilterOn property to True for the filter to take effect. If you change the Filter property programmatically at any time while a form is open, Access will not save the Filter property when you close the form.

The FilterOn Property

When you open a form that has a non-null Filter property, Access doesn't filter the data automatically. To cause Access to make the filtering active, set the FilterOn property of the form to True. This read/write property allows you to both set the filtering to be active or not and to find out whether filtering is active. (Remember, changing the filter via the UI might set this property without your knowing about it.) For example, you could use code like this:

```
' Make a label on the form visible if filtering is active
Me!lblWarning.Visible = Me.FilterOn
' or
' Force filtering to be inactive.
Me.FilterOn = False
```

When you set the FilterOn property to True, Access applies the existing filter; it works the same as clicking the Apply Filter toolbar button. (As a matter of fact, if you set the FilterOn property for a form to True, Access will also select the Apply Filter toolbar button for you.) Setting the FilterOn property to False, if it's currently True, is the same as deselecting the Apply Filter toolbar button. (Actually, the tool tip for the button says "Remove Filter" when it's already selected.)

If you set the FilterOn property to True for a form with no Filter property, Access does not complain. The FilterOn property will be True; there just won't be any active filter. If you then subsequently set the Filter property, that filter will take effect immediately (because the FilterOn property is already set to True).

Changing the value of the FilterOn property does not trigger the ApplyFilter event (discussed in the next section). You must use the user interface to trigger that event.

The Filter Event

Access triggers a form's Filter event whenever you select Filter by Form or Advanced Filter/Sort but before it actually goes into the filtering UI mode. Access passes two parameters to your event procedure: Cancel, which you can set to True to cause Access to cancel the filter activity that triggered the Filter event; and Filter-Type, which will be either 0 (acFilterByForm) for Filter by Form or 1 (acFilterAdvanced) for Advanced Filter/Sort.

You can use the Filter event to control what happens before a filtering session gets started. You could

- Make certain controls on the form invisible or disabled. If you do disable or hide controls, you'll want to reset them in the ApplyFilter event procedure. (See the next section for more details.)

- Clear out a previous Filter property so the filter starts "clean" every time. (Of course, changing the Filter property programmatically will prohibit its being saved with the form when you next close the form.)

- Cancel the event completely (set the Cancel parameter to True) or replace the standard Access interfaces with your own.

The sample form, frmQBFExample, uses the first technique to hide the button on the form that starts the Filter by Form session. The button, cmdQBF, uses DoMenuItem to switch into Filter by Form mode. When you're in Filter by Form mode, Access disables all buttons but doesn't change their appearance. To make the current mode clearer, the example hides the button, as well. It also disables the Address field, just to show that it's possible. This is the code attached to the form's OnFilter event property; it reacts only to requests to start a Filter by Form session:

```
Private Sub Form_Filter(Cancel As Integer, _
  FilterType As Integer)
    ' Disabling controls, and moving to the previous control,
    ' could trigger run-time errors. Just disregard them.
    On Error Resume Next
    If FilterType = acFilterByForm Then
        ' Move to the previous control so you
        ' can hide the filter button. Also,
        ' disable the Address field, which doesn't
        ' make much sense for a QBF. Of course, if
        ' the Address field WAS the previous control,
        ' this is going to cause a little trouble
        ' (It just won't disable the address field.)
        Screen.PreviousControl.SetFocus
        Me!cmdQBF.Visible = False
        Me!Address.Enabled = False
    End If
End Sub
```

The ApplyFilter Event

Once you've created your filter and wish to apply it to your form, Access triggers the ApplyFilter event. Access calls this event procedure for all user-initiated filtering (Filter by Form, Filter by Selection, Advanced Filter/Sort) and most program-initiated filtering. As with other events (BeforeUpdate/AfterUpdate), Access triggers the event procedures only if the event happens as a result of user interaction. If you apply or clear the filter through code, Access will not trigger the Apply-Filter event; you'll need to do that yourself.

Access calls the ApplyFilter event procedure at different points, depending on the filtering action you've taken, but the event is always triggered before Access modifies the Filter property, and it is a cancelable event. Using this event, you could

- Trap attempts to remove a filter, or set a new one, and request confirmation
- Modify the filter expression manually, before Access applies it (Of course, modifying the filter in code prohibits Access from saving the new filter with the form when you close the form.)
- Reset the display of the form, putting things back the way they were before you modified them in the Filter event
- Change or update the display of the form before Access applies the filter

Again, Access allows you to cancel the ApplyFilter event by setting the Cancel parameter it sends to your event procedure to True. In addition, Access sends you the ApplyType parameter, which can be 0 (acShowAllRecords) to remove the filter, 1 (acApplyFilter) to apply a new filter, or 2 (acCloseFilterWindow) if you attempted to close the filter window without specifying a new filter.

The example form, frmQBFExample, uses this event to reset the form to its previous state and to confirm changes. The event procedure, shown below, first makes the command button visible again and makes the Address field enabled. Then, if you are attempting to set a new filter and that filter isn't null, the form displays the filter string to be applied and requests confirmation. If you're trying to show all records or the filter you're applying is null, the form requests confirmation to show all the rows:

```
Private Sub Form_ApplyFilter(Cancel As Integer, _
  ApplyType As Integer)
    Dim strMsg As String
    Dim strFilter As String
    ' Put things back the way they were before the
    ' Filter event changed them.
    Me!cmdQBF.Visible = True
    Me!Address.Enabled = True
    ' Get the filter, and convert it to a string
    ' (if it's Null, tacking on "" will convert it
```

```
     ' to an empty string)
     strFilter = Me.Filter & ""
     If ApplyType = acApplyFilter And Len(strFilter) > 0 Then
         strMsg = "You've asked to filter the form " & _
          "given the condition:"
         strMsg = strMsg & vbCrLf & vbCrLf & strFilter
         strMsg = strMsg & vbCrLf & vbCrLf & "Continue?"
         If MsgBox(strMsg, vbYesNo Or vbQuestion, _
          "Apply Filter") = vbNo Then
             Cancel = True
         End If
     ElseIf ApplyType = acShowAllRecords Or _
      Len(strFilter) = 0 Then
         strMsg = "You've asked to show all records."
         strMsg = strMsg & vbCrLf & vbCrLf & "Continue?"
         If MsgBox(strMsg, vbYesNo Or vbQuestion, _
          "Apply Filter") = vbNo Then
             Cancel = True
         End If
     End If
End Sub
```

TIP

Because the ApplyFilter event can be canceled, you must now place error handling around calls to the ShowAllRecords and ApplyFilter actions when called from VBA. If you don't handle the error, Access will trigger a run-time error if you cancel the filter, and your code will halt. This is similar to the way the Print action has always worked in Access: if you didn't handle errors and the user clicked the Cancel button while printing, your code would halt with a run-time error.

Fine-Tuning Filter by Form

When you enter Filter by Form mode, Access attempts to convert every text box on your form into a drop-down list, showing each unique item already in that field. In general, this is very useful, but with large datasets it can be inordinately slow. You can control whether or not Access fills those lists with values in two ways:

- Find the text box in the Tools ➤ Option ➤ Edit/Find dialog that's labeled, "Don't display lists where more than this number of records read." You can set that value to any number between 0 and 32766. Once you set the value, Access will read rows to fill your lists only until it reaches that number of rows. Once it has run out of rows, it knows not to display the list of values, but instead supplies only Is Null and Is Not Null as choices in the drop-down list. In other words, you're telling Access: "If you can't get all the unique values by reading fewer than this many rows, then just stop trying."

- You can also set the FilterLookup property for each control on your form. This property has three possible values: Never, if you never want Access to supply a list of values; Default, if you want to use the maximum number of rows described in the previous bullet point; or Always, if you always want Access to create the list, even if Access will have to read more rows than specified in the Options dialog.

The only remaining issue, then, is how many rows Access actually reads. The answer to this question is related to whether or not the field in question is indexed. If it is indexed, Access needs to read only unique values, so there's a much better chance you'll find all the unique values within the specified number of rows to be read. If the field is not indexed, Access has to look at every single row in order to create a unique list of values. Because Access will stop reading when it has reached the number of rows you specified in the Options dialog, you'll need to plan ahead before specifying that value. If you want Access to always pull up a list of unique values, set the option value to be at least as large as the number of rows in any non-indexed field in the underlying table. If, however, Access manages to build the full list of unique values before reaching the maximum number of rows to be read, it always displays just unique values, regardless of whether the field was indexed.

Ordering Your Rows

Just as with the Filter property, you can specify an OrderBy property for a form, report, query, or table and then make that order active by setting the OrderByOn property to True. This functionality corresponds to the quick-sort toolbar buttons: if you open frmQBFExample, choose the City field, and then click the Sort

Ascending or Sort Descending toolbar button, you're actually setting the form's OrderBy property. To see this, check it out in the Debug window:

```
? Forms!frmQBFExample.OrderBy
```

will show you the current OrderBy value.

Just as it does the Filter property, Access saves the OrderBy property of the form when you close the form. If you want to make the sort order active, set the Order-ByOn property to True. And just as with the Filter property, if you set the OrderBy property programmatically, Access will not save the setting when you close the form; it only does that if you set the ordering using the user interface.

If you want to sort on multiple fields, set the property to be the names of the fields, separated with commas:

```
Forms!frmQBFExample.OrderBy = "Country,City"
```

To make one or more of the fields sort in descending order, append DESC to the field name (just as you would in a SQL string, which is, of course, where this all comes from—you're just building the SQL ORDER BY clause):

```
Forms!frmQBFExample.OrderBy = "Country,City DESC"
```

When you open a form, Access does apply the OrderBy setting automatically (as opposed to the Filter property, which you must apply manually). Regardless of whether the OrderBy setting is active, it's stored with the form, and you can activate and deactivate it with the form's OrderByOn property.

Creating Popup Forms

If you write many applications, you will begin to notice a class of tool that is needed over and over—for example, popup calendars to select dates or popup calculators to calculate values. Once you create these items, you'd like to be able to use them in multiple applications.

The technique for providing a popup tool that returns a value is really simple in Access:

- Open the form using OpenForm, using the acDialog flag for the Window-Mode parameter. This forces all VBA code that follows the OpenForm action to pause, waiting for the form to be either closed or hidden.

- Pass parameters, as necessary, to the form in the OpenArgs parameter. (See the sidebar "Sending Multiple Values in OpenArgs" later in this chapter for information on passing multiple items in the single OpenArgs string.)

- In the form's Open event procedure, retrieve items from the OpenArgs property, as necessary. Using the code in basParse, and specifically glrGetItem(), your form can retrieve specific items from a delimited list. (Again, see the sidebar for more information on using glrGetItem().

- On the form itself, provide OK and Cancel buttons (or their equivalents). The OK button should make the form invisible, and the Cancel button should actually close the form.

- Once back in your original procedure, you know that the form has been either closed or hidden. To check which, use a function such as IsLoaded(), as in the section "Is a Specific Form Loaded?" earlier in this chapter, to check whether the form is still open. If it is, you know the user clicked OK and wants to use the data from the form. If the form is not loaded, you know the user clicked Cancel and you should disregard anything the user did with the form open.

- If the form is still loaded, retrieve the value(s) as necessary from the form (which is currently invisible), and then close the form.

Sending Multiple Values in OpenArgs

When working with popup forms, you'll often find it useful to be able to send multiple values to the newly opened form in the OpenForm OpenArgs parameter. You're allowed to pass only a single string value, however, so how are you going to send multiple values? You'll use the delimited text technique we discussed in Chapter 7, of course! The basParse module includes just the two functions you need: glrSetItem() and glrGetItem(). In Chapter 7 you used this technique to place multiple values into the Tag property. In this case you'll just want to build up a string containing multiple values, pass it to the popup form in the OpenArgs parameter, and have the popup form retrieve the various items from its OpenArgs property.

For example, imagine you need to pass two values to a form as it opens: the initial date to be displayed and the background color to use. You'll need to build up a string that looks something like this:

```
Date=5/16/56;Color=255;
```

You can either do that by hand or use glrPutItem() to do it:

```
Dim varItems As Variant
varItems = glrPutItem(varItems, "Date", "5/16/56")
varItems = glrPutItem(varItems, "Color", 255)
```

Once you've done that, you can send varItems to your popup form in the OpenArgs parameter:

```
DoCmd.OpenForm "YourForm", WindowMode:=acDialog, _
 OpenArgs:=varItems
```

On the receiving end, from the popup form, you can have code in the Open event that retrieves items from the OpenArgs parameter:

```
Dim mvarDate As Variant
Dim mvarColor As Variant
Sub Form_Open()
    ' Get the date, or use today's date if it's Null.
    mvarDate = Nz(glrGetItem(Me.OpenArgs, "Date"), Date)
    ' Get the color, or use black (0) if it's Null.
    mvarColor = Nz(glrGetItem(Me.OpenArgs, "Color"), 0)
End Sub
```

TIP

You don't actually have to close the form once you're done with it: if you want to leave it open but hidden, then the next time you open the form, Access will just make it visible, and it will still show the state in which the user last left it. Unfortunately, Access will not send the OpenArgs property unless it actually opens the form, so this technique will work only if you are not sending any parameters to the form.

Using Popup Tools

We've provided two popup tools, a calendar and a calculator, that fit into your application in the manner described in the previous section. In both cases you make a single function call that returns to your application the value returned from the popup form. In the case of the calendar, the return value will be the chosen date (or Null, if none was chosen). For the calculator, the function will return the result of the user's calculations. The inner workings of these tools aren't the issue here, but rather their interface to your application. Once you've seen how these forms work, you should be able to use the techniques from the previous section to create your own popup tools.

How Do the Sample Forms Work?

Both the calendar and calculator popup forms use a new technique, Property Let/Get/Set procedures, to set and retrieve user-defined properties of forms. (See the section "Using Property Let/Set/Get Procedures" later in this chapter for more information.) In this simple case, glrDoCalc() retrieves the Value property of the popup form to return the result of the calculation.

Here is the code for the glrDoCalc() function:

```
Const glrcCalcForm = "frmCalc"
Function glrDoCalc()

    ' Load frmCalc in dialog mode, and return the
    ' calculated value at the end of the session.

    DoCmd.OpenForm FormName:=glrcCalcForm, _
     WindowMode:=acDialog
    If isOpen(glrcCalcForm) Then
        ' Retrieve the return value
        ' then close the form.
        glrDoCalc = Forms(glrcCalcForm).Value
        DoCmd.Close acForm, glrcCalcForm
    Else
        glrDoCalc = Null
    End If
End Function
```

The code used to pop up the calendar is very similar to that used for the calculator. Again, in this case you'll check the Value property of the Calendar form (supplied by a Property Get procedure in the Calendar form) to see what date the user chose:

```
Const glrcCalendarForm = "frmCalendar"
Function glrDoCalendar(Optional varPassedDate As Variant) _
 As Variant
    '
    ' If the passed-in date is missing (as it will
    ' be if someone just opens the Calendar form
    ' raw), start on the current day.
    ' Otherwise, start with the date that is passed in.
    '
    Dim varStartDate As Variant

    ' If the user passed a value at all, attempt to
    ' use it as the start date.
    varStartDate = IIf(IsMissing(varPassedDate), _
     Date, varPassedDate)
    ' OK, so the user passed a value that wasn't a date.
    ' Just use today's date in that case, too.
    If Not IsDate(varStartDate) Then varStartDate = Date
    ' Open the form, and stand back!
    DoCmd.OpenForm FormName:=glrcCalendarForm, _
     WindowMode:=acDialog, OpenArgs:=varStartDate

    ' You won't get here until the form is
    ' closed or hidden.
    '
    ' If the form is still loaded, then get the
    ' final chosen date from the form. If it isn't,
    ' return Null.
    If isOpen(glrcCalendarForm) Then
        glrDoCalendar = Forms(glrcCalendarForm).Value
        DoCmd.Close acForm, glrcCalendarForm
    Else
        glrDoCalendar = Null
    End If
End Function
```

In this case you can pass to the function the date you want to have displayed on the calendar when it first appears. You can also pass a null value to have it use the current date or just leave the parameter out. (It's optional, so you don't have to supply a value at all.)

> **TIP**
>
> If you include more than one module from this book in your own application, you may find duplicated private functions or subroutines. Since we can't guarantee which combinations of modules and forms you'll want to include in your own applications, we've placed these small helper functions in the particular modules where they're needed. You may want to remove the Private keyword from one such instance, move it to a global module, and delete the other local instances; there's no need to carry around multiple copies of the same function.

Using the Sample Forms

You can easily include the popup calendar, the calculator, or both in your own applications. Follow these steps to include one or both:

1. From CH08.MDB, include the module basCalc or basCalendar.

2. Include the form frmCalc or frmCalendar.

3. When you want to pop up the calendar, call it with code like this:

   ```
   varDate = glrDoCalendar(varStartDate)
   ```

   where varStartDate is either null or a specific date/time value. The function returns the date the user selected by either double-clicking or pressing ↵ (see Figure 8.14).

FIGURE 8.14:
Calendar (frmCalendar), called from frmTestPopup (also in CH08.MDB)

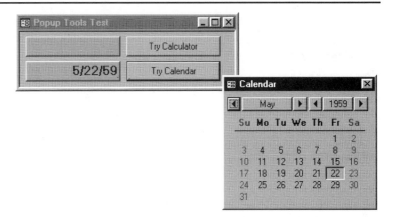

4. When you want to pop up the calculator, call it with code like this:

```
varValue = glrDoCalc()
```

The function returns the result of the user's calculations (see Figure 8.15).

FIGURE 8.15:

Popup calculator (frmCalc) in action

> **TIP**
>
> You might want to add the code discussed in the section "Saving and Restoring Form Locations" earlier in this chapter, which will preserve the location of the popup forms from one session to another. That way, once you place the Calendar form, for example, where you want it, that's where it will pop up the next time you invoke it. (See the earlier section for more information on adding that technique to your popup forms.)

Creating User-Defined Properties

In Access 95, you can create properties and methods of forms that "feel" just like built-in properties and methods from outside the form. The next few sections explain how you can create your own properties and methods. You'll use the Calendar form, presented earlier in this chapter, as an example.

Using a Public Form Variable

If the property you'd like to expose equates directly with a public module-level variable in the form's module, then there's no problem: just refer to the variable as though it were a property of the form. For example:

```
' In the module's declarations area
Public Value As Variant

' somewhere in your code
Forms!YourForm.Value = 5
```

will set the form's Value property to 5.

Using Property Let/Set/Get Procedures

If, on the other hand, you want to provide a property that requires some code to set or retrieve, you'll need to use VBA's Property Let/Get/Set procedures. Property Get procedures retrieve the value of a form property. Property Set procedures set the value of an object property of a form, and Property Let procedures allow you to set the value of a simple (nonobject) form property. These names, of course, correspond to the VBA Set and (seldom-used) Let keywords. (For example, for a form, you might want to create a ParentForm property that refers to the form that was active when you loaded the current form. That way you'd know which form to make current when you closed the current form again.) These procedures allow you to do any necessary work to set or retrieve information about the form. For example, in the calendar, this code allows you to set the FirstDay property:

```
Property Let FirstDay(intNewStartDay As Integer)
    ' Set the first day of the week.
    ' Fix up errant values.
    If intNewStartDay < 0 Or intNewStartDay > 7 Then
        intNewStartDay = 1
    End If
    intFirstDay = intNewStartDay
    RedisplayCalendar
End Property
```

You don't actually call Property Let procedures. Instead, you set the value of the property as though it were a built-in property. Given the code in the previous example, setting the form's FirstDay property looks like this:

```
Forms!frmCalendar.FirstDay = 2
```

If you want to try this, load frmCalendar in Form view. In the Debug window, type the previous line (setting the FirstDay property to 2). The Calendar form will immediately redisplay itself with Monday as the first day of the week.

You can supply either the Property Let or Get procedure or both, but if you do supply both, the input datatype to the Let routine must match the output type for the Get routine. For example, the Calendar form supplies Let and Get procedures for the form's Value property:

```
Property Get Value() As Date
    ' Return the current value of this form,
    ' the selected date.
    Value = DateSerial(Me!Year, Me!Month, Me!Day)
End Property

Property Let Value(datNewDate As Date)
    ' Set the value of the form: the
    ' selected date.
    mdatStartDate = datNewDate
    RedisplayCalendar
End Property
```

To test this out, with frmCalendar open, enter the following statement in the Debug window:

```
Forms!frmCalendar.Value = #5/16/56#
```

This moves the calendar so that it has the specific date selected. To use the Property Get procedure, use standard property retrieval syntax:

Debug.Print Forms!frmCalendar.Date

The following table lists all the properties exposed by frmCalendar:

Property	Description
Value	Gets or sets the selected date
FirstDay	Gets or sets the first day of the week (1=Sunday, 2=Monday, and so on)

Using Form Procedures as Methods

VBA allows Access 95 to expose any public function or subroutine as a method of that form. By using the Public keyword, you can create methods any other object can use to manipulate the form. The Calendar form does just this, making it a completely reusable, embeddable "object."

If you use form procedures as methods, no object outside the form needs to know anything about the form except its exposed methods and properties. For example, the Calendar form exposes the methods shown in Table 8.5. When your code calls these methods (for example):

```
Forms!frmCalendar.PreviousMonth
```

the Calendar form knows what to do and reacts by moving to the previous month.

TABLE 8.5: Methods Exposed by frmCalendar

Method	Description
NextDay	Moves selection to the next day
NextWeek	Moves selection to the next week
NextMonth	Moves selection to the next month
NextYear	Moves selection to the next year
PreviousDay	Moves selection to the previous day
PreviousWeek	Moves selection to the previous week
PreviousMonth	Moves selection to the previous month
PreviousYear	Moves selection to the previous year
Today	Moves selection to the current date

If you write reusable objects so that they expose as many properties and methods as you need, you should be able to pick them up and move them from application to application, with no rewriting at all.

To create a method for a form, all you need to do is add the Public keyword in front of the subroutine or function definition. Since the procedure is public, you can call it from anywhere else. For example, the code for the form's NextMonth method looks like this:

```
Public Sub NextMonth()
    ' The subroutine ChangeDate and the two
    ' constants tell the calendar what to do.
    ChangeDate glrcMonthStr, glrcMoveForward
End Sub
```

To test this from the Debug window, open frmCalendar in Form view, and type

```
Forms!frmCalendar.NextMonth
```

This moves the calendar to the next month after the one it's currently displaying.

To test this functionality, check out frmCalendarTest in CH08.MDB, shown in Figure 8.16. Clicking any of the buttons calls one of the exposed methods for the subform. For example, clicking the Next Month button calls this code:

```
Private Sub cmdNextMonth_Click()
    Me!Calendar.Form.NextMonth
    ' Make sure the screen repaints so
    ' the user sees the cursor move.
    Me.Repaint
End Sub
```

FIGURE 8.16:

Because frmCalendar exposes methods and properties, you can embed it and use it as a single entity.

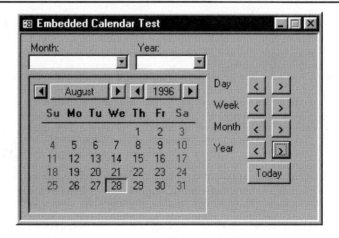

Form-Level Error Handling

Many errors can occur while your form is active. Some of these are standard run-time errors: perhaps a file is missing, a query your form expects to find isn't actually there, or the user does something you hadn't expected. Other errors are errors in the Access engine itself, and they can't be caught with normal error trapping. (For information on handling run-time errors, see Chapter 16.) You may find that you want to replace the standard Access behavior when these engine errors occur with behavior that is a little friendlier toward the user.

Access provides a form event to handle these errors. If you attach code to the Error event of a form, your procedure will be called whenever a trappable error occurs while the form is running. If you place your code in the CBF, Access sends you two parameters. The syntax for the call is

Sub Form_Error (*DataErr* As Integer, *Response* As Integer)

The value *DataErr* will contain the error number for the error that just occurred, and *Response* allows you to specify how you want Access to handle the error. If your code handles the error to your satisfaction and you don't want Access to intervene or display its own message, place the value acDataErrContinue in *Response*. If you want Access to display its own error message, place acDataErrDisplay in *Response*.

The sample Form_Error() subroutine shown in Listing 8.14 traps four errors that might pop up. In each case the procedure replaces the standard Access error message with its own. If an error occurs that it hadn't planned on, the subroutine just passes the responsibility back to Access. The form frmErrorSample in CH08.MDB includes this particular error handler. In this example, the following special conditions occur:

- The State field has a table-level validation rule. (Only "TX" will be allowed as the state.)

- The Age field is set up to accept numeric input only, between 0 and 255.

- The LastName field is set up as the key field.

The error-handling procedure reacts to any of the following events:

- The user enters a state other than "TX" in the State field.
- The user enters a non-numeric value in the Age field or a value out of range.
- The user creates or modifies a record such that the LastName field is empty.
- The user creates or modifies a record such that the LastName field (the primary key) is not unique.

In any of these cases the error-handling procedure takes over and displays the prepared message. If any other engine-level error occurs, Access' own error handling prevails.

NOTE   If any VBA error occurs within the Form_Error( ) subroutine, Access just disregards the procedure and handles any engine-level errors itself. That is, you won't get any error messages dealing with your coding error, but your procedure just won't get called.

Chances are you'll find a number of uses for form-level error handling. You could replace the error handling for these and other engine errors with your own, more personal, error handler. In previous versions of Access, the Error event was not as powerful as it might have been in that it did not, in general, allow you to handle multiuser errors. Access 95 does handle these errors correctly. (For more information on trapping multiuser errors with the Form Error event, see Chapter 12.)

NOTE   The form error handler will not trap VBA run-time errors. If your code causes an error to occur or if the user is executing your code when an error occurs, your code should deal with those errors. The form-level error handler is meant to deal with errors that occur while the form has control and you're just waiting for the user to choose some action that will place your code into action again.

Listing 8.14

```
Private Sub Form_Error(DataErr As Integer, _
 Response As Integer)

    Const glrcErrDataValidation = 3317
    Const glrcErrDataType = 2113
    Const glrcErrDuplicateKey = 3022
    Const glrcErrNullKey = 3058

    Dim strMsg As String
    Select Case DataErr
    Case glrcErrDataValidation, glrcErrDataType
        strMsg = "The data you entered does not " & _
            "fit the requirements for this field."
        strMsg = strMsg & vbCrLf & "Please try again, " & _
            "or press Escape to undo your entry."
        MsgBox strMsg, vbExclamation
        Response = acDataErrContinue
    Case glrcErrDuplicateKey
        strMsg = "You've attempted to add a record " & _
            "which duplicates an existing key value."
        strMsg = strMsg & vbCrLf & "Please try again, " & _
            "or press Escape to undo your entry."
        MsgBox strMsg, vbExclamation
        Response = acDataErrContinue
    Case glrcErrNullKey
        strMsg = "You've attempted to add a new " & _
            "record with an empty key value."
        strMsg = strMsg & vbCrLf & "Please supply " & _
            "a key value, or press Escape to undo your entry."
        MsgBox strMsg, vbExclamation
        Response = acDataErrContinue
        ' You can even place them on the right field!
        Me!txtLastName.SetFocus
    Case Else
        ' It's an unexpected error. Let Access handle it.
        Response = acDataErrDisplay
    End Select
End Sub
```

Using Subforms in Your Applications

Subforms are useful for at least two unrelated purposes: they are perfect for displaying data from one-to-many relationships, and you can use them to group together otherwise disparate groups of controls on a form. Both of these uses have some facets that aren't usually discussed, so the next few sections deal with areas of subform use that may be giving you difficulty.

Nested Subforms versus Separate, Synchronized Subforms

As long as you're interested in displaying one-to-many relationships, you'll find it easy to drag-and-drop a form onto another form. If you've defined relationships for the tables involved, it becomes even easier, since Access fills in the LinkChildFields and LinkMasterFields properties for you.

This method has its good and bad sides, however. If you nest subforms, you're limited to having at most three levels of data: the main form plus two levels of nested subforms. On the other hand, forms involving nested subforms are simple to set up. Figure 8.17 shows an example from CH08.MDB, frmNestedMain, which draws on frmNestedOrders, which in turn includes frmNestedOrderDetail. The two inner forms are linked on OrderId, and the two outer forms are linked on CustomerID. This example requires absolutely no macros or VBA code.

Although you'll find it easy to create examples like frmNestedOrders, you'll also run into some limitations if you want the form to look much different from the example. You can't, for example, make any form except the lowest-level form appear in Datasheet or Continuous Forms view, and you can't use more than two subforms. If you want any of the intermediate forms to appear in Datasheet or Continuous Forms view or if you need more than three levels of data displayed, you'll have to consider some other method.

The syntax for referring to objects on subforms, in its most complete form, is daunting. For example, to retrieve a value from txtName on the subform for which the

FIGURE 8.17:

Access makes it easy to create a form with two nested subforms, as long as you need only three levels and don't need to display any but the lowest-level forms in Form view.

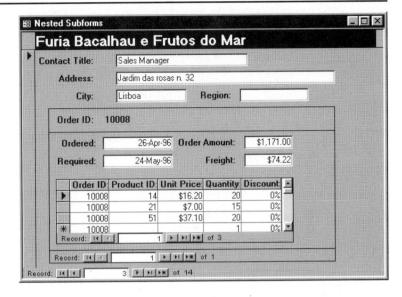

ControlName property is frmSub1, which lives on frmMain, you could use the syntax

varName = Forms!frmMain!frmSub1.Form.Controls!txtName

The reference to frmSub1 takes you to the control that contains the subform. The ".Form" gets you to the actual form property of that control, from which you can access any control on the form through the Controls collection.

Referencing controls on nested subforms follows the same pattern. To reference a check box named chkAlive on frmSub2, which is a control on frmSub1, which is a control on frmMain, you'd use the syntax

```
fAlive = Forms!frmMain!frmSub1.Form.Controls!frmSub2. _
  Form.Controls!chkAlive
```

Fortunately, Access 95 makes this all a lot easier. The Controls collection reference is completely optional, and VBA code runs more quickly if you don't use the explicit reference. In addition, in direct contrast to the syntax required by Access 2, Access 95 does not require the Form property reference! Finally, you can refer to objects on subforms with a simple syntax. For example, the previous reference to a control on a subsubform could be condensed to:

```
fAlive = Forms!frmMain!frmSub1!frmSub2!chkAlive
```

Yes, it's true: if you've struggled with subform references in Access 2, you can disregard all you've learned. The Form property is now the default property for the subform control, and the default collection for a form object is the Controls collection. Both references are therefore optional.

One more concern: the expression might be able to be abbreviated, depending on the current scope when you need to retrieve the value. For example, if you were trying to retrieve the value on frmSub2 as part of the ControlSource expression for a text box on frmSub1, you'd only need to refer to:

```
frmSub2!chkAlive
```

since you're already on the form contained in frmSub1.

TIP
The Access Expression Builder can help you create these complex references. Once in the Expression Builder, if you double-click the Forms item in the first list box, then double-click Loaded Forms, and then double-click the name of your main form, you should see the subform name. Double-click that subform name, and you see the name of the nested subform, if there is one. Once you've navigated to the form you want to reference, choose the appropriate control or property, and the Expression Builder builds up the necessary reference for you. The Expression Builder does include the Form property references, however, as if this were still Access 2.

Using Synchronized Subforms

Creating synchronized subforms in early versions of Access was a complicated process, due to some strange interactions between events on the different forms. In Access 2 the process became more straightforward, and it continues to work well. Figure 8.18 shows frmSyncMain with its included subforms, frmSyncOrders and frmNestedOrderDetail. Instead of nesting the two subforms, frmSynchMain synchronizes the two subforms. The mechanism is simple: in the "primary" subform's

FIGURE 8.18:

frmSyncMain with its included subforms

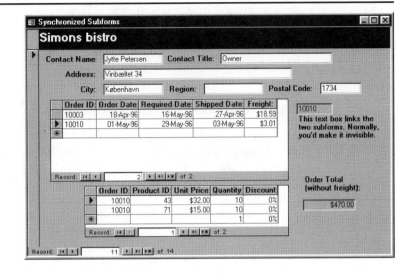

Current event, fill in a (normally) hidden text box. The code might look something like this:

```
Private Sub Form_Current()
    ' Disregard errors that would occur if you
    ' opened this subform as a normal form, without
    ' a parent property or without a text box
    ' named txtLink.
    On Error Resume Next

    ' Using the Parent property allows this form to
    ' be used as a subform on any form which happens
    ' to use a text box named txtLink to link it with
    ' other subforms.
    Me.Parent!txtLink = Me![Order ID]
End Sub
```

The error handler takes care of the case in which you might try to open the form on its own (without its being a subform of a form that contains a linking text box named txtLink).

The "secondary" subform's LinkMasterFields property is set to that same text box, with its LinkChildFields property set to the control name of the text box ([Order ID] in this example). Therefore, as the user moves from row to row in frmSynchOrders, frmNestedOrderDetail will show only the orders with the same Order ID field as the chosen row in frmSynchOrders. This concept could be extended even further. If there were a one-to-many relationship starting from frmNestedOrderDetail, its Current event could fill in a text box to which yet another form could be linked with its LinkMasterFields property.

Is It Loaded as a Subform?

You may have instances in which you'll want a form to work a certain way if loaded as a subform but a different way when loaded as a stand-alone form. For example, you may want to hide certain controls if the form is currently a subform.

There's no built-in function or property to get this information for you, but it's easy to write one yourself. The trick is that subforms always have a Parent property that refers to a real form, and stand-alone forms do not. Attempting to retrieve the Parent property of the form when it's not being used as a subform will always trigger a run-time error, and you can count on this error as you perform your test.

The following function, IsSubForm(), from basFormGlobal, returns True if the form you inquire about is currently loaded as a subform and False if it's a stand-alone form. It does its work by attempting to retrieve the Name property of its parent. If that triggers a run-time error, you can be assured the form is not a subform.

```
Function IsSubForm(frm As Form) as Boolean
    ' Is the form referenced in the
    ' parameter currently loaded as a subform?
    ' Check its Parent property to find out.
    ' In:
    '     frm: a reference to the form in question
    ' Out:
    '     Return value: True if the form is a subform
    '                   False if it's a stand-alone form
    Dim strName As String
    On Error Resume Next
    strName = frm.Parent.Name
    IsSubForm = (Err = 0)
    On Error GoTo 0
End Function
```

To call the function, you could use code like this in your form's event procedures:

```
If IsSubform(Me) Then
    ' It's a subform.
```

```
Else
     ' You know it's not a subform.
End If
```

Using Subforms to Replace Multiple-Page Forms

Although Windows 95 uses tabbed dialogs as often as it can, Access doesn't support this same functionality. (Of course, if you have the Access Developer's Toolkit, you do have access to the TabStrip OLE control, and you can use it to design tabbed interfaces. See Chapter 15 for an example.) Access doesn't directly support this look, but you can emulate its most important features: you provide a series of buttons, each of which displays a different page, or subform, loaded with other controls. Many programmers use multipage forms for this purpose (as do the Access Wizards, for the most part), and you'll find pros and cons for using this method:

- Multipage forms can be difficult to handle in Design view because you end up with a form that you must scroll vertically to view.

- Multipage forms are limited to a maximum of 22 inches for the Detail section. This just may not be enough for your application. Using several subforms would alleviate this problem, since each could be as long as necessary, up to 22 inches.

- If you use multipage forms, buttons that apply to the entire form must be in either the form header or the footer. This may not match the style of other forms in your application.

- If users tab through your controls, you must take care that tabbing past the end of one page doesn't scroll part of a second page into view. (The new Cycle property, discussed in the section "Using the Cycle Property" later in this chapter, will help with this.)

- Because Access provides no way to know which page is the current page, you must control movement from one page to another yourself. In Access 2, this required loading the form using the dialog window mode (which disabled the PgUp and PgDn keys). In Access 95, the form's KeyPreview property makes it possible to handle those keystrokes yourself.

Look at the two examples in this chapter before making up your mind. We've found that working with a single multipage form makes the most sense, most of the time.

With the addition of the Cycle and KeyPreview properties in Access 95, almost all the complaints about multipage forms from Access 2 have been alleviated. Figure 8.19 shows an example of a multipage form in Design view (frmOptionsMulti-Page from CH08.MDB).

Figure 8.20 shows an example of the same two pages as they might be designed to be used as subforms on a main form. Of course, this method has its drawbacks, too:

- Having multiple forms adds to the overhead of your application—you'll have more objects to maintain.

- Using multiple forms requires more system resources than using a single multipage form.

- Loading multiple forms takes longer than loading a single form.

FIGURE 8.19:

The first two pages of a multipage example (frmOptionsMultiPage) in Design view

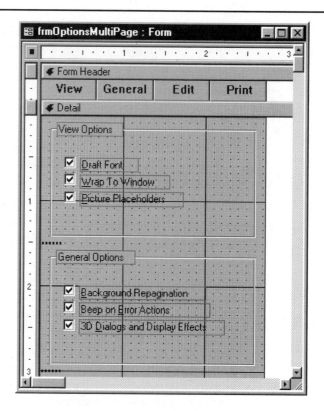

FIGURE 8.20:

Two subforms, destined to appear in frmOptionsSubForms in CH08.MDB

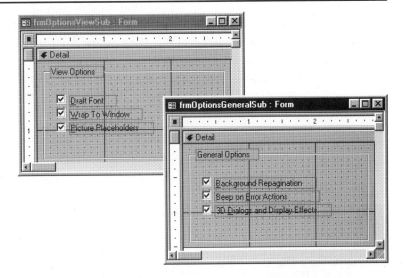

- Using subforms, you'll find it more difficult to track data from one page to the next. On a single form with multiple pages, all the controls have the same scope. On multiple subforms, the code necessary to access each control becomes more complicated.

- Designing the separate forms that will become the subforms can be complex, since it's more difficult to display them all at once than it is to just change pieces of one big form.

- Sizing and placing the forms exactly require more patience than when you are working with multipage forms.

For your own application you must decide which is the better alternative. If you need more than 22 inches of form space, you have no choice; you'll need to opt for multiple subforms. Otherwise, make your choice after studying the examples in the next few sections.

Creating Multipage Forms

If you wish to use a single multipage form, you'll need one or more evenly spaced page-break controls, and you'll need to either set the form's AutoSize property to Yes or set the form's size to show just one of those pages. Your users can easily move from page to page, either using the PgUp and PgDn keys or by clicking the buttons you provide to move them from page to page (using the GotoPage method). As mentioned earlier in this chapter, the total length of the Detail section can be no more than 22 inches (due to limitations of the 16-bit integers Access uses to store positions). The example form, frmOptionsMultiPage in CH08.MDB, places four buttons in the form's header, all part of an option group named grpButtons. The AfterUpdate event for the option group contains just a single line of code:

```
Me.GotoPage Me!grpButtons
```

which sets the current page to match the value of the button the user just clicked. Notice that since the whole Detail section moves from page to page, you must place any form-wide buttons (the option group and the OK and Cancel buttons) in either the form header or the footer.

TIP

To keep the user from moving from page to page using the PgUp and PgDn keys, you can either open your multipage form using the dialog window mode or trap the keys yourself. If you decide on the first method, it's not enough to set the form's Popup property to Yes. You must actually use the OpenForm macro action, setting the Window-Mode parameter to Dialog (or acDialog, if called from VBA). If you decide to open the form normally, you can use the KeyPreview property along with the KeyDown event to trap and disregard the keystrokes. (See the section "Trapping Keys Globally: The KeyPreview Property" later in this chapter for more information.)

Setting the Tab Order

When you create your multipage form, don't forget to check the tab order of the controls. Use the View ➤ Tab Order menu item to set the order such that a control on the first page is first in the tab order. Otherwise, when you first open the form, Access scrolls the first control in the tab order into view. This may make your form display rather oddly.

Using the Cycle Property

In previous versions of Access, as you moved past the last field on a bound form, Access automatically moved to the next row of data. Moving backward (Shift+Tab) past the first control moved you to the previous row. You could work around this through a bit of work, using hidden controls and a little bit of code, but it wasn't simple, and you had to do it on each and every form for which you wanted to restrict row movement.

Finally, in Access 95, you can restrict movement to the current row. The Cycle property of a form allows you to cause the cursor to wrap around the current form, or the current page of the form. The options for the Cycle property are listed in the following table:

Setting	Description	Value
All Records	Pressing Tab on the last control or Shift+Tab in the first control in the tab order moves to the next or previous row in the underlying data	0
Current Record	Wraps around to the first control on the form after pressing Tab on the last control, or to the last control after pressing Shift+Tab on the first control	1
Current Page	Wraps around to the first control on the page after pressing Tab on the last control, or to the last control after pressing Shift+Tab on the first control	2

Setting the Cycle property to 1 (Current Record) will handle the most common case: you'd like Access not to change the current row unless you tell it to. The sample form, frmCustomers in CH08.MDB, has its Cycle property set this way. Load it and give it a try. You'll see that you can't move to a new row using the Tab or Shift+Tab keys—you must use the navigation buttons or the PgUp or PgDn key. (If you wish to disable the PgUp and PgDn keys, as well, see the next section, "Trapping Keys Globally: The KeyPreview Property.")

For multipage forms, you'll always want to set the Cycle property to 2 (Current Page). In this situation, having the user move from page to page inadvertently, using the Tab or Shift+Tab keys, can ruin the look of your form. The sample form, frmOptionsMultiPage, allows you to try the form with the Cycle property set to 2 (Current Page) or 0 (All Records). Uncheck the Cycle Controls check box to try this form without cycling through the current page, and you're likely to end up with an unfortunate situation— controls displayed half visible—as shown in Figure 8.21.

FIGURE 8.21:

Using multipage forms without setting the Cycle property to 2 can be hazardous.

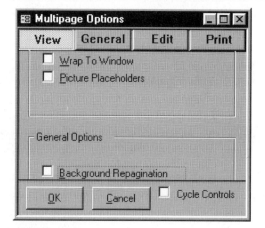

Trapping Keys Globally: The KeyPreview Property

There are probably many situations in which you'd like to be able to trap keystrokes before Access sends them on to the controls on the form and perhaps react to them on a form-wide basis—for example, disabling the PgUp and PgDn keys. Without some global key-trapping mechanism, you'd have to attach code to the KeyDown event of each and every control on the form, watching for those particular keystrokes.

Access 95 provides a mechanism to allow you to trap keystrokes before Access sends them to controls on the form: the KeyPreview property of a form routes all keys you press while that form is active to the form's key-handling events before the active control's events get them. This way, you can react to, alter, or discard the keypresses at the form level.

Keep Users on a Single Page

For example, imagine you've set the form's Cycle property to 1 (Current Form) and you'd also like to make sure the user can't move from row to row by pressing the PgUp or PgDn key. In Access 2, this would have been inordinately difficult, requiring you to attach code to each control's KeyDown event. In Access 95, you can set the form's KeyPreview property to Yes and attach code like this to the form's KeyDown event:

```
Private Sub Form_KeyDown(KeyCode As Integer, _
  Shift As Integer)
    If KeyCode = vbKeyPageDown Or KeyCode = vbKeyPageUp Then
        KeyCode = 0
    End If
End Sub
```

By setting the value of KeyCode to 0, you're telling Access to disregard the keystroke altogether. The sample form frmOptionsMultiPage is set up just this way. The only way to move from page to page on that multipage form is to use the buttons at the top of the form.

Navigate Continuous Forms as Spreadsheets

Perhaps you'd like to make your continuous forms navigable as though they were spreadsheets. Out of the box, Access treats the → and ↓ keys the same way on a continuous form if an entire field is selected: it moves the highlight to the next field on the row, or to the first field on the next row if you're on the last field of the current row. However, you might want the ↓ key to move you to the current field in the next row, instead.

The KeyPreview property makes this possible. Once you've set the KeyPreview property to Yes, Access routes all keystrokes to the form's Key events first. Using a KeyDown event procedure such as the following causes Access to move to the previous row when you press the ↑ key or the next row if you press the ↓ key. In either case, the code sets the value of KeyCode to 0 once it's done so Access doesn't try to handle the keypress itself once this procedure has done its work.

```
Private Sub Form_KeyDown(KeyCode As Integer, Shift As Integer)
    ' Of course, pressing up or down could cause an
    ' error, when you get to the top or bottom of the
    ' set. Make sure to trap for errors, to avoid
```

```
        ' unsightly error alerts!
        On Error GoTo Form_KeyDown_Err
        Select Case KeyCode
            Case vbKeyDown
                DoCmd.GoToRecord Record:=acNext
                KeyCode = 0
            Case vbKeyUp
                DoCmd.GoToRecord Record:=acPrevious
                KeyCode = 0
            Case Else
                ' Do nothing at all!
        End Select

Form_KeyDown_Exit:
        Exit Sub

Form_KeyDown_Err:
        Select Case Err.Number
            Case glrcErrInvalidRow
                KeyCode = 0
            Case Else
                MsgBox "Error: " & Err.Description & " (" & _
                    Err.Number & ")"
        End Select
        Resume Form_KeyDown_Exit
End Sub
```

To see this procedure in action, take a look at frmCustomersTabular, shown in Figure 8.22. This form allows you to toggle the key handling on and off so you can see how it feels both ways.

FIGURE 8.22:

Use the form's KeyPreview property to handle keystrokes on a form-wide basis.

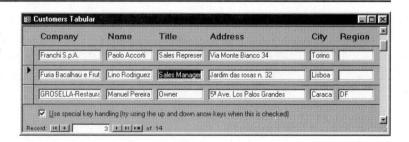

TIP

Access includes intrinsic constants representing most of the key-strokes you'd ever want to use in your applications. (CH08.MDB uses these constants in several of its examples, including frmCustomersTabular, frmCalendar, and frmCalc.) To see the list yourself, open the Object Browser window (press F2 from the module editor), choose Access—Microsoft Access for Windows 95 from the list of libraries/databases, and then choose Constants from the list of modules/classes. The Object Browser will show, in its right-hand window (see Figure 8.23), a list of all the constants Access provides. At the bottom of the list you'll find a list of constants starting with "vbKey". Those are the key constants you'll use in your key-handling event procedures.

FIGURE 8.23:

The Object Browser allows you to find a list of all the key constants.

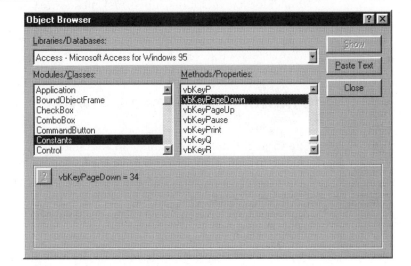

Creating Multi-Subform Forms

If your form requires more than 22 inches for the Detail section or if managing a very long form intimidates you, you might find the multiple-subform method a useful change. To make the multiple subforms work correctly, attach code to the AfterUpdate event of the option group containing the page-selection buttons that will make the correct subform visible and the rest invisible. The code used in frmOptionsSubForms looks like this:

```
Me!frmOptionsViewSub.Visible = (Me!grpButtons = 1)
Me!frmOptionsGeneralSub.Visible = (Me!grpButtons = 2)
Me!frmOptionsEditSub.Visible = (Me!grpButtons = 3)
Me!frmOptionsPrintSub.Visible = (Me!grpButtons = 4)
```

The expression on the right side of each equal sign will evaluate to either True or False, causing each subform to be made visible or invisible, depending on the button you've pressed.

Prepare the subforms just as you would the separate pages for a multipage form. Try to lay out each subform with major controls in the same location (the group boxes on these forms all have the same upper-left corner), and clearly label each "page" so the user understands which page is current. When you design the container form (frmOptionsSubForms), make sure you assign a default value to the option group containing the buttons, set the matching subform's Visible property to Yes, and set the rest of the subforms' Visible properties to No. This ensures that Access displays the correct page when you first open the main form.

One More, Even Slower, Option

If you just can't know which subform will be loaded until run time, you can place just a single subform container on your main form. Then, when you do know which subform to display, set the SourceObject property of the subform control. When you change the source object, Access loads the new form and displays it in the subform container. This is the slowest possible solution, however, because Access must read the new form from disk before it can display the form, so avoid this technique if at all possible.

Compare and Decide

Neither multiple pages nor multiple subforms are a perfect solution, and both have inherent limitations. Experiment with the two examples (frmOptionsSubForms and frmOptionsMultiPage in CH08.MDB) and decide for yourself which method will work best in your application. Remember that multipage forms have a limited page length, while multiple subforms are, for all intents and purposes, limited only by the maximum number of controls you can place on a form. Neither method will replace the built-in tabbed dialogs you'll find in other Microsoft products, but these methods do provide a similar metaphor for your own Access applications, without the need to add the extra overhead OLE controls incur. As mentioned earlier in this chapter, we tend to use multipage forms whenever possible, now that Access has added the Cycle and KeyPreview properties.

Displaying Multiple Instances of Forms

In Access 2, if you wanted to display a form more than once in a given session, you needed to create as many physical copies of the actual form as you wanted to display. Now, in Access 95, you can open multiple instances of the same form (or report—the mechanism works the same for either) without making physical copies. There is no user interface for this functionality. If you want to display multiple instances, you'll need to write VBA code to make it happen.

NOTE
We could just as easily have placed this section of the chapter in Chapter 9, which discusses reports, but we feel you're more likely to need multiple instances of forms than reports, so we decided to place this material here.

Although you can create multiple instances of a master form, the original form is the only one for which you can permanently alter the properties. Access will not save any changes you make to the instances of the original form, although you are allowed to make programmatic changes to the properties of any instance. You won't be able to switch the form instances into Design view, so any changes you wish to make to the instances will be through code, and they'll be temporary.

What Happens When You Create a New Instance?

When you create multiple instances of forms or reports, each new instance has its own set of properties, its own current row (if it's bound), and its own window. All instances of the same form or report share the same *name*, however, and this is a concept that takes some getting used to. Any place in VBA that requires you to supply a form or report name, therefore, will be generally useless when you are working with multiple instances. A side issue here is that because all the instances share the same name, you won't be able to use syntax like this:

```
Debug.Print Forms!frmCustomer.Caption
```

and expect to find any of the extra instances of frmCustomer. (On the other hand, Access does add an item to the Forms collection for each form instance you create, and you can always refer to these items by number. See Chapter 6 for information on the different ways you can refer to objects in collections.) Although Access does not create a named element of the Forms or Reports collection for each instance, it does add a reference in the collection, so this code will still work, even if several instances of forms are open:

```
For Each frm In Forms
    Debug.Print frm.Caption
Next frm
```

Because each form instance can (and should) have a unique caption, the previous example can actually be useful if you want a list of all the open forms, regardless of whether they're "real" forms or instances of real forms.

How Do You Create a New Instance?

Creating a new instance is simple: just declare a form variable and set it equal to a new form:

```
Dim frm As Form
Set frm = New Form_frmCustomers
```

That "Form_" syntax indicates to Access that you want a new member of the form class that's described by "Form_frmCustomers". The name of the form after the "Form_" must be a real, existing form, and by using the New keyword, you are asking Access to create a new instance for you. As soon as the variable referring to the new form goes out of scope, Access destroys the new form instance. What's more, you are asking Access to create the new form with its Visible property set to False; if you want to actually *see* the form, you'll need to set its Visible property to True.

It should be pretty clear, at this point, that if you write a procedure like this one:

```
Sub BadIdea()
    Dim frm As Form
    Set frm = New Form_frmCustomers
    frm.Visible = True
End Sub
```

you're never going to actually see that new form. Because Access will destroy the form when the reference to it goes out of scope, as soon as this procedure is complete, the form you created in it is history. What's the solution, then? You need to find some place to store that form reference until you're finished with it.

A simple solution is to make frm a static, or global, variable. That way it simply will never go out of scope. If you want to close it manually, you can always use code like this:

```
frm.SetFocus
DoCmd.Close
Set frm = Nothing
```

which sets focus to the form, closes it, and then releases the connection between the form variable and the object it was referring to. (Remember, you can't use the name of the object to close it, so you'll first have to make it the current form.)

A Better Solution

If you're going to be working with more than one extra instance of a form, you'll need a better way to manage the references to those new instances. One solution is to store the form references in a user-defined collection. (See Chapter 2 for more information on user-defined collections.)

For example, try out frmCustomers in CH08.MDB. Open the form itself, and then click the New Instance button a few times. Each time you click the button, you're running code that's creating a new form instance and placing a reference to it in a user-defined collection. If you want a list of all the extra instances, click the List Instances button on any of the forms, which will write a list of instance captions to the Debug window. Figure 8.24 shows what such a test might look like.

Use the New Instance button to create multiple instances of the main form.

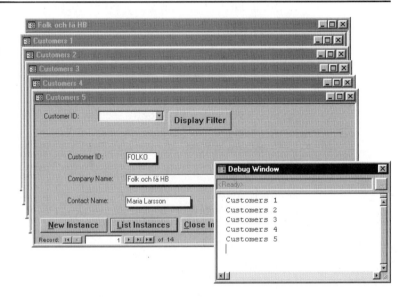

Every time you click the New Instance button, you're calling the NewCustomer-Form procedure, which creates a new instance for frmCustomers and adds that new form reference to colForms, the collection of form instances:

```
Dim colForms As New Collection

Sub NewCustomerForm(frmOld As Form)
    Dim frm As Form

    Set frm = New Form_frmCustomers
    mintI = mintI + 1
    ' The Key value must be a string, so tack on an empty
    ' string to force the conversion. You'll
    ' use the hWnd later when you try to
```

```
' remove the window from the collection of windows.
colForms.Add Item:=frm, Key:=frm.hwnd & ""
frm.Caption = "Customers " & mintI
' These numbers are completely arbitrary.
DoCmd.MoveSize (mintI + 1) * 80, (mintI + 1) * 350
' Preserve the original form's filter and whether or not
' that filter's active.
frm.Filter = frmOld.Filter
frm.FilterOn = frmOld.FilterOn
frm.Visible = True
End Sub
```

NewCustomerForm increments a global variable, mintI, to keep track of which instance is the newest. That integer becomes part of the new instance's caption. When NewCustomerForm adds the new form reference to colForms, it stores the form reference itself, along with the hWnd (the window handle, guaranteed to be unique) as the key for the item. That way, later code can retrieve an item from the collection, given its window handle. (Remember, each form instance you create has the same name, so you can't refer to any instance individually by name.) The procedure also places the new form at a convenient location, sets its Filter and FilterOn properties to match the original form's, and then makes the new form visible.

Now that you've created these new form instances, you have a collection (colForms) that contains a reference to each of the forms. You can iterate through that collection (as you'll do when you attempt to close them all) or refer to a single form, given its hWnd.

Closing a Form Instance

If you close one of the form instances, you'll want to make sure the collection of form references is up to date. To make that happen, we've attached code to the form's Close event that removes the particular form from the collection:

```
Sub RemoveInstance(frm As Form)
    ' Each form calls this code when it closes itself.
    ' This is also hooked to the main
    ' form's Close event, so skip over the
    ' error that occurs when you try to close the
    ' main form (which doesn't have an entry in the
    ' collection!)
```

```
      On Error Resume Next
      colForms.Remove frm.hwnd & ""
End Sub
```

Each form calls

```
Call RemoveInstance(Me)
```

in its Close event. That way, the collection of instances always accurately reflects the current group of form instances.

> **NOTE**　The original form isn't in the collection of form instances—it never added itself, only the new instances. On the other hand, it has the call to RemoveInstance in its Close event, and its form reference is not in the collection. To avoid the error that would occur when trying to remove the form itself from the collection of instances, we just set up RemoveInstance so it doesn't complain about errors.

Closing All the Instances

If you want to close all the instances of the main form, you have a few choices. Here are two options:

- Remove each form reference from the collection. This forces each one to go out of scope and thus will close the instances.

- Set the focus to each instance in turn and then explicitly close each form.

We chose the second method, for a very specific reason. (The first method works fine in this simple example, and the code to do it appears in the CloseInstances procedure, although it's commented out.) If your forms were complex and perhaps had validation rules that had to be met, it's possible that the form wouldn't be allowed to close; imagine, for example, that you'd not fulfilled a validation rule. The second method, closing each form explicitly, guarantees that Access doesn't close the form before removing its form reference from the user-defined collection. It's just a cleaner way to close the forms, even though it does require physically setting the focus to each form in turn.

The code that's called from the Close Instances button, therefore, is quite simple (it's mostly comments):

```
Sub CloseInstances()
    Dim varItem As Variant
    ' The user may have closed some or all of the
    ' forms by hand. Skip any errors that
    ' occur because the collection count
    ' doesn't match reality.
    On Error GoTo CloseInstancesErr
    Application.Echo False
    For Each varItem In colForms
        ' Go to the form, and then close it.
        ' You can't close it given the name, because
        ' all the form instances have the same name.
        varItem.SetFocus
        DoCmd.Close
        ' You could also use
        '    colForms.Remove 1
        ' to remove the first element
        ' of the collection, over and over,
        ' but what happens if you can't close
        ' the form for some reason (Key violation,
        ' for example)? Explicitly closing
        ' the form is safer.

    Next varItem
    mintI = 0

CloseInstancesExit:
    Application.Echo True
    Exit Sub

CloseInstancesErr:
    Resume CloseInstancesExit
End Sub
```

All the example code for this simple test case is in basFormInstance. You'll need to modify it for any example in which you use it (because it requires the actual name of the form you're working with as part of its code), but the example ought to at least get you started.

> **NOTE**
>
> In this example, one form was different from all the rest: the original form. This needn't be the case. That is, you don't have to actually open the "seed" form in order to make instances of it. The form you refer to when you create the new instance can be closed, and as long as it's in the current database, Access can find it and create a new instance of it. If you follow this technique, then all open forms with the same name are equivalent—they're "clones" of the master.

Summary

Through the use of Windows API calls and VBA code, you can exact a great deal of control over the appearance and actions of your forms. In particular, you can control

- The border controls, individually or collectively
- The modality of the form
- When or whether your form gets closed
- The size and position of forms from one Access session to the next
- Form-level error handling

You've learned to create various Access tools, including

- Toolboxes
- Popup utilities
- Auto-sizing forms
- Self-disabling navigation buttons
- Multipage and multi-subform forms, emulating tabbed dialogs

You've seen some useful techniques, including

- Working with multiple instances of forms
- Controlling form filtering

And finally, along the way, you've encountered some useful tidbits, such as

- Reading and writing items in the System Registry
- Using the RecordsetClone property of bookmarks and forms
- Determining whether a specific form is loaded
- Detecting record position states
- Moving and sizing windows
- Enabling/disabling control menu items
- Resizing forms for various screen resolutions
- Using the Cycle and KeyPreview properties to control form behavior

CHAPTER

NINE

Topics in Report Design

- Using report and section events and properties

- Controlling sorting and grouping programmatically

- Altering the report layout programmatically

Designing reports ought to be a simple task. In theory, you never have to worry about data input, validation, movement from field to field, or capturing an endless number of different fields on the same form. On the other hand, designing a report that is both functional and aesthetically pleasing can be difficult. You may be attempting to simulate an existing report that exists on paper or in some other database system, or you may be designing your own reports. In this chapter we cover some of the basics involved in designing creative reports, focusing on the issues that elude or confuse many developers: report and section events and sorting and grouping. You won't find many Windows API calls in this chapter, since they won't normally help much when you're creating reports. Access gives you all the flexibility you need.

Learning to harness that flexibility is the challenge you face when you create reports. This chapter assumes you've already managed to create simple reports and now need to work with the various events and properties to add functionality. In addition, the chapter covers some common problem areas and suggests interesting solutions to those problems.

New Report Properties

Reports expose a number of properties you can manipulate at design time to get just the output you want. Access 95 adds a few new properties, and this section focuses on those new properties.

Filtering and Sorting

The Filter, FilterOn, OrderBy, and OrderByOn properties for reports work very much the same way they work for forms. To see these properties in action, take a look at frmCustomers in CH09.MDB. This form allows you to filter your data any way you wish (using Filter by Selection, Filter by Form, or Advanced Filter/Sort) and, once you're ready, click the Preview Report button. That button's Click event executes this code:

```
Sub cmdPreview_Click()
On Error GoTo Err_cmdPreview_Click

    Dim strDocName As String
```

```
    strDocName = "rptPhoneBook"
    ' There are three possible scenarios:
    ' 1. No filter
    ' 2. Filter, but not applied
    ' 3. Filter, applied
    If Me.FilterOn And Len(Me.Filter & "") > 0 Then
        DoCmd.OpenReport ReportName:=strDocName, _
          View:=acPreview, WhereCondition:=Me.Filter
    Else
        DoCmd.OpenReport ReportName:=strDocName, View:=acPreview
    End If

Exit_cmdPreview_Click:
    Exit Sub

Err_cmdPreview_Click:
    MsgBox Err.Description
    Resume Exit_cmdPreview_Click

End Sub
```

This code checks the form's Filter and FilterOn properties and, assuming all is correct, opens the report with either the form's current filter or no filter at all.

To see the OrderBy property at work, open rptOrderByProperty and frmOrderByProperty in CH09.MDB. When you make a choice on the sample form, code attached to the AfterUpdate event of the option group on the form sets the OrderBy property of the report:

```
Private Sub grpSort_AfterUpdate()
    On Error Resume Next
    Dim strOrderBy As String
    With Reports(glrcReportName)
        strOrderBy = Choose(Me!grpSort, _
          "[Company Name]", "Sales")
        If Me!chkDescending Then
            strOrderBy = strOrderBy & " DESC"
        End If
        .OrderBy = strOrderBy
        .OrderOn = True
    End With
End Sub
```

The OrderBy property becomes the highest-level sort, added on to the normal sorting applied in the Grouping/Sorting dialog box. You'll find you cannot override the sorting that's been done at design time, so you'll have the best luck using this property with reports that aren't currently sorted.

> **WARNING** Setting the OrderBy property for a report triggers that report's Close and Open events. If you have code attached to either of those events, be aware that changing the sort order for the report will run those event procedures as though you'd closed and then reopened the report.

To set the ordering based on multiple fields, separate their names with commas. To force one or more of the fields to sort descending, append DESC to the field name. The OrderBy expression works in addition to (that is, *after*) any sorting applied by the report's internal sorting. (See the section "Controlling Sorting and Grouping" later in this chapter for detailed information on controlling the report's internal sorting and grouping from your applications.)

Keeping Groups Together across Columns–The GrpKeepTogether Property

In previous versions of Access there really was no reasonable way to ensure that your sections didn't break across columns if you created a multicolumn report. Access 95 adds the GrpKeepTogether property for reports, which allows you to specify that you want group data for which you've specified either Whole Group or With First Detail kept together in a single column (Per Column) or on the whole page (Per Page).

To see this property in action, take a look at rptPhoneBook in CH09.MDB. This report prints in a phone book–type layout and is the subject of several examples in this chapter. The report's GrpKeepTogether property is set to Per Column so that groups aren't broken across columns. Try it out this way, and then change the setting to Per Page to see what a difference it makes in the printout.

Is Anyone Home? The HasData Property

At times you need to know, after the report has opened, whether or not the report is showing any rows. Knowing this can be useful in places where you still want to view the report (or subreport) even if there are no rows, but you want to keep "#Error?" from displaying on your reports in places where you were performing calculations based on rows in the report.

The HasData property of a report, available only at run time, returns one of three possible values:

Value	Description
−1	Bound report with records
0	Bound report with no records
1	Unbound report

The sample report, rptBankInfo, uses this property to avoid showing incorrect summary data if rptBankInfoSub2 doesn't contain any rows. The subreport contains a list of all the computers in use at the company, and it includes a total value in its footer. The main report extracts that value and displays it in the text box, txtSummary. If there are no rows in rptBankInfoSub2, however, you don't want an error message in txtSummary. To avoid this problem, txtSummary's ControlSource is

```
=[Company] & " uses " & _
 IIf([rptBankInfoSub2].[Report].[HasData]=-1, _
 [rptBankInfoSub2].[Report]![txtSum], 0) & " computers."
```

In other words, if the company's list of computers includes some items, the control will indicate that. If not, it just indicates that the company uses 0 computers. Figure 9.4, shown later in this chapter, shows this report in use.

Controlling Sorting and Grouping

After layout of the controls on the report, the highest-level control you have over the results from a report are the sorting/groupings. It's impossible to completely separate these two issues, since grouping is so dependent on the sort order. Figure 9.1 shows a typical report layout, with groups set up based on the Company-Name and ContactName fields. If you've created any reports up to this point, you're probably well aware of the possibilities involved with using group headers and footers. What you might not have noticed is that group headers and footers, as well as every other section on the report, supply event hooks; you can use the "break" in the processing as a signal to your program code, which might need to react to the new group that is about to be printed or has just been printed. (We discuss report and section events throughout this chapter.)

You also may be unaware that you can control the sorting and grouping properties of reports programmatically. You can create new reports or modify existing ones, creating new sections as necessary, and you can modify the sort information, as well. The next few sections suggest methods for controlling the sorting and grouping characteristics of your reports from your VBA code.

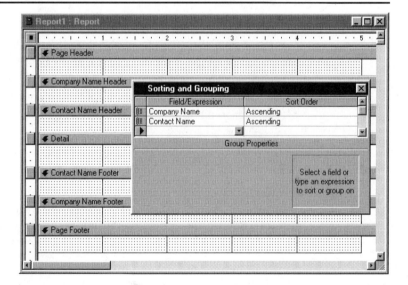

FIGURE 9.1:

The sample report is grouped on the CompanyName and ContactName fields.

The Section Property

Forms, reports, and all controls expose the Section property. For controls, it's just an indication of which section of the parent form or report it appears on, and this isn't the issue here (although the value returned from a control's Section property corresponds with the numbers used in specifying a form or report's section). For forms and reports, the Section property provides an array of all the sections contained in the given object, referred to by number, as shown in Table 9.1. To refer to any specific section, you treat it as an element from an array of sections, as in the following:

```
Reports!rptExample.Section(1).Visible = False
' or, because Access defines the constant acHeader to be 1:
Reports!rptExample.Section(acHeader).Visible = False
```

which makes the Report Header section invisible for rptExample.

Here are two more items to remember about sections:

- Aside from the sections listed in Table 9.1, group-level section headers and footers are numbered consecutively, starting with 9.

- Forms never contain more than five sections (numbered 0 through 4).

There's not much you can do with the Section property on its own; anytime you deal with the Section property, you'll be interested in the properties of that particular section. Unlike other property arrays in Access (the Column property, for example), the Section property does not ever return a value on its own—it just returns a reference to the section in question.

TABLE 9.1: Section Numbers and Their Descriptions

Setting	Description	VBA Constant
0	Detail section	acDetail
1	Form or Report Header section	acHeader
2	Form or Report Footer section	acFooter
3	Form or Report Page Header section	acPageHeader
4	Form or Report Page Footer section	acPageFooter
5	Group-level 1 Header section (reports only)	
6	Group-level 1 Footer section (reports only)	
7	Group-level 2 Header section (reports only)	
8	Group-level 2 Footer section (reports only)	

Referring to Sections by Name

Access 95 allows you to refer to form and report sections by name, as well as by number. For example, if you create a new report, its Detail section's Name property will be "Detail", and you can use that name in expressions:

```
Debug.Print Reports!rptSample.Detail.Height
```

That is, Access exposes a property of the report that matches the name of the section, through which you can access any property of that section. The name you type in your expression must match the name of the section, exactly as Access sees it in the property sheet for that section. Names of sections depend on the order in which they were created and are unique. To use the name in this context, you'll need to look in the property sheet to find the name of the section and then use that name (or change the name to one of your choosing) to refer to the section.

At the time of this writing, the default names for the Page Header and Page Footer sections were PageHeader and PageFooter, respectively. Reports already expose PageHeader and PageFooter properties, so these names will conflict with the built-in property names. You won't be able to check the Page Header section's height using an expression like this:

```
Debug.Print rpt.PageHeader.Height
```

You'll need to either rename the section (change its Name property in the property sheet) or use the standard syntax:

```
Debug.Print rpt.Sections(acPageHeader).Height
```

Setting Physical Characteristics Using the Section Property

In addition to setting the visibility of a specific section, you often need to set the height of a section. For example, perhaps you need to create a Footer section on a form, if one doesn't already exist, and then set its height. The code fragment in Listing 9.1 makes sure the Report Footer section is visible. To do this, it checks to see whether the report is already showing a footer section and, if not, creates one, setting the height of both the header and footer to 0. (Setting the height to 0 makes the section as small as possible, given the existing controls on the section. If there are no controls, the section shrinks to nothing.) Code later in the function might set the particular height for the footer. Note that if you create a report or page footer, you also create a header. This code sets the height of the header to 0 and sets its Visible property to False, ensuring that it won't be visible in the running report. This code fragment calls the isSection() function, which is discussed in the following section.

Listing 9.1

```
' If there isn't already a report footer,
' turn on headers and footers, and then
' hide the header.
If Not isSection(Me, acFooter) Then
     ' Report Design/View/Report Header/Footer
    DoCmd.DoMenuItem 3, 2, 11, , acMenuVer70
    Me.Section(acHeader).Height = 0
    Me.Section(acFooter).Height = 0
End If

' Make SURE the footer is visible, and the
' header's invisible.
Me.Section(acHeader).Visible = False
Me.Section(acFooter).Visible = True
```

TIP

If you want a section to be as short as possible (just tall enough to include the controls inside it, with no extra vertical space), set the height to 0. A section can never obscure controls it contains, and setting its height to 0 is the quick and easy way to make the section just big enough.

Determining Whether a Particular Section Exists

Access provides no simple way of determining whether a given section has been created on a form or report. The following function (from basSections in CH09.MDB) demonstrates one method: it attempts to retrieve the height of the section in question. If this attempt doesn't trigger a run-time error, the section must have existed. Just pass to it a reference to the form or report you're interested in, along with a number or constant representing the section on which you need to check.

```
Function IsSection(obj As Object, intSection As Integer)
    ' Returns TRUE if there currently is a form/report
    ' footer section, FALSE otherwise.
    ' Call as:
    '     If IsSection(Reports!Report1, acFooter) Then...
    ' to see if Report1 includes a footer section.
    Dim varTemp as Variant

    On Error Resume Next
    varTemp = obj.Section(intSection).Height
    isSection = (Err = 0)
End Function
```

Determining How Many Sections Exist

Forms are guaranteed to have no more than 5 sections but may have fewer. Reports may have up to 25 sections (5 standard, plus up to 10 groups with both a header and a footer). Access provides no built-in way to determine how many sections an object contains, and you may need to know this information. The function in Listing 9.2 demonstrates one solution to this problem: loop through the report, retrieving section heights and counting all the sections for which you don't trigger a run-time error. Since no report can contain more than 25 sections, that's as far as you need to look. You're also guaranteed that every form or report contains at least one section, Section(0) (the Detail section). You use that fact, in the function shown in Listing 9.2, to verify that the requested form is, in fact, loaded at the time you call the function.

NOTE   It was tempting, when trying to optimize this function, to make assumptions about the existence of sections. Unfortunately, all the sections aside from the paired page header/footer and report header/footer are individually selectable. This means you really do need to check out every section from 0 through 24.

Listing 9.2

```
Function glrCountSections(rpt As Report) As Integer
    ' Count the number of sections in a report.

    Dim intCount As Integer
    Dim intI As Integer

    On Error Resume Next
    intCount = 0

    ' Loop through all the sections,
    ' counting up the ones that exist.
    For intI = 0 To glrcMaxSections - 1
        If isSection(rpt, intI) Then
            intCount = intCount + 1
        End If
    Next intI

glrCountSectionsExit:
    glrCountSections = intCount
End Function
```

Creating New Report Sections

Aside from the method included in Listing 9.1 (using DoMenuItem), Access doesn't provide a method for creating Page or Report Header or Footer sections. For creating group headers and footers, though, Access provides the CreateGroupLevel() function. Since sections beyond the Detail section and the page and report headers and footers are all manifestations of groupings, this function allows you to create all sections except the standard five (Detail, Report Header, Report Footer, Page Header, and Page Footer). This function takes four parameters:

intLevel = CreateGroupLevel(*strReport*, *strExpr*, *fHeader*, *fFooter*)

The following list describes the parameters:

- *strReport* is a string expression containing the name of the report on which to create the group.

- *strExpr* is the expression to use as the group-level expression.

- *fHeader* and *fFooter* indicate whether or not to create sections for the header and/or footer. Use True (–1) to create the section, False (0) otherwise.

The function returns an index into the array of group levels on your report. (See the next section for more information.) Access supports no more than ten group levels, so run-time error 2153, "You can't specify more than 10 group levels," occurs if you attempt to create more groups than that. If you try to call the function with the Sorting/Grouping dialog box open, Access slaps your wrist with run-time error 2154, "You can't call this function when the Sorting and Grouping box is open." If you receive this error in your code, you can simply use DoMenuItem to hide the Sorting and Grouping box and then call CreateGroupLevel() a second time.

Accessing Group Levels

Access treats group levels in the same manner as sections: it maintains an array of group levels, which you access like this:

```
intOrder = Reports!Report1.GroupLevel(0).SortOrder
```

Just as with the array of sections, you cannot access the GroupLevel array directly; rather, you must access one of its properties. The expression

```
varTemp = Reports!Report1.GroupLevel(0)
```

generates compile-time error 438, "Object doesn't support this method or property," since you've attempted to retrieve information about the group level itself rather than one of its properties. Just as with sections, Access externalizes no information about the number of group levels.

Although you can't access any properties of GroupLevel or Section objects, you can declare an object variable to refer to one and use that object variable in further references (just as you can with any other object type). This functionality is new in Access 95. For example, you can use code like this:

```
Dim objGL As GroupLevel
Set objGL = Reports!Report1.GroupLevel(0)
Debug.Print "Sort Order: "; objGL.SortOrder
Debug.Print "Group Header: "; objGL.GroupHeader
Debug.Print "Group Footer: "; objGL.GroupFooter
```

to list information about a specific group level. (The next few sections provide details about various GroupLevel properties.) And because you can refer to group-level objects using object references, you can also rewrite the previous example, like this:

```
With Reports!Report1.GroupLevel(0)
    Debug.Print "Sort Order: "; .SortOrder
    Debug.Print "Group Header: "; .GroupHeader
    Debug.Print "Group Footer: "; .GroupFooter
End With
```

To enumerate the group levels in a report, you need a function similar to that found in Listing 9.2 to count or walk through the array of GroupLevels. See Listing 9.3 for such a function. Note that this function is much simpler than the similar one in Listing 9.2, since groups must be consecutively numbered. Removing a section bumps all the sections that follow it up the list. You can find the functions presented in both Listing 9.2 and Listing 9.3 in basSections in CH09.MDB.

Listing 9.3

```
Function glrCountGroups(rpt As Report) As Integer
    ' Count the number of groups in a report.

    Dim intI As Integer
    Dim intOrder As Integer

    On Error Resume Next
    For intI = 0 To glrcMaxGroups - 1
        intOrder = rpt.GroupLevel(intI).SortOrder
        If Err.Number <> 0 Then
            Exit For
        End If
    Next intI
    glrCountGroups = intI
End Function
```

GroupLevel Properties

Just as with sections, you can access only properties of group levels, not the group levels themselves. To that end the GroupLevel array exposes these properties: GroupFooter, GroupHeader, GroupInterval, GroupOn, KeepTogether, SortOrder, and ControlSource. The following sections describe each of these properties and its use.

GroupHeader and GroupFooter Properties

The GroupHeader and GroupFooter properties tell you whether or not a specific group level shows a Header and/or Footer section. In either case the property returns True (−1) if the section exists and False (0) otherwise. The property is read-only, so you can't use it to create new Header/Footer sections. You must use the CreateGroupLevel() function mentioned earlier in this chapter to create new sections.

This code fragment determines whether or not there is a group header for group 0:

```
If Reports!rptTest1.GroupLevel(0).GroupHeader Then
    ' Do something
End If
```

The GroupOn Property

The GroupOn property specifies how data is to be grouped in a report. The values for the property depend on the datatype of the field or expression on which the GroupLevel is grouped. None of the settings except 0 (Each Value) is meaningful unless you have a group header or group footer selected for the group.

Table 9.2 displays all the possible values for the GroupOn property.

TABLE 9.2: Possible Values for the GroupLevel's GroupOn Property

Setting	Value
Each Value	0
Prefix Characters	1
Year	2
Qtr	3
Month	4
Week	5
Day	6
Hour	7
Minute	8
Interval	9 (see the GroupInterval property)

The GroupInterval Property

The GroupInterval property defines an interval that is valid for the field or expression on which you're grouping. You can set the property only when the report is in Design view, and its value is dependent on the value of the GroupOn property. As with the GroupOn property, the Access documentation states that you must have created a group header or footer before setting the value of this property to anything other than its default value (1). Actually, you can change it if you wish, but unless you have a group header or footer created, it won't have any effect. If the GroupOn value is 0 (Each Value), the GroupInterval property is treated as though it were 1, no matter what its value.

Set the GroupInterval property to a value that makes sense for the field or expression on which you're grouping. If you're grouping on text, the GroupInterval property defines the number of characters on which to group. If you're grouping on dates and you set the GroupOn property to 5 (Grouping on Weeks), setting the GroupInterval property specifies how many weeks to group together.

The following example creates a group, grouping on a date/time field and breaking every five minutes:

```
Dim intLevel As Integer

intLevel = CreateGroupLevel("rptTest", "DateField", _
 Header:=True, Footer:=False)
With Reports!rptTest.GroupLevel(intLevel)
    .GroupOn = 8
    .GroupInterval = 5
End With
```

TIP

Although you'll almost always set the GroupOn and GroupInterval properties when you're creating a report programmatically, you can also set these properties from the report's Open event. You cannot create a group level, except in Design view, but you can set properties for existing group levels from the report's Open event (and no other event).

The KeepTogether Property

The KeepTogether property specifies whether the data in the group level is to be kept together when printed. You can set the property only when the report is in Design view or, as with the GroupOn/GroupInterval properties, from the report's Open event. As with the other properties mentioned above, the Access documentation states that you must have created a group header or footer before setting the value of this property to anything other than its default value (0). Actually, you can change it if you wish, but unless you have a group header or footer created, it won't have any effect. The possible values for the KeepTogether property are shown in Table 9.3.

TABLE 9.3: Possible Values for the GroupLevel's KeepTogether Property

Setting	Value	Description
No	0	Makes no attempt to keep header, detail, and footer on the same page
Whole Group	1	Attempts to print header, detail, and footer all on same page
With First Detail	2	Attempts to print the header and the first detail row on the same page

Under some circumstances Access is forced to ignore this setting. For example, if you've specified Whole Group (1), Access attempts to print the Group Header, Detail, and Footer sections on the same page. If that combination will not fit on a single page, Access is forced to ignore the setting and print it as best it can. The same concept can hold true if you've chosen With First Detail (2). In that case Access attempts to place the group header and the first detail row on the same page. If the combination of the two is larger than a single page, all bets are off and Access prints as best it can.

As with all the rest of the GroupLevel properties, you set the KeepTogether property through the GroupLevel array. For example, the following code fragment asks Access to attempt to print all of GroupLevel 0 on the same page:

```
Reports!rptTest.GroupLevel(0).KeepTogether = 2
```

NOTE

As useful as it would be, Access does not provide a method for preventing a group footer from being the first line on a page. There is a With First Detail setting for headers but no With Last Detail setting for footer sections.

The ControlSource and SortOrder Properties

The ControlSource property specifies the field or expression on which the group is to be grouped and/or sorted. By default, the ControlSource property matches the value you used to create the group level and should be identical to the second parameter you passed to the CreateGroupLevel() function. Although you cannot use CreateGroupLevel() to alter the field on which a group is based, you can change the group's ControlSource property. Like all the rest of the group-level properties, you change the ControlSource and SortOrder properties only when the report is in Design view or in the report's Open event.

Use the SortOrder property to set the sorting order of rows in the Detail section of a group level. Table 9.4 shows the possible values for the SortOrder property. You use this property in combination with the ControlSource property to define the sorting characteristics of the group.

TABLE 9.4: Possible Values for the GroupLevel's SortOrder Property

Setting	Value	Description
Ascending	0	Sorts values in ascending order (0–9, A–Z) (default)
Descending	−1	Sorts values in descending order (9–0, Z–A)

Using the GroupLevel Properties

In your application you may need to change the GroupLevel properties of an existing report. For example, you might want to allow the user to choose, from two or more fields, the field that's displayed on your report and still group rows correctly on the chosen field. CH09.MDB contains such an example, frmSortOrder and rptPhoneBook. Figure 9.2 shows the form and report in action.

FIGURE 9.2:

Changing the sort order requires changing the GroupLevel's ControlSource property.

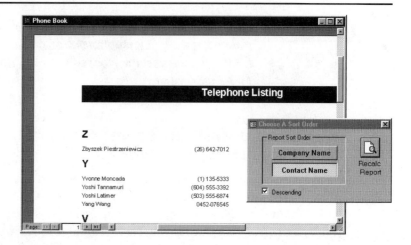

In this example, frmSortOrder loads rptPhoneBook. Depending on which of the option buttons you've selected, it sets up the report to group on either CompanyName or ContactName, setting the header information appropriately. The code in Listing 9.4 does the work.

Listing 9.4

```
Private Sub cmdPreview_Click()
    On Error GoTo Err_cmdPreview_Click

    Dim strDocName As String

    strDocName = "rptPhoneBook"
    Reports(strDocName).Painting = False

    DoCmd.OpenReport strDocName, acDesign
    ResetSort strDocName, IIf(Me!grpSort = 1, _
      "Company Name", "Contact Name")
    DoCmd.OpenReport strDocName, acPreview

    Reports(strDocName).Painting = True

Exit_cmdPreview_Click:
    Exit Sub

Err_cmdPreview_Click:
    MsgBox Error$
```

```
        Resume Exit_cmdPreview_Click

End Sub

Private Sub Form_Close()
    On Error Resume Next

    ' Close, don't save changes.
    DoCmd.Close acReport, "rptPhoneBook", acSaveNo
End Sub

Private Sub Form_Open(Cancel As Integer)
    Dim intSortOrder As Integer
    Dim strControlSource As String

    On Error Resume Next
    DoCmd.OpenReport "rptPhoneBook", acPreview
    If Err <> 0 Then
        MsgBox "Unable to open 'rptPhoneBook'"
        Exit Sub
    End If

    ' Set the controls on the form to match the report
    ' itself, as it was last saved.
    With Reports!rptPhoneBook
        intSortOrder = .GroupLevel(0).SortOrder
        strControlSource = .GroupLevel(0).ControlSource
    End With
    Me!grpSort = IIf(strControlSource = "Company Name", 1, 2)
    Me!chkDescending = intSortOrder
End Sub

Private Sub ResetSort(strDocName As String, strField As String)
    With Reports(strDocName)
        !txtName.ControlSource = strField
        !txtLetter.ControlSource = "=Left([" & strField & _
        "], 1)"
        .GroupLevel(0).ControlSource = strField
        .GroupLevel(1).ControlSource = strField
        .GroupLevel(0).SortOrder = Me!chkDescending
        .GroupLevel(1).SortOrder = Me!chkDescending
    End With
End Sub
```

CmdPreview_Click() either opens the report (if it isn't already open) or switches it to Design view and then calls the ResetSort procedure to change the grouping and sorting expressions and the sort order. In addition, Listing 9.4 includes the form's Open event procedure, which not only opens the report but retrieves the current GroupLevel settings from the report so it can set its own controls accordingly.

NOTE Because the example changes properties of the report in Design view, Access prompts you to save changes when you close the report unless you take steps to avoid this. In Access 95, you can add the acSaveNo constant as the third parameter to the Close action. This causes Access to close the object and save no changes, without asking your permission. The example demonstrates this technique.

Events of Reports and Their Sections

As in all the other areas of Access, it's the events that drive the application. As your users interact with Access' user interface, it's up to your application to react to the events Access fires off. Reports themselves support only a few events besides the standard load/unload events (Open, Activate, Close, Deactivate, and Error)—that is, the Error, Page, and NoData events—but their sections react to events that occur as Access prints each record.

Report Events

Table 9.5 lists the events reports can initiate. As indicated in the table, when you open a report, Access fires off the Open and then the Activate event. When you close the report, Access executes the Close and then the Deactivate event.

TABLE 9.5: Report Event Properties

Event	Event Property	Occurs When
Open	OnOpen	You open a report but before the report starts printing or becomes visible (before the Activate event)
Close	OnClose	You close the report (before the Deactivate event)
Error	OnError	A Jet error occurs while the report is printing
Activate	OnActivate	The report becomes the active window or starts printing (after the Open event)
Deactivate	OnDeactivate	You move to another Access window or close the report (after the Close event)
NoData	OnNoData	You attempt to open a report for printing or previewing, and its underlying recordsource provides no rows
Page	OnPage	The current page has been formatted but hasn't yet been printed

Activation versus Deactivation

When you switch from one report to another (in Preview view), the report you're switching away from executes its Deactivate event before the new report executes its Activate event. If you switch to any other Access window from a report, the report's Deactivate event still executes. If you switch to a different application or to a popup window within Access, the Deactivate event does not fire; that is, the Deactivate event fires off only when you switch to another window for which the parent is also the Access MDI Client window. (See Chapter 8 for more information on the MDI client window.) This makes sense; the main reason you use the Activate/Deactivate events is to set up menus and toolbars for the specific report, as opposed to any other Access window. Since popup Access windows do not have their own menus or toolbars, you don't need to execute the event code.

Using the Open and Activate Events

When Access first opens the report, it runs the code attached to the report's Open event before it runs the query that supplies the data for the report. Given this fact, you can supply parameters to that query from the report's Open event. You might, for example, pop up a form that requests starting and ending dates or any other information your query might need. To see this in action, open rptPhoneBookParam in CH09.MDB. (See Figure 9.3, although this figure is somewhat misleading—the form and the report would never actually be visible at the same time.)

In this example, rptPhoneBookParam's Open event executes the code found in Listing 9.5.

Listing 9.5

```
Private Sub Report_Open(Cancel As Integer)

    ' Set the global variable.
    strForm = "frmParam"

    DoCmd.OpenForm FormName:=strForm, WindowMode:=acDialog

    ' Set the Cancel flag if the form isn't still open.
    ' That would mean the user pressed the Cancel button.
    Cancel = Not isFormOpen(strForm)
End Sub

Private Sub Report_Activate()
    DoCmd.Close acForm, strForm
End Sub
```

FIGURE 9.3:

The report's Open event loads the parameter-gathering form, which, in turn, provides a parameter for the report's underlying query.

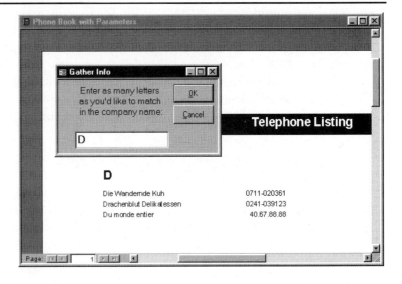

This code first opens frmParam modally so that code execution halts until you either hide or close the form. Just as described in Chapter 8, the OK button hides the form and the Cancel button closes the form altogether. On return from the OpenForm action, the code checks to see whether the form is still open, using the SysCmd() function, and if not it uses the Cancel parameter to indicate that Access should abort the attempt to load the report.

Once Access has executed the Open event, it can go ahead and load the data that's going to populate the report. Because Access wouldn't be at this point at all for this report unless the parameter-providing form were still open (but hidden), you're assured that Access will be able to find the form it needs to supply the parameter for qryCustomerNameParam. The query uses the expression

```
Like Forms!frmParam!txtName & "*"
```

to filter its rows.

Finally, once the report executes its Activate event, the query no longer needs the form, and the code attached to the Activate event can close the form.

Avoiding Empty Reports—Using the NoData Event

There's nothing stopping you from choosing a filter for the report that returns no rows at all. In this case the report prints "#Error" in the Detail section. If you want to avoid this problem, you can add code to the NoData event of your report that reacts to this exact situation and cancels the report if there's no data to be printed. If you want to cancel the report if there aren't any rows, you can use code like this, from rptPhoneBookParam:

```
Private Sub Report_NoData(Cancel As Integer)
    MsgBox "There aren't any rows to display!"
    ' Close the parameter form, as well.
    DoCmd.Close acForm, strForm
    ' Tell Access to just skip it.
    Cancel = True
End Sub
```

To test this code, try entering a value that is guaranteed to return no rows, such as "ZZ", when rptPhoneBookParam requests a value from you.

> **NOTE**
> Unsurprisingly, Access doesn't even bother with the NoData event for unbound reports. Finding out that an unbound report's recordset (which doesn't exist) doesn't contain any rows wouldn't be very useful information.

Using the Error Event

Access triggers a report's Error event when an error occurs in the Jet engine while the report is either formatting or printing. Although this eventuality is less likely with a report than it might be for a form, it can still occur. For example, if a table is opened exclusively by some user or a report is bound to a recordset that doesn't exist, Access triggers this error.

As with most other form and report events, you're far better off using the built-in module (CBF) to handle the Error event. In this case Access provides two parameters to your event handler, allowing you some functionality you'd be missing if you called a macro or an external routine to handle this event. By using CBF you can control how Access handles the error once you've investigated it. (For details, see Chapter 8.)

Listing 9.6 shows a simple error-handling routine. Although this example does little more than display a message box in response to the error that can occur when a user has removed the query or table to which a report has been bound, it should provide a starting place for your own error handlers.

> **NOTE**
> Because of the separation of VBA, the Access report engine, and Jet, you can't use the Error$ function to return information on Jet errors. In this case you'll need to use the AccessError method of the Access Application object. This is just one of the many ways Access has changed due to the addition of the VBA shared component.

Listing 9.6

```
Private Sub Report_Error(DataErr As Integer, _
  Response As Integer)
```

```
    Const glrcErrNoRecordSource = 2580

    Select Case DataErr
        Case glrcErrNoRecordSource
            MsgBox "This report is bound to a table or " & _
                "query that doesn't exist: '" & _
                Me.RecordSource & "'", vbExclamation
        Case Else
            MsgBox Application.AccessError(DataErr)
    End Select
    ' Close the parameter lookup form.
    DoCmd.Close acForm, strForm
    Response = acDataErrContinue
End Sub
```

The Page Event

You'll find there are some actions you just can't take at any time except when Access
has finished formatting a page but before it actually prints the page. You can most
easily draw a border around the page, for example, right before Access prints the
page. The new Page event gives you the flexibility you need to make any last-minute
changes just before Access sends the formatted page to the printer.

The following code, from the Page event of rptBankInfo in CH09.MDB, draws a rectangle surrounding the entire printed page once Access has formatted the page (see
Figure 9.4):

```
Private Sub Report_Page()
    Me.Line (0, 0)-(Me.ScaleWidth, Me.ScaleHeight), , B
End Sub
```

NOTE
You may find that printing a border all the way around the printable
region causes the border to extend past the printable region on your
printer. In that case you may need to experiment with subtracting a
few twips from the value in Me.ScaleHeight until the entire border
prints.

FIGURE 9.4:

Use the Page event to draw on the report page once all the data for the page has been placed on the page.

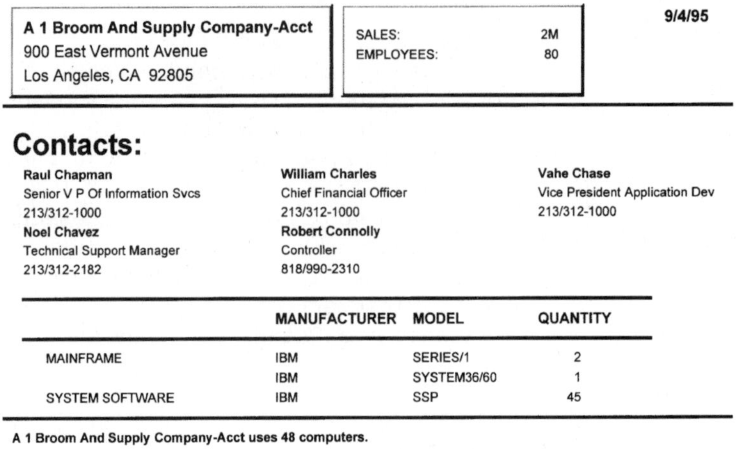

A 1 Broom And Supply Company-Acct		9/4/95
A 1 Broom And Supply Company-Acct 900 East Vermont Avenue Los Angeles, CA 92805	SALES: 2M EMPLOYEES: 80	

Contacts:

Raul Chapman Senior V P Of Information Svcs 213/312-1000	William Charles Chief Financial Officer 213/312-1000	Vahe Chase Vice President Application Dev 213/312-1000
Noel Chavez Technical Support Manager 213/312-2182	Robert Connolly Controller 818/990-2310	

	MANUFACTURER	MODEL	QUANTITY
MAINFRAME	IBM	SERIES/1	2
	IBM	SYSTEM36/60	1
SYSTEM SOFTWARE	IBM	SSP	45

A 1 Broom And Supply Company-Acct uses 48 computers.

Section Events

Just as report events focus mainly on loading and unloading the report itself and on setting up the overall data that will populate the report, section events deal with the actual formatting and printing of that data. The following table lists the three events that apply to report sections:

Event	Event Property	Occurs When
Format	OnFormat	Access has selected the data to go in this section but before it formats or prints the data
Print	OnPrint	Access has formatted the data for printing (or previewing) but before it prints or shows the data
Retreat	OnRetreat	Access needs to move to a previous section while formatting the report

The Format Event

Access executes the code attached to a section's OnFormat event property once it has selected the data to be printed in the section but before it actually prints it. This allows you to alter the layout of the report or to perform calculations based on the data in the section at this particular time.

For a report's Detail section, Access calls your code just before it actually lays out the data to be printed. Your code has access to the data in the current row and can react to that data, perhaps making certain controls visible or invisible. (See the example in the section "Altering Your Report's Layout Programmatically" later in this chapter for more information on this technique.)

For group headers, the Format event occurs for each new group. Within the event procedure, your code has access to data in the group header and in the first row of data in the group. For group footers, the event occurs for each new group, and your code has access to data in the group footer and in the last row of data in the group. (For an example of using this information, see the section "The Sales Report" later in this chapter.)

For actions that don't affect the page layout or for calculations that absolutely must not occur until the section is printed, use the Print event. For example, if you're calculating a running total, place the calculation in the Print event, since doing so avoids any ambiguities about when or whether the section actually printed.

If you've placed code for the Format event in the report's code module, Access passes you two parameters: Cancel and FormatCount. The FormatCount value corresponds to the section's FormatCount property. The Cancel parameter allows you to cancel the formatting of the current section and move on to the next by setting its value to True. This parameter corresponds to using

```
DoCmd.CancelEvent
```

from within your code.

The Print Event

Access executes the code attached to a section's OnPrint property once it has formatted the data to be printed in the section but before it actually prints it. For a report's Detail section, Access calls your code just before it actually prints the data. Your code has access to the data in the current row. For group headers, the Print event occurs for each new group. Within the event procedure, your code has access to data in the group header and in the first row of data in the group. For group footers, the event occurs for each new group, and your code has access to data in the group footer and in the last row of data in the group.

For actions that require changing the report's layout, use the Format event. Once you've reached the Print event, it's too late to change the report's layout.

Just as it does for the Format event, Access passes two parameters to your code for the Print event if you place your code in the report's module. The PrintCount parameter corresponds to the section's PrintCount property. The Cancel parameter allows you to cancel the formatting of the current section and move on to the next by setting its value to True.

The Retreat Event

Sometimes Access needs to move back to a previous section while it's formatting your report. For example, if your group level's KeepTogether property is set to With First Detail Row, Access formats the group header and then the first row and checks to make sure they'll both fit in the space available on the current page. Once it has formatted the two, it retreats from those two sections, executing the Retreat event for each. Then it again formats the sections and finally prints them.

If you've made any changes during the Format event, you may wish to undo them during the Retreat event. Since you really can't know during the Retreat event whether the current section will actually be printed on the current page, you should undo any layout changes made during the Format event.

Counting rows from the Format event makes a very simple example. If you include code attached to a section's Format event procedure that increments a counter for each row, include code in the Retreat event that decrements the counter. Otherwise the Format event may be fired multiple times for a given row, and the count will be incorrect. (Of course, there are several other ways to take care of this problem, including checking the FormatCount property. This example is intended only to explain why you might need to use the Retreat event.)

TIP

Access triggers the Retreat event in two very predictable places, among others. If you've created a group and set its KeepTogether property to With First Detail, Access triggers the Format event, then the Retreat event, and then the Format and Print events for the first row in the group as it attempts to fit the header and the first row on the same page. The same concept applies to groups in which you've set the KeepTogether property to All Rows, in which case Access formats each row, retreats from each row, and then formats the ones that will fit on the current page. Although there are many other circumstances in which Access will fire off the Retreat event, you can be assured that setting the group's KeepTogether property will force it.

Section Design-Time Properties

Report sections maintain a set of properties different from any other Access objects. Table 9.6 lists those properties, and the following sections discuss some of them and give examples and hints for their use in designing your reports. Each of the properties in Table 9.6 applies to all report sections except the page header and footer.

The CanGrow/CanShrink Properties

Setting either the CanGrow or CanShrink property causes other controls on the report to move vertically to adjust for changes in the sections' heights. Sections can grow or shrink only across their whole widths, so they must account for the maximum size needed within themselves. If you have a text box horizontally aligned with an OLE object that cannot shrink, the section will not shrink, no matter how little text is in the text box. If you set a control's CanGrow property to Yes, Access sets the CanGrow property for the control's section to Yes, also. You can override this setting by changing the section's CanGrow property back to No if you need to.

TABLE 9.6: Report Section Properties

Property	Description	Settings
CanGrow	Determines whether the size of a section will increase vertically so Access can print all its data	True (−1); False (0)
CanShrink	Determines whether the size of a section will shrink vertically to avoid wasting space if there is no more data to print	True (−1);False (0)
NewRowOrCol	Specifies whether Access always starts printing a section in a multicolumn layout at the start of a new row (Horizontal layout) or column (Vertical Layout)	None (0); Before Section (1); After Section (2); Before & After (3)
ForceNewPage	Determines whether Access prints a section on the current page or at the top of a new page	None (0); Before Section (1); After Section (2); Before & After (3)
KeepTogether	Determines whether Access attempts to print an entire section on a single page	True (−1); False (0)
RepeatSection (Group Header sections only)	Specifies whether Access repeats a group header on the next page or column when a group spans more than one page or column	True (−1); False (0)

Why CanShrink Doesn't and CanGrow Won't

Microsoft Product Support Services suggests the following reasons why the Can-Grow and CanShrink properties might not always do what you think they ought:

- Overlapping controls will not shrink, even when you've set the CanShrink property to Yes. If two controls touch at all, even by the smallest amount, they won't grow or shrink correctly.

- Controls shrink line by line (vertically). This means, for example, that if a group of controls is placed on the left side of a page and a large control (for example, an OLE picture) on the right side of the page, the controls on the left side will not shrink unless the picture is blank and hidden.

- Space between controls is not affected by the CanShrink or CanGrow property.

- Controls located in the page header or page footer will grow to, at most, the height of the section. Neither the Header nor the Footer section itself can grow or shrink.

The NewRowOrCol Property

The NewRowOrCol property applies only when your report uses multiple columns for its display. When you choose to use multiple columns in the Print Setup dialog (selecting the More options button), you can select either a horizontal or vertical layout for your items. Choosing Vertical prints items down the first column, then down the second, and so on. Choosing Horizontal prints across the first row, in the first column, the second column, and so on, and then goes on to the second row, printing in each column. You might use the Vertical layout for printing phone book listings and the Horizontal layout for printing mailing labels.

The NewRowOrCol property allows you to maintain fine control over how the Detail section of your report prints when it's using multiple columns. Table 9.7 describes each of the property's possible settings and how you can use it to control the layout of your report.

You'll want to experiment with the NewRowOrCol property if you're working with multicolumn reports. You can find an example of its use in the section "Company, Contacts, and Hardware" later in this chapter.

TABLE 9.7: NewRowOrCol Property Settings

Setting	Value	Description
None	0	Row and column breaks occur naturally, based on the settings in the Print Setup dialog and on the layout of the current page so far (default)
Before Section	1	The current section is printed in a new row or column. The next section is printed in the same row or column
After Section	2	The current section is printed in the same row or column as the previous section. The next section is printed in a new row or column
Before & After	3	The current section is printed in a new row or column. The next section is also printed starting in a new row or column

The ForceNewPage Property

The ForceNewPage property allows you to control page breaks in relation to your report sections. Table 9.8 details the four options that are available for this property. Since you can control this option while the report is printing, you can, for example, decide, based on a piece of data in a particular row, to start the section printing on a new page. You can accomplish the same effect, although not quite as elegantly, by including a page break control on your report and setting its Visible property to Yes or No, depending on the data in the current row.

TABLE 9.8: ForceNewPage Property Settings

Setting	Value	Description
None	0	Access starts printing the current section on the current page (default)
Before Section	1	Access starts printing the current section at the top of a new page
After Section	2	Access starts printing the next section at the top of a new page
Before & After	3	Access starts printing the current section at the top of a new page and prints the next section starting on a new page, too

In addition, the ForceNewPage property is now settable at run time, so you can insert page breaks easily from the Format or Print events of your sections. This ability should all but eliminate the need for setting the visibility of page break controls (a hokey hack, at best).

For example, to change the ForceNewPage behavior after printing a specific value, you could place code like this in your group header's Print event (in this case, the group header's name is GroupHeader2):

```
If Me!txtLetter > "C" Then
    Me.GroupHeader2.ForceNewPage = 2
Else
    Me.GroupHeader2.ForceNewPage = 0
End If
```

The KeepTogether Property

The KeepTogether property simply asks Access to try to print a given section all on one page. If it won't fit on the current page, Access starts a new page and tries printing it there. Of course, if it can't fit on one page, Access must continue printing on the next page, no matter how the property is set.

The KeepTogether property for sections is much simpler than the KeepTogether property for groups. The Section property doesn't attempt to keep together different sections, as does the GroupLevel property. It just refers to the "togetherness" of each individual section.

The RepeatSection Property

Often, when you print a group on your report, Access has to start a new page or column in the middle of the group. In that case you may decide you'd like Access to reprint the group header for you on the new page or column. The RepeatSection property for group headers controls whether or not Access repeats the group header at the top of the new page or column. The sample report, rptPhoneBook in CH09.MDB, uses this property to force Access to reprint the group header at the top of the column if a group has been broken across a column.

This property is available only for group headers, not the report header. For report headers you don't really need this—you can just use a page header instead. If you're printing a subreport, however, and you'd like to emulate this behavior, you can fake it:

- In the subreport, create a group that's grouped on the string expression "=1". This creates a static grouping that won't change from row to row of data.

- Use this group header as the report header. (That is, don't show the Report Header section; use this group header instead, since it won't change throughout the report.) Because it's a group header, it will have a RepeatSection property, and Access will repeat it at the top of a new page.

Section Run-Time Properties

Some section events occur only while Access is formatting or printing the report (for example, the Format and Print events, discussed earlier in this chapter). Table 9.9 lists the run-time properties, and the following sections present more information and suggestions for their effective use.

TABLE 9.9: Section Run-Time Properties

Property	Description	Settings
MoveLayout	Specifies whether Access should move to the next printing location on the page	True (−1): the section's Left and Top properties are advanced to the next print location; False (0): the Left and Top properties are unchanged
NextRecord	Specifies whether a section should advance to the next record	True: advance to the next record; False: stay on the same record
PrintSection	Specifies whether a section should be printed	True: the section is printed; False: the section isn't printed
FormatCount	Indicates the number of times the Format event has occurred for the current section	Read-only while the report is being formatted; not available in Design view
PrintCount	Indicates the number of times the Print event has occurred for the current section	Read-only while the report is printing; not available in Design view
HasContinued	Indicates whether the current section has been continued from the previous page	True (−1) or False (0): available in the section's Format event
WillContinue	Indicates whether the current section will continue on the next page	True (−1) or False (0): available in the section's Print event

The MoveLayout, NextRecord, and PrintSection Properties

The MoveLayout, NextRecord, and PrintSection properties, when combined, control exactly how Access moves from row to row in the underlying data and whether or not the current row will be printed. Table 9.10 presents all the possible combinations of the three properties and how they interact. By combining these three layout properties, you'll have a great deal of flexibility in how you lay out your reports. The examples in the sections "Printing Multiple Labels" and "Inserting Blank Lines" later in this chapter demonstrate the use of these properties.

TABLE 9.10: Section Run-Time Properties and Their Interactions

MoveLayout	NextRecord	PrintSection	Results
True	True	True	Moves to the next print location, moves to the next row, and then prints the row (default)
True	True	False	Moves to a new row and moves to the next print location, but it doesn't print the row (It leaves a blank space where the row would have printed.)
True	False	True	Moves to the next print location, stays on the same row, and prints the data
True	False	False	Moves to the next print location but doesn't skip a row and doesn't print any data. This effectively leaves a blank space on the paper without moving to a new row in the data
False	True	True	Doesn't move the print location but prints the next row right on top of the previous one. This allows you to overlay one row of data on another
False	True	False	Doesn't move the print location and doesn't print anything, but it skips a row in the data. This allows you to skip a row without leaving any blank space on the page
False	False	True	Not allowed
False	False	False	Not allowed

The FormatCount Property

Access increments a section's FormatCount property each time it executes the Format event for that section. Once it moves to the next section, it resets the FormatCount property to 1.

In some circumstances Access must format a section more than once. For example, as Access reaches the end of a page, it's possible that the current section won't fit. Access attempts to format the section and, if it doesn't fit, formats it again on the next page. It calls the Format event code twice, first with a FormatCount value of 1 and then with a FormatCount value of 2.

If you're performing some calculation or action from your Format event code, pay careful attention to the FormatCount value. For example, you want to increment only counters if the FormatCount value is 1. If you normally take an action in the Format event code, you must skip the action if the FormatCount value is greater than 1.

The PrintCount Property

Access increments a section's PrintCount property each time it executes the Print event for that section. Once it moves on the next section, it resets the PrintCount property to 0.

Access attempts to print a section more than once when a specific section spans more than one page. For example, if a section requires more than a single page for its output, Access calls the Print event code once for each page, incrementing the PrintCount property. If you're attempting to maintain running totals, adding in an amount each time a report section prints, you need to check the PrintCount property and add in the value only once. The following code might be used in a section's Print event code. (If you place the code in the report's attached module, Access passes the PrintCount property to the code as a parameter. If not, you need to refer to the PrintCount property using the standard syntax.)

```
If PrintCount = 1 Then
    lngRunningTotal = lngRunningTotal + Me!OrderAmount
End If
```

The WillContinue/HasContinued Properties

The two new report properties, HasContinued and WillContinue, are intended to allow code in your event procedures to react to the fact that a given section has continued from the previous page or will continue on the next page. These are both properties of sections, and they return either True or False. Each works a bit differently, and the following sections explain the details of using them. Unfortunately, they're both constructed in such a way that we were unable to find a use for either in any but the most trivial situations or by employing some difficult work-arounds. For the sake of completeness, however, the next few sections explain how they work.

The WillContinue Property

Access sets the WillContinue property during a section's Print event, and the property returns True if any portion of the current section will print on the next page. Therein lies the problem: Access' "trigger" is wound a bit too tightly. Access doesn't distinguish between white space and controls when setting this property, so it sets the WillContinue property to True for almost every page. All you care about is whether text has been printed on one page and continued on the next, not whether white space from the next row to be printed has touched the current page, but Access can't discern between these two situations.

Once Access has set the property to True for a given section, it remains True until the same section's next Print event (PrintCount > 1, on the next page). Therefore, you can use the value of the section's WillContinue property from the Format or Print event procedures of any section that will print before Access prints your section again. (For Detail sections, this means you could check in the current page's Page Footer section or the next page's Page Header section, for example.) In our experimentation, the WillContinue property returned True for every single page of all our test reports except the last page, whether or not the rows actually carried over to the next page—even if the data occupied only a single row on the printed page! The only way we were able to avoid this situation was to print a report in which the Detail section's height was an integral factor of the printed page's height (1 inch, for example, on a 10-inch print area) and in which we didn't include any headers or footers. In that case, Access correctly did *not* set the WillContinue property for each page.

The HasContinued Property

Access sets a section's HasContinued property during the section's Format event, and it sets the property to True only if the FormatCount property is greater than 1 (which is, of course, exactly what it should do). As a matter of fact, our experiments found that Access always sets the HasContinued property correctly, even when it has incorrectly set the WillContinue property on the previous page.

The problem with the HasContinued property is that you can't check it from the location where it would be the most useful—when you're printing the page header. At that point Access hasn't yet set the FormatCount property for the section to a number greater than 1, so the HasContinued property will still be False if you examine the Detail section's properties from the page header. By the time you start printing the second portion of the Detail section (with its FormatCount property now set to 2), it's too late to do anything useful with the HasContinued property.

Of course, even though you can't set the visibility of a control based on the HasContinued property, you can use the report's Print method to write text directly onto the report if you find the Detail section's HasContinued property is True. You may find this useful, but in our testing it appeared to be more work than it was worth.

Perhaps you can tell from the tone that we're a bit disappointed in the functionality these properties provide. They *sound* good, but they just don't provide the right results in the cases where they'd be most useful. We hope the properties will work correctly, or at least better, in future releases of the product.

Examples Using Report and Section Events and Properties

The following sections contain examples and solutions to some common problems. Each example refers to a specific report or form in CH09.MDB. In each case you might find it useful to open the specific report in Design view and follow along with the description you find here. Change properties and see what happens. Experimentation is the best way to find out how each of the report and section properties affects the printed output.

Printing Multiple Labels

Printing multiple labels based on a count stored with the label data makes a perfect example of the use of the MoveLayout, NextRecord, and PrintSection properties. In this example the user has stored, in the LabelCount column of a table, the number of copies of the row to be printed. Listing 9.7, which would be called from the Print event of the Detail section containing the label, shows the code necessary to print the correct number of labels. (See rptMultiLabel in CH09.MDB to test this example.) Given the data shown in Figure 9.5, the design surface shown in Figure 9.6 creates the labels shown in Figure 9.7.

Listing 9.7

```
Sub Detail1_Print(Cancel As Integer, PrintCount As Integer)
    If Me!txtLabelCount = 0 Then
        Me.NextRecord = True
        Me.MoveLayout = False
        Me.PrintSection = False
    Else
        If PrintCount < Me!txtLabelCount Then
```

```
            Me.NextRecord = False
        End If
    End If
End Sub
```

To make this technique work, you must create a text box on your report for the field that contains the count. You can make it invisible, but it has to be on the report for the code to be able to get to it. (In this example the text box control is named txt-LabelCount.) Unlike forms, reports must contain a control bound to any column they reference. Forms can reference any column in the underlying data without actually having to contain a control bound to that field.

This example does its work quite simply. If the user has requested no labels at all for the particular row, the code tells Access to move to the next record (Next-Record = True) but not to move to the next print position (MoveLayout = False) and not to print anything at all (PrintSection = False). Otherwise, if the PrintCount value is less than the number of labels to be printed (Me!txtLabel-Count), don't move to the next record (NextRecord = False), but use the default value for the other properties. This causes Access to print the data from the current row and move to the next print location.

FIGURE 9.5:

Each row in the table contains a column indicating the number of labels to be printed.

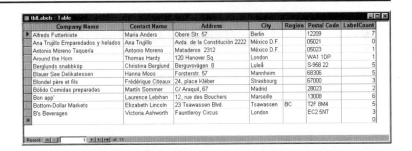

FIGURE 9.6:

The report design includes a visible control containing the LabelCount column. In your labels, this could be made invisible.

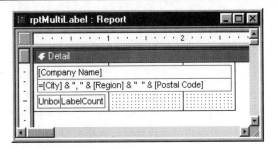

FIGURE 9.7:

The labels will contain as many multiples as you requested in your table.

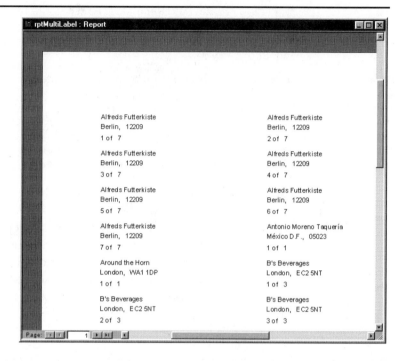

Although you might be tempted to attach this code to the Format event, it won't work correctly. Because Access must decide at format time how to lay out the labels on the page, the FormatCount value to which the Format event has access won't always be correct, especially when you've filled a page without completing the run of a particular row.

Printing Mailing Labels
Starting at a Specific Location

If you print mailing labels on full sheets of paper (as do most people with laser printers), you've probably needed, at one point or another, to start a printout at the first unused label on the page rather than on the first label. The technique to make this happen is very simple and uses the same properties used in the previous example: NextRecord and PrintSection. If you want to try out this technique, load rptSkipLabels in Preview view. This causes frmSelectLabel to pop up, requesting you to choose the first label on which to print. Once you've made a selection, the form disappears and the report prints, starting on the label you chose.

How Does it Work?

The basic idea is this: you call a function, glrGetLabelsToSkip() (in basSelectLabel), that pops up a form requesting you to click the first label you want printed (see Figure 9.8). You send to this function information about the number of rows and columns for your labels, which label to choose by default, and whether you're printing across and then down or down and then across. Given that information, that form configures itself for your label situation and allows you to select the label on which you'd first like to print. When you click the form's OK button, the form hides itself, and the calling function in your report then knows how many labels to skip on the page. (For more information on creating popup forms that return values, see the section "Using Popup Tools" in Chapter 8.)

Your call to glrGetLabelsToSkip() returns the first label you want printed, and it's up to your report to skip all labels before that one, but only on the first page. Figure 9.9 shows how rptSkipLabels will print after you've chosen to start on label 11,

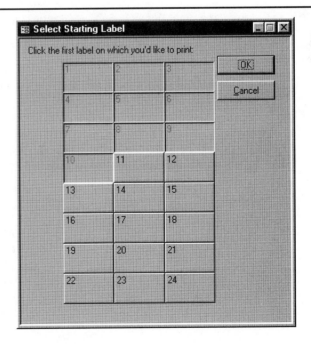

FIGURE 9.8:
Choose a label from frmSelectLabel on which to start printing.

FIGURE 9.9:

Once you've selected a starting label, the report will skip labels up to that label number.

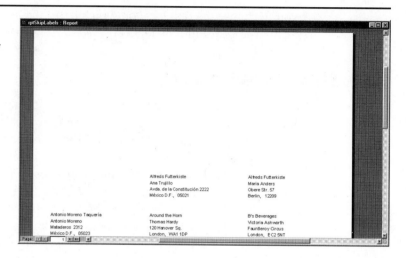

as in Figure 9.8. To do its work, rptSkipLabels calls the code shown here in reaction to the Report Header and Detail sections' Format events:

```
Dim intSkipped As Integer
Dim intToSkip As Integer

Private Sub Detail_Format(Cancel As Integer, _
  FormatCount As Integer)
   If intSkipped < intToSkip Then
      Me.NextRecord = False
      Me.PrintSection = False
      intSkipped = intSkipped + 1
   End If
End Sub

Private Sub ReportHeader_Format(Cancel As Integer, _
  FormatCount As Integer)
   intSkipped = 0
   intToSkip = glrGetLabelsToSkip(FormName:="frmSelectLabel", _
     Rows:=10, Cols:=3, Start:=1, PrintAcross:=True)
End Sub
```

Every time you print or preview the report, Access triggers the report header's Format event. There, you'll need to reset the count of skipped labels, intSkipped, back to 0 and then call glrGetLabelsToSkip(). Pass glrGetLabelsToSkip() information on the form to pop up; the number of rows and columns on your label sheets; which label to choose, by default; and whether you're printing across first (as opposed to down first). The function pops up the requested form, waits for a response, and returns the number of labels your printout should skip.

From the Detail section's Format event, the code keeps track of how many labels it has skipped. Once it reaches the value in intSkipped, it actually starts printing labels. Up to that point, however, it sets the NextRecord and PrintSection properties to False, stalling until it reaches the right label.

As you can see from the previous two examples, you can use the MoveLayout, PrintSection, and NextRecord properties to create reports that would be difficult by any other means. Don't be put off by their apparent complexity; once you get the hang of it, you can make them do exactly what you need.

TIP

To use this technique in your own applications, import frmSelectLabel and basSelectLabel from CH09.MDB. Copy all the event code from rptSkipLabels (it's easier to do if you set the Tools ➤ Options ➤ Module ➤ Full Module View option) into your own report's module, and modify the call to glrGetLabelsToSkip() to reflect your report's geography. Finally, make sure your report's property sheet has the Detail and Header sections' Format properties set to [Event Procedure]. When you open your report, it will pop up the form and request a starting label.

Handling Odd and Even Pages

Perhaps you print your reports double sided (either on a duplex printer or by using a printing utility such as *Click*Book, from BookMaker Corporation). In general, given that the first page of a document prints on the front of a piece of paper, odd-numbered pages appear on the right and even-numbered pages appear on the left when you bind the document. Quite often, in published documents, you'll want the page numbers to appear flush right on odd-numbered pages and flush left on even-numbered pages. Although Access doesn't provide a built-in method to accomplish this, it's easy to do. (See rptPhoneBook or rptPhoneBookParam for this example.)

To alternate left and right alignment for alternating pages, take these two steps:

1. Create your page footer control so that it spans the entire width of your report (see Figure 9.10). Enter the ControlSource value you'd like.

2. Attach the code in Listing 9.8 to the Format event of the Page Footer section. This handles setting the TextAlign property for the Footer section as each page gets printed. For every page, the code checks the page number MOD 2, which is 0 for even pages and 1 for odd pages. It sets the TextAlign property to acAlignRight for odd pages and acAlignLeft for even pages.

FIGURE 9.10:

Your footer can alternate alignments easily if it spans the entire page.

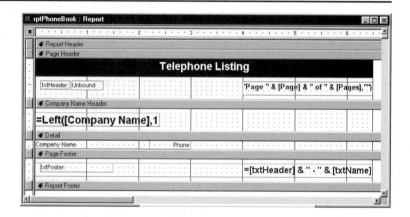

If you haven't used the MOD operator, this might appear confusing. Basically, the MOD operator returns the remainder you get when you divide the first operand by the second. That is, if you have

```
? 5 MOD 2
```

the result would be 1, since the remainder when you divide 5 by 2 is 1. The MOD operator is most useful for determining whether one number is a multiple of another since, if it is, the result will be 0. To tell whether a number is even, you can use the expression

```
If x MOD 2 = 0 Then ...
```

Listing 9.8

```
Private Function IsEven(intValue As Integer) As Boolean
    ' Is intValue even, or not?
    IsEven = (intValue Mod 2 = 0)
End Function

Private Sub PageFooter2_Format(Cancel As Integer, _
 FormatCount As Integer)

    ' Constants Access should supply, but doesn't.
    Const acAlignLeft = 1
    Const acAlignRight = 3

    Me!txtFooter.TextAlign = IIf(IsEven(Me.Page), _
      acAlignLeft, acAlignRight)
End Sub
```

Controlling the Starting Page Number

Every report supports a read/write property that indicates and/or sets the current page number. By inspecting the Page property of the current report, you can determine which page is currently active. You can also set the Page property, effectively resetting Access' understanding of the current page number. You could, if you had a reason to, set the Page property to 1 in the page header's Format event. Then, every time Access formatted a page header (once per page), it would reset the report's Page property to 1.

A more useful trick involving the Page property is the ability to set the starting page number to some value other than 1. This is especially useful if you need to chain reports or number chapters with a page number including the chapter number, with each chapter starting at page 1. The only tricky issue here is deciding when to reset the page number. If you want to print an entire report, starting at a particular page number, set the Page property in the report header's Format event. If you need to set the Page property based on data that could occur at the top of any given page, set the value in the page header's Format event.

For an example, see rptSales in CH09.MDB. This report sets the first page number to 6 in the report header's Format event. Numbers increase consecutively from there. The code to make this change is minimal, of course:

```
Sub ReportHeader0_Format(Cancel As Integer, _
 FormatCount As Integer)
    Me.Page = 6
End Sub
```

Because the report's Open event occurs before any of the formatting events, you could also use that hook to retrieve the starting page number, store it in a variable, and then assign the value of that variable to the Page property in the report header's Format event. (We discuss the other interesting features of this report, including the alternate gray bars, in the section "The Sales Report" later in this chapter.)

Numbering Items on a Report

Access makes it simple to number rows on a report. By changing two properties of a text box, you can create a row counter that will count rows either over the total report or just within a group. The report rptNumberRows in CH09.MDB demonstrates both types of row counters, as you can see in Figure 9.11.

To create a row counter on a report, set a text box's properties as follows:

Property	Setting
RunningSum	Over Group (1) or Over All (2)
ControlSource	=1

This technique takes advantage of the fact that setting the RunningSum property causes the current row's value to be the sum of all the previous rows' values plus the current row's value. Since the current row's value in this case is always 1, the running sum just increments by 1. You could, of course, place some other value in the ControlSource property to force it to increment by a different value.

You can examine rptNumberRows to see how it works, but the most important setting is that for the RunningSum property of the text boxes. If set to Over Group, it continues to sum only over the current group. Every time Access starts a new group, its value gets reset to 0. If set to Over All, the value gets reset only at the beginning of the report and continues to increment for the rest of the report.

FIGURE 9.11:

Use the RunningSum property to create a row counter in a report.

Numbering Rows Report

A.1	1	Alfreds Futterkiste	L.6	46	Lehmanns Marktstand
A.2	2	Antonio Moreno Taquería	L.7	47	Let's Stop N Shop
A.3	3	Around the Horn	L.8	48	Lonesome Pine Restaurant
A.4	4	Alfreds Futterkiste	L.9	49	LILA-Supermercado
B.1	5	B's Beverages	M.1	50	Magazzini Alimentari Riuniti
B.2	6	Berglunds snabbköp	M.2	51	Maison Dewey
B.3	7	Blauer See Delikatessen	M.3	52	Mère Paillarde
B.4	8	Blondel père et fils	M.4	53	Morgenstern Gesundkost
B.5	9	Bólido Comidas preparadas			
B.6	10	Bon app'	N.1	54	North/South
B.7	11	Bottom-Dollar Markets			
			O.1	55	Old World Delicatessen
C.1	12	Consolidated Holdings	O.2	56	Ottilies Käseladen
C.2	13	Comércio Mineiro	O.3	57	Océano Atlántico Ltda.
C.3	14	Chop-suey Chinese			
C.4	15	Cactus Comidas para llevar	P.1	58	Pericles Comidas clásicas
C.5	16	Centro comercial Moctezuma	P.2	59	Piccolo und mehr
			P.3	60	Princesa Isabel Vinhos
D.1	17	Die Wandernde Kuh	P.4	61	Paris spécialités
D.2	18	Drachenblut Delikatessen			
D.3	19	Du monde entier	Q.1	62	Que Delícia
			Q.2	63	Queen Cozinha
E.1	20	Eastern Connection	Q.3	64	QUICK-Stop
E.2	21	Ernst Handel			
			R.1	65	Ricardo Adocicados
F.1	22	FISSA Fabrica Inter. Salchichas S.A.	R.2	66	Richter Supermarkt
F.2	23	Furia Bacalhau e Frutos do Mar	R.3	67	Rattlesnake Canyon Grocery
F.3	24	Franchi S.p.A.	R.4	68	Rancho grande
F.4	25	France restauration	R.5	69	Reggiani Caseifici
F.5	26	Folies gourmandes	R.6	70	Romero y tomillo
F.6	27	Familia Arquibaldo			
F.7	28	Frankenversand	S.1	71	Santé Gourmet
F.8	29	Folk och fä HB	S.2	72	Save-a-lot Markets
			S.3	73	Seven Seas Imports
G.1	30	Galería del gastrónomo	S.4	74	Simons bistro
G.2	31	Godos Cocina Típica	S.5	75	Spécialités du monde
G.3	32	Gourmet Lanchonetes	S.6	76	Split Rail Beer & Ale
G.4	33	Great Lakes Food Market	S.7	77	Suprêmes délices
G.5	34	GROSELLA-Restaurante			
			T.1	78	The Big Cheese
H.1	35	Hanari Carnes	T.2	79	Trail's Head Gourmet Provisioners
H.2	36	Hungry Owl All-Night Grocers	T.3	80	Tradição Hipermercados
H.3	37	HILARIÓN-Abastos	T.4	81	Tortuga Restaurante
H.4	38	Hungry Coyote Import Store	T.5	82	The Cracker Box
			T.6	83	Toms Spezialitäten
I.1	39	Island Trading			
			V.1	84	Vaffeljernet
K.1	40	Königlich Essen	V.2	85	Victuailles en stock
			V.3	86	Vins et alcools Chevalier
L.1	41	LINO-Delicateses			
L.2	42	La corne d'abondance	W.1	87	Wolski Zajazd
L.3	43	La maison d'Asie	W.2	88	Wartian Herkku
L.4	44	Laughing Bacchus Wine Cellars	W.3	89	Wellington Importadora
L.5	45	Lazy K Kountry Store	W.4	90	White Clover Markets
			W.5	91	Wilman Kala

Inserting Blank Lines

If your report consists of a long list of values, you may wish to insert a blank line at regular intervals. Figure 9.12 shows such a report, with a blank line inserted after each group of five rows.

FIGURE 9.12:
Insert a blank line to separate large groups into readable chunks.

Blank Every N Lines Report

Alfreds Futterkiste	Maria Anders	030-0074321
Ana Trujillo Emparedados y helados	Ana Trujillo	(5) 555-4729
Antonio Moreno Taquería	Antonio Moreno	(5) 555-3932
Around the Horn	Thomas Hardy	(71) 555-7788
B's Beverages	Victoria Ashworth	(71) 555-1212
Berglunds snabbköp	Christina Berglund	0921-12 34 65
Blauer See Delikatessen	Hanna Moos	0621-08460
Blondel père et fils	Frédérique Citeaux	88.60.15.31
Bólido Comidas preparadas	Martín Sommer	(91) 555 22 82
Bon app'	Laurence Lebihan	91.24.45.40
Bottom-Dollar Markets	Elizabeth Lincoln	(604) 555-4729
Cactus Comidas para llevar	Patricio Simpson	(1) 135-5555
Centro comercial Moctezuma	Francisco Chang	(5) 555-3392
Chop-suey Chinese	Yang Wang	0452-076545
Comércio Mineiro	Pedro Afonso	(11) 555-7647
Consolidated Holdings	Elizabeth Brown	(71) 555-2282
Die Wandernde Kuh	Rita Müller	0711-020361
Drachenblut Delikatessen	Sven Ottlieb	0241-039123
Du monde entier	Janine Labrune	40.67.88.88
Eastern Connection	Ann Devon	(71) 555-0297
Ernst Handel	Roland Mendel	7675-3425
Familia Arquibaldo	Aria Cruz	(11) 555-9857
FISSA Fabrica Inter. Salchichas S.A.	Diego Roel	(91) 555 94 44
Folies gourmandes	Martine Rancé	20.16.10.16
Folk och fä HB	Maria Larsson	0695-34 67 21
France restauration	Carine Schmitt	40.32.21.21
Franchi S.p.A.	Paolo Accorti	011-4988260

This technique again involves the NextRecord and PrintSection properties. The code in Listing 9.9 does the work for you, and you can copy it into any of your own report's modules. (Look in rptBlankEveryNLines in CH09.MDB.) It does its work by counting up the lines that have been printed so far on each page; when the number is an even multiple of the group size plus 1 (that is, if you're breaking after five lines, you'll be looking for lines that are a multiple of 6), the report skips to the next print location but does not move to the next record (NextRecord = False) and doesn't print anything (PrintSection = False). This inserts a blank row.

> **NOTE**
> The HandleLine subroutine checks each control's Visible property before it sets it as visible or invisible. Although this may seem redundant, it might actually speed up the report. Because checking a control's state is faster than actually setting a property for the control, checking first saves some property setting if the control is already in the right state, as it is 80 percent of the time in this example.

Listing 9.9 shows the HandleLine procedure.

Listing 9.9

```
Private Sub HandleLine()
    Dim fShowLine As Boolean
    Dim intI As Integer
    Dim ctl As Control

    Const glrcBreakCount = 5

    fShowLine = ((mintLineCount Mod (glrcBreakCount + 1)) <> 0)

    For Each ctl In Me.Controls
        ' Walk through all the controls
        ' in the Detail section, setting
        ' them all either visible or invisible.
        If ctl.Section = 0 Then
            ' It's always faster to check first, then
            ' set a property, since there's nothing slower
            ' than setting a property.
            If Not ctl.Visible Eqv fShowLine Then
                ctl.Visible = fShowLine
```

```
            End If
        End If
    Next ctl

    If Not fShowLine Then
        ' If you're not showing the current
        ' row, then don't move to the next record,
        ' and don't print the section.
        Me.NextRecord = False
        Me.PrintSection = False
        mintLineCount = 0
    End If
    mintLineCount = mintLineCount + 1
End Sub
```

TIP If you just want to insert a blank line between your groups and don't care about breaking specific-sized groups, you can set up a group footer that's blank (with its CanShrink property set to No). Then, when the group breaks, Access inserts a blank space between groups.

Some Simple Sample Reports

The following three reports show off some of the effects various properties can make on the printed output of an Access report. Each was designed to show off specific techniques:

- **Sales report:** Alternating gray bars, displaying report properties on the report, creating page totals

- **Telephone book:** Using multiple columns with full-page-width title, section titles, and footer page-range listing

- **Companies, contacts, and hardware:** Using multiple subreports and report properties to link separate reports

The Sales Report

The sales report (see Figure 9.13) lists companies in reverse order of sales and, within sets of equal sales, in alphabetical order by company name. For visibility, every other line is printed in gray, and each page contains a total sales amount for the companies printed on that page.

We'll take this in steps:

1. Create the basic report, with no gray and no totals.

2. Add the page totals (using the Print event).

3. Add the alternate gray lines (using the Format event).

Step 1: Creating the Basic Report—No Gray, No Totals

Figure 9.14 shows the design surface for the basic, no-frills sales report. The sorting and grouping have already been performed, using the setup shown in Figure 9.15. For this report, Access prints information from the Report Header section once, on the first page. It prints the information in the Page Header and Page Footer sections once on each page and prints the Detail section once for each row of data.

TIP

If you're using a calculated expression as the ControlSource property for a text box on a report, make sure its Name property does not match one of the fields in your expression. If the Name property is the same as one of the fields used to fill the control, Access can't know whether you want it to get the value from the field or from the control with that particular name. Confused, Access will place #Error into the text box when you run the report. This is a common occurrence when you create reports using the Report Wizards and then customize them. The Wizards use the field name as the Name property for each control, which can lead to just this sort of problem.

FIGURE 9.13:

Company names in decreasing order of sales, with added alternate gray bars

COMPUTER SURVEY DATA

COMPANY NAMES IN DECREASING ORDER OF REVENUE
(Actual values have been altered to protect confidentiality)

COMPANY NAME	SALES (In Millions of $'s)
Bottom-Dollar Markets	4654
QUICK-Stop	675
Old World Delicatessen	454
Berglunds snabbköp	434
Galería del gastrónomo	356
GROSELLA-Restaurante	356
Hungry Coyote Import Store	356
Split Rail Beer & Ale	356
North/South	68
Morgenstern Gesundkost	57
Mère Paillarde	56
Océano Atlántico Ltda.	56
Suprêmes délices	56
Trail's Head Gourmet Provisioners	56
Bon app'	54
Que Delícia	54
Spécialités du monde	54
La maison d'Asie	46
B's Beverages	45
France restauration	45
La corne d'abondance	45
Laughing Bacchus Wine Cellars	45
Rancho grande	43
LINO-Delicateses	36
Maison Dewey	36
Magazzini Alimentari Riuniti	35
Blauer See Delikatessen	34
Cactus Comidas para llevar	34
FISSA Fabrica Inter. Salchichas S.A.	34
	8630

Report: rptSales (tblCustomers)   Page 6

FIGURE 9.14:

Plain sales report's design surface

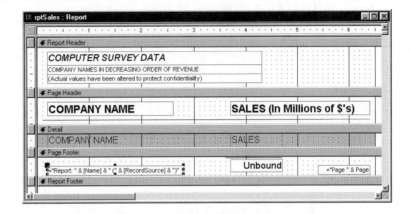

FIGURE 9.15:

Sorting and Grouping dialog for the sales report

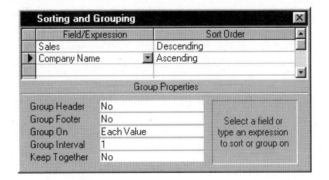

Using Report Properties

If you look carefully at the Page Footer section of the report, you'll notice that it's using some of the report's properties—Name, RecordSource, and Page—as values that are shown on the report. You can use any of the report's properties as built-in variables on the report printout. This same feature applies to forms, although it's not as useful in that context, since form properties aren't nearly as interesting as report properties. (Forms don't support the Page property except when printing, for example.)

Step 2: Adding Page Totals

Unlike the Report and Group Header/Footer sections, page Header/Footer sections don't support aggregate functions, so you have to "fake out" Access in order to create page totals. Our solution (only one of many possible solutions) has two parts:

- As each page header is printed, reset the running total to 0 in preparation for accumulating the value for the current page.

- As each row is printed, accumulate the running total in a control in the page footer.

Each of these refers to a control in the page footer, necessary for accumulating the running total. In this sample report (rptSales), that text box is named txtPageTotal.

Because you surely do not want a value added into the running total unless that particular row has been slated to be printed on the current page, you should attach the code that updates the totals to the section's Print event. (If you insisted on using the Format event, you would need to add code to the matching Retreat event that would back out of the addition if the row were not to be printed.) In this simple example there's no chance that the Print and Format events will be fired off independently (since there's only one printed row per row in the data), but you need to think about the differences between the Print and Format events when deciding how to attach actions to events. Access fires off the Format event when it's formatting a section but isn't yet sure whether it will get printed. It fires off the Print event only when it's about to actually print the row.

Resetting the Total for Each Page

In the Page Header's Format event (which occurs only as each page starts its formatting process), call the following code:

```
Me!txtPageTotal = 0
```

This resets the text box in the page footer that will accumulate the total for each page.

Accumulating the Sales as You Go

In the Detail section's Print event, call the following code:

```
Me!txtPageTotal = Me!txtPageTotal + Nz(Me!txtSales)
```

(For more information on the Nz() function, see the sidebar entitled "The Helpful Nz() Function" in Chapter 8.)

This code adds the current row's sales value to the current page total. Remember that the Print event handler is the only event procedure that can access each and every row's data, once you're sure the data is to be printed on the current page. It's here that you need to place any code that must react to each row as it gets printed. When each page is finally pushed out of the printer, this total will be correct, since you've been maintaining it while Access has printed each row.

Step 3: Alternating White and Gray Bars

Although this sort of maneuver was tricky in previous versions of Access, in Access 95 you can easily create alternate gray and white bars. You can find the procedure AlternateGray (Listing 9.10) in CH09.MDB, in the report module for rptSales. Because Access 95 allows text boxes to be transparent, showing the background color through them, the exercise is trivial: every alternate row, change the background color of the section. The controls are transparent, and the background color for the section will be the background color for the row.

The routine uses a module-global variable, fGray, to keep track of whether or not the current row should be printed. The procedure switches the variable between True and False:

```
fGray = Not fGray
```

If you want to ensure that the first row on each page is printed in white, set the value of fGray to False in the page header's Format event code.

Listing 9.10

```
Private Sub AlternateGray()

    Const glrcColorGray = &HCOCOCO
    Const glrcColorWhite = &HFFFFFF

    ' If the current section is to be printed in gray, then set
    ' the BackColor property for the section. This works, since
    ' the controls on the section are all set to be transparent.
    Me.Section(0).BackColor = IIf(fGray, glrcColorGray, _
```

```
    glrcColorWhite)

    ' Next time, do it the opposite of the way you did
    ' it this time.
    fGray = Not fGray
End Sub
```

TIP

To include this functionality in your own reports, copy the subroutine named AlternateGray from rptSales to your own report, declare the fGray integer variable in your module's declarations area, and add the necessary call to AlternateGray to the Format event of the Detail section. You might also set the value of fGray to False (or True) in the page header's Format event handler (to reset the first row on each page to a known color).

The Phone Book

Many people use Access to maintain their phone books and address lists. The report you'll see in this section creates a phone book–like listing of names and telephone numbers and adds a few twists. It incorporates large group separators, prints in two vertical columns, and puts a "names on this page" indicator at the bottom of the page. Figure 9.16 shows the layout of the first page of rptPhoneBook, in CH09.MDB.

Again, we'll take this in steps:

1. Create a basic list, sorted and grouped on Company Name, with a page number on each page.

2. Print the list in two columns, with a full-span page header and page footer.

3. Add the "names on this page" indicator with alternating alignment, and hide the page number on the first page.

FIGURE 9.16:

Multicolumn, grouped phone book

Telephone Listing

A

Alfreds Futterkiste	030-0074321
Ana Trujillo Emparedados y helados	(5) 555-4729
Antonio Moreno Taquería	(5) 555-3932
Around the Horn	(71) 555-7788

B

B's Beverages	(71) 555-1212
Berglunds snabbköp	0921-12 34 65
Blauer See Delikatessen	0621-08460
Blondel père et fils	88.60.15.31
Bólido Comidas preparadas	(91) 555 22 82
Bon app'	91.24.45.40
Bottom-Dollar Markets	(604) 555-4729

C

Cactus Comidas para llevar	(1) 135-5555
Centro comercial Moctezuma	(5) 555-3392
Chop-suey Chinese	0452-076545
Comércio Mineiro	(11) 555-7647
Consolidated Holdings	(71) 555-2282

D

Die Wandernde Kuh	0711-020361
Drachenblut Delikatessen	0241-039123
Du monde entier	40.67.88.88

E

Eastern Connection	(71) 555-0297
Ernst Handel	7675-3425

F

Familia Arquibaldo	(11) 555-9857
FISSA Fabrica Inter. Salchichas S.A.	(91) 555 94 44
Folies gourmandes	20.16.10.16
Folk och fä HB	0695-34 67 21
France restauration	40.32.21.21
Franchi S.p.A.	011-4988260
Frankenversand	089-0877310
Furia Bacalhau e Frutos do Mar	(1) 354-2534

G

Galería del gastrónomo	(93) 203 4560
Godos Cocina Típica	(95) 555 82 82
Gourmet Lanchonetes	(11) 555-9482
Great Lakes Food Market	(503) 555-7555
GROSELLA-Restaurante	(2) 283-2951

H

Hanari Carnes	(21) 555-0091
HILARIÓN-Abastos	(5) 555-1340
Hungry Coyote Import Store	(503) 555-6874
Hungry Owl All-Night Grocers	2967 542

I

Island Trading	(24) 555-8888

K

Königlich Essen	0555-09876

L

La corne d'abondance	30.59.84.10
La maison d'Asie	61.77.61.10
Laughing Bacchus Wine Cellars	(604) 555-3392
Lazy K Kountry Store	(509) 555-7969
Lehmanns Marktstand	069-0245984
Let's Stop N Shop	(415) 555-5938
LILA-Supermercado	(9) 331-6954
LINO-Delicateses	(8) 34-56-12
Lonesome Pine Restaurant	(503) 555-9573

M

Magazzini Alimentari Riuniti	035-640230
Maison Dewey	(02) 201 24 67
Mère Paillarde	(514) 555-8054
Morgenstern Gesundkost	0342-023176

N

North/South	(71) 555-7733

O

Océano Atlántico Ltda.	(1) 135-5333
Old World Delicatessen	(907) 555-7584

Alfreds Futterkiste - Old World Delicatessen

Step 1: Creating the Basic List

Because reports do their own sorting, based on the choices made in the Sorting and Grouping dialog box, this report is based on a table rather than on a query. (There would be no point in basing this report on a query: if the query sorted the data, the report would then just sort it again!) If you look at the report design (Figure 9.17), you'll notice that the list is grouped on [Company Name] (Prefix Characters:1), which means Access will start a new group every time the first letter of the last name changes. When that happens, it prints out the current value's group footer and the next value's group header. To get Access to sort the companies within the group, you must add [Company Name] to the Sorting and Grouping dialog again.

Each time Access starts a new group, it prints out the Company Name Header section, which consists of a large copy of the first letter of the company name at that moment. (Remember that the group header has access to the data from the first row of its section and the group footer has access to the last row of data in the section.)

FIGURE 9.17:

Phone book's design surface

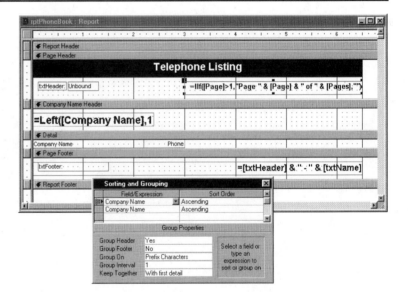

Step 2: Printing the Multicolumn Report

Setting up reports to print in multiple columns requires digging around in a dialog box buried in the Page Setup dialog. Choose the Layout tab to find the options that control the number and type of columns you use in your report. Figure 9.18 shows the Page Setup dialog. Table 9.11 shows the items you'll be concerned with when creating a multicolumn report.

FIGURE 9.18:
Choose the Layout tab in the Page
Setup dialog to control the column
settings for your report.

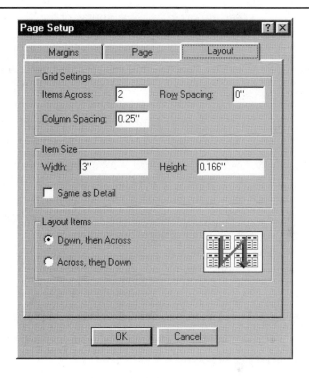

TABLE 9.11: Multicolumn Report Option Settings

Item	Description	Setting for the Phone Book
Items Across	Number of columns	2
Same as Detail	Determines whether each column is the same width as the Detail section in the report design	No (unchecked)
Width	Width of each column	3
Layout Items	Determines whether your columns will go across (Across, then Down) or up and down (Down, then Across)?	Down, then Across

Making the changes outlined in the table should transform your report from a one-column list to a phone book–style layout.

One important point: if you want the header and footer to span the entire report (as you do in this case), you must set the report design surface width to the width of the entire report. Then, place controls in the Detail section (and its Header/Footer sections) only as wide as your columns will be. Finally, make sure the Same as Detail option is unchecked, with the Width option set to the width each column will fill. This way the report's width determines the width of the Report Header and Footer sections, but the Width setting in the Print Setup dialog controls the width of each column.

You might also find it interesting to try setting the Item Layout property to print horizontally rather than vertically. In that case Access prints each row and then moves horizontally to the next print location. When all the columns are full across the page, it moves to the next row. You'll most likely want to try setting the New-RowOrColumn property for the group header to Before & After Section. This places each section header on a new row, by itself, with the data beginning on the following row. Figure 9.19 shows the horizontally arranged phone book.

Step 3: Indicating the Group Names and Hiding the First-Page Page Number

You have two final challenges in creating this report:

- Provide an indication of the group of names that are shown on the current page.
- Hide the page number on the first page. (Okay, Access will do this for you if you choose the Insert ➤ Page Number command, but it's worth understanding the details.)

Gathering Information, but Only in the Footer

To create a text box that displays the range of names on the current page, you need a bit more trickery. By the time Access formats the page footer, it has access to only the current row, which is the last row to be printed on the page. But you need to know the *first* name on the page, also. The trick here is to store away the first name when you can get it—when Access is formatting the page header. The easiest way to use it is to place it in a hidden text box in the report's page header during the page header's Format event. Then, as the control source for a text box on the page footer,

FIGURE 9.19:
Setting the Item Layout property to Horizontal changes the look of the phone book.

Telephone Listing

A

| Alfreds Futterkiste | 030-0074321 | Ana Trujillo Emparedados y helados | (5) 555-4729 |
| Antonio Moreno Taquería | (5) 555-3932 | Around the Horn | (71) 555-7788 |

B

B's Beverages	(71) 555-1212	Berglunds snabbköp	0921-12 34 65
Blauer See Delikatessen	0621-08460	Blondel père et fils	88.60.15.31
Bólido Comidas preparadas	(91) 555 22 82	Bon app'	91.24.45.40
Bottom-Dollar Markets	(604) 555-4729		

C

Cactus Comidas para llevar	(1) 135-5555	Centro comercial Moctezuma	(5) 555-3392
Chop-suey Chinese	0452-076545	Comércio Mineiro	(11) 555-7647
Consolidated Holdings	(71) 555-2282		

D

| Die Wandernde Kuh | 0711-020361 | Drachenblut Delikatessen | 0241-039123 |
| Du monde entier | 40.67.88.88 | | |

E

| Eastern Connection | (71) 555-0297 | Ernst Handel | 7675-3425 |

F

Familia Arquibaldo	(11) 555-9857	FISSA Fabrica Inter. Salchichas S.A.	(91) 555 94 44
Folies gourmandes	20.16.10.16	Folk och fä HB	0695-34 67 21
France restauration	40.32.21.21	Franchi S.p.A.	011-4988260
Frankenversand	089-0877310	Furia Bacalhau e Frutos do Mar	(1) 354-2534

G

Galería del gastrónomo	(93) 203 4560	Godos Cocina Típica	(95) 555 82 82
Gourmet Lanchonetes	(11) 555-9482	Great Lakes Food Market	(503) 555-7555
GROSELLA-Restaurante	(2) 283-2951		

H

| Hanari Carnes | (21) 555-0091 | HILARIÓN-Abastos | (5) 555-1340 |
| Hungry Coyote Import Store | (503) 555-6874 | Hungry Owl All-Night Grocers | 2967 542 |

I

| Island Trading | (24) 555-8888 | | |

Alfreds Futterkiste - Island Trading

the first name can be retrieved from its storage place and concatenated to the current (last) name. This works fine, except for one small problem: it can work only from the page footer. Because Access formats the page in a linear fashion (from the top section to the bottom), your names will be off by one page, one way or another, if you try this in any other sequence.

Printing the Page Range Anywhere

The Solutions database that ships with Access suggests an alternate method for gathering and printing the page range information, but it's quite complex and works only if you follow their rules exactly. On the other hand, it does allow you to print the information anywhere you like on the page.

The suggested solution requires that you use the Pages property somewhere on the report, which forces Access to make two passes through the report. Once you've done that you can calculate, during the first pass, the name ranges for each page and store them in an array. Then, on the second pass, you can retrieve the values in the array and use them on the report. If you absolutely must place the page range somewhere besides the page footer, this may be the best solution. See SOLUTION.MDB (shipped with Microsoft Access) for more information.

Therefore, in the report's Page Header section, call the following code from the Format event. In this example the text box txtName contains the current row's [Company Name] field, and txtHeader is the text box in the page header that's used for storage:

```
Me![txtHeader] = Me![txtName]
```

Then, as the ControlSource for a control in the page footer, use this expression:

```
=[txtHeader] & " - " & [txtName]
```

This concatenates the stored first name and current final name in the control.

Hiding the Page Number

Hiding the page number on the first page requires a single step: set the Control-Source property of the text box such that it prints an empty string on the first page and the page number on all the rest:

```
=IIf([Page] > 1, "Page " & [Page] & " of " & [Pages],"")
```

That is, all reports support the Page and Pages properties, and you can use them on your reports, as you can from your event procedures. (See the section "Controlling the Starting Page Number" earlier in this chapter.) In this case, if the current page number is larger than 1, display the current page number along with the total number of pages; otherwise, display nothing.

Avoiding Widows

In previous versions of Access, it was difficult to ensure that groups didn't break across columns, leaving "widows"—headers with no matching detail rows in the same column. In Access 95, it's simple: use the report's GrpKeepTogether property (set to "Per Column") to have your groups' settings take effect over columns. (That is, how you've set your groups' KeepTogether property will be affected either by page breaks [Per Page] or by column breaks, as well [Per Column].) It is confusing that this is a *report* property, not a group property, because it applies to all groups and therefore must be a global property.

Companies, Contacts, and Hardware

Sometimes you'll find that one complex report really requires several smaller, linked reports. The report in Figure 9.20 is one such report. It shows a single company site, the listed contacts for that site, and the computer hardware and software the company uses at that site. The data comes from three different tables:

- A list of companies' sites (with siteID as the primary key)
- A list of names, with each row also containing a siteID field—a foreign key from the site table

- A list of hardware and software items, one row per item, again with a siteID field as a foreign key from the site table.

Figure 9.20 shows the required output, created with almost no code at all.

FIGURE 9.20:

Subreports make this complex report possible.

A B C Unified School District	SALES:	7M	9/5/95
1110 North Lemon Street	EMPLOYEES:	130	
Agoura, CA 92801			

Contacts:

Linda Allen	**Geoffrey Bailey**	**Jim Bailey**
Assistant Principal Director	Director Of Data Processing	Vice President Of Finance
213/336-6016	213/323-7315	213/323-7315
Larry Bailey	**Alan Barton**	**Carl Bashir**
Manager Programming/Tech Spt	Vice President Computer Svcs	Vice President Of Finance
213/323-7315	213/543-3315	213/543-6200
Wayne Bass		
Systems/Programming Director		
213/543-3329		

	MANUFACTURER	MODEL	QUANTITY
MAINFRAME	IBM	SYSTEM36/60	2
SYSTEM SOFTWARE	IBM	SSP	4
APPLICATION SOFTWARE	HARRIS-DAT	GEN-LEDGER	12
	IBM	PC/SUPPORT	4
	IBM	QUERY/36	3
	IN-HOUSE	A/P	6
	IN-HOUSE	A/R	5
	IN-HOUSE	INVENTORY	3454
	IN-HOUSE	PAYROLL	334

A B C Unified School District uses 3824 computers.

Designing the Report

Looking at the report, you see three distinct sections: the site information, the contact information, and the hardware/software list. Since there isn't any way to create those three different sections within the confines of a single report, this situation is a perfect candidate for using subreports. You create this report in three steps, by creating three separate reports and then combining them:

1. Contact Information

2. Hardware/Software List

3. Site Information (the main report)

The main report will contain the site information, and its siteID will link it with the two subreports. As the report prints, moving from siteID to siteID, Access will display only the contacts and hardware/software for the specific siteID. You should be able to create each of the subreports independently, as long as you plan ahead and include the linking field, siteID, somewhere on the report surface (and it can be invisible, of course). Although the final report is rather complex, each piece is simple.

The Multicolumn Contact List

After building the phone book list in the previous example, creating the multicolumn contact list should be trivial. The only differences in this case are that the items are to increment horizontally rather than vertically and that each item is in a vertical clump of data rather than a horizontal one. Figure 9.21 shows the design surface for this report (rptBankInfoSub1 in CH09.MDB).

FIGURE 9.21:

Design surface for the three-column contact list

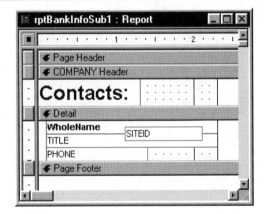

Pertinent Properties

To get the report just right, you set the properties for the Header section as follows:

Property	Value
NewRowOrCol	After Section
ForceNewPage	Before Section (necessary only when the report is not used as a subform)

You set the Sorting and Grouping dialog so that the report is sorted/grouped on Company, then Last, and then First, with the properties on the first grouping as shown here:

Property	Value
GroupHeader	Yes
GroupFooter	No
GroupOn	Each Value
GroupInterval	1

Finally, you open the Page Setup dialog and set the properties there, as shown in the following table, so the report will print in three columns:

Property	Value
Items Across	3
Same As Detail	Yes (checked)
Layout Items	Across, then Down

As you set these properties, try variations and run the report. The best way to learn what each property does is to experiment with an existing report, changing properties and seeing how the output changes. Use Print Preview, of course, to save a few trees.

Hardware/Software List

The hardware/software report should seem simple compared with the other reports you've been creating. Figure 9.22 shows the design surface for this simple report (rptBankInfoSub2 in CH09.MDB).

The only interesting feature of this report is its use of a simple function to convert the code representing the class type into an English word for that class. You can call any function to provide the contents of a report control: just assign the function you want placed in the control as the return value from the function. In the property sheet entry for the ControlSource property, enter

```
=ConvertClass([Class])
```

FIGURE 9.22:

Design surface for the simple list of hardware and software

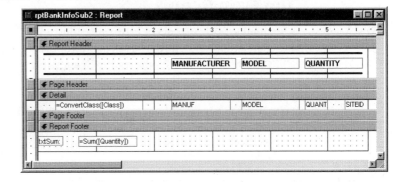

Access calls the ConvertClass() function shown in Listing 9.11 and places the return value from the function in the text box. The function itself can reside in either the report's module or a stand-alone module.

Listing 9.11

```
Function ConvertClass(varClass As Variant)
    Select Case varClass
        Case "CPU"
            ConvertClass = "MAINFRAME"
        Case "OPR"
            ConvertClass = "SYSTEM SOFTWARE"
        Case "PRG"
            ConvertClass = "APPLICATION SOFTWARE"
        Case Else
            ConvertClass = "UNKNOWN"
    End Select
End Function
```

TIP   To avoid repetitions of the same class name, you can set the Hide-Duplicates property of the Class Name text box to Yes. In that case Access won't display the class name if it matches the one used in the previous row.

The Main Report

The main report consists of little more than a few fields showing information about the particular site, and the two subreports you just created (rptBankInfo in CH09.MDB). Figure 9.23 shows the design surface for the main report.

The simplest way to create a report with subreports is to make the main report design surface and the Database Container window visible at the same time. Then, drag the subreport from the Database Container window directly onto the report. In this case you want to remove the labels Access attaches to the subreports.

FIGURE 9.23:

Design surface for the main report

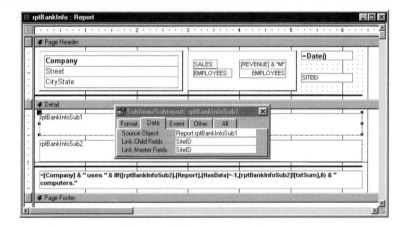

> **TIP**
> Although it is not necessary for this report, you may sometimes need to embed an existing form in a report. Access allows this, treating the form as though it were a subreport. You can drag a form from the database container onto the report's surface to create a subreport just as easily as you can drag a report.

Linking It All Up

Once you've created the main report, the only job left is to link it all up. To do this you set some properties for the newly created subreports. From the main report's point of view (and that's where you are now—on the main report), these subreports are just controls, like any other report control. They have properties just like all other controls. In Figure 9.23 you can see the property sheet for the first subform, showing just the data properties for the subform.

To link the master and child reports, Access uses the LinkMasterFields and Link-ChildFields properties in the subreport control. The LinkMasterFields property tells Access the name of the field(s) from the main report that must match the value(s) of the field(s) specified in the LinkChildFields property. In this case, as the report moves from siteID to siteID, you want to display just the rows in the two subreports for which the siteID fields match the current siteID on the main report. It's important to remember that Access needs the actual name of the field, not the name of the control that displays that field, in the LinkChildFields property. Control names are acceptable in the LinkMasterFields property. (For more information on subforms and subreports and how Access links them with their parents, see the section "How and When to Use Subforms" in Chapter 7.)

Other Important Properties

Before leaving this report, you need to concern yourself with a few other properties, as described in the following sections.

The CanGrow Property

In this example there's no way to know ahead of time how much vertical space the two subreports will require. Access provides the CanGrow property so you can decide whether or not to allow the subreport control to grow as necessary. Sometimes you'll want a fixed-size subreport. Here, though, you set the CanGrow property to Yes so all the information will be visible.

CanShrink Property

Some of the sites might not list any contacts. In that case you'll want the contacts subreport to take up no space at all. To make that happen, you set the CanShrink property for the subreport control to Yes. (For details about when Access restricts the functionality of the CanShrink and CanGrow properties, see the section "Why CanShrink Doesn't and CanGrow Won't" earlier in this chapter.)

Altering Your Report's Layout Programmatically

In some instances you may need to alter the complete layout of the Report Detail section on a row-by-row basis. Imagine, for example, you're printing a questionnaire and each question can be a yes/no, multiple-choice, write-in, or 1-through-10 type question. Your table containing the questions includes a column that indicates which question type to use on the report. RptQuestions in CH09.MDB is such a report; it makes different controls visible, depending on which question type is currently being printed. Figure 9.24 shows the printed report.

The concept here is simple. The report has several controls that always show up: dsptxtQuestion, dsptxtCount, and dsplblCount. (We're using the "dsp" prefix to indicate that these controls display for each row.) In addition, it contains five controls (four text boxes and a line) that Access displays or hides, depending on the question type. Figure 9.25 shows the design surface, with the controls spread out. Normally, all the user-response controls overlay one another. To make them easier to see, we've spread them out vertically.

Listing 9.12 contains the code that controls which of the user-response controls are visible in each printed row. Because Access calls this code for each row in the Detail section, it must first hide all the user-response controls and then enable the ones that apply to this particular row. Once it has hidden all the nonessential controls, it shows the controls that are necessary for this particular question type.

FIGURE 9.24:

The printed survey shows different controls, depending on the question type.

Survey Printed from tblQuestions

	Please circle one	
1.)	1...2...3...4...5...6...7...8...9..10	On a scale of 1 to 10, how would you rate your satisfaction with this book?
2.)	Yes / No	Are you a corporate developer?
3.)	_____	What percentage of your sales are to end users?
	Please circle one	
4.)	A B C D	How many users do you support? Choose A for 1-10, B for 11-100, C for 101-999, D for 1000-9999.

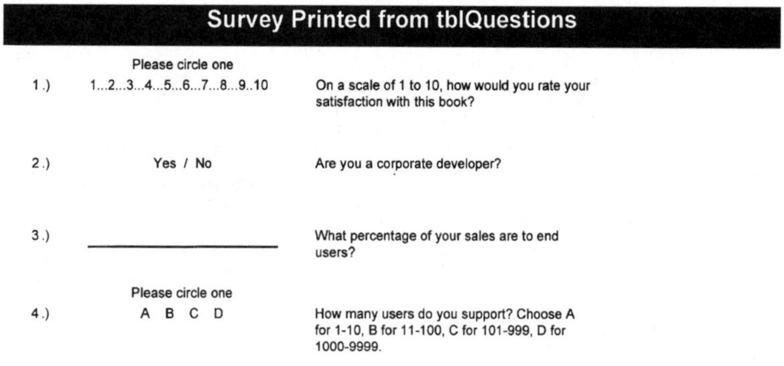

FIGURE 9.25:

Design surface for the questionnaire

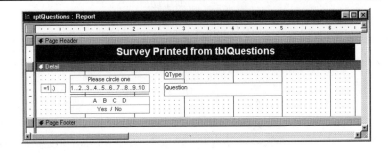

Listing 9.12

```
Private Sub Detail0_Format(Cancel As Integer, _
 FormatCount As Integer)
    Const glrcTypeFillIn = 1
    Const glrcType1To10 = 2
    Const glrcTypeABCD = 3
    Const glrcTypeYesNo = 4

    Dim intI As Integer
    Dim ctl As Control

    ' Turn off all the controls in the Detail section,
    ' except the question and its counter, which never go away.
    For Each ctl In Me.Controls
        If ctl.Section = 0 Then
            If Left(ctl.Name, 3) <> "dsp" Then
                If ctl.Visible Then
                    ctl.Visible = False
                End If
            End If
        End If
    Next ctl

    Select Case Me!QType
        Case glrcType1To10
            Me!lbl1To10.Visible = True
            Me!lblCircleOne.Visible = True

        Case glrcTypeABCD
            Me!lblABCD.Visible = True
            Me!lblCircleOne.Visible = True

        Case glrcTypeYesNo
```

```
            Me!lblYesNo.Visible = True

        Case glrcTypeFillIn
            Me!linFillIn.Visible = True

        Case Else
            ' Do nothing, right now.
    End Select
End Sub
```

Of course, this isn't the only solution to this problem. If you knew the user-response controls could all be labels, you could just as easily change the Caption property of the labels, based on the question type. In this case, though, since one of the controls is a line, that method isn't workable.

If you expand on the "questionnaire" method, you can create very complex reports that, in Design view, take up just a very small amount of space. This can be particularly useful when you remember that your reports are limited to 22 inches of design space! Rather than iterate through your questions by hand, create a report to create the questionnaire for you.

Summary

In this chapter we've taken a look at reports from several angles. We covered these issues:

- New report properties
- Programmatically controlling sorting and grouping
- Report events and properties
- Section events and properties
- A series of tricky report issues
- A group of sample reports, using events and properties

We've worked through some problematic issues in report design, but we've barely scratched the surface. Once you get deeply into it, you'll find that report design can be even more complex, challenging, and rewarding than forms design. As long as you keep forward motion of the report engine in mind, you can learn to control the flow of events on your reports.

CHAPTER

TEN

Controlling Your Printer

- Retrieving information about your printer

- Creating a list of available output devices

- Changing print destinations programmatically

- Using the Windows printing mechanisms to control printed output

10

Although Access provides a standardized Print Setup dialog box, you'll find it difficult to programmatically control printing options using the standard means. You might be tempted to try using SendKeys to control the print settings, but you'll quickly run into obstacles when you try to control specific printer settings, such as paper size, for which each printer driver provides a list. Even worse, every printer's Options dialog box is different, making the control of that portion completely impossible with SendKeys.

Controlling Print Setup Information

Luckily, Windows provides a standardized mechanism for conversing with the printer driver to retrieve and set information. The Windows API defines two user-defined types, generally referred to as the DEVMODE and DEVNAMES structures by the Windows SDK documentation. Listing 10.1 shows the VBA–type declarations for appropriate user-defined types to contain the information stored in the DEVMODE and DEVNAMES structures, as well as the Access-defined prtMip information, described later in this section. You can find all these declarations in basPrtGlobal, in CH10.MDB.

Access makes all this information available to you so you can retrieve and change very specific printer settings. All reports and forms provide three properties: prtDevMode (associated printer-specific settings), prtDevNames (associated with the specific chosen printer), and prtMip (defined only in Access to support margin settings and page layout information). Later in this chapter we discuss methods for retrieving all the information, setting new values, and replacing the values in the properties. Listing 10.1 shows the user-defined data structures we use throughout this chapter when we refer to each of the different (prtDevMode, prtDevNames, and prtMip) properties.

The Access Wizards use structures very similar to those shown in Listing 10.1. We could have used those exact structures throughout the book and not have bothered to create our own. Since you can't distribute the Wizard code with applications you create with the run-time version of Access, however, we wanted to enable you to write code you could distribute. If you use the declarations and examples from this chapter, there's no limitation on distribution.

Listing 10.1

```
Const glrcDeviceNameLen = 32
Const glrcFormNameLen = 32
' This is an arbitrary value. Based on experience,
' it ought to be large enough.
Const glrcExtraSize = 1024

' Structure for prtDevMode
Type glr_tagDevMode
    strDeviceName(1 To glrcDeviceNameLen) As Byte
    intSpecVersion As Integer
    intDriverVersion As Integer
    intSize As Integer
    intDriverExtra As Integer
    lngFields As Long
    intOrientation As Integer
    intPaperSize As Integer
    intPaperLength As Integer
    intPaperWidth As Integer
    intScale As Integer
    intCopies As Integer
    intDefaultSource As Integer
    intPrintQuality As Integer
    intColor As Integer
    intDuplex As Integer
    intYResolution As Integer
    intTTOption As Integer
    intCollate As Integer
    strFormName(1 To glrcFormNameLen) As Byte
    intLogPixels As Integer
    lngBitsPerPixel As Long
    lngPelsWidth As Long
```

```
        lngPelsHeight As Long
        lngDisplayFlags As Long
        lngDisplayFrequency As Long
        lngICMMethod As Long
        lngICMIntent As Long
        lngMediaType As Long
        lngDitherType As Long
        lngICCManufacturer As Long
        lngICCModel As Long
        bytDriverExtra(1 To glrcExtraSize) As Byte
End Type


' Structure for prtDevNames
Type glr_tagDevNames
        intDriverPos As Integer
        intDevicePos As Integer
        intOutputPos As Integer
        intDefault As Integer
End Type


' Structure for prtMip
Type glr_tagMarginInfo
        lngLeft As Long
        lngTop As Long
        lngRight As Long
        lngBottom As Long
        lngDataOnly As Long
        lngWidth As Long
        lngHeight As Long
        lngDefaultSize As Long
        lngItemsAcross As Long
        lngColumnSpacing As Long
        lngRowSpacing As Long
        lngItemLayout As Long
        lngFastPrinting As Long
        lngDataSheet As Long
End Type
```

NOTE
The main job of a visual development tool such as Access is to shield you from the details of the operating system. In a perfect world it would be impossible to do anything from VBA that could cause you to halt Access or Windows or that could cause any sort of data loss. In general, that's true. Access usually buries most of the workings of Windows under a thick layer of protective wrapping. The properties we're discussing here, however, are extremely "raw." That is, there's almost no protective layer between you and the operating system when you're modifying Access' prtDevMode or prtDevNames property. If you set the values incorrectly or place an inappropriate value into one of the properties, you're likely to cause Access to crash. The routines we've provided here make the use of these properties as painless as possible, but be aware that there's not much of a net underneath you when you're working this close to the surface.

Introducing the prtDevMode Property

The prtDevMode property contains information about the printing device that is to print the object. It contains, among other things, the name of the device, information about the driver, the number of copies to print, the orientation of the printout, the paper tray to use when printing, and the print quality to use. All this information corresponds directly with Windows' DEVMODE structure, used by every single Windows program that ever intends to do any printing.

Although Access makes all this information available to you so you can retrieve and set print properties for reports and forms, it doesn't make it easy. The prtDevMode property is nothing more than a text string with all the information from the DEVMODE structure strung together. It's up to your code to pick apart the text string, make changes as necessary, and reassign the property. And unlike almost every other property in Access, the prtDevMode property is only read/write when the report or form is in Design view. You won't be able to make changes to the prtDevMode property while running the report—which makes sense, since you really can't be changing such things as the printer name or margins while printing the report. Table 10.1 lists each field in the DEVMODE structure, its datatype, and a short description. Some of the fields contain enumerated data, and the choices for those items are listed in Tables 10.2 through 10.6.

TABLE 10.1: prtDevMode Fields and Their Contents

Setting	Datatype	Description
Device Name*	32-byte string	Name of the device supported by the driver: "HP LaserJet 4", for example
Specification Version*	Integer	Version number of the DEVMODE structure in the Windows SDK
Driver Version*	Integer	Driver version number assigned by the driver developer
Size*	Integer	Size, in bytes, of the DEVMODE structure
Driver Extra*	Integer	Size, in bytes, of the optional driver-specific data, which can follow this structure
Fields	Long	Specifies a set of flags that indicate which of the members of the DEVMODE structure have been initialized. It can be 0 or more of the values in Table 10.2, added together
Orientation	Integer	Paper orientation. It can be either 1 (Portrait) or 2 (Landscape)
Paper Size	Integer	Size of the paper on which to print. The value can be chosen from Table 10.3. If you choose 256 (User-Defined Size), the length and width of the paper are specified in the Paper Length and Paper Width members
Paper Length	Integer	Paper length in tenths of a millimeter. Overrides the setting in the Paper Size member
Paper Width	Integer	Paper width in tenths of a millimeter. Overrides the setting in the Paper Size member
Scale	Integer	Factor by which the printed output is to be scaled. The apparent page size is scaled from the physical page size by a factor of Scale/100
Copies	Integer	Number of copies printed if the printing device supports multiple-page copies
Default Source	Integer	Default bin from which paper is fed. See Table 10.4 for a list of possible values

TABLE 10.1: prtDevMode Fields and Their Contents (continued)

Setting	Datatype	Description
Print Quality	Integer	Printer resolution. See Table 10.5 for a list of device-independent values. If you specify a positive value, it's treated as the x-resolution, in dots per inch (DPI), and is not device independent. In this case the Y-Resolution field must contain the y-resolution in DPI
Color	Integer	Specifies Color (1) or Monochrome (2) printing if the device supports color printing
Duplex	Integer	Specifies Simplex (1), Horizontal (2), or Vertical (3) print mode for printers that support duplex printing
Y-Resolution	Integer	Specifies the y-resolution for the printer, in dots per inch (DPI). If this value is specified, you must also specify the x-resolution in the Print Quality member. These values are device specific
True Type Option	Integer	Specifies how TrueType fonts should be printed (See Table 10.6 for a list of possible values.)

*Read-only for any specific printer.

TABLE 10.2: Initialized Field Flags for prtDevMode

Constant	Value
glrcDMOrientation	&H0000001
glrcDMPaperSize	&H0000002
glrcDMPaperLength	&H0000004
glrcDMPaperWidth	&H0000008
glrcDMScale	&H0000010
glrcDMCopies	&H0000100
glrcDMDefaultSource	&H0000200
glrcDMPrintQuality	&H0000400
glrcDMColor	&H0000800
glrcDMDuplex	&H0001000
glrcDMYResolution	&H0002000
glrcDMTTOption	&H0004000

TABLE 10.3: Available prtDevMode Paper Sizes

Value	Paper Size
1	Letter (8.5 × 11 in.)
2	Letter Small (8.5 × 11 in.)
3	Tabloid (11 × 17 in.)
4	Ledger (17 × 11 in.)
5	Legal (8.5 × 14 in.)
6	Statement (5.5 × 8.5 in.)
7	Executive (7.25 × 10.5 in.)
8	A3 (297 × 420 mm)
9	A4 (210 × 297 mm)
10	A4 Small (210 × 297 mm)
11	A5 (148 × 210 mm)
12	B4 (250 × 354)
13	B5 (182 × 257 mm)
14	Folio (8.5 × 13 in.)
15	Quarto (215 × 275 mm)
16	11 × 17 in.
18	Note (8.5 × 11 in.)
19	Envelope #9 (3.875 × 8.875 in.)
20	Envelope #10 (4.125 × 9.5 in.)
21	Envelope #11 (4.5 × 10.375 in.)
22	Envelope #12 (4.25 × 11 in.)
23	Envelope #14 (5 × 11.5 in.)
24	C size sheet
25	D size sheet
26	E size sheet
27	Envelope DL (110 × 220 mm)
28	Envelope C5 (162 × 229 mm)
29	Envelope C3 (324 × 458 mm)
30	Envelope C4 (229 × 324 mm)
31	Envelope C6 (114 × 162 mm)

TABLE 10.3: Available prtDevMode Paper Sizes (continued)

Value	Paper Size
32	Envelope C65 (114 × 229 mm)
33	Envelope B4 (250 × 353 mm)
34	Envelope B5 (176 × 250 mm)
35	Envelope B6 (176 × 125 mm)
36	Envelope (110 × 230 mm)
37	Envelope Monarch (3.875 × 7.5 in.)
38	6-3/4 Envelope (3.625 × 6.5 in.)
39	US Std Fanfold (14.875 × 11 in.)
40	German Std Fanfold (8.5 × 12 in.)
41	German Legal Fanfold (8.5 × 13 in.)
256	User-defined

TABLE 10.4: Available Paper Source Values for prtDevMode

Value	Paper Source
1	Upper or only one bin
2	Lower bin
3	Middle bin
4	Manual bin
5	Envelope bin
6	Envelope manual bin
7	Automatic bin
8	Tractor bin
9	Small-format bin
10	Large-format bin
11	Large-capacity bin
14	Cassette bin
256	Device-specific bins start here

TABLE 10.5: Available Print Quality Values for prtDevMode

Value	Print Quality
−4	High
−3	Medium
−2	Low
−1	Draft

TABLE 10.6: Available True Type Options for prtDevMode

Value	True Type Option
1	Print TrueType fonts as graphics. This is the default for dot-matrix printers
2	Download TrueType fonts as soft fonts. This is the default for Hewlett-Packard printers that use Printer Control Language (PCL)
3	Substitute device fonts for TrueType fonts. This is the default for PostScript printers

We'll show now to retrieve and modify the prtDevMode property in the next section. For now, here are some ideas to keep in mind as you peruse the tables that describe the DEVMODE information:

- Not all forms or reports will necessarily have a non-null prtDevMode property. Any code you write should be able to handle this situation.

- Before providing your user with a list of choices (paper sizes, TrueType options, and so on), check the capabilities of the current device and limit your choices to options the device supports. Although Access does not provide this capability, you can use the Windows API to retrieve the information. We cover this functionality (calling the DeviceCapabilities() API function) in the section "Retrieving Printer Capabilities" later in this chapter.

- Many printer drivers store additional information immediately following the DEVMODE structure. Therefore, when retrieving and setting the prtDevMode property, be aware that most often it will require more than the documented size. Plan on 512 bytes or more, and check the intDriverSize and intExtraSize fields when manipulating the values. (The code in our examples does all this for you.)

Retrieving the prtDevMode Information

Actually retrieving the prtDevMode information is, of course, trivial. Since prtDevMode is a property of forms and reports, you can retrieve the information by simply copying it from the object into a string variable. Once it's there, though, you must somehow get it into a structure with the appropriate fields set up for you. The glr_tagDevMode structure shown here is what you need:

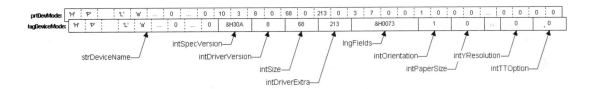

However, you also need a method for getting the string you've read directly from the object's property into the structure. The answer is VBA's LSet statement.

LSet allows you to copy bytes of data from one variable to another, even if they are of different datatypes. Normally, Access allows you to copy information between two variables of the same datatype. In this case you need to copy data from a string datatype to a variable of type glr_tagDevMode. The value returned by the prtDevMode property is laid out perfectly, so performing a byte-by-byte copy into the glr_tagDevMode structure fills in all the fields correctly. The previous graphic shows this "overlay" in progress. In the graphic, the top row represents the prtDevMode string, and the bottom row represents the variable of type glr_tag-DevMode into which you've copied that data. The LSet command makes it easy to perform this operation, although there are a few issues you need to understand first, as described in the following sections.

Using LSet to Copy Unformatted Data

The LSet command has two variations. In one context LSet allows you to left-align text within a string variable type, padding the extra room with spaces. In a different context LSet overlays the data stored in one user-defined type into a variable of a different user-defined type. This is the functionality you'll need. Note, however, the use of the term *user-defined*. Both variables must be of a user-defined type. Since your goal here is to move data from a string variable (the data retrieved directly from the object's prtDevMode property) into a user-defined variable, you must first take one intermediate step: place the data into a user-defined type that is nothing more than a fixed-length string:

```
' This is the number of bytes in the fixed portion of
' the DEVMODE structure. We've just broken the
' two sizes apart in case the fixed portion of
' the structure changes.
```

ANSI versus Unicode

The 32-bit versions of Windows (Windows 95 and Windows NT) support two separate character sets: ANSI, in which each character takes 1 byte of storage and there are only 256 different possible characters; and Unicode, in which each character takes up 2 bytes of storage and there are 65,536 different possible characters. VBA, Access' programming language, supports Unicode only. In general, this works in your favor, allowing support for many languages, including those that use character sets different from the English ones.

There's one area of Access in which the Unicode support causes trouble: the prtDevMode and prtDevNames properties return the character strings in their values in ANSI format. This means that if you attempt to view the pieces of those properties directly, you'll just see garbled characters, since Access is attempting to convert them to Unicode as it displays them.

This is why you'll find the ANSI ToUni( ) and UniToANSI( ) functions in basStrings, in CH10.MDB. These functions handle each byte in the ANSI strings and convert back and forth between ANSI and Unicode, calling the built-in StrConv() function. You shouldn't need these routines anywhere in Access aside from working with prtDevMode and prtDevNames, but it's important that you understand their purpose, should you ever want to write your own functions to handle these properties.

```
Const glrcDevModeSize = 148
Const glrcDevModeMaxSize = glrcDevModeSize + glrcExtraSize

' Temp structure for prtDevMode info.
Type glr_tagDevModeStr
    strDevMode As String * glrcDevModeMaxSize
End Type
```

Given a type declaration for such a datatype, you could retrieve the prtDevMode property and assign it to a variable of type glr_tagDevMode, as in the following code fragment:

```
Dim DM as glr_tagDevMode
Dim DMStr as glr_tagDevModeStr

DMStr.strDevMode = Reports!Report1.prtDevMode
LSet DM = DMStr
```

That code overlays the value retrieved from the prtDevMode property of Report1 into the glr_tagDevMode variable, DM. You should now be able to access any member of DM, just as you would with any other user-defined type. For example,

```
Debug.Print ANSIToUni(DM.strDeviceName)
```

should print the name of the printer assigned to print this particular report. (See the sidebar in this section for information on converting from ANSI to Unicode.)

Using LSet to Replace the Data

Once you've made the necessary changes to the glr_tagDevMode structure, you'll want to replace the value of the prtDevMode property. To do so, use the LSet command again:

```
Dim dm as glr_tagDevMode
Dim dmStr as glr_tagDevModeStr

dmStr.strDevMode = Reports!Report1.prtDevMode
LSet dm = dmStr
'
' Do work here, manipulating dm.
'
LSet dmStr = dm
Reports!Report1.prtDevMode = dmStr.strDevMode
```

A Simple Example Using prtDevMode

Anytime you want to manipulate the values in the prtDevMode property, follow these steps:

1. Declare variables of type glr_tagDevMode and glr_tagDevModeStr.

2. Copy the prtDevMode property from the report or form into the strDevMode member of the glr_tagDevModeStr variable.

3. Use LSet to copy the bytes into the glr_tagDevMode variable.

4. Make whatever changes you wish. You must inform Windows of the changes you've made, using the Or operator to set the appropriate bits in the lngFields member of the DEVMODE structure. (See the examples in the next few sections for more information.)

5. Use LSet to copy the bytes back into the glr_tagDevModeStr variable.

6. Replace the value of the prtDevMode property for the form or report from the glr_tagDevModeStr variable. Note the use in our examples of the MidB() function, which treats the string as a series of single bytes (ANSI) instead of 2-byte values.

For example, Listing 10.2 demonstrates changing the number of copies of a given report to be printed. (Look in basSetCopies in CH10.MDB for SetCopies() and Set-Copies2(), presented in the next section of this chapter.)

Listing 10.2

```
Function SetCopies(obj As Object, intCopies As Integer)

    ' This simple function would require
    ' error checking for real use. In addition,
    ' it requires that the report in question be
    ' already open in Design view (you can't set the
    ' prtDevMode property except in Design view).
    ' For example:
    ' retval = SetCopies(Reports!rptCompany, 3)

    ' 1. Declare variables of type glr_tagDevMode and
    '       glr_tagDevModeStr.
    Dim DM As glr_tagDevMode
```

```
Dim DMStr As glr_tagDevModeStr
Dim dr As glr_tagDeviceRec

' Some objects may have a null prtDevMode property
' (if you've never touched their printer settings).
' In that case, use the default printer's
' DEVMODE structure instead.

If IsNull(obj.prtDevMode) Then
    If glrGetCurrentDevice(dr, ",") Then
        DMStr.strDevMode = glrGetDefaultDM(dr)
    End If
Else

    ' 2. Copy the prtDevMode property from the
    '       report or form into the
    '       glr_tagDevModeStr variable.
    DMStr.strDevMode = obj.prtDevMode
End If

' 3. Use LSet to copy the bytes into the
'       glr_tagDevMode variable.
LSet DM = DMStr

' 4. Make whatever changes you like, and set
'       the lngFields entry accordingly.
DM.intCopies = intCopies
DM.lngFields = DM.lngFields Or glrcDMCopies

' 5. Use LSet to copy the bytes back into the
'       glr_tagDevModeStr variable.
LSet DMStr = DM

' 6. Replace the value of the prtDevMode
'       property for the form or report from the
'       glr_tagDevModeStr variable.
obj.prtDevMode = MidB(DMStr.strDevMode, 1)
End Function
```

And a Bit Simpler

To make it a bit easier for you to retrieve and set values in the prtDevMode property, we've provided functions in basDevMode (in CH10.MDB): glrRetrieveDevMode()

and glrSetDevMode(). Each takes two parameters:

- A reference to the form or report to use
- A variable of type glr_tagDevMode (glrRetrieveDevMode() will fill this in from the object's prtDevMode property, and glrSetDevMode() will place its value into the object's prtDevMode property.)

Each function returns either True or False, indicating the success of the operation.

Using these functions you could rewrite SetCopies as follows:

```
Function SetCopies2(obj As Object, intCopies As Integer)

    ' For example:
    ' retval = SetCopies2(Reports!rptCompany, 3)
    Dim DM As glr_tagDevMode

    ' Assume failure.
    SetCopies2 = False
    If glrRetrieveDevMode(obj, DM) Then
        DM.intCopies = intCopies
        DM.lngFields = DM.lngFields Or glrcDMCopies
        SetCopies2 = glrSetDevMode(obj, DM)
    End If
End Function
```

An Important Reminder

Remember, all the properties mentioned in this section (prtDevMode, prtDevNames, and prtMip) are available only in *Design view.* You must make sure your report or form is open in Design view before attempting to set any of these properties. (You can *retrieve* the properties, of course, no matter what the mode.)

Changing Paper Size

Contrary to the information presented above, many printers do not allow you to specify a user-defined page size. In addition, some printers use a page size of 0 to indicate a user-defined size, and some use 256. You need to retrieve information about the specific printer (see the section "Retrieving Printer Capabilities" later in this chapter for information on this) before trying to set a specific nonstandard page size.

If you find that you can change the size, you must change a number of fields in the prtDevMode string. You not only need to inform the printer that you're setting a user-defined size, you need to send the coordinates. The code listed here changes the paper size to 1000×1000 units (10 cm × 10 cm):

```
DM.intPaperSize = 256
DM.intPaperLength = 1000
DM.intPaperWidth = 1000
DM.lngFields = DM.lngFields Or glrcDMPaperSizeOr _
 glrcDMPaperLengthOr glrcDMPaperWidth
```

You must set the lngFields value so that the driver knows you've changed the paper size values.

Using the prtDevMode Property in Your Applications

If you want to use any of the procedures discussed in the preceding sections in your own applications, you should import basDevMode, basPrtDest, and basStrings from CH10.MDB. Once you have those modules in your application, you should be able to call the functions you need in order to manipulate the prtDevMode property effectively.

Controlling Print Layout Information

Access makes the print layout information for a given report or form available to you through the object's prtMip property. This information includes margin settings, number of columns, spacing between columns, and the layout (horizontal or vertical) of those columns. Just as with the prtDevMode property, Access provides this information as a single string value, which you must pick apart yourself. Table 10.7 shows the elements of this property and their possible values. Listing 10.1, presented earlier in this chapter, shows an Access user-defined type you can use to extract and set information in the prtMip property.

TABLE 10.7: prtMip Fields and Their Contents

Setting	glr_tagMarginInfo Field	Description	Possible Values
Left	lngLeft	Left margin, in twips ($\frac{1}{1440}$ inch)	Limited logically by the paper dimensions
Top	lngTop	Top margin, in twips	Limited logically by the paper dimensions
Right	lngRight	Right margin, in twips	Limited logically by the paper dimensions
Bottom	lngBottom	Bottom margin, in twips	Limited logically by the paper dimensions
Data Only	lngDataOnly	Print only the data, without gridlines, borders, or graphics	True (−1) or False (0)
Item Size Width	lngWidth	Width, in twips, for each column	Limited logically by the paper dimensions
Item Size Height	lngHeight	Height, in twips, for each column	Limited logically by the paper dimensions
Default Size	lngDefaultSize	Specifies whether each column should be the same size as the Detail section or use the Width and Height settings	True (−1), use the width of the Detail section; or False (0), use the Width and Height settings
Items Across	lngItemsAcross	Number of columns across for multicolumn reports or forms	Limited logically by the paper dimensions
Column Spacing	lngColumnSpacing	Space between detail columns, in twips	Limited logically by the paper dimensions
Row Spacing	lngRowSpacing	Space between detail rows, in twips	Limited logically by the paper dimensions
Item Layout	lngItemLayout	Specifies vertical or horizontal layout	1953 for Horizontal, 1954 for Vertical
Fast Printing	lngFastPrinting	Undocumented, and perhaps unused in this version?	
Print Headings	lngDataSheet	Print page headings for datasheets?	True, False

Just as with the prtDevMode property, the steps you use when modifying one or more prtMip options are as follows:

1. Declare variables of type glr_tagMarginInfo and glr_tagMarginInfoStr.
2. Copy the prtMip property from the report or form into the glr_tagMargin-InfoStr variable.
3. Use LSet to copy the bytes into the glr_tagMarginInfo variable.
4. Make whatever changes you like.
5. Use LSet to copy the bytes back into the glr_tagMarginInfoStr variable.
6. Replace the value of the prtMip property for the form or report from the glr_tagMarginInfoStr variable.

For example, Listing 10.3 demonstrates changing the number of columns and the column width for a given report. (Look in basSetColumns in CH10.MDB for SetColumns() and SetColumns2(), presented in the next section.)

Listing 10.3

```
Sub SetColumns(rpt As Report, intCols As Integer, _
sglWidth As Single)
    ' Set the number of columns for a specified
    ' report. Pass in a reference to the report, the
    ' number of columns to print, and the width of
    ' each, in inches.
    ' For example,
    ' SetColumns Reports!rptPhoneBook, 3, 2.25

    ' To keep this example simple, all error checking
    ' has been removed.

    ' 1. Declare variables of type glr_tagMarginInfo
    '      and glr_tagMarginInfoStr.
    Dim MIP As glr_tagMarginInfo
    Dim mipTemp As glr_tagMarginInfoStr

    ' 2. Copy the prtMip property from the report or
    '      form into the glr_tagMarginInfoStr variable.
    mipTemp.strMIP = rpt.prtMip

    ' 3. Use LSet to copy the bytes into the
```

```
'      glr_tagMarginInfo variable.
LSet MIP = mipTemp

' 4. Make whatever changes you like.
MIP.lngItemsAcross = intCols
' Convert inches to twips.
MIP.lngWidth = glrcTwipsPerInch * sglWidth
' Tell the report not to use the detail section
' width.
MIP.lngDefaultSize = False

' 5. Use LSet to copy the bytes back into the
'      glr_tagMarginInfoStr variable.
LSet mipTemp = MIP

' 6. Replace the value of the prtMip property for
'      the form or report from the
'      glr_tagMarginInfoStr variable.
rpt.prtMip = mipTemp.strMIP
End Sub
```

Making It a Bit Simpler

To simplify your interactions with the prtMip property, we've supplied the glrRetrieveMIP() and glrSetMIP() functions, in basPrtMip (CH10.MDB). These two functions operate exactly like the glrRetrieveDevMode() and glrSetDevMode() functions described earlier in this chapter. You pass in an object reference and an appropriate structure to fill in. In this case you'll pass a glr_tagMarginInfo structure. Using these two functions, you could rewrite the procedure SetColumns like this:

```
Sub SetColumns2(rpt As Report, intCols As Integer, _
 sglWidth As Single)
    ' For example,
    ' SetColumns2 Reports!rptPhoneBook, 3, 2.25
    Dim MIP As glr_tagMarginInfo

    If glrRetrieveMIP(rpt, MIP) Then
        MIP.lngItemsAcross = intCols
        MIP.lngWidth = glrcTwipsPerInch * sglWidth
        MIP.lngDefaultSize = False
        glrSetMip rpt, MIP
    End If
End Sub
```

Using these functions relieves you of dealing with LSet or the intermediate glr_tag-MarginInfoStr structure.

Using prtMip in Your Own Applications

To retrieve or modify settings in an object's prtMip property, you need to import the basPrtMip and basPrtGlobal modules from CH10.MDB. Once you have that code in your application, you should be able to use the functions there to manipulate all the margin settings you need.

Introducing the prtDevNames Property

Both reports and forms support a property that contains information about the current output device associated with that form or report. That is, if you use the Print Setup menu option to select a specific printer for a form or report, that information is stored with the object. When you print the form or report, Access attempts to send the printout to the specified device, based on what it finds in the prtDevNames property of the object. To momentarily change the output device (to send the report to the fax instead of to the printer, for example), you need to retrieve the prtDevNames property, set it to the fax device, print the document, and then set it back.

The prtDevNames property stores three pieces of information about the specific output device in a manner that's convenient for programmers working in C or C++ (the standard Windows programming languages) but not as convenient for Access programmers. The property itself is just an exact copy of the DEVNAMES structure that's used as part of the Windows SDK. The DEVNAMES structure contains the device name, the driver, and the output port in a variable-length string, with each piece of information followed by a null character (CHR$(0)). In addition, the property starts out with a group of four integers. Each of the first three integers contains the offset of one of the three strings that follow, and the fourth contains a 0 or a 1, depending on whether the current device is the Windows default output device. Table 10.8 lists the members of the DEVNAMES structure, stored in the prtDevNames property. The order of the three strings in the structure is not important, as long as

TABLE 10.8: prtDevNames Fields and Their Contents

Member	Description
Driver Offset	Offset from the beginning of the structure to a null-terminated string that specifies the file name (without the extension) of the device driver
Device Offset	Offset from the beginning of the structure to a null-terminated string that specifies the name of the device
Output Offset	Offset from the beginning of the structure to a null-terminated string that specifies the MS-DOS device name for the physical output port
Default	Specifies whether the strings in this structure identify the default Windows printer (1 if True, 0 if False)
Device Name	Specified device name. It cannot be longer than 32 characters (including the trailing null) and must match one of the items from WIN.INI in the [devices] section
Driver Name	Specified driver name. It cannot be longer than 9 characters (including the trailing null)
Output Name	Specified output port. It cannot be longer than 9 characters (including the trailing null)—for example, "LPT1:"

the offsets are consistent with that ordering. In the examples, you'll find the device name, then the driver name, and finally, the output port. You'll discover that the three pieces of information the prtDevNames structures need are the same three pieces of information we'll gather from WIN.INI (or the system registry) in the section "Controlling Your Destination" later in this chapter. Therefore, it should be simple to build up a new prtDevNames property based on the user's choice from the list of possible output devices. Here is an example prtDevNames string, using the Generic/Text Only driver:

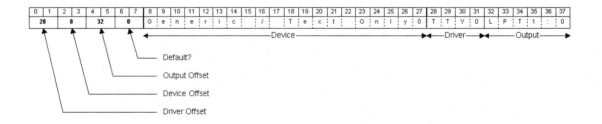

Using the prtDevNames Property

To use the prtDevNames property, you must be able to perform two basic manipulations: build up the string and break it apart. The module basPrtNames in CH10.MDB contains two functions that perform these tasks. The function glrBuildDevNames() takes as a parameter a structure of type glr_tagDeviceRec, containing the device name, the driver name, and the output location, and builds up an appropriate string. This function just takes the three strings, concatenates them with a null character inserted between them and at the end, and calculates the offsets for each.

To store away the offsets, you'll find it easiest to store them as integers in a user-defined type with four elements:

```
Type glr_tagDevNames
    intDriverPos As Integer
    intDevicePos As Integer
    intOutputPos As Integer
    intDefault As Integer
End Type
```

Once you've filled in all the values, you can use the LSet command to copy the structure, byte by byte, into a string-type variable. Once you have the four integers in the string variable, you can concatenate the list of three strings onto the end of the string variable. Just as before, you must create a simple user-defined type, consisting of just the string you want, into which you can LSet the values in the glr_tagDevNames structure. That is, given the user-defined type

```
Type glr_tagDevOffsets
    strDevInfo As String * 4
End Type
```

you can use the LSet command to copy the 8 bytes of information into that string. (Each character in a string is 2 bytes, so the structure has room for all 8 bytes.) The code might look like this:

```
Dim devNames As glr_tagDevNames
Dim devStr As glr_tagDevOffsets
.
. ' Fill the values in devNames here
.
LSet devStr = devNames
```

645

Listing 10.4 contains the glrBuildDevNames() function, which creates the prtDevNames string, given the three pieces of information it needs.

Listing 10.4

```
Function glrBuildDevNames(dr As glr_tagDeviceRec) As Variant

    ' Given the printer's device name, driver name, and port,
    ' create an appropriate prtDevNames structure.

    ' In:
    '     dr: A filled-in dr structure
    ' Out:
    '     Return Value: the resulting prtDevNames structure

    Dim DN As glr_tagDevNames
    Dim devStr As glr_tagDevOffsets
    Dim varTemp As Variant

    ' Check for maximum length for the device name
    ' (leaving room for the null terminator)
    If Len(dr.strDeviceName) > glrcMaxDevice - 1 Then
        MsgBox "Invalid Device Name!", vbCritical, _
          "glrBuildDevNames()"
        Exit Function
    End If

    ' The first offset is always offset 8
    DN.intDriverPos = glrcDevNamesFixed
    DN.intDevicePos = DN.intDriverPos + _
      Len(dr.strDriverName) + 1
    DN.intOutputPos = DN.intDevicePos + _
      Len(dr.strDeviceName) + 1

    ' Since you're forcing a new printer setting, tell
    ' Windows that it's not the default printer.
    DN.intDefault = 0

    ' Both sides of the LSet need to be user-defined types,
    ' so use devStr (of type glr_tagDevOffsets) instead of
    ' just a plain ol' string.
    LSet devStr = DN
```

```
        ' Copy array to a variant, so it's easy to
        ' concatenate into output string.
        varTemp = devStr.strDevInfo

        ' The prtDevNames property is ANSI, so we've got
        ' to now convert these three strings BACK from
        ' Unicode to ANSI.
        glrBuildDevNames = varTemp & _
          UniToAnsi(dr.strDriverName) & ChrB$(0) & _
          UniToAnsi(dr.strDeviceName) & ChrB$(0) & _
          UniToAnsi(dr.strPort) & ChrB$(0)
End Function
```

Pulling apart the pieces of the prtDevNames property is easier. The function glrParseDevNames() (in basDevNames in CH10.MDB) takes in a prtDevNames string and fills in the appropriate pieces of the glr_tagDeviceRec structure. In addition, the function returns True if the selected device is the default Windows output device and False otherwise. Once the function has used LSet to copy the four integer values into the glr_tagDevNames structure, it can use the offsets in the structure to pull apart the pieces. Note that the function uses the glrTrimNull() function to get rid of everything past the first null character in the string that's past the beginning of the output port string. Listing 10.5 shows the entire glrParseDevNames() function.

NOTE   Access is not neat about the value returned in the prtDevNames property. You will often find trailing "junk" after the information you're interested in. Since you can't count on its length, you must be careful to copy out only the parts that are of interest to you. When you're retrieving the property from a form or a report, be sure to throw away all but the first 58 characters of the string. (That gives you room for 8 bytes of offsets, 32 bytes for the device, and 9 bytes each for the port and the driver name.) Note the use of the ANSIToUni() function, since the prtDevNames property stores its strings internally in ANSI format, just like the prtDevMode property.

Listing 10.5

```
Function glrParseDevNames(ByVal varDevNames As Variant, _
 dr As glr_tagDeviceRec) As Boolean

    ' In:
    '    varDevNames: string containing the devNames info
    '    dr: tagDeviceRec structure to fill in
    ' Out:
    '    dr: Filled in with the information from varDevNames
    '    Return value: True if this dr is the default printer,
    '        False otherwise

    Dim DN As glr_tagDevNames
    Dim temp As glr_tagDevOffsets

    ' To use LSet, both sides must be user-defined types.
    ' Therefore, copy the string into a temporary
    ' structure so you can LSet it into dn.
    temp.strDevInfo = LeftB(varDevNames, glrcDevnamesFixed)
    LSet DN = temp

    dr.strDriverName = ANSIToUni( _
     MidB(varDevNames, DN.intDriverPos + 1, _
     DN.intDevicePos - DN.intDriverPos - 1))
    dr.strDeviceName = ANSIToUni( _
     MidB(varDevNames, DN.intDevicePos + 1, _
     DN.intOutputPos - DN.intDevicePos - 1))
    dr.strPort = ANSIToUni(glrTrimNull( _
     MidB(varDevNames, DN.intOutputPos + 1)))
    glrParseDevNames = CBool(DN.intDefault)
End Function
```

Controlling Your Destination

Windows allows you to print a document to any of the installed printer devices just by changing the current printer selection, using the Print Setup dialog. You can install a fax printer driver that will intercept your printing and send your document out the fax modem, for example, or just have multiple printer choices installed for various printing jobs.

Almost every Windows application uses the standard Print Setup dialog provided with Windows. This works fine in an interactive environment. But under program control you must find some other way to specify a list of possible devices and provide a method for the user to choose a new output destination. Then, once you've changed the document's destination and told your application to send the document to that device, you need to set things back the way they were.

CH10.MDB contains a form demonstrating the use of the prtDevNames (and prtDevMode) property, allowing you to choose a form or report from your database and print it to any of the installed print devices. The form, zfrmPrintDest, displays a list of all the forms and reports and a list of the installed printer devices (see Figure 10.1 later in the chapter). Once you select an object and an output device, you can print either to the original device or to the chosen device. The code in zfrmPrintDest accomplishes this goal by changing the value of the prtDevNames property for the chosen object, and it changes it back once it's been printed.

WARNING It is imperative that you set the prtDevMode property at the same time you set the prtDevNames property if you are changing the output destination. Changing just the prtDevNames property will cause your system to crash unless you happen to be very lucky. In the examples that follow, you'll see that before you change the prtDevNames property, you should request the default DevMode structure from the printer driver, perhaps copy over the current user settings, and set the object's prtDevMode property before changing the prtDevNames property. Failure to follow these steps will, sooner or later, cause Windows to crash.

The problem of providing your users with a means of selecting a specific output device and sending the current document to that device has two parts. First of all, you must be able to build a list of all the installed output devices. Then, once your user has chosen one from the provided list, you must be able to use the prtDevNames property to control the destination of the particular document. Neither of these steps is terribly difficult, once you know the tricks.

Providing a List of Output Devices

Windows maintains a list of all the installed output devices in WIN.INI, under the "[devices]" heading. For example, the [devices] section in your WIN.INI might look like this:

```
[devices]
Microsoft Fax=WPSUNI,FAX:
Rendering Subsystem=WPSUNI,PUB:
HP LaserJet 4=HPPCL5MS,\\GATEWAY\HPLJ4
HP LaserJet III=HPPCL5MS,LPT1:
```

Each line represents one device, and the syntax of each line can be represented as

> *Device Name=Driver,Output*

> **NOTE**   Although Windows 95 and Windows NT store all the printer output information in the system registry, all the Microsoft Office 95 products still rely on WIN.INI for information about the current printer, since this is the method recommended in the Windows SDK. Although the Win32 API provides methods for enumerating the list of installed printers, with more flexibility than the method we're using, this method is much simpler.

To provide your users with a list of devices, you need to read all the items from WIN.INI and create an array of these items in Access. Luckily, Windows provides a mechanism for reading one (GetProfileString()) or all (GetProfileSection()) of the items within a section at once. In general, the syntax for GetProfileString() is this:

> GetProfileString(*strSection, strEntry, strDefault,*
>
> *strReturnBuffer, lngReturnBufferSize*) As Long

where the following is true:

- *strSection* is the name of the section in WIN.INI from which to read. In this case the section will be "devices".

- *strEntry* is the item within the section to retrieve. Windows places the portion of the matching entry to the right of the equal sign in *strReturnBuffer.*

- *strDefault* is the value to return in *strReturnBuffer* if no match can be found. This value must never be null. You know that your search didn't find any matches if *strReturnBuffer* is the same as *strDefault* after the function call.

- *strReturnBuffer* is the string buffer into which Windows will place the text the function call finds. If *strEntry* is a single item, *strReturnBuffer* will contain either the portion of that specified entry to the right of the equal sign (if it's found) or the string in *strDefault* (if it's not).

- *lngReturnBufferSize* is the size, in characters, of *strReturnBuffer.* As with all Windows API calls, you must specify the width of the buffer before passing it to the Windows DLL. For example, to create a 1024-character buffer, you can use either

```
Dim strReturnBuffer as String * 1024
```

or

```
Dim strReturnBuffer as String
strReturnBuffer = Space$(1024)
```

The function returns the number of characters returned in *strReturnBuffer.*

On the other hand, to get a string containing all the different installed output devices, you would instead use the GetProfileSection() function. To call this function, pass to it the section name, a buffer, and the size of that buffer. (We've provided the glrGetProfileSection() function in basSetPrinter to handle all the details for you.)

```
Dim strMatch as String * 2048
lngCount = GetProfileSection("devices", strMatch, 2048)
```

You'd then need code to pull apart this string, breaking it at each null value and placing the values into an array. You can find the code to do this in the function glrGetDevices() (in basSetPrinter in CH10.MDB). glrGetDevices() fills the array passed to it with information about each of the devices found in WIN.INI, using the brute-force method of walking through the string returned from GetProfileString(), pulling off pieces until it runs out of characters.

Your final goal, then, is to create an array of information about output devices. Each element of this array will contain a specific output device name, its driver name, and a specific output port. The user-defined type used as the basis for this array is declared in the module basPrtGlobal—the glr_tagDeviceRec:

```
Type glr_tagDeviceRec
    strDeviceName As String
    strDriverName As String
    strPort As String
End Type
```

On return from glrGetDevices(), the application will have a global array of structures, each containing a specific combination of device, driver, and port.

Armed with this array, you now have all the information you need. Given an array that you want to present to the user as a list or combo box, your best solution in Access is to write a list-filling callback function. The function glrFillDeviceList() calls the functions mentioned above to fill the array in its initialization case and then uses the values from that array when asked to provide data. Figure 10.1 shows the sample form in use with the list of devices visible. You should be able to easily use the code provided in basSetPrinter in your own applications by just importing the entire module. Listing 10.6 shows the function that fills the list of devices. You can call this function directly from your own applications once you've imported basPrt-Global and basSetPrinter. (For more information on filling list or combo boxes programmatically, see Chapter 7.)

FIGURE 10.1:

The sample form, zfrmPrintDest, shows the list of all available output devices and their ports.

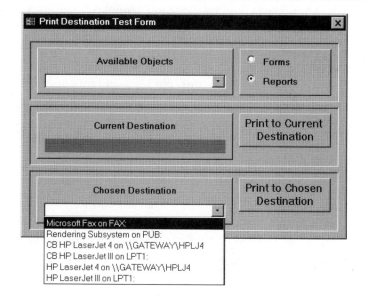

Listing 10.6

```
Function glrFillDeviceList(ctlField As Control, _
 varID As Variant, varRow As Variant, varCol As Variant, _
 varCode As Variant)

    Static intCount As Integer
    Dim varRetval As Variant

    Select Case varCode
        Case acLBInitialize
            ' Initialize
            ' Go fill the array aDevList() with
            ' all the devices.
            intCount = glrGetDevices(aDevList())
            varRetval = (intCount > 0)
        Case acLBOpen
            ' Get ID
            varRetval = Timer
        Case acLBGetRowCount
            ' Number of rows
            varRetval = intCount
        Case acLBGetValue
            varRetval = aDevList(varRow).strDeviceName & _
                " on " & aDevList(varRow).strPort
        Case acLBEnd
            Erase aDevList
    End Select
    glrFillDeviceList = varRetval
End Function
```

Providing a List of Reports or Forms

Although it's not a primary concern of this example, you'll also find a list of available forms or reports on the sample form. This allows your users to choose an object from the existing items in the Database Container window. The example uses DAO and a list-filling function to provide the list of items (see Figure 10.2). (For more information on retrieving information from the current database's Container collections, see Chapter 6. For information on filling a list box programmatically, see Chapter 7.)

FIGURE 10.2:

The Available Objects combo box uses DAO to provide the user with a list of objects.

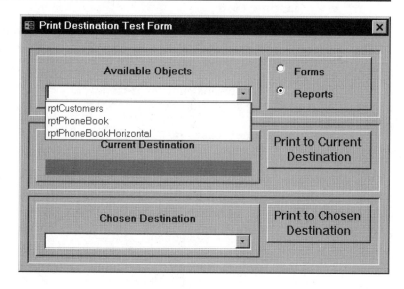

Retrieving the Default DevMode Structure

Before you attempt to change the values stored in the prtDevNames property, you must also be able to retrieve a particular printing device's default DEVMODE structure. This really has nothing to do with Access, but rather with the fact that Access has exposed some rather low-level functionality. If you change the prtDevNames settings, you're in effect telling Access to use a different printing device. If you don't also change the prtDevMode property to match that new device, it's guaranteed that the two properties will collide. (Remember, the prtDevMode property also contains the name of the printing device.) In many cases this isn't catastrophic, and you'll never notice the difference. Switching between some pairs of printers, on the other hand, can be detrimental to the health of your application, Windows, and any other applications that are currently running.

Every printer maintains default values for each of the fields, and you can retrieve the default DEVMODE from the driver, using the OpenPrinter() and DocumentProperties() API functions. Once you have the default values, you can copy the user-modifiable values from your form or report's prtDevMode property into your copy of the default DEVMODE structure. Then you can use this new combined DEVMODE structure as the prtDevMode property for your object. The read-only fields (device name, DEVMODE size and extra size, and so on) must not be changed, however. Given a glr_tagDeviceRec structure containing information about the specific printer driver, the glrGetDefaultDM() function, shown in Listing 10.7, retrieves the DEVMODE structure associated with that driver and returns it as a string.

Listing 10.7

```
Function glrGetDefaultDM(dr As glr_tagDeviceRec) As Variant
    Dim dmDefault() As Byte
    Dim hPrinter As Long
    Dim lngSize As Long
    Dim dmTemp As glr_tagDevModeStr
    Dim DMFull As glr_tagDevMode
    Dim varTemp As Variant
    Dim bytTemp As Byte

    Const glrcDMOutBuffer = 2

    If glr_apiOpenPrinter(dr.strDeviceName, hPrinter, 0) Then
        ' This test shouldn't be necessary, but sanity
        ' checks never hurt!
        If hPrinter > 0 Then
            ' Call glr_apiDocumentProperties to get
            ' the size of the default devmode structure.
            lngSize = glr_apiDocumentProperties(0, hPrinter, _
              dr.strDeviceName, bytTemp, bytTemp, 0)
            If lngSize > 0 Then
                ReDim dmDefault(1 To lngSize)
                If glr_apiDocumentProperties(0, hPrinter, _
                  dr.strDeviceName, dmDefault(1), _
                    dmDefault(1), glrcDMOutBuffer) > 0 Then
                    ' A few tricks here.
                    ' First, copy the whole byte array to the
                    ' variant, which moves all the bytes.
                    varTemp = dmDefault()
                    ' Next, copy the variant to the string
                    ' portion of a DevModeStr structure
                    ' so you can LSet it into a real DevMode
                    ' structure. That way, you can pull
                    ' it apart and get the full size from
                    ' two of its member elements.
```

```
                            dmTemp.strDevMode = varTemp
                            LSet DMFull = dmTemp

                            glrGetDefaultDM = LeftB(varTemp, _
                             DMFull.intSize + DMFull.intDriverExtra)
                        End If
                    End If
                End If
                glr_apiClosePrinter (hPrinter)
            End If
End Function
```

Copying Values from One DEVMODE to Another

Once you've retrieved the printer driver's default DEVMODE structure, you copy the settings for the current document that apply to the new printer into that DEVMODE structure. We've provided a function in basDevMode, glrCopyDMValues(), that does the work for you. It looks at each bit in the lngFields member of the structure, and for each field that has been initialized by the new driver, it copies the data from the original prtDevMode property. Listing 10.8 shows the entire function.

Listing 10.8

```
Sub glrCopyDMValues(varOldDM As Variant, varNewDM As Variant)
    ' In:
    '     varOldDM: source devMode structure
    '     varNewDM: output devMode structure
    ' Out:
    '     varNewDM: Filled in with the non-essential values
    '          from varOldDM.

    Dim dmOld As glr_tagDevMode
    Dim dmNew As glr_tagDevMode
    Dim dmTemp As glr_tagDevModeStr
    Dim intI As Integer

    ' Copy the string into a structure, using LSet.
    ' Since both sides of LSet must be user-defined types,
    ' copy the string into a temporary structure first.
```

```
dmTemp.strDevMode = varOldDM
LSet dmOld = dmTemp
dmTemp.strDevMode = varNewDM
LSet dmNew = dmTemp

' Copy all the old settings.
' Some of these may not apply to the newly chosen printer.
' Check the flags so only applicable ones get copied over.
If dmNew.lngFields And glrcDMOrientation Then
    dmNew.intOrientation = dmOld.intOrientation
End If
If dmNew.lngFields And glrcDMPaperSize Then
    dmNew.intPaperSize = dmOld.intPaperSize
End If
If dmNew.lngFields And glrcDMPaperLength Then
    dmNew.intPaperLength = dmOld.intPaperLength
End If
If dmNew.lngFields And glrcDMPaperWidth Then
    dmNew.intPaperWidth = dmOld.intPaperWidth
End If
If dmNew.lngFields And glrcDMScale Then
    dmNew.intScale = dmOld.intScale
End If
If dmNew.lngFields And glrcDMCopiesThen
    dmNew.intCopies = dmOld.intCopies
End If
If dmNew.lngFields And glrcDmDefaultSourceThen
    dmNew.intDefaultSource = dmOld.intDefaultSource
End If
If dmNew.lngFields And glrcDMPrintQualityThen
    dmNew.intPrintQuality = dmOld.intPrintQuality
End If
If dmNew.lngFields And glrcDMColorThen
    dmNew.intColor = dmOld.intColor
End If
If dmNew.lngFields And glrcDMDuplexThen
    dmNew.intDuplex = dmOld.intDuplex
End If
If dmNew.lngFields And glrcDMYResolutionThen
    dmNew.intYResolution = dmOld.intYResolution
End If
If dmNew.lngFields And glrcDMTTOptionThen
    dmNew.intTTOption = dmOld.intTTOption
End If
If dmNew.lngFields And glrcDMCollateThen
```

```
        dmNew.intCollate = dmOld.intCollate
    End If

    ' Copy the value back into a string. Again,
    ' this must go through the temp structure, since that's
    ' the only way LSet can work.
    LSet dmTemp = dmNew

    varNewDM = LeftB(dmTemp.strDevMode, _
      dmNew.intSize + dmNew.intDriverExtra)
End Sub
```

> **TIP**
>
> Manually changing printer drivers using Access' Print Setup dialog doesn't necessarily preserve settings as the glrCopyDMValues( ) procedure does. If, for example, you had set up your report to print in landscape mode and then changed printer drivers manually, that value would be reset to the new driver's default orientation. This is yet another reason to use the functionality demonstrated here rather than use SendKeys to do the work.

Saving, Printing, and Restoring

Once you know how to put together and break apart the prtDevNames string and how to retrieve the default DEVMODE structure for the new driver, you're ready to control print destinations for forms and reports. The code to do this is embedded in the cmdChosen_Click() procedure in the form module attached to zfrmPrint-Dest, and it breaks down into seven steps:

1. Get the old prtDevNames and prtDevMode properties.
2. Create the new prtDevNames string, based on the chosen output device.
3. Retrieve the default prtDevMode string for the newly selected printer.
4. Copy the current printer settings into the new prtDevMode string.
5. Set the new prtDevNames and prtDevMode strings for the form or report.
6. Print the form or report.

7. Replace the old prtDevNames string. (If you're not planning on saving your changes, this step is unnecessary.) Also, replace the original prtDevMode string.

Retrieving the Old Properties

To retrieve the old prtDevNames property, the sample application calls the glrRetrieveDevNames() function, passing to it an object name and that object's type (acForm for forms or acReport for reports). The glrRetrieveDevNames() function attempts to open the appropriate object, retrieves its prtDevNames property, and leaves the object open in Design view so later code can alter its properties. It also fills in the strOldDM variable so you can both replace the value of the prtDevMode property when you're done and copy values from it to the new DEVMODE structure you'll retrieve from the new output device:

```
strOldDevName = glrRetrieveDevNames(strName, _
 intType, strOldDM)
```

Creating the New prtDevNames String

Before you can print to a new destination, you must have chosen an item from the list of output devices. Since the combo box showing the list of devices, cboDestination, has its BoundColumn property set to 0, the value of the control is the index of the chosen item. That number corresponds to an element in the array that filled the combo. So given the value of the control, your code knows the specific device that was chosen. Passing the chosen item number to glrFillStructure returns a glr_tagDeviceRec structure filled in with the information from the array of installed output devices. Once you have the glr_tagDeviceRec structure filled in, you can call glrBuildDevNames() to build the appropriate value to be used as a new prtDevNames string:

```
dr = glrFillStructure(ctl)
varNewDevName = glrBuildDevNames(dr)
```

Retrieving the Default DEVMODE Structure for the New Printer

As mentioned earlier, before you can change the output device you need to have the default DEVMODE structure for the new device to which you're switching. You can call the glrGetDefaultDM() function to retrieve that information. You can then use the glrCopyDMValues procedure to copy the values from the current DEVMODE structure to the new one:

```
varDM = glrGetDefaultDM(dr)
glrCopyDMValues strOldDM, strDM
```

Setting the New Properties

To set the new prtDevNames string, your application must open the form or report in Design view and assign the newly created string to its prtDevNames property. (Remember that none of the prtDevMode, prtDevName, or prtMip properties are modifiable at run time.) To avoid problems when switching printer drivers, you must also assign the new printer's DEVMODE structure to the object's prtDevMode property at this point.

The simple matter of assigning the prtDevNames and prtDevMode properties is complicated in this application only because the object to be printed can be either a form or a report. The subroutine glrSetDevName (in basPrtDest) does the work for you in this case:

```
glrSetDevName strName, intType, varNewDevName, varDM
```

Listing 10.9 shows the glrSetDevName subroutine. Note the use of the MidB() function to copy the data from the input values to the properties of the object. Unless you take steps to convince Access that these are just streams of bytes, as opposed to strings, Access will convert them to Unicode strings, which will make a mess of your prtDevNames and prtDevMode properties. Using MidB() leaves the values intact as ANSI strings.

Listing 10.9

```
Sub glrSetDevName(strName As String, intType As Integer, _
  varDevNames As Variant, varDevMode As Variant)

    Dim obj As Object
    Select Case intType
        Case acForm
            DoCmd.OpenForm strName, acDesign
            Set obj = Forms(strName)
        Case acReport
            DoCmd.OpenReport strName, acDesign
            Set obj = Reports(strName)
    End Select
```

```
      ' Use the MidB() function to convert
      ' the variant into a string of bytes. Otherwise,
      ' Access assumes you're sending in a string
      ' and converts it from Unicode to ANSI, which ISN'T
      ' what you want here.
      obj.prtDevMode = MidB(varDevMode, 1)
      obj.prtDevNames = MidB(varDevNames, 1)
End Sub
```

Printing the Object (Finally!)

To print the object, you can use the PrintOut macro action. You'll probably want to switch to Normal view (instead of Design view) for printing. In addition, you may or may not want to close the object when you're done printing. (If you do close it without saving, you needn't worry about resetting the prtDevNames and prtDevMode properties.) The DoPrint subroutine in the basFormEvents module takes care of the printing and closing details for you. It opens the object in an appropriate view for printing, does the printing, and then either puts it back into Design view, so the caller can restore its state, or closes it. If you asked DoPrint to close the object, it calls the DoClose subroutine to do the work. (You'll find both procedures in the module attached to zfrmPrintDest.) This procedure uses the third parameter of the Close macro action, indicating that Access shouldn't ask whether or not to save the object; this code just closes it without saving. It also resets some objects on the main example form, cleaning up after the print job.

Replacing the Old Properties

Finally, to reset the prtDevNames property to its original state, you can call the glrSetDevName subroutine again, this time passing the old prtDevNames value. This restores the original state of the form or report's prtDevNames and prtDevMode properties, allowing you to print to the originally chosen device:

```
glrSetDevName strName, intType, varOldDevName, varOldDM
```

All the rest of the code in the sample application deals with manipulating the form or report object you've selected to print and with the user interface of the application itself. You may find it useful to study the code in the application, but in any case you should be able to adopt it to your own needs quite easily.

Retrieving Printer Capabilities

To use the prtDevMode property to its fullest, you'll want to provide a means of allowing your users to make choices about their printed output. You might want to allow them to programmatically choose a particular page size, the number of copies, or the paper source. Access, though, does not provide a means of determining your printer's capabilities. Windows, of course, does provide just such a mechanism, although using this mechanism from within Access requires a bit of effort.

When Access (or any other Windows application) presents you with a Print dialog box, it has requested information from the printer driver to know which options to make available to you. Windows exposes information directly from the printer driver, using the DeviceCapabilities() API function. You can call this function from your own applications, retrieving information about which features the printer supports.

In the next few sections we first describe the DeviceCapabilities() function as Windows implements it and then discuss how you can use it in your own applications. You have choices as to how to interact with the DeviceCapabilities() API function. You can, of course, call it directly. Table 10.9 lists the various capabilities for which you can query DeviceCapabilities(), along with the associated high-level function we've provided (see Table 10.10) to get the information for you.

TABLE 10.9: Options Available When Calling DeviceCapabilities()

Value	High-Level Function in basPrintCap	Meaning
glrcDCBinNames	glrGetBinNames()	Copies an array containing a list of the names of the paper bins into the strOutput parameter. To find the number of entries in the array, call glr_apiDeviceCapabilitiesLng with the lngOutput parameter set to 0; the return value is the number of bin entries required. (Each bin name can be up to 24 [glrcBinNameSize] bytes long.) This allows you to make sure your output string is long enough to hold all the entries. Otherwise the return value is the number of bins copied

TABLE 10.9: Options Available When Calling DeviceCapabilities() (continued)

Value	High-Level Function in basPrintCap	Meaning
glrcDCBins	glrGetBins()	Retrieves a list of available bins. The function copies the list to lngOutput as an array of integers. If you call glr_apiDeviceCapabilitiesLng with lngOutput set to 0, the function returns the number of supported bins, allowing you to allocate a buffer with the correct size. (See the description in Table 10.1, earlier in this chapter, of the Default Source member of the DEVMODE structure for information on these values.)
glrcDCCopies	glrGetCopies()	Returns the maximum number of copies the device can produce
glrcDCDriver	glrGetDriverVersion()	Returns the printer-driver version number
glrcDCDuplex	glrGetDuplex()	Returns the level of duplex support. The function returns 1 if the printer is capable of duplex printing. Otherwise the return value is 0
glrcDCEnum Resolutions	glrGetEnumResolutions()	Returns a list of available resolutions. If lngOutput is 0, glr_apiDeviceCapabilitiesLng returns the number of available resolution configurations. Resolutions are represented by pairs of long integers representing the horizontal and vertical resolutions
glrcDCExtra	glrGetExtraSize()	Returns the number of bytes required for the device-specific portion of the DEVMODE structure for the printer driver
glrcDCFields	glrGetFields()	Returns the lngFields member of the printer driver's DEVMODE data structure. The lngFields member indicates which members in the device-independent portion of the structure the printer driver supports
glrcDCFile-Dependencies	glrGetFileDependencies()	Returns a list of files that also need to be loaded when a driver is installed. Call glr_apiDeviceCapabilitiesLng() with lngOutput set to 0 to return the number of files. Call glrDeviceCapabilities() to fill a string buffer with an array of file names. Each element in the array is exactly 64 (glrcFileDependencySize) characters long
glrcDCMaxExtent	glrGetMaxExtent()	Returns a typePOINT variable containing the maximum paper size the intPaperLength and intPaperWidth members of the printer driver's DEVMODE structure can specify
glrcDCMinExtent	glrGetMinExtent()	Returns a typePOINT variable containing the minimum paper size the intPaperLength and intPaperWidth members of the printer driver's DEVMODE structure can specify

TABLE 10.9: Options Available When Calling DeviceCapabilities() (continued)

Value	High-Level Function in basPrintCap	Meaning
glrcDCOrientation	glrGetOrientation()	Retrieves the relationship between portrait and landscape orientations in terms of the number of degrees portrait orientation is to be rotated counterclockwise to get landscape orientation. It can be one of the following values: 0 (no landscape orientation); 90 (portrait is rotated 90 degrees to produce landscapes—for example, PCL); 270 (portrait is rotated 270 degrees to produce landscape—for example, dot-matrix printers)
glrcDCPaperNames	glrGetPaperNames()	Retrieves a list of the paper names supported by the model. To find the number of entries in the array, call glr_apiDeviceCapabilitiesLng() with the lngOutput parameter set to 0: the return value is the number of paper sizes required. (Each paper size name can be up to 64 [glrcPaperNameSize] bytes long.) This allows you to make sure your output string is long enough to hold all the entries. Otherwise, the return value is the number of paper names
glrcDCPapers	glrGetPapers()	Retrieves a list of supported paper sizes. The function copies the list to lngOutput as an array of integers and returns the number of entries in the array. If you call glr_apiDeviceCapabilitiesLng() with lngOutput set to 0, the function returns the number of supported paper sizes. This allows you to allocate a buffer with the correct size. (See the description in Table 10.1 of the Paper Size member of the DEVMODE data structure for information on these values.)
glrcDCPaperSize	glrGetPaperSize()	Copies the dimensions of supported paper sizes in tenths of a millimeter to an array of typePOINT structures pointed to by lngOutput. This allows an application to obtain information about nonstandard paper sizes
glrDCSize	glrGetDMSize()	Returns the Size member of the printer driver's DEVMODE data structure
glrDCTrueType	glrGetTrueType()	Retrieves the driver's capabilities with regard to printing TrueType fonts. The return value can be one or more of the following capability flags: glrCDCTTBitmap (1): device is capable of printing TrueType fonts as graphics; glrcDCTTDownload (2): device is capable of downloading TrueType fonts; glrcDCTTSubdev (4): device is capable of substituting device fonts for TrueType. In this case the strOutput parameter should be 0
glrcDCVersion	glrGetSpecVersion()	Returns the specification version to which the printer driver conforms

TABLE 10.10: High-Level Functions for Retrieving Printer Driver Capabilities

Function Name	Parameters	Return Values
glrGetBinNames()	dr As glr_tagDeviceRec, astrBinNames() As String	Fills in astrBinNames(), returns the number of bins
glrGetBins()	dr As glr_tagDeviceRec, aintList() As Integer	Fills in aintList(), returns the number of bins
glrGetCopies()	dr As glr_tagDeviceRec	Returns the number of copies
glrGetDMSize()	dr As glr_tagDeviceRec	Returns the size of the DEVMODE structure for the specified device
glrGetDriverVersion()	dr As glr_tagDeviceRec	Returns the driver version number
glrGetDuplex()	dr As glr_tagDeviceRec	Returns 1 if duplex allowed, otherwise 0
glrGetEnum-Resolutions()	dr As glr_tagDeviceRec, aptlngList() As typePOINT	Fills in aptlngList(), returns the number of resolutions
glrGetExtraSize()	dr As glr_tagDeviceRec	Returns the "extra" size of the DEVMODE
glrGetFields()	dr As glr_tagDeviceRec	Returns the DEVMODE lngFields value
glrGetFile-Dependencies()	dr As glr_tagDeviceRec, astrList() As String	Fills in astrList(), returns the number of file dependencies
glrGetMaxExtent()	dr As glr_tagDeviceRec, ptValue As typePOINT	Fills in ptValue with the max X and Y dimensions
glrGetMinExtent()	dr As glr_tagDeviceRec, ptValue As typePOINT	Fills in ptValue with the min X and Y dimensions
glrGetOrientation()	dr As glr_tagDeviceRec	Returns the orientation (see Table 10.9)
glrGetPaperNames()	dr As glr_tagDeviceRec, astrNames() As String	Fills in astrNames(), returns the number of paper names
glrGetPapers()	dr As glr_tagDeviceRec, aintList() As Integer	Fills in aintList(), returns the number of papers
glrGetPaperSize()	dr As glr_tagDeviceRec, aptList() As typePOINT	Fills in aptList(), returns the number of paper sizes
glrGetDMSize()	dr As glr_tagDeviceRec	Returns the size of the DEVMODE structure
glrGetTrueType()	dr As glr_tagDeviceRec	Returns the TrueType flag (see Table 10.9)
glrGetSpecVersion()	dr As glr_tagDeviceRec	Returns the driver spec version

You could also call the higher-level functions we've provided, which shield you from having to worry about many of the details involved in calling the API directly. We strongly recommend that you use the higher-level functions, since they make your use of this information much, much simpler. Table 10.10 lists all the high-level functions, the parameters to each, and the return values.

The Printer Driver's DeviceCapabilities() Function

To request information about the capabilities of the printer driver, you call the DeviceCapabilities() API function. In Listing 10.10 you'll find three Declare statements for the function, since you need to call DeviceCapabilities() in different ways. If you pass 0 for the fourth parameter, the driver returns the number of items in the array you're requesting. If you pass it the address of a string buffer in the fourth parameter, it returns the actual data. To make it possible to call the function both ways, we've provided two ways of calling it. If you call glr_apiDeviceCapabilitiesLng(), you pass a Long Integer in the fourth parameter. If you call glr_apiDeviceCapabilitiesStr( ), you pass the address of a string buffer in the fourth parameter. In addition, we've provided the declaration for glr_apiDeviceCapabilitiesAny(), which allows you to pass anything you wish in that fourth parameter. You use this declaration when you need to pass a user-defined datatype to the API call, for example. This difference in calling conventions points out one more reason why you'd be better served in using the high-level functions discussed below.

Listing 10.10

```
Declare Function glr_apiDeviceCapabilitiesStr _
 Lib "winspool.drv" Alias "DeviceCapabilitiesA" _
 (ByVal strDeviceName As String, ByVal strPort As String, _
 ByVal lngIndex As Long, ByVal strOutput As String, _
 lngDevMode As Long) As Long
Declare Function glr_apiDeviceCapabilitiesLng _
 Lib "winspool.drv" Alias "DeviceCapabilitiesA" _
 (ByVal strDeviceName As String, ByVal strPort As String, _
 ByVal lngIndex As Long,  ByVal lngOutput As Long, _
 lngDevMode As Long) As Long
Declare Function glr_apiDeviceCapabilitiesAny _
 Lib "winspool.drv" Alias "DeviceCapabilitiesA" _
```

```
(ByVal strDeviceName As String, _
ByVal strPort As String, ByVal lngIndex As Long, _
lpOutput As Any, lngDevMode As Long) As Long
```

No matter which way you call DeviceCapabilities(), it requires five parameters. Table 10.11 lists those parameters and gives information about each.

TABLE 10.11: Parameters for DeviceCapabilities()

Parameter	Description
strDeviceName	The device name, as listed in Win.INI ("HP LaserJet 4/4M")
strPort	The output port, as listed in Win.INI ("LPT1")
lngIndex	An item chosen from the first column of Table 10.9, indicating the capability about which to inquire
strOutput, lngOutput, lpOutput	A string buffer or a user-defined type to be filled, or 0 to indicate that you're requesting the number of elements the function will return
lngDevMode	By definition, the address of a DEVMODE variable, 0 for your purposes

An Example of Calling glrDeviceCapabilities() Directly

This example calls DeviceCapabilities() directly. You will most likely find it easier to call the high-level functions (listed in the second column of Table 10.9) than to use this example's code directly. We started out using code like this but quickly realized that much of the code was the same among the different capabilities. Although you might never use this code, it does demonstrate how to use Device-Capabilities() in case you need it for purposes we haven't considered.

Retrieving a List of Paper Names

The code in Listing 10.11 requests a list of the supported paper names from a specific printer driver. You pass to it a filled-in glr_tagDeviceRec variable, along with a dynamic array that it can fill with the list of names. It returns the total number of items it received from the driver. The function that called GetPaperNames() would need to fill in the glr_tagDeviceRec structure, create the dynamic array, and then call the function (see Listing 10.11).

GetPaperNames() must first retrieve the number of items in the array DeviceCapabilities() will be returning so you can allocate enough space in the string buffer it will fill in. To do this, call glr_apiDeviceCapabilitiesLng(), passing a 0 in the fourth parameter and the capability ID in the third parameter. If this call succeeds, it returns to you the number of elements in the array of names:

```
lngItemCount = glr_apiDeviceCapabilitiesLng( _
  dr.strDeviceName, dr.strPort, glrcDCPaperNames, 0, 0)
```

Once you know how many elements there will be, you can use ReDim to resize the output array to fit them all. Given a known size for each element you'll be retrieving from the driver (glrcPaperNameSize, in this case), you can use Access' String() function to make sure the string buffer is large enough. Failure to execute this step will surely cause Access to crash, since it might very well overwrite code or data with the output values when you call DeviceCapabilities(). Finally, you can call grlDeviceCapabilities() to retrieve the necessary string buffer full of information from the driver:

```
' Reset the size of the array to fit all the items.
ReDim astrList(0 To lngCount - 1)

strItemName = String(glrcPaperNameSize * lngCount, 0)

lngTemp = glr_apiDeviceCapabilitiesStr(dr.strDeviceName, _
  dr.strPort, glrcDCPaperNames, strItemName, 0)
```

You're still missing the final step at this point, though. You need to pull apart the pieces of the array. (They're stored in one big, continuous stream in strItemName.) This is simple enough, of course, since you know the length of each piece. It's just a matter of pulling out each piece with the Mid() function, trimming off trailing nulls (using the glrTrimNull() function), and assigning the substring to the current row in astrList():

```
If lngTemp <> -1 Then
    For intI = 0 To lngCount - 1
        astrList(intI) = glrTrimNull( _
          Mid(strItemName, intI * _
          glrcPaperNameSize+ 1, glrcPaperNameSize))
    Next intI
End If
```

As you'll see in the next section, we've done all this work for you. You should be able to retrieve any of the printer's capabilities easily with the high-level functions listed in the second column of Table 10.9.

Listing 10.11

```
Function GetPaperNames(dr As glr_tagDeviceRec, _
 astrList() As String) As Long

    ' Retrieve a list of strings from the driver, returning
    ' the number of strings in the output list.

    Dim lngCount As Long
    Dim strItemName As String
    Dim lngTemp As Long
    Dim intI As Integer

    On Error GoTo GetPaperNamesErr

    ' Find out how many items there are in the list.
    LngCount = glr_apiDeviceCapabilitiesLng( _
     dr.strDeviceName, dr.strPort, glrcDCPaperNames, 0, 0)
    If lngCount <> -1 Then
        ReDim astrList(0 To lngCount - 1)

        If lngCount > 0 Then
            ' This code places the entire string list in one
            ' string buffer and then parses it out later.
            strItemName = String( _
             glrcPaperNameSize * lngCount, 0)
            lngTemp = glr_apiDeviceCapabilitiesStr( _
             dr.strDeviceName, dr.strPort, _
             glrcDCPaperNames, strItemName, 0)
            If varTemp <> -1 Then
                For intI = 0 To lngCount - 1
                    astrList(intI) = glrTrimNull( _
                    Mid(strItemName, intI * _
                    glrcPaperNameSize + 1, _
                    glrcPaperNameSize))
                Next intI
            End If
        End If
    End If
```

```
GetPaperNamesExit:
    ' Set the return value now.
    GetPaperNames = IIf(lngTemp = -1, 0, lngCount)
    Exit Function

GetPaperNamesErr:
    lngTemp = -1
    Resume GetPaperNamesExit
End Function
```

Saving Effort by Calling the High-Level Interfaces

To save you some time (and us, as well), we've provided a high-level interface to each of the printer capabilities. We've listed the name of each of these functions in Table 10.10. The second column of this table lists the parameters you need to pass to each function, and the third column lists the return values. You'll probably find it much simpler to call these functions directly, since they perform for you almost all the work shown in Listing 10.11. The code in Listing 10.12 is quite similar to the code you'd need to retrieve any of the printer's capabilities.

GetPaperNameList(), in Listing 10.12 (from basPaperNameList in CH10.MDB), first fills in a glr_tagDeviceRec structure. This example pulls its information from the default printer listed in WIN.INI, using the glrGetCurrentDevice() function (see basSetPrinter in CH10.MDB):

```
' Set up the device rec.
If glrGetCurrentDevice(dr, ",") Then
'   ...
End If
```

Once GetPaperNameList() has the device information, it can call glrGetPaper-Names() directly. This fills in the dynamic array, astrSizes, and returns the number of elements in the array:

```
' Get the list of paper sizes.
lngCount = glrGetPaperNames(dr, astrNames())
```

Finally, once you have the array of paper names, you can use it however you wish. This simple example just displays the list in the Immediate window:

```
' You might use astrNames() to fill a list box, for example.
For intI = 0 To lngCount - 1
```

```
        Debug.Print astrNames(intI)
    Next intI
```

Listing 10.12

```
Function GetPaperNameList()
    Dim dr As glr_tagDeviceRec
    Dim astrNames() As String
    Dim lngCount As Integer
    Dim intI As Integer

    ' Set up the device rec.
    If glrGetCurrentDevice(dr, ",") Then
        lngCount = glrGetPaperNames(dr, astrNames())

        ' You might use astrNames() to fill a list box,
        ' for example.
        For intI = 0 To lngCount - 1
            Debug.Print astrNames(intI)
        Next intI
    End If
End Function
```

A Major Example

To see an example of all this technology in action, check out frmDevCaps in CH10.MDB (see Figure 10.3). This form displays all the information it can retrieve from the printer driver you select from the list of installed drivers. The code you'll find in the form module deals mostly with displaying the information, but in it you'll find lots of calls to the functions listed in Table 10.10. Although it's doubtful you'll need all this information in any of your applications, you may well need one or more of the items from frmDevCaps when you present lists of formatting options to your users.

FIGURE 10.3:

The form frmPrtCaps demonstrates all the values available by calling DeviceCapabilities().

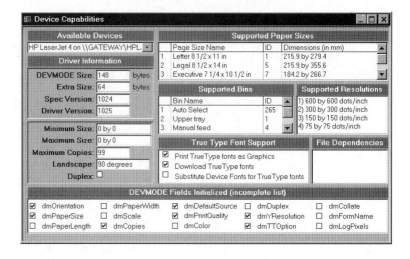

Summary

In this chapter we've taken a look at printing from several angles. We covered these issues:

- Using the prtDevMode property of objects to control printing details
- Using the prtMip property to control margins, columns, and so on
- Using the prtDevNames property to control the output device
- Retrieving printer capabilities using the DeviceCapability() Windows API function

Although the information presented here is relevant to all of Windows, Access is alone in the manner in which it presents this information (unlike Word, Excel, or any of the other Microsoft products). Getting at and changing printer characteristics isn't easy with Access, but you have enough generic routines under your belt now to at least make it possible. You should be able to use the prtDevMode, prtDevNames, and prtMip properties in your own applications, given the sample routines in this chapter.

CHAPTER

ELEVEN

Menus, Toolbars, and Macros

- Knowing how and when to use macros

- Setting and retrieving global options

- Using Access' toolbars

- Manipulating Access' menus programmatically

This chapter covers the areas of Access in which you will often use macros. You'll learn about menus and toolbars, as well as the AutoKeys and AutoExec macros. In addition, we cover how to manipulate Access menus using the Windows API. And since you'll be modifying global options settings in this chapter, we also cover the Application object's GetOption() and SetOption methods.

Just as a point of reference, macros in Access work differently from macros in any other Microsoft product: unlike the macros of Word or Excel, they're not recordable and they don't create VBA code. They do, however, provide a simple front end to programming for novice users and, as this chapter outlines, are required for some operations in Access.

To Macro or Not to Macro

When creating Access applications, you usually have a choice as to the method you employ when automating actions. Access supplies a group of more than 40 macro actions, from which you can create simple (and perhaps not-so-simple) applications without writing any code at all. In their attempt to provide a database program "for the masses," the Access development team has done an excellent job. With the macro actions in Access, you really can do a great deal using only macros.

But it should be clear from the preceding chapters that the authors of this book do not subscribe to the "macros only" school of application development. We do, however, have a short list of situations in which you would choose macros rather than VBA.

Choose macros if you:

- Need to prototype your application quickly. Because macros make it simple to open, close, and manipulate forms and reports, you'll find it easy to mock up the flow of an application using macros.

- Don't really care about complete bulletproofing. Since macros can't trap for errors, Access itself handles any run-time errors that occur while your application is running. If you're providing an application for your own purposes or for in-house use, then perhaps it's not worth the time trapping for errors.

- Need to use user-defined menus, trap keystrokes globally, or provide a macro that runs automatically, without any command-line interference. Each of these actions requires a macro and is discussed later in this chapter.

Otherwise, use VBA. Since you can more easily comment, document, and control VBA code, it seems the wiser choice for large applications. In fact, you must use VBA if you need to

- Call functions in DLLs, including all the Windows API functions
- Control transaction processing (allowing rollbacks of partially completed sets of actions)
- Use scoped variables (variables that are visible only from specific areas of your application)
- Provide commented printouts of your application code (Although you can print macros, it's much more difficult to document them carefully than it is to document VBA code.)

Actually, most applications use a combination of VBA and macros. Since menus and global key trapping require macros, these macros are a part of almost every application. You may also find that some actions are just easier using macros and that their use doesn't compromise the robustness of your application. You need to make these decisions yourself, based on your own needs.

NOTE In previous versions of Access, the only way you could get your application to do something automatically when you opened it was to use an AutoExec macro. In Access 95, this is no longer necessary for most applications. Instead of using a startup macro, you can specify a form for Access to load automatically at startup, and code in that form's Open event can replace actions you would have called from the AutoExec macro in previous versions. See the section "Controlling Startup Options" later in this chapter for more information.

In addition, you'll find that your VBA programming will be enhanced if you completely understand all the macro actions. Since there are some operations in Access that require macro actions (opening and closing forms, for example), you need to know which of the hundreds of Access operations supported by VBA require macro actions (and the DoCmd object) and which are directly supported by VBA. It's to your benefit to experiment with macros first, learning their capabilities, before moving on to VBA.

The following sections detail the three areas of Access that require macros:

- Trapping keystrokes globally
- Providing user-defined menus
- Executing a macro from the command line

In addition, this chapter covers the use of toolbars, since they fit so neatly into this group of topics, if for no other reason than that they usually call macros to do their work.

The AutoKeys Macro

You may find in some instances that your application would work better if you could map certain keystrokes to actions of your choosing. Access provides a global key-remapping interface, centered around the AutoKeys macro. The next few sections discuss how and why you'd use this special macro.

Creating Your Key Actions

To create your key mappings, you need to create a new macro item within the AutoKeys macro. In Design view, make sure the macro names are visible by clicking the Macro Names button on the toolbar, choosing the View ➤ Macro Names menu option, or choosing the Tools ➤ Options ➤ View dialog and checking the Show in Macro Design ➤ Names Column check box. (Choosing this option from the Tools ➤ Options menu makes the setting persistent and is probably a good idea for most programmers.) Enter a key name formatted like the examples in the first column of Table 11.1 into the Macro Name column of the design grid. Enter an action to take when that key is pressed into the Action column of the design grid. Just as with any other macro you create, the Action column can contain any of the standard macro actions and can use the RunCode action to run VBA code.

TABLE 11.1: AutoKeys Macro Names Syntax

SendKeys Syntax	Key Combinations
^A or ^2	Ctrl + any letter or number
{F11}	Any function key, 1 through 12
^{F11}	Ctrl + any function key
+{F11}	Shift + any function key
^+{F11}	Ctrl+Shift + any function key
{Insert}	Ins
^{Insert}	Ctrl+Ins
+{Insert}	Shift+Ins
^+{Insert}	Ctrl+Shift+Ins
{Delete} or {Del}	Del
^{Delete} or ^{Del}	Ctrl+Del
+{Delete} or +{Del}	Shift+Del
^+{Delete} or ^+{Del}	Ctrl+Shift+Del

To separate your key mappings, just place a new macro name (actually, the key name to map) on a new row. Access stops playing back each macro when it runs across a new name in the macro group. You might want to separate each macro from the next with a blank line and perhaps some comments.

Figure 11.1 shows the macro editor in use, with two key mappings already laid out. In this case, if the user presses the Ctrl+S key and if the current object is a form (see the section "Restricting Key Playback to the Desired Environment" later in this chapter), Access puts up a message box. If the user presses Shift+Ins, Access

FIGURE 11.1:

The macro editor in action, modifying the AutoKeys macro

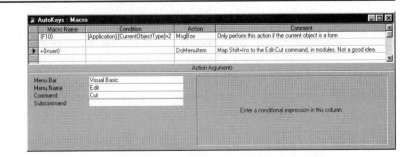

performs the Edit ➤ Cut menu item (just a little practical joke, since the user is probably expecting this combination to paste the contents of the clipboard instead).

Not All Keystrokes Are Created Alike

Table 11.1 lists the only keystrokes that are valid within your AutoKeys macro. Access really must restrict the values to those in this list; think what would happen if you reassigned the A key, for example, in your AutoKeys macro! On the other hand, it would be nice if Access made it possible to trap certain untrappable keys, such as the PgUp and PgDn keys, as well as the Esc key. If you use any keys not listed in this table, Access gives you a warning message when you attempt to save the macro. (All keys are trappable using a form's KeyDown event if you've set the KeyPreview property of the form to True. If you can trap keystrokes at that level, these restrictions won't apply. See the section "Trapping Keys Globally: The KeyPreview Property" in Chapter 8 for more information.)

The following key combinations are noticeably absent from the list in Table 11.1:

- Alt + function keys
- Alt+Ins
- Alt+Del
- Esc
- Cursor movement keys (in any combination with Ctrl, Shift, or Alt)
- Alt+A through Alt+Z (reserved for hot-key usage)

Hierarchy of AutoKeys Mappings

Access always looks in the AutoKeys macro first, before looking into its own internal key mappings. That is, if you have a standard Access key remapped, your mapping will take precedence. If you've remapped Shift+Ins in your AutoKeys macro, the standard Access use of this key (to paste text from the clipboard) will no longer work. Your macro could, of course, trap these built-in keys for its own use and then perform the standard action when it was done (using DoMenuItem, since you can't recursively call SendKeys from within your AutoKeys macro).

WARNING Do not attempt to trap a standard keystroke, performing some action when you press that particular key, followed by a call to SendKeys to perform the original keystroke. Once Access has remapped the key, it's completely remapped. Using SendKeys to perform the same key that's mapped will cause an infinite loop in your macro. Instead of using SendKeys to perform the original keystroke, use DoMenuItem.

Restricting Key Playback to the Desired Environment

Although keys assigned in the AutoKeys macro normally take effect anyplace in the Access environment, you can limit that. If you set a condition in the macro sheet's Condition column, the macro attached to the particular keystroke will be played out only if the condition is met. For example, in Figure 11.1 the macro attached to Ctrl+S will be skipped unless the current object is a form. If you press the key combination anywhere else, Access will see that the condition isn't met and just skip the action.

You can also skip the action from VBA code that the macro calls (using the Run-Code macro action). Once your code gets control, it can check the necessary condition. If that condition isn't met, it can either use the CancelEvent action or just exit the current function. To match the macro condition in Figure 11.1, you need code like that shown in Listing 11.1.

Listing 11.1

```
Function DoMsgBox()
    If Application.CurrentObjectType = acForm Then
        MsgBox "AutoKeys got you here!"
    End If
End Function
```

Allowing for Multiple AutoKeys "Sets"

Access makes it simple for you to change the current key assignment macro. Although it assumes you want to use a macro named AutoKeys unless you've told it otherwise, your application can change that value at run time. You can use the Get-Option() and SetOption methods of the Application object to retrieve and set the name of the macro. (See the section "Controlling Global Options" later in this chapter for more information on the GetOption() and SetOption methods.) To change the current key assignment macro, use this code:

```
Application.SetOption "Key Assignment Macro", _
  "YourNewMacroName"
```

To retrieve the current setting (so you can store away its value to reset later, perhaps), use this code:

```
strOldMacroName = Application.GetOption( _
  "Key Assignment Macro")
```

In CH11.MDB you'll find the example form frmAutoKeys, which demonstrates the method of changing the key assignment macro while your application is running.

> **NOTE**   Like several other options available through the Application.SetOption method, the Key Assignment Macro option doesn't have a corresponding option in the Tools ➤ Options dialog box. For these options, you can use only VBA to set the values you need.

Although it might not at first be completely obvious why you'd need to change key assignments midstream, think about the following scenario. Imagine that your application consists of several completely distinct portions, each with its own set of tables and activities. You'd like to supply consistent key mappings for all the pieces, but the actions those keystrokes must produce are very different, depending on the section of the application that's currently active. Your macros could, of course, detect the current portion of the application that's running and react differently in each instance. Because complex macros are very difficult to maintain and debug, a better solution would be to use separate key assignment macros for each section of your application. The macros are global throughout Access, and you can have only one loaded at a time, so you need to use Application.GetOption() to retrieve the current macro setting, store it away, set your new value with Application.SetOption (which takes effect immediately), and restore the old value when you leave.

AutoKeys versus Keypress Events

Although the use of AutoKeys macros and Keypress events (KeyPress, KeyDown, and KeyUp) might seem somewhat overlapping, they really are designed for different uses altogether. The following table lists some comparisons between the two:

Feature	AutoKeys	Keypress Events
Scope	Global throughout Access	Local to the specific control (or form)
Keystroke Trapping	Limited to very specific keys	Can trap any key on the keyboard (KeyDown/KeyUp)
Precedence	Take precedence over Access' built-in keystrokes	Take precedence over *all* keystrokes (including AutoKeys')

You use AutoKeys mappings when you want to supply a quick way to activate some action in your applications. That is, if you want Ctrl+B to start a backup, you could assign the Ctrl+B key mapping to perform the necessary action. Unless your macro restricted the use of the key, you'd be able to press Ctrl+B anywhere while your application was running and have the action take place.

You use KeyDown/KeyUp/KeyPress events when you need to react to a key the user has pressed while interacting with a particular control or form. Rather than using them to cause some action to take place, you can use KeyPress events to react to each keystroke in a stream of keystrokes. You can trigger other events, depending on the keystroke that's been pressed; convert the keystroke to a different keystroke; or even disregard the keystroke.

The interaction between the KeyDown event and the mappings in the AutoKeys macro is somewhat difficult to pin down. The sample form, frmKeyDownTest in CH11.MDB (see Figure 11.2) helps demonstrate that interaction. In Access 2, the AutoKeys macro trapped the keystrokes before the current form received them. In Access 95, this appears to have been reversed: Access routes keystrokes to the form's KeyDown event before the AutoKeys macro gets them. Following the directions on that form will demonstrate this relation.

FIGURE 11.2:

frmKeyDownTest proves that the KeyDown event takes precedence over AutoKeys mappings.

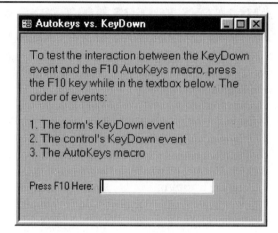

AutoKeys mapping and the use of the KeyPress event are complementary: the KeyPress event can trap and react only to "typable" characters, and AutoKeys can trap and react only to characters that KeyPress skips. For example, if a control has code that reacts to the KeyPress event and the application has an AutoKeys macro that traps for Ctrl+Z, the KeyPress event code won't even notice that particular keystroke. Because the KeyPress event can trap only typeable keys (A–Z, a–z, 0–9, and Backspace), it will live harmoniously with any settings you've made in your AutoKeys macro.

AutoKeys in Competition with SendKeys

Be very careful when mixing SendKeys actions with AutoKeys key mappings. Unless you keep careful track of the keys you're trapping with AutoKeys mappings, you can find things not going the way you'd planned. Because SendKeys sends its keystrokes through Access' key handler as though the user had typed them from the keyboard, the AutoKeys mappings intercept and alter them as they've been told. This is especially important when your code resides in a library database that needs to work with various user databases. Since there's no way you can know how the user has remapped the keyboards with the AutoKeys macro, you should never use SendKeys in a library database except for keys that cannot be remapped using the AutoKeys macro.

NOTE
If you need keystroke mapping at a form level rather than globally or at a control level, you can use the form's KeyPreview property. If you've set this property, keystrokes typed anywhere on the form are filtered through the form's KeyPress/KeyDown/KeyUp event procedures, rather than through the controls' event procedures. The combination of control, form, and global key events give you a great deal of flexibility. (For more information on the KeyPreview property, see the section "Trapping Keystrokes Globally" in Chapter 8.)

Controlling Startup Options

For most applications you want Access to take a specific action automatically every time a user loads your application. Fortunately, Access provides the Tools ➤ Startup menu item, allowing you to specify most settings you will ever need to set at your application's startup. Table 11.2 shows the options you can set, with a short description of each.

TABLE 11.2: Automatic Startup Options

Option	Description	Database Property
Application Title	Main Access' window title bar caption	AppTitle
Application Icon	File name for icon to be displayed when Access is minimized	AppIcon
Display Form	Name of the form to be displayed automatically on startup. Code attached to the form's Open events (Open, Load, Activate, and so on) runs, of course	StartupForm
Display Database Window	If unchecked, Access automatically hides the Database container when your application loads (If you choose this option, the database window is still available—you must use the Window ➤ Unhide menu or press the F11 key to display it.)	StartupShowDBWindow
Display Status Bar	If unchecked, Access hides the status bar that normally appears at the bottom of the Access window	StartupShowStatusBar
Menu Bar	Name of the macro containing the default menu bar to be used when not overridden by a specific form or report menu bar	StartupMenuBar

TABLE 11.2: Automatic Startup Options (continued)

Option	Description	Database Property
Shortcut Menu Bar	Name of the macro containing the default shortcut menu to be used when not overridden by a specific form, report, or control menu	StartupShortcutMenuBar
Allow Full Menus	If unchecked, Access will not allow the full menus to be used	AllowFullMenus
Allow Default Shortcut Menus	If unchecked, Access will not display the default shortcut menus	AllowShortcutMenus
Allow Built-In Toolbars	If unchecked, Access hides the built-in toolbars (If you're using the run-time version of Access, default toolbars are never available.)	AllowBuiltInToolbars
Allow Toolbar Changes	If unchecked, users cannot make changes to toolbars	AllowToolbarChanges
Allow Viewing Code After Error	If unchecked, Access treats code errors as though you were running the run-time version. That is, it unceremoniously dumps your application back to Windows	AllowBreakIntoCode
Use Access Special Keys	If unchecked, Access disregards the special keys it normally traps (Ctrl+Break to break executing code, F11 to select the database container, and so on). This makes your running application simulate the run-time environment	AllowSpecialKeys

Setting Startup Options Programmatically

You can change any of the options in Table 11.2 programmatically, but it's not as easy as you might wish. All the items in that table are properties of a database, and as such, Jet is in charge of the properties. As with all other properties that aren't built in, you must create the database properties if they don't already exist. For example, if you try to set the AppTitle property for the current database, it may fail because that property doesn't yet exist. (If you haven't yet created the property in the Tools ➤ Startup dialog box, it won't exist.) (See the section "Creating Your Own Property Dialogs" in Chapter 6 for more information on creating these database properties.)

The simplest possible code for setting a database property might look like this:

```
Const glrcErrPropNotFound = 3270
On Error Resume Next
Dim db As Database
Dim prp As Property
Set db = CurrentDb()
```

```
db.Properties("AppTitle") = "Paul's Pizza"
If Err.Number = glrcErrPropNotFound Then
    Set prp = db.CreateProperty("AppTitle", _
      dbText, "Paul's Pizza")
    db.Properties.Append prp
End If
Application.RefreshTitleBar
```

This is one place in Access where it might be simpler to use the Windows API to accomplish a task. Setting the title bar with the Windows API requires a single call:

```
Declare Function SetWindowText Lib "user32" _
 Alias "SetWindowTextA" (ByVal hwnd As Long, _
 ByVal lpString As String) As Long
' To call it:
Call SetWindowText (Application.hwndAccessApp, "Paul's Pizza")
```

It sure seems easier from here. The difference, of course, is that by setting the database's property, you have to do it only once. If you use the Windows API, you'll need to call the code every time you start up your database.

Running Code at Startup

Most often, the options Access provides in the Tools ➤ Startup menu will give you all the flexibility you need. On the other hand, you may still need to specify a set of steps you'd like executed when your application starts up. (Perhaps you need to perform some steps not associated with any form.) Although it would be helpful if Access provided a facility for executing a VBA procedure at startup, it does not. Instead, you must use a macro if you don't want to display a form. Therefore, you have two choices:

- If your application contains a macro named AutoExec, Access executes that macro after it loads the database. Because of the limitations of macros, we suggest that this macro do nothing more than use the RunCode action to execute a VBA procedure.

- A better alternative, because almost all Access applications start up by displaying a form, is to call any startup code you need to execute from the Open event of your startup form. You can specify a form that will be loaded automatically when a user opens your database (see Table 11.2), and Access will execute your code as it loads that form. In almost all cases, this is the preferable method.

Choosing Your Own Startup Macro

If you'd like to be able to specify a particular macro to be run when your application loads, you have another choice. You may have a particular application you use for varying circumstances. In one instance you'd like to start it and run Macro1. In other instances you'd like to start it and run a different macro, Macro2. To make this happen, you need to tell Access, from the command line, which macro to run. You can specify both a database and a startup macro from the command line, as in:

MSACCESS *YourApp*.MDB /x*YourMacro*

Access runs the macro name that follows the /x (with or without a separating space) as soon as it loads the application. By setting up different icons that run Access with various startup macros, you can control exactly which portion of your application gets executed when the user clicks a given icon.

WARNING If your application includes an AutoExec macro and your command line tells Access to run a different macro when it loads your application (using the /x option), Access first runs the AutoExec macro and then your specified macro. This certainly isn't a bug, but it is something to be aware of. In addition, if the application's startup options indicate a form to open automatically, that form's Open event procedure will run before either macro.

Skipping the AutoExec Macro

If you have a macro running automatically every time you start your application, sooner or later you're going to want to run the application *without* running that macro. To bypass the AutoExec macro, press and hold the Shift key when you load the database. This is a standard keypress, used in (at least) Access, Word, and Excel to bypass autoexecuting code, and in Windows itself to bypass the Startup group/folder.

If your application is running in the Access run-time environment, your users won't be able to bypass the AutoExec (or the command line–specified) macro at all. The run-time environment disregards the Shift key at load time.

Using Custom Toolbars in Your Application

Toolbars provide another means of communication between your application and its users. By providing carefully planned toolbars, you can make your application far easier for your users to work with and to find their way through. As we discuss in Chapter 15, a well-designed application provides an explicit means to accomplish every action that will occur often. Although you might allow a double-click on a control to start an action, this isn't an explicit action; the user has to know about the double-click. You might include a menu item to start the same action, but the user must still search through the menus to find the item. A better alternative would be to provide a toolbar button for each commonly used activity.

Access provides two types of toolbars: built-in and custom. Access itself ships with 19 toolbars, 2 of which (Utility1 and Utility2) are left empty for your use. In addition, you can create as many toolbars as you like for each application. The discussion in the following sections focuses on using toolbars in your applications.

Using Your Own Toolbars with Forms

To use custom toolbars in your application, you take two steps:

1. Turn off the standard toolbars, if you don't want them to be visible.

2. Turn on your own custom toolbars.

To perform these actions, use the ShowToolbar macro action. The VBA syntax for the action is

DoCmd.ShowToolbar *strToolbarName*[, *fShow*]

where *strToolbarName* is the actual name of the toolbar to act upon and *fShow* is one of the following:

acToolbarYes	Always display this toolbar
acToolbarNo	Never display this toolbar
acToolbarWhereApprop	Display this toolbar only when it's appropriate

If you leave off the *fShow* argument, Access assumes you want to turn on the toolbar (acToolbarYes).

Using the ShowToolbar macro action is similar to choosing the View ➤ Toolbars dialog box, except that by using the macro action you can specify whether to display a toolbar in all views, as opposed to only the view in which it's appropriate. You could, if you liked, use the following code to make the form design toolbar visible, no matter what you were doing in Access:

```
DoCmd.ShowToolbar "Form Design", acToolbarYes
```

Therefore, you could create a function like this one, which turns on or off the specified toolbar and does the opposite with the standard Form view toolbar:

```
Sub ShowYourToolbar(strToolbar As String, fTurnOn as Boolean)
    DoCmd.ShowToolbar strToolbar, IIf(fTurnOn, acToolbarYes, _
    acToolbarNo)
    DoCmd.ShowToolbar "Form View", IIf(fTurnOn, acToolbarNo, _
    acToolbarWhereApprop)
End Sub
```

If you want to display only a single toolbar for every form in your application, the steps are simple: as part of your application's startup, call the ShowToolbar macro actions to set the visibility of the appropriate toolbars.

If you want different forms to display different toolbar configurations, call

```
ShowYourToolbar "YourToolbar", True
```

from your form's Activate event handler, and call

```
ShowToolBar "YourToolbar", False
```

from your form's Deactivate event handler. The form frmTestToolbar, shown in Figure 11.3, in CH11.MDB demonstrates these concepts.

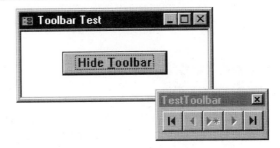

FIGURE 11.3:
You can load a toolbar in your form's Activate event and hide it in the Deactivate event.

Allowing Users to Change Toolbars

You can use a global option setting (using the Tools ➤ Options menu) to control whether or not your users can change the toolbars. If this option is set to Yes, users can add or delete toolbar buttons. If it's set to No, they won't be able to make changes to the toolbars. In either case they'll be able to move, size, hide, or show them. To change the value at run time, you can use the SetOption method of the Application object, along with the toCustomizeToolbars constant. (See the section "Controlling Global Options" later in this chapter for more information.)

Where Are Those Toolbar Changes?

If you allow your users to change the toolbars, you need to be aware of where those changes are stored. Changes to the appearance of a toolbar (where it's located and its size and position) are stored in the system database (SYSTEM.MDW, by default). Each logged-in user maintains a different group of settings for toolbars in the system database. As long as each user logs in under a unique name, each can have a distinct workspace environment.

Changes to the content of the toolbars (the buttons displayed on the toolbar) are stored in one of two places, depending on whether the toolbar is built in or custom. Content changes for built-in toolbars are stored in the system database, under the name of the user who made the change. Again, as long as users log in using unique names, they should each see their own toolbars. Content changes for custom toolbars, however, are stored with the particular application that contains the toolbar. If you want your users to be able to change your custom toolbars, make sure each user owns a copy of the application database locally. Otherwise, each person's changes will overwrite other changes that had been previously made.

Using Toolbars in the Run-Time Environment

The Access run-time executable does not support Access' built-in toolbars. If you're developing an application that will be distributed with the run-time version of Access, you must supply your own set of toolbars for every circumstance in which you'd like your users to see a toolbar. In addition, the run-time version does not automatically display the toolbars based on the current context. You must explicitly use the ShowToolbar macro action each time you want to show or hide a particular toolbar. The run-time version turns off all toolbars, by default. If you want a toolbar visible when your application starts up, you must place a call to the ShowToolbar macro action in your application's startup code.

Don't Try This at Home—What You Can't Do with Access Toolbars

Even after several versions of Access, quite a few "holes" still exist in its support of toolbars. To keep you from spending time trying to find these features, here's a list of things you *can't* do with Access toolbars:

- You can't easily import your own bitmaps. You can copy existing images and then edit them to create "new" images. Access provides no simple mechanism for importing existing bitmaps or icon files. You can, however, paste images from the clipboard into button faces, and Access will scale them appropriately. You'll need to copy them to the clipboard in some fashion (using Paintbrush, for example), but at least this supplies you with *some* way to import images.

- You can't modify the functionality of the buttons Access does provide. Although you can attach a button that calls your own macro or function to a toolbar, you can't change what the built-in buttons do when they're pressed.

- You can't modify toolbars programmatically. There's no interface for adding or deleting buttons from your applications' code.

- You can't dock/undock or move toolbars from within your applications. (You actually can move them, if you're terrifically adventurous, using Windows API calls. You'll need to first retrieve their window handles using the code shown in the section "Determining Which Toolbars are Open" later in this chapter.)

- You can't provide custom help topics for your toolbars.

- You can't trap any events that occur because of the user's interactions with toolbars. That is, you won't know when they've opened, closed, clicked, docked, or hidden your toolbar.

We all hope that future versions of Access give us more programmatic control over the toolbars.

What Access 95 Adds to the Toolbar Picture

True, you still can't control toolbars progammatically in Access 95, but there are two new operations you can perform. Both are undocumented, but the first, calling expressions from toolbars, is at least endorsed by Microsoft. The second, determining which toolbars are currently open, is possible because of one new piece of information that Access makes available about its toolbars: the window text for each toolbar.

Calling Expressions from Toolbars

As it's documented, you can call macros only from toolbar buttons that you create yourself. If you know the special trick (sort of like knowing the secret handshake to get into a club), you can also have toolbar buttons call functions in your application.

To make this happen, you take two steps. First, in your Registry, add a value under this subkey:

```
HKEY_LOCAL_MACHINE\SOFTWARE\Microsoft\Access\7.0\Options
```

The name of the item should be ExprsInToolbars, and its value should be 1 (DWORD). Figure 11.4 shows RegEdit (RegEdt32 on Windows NT) editing this value.

Second, once you've added the Registry setting, you can use expressions in toolbars. Customize toolbars as you normally would, but notice that there's a new entry at the bottom of the list of categories: Expression. If you choose that option, as

FIGURE 11.4:

Add ExprsInToolbars to enable
using function calls in Access
toolbars.

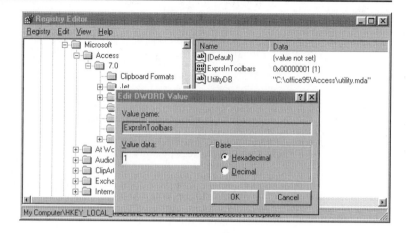

shown in Figure 11.5, you can enter any function name (without a preceding =
(equal sign) but including parameters) to call when you click that toolbar button.
This makes it a bit simpler to call VBA from toolbars: you needn't have the intermediate macro, whose only purpose in life was to call the RunCode macro action.

FIGURE 11.5:

Enter an expression in the
Customize dialog to be able to call
functions from your toolbar buttons.

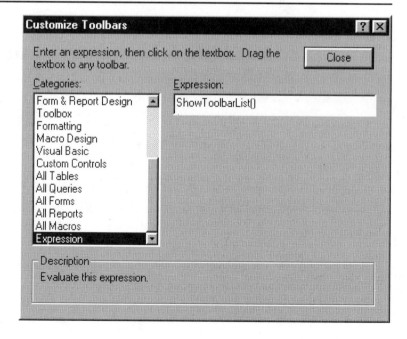

> **NOTE**
>
> Although Microsoft has made this information public knowledge, they do not support this technique. That is, their stance on this is, "If it works, great. If not, use a macro instead." They have not devoted any testing resources to verify that it works in all cases, as they do for all documented features. In our test cases it has worked very well, and Microsoft intends, as far as we can tell, to continue to support this functionality.

Determining Which Toolbars Are Open

Although Microsoft supplies no programmatic support for toolbars in Access 95, you can play one trick: you can get a listing of all the open toolbars and whether or not each is docked. This exercise requires some understanding of window classes and their hierarchy. (See the section "Windows Handles, Classes, Access Forms, and MDI" in Chapter 8 for more information on window classes.) In Access, all toolbar containers are part of the OTBDock window class, and within each toolbar container, you'll find the actual toolbars, each of the OToolbar window class. (Docked toolbar containers can contain multiple toolbars and are children of the Access window; floating containers can contain only one and are children of the main Windows screen window.) Each toolbar container makes its window text available to Windows, and the code you'll use retrieves that text, which contains the name of the toolbar.

Listing 11.2 shows the code that collects information about the open toolbars. The goal of the main routine, glrGetToolbarList(), is to fill an array of user-defined data structures with one element for each open toolbar. The structure contains the name of the toolbar, its window handle, and a Boolean value indicating whether or not it's docked.

Listing 11.2

```
Function glrGetToolbarList(aToolbars() As typTBInfo) _
 As Integer

    Dim hWnd As Long
    Dim intCount As Integer
```

```
    ' First do undocked toolbars, which are top-level
    ' windows. Use FindWindow to find the first,
    ' and then loop around until you get them all.
    hWnd = glr_apiFindWindow(glrcToolbarClassContainer, 0&)
    Do While hWnd <> 0
        intCount = HandleContainers(hWnd, aToolbars(), _
         intCount, False)
        hWnd = glr_apiGetWindow(hWnd, glrcGW_HWNDNEXT)
    Loop

    ' Repeat the operation for Access child windows (the
    ' docked toolbars).

    hWnd = glr_apiGetWindow(Application.hWndAccessApp, _
     glrcGW_CHILD)
    Do While hWnd <> 0
        intCount = HandleContainers(hWnd, aToolbars(), _
         intCount, True)
        hWnd = glr_apiGetWindow(hWnd, glrcGW_HWNDNEXT)
    Loop
    glrGetToolbarList = intCount
End Function

Function glrGetClass(hWnd As Long) As String

    ' Get the window class name for a given window handle.
    ' Useful enough to be made a public function.

    Dim lngStyle As Long
    Dim lngLen As Long
    Dim strBuffer As String * glrcMaxSize

    ' Is this window visible? If so, check its class.
    lngStyle = glr_apiGetWindowLong(hWnd, glrcGWL_STYLE)
    If (glrcWS_VISIBLE And lngStyle) Then
        lngLen = glr_apiGetClassName(hWnd, strBuffer, _
         glrcMaxSize - 1)
        glrGetClass = Left(strBuffer, lngLen)
    End If
End Function

Private Function HandleContainers(hWndContainer As Long, _
 aToolbars() As typTBInfo, intCount As Integer, _
 fDocked As Boolean)
```

```
        Dim strClass As String
        Dim hWnd As Long

        strClass = glrGetClass(hWndContainer)
        If strClass = glrcToolbarClassContainer Then
            ' OK, so you found a toolbar container.  If it's
            ' undocked, it can only contain one toolbar.  If it's
            ' docked, it can contain many toolbars. Either way,
            ' loop through all the children of this window.

            hWnd = glr_apiGetWindow(hWndContainer, glrcGW_CHILD)
            Do While hWnd <> 0
                intCount = AddToolbar(hWnd, aToolbars(), _
                  intCount, fDocked)
                hWnd = glr_apiGetWindow(hWnd, glrcGW_HWNDNEXT)
            Loop
        End If
        HandleContainers = intCount
End Function

Private Function AddToolbar(hWnd As Long, _
  aToolbars() As typTBInfo, _
  intCount As Integer, fDocked As Boolean)
    Dim lngLen As Long
    Dim strBuffer As String * glrcMaxSize
    Dim strText As String

    lngLen = glr_apiGetWindowText(hWnd, strBuffer, _
      glrcMaxSize - 1)
    strText = Left(strBuffer, lngLen)
    ReDim Preserve aToolbars(0 To intCount)
    With aToolbars(intCount)
        .strTBName = strText
        .hWnd = hWnd
        .fDocked = fDocked
    End With
    intCount = intCount + 1
    AddToolbar = intCount
End Function
```

To do its work, glrGetToolbarList() follows these basic steps:

1. It loops through all the top-level windows of class OTBDock.

2. For each matching window, it calls HandleContainers to add information to the array for each toolbar in the container. (Of course, for these undocked toolbar containers, there will be only one toolbar inside the container.)

3. It then looks at all the windows that are children of the main Access window. It calls HandleContainers for each child window.

Every time glrGetToolbarList() finds a new window, it calls HandleContainers to do its work. HandleContainers loops through all the child windows of the main window, and for each child whose class name is OToolbar, adds information to the array of data structures. That way, when glrGetToolbarList() is done, it returns to you an array filled with the information you need. (For the details, see Listing 11.2.)

To test this out, open the Debug window and type

`Call ShowToolbarList`

This procedure, shown below, first calls glrGetToolbarList(), passing to it a dynamic array of structures, aToolbars(). Once that function returns, ShowToolbarList just loops through all the elements of the array, printing out the information stored there.

```
Sub ShowToolbarList()

    ' This sample routine just prints out information
    ' about the currently open toolbars to the Debug window.

    Dim varItem As Variant
    Dim intCount As Integer
    Dim aToolbars() As typTBInfo
    Dim intI As Integer

    intCount = glrGetToolbarList(aToolbars())
    For intI = LBound(aToolbars) To UBound(aToolbars)
        With aToolbars(intI)
            Debug.Print .strTBName, Hex(.hWnd), .fDocked
        End With
    Next intI
End Sub
```

If you want to do something with all the toolbars—for example, to close them all except the main Database toolbar—you could use code like the following example, CloseAllExceptDatabase(). This function loops through all the values returned by glrGetToolbarList() and for each toolbar, if the name isn't Database, closes the toolbar.

```
Function CloseAllExceptDatabase()

    ' Close all the currently opened toolbars, except
    ' the one whose name is Database (the main database
    ' toolbar)

    Dim aToolbars() As typTBInfo
    Dim intI As Integer

    ' Get the list of toolbars, then loop through them all.
    glrGetToolbarList aToolbars()
    For intI = LBound(aToolbars) To UBound(aToolbars)
        With aToolbars(intI)
            ' If this toolbar isn't the Database toolbar,
            ' then close it.
            If .strTBName <> "Database" Then
                DoCmd.ShowToolbar .strTBName, acToolbarNo
            End If
        End With
    Next intI
End Function
```

You'll find all the examples and code for working with toolbars in basToolbars, in CH08.MDB. Import that module into your own database if you'd like to use the functionality. You can delete the sample routines, ShowToolbarList and CloseAll-ExceptDatabase, if you wish to conserve space.

Controlling Global Options

Access provides two methods of the Application object, GetOption() (a function) and SetOption (a subroutine), that can set and retrieve global options. The syntax necessary to call them is

Application.SetOption *optionName*, *Setting*

Setting = Application.GetOption(*optionName*)

The only catch is that the *optionName* value must be the exact text shown in the first column of Table 11.3. (Misspellings and abbreviations will fail.) In addition, Table 11.3 lists all the possible values for each option, as well as constants (defined in basToolOpts) you can use to refer to each option instead of having to type the text strings explicitly.

TABLE 11.3: Application.GetOption/SetOption Options and Constants

Undocumented (No UI Equivalents)

Menu Option	Constant	Allowable Values
Built-In Toolbars Available	toBuiltInToolbars	−1 (True); 0 (False)
Can Customize Toolbars	toCustomizeToolbars	−1 (True); 0 (False)
Key Assignment Macro	toKeyAssignment	(Any valid macro name)
Show Ruler	toShowRuler	−1 (True); 0 (False)
Objects Snap To Grid	toSnapToGrid	−1 (True); 0 (False)
Show Grid	toShowGrid	−1 (True); 0 (False)
Move Enclosed Controls	toMoveEnclosed	−1 (True); 0 (False)
Control Wizards	toControlWizards	−1 (True); 0 (False)

View Tab

Menu Option	Constant	Allowable Values
Show Status Bar	toShowStatusBar	−1 (True); 0 (False)
Show Startup Dialog	toStartupDialog	−1 (True); 0 (False)
Show Hidden Objects	toShowHidden	−1 (True); 0 (False)
Show System Objects	toShowSystemObjects	−1 (True); 0 (False)
Show Macro Names Column	toMacroNames	−1 (True); 0 (False)
Show Conditions Column	toMacroConditions	−1 (True); 0 (False)
Large Toolbar Buttons	toLargeButtons	−1 (True); 0 (False)

TABLE 11.3: Application.GetOption/SetOption Options and Constants (continued)

Color Buttons on Toolbars	toColorButtons	−1 (True); 0 (False)
Show ToolTips	toToolTips	−1 (True); 0 (False)

General Tab

Menu Option	Constant	Allowable Values
Left Margin	toLeftMargin	0 to the width of the printed page, as a string, including units ("3 cm" or "1 in", for example)
Right Margin	toRightMargin	0 to the width of the printed page (see Left Margin)
Top Margin	toTopMargin	0 to the height of the printed page (see Left Margin)
Bottom Margin	toBottomMargin	0 to the height of the printed page (see Left Margin)
Default Database Directory	toDefaultDirectory	(Any valid path, including ".")
New Database Sort Order	toSortOrder	0 (General); 1 (Traditional Spanish); 2 (Dutch); 3 (Swedish/Finnish); 4 (Norwegian/Danish); 5 (Icelandic); 6 (Czech); 7 (Hungarian); 8 (Polish); 9 (Russian); 10 (Turkish); 11 (Arabic); 12 (Hebrew); 13 (Greek)

Edit/Find Tab

Menu Option	Constant	Allowable Values
Default Find/Replace Behavior	toFindReplace	0 (Fast Search); 1 (General Search); 2 (Start of Field Search)
Confirm Record Changes	toConfirmChanges	−1 (True); 0 (False)
Confirm Document Deletions	toConfirmDeletions	−1 (True); 0 (False)
Confirm Action Queries	toConfirmQueries	−1 (True); 0 (False)
Show Values in Indexed	toShowLocalIndexed	−1 (True); 0 (False)

TABLE 11.3 : Application.GetOption/SetOption Options and Constants (continued)

Show Values in Non-Indexed	toShowLocalNonIndexed	-1 (True); 0 (False)
Show Values in Remote	toShowRemote	−1 (True); 0 (False)
Show Values Limit	toShowValuesLimit	0 to 32766

Datasheet Tab

Menu Option	Constant	Allowable Values
Default Font Color	toFontColor	0 (Black); 1(Maroon); 2(Green); 3(Olive); 4 (Navy); 5 (Purple); 6 (Teal); 7 (Gray); 8 (Silver); 9 (Red); 10 (Lime); 11 (Yellow); 12 (Blue); 13 (Fuchsia); 14 (Aqua); 15 (White)
Default Background Color	toBackgroundColor	0 to 15 (see Default Font Color)
Default Gridlines Color	toGridlinesColor	0 to 15 (see Default Font Color)
Default Font Name	toFontName	(Any installed font name)
Default Font Weight	toFontWeight	0 (Thin); 1 (Extra Light); 2 (Light); 3 (Normal); 4 (Medium); 5 (Semi-Bold); 6 (Bold); 7 (Extra Bold); 8 (Heavy)
Default Font Size	toFontSize	(Any integer value between 1 and 127, inclusive)
Default Font Italic	toFontItalic	−1 (True); 0 (False)
Default Font Underline	toFontUnderline	−1 (True); 0 (False)
Default Gridlines Horizontal	toGridlinesHorizontal	−1 (True); 0 (False)
Default Gridlines Vertical	toGridlinesVertical	−1 (True); 0 (False)
Default Column Width	toColumnWidth	0.1 to 22.75 inches (up to 32,767 twips), as a string, including units ("1 in", for example)
Default Cell Effect	toCellEffect	0 (Sunken); 1 (Raised); 2 (Flat)
Show Animations	toShowAnimations	−1 (True); 0 (False)

TABLE 11.3: Application.GetOption/SetOption Options and Constants (continued)

Table/Query Design Tab

Menu Option	Constant	Allowable Values
Default Text Field Size	toDefaultTextField	1 to 255
Default Number Field Size	toDefaultNumberField	0 (Double); 1 (Integer); 2 (Long Integer); 3 (Single); 4 (Byte); 5 (Replication ID)
Default Field Type	toDefaultFieldType	0 (Text); 1 (Memo); 2 (Number); 3 (Date/Time); 4 (Currency); 5 (AutoNumber); 6 (Yes/No); 7 (OLE Object)
AutoIndex on Import/Create	toAutoIndex	(A semicolon-delimited list of field names)
Show Table Names	toShowTableNames	−1 (True); 0 (False)
Output All Fields	toOutputAllFields	−1 (True); 0 (False)
Enable AutoJoin	toEnableAutoJoin	−1 (True); 0 (False)
Run Permissions	toRunPermissions	0 (User's); 1 (Owner's)

Form/Report Design Tab

Menu Option	Constant	Allowable Values
Selection Behavior	toSelectionBehavior	0 (Partially enclosed); 1 (Fully enclosed)
Form Template	toFormTemplate	(Name of any form in the current database)
Report Template	toReportTemplate	(Name of any report in the current database)

Keyboard Tab

Menu Option	Constant	Allowable Values
Move After Enter	toMoveAfterEnter	0 (Don't move); 1 (Next field); 2 (Next record)
Arrow Key Behavior	toArrowKeys	0 (Next field); 1 (Next character)
Behavior Entering Field	toEnterField	0 (Entire field); 1 (End of field); 2 (Beginning of field)
Cursor Stops at First/Last Field	toCursorStops	−1 (True); 0 (False)

TABLE 11.3: Application.GetOption/SetOption Options and Constants (continued)

Module Tab		
Menu Option	**Constant**	**Allowable Values**
Break On All Errors	toBreakOnErrors	−1 (True); 0 (False)

Advanced Tab		
Menu Option	**Constant**	**Allowable Values**
Default Record Locking	toRecordLocking	0 (No locks); 1 (All records); 2 (Edited record)
Default Open Mode for Databases	toOpenMode	0 (Shared); 1 (Exclusive)
Ignore DDE Requests	toIgnoreDDE	−1 (True); 0 (False)
Enable DDE Refresh	toEnableDDERefresh	−1 (True); 0 (False)
OLE/DDE Timeout (sec)	toOLEDDETimeout	0 to 300
Number of Update Retries	toRetryCount	0 to 10
ODBC Refresh Interval (sec)	toODBCRefresh	1 to 3600
Refresh Interval (sec)	toRefreshInterval	1 to 32766
Update Retry Interval (msec)	toRetryInterval	0 to 1000

> **NOTE** Although this feature doesn't appear to be documented, translated (non-English) versions of Access will understand the English values, shown in Table 11.3, for SetOption and GetOption( ).

TIP

If you're developing applications for other people to use, there's one setting in Table 11.3 that you'll want to incorporate into every application you write: You'll need to set the "Break On All Errors" (toBreakOnErrors) option to False (0) when you start up and put it back the way it was when you're done. Otherwise, anytime your application triggers any sort of run-time error, whether or not you've trapped for and handled that error, your code will halt. This option is great for developers who want to watch every error occur, but for end-users it's the fastest way there is to kill any application. Do not bypass this step, or sooner or later you'll be sorry.

Remember that the options settings are both global and persistent. If you make a change, be sure to set it back. Certainly, if you change any settings using Application.SetOption, you must make an effort to reset the values when your application exits. Whether your user exits through an error handler or through the normal shutdown procedures, you should reset any options your application changed. That is, your application might contain code to set the value for the OLE/DDE Timeout to be 100 seconds. In the application's startup routine you might include code like this (the variable gintTimeOut is global):

```
gintTimeOut = Application.GetOption("OLE/DDE TimeOut (sec)")
Application.SetOption "OLE/DDE TimeOut (sec)", 100
```

Then, in the code that's executed when your application shuts down, include a statement like this:

```
Application.SetOption "OLE/DDE TimeOut (sec)", gintTimeOut
```

If you don't reset the value when your application shuts down, your user will find the settings as your application left them the next time Access starts up. This is especially frustrating if your application disables the default toolbars—many applications do this and then forget to reenable them when they quit. The next time a user starts Access, the toolbars are disabled, and the user is left wondering where the toolbars went.

Making It a Bit Simpler

To make it a bit simpler for you to use the GetOption() and SetOption methods, we've supplied a module containing all the possible options, with associated constants. This way, rather than use the exact strings each time you set or retrieve options, you can use the constants. This saves your typing the strings, which can introduce errors. Instead of using this expression:

```
Application.SetOption "Update Retry Interval (msec)", 100
```

you can use

```
Application.SetOption toRetryInterval, 100
```

Table 11.3 includes a list of all the options, their associated constants, and the allowed values for each. To use these in your own applications, import basToolsOpts from CH11.MDB.

A Few More Undocumented Options

Besides the documented options for Application.SetOption and GetOption() that correspond to settings in the Tools ➤ Options dialog, Access supports a few extra options that have no user-interface equivalents. As a matter of fact, these options offer the only way in Access to change the associated settings! We've included these undocumented option settings at the top of Table 11.3.

In addition, there are several other undocumented settings you can use with GetOption() and SetOption. Because they're of limited use and have never been mentioned in any version of Access, we've pulled them out into their own table. The 12 settings in Table 11.4 are part of a larger set of undocumented values, but these are the only ones we could reverse-engineer.

The first four items in Table 11.4 allow you to retrieve the most recently used files from the File menu. These are all read-only (that is, you cannot use Application.SetOption to change the values) but may be of interest to add-in developers.

The second group of items allows you to retrieve and set the coordinates of various windows Access uses. In each set of coordinates, the first position indicates whether

TABLE 11.4: Undocumented GetOption ()/SetOption Values,

Value	Description
_2	First item in the Most Recently Used (MRU) list on the File menu (read-only)
_3	Second item in the MRU list (read-only)
_4	Third item in the MRU list (read-only)
_5	Fourth item in the MRU list (read-only)
_16	Coordinates for the Table property sheet, in the format: Open?;Left;Top;Width;Height. For example: 0;275;150;650;325
_17	Coordinates for the Index List window
_18	Coordinates for the Sorting/Grouping window
_19	Coordinates for the Fields List window
_24	Coordinates for the Form property sheet
_25	Coordinates for the Query property sheet
_26	Coordinates for the Report property sheet
_28	Coordinates for the Debug window

or not the window is visible by default, and the other coordinates indicate the left, top, width, and height for the window. In each case, Access reads these values only the first time it loads each of the windows. Once you've loaded each of the windows so it's visible, Access no longer notices the settings in these options, and changing them once the window is open would be a waste of time.

So, you ask, what's the point? For the most part, these are interesting factoids, but they're not terribly useful. One very important use for these, however, is the ability they give you to ensure that the Report property sheet isn't visible when you open a report in Design view. You can't open a report invisibly, and if you want to perform some modifications to a report in Design view, you'll want to hide the property sheet while you're working. You can use option _26 to make sure that when you first open a report in your application, Access won't display the property sheet, and your application will look much smoother because of it.

To make this change, you could use code like this:

```
Dim strOpt As String
strOpt = Application.GetOption("_26")
' Make sure the first character is a 0.
strOpt = "0" & Mid(strOpt, 2)
```

```
Application.SetOption "_26", strOpt
' Now, open the report in Design view.
```

Certainly, this technique is not for everyone, and it is subject to change. But if you're attempting to write a clean add-in that works on reports in Design view, this could finally make your application appear seamless.

Don't forget, the leading underscore is crucial. In addition, remember that Access will look at the coordinate settings in Table 11.4 only before it has actually opened the window in question. Changing option _26 will be fruitless once you've opened a report.

Menus in Access

Access ships with a number of prebuilt menu layouts, and you can create your own. Unlike most of the other Windows desktop applications from Microsoft, however, you cannot add items to the existing menu structures in Access. All menus in Access are either prebuilt or user defined. You must use Access' macros to create your own menus, and if you want to modify an existing menu tree, you need to re-create all the pieces of it yourself, adding or removing the items you need.

The following sections discuss how you can create, modify, and use user-defined menus in Access. In addition, we provide examples and code for using the Windows API to manipulate the menus in ways that Access itself doesn't support. You'll be able to modify text on menus, place or remove a check mark next to menu items at any level, and disable and enable specific menu items or entire pull-down menus, all while your application is running.

Creating Menus

Access provides only a single menu at any given time. Unlike other MDI applications (such as Visual Basic), you cannot attach a menu to a specific form, although you can attach a menu tree to a form as its shortcut menu (available by right-clicking while that form has the focus). All menus aside from shortcut menus are attached to the main Access window, and their parent is the running instance of Access itself. (You can, of course, have each form *invoke* a different set of menu items. Using the form MenuBar property, you can have Access display a specific menu for each form or report in your application.) In addition, Access maintains only a single instance of each menu layout. If you make changes using the Windows API to a menu layout (modifying text, for example), every place in Access where that layout might be used will also see your changes. Your changes will also be persistent thoughout your Access session until you either change them back or restart Access. None of your changes to Access menus, using the API, will remain across sessions.

Because Access provides no mechanism at all for modifying the built-in menus, you must create an entirely new replacement menu system if you need to change or remove even a single menu item from the standard menus. Luckily, Access includes a Menu Builder that makes it slightly easier to create your own menus than it would be to create them by hand, one macro at a time.

> **TIP**
>
> If you're going to create a new menu system, your best bet is to base it on an existing menu tree. The Menu Builder Wizard provides a list of all the existing menus. You'll find it much simpler to choose one of these and remove or modify items than to start from scratch and build your own. If you must create a new menu system from scratch, plan it carefully before starting.

> **TIP**
>
> Using the Windows API, you can remove menu items manually from the standard Access menus rather than having to create a whole new menu system. Although removing menu items using the API is too much work if you need to remove many of them, for just a few it works well. You can easily remove menu items at startup and replace them when you're done. See the sections later in this chapter, starting with "Manipulating Menus," covering modifications to the menu structure using Windows API calls.

Using the Menu Builder Wizard

In this section we walk through the steps for modifying the Database menu bar to remove the View ➤ Database Objects ➤ Modules menu item, and we add a new item to the File menu to run your (imaginary) VBA function, ZipItUp(). To get started, choose Tools ➤ Add-ins ➤ Menu Builder. The Add-in gives you four choices: Edit, New, Delete, and Cancel. For this exercise, choose New. Figure 11.6 shows the list of available menu bars.

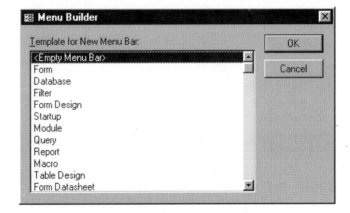

FIGURE 11.6:

When creating a new menu, start by selecting an existing menu on which to base it.

Since you want to modify the standard Database menu bar, choose that option. Once you do, you see a dialog box like the one in Figure 11.7. Your first step is to remove the View ➤ Database Objects ➤ Modules menu item. To do so, select that item and click the Delete button. Your new menu system will not include that particular menu item. Figure 11.8 shows this action.

Next, to add the Zip It Up menu item right above the Exit menu item, scroll down until you've highlighted the Exit menu item. Click the Insert button (which inserts a new row above the current cursor location) and enter the new command, &Zip It Up, filling in the Action item by selecting RunCode. (The Menu Builder supports only RunCode, RunMacro, and DoMenuItem actions.) Finally, enter the name of the VBA procedure (ZipItUp()) to execute when you choose the menu item, and fill in the status bar text. You've now added the new menu item you needed, and the dialog should look like the one in Figure 11.9.

Once you're satisfied with your modified menu, click the OK button on the Menu Builder. This saves your modified menu tree, with one macro group for each main menu item or submenu. Access requests a name for the group of menus.

FIGURE 11.7:

The Menu Builder allows you to visually create your menu trees.

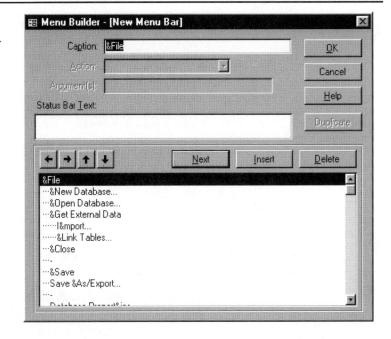

FIGURE 11.8:

You delete a menu item by selecting it and then deleting it. The View ➤ Database Objects ➤ Modules menu item in this example is now deleted.

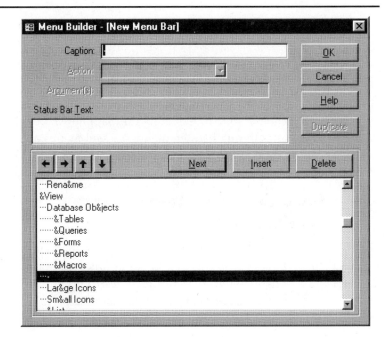

FIGURE 11.9:

The Menu Builder after you've
added your new items

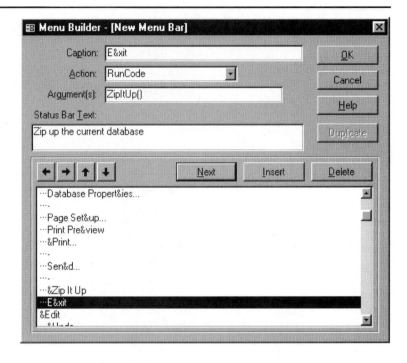

For this example, choose Sample_MenuBar. The Menu Builder will create all the macros for you. Figure 11.10 shows the macro list after you've created the menu system in this example.

You can modify your menu system at any time. Just choose Menu Builder from the Tools ➤ Add-ins menu, and when it requests the name of the menu to modify, choose your top-level menu (Sample_MenuBar in this case). The Menu Builder goes through all the menus and submenus and presents them to you in the same editing form, for modification.

Situations the Menu Builder Can't Handle

If you modify your menu macros manually between sessions with the Menu Builder, you might add some functionality the Menu Builder just can't handle. There are two possible outcomes: the Menu Builder won't be able to load your macros at all, or it will warn you that it has to lose some of your changes.

FIGURE 11.10:

The macro list after you've created your menu bar

The Menu Builder won't be able to open your macros if

- You've added rows to the menu bar macro that contain actions besides AddMenu

- You've used actions other than DoMenuItem, RunCode, or RunMacro for any row in any of the menu macros

The Menu Builder warns you, when it attempts to load the menu structure, that it will delete any of the following characteristics when it saves your menu macros:

- Blank rows, or rows with comments only

- Names that don't follow the Menu Builder's naming conventions (Don't rename the macros!)

- Expressions in the Conditions column in a menu bar macro

> **NOTE**
>
> You can use a condition in any menu macro, on the line that contains the AddMenu action. The decision to show or not show the menu item is checked only when the form in question is loaded. (That is, you can't use the condition to dynamically add or remove the menu item.) You cannot use a condition on the macro that actually performs the action for the specific menu item.

Some Tips on Using the Menu Builder

The following group of tips will help you in your Menu Builder menu creations:

- You can't fill in Action or Arguments for any menu item that has menu items indented beneath it. If you change a menu item from a "child" item to a "parent" item, the Menu Builder removes the Action and Arguments fields for that item.

- Since the Menu Builder can edit only menus for which the macro action is DoMenuItem, RunCode, or RunMacro, if you have any menus built that run other actions, you won't be able to edit that menu tree with the Menu Builder. For example, if your menu contains the Close macro action, the Menu Builder will refuse to load your menu tree.

- Remember that inserting a new item places it above the current cursor location. To change the level of the chosen item, use the arrow buttons. Access allows you to indent a menu to any level you like, but when it tries to save the menu, it complains and refuses to save if you've skipped a level.

- If you want to use DoMenuItem as the action for a menu item, be sure to use the builder provided to supply the arguments. Click the "…" button to the right of the text box, and Access provides an easy means for you to fill in the required list of arguments.

Examining Menu Macros

Whether you create menus using the Menu Builder or by hand (from scratch), you need to understand how Access uses and stores menu macros. The top-level menu bar, each item on the main menu, and each submenu exist in their own macro group. Within that group you'll find an entry for each menu item that appears on the specific menu. For menus attached to the given item, Access uses the AddMenu macro action to specify the menu to pop up if you choose the particular item. For menu items that perform an action, the macro specifies the action to take when the user clicks the item.

For example, frmModifyMenuItems in CH11.MDB uses a sample user-defined menu layout. This menu tree includes two top-level menu items, each with a pull-down menu. The File ➤ New item includes a submenu. (To see this menu in action, run frmModifyMenuItems in CH11.MDB and choose the Use Custom Menu Bar button.)

In Outline view, the menus lay out as shown in Table 11.5.

TABLE 11.5: The Menu in Outline View

File	New	Form
		Module
		Query
	Close	
Utilities	Run NotePad	
	Run Calculator	
	Save Settings	

Although not a perfect representation, Figure 11.11 shows a schematic diagram of how the simple menu lays out. The macro mcrNewMenu is the top-level menu and points to mcrNewMenu_File and mcrNewMenu_Utilities. The one menu item that loads a submenu, the File ➤ New item, points to the mcrNewMenu_File_New macro.

At each level Access uses the AddMenu macro action to add a new menu item. For these actions you must specify the AddMenu action in the Action field, telling Access to add a new menu item here. You must also specify the Macro Name parameter. Its specific value doesn't matter, since the Menu Name parameter tells Access the name to display on the menu. If you leave the Menu Name field blank, however, Access will not display the menu item at all. You must also specify the

FIGURE 11.11:

Schematic diagram of the menu

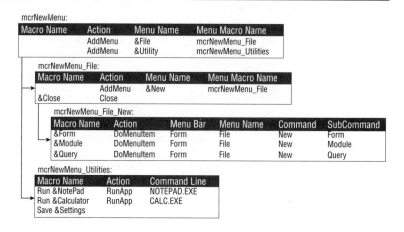

Menu Macro Name parameter, which tells Access which macro to look in for the next menu level. If you leave this item blank, Access triggers a run-time error.

If your macro describes an action instead of a submenu, you must specify the menu text (in the Macro Name field), the action to take (in the Action field), and the specific parameters describing that action (which are different for each of the actions). Although the menu item is not very useful if you don't specify an action, you needn't. The menu will display correctly, but it won't do anything.

Attaching the Menu to a Form

Once you've created your menu structure, you need some way to attach it to a form. To do this, you specify the name of the main, top-level menu macro in the form's MenuBar property (in the Other group on the property sheet). If you leave this property blank, the form displays either the Access default menu bar or the application's Global menu bar, if you've assigned one. (See the section "The Global Menu Bar" later in this chapter.) In addition, your application can easily change the menu bar your form uses. The code in Listing 11.3 shows a way to attach a different menu bar while your application is running. This code is from frmModifyMenuItems in CH11.MDB. You'll also see examples later in this chapter of using the Windows API to modify existing menus at run time.

Listing 11.3 changes the MenuBar property of the current form from a user-defined menu bar back to the default menu bar by setting the MenuBar property to a macro name or to Null. Setting the property to Null causes the form to use the Access default or Application Global menu bar.

Listing 11.3

```
Sub cmdCustomMenuBar_Click()

    Const glrcTextCustom = "Use &Custom Menu Bar"
    Const glrcTextStandard = "Use &Standard Menu Bar"

    If IsNull(Me.MenuBar) Then
        Me.MenuBar = "mcrNewMenu"
        Me!cmdCustomMenuBar.Caption = glrcTextStandard
    Else
        Me.MenuBar = Null
        Me!cmdCustomMenuBar.Caption = glrcTextCustom
    End If
    ' Refill the list box showing the top-level menus.
    FillTopLevelList
End Sub
```

Using Shortcut Menus

Just as you can attach your own menu to a form or report, you can attach a shortcut menu to any report, form, or form control. These menus are constructed just as though they were menu bars (and you can share macros between menu bars and shortcut menus). By setting a form's ShortCutMenu property to Yes and supplying the name of a menu macro in the ShortCutMenuBar property, you can supply your own shortcut menus that can be different for every object in your application. For the shortcut menus, you'll want to choose the "second-tier" macros—that is, the macros that supply the menus that hang off your menu bar if you're reusing existing menu macros. For an example, see the Change Text button on frmModify-MenuItems. If you click this button with the right mouse button, Access displays the menu stored in mcrNewMenu_File. Using the right mouse button anywhere else on the form pops up the standard Access shortcut menus.

NOTE

Unless a control is enabled, Access will use the built-in shortcut menu, whether or not you've chosen a shortcut menu of your own. To see this, right-click the Change Text button on frmModifyMenuItems before it's enabled. You'll get the standard shortcut menu. Once you choose a menu item to alter and the code enables the button, you'll get the user-defined shortcut menu instead. You can use the Tools ➤ Startup dialog to disable the default shortcut menus (remove the check from Allow Default ShortCut Menus) for your application, if you wish. If you do that, you'll see no shortcut menu at all if you right-click a disabled control and your custom shortcut menu, once it's enabled.

Menu Tips

Keep the following tips in mind when creating your menus:

- You can nest menus as deeply as you like, although nesting more than two levels deep is probably not a very good idea; it makes it difficult for users to find the menu items they need. To nest menus, just add an AddMenu action within your menu macro. If you nest more than two levels deep, you won't be able to use the DoCmd.SetMenuItem macro action to modify the state of your menu items. In that case you'll be forced to use the Windows API if you wish to enable/disable or check/uncheck menu items. (See the section "Manipulating Menus" later in this chapter.)

- To add a menu hot key (an underlined character in the text, providing access via the Alt key and the specified letter), place an ampersand (&) in front of the character you want to have underlined. To actually place an ampersand in your menu item, use two together (&&). Figures 11.7, 11.8, and 11.9 show the Menu Builder in action, with ampersands included in each menu item.

- To place a menu divider in your menu, use a single hyphen in the Macro Name column.

TIP

You've probably noticed that many menu items in Windows have a shortcut key name to the right of the menu item. For example, the File ➤ Print menu item has Ctrl+P on its right. You can reproduce this effect, although you'll need to go outside Access to do it. In a text editor (such as Notepad), enter the name you want, followed by a tab character and then the text you want on the right side of the menu item. Copy that to the clipboard (using the Edit ➤ Copy menu in Notepad), and paste it into your macro definition in Access using Ctrl+V or Shift+Ins. (You'll see a vertical bar where the tab character is.) It's the tab character that tells Windows to display the following text to the right in the menu, and the Access macro editor won't allow you to enter a tab character. This still leaves the problem, however, of reacting to the keystroke you specify. Unless you choose a keystroke that Access already traps, you must supply an AutoKeys macro to trap the keystroke.

The Global Menu Bar

In addition to the specific Form and Report menu bars, you can specify a menu bar that Access will display for all windows. Access allows you to specify a single menu bar that can be used globally, such as when you're in the database container, in Query Design view, or in Macro Design view. Any form or report's specifically designated menu bar always takes precedence over the Global menu bar, and setting a form or report's MenuBar property to Null causes it to display the Application Global menu bar, if one exists. Therefore, the default Access menu bar has the lowest priority for display. The Application Global menu bar has a higher priority and displays for all areas of Access that don't maintain their own user-defined menus. Finally, forms or reports for which you've specified a macro in the MenuBar property always display their own menus, independent of the global settings.

To assign the Global menu bar, set the Application object's MenuBar property to the name of the macro that defines the menu bar you'd like to make global. Most often you do this from the Tools ➤ Startup dialog box. On the other hand, you may need to change this value from within your application. This fragment sets the Application menu bar to mcrYourGlobalMenu:

```
Application.MenuBar = "mcrYourGlobalMenu"
```

Your application can change the global menu at any time, of course, by just resetting the application's MenuBar property. If you watch Access' menus carefully, you'll see that's exactly what it does: it changes the menu tree based on the current context. Your applications can do that, too, by changing the Application.MenuBar property to a macro that contains the menu you'd like to have displayed in the current situation.

All of the previous information dealing with Global menu bars applies, as well, to global shortcut menus. You can supply, in the Tools ➤ Startup dialog box, the name of a macro containing the shortcut menu you'd like to see for all your reports, forms, and form controls, unless the object sets up its own shortcut menu. Figure 11.12 shows the Startup dialog box filled in with settings for default menu bars and shortcut menus.

FIGURE 11.12:

Use the Startup dialog box to specify the global menu bar and shortcut menu settings.

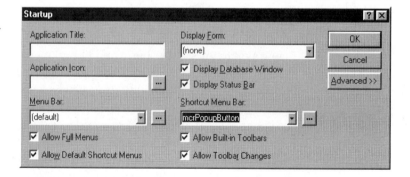

Manipulating Menus

In Access 95, you can use the new SetMenuItem macro action to gray/ungray or enable/disable a menu item. The next section discusses using this interface to modify Access menu states. For many applications, the SetMenuItem macro will be sufficient. On the other hand, it's quite limited, and you may find you need more control. The Windows API can give you the control you need, and we'll discuss that issue in later sections of this chapter.

Getting the Names Right

Although there may be other terminologies in use, we discuss menus at three basic levels: the menu bar, the top-level menu, and the submenu. Figure 11.13 shows what we mean when we refer to each menu level.

FIGURE 11.13:
To use GetMenuItem, you'll need to understand the three levels of menus.

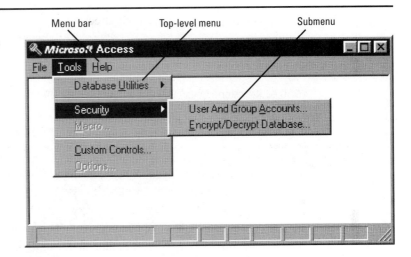

Using SetMenuItem to Control Menus

Access supplies the SetMenuItem macro action, which allows you to control the checked and enabled states of custom menu items. The general syntax is

DoCmd.SetMenuItem *intTopLevel*, [*intCommand*],

[*intSubCommand*], *intFlag*

The parameters *intTopLevel, intCommand,* and *intSubCommand* contain zero-based positions of your menu items, starting at the menu bar. The *intFlag* parameter indicates to Access what you want to do. Choose an item from the Constant column in the following table to tell SetMenuItem what to do:

Action	Constant
Gray	acMenuGray
Ungray	acMenuUngray
Check	acMenuCheck
Uncheck	acMenuUncheck

For example, using the menu structure described in the preceding table, the following statement would gray out the File ➤ New ➤ Query menu item:

```
DoCmd.SetMenuItem 0, 0, 2, acMenuGray
```

> **NOTE**
>
> Debugging code that uses DoCmd.SetMenuItem can be difficult because SetMenuItem works only with user-defined menus. Once you switch to the Debug window, unless you've set up a global menu bar, you've switched to a built-in menu, and calls to SetMenuItem will fail with a run-time error. Debugging will be simpler if you include error handlers in any code that manipulates menus (see Chapter 16 for more information on error handlers) and if you don't go into debugging mode until menu changes have been made.

Limitations of SetMenuItem

As handy as it is to use SetMenuItem, the macro action has some severe limitations:

- There's no way, using SetMenuItem, to test the state of a menu item. If you want to know the current setting of a menu item (whether it's currently checked or enabled), you'll need to use the Windows API.

- SetMenuItem allows you to control only the enabled and checked states of the menu items. You can't remove menu items with this action. You can remove menu items with the Windows API.

- SetMenuItem works only two levels deep. That is, you can work with menu items on submenus of the menus hanging off the menu bar, but that's as far as SetMenuItem can look. Of course, you'll seldom have menus nested more deeply than that, but if you do, SetMenuItem won't help you.

- SetMenuItem won't work at all with built-in menus. As you'll discover in the next section, you can't really control the enabled or checked state of most built-in menu items using the Windows API either, but you can modify some of them. SetMenuItem triggers a run-time error if you even try to work with built-in menus.

Using the Windows API (and the wrapper functions we've provided to shield you from the intricacies of the API) will give you complete control, as you will see in the following sections.

NOTE　When providing arguments for the SetMenuItem macro action, do not count dividing lines on your menus. SetMenuItem skips those dividers when it counts the items, and because you use numeric positions on your menus to indicate to SetMenuItem which menu item you want affected, you must count items the same way it does. This is different from the way the Windows API works; there, you *must* count the dividing lines when telling Windows what to do. Chapter 19 provides yet another method for working with menus. There you have a choice of whether or not to include separators.

Providing a Simple API Interface

Windows provides many functions you can use to set and retrieve information about menus. There are so many of them, with so many intricacies, that we've provided a set of wrapper functions in this chapter, shielding you from most of the details. You can find these functions in basMenuHandling in CH11.MDB. You'll need to import this module into any application you write that includes any of the menu-handling functionality. Table 11.6 lists all the public procedures in that module, along with a short description of each. The discussions in the following sections refer to procedures in this table instead of using the Windows API functions directly.

TABLE 11.6: Windows API Menu-Handling Wrapper Procedures

Procedure Name	Description
glrCheckMenuItem	Places or removes a check mark before a specific menu item, given the top-level menu number and the item number within that menu
glrCheckSubMenuItem	Places or removes a check mark before a menu item, given the menu handle and the ordinal menu item number
glrEnableMenuBarItem	Enables or disables a menu item on the menu bar
glrFindAccessHWnd	Retrieves the window handle for the main Access Window
glrGetMenuBar	Retrieves the menu handle for the main Access menu bar
glrGetMenuBarText	Retrieves the menu text from any of the menu bar items
glrGetMenuBarTitles	Fills a passed-in array with all the menu text on the menu bar
glrGetMenuHandles	Retrieves the menu handle for the menu bar and a specific submenu (attached to the main menu bar)
glrGetMenuText	Retrieves the menu text from any menu item, given the menu handle and the ordinal menu item number
glrGetMenuTitles	Fills a passed-in array with all the menu text on any menu, given the menu handle
glrGetSystemMenu	Retrieves the menu handle of the system menu for a given window
glrGrayMenuItem	Enables or grays a user-defined menu item on any menu attached to the menu bar
glrGraySubMenuItem	Enables or grays a user-defined menu item on any menu, given a menu handle and the ordinal menu item number
glrHiliteMenuBarItem	Highlights a specific menu bar item (not terribly useful)
glrInsertMenuBarItem	Inserts a menu item in the menu bar at a specific location
glrInsertMenuItem	Inserts a menu item in any menu at a specified location
glrIsItemChecked	Determines whether an item "on" a top-level menu is checked
glrIsItemDisabled	Determines whether an item "on" a top-level menu is disabled
glrIsItemGrayed	Determines whether an item "on" a top-level menu is grayed
glrIsMenuBarItemDisabled	Determines whether a menu bar item is disabled
glrIsSubItemChecked	Determines whether an item on any menu is checked, given a menu handle and the ordinal menu item number
glrIsSubItemDisabled	Determines whether an item on any menu is disabled, given the menu handle and the ordinal menu item number

TABLE 11.6: Windows API Menu-Handling Wrapper Procedures (continued)

Procedure Name	Description
glrIsSubItemGrayed	Determines whether an item on any menu is grayed, given a menu handle and the ordinal menu item number
glrRemoveMenuBarItem	Removes an item from the main menu bar
glrRemoveMenuItem	Removes an item from any menu, given a menu handle and the ordinal menu item number
glrResetSystemMenu	Resets the system menu back to the Windows default for a given window
glrSetMenuBarText	Sets the text of any menu bar item
glrSetMenuText	Sets the text of any menu item, given a menu handle and the ordinal menu item number

In this chapter we shield you from needing to know how the API calls work. You are welcome to load basMenuHandling and study the calls to the API, but you can do a great deal of work without ever digging very deeply. The layer we've provided makes it simple to do the work you need without your having to know anything about the details of the API calls themselves.

NOTE Some of the API functions declared in basMenuHandling are so seldom used that we didn't provide interfaces for them. (You just call them directly.) We discuss them as needed throughout the rest of this chapter. In addition, some added functionality is available if you want to push the API just a little harder. You can, for example, change a horizontal dividing line into a vertical dividing line, giving you a two-column menu, using the glr_apiModifyMenu() function, but we leave this esoteric functionality for you to explore.

Knowing Your Limitations

Although the Windows API provides all the control you could possibly want, Access limits that control by grabbing some of its own. For any built-in menu item or any user-defined menu item that maps to an Access menu item, Access maintains strict control over the status of the menu item. At the time you pull down a menu, Access decides whether each item in the menu is to be available and whether it is to be checked. No matter what you did while the menu was closed, Access controls how it looks once it's dropped down.

This scenario becomes clearer if you envision the menus as a large data structure in memory. This data structure contains information about the menu hierarchy, the text of each item, a command ID or a submenu handle, and the state of each item. When you ask the Windows API to enable or disable a particular item, for example, you're storing specific information in that data structure in memory. When Access displays one of its own menus, it decides, just before it shows you the menu, what the status of each item in the menu ought to be. It might check to see whether you've done anything that might require undoing or whether you've displayed the Debug window. In any case, no matter how you've changed that data structure in memory, Access can and does override your changes with its own decisions about how those menus ought to appear. Given this information, there's no way you can, for example, make the Edit ➤ Undo menu item available if Access has decided it should be grayed. In addition, if you perform some action and then use the Windows API to inquire whether or not the Edit ➤ Undo menu item is grayed out, you will not receive current information. Since Access doesn't bother updating the menu data structure until it's just about to display the menu, you'll retrieve out-of-date information.

User-defined menus, however, don't normally have these limitations. If the menus you create don't replace built-in Access menu items, you can control their state completely using API calls (or the SetMenuItem macro action). Since Access doesn't care about your menus, it won't interfere with their availability or checked state. If your user-defined menus call the DoMenuItem action, however, Access will control their state as though they were built-in menu items.

In case you're determined to retrieve information from the Access built-in menus, we've provided an interface to a function from the Windows API that will help you. To retrieve the state of an internal menu, you first pull down the menu and then retrieve its state. This result will be unattractive in your application since there's no way to hide that menu's flopping down. Windows does provide a method, the LockWindowUpdate() function, for turning off all screen updates. Therefore, you can turn off the screen updating, pull down the necessary menu, turn screen updating back on, and then go about your business, retrieving the state of the menu item you care about. Access' own Application.Echo won't ever hide menu actions from you.

You can use the subroutine glrEchoOff in basMenuHandling (CH11.MDB) to control the screen updating. Pass it True to turn off the Access screen updating and False to turn it back on. You can use it with a SendKeys action to turn off the display, pull down the necessary menu that needs to have its states set by Access, and then turn it back on.

For example, if you need to know whether or not the Edit ➤ Undo menu item is currently available, you could use code like this:

```
glrEchoOff True
SendKeys "%E{Esc 2}"
glrEchoOff False
```

to turn off the screen display, pull down the menu and immediately close it up, and then turn on the screen display again. After that you can call glrIsItemGrayed() (see the section "Retrieving Top-Level Information" later in this chapter) to check the state of the menu item.

WARNING Because it's possible for an error to occur while screen updating has been disabled, leaving the user to believe that the system has completely hung, you'll always want to use an error handler that turns screen updating back on should an error of any sort occur. Never use glrEchoOff without an appropriate error handler set up to reset the screen display.

API or Not?

With many menu issues you don't have much choice as to whether or not to use the Windows API. If you want to retrieve the current state of a menu item, you have to use the Windows API. On the other hand, if you want to create a menu tree that replicates the entire Access menu tree with just a few items missing, you have a choice. You can use the Menu Builder to create the macros for you since it's so easy to duplicate an entire menu system using that tool. You may find it easier, though, if you're just going to change or remove a few of the standard Access menu items, to modify the existing menus rather than create your own full set with macros. There are some caveats to this method, of course, since Access doesn't know about or support changes made to its menus with the Windows API. In any case, if you're careful about controlling the menus, you should be able to do a great deal using the rich set of menu-manipulation functions included in the Windows API.

NOTE   Chapter 19 provides an alternate set of limited wrapper functions. For a different viewpoint, check out the menu functions from MSAU7032.DLL.

Running the Example

The menu state example form, frmModifyMenuItems, demonstrates many of the topics covered in the following sections. It shows how to retrieve a list of menu items; modify a menu item's text; disable, gray, and check a menu item; retrieve the state of a given menu item; and change a form's menu while the form is running. If you experiment with the form, you'll notice you don't get much control over the standard menu items. You can tell the form to make a specific item grayed, but once you pull down the menu, it still appears normal. This is just the way Access handles menus. You'll get a better response if you switch to the custom menu bar. Using the custom menu bar, you should be able to modify any menu item any way you wish. Figure 11.14 shows the sample form in action. In this case the user has disabled the File menu and has tried to pull down the File pull-down menu. Note that in this case the File menu is highlighted, but there's no pull-down portion. Because the item has been disabled, you can't pull down the menu.

Getting a Handle on Menus

As with almost every other data structure in Windows, to manipulate a menu you must have some way to address it. To do so, you must know the handle for that menu. A *handle* is simply a unique number (a Long Integer) you use to refer to a Windows object—in this case, a menu. In many ways a handle is analogous to a primary key of type Counter in an Access table. The number itself has no significance, but you can use its value in order to refer to a row in an Access table. In the same

FIGURE 11.14:

frmModifyMenuItems in action. The File menu has been disabled.

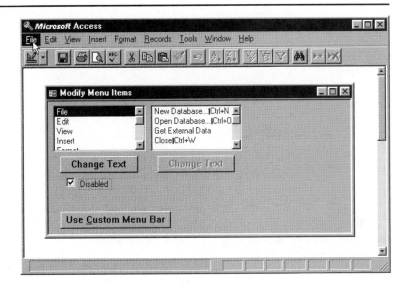

way, you don't really care what the value of the menu handle is; you just need to know that it refers to a particular menu.

You need a menu handle to use Windows API procedures with any menu. To retrieve a menu handle, you have three choices:

- You can call glrGetMenuBar(), which returns the handle of the main Access menu bar:

```
hMenuBar = glrGetMenuBar()
```

- You can call glrGetMenuHandles (which itself calls glrGetMenuBar()), which fills in the handle of the main menu bar in addition to the handle of a specific menu attached to the menu bar:

```
Dim hMenuBar as Long
Dim hMenu as Long
Dim lngMenu as Long

lngMenu = 1
' Get the handle to the menu bar and the 2nd menu
' (since the menus start counting at 0).
glrGetMenuHandles lngMenu, hMenuBar, hMenu
```

- You can call glrGetSystemMenu(), which returns a handle to a system menu:

```
' Retrieve a handle for the current form's system menu.
hSystemMenu = glrGetSystemMenu(Screen.ActiveForm.hWnd)
```

To obtain the handle to a specific menu, you need to call the API directly. The following example retrieves the menu handle of the menu attached to the fourth menu item on the menu referred to by hMenu:

```
newHandle = glr_apiGetSubMenu(hMenu, 3)
```

Once you know the handle for a specific menu, you can retrieve the handle to any menu attached to that menu by calling the glr_apiGetSubMenu() function.

Handling the System Menu

The system menu (sometimes called the control menu) is a standard piece of the Windows interface. Unless you specifically remove the system menu, it's always there, in the upper-left corner of each window. Figure 11.15 shows a standard form with its system menu opened.

The system menu is, for your purposes, a normal menu that just happens to be attached to each and every form. You can retrieve its menu handle by calling glrGetSystemMenu(). Once you have that handle, you can treat it just as you do any other menu, following the techniques outlined in the rest of this chapter. The major difference you'll find when dealing with the system menu is that Windows knows the default state of the menu. If you make changes to the system menu on any form (or on the main Access window itself), you can reset it to its original state by calling glrResetSystemMenu().

FIGURE 11.15:

Access forms use the standard
system menu.

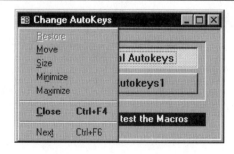

In addition, you most often refer to items on the system menu differently than you might on normal menus. When working with most menus, you refer to menu items by their position in the menu. Starting with 0, you count from the top of the pull-down menu (including the menu dividing lines) to refer to any specific menu item. On the system menu, however, you often refer to menu items by their action instead of their position. Since all the items on the system menu are standard, Windows provides built-in values that refer to their functionality as opposed to their position. See Listing 8.1 in Chapter 8 for more information on modifying the system menu.

The Grayed/Checked/ Disabled Status

A specific menu item may be in one of a number of different states at any given time. It can be disabled, in which case it looks normal but can't be selected. It can be grayed, in which case it both looks disabled and can't be chosen. Finally, Windows can place or remove a check mark next to the menu item. The functions presented in the following sections will help you control all these states.

Retrieving the Current Status

To retrieve the current state of a menu item, you can call one of seven functions from basMenuHandling. You decide which function to use based on the location of the item and which state you want to retrieve.

Retrieving Top-Level Information

The functions glrIsItemChecked(), glrIsItemDisabled(), and glrIsItemGrayed() all work the same way, returning a True/False value indicating whether or not the specified menu item is checked, disabled, or grayed:

```
fChecked = glrIsItemChecked(2, 6)
```

After this function call, fChecked will contain True or False, depending on the state of the seventh item on the third pull-down menu. (All menu items start counting at 0 and include any menu dividers in the count.)

Each of these functions uses the ordinal menu item number (the first parameter) to retrieve the handle for the correct menu. They use the second parameter to indicate the item on the menu in which you're interested. This makes these functions simple to use as long as you care only about items on the first level of menus.

Retrieving Information for Any Menu Item

To inquire about the state of any arbitrary menu item, on any level, you must supply the menu handle yourself. The module basMenuHandling also includes the functions you use to retrieve the handle, so this requirement shouldn't be a real drawback. You can use glrIsSubItemChecked(), glrIsSubItemDisabled(), and glrIs-SubItemGrayed() to check the state of any menu item. You could always use these functions in place of the corresponding glrIsItem...() functions, but the other functions are simpler to use when dealing with top-level menus.

These functions expect to receive a menu handle and an item number within the menu as parameters. Given those items, the functions can retrieve the information you need from the specific item on the specific menu.

Imagine you want to check the disabled state of the fourth menu item on the sub-menu attached to the third menu item on the menu attached to the second item on the menu bar. You could use code similar to this:

```
Dim hMenuBar As Long
Dim hMenu As Long
Dim hSubMenu As Long
Dim fIsDisabled As Boolean

' Get the handles to the menu bar and the 2nd pull-down menu
glrGetMenuHandles 1, hMenuBar, hMenu
' Get the handle to the third item on the 3rd submenu.
hSubMenu = glr_apiGetSubMenu(hMenu, 2)
' Get the information about the 4th menu item.
fIsDisabled = glrIsSubItemDisabled(hSubMenu, 3)
```

Retrieving Menu Bar Information

Unlike normal menu items, menu bar items can be neither checked nor grayed. The only allowed attribute change for them is to be disabled. To make it as simple as possible to inquire about this state, you can use the glrIsMenuBarItemDisabled()

function. It takes one parameter, the ordinal value of the menu item to check. To see whether the fourth menu bar item is disabled, you could use this code:

```
fIsDisabled = glrIsMenuBarItemDisabled(3)
```

One More Reminder

It never hurts to reiterate this issue: you really can't retrieve current information about the Access built-in menus using these tools (unless you go through the hoops mentioned above, pulling down the menus first). Since Access doesn't ensure that the menus are current until you pull them down, the states you retrieve with these function calls may or may not be current. For values that can change only because the user pulled down the menu and made a choice, you can safely retrieve the state. For values that might change because of something the user has done in the user interface, the menus are destined to be out of sync.

Setting the Status

Just as you can retrieve information about a menu's state, you can set the state of many menu items. You can set the grayed, enabled, and/or checked status of items on menus. You can set only the enabled status of menu bar items. (See the section "Using SetMenuItem to Control Menus" earlier in this chapter for information on using the SetMenuItem macro action to control your menu items' states.) Keep in mind that since Access controls its own menu items, your attempts to set the state of most of the Access menu items will appear to succeed, but your changes will be overridden when Access needs to redisplay the particular menu. You'll have more success setting the status of your own menu items.

To get a feel for how these status settings work, try out frmModifyMenuItems. It allows you to change the enabled state of menu bar items and the checked/grayed state of first-level menu items.

Setting Top-Level Menu Status

You can use the functions glrCheckMenuItem() and glrGrayMenuItem() to set the state of a menu item in a top-level menu. These functions return the previous state of the menu item. Here is an example using glrCheckMenuItem():

```
fChecked = glrCheckMenuItem(2, 6, True)
```

After this function call, fChecked will contain True or False, depending on the previous state of the seventh item on the third pull-down menu (all menu items start counting at 0), and the menu item will currently be checked.

Setting Any Level Menu Status

To set the state of any arbitrary menu item, on any level, you must supply the menu handle yourself. You can use glrCheckSubItem() and glrGraySubItem() to set the state of any arbitrary menu item. There's no reason not to use these functions in every case, in place of the corresponding glrCheckMenuItem() and glrGrayMenuItem() functions, but the other functions are simpler to use when you're dealing with top-level menu items.

Each of the two functions grlCheckSubItem() and glrGraySubItem() accepts a menu handle, an item number within that menu on which to act, and a logical value telling the function whether to set the state or clear it. You use the glrGetMenuHandles and glr_apiGetSubMenu() procedures to retrieve the appropriate menu handles before you can call these functions.

Imagine you want to set the fourth menu item on the submenu attached to the third menu item on the menu attached to the second item on the menu bar to be grayed out. You could use code similar to this:

```
Dim hMenuBar As Long
Dim hMenu As Long
Dim hSubMenu As Long
Dim fWasGrayed As Boolean

' Get the handles to the menu bar and the 2nd menu item.
glrGetMenuHandles 1, hMenuBar, hMenu
' Get the handle to the third item on the 3rd submenu.
hSubMenu = glr_apiGetSubMenu(hMenu, 2)
' Get the state of the 4th menu item.
fWasGrayed = glrGraySubItem(hSubMenu, 3, True)
```

Setting the Menu Bar Status

Although you can theoretically disable menu items, your users won't be very happy if you do. Your applications will be much clearer if you gray out items instead. There's little more frustrating than clicking a menu item that looks perfectly normal but does nothing. On the menu bar itself, you have no choice. Windows doesn't allow you to gray out items there, so your only choice is to disable items.

This is why we've included a function, glrEnableMenuBarItem(), that works on menu bar items but have not included a corresponding function for other menu items.

To use the glrEnableMenuBarItem() function, pass it two pieces of information: the menu item number (starting with 0) and a logical value indicating whether to enable (True) or disable (False) the menu item. For example, to disable the File menu item while a form is active, you would use this:

```
fSuccess = glrEnableMenuBarItem(0, False)
```

When you've disabled a menu bar item, it looks normal until you click it. At that point Access highlights the menu bar item, but it doesn't drop down the attached menu. You've effectively blocked the user from choosing that menu item. Figure 11.14, presented earlier in this chapter, shows frmModifyMenuItems after it has just disabled the File menu and you've attempted to choose that menu item.

Retrieving Menu States

All the functions in basMenuHandling that retrieve information about a specific menu item's state go through a single utility function, GetSpecificItemState() (see Listing 11.4). The function is very simple. It just calls the Windows API function GetMenuState(), passing in the menu handle and the position of the menu item on the menu in which you're interested.

GetMenuState() (aliased here as glr_apiGetMenuState()) returns a Long Integer, with different pieces of information coded into each of its 32 bits. To retrieve just one piece of information, you can perform a bitwise And of the returned value with a predefined constant. (In this case the calling function passes that constant down to GetSpecificItemState().) Perform the bitwise comparison using the following syntax:

fTrueOrFalse = ((*CodedLongInteger* And *Constant*) = *Constant*)

If the bit of interest is set (equal to 1), fTrueOrFalse will be nonzero. In GetSpecificItemState() it's the last line that does this test for you. The function returns True if the bitwise comparison returns a nonzero value and False otherwise. (For more background on using bitwise operators, see the section "Changing the Window Style" in Chapter 8. That section uses bitwise operations to perform a similar task: modifying window styles.)

Listing 11.4

```
Private Function GetSpecificItemState(hMenu As Long, _
 lngItem As Long, lngFlag As Long)

    Dim lngTemp As Long

    lngTemp = glr_apiGetMenuState(hMenu, lngItem, _
     glrcMF_BYPOSITION)
    GetSpecificItemState = ((lngTemp And lngFlag) = lngFlag)
End Function
```

Understanding the Low-Level Activity

As part of our interface between your application and the Windows API functions that deal with menus, we've provided functions to set the checked and/or grayed status of any menu item. The functions are glrCheckMenuItem(), glrCheckSub-MenuItem(), glrGrayMenuItem(), and glrGraySubMenuItem(). All four functions work in basically the same manner. Windows provides a function to set or clear the check (CheckMenuItem()) and a function to gray or enable a menu item (Enable-MenuItem()). In either case the function accepts a handle to a menu, an ordinal number representing the position of the item in question on that menu, and a flag telling Windows what action to take. The choice of whether you call glrCheck-MenuItem() or glrCheckSubMenuItem() is dictated by whether or not you wish to find the menu handle yourself. If you call glrCheckMenuItem() or glrGray-MenuItem(), the function finds the menu handle but can do so only for top-level menus. If you call glrCheckSubMenuItem() or glrGraySubMenuItem(), you can work with any menu item on any menu, but you'll need to find the menu handle yourself, using the glr_apiGetSubMenu() function.

To illustrate, look at the two functions glrGrayMenuItem() and glrGraySub-MenuItem() in Listing 11.5. Notice that the only difference between them is that glrGrayMenuItem() calls glrGetMenuHandles() first, to retrieve the handle to the requested menu. From that point on, they do the exact same work. (The corresponding functions, glrCheckMenuItem() and glrCheckSubMenuItem(), work in exactly the same manner.)

Both functions call glr_apiEnableMenuItem() to gray or enable a menu item. This function takes the menu handle, the item number on that menu, and a flag telling the function what to do. In this case you pass to it either the glrcMF_GRAYED or the glrcMF_ENABLED constant (defined by the Windows API). In addition, you need to tell Windows whether you're referring to the menu item by position or by menu ID. Every menu item has a menu ID associated with it, assigned at the time the program is written. When you're referring to menu items from code, you can either refer to them by their position (in which case the API call must know the exact menu handle for the menu that contains the item) or by command (in which case Windows searches the menu whose handle you pass to the API call and descends into all subordinate menus).

For your purposes, since you have no way of knowing the menu IDs, you'll almost always want to refer to menu items by position. To tell that to Windows, you add in the glrcMF_BYPOSITION constant every time you're telling Windows what to do with your menu items. If you call our middle-level functions in basMenuHandling, you won't have to worry about this issue. If you modify those functions or need to add some more of your own, it will be a concern. If you're working with the system menu, by the way, you'll want to use the glrcMF_BYCOMMAND flag since in that case you do know the menu IDs. (See the section "Disabling the Close Menu Item" in Chapter 8 for more information.)

Finally, each of the low-level menu-state functions returns the previous state of the menu item. That is, if you're attempting to set an item to gray, glrGrayMenuItem() will return True if it was previously grayed or False if it wasn't. Because the API function EnableMenuItem() returns the previous status of the menu item, it's a simple task to check the particular bit in the status that you care about (see the preceding section) and return True or False.

Listing 11.5

```
Public Function glrGrayMenuItem(lngMenu As Long, _
  lngItem As Long, fDisableIt As Boolean) As Boolean

    ' Gray/UnGray a user-defined menu item
    ' (this won't work with Access-controlled menu items!)
    Dim lngOldState As Long
    Dim hMenu As Long
    Dim hMenuBar As Long
```

```
      glrGetMenuHandles lngMenu, hMenuBar, hMenu
      lngOldState = glr_apiEnableMenuItem(hMenu, lngItem, _
       IIf(fDisableIt, glrcMF_GRAYED, glrcMF_ENABLED) _
       Or glrcMF_BYPOSITION)
      glrGrayMenuItem = Not ((lngOldState And _
       glrcMF_GRAYED) = glrcMF_GRAYED)
End Function

Public Function glrGraySubMenuItem(hMenu As Long, _
 lngItem As Long, fDisableIt As Boolean) As Boolean

      ' Gray/UnGray a user-defined menu item
      ' (this won't work with Access-controlled menu items!)
      Dim lngOldState As Long

      lngOldState = glr_apiEnableMenuItem(hMenu, lngItem, _
       IIf(fDisableIt, glrcMF_GRAYED, glrcMF_ENABLED) _
        Or glrcMF_BYPOSITION)
      glrGraySubMenuItem = Not ((lngOldState And _
       glrcMF_GRAYED) = glrcMF_GRAYED)
End Function
```

Retrieving or Modifying Menu Text

In addition to being able to retrieve or modify the state of any menu item, you can retrieve or modify the actual text of any menu item. Access uses this trick when it changes the Edit ➤ Undo menu item to Can't Undo when there's nothing to undo. You can use this same principle in your own applications, changing menu items to match the current situation. In basMenuHandling, we've included functions to retrieve a single menu item (glrGetMenuBarText() and glrGetMenuText()), to retrieve all the menu text in a specific menu into an array of strings (glrGetMenuBarTitles() and glrGetMenuTitles()), and to set a specific menu item's text (glrSetMenuBarText() and glrSetMenuText()).

Retrieving Menu Item Text

To retrieve a single menu item's text, you can call glrGetMenuBarText(), passing it an ordinal number, starting with 0, that represents the position of the item on the menu bar. Or you can call glrGetMenuText(), passing it a menu handle for the menu in question and the ordinal position of the menu item whose text you want to retrieve. For example, the following code retrieves the text from the third item on the second menu hanging off the menu bar:

```
Dim hMenuBar As Long
Dim hMenu As Long
Dim strText As String

glrGetMenuHandles 1, hMenuBar, hMenu
strText = glrGetMenuText(hMenu, 2)
```

Retrieving the Number of Menu Items

To retrieve the number of menu items, you can call the Windows API function glr_apiGetMenuItemCount(), passing to it the handle of the menu. All the API wrapper functions in this chapter assume you know how many menu items there are and won't pass a value that's outside the reasonable range. If you aren't sure, check first. The following code retrieves the number of menu items in the third menu and prints out their text:

```
Dim hMenuBar As Long
Dim hMenu As Long
Dim lngCount As Long
Dim lngI As Long

glrGetMenuHandles 2, hMenuBar, hMenu
lngCount = glr_apiGetMenuItemCount(hMenu)
For lngI = 0 To lngCount - 1
     Debug.Print glrGetMenuText(hMenu, lngI)
Next lngI
```

Retrieving All the Text from a Menu

Sometimes you want to retrieve all the items from a menu in one function call. Although the Windows API doesn't support this directly, we've provided two functions to make it simple for you. You can call glrGetMenuBarTitles() or glrGetMenuTitles() to fill an array with all the items on a specific menu. Your only obligation is to provide a dynamic array for the function to resize and fill in.

For example, the following code retrieves all the items from the File menu and prints them to the Debug window.

```
Dim astrMenuItems() as String
Dim hMenuBar As Long
Dim hMenu As Long
Dim intCount As Integer
Dim intI As Integer

glrGetMenuHandles 0, hMenuBar, hMenu
intCount = glrGetMenuTitles(hMenu, astrMenuItems())
For intI = 0 To intCount - 1
    Debug.Print astrMenuItems(intI)
Next intI
```

The sample form, frmModifyMenuItems, uses this technique to show all the menu items in a list box.

Changing Menu Item Text

Changing the text of a menu item is no more difficult than retrieving it. You can call glrSetMenuBarText(), passing to it the position to change and the new text, to change an item on the menu bar. Or you can call glrSetMenuText(), passing in a menu handle, the position of the menu item you want changed, and the new text. In either case Windows takes care of the details, and you end up with a changed menu item. If you're working with the standard Access menus, you'll want to use one of the functions in the preceding sections to retrieve the menu items before you change them so you can change them back when you're done. Remember that Access maintains only one copy of each of its menu bars and associated menu items, so if you change the text of an item on the Forms menu bar, every other form (unless it has its own menu bar defined) will also see the same change. Even after your application is finished, any other application opening a form will see your changes. So, as in so many other areas of programming, *if you change a menu item, put it back the way it was.*

The following code retrieves the text from the fourth item on the Edit menu (Paste Special) and replaces it with "Glue":

```
Dim hMenuBar As Long
Dim hMenu As Long
```

```
' Get the menu handle for the Edit menu.
glrGetMenuHandles 1, hMenuBar, hMenu
' Return the previous text in the sixth slot on the Edit menu,
' and set the text to be "Glue"
Debug.Print glrSetMenuText(hMenu, 6, "Glue")
```

The sample form, frmModifyMenuItems, uses this same method when it allows you to modify menu items. Figure 11.16 shows the menus altered as in the previous example. (Because menu items start numbering at 0 and skip dividers, the fifth menu item in Figure 11.16 has an ordinal position number of 6.)

FIGURE 11.16:

The text of the Paste Special menu item on the Edit menu has been changed to "Glue".

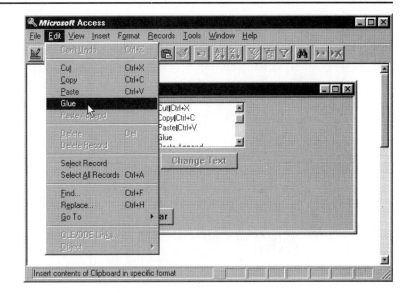

NOTE

You won't be able to use this method to alter the text of user-defined menu items. Access must correlate the menu text with matching macro items, and altering the menu text will confuse Access. If you must change the text of user-defined menu items, your best bet is to create multiple items, one for each caption you require, and remove and reinsert the various items, using the methods described in the next section, "Removing Menu Items."

739

Removing Menu Items

Many Access applications' menuing systems consist mainly of the standard Access menus with some items removed. Even removing a single menu item, using the standard Access menu macros, requires you to create the full Access menuing system in macros, minus the single item you don't want on your menus. You can use the functions from basMenuHandling, glrRemoveMenuBarItem() and glrRemove-MenuItem(), to remove menu items one by one, without going through all the work of maintaining extra macros.

Preserving Information

Every menu item carries around with it information about what to do when you select that item. If choosing the item causes another menu to be displayed, the item you chose stores the handle for that menu. If choosing the item causes an action to occur, the item stores an action ID. (The program you're running knows what to do with that action ID. This explains why you can't add a completely new menu item from within your running Access application. Access wouldn't have any idea what to do when you chose the item.) When you remove a menu item, it's up to you to preserve those pieces of information so you can put them back when you restore the menu item. The functions in basMenuHandling help you with this process.

Calling the Functions

To remove a menu item on the menu bar, you call glrRemoveMenuBarItem(). You pass it three parameters: the item number to remove, a variable in which to store the handle to the submenu attached to it, and a variable to hold the text of the item. The function fills in the last two parameters, so your code can preserve them and later restore them. For example, the following code removes the Edit menu from the Access menu bar:

```
Dim hMenu As Long
Dim strMenuText As String
Dim fSuccess As Boolean

fSuccess = glrRemoveMenuBarItem(1, hMenu, strMenuText)
MsgBox "You removed the '" & strMenuText & _
  "' menu (its submenu handle was: " & hMenu & ")"
```

To call glrRemoveMenuItem() you must also pass in the handle to a menu as the first parameter. In addition, since a menu item might have either an action ID or a menu handle (but not both), you pass in a variable for each. On return, one of the parameters will contain 0 and one will contain a useful value. For example, to remove the Undo item on the Edit menu, you could use this code:

```
Dim hMenu As Long
Dim hMenuBar As Long
Dim hSubMenu As Long
Dim lngActionID As Long
Dim strMenuText As String
Dim fSuccess As Boolean
Dim strText As String

' Get a handle to the Edit menu.
glrGetMenuHandles 1, hMenuBar, hMenu
' Remove the first item.
fSuccess = glrRemoveMenuItem(hMenu, 0, lngActionID, _
 hSubMenu, strMenuText)
strText = "You removed the '" & strMenuText & "' menu "
If lngActionID > 0 Then
    strText = strText & "(its action ID was: " & _
      lngActionID & ")"
Else
    strText = strText & "(its handle was: " & hMenu & ")"
End If
MsgBox strText
```

Later, when you needed to restore the menu item, you could use the values stored in lngActionID, hSubMenu, and strMenuText to set everything back the way it was originally.

The Good, the Bad, and the Ugly–Removing Menu Items

The good part of removing menus in code (rather than by creating an entire set of macros to replace part of the standard Access menuing scheme) is that it requires a lot less overhead both in preparation and in terms of objects your application must carry around. Rather than have one macro for each menu bar, you can use a single module to manipulate your menus directly. In addition, Access appears to be able to use DoMenuItem to access the menu items you've removed, even though they're no longer visible. On the other hand, using SendKeys to access the menu items will no longer work. (This isn't a terrible loss, since you ought to avoid using SendKeys to access menu items at all costs. It makes your code nearly impossible to read and, even worse, unless you're just using SendKeys to send arrow keys, makes it impossible to run in versions of Access translated to other languages.)

The bad part of removing menus in code is that you're ultimately responsible for undoing everything you do. If you create menus using macros, Access takes care of all the details for you. If you remove a top-level menu item, for example, it's up to your application to put it back when it's done. Generally, you'll want to remove menu items in the Activate event and replace them in the Deactivate event for forms. This way you're guaranteed that whenever focus moves away from the particular form, the menus revert to their normal state.

The ugly part of removing menus in code is that Access doesn't have a clue as to what you're doing behind its back. You're treading on very thin ice when you change Access' menu structure using Windows API calls. Be very careful, and test your work strenuously before handing it out to end users. Make sure all the remaining menus work correctly and any DoMenuItem calls you make from your code still work as designed.

NOTE Access maintains only a single copy of its own menu bars. That is, each different state in Access has its own menu bar and only one copy of that menu bar. If your code changes an Access menu bar, every other instance in Access that shares that menu bar sees the change, as well. For instance, if you remove a menu item from a running form's menu bar, any other running form that doesn't maintain its own menu bar will see the same change. Therefore, if your code makes changes to any built-in menu bar, you absolutely must undo your changes, normally in the form's Deactivate event procedure. Then reset the changes in the form's Activate event procedure.

As you remove items from menu bars, the ordinal position value of the following menu items moves up to fill the space you just created. Therefore, if you're deleting more than one menu item, you may be better served by deleting from the bottom up. Otherwise, as you delete, the positions of the items you need to delete later change. This can make the process somewhat confusing (to say the least). And remember: if you delete a menu item, you need to put it back later.

Inserting Menu Items

Although you can insert your own menu items into the Access menu bars at run time, doing so is generally a waste of time. Since you have no way to attach an action ID to the new menu that means anything to Access, any newly created menu items wouldn't be able to actually do anything. The only useful purpose we can find for inserting new menu items is to replace menu items you've previously removed. If you store away the text, the ID, and/or the submenu handle for a given menu item, you can easily place that menu item back where it came from on the menus. In fact, this action is imperative if you intend to allow your users to go back to the standard Access menus after you've modified any of those menu bars. It would be rude, indeed, to modify the Access menu bars and leave them modified when your application exits.

We've provided two functions to handle inserting menu items: glrInsert-MenuBarItem() and glrInsertMenuItem(). To insert an item into the menu bar, use glrInsertMenuBarItem(), passing to it the position in which to insert the item, the handle to the pull-down menu for this item, and the text to use. Remember that every item on the menu bar must drop down a menu when it's selected, so you need to supply a menu handle. The following code demonstrates how you might use this function. It removes the Edit menu and later restores it:

```
Dim hMenu As Long
Dim hMenuBar As Long
Dim strMenuText As String
Dim fSuccess As Boolean
```

```
' Fill in hMenu and strMenuText
fSuccess = glrRemoveMenuBarItem(1, hMenu, strMenuText)
' Now the menu's gone. Do whatever your application requires
' here.
'
'
' Now put the menu back.
fSuccess = glrInsertMenubarItem(1, hMenu, strMenuText)
```

To insert a menu item on a pull-down menu, you must provide the same information as before, but now you also need to provide an action ID, which might be 0 (if the menu item has a submenu attached). You also need to supply the handle to the menu on which the item is to be inserted. The following code removes the Toolbars item from the View menu (when you have a form loaded) and later restores it. In this case the hSubMenu variable will always be 0, since this particular item has an action ID, not a submenu.

```
Dim hMenuBar As Long
Dim hMenu As Long
Dim hSubMenu As Long
Dim lngActionID as Long
Dim strMenuText As String
Dim fSuccess As Boolean

' Get a handle to the View menu.
glrGetMenuHandles 2, hMenuBar, hMenu
' Remove the 6th item (Toolbars) from the View menu.
fSuccess = glrRemoveMenuItem(hMenu, 5, lngActionID, _
 hSubMenu, strMenuText)
' Now the menu item's gone. Do whatever your application
' requires here.
'
'
' Now put the menu back.
fSuccess = glrInsertMenuItem(hMenu, 5, lngActionID, _
 hSubMenu, strMenuText)
```

Highlighting a Menu Bar Item

Although we haven't found a good use for this functionality, Windows does provide a method of highlighting a particular menu bar item. Since it's your imagination doing the driving here, we've included a function you can call that highlights an item on the menu bar. The example form frmTestPopup demonstrates this functionality.

To use the function glrHiliteMenuBarItem(), you need only pass to it a menu bar item number and a logical value indicating whether to turn the highlight on or off. For example, the following code highlights the Edit menu bar item, allows you to take some actions, and then turns off the highlight:

```
Dim fSuccess As Boolean

fSuccess = glrHiliteMenuBarItem(1, True)
'
' Do whatever your application requires here.
'
' Then turn off the highlight.
fSuccess = glrHiliteMenuBarItem(1, False)
```

Summary

Although you won't be using macros for a large part of your applications, they do have their uses. Since you must use macros to create menus and to trap global keystrokes, they do have their place in your database. They can't, however, replace carefully written, error-trapped VBA code.

In addition, the standard Access menu engine gives you very little control over your menus. We've presented a number of uses for the Windows API in terms of manipulating, modifying, and controlling your user-defined menus. Armed with the routines covered in this chapter, you should be able to do most of what you need to do with menus. You can

- Remove and insert menu items

- Gray and ungray menu items

- Disable and reenable menu items

- Change the text of menu items

- Retrieve the number of menu items

- Retrieve an array filled with menu text

Access toolbars provide a nice medium for simplifying your applications, although their lack of programmatic control can make them difficult to manage. If you don't need to modify or move them under program control or add your own button images, Access provides all the tools you need.

Throughout this part of the book, we've focused on the user-interface elements in Access—controls, forms, reports, and user-interface macros. Armed with your basic knowledge and the tricks you've found here, you should be set to create some inventive interfaces for your applications.

PART IV

Multiuser Issues

CHAPTER

TWELVE

Developing Multiuser
Applications

- Understanding page locking

- Contrasting optimistic and pessimistic locking

- Splitting a database to improve performance

- Handling multiuser errors with the Form Error event

- Determining who's logged on to a database

- Managing linked tables

Developing Access applications for multiuser systems requires extra planning and a shift from single-user application thinking, but it's not especially difficult to learn. In this chapter we explore the behavior of networked applications in Access. We don't cover network hardware or operating systems, but the good news is that you don't need to become a network administrator or a specialist in cabling and hubs to develop multiuser applications. Let your network administrator or hardware specialist worry about those aspects. (Of course, it can't hurt to communicate with this person and learn a bit about network hardware and operating systems over time.) We do, however, discuss how to *plan* and *think* multiuser and how to avoid the common pitfalls of multiuser development.

> **NOTE**
>
> There are three sample databases for Chapter 12 and one supporting .DLL file. CH12APP.MDB is the "application" database—it contains all the user interface objects and supporting code, including code that manages links to CH12DAT.MDB. CH12DAT.MDB is the "data" database—it contains only the tables. CH12AUTO.MDB contains the custom AutoNumber table discussed in the section "Using a Custom AutoNumber Routine." The frmViewUsers form in CH12APP.MDB calls the MSLDBUSR.DLL file, which can also be found on the companion CD in the \Other\Msft\Jetlock folder. Make sure you copy this file to your \Windows\System folder prior to using this form.

Setup on a Network

Before installing Access on a network, you need to decide whether Access will be installed only on the file server or on each workstation.

The first option, installing a single copy of Access on the file server, has several advantages:

- The network administrator has central control of the executables, minimizing maintenance chores.

- Hard-disk-space usage is kept to a minimum on workstations.

- Users with diskless workstations can run Access.

This scenario also has several disadvantages:

- Each time a workstation runs Access, the Access .EXE, DLLs, and other files are sent over the network cable to each workstation. Since Access is much more than a single executable (it may call over 20 DLLs during execution, swapping portions of itself to and from memory), network traffic will be very high.

- Performance can vary from acceptable to abysmal.

A better alternative is to install a copy of Access on each workstation on the network. The major advantage of this scenario is performance. Access startup and execution will be significantly faster. Of course, this scenario does carry with it a disadvantage when compared with the file server–only scenario: you (or the network administrator) will have to maintain multiple copies of Access rather than just one. Still, we feel strongly that any added maintenance burden under this scenario is greatly overshadowed by the substantial increase in performance.

TIP

Access provides an option for installing a special administrator version on the file server you can use to install individual copies of Access on each workstation. With this install technique, you need to use the disks or CD only once, and the installation process is much faster. (For more information on using the administrator setup options, see the NETWORK.TXT file on disk 1 of the Access disks or in the root directory of the Office Professional CD.)

Access Locking and Novell NetWare 3.11

When using data from a server, Access uses the locking facilities the server's operating system provides. There is a bug in NetWare 3.11 TTS (Transaction Tracking System) that can result in a server crash when you run certain Access queries or otherwise request a large number of locks. Each page of records Access locks uses one or more locks from the NetWare TTS. The defaults in NetWare allow a single workstation to have 500 locks at any given time. This results in a limit of 1MB of data that Access can deal with in a single transaction. Since Access tries to lock every record involved in either an update or a delete query before actually carrying out the update or delete, it is quite possible to bump into this limit on a moderately large database.

The problem is that NetWare 3.11 reacts rather poorly to having its lock limit exceeded. It appears to count a lock violation every time it looks at the connection in question, which is still trying to lock more records. Eventually (in about 3–5 minutes) some internal table overflows and the entire server goes down, with a frightening message that instructs you to cycle the power. There are two things you can do if this happens to you. The first is to increase the number of locks available, and the second is to apply the NetWare patch that prevents the abend of the server. (Very large queries can still fail, but at least the server won't fail along with them.) To increase the number of locks available, enter the following commands at the file server console or in your AUTOEXEC.NCF file:

```
set maximum record locks per connection = 10000
set maximum record locks = 200000
```

The first parameter is the most locks any single connection can have, and the second is the most the entire server can keep track of. These values (10,000 and 200,000) are the maximums NetWare 3.11 can accommodate. If you set the maximum record locks per connection to 10,000, Access can handle a transaction up to 20MB. To fix the server abend problem, you need to download the latest NetWare 3.11 patch file. You can find it on CompuServe, in the

NOVFILES section. You will need to load two of the NLMs from this file, either directly from the server console or in your AUTOEXEC.NCF file:

```
load patchman.nlm
load ttsfix.nlm
```

This problem is specific to NetWare version 3.11 and has been fixed in later versions of NetWare.

Multiuser Settings

Several options and settings in Access affect how your applications behave in a multiuser environment, as described in the following sections.

Database Open Modes

You can affect the way a database is opened in Access in three ways:

- When you start Access, you can include a database name on the command line and either the /Excl or /Ro parameter to open that database in exclusive or read-only mode, respectively.

- You can check or uncheck the Exclusive check box or use the Open Read Only property when using the File ➤ Open Database dialog.

- You can change the default database open mode using the Tools ➤ Options command by changing the Default Open Mode setting on the Advanced tab of the Options dialog. The setting can be Exclusive for single-user access or Shared for multiuser access to the database.

TIP   You can prevent a user from opening a database in exclusive mode by using the Tools ➤ Security ➤ User and Group Permissions command to uncheck the OpenExclusive permission of the database.

The Refresh Interval

Using the Tools ➤ Options command, you can also set the refresh interval. Access automatically checks the recordsets of open forms and datasheets to see whether changes have occurred at the frequency set by the refresh interval. The default refresh interval is 60 seconds, which may be too long for some applications. If you set the refresh interval to too small a value, however, you may create excessive network traffic. Finding the proper setting for your application may require some experimentation. In general, the smaller the network, the smaller you can set the refresh interval without adverse effect.

You can override the default refresh interval in your applications by using the Refresh method, the Requery method, or the Requery action. Record *refreshes*—either automatic refreshes by Access using the refresh interval or manual refreshes using the Refresh method—are faster than requeries. New records added by other users, however, appear only during a requery, and records deleted by other users vanish from your copy only after a requery. (All the values in the fields of deleted records, however, are replaced with the string "#DELETED" when the record is refreshed.)

Given the choice, you should use the Requery *method* rather than the almost equivalent Requery *action.* The method reruns the query that's already in memory, while the action reloads it from disk.

> **TIP**
>
> Even if you set the refresh interval to a long value, Access automatically refreshes the current record whenever a user attempts to edit it. The benefit of a shorter refresh interval lies chiefly in providing quicker visual feedback that someone else has locked or changed a record while you are viewing it.

Locking Options

To provide concurrent access to records by multiple users, Access locks records. Unlike some other databases, however, Access doesn't lock individual records; instead it locks a 2K (2048 bytes) page of records. The advantage of page locking is that there's less overhead and thus generally better performance over true record locking. Unfortunately, this also means that Access usually locks more records than you would like. This is especially an issue when you employ pessimistic locking, since this type of record locking allows users to keep records locked for long periods of time.

In a multiuser environment, you can open recordsets in one of three modes:

- **No Locks:** This is often called *optimistic locking* and is the default setting. With the No Locks setting, the page of records that contains the currently edited record is locked only during the instant when the record is being saved, not during the editing process. This allows for concurrent editing of records with fewer locking conflicts.

- **Edited Record**: As soon as a user begins to edit a record, the page containing the currently edited record is locked until the changes are saved. This is known as *pessimistic locking*.

- **All Records:** This setting causes all the records in the entire recordset to be locked. You won't find this option very useful except when doing batch updates or performing administrative maintenance on tables.

You can adjust locking options for database objects that manipulate recordsets. Table 12.1 shows which locking options (No Locks, Edited Record, or All Records) are available for each database object. The point at which records are actually locked is also shown in Table 12.1. The default RecordLocks setting for most of these objects is taken from the Default Record Locking option established through the Tools ➤ Options dialog.

TABLE 12.1: Available RecordLocks Settings for Various Access Objects

Access Object	No Locks	Edited Record	All Records	Default	When Records Are Locked
Table datasheets	Yes[1]	Yes[1]	Yes[1]	DRL	Datasheet editing
Select query datasheets	Yes	Yes	Yes	DRL	Datasheet editing
Crosstab query datasheets	Yes	Yes	Yes	DRL	Query execution
Union query datasheets	Yes	Yes	Yes	DRL	Query execution
Update and delete queries	No	Yes	Yes	DRL	Query execution
Make-table and append queries	No	Yes	Yes	DRL	Query execution[2]

TABLE 12.1: Available RecordLocks Settings for Various Access Objects (continued)

Access Object	No Locks	Edited Record	All Records	Default	When Records Are Locked
Data definition queries	No	No	Yes	All Records[3]	Query execution
Forms	Yes	Yes	Yes	DRL	Form and datasheet modes
Reports	Yes	No	Yes	DRL	Report execution, preview, and printing
OpenRecordset	Yes	Yes	Yes	Edited Record[4]	Between Edit and Update methods

Yes = available option

No = option not available for this object

DRL = Default Record Locking option setting for the database

[1]There is no RecordLocks property for table datasheets. Datasheets use the Default Record Locking option setting for the database.

[2]For make-table and append queries, the target tables are locked.

[3]There is no RecordLocks property for data definition queries. Access locks the entire table.

[4]Changed using the LockEdits property of recordsets. Edited Record is the default unless you use the dbDenyWrite or dbDenyRead option of the OpenRecordset method, in which case the entire table is locked.

The Default Record Locking option is ignored when you use code to open recordsets using the OpenRecordset method. In this case Access employs pessimistic locking (Edited Record) unless you either set the option of the OpenRecordset method to dbDenyWrite or dbDenyRead or alter the LockEdits property. You use the dbDenyWrite option to lock all records for updates. You can go one step further and deny write *and* read access to table-type recordsets (only) by using the more restrictive dbDenyRead option. (These options apply only to native Access tables.)

NOTE No record locking is performed for snapshot-type recordsets, since they are read-only.

If you haven't used either the dbDenyWrite or dbDenyRead constant when opening the recordset, you can use the LockEdits property of recordsets to specify the type of locking to be used. The default of True uses pessimistic (Edited Record) locking. You can force optimistic (No Locks) record locking by setting this property to False.

For example, the following piece of code opens a recordset against the tblCustomer table using pessimistic locking:

```
Set rstPessimistic = db.OpenRecordset("tblCustomer")
' This recordset will employ pessimistic locking
With rstPessimistic
    ' This next line isn't really needed
    ' since LockEdits defaults to True
    .LockEdits = True

    .MoveFirst
    ' This next statement will produce Error 3260
    ' if another user has locked this page of records.
    .Edit
        '   ...
        ' This record will be locked
        ' for every statement between
        ' the Edit and Update methods
        '   ...
        !ZipCode = !ZipCode + 1
    .Update

    .Close
End With
```

Similarly, the next piece of code also opens a recordset against the tblCustomer table, this time using optimistic locking:

```
Set rstOptimistic = db.OpenRecordset("tblCustomer")
' This recordset will employ optimistic locking
With rstOptimistic
    .LockEdits = False

    .MoveFirst
    .Edit
        '   ...
        ' This record will not be locked
        ' until the Update method is executed.
        '   ...
```

```
     !ZipCode = !ZipCode - 1
  ' This next statement will produce Error 3197
  ' if another user has saved changes to this
  ' record since the Edit method was executed.
  .Update

  .Close
End With
```

Choosing a Locking Strategy

The *advantages* of *pessimistic* locking are

- It is simple for the developer.
- It prevents users from overwriting each other's work.
- It may be less confusing to the user than optimistic locking.

The *disadvantages* of *pessimistic* locking are

- It will usually lock multiple records. (How many depends on the size of the records.)
- Concurrency—the ability of multiple users to have simultaneous (concurrent) access to records—is worse than for optimistic locking because locks are held for longer time periods.

Because Access locks pages of records, optimistic locking is usually the better choice. The *advantages* of *optimistic* locking are

- It is simple to use.
- It provides better concurrency than pessimistic locking.
- It is less likely to lock other users out of editing multiple records.

The *disadvantages* of using *optimistic* locking are

- It may be confusing to the user when there's a write conflict.
- Users can overwrite each other's edits.

Unless you have a compelling reason to use pessimistic locking, we strongly recommend you consider optimistic locking. In most applications you don't want your users prevented from being able to edit records for potentially long periods of time.

NOTE   Several changes have been made to the Jet engine (Jet 3.0) for Access 95 that improve multiuser performance and reduce locking problems. The most important change is that Jet will no longer prevent users from adding new records when the last page of records in a table has been locked. (See Chapter 4 for more details on this and other Jet 3.0 enhancements.)

In some applications you may need to use both strategies on different forms. For example, in an inventory application you must ensure that the QuantityOnHand column is pessimistically locked so that salespeople don't try to post a sale beyond QOH without invoking back-order processing. On the other hand, you might use optimistic locking on a vendor address form, since it's unlikely that two change-of-address requests for the same vendor will be given to two different users for posting at the same time.

Default Optimistic Locking Behavior

As already mentioned, the main problem with optimistic locking is the potential for write conflicts. A *write conflict* occurs when:

1. A user begins to edit a record.

2. A second user saves changes to the record.

3. The first user then attempts to save his/her changes.

When a write conflict occurs in bound forms, Access displays the Write Conflict dialog, as shown in Figure 12.1 for the frmCustomerOptimistic1 sample form in the CH12APP.MDB database.

FIGURE 12.1:

FIGURE 12.1:

Under optimistic locking, users may
encounter the Write Conflict dialog
when attempting to save a record
that has been changed by another
user.

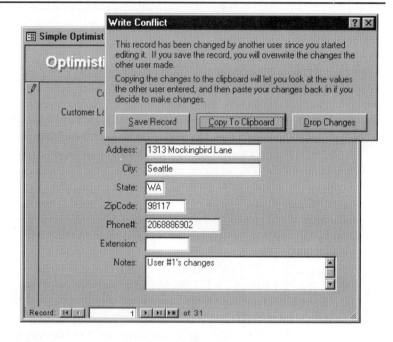

This dialog offers the user three options:

- **Save Record:** If the user selects this option, changes the user makes will overwrite changes made by the other user. In most cases a user should not use
  this option; it blindly discards the other user's changes.

- **Copy to Clipboard:** This option copies the user's changes to the clipboard
  and refreshes the record with the other user's changes. This option is a good
  choice for the sophisticated user but requires too much understanding for
  the naive user. If you used this option in Access 2.0, you'll be happy to know
  that the bug that prevented formatted data from being pasted back to the
  form has been fixed in Access 95.

- **Drop Changes:** If the user selects this option, his or her changes are dropped
  and the record is refreshed with the other user's changes.

> **WARNING**
>
> A bug in Access 95 (it was also in Access 2) occurs when you have a one-to-many relationship defined for two tables *without* cascading updates turned on and you choose Save Record in the Write Conflict dialog for a record on the "one" side of the relationship. You will get a spurious referential integrity violation message even if you have not updated the primary key value (see Figure 12.2). (This message occurs because Access blindly copies values for all your fields over the values that have been saved by the other user, without bothering to check whether each field was actually changed. Since the fields include the primary key field, Jet thinks the primary key value has changed and displays the spurious error message.)

FIGURE 12.2:
This spurious error message can occur when you choose Save Record from the Write Conflict dialog.

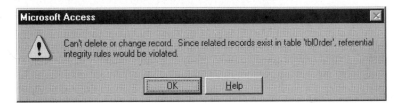

Optimistic Locking with Custom Error Handling

With the introduction of Access 95, Microsoft has corrected a major design flaw that was present in prior versions of Access: the inability to trap and handle locking errors when using bound forms. Using the improved Form Error event, you can now intercept write conflict errors and handle them using VBA code by creating an Error event procedure.

Access passes to your event procedure the DataErr and Response parameters. The two most common optimistic locking DataErr values are described in Table 12.2.

Error 7787 is the standard Write Conflict dialog error. It occurs when a user attempts to *save changes* to a record that has changed. Error 7878 occurs when a user

TABLE 12.2: Optimistic Locking Errors in Forms

Error Number	Access Error Message	Comment
7787	Write Conflict: This record has been changed by another user since you started editing it...	A second user saved changes while the first user was editing the record
7878	The data has been changed...	A second user saved changes while the first user was viewing the record

begins to edit a record that has changed; this error is more likely to occur with long refresh intervals.

> **NOTE**
>
> The Error event (which was discussed in Chapter 8) is triggered anytime a data access error is generated, so any event procedure you create must also be prepared to deal with non-locking data access errors.

You can set the Response parameter to one of two built-in constants:

Response	When Used
acDataErrContinue	To tell Access to continue without displaying the error message; in the case of optimistic errors, this causes a refresh of the record, with the current user's edits discarded
acDataErrDisplay	To tell Access to display the normal error message; use this constant for errors you are not handling

You'll notice that there's no way to tell Jet to overwrite the record with "your" changes. Aside from choosing the built-in error message, your only option is to allow Jet to refresh the user's edits with those the other user has already saved to disk. The built-in Save Record functionality is provided by the Access UI and is, thus, not one of the options available programmatically. However, we have come up with a work-around that produces the same effect—without causing the bug mentioned in the preceding section.

The event procedure attached to the Error event of the frmCustomerOptimistic2 form in the CH12APP.MDB sample database demonstrates this work-around. Listing 12.1 includes this event procedure, as well as supporting code found in the Current event procedure of frmCustomerOptimistic2.

Listing 12.1

```
Dim mvarCustomerId As Variant

Const glrcErrWriteConflict = 7787
Const glrcErrDataChanged = 7878

Private Sub Form_Current()

    ' Store away primary key value.
    ' It may be needed later in the
    ' error handler for the form

    ' Value won't exist for a new record,
    ' so just ignore error that may occur
    On Error Resume Next
    mvarCustomerId = Me![Customer#]

End Sub

Private Sub Form_Error(DataErr As Integer, Response As Integer)

    ' Handle form-level errors

    On Error GoTo Form_ErrorErr

    Dim strMsg As String
    Dim intResp As Integer
    Dim rst As Recordset
    Dim fld As Field
    Dim db As Database

    ' Branch based on value of error
    Select Case DataErr

    Case glrcErrWriteConflict
```

```
' Write conflict error
strMsg = "Another user has updated this record " & _
 "since you began editing it. " & vbCrLf & vbCrLf & _
 "Do you want to refresh your record with " & _
 "the other user's changes?" & vbCrLf & vbCrLf & _
 "Choose Yes to refresh your record, " & vbCrLf & _
 "or No to replace the record with your version."
intResp = MsgBox(strMsg, _
 vbYesNo + vbDefaultButton1 + vbQuestion, _
 "Overwrite Conflict")

' Jet only allows the other user's changes to
' be saved, so we need to trick Jet into using our
' changes by writing our changes out to the underlying
' record, which Access will then copy over our changes.
If intResp = vbNo Then

    Set db = CurrentDb

    ' Create recordset of one record that matches the
    ' PK value of the record when we began editing it.
    ' This value was stored away by the Current event
    ' procedure. This is necessary since we could've
    ' changed the PK value.
    Set rst = db.OpenRecordset("SELECT * FROM " & _
     "tblCustomer WHERE [Customer#] = " _
     & mvarCustomerId)

    ' Make sure PK value wasn't changed by other user.
    If rst.RecordCount = 0 Then
        strMsg = "Another user has changed the " & _
         "Customer# for this record. " & _
         "The record will need to be refreshed " & _
         "before continuing."
        MsgBox strMsg, vbOKOnly + vbInformation, _
         "Overwrite Conflict"
    Else
        ' Update values in underlying record with
        ' any changed values from form.
        ' Since Null comparisons will always return
        ' False, temporarily convert Nulls to zero-
        ' length strings for comparison.
        DoCmd.Hourglass True
        For Each fld In rst.Fields
            rst.Edit
```

```
                    If Nz(fld) <> Nz(Me(fld.Name)) Then
                        fld.Value = Me(fld.Name).Value
                    End If
                rst.Update
            Next fld
        End If
    End If

    ' This will cause record refresh
    Response = acDataErrContinue

Case glrcErrDataChanged
    ' This error occurs if Access detects that
    ' another user has changed this record when we
    ' attempt to dirty the record. Fairly harmless since
    ' we haven't actually made any changes.
    strMsg = "Another user has updated this record " & _
        "since you began viewing it. " & vbCrLf & vbCrLf & _
        "The record will be refreshed with the other " & _
        "user's changes before continuing."
    MsgBox strMsg, vbOKOnly + vbInformation, _
        "Record Refresh"

    ' This will cause record refresh
    Response = acDataErrContinue
Case Else
    ' Otherwise, let Access display standard error message
    Response = acDataErrDisplay
    Debug.Print DataErr, Error(DataErr)
End Select

DoCmd.Hourglass False

Form_ErrorEnd:
Exit Sub

Form_ErrorErr:
    ' It's possible to hit our own error while handling a
    ' data error. For example, someone could pessimistically
    ' lock the record while we are trying to update it.
    ' Report the error to the user and exit.
    MsgBox "Error " & Err.Number & ": " & Err.Description, _
        vbOKOnly + vbCritical, "Error Handler Error"

End Sub
```

The frmCustomerOptimistic2 form displays a custom write conflict message when error 7787 has been detected (see Figure 12.3). If the user chooses Yes, Response is set to acDataErrContinue and the event procedure exits. If the user chooses No, however, the event procedure takes the values from the form's current record and writes them out to a newly created recordset based on the conflict record. Then, when the event procedure sets Response to acDataErrContinue and exits, Jet copies "our" values back over the current record, thus providing the equivalent of the Save Record option. However, by copying only the values of fields that differ from the values the other user has saved, the code avoids the referential integrity error message:

```
For Each fld In rst.Fields
    rst.Edit
        If Nz(fld) <> Nz(Me(fld.Name)) Then
            fld.Value = Me(fld.Name).Value
        End If
    rst.Update
Next fld
```

FIGURE 12.3:

The frmCustomerOptimistic2 form displays a custom write conflict message.

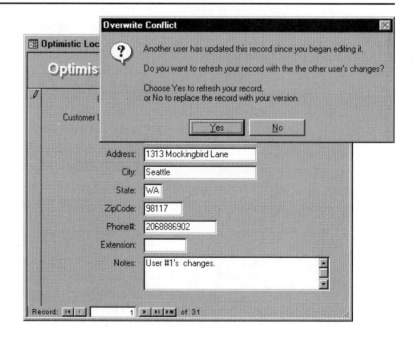

This work-around depends on storing the primary key field value for the current record in a module-level global variable, mvarCustomerId, using an event procedure attached to the Current event. This is necessary because you need to be able to open a recordset based on the current record, but you have no guarantee that the user hasn't changed the primary key value. Thus, this technique uses the value of the PK field that was stored away during the Current event. An alternative way to handle this would be to make the PK field read-only or to use the inherently read-only AutoNumber datatype for your PK.

If your form uses a compound primary key field or a query based on multiple tables, you will have to store away each primary key field value.

NOTE In many applications, you may not wish to offer your users the ability to save their changes without first viewing the other user's changes. In these cases you may wish to use a much simpler optimistic locking error handler that simply informs the user that another user has saved changes to the record and then perform a record refresh. An example of this simpler event handler is also included in the sample database attached to the frmCustomerOptimistic3 form.

Default Pessimistic Locking Behavior

Forms that use pessimistic locking avoid write conflicts because only one user at a time is allowed to edit a record. The presence of the slashed-O icon in the record selector notifies other users that a record has been locked, as demonstrated by the frmCustomerPessimistic1 form from the sample database (see Figure 12.4).

FIGURE 12.4:

Under pessimistic locking, the slashed-O icon in the record selector notifies users that the current record is locked.

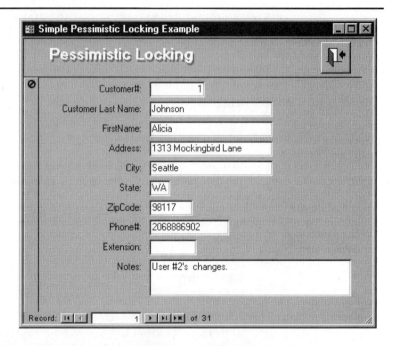

TIP

If you have set the RecordSelector property of a form to No, the slashed-O icon does not appear when a record is pessimistically locked. Access beeps at the user, but other than this audible signal, users won't have any clue as to why they can't edit the values in the record. No trappable error is generated, either, since this really isn't an error state. Thus, it's important to leave the RecordSelector property set to Yes when using pessimistic locking unless you create some custom mechanism for notifying users of the lock, as described in the next section.

Pessimistic Locking with Custom Lock Notification

While the default slashed-O lock icon works, it suffers from two shortcomings:

- It requires you to display the form's record selector.
- It doesn't tell you who locked the record.

Unfortunately, there's no event or error that occurs when the currently displayed record has been locked. You can simulate such an event, however, by using the form's Timer and Current events to check whether another user has locked the current record. We've included a form, frmCustomerPessimistic2, in the sample database that uses the Timer event to provide a custom lock notification message (see Figure 12.5). The code behind the frmCustomerPessimistic2 form is shown in Listing 12.2.

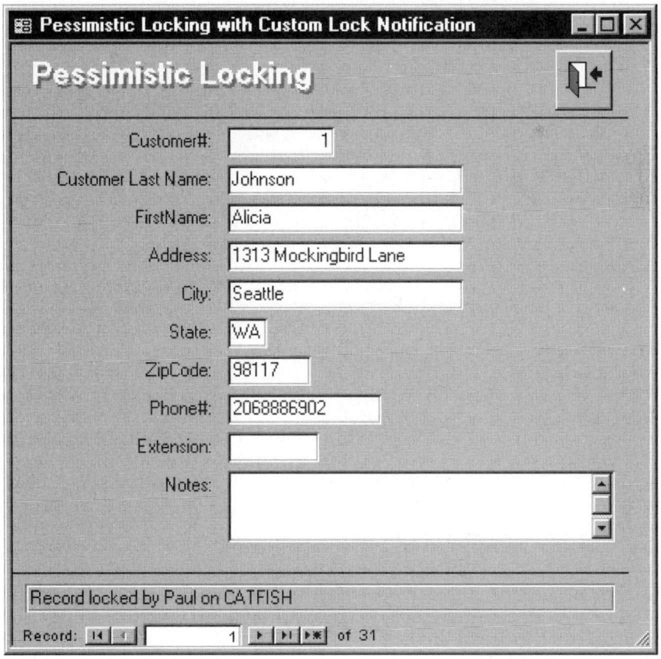

FIGURE 12.5:

The frmCustomerPessimistic2 form uses VBA code attached to the Timer and Current events to report whether a record is locked and by whom.

Listing 12.2

```
Const glrcRefreshInterval = 5

Private Sub Form_Current()
    Me!txtLockStatus = glrGetLockMsg(Me)
End Sub

Private Sub Form_Load()
    Me.TimerInterval = glrcRefreshInterval * 1000
End Sub

Private Sub Form_Timer()
    Me!txtLockStatus = glrGetLockMsg(Me)
End Sub
```

The Timer and the Current event procedures call the glrGetLockMsg() function, which is located in the basLockingError module. glrGetLockMsg() is shown in Listing 12.3.

Listing 12.3

```
Function glrGetLockMsg(frm As Form) As String

    On Error GoTo glrGetLockMsgErr

    Dim rst As Recordset
    Dim strUser As String
    Dim strMachine As String

    Set rst = frm.RecordsetClone
    rst.Bookmark = frm.Bookmark

    rst.Edit
        ' do nothing
    rst.Update

    glrGetLockMsg = "Record isn't locked by another user"

glrGetLockMsgDone:
    DoCmd.Hourglass False
    On Error GoTo 0
    Exit Function

glrGetLockMsgErr:
```

```
Call glrGetLockInfo(Err.Number, Err.Description, _
 strUser, strMachine)
If Len(strUser) = 0 And Len(strMachine) = 0 Then
    glrGetLockMsg = "Record isn't locked by another user"
Else
    glrGetLockMsg = "Record locked by " & strUser & _
     " on " & strMachine
End If
Resume glrGetLockMsgDone

End Function
```

glrGetLockMsg() works by cloning the form's recordset and synchronizing the current record pointer of the clone with the currently displayed record on the form. Then, the function attempts to lock the record by using the Edit method of the recordset. If no error is generated, the record isn't locked, and glrGetLockMsg() returns a message indicating that this is the case.

If an error is generated, code in the function's error handler passes the error number and message to the glrGetLockInfo subroutine, which checks whether the error is a standard locking error number and, if it is, parses the user and machine names from the error message. If the error is not a locking error, glrGetLockInfo returns empty user and machine names, which glrGetLockMsg() interprets to mean that the record is not locked.

There's not much to the glrGetLockInfo subroutine, which is also located in the basLockingError module of CH12APP.MDB. It uses a brute-force algorithm to determine the user and machine names based on landmarks in the error message. The key part of this subroutine is shown here:

```
intUserStart = InStr(1, strErr, "by user") + _
 glrcLenByUser
intUserLen = InStr(intUserStart + 1, strErr, "'") - _
 intUserStart + 1
intMachineStart = InStr(1, strErr, "on machine") + _
 glrcLenOnMachine
intMachineLen = InStr(intMachineStart + 1, _
 strErr, "'") - intMachineStart + 1
strUser = Mid$(strErr, intUserStart + 1, intUserLen - 2)
strMachine = Mid$(strErr, intMachineStart + 1, _
 intMachineLen - 2)
```

The code attached to the Timer event of frmCustomerPessimistic2 uses the glrc-RefreshInterval constant to determine how often to check whether the record is locked. We have set this constant to 5 seconds, but you may wish to lengthen it to reduce network traffic.

Forcing Access to Lock Records

The main disadvantage of using pessimistic locking with bound forms is that Jet locks pages of records, not individual records. You can, however, force Access to lock individual records by creating record sizes that are larger than half a page—that is, larger than 1024 bytes. This works because Access won't begin storing a new record on a partially filled page if it can't fit the entire record on that page. You can estimate the size of your records by using Table 12.3 and summing the size of each column.

The contents of Memo and OLE-type columns are stored elsewhere in the .MDB file, so you need to count the overhead only for their address pointers. Text columns require 1 byte for each actual stored character, with zero-length strings using 1 byte and null strings using 0 bytes. If your table is in a replicated database, you must also be sure to include the sizes of the system columns, which are visible only when you've used Tools ➤ Options ➤ View to make system objects visible.

TABLE 12.3: Number of Bytes (Not Counting Overhead) Used by Each Access Datatype

Field Datatype	Storage Size
Byte	1 byte
Integer	2 bytes
Long Integer	4 bytes
Single	4 bytes
Double	8 bytes
Currency	8 bytes
Counter	4 bytes
Yes/No	1 bit
Date/Time	8 bytes
Text	*variable*
Memo	14 bytes
OLE	14 bytes
Replication ID	16 bytes

You also have to account for overhead, which includes the following:

- Seven bytes per record for record overhead
- One byte variable-length column overhead for each Text, Memo, and OLE column
- One additional byte for every 256 bytes of the total space occupied by all Text, Memo, and OLE datatype columns
- One byte fixed-column overhead for each Yes/No, Byte, Integer, Long Integer, Counter, Single, Double, Date/Time, and Replication ID column

NOTE   These numbers were derived from a Microsoft Knowledge Base article (Q114215 INF: Estimating Microsoft Access Table Sizes), which states that these numbers can be used to calculate only an *estimated* record size.

An Example

The easiest way to pad a record to exceed 1024 bytes is to create one or more dummy Text columns in the table with long default values. For example, if you estimated your record size to be at least 130 bytes (considering the minimal size of any text fields), you would calculate the needed dummy fields as follows:

- Bytes you will need to pad = (1025 − 130) = 895 bytes.
- Each whole dummy text field occupies = (255 + 2 bytes overhead) = 257 bytes.

Thus you would need three completely filled dummy fields (257 * 3 = 771) of 255 x's plus one partially filled dummy field of (895 − 771 − 1 overhead byte) = 123 x's.

Don't place these dummy fields on your forms. Whenever a new record is created, Access automatically creates a record with the four x-filled dummy fields, which forces it into record-locking mode.

The sample database includes a simple table named tblForceRecordLocking (see Figure 12.6) and an accompanying form, frmForceRecordLocking, that uses this technique. Try it out with two machines on a network, and you will notice that Access locks individual records.

FIGURE 12.6:

tblForceRecordLocking form in Design view. Notice that the default value for the Dummy1 field is made up of a series of x's—in this case, 255 of them.

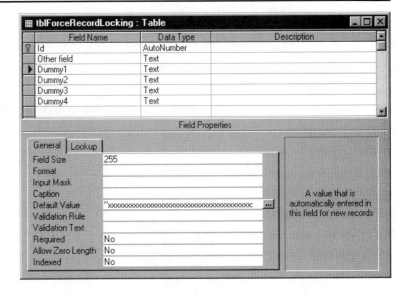

The Caveat

Now for the main caveat: this strategy wastes a lot of disk space and increases network traffic. Still, if you decide to use pessimistic locking and absolutely must have record locking, you may wish to consider this technique.

Alternative Locking Strategies

If you're not happy using either optimistic or pessimistic locking using bound forms—and this is less likely to be the case in Access 95 due to its much improved support for custom error handling of optimistic locking errors—and you don't wish to pad your record size to force the locking of records, you can choose one of the following alternative strategies:

- Use unbound forms to collect data, along with VBA code behind the unbound forms to handle the updating of records.

- Use forms bound to local transaction tables that are used to collect data offline. Then, create a system for downloading and posting transactions to the master data tables.

These strategies work best when you've split your database into data and application databases. (See the section "Splitting Databases" later in this chapter.) If you take either of these routes, be prepared for a lot of work; you'll have to handle everything Access bound forms normally handle for you (for example, reading records, navigating, writing records, and so on) and trap for and handle all the possible errors that might occur (both locking and other kinds of errors). It's not an easy task.

Recordset Error Handling

When using recordsets in a multiuser environment that are not bound to Access forms, you'll need to trap for any multiuser errors that may occur. The three most common errors are summarized in Table 12.4. Error 3197 is equivalent to the write conflict error code 7787 that occurs on bound forms.

When manipulating recordsets, you'll need to anticipate and handle each of the errors found in Table 12.4. To handle locked records, you will probably want to include some form of a retry loop that makes several attempts at gaining access to locked records. There's a good example of how to do this in the section "Using a Custom AutoNumber Routine" later in this chapter.

TABLE 12.4: Common VBA Multiuser Error Codes

Error Code	Error Message	Comment
3186	Couldn't save; currently locked by user *username* on machine *machinename*	Usually occurs when you use the Update method with optimistic locking
3197	Data has changed; operation stopped	Usually occurs when you use the Edit or Update method with optimistic locking and another user changed the record while you were editing it. Following this message you get the Write Conflict dialog
3260	Couldn't update; currently locked by user *username* on machine *machinename*	Usually occurs when you attempt to use the Update method on a record that has been locked. This is most commonly encountered using pessimistic locking but may also occur with optimistic locking

Transaction Processing

Transaction processing is a database term that refers to the process of grouping changes to your data into batches that are treated as single atomic units. Either the entire batch of *transactions* succeeds or they all fail. For example, when moving data from one account to another in a banking application, you wouldn't want to credit the new account without debiting the old account. Thus, you'd wrap this pair of up-dates in a transaction.

Transaction processing is useful in any application where one action *must* occur in concert with one or more other actions. Transaction processing is commonly required in banking and accounting applications, as well as in many others.

Access supports transaction processing with the BeginTrans, CommitTrans, and Rollback methods of the Workspace object. BeginTrans allows you to mark the start of a series of operations that should be considered as a single unit. CommitTrans takes everything since the most recent BeginTrans and writes it to disk. Rollback is the opposite of CommitTrans; it undoes all your changes back to the last Commit-Trans. In skeletal form, transaction processing usually looks something like this:

```
On Error GoTo Err_Handler

Dim wrkCurrent As WorkSpace
Dim fInTrans As Boolean

fInTrans = False
Set wrkCurrent = DBEngine.Workspaces(0)
' ...
wrkCurrent.BeginTrans
    fInTrans = True
    ' (Any series of data changes here)
wrkCurrent.CommitTrans
fInTrans = False
' ...
Err_Handler:
    if fInTrans Then
        wrkCurrent.Rollback
    End If
    ' (further error processing)
```

Here are some issues you need to be aware of when using transaction processing:

- Not all recordsets support transaction processing. None of the non-native ISAM formats support transactions, but most ODBC data sources do. You can check the Transactions property of a Recordset object to see whether it supports transaction processing.

- Transactions affect *all* changes to data in the workspace. Everything you do after a BeginTrans method is committed or rolled back as a single unit. This applies even to changes across multiple databases open within a single workspace.

- You can nest transactions in Access databases up to five levels deep. Inner transactions must be committed or rolled back before the surrounding ones. You cannot nest transactions for ODBC tables. To maintain two independent transactions, you can use two separate workspaces.

- If you close a workspace without explicitly committing its transactions, all pending transactions are automatically rolled back.

- Access handles its own transaction processing on bound forms. You cannot use transaction processing in event procedures to group together changes made via bound forms.

Transaction Processing in a Multiuser Setting

Transaction processing has extra importance in multiuser applications. When more than one user is modifying the database, you can no longer depend on the results of one change being present when you start another unless you wrap the set of updates in a transaction. Thus, you may wish to use transactions in a multiuser setting.

NOTE   When you use transactions, you increase the *integrity* of one user's set of changes at the expense of reduced *concurrency* of the entire application, because locks on multiple records are maintained for longer periods of time. Extensive use of transactions will likely cause an increase in the number of locking errors in your application.

When you use transaction processing in a multiuser setting, Access treats the entire transaction as a single disk write but otherwise respects your specified locking setting. Thus, if you're using pessimistic locking (LockEdits = True), Access locks a record when an Edit or AddNew method is encountered. If you're using optimistic locking (LockEdits = False) instead, Access doesn't lock the record until it encounters an Update method. Within the confines of a transaction, however, Access accumulates these locks without releasing them until the entire transaction has been either committed or rolled back.

If Access encounters a locked record within a transaction, the standard set of trappable errors occurs. For example, if a record needed by a transaction is locked by another user when the transaction process attempts to lock the record, the transaction fails with a 3260 error, "Couldn't update; currently locked by user *username* on machine *machinename*." In this case you need to either obtain the necessary lock or roll back the transaction.

Implied Transactions

In addition to *explicit transactions* that you create using the BeginTrans, CommitTrans, and Rollback methods, Jet 3.0 creates *implicit transactions* to improve the performance of recordset operations. In an exclusively used database, by default, Jet commits implicit transactions every 2 seconds; in a shared environment, Jet commits these transactions every 50 milliseconds. The default setting of 50 milliseconds should ensure no noticeable change in concurrency in a multiuser setting.

The exact effect implicit transactions have on concurrency depends on the values of several optional Registry settings. These settings, which are not created by default, are described in Table 12.5. To use non-default settings, you need to create the Registry keys under the following node:

```
HKEY_LOCAL_MACHINE\SOFTWARE\Jet\3.0\Engines\Jet
```

There may be some applications for which you wish to sacrifice concurrency for increased performance. In these cases you may want to increase the value of the SharedAsyncDelay key.

TABLE 12.5: Transaction Registry Settings

Key	Datatype	Effect	Default
UserCommitSync	String	Determines whether explicit transactions are executed synchronously (unnested transactions are performed one after the other)*	Yes
ImplicitCommitSync	String	Determines whether Jet creates implicit transactions for recordset updates. A setting of No causes implied transactions to be used*	No
ExclusiveAsnycDelay	DWORD	Determines the maximum time (in milliseconds) before Jet commits an implicit transaction when the database is opened exclusively	2000
SharedAsyncDelay	DWORD	Determines maximum time (in milliseconds) before Jet commits an implicit transaction when the database is opened in shared mode	50

*There's a bug in Jet 3.0 that reverses the meaning of this setting. If you want this setting to be True, you must set this string to No. (This bug has no effect if the key was never created; in this case Jet correctly defaults to synchronous transactions.)

Multiuser Action Queries

Access 1.x provided no means of determining programmatically whether an action query failed. If any records failed to be updated because of locking conflicts or other errors, no trappable run-time error was triggered. With the introduction of Access 2.0, Microsoft improved the situation by adding an option (dbFailOnError) to the Execute method of querydefs. In Access 2, if an error was encountered, you could trap the error, but you still couldn't determine how many records were prevented from being updated, deleted, or appended.

With Access 95 you can now determine how many records were affected by the action query by checking the RecordsAffected property of the querydef after the query has executed. When executing a SQL statement rather than a stored query, you can use the RecordsAffected property of the DBEngine object to retrieve the same information. Unfortunately, you can't programmatically determine how many records were prevented from being updated because of locking conflict, key violation, or other reasons. (The Access UI provides this information when queries are executed interactively.)

Listing 12.4 shows an example of using the dbFailOnError option and the Records-Affected property.

Listing 12.4

```
Function DeleteTempOrders()

    On Error GoTo DeleteTempOrdersErr

    Dim db As Database
    Dim wrk As Workspace
    Dim qdf As QueryDef
    Dim lngRecsEstimated As Long
    Dim lngRecsAffected As Long
    Dim intResp As Integer
    Dim strWhere As String
    Dim fInTrans As Boolean

    DeleteTempOrders = False
    fInTrans = False

    Set db = CurrentDb
    Set wrk = DBEngine.Workspaces(0)

    strWhere = "[Order#] BETWEEN 1 AND 100"

    lngRecsEstimated = DCount("*", "tblTempOrders", strWhere)
    Set qdf = db.CreateQueryDef("", _
      "DELETE * FROM tblTempOrders WHERE " & strWhere)

    intResp = MsgBox("About to delete " & lngRecsEstimated & _
      " records." & vbCrLf & _
      "Fail if any record can't be deleted?", _
      vbYesNo + vbInformation + vbDefaultButton1, _
      "Action Query Example")

    wrk.BeginTrans
        fInTrans = True
        If intResp = vbYes Then
            qdf.Execute (dbFailOnError)
```

```
        Else
            qdf.Execute
        End If
        lngRecsAffected = qdf.RecordsAffected
        If lngRecsAffected < lngRecsEstimated Then
            intResp = MsgBox("Only " & lngRecsAffected & _
            " out of " & lngRecsEstimated & _
            " records will be deleted." & vbCrLf & _
            "OK to continue?", _
            vbOKCancel + vbInformation, "Action Query Example")
            If intResp = vbCancel Then
                MsgBox "Transaction rolled back!", _
                 vbOKOnly + vbCritical, "Action Query Example"
                wrk.Rollback
                GoTo DeleteTempOrdersDone
            End If
        End If
    wrk.CommitTrans
    fInTrans = False

    DeleteTempOrders = True

DeleteTempOrdersDone:
    Exit Function

DeleteTempOrdersErr:
    If fInTrans Then
        wrk.Rollback
        MsgBox "Error occurred. Rolled back.", _
         vbOKOnly + vbCritical, "Action Query Example"
    Else
        MsgBox "Error#" & Err.Number & ": " & Err.Description, _
         vbOKOnly + vbCritical, "Action Query Example"
    End If
    Resume DeleteTempOrdersDone

End Function
```

In this example, which can be found in the basActionQueryExample module of CH12APP.MDB, DeleteTempOrders() calculates the estimated number of records to be deleted by a delete query prior to its execution. Next, the function asks the user whether to use the dbFailOnError option.

If the user chooses Yes, the query is run using the dbFailOnError option. If a record is locked or if some other problem prevents one or more records from being deleted, the entire transaction is rolled back.

If the user chooses No, the query is run without the dbFailOnError option. If a record is locked or if some other problem prevents one or more records from being deleted, the query executes within a transaction, but the user is warned of the incomplete results and given the opportunity to roll back the transaction.

The addition of the RecordsAffected property to Access 95 gives you more flexibility in dealing with action queries in a multiuser environment.

Splitting Databases

No matter which locking scheme you employ, you are still left with the fact that, by default, Access puts all objects in a single database file. Performance can suffer considerably because every time an object (for example, a form) is used, it must be sent across the network to the user. In a production setting, where nothing but the data is updated, much of this network traffic is unnecessary.

You can eliminate this unnecessary traffic by splitting the database into an "application" database and a "data" database. Install the data database (with tables only) on the file server and a copy of the application database (containing all other objects) on each workstation. From each copy of the application database, use the File ➤ Get External Tables ➤ Link Tables command to link to the set of tables in the data database.

The *advantages* of this approach are

- Performance (especially user interface performance) is improved considerably.

- You can create temporary tables on each workstation and not worry about naming and locking conflicts for temporary objects.

- Splitting the database makes the updating of applications easier since the data and application are kept separate. Changes to the application can be made off site and easily merged back into the application database without disturbing the data.

The *disadvantages* of this approach are

- Access can't enforce referential integrity between local and remote tables. Fortunately, Access enforces referential integrity between tables in the remote database.
- Access hard-codes the paths to linked tables. This means that if you move the data database, you have to fix up the table links.

Managing Linked Tables

Because Access hard-codes linked table paths, their use requires extra maintenance. If you move the data database with linked tables, you have three options for fixing the broken links:

- Delete and reestablish the link from scratch.
- Use the Access 95 Linked Table Manager Add-In to fix up the references and refresh the links.
- Create VBA code to manage links programmatically.

TIP

If you use universal naming convention (UNC) names when establishing your links, you won't have to bother with fixing up links when you copy or move the application database from one computer to another on your LAN.

The sample database includes a module, basLinkedTables, that contains reusable code for managing linked tables. The entry point to the code is through the glrVerifyLinks() function, which is shown in Listing 12.5.

Listing 12.5

```
Function glrVerifyLinks(strDataDatabase As String, _
  strSampleTable As String) As Integer

    On Error GoTo glrVerifyLinksErr

    Dim varReturn As Variant
```

```
Dim strDBDir As String
Dim strMsg As String
Dim db As Database
Dim varFileName As Variant
Dim tdf As TableDef
Dim intI As Integer
Dim intNumTables As Integer
Dim strProcName As String
Dim strFilter As String
Dim lngFlags As Long

strProcName = "glrVerifyLinks"

' Verify Links using one sample table.
varReturn = CheckLink(strSampleTable)

If varReturn Then
    glrVerifyLinks = True
    GoTo glrVerifyLinksDone
End If

' Get name of folder where application database is located
strDBDir = GetDBDir()

If (Dir$(strDBDir & strDataDatabase) <> "") Then
    ' Data database found in current directory.
    varFileName = strDBDir & strDataDatabase
Else
    ' Let user find data database using common dialog
    strMsg = "The required file '" & strDataDatabase & _
    "' could not be found."
    strMsg = strMsg & " You can use the next dialog " & _
    "box to locate the file on your system."
    strMsg = strMsg & " If you cannot find this file " & _
    "or are unsure what to do choose CANCEL"
    strMsg = strMsg & " at the next screen and call " & _
    "the database administrator."
    MsgBox strMsg, vbOKOnly + vbCritical, strProcName

    ' Display Open File dialog using the GetOpenFile
    ' function in the basFileOpen module
    strFilter = glrAddFilterItem( _
    strFilter, "Access (*.mdb)", "*.mdb")
    lngFlags = glrOFN_HIDEREADONLY Or _
    glrOFN_HIDEREADONLY Or glrOFN_NOCHANGEDIR
```

```
        varFileName = glrCommonFileOpenSave( _
            OpenFile:=True, _
            Filter:=strFilter, _
            Flags:=lngFlags, _
            DialogTitle:="Locate Data database file")

    If IsNull(varFileName) Then
        ' User pressed Cancel.
        strMsg = "You can't run database until you can " & _
         "locate '" & strDataDatabase & "'."
        MsgBox strMsg, vbOKOnly + vbCritical, strProcName
        glrVerifyLinks = False
        GoTo glrVerifyLinksDone
    Else
        varFileName = glrTrimNull(varFileName)
    End If
End If

'Rebuild Links. Check for number of tables first.
Set db = CurrentDb
intNumTables = db.TableDefs.Count
varReturn = SysCmd(acSysCmdInitMeter, "Relinking tables", _
 intNumTables)

' Loop through all tables.
' Reattach those with nonzero-length Connect strings.
intI = 0
For Each tdf In db.TableDefs
    ' If connect is blank, it's not a Linked table
    If Len(tdf.Connect) > 0 Then
        intI = intI + 1
        tdf.Connect = ";DATABASE=" & varFileName

        ' The RefreshLink might fail if the new path
        ' isn't OK. So trap errors inline.
        On Error Resume Next
        tdf.RefreshLink
        'If one link bad, return False
        If Err <> 0 Then
            glrVerifyLinks = False
            GoTo glrVerifyLinksDone
        End If
    End If
```

```
        varReturn = SysCmd(acSysCmdUpdateMeter, intI + 1)
    Next tdf

    glrVerifyLinks = True

glrVerifyLinksDone:
    On Error Resume Next
    varReturn = SysCmd(acSysCmdRemoveMeter)
    On Error GoTo 0
    Exit Function

glrVerifyLinksErr:
    Select Case Err
    Case Else
        MsgBox "Error#" & Err.Number & ": " & Err.Description, _
            vbOKOnly + vbCritical, strProcName
    End Select
    Resume glrVerifyLinksDone
End Function
```

The glrVerifyLinks() function takes two parameters: strDataDatabase, the name of
the data database containing the linked tables, and strSampleTable, the name of one
of the linked tables. glrVerifyLinks() starts by checking the validity of this sample
linked table. It assumes that if this table's link checks out okay, then all the links are
fine. (You can modify the code to check the integrity of all links instead.) The function verifies the links by calling the private function CheckLink(), which is shown
in Listing 12.6.

Listing 12.6

```
Private Function CheckLink(strTable As String) As Integer

    Dim db As Database
    Dim rst As Recordset

    Set db = CurrentDb

    On Error Resume Next
    Set rst = db.OpenRecordset(strTable, dbOpenDynaset)

    ' Check for failure. If the OpenRecordSet failed, then
    ' the link must be bad.
    If Err <> 0 Then
        CheckLink = False
```

```
    Else
        rst.Close
        CheckLink = True
    End If

End Function
```

This simple function checks the validity of a link by attempting to open a recordset on the table. If this operation succeeds, the link is good; if it fails, it's assumed to be bad and the function returns False.

If CheckLink() returns False, glrVerifyLinks() attempts to find the data database in the same folder as the application database. If the database is found there, the function relinks all the tables using this database. If the data database isn't in the application folder, however, the function prompts the user with a common open file dialog.

glrVerifyLinks() relinks the tables by modifying the Connect property of the tabledef and using the RefreshLink method.

Integrating Linked Tables into Your Applications

When you split an existing single-database application into data and application databases, you may be required to alter some of your VBA code. You can't use table-type recordsets or the Seek method on linked tables. You can, however, use one of two alternative methods instead:

- Create dynaset-type recordsets and use the slower FindFirst method.
- Use the OpenDatabase method to open the data database directly. You can then create table-type recordsets and use the Seek method just as though the tables were local.

Whichever method you choose, you'll almost certainly have to make changes to your application code.

> **TIP**
>
> Access 95 includes a new add-in called the Database Splitter that makes it easy to split a single database into data and application databases.

Using a Custom AutoNumber Routine

Access 95 offers a great deal of flexibility in choosing AutoNumber fields (called Counter fields in prior versions of Access). You can choose an AutoNumber field with Long Integer values that are made up of sequentially incremented or randomly chosen numbers, or you can use a 16-byte globally unique identifier (GUID) instead. (See Chapter 13 for more on GUIDs.) At times, however, you may prefer to use a custom routine for assigning some type of incremented value for one of the following reasons:

- You need to use an alphanumeric string.
- You need to use an increment greater than 1.
- You wish to recover values for discarded records.
- You need to create values that are computed using other fields in the record.
- You have the data stored in a non-native ISAM format that has no support AutoNumber fields.

> **NOTE**
>
> It's important that you not place too much faith in surrogate primary keys, such as those that can be generated using AutoNumber fields. While these fields can certainly guarantee uniqueness of the record, you still have to ensure, through the use of additional indexes or event procedures, that a user can't create five records for a single customer.

Custom AutoNumber Setup

You can implement your own custom AutoNumber fields for an Access database by maintaining a separate table to hold the next AutoNumber value. You must lock this table when you need an AutoNumber value and trap for errors that may occur when more than one user attempts to assign a new value simultaneously.

We have created a custom AutoNumber routine for the Menu# field of tblMenu in the CH12APP.MDB sample database. The routine is called from the frmMenu form; the table that holds the AutoNumber value is kept in the CH12AUTO.MDB database.

Implementing a Custom AutoNumber

We have split the activity of obtaining a new AutoNumber value into two parts. A low-level routine handles the AutoNumber increment or returns −1 if an AutoNumber value cannot be retrieved. A high-level routine handles the assignment of this AutoNumber to a new record and determines what to do about any errors. Both routines are contained in the module basAutoNumber in the CH12APP.MDB database.

glrGetNextAutoNumber() is the low-level routine that interfaces directly with the AutoNumber database. It takes a single parameter—the name of the table that will use the AutoNumber value. The next AutoNumber value is obtained from a table (in the glrcAutoNumDb database) with _ID appended to the base table name. For example, the AutoNumber for tblMenu is stored in tblMenu_ID. This table has a simple structure: it consists of a single Long Integer field named NextAutoNumber. glrGetNextAutoNumber() is shown in Listing 12.7.

Listing 12.7

```
' Database storing autonumber values
Global Const glrcAutoNumDb = "Ch12Auto.Mdb"
Global strAutoNumDbName As String

' Number of times to retry in case of locking conflicts
Global Const glrcMaxRetries = 5

'Error constants
Const glrcErrRI = 3000
```

```
Const glrcLockErrCantUpdate2 = 3260
Const glrcLockErrTableInUse = 3262

Function glrGetNextAutoNumber(ByVal strTableName As String) _
  As Long

    On Error GoTo glrGetNextAutoNumber_Err

    Dim wrkCurrent As Workspace
    Dim dbAutoNum As Database
    Dim rstAutoNum As Recordset
    Dim lngNextAutoNum As Long
    Dim lngWait As Long
    Dim lngX As Long
    Dim intLockCount As Integer
    DoCmd.Hourglass True

    intLockCount = 0

    ' Open a recordset on the appropriate table in the
    ' autonumbers database, denying all reads to others
    ' while it is open
    Set wrkCurrent = DBEngine.Workspaces(0)
    Set dbAutoNum = wrkCurrent.OpenDatabase(strAutoNumDbName, _
      False)
    Set rstAutoNum = dbAutoNum.OpenRecordset(strTableName _
      & "_ID", dbOpenTable, dbDenyRead)

    ' Increment and return the autonumber value
    rstAutoNum.MoveFirst
    rstAutoNum.Edit
        lngNextAutoNum = rstAutoNum![NextAutoNumber]
        rstAutoNum![NextAutoNumber] = lngNextAutoNum + 1
    rstAutoNum.Update

    glrGetNextAutoNumber = lngNextAutoNum

    rstAutoNum.Close
    dbAutoNum.Close

glrGetNextAutoNumber_Exit:
    DoCmd.Hourglass False
    Exit Function

glrGetNextAutoNumber_Err:
```

```
      ' Table locked by another user
     If Err = glrcErrRI Or Err = glrcLockErrCantUpdate2 Or _
      Err = glrcLockErrTableInUse Then
          intLockCount = intLockCount + 1
          ' Tried too many times, give up
          If intLockCount > glrcMaxRetries Then
              glrGetNextAutoNumber = -1
              Resume glrGetNextAutoNumber_Exit
          ' Otherwise, let Windows process and try again
          Else
              ' Let Windows catch up
              DoEvents
              ' Calculate the wait time based on
              ' the number of retries and a random number
              lngWait = intLockCount ^ 2 * Int(Rnd * 20 + 5)
              ' Waste time, but let Windows
              ' multitask during this dead time
              For lngX = 1 To lngWait
                  DoEvents
              Next lngX
              Resume
          End If
     ' Unexpected error
     Else
          MsgBox "Error " & Err.Number & ": " & Err.Description, _
           vbOKOnly + vbCritical, "glrGetNextAutoNumber"
          glrGetNextAutoNumber = -1
          Resume glrGetNextAutoNumber_Exit
     End If

End Function
```

When there is no contention for AutoNumber values, glrGetNextAutoNumber() does its work by simply retrieving and incrementing the NextAutoNumber field. In a multiuser situation, however, it is possible for one user to request an AutoNumber value while another user already has the table locked. glrGetNext-AutoNumber() handles these types of errors using the following code:

```
intLockCount = intLockCount + 1
' Tried too many times, give up
If intLockCount > glrcMaxRetries Then
    glrGetNextAutoNumber = -1
    Resume glrGetNextAutoNumber_Exit
' Otherwise, let Windows process and try again
Else
```

```
    '  ...
End If
```

You'll need to set glrcMaxRetries to balance between potential failure and potential delays to the user. Depending on your network, you may find a value between 3 and 20 is appropriate. If the table is not free after a number of retries, it generally means that someone else has it locked for a reason unrelated to assigning AutoNumber values (for example, as a side effect of a GPF [General Protection Fault] encountered when assigning an AutoNumber).

The second part of the preceding If...Then...Else statement contains the code that forces the retry of the operation that encountered the lock:

```
Else
    ' Calculate the wait time based on
    ' the number of retries and a random number
    lngWait = intLockCount ^ 2 * Int(Rnd * 20 + 5)
    ' Waste time, but let Windows
    ' multitask during this dead time
    For lngX = 1 To lngWait
        DoEvents
    Next lngX
    Resume
End If
```

Rather than immediately retrying to obtain the lock, glrGetNextAutoNumber() includes some time-wasting logic. It's useful to review this logic since it's likely you'll want to include similar code in all your routines that may experience locking conflicts. A Long Integer, lngWait, is calculated based on a formula that squares the number of retries and multiplies the result by a random number between 5 and 25. Then, a For...Next loop is executed for lngWait iterations to waste time. The inclusion of the DoEvents statement ensures that any other Windows tasks are given processor time during this "dead" period. By including a random number and squaring the time for each retry, glrGetNextAutoNumber() attempts to separate out any users who were requesting locks at the same time.

After the For...Next loop, the actual retry is accomplished with the Resume statement.

The function glrAssignID(), also located in basAutoNumbers (and not shown here), handles the high-level AutoNumber assignment. It is called from the BeforeInsert event of the form and is passed three parameters: the Form object, the name of the underlying table that holds the custom-AutoNumber field, and the name of the custom-AutoNumber field. glrAssignID() deletes any record that cannot be assigned an AutoNumber. Depending on your particular circumstances, you may need a more sophisticated high-level control routine. For example, you might want to save records that couldn't be assigned a value to a temporary local table rather than discard them entirely.

You may wish to modify glrGetNextAutoNumber() to return an AutoNumber in some custom format that uses an increment other than 1 or that uses an alpha-numeric string.

Security

Although security is not really a multiuser-specific concern, it certainly becomes more necessary in a multiuser environment. As the number of workstations running your application increases, the more likely it is you'll want to prevent unauthorized users from gaining access to either the data *or* the application.

Using security also allows Access to accurately inform you as to who has locked a record in its error messages. Even if you intercept Access' built-in locking-error messages, you still may want to parse out the user name and use it in any custom error messages. If you don't use security, every user will be named Admin. (See Chapter 24 for more details on security.)

Determining Which Users Have a Database Open

We've included on the CD that accompanies this book an unsupported DLL, MSLDBUSR.DLL, from Microsoft's Kevin Collins and Bob Delavan (along with documentation) that allows you to determine which users have a database open. This DLL works by reading information directly out of the .LDB file that Jet uses to maintain locking information.

To use the DLL you must include the following Declare statement in the Declarations section of a module:

```
Private Declare Function LDBUser_GetUsers Lib "MSLDBUSR.DLL" _
  (strUserBuffer() As String, ByVal strFilename As String, _
  ByVal lngOptions As Long) As Integer
```

When you call the DLL, you pass it an array, the name of the database to check, and an options parameter; it returns the number of users and fills the passed array with the machine names of the users who have the database open. The lngOptions parameter can be any of the following:

Value	Purpose
&H1	Returns all users who ever had the database open during this session
&H2	Returns only currently active users
&H4	Returns users marked as corrupted only
&H8	Returns only the count of users

We've created a form, frmViewUsers, that calls MSLDBUSR and displays the machine names of active users in a list box control. frmViewUsers is shown in Figure 12.7.

For additional information on Jet locking issues and MSLDBUSR, including a discussion of an accompanying API call that returns various error conditions, see the white paper, JETLOCK.DOC, included on this book's CD with the DLL.

TIP

Access automatically creates an .LDB file of the same name as the database whenever it finds that one does not exist. This file keeps track of record locks. If you experience a GPF or power failure or you reboot while a record is locked, the .LDB file will be left in a state that reports which records were locked at the time of the problem. Since this lock would now have no owner, the effect is a permanent lock of the record. The solution to this problem is to close the database (in a multiuser environment, all users must close it) and delete the .LDB file. Access creates a new .LDB file whenever none is found.

FIGURE 12.7:

This form calls MSLDBUSR.DLL to determine the machine names of all users who have the specified database opened.

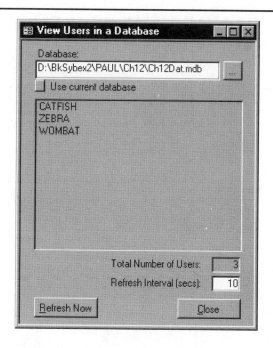

The Wire

When moving from single-user to multiuser applications, you need to start thinking about potential data bottlenecks. Remember that every time your application requests data, it is sent over the network (also know as *the wire*) to the workstation. Thus, you'll want to minimize sending large amounts of data over the wire, for the sake of both the user requesting the data and the network traffic.

One Record at a Time

One area that demands special attention is how *much* of a recordset you offer your users in a form. Although Access makes it easy to bind a form to an entire table or query, letting users navigate to their hearts' content, you'll quickly find this doesn't work well with even moderately large tables (more than 30,000–50,000 rows) on a network. You're better off presenting each user with a single record at a time and programmatically changing the record source of the form rather than using the FindFirst method to move to a specific record.

The frmOrderOneRec Sample Form

In CH12APP.MDB we've included a form, frmOrderOneRec, that demonstrates the technique of displaying only one record at a time to minimize network traffic. The form (see Figure 12.8) is bound to the tblOrder table. It also contains a subform bound to tblOrderDetails. frmOrderOneRec includes these features:

- It's bound to a SQL statement that initially returns no records:

  ```
  SELECT DISTINCTROW * FROM tblOrder where [Order#] = 0;
  ```

- The user navigates to another order by entering a different order number in a text box control, txtGotoOrder, located in the form header, and clicking the cmdGoto command button. This triggers an event procedure that builds a new SQL statement based on the value entered in the text box and changes the record source accordingly.

- The form switches among four modes (NoRecord, Browse, Edit, and AddNew); the current mode is indicated in the form's caption. Users switch among modes using buttons located in the form's header. When a record is made current, it's pulled up in Browse mode to minimize inadvertent changes to the data.

FIGURE 12.8:

frmOrderOneRec form in edit mode

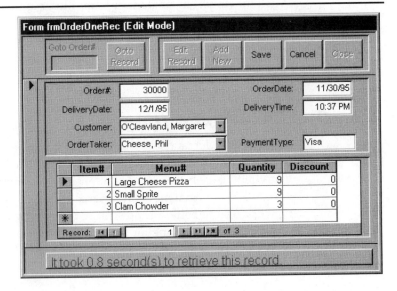

- When in Edit or AddNew mode, users are prevented from closing the form or navigating to a new record until they explicitly choose to save or cancel their changes.

You may wish to examine the code behind frmOrderOneRec and compare it with the code behind another form in the database, frmOrderAllRecs, which takes the default approach of offering the user all records at the same time.

NOTE There is some overhead associated with dynamically changing the form's record source. Thus, frmOrderOneRec will be slower in locating records than frmOrderAllRecs for recordsets with fewer than about 30,000–50,000 records. (The sample database contains far fewer records than this.) If you wish to add records to the sample database for the purpose of comparing these two techniques, you can use the frmCreateRandomRecords form that we've provided to generate thousands of order and order detail records.

Test, Test, Test!

You need to test your applications more thoroughly if they will be used on a network. The rule to remember here is, if something *can* go wrong, it will. This means you must set aside a significant amount of time for testing and debugging your multiuser applications.

One advantage of developing in the Windows environment is that you can develop, test, and debug multiuser applications on a single machine by starting two instances of Access and switching back and forth between the instances. While this should allow you to test for and fix many potential problems, you'll still need to test the application on the target network under a typical load of users to find all potential problems. In other words, there's no substitute for the real thing.

Summary

The important point to remember when writing multiuser applications is to anticipate problems. Multiuser applications need to handle—that is, recover from—the errors that occur when locks are placed on pages of records. In general, there is no set of perfect answers that applies to all multiuser applications. You'll have to develop the appropriate solution for your particular database and consider each of the following:

- Balance network security and maintenance against efficiency and speed when choosing whether to install Access on each workstation.
- Adjust your multiuser settings to achieve optimum performance for your particular application.
- Balance ease of use, data integrity, and ease of programming in developing your locking strategy.
- Be aware of the errors that can occur when multiple users share data.
- Use custom error-handling code when using bound forms with optimistic locking.
- Use custom lock notification code when using bound forms with pessimistic locking.
- Split your database into separate data and application databases for increased performance.
- Use VBA code to manage the linked tables in a split database architecture.
- Use transactions to ensure the integrity of your data when multiple operations must occur in concert.
- Use MSLDBUSR.DLL to see who has a database open.
- Minimize data going across the network wire.
- Be sure to adequately test your applications.

CHAPTER

THIRTEEN

Mastering Replication

- Understanding how replication works

- Using Replication Manager

- Creating a custom conflict resolution function

- Deciding on a replication topology

Of all the changes made to the product with the introduction of Access 95, replication has got to be the most significant. If you wanted to keep two or more copies of a database synchronized using prior versions of Access, you faced many hurdles. In fact, this functionality required so much coding that few developers attempted it. With the support for replication and synchronization built right into both Access 95 and Jet 3.0, replication is finally a reality for many developers. In this chapter we discuss Jet replication in detail, including how replication works and when to use it. In addition, we discuss how to replicate and synchronize databases and manage replication conflicts and errors—both through the built-in user interfaces and programmatically.

NOTE There are two sample databases for this chapter: CH13A.MDB and CH13B.MDB. CH13A.MDB contains a series of forms and generic code that can be used to manage replicated databases, but this database is not replicated. CH13B.MDB is the pre-replicated design master for a sample replicated database that includes custom conflict and error resolution code. You'll need to replicate CH13B before you can start experimenting with the special replication code in that database.

Replication: What Is It and How Does It Work?

Replication is the act of making special copies of a regular Access database that are enabled in such a way that you can easily transfer changes made in one copy to each of the other copies. There are three basic steps to Jet replication:

1. Replication
2. Synchronization
3. Conflict and error resolution

Replication

When you replicate a normal Access database, Jet makes many changes to the schema of the database that enables it to exchange updates with other databases. These schema changes, which are discussed in more detail later in the chapter, include the addition of system tables, the modification of existing tables, and the creation of new properties of the database and many of its objects.

When you convert a nonreplicated database into a replicated database, you end up with the *design master* of a new *replica set*. A replica set of one, however, is not very useful since you wouldn't have anyone to exchange changes with, so you normally create a second member of the replica set by immediately cloning (or replicating) the design master. You can create additional members of a replica set by replicating any of its existing replicas.

Two replicas can exchange updates only if they are descendants of the same design master; that is, members of the same replica set.

The design master is a special member of a replica set. You can make schema changes only in the design master. You can, however, make changes to data in any replica of a replica set (unless you elect to make a replica read-only).

Synchronization

When you make updates to a replica that's a member of a replica set, Jet tracks the updates using the extra tables and fields it added to the database when you first replicated it. Jet does not, however, send changes to the other members of the replica set without your intervention. In fact, unlike networked databases in a multi-user file-server or client-server environment, replicas are not connected except when you temporarily connect them—two at a time—during a *synchronization exchange*.

When you synchronize two replicas, Jet sends updates from one replica to another. What makes replication so useful is that Jet has to send only the *updates*. This makes synchronization much more efficient than importing and exporting records between two nonreplicated databases. Normally, synchronization occurs in both directions, but you can elect to synchronize in only one direction if you wish. It's up to you to control when synchronization occurs and between which replicas. In addition, you must first establish a physical connection between the two replicas (or between two Replication Manager transporters) before you can make a synchronization exchange.

Conflict and Error Resolution

It's possible that, in between synchronization exchanges, two users might modify the same row in two different replicas. When this occurs, Jet flags a conflict the next time the replicas are synchronized. Jet uses a simple algorithm to determine which record's changes are preserved that is based on which replica modified the record the greatest number of times. Access includes the Conflict Resolution Wizard, which you can use to alter this automated decision and swap the winning and losing records. In addition, you can write a custom conflict resolution function to use instead of Access' built-in Wizard.

The Many Faces of Replication

You can replicate and synchronize Jet databases through a variety of means, as shown in Table 13.1.

Each method has its own set of advantages and disadvantages, as described in more detail in the next few sections. Your situation will usually dictate which method to choose. For example, if you're developing an application that will be run by sophisticated power users, you may wish to employ Briefcase replication or the Access menus. On the other hand, if you're developing an application for naive users, you'll need to use DAO or Replication Manager or some combination of the two.

Briefcase Replication

The Windows 95 Briefcase is an operating system utility that makes it easy for users to manage files on multiple PCs. Typically, you drag files to and from the Briefcase on your laptop. The Briefcase makes it easy to keep multiple copies of the same files synchronized. Normally, the Briefcase works at the file level, performing simple file date/time comparisons to ensure that the most recent copy of a file is never overwritten.

TABLE 13.1: Various Mechanisms for Managing Jet Replication

Method	Advantages	Disadvantages	Comments
Windows 95 Briefcase	Simple drag-and-drop action; can be performed by users	Requires user intervention; cannot be controlled programmatically; requires Windows 95 Briefcase	Not as simple as it seems; can be confusing for some users; can't be used on Windows NT 3.51 (no Briefcase)
Access menus	Simple; can be performed by users; can be used on Windows NT; includes basic conflict management facility	Requires user intervention and the understanding of basic replication terminology	Requires retail copy of Access on each desktop
DAO methods and properties	Can be automated; insulates user from process. Can be used on Windows NT. No need for Access; can be used with the Access run-time, Visual Basic, and Visual C++	Requires programming; no built-in conflict management mechanism	Probably the best solution for most developers
Replication Manager	Can be automated. Can be used on Windows NT and with the Access run-time	Not all aspects of replication can be handled with Replication Manager. Not included with Visual Basic or Visual C++	Only a partial solution; you will need to supplement with DAO or the Access menus

If you choose the replication option when you install Access 95, Access registers a special Jet replication reconciler to be used instead of Briefcase's normal reconciler when an .MDB file is dragged to and from the Briefcase. With the Jet replication reconciler installed and registered, the first time you drag an .MDB file to the Briefcase, the .MDB file is converted into a replication design master, and on your laptop, a replica of the database is made. Finally, when you choose the Update option within the Briefcase, the two replicas of the database are synchronized using the Jet replication reconciler.

To use the Windows 95 Briefcase-based replication facilities, you must have

- Windows 95 on the laptop with the Briefcase installed
- Access 95 on the laptop with the replication option installed

There's no way to automate Briefcase replication or integrate it into an existing application, so its use for the professional developer is limited.

WARNING Once the special Jet replication reconciler has been registered, the Briefcase will attempt to replicate or synchronize all .MDB files, even if the .MDB file is an Access 2.0 database. There's no way to direct the Briefcase to perform file date/time comparisons only for certain .MDB files.

Access Menu-Based Replication

The Access user interface includes a set of menus found under Tools ➤ Replication that expose most of the Jet replication functionality to the Access user. You won't be able to use the Access replication menus from a custom Access application—you aren't able to use DoCmd.DoMenuItem with these special menus—but you'll likely find them useful for setting up and maintaining your replicated databases.

The Access replication menus are summarized in Table 13.2.

TABLE 13.2: Access Replication Menus

Menu	Description
Synchronize Now	Specifies another replica with which to synchronize; can also be used to transfer design master status to another replica
Create Replica	For nonreplicated databases, creates a design master and one replica; for replicated databases, creates an additional replica
Resolve Conflicts	If there are synchronization conflict or error records in the currently open replica, this command opens the Resolve Replication Conflicts dialog, which allows you to resolve conflict records (This command is automatically executed when you open a replica that contains synchronization conflicts or errors.)
Recover Design Master	If the currently open replica is not the design master, you can use this command to make this replica the design master for the replica set. You should use this command only if the design master has been damaged or destroyed

DAO Replication

While Briefcase replication and replication through the Access menus are useful, if you're a developer, you're probably most concerned about how to programmatically manipulate replication from DAO and VBA. The good news is that it's all there. Everything you can do from the Windows Briefcase or the Access menus is programmable through DAO—from Access, Visual Basic, and Visual C++. The only bad news is that the Access Conflict Manager Wizard is not accessible from DAO; it's available only through the Access UI. Fortunately, you can use your own conflict management routine to replace Access' Wizard.

The DAO replication properties and methods are summarized in Tables 13.3 and 13.4, respectively.

TABLE 13.3: DAO Replication Properties

Object	Property	Description	Read/Write Status
Database	DesignMasterID	Unique identifier assigned to the design master of a replica set	Read/write
	ReplicaID	Unique identifier for replica	Read-only
All document objects	KeepLocal	Property you set to the string "T" *before* the database is first replicated to make an object nonreplicated (local)	Read/write before the database has been replicated
	Replicable	Property you set to the string "T" *after* the database is replicated to start replicating an object that was local; or to "F" to stop replicating an object	Read/write
Table document objects only	CollsGuid	The column in the table that serves as the globally unique identifier (GUID); usually s_GUID, but Jet will use a user-created field of type GUID if the table already contains one	Read-only
MSysDB document of the Databases container	ReplicaId	GUID that identifies this replica	Read-only
	DefaultPartner	GUID that identifies the replica that's the default synchronization partner	Read-only
	RepVersion	Tracks whether VBA code at a replica needs to be recompiled	Read-only
	LastUpdater	GUID of the replica that last updated data in the replica set	Read-only

TABLE 13.3: DAO Replication Properties (continued)

Object	Property	Description	Read/Write Status
	MostRecentSync-Partner	GUID of the replica that last made a synchronization exchange with this replica	Read-only
UserDefined document of Databases container	ReplicationConflict-Function	Name of a custom function that's called when synchronization conflicts or errors are detected; called only when the database is opened; to reset to default conflict resolution, you must delete this property	Read/write

TABLE 13.4: DAO Replication Methods of the Database Object

Method	Description
MakeReplica	Makes a new replica from the current replica
Synchronize	Synchronizes the current database with another replica

Replication Manager

If you've purchased a copy of the Microsoft Access Developer's Toolkit for Windows 95 (the Access 95 ADT), you have an additional mechanism for managing replication and synchronization: Replication Manager and its companion program, the Transporter. Replication Manager is shown in Figure 13.1.

Using Replication Manager, you can

- Replicate a database
- Create additional replicas for a replica set
- Synchronize replicas
- Create a regular synchronization schedule for a replica set
- Review the synchronization history of a replica
- Manage various replica properties
- Set up a synchronization scheme for remote sites

FIGURE 13.1:

FIGURE 13.1:

Replication Manager is managing a replica set on the computer WOMBAT.

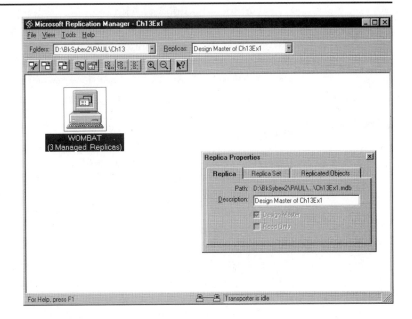

Managed Folders

In contrast to Access, Replication Manager takes a more global approach to managing replication. When you install Replication Manager, it asks you to designate one or more managed folders. Replication Manager and its companion program, the Transporter, work only with replicas residing in these managed folders (directories). To manage additional folders after setup, use the File ➤ Begin Managing Folder command.

We recommend using a different managed folder for each replica. Thus, if you had two applications replicated across a local area network, you'd use Replication Manager to create two managed folders on each desktop on the network.

Replication Manager makes it easy to plan your replication topology and manage the synchronization schedules for a replica set. This allows you to set up a regular synchronization schedule without programming. It also comes in handy if you need to review the synchronization history for a replica set.

You use Replication Manager to create replicas, design replication topologies, and set up synchronization schedules, but it is the Transporter program that actually carries out the scheduled synchronization exchanges, moving data between replicas at the times you have designated using Replication Manager. When you install Replication Manager, it defaults to loading the Transporter when you start Windows. If you don't plan on using Replication Manager and the Transporter to perform synchronization, you'll want to remove the Transporter icon from your startup group. Otherwise, you should leave this default behavior as is.

Transporters

When you use Replication Manager and the Transporter to manage synchronization of replicas on your LAN, you need to decide which PC will host the Transporter program. This machine will need to load the Transporter upon bootup and allow it to remain running in the background. If your LAN server runs under Windows 95 or Windows NT, you can run the Transporter directly on the server. If your server runs under NetWare, Windows for Workgroups, or some other network operating system, however, or you'd rather not increase the load on an already-overburdened server, you can elect to run the Transporter program from some other PC on the network.

You use a single transporter to manage the synchronization of all replicas on a LAN. On a WAN, however, or in a distributed system of workgroups occasionally connected by modem, you need to use multiple transporters, one for each workgroup (site). Each transporter would manage the synchronization schedule of the local workgroup's replicas and would cooperatively manage (along with the other site's transporter) the synchronization between workgroups.

The Replication Manager Map

The Replication Manager user interface can be a bit confusing. For locally managed replicas, Replication Manager draws a single machine icon on the screen (the map) to represent a replica set with the machine name, with the total number of local replicas this transporter manages appearing below the icon.

If you're using Replication Manager to manage multiple replica sets, you need to use the Folders and Replicas combo boxes to select a replica in the replica set you wish to manage before proceeding.

If replicas in the selected replica set are being managed by multiple transporters, Replication Manager draws an icon for each transporter site (see Figure 13.2).

FIGURE 13.2:

This replica set is managed by two transporters: one on the local PC (WOMBAT) and one on a remote PC (ZEBRA).

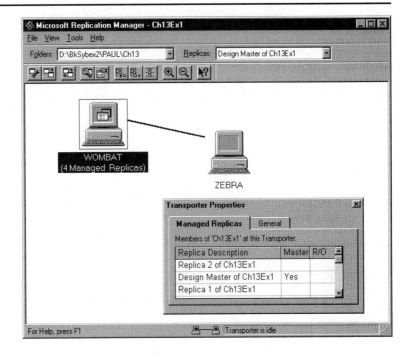

When to Use Replication

You may benefit from Jet replication in many situations. In general, anytime you need to keep multiple copies of the same database synchronized, Jet replication is a good candidate. Table 13.5 offers several scenarios under which replication might be considered and the relative merits of using a traditional file-server system, a traditional client-server system, or Jet replication for each scenario.

Local Area Networks

When designing a system for a local area network (LAN), you may have difficulty deciding whether to share a single copy of a nonreplicated database (or at least a single copy of a "data" database in a classic split Access database system—see Chapter 12 for more details) across a workgroup or to distribute replicated copies of the database to each user and regularly synchronize changes between the replicated copies. In most cases the more traditional file-server approach makes more

TABLE 13.5: Various Scenarios in Which Replication Might Be Considered

Scenario	Example	Candidate for File-Server?	Candidate for Client-Server?	Candidate for Replication?	Comments
Only one user needs access to data	Personal inventory database	No	No	No	No need for data sharing
Multiple users need read/write access to data across LAN; updates must be shared with other users immediately	Order-entry system for small business	Yes	Yes	No	Because employees and customers need up-to-the-minute status of an order, replication is ruled out
Multiple users need read/write access to data across LAN; updates don't need to be shared with other users immediately	Subscriber database for newsletter or magazine	Yes	Yes	Yes	Each employee covers a specific territory and rarely needs to see data for other territories. Hourly or daily updates of data from other territories would be adequate
Multiple users need read/write access to data, some of whom are remote on laptops; updates don't need to be immediately disseminated	Contact management/sales system for traveling sales representatives	No	No	Yes	Laptop users can synchronize changes when they plug back into the office
Multiple workgroups of users need read/write access to data spread out across a large company's WAN	Policyholder system for insurance company	No	Yes	Yes	The choice of client-server versus a replicated Access database would depend on the speed of the WAN connection and how up-to-date data needed to be

TABLE 13.5: Various Scenarios in Which Replication Might Be Considered (continued)

Scenario	Example	Candidate for File-Server?	Candidate for Client-Server?	Candidate for Replication?	Comments
Multiple sites need read/write access to data; sites are connected by modem spread out across the country or the globe	International medical research study with data collection performed at distributed clinics	No	No	Yes	Databases could be synchronized over modem lines on a regular schedule
Multiple sites connected by modem spread out across the country or the globe, each needing read-only access to the data	Corporate product information database	No	No	Yes	Databases could be one-way synchronized over modem lines on a regular schedule

sense because of the need for the immediate dissemination of updates to all users. In a replicated system, there is a greater time lag between the dissemination of updates. This lag period may vary from an hour to several hours or days, depending on the number of users, the volume of updates, the frequency of conflicts, the synchronization topology, and the synchronization schedule.

On the other hand, using replication in this scenario might make sense in one of the following situations:

- If data is updated infrequently
- If updates do not usually affect other users
- If the network is already overloaded
- If the network is often down

In these cases it might make sense to use a replicated database instead of the traditional file-server approach.

Another alternative, especially when you have an overloaded network and can't afford to move to a client-server system, might be to create a hybrid system that uses replication *and* file-server sharing. Create multiple workgroups, each tied to a workgroup server machine. Users within a workgroup would use a split database system with the data database residing on the workgroup's file server. The data database would be replicated across workgroup servers, which would be synchronized on a regular schedule. This hybrid system would distribute the load over multiple servers.

Update latency—the time it takes for an update to be propagated to all replicas in the replica set—would be small within a workgroup but would be greater between machines in different workgroups.

Wide Area Networks

Wide area networks (WANs) are usually larger than LANs (have more nodes) and are spread out across greater distances. Perhaps most important, the speed of the connection between two nodes (computers) on a WAN is slower than on a LAN. These factors usually rule out the use of a file-server sharing model on a WAN in favor of a client-server system. With the introduction of replication, however, you may wish to consider using replication instead of a classic client-server system when using a WAN. Recall that synchronization exchanges transfer only the changed records, not whole tables, which makes replication well suited for WANs.

Replication may make sense on a WAN in the following situations:

- If data is updated infrequently
- If updates do not usually affect other users
- If the network is already overloaded
- If the network is often down
- If the move to a client-server system is considered too expensive

On the other hand, replication is probably not a good candidate in the following situations:

- If there are a great many updates, especially if multiple users will be updating the same records (large number of conflicts)

- If there is a need for the immediate dissemination of updates to all users

- If data consistency is critical

In these situations you'd be better off using a more classic client-server, transaction-oriented approach or the replication services of a server database.

Contrasting Access Replication with Microsoft SQL Server 6.0 Replication

Microsoft has added replication capabilities to Microsoft SQL Server 6.0, as well as to Access. However, there are substantial differences in the way the two products handle replication.

On the most fundamental level, Access replication treats the data in every replica equally. You can make a change to data anywhere, and it will eventually propagate around the entire replica set. In contrast, SQL Server replication employs a "publish and subscribe" metaphor. One copy of the database publishes a table; many others may subscribe to it. Replication is a one-way-only process. (Multiple SQL Server databases may publish parts of the same table using horizontal or vertical partitioning, but these multiple publications may not overlap).

Since SQL Server replication operates on a table rather than a database level, it's easy to replicate tables from one database into a second, otherwise dissimilar database.

SQL Server offers much richer scheduling options than Access does for maintaining synchronization between replicas. Since the server keeps a transaction log, it has the ability to synchronize every time a specified number of transactions has taken place in a table. Thus, you can ensure that SQL Server replicas differ by no more than a maximum number of changed records from the publishing database without resorting to frequent, possibly unneeded synchronizations. Text and Image columns—the SQL Server rough equivalents of memo and OLE fields—cannot participate in transaction-based replication. They must be replicated using schedule-based replication instead.

SQL Server does not replicate schema changes to a published table. If you need to change the design of a table in a replicated SQL Server database, you must delete the old publication, create a new one, and manually synchronize the new table into every replica.

SQL Server replication offers an additional level of flexibility through the use of stored procedures to customize replication. A subscribing database can call a stored procedure on any replicated insert, delete, or update. This capability allows you to design replication schemes in which the data on the subscriber is stored differently than it is on the publisher.

Although SQL Server uses ODBC to move data into subscribing databases, neither Access nor SQL Server is yet capable of heterogeneous replication (replication between tables in databases of two different types). Microsoft has announced that future versions of SQL Server will have this capability. In the meanwhile, if you have a client-server database using Access for the front end and SQL Server for the back end (as we discuss in Chapter 14), you'll need to use the replication capabilities of both products to maintain multiple copies in synchronization. You might, for example, use Access replication to ensure that geographically diverse users all have the same forms and reports while using SQL Server replication to publish the data to servers to which those same users connect.

Loosely Connected Networks

Mobile users on laptops connected to either a LAN or a WAN either infrequently or over slow modem lines do not fit well into either the classic file-server or client-server system, especially when two-way transfer of updates is needed. This type of system is often ideally suited for Jet replication.

There at least two potential stumbling blocks, however, to the use of Jet replication on laptops:

- Laptops must have at least 12MB of RAM.

- There's no support for the replication of partial tables; that is, there's no support for a salesperson to have only the records for his or her region on his or her laptop. (We discuss several potential work-arounds for this shortcoming in the section "Partial Replication" at the end of this chapter.)

If you use Visual Basic instead of Access to develop your applications, you may be able to create replicated databases that run on systems with as little as 8MB of RAM.

Other Replication Uses

Replication may also be useful in the following situations:

- Warm backups
- Distribution of application updates

Even if you decide not to use replication to share data in a file-server environment, you may wish to consider using it for maintaining warm backups. By replicating a database and regularly (perhaps every 15 minutes or hourly) synchronizing it with another replica, you'll be ready in the event of a disaster that corrupts or destroys your main database. And if the backup replica is located on a different machine—perhaps even in another building—you're insulating yourself even further if the server itself goes down.

You may also wish to consider using replication to distribute application updates. This could significantly reduce the maintenance burden associated with updating an application that has been distributed to tens or hundreds of workstations. In this situation you'd synchronize with each workstation to distribute your update.

In both these scenarios, you'd have to weigh the potential benefits of using replication against the extra overhead replication adds to a database. (See the section "Changes Made to a Database When It Is Replicated" later in this chapter for more on replication overhead.)

Replication Topologies

When replicating a database, you must decide on a synchronization topology and schedule for the replica set. The *topology* defines which replicas exchange updates with which other replicas and the direction of these exchanges. The *schedule* defines when the exchanges occur and who initiates the exchanges. The topology and schedule you choose for your replica set affect the update latency.

LAN Topologies

Various topologies that might be used on a LAN are depicted in Figure 13.3 and contrasted in Table 13.6.

Which synchronization topology you choose will depend on the importance of latency, network load, and synchronization reliability. If a very short latency is of utmost importance, network traffic is not a concern, and you don't have many nodes, then you may wish to use the fully connected topology. Otherwise, the star usually works best, with the ring topology another common choice. Replication Manager uses the star topology for locally managed replicas. The replica in the middle of a star topology is called the hub replica, and the other replicas are called satellite replicas.

FIGURE 13.3:

Common replication topologies for a local area network

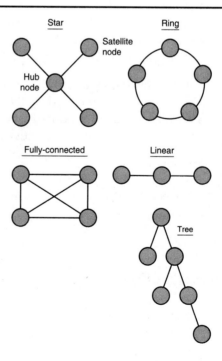

TABLE 13.6: Contrasting Various Replication Topologies

Topology	Latency	Load Distribution	Network Traffic	Reliability	Comments
Star	Moderate	Uneven	Low	Good as long as hub doesn't fail; bad if hub fails	Appropriate for many situations. Two rounds of synchronization exchanges may be necessary to fully propagate updates
Ring	Moderate	Even	Low	Good if direction can be reversed in the event of a node failure	Appropriate for many situations, especially when you need to evenly distribute the load
Fully connected	Low	Even	High	Good	Best latency but the most network traffic since every replica must exchange with every other replica in the replica set. Appropriate for applications with a small number of nodes where latency must be kept to a minimum
Linear	High	Even	Low	Bad; if any node fails, synchronization is disrupted	Simple to implement but worst update latency. May be appropriate for single-master model (data updates made only to the design master)
Tree	Variable	Uneven	Low	Depends on where the failure occurs	May be most efficient for applications where data updates occur only in selected nodes

WAN Topologies

All the topologies shown in Figure 13.3 are also possible on a WAN or a loosely connected network. More likely, however, you'll use a topology that interconnects several stars or rings, as depicted in Figure 13.4.

FIGURE 13.4:

Common replication topologies for a wide area network

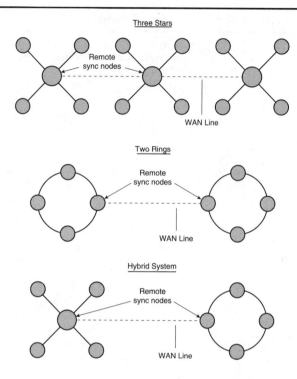

In a WAN or loosely connected network, each replica that exchanges updates with remote replicas is called a remote sync node. (This is our terminology, not Microsoft's.) If you're using Replication Manager, the transporters will most likely be located on these machines. WANs and loosely connected networks actually have two sets of topologies: the topology that connects the remote sync nodes (this topology shows up in the Replication Manager map) and the topology used at each workgroup site. In a topology that consisted of several interconnected stars, the hubs of each star would also be remote sync nodes.

Design Master Location

We recommend placing the design master for a replica set on a non-hub computer when using the star topology. In addition, the design master should not be a remote sync node. This allows you to insulate the design master from the rest of the replicas and to better control when design changes are rolled out to the other members of the replica set.

When you will be making design changes over an extended time period, you should remove the design master from the normal synchronization schedule so that inconsistent design changes are not propagated to other members of the replica set.

Changes Made to a Database When It Is Replicated

When you replicate a database, Jet makes a number of changes to the database. These changes include

- Adding fields to each replicated table in the database
- Changing sequential AutoNumber fields to random AutoNumber fields
- Adding several system tables to the database
- Adding properties to database document objects

These changes, which can significantly increase the size of your database, are explored in the next few sections.

New Tables

Several new system tables are added to the database when it is replicated. These tables track the names and locations of replicas and replicated tables in the replica set, log synchronization exchanges, track deleted records, and log synchronization conflicts and errors. The replication system tables are summarized in Table 13.7.

TABLE 13.7: System Tables Added to a Replicated Database

Table	Present When	Purpose	Replicated?*
MSysErrors	Always	Tracks unresolved data synchronization errors for this replica set. This table is empty when all errors have been resolved	Yes
MSysExchangeLog	Always	Logs information on each synchronization exchange with this replica	No

TABLE 13.7: System Tables Added to a Replicated Database (continued)

Table	Present When	Purpose	Replicated?*
MSysGenHistory	Always	Logs the history of every generation of updates in the replica set of which this replica is aware. Used to avoid sending unchanged records during synchronization exchanges	No
MSysOthersHistory	Always	Logs the generations received from other replicas in the replica set	No
MSysRepInfo	Always	Stores information about the replica set, including the GUID of the design master	Yes
MSysReplicas	Always	Stores the GUID of each replica in the replica set	No
MSysRepLock	Always	Used to log failed attempts to lock rows during a synchronization exchange	No
MSysSchChange	Always	Stores all schema changes made to the design master. Jet deletes records in this table periodically to minimize the size of this table	No
MSysSchedule	Always	Schedule information used by Replication Manager and the Transporter. Used only with these utilities	Yes
MSysSideTables	After first conflict has occurred	Stores the name of the conflict table and GUID of the user table to which it applies. Contains one record for each table with outstanding conflicts	No
MSysTableGuids	Always	Stores the name of all replicated tables in the database and their GUIDs	No
MSysTombstone	Always	Stores the table and row GUIDs for all deleted rows in the replica	No
MSysTransp-Address	Always	Stores settings used by the Transporter	Yes
MSysTransp-Coords	Replication Manager–managed replicas	Stores the x, y coordinates of the topology map used in Replication Manager	No

*Even though many of these tables are not replicated, the records in many of them are kept up to date across all replicas of a replica set.

All the replication system tables are read-only. Most of the fields in these tables are readable, although some of the fields are not because the data is stored in binary form as OLE objects. An example of one of the system tables, MSysRepInfo, is shown in Datasheet view in Figure 13.5.

FIGURE 13.5:

MSysRepInfo table in Datasheet view

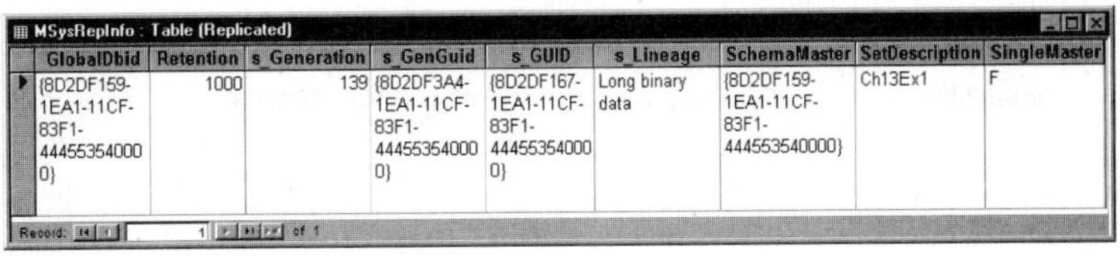

GlobalDbid	Retention	s_Generation	s_GenGuid	s_GUID	s_Lineage	SchemaMaster	SetDescription	SingleMaster
{8D2DF159-1EA1-11CF-83F1-44455354000 0}	1000	139	{8D2DF3A4-1EA1-11CF-83F1-44455354000 0}	{8D2DF167-1EA1-11CF-83F1-44455354000 0}	Long binary data	{8D2DF159-1EA1-11CF-83F1-444553540000}	Ch13Ex1	F

In addition to the hidden system tables outlined in Table 13.7, Jet creates local (non-replicated) conflict tables whenever there are outstanding conflicts in a database table as a result of a synchronization exchange. Jet constructs the name of the conflict table by appending "_Conflict" to the end of the table that contains conflicts. For example, the conflict table for tblCustomer would be tblCustomer_Conflict. The schema of the conflict table is the same as that of the original database table with which it is associated, except that the conflict table doesn't contain indexes (other than an index on the s_GUID field) or most field properties.

When a conflict occurs during synchronization because a row has been updated in both replicas, Jet creates a row in the conflict table (if this is the first conflict for a table, Jet first creates the conflict table) and stores in it the losing row. The algorithm used to determine the losing row is discussed in the section "Conflicts" later in this chapter.

When you use the Access UI to resolve conflicts, Access deletes the conflict table once you've resolved all the conflicts for a table. Thus, it's a good idea to do the same when using DAO code to resolve conflicts.

Table Changes

Jet makes two types of changes to each replicated table when a database is replicated or a local table is made replicable:

- It adds new replication fields.
- It changes existing AutoNumber fields.

Additional Replication Fields

Jet adds several fields to each replicated table. The additional replication fields are summarized in Table 13.8. All the replication fields are read-only.

TABLE 13.8: Replication Fields Added to Each Table

Field	Datatype	Purpose	Comments
s_Generation	Long Integer	Tracks changes (generations) to a row	Always present in replicated tables. If the s_Generation field value is 0, it represents an added row or a changed row that needs to be sent to other replicas during the next synchronization exchange. If it is a nonzero value, it represents the generation of the replica during which this change was made
s_GUID	AutoNumber—Replication ID	Added to most tables to uniquely identify the row across replicas, even if the primary key values change	This field will not be added to the table if the table contains an existing AutoNumber field with a field size of Replication ID. The CollsGuid property of the TableDef identifies which field is the GUID for the table—either s_GUID or a user-defined GUID field
s_Lineage	OLE Object	Tracks the history of changes to the record	
Gen_*Field*	Long Integer	One Gen field is added for each large object (memo or OLE object) user field in the table. This field tracks changes (generations) to the large object field independent of the other fields in the row	Its name takes the format Gen_*Field*, where *Field* is the name of the large object field. If this name is not unique, the rightmost characters are changed until a unique name is produced. The ColGeneration property of the large object field identifies the exact name of the accompanying Gen field

AutoNumber Fields

In addition to adding the fields from Table 13.8 to each database table, Jet alters the behavior of existing AutoNumber fields. If a table contains a Long Integer AutoNumber field with a NewValues property setting of Increment, Jet changes the property to Random. This significantly reduces the chance that two replicas have assigned the same AutoNumber value, because each AutoNumber field will be based on a randomly selected number between −2 billion and +2 billion. If for some reason this still produces too many duplicate values across a replica set, you may wish to use an AutoNumber field of type Replication ID instead. When you use an AutoNumber field with a Replication ID field size, Jet assigns numbers using a globally unique identifier.

Globally Unique Identifiers (GUIDs)

While no system can ever guarantee that a number will *always* be unique, globally unique identifier (GUID) numbers have been designed with *global* uniqueness in mind. (These numbers are also sometimes referred to as universally unique identifiers, or UUID.) A Jet-generated GUID is a 16-byte string made up of several parts that, when concatenated, have an infinitesimal chance of ever generating duplicate values. And the *global* in GUID means that each GUID will be unique throughout the world, regardless of where or when it was generated. The datasheet for a replicated table with a GUID row identifier field (s_GUID) is shown in Figure 13.6.

FIGURE 13.6:

The replication fields can be seen in the tblCustomer table.

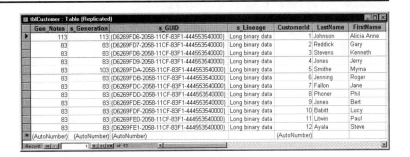

GUIDs are used in several places in a replicated database to uniquely identify many parts of a replicated system, including:

- Rows in a replicated table
- Each table in a replicated database
- Each replica in a replica set
- Each synchronization exchange

- Each database generation
- Each schema change
- Each transporter

New Properties

Replicating a database adds properties to database objects. Earlier in the chapter, in Table 13.3, we described the DAO properties added to the database itself and its document objects, including the MSysDB and UserDefined documents of the Databases container. Each of the properties added to Table document objects of the Tables collection (KeepLocal, Replicable, and CollsGuid) is also added to the Properties collection for each TableDef object.

Jet adds properties to some TableDef *fields* also: the ColGeneration property is added to memo and OLE object fields. ColGeneration identifies the name of the field used to track generations for these large object fields.

Replicating a Database

The first step in employing Jet's replication services is to convert an existing non-replicated database into a replicated design master. You can do this using the Access menus, the Windows 95 Briefcase, Replication Manager, or DAO.

Regardless of which method you employ, you'll notice several Access UI changes in the look and behavior of the database that are a result of the underlying changes Jet makes to the database schema. (See the section "Changes Made to a Database When It Is Replicated" earlier in this chapter.)

One of the first changes you will notice is to the title bar of the Database Explorer. Nonreplicated databases have title bars of the form *database_name*: Database. After replication, the title bar changes to either *database_name*: Design Master or *database_name*: Replica.

In addition, when you save new database objects other than tables in a design master, the Save As dialog will include a new Make Replicable check box, as shown in Figure 13.7. This is not the case for new tables. When you save a new table in a design master, you don't have the option of making it replicable; instead, Access

FIGURE 13.7:

Saving a form in a replicated database

displays a warning dialog after you save a new object. To make a local object replicable in a design master, open the object's property dialog by using the View ➤ Properties menu command (or by using the equivalent right-click shortcut menu command) and check the Replicated check box.

All saved objects in non–design master replicas will automatically be local. You can't change this. The only way you can make a local object replicable in a non–design master replica is to import that object into the design master, delete it from the replica, and then make it replicable in the design master by using the View ➤ Properties command.

Replicating a Database Using the Access Menus

You use Tools ➤ Replication ➤ Create Replica to convert an existing nonreplicated database into a replication design master. After executing this command, you are met with a warning dialog explaining that Access will close the database and then convert it into a replicated design master.

If you choose to proceed, you will see a second dialog asking whether you want Access to create a backup of your database before converting it. If you haven't already backed up the database, do so now, because there's no simple way to "un-replicate" a database. Access names the backup database name with the same root name and the extension .BAK. You won't have a chance to change this now, but you can always rename the backup later using the Explorer. If you choose Yes or No, Access converts the database to the design master of the new replica set; if you choose Cancel, the database will not be replicated. After the database has been converted, you will see a File Save As dialog, which asks for a name for the second replica of the replica set (see Figure 13.8). It's important to realize that the design master has already been created, assuming the name of the database you chose to convert. This dialog, however, refers to the name for a second replica of the replica set, not the

FIGURE 13.8:

After converting your database to the design master for the replica set, Access asks you to name a second replica.

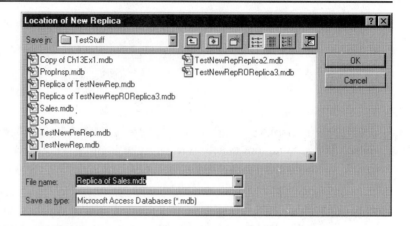

design master. If you don't wish to create a second replica at this time, you can click the Cancel button; otherwise, name the replica (or accept the default "Replica of *database_name*" name) and click OK to create the replica.

You can create additional replicas from any existing replica using the same command (Tools ➤ Replication ➤ Create Replica) you used to convert a database to a replicated design master.

Replicating a Database Using Replication Manager

You use the File ➤ Convert Database to Design Master command to convert a non-replicated database into a replicated design master. Executing this command launches the Convert Database to Design Master Wizard. Like the Access menus, Replication Manager gives you the option of creating a backup with the .BAK extension when it converts the database. Unlike the Access menus, Replication Manager does not create a second replica for the replica set during the conversion process.

In creating and managing replicas, Replication Manager offers two features that are not exposed to you through either the Access UI or Jet DAO:

- Single design master replica sets
- Replica retention period

Single Master Replica Sets

When converting a database to a design master, Replication Manager gives you the option of creating a replica set based on the *single master model* (see Figure 13.9). In this model, schema *and* data changes can be made only at the design master. If you choose the single master model (the second radio button option shown in Figure 13.9), all replicas other than the design master will be read-only (even if you specify otherwise when creating replicas using DAO). When you choose this option, Jet sets the SingleMaster field in the MSysRepInfo table to "T". Of course, you can get the equivalent effect in DAO by always creating read-only replicas, but there is no documented way to create a single master replica set from the Access UI or DAO.

WARNING   Take care before creating a single master replica set. There's no way to reverse this operation.

FIGURE 13.9:

Using Replication Manager, you can create replica sets that allow data changes only in the design master. The default setting is to allow data changes in all replicas.

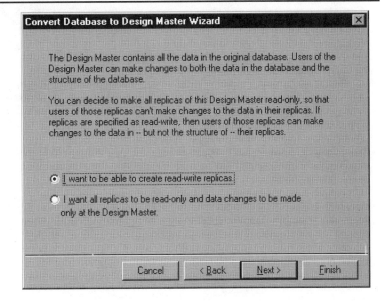

Convert Database to Design Master Wizard

The Design Master contains all the data in the original database. Users of the Design Master can make changes to both the data in the database and the structure of the database.

You can decide to make all replicas of this Design Master read-only, so that users of those replicas can't make changes to the data in their replicas. If replicas are specified as read-write, then users of those replicas can make changes to the data in -- but not the structure of -- their replicas.

   ⦿ I want to be able to create read-write replicas.

   ○ I want all replicas to be read-only and data changes to be made only at the Design Master.

Cancel   < Back   Next >   Finish

Replica Retention Period

Replication Manager exposes the ability to set the replica retention period. This value, which is stored in the MSysRepInfo table in the Retention field, controls how long Jet maintains schema changes and deleted records for replicas that have not been synchronized. This Integer value must be between 5 and 32,000 days and can be set only for the design master.

Even though you cannot set the retention value from Access, when you create a new replica set using the Access UI, the retention period is set to 1000 days. If you use Replication Manager or Jet DAO to create the replica set, however, the retention period is set to a much shorter time period: 60 days. Regardless of which of these methods you used to create the design master, you can use Replication Manager's Replica property sheet to alter the value at any time (see Figure 13.10).

FIGURE 13.10:

You can adjust the replica retention period for a replica set using Replication Manager.

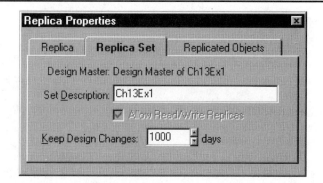

When you open a replica in Access or Replication Manager that is within 5 days of expiring, you are reminded of the impending replica expiration with a warning message. If the retention period expires for a replica, Replication Manager will refuse to synchronize changes between this replica and other replicas in the replica set. (Access also tells you that you will no longer be able to synchronize the expired replica, but our testing has revealed that the Tools ➤ Replication ➤ Synchronize Now command still works.)

Selectively Replicating Database Objects

The Convert Database to Design Master Wizard includes a page that allows you to selectively exclude objects from being replicated when the database is first converted (see Figure 13.11). These objects will still be present in the design master, but they will not be replicated to other members of the replica set. This feature is equivalent to setting the KeepLocal property of objects to "T" using DAO.

FIGURE 13.11:
You can use the Select Replicated Objects dialog to keep objects from being replicated.

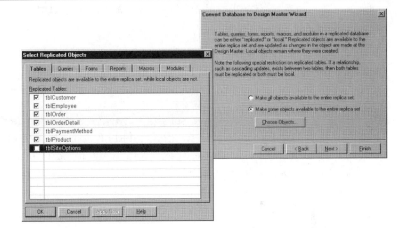

Once a database has been replicated, you can use the Modify Object Status command button on the Replicated Objects tab of the Replica property sheet to make selected design master objects replicated or local. (This command button's label changes to View Object Status for non–design master replicas.) This feature is equivalent to setting the Replicable property of objects to "T" or "F" using DAO.

Replicating a Database Using DAO

Using DAO, you convert a nonreplicated database into a replicated design master by setting the Replicable property of the database to "T". In an odd stroke of inconsistency with the rest of Access and Jet, Microsoft has given this and other true/false replication properties a String datatype that must be set to the literal String value of "T".

Since the Replicable property of the database will not exist until you set it for the first time, you'll need to add the property to the database's Properties collection in order to set it. For example, you could use the following code to make a new design master from the nonreplicated DatabaseToBeReplicated.MDB database:

```
Sub CreateNewReplicaSet()

    Dim db As Database
    Dim prp As Property

    Set db = DBEngine.Workspaces(0). _
     OpenDatabase("DatabaseToBeReplicated.MDB", _
     Exclusive:=True)

    Set prp = db.CreateProperty("Replicable", dbText, "T")
    db.Properties.Append prp

End Sub
```

Note that we have set the Exclusive parameter of the OpenDatabase method to True. To convert a nonreplicated database to a replicated design master, you must have the database open exclusively. In addition, you *can't* convert the currently open database.

Creating Additional Replicas Using DAO

To create additional replicas, you use the CreateReplica method of the database object. The syntax of CreateReplica is

database.MakeReplica *replica_name, description*

[, dbRepMakeReadOnly]

For example, you could use the following subroutine to create a new read/write replica based on the current database:

```
Sub MakeReplica()

    Dim db As Database

    Set db = CurrentDb()

    db.MakeReplica "Replica1.MDB", _
```

```
    "Replica of DatabaseToBeReplicated"

End Sub
```

The value of the description parameter is stored in the Description field of MSys-Replicas, and you can view and change it using Replication Manager. In fact, when you use Replication Manager, the description—not the replica name—appears in the Replicas drop-down box, so you may wish to create succinct but informative descriptions.

If you include the optional dbRepMakeReadOnly property, the created replica will be read-only.

The basReplicationTools module in the CH13A.MDB database includes the glrCreateReplicaSet() and glrCreateReplica() functions, which you can use to create new design masters and additional replicas, respectively.

Selectively Replicating Database Objects Using DAO

Prior to converting a database into a replicated design master, you can prevent objects from being replicated by setting their KeepLocal property to "T". By default, this property doesn't exist until you create it. If you wish to change your mind and replicate a local object before converting the database, set KeepLocal to "F". You can use the glrGetKeepLocal() and glrSetKeepLocal() functions in basReplicationTools to get and set the KeepLocal property of objects, respectively. glrSetKeepLocal() is shown in Listing 13.1.

Listing 13.1

```
Function glrSetKeepLocal(ByVal intObjType As Integer, _
  ByVal strObjectName As String, ByVal fKeepLocal As Boolean) _
  As Boolean

      ' Prevent an object from being replicated when
      ' the database is converted into a replicated design master.
      ' Can only be used on nonreplicated databases.
      ' First parameter should be one of the acObject constants.

      On Error GoTo glrSetKeepLocal_Err

      Dim db As Database
      Dim con As Container
```

```
        Dim doc As Document
        Dim varCon As Variant
        Dim varProp As Variant
        Dim strMsg As String

        Const glrcProcName = "glrSetKeepLocal"

        glrSetKeepLocal = False

        varCon = glrIntObjType2Container(intObjType)

        If Not IsNull(varCon) Then
            Set db = CurrentDb()
            Set con = db.Containers(varCon)
            Set doc = con.Documents(strObjectName)

            If fKeepLocal Then
                varProp = glrSetProp(doc, "KeepLocal", "T")
            Else
                varProp = glrSetProp(doc, "KeepLocal", "F")
            End If
        End If

        glrSetKeepLocal = True

glrSetKeepLocal_Exit:
    On Error GoTo 0
    Exit Function

glrSetKeepLocal_Err:
    Select Case Err
    Case Else
        strMsg = "Error#" & Err.Number & "--" & Err.Description
        MsgBox strMsg, vbCritical + vbOKOnly, "Procedure " & _
          glrcProcName
        Resume glrSetKeepLocal_Exit
    End Select

End Function
```

glrSetKeepLocal() returns True if it succeeds. The intObjType parameter takes one of the acObject constants (acTable, acQuery, acForm, acReport, acMacro, or acModule). The strObjName parameter is the object name. You set the fKeepLocal parameter to True to keep an object local or False to make it replicable. This function uses the glrSetProp() function from Chapter 6, as well as a private function, glrInt-ObjType2Container(), which converts the acObject constants into the proper container name.

After you have replicated a database, the KeepLocal property becomes read-only. You can, however, use the Replicable property of objects to make an object local or replicated. You can set this property to "T" or "F" in the design master, but you can't set this property to "T" for local objects in non–design master replicas. The glrGetReplicable() and glrSetReplicable() functions get and set the Replicable property of objects, respectively. glrSetReplicable() is shown in Listing 13.2.

Listing 13.2

```
Function glrSetReplicable(ByVal intObjType As Integer, _
 ByVal strObjectName As String, ByVal fKeepLocal As Boolean) _
 As Boolean

    ' Make an object replicated or local.
    ' Can only be used on a replicated database.
    ' First parameter should be one of the acObject constants.

    On Error GoTo glrSetReplicable_Err

    Dim db As Database
    Dim con As Container
    Dim doc As Document
    Dim varCon As Variant
    Dim varProp As Variant
    Dim strMsg As String

    Const glrcProcName = "glrSetReplicable"

    glrSetReplicable = False

    varCon = glrIntObjType2Container(intObjType)

    If Not IsNull(varCon) Then
        Set db = CurrentDb()
        Set con = db.Containers(varCon)
        Set doc = con.Documents(strObjectName)

        If fKeepLocal Then
            varProp = glrSetProp(doc, "Replicable", "T")
        Else
```

```
            varProp = glrSetProp(doc, "Replicable", "F")
        End If
    End If

    glrSetReplicable = True

glrSetReplicable_Exit:
    On Error GoTo 0
    Exit Function

glrSetReplicable_Err:
    Select Case Err
    Case Else
        strMsg = "Error#" & Err.Number & "--" & Err.Description
        MsgBox strMsg, vbCritical + vbOKOnly, "Procedure " & _
         glrcProcName
        Resume glrSetReplicable_Exit
    End Select

End Function
```

When you change the Replicated property of an object from "T" to "F", Jet makes the object local to the design master and deletes it from other replicas during the next synchronization.

When to Convert a Database

Because Jet must track all schema changes in a replicated database and maintain each version in the MSysSchChange table, we recommend delaying the conversion process until you think you have finalized the design of the database and have an application that is close to final. Of course, database and application design is a dynamic process, so it's impossible to say with any reasonable certainty when a database is complete. Still, your replicated database will be smaller and faster if you replicate it later rather than sooner in the design process. We suggest the following order when building a database that will be replicated:

1. Design and create the database tables.

2. Build the application.

3. Test, debug ,and refine all application components with the exception of any involving replication. This should include the usual multiuser testing if you plan on having at least some replicas shared by multiple concurrent users.

4. Convert the database into a replicated design master and one additional replica.

5. Add the replication components to your application.

6. Test, debug, and refine the application, including the new replication components.

7. Synchronize and compact the replicas.

8. Create additional replicas as necessary for the application.

9. Perform final testing and debugging.

10. Roll out the final application.

Preventing Replication

Only users with the Administer permission for a database can convert it to a replicated design master. However, any user who can open a replica has the necessary permissions to create additional replicas from an existing replica. This is unfortunate because each replica in a replica set takes some overhead to track. Of course, this may not be a problem if you do not give users the ability to create replicas in your application, but these users will still be able to create replicas if they can open the database outside the confines of your application using Access or Replication Manager.

Reversing Replication

Once replicated, a database can't be un-replicated—at least not directly. You can follow these steps, however, to create a nonreplicated version of a replicated database:

1. Open the design master and document the existing relationships—either manually or by using the Database Documentor Add-In.

2. Delete all relationships in the design master.

3. Select a table in the Database Explorer and choose View ➤ Properties (or the equivalent shortcut menu). Uncheck the Replicated property and click the OK button. Repeat for all other replicated tables.

4. Create a new empty database and import all objects from the design master to the new database.

5. Open the new database created in step 4, which should now contain all the objects from the replicated database. Using the relationship documentation created in step 1, re-create all relationships in the new database.

Synchronizing Replicas

When you make a synchronization exchange between two replicas, Jet copies schema changes and data updates between the two replicas. The default exchange method is two way, which means that data updates move in both directions. If you are using DAO or Replication Manager to perform the synchronization exchange, you can also opt for a one-way data exchange between two replicas, but regardless of whether you choose two-way or one-way exchanges, Jet always propagates schema changes.

Synchronizing two databases is simple—Jet does all the work. It's up to you, however, to decide when to synchronize, with whom, and whether to use two-way or one-way synchronization. You're also responsible for making sure the two replicas are connected when you wish to synchronize them. In addition, you must be aware of how your replication topology affects the propagation of updates through your replica set. (See the section "Replication Topologies" earlier in this chapter.) Finally, you must manage any conflicts or errors that occur as a result of the synchronization exchange. This last item is discussed in the section "Managing Conflicts and Errors" later in this chapter.

Synchronizing Using the Access Menus

To synchronize two replicas using the Access menu commands, select Tools ➤ Replication ➤ Synchronize Now. Access responds with the Synchronize Database dialog, as shown in Figure 13.12. (This dialog will look different if you've used Replication Manager to distribute replicas to multiple transporters.) Access fills the Synchronize With combo box with the list of all known replicas from MSysReplicas. It also sets the default replica to the one you last synchronized with using Access. (This information is stored in the MostRecentSyncPartner property of the MSysDb document of the Databases container.)

FIGURE 13.12:

Synchronize Database dialog

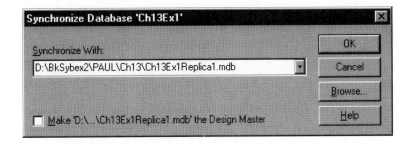

When the synchronization is complete, Access displays a dialog informing you that some changes (schema changes) won't be visible until you close and reopen the database and offering to do this for you.

Synchronizing Using Replication Manager

In addition to using the capabilities previously discussed in the area of replica management, you can use Replication Manager (and its companion Transporter program) to create synchronization schedules, perform the synchronizations, and view the results of synchronization exchanges. Although you can do all of this using DAO, you may ask yourself, "Why bother?" Replication Manager is Microsoft's preferred method for managing and automating synchronization exchanges, and for good reason: it makes the synchronization management process very easy.

You can synchronize a replica set using the Tools ➤ Synchronize Now command. When you execute this command, Replication Manager displays a dialog similar to the one shown in Figure 13.13. At this time you can choose to synchronize the selected replica with one of the following:

- All local members of the replica set managed at this location

- All members of the replica set at all locations

- The replicas at a specified remote site

FIGURE 13.13:

Synchronize Now dialog box

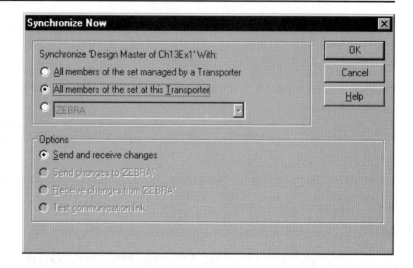

Scheduled Synchronizations

While the ability to synchronize replicas on demand is certainly useful, Replication Manager's scheduling abilities are its strong suit. You can set up a local synchronization schedule for all replica sets managed by the local transporter by right-clicking the local machine icon on the Replication Manager map and choosing Edit Locally Managed Replica Schedule from the shortcut menu. When you do this, Replication Manager displays the dialog shown in Figure 13.14. You can schedule synchronizations on a weekly basis in 15-minute increments. This schedule applies to all local replicas managed by this Transporter; there's no way to create individual schedules for different replica sets.

Remote Synchronizations

In addition to scheduling the synchronization of local replicas, you can use Replication Manager to manage synchronizations between *remote* sites. Once you have set up the replica on the remote site (see the sidebar "Setting Up Remote Synchronization Sites Using Replication Manager"), both sites will appear on the Replication Manager map (see Figure 13.15). If you right-click the line connecting the local and remote sites, a shortcut menu appears. To immediately synchronize the replicas at the two sites, choose Synchronize Now, which brings up the Synchronize Now dialog shown in Figure 13.13.

FIGURE 13.14:

Use this dialog to edit the synchronization schedule for locally managed replicas.

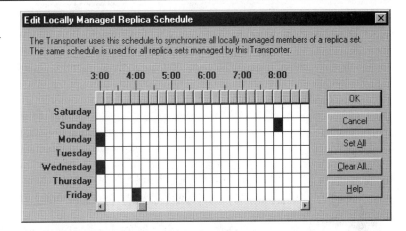

Setting Up Remote Synchronization Sites Using Replication Manager

While the Replication Manager documentation and online help system include plenty of references to synchronization topologies involving remote sites, they actually never discuss how to move a replica to a remote site and set up the remote synchronization site. Fortunately, the process is simple. Here are the steps to create a remote replica:

1. If you haven't already done so, install Replication Manager at the remote site and create a managed folder where the remote replica will reside.

2. At your local site, create a new replica in a local managed folder.

3. Establish a direct connection to the remote site. This connection can be by any means—modem or network—as long as you can open the managed folder at the remote site.

4. From your local site, select File ➤ Move Replica. Select the replica created in step 2 at the Move Replica dialog. Navigate to a managed replication folder at the remote site when prompted with the Move To dialog.

5. From the remote site, start Replication Manager and select the moved replica. Because the replica will know that it came from a machine that is managed by a different transporter, icons representing the local and remote sites should appear on the Replication Manager map.

6. From the remote site, establish a connection to the local site, right-click the line connecting the two sites, and select Synchronize Now from the shortcut menu.

7. Back at the local site, select Tools ➤ Refresh Managed Folder Information. The remote site should now appear on the local Replication Manager map.

Note that you're responsible for establishing the connections between the transporters at the two sites. You can use a wide area network, Windows 95 or Windows NT Dial-Up Networking, LapLink, or some other third-party connectivity program.

FIGURE 13.15:

The Replication Manager screen displays a map of the local and remote replicas.

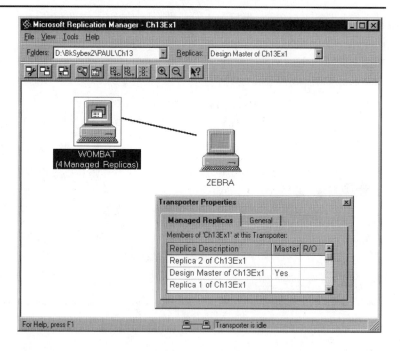

To edit the schedule for remote synchronization exchanges between two sites, right-click the line connecting the two sites and choose Edit Schedule. The Edit Schedule dialog appears, as shown in Figure 13.16. The shading of each box indicates which transporter initiates the exchange; if the same time point is selected by both sites, both sites will attempt to initiate the exchange at the same time.

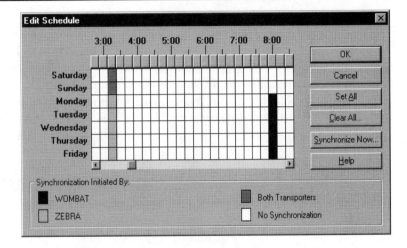

FIGURE 13.16:
You can use this dialog to edit the synchronization schedule between the local and remote replicas.

Once you have scheduled remote exchanges, it's up to you to ensure that the connection will be made prior to the synchronization exchange. If it's not, the Transporter will log the changes to a temporary database located in the drop-box folder for that transporter. (This was the location specified when you first configured Replication Manager; you can change it using the Tools ➤ Configure Microsoft Replication Manager command.) The Transporter then continues to check whether it can connect to the remote site every 15 minutes. When it eventually connects to the remote transporter, it transfers the changes that have accumulated in the drop-box to the target transporter.

This feature allows you to easily configure laptop copies of a database to be synchronized each time the laptop is connected to a network. Simply designate a dedicated drop-box folder for each laptop, which will receive all changes intended for that replica while the laptop is off the network. When the laptop returns, it will automatically be brought up to date.

Reviewing Synchronization History

Replication Manager includes the ability to view three types of activity logs:

- The local synchronization history
- The synchronization history with a remote site
- The transporter log

If you right-click the local machine icon and choose View Local Synchronization History, you'll be able to view the history of all local synchronization exchanges. Similarly, if you right-click a remote computer icon and choose View Synchronization History, you'll be able to view the history of exchanges between the local and remote replicas. A sample of a remote synchronization history log, which is sorted in descending order by the time the exchange was initiated, is shown in Figure 13.17.

FIGURE 13.17:

The remote synchronization history lists each exchange in descending time order.

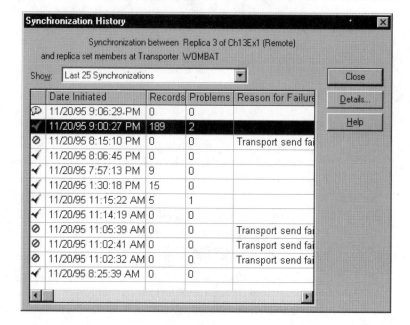

If you double-click a record (or click the Details button), a wealth of information regarding the selected exchange is revealed (see Figure 13.18), including:

- The direction of the exchange
- Whether the exchange was successful
- The number of data errors
- The number of conflicts
- The number and type of updates sent
- The number and type of updates received
- The number of design changes sent or received

In an unfortunate omission, Replication Manager fails to list the names of the replicas involved in the exchange; it tells you only the name of replica set.

FIGURE 13.18:

The Synchronization Details dialog reveals a wealth of detail regarding a particular exchange.

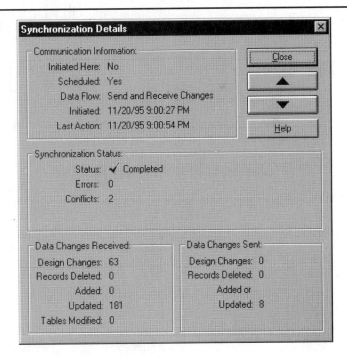

When you browse the local or remote synchronization history logs using Replication Manager, you are actually viewing the history of all synchronization exchanges, not just those initiated by Replication Manager or the Transporter program. Thus, even if you use the Access menus or DAO to synchronize replicas, you can still use Replication Manager to browse the exchange histories.

In addition to browsing the synchronization histories, you can view a cruder log of transporter activity by selecting the View ➤ Transporter Log command. The information in this log pertains only to activities involving the local transporter; it lacks the level of detail the Synchronization History commands reveal. Here's a sample of the information from a transporter log:

```
Time = 11/20/95 9:00:24 PM
Log Type = Start exchange
Replica = D:\BkSybex2\PAUL\Ch13\CH13B.mdb
Exchange ID = {B2D550EB-236F-11CF-83F1-444553540000}
Initiated Locally = Yes
Exchange Type = 131076
Destination Transporter = {7E1F04E0-F1C0-11CE-8F92-0080C786917E}
Destination ReplicaID = {EE30AE00-232A-11CF-8F93-0080C786917E}
Transport = YOUPICK
```

You may find this information useful when trying to debug a failed synchronization.

Synchronizing Using DAO

You can programmatically initiate synchronization exchanges using the Synchronize method of the database object. The syntax for this method is shown here:

database.Synchronize *DbPathName* [, *ExchangeType*]

where *DbPathName* is the path and name of the other replica you wish to exchange with and ExchangeType is one of the following constants:

Constant	Purpose
dbRepExportChangesSend	Only send changes to the other replica

Constant	Purpose
dbRepImportChangesReceive	Only receive changes from the other replica
dbRepImpExpChanges	Send and receive changes between both replicas (the default)

Just as when using Replication Manager, you're responsible for ensuring that any remote connections are made prior to initiating a synchronization exchange using DAO.

In basReplicationTools, we've created the glrDbSynch() function, which you can use to synchronize any two replicas programmatically. Listing 13.3 shows this function.

Listing 13.3

```
Function glrDbSynch(ByVal strToDb As String, _
 Optional ByVal varFromDb As Variant, _
 Optional ByVal varExchType As Variant) As Variant

    ' Synchronizes two databases
    ' If varFromDb is Null, current database is used
    ' varExchType must be one of following constants:
    '    dbRepImpExpChanges (the default), dbRepExportChanges,
    '    dbRepImportChanges
    ' Returns True if successful; otherwise returns error code

    On Error GoTo glrDbSynch_Err

    Dim dbFrom As Database
    Dim strMsg As String
    Const glrcProcName = "glrDbSynch"

    If IsMissing(varFromDb) Then
        Set dbFrom = CurrentDb()
    Else
        Set dbFrom = DBEngine.Workspaces(0). _
         OpenDatabase(varFromDb)
    End If

    If IsMissing(varExchType) Then varExchType = _
     dbRepImpExpChanges
```

```
    dbFrom.Synchronize strToDb, varExchType

    glrDbSynch = True

glrDbSynch_Exit:
    On Error GoTo 0
    Exit Function

glrDbSynch_Err:
    Select Case Err
    Case Else
        glrDbSynch = CVErr(Err.Number)
    End Select

End Function
```

NOTE If you execute synchronization code from a replica that has received design changes from a design master replica, you'll have to close and reopen the database for the changes to be incorporated into the schema of the open replica. Also, any conflict resolution code (either the built-in Access Conflict Resolution Wizard code or your custom code) will not automatically execute until you close and reopen the database. Unfortunately, there's no way to close and reopen the currently open database from code that is running from the open database.

Scheduling Synchronizations Using DAO

If you need to synchronize replicas on a regular basis and you've purchased the ADT, you may wish to use it instead of DAO to schedule synchronizations. It's easier to use, requires no programming, and maintains an excellent history of the exchanges. Creating your own synchronization schedule using DAO, however, does have some advantages:

- It allows you to deliver an Access-only solution; you don't have to install and use Replication Manager and the Transporter.

- You're not limited to a day-of-week schedule. For example, you could create a schedule based on the day of the month.

- You can synchronize at times other than at 15-minute intervals beginning on the hour.

- You can create a hybrid synchronization system that is based on both a regular timed schedule and update load. (See the next section.)

If you decide to implement a synchronization system using DAO, you'll need to decide how the process will be driven. Most likely you'll employ a hidden form that's automatically loaded when the database is started with code attached to the form's Timer event. This form would likely follow a schedule that was stored in a table in the database. But where will this hidden form and table reside? Should it be part of the normal application database that runs on each desktop, or should it perhaps run only on selected desktops? One alternative might be to keep this form and table in a utility database that's kept separate from the rest of your application. This application could run off the file server or the database administrator's desktop.

Synchronization Based on Number of Updates

You may wish to implement a synchronization system that is based on update load rather than (or in addition to) a regular schedule. You can ascertain the update load by counting the number of records in each replicated table in the database where the s_Generation field equals 0. This number represents the number of records that have been updated or added since the last synchronization exchange. The sample form frmUpdateVolume in the CH13B sample database contains code that does just that. If you open this form and click its command button, the code in Listing 13.4 executes. After a brief delay, the number of updated records in the replicated tables in the database is displayed in a text box on the form (see Figure 13.19).

FIGURE 13.19:
frmUpdateVolume counts the number of updated records since the last synchronization exchange.

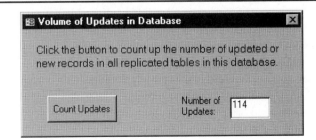

Listing 13.4

```
Private Sub cmdCount_Click()

    ' Count the number of updated/new
    ' records in any replicated tables
    ' in this database

    Dim lngCount As Long
    Dim ctlCount As TextBox
    Dim db As Database
    Dim tdf As TableDef

    DoCmd.Hourglass True

    Set ctlCount = Me!txtCount
    Set db = CurrentDb()
    lngCount = 0

    For Each tdf In db.TableDefs

        If glrGetReplicable(acTable, tdf.Name) = "T" Then
            lngCount = lngCount + DCount("*", tdf.Name, _
            "[s_Generation]=0")
        End If

    Next tdf

    ctlCount = lngCount
    ctlCount.Enabled = True

    DoCmd.Hourglass False

End Sub
```

Of course, this example doesn't do anything with the value, but once you've determined the number of updated or new records, you can easily decide whether it's time to synchronize. It's likely you'd call this code from a hidden form that is used to maintain a synchronization schedule for your application. (See the previous section, "Scheduling Synchronizations Using DAO.")

Managing Conflicts and Errors

Three types of problems can occur as the result of a synchronization exchange (or an attempted synchronization exchange) between two replicas:

- Conflicts
- Data errors
- Design errors

Conflicts

Synchronization conflicts can arise when the same record has been modified in more than one replica since the last synchronization exchange. When this happens, Jet must declare one of the changes the winner in order to keep the replicas in agreement. In determining which update "wins" the exchange, Jet follows a fairly simple algorithm:

- If the row was updated more times in one replica than the other, its changes win.
- If rows were updated an equal number of times in the two replicas, Jet chooses a winner randomly.

When designing Jet replication, Microsoft realized that you may not want to resolve conflicts in this fashion, so Jet logs each losing row to a conflict resolution table. As mentioned in the section "Changes Made to a Database When It Is Replicated" earlier in this chapter, the conflict table name is constructed by appending "_Conflict" to the end of the name of the table that contains the conflicts.

Jet makes two other changes to the database when it creates a conflict table: it logs the name of the conflict table and its GUID to the MSysSideTables system table. In addition, it adds the ConflictTable property to the Properties collection of the user TableDef object, setting it equal to the name of the conflict table for that table.

> **NOTE**　Unlike the way it handles many other properties of tables, Jet adds the ConflictTable property only to the TableDef object's properties collection, not the Table document object for the table.

Data Errors

A data error occurs whenever a record in one replica causes some type of error state in another replica. The different types of data errors are summarized in Table 13.9.

Data errors are stored in MSysErrors until they have been resolved. Unlike conflict records, data errors are replicated throughout the replica set, so MSysErrors will often contain multiple records for a given error. For example, information on both inserted records will be logged into MSysErrors for a duplicate key error. To resolve

TABLE 13.9: Data Errors That Can Occur in a Replica Set

Error	Occurs When	How to Resolve
Duplicate keys	A record with the same primary key value or values is inserted in two or more replicas. Usually occurs for non-AutoNumber primary keys, but it can occur when two random AutoNumber values have been assigned to different records	Delete one of the duplicate records or change the value of its primary key so it's no longer a duplicate
Validation rules	You change a table-level validation rule in one replica while at the same time, a user adds or updates records in another replica that fail to satisfy the new rule	Correct the new records so they meet the new rule
Referential integrity	A user inserts a new record in one table that references a primary key value in another table while at the same time, a second user deletes the referenced record in a second replica	Delete the record that references the deleted key (If you've enabled cascading deletes, this situation will correct itself during the next synchronization exchange.)
Locked records	A record that needs to be updated during a synchronization exchange is locked by another user	Release the lock (This is usually just a temporary problem that will correct itself during the next synchronization exchange.)

a data error, you must correct the offending situation and resynchronize. Sometimes you may have to synchronize more than once to completely resolve the data error. Jet deletes the row from MSysErrors when the data error has been resolved.

> **WARNING** Because of the inherent complexities, only the database administrator or technically adept users should attempt data error resolution. At the very least, the database administrator should be contacted as soon as a data error occurs so it can be corrected quickly.

You can prevent many data errors by following these rules:

- Divide up the responsibility for adding new records by territory or some other criteria so it's unlikely that multiple users will be inserting the same records. If it's likely there will be some overlap, assign one user responsibility for okaying the new records.

- Make table validation rule changes and referential integrity rule changes only after you have synchronized all replicas in the replica set, and immediately synchronize the replicas after making the change. Also, you may wish to make these schema changes only during off hours.

Design Errors

Design errors can occur when a design change made at the design master replica conflicts with the design state of another replica. For example, if you add a table at the design master replica and make it replicable, but a user has previously created a local table at another replica with the same name, a design error will occur when these replicas attempt to synchronize.

Design changes are always applied first, before data changes are exchanged, during a synchronization exchange. Because of this, a design error will cause a synchronization exchange to fail.

> **WARNING** Since design errors prevent data from being exchanged, the database administrator must attend to them immediately.

Design errors are logged into the MSysSchemaProb system table at the replica where the design change could not be applied. This means that the design master replica will never be notified of the design error since, unlike MSysErrors, MSysSchemaProb is not replicated. MSysSchemaProb is deleted once all design errors have been corrected. Like data errors, design errors require immediate attention by a database administrator, who should carefully review the records in MSysSchemaProb in order to determine how to fix the errors. This will require removing the blocking object at the non–design master replica. You'll need to make the change at the non–design master replica even if you plan to remove the design master change. (If this is the case, you may wish to export the object to another database before you delete it so you can easily re-create the local object after the design error has been resolved.)

Resolving Conflicts Using Access Menus

When a user opens a database in Access that has lost at least one conflict during the synchronization exchange, Access displays a message and asks whether the user would like to resolve conflicts now. This message is displayed right after the execution of the database's AutoExec macro or the opening of the database's startup form. If the user answers Yes to this message box dialog, Access displays the Resolve Replication Conflicts dialog, as shown in Figure 13.20.

FIGURE 13.20:

Resolve Replication Conflicts dialog

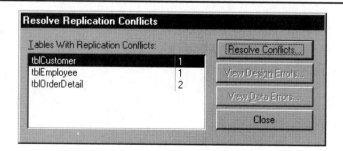

If the user highlights a conflict table and clicks the Resolve Conflicts button, Access launches the Conflict Resolution Wizard, which creates a custom conflict resolution form for the selected conflict table (see Figure 13.21). Using this form, the user can review and possibly reverse the automated decision as to which version of the record was declared the winner. The custom conflict resolution form is deleted as soon as it is closed and re-created, if necessary, the next time the user clicks the Resolve Conflicts button for that table.

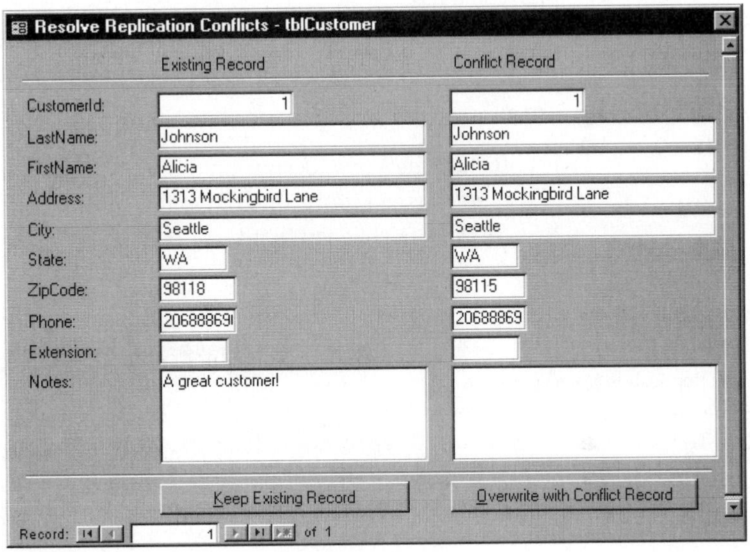

FIGURE 13.21:

The Conflict Resolution Wizard creates a custom conflict resolution form for each table with conflicts.

Once the user has either kept or overwritten each record in a conflict table, Access deletes the conflict resolution table, removes the entry from MSysSideTables, sets the ConflictTable property to Null, and displays a message box stating that all conflicts have been resolved.

Resolving Errors Using Access Menus

If either data or design errors are present in the database, the appropriate button will be enabled on the Resolve Replication Conflicts dialog (see Figure 13.20).

If data errors are present and you click the View Data Errors button, Access displays the Replication Data Errors form (see Figure 13.22). You can use this form to view the pertinent information regarding the data errors. Because this form (and its source of information, MSysErrors) does not log the primary key values for the offending records, you'll need to note the RecordId field. (This is the value of the s_GUID field) for each record (as well as the table in which the error occurred and the nature of the error). You may wish to write down or copy this information to the Windows clipboard. (The ability to print a record from this form would be a nice enhancement.) With this information in hand, you'll next need to use the Tools ➤ Options command to turn on the display of system objects and then use a filter or the Edit ➤ Find dialog to locate the offending records in the tables based on the s_GUID value. See Table 13.9 for some hints on how to resolve certain types of data errors.

If you click the View Design Errors button, Access displays the Replication Design Errors form (see Figure 13.23), which, unlike the more cryptic Replication Data Errors form, is fairly easy to interpret.

FIGURE 13.22:

The Replication Data Errors form reveals the offending data errors.

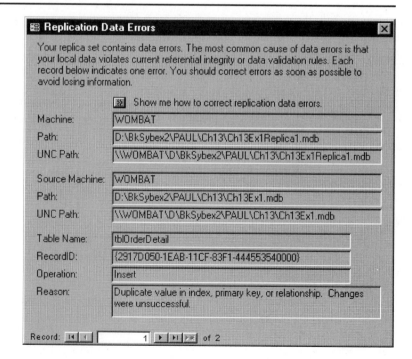

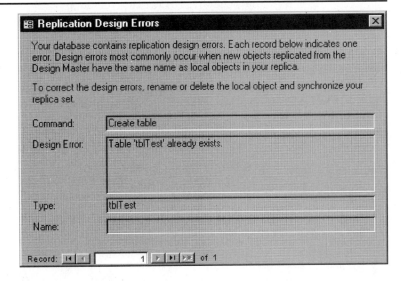

The Replication Design Errors form describes design errors that are preventing this replica from synchronizing with another replica in the replica set.

Resolving Conflicts and Errors Using DAO

If you are using the Access Developer's Toolkit or a Visual Basic application, the Access Conflict Resolution Wizard will not be available. You will have to create your own facility for reviewing and resolving conflicts. Even if you are using Access, you may wish to resolve conflicts using a custom resolution algorithm rather than depend upon users to resolve conflicts.

Creating a Custom Conflict and Error Resolution Function

A custom conflict and error resolution function must take care of the resolution of conflicts, data errors, and design errors, so it's best to write a single high-level function that first determines the number of conflicts and errors in the database and then dispatches the appropriate procedure to deal with any problems that are present. For example, you might create a high-level function such as this:

```
Function glrResFun()

    ' Ignore errors in case MSys tables doesn't exist
    On Error Resume Next
```

```
Dim lngConflictTables As Long
Dim lngDataErrors As Long
Dim lngDesignErrors As Long
Dim fOK As Boolean
Dim db As Database

Set db = CurrentDb()

lngConflictTables = _
 db.TableDefs("MSysSideTables").RecordCount
lngDataErrors = db.TableDefs("MSysErrors").RecordCount
lngDesignErrors = _
 db.TableDefs("MSysSchemaProb").RecordCount"

If lngDataErrors = 0 And lngDesignErrors = 0 Then
    If lngConflictTables > 0 Then
        ' Call conflict resolution function
    End If
Else
    ' Call data error/design error processing function
End If

End Function
```

Setting the ReplicationConflictFunction Property

If you're using Access or the ADT, you can tell it to call your custom conflict and error resolution function (when there are conflicts or errors in the replica) at application startup by setting the ReplicationConflictFunction property of the UserDefined document of the Databases container to the name of your custom function. You must set this property to a string of the following format:

CustomFunction()

You must include the parentheses. To reset the conflict resolution facility to point to the default Access Wizard, you must remove this property from the UserDefined document's Properties collection; you can't set it to an empty or null string.

Besides having to create the ReplicationConflictFunction property before you can set its value, you must pass the CreateProperty method a True value for the usually optional fourth parameter, DDL. This Boolean parameter indicates that this property can't be changed or deleted unless the user has dbSecWriteDef permission. If you don't set this property to True, no error will occur, but your function will never be called.

The basReplicationTools module includes a function, glrSetConflictFunction(), you can use to programmatically set this property. You can find this function in Listing 13.5.

Listing 13.5

```
Function glrSetConflictFunction(strFunName As String) As Boolean

    ' Use properties code to set this function

    On Error GoTo glrSetConflictFunction_Err

    Dim db As Database
    Dim doc As Document
    Dim prp As Property
    Dim varProp As Variant
    Dim strMsg As String

    Const glrcProcName = "glrSetConflictFunction"

    glrSetConflictFunction = False

    Set db = CurrentDb()
    Set doc = db.Containers!Databases.Documents!UserDefined

    If Len(strFunName) > 0 Then
        ' First attempt to set the existing property
        On Error Resume Next
        doc.Properties!ReplicationConflictFunction = strFunName
        ' If that failed, must create property
        If Err.Number <> 0 Then
            Set prp = doc.CreateProperty( _
```

```
                Name:="ReplicationConflictFunction", _
                Type:=dbText, Value:=strFunName, DDL:=True)
            doc.Properties.Append prp
        End If
        On Error GoTo glrSetConflictFunction_Err
    End If

    glrSetConflictFunction = True

glrSetConflictFunction_Exit:
    On Error GoTo 0
    Exit Function

glrSetConflictFunction_Err:
    Select Case Err
    Case Else
        strMsg = "Error#" & Err.Number & "--" & Err.Description
        MsgBox strMsg, vbCritical + vbOKOnly, "Procedure " & _
         glrcProcName
        Resume glrSetConflictFunction_Exit
    End Select

End Function
```

There are related functions in basReplicationTools that you can use to get the name of the current conflict and error resolution function (glrGetConflictFunction()) and reset the function back to the Access default (glrRemoveConflictFunction()).

Resolving Errors

It's unlikely that users will be able to understand and fix data or design errors, so you may wish to simply alert users of the number and type of errors and ask them to call the database administrator when this type of error occurs. For example, you might call a simple function such as glrProcessErrors(), which is shown in Listing 13.6.

Listing 13.6

```
Sub glrProcessErrors(lngDataErrors As Long, _
 lngDesignErrors As Long)

    Dim fOK As Boolean
    Dim strTitle As String
```

```
    Dim strMsg As String
    Dim strSol As String

    If lngDataErrors > 0 Or lngDesignErrors > 0 Then
        strTitle = "Database Synchronization Errors"
        strMsg = "* There are " & lngDataErrors & _
        " data errors." & vbCrLf & _
        "* There are " & lngDesignErrors & _
        " design errors."
        strSol = _
        "Contact your database administrator immediately!"
        MsgBox strTitle & "@" & strMsg & "@" & strSol, _
        vbCritical + vbOKOnly, "Serious Error"
    End If

End Sub
```

glrProcessErrors, which you can find in basConflictMng in the CH13B.MDB database, uses the special formatting capabilities of MsgBox that are new for Access 95. (For further details on these capabilities, see Appendix D on the companion disk.)

Resolving Conflicts

The basic idea behind a custom conflict resolution function is to iterate through each of the records in a conflict table, make a decision on how to resolve the conflict, resolve the conflict, and then delete the conflict record. The shell for a custom conflict resolution function might look the function shown in Listing 13.7.

Listing 13.7

```
Function CustomConflictResolver()

    Dim db As Database
    Dim tdf As TableDef
    Dim rstResolve As Recordset
    Dim strTable As String
    Dim strConflict As String

    Set db = CurrentDb()

    ' Iterate through all TableDefs looking for tables
    ' with conflict tables
    For Each tdf In db.TableDefs
        strTable = tdf.Name
```

```
        strConflict = Nz(tdf.ConflictTable)

        If (strConflict <> "" And Not strTable Like "~TMPCLP*") _
          Then
            Set rstResolve = db.OpenRecordset(strSQL)

            rstResolve.MoveFirst
             Do While Not rstResolve.EOF
                 '   Resolve conflict
                 rstResolve.MoveNext
            Loop

            rstResolve.Close
            db.TableDefs.Delete strConflict
        End If
    Next tdf

    MsgBox "Conflicts have been logged!", _
       vbInformation + vbOKOnly
End Function
```

This function uses the ConflictTable parameter of the TableDef object to determine whether a conflict table exists for each TableDef in the database. It also compares the table name with "~TMPCLP*" to skip any deleted tables.

The difficult part of this process is deciding how to resolve the conflict. The Access Conflict Resolution Wizard leaves the onus on the user, which isn't a bad approach for a built-in UI tool, but it's arguable whether a professional application should leave conflict resolution up to the user.

In creating a custom conflict resolution routine, the simplest approach would be to simply delete the conflict tables and take for granted that the automated decision based on the number of times the record was updated is correct, or at least good enough. Other approaches might include

- Logging all conflict records to a table and then deleting them
- Determining the winning record based on who (the user's security level) made the change
- Making the last update always the winning update
- Offering some user control, such as the built-in Wizard

- A hybrid approach that would let users of a certain security level decide on the winning record, while the resolution for all other users would follow some other scheme

The sample database CH13B.MDB includes a form, frmConResFun, that uses the glrGetConflictFunction(), glrSetConflictFunction(), and glrRemoveConflictFunction() functions to switch between the default Access Conflict Resolution Wizard and two different custom conflict and error resolution functions. This form is shown in Figure 13.24. If you choose the third choice on the form, it sets the ReplicationConflictFunction property to "glrResSecurity()". This function, which is part of the basConflictMng module, is shown in Listing 13.8.

FIGURE 13.24:
You can use frmConResFun to alter the ReplicationConflictFunction property.

Listing 13.8

```
Function glrResSecurity()

    ' This conflict resolution function
    ' inventories the conflicts and errors
    ' in the database and then dispatches
    ' the appropriate procedure.
    ' It calls the glrConflictSecurity function
    ' for resolution of conflicts.

    Dim lngConflictTables As Long
    Dim lngDataErrors As Long
    Dim lngDesignErrors As Long
    Dim fOK As Boolean
```

```
Call glrSynchInventory(lngConflictTables, _
  lngDataErrors, lngDesignErrors)

If lngDataErrors = 0 And lngDesignErrors = 0 Then
    If lngConflictTables > 0 Then
        fOK = glrResolveConflicts(True)
    End If
Else
    Call glrProcessErrors(lngDataErrors, lngDesignErrors)
End If

End Function
```

glrResSecurity() calls the glrResolveConflicts() function with a parameter of True, which tells the function to use security to resolve conflicts. The security algorithm is fairly simple:

- If the losing user has a security level that's the same or lower than the security level of the winning user, accept the default winner and delete the conflict record.

- Otherwise, if the losing user's security level is higher than the winning user's security level, replace the default winning record with the losing record.

To use this technique you must have

- Enabled workgroup-based security

- Added three fields to each table—LastModUser, LastModTime, and Last-ModDB—and added VBA code to each form so these fields are updated every time a record is saved

- Added the USystblConflictPriority table (see Figure 13.25)

The glrResolveConflicts() function and two related procedures from basConflictMng, glrGetConflictPriority and UpdateLogValues, are shown in Listing 13.9.

Listing 13.9

```
Public Const glrcCnflctLogTbl = "USystblConflictLog"
Public Const glrcCnflctPrtTbl = "USystblConflictPriority"
```

FIGURE 13.25:

The USystblConflictPriority table

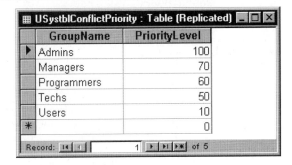

```
Function glrResolveConflicts(fUseSecurity As Boolean)

' Iterates through conflict records
' and logs them to a table (glrcCnflctLogTbl).
' Optionally uses LastModUser field and
' a security table (glrcCnflctPrtTbl) to
' change the winner of the exchange.

On Error GoTo glrResolveConflicts_Err

Dim db As Database
Dim tdf As TableDef
Dim rstResolve As Recordset
Dim rstLog As Recordset
Dim strSQL As String
Dim fInTrans As Boolean
Dim strTable As String
Dim strConflict As String
Dim strGUID As String
Dim strTemp As String
Dim strsPKFields As New Collection
Dim fld As Field
Dim fOK As Variant
Dim strMsg As String
Dim varRet As Variant
Dim lngConflicts As Long
Dim lngCounter As Long
Dim intI As Integer
Dim fChangeWinner As Boolean

Const glrcProcName = "glrResolveConflicts"
```

```
DoCmd.Hourglass True
varRet = SysCmd(acSysCmdSetStatus, _
 "Logging conflict records...")

Set db = CurrentDb()

' Check if log table exists. If not, create it.
If Not glrTableExist(glrcCnflctLogTbl) Then
    fOK = glrCreateConflictLogTbl()
    If Not fOK Then
        MsgBox "Conflict log table could not be created.", _
          vbCritical + vbOKOnly, glrcProcName
        GoTo glrResolveConflicts_Exit
    End If
End If

' Create recordset for log table
Set rstLog = db.OpenRecordset(glrcCnflctLogTbl, _
 dbOpenDynaset, dbAppendOnly)

' Iterate through all TableDefs looking for tables
' with conflict tables
For Each tdf In db.TableDefs
    strTable = tdf.Name

    varRet = SysCmd(acSysCmdSetStatus, "Scanning " & _
      strTable & "...")

    strConflict = Nz(tdf.ConflictTable)

    If (strConflict <> "" And _
     Not strTable Like "~TMPCLP*") Then

        lngConflicts = _
         db.TableDefs(strConflict).RecordCount

        varRet = SysCmd(acSysCmdClearStatus)
        varRet = SysCmd(acSysCmdInitMeter, _
         "Logging " & strTable & " conflicts...", _
         lngConflicts)

        ' Grab name of GUID field for table
        strGUID = tdf.Properties!ColIsGuid

        ' Clear out any existing collection if it exists
```

```
For intI = strsPKFields.Count To 1 Step -1
    strsPKFields.Remove intI
Next intI

' Create collection of primary key fields
For Each fld In tdf.Indexes!PrimaryKey.Fields
    strsPKFields.Add Item:=fld.Name
Next fld

' Create a recordset that joins the conflict table
' and data table together.
strSQL = "SELECT DISTINCTROW "
strSQL = strSQL & "[" & strTable & "].*, "
strSQL = strSQL & "[" & strConflict & "].* "
strSQL = strSQL & "FROM ([" & strConflict & "] "
strSQL = strSQL & "LEFT OUTER JOIN "
strSQL = strSQL & "[" & strTable & "] ON "
strSQL = strSQL & "[" & strConflict & "].["
strSQL = strSQL & strGUID & "] = "
strSQL = strSQL & "[" & strTable & "].["
strSQL = strSQL & strGUID & "]);"
Set rstResolve = db.OpenRecordset(strSQL)

lngCounter = 0
rstResolve.MoveFirst
Do While Not rstResolve.EOF
    lngCounter = lngCounter + 1
    varRet = SysCmd(acSysCmdUpdateMeter, lngCounter)

    ' By default, keep winning record
    fChangeWinner = False
    If fUseSecurity Then
        ' Compare security level of winning and
        ' losing users and set fChangeWinner to True
        ' if losing user has higher priority
        If glrGetConflictPriority(rstResolve("[" & _
        strTable & ".LastModUser]")) < _
        glrGetConflictPriority(rstResolve( _
        "[" & strConflict & ".LastModUser]")) Then
            fChangeWinner = True
        End If
    End If
    If fChangeWinner Then
        ' Swap winner & loser in log
        Call UpdateLogValues(rstLog:=rstLog, _
```

```
                    rstData:=rstResolve, _
                    strTable:=strTable, _
                    strGUID:=strGUID, _
                    strsPKFields:=strsPKFields, _
                    strWinTbl:=strConflict, _
                    strLoseTbl:=strTable, _
                    strReason:="Security check caused " _
                    & "swap of original winning & " _
                    & "losing records")
        ElseIf fUseSecurity Then
            ' Maintain original winner in log
            Call UpdateLogValues(rstLog:=rstLog, _
                    rstData:=rstResolve, _
                    strTable:=strTable, _
                    strGUID:=strGUID, _
                    strsPKFields:=strsPKFields, _
                    strWinTbl:=strTable, _
                    strLoseTbl:=strConflict, _
                    strReason:="Security check did not " _
                    & "cause change of winning record ")
        Else
            ' Maintain original winner in log
            Call UpdateLogValues(rstLog:=rstLog, _
                    rstData:=rstResolve, _
                    strTable:=strTable, _
                    strGUID:=strGUID, _
                    strsPKFields:=strsPKFields, _
                    strWinTbl:=strTable, _
                    strLoseTbl:=strConflict, _
                    strReason:="Automatic logging of " _
                    & "conflict")
        End If

        ' If changing winners, then need to copy data
        ' from conflict record over winning record
        If fChangeWinner Then
            rstResolve.Edit
                For Each fld In rstResolve.Fields
                        ' SourceTable property gives you the
                        ' field's underlying table
                        If fld.SourceTable = strTable Then
                            ' This will fail for read-only
                            ' fields which we can ignore
                            On Error Resume Next
                            ' Copy conflict field value
```

```
                              ' over data table field value.
                              ' This works because recordset
                              '  is updatable.
                              fld.Value = rstResolve("[" & _
                               strConflict & "." & _
                               fld.SourceField & "]")
                              ' Reset error handler
                              On Error GoTo _
                               glrResolveConflicts_Err
                          End If
                       Next fld
                   rstResolve.Update
               End If
               rstResolve.MoveNext
           Loop

           rstResolve.Close
           DoEvents
           ' If we got to this point, then
           ' it should be OK to delete table.
           db.TableDefs.Delete strConflict
        End If
        varRet = SysCmd(acSysCmdRemoveMeter)
    Next tdf
    rstLog.Close

    strMsg = "Conflicts have been logged!"
    MsgBox strMsg, vbInformation + vbOKOnly, glrcProcName

glrResolveConflicts_Exit:
    On Error Resume Next
    varRet = SysCmd(acSysCmdClearStatus)
    varRet = SysCmd(acSysCmdRemoveMeter)
    DoCmd.Hourglass False
    If Not rstResolve Is Nothing Then rstResolve.Close
    If Not rstLog Is Nothing Then rstLog.Close
    On Error GoTo 0
    Exit Function

glrResolveConflicts_Err:
    Select Case Err
    Case Else
        strMsg = "Error#" & Err.Number & "--" & Err.Description
        MsgBox strMsg, vbCritical + vbOKOnly, _
         "Procedure " & glrcProcName
```

```
        Resume glrResolveConflicts_Exit
    End Select

End Function


Function glrGetConflictPriority(strUser As String) As Long

    Dim wrk As Workspace
    Dim db As Database
    Dim lngPriority As Long
    Dim rstPriorities As Recordset
    Dim strTemp As String

    Set wrk = DBEngine.Workspaces(0)
    Set db = CurrentDb()
    Set rstPriorities = db.OpenRecordset("SELECT GroupName, " _
     & "PriorityLevel " & "FROM [" & glrcCnflctPrtTbl & "] " _
     & "ORDER BY PriorityLevel DESC")

    With rstPriorities
        .MoveFirst
        lngPriority = 0
        Do While Not .EOF
            On Error Resume Next
            strTemp = wrk.Users(strUser).Groups(!GroupName).Name
            If Err = 0 Then
                lngPriority = !PriorityLevel
                Exit Do
            End If
            .MoveNext
        Loop
    End With

    glrGetConflictPriority = lngPriority

End Function


Private Sub UpdateLogValues(rstLog As Recordset, _
 rstData As Recordset, strTable As String, strGUID As String, _
 strsPKFields As Collection, strWinTbl As String, _
 strLoseTbl As String, strReason As String)

    Dim strPKValues As String
```

```
Dim varItem As Variant

With rstLog
    .AddNew
        ' Update header fields
        !LogTime = Now()
        !TableName = strTable
        !RowGuid = rstData("[" & strTable _
        & "." & strGUID & "]")

        ' Build up expression representing primary key
        ' values for winning record separated by semicolons
        strPKValues = ""
        For Each varItem In strsPKFields
            strPKValues = strPKValues & varItem & "=" & _
            rstData("[" & strWinTbl & "." & varItem _
            & "]") & "; "
        Next varItem
        ' Remove trailing semicolon and space
        !WinPKValues = Left$(strPKValues, _
        Len(strPKValues) - 2)
        !WinTime = rstData("[" & strWinTbl _
        & ".LastModTime]")
        !WinUser = rstData("[" & strWinTbl _
        & ".LastModUser]")
        !WinDB = rstData("[" & strWinTbl & ".LastModDB]")

        ' Build up expression representing primary key
        ' values for losing record separated by semicolons
        strPKValues = ""
        For Each varItem In strsPKFields
            strPKValues = strPKValues & varItem & "=" & _
            rstData("[" & strLoseTbl & "." & varItem _
            & "]") & "; "
        Next varItem
        ' Remove trailing semicolon and space
        !LosePKValues = Left$(strPKValues, _
        Len(strPKValues) - 2)
        !LoseTime = rstData("[" & strLoseTbl _
        & ".LastModTime]")
        !LoseUser = rstData("[" & strLoseTbl _
        & ".LastModUser]")
        !LoseDB = rstData("[" & strLoseTbl & ".LastModDB]")

        ' And the reason record logged
```

```
            !ReasonText = strReason
        .Update
    End With

End Sub
```

The glrResolveConflicts() function begins by checking to see whether the log table, the name of which is stored in the glrcCnflctLogTbl constant, exists. If not, it calls glrCreateConflictLogTbl(), which creates it using a CreateTable DDL query. Next, it opens an append-only recordset based on the this table, where it will log its activity.

glrResolveConflicts() then sets up a For Each loop to iterate through the TableDefs in the database, just like the code for the CustomConflictResolver() function from Listing 13.7, and uses an If…Then statement to disregard tables without any conflicts and any deleted tables.

The next part of the function determines the GUID field for the table and then adds the names of each of the primary key fields to a user-defined collection, strsPKFields. Because this code can be called for multiple tables, the collection is first cleared out.

Next, a recordset is created from a SQL statement that joins the conflict and user tables on the GUID field using a left outer join, and the function iterates through the records in this recordset.

If the fUseSecurity parameter is False, Jet's automatic determination of the winning record is left unchanged. If fUseSecurity is True, however, the following piece of code is executed, comparing the security levels of the winning and losing users:

```
If fUseSecurity Then
    ' Compare security level of winning and
    ' losing users and set fChangeWinner to True
    ' if losing user has higher priority
    If glrGetConflictPriority(rstResolve("[" & _
      strTable & ".LastModUser]")) < _
      glrGetConflictPriority(rstResolve( _
      "[" & strConflict & ".LastModUser]")) Then
        fChangeWinner = True
    End If
End If
```

This code calls the glrGetConflictPriority() function to check the security level of each user. glrGetConflictPriority(), which is also shown in Listing 13.9, determines the highest level of security by creating a recordset on USystblConflictPriority (see Figure 13.25) sorted in descending order by PriorityLevel and then checking the first record (the record with the highest priority level) to see whether the user is a member of the group for that priority level. If so, the Do loop is exited, returning the PriorityLevel value of the record. If not, the next highest group is checked, and so on. Thus, by calling glrGetConflictPriority() with both the winning and losing user names, the code is able to determine whether the losing user has a higher priority level than the winning user. If this is the case, fChangeWinner is set to True. Otherwise, if the losing user has the same or a lower priority level than the winning user or, if fUseSecurity is False, fChangeWinner is set to False.

NOTE While glrResolveConflicts() uses security levels to resolve conflicts, it could easily be adapted to resolve conflicts based on the date and time of the last update, the name of the replica where the update was last made, or some combination of these fields.

Next, glrResolveConlficts() calls UpdateLogValues, which is also shown in Listing 13.9, passing it one set of parameters if fChangeWinner is False and a different set if it is True. (If fChangeWinner is True, it switches the names of the winning and losing tables and changes the "reason" text from "Security check did not cause change of winning record" to "Security check caused swap of original winning & losing records".) UpdateLogValues adds a new log record to rstLog for each conflict record, with the fields listed in Table 13.10 logged.

TABLE 13.10: The rstLog Fields

Field	Source	Description
LogTime	=Now()	Date/time
TableName	User record	User table name
RowGUID	User record	Usually the value of s_GUID
WinPKValues	Winning record	Primary key values of winning record
WinTime	Winning record	Date/time when winning record was last saved
WinUser	Winning record	User name when winning record was last saved
WinDB	Winning record	Name of replica where winning record was last saved

TABLE 13.10: The rstLog Fields (continued)

Field	Source	Description
LosePKValues	Losing record	Primary key values of losing record
LoseTime	Losing record	Date/time when losing record was last saved
LoseUser	Losing record	User name when losing record was last saved
LoseDB	Losing record	Name of replica where losing record was last saved
ReasonText	N/A	Determined by glrResolveConflicts()

Finally, if fChangeWinner is True, the following code swaps the values in the winning and losing records:

```
' If changing winners, then need to copy data
' from conflict record over winning record
If fChangeWinner Then
    rstResolve.Edit
        For Each fld In rstResolve.Fields
            ' SourceTable property gives you the
            ' field's underlying table
            If fld.SourceTable = strTable Then
                ' This will fail for read-only
                ' fields which we can ignore
                On Error Resume Next
                ' Copy conflict field value
                ' over data table field value.
                ' This works because recordset is
                ' updatable.
                fld.Value = rstResolve("[" & _
                 strConflict & "." & _
                 fld.SourceField & "]")
                ' Reset error handler
                On Error GoTo _
                 glrResolveConflicts_Err
            End If
        Next fld
    rstResolve.Update
End If
```

Learning from the Access Conflict Resolution Wizard Code

The Access Conflict Resolution Wizard code is stored in the WZCNF70.MDA library. While the Wizard libraries are normally secured, Microsoft, on a limited basis, provides an unsecured copy of most of the Wizards, including WZCNF70.MDA, for use by advanced developers. (Microsoft has graciously allowed us to include a copy of the unsecured Wizards on the CD that comes with this book.) If you wish to create a custom conflict and error resolution function that works similarly to Access' built-in functionality, you may wish to load a copy of WZCNF70.MDA and pore through its code. You'll undoubtedly learn quite a bit by looking at the Wizard code—we did.

Other Issues to Consider

When developing database applications that will be replicated, you need to consider several other issues, as described in the next few sections.

Moving the Design Master

Normally, you won't need to change the design master status, but there may be times when you wish to designate another replica as the new design master. For example, say you are the database administrator for a replicated database and you will be going on vacation or transferring to another job. In cases like this you may wish to transfer design master status to your assistant, who normally uses a non–design master replica on the network.

Before you transfer design master status from one replica to another, compact the design master and synchronize all replicas with the current design master so they are at the same generation.

To transfer design master status from one replica to another using the Access menus, open the current design master and select Tools ➤ Replication ➤ Synchronize Now. In the Synchronize With combo box, choose the replica to which you wish to transfer design master status, and check the check box labeled "Make *database*' the Design Master." (See Figure 13.12 earlier in this chapter.) Alternatively, you can use the Tools ➤ Designate New Design Master command in Replication Manager to accomplish the same task.

To transfer design master status using DAO code, follow these steps:

1. Exclusively open both the current design master and the replica you wish to make the new design master.

2. Set the current design master's DesignMasterID property to the ReplicaId property of the new design master.

3. Synchronize the two replicas.

You can use the glrDbTransferMaster() function from basReplicationTools to transfer the design master status from one replica to another. It's shown in Listing 13.10.

Listing 13.10

```
Function glrDbTransferMaster(Optional ByVal varReplicaFrom _
 As Variant, Optional ByVal varReplicaTo As Variant) As Boolean

    On Error GoTo glrDbTransferMaster_Err

    Dim dbFrom As Database
    Dim dbTo As Database
    Dim strMsg As String

    Const glrcProcName = "glrDbTransferMaster"
    glrDbTransferMaster = False

    If IsMissing(varReplicaFrom) And _
      IsMissing(varReplicaTo) Then
        strMsg = "Error. You must specify at least _
          one database."
        MsgBox strMsg, vbCritical + vbOKOnly, "Procedure " & _
          glrcProcName
        GoTo glrDbTransferMaster_Exit
    End If

    If IsMissing(varReplicaFrom) Then
        Set dbFrom = CurrentDb()
        varReplicaFrom = dbFrom.Name
```

```
    Else
        Set dbFrom = DBEngine.Workspaces(0). _
        OpenDatabase(varReplicaFrom, True)
    End If

    If IsMissing(varReplicaTo) Then
        Set dbTo = CurrentDb()
        varReplicaTo = dbTo.Name
    Else
        Set dbTo = DBEngine.Workspaces(0). _
        OpenDatabase(varReplicaTo, True)
    End If

    dbFrom.DesignMasterID = dbTo.ReplicaID
    dbFrom.Synchronize varReplicaTo, dbRepImpExpChanges

    glrDbTransferMaster = True

glrDbTransferMaster_Exit:
    On Error GoTo 0
    Exit Function

glrDbTransferMaster_Err:
    Select Case Err
    Case Else
        strMsg = "Error#" & Err.Number & "--" & Err.Description
        MsgBox strMsg, vbCritical + vbOKOnly, "Procedure " & _
        glrcProcName
        Resume glrDbTransferMaster_Exit
    End Select

End Function
```

In some cases you may have to designate a new design master without the luxury of having the old design master around. This may be necessary, for example, if the design master becomes corrupted or was inadvertently deleted. In these cases you need to assign design master status to some other replica. You can do this by using Access' Tools ➤ Replication ➤ Recover Design Master command or Replication Manager's Tools ➤ Recover Design Master command.

You can recover the design master using DAO code by opening the new design master database exclusively and setting its DesignMasterID property to its ReplicaId property. You can use the glrDbRecoverMaster() function in basReplicationTools to do this.

After changing the design master, synchronize all replicas with the new design master.

Linked Tables

When you synchronize two replicas, Jet will exchange only the data in native Access tables, not in linked tables. You can, however, separately replicate and synchronize the database that contains the linked tables. If you're using a typical split database architecture (see Chapter 12), where users run an application from a local "application" database on their workstations linked to tables stored in a shared "data" database stored on the file server, you could choose to replicate the application database, the data database, or both.

NOTE   You cannot replicate data stored in external non-Access tables.

Design Considerations

If the application is to be used on a LAN only, you might keep a single nonreplicated data database on the file server with the application database replicated across the LAN, using a star topology with the file server as the hub node. As an alternative, you might wish to abandon the split database design and replicate the single database across the LAN using a star, ring, or fully connected topology.

If you wished to move a split application to a WAN or loosely connected network with, for example, multiple stars interconnected at their hub nodes, it may make sense to create two replica sets: one for the application databases that would be replicated to every desktop on the WAN, and a distinct replica set for the data databases that would remain on the file server hubs of each workgroup. Since application updates would be rare, you'd probably synchronize the application databases only when you needed to roll out a new version of the application. On the other hand, the data databases would be on a more regular synchronization schedule.

NOTE
When moving a replicated database with linked tables to another site, you'll have to update the Connect property of the TableDef and use the RefreshLink method at each site to fix up the linked tables so they point to the tables using a path that's valid for that site. (You can use either the Linked Table Manager Add-In or your own VBA linked table management code—see Chapter 12 for an example of such code—to fix up the links.) Jet doesn't consider making changes to the Connect property a design change, so you can make these changes at each replica.

Resolving Conflicts for "Data" Databases

Whenever you replicate a database that users will not normally open, you need to have in place some automated system for detecting and resolving conflicts and errors that might occur from synchronization exchanges between these replicas. This is necessary because the built-in Access Conflict Resolution Wizard or custom conflict resolution code will never be called, since the database won't be normally be opened by a user. Thus, you'd have to create a VBA routine to automatically run after each synchronization exchange, logging and resolving conflicts and alerting the database administrator to any errors.

Security Issues

Jet doesn't support replicating the workgroup file (SYSTEM.MDW) in a secured workgroup environment. Thus, on a LAN you must either connect each replica to the workgroup file or copy the workgroup file to each workstation. For a WAN you'll need to copy the workgroup file to each remote synchronization replica.

NOTE
You can't replicate a database that has a database password. You must remove the password before proceeding. Similarly, you can't create a database password for a replicated database.

In a secured system that's normally centrally controlled by a single database administrator, this shortcoming shouldn't affect you. However, in situations where you would normally distribute security responsibilities among users, you will have to address the following issues:

- Since permission changes are considered design changes, they can be made only at the design master.

- Unless you restrict user access to the account management features, users will be able to make changes to user and group accounts (including the changing of passwords) from any replica.

NOTE Security information is stored in two places. Account information is stored in the workgroup file (SYSTEM.MDW), and permission information is stored along with the objects in each user database. Thus, only permission information will be replicated in a replicated database.

Because you are restricted from making permission changes and these changes are kept in the user database, coordination of updates should not be a problem—they must be done at the design master and then propagated using the normal synchronization schedule. Changes to user accounts, however, present a problem: local account changes won't be replicated, since they are stored in the workgroup file. The best approach may be to limit these types of security changes to one database administrator who can see that the multiple workgroup files are kept synchronized (that is, manually synchronized without the aid of replication).

WARNING It's important that any permission changes that are dependent on changes to accounts be made only *after* updated workgroup files have been copied to each workstation. Otherwise you run the risk of the replicated databases being out of sync with the workgroup files.

Compacting Replicas

When you make a number of schema changes at the design master, you should compact the database before synchronizing it with other replicas. This reduces the number of design changes that need to be transferred between replicas. In addition, it's a good idea to compact all replicas on a regular—perhaps daily or weekly—basis because replication will tend to bloat the databases.

TIP
> When you compact replicated databases, you should compact each database *twice*. Jet performs the compact in two phases: first it performs the normal consolidation and recovery of deleted space, and *then* it goes through replicated objects and decides which ones to mark for deletion. However, since it has already finished reclaiming space from deleted objects, you need to compact a second time to finish the job. It won't hurt the replica to compact only once, but you will save additional space and make your replicas more efficient by compacting an extra time.

Partial Replication

Partial replication is the ability to partition a table so that only part of it gets synchronized with one replica, part with another replica, and so on. Partial replication would be ideal for a sales database where salesperson A only needs to get data relating to his or her territory rather than the whole sales table, which might be quite large. Partial replication could be useful when:

- A table has a very large number of rows and some workstations (for example, laptops) don't have enough hard disk space to hold the entire table

- You don't want users at one site to be able to see or modify data that is not theirs

Jet 3.0 does not support partial replication. (Partial replication is an often-requested enhancement, however, that may be added at a later date.) In the meantime, you may be able to use one of the following work-arounds to simulate partial replication:

- Employ security so that users can see and change only data belonging to them. The main disadvantage of this option is that each replica will still have to hold the entire table.

- Use a star topology and make normal replicas, and then delete rows from each satellite replica that do not apply to that site. Only synchronize one way, from the satellite replicas *to* the hub replica. The main disadvantage of this option is that the satellite nodes will never get changes to their data made at the hub replica.

- Use a star topology and split the main table into separate satellite tables. Move each satellite's tables into separate databases. Attach each of these tables to the master database, which also contains the common tables. Create replicas from this master database and distribute them to each of the satellite nodes. Now create a replica set for each satellite database that contains the satellite's tables, and place a replica of this database on the appropriate satellite node. At the hub, then, you'll have the master database and one satellite database for each satellite replica. At each site you'll have a replica of the master database and a replica of the satellite replica for that site. Set up a synchronization schedule so that all the master databases two-way synchronize with each other on a regular basis. Set up individual synchronization schedules for the individual satellite replica sets so that they two-way synchronize with each other regularly. The main disadvantage of this work-around is that in order to combine the data from all sites for an analysis, you'll need to use a union query or a temporary table in which you combine the data from each of the satellite tables into one.

None of these options is without its disadvantages, but this is the best you can do until Jet includes support for partial replication.

NOTE   When you use one-way synchronization, data changes are transferred in only one direction, but design changes are always replicated from the design master to other replicas, regardless of the synchronization direction.

Summary

Replication is an exciting technology that's new for Access 95. In this chapter we've explored replication in detail and covered the following topics:

- How replication works
- All the tools you can use to manage replication: Windows 95 Briefcase, Access menus, Replication Manager, and DAO code
- When you should consider using replication
- Replication topologies
- The changes Jet makes to a replicated database
- Replicating a database
- Synchronizing replicas
- Resolving conflicts and errors
- Creating a custom conflict and error resolution function
- Moving the design master
- Replicating databases with linked tables
- Replicating secured databases
- Compacting replicas
- Partial replication

CHAPTER

FOURTEEN

Developing Client-Server Applications

- Using Access as a client

- Setting up and controlling ODBC and using ODBC data efficiently

- Managing connections to your server

- Controlling the flow of data

- Testing client-server applications

- Upsizing your Access application

The term *client-server* has come to represent many types of processing. The basic idea is that the computational elements of some task are split between a client computer and a larger server computer. Within the database market, most client-server work focuses on the use of database servers, usually SQL based. These servers provide database access and management services for client programs or workstations. Clients and servers can also communicate by means of several different methods, such as Remote Procedure Calls (RPC), ODBC, Network DDE, and in the future, Remote OLE Automation. (Visual Basic 4.0 includes a preliminary version of Remote OLE Automation.) Whatever the communications link, using client-server computing from Access generally involves offloading the actual storage and retrieval of data entirely to another program.

In this chapter we discuss the use of Access as a front end to SQL-based database management servers. We focus on the use of ODBC as the method of communication between Access and the database server. Because every server and every network are different, we can't give you complete advice on what to do in every client-server situation. However, we will show you the basic guidelines for understanding how Access functions as a client and demonstrate a method for testing with your own hardware and software.

The Difference between File-Server and Client-Server

Figure 14.1 shows schematically the four methods of retrieving data from a server we'll be discussing in this chapter:

- File-server
- Open Database Connectivity (ODBC)
- SQL pass-through (SPT)
- Remote Data Objects (RDO)

ODBC, SQL Pass-through, and RDO are variants of client-server computing.

File-server Access is what you get when you simply move your database to a server's hard drive. In this case no active components at all are running on the server.

Methods of data access. The Client-Server methods are distinguished by having a program that runs on the server.

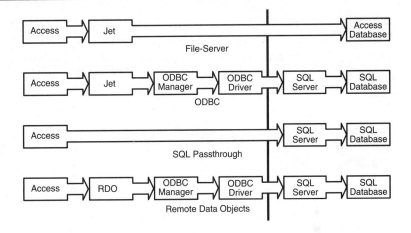

(The heavy black line in Figure 14.1 indicates the boundary between client and server components.) For example, suppose you need to retrieve all the customers in Alaska. In this case, assuming the State field of the customers table was indexed, the Jet engine would read the entire index for this field from the server. It would then retrieve the records it required. This type of data access tends to be inefficient because the Jet engine needs to bring every piece of data it wishes to view across the relatively slow network connection.

Open Database Connectivity (*ODBC*) takes a more complex route to retrieve server data. In this case the Jet engine translates the original SQL for your query into a universal SQL dialect. This SQL, together with information on which server contains the data, is passed to the ODBC manager. The ODBC manager locates the appropriate driver and hands it the SQL statement. The ODBC driver then translates the universal SQL to a SQL dialect understood by the particular database server and hands it to that server to process. In this scenario the only network traffic is the SQL statement going out and the final result set coming back.

SQL pass-through adds another wrinkle to this means of communication. Although the "plumbing" components are still present, none of them will perform any translation on a SQL pass-through query. Instead, you must write the exact SQL statement that the server will execute within Access itself. SQL pass-through is mainly of use when you need to use some advanced feature of your database server that ODBC SQL is incapable of understanding.

Finally, *Remote Data Objects,* or *RDO* (which ships with the Enterprise Edition of Visual Basic 4.0), add another wrinkle to the standard ODBC connection. With RDO, instead of sending your query to Jet to be translated, you set it directly as properties of an object. The RDO layer provides very thin wrapper functions around native ODBC calls and can produce additional speed at the expense of more coding.

Using Client-Server versus File-Server

When you first look at using Access in a client-server system, you may think it's an easy task. After all, if you bought this book, you've probably developed in Access for a while. Migrating to client-server should just mean loading your data tables onto the server and changing the links, right?

Wrong. As you just saw, client-server systems are a completely different architecture from native Access. Migrating from one to the other often requires many changes in the design, implementation, and support of your application. Before you convert your application, you should understand the differences and the impact they will have on your application. Above all, if you're writing your first client-server application, be sure to leave plenty of time for testing in a nonproduction environment.

When you use Access in file-server mode, each instance of Jet manages its own cache of physical pages from the file, updates the pages on each client's machine, and sends the updated physical pages back over the network. Each copy of Jet performs the index updating, system table maintenance, and other database management functions required to process your application's work.

In marked contrast, when you use Access as a front-end application and the database resides on a database server, the database server provides all the data management functions for the application. Only the *database server* updates the physical file and sees the physical pages in the database. Each user's copy of Access sends requests to the database server and gets data, or pointers to the data, back from the server. It's this single point of control that makes client-server computing more robust than file-server computing, and that makes it a better choice for mission-critical applications.

Table 14.1 shows some of the key differences in processing between an Access-only multiuser application and a client-server application using Access and a database server.

TABLE 14.1: Key Differences between File-Server and Client-Server Access Applications

Process	Native Access (File-Server) Processing	Client-Server Access Processing
Updating data	Each user's machine retrieves the physical pages over the network, updates them, and writes them back to the shared drive. Because of this, a failure on any client machine has a good chance of corrupting the database and requiring shutdown and repair	The server database engine manages all updates of the physical database. Because of this, management problems with the network and individual machine failures are greatly reduced
Security	The Access security model covers all portions of a multiuser Access application	The Access security model is applied to the Access application portions of the application (forms, reports, modules, and macros). The security system of the database server controls accessing and updating the actual data. You still use Access security for forms, reports, modules, and queries, so both security systems must be kept current
Validation rules	Validation rules are part of native Access and the data engine	Validation rules and triggers must be defined at the server. They will not display the Access-defined error message when triggered. Your application will need to handle notifying the user appropriately
Support for special datatypes	Supports Counter, OLE, and Memo datatypes	Server dependent
Referential integrity	Defined within Access	Referential integrity must be defined directly at the server if the server supports it. You cannot establish referential integrity rules across servers or between server data and Access stored data
Updatable queries/views	Access allows update of almost any type of join. Access allows update of both sides of a one-to-many join	Most servers prohibit updates to joined queries. Using ODBC will sometimes work around this by sending multiple updates. Using pass-through limits you to updates the server allows

By now you are probably wondering whether client-server is such a good idea after all. This is a good frame of mind from which to approach the native-Access versus client-server decision, because moving to a client-server implementation requires learning a new approach to application programming. It also requires giving up many of your familiar tools and losing some of the strong integration you find in Access. There are, however, several compelling reasons why you might choose to use a database server as a back end to Access applications:

- Reliability
- Transaction and data integrity
- Performance
- Improved management
- Unique server capabilities

NOTE

Each of the preceding reasons assumes you have a choice as to where to store the data. However, often you will consider using Access in a client-server environment simply because the data already resides on a database server and you wish to use Access to gain access to the data while continuing to keep the data on the server to support existing applications.

Reliability and Data Protection

Access runs a copy of the database engine on every client machine and has no synchronized transaction log or distributed transaction commit system. A failure of any single client machine or network component, therefore, has the potential to corrupt the entire database. Usually the database can be fixed, but repairing an Access database requires all users to log off the database. Repair of a large database can take several hours, and no user can be using the database during the repair. On the other hand, since all updating and data management on a server occur at the *server*, failures on the network or client machines rarely affect the database. Also, most database servers have fast and robust recovery facilities.

Transaction Processing and Data Integrity

The transaction support built into Jet has access to the data only for its own current session. It cannot resolve problems left from a previous failed session or from another copy of Jet that failed somewhere else on the network. This transaction support also does not have full protection for the database if a failure occurs while Jet is committing a transaction. In addition, the current implementation of Jet can leave locks orphaned in the shared locking (.LDB) file, requiring a shutdown and purge of the shared locking file before anyone can access or repair the data. As a result, failures that occur while a copy of Access is committing a transaction can result in data loss, data lockout, or database corruption. The windows are small, but they may be sufficient to cause you to seriously consider client-server if you are implementing systems that, for example, process real-funds transactions. In this case money will not be properly transferred or accounted for if the transaction partially commits. In contrast, most database servers are capable of maintaining a full audit trail, enabling the database administrator to reconstruct the state of the database at any time. Popular servers, such as Microsoft SQL Server, also offer hot backup facilities, letting you save a second copy of critical data in real time without needing to suspend database operations.

Performance Considerations

Performance is another important reason to consider client-server, but one that is often misrepresented. Unlike the reliability issues, there are many approaches to providing good performance from a native Access multiuser system. However, there are cases in which a server is the only way to achieve appropriate performance. Generally speaking, if you often need to find small amounts of data in a sea of records, client-server will provide a speed boost. On the other hand, if you're frequently analyzing records from the bulk of your database or running multiple reports with only slight variations between them, a client-server environment might prove slower than the equivalent file-server system.

System Management

One often-overlooked area in client-server is overall system management and administration. Windows and the Access Workgroup Administrator program offer only very limited management services compared to a Windows NT Advanced

Server or a UNIX server machine. Adding a robust, modern server database to the package further increases the management tools. Microsoft SQL Server, for example, is capable of monitoring its own operation and sending e-mail or even electronic pages to the database administrator in case of trouble.

Unique Server Capabilities

Sometimes you will need to use a server for your database simply because it offers some capabilities that Access doesn't. Here is a list of the most important features built into SQL Server that might make it the right choice for your applications:

- Data replication triggered by a specific transaction load.

- Central management of distributed servers.

- Scalability to high-performance machines. (SQL Server will make use of multiple processors; Access will not.)

- Support for very large databases (up to multiple gigabytes of data).

- Querying via Microsoft Mail.

- Deadlock and livelock resolution, ensuring that two users cannot lock each other out of needed data.

- Dynamic backup, even while the database is in use.

- Automatic recovery—backups plus log files can be used to regenerate a database lost to hardware failure.

- Device mirroring—your data can be written to multiple drives at one time, for instantaneous backups.

- Integrated security resulting in a single logon for both the network and the database.

When you think about the amount of code you would have to write to get most of these capabilities in Access itself, you can see that a database server can save considerable development time and expense.

The Role of Access in Distributed Applications

Because Access is a full database management product, you have a great deal of flexibility in establishing the role of Access in your distributed application. The three main approaches we cover are

- Using Access as a true front-end process
- Using Access with both Jet tables and linked server tables
- Using Access as a store-and-forward application

NOTE You can also use ODBC to import data into an Access system and use the system as though there were no link to an outside data source. While we do not cover this approach in this chapter, it is often useful for data analysis and some decision-support systems, where up-to-the-second data is not necessary. It allows the use of outside data with the least impact on your Access development style. This approach is obviously dependent on having no more than a few hundred megabytes of data to deal with. If there is more data than that, the time it takes to move the data to your local computer and the storage space it requires become prohibitive.

Using Access as a True Front-End Process

You can implement a pure client-server application using Access as a front-end process, storing all data on the server, and implementing all queries so that they run using the server's SQL engine. By doing this you centralize all the data administration functions on the server. All table maintenance and associated work are performed in a single environment. You can implement this approach by using SQL pass-through (SPT) or Remote Data Objects (RDO) for all your queries, an approach we cover later in this chapter.

The biggest disadvantage to this approach is performance. Access is a complete database product. You cannot really disable all the database-related processing and have only a forms and reports engine, so you are paying for a lot of overhead from which you get no benefit. Another disadvantage is the loss of all of Access' native processing capabilities. You may be better off using an application development tool such as Visual Basic if you are planning to build a system using this approach for which the desktop portion of the application performs no data management.

Using Access with Both Jet Tables and Linked Server Tables

The most common approach to client-server with Access is to have a mix of local (Access-owned) and server-based data. The local data may be copies of relatively static data from the servers, or it may be data no one outside your workgroup needs to access. Common techniques that fall under this general approach are

- Downloading lookup tables to each client machine at login time
- Maintaining custom or auxiliary data in local databases
- Downloading bulk data to client machines for processing a series of reports or performing extended interactive analysis

Each of these areas is covered in more detail in the section "Partitioning Work between Client and Server" later in this chapter.

Using Access as a Store-and-Forward Application

An approach related to the preceding one is to use Access to perform store-and-forward processing to a server. In *store-and-forward processing*, Access is acting as a full database product for the user and then turning around and acting as a client to the database server to update the shared database. This approach is useful if your server is over a wide area network (WAN) rather than a high-speed local area network (LAN) but may be useful in some cases even for local (non-WAN) processing.

One example of store-and-forward is an order entry application. In a pure client-server system, every detail item goes back to the server, perhaps multiple times, to validate and enter the item. In a store-and-forward approach, you use a set of local

Access data tables to store the detail data as the order is entered and initial validation is made. After Access captures the entire order, it sends it to the server in a single transaction for final validation and loading into the shared database.

With Microsoft SQL Server 6.0 and Access 95, you can also use database replication to your advantage in store-and-forward designs. You could, for example, set up multiple servers around your WAN and use replication between the servers to make sure every client has access to a local copy of the data. Alternatively, you could use Access's own replication to forward all the data to a single Access database located on the same LAN as the server and have it perform all the server updates.

Understanding ODBC

Access uses the Open DataBase Connectivity (ODBC) standard to connect to servers. ODBC is a common language definition and a set of protocols that allow a client to interactively determine a server's capabilities and adapt the processing to work within the functions the server supports. You implement ODBC using components within Access, on each client machine running separately from Access, and on the database server machine. To use ODBC to connect from Access to a back-end database, you need three things:

- A network that allows communications between the client machine and the machine that holds the back-end database
- The ODBC driver manager that comes with Access
- An ODBC driver that can work with your back-end database

Many sources exist for ODBC-compliant drivers. Many database and hardware vendors now provide them, and there are several third-party sources for drivers. If you have CompuServe access, you can find information on the latest ODBC drivers on the WINEXT forum.

ODBC processing consists of three major activities:

- Establishing connections
- Parsing queries

- Managing record sources

The key to getting reliable performance lies in understanding all three of these areas and how your specific ODBC driver and back-end server handle each.

Establishing Connections

ODBC processing revolves around *connections*. When a client needs access to data on a server, the ODBC software at the client end (in the case of Access, Jet and the underlying ODBC drivers) performs a number of steps to establish a connection. It

1. Finds the system and path information for the appropriate connection
2. Connects over the appropriate network(s) to the database server
3. Checks for a stored login for the database
4. Prompts the user (if required) for login and password information
5. Gathers information about the capabilities of the server
6. Gathers information about the capabilities of the ODBC driver
7. Gathers information about the table(s) that are being connected

Jet uses all this information to determine the best way to process your query using the server's SQL engine. This information comes from the Connect string of the linked table and from the ODBC.INI file.

Because of the cost of performing this work, you generally want to make connections only once for each session. This is what happens when you use linked tables, because Access caches connection information for linked tables locally. This in turn allows Jet to connect to the table when you reference it without all the overhead of a dynamic connection. When converting your Access application to a client-server application, try to remove all uses of the OpenDatabase() function or method and open recordsets only against queries or linked tables. Anytime you use a connect string directly in your code or in a query property, you're forcing ODBC to make another connection, taking up processing time.

With the current release of ODBC (2.10), some drivers include a "fast connect" option. When you invoke this option (during the driver setup), the driver defers as much of the connection processing as possible until you actually request records from the data source. Using this option can speed the initial load of your application, at the cost of making the first access to each table slower.

Query Parsing

Jet handles a query for an ODBC connection in one of three ways. You can use any of the following:

- A regular Jet-optimized Access query
- A SQL pass-through (SPT) query
- A query performed by the Remote Data Object (RDO)

If you use an SPT or RDO query, Access does no parsing of the query and passes the SQL string directly to the database server for processing. It is your responsibility to ensure that the string is a valid SQL statement. On the other hand, you can also use a regular Access query, whereupon Jet interprets and optimizes the query locally, determining the best execution path. During the optimization step, Jet partitions the query execution into a Jet-executed component and a server-executed component.

When you use SPT queries, minimal overhead is introduced on the Access side, but there is also minimal control and no assistance from Access. Do not, however, assume that this low overhead will result in faster queries. In many cases you'll find that the server query execution time and network overhead wash out any difference among the various querying methods. The only sure way to know which way to run a query is best is to time the alternatives, as discussed in the section "Evaluating Query Alternatives" later in this chapter.

When you use RDO querying, there's no Jet query overhead at all. The Remote Data Object is just another OLE object as far as Access is concerned, with its own methods and properties. You execute queries through RDO by setting a property to the appropriate back-end SQL and using methods to retrieve rows of the results. Although this gives you querying performance very close to writing to the raw ODBC API, the OLE libraries introduce their own overhead, and of course the server is doing as much work as it does with SPT.

SQL pass-through and RDO querying generally work best for activities during which the server can do a large amount of processing or for which Access is incapable of expressing the query in native SQL. You might consider using one of these techniques in the following situations:

- To perform data definition language (DDL) operations or other administrative actions on the server. Often, there is no Jet equivalent for these queries
- To execute SQL when the SQL syntax is not supported by Access
- To execute very short SQL actions, such as single row retrievals or updates
- To process SQL statements that join tables from two different databases on the same server
- To process SQL updates when you need to check on the number of rows updated
- To process large action queries within transactions

Even in these cases it may be more efficient to use Jet-optimized Access queries, depending on your particular server and network load. Only convert to pass-through queries if you encounter a significant performance problem, such as a query that Jet fails to optimize properly. The normal SQL parsing for ODBC processing is similar to the Jet processing for native Access tables. The major difference is that once the Jet engine has isolated the commands that need to be processed at the server, it generates a SQL string in the common ODBC SQL dialect. This in turn is translated by your server-specific ODBC driver into your server's SQL dialect. When Jet executes the query, it executes all the portions of a query that are local and sends the translated SQL strings to the server for processing.

Managing Record Sources

When you convert to ODBC from native Access, you may find that complex forms open slowly compared to other forms. When you built your forms in native Access, you probably didn't worry about how many different sources of data the form used, because the data all came from one place anyway. When you use ODBC you need to limit the number of different record sources on a form to ensure reasonable performance and usability.

As mentioned earlier in this chapter, ODBC uses connections to talk to the server. Depending on the server, a single physical connection may be opened or a separate physical connection may exist for each active recordset. In some cases, such as with the Microsoft or Sybase SQL Servers, a single recordset can have two connections (except when there are fewer than 100 records when only one connection is used). Whether they are physical links or logical links over a shared path, all connections use memory and processing resources. In addition, some servers impose a licensing limit on the number of open connections. Thus, to work efficiently under ODBC, you need to be careful about the number of active recordsets your application uses. Each row source on your form (whether for the form itself or a combo or list box) is a separate connection. Each bound subform will have one or more connections. A connection is in use in each of these situations:

- Until all associated data has been returned from the server

- While any transactions are outstanding

Jet may cache a connection, once made, to avoid the cost of reestablishing the connection the next time it requires the data. You can control this caching process by way of ODBC parameters in the Registry. (See Table 14.2 later in this chapter.)

Using the Sample Database

Unlike the other sample databases for this book, the database for this chapter is not completely self contained. Because it contains attached Microsoft SQL Server tables, you can use it without modification only if you have installed Microsoft SQL Server (either version 4.2 or version 6.0). The sample database also assumes you have installed the pubs sample database that comes with SQL Server. In addition, to make sure the database works seamlessly, you'll need to create an ODBC data source named SQLPUBS that points to this database. Depending on which versions of SQL Server and ODBC you have, this data source name may be case sensitive. If you have problems reading data from the attached tables even after defining a proper DSN, it's worth deleting the tables and reattaching them as a check.

Also, the sample database uses the default login of "sa" with no password throughout. If this is not a valid login on your SQL Server, you'll need to take two steps. First, drop and reattach the three tables in the sample. Second, open up frmTestbed in Design view and change the embedded login and password strings in the code to match your actual login.

Finally, to execute the RDO examples, you'll need to have Visual Basic 4.0, Enterprise Edition, installed on your machine.

Using the Three Methods of Getting Data

You can retrieve data in each of the three ways we've been considering—the native Jet query, SQL pass-through, and RDO—using VBA code. Let's look at the syntax for each of the three alternatives in turn, using the query shown in Design view in Figure 14.2. This query uses three of the tables from the pubs database shipped with Microsoft SQL Server to retrieve information on authors and the books they have written.

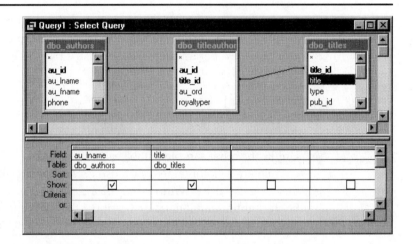

Native Jet Query

Finding the proper SQL for a native Jet query is simple: just construct the query on the QBE grid and switch to SQL view. Here's the Jet SQL for the sample query:

```
SELECT dbo_authors.au_lname, dbo_titles.title
FROM (dbo_titleauthor INNER JOIN dbo_authors
ON dbo_titleauthor.au_id = dbo_authors.au_id)
INNER JOIN  dbo_titles ON dbo_titleauthor.title_id =
dbo_titles.title_id;
```

frmTestbed in the sample database has CBF procedures to execute each of the query variations we're discussing here. For the native Jet query, we create a QueryDef object using the linked tables directly and then base a recordset on this querydef.

Here's the relevant portion of the code:

```
Private Sub cmdExecuteLinked_Click()
    ' Execute a query directly on a linked table
    '

    Dim dbCurrent As Database
    Dim qdfLinked As QueryDef
    Dim rstLinked As Recordset
    On Error GoTo cmdExecuteLinkedErr
...
    Set dbCurrent = DBEngine.Workspaces(0).Databases(0)

    ' This should set a global timeout for all queries run
    ' from this database. Unfortunately, a bug that persists
    ' from Access 2.0 ignores this property entirely. This
    ' is why we need to create a QueryDef object instead
    ' dbCurrent.QueryTimeout = 0
    Set qdfLinked = dbCurrent.CreateQueryDef _
    ("", Me!txtLinkedSQL)
    ' Tell Access to wait as long as the query takes
    qdfLinked.ODBCTimeout = 0
...
    Set rstLinked = qdfLinked.OpenRecordset()
...
cmdExecuteLinkedErr:
    If Err.Number = DBEngine.Errors(0).Number And _
    DBEngine.Errors.Count > 1 Then
        For Each errX In DBEngine.Errors
            MsgBox "Error " & errX.Number & " raised by " _
            & errX.Source & ": " & errX.Description, _
            vbCritical, "cmdExecuteAttached()"
        Next errX
    Else
        MsgBox "Error " & Err.Number & " raised by " _
        & Err.Source & ": " & Err.Description, _
        vbCritical, "cmdExecuteAttached()"
    End If
    Resume cmdExecuteLinkedExitEnd Sub
```

(For more information on using Data Access Objects, such as the QueryDef and Recordset objects discussed here, see Chapter 6.)

The only major complication here is setting the query timeout. By default, Jet will wait only 60 seconds for a query to execute before deciding that the server is down and aborting all processing on that query. You can use the query's ODBCTimeout property (available through code, as shown here, or on any query's property sheet) to increase this time. If you set the timeout to 0, Jet will wait until either the server returns data or you give up and press Ctrl+Break to abort the query.

You should also note the error handling in this function. Because we're dealing with multiple components (Access, Jet, ODBC, and SQL Server), it's possible for a single operation to produce more than one error. If multiple errors occur in any Jet operation, Jet will populate the Errors collection of the DBEngine object with Error objects—one for each component to report an error. Jet will also put the last error into the Err object, which belongs to Access. However, if an error occurs in some non-data component (for example, VBA), Jet will not be notified, and consequently the Errors collection won't match the actual error. In this case you must retrieve the information from the Err object.

When it senses an error, the code checks to see whether there are multiple errors in the Errors collection, and if so checks to see whether the first member of this collection matches the one stored in Err. If so, it dumps every member of the collection using a For Each loop. If not, it simply dumps the error information from the Err object.

SQL Pass-Through

To execute the same query using SQL pass-through, you must rewrite it in SQL the server can understand directly—which means you need to know the dialect of SQL used on your server. To translate this query to Microsoft SQL Server, you need to change the underlines in the table names back to dots and modify the join syntax, as shown here:

```
SELECT dbo.authors.au_lname, dbo.titles.title
FROM dbo.authors, dbo.titleauthor, dbo.titles
WHERE (dbo.titleauthor.au_id = dbo.authors.au_id)
AND (dbo.titleauthor.title_id = dbo.titles.title_id)
```

TIP   If you're unsure of the proper SQL but have a sniffer tool such as SQLEYE (available on Microsoft TechNet), you can execute your query using the regular QBE grid and then inspect the trace of the conversation with the server to see how ODBC chose to translate it for you.

Executing a pass-through query in code also requires creating a QueryDef object:

```
Private Sub cmdPassthroughExecute_Click()
    ' Execute a query via SQL pass-through

    Dim dbCurrent As Database
    Dim qdfPassthrough As QueryDef
    Dim rstPassthrough As Recordset
...
    Set dbCurrent = DBEngine.Workspaces(0).Databases(0)

    Set qdfPassthrough = dbCurrent.CreateQueryDef("")

    qdfPassthrough.Connect = _
      "ODBC;DSN=SQLPUBS;UID=sa;DATABASE=pubs"
    qdfPassthrough.SQL = Me!txtPassthroughSQL
    qdfPassthrough.ReturnsRecords = True
    ' Tell Access to wait as long as the query takes
    qdfPassthrough.ODBCTimeout = 0
...
    Set rstPassthrough = qdfPassthrough.OpenRecordset()
...
End Sub
```

To create a pass-through query in code, you need to take the following steps in order. (Setting properties in the wrong order will result in a run-time error.)

1. Create the querydef.

2. Set the querydef's Connect property. If you're unsure of the syntax for the Connect property, check the Description of a linked table from the same database.

3. Assign the proper server SQL to the query's SQL property.

4. Set the ReturnsRecords property to True if the query returns records. (You would set this to false for queries that don't return records, such as DDL queries.)

Once you have created the proper querydef, a pass-through query behaves largely like a native query in Jet—with one significant difference. Because Jet can't know how the server is retrieving these records, a pass-through query is always read-only. (If you need to update records in a pass-through query, you can write an update query and execute it by means of pass-through, as well.)

Remote Data Objects

Because Remote Data Objects also send their SQL directly to the server, they use the same SQL syntax as pass-through queries. The code needed to execute an RDO query, however, is quite different:

```
Private Sub cmdRDOExecute_Click()
    ' Execute a query via Remote Data Objects
...
    Dim rdoEnv As RDO.rdoEnvironment
    Dim rdoConn As RDO.rdoConnection
    Dim rdoResults As RDO.rdoResultset
    Dim rdoColumn As RDO.rdoColumn
    rdoEngine.rdoDefaultCursorDriver = rdUseOdbc
    Set rdoEnv = rdoEngine.rdoCreateEnvironment _
      ("", "", "")
    Set rdoConn = rdoEnv.OpenConnection _
      ("SQLPUBS", rdDriverNoPrompt, False, _
      "UID=sa;DATABASE=pubs")
    rdoConn.QueryTimeout = 0
...
    Set rdoResults = rdoConn.OpenResultset _
      Me!txtRDOSQL, rdOpenForwardOnly, rdConcurReadOnly)
    Set rdoColumn = rdoResults.rdoColumns.Item(0)
...
        rdoResults.Close
        Set rdoResults = Nothing
...
    rdoConn.Close
    rdoEnv.Close
End Sub
```

RDO provides an object model as a layer on top of the ODBC connection. The full RDO object model is much richer than the simple example shown here indicates; for full details, refer to the online help and examples that come with Visual Basic 4.0, Enterprise Edition. To use RDO, you need to set up an environment and a connection. The SQL statement is a property of the connection. Using the Open-ResultSet method of the Connection object causes RDO to execute the query.

WARNING To develop applications using RDO (or using the sample RDO function), you'll need Visual Basic 4.0, Enterprise Edition, installed on your computer. Although Visual Basic programs using RDO can be distributed to other computers without the Enterprise Edition, Access applications using RDO will function only if this edition is actually installed on the computer where the application is executing.

Evaluating Query Alternatives

Choosing a query strategy blindly is unlikely to get you the best possible query performance. In any sizable application, you'll need to test at least Jet against pass-through for your important queries, and if your user base has Visual Basic 4.0 Enterprise Edition installed, you should test RDO, as well. The sample database, in CH14.MDB, includes code to use the Windows API call GetTickCount() to do precise timings.

On frmTestbed, you can type a SQL statement to be executed by any of the three methods of querying we've discussed. You can also choose the number of iterations of testing you wish to run for each query. Always test a query multiple times when you're evaluating its performance because during a working session, data may end up cached on both the server and the client. You want your test to be extensive enough to get an average time, without the initial load of getting tables into memory.

Figure 14.3 shows some sample timings made on a copy of the pubs database with a 90,000-row authors table on a lightly loaded network. You certainly shouldn't take the times in the figure to indicate that Access is always faster than RDO. The actual times in any situation will depend on many factors, including the type of query (Jet is very good at single-table select queries but tends to fall behind on complex joins or update queries, for example), the load on the network, the size of the server database, and the number of simultaneous users.

FIGURE 14.3:

Sample query timings

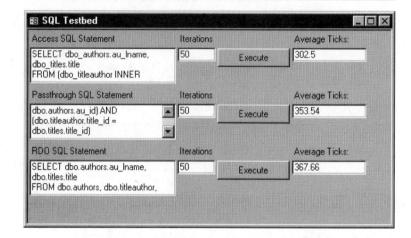

Configuring ODBC for Your System

Access provides a wide range of configuration options for controlling ODBC. These settings were contained in the MSACC20.INI file in Access 2.0, but in Access 95 they are in the Registry. All the settings in Table 14.2 are made in the \HKEY_LOCAL_MACHINE\SOFTWARE\Microsoft\Jet\3.0\Engines\ODBC Registry key. Table 14.2 contains descriptions of each configuration option and points out some potential settings for various conditions.

TABLE 14.2: Registry Settings for ODBC

Key Name	Value	Use
.TraceSQLMode (or SQLTraceMode)	0	Turns off tracing of the Jet-to-server SQL dialog (default)
	1	Traces all dialog of SQL between Jet and the ODBC interface. The output will be in a file named SQLOUT.TXT

TABLE 14.2: Registry Settings for ODBC (continued)

Key Name	Value	Use
.TraceODBCAPI	0	Disables tracing the ODBC API-level interface (default)
	1	Traces ODBC API calls into file ODBCAPI.TXT. You would use this only for debugging an ODBC driver or resolving a problem when working with a vendor. Normally, for working on your application's perform-ance or debugging your SQL, use a SQL trace instead
.DisableAsync	0	Allows Access to continue processing while the server processes an ODBC request (default)
	1	Forces Access to wait for each ODBC request to complete before proceeding. You should set this only for debugging purposes or when dealing with a server that has problems with asynchronous queries, because it can have severe performance problems
.LoginTimeout	s	Aborts a login attempt if the server has not responded in s seconds (default: 20)
.QueryTimeout	s	Provides a default value for query-processing timeouts in seconds. Individual queries can override this with the ODBCTimeout property of the querydef. If you set this to 0, queries will not time out; instead, they will wait forever for data (default: 60)
.ConnectionTimeout	s	Sets the length of time in seconds during which Jet will maintain an inactive connection before releasing it. If your server is not licensed on a per-connection basis, setting this higher may improve response time. If you frequently run out of connections, lower this value (default: 600)
.AsyncRetryInterval	m	Sets the length of time, in milliseconds, Jet waits each time it checks on the progress of an async query (default: 500)
.AttachCaseSensitive	0	Does not use case when matching table names (default). If you use this setting, the first matching table that ODBC finds is attached
	1	Performs a case-sensitive search when opening tables
.SnapshotOnly	0	Allows processing that uses updatable recordsets (default)
	1	Forces the use of read-only Snapshot recordsets

TABLE 14.2: Registry Settings for ODBC (continued)

Key Name	Value	Use
.AttachableObjects	*string*	Includes the server's system objects in the selection list for attaching tables. *string* is a list of all the system objects to include in the selection list (default: TABLE, VIEW, SYSTEM TABLE, ALIAS, and SYNONYM)
.JetTryAuth	1	Try Jet Userid & Password before prompting the user for a different ID and password (default). You can use this setting if you keep IDs and passwords in sync between Access and the server
	0	Prompts the user for a different ID and password. Use this setting if your Access IDs are not kept in sync with the server
.PreparedInsert	0	Generates data-specific inserts that reflect only the supplied columns (default). You should normally use this setting
	1	Uses a predefined INSERT that uses all columns in the table. Using prepared INSERT statements can cause nulls to overwrite server defaults and can cause triggers to execute on columns that weren't inserted explicitly
.PreparedUpdate	0	Generates data-specific updates that reflect only the supplied columns (default). You should normally use this setting
	1	Uses a predefined UPDATE that updates all columns. Using prepared UPDATE statements can cause triggers to execute on unchanged columns
FastRequery	0	Uses a new SELECT statement each time a parameterized query is executed (default)
	1	Uses a prepared SELECT statement on the server when executing a parameterized query

Editing the Registry

If you're new to Windows 95 or Windows NT, you may not yet have had cause to edit the System Registry. The Registry is a replacement for the plethora of .INI files that controlled the operation of Windows 3.1. Configuration information is now stored for the most part in a single database, which you can edit with a tool called

RegEdit. Although you won't find this tool on your menus by default, it's installed in C:\Windows\Regedit.exe when you set up your system.

To make any changes to the parameters that control the operation of Access, you'll need to master two skills: adding a key and adding a value. The first sets up a storage location in the Registry; the second puts information there that applications can retrieve.

To add a key:

1. Launch RegEdit.

2. Expand the tree on the left-hand side of Regedit until you find the parent folder for your new key. (In Figure 14.4, we've chosen \HKEY_LOCAL_ MACHINE\SOFTWARE\Microsoft\Jet\3.0\Engines as our starting point, as you can see on the status bar.)

3. Select Edit ➤ New ➤ Key.

4. Type a name for your new key directly in the window. Here we've set up a key called ODBC.

FIGURE 14.4:

Inserting a new key and value with Regedit

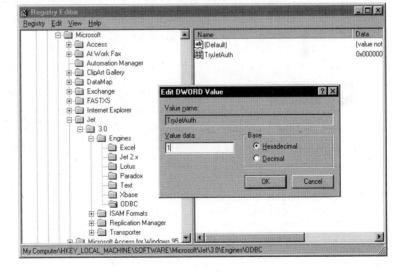

To add a new value within a key:

1. Select Edit ➤ New ➤ DWORD Value (or choose the appropriate datatype for the value you wish to add).
2. Name the new value when it appears in the right-hand window.
3. Double-click the new value to set it, as shown in Figure 14.4, where we're assigning the value of 1 to the TryJetAuth value.

Be very careful when adding values to the Registry or editing existing values. Since the Registry contains all the device and software configuration information for Windows, a mistake here could render your machine inoperable.

Configuring Your Server for Access

You can provide additional information Access uses to manage your server connections in an optional table, MSysConf. You must add this table to each *server* database. It provides Access-specific information to assist in managing connections. The table should be defined as described in Table 14.3. Table 14.4 describes each of the settings for the MSysConf table.

WARNING If you include an MSysConf table on the server, it must have the proper format and data, or you won't be able to connect to that server at all.

TABLE 14.3: Structure of the MSysConf Table

Column Name	Data Type	Allows Nulls?
Config	2-byte integer	No
chValue	VARCHAR(255)	Yes
nValue	4-byte integer	Yes
Comments	VARCHAR(255)	Yes

TABLE 14.4: Settings in Your MSysConf Table

chValue	nValue	Use
101	0	Does not store user IDs and passwords for attached tables. This value prompts the user for ID and password information each time the tables are attached
	1	Stores the user ID and password information with the connect string information for attached tables (default)
102	d	Sets the data retrieval delay time. Jet will delay d seconds between each retrieval of a block of rows from the server (default: 10; range: not documented [appears to be 1–32767])
103	n	Sets the number of rows to fetch from the server at each interval. You use these two settings (102 and 103) to control the rate at which data is brought from a server to Access during idle time (default: 100; range: not documented [appears to be 1–32767])

Editing ODBC Data

You may on occasion link a server table only to discover that Access is treating it as a read-only data source. The Jet Engine requires a primary key for every non-Access table it will allow you to edit. When you link a table from an ODBC data source, Access chooses the clustered unique index as the primary key. If there is no clustered unique index, Access chooses the (alphabetically) first unique index as the primary key of the table. This has a couple of implications:

- A table with no unique index will always be read-only.
- If you have an index on the server that you wish to use as the primary key, you must make sure it is named something like AAA_PrimaryKey so that it will alphabetize before any other unique indexes, or you must make it a clustered unique index.

Should you have a table with no indexes, you can fix the problem in two ways. First, you can use whatever tools your server provides to create an index and then delete and relink the table. (Doing this forces Access to requery the server for the new structure of the table.) If someone other than yourself is maintaining your server database, this method may be the best way to go, since changing the table on the server will make it read-write for all users.

You can also correct the problem in Access by creating a pseudo-index. Access 95 automatically offers to do this for you when you link a table without a unique index on the server. You'll see the dialog box shown in Figure 14.5, and you can choose any combination of fields that you know is unique on the server.

Alternatively, you can use a DDL (Data Definition Language) query in Access to create the pseudo-index. This has the general form

CREATE UNIQUE INDEX *index* ON *table* (*field* [ASC | DESC][, *field* [ASC | DESC], ...])

Using either the automatic method or the CREATE INDEX method causes Access to maintain a local index on the linked table, enabling it to update the data in the table.

Although any table with a unique index is updatable, you can make another optimization to speed updates on some servers. If your server supports a Timestamp datatype (a date/time field the server updates whenever any value in the record is changed), tables with a Timestamp field can be updated much more efficiently. Whenever Jet goes to update a row using ODBC, it has to ensure that the record was not changed by another user while you were editing it. Normally it will check by retrieving all non-memo and non-OLE fields from the table and comparing them to the locally cached values, to make sure there were no changes to any field. If the table has a timestamp, it can just check to make sure the timestamp hasn't changed since you started editing the record.

FIGURE 14.5:

Linking a table without a unique index

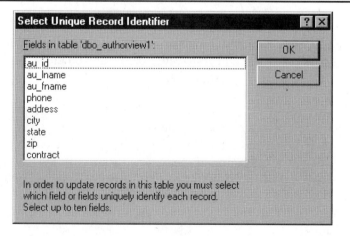

910

Understanding Your Server

Part of the promise of ODBC is that you can develop applications that are server independent. It turns out, though, that while ODBC certainly makes it easier to move from server to server, it is still important to write your application with the target server in mind. Both the server and the connecting software will affect the processing of your SQL. The SQL language used in Access is far from any specific ANSI standard. (Chapter 5 outlines most of the differences.) Access has several features not supported by most servers and lacks features present in some servers.

ANSI SQL standards define datatypes differently from Access. You need to understand how ODBC maps datatypes, both from the server to Access and from Access tables to the server.

Some important areas to check for different servers are security, counter fields or their equivalent, joins, support for the use of multiple indexes within a single query, declarative referential integrity (DRI), and transaction processing support. The level of transaction support is a function of both the server and the ODBC driver. You need to match the features of your server with the features of Access that your application uses. If your application functionality is dependent on features your server does not support, you should look at a different server, rework your application, or consider not migrating the application. You will often end up splitting your application's logic between parts that can be performed on the server and parts that must be performed locally in the front end.

Consider the following server characteristics when picking a server and developing your Access applications:

- Does the server support SQL-92 Join syntax?
- What Join syntax is supported?
  - Inner joins only
  - Outer joins
  - Nested inner and outer joins (Note that this would require SPT or RDO queries.)
- Does the server support subqueries?
- Does the server support auto-incrementing or identity fields (counters)?
- Does the server support referential integrity?

- Does the server allow updates on any joined queries? If so, which updates and deletes are supported?

- Does the server support stored procedures or triggers?

- Does the server support cascading updates or deletes?

- Which built-in functions does the server support?

- Which date/time functions does the server support?

Designing an Efficient Client-Server Application

When implementing client-server systems, you need to address several design areas that you typically do not need to deal with in a stand-alone Access application. The next few sections cover each of these design areas in detail.

Establishing Rules for Transactions

You must clearly define and document all your data activity that is to be grouped together so that the transaction protection and recovery features of your server can work correctly.

Jet applies the following rules regarding transactions when processing against an ODBC data source:

- Forms must use optimistic locking.

- Recordsets must use optimistic locking.

- Only the outermost transaction is used if nested transactions are encountered.

- Only a single workspace is used for an ODBC connection. Multiple workspaces are consolidated.

- Action queries are processed in a single transaction.

- Recordsets created inside a VBA transaction are processed under that transaction.

Because of the limitations of locking choices and lack of control over transactions (see Chapter 12), bound forms are usually not useful if you are doing standard client-server processing with Access. On the other hand, you can use bound forms in store-and-forward implementations or against downloaded data with good results. In addition, you may be able to successfully use bound forms directly against server tables or views in the following circumstances:

- When the form is based on a single table
- When the system is coded to handle update contention that will occur from optimistic locking
- When the data being updated does not need to be kept private while a set of changes is completed
- When the amount of data shown on the form at any one time is strictly limited

Forms that will usually meet these criteria include

- Inquiry-only forms (based on read-only recordsets)
- Master table maintenance forms
- Browse forms that accept a key value from the user and then change their record source to fetch only the record with that key

Processing that generally does *not* work well using bound forms in the client-server setup includes

- Updates or inserts of master/detail combinations, such as orders
- Updates in which multiple rows of a table must be changed at once

Using Local Tables

At times you will want to keep a local copy of some of your server database within the Access client application. When splitting the workload between Access and the server, always remember that Access is a complete database system. You can take advantage of this by caching data locally on each client machine as it is first used or even at login time, refreshing your local tables during your AutoExec or Startup-Form FormOpen procedure. This way you can reduce both network traffic and the load on your server, allowing you to support many more concurrent users on the same server and network. This procedure is especially easy to implement if you are converting an existing application, since you already have the native Access processing coded.

Review all your data requirements and identify the data that matches the following conditions:

- Data is static or relatively static.
- Users do not need to see each other's changes immediately.
- Data is always used together as a set, with each set needing to be used together exclusively.

Also, review your processing requirements to look for the following situations:

- Data entry systems in which several detail records are entered to build a complete transaction. This may be an order, an invoice, a parts list, or one of several other cases matching the traditional header-detail data pairing.
- Reports showing several aspects of the same data.
- Reports that do a great deal of data consolidation.

When you have processing needs matching the above types, you can benefit by downloading the data onto the client machine for processing or, when going the other way, by capturing the user's activity locally and uploading data to the server only when the user's session or activity is complete.

If your application uses a number of lookup tables, set up your system to load these at startup time. You can then design your forms and reports to use the local data in pick lists, in combo boxes, or when displaying descriptive lookup text instead of codes.

If your users typically work on a particular set of data for an extended period and other users should not work on this same data concurrently, you have a prime candidate for downloading the data and processing it locally—for example, a problem management system or an order processing system.

Note that you'll have to choose carefully when to use the client copy of a table and when to use the server copy. A table of U.S. states used as the row source for a combo box, for example, should be the local copy because opening the combo will cause it to be requeried multiple times. On the other hand, when you're writing a query that joins that table with other server tables, you'll want to use the server copy, to avoid the heavy network traffic of doing a join between two different data sources.

Creating Efficient Client-Server Applications

Creating efficient client-server applications requires that you follow certain principles: try to move data only once, and make sure the server gives you only what you need.

Remember, your major benefits from a client-server application come when you move less data over the network cable than you would in a file-server application. These principles are discussed in the next two sections.

Try to Move Data Only Once

Access has a penchant for allowing the user to examine data in several formats, views, and orders. It is very costly to reload the data to the client when processing in a client-server environment. In situations in which a dataset will be used for analysis, you should consider downloading the data into working tables on the client.

Make Sure the Server Gives You Only What You Need

It is important to avoid recordsets based on all fields and all rows of a table. If you really need this level of data, consider importing or downloading the data from the server instead of linking to it. You can always refresh the data from the server by dropping your local table and reimporting. For forms, always define a query for the record source, and always include a WHERE clause that is as restrictive as possible—one row is usually best. Avoid the use of the all-fields identifier (*) in your queries. Create form-specific queries that contain only the fields required for that form.

When you're writing queries to serve as the record source for a form, start with an impossible condition. For example, if all your customer numbers are greater than 0, you might open a form with a record source of

```
SELECT CustomerName, CustomerID FROM Customers WHERE
    CustomerID = -1
```

Because this returns no rows, the server can evaluate it very quickly. For most efficient processing, be sure the impossible condition refers to a nonexistent value in a primary key or uniquely indexed field. If you just use "WHERE False", the processing will be much slower. If you then provide your users with an input control to supply a customer number, you can dynamically change the RecordSource property at run time and requery the form. (This strategy was also discussed for file-server applications in Chapter 12.) You can accomplish this by using an event procedure similar to this one:

```
Sub txtCustomerNumber_AfterUpdate ()
Dim strSQL As String
    If Not IsNull(Me![txtCustomerNumber]) Then
        strSQL = "SELECT CustomerName, CustomerID "
        strSQL = strSQL & "FROM Customers WHERE "
        strSQL = strSQL & "CustomerID = "
        strSQL = strSQL & Me![txtCustomerNumber]
        Me.RecordSource = strSQL
    End If
End Sub
```

In the sample database, frmAuthors demonstrates this same technique with the authors table from the SQL Server pubs database. Be particularly careful about retrieving memo or OLE fields from the server. Because these tend to involve a substantial amount of data, they will vastly increase your network traffic. If you have an employees table with a picture of the employee, for example, you might start by bringing back only the text data and including a command button to retrieve the picture only if the user wants to see it.

For reports, consider defining the base data for the report as a table and running an append query to load it from the server. Doing so avoids many of the pitfalls you will find when trying to interpret all the data access requirements of a report. It will also allow you to base multiple reports on the same set of data and yet query the server only once.

Partitioning Work between Client and Server

Some of your most critical decisions during the design process will be splitting, or partitioning, the work between Access and the server. When using Access as a front end, you need to use client hardware that has almost as much memory and processing power as a machine used for stand-alone Access. Access differs from many front-end clients (for example, PowerBuilder and ObjectView) in this respect because Access *always* creates an entire application. To end up with an efficient client-server system, you must leave appropriate portions of the application in native Access.

Data Entry Systems

Many data-entry systems feature an operator doing heads-down, high-speed entry of a lot of detail data for an order and then committing the entire order to the system. The partial order is of no use to others in the system. In fact, you do not want other groups to see a partially entered order because it could skew results of their work. Thus, it makes sense in these cases to use local Access tables to capture the order and then upload the data to the server only when the entire order is complete.

Reporting Systems

Reporting itself is rarely a good reason for considering a move to client-server. Often the reports are the hardest part of an Access application to convert to client-server use. Usually, the most flexible way to implement reporting in a client-server environment is to either download the data used by reports to local tables on which the reports are then based or to base reports on stacked queries. With stacked queries, the report's query uses a query based on the server's tables rather than directly referencing the tables. This helps avoid problems where Jet is unable to produce an efficient partitioning of work, particularly for reports using crosstabs or extensive aggregate processing. Initially, you should probably just download temporary tables for your reports. Convert reports to server-based record sources only if you encounter severe performance problems downloading the data.

Danger Signs for Queries

When using "regular" (non-SPT) Access queries, there are many things to keep in mind. The key point is to make sure as much processing as possible is transferred to the server. To do this you need to have gathered the information from the section "Understanding Your Server" earlier in this chapter to know what can be processed there. You also need to understand which types of query processing Access will never attempt to send to a server.

While the details will vary from server to server, in general the query features listed here will require at least part of the processing to be done locally. Because this means that Access will not be able to restrict the server dataset only to the records you need, this condition will increase your network traffic and decrease performance.

- User-defined functions and functions not supported by your server, especially in the WHERE clause
- Multiple-level GROUP BYs
- GROUP BYs including DISTINCT
- Joins over GROUP BYs
- Joins over DISTINCT clauses
- Certain combinations of outer and inner joins
- Queries stacked on unions
- Subqueries that include data from more than one source

You should consider crosstab queries a special case when developing queries. While no server supports crosstabs directly, most servers will process the underlying aggregate query if the following conditions are met:

- Row and column headers may not contain aggregates.
- The value field must contain only one aggregate.
- There can be no user-defined ORDER BY clause.

If you meet these conditions, your crosstab query will be processed on the server, and the local Jet engine will only have to do the final formatting to present the crosstab.

Building Your Forms

Building forms for client-server applications requires some special considerations beyond those covered in Chapter 8. You must pay special attention to how your searching and navigation processes work. You must also be closely aware of your data sources.

Choosing Bound and Unbound Fields

After you have identified all the data requirements and data sources for your forms, you need to create the forms and link all the fields to their data sources. Whenever possible, link bound fields to a field from the record source of the form rather than creating a separate row source for each control. In a client-server environment, each row source will result in a separate connection to the server.

If you do use controls bound to separate data sources (including subforms, list boxes, or combo boxes), make sure either that they are set to be hidden when the form opens or that the fields used to link to them or provide criteria for them are filled in during the form's Open event. Firing off the query for a subform with null criteria can create a major, unneeded workload for your network. This is especially important for subforms because they tend to be more complex than list boxes or combo boxes.

Choosing an Appropriate Design for Your Forms

Often an Access form allows a user both to navigate to a specific record and to then perform detailed work on the record. Several approaches to form design provide good performance for these situations. The goal of each approach is to present the user with a small subset of the fields to use to select the records they need and a separate recordset for the detail. The form should be set up to fill the detail recordset only *after* the user selects the criteria.

Using an Unbound Main Form and a Subform for Detail

One of the simplest approaches you can use for forms mainly used to search or edit data is to create your edit form as though it would be used directly and then embed it as a subform on an unbound form. You can set the record source of the subform based on a query that references fields on the unbound main form rather than using the master and child linking fields. On the main form, create the controls users will use to establish the criteria for their final recordset. You should set the default value on each of the criteria fields to a value that will cause the subform to return no rows when the form is first opened. If you use a combo box, list box, or other pick-list mechanism to allow the user to find records, use a hidden field to hold the criteria and fill it in the AfterUpdate event procedure of the pick-list type control. Provide a command button, toolbar button, or menu selection for users to indicate that they are finished setting criteria. If the pick lists are based on fairly static data, such as order types, lists of valid codes, or processing status codes, this data should be downloaded to the client at startup. For more volatile data, you should accept the overhead of retrieving it from the server each time the form is opened to ensure that users receive the most current data.

Using a Dynamic Record Source

You can provide more flexibility by using a modified version of the form/subform model presented in the preceding section. Create the SQL for the detail form dynamically, based on the values filled in on the unbound main form. This eliminates the need for hidden fields for criteria and helps ensure that the most efficient SQL can be used for each alternative set of criteria. You must use dynamic SQL instead of a fixed query with parameters if you are using LIKE in your criteria and appending wildcard characters to the user's selections. If you use fixed criteria, you will end up with a full table scan because the optimizer cannot predict how to use the indexes. You should also use dynamic SQL instead of a fixed query if your table has multiple indexes but your server can use only a single index for each table in a query. By building the SQL based on the fields the user selects, you have the best chance of using the most restrictive index each time.

Using Unbound Controls in the Header or Footer

On a single form, you can use a variation on the approach just described. Place the unbound controls that are used for criteria entry in the header or footer, and at run time, either filter the form using the ApplyFilter action or reset the form's record source using the form's RecordSource property. (See the frmAuthors form in CH14.MDB for an example of this technique.) This approach has the advantage of using only a single bound form, but it offers fewer user interface design alternatives because the header and footer must always appear at a specific location.

Using FindFirst

One approach to record navigation and searching that works much better in client-server than in native Access is the FindFirst method. In Access this method always results in a scan, but with servers, Jet will often use a new query, and the server can process an efficient search. You can take advantage of this by placing your search criteria in the header or footer area of a form and using FindFirst to move the Detail section to the desired data.

Building Reports

Reports often cause problems for client-server work in Access. Access has a powerful reporting module that offers many data-analysis tools. Most of these tools assume that the data with which they are working is local and that retrieving the data multiple times will not cause unacceptable overhead.

You may find that the easiest solution is to split your report processing into two parts. First, set up a query that extracts all the required data from your server. While building this query, do not worry about obtaining totals, grouping, or other reporting requirements. After you have isolated the data for the report, build the query or queries used by the report based on the server query. When you need to run multiple reports from a single data source, you should download the data into local Access tables and base the reports on these temporary tables.

Exceptions to this general approach are

- Generating a summary report from a very large database
- Generating a report using statistics (such as median) that are supported by your server directly but are not supported in Access

Effects of Grouping and Sorting

Access cannot send multiple-field GROUP BYs directly to servers. If you do not download the data into an Access table with indexes that support the GROUP BYs, the recordset is sorted on the client machine. The grouping and sorting in the report design will override the grouping and sorting in a query, so do not use grouping and sorting in the query when you are grouping and sorting data within the report.

Selecting Data Sources for Fields

Because reports represent a read-only snapshot of a database, you will find more cases in which downloaded data can be used than for forms. Applying all formatting on the report fields instead of the query fields also helps with query optimization.

Creating Header and Footer Fields and Expressions

You should try to base the summary fields in your headers and footers on fields from the Detail sections of your reports instead of on expressions against the tables.

Graphs

When including graphs in a report, you must pay close attention to the data source and the location of the OLE server. You usually use a separate record source for each chart on a report. Make sure the record source is restricted to exactly what should be graphed. Do not use the query to add formatting or titles or to provide anything other than the raw data for the graph. Provide all legends, titles, and formatting by means of OLE automation. Allowing the server to do what it does best—provide data from its tables—should keep your reports working smoothly.

Common Client-Server Migration Problems

It's likely you will encounter problems when moving existing file-server applications to a client-server environment. While much of this chapter has provided useful information for this process, the following sections offer additional trouble-shooting assistance.

Nonupdatable Queries

One of the first problems you may run into is that queries (or views) that are updatable in Access will be read-only on your server. In these cases Jet processes the join operation locally and manages the retrievals and updates to the server's tables on the client side. This is not as efficient as handling the updates solely on the server, and it may also introduce increased contention problems, depending on how Access and your server define the transactions for these updates. You may want to consider redesigning your system to avoid doing updates on joined data. Typically, as long as your network is well designed, the server will be fast enough to allow the split in updating that Jet produces. The major problem comes with the increased network load that sometimes occurs with this type of system.

Converting Validation Rules

Validation rules are another area that requires special consideration during migration. Access-defined validation rules cannot be used by any current server. If your server supports triggers and stored procedures, you should be able to convert most Access rules to server-based triggers. If you do this, you will need to add in your own error handling to replace the validation text and error trapping you had in your native Access application. You will also need to test your specific server to determine the error processing related to stored procedures and triggers. Take extra care when converting table-level validation rules and validation rules that use Access functions. Most servers will not have the same set of predefined functions as Access, so you may need to have stored procedures written to replace them. In some cases you may need to do the validation locally in VBA before the data is sent to the server.

User-Defined Functions

Any queries that make use of user-defined functions or built-in Access functions also require special attention. Since the server will not support them, Jet returns them to your application to perform locally. This may not be too much of a problem if the functions are only on the final output, because they will be applied only as the data is sent from the server to the client. You will experience severe performance problems, however, if they are part of query criteria, ORDER BY, GROUP BY, or aggregate expressions. If you have any of these cases, look at converting the functions to stored procedures on the server. You could also split your query to allow all the server processing that doesn't involve the Access function to occur in one server query, returning a recordset that is then processed locally.

Counter, OLE, and Memo Fields

The presence of counter fields in your database requires the use of a stored procedure or special field datatype on many servers to provide a similar function. Most servers now support equivalents of OLE and memo fields, but if you use either of these, make sure you understand exactly *how* the server supports them.

Combo and List Boxes

Combo and list boxes that reference large numbers of server rows will be a problem. You'll get much better performance if you either cache the data locally or use appropriate criteria to restrict the list to a small number of entries.

The Upsizing Wizard

There is one special case in which you will find the mechanics of moving from Access to a server database to be considerably simplified: when you're moving from Access to Microsoft SQL Server. Microsoft has designed a separate product called the Access Upsizing Tools to make this transition easier. The original version was intended to convert an Access 2.0 database to use Microsoft SQL Server 4.21 tables. A new version, due out in early 1996, will simplify the transition from Access 95 to SQL Server 6.0.

The Upsizing Wizard runs as an Access add-in. When you run it, it accomplishes the following tasks:

- Exports the structure of all tables to the SQL Server
- Creates indexes on the server
- Exports as many validation rules as possible to the server
- Creates stored procedures (for SQL 4.21) or Identity fields (for SQL 6.0) to replace counters
- Creates stored procedures (for SQL 4.21) or uses Declarative Referential Integrity (for SQL 6.0) to enforce your referential integrity on the server
- Renames tables and fields as necessary to conform with the SQL Server naming limits
- Exports your Access data to the server
- Links the SQL Server tables back to your Access application
- Creates queries as necessary to alias changed field and table names back to their original names

You can think of the Upsizing Wizard as the client-server equivalent of the Database Splitter that's included with Access 95. While it won't do anything to make the changes we've discussed above to make your application more efficient in a client-server environment, it will eliminate most of the tedious work, leaving you free to concentrate on the fine-tuning.

NOTE Bunker Hill Software (800-676-8007 or 510-734-8007, fax 510-734-9443, e-mail 76620.1501@compuserve.com) sells a similar tool for upsizing Access 2.0 applications to Oracle called Scriptoria. It's likely they will be creating an Access 95 version of their product, too.

Resources

This chapter has merely scratched the surface of the issues involved in client-server development. *Developing Client-Server Solutions with Access95 and SQL 6.0*, by John Viescas, Mike Gunderloy, and Mary Chipman (available in Spring 1996 from SYBEX) concentrates exclusively on client-server issues within the Microsoft product line. Several other sources of information may help further in this process. The Access Developer's Toolkit for Access 95 comes with the *Advanced Topics* manual, which includes chapters on ODBC and client-server applications. Many Microsoft knowledge-base articles are also available from Microsoft on specific issues, problems, and work-arounds for both ODBC and client-server. Microsoft's *Jet Database Engine ODBC Connectivity* white paper also contains excellent information on using Access in a client-server environment. (You can access knowledge-base articles and the white paper on CompuServe, MSN, the MSDN, and TechNet CDs and through Microsoft's download services.) Your ODBC driver vendor and your database server vendor should be able to supply help in configuring the server and getting the ODBC links running properly.

Summary

In this chapter we have covered the basics of implementing a client-server system using Access. We introduced the major areas to consider when planning a client-server system or planning a migration to client-server. More specifically, we covered these issues:

- Selecting a server to match your processing needs
- Understanding the mechanics of ODBC processing
- Choosing a query strategy for client-server applications
- Configuring Access for ODBC
- Mapping your transactions in client-server systems

- Taking advantage of Access' strengths in creating client-server applications
- Choosing the best form and control design for efficient processing
- Building efficient reports
- Identifying problem areas when migrating an application to client-server
- Using the Access Upsizing Tools

PART V

Building Applications

CHAPTER

FIFTEEN

Providing an Elegant Interface

- Designing consistent, user-aware applications

- Identifying the best interface for your application

- Exploiting Windows 95's interface features

- Creating your own property dialogs

When you have your application running perfectly on the computer on your desk, you're still a long way from being finished. An application's user interface is at least as important as, and often more important than, the functionality "under the covers." A well-designed user interface facilitates user learning and acceptance, acts as a visible representation of your style as a developer, and, if you market your application commercially, provides a competitive advantage over other applications. One of the challenges facing designers of today's applications is creating user interfaces that are simultaneously functional, intuitive, and aesthetically pleasing and that perform well on users' hardware configurations.

Unfortunately, most programmers put the functionality together first and worry about the interface last, if at all. If you just create a switchboard form and throw on a few buttons to launch other forms and reports, you're not doing your users much of a service. You need to take time up front to think about user interface design. Your goal should be to come up with a design that is useful and elegant and that empowers users to get the most out of your application. This chapter focuses on some principles of user-interface design that may help your applications meet these goals.

Methods for Approaching Interface Design

Like many aspects of application design, creating a user interface is part art, part science. There is no one best way to build a user interface, but there are a number of guidelines you can use to help choose a direction for development. The following sections describe a variety of issues facing the interface designer and include suggestions for making your user interfaces consistent and useable.

Designing for the User, Not the Developer

There's a difference between "useful and elegant" and "clever and unique." You may have revolutionary ideas for reworking the way Windows applications are presented to the user. In the real world of useful applications, though, cleverness is far less important than ease of use. The flashiest interface in the world is worthless if it forces users to learn new techniques for skills they already have. Use the Windows interface and the Windows way of doing things, even if you think you might have a better way. This means, for example, that you should indicate accelerator keys with underlining, that you should avoid hiding important actions behind double-clicking fields, and that you should present lists in a scrolling vertical column.

Keep in mind, too, that Windows 95 is changing the standard in some respects, introducing new features and conventions, such as the increased use of the right mouse button. As your users become familiar with these methods in Windows, they will come to expect them in your applications. Still, despite the recent change in operating system interfaces, there are close to 60 million desktops running the standard Windows 3.x interface. Those users will expect you to provide a smooth transition in your applications, just as Microsoft is attempting to do with Windows 95.

Providing Multiple Access Methods

As part of the notion of user control, it's important to provide multiple ways to get to any particular activity. For example, if you have a form for entering new complications in a medical procedure, it's not enough to provide a command button on your switchboard to open the form. Different users think in different ways. Some like to choose items from menus, while others look only for buttons. Your program must accommodate all the standard ways to perform actions in Windows.

Also be sure the different interfaces are consistent. If you have a command button for an action, you should also have

- An accelerator key for that command button
- A menu item that performs the same action
- A toolbar button that performs the action (if you've implemented custom toolbars)
- A status bar that indicates which operation will be performed in response to any of these actions
- A Help file topic offering further information

Yes, it's a lot of work, but work spent here in bulletproofing the user interface is just as important as work spent bulletproofing your code.

Allowing for Nonlinear Use

Don't expect or try to force linear movement through your application. You have to remember that this is *Windows,* and your users for the most part are going to be armed with mice. Even if your application itself has a straightforward linear flow, users will step outside it to other running applications—to cut and paste data (incidentally destroying anything you might have stored on the clipboard), click everywhere, and in general make a nuisance of themselves.

Very few applications have a linear flow (although many programmers seem happiest thinking in linear terms). Almost any application has multiple actions that could be performed all at once: editing a lookup table to bring a new choice into a combo box, putting up a report in Print Preview view and then hopping back to data entry without closing it, and so on. Make sure users can jump around and have multiple parts of your application open at once. This is more consistent with the way the real world works, in all its wonderful confusion; more important, it's consistent with the way the rest of the Windows world works.

Supporting Multiple Data Interaction Modes

You may find you need two different forms for each table of your application to accommodate the two typical ways users work with data. In general, you'll find that there is both a data-entry mode and a data-browsing mode and that working with both on the same form is difficult unless you're prepared to manipulate the visible properties of many controls.

Data-entry mode allows users to fill tables with little hand-holding. The goal is simply to get in the new data quickly. You must allow for verification and easy changes, but in data-entry mode you don't have to deal with searching and sorting the data. Forms designed for data-entry mode typically rely heavily on input masking, tab order, defaults, and status bar messages to move the experienced user through quickly. Whenever possible, data-entry–mode forms should perform immediate data validation on a field rather than record basis and offer auditory feedback for users who may be working in a "heads-down" fashion.

Less sophisticated users who need to look up things and work with them but don't do any heavy data entry often use data-browsing mode. Data-browsing forms tend to feature combo boxes for selecting records quickly from a list already prepared by the application. On-screen help may need to be more detailed. If the primary use of your data-browsing forms is for extracting information from your application, the data needs to be protected from casual changes. Often, such browsing forms will be opened in read-only mode or with most of their controls locked and disabled, perhaps with an Edit button to enable editing for those users who are allowed to do so. One very useful feature added to Access 95 is Filter-by-Form, which lets users create queries and filters using the very same forms they use for data entry.

Your design decisions are made even more complicated because there are different classes of data-entry persons and data browsers. For example, data entry runs the gamut of users, from the legendary heads-down data-entry person to the person taking orders over the phone, with every level in between. The person taking orders over the phone will probably appreciate the days you spent getting the look and feel of that form just right. Give that same form to heads-down data-entry operators and they will immediately complain that your pretty form is getting in the way of the job. Similarly, you would probably design a form for executives to use occasionally to look up data differently than an analyst would on a daily basis. The key point is to get to know who your users are and how they will be using the program. By using Access' security system, you can easily detect the class of user and change the user interface accordingly.

Testing and Refining Your Design

Just as an application must be tested to ensure functional performance, it must be tested to be sure the interface works. This means making sure users can access all the available functionality easily with minimum training. You should make interface testing part of your overall test plan for your application (you do have a test plan, don't you?) and conduct testing as early as possible to work out any quirks in the way it operates. Performing user interface testing early lets you freeze the interface, which, in turn, allows you to concentrate on the functional aspects of the application. Early testing also lets you begin the normally time-consuming documentation process without having to worry about last-minute changes invalidating printed procedures and user manuals.

Formal testing of the user interface, often called *usability testing*, normally requires a dedicated lab area with two-way mirrors and recording equipment. Having said this, however, we're not suggesting you make interface testing an overly complex and burdensome task. Simply spending a few hours with a representative sample of your users can prove invaluable. When conducting tests of your application's user interface, consider the following items:

- Be sure to select test subjects who represent the level of sophistication your users are likely to possess.

- Present your users with a list of general tasks to perform, such as "Open the Customer form, find Joe Smith's record, and display a list of his outstanding invoices." Avoid giving your users specific methods to accomplish tasks.

- Use a stopwatch to measure the amount of time it takes to perform each task. As you refine the interface, use subsequent timings to judge how much you've improved.

- If you use testers more than once, make sure they're assigned different tasks to perform. This eliminates test bias from their knowledge of the application.

- Survey your testers for their subjective feedback on the application. Ask them if they understand fully any specific terminology the application uses. You might learn, for example, that users can more easily understand the phrase "Reorganize and shrink data file" than "Compact database."

Interface design is a constant process of testing and refinement. As you work toward the "perfect interface," however, conduct testing early enough in the development process so you can make changes before a large investment is made in development. After deciding on a particular design, avoid the urge to make modifications late in the game, even seemingly minor ones.

Coexisting with the Windows 95 Interface

Microsoft Windows 95 represents the most significant overhaul of the operating system's user interface in its long history. In addition to a major paradigm shift in how data and applications are represented and organized, Windows 95 offers users more control over their environment than ever before. On the one hand, this presents application developers with the challenge of adapting their programs to this new paradigm, integrating new and different interface elements in an effort to maintain consistency and increase functionality. On the other hand, the new Windows interface also provides an opportunity to enhance applications with usability features that are the result of numerous hours of testing by Microsoft. In effect, Microsoft is setting a new standard for what users want in an interface. Those who adopt its conventions are likely to prosper. This section explains a number of key features of the new interface that should be of interest to Access developers. Later in the chapter you will see an example of how you can put them to use in your applications.

Underlying the numerous clever enhancements to the user interface—"gee whiz" items such as the What's This button and shortcuts—is an approach to interface design that further blurs the line between programs and the data they manipulate. Microsoft has long been promoting a document-centric view of computing, one in which users focus on their data rather than on application programs. Keep this in mind when designing your applications, and don't let the challenges of using your system outweigh its benefits.

Font and Color Usage

Windows 95 brings with it some changes to the way fonts and colors are used within the graphical environment and individual applications. You should consider how some of these changes will affect existing applications, as well as those you create from scratch using Access 95.

First off is the abandonment of boldface type as a standard text style for dialog controls and informational text. Figure 15.1 shows the Windows 95 System Properties dialog. You'll notice there isn't a single piece of boldface type anywhere on the dialog.

This represents a change from Windows 3.x, which used bold type almost exclusively for dialog and button text. In fact, Microsoft's own design guide for Windows recommended the use of boldface so that text remained legible even if it was dimmed to indicate unavailability. (Windows 95 uses a subdued, three-dimensional effect to indicate a disabled object, eliminating the need for bold type.) Perhaps Microsoft is using this new standard to create a "kinder and gentler" impression of Windows. Regardless of the motivation, you may want to consider adopting this approach with your Access forms, changing boldface type on labels, text boxes, and buttons to regular type to remain consistent with the "lighter" interface of Windows 95.

FIGURE 15.1:

Example of Windows 95's use of nonbold type for dialog and button text

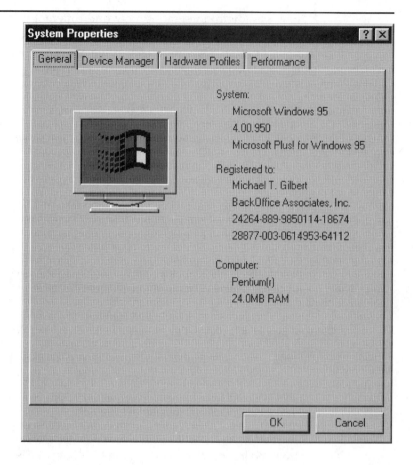

In addition to the move toward regular-weight type in dialogs, Windows 95 gives users more control over the typefaces they can use in system objects. For example, Windows 3.x used the System font for window captions, message box text, and menus, and it used MS Sans Serif for icons and dialog text. Although it was, in fact, possible to change the font used (by modifying the SYSTEM.INI file), it was not at all straightforward. Windows 95, on the other hand, includes an extensive property dialog for the video display, allowing users to change the typeface and size of text used by the interface elements mentioned above. Users will come to expect this type of flexibility in application interfaces, as well. You may want to consider adding a font-customization feature to your Access applications.

Another significant change involves color usage. Windows 95 features enhanced palette manipulation that allows users to select from a broad range of color choices for interface elements, such as window titles, borders, and text. These colors, known as the *system colors*, have been around for many years (and numerous Windows versions) and can be used as foreground and background colors of Access objects. In fact, in Access 95 the default background color of new forms is the color of 3-D objects, such as buttons and dialog boxes in Windows 95. This means that unless you change the BackColor property of a form you create with Access 95 to a nonsystem color, its background color is likely to change with the whims of your users. If you choose a color scheme for your application that is not responsive to system color changes, you may end up with an extremely ugly interface.

TIP

When designing forms in Access 95, make sure you use a BackStyle property of Transparent or a BackColor property of –2147483633 (&H8000000F hexadecimal), the system color for dialogs, for label controls. Otherwise, these controls may stand out unattractively if the user switches to a different system color scheme.

New Interface Controls

Windows 95 provides developers with the same standard visual controls that have been creeping into Windows applications for years. Visual elements such as tabbed dialogs, toolbars, and multicolumn lists are standard parts of the operating system available to developers using tools such as Microsoft Visual C++. As an Access developer, you can implement these features in your applications either by faking them (using multiple command buttons in place of a tabbed dialog, for example) or by using an OLE control such as COMCTL32.OCX, which ships with the Access Developer's Toolkit. Not only do these elements offer advances in ease of use, your users will expect to find them in your applications that are "built for Windows 95."

Increased User Control

Finally, Windows 95 tries more than any other version to put users in control of their own environment. It seems as though everything has a property sheet users can expose in one way or another, and there are usually multiple ways to perform any given task. As you design your application, try to provide this kind of flexibility to your users. Give them options, even simplistic ones, that provide them with a sense of control. As an example, the section "Allowing Users to Choose Custom Color Schemes" later in this chapter demonstrates how to create dialogs and procedures that let users choose their own color schemes for the user interface. Don't limit users to strict procedures for accomplishing tasks. Take advantage of Access' MDI design and event-driven programming model to provide users with many different ways to interact with information. *Empowerment* is an overused term these days, but giving careful thought to how people will try to use your application (and allowing them to use it those ways) will pay you back in satisfied users.

Basics of Interface Design with Access

Despite the fact that Access offers you a near-limitless number of options for interface design, only a few basic form styles and control layouts actually make sense for the vast majority of Access applications. If you're in the process of planning or building a mainstream application that must coexist with other Access and Windows programs, this section will help you make the right choices when putting together your forms.

Choosing the Right Form Design

Access lets you create forms with a variety of attributes. For example, you can choose from different border styles (none, sizable, thin, or dialog), system controls (Minimize, Maximize, and Close buttons), and navigation tools (navigation buttons, record selectors ,and scroll bars). Not all styles make sense for every situation, however. Table 15.1 lists a number of general classes of forms and the most appropriate set of attributes for each. If you are new to Windows application development, consult this list when designing forms, since the guidelines represent, for the most part, standard Windows conventions.

TABLE 15.1: Suggested Styles for Forms Based on Usage

Style	Attributes
Single Form (Bound)	Form with a sizable border, record selectors, a horizontal scroll bar, and all system controls
Single Form (Unbound)	Form with a sizable border and all system controls
Continuous Form (Bound)	Form with a sizable border, record selectors, a vertical scroll bar, and all system controls, plus header and footer sections
Floating Toolbox	Popup form with a thin border, a control menu, and Minimize and Close buttons
Dialog Box	Popup modal form with a dialog border and a Close button
Splash Screen	Popup form with no border
Status Dialog	Popup form with a dialog border and no control menu or Minimize, Maximize, or Close button

To aid you in form design, CH15.MDB contains a form that displays the listed styles, as well as their associated attributes. The form, called frmFormBuilder, is shown in Figure 15.2. You can use the form to create new, blank forms by selecting a style, modifying any attributes you wish, and clicking the Build! button.

FIGURE 15.2:

frmFormBuilder form showing options for a continuous bound form

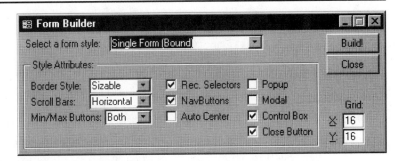

Using Appropriate Controls

After you create a form with characteristics that are consistent with its usage, the next step is to place controls on the form. When deciding on which controls to use, remember that there are commonly accepted standards as to which controls you should use to represent different types of information. Once again, your users will expect your applications to look and work like other Windows programs. The following table describes a number of datatypes and the most appropriate control for each case:

Data Represented	Control to Use
Binary (yes/no)	Check box
Small list of mutually exclusive options	Option group and radio buttons
Small, finite list of nonexclusive options	Rectangle and check boxes (see Chapter 7)
Small, indeterminate list of options	List box
Large, indeterminate list of options	Combo box
Indeterminate data	Text box

Although there may be cases in which another control type makes sense, those listed in the table are generally very consistent with Windows and other Windows applications.

Applying Fonts and Colors Thoughtfully

Do you remember when Microsoft shipped Windows 3.1 with its support for True-Type fonts? Did you rush out and purchase one of the cheap, multiple-font add-on packages that appeared shortly thereafter? An examination of laser-printed reports, personal letters, and corporate memos produced around the same time will show that many people did. The ease with which multiple typefaces could be applied to a single document caused some people to simply lose control! Choosing fonts and colors for an application has always presented a similar dilemma for developers. Used effectively, they can convey additional information to the user, above and beyond the data displayed. Unfortunately, many developers can't—but should—control the urge to use all the font and color options a development tool provides.

Access' visual design tools make it easy to customize the look of your application. With a few mouse clicks you can turn a bland form into a well-organized, informative display of critical data. Alternatively, you can produce something that resembles a cross between the technical schematic for a nuclear submarine and an accident involving a truck loaded with crayons. Figure 15.3 shows such a form.

FIGURE 15.3:

An Access form gone bad

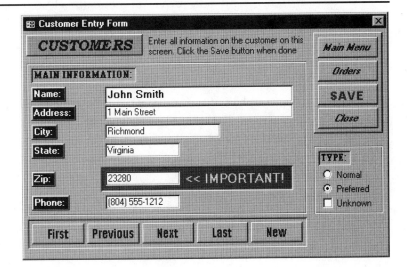

As with almost every aspect of interface design, *simple is better.* You might want to consider the following guidelines when selecting fonts and colors for your application:

- Choose one typeface for your forms and controls. (Reports allow for somewhat more flexibility.) Use regular-weight type for all text except where you need to show emphasis, and then use boldface. Avoid having more than two different point sizes on the same form, and use the same size type for all your forms.

- Use a bitmap font, such as MS Sans Serif, for maximum readability on screen. Typefaces without serifs tend to make text easier to read on screen. Serif fonts, such as Times Roman, are more suited to large blocks of printed text.

- Unless you have a license to distribute custom fonts, stick with those installed as part of Windows: Arial, Courier New, MS Sans Serif, MS Serif, System, and Times New Roman. This will ensure that your forms will be displayed correctly on every user's PC.

- Avoid large regions of bright colors, especially for form backgrounds. Subdued hues are easier on the eyes and less distracting. Use bright colors to highlight data such as numbers (bright red for negative numbers, for instance).

- If you want to use color, choose only one or two besides the form's background color, and use them sparingly. Use dark and light shades of the same color to contrast related items.

- Graphics often only confuse and distract users. They also slow down your form's display speed. If you want to use graphics images for command buttons or to provide feedback to the user, make sure they are simple and easily understood.

Most developers (and almost *all* users) can recognize an application that abuses colors and fonts. It takes a great deal more thought, however, to actually create one that doesn't. If, after following the guidelines listed above, you're still unsure whether you've got the hang of it, ask a few users for their opinions. They'll know whether you've got it right.

Controlling Form-to-Form Navigation

When you are designing your interface, the least restrictive design is one that allows users to open a form or report whenever they want and switch freely between them. This is essentially what you can accomplish by using Access' database container as a main switchboard form. Under some circumstances, however, this may not be desirable. For example, your users might be new to Windows and not feel comfortable using a true MDI application. In situations like this, you might want to provide a simpler interface, one that lets your users work on one form at a time. CH15.MDB demonstrates this technique, called *form chaining*, using several forms and two global procedures, glrChainForm and glrUnchainForm. Listing 15.1 shows the declarations of the two procedures.

Listing 15.1

```
Sub glrChainForm(frmCalling As Form, strCalled As String, _
 Optional varFilter As Variant, _
 Optional varWhere As Variant, _
 Optional varDataMode As Variant, _
 Optional varOpenArgs As Variant)

    Dim strOpenArgs As String

    ' If the user supplied OpenArgs capture them now
    If Not IsMissing(varOpenArgs) Then
        strOpenArgs = varOpenArgs
    End If

    ' If the called form is already open, just make
    ' it visible and active
    If SysCmd(acSysCmdGetObjectState, acForm, strCalled) = _
     acObjStateOpen Then

        Forms(strCalled).Visible = True
        Forms(strCalled).SetFocus
    Else
        ' Otherwise, open it, putting the name of the calling
        ' form in the OpenArgs property
        If glrPutTag(strOpenArgs, "CallingForm", _
         frmCalling.Name) Then

            DoCmd.OpenForm FormName:=strCalled, _
             FilterName:=varFilter, _
             WhereCondition:=varWhere, _
             DataMode:=varDataMode, _
             OpenArgs:=strOpenArgs

            frmCalling.Visible = False
        End If
    End If
End Sub

Sub glrUnchainForm(frmCalled As Form)
    Dim varCalling As Variant

    ' Get the name of the form that called this one
    ' from the OpenArgs property
    varCalling = glrGetTag(frmCalled.OpenArgs, "CallingForm")
```

```
' If a name of the form was found see if it is already
' open--if so, just make it visible and active, otherwise
' open it
If Not IsNull(varCalling) Then
    If SysCmd(acSysCmdGetObjectState, acForm, _
     varCalling) = acObjStateOpen Then

        Forms(varCalling).Visible = True
        Forms(varCalling).SetFocus
    Else
        DoCmd.OpenForm varCalling
    End If
End If
End Sub
```

GlrChainForm accepts a pointer to an open form and the name of a form to open as its first two arguments; you can use the procedure in place of Access' OpenForm method. Its optional arguments allow you to pass in a filter name, a where condition, a data mode, and an OpenArgs value. You call this procedure using this syntax:

Call glrChainForm(Me, "frmCategories")

The procedure stores the name of the calling form in the OpenArgs argument passed to the called form when it opens and then immediately hides the calling form.

GlrUnchainForm works in a way exactly the opposite of grlChainForm. It retrieves the name of the calling form from the current form's OpenArgs property and either makes the form visible (if it's still open) or opens it. You should call glrUnchain-Form from the Close event of the called form. The net result is an interface in which users move from form to form without cluttering their screens or having to deal with window management. To see this in action, open the main switchboard form in CH15.MDB (frmMenu_MainSwitchboard) and click the Data Entry button. This displays the data-entry menu from which you choose from two additional forms. As each form is displayed, the one that called it is hidden until the called form is, itself, closed.

Application Consistency and Certified Compatibility

Consistency is important in any application, whether it's internal to the application itself or in relation to other products or even Windows. A consistently designed application facilitates learning and user acceptance. These days, Microsoft is taking consistency one step further, by offering official compatibility certifications that let developers identify their applications with Windows 95 and Microsoft Office 95. The following sections discuss the relevant aspects of consistency as they relate to designing an Access application and briefly describe two Microsoft compatibility certification programs.

Maintaining Consistency

Visual consistency is an important part of user interface design, both within your application and as it relates to other programs. No longer can you assume that your application is the only one your users will use on a regular basis, so you don't have the luxury of making up your own standards and conventions. Users will expect your application to conform to certain customs set by Windows and other programs. With this in mind, consider three different classes of consistency you should try to achieve when designing your user interfaces:

- Internal consistency
- Suite consistency
- Environmental consistency

Internal consistency refers to consistency among form and control styles within your application. Think carefully about how you are going to present visual cues to your users and apply styles consistently. For example, you may decide to use sunken text boxes with white backgrounds to denote fields that can accept user input. Read-only fields, on the other hand, might utilize gray backgrounds. Whatever convention you choose, be sure to use it throughout your application.

Suite consistency refers to consistency among multiple applications. These could be applications you develop yourself, such as those for commercial sale or delivered to corporate customers. In this case, consistency can readily identify your applications and distinguish them from others. It also makes it easier for users to move between applications, enhancing demand for similar programs. Suite consistency also applies to programs developed by others whose example you wish to follow. Microsoft, for instance, is promoting the development of applications that look and work like those in the Microsoft Office suite. You can benefit by creating an application that resembles mass-market products through faster recognition and accelerated user acceptance.

Environmental consistency refers to how well your application fits in with Microsoft Windows standards and conventions. These include not only those embodied in the operating system and shell, but the population of Windows applications, as well. Obviously, not all Windows programs are perfect models of consistent behavior, due to the many varied tasks they perform. Nonetheless, users have come to expect certain things, such as the ability to customize their work environment, common file-manipulation dialogs, and consistent shortcut keys. Any application that strays too far from Windows standards will likely become the subject of user complaints.

As mentioned above, a new phenomenon concerning consistency that is gaining momentum is the idea of certified compatibility with either Windows or an application suite such as Microsoft Office. Microsoft has developed two programs that aim to set a standard for compatibility with both Windows and Office. These programs feature consistency guidelines that, if followed, allow developers to promote their products as working similarly to programs that users in their target audience use every day. To companies that create and sell commercial applications, the marketing benefits are obvious. Even corporate developers can gain from certification by leveraging the experience their users have with operating complex computer programs. The sections that follow detail how Access applications fit (or don't fit) into the equation should you decide to seek a compliance certification for your programs.

Creating Windows 95– Compatible Programs

Developing an application that complies with Windows 95 Compatible program guidelines involves implementing a number of obvious (and not so obvious) features that take advantage of the Windows 95 user interface enhancements described in previous sections, as well as other behind-the-scenes functionality. For Access developers, the quest for Windows 95 compatibility holds both good news and bad news. First the good news. Because Access itself is Windows 95 compatible, much of the work has already been done for you. For example, according to Microsoft, Windows 95–compatible programs must supply both 32x32-pixel and 16x16-pixel icons, the latter being used in places like Explorer and the application's title bar. Access provides icons for itself and its child windows (forms, reports, and so on), eliminating the need for you to be concerned about it.

Now for the bad news. Certain Windows 95 Compatible program requirements cannot be met using Access as a development tool. One example of this is required support for dynamic screen resolution—the ability to change screen resolution on the fly in Windows 95. In this situation, Windows issues a WM_SETTINGCHANGE message to all running applications that can, in turn, take action regarding the new resolution, the most likely action being moving any child windows that would appear off the screen to a region in the new screen area. Since Access does not pass along this message to you as a developer (via a form event, for instance), you cannot take any action yourself. This violates one of the requirements for Windows 95 compatibility certification.

When this book was written, Microsoft was shipping a new OLE Custom Control with Visual Basic 4.0, called the Plug-and-Play control, that passed on the WM_SETTINGCHANGE message through a control event. This allows Visual Basic developers to create Windows 95–compatible applications. You can find this control, called SYSINFO.OCX, in the Tools\Sysinfo directory of the Visual Basic CD ROM. Due to time constraints, we were not able to test this control fully with Access, but it appears as though it might provide at least one solution to the problem of satisfying Windows 95 Compatible program requirements.

What does this mean for you? Despite the fact that you can't officially certify your application, you should still endeavor to make it look and act as much like Windows 95 as possible. Your users are unlikely to care very much about certifications if you make your applications easy for them to learn and use.

Creating Office 95–Compatible Programs

Just as the Windows 95 Compatible program aims to identify applications that coexist well with Windows, Microsoft's Office 95 Compatible program is a way to distinguish programs that resemble and act like those in the Microsoft Office 95 suite. Access applications are natural candidates for this rating since they are, after all, created with one of the Office programs. In fact, the requirements for Office 95–compatible programs are not very hard to meet.

To be considered compatible with Office 95, your program must focus on consistency with the Office applications in three key areas: toolbars, menus, and shortcut keys.

NOTE For the most part, the applications in Office 95 are oriented toward the creation and manipulation of document files. A database, on the other hand, does not follow this paradigm. Microsoft clearly states that the guidelines presented below are to be applied in a manner consistent with the overall purpose of a given application. We've purposely interpreted the guidelines in a way that makes sense for an Access application. For more information, you can obtain the complete guidelines for the Office 95 Compatible program from Microsoft. It is also one of the options available when you install the Access 95 Developer's Toolkit.

Toolbars

To begin with, your application must feature at least one toolbar with a requisite number of common toolbar buttons. The specifications dictate a standard for toolbar and toolbar button size and also require that your application be able to display both large and monochrome buttons. Since Access supplies the toolbar mechanism for you to use, you can be sure these standards will be met. Microsoft has designated three portions of the toolbar that you must consider. Here is a custom toolbar called Office Compatible, included with CH15.MDB, that demonstrates the three regions:

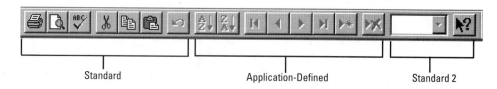

Standard   Application-Defined   Standard 2

The first region of the toolbar, called the Standard region, includes buttons for basic file and editing commands, such as New, Open, Save, Cut, Copy, Paste, and so on. Some of these, such as New, Open, and Save, have different connotations to database users who are manipulating records instead of files. The right-hand section of the toolbar is called Standard 2 and holds the Zoom Control and Help buttons.

The middle region is reserved for application-specific buttons. You can see from Figure 15.4 a little later in this chapter that we've included buttons for record sorting and navigation. You can add buttons to this toolbar as appropriate for your application.

TIP

> You can copy custom toolbars such as the one described here between databases. To do this, make sure System Objects are displayed; then open the MSysToolbars table in the source database and look for the name of the toolbar in the TbName field. Copy the entire row of data to the MSysToolbars table in the destination database. You must then close and reopen the destination database to make the new toolbar available.

Menus

The second area of consistency required for Office-compatible applications is menu command structure. As much as possible, you should supply the minimum menu structure shown in Table 15.2, which is a superset of the standard Windows menus. Obviously, some items (the View ➤ Ruler command, for instance) will make no sense in the context of an Access application, but many do apply if you think of Access forms and the data they display as the "files" that standard Office applications manipulate. For example, using Access 95's ability to create multiple instances of forms, you might use the File ➤ New command to open another instance of the current form in data-entry mode.

TABLE 15.2: Office-Compatible Menu Commands

Menu Name	Command Name	Description
File	New	Opens a new file
	Open	Displays the standard File Open dialog box
	Close	Closes the currently active window. Prompts the user to save changes if appropriate. Not displayed unless a file is open
	Save	Saves changes made to the current file. Not displayed unless a file is open
	Save As	Displays the Save As dialog box. Not displayed unless a file is open
	Save All	Saves all currently open files. Not displayed unless a file is open
	Find File	Displays the standard Find File dialog box
	Properties	Displays the properties of the current file
	Templates	Displays the Template dialog box
	Page Setup	Displays the Page Setup dialog box. Not displayed unless a file is open
	Print Preview	Displays the file as it will look when printed. Not displayed unless a file is open
	Print	Displays the Print dialog box. Not displayed unless a file is open
	MRU List	Lists the most recently used (that is, opened) files
	Exit	Terminates the application, closing all open files and prompting the user to save files as appropriate
Edit	Undo	Nullifies the last command the user performed
	Repeat	Reexecutes the last command
	Cut	Deletes the current selection but retains a copy on the clipboard
	Copy	Copies the current selection to the clipboard
	Paste	Inserts a copy of the clipboard's contents at the insertion point
	Paste Special	Displays the OLE 2.0 Paste Special dialog box
	Clear	Deletes the current selection

TABLE 15.2: Office-Compatible Menu Commands (continued)

Menu Name	Command Name	Description
	Select All	Selects the entire contents of the active file
	Find	Displays the Find dialog box
	Replace	Displays the Replace dialog box
	Links	Displays the OLE 2.0 Links dialog box
	Object	Provides access to OLE 2.0 objects
View	General File Views	Displays the current view mode the user has selected
	Full Screen	Changes the view to maximize screen space available for editing
	Toolbars	Displays the Toolbars dialog box
	Ruler	Alternately displays (or hides) the Word 95 ruler
	Zoom	Displays the Zoom dialog box
Insert	File	Displays a variation of the File Open dialog box
	Picture	Same as Insert ➤ File, or may bring up a clip art viewer
	Object	Displays the OLE 2.0 Insert Object dialog box
	Other special objects	Display dialog boxes for inserting other application-specific objects
Format	Font	Displays the Font dialog box
	Paragraph	Displays the Paragraph dialog box
	Application-specific formattable properties	Display dialog boxes that are specific to the application
Tools	Application-specific tools	Display other tools specific to the current application
	Macro	Displays the Macro dialog box
	Customize	Displays the Customize dialog box
	Options	Displays the Options dialog box
Window	New Window	Opens a new window and displays the current file in it
	Arrange All	Arranges all currently opened windows on the screen
	Split	Lets the user split the window into two parts
	Window List	Numbered list of all currently open files. If the user chooses one of these, it becomes the active file

TABLE 15.2: Office-Compatible Menu Commands (continued)

Menu Name	Command Name	Description
Help	Product Name Help	Displays the Windows 95 Help Tab dialog box
	Application-specific entries	Display help topics, tutorials, and related items that are specific to the application
	Office Compatible	Displays a Microsoft-provided help topic that describes the Office Compatible program
	About Product Name	Displays the standard About dialog box

Shortcut Keys

The third and final area of compatibility with Office applications concerns the use of shortcut keys. The section "Using an AutoKeys Macro to Provide Keyboard Shortcuts" later in this chapter lists Access-specific shortcut keys, but Microsoft has published its own list of Office-compatible keyboard shortcuts. Table 15.3 shows a short list of key combinations that developers are strongly urged to support.

TABLE 15.3: Office-Compatible Shortcut Keys

Shortcut	Menu/Command
Ctrl+N	File ➤ New or its equivalent
Ctrl+O	File ➤ Open
Ctrl+S	File ➤ Save
Ctrl+P	File ➤ Print
Ctrl+Z	Edit ➤ Undo
Ctrl+Y	Edit ➤ Repeat
Ctrl+X	Edit ➤ Cut
Ctrl+C	Edit ➤ Copy
Ctrl+V	Edit ➤ Paste
Delete	Edit ➤ Clear
Ctrl+A	Edit ➤ Select All
F1	Context Help

NOTE A more extensive list is also available in the Office 95 Compatible program documentation, but it is highly detailed and specialized and therefore beyond the scope of this book.

As companies buy more and more copies of Access as part of the Office suite of products, users will come to expect consistency among applications you develop. Even if you don't plan on marketing your application commercially, your users will nonetheless come to recognize the designation *Office 95–Compatible*.

Taking Advantage of AutoExec and AutoKeys Macros

Access provides you with two opportunities to take action on behalf of your users. The first is when your users first open the database, and the second is when they press a predetermined keyboard combination. You can tap into these occurrences using AutoExec and AutoKeys macros, special-case macros that Access executes automatically. The following sections explain how to make the most of each.

Readying the Interface with the AutoExec Macro

The first chance you get to interact with your users is in your AutoExec macro, which runs whenever your database is opened. To avoid potential error-trapping problems, keep your AutoExec macro as simple as possible. In fact, one line will do, with the express purpose of throwing further execution to Access Basic. Figure 15.4 shows a sample AutoExec macro that does nothing more than transfer its execution to a VBA function.

FIGURE 15.4:

Use the AutoExec macro to run an extended AutoExec() function.

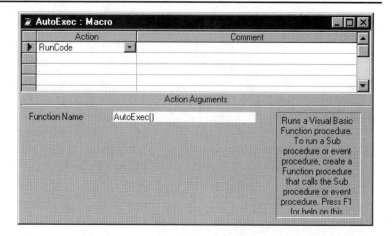

> **NOTE**   If you prefer, you can dispense with the AutoExec macro altogether and place the code in the Load event of a database's Startup form. This has the added benefit of being portable, in that you can copy your form from one database to another and keep the initialization code intact.

The AutoExec() function can then proceed with the task of initializing your user environment, as well as your data structures. Listing 15.2 shows an AutoExec() function that starts by giving the user some immediate feedback and then proceeds to load forms and initialize variables behind the scenes. (The AutoExec() function is contained in the basAutoExec module of CH15.MDB.) AutoExec() uses a table called tblPreload and a query called qryPreload to store and retrieve names of forms that should be loaded during the startup process. By preloading forms in this fashion with the acHidden attribute, you can trade off a slightly longer initialization period for snappier operation later in the application. Users generally notice one lengthy delay less than a series of small but annoying ones.

Listing 15.2

```
Function AutoExec()
    ' Runs at database initialization only. Called directly
    ' from the AutoExec macro in order to transfer processing
```

```
' immediately into VBA.

' Make up some menu and form constants...
Const glrcMenuBarDB = 1
Const glrcMenuWindow = 5
Const glrcMenuCmdHide = 4
Const glrcFrmSwitchboard = "frmMenu_MainSwitchboard"
Const glrcFrmSplash = "frmSplash"

On Error GoTo AutoExec_Err

Dim rstPreload As Recordset
Dim intPreload As Integer

' If not running under the Access runtime,
' hide the database window and provide a splash form.
' If you're using the runtime, specify a bitmap
' to be used as a splash screen in the registry.
If Not SysCmd(acSysCmdRuntime) Then
    DoCmd.SelectObject acMacro, "AutoExec", True
    DoCmd.DoMenuItem glrcMenuBarDB, glrcMenuWindow, _
      glrcMenuCmdHide, , acMenuVer70
    DoCmd.OpenForm glrcFrmSplash
    DoEvents      ' This lets the screen catch up
End If

DoCmd.Hourglass True

' Remove the toolbar to keep users out of mischief
' (Uncomment the next line after testing your app)
' Application.SetOption "Built-In Toolbars Available", False

' Now get the list of forms to preload
Set rstPreload = CurrentDb.OpenRecordset("qryPreload", _
 dbOpenSnapshot)

' If the table has records in it, load those forms
If Not rstPreload.EOF Then

    ' Initialize the status bar
    rstPreload.MoveLast
    Call SysCmd(acSysCmdInitMeter, "Initializing...", _
      rstPreload.RecordCount)
    intPreload = 1
```

```
            ' Open all the forms in the list.
            ' This example assumes a field named FormName that
            ' contains the names of the forms to load.
            rstPreload.MoveFirst
            Do Until rstPreload.EOF
                DoCmd.OpenForm FormName:=rstPreload![FormName], _
                 WindowMode:=acHidden
                Call SysCmd(acSysCmdUpdateMeter, intPreload)
                intPreload = intPreload + 1
                rstPreload.MoveNext
            Loop
        End If

        ' Open the switchboard as a visible form
        DoCmd.OpenForm glrcFrmSwitchboard

        ' Unload the splash screen if its timer event
        ' hasn't closed it already
        If SysCmd(acSysCmdGetObjectState, acForm, glrcFrmSplash) _
         = acObjStateOpen Then
            DoCmd.Close acForm, glrcFrmSplash
        End If

AutoExec_Exit:
    ' Clean up and exit
    On Error Resume Next
    rstPreload.Close
    Call SysCmd(acSysCmdRemoveMeter)
    DoCmd.Hourglass False
    Exit Function
AutoExec_Err:
    MsgBox "Error " & Err.Number & ": " & Err.Description, _
     vbExclamation, "AutoExec"
    Resume AutoExec_Exit
End Function
```

You should store the list of forms to be opened in tblPreload, but you can use qryPreload to reorder this table to include an explicit load order. This allows for dependencies between forms; for example, if you design one that contains controls that reference another, it is critical that you load the latter form first.

AutoExec() also opens a splash screen form as one of its first actions. This form, called frmSplash in the sample database, is a borderless form that remains on the screen while the rest of the initialization process takes place. Figure 15.5 shows what the form looks like when it opens.

Splash screens are useful in that they add to the *perceived* performance of an application by distracting the user during lengthy operations. Although the AutoExec() function closes the form after completing the initialization process, the form also has code attached to the Timer event that automatically closes the form after two seconds. Since the splash screen form has no border or other obvious controls the user can use to close it, the timer code acts as a safeguard if the AutoExec() function fails and also determines the maximum length of time the form will remain open.

FIGURE 15.5:
Splash screen form displayed during the initialization process

Using an AutoKeys Macro to Provide Keyboard Shortcuts

Another aspect of a user-friendly interface is support for keyboard shortcuts. Shortcuts allow users to perform some action quickly by pressing a combination of keys, usually a letter or number in conjunction with the Ctrl, Alt, or Shift key—for example, the keyboard shortcut for copying objects, Ctrl+C. You can add your own custom shortcuts or replace the standard shortcuts Access defines by using an AutoKeys macro. AutoKeys, like AutoExec, is a special-case macro that is automatically processed when a database is opened.

Figure 15.6 shows an AutoKeys macro you can find in CH15.MDB. It defines two keyboard shortcuts, Ctrl+Shift+H and Ctrl+Shift+D, which open the main (home) switchboard and data-entry switchboard forms, respectively. You define the

FIGURE 15.6:

Sample AutoKeys macro with keyboard shortcuts to the switchboard forms

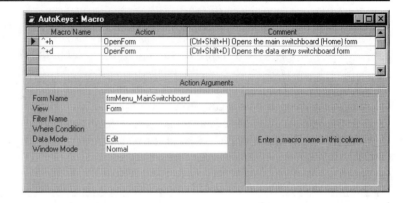

shortcut key combinations using codes in the Macro Name column. You can combine alphanumeric characters, as well as function keys, with the Ctrl (^), Shift (+), and Alt (%) keys to specify which macro actions to run. For example, Ctrl+Shift+H is represented by the code ^+h.

Tables 15.4 and 15.5 list Access' global and form/datasheet shortcut keys, respectively. When creating shortcut keys for your users using the AutoKeys macro, consult these lists to make sure you're not overriding any existing combinations (unless, of course, that is your intent). (See Chapter 11 for more on AutoKeys macros.)

TABLE 15.4: Global Shortcut Keys

Shortcut Key	Purpose
Alt+F4	Quits Microsoft Access or closes a dialog box
Alt + spacebar	Displays the Control menu
Ctrl+C	Copies the selection to the clipboard
Ctrl+F	Opens the Find dialog box
Ctrl+F4	Closes the active window
Ctrl+F6	Cycles between open windows
Ctrl+H	Opens the Replace dialog box
Ctrl+N	Opens a new database
Ctrl+O	Opens an existing database
Ctrl+V	Pastes the contents of the clipboard at the insertion point
Ctrl+X	Cuts the selection and copies it to the clipboard

TABLE 15.4: Global Shortcut Keys (continued)

Shortcut Key	Purpose
Ctrl+Z	Undoes typing
F1	Displays context-sensitive help about the selected menu command, dialog box option, property, control, action, Visual Basic keyword, or window
F10	Displays the menu for the active object
F11 or Alt+F1	Brings the Database window to the front
F12 or Alt+F2	Opens the Save As dialog box
Shift+F1	Displays context-sensitive help using the question mark pointer
Shift+F10	Displays the shortcut menu for the active object
Shift+F12 or Alt+Shift+F2	Saves a database object

TABLE 15.5: Shortcut Keys in Form and Datasheet Views

Shortcut Key	Purpose
Ctrl+− (minus sign)	Deletes the current record
Ctrl++ (plus sign)	Adds a new record
Esc	Undoes changes in the current field or current record or cancels extend mode
F2	Switches between Edit view (with the insertion point displayed) and Navigation view
F4	Opens a combo box
F5	Moves to the record number box
F6	Cycles forward through sections of a record
F7	Checks spelling
F8	Turns on extend mode
F9	Recalculates the fields in the window
Shift+↵	Saves changes to the current record
Shift+F2	Opens the Zoom box
Shift+F4	Finds the next occurrence of the text specified in the Find or Replace dialog box when the dialog box is closed
Shift+F6	Cycles back through sections of a record
Shift+F8	Reverses the F8 selection
Shift+F9	Requeries the underlying tables in a form or subform

Designing a Responsive Interface

When you design your application, you must take care to be responsive to your users. This means keeping them informed of progress during long processing tasks and trying to aid them as much as possible while browsing or editing data. In this section we'll offer a number of helpful tips on how you can make your application respond to the user's actions and keep them informed of events as they happen.

Using Default Values to Your (Users') Advantage

One convenience Access provides is the ability to set default values for controls. Not only can this speed up data-entry applications by eliminating the need to enter data in every control on a form, it can aid users in selecting other application options. Be sure to use default values wherever possible. Remember that you can set these at design time and change them at run time through code. For example, it may make sense to set the DefaultValue property of a control to the Date() function at design time if the current date is the most likely entry. In other situations you may want to change the property dynamically.

As an example of changing the DefaultValue property in response to user input, the sample database for this chapter contains a form called frmCheckBook, which is a simple mock-up of a personal checkbook (see Figure 15.7).

FIGURE 15.7:

The frmCheckBook form

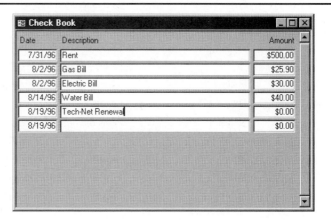

962

Code behind the form's AfterInsert event changes the DefaultValue property of the Date text box to whatever the user entered. The code that accomplishes this is shown here:

```
Private Sub Form_AfterInsert()
    Me![txtTransDate].DefaultValue = CLng(Me![txtTransDate])
End Sub
```

The assumption here is that as a user enters each new record, the date for the next record entered will likely be the same. You can use this technique whenever you expect users to enter a series of related records.

Providing Users with Ample Feedback

Your users deserve plenty of feedback in your application and on your application's forms. Be sure to use the status bar property on your controls. It's a simple-to-implement solution to providing front-line help for users. Although this is an easy point to skip, it's worth the care it takes to set the StatusBarText property for each and every control. By implementing complete status bar messages, you move your applications one step closer to matching the polish shown in mainstream applications. In cases in which your users might not be interacting directly with forms and controls, you can write custom messages to the status bar with the SysCmd() function.

Additionally, anytime your application is going to take over the screen for two seconds or more, you should turn on the hourglass cursor and, if necessary, provide other feedback, such as a status dialog (discussed in the next section). If the operation will take more than a few seconds, use the SysCmd() function to provide visual cues as to how much longer the user will have to wait. You can also customize your feedback through custom error handling so that any error messages your users see are tailored to your own application (see Chapter 16).

Using Pop-Up Status Dialogs

Another way to provide your users with visual feedback is by using a pop-up status dialog. Although the trend these days is to display progress using the status bar, this is not always obvious to users, and there are limitations on the amount and type of data you can display this way. By creating your own status dialog, which is displayed in the center of the screen, you can customize the way it looks and provide the user with more information. Figure 15.8 shows an example of a status dialog using the frmStatus form contained in CH15.MDB.

FIGURE 15.8:

Sample status dialog showing progress information

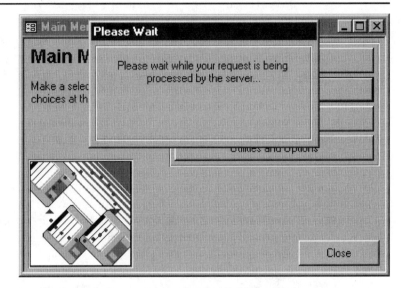

You use the status form in conjunction with a subroutine called glrStatus, declared in the basUserInterface module. The glrStatus procedure, shown in Listing 15.3, accepts three optional arguments, representing the message to display in the center of the dialog, the dialog's caption, and a third argument, which we'll explain shortly.

Listing 15.3

```
Sub glrStatus(Optional varMessage As Variant, _
 Optional varCaption As Variant, _
 Optional varCurrStatus As Variant)

    Dim fClose As Boolean
    Const glrcStatusForm = "frmStatus"

    ' If the user called Status with no arguments
    ' then the user wants to close the form, otherwise
    ' the user wants to display a message or determine
    ' whether the Cancel button was clicked
    If IsMissing(varMessage) _
```

```
    And IsMissing(varCaption) _
    And IsMissing(varCurrStatus) Then

        fClose = True
    Else
        fClose = False
    End If

    ' If the form's already open and the user wants to close
    ' it, then do that and exit; otherwise open it
    If SysCmd(acSysCmdGetObjectState, acForm, glrcStatusForm) _
    = acObjStateOpen And fClose Then

        DoCmd.Close acForm, glrcStatusForm
        Exit Sub
    Else
        DoCmd.OpenForm glrcStatusForm
    End If

    ' Set the form's message if that argument was supplied
    If Not IsMissing(varMessage) Then
        Forms(glrcStatusForm)![lblMessage].Caption = varMessage
    End If
    ' Set the form's caption if that argument was supplied
    If Not IsMissing(varCaption) Then
        Forms(glrcStatusForm).Caption = varCaption
    End If
    ' If the varCurrStatus argument was supplied and its
    ' value was not "False" then display the
    ' Cancel button, issue a DoEvents, and see if the button
    ' was clicked by returning the value of the form's
    ' Canceled property in the varCurrStatus argument--
    ' if varCurrStatus is False then hide the button
    If Not IsMissing(varCurrStatus) Then
        If varCurrStatus = acHidden Then
            Forms(glrcStatusForm)![cmdCancel].Visible = False
        Else
            Forms(glrcStatusForm)![cmdCancel].Visible = True
            DoEvents
            varCurrStatus = Forms(glrcStatusForm).Canceled
        End If
    End If
```

```
    ' Update the form
    Forms(glrcStatusForm).Repaint
End Sub
```

You initiate the status dialog by calling the glrStatus procedure, supplying either of the first two arguments (most likely the varMessage argument, since a dialog with a caption and no message is not very helpful). The procedure opens the form and displays your message by setting the Caption property of label control (and, optionally, the caption of the form). You can call glrStatus multiple times to update the dialog while it remains on the screen. When you are ready to close the dialog, simply call glrStatus with no arguments.

You can also use popup status dialogs as alternatives to message boxes to show progress during a long process and solicit user input regarding whether the process should continue. That is, some developers precede each step in a long process with a prompt such as, "About to purge temporary tables. Okay?" Users must continually answer questions to complete the process. The glrStatus procedure lets you display an optional Cancel button on the status form and determine whether the user has clicked it. To do this, you must declare a Boolean variable and pass it as the third argument to glrStatus (varCurrStatus). The procedure will display the Cancel button, issue a DoEvents command to allow the user to click it, and then return the value of the form's Canceled property (a public variable declared in the status form's module and set by the Cancel button) in the varCurrStatus argument. You can also hide the Cancel button without closing the form by passing the acHidden constant in varCurrStatus.

During long operations you should display the status dialog and the Cancel button and then periodically call glrStatus with the varCurrStatus argument, inspecting its value after the procedure returns. If you find the value returned in varCurrStatus to be True, take appropriate measures to shut down your process.

Creating Your Own Property Dialogs

One prevalent user interface innovation in Windows 95 is the property dialog. Spend a few minutes with the right mouse button on the Windows desktop, and you'll expose a plethora of property dialogs for everything from the video display (see Figure 15.9) to each and every shortcut icon. A property dialog is, in effect, the

FIGURE 15.9:
Property dialog for the system display

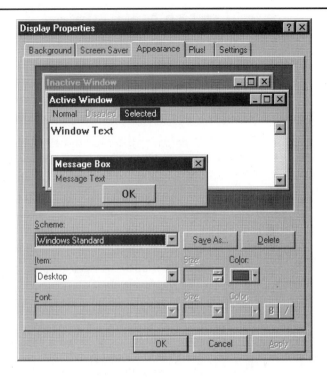

equivalent of an About dialog for objects. Property dialogs display (and even allow updating of) an object's characteristics. The following sections explain how you can create your own custom property dialogs using Access forms. You can use these dialogs to display information regarding your application's options or data.

NOTE   The example in this section requires the TabStrip control provided by the Windows 95 Common Control OCX (COMCTL32.OCX). Attempting to open the main dialog form without first installing and registering the control will result in an error. You can find this OLE custom control, which implements the multiple tab interface found on property dialogs, in the ADT or Visual Basic 4.0. Although you could construct a property dialog using simple command buttons, it would not have the exact look and feel of those provided with Windows 95.

Designing the Main Dialog

Property dialogs have a fairly standardized look and feel. They're about 370 pixels wide by 420 pixels tall and feature a tabbed interface that lets users see various groups of related properties without cluttering the dialog. Most property dialogs also have OK, Cancel, and Apply buttons. The purpose of the Apply button is to make permanent any changes to displayed properties without closing the dialog.

CH15.MDB contains a template called frmTmpPropDialog for creating tabbed property dialogs. It already has the tab strip control and appropriate buttons and VBA code. You can use this template as the basis for your own property dialogs. Simply make a copy with a different name. Listing 15.4 shows all the code in the template form.

Listing 15.4

```
Private Sub cmdApply_Click()
    Dim ctlAny As Control

    ' Loop through controls looking for subforms
    For Each ctlAny In Me.Controls
        ' If found, and if values have changed,
        ' call its Apply method
        If ctlAny.ControlType = acSubForm Then
            If ctlAny.Form.PropsChanged Then
                Call ctlAny.Form.Apply
            End If
        End If
    Next
    Me![cmdOK].SetFocus
    Me![cmdApply].Enabled = False
End Sub

Private Sub cmdCancel_Click()
    DoCmd.Close acForm, Me.Name
End Sub

Private Sub cmdOK_Click()
    Call Me.cmdApply_Click
    DoCmd.Close acForm, Me.Name
End Sub
```

```
Private Sub oleOptionsTab_Click()
    Dim ctlAny As Control

    ' Loop through controls looking for subforms
    For Each ctlAny In Me.Controls
        ' If found hide or display it according
        ' to the tab selected
        If ctlAny.ControlType = acSubForm Then
            ctlAny.Visible = (ctlAny.SourceObject = _
            Me![oleOptionsTab].SelectedItem.Tag)
        End If
    Next
End Sub
```

Using Subforms for Dialog Pages

The secret of the property dialog in CH15.MDB is its use of subforms to hold the controls for each tab. Using subforms lets you switch "pages" easily and lets you design and test the logic for each page independently. Listing 15.4 above shows the oleOptionsTab_Click procedure, which hides or displays each embedded subform according to the selected tab. It does this by comparing each control's SourceObject property with the Tag property of the selected tab. Each tab's Tag property holds the name of the form to use for the source object.

CH15.MDB also includes a template property page called sbfTmpPropDialogPage. It's nothing more than an unbound form of the right size, with two functions declared, that brings up another link between the property dialog form and the subform. The subform declares a public function called Apply, which applies any changes users made to properties. (The version in the template simply displays a message box.) The main form calls this function in each embedded subform when the user clicks the Apply button, as seen in the cmdApply_Click procedure in Listing 15.4. By taking advantage of VBA's ability to externalize procedures declared in a form's module, the code in Listing 15.4 can call a function with the same name in each subform. Each subform also declares a private function called MakeDirty that enables the parent form's Apply button. You should call this function in response to any event that changes the data displayed in the dialog. The section "Creating a Color Choice Dialog" later in this chapter presents a more complete example.

Triggering Property Dialogs from Shortcut Menus

Property dialogs can be displayed using a variety of means, including buttons, menu commands, and shortcut menus. For example, the Tools ➤ Options command displays the Access Options dialog, which is essentially a property sheet for Access. Using shortcut menus, however, has become the preferred approach in Windows 95, and users will eventually come to expect a Properties command on most shortcut menus they use. You can add this capability to your application, at least for forms, by using the ShortCutMenubar property and an appropriately designed menu macro.

CH15.MDB contains two macros called mcrMenuPropPopup and mcrMenuProp-Popup_Commands. The former is referenced in the frmCategories form's ShortCutMenubar property, and the latter is called by mcrMenuPropPopup to provide it with the menu commands to display. Figure 15.10 shows the menu commands defined in mcrMenuPropPopup_Commands, including a Properties command at the bottom of the list.

FIGURE 15.10:

The mcrMenuPropPopup_
Commands macro listing menu
commands for a form's shortcut
menu

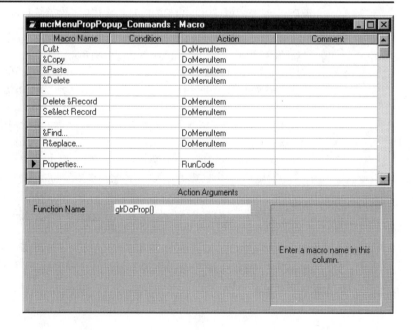

When a user clicks the right mouse button on a record displayed in the frmCategories form, a shortcut menu appears. If the user then selects the Properties command from the shortcut menu, the macro called by the menu, mcrMenuPropPopup_Commands, calls glrDoProp(), a function defined in basUserInterface and shown in Listing 15.5. Based on the active form, glrDoProp() opens a property dialog, frmProperties, passing the name of a unique subform, frmPropCategories in this case, in the OpenArgs argument of OpenForm. Code in frmProperties' OnLoad event sets the SourceObject of its subform control to the form name passed in the OpenArgs property.

Listing 15.5

```
Public Function glrDoProp()
    ' Error handling in case no form is active
    On Error GoTo glrDoProp_Exit

    ' Determine which property dialog to open based
    ' on the active form
    Select Case Screen.ActiveForm.Name
        Case "frmCategories"
            DoCmd.OpenForm FormName:="frmProperties", _
            WindowMode:=acDialog, _
            OpenArgs:="sbfPropPageCategories"
        Case Else
            ' Add other forms here
    End Select
glrDoProp_Exit:
    Exit Function
End Function
```

Using Property Dialogs to Edit Data

One potential use for property dialogs is to edit data in your database. After all, the values in a particular record can be thought of as the properties of that record. When a user calls glrDoProp() from the frmCategories form, a property dialog opens showing details for the current record (see Figure 15.11). The form contained in the property dialog's subform control, sbfPropPageCategories, uses a RecordSource that restricts records to the one selected in frmCategories. Since sbfPropPageCategories is a bound form, the user can edit data directly on the property

FIGURE 15.11:

Property dialog showing details of a category record

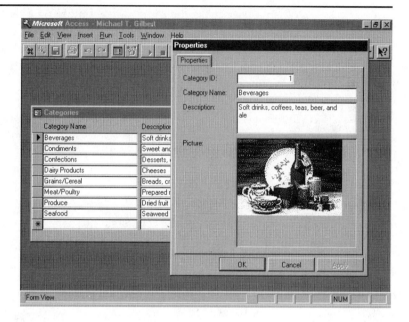

dialog. You could also use an unbound form, but you would have to write the code to populate the controls and save back any changes.

When would you use a form like the one shown in Figure 15.11? Whenever you have a continuous form and cannot display all the fields in the underlying dataset, you can use a popup property dialog to show fields of minor importance, reserving space on the main form for critical information.

Allowing Users to Choose Custom Color Schemes

Another use for property dialogs is for setting custom application options, providing yet another way to put your users in control of their own environment. You might consider this approach as an alternative to the default Access Options dialog. Creating your own version lets you control the options to which your users have access. In the following sections we'll explain how to implement a custom color selection dialog that lets users create, save, and apply their own color schemes to your application at run time. Figure 15.12 shows the color selection dialog form in action.

FIGURE 15.12:

Use the Colors page of a custom Options dialog to select a color scheme for your application.

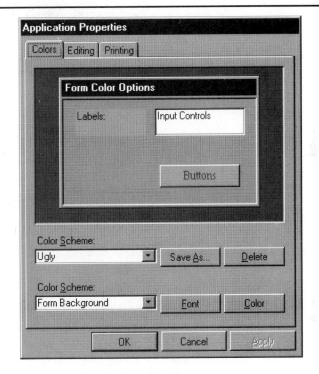

Creating a Color Choice Dialog

The color selection dialog shown in Figure 15.12 is implemented using a parent property dialog, frmOptions, and several subforms; it works similarly to the Windows 95 Display Properties dialog. The sbfOptionsColors form handles color selection. Figure 15.13 shows this form in Design view.

A number of controls on the form make selecting colors easy for users. In the top half of the form are controls that represent various form elements, including a label, a text box, and a command button. Covering each control is a transparent command button that, when the user clicks it, sets the active screen element in the combo box at the bottom of the form. Driving the combo box is a table, tblColorItems, which

FIGURE 15.13:
sbfOptionsColors form in Design view, showing controls used to define custom colors

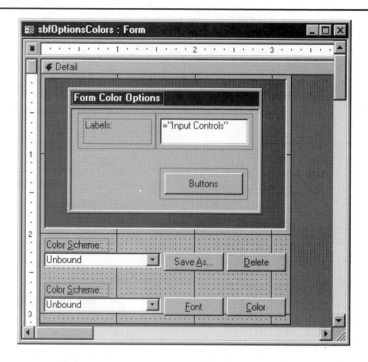

contains the various screen elements and the options that are applicable to each. Clicking the Font and Color buttons opens common dialogs that let users select typeface and color attributes. Users can save and retrieve color schemes by using the combo box and buttons in the center of the form. There is not enough room to show all the VBA code in sbfOptionsColors here, but you can browse it easily by opening the form in Design view.

Implementing an Apply Feature

The section "Using Subforms for Dialog Pages" earlier in this chapter commented briefly about encapsulating the logic that applies a property dialog's settings in the subforms that act as individual property pages. The Apply() function defined in sbfOptionsColors, which transfers the current color properties to all open forms, is shown in Listing 15.6.

Listing 15.6

```
Public Function Apply() As Boolean
    Dim frmAny As Form
    Dim fci As glrFormColorInfo

    ' Get current color selections
    fci.lngFrmBackGrnd = Me![shpForm].BackColor
    fci.lngLblForeGrnd = Me![lblSample].ForeColor
    fci.lngCtlForeGrnd = Me![txtSample].ForeColor
    fci.lngBtnForeGrnd = Me![cmdSample].ForeColor
    fci.strLblFontName = Me![lblSample].FontName
    fci.strCtlFontName = Me![txtSample].FontName
    fci.strBtnFontName = Me![cmdSample].FontName
    fci.intLblFontSize = Me![lblSample].FontSize
    fci.intCtlFontSize = Me![txtSample].FontSize
    fci.intBtnFontSize = Me![cmdSample].FontSize
    fci.fInitialized = True

    ' Apply to all open forms
    For Each frmAny In Forms
        Call glrApplyColors(frmAny, fci)
    Next

    ' Disable parent form's Apply button
    On Error Resume Next
    Me.Parent![cmdOK].SetFocus
    Me.Parent![cmdApply].Enabled = False
End Function
```

The subform's Apply() function captures properties of individual controls and places them into a user-defined type called glrFormColorInfo. It then iterates through all open forms, calling glrApplyColors, a procedure in basUserInterface. The declarations for glrFormColorInfo and glrApplyColors are shown in Listing 15.7.

Listing 15.7

```
Option Compare Database
Option Explicit

Type glrFormColorInfo
    lngFrmBackGrnd As Long      ' Form background color
    lngLblBackGrnd As Long      ' Label background color
    lngCtlBackGrnd As Long      ' Control background color
```

```
        lngLblForeGrnd As Long        ' Label text color
        lngCtlForeGrnd As Long        ' Control text color
        lngBtnForeGrnd As Long        ' Button text color
        strLblFontName As String      ' Label font name
        strCtlFontName As String      ' Control font name
        strBtnFontName As String      ' Button font name
        intLblFontSize As Integer     ' Label font size
        intCtlFontSize As Integer     ' Control font size
        intBtnFontSize As Integer     ' Button font size
        intAction As Integer          ' Action indicator:
                                      '   0 = uninitialized
                                      '   1 = change colors
                                      '   2 = don't change
End Type

Global ggfiGlobalColors As glrFormColorInfo

Sub glrApplyColors(frmAny As Form, fci As glrFormColorInfo)
    Dim ctlAny As Control
    Dim varTag As Variant

    ' If color info hasn't been initialized then do it now
    Select Case fci.intAction
        Case 0      ' Uninitialized
            If Not glrInitColors(fci) Then
                Exit Sub
            Else
                Call glrApplyColors(frmAny, fci)
            End If
        Case 2      ' Don't change colors
            Exit Sub
    End Select

    ' Set values for form and each control
    On Error Resume Next
    frmAny.Section(0).BackColor = fci.lngFrmBackGrnd
    frmAny.Section(1).BackColor = fci.lngFrmBackGrnd
    frmAny.Section(2).BackColor = fci.lngFrmBackGrnd

    For Each ctlAny In frmAny.Controls
        ' Check protection of control
        varTag = glrGetTag(ctlAny.Tag, "Protect")
        If IsNull(varTag) Or Not varTag Then
            Select Case ctlAny.ControlType
                ' Special case: subforms
```

```
            Case acSubForm
                Call glrApplyColors(ctlAny.Form, fci)
            ' Labels
            Case acLabel
                ctlAny.BackColor = fci.lngLblBackGrnd
                ctlAny.ForeColor = fci.lngLblForeGrnd
                ctlAny.FontName = fci.strLblFontName
                ctlAny.FontSize = fci.intLblFontSize
            ' Input Controls
            Case acTextBox, acComboBox, acListBox
                ctlAny.BackColor = fci.lngCtlBackGrnd
                ctlAny.ForeColor = fci.lngCtlForeGrnd
                ctlAny.FontName = fci.strCtlFontName
                ctlAny.FontSize = fci.intCtlFontSize
            ' Buttons
            Case acCommandButton, acToggleButton
                ctlAny.ForeColor = fci.lngBtnForeGrnd
                ctlAny.FontName = fci.strBtnFontName
                ctlAny.FontSize = fci.intBtnFontSize
            End Select
        End If
    Next
End Sub
```

When glrApplyColors is called, it iterates through every control on the form specified by the frmAny argument, setting property values to those stored in the fci structure. You can use this procedure to set the attributes of controls on any form. If you don't want a particular control to be altered, simply append the text "Protect=True;" to the control's Tag property. GlrApplyColors excludes controls that have this Tag value set.

Applying Color Choices to Forms Dynamically

After you've defined and applied a custom color scheme to your forms, it would be nice if the scheme were automatically applied to forms when they were opened. You can do this by placing a call to glrApplyColors in the OnLoad event of each form you want changed. Before calling the procedure, however, you should call glrInitColors(), shown in Listing 15.8, which loads color information from tblColorSchemes into a passed glrFormColorInfo structure. If you call glrInitColors() with no scheme name argument, it will automatically prompt the user to select one.

Note, however, that if you choose not to do this, glrApplyColors will call glrInit-Colors() automatically if the data structure has not been initialized. Forms in CH15.MDB call glrApplyColors using a global structure, gfciGlobalColors.

Listing 15.8

```
Public Function glrInitColors(fci As glrFormColorInfo, _
  Optional varScheme As Variant) As Boolean

    Dim rstScheme As Recordset
    Dim strSQL As String

    ' If the scheme name is missing then prompt
    ' the user to enter one using glrGetColorScheme()
    If IsMissing(varScheme) Then
       varScheme = glrGetColorScheme()
       If IsNull(varScheme) Then
          Exit Function
       End If
    End If

    ' Get all the colors
    strSQL = "SELECT * FROM tblColorSchemes WHERE " & _
     "SchemeName = '" & varScheme & "' AND " & _
     "UserName = '" & CurrentUser() & "';"
    Set rstScheme = CurrentDb.OpenRecordset(strSQL, _
     dbOpenDynaset)

    Do Until rstScheme.EOF
       Select Case rstScheme![Item]
          Case "Form Background"
             fci.lngFrmBackGrnd = rstScheme![BackColor]
          Case "Labels"
             fci.lngLblBackGrnd = rstScheme![BackColor]
             fci.lngLblForeGrnd = rstScheme![ForeColor]
             fci.strLblFontName = rstScheme![FontName]
             fci.intLblFontSize = rstScheme![FontSize]
          Case "Input Controls"
             fci.lngCtlBackGrnd = rstScheme![BackColor]
             fci.lngCtlForeGrnd = rstScheme![ForeColor]
             fci.strCtlFontName = rstScheme![FontName]
             fci.intCtlFontSize = rstScheme![FontSize]
          Case "Buttons"
             fci.lngBtnForeGrnd = rstScheme![ForeColor]
```

```
                    fci.strBtnFontName = rstScheme![FontName]
                    fci.intBtnFontSize = rstScheme![FontSize]
        End Select
        rstScheme.MoveNext
    Loop
    rstScheme.Close

    fci.fInitialized = True
    glrInitColors = True
End Function

Function glrGetColorScheme() As Variant
    Const SCHEME_FORM = "frmGetColorScheme"

    DoCmd.OpenForm FormName:=glrcSchemeForm, _
     WindowMode:=acDialog
    If SysCmd(acSysCmdGetObjectState, acForm, glrcSchemeForm) _
     = acObjStateOpen Then

        glrGetColorScheme = Forms(glrcSchemeForm)![lstScheme]
        DoCmd.Close acForm, glrcSchemeForm
    Else
        glrGetColorScheme = Null
    End If
End Function
```

Dealing with Different System Hardware

In some cases you may be able to completely ignore hardware issues. If you are installing a custom application to a small base of computers and you have access to all of them, you can survey the hardware installed and act accordingly. However, if you gain any significant market penetration, you need either to specify precisely the requirements for your package or to deal with differing hardware on differing systems. You need to consider, in particular, the screens, mice, and printers you are likely to run into.

Designing for Display Differences

Screen issues revolve around size and color depth. As discussed in Chapter 8, you can retrieve the screen dimensions via the Windows API and resize your forms dynamically, depending on the ratio between your current screen size and design screen size. This technique allows you to fill your customers' screens properly despite hardware differences between their systems and your own.

To add to the video confusion, users employ different Windows video drivers. If you prosper in your work, you may well be running the latest 16-million-color driver on your system. Before you release your forms with the colors lovingly tweaked for your system, investigate their look in 256-, 16-, and 2-color mode, for customers who may be a bit more hardware impaired than you. Use the Display properties applet in the Windows Control Panel to temporarily switch to standard VGA and LCD screen drivers and see how your masterpiece looks with them. You may discover a sudden need to redesign if green on blue turns into amber on amber.

Also be aware of the position of your forms when you distribute your applications. If you use the AutoCenter property of the form and if it fits on your users' screens, you'll do fine. If you don't have Access position the form for you and you've done your development work on a driver with a resolution different from the one on which your users run the application, you may have a problem with forms appearing off the edge of your users' screens. This issue gets even more confusing under Windows 95 because of the space the taskbar takes up. Not only can you not predict how large the taskbar will be, you can't predict where on the screen it will appear. You'd be wise to play it safe and avoid overly large forms and either use AutoCenter or make sure the forms appear in the upper left-hand corner of your screen when you save them.

> **NOTE**
>
> You can use the SystemParametersInfo( ) API function to determine how much screen real estate is available after factoring in the size and position of the taskbar. CH15.MDB contains code in the basSysParam module that demonstrates how to do this. To experiment, try moving or resizing the taskbar and running the glrShowTrueSize procedure.

TIP

Windows 95 supports dynamic screen resolution. If you develop your applications using a high-resolution driver, you can quickly switch back to 640x480 mode without shutting down Windows. Right-click the Desktop and select Properties from the shortcut menu. Select the Settings tab and use the slider bar to reduce your display's resolution.

Supporting the Mouseless

Hard though you may find it to believe, not everyone has (or wants to use) a mouse. Be sure your application is friendly to keyboard users, as well as mouse users:

- Use accelerator keys liberally.
- Make sure your menus have all the options your forms do.
- Check your tab order after every form redesign.

Don't assume that built-in properties in Access will take care of you; Access itself is guilty of not allowing all actions to be performed without a mouse. (Try editing relationships without a mouse, for example.)

Different Printers for Different Clients

The final critical piece of hardware you need to deal with is your user's printer. Chapter 9 discussed the techniques involved in switching printers at run time and allowing users to choose a printer for each report as they print it. To maintain flexibility and compatibility with other Windows products, you should implement these techniques in your own applications.

Summary

This chapter has explained a number of issues related to the design of elegant and user-friendly interfaces. We covered a number of topics you should keep in mind when designing your applications:

- Design for the user's needs, not your own.
- Aim for a design that's flexible and responsive to the way your users work.
- Use the Windows 95 interface as a guide for look, feel, and features.
- When appropriate, follow the guidelines for Windows 95– and Office 95– compatible programs.
- Remember that not all users have the same hardware.

We also offered several examples of interface features you can import into your applications:

- A sample AutoExec macro and function that implement preloading of forms
- Templates for custom Windows 95–like property dialogs
- Color customization form and code that lets users choose the look of their forms

Overall, remember that interface design is often as much an art as it is a science. What might be a perfect design for some users may be unusable by others.

CHAPTER

SIXTEEN

Error Handling and Debugging

- Dealing with compile-time errors

- Handling run-time errors

- Avoiding and resolving logic errors

- Techniques and strategies for debugging

In any programming environment, you have to deal with errors, and Access is no different. These errors fall into three categories:

- Compile-time errors
- Run-time errors
- Logic errors

Compile-time errors occur when your code contains incorrect syntax. The compiler requires that these errors be fixed before the code will run. Access flags the error either when you enter the improper syntax or when the code is compiled, depending on an option you set for the database.

Run-time errors occur when some condition makes your code invalid. For example, trying to open a table that doesn't exist will trigger a run-time error. If you don't trap run-time errors, Access displays an error message and stops your code at that point. Access provides a mechanism using the On Error statement that allows you to trap a run-time error and handle the problem.

Logic errors occur when your code doesn't do what you intended because of improper logic, a misunderstanding of how certain statements and functions work, or outright mistakes. For example, if you use a less-than operator (<) when you mean to have a less-than-or-equal-to operator (<=), you have a logic error. Logic errors are commonly known as *bugs*.

This chapter shows you how to reduce the number of each of these types of errors and how to deal with them when they do occur.

Dealing with Syntax Errors

Access can report syntax errors at two points. If you select Tools ➤ Options and then look in the Module tab, you see a check box called Display Syntax Checking. This option controls when Access will report syntax errors to you. If it is checked, Access displays a message box as soon as you leave a line of code that has a syntax error in the module editor. If the option is unchecked, Access merely changes the color to indicate that it doesn't understand the line. In either case, when Access compiles the code, it reports the message again.

Often you will write half a line of code and then discover you need to move up to the top of the module to declare the variable you are using. At this point Access reports the line as having a syntax error if the Display Syntax Checking option is on. Since Access shows lines with syntax errors in red, you already have immediate feedback that there is a problem, so you may prefer to turn off the option. You can always get complete details on the error by clicking the Compile All Modules button on the toolbar.

Dealing with Run-time Errors

When a run-time error occurs, you have several ways of dealing with it. If you do nothing, Access responds by displaying an error message and stopping the execution of your code. Resolving errors requires three steps:

- Setting an error trap
- Reacting to the error
- Exiting the error handler

The following sections discuss these steps.

The On Error Statement

You invoke an error handler with the On Error statement, which comes in several varieties, as described in the following sections. Each procedure can have as many On Error statements as you wish. However, only the most recently executed On Error statement remains in force.

The On Error GoTo Label Statement

Use the On Error Goto *Label* statement to cause Access to jump to a specific location in your code if an error occurs. When an error occurs in code after an On Error GoTo *Label* statement, control passes to the assigned label. Listing 16.1 shows the most common format for an error handler.

Listing 16.1

```
Sub GenericSubWithHandler()
    ' Stub showing standard way to construct an error handler

    On Error GoTo GenericSubWithHandlerErr

    ' Some code that might generate a run-time error

GenericSubWithHandlerDone:
    Exit Sub
GenericSubWithHandlerErr:
    ' Error Handler
    Resume GenericSubWithHandlerDone
End Sub
```

When an error occurs, control immediately passes to the label specified in the On Error GoTo *Label* statement. The label must appear in the same procedure as the On Error GoTo *Label* statement. By convention, the error handler appears at the end of the procedure.

Unlike previous versions of Access, VBA no longer requires that label names be unique across the entire module.

Use an Exit Sub or Exit Function statement to keep the normal flow of control from passing into the error handler.

Once an error has occurred and control has passed into the error handler, the code is treated as being in a special state. While the code is in this state, the following is true:

- The error handler defined by the On Error Goto *Label* statement is no longer in effect. This means any run-time error that occurs within the error handler is treated as though no error handler exists in this procedure.

- You can use a Resume statement (described in the section "Error Handling" later in this chapter) to return control back to the main procedure and re-sume normal error handling.

- You cannot execute an End Sub or End Function statement to "fall out" of an error handler. You must explicitly use an Exit Sub or Exit Function statement to exit the procedure. Commonly accepted software engineering practice says a procedure should have only one entry point and one exit point, so an even better idea is to use Resume *Label* to return control to the main code, where the procedure can be exited at a common point.

The On Error Resume Next Statement

Creating an error handler with the On Error GoTo *Label* statement can require a considerable number of lines of code. Sometimes you want to ignore errors. Other times you know exactly which error to expect and want to handle it without having to write a full error handler. The On Error Resume Next statement informs Access that you want control to resume at the statement immediately after the statement that generated the error, without any visible intervention from Access. For example, if you are attempting to delete a file and don't care whether the file actually exists, you might have some code like that shown in Listing 16.2.

Listing 16.2

```
Sub Delfile(ByVal strFileName As String)
    ' Example showing an On Error Resume Next
    'Deletes a file if it exists

    On Error Resume Next

    Kill strFileName
End Sub
```

Normally, the Kill statement generates a run-time error if the file specified as its argument doesn't exist. However, the On Error Resume Next statement in this example causes the run-time error to be ignored, and control passes to the next line (in this case, the End Sub statement).

A slightly more complex example is shown in Listing 16.3.

Listing 16.3

```
Sub SetControlColors(frm As Form, ByVal lngColor As Long)
    ' Changes the color of all the controls on the
    ' form to the color specified by lngColor

    Dim ctl As Control

    On Error Resume Next

    For Each ctl In frm.Controls
```

```
        ctl.BackColor = lngColor
    Next
End Sub
```

This procedure loops through all the controls on a form specified by a form variable and changes the BackColor property of the controls to the value specified by the lngColor argument. Some controls, such as command buttons, do not have a Back-Color property. When the code reaches these controls, a run-time error is normally generated. The On Error Resume Next statement lets the program ignore the error and continue. See the section "Inline Error Handling" later in this chapter for more on using On Error Resume Next.

The On Error GoTo 0 Statement

When you use an On Error GoTo *Label* or On Error Resume Next statement, it remains in effect until the procedure is exited, another error handler is declared, or the error handler is canceled. The On Error GoTo 0 statement cancels the error handler. Access (or an error handler in a calling procedure, as described in the section "Hierarchy of Error Handlers" later in this chapter) again traps subsequent errors. This statement also resets the value of the Error object, so if you need the values it contains, you must store away its properties.

Error Handlers

After trapping an error with the On Error GoTo *Label* statement, you will want to take some action. What you do depends on your application. If you are trying to open a table and the table doesn't exist, you might want to report an error to the user. On the other hand, you might decide instead to go ahead and create the table by executing a make-table query.

Determining Which Error Has Occurred

Visual Basic for Applications (VBA) in Access 95 has a new method of dealing with errors: the Err object. The Err object has the properties listed in Table 16.1. By using the properties of the Err object, you can determine exactly which error has occurred.

TABLE 16.1: Err Object Properties

Property	Description
Description	Returns a descriptive string associated with an error
HelpContext	Returns a context ID for a topic in a Microsoft Windows Help file
HelpFile	Returns a fully qualified path to a Microsoft Windows Help file
LastDLLError	Returns a system error code produced by a call into a dynamic-link library (DLL). The GetLastError() Windows API call gives the error code for the most recent Windows API call. When you are calling Windows API calls from VBA, though, you have a problem: VBA itself will make several Windows API calls between the time you make the call through VBA code and you try to call GetLastError(). When VBA does this, it wipes out the information that GetLastError() returns. To get around this situation, VBA calls GetLastError() for you after every API call
Number	Returns a numeric value specifying an error. Number is the Err object's default property
Source	Returns the name of the object or application that originally generated the error

NOTE In future versions of Access, Microsoft may change the text appearing in the Err.Description property for any given error number. Also, if your program is ever run on an international version of Access, the error message will appear in the local language of the version of Access. For these reasons you should always compare the Err.Number property to constants in your code rather than compare the description strings from the Err.Description property.

If you are using a full error handler at the bottom of the procedure, you can use the general construction shown in Listing 16.4.

Listing 16.4

```
Sub TypicalErrorHandlerSub()
    ' Example showing the construction of a procedure with an
    ' error handler.

    Dim rst As Recordset
```

```
        On Error GoTo TypicalErrorHandlerSubErr

        ' Some code that might generate a run-time error
        Set rst = CurrentDb.OpenRecordset("tblTable", dbOpenTable)

        ' You would do some processing with rst here

TypicalErrorHandlerSubDone:
        On Error Resume Next
        rst.Close
        Exit Sub
TypicalErrorHandlerSubErr:
        Const glrcErrCannotFindObject = 3011
        Select Case Err.Number
        Case glrcErrCannotFindObject    'Cannot find object
            MsgBox "tblTable doesn't exist. " _
            & "Call the database administrator."
        Case Else
            MsgBox "The application encountered unexpected " & _
            "error #" & Err.Number & " with message string '" & _
            Err.Description & "'", _
            vbOKOnly Or vbExclamation _
            Or vbDefaultButton1 Or vbApplicationModal, _
            "TypicalErrorHandlerSub"
        End Select
        Resume TypicalErrorHandlerSubDone
End Sub
```

The Select Case statement uses the value in Err.Number to determine which error has occurred. You should use a Select Case statement even if you have only one case you want to handle, since this makes it easy for you to handle other errors later just by inserting another Case statement. Always use a Case Else to trap unexpected errors. You can use a MsgBox statement in the Case Else, an Error statement, or an error-reporting routine, as shown in the section "Creating an Error-Reporting Subroutine" later in this chapter.

It's important to realize that two or more statements in your main code can generate the same error. If you want different things to happen in your error handler for each of those statements, you must set a flag in your main code and use If statements within the Case statement (or a nested Select Case statement) in your error handler. A more complicated method would define several different error handlers with On Error statements as you reached different parts of your code. Fortunately, most code doesn't require this complexity. If it does, it might be time to consider splitting the procedure into several smaller procedures.

Listing 16.5 shows an example of the use of flags.

Listing 16.5

```
Sub AddLineNumbers()
    ' Opens C:\FILE1.TXT and writes a new file C:\FILE2.TXT.
    ' Reports any errors opening the file
    '
    Dim fState As Integer
    Dim strInput As String
    Dim lngLineNumber As Long

    Const glrcFStateNone = 0
    Const glrcFStateOpeningFile1 = 1
    Const glrcFStateOpeningFile2 = 2

    On Error GoTo AddLineNumbersErr

    fState = glrcFStateOpeningFile1
    Open "c:\file1.txt" For Input As #1

    fState = glrcFStateOpeningFile2
    Open "c:\file2.txt" For Output As #2

    fState = glrcFStateNone

    lngLineNumber = 1
    Do Until EOF(1)
        Input #1, strInput
        Print #2, lngLineNumber, strInput
        lngLineNumber = lngLineNumber + 1
    Loop
    Close #2
AddLineNumbersCloseFile1:
    Close #1
AddLineNumbersDone:
    Exit Sub
AddLineNumbersErr:
    Const glrcErrPermissionDenied = 70
    Const glrcErrPathFileError = 75
    Select Case Err.Number
    Case glrcErrPermissionDenied, glrcErrPathFileError
```

```
            ' Permission denied or Path/File access error
            Select Case fState
            Case glrcFStateOpeningFile1
                MsgBox "Could not open 'c:\file1.txt'. " & _
                 "Something probably has the file locked.", _
                 vbOKOnly Or vbExclamation Or vbDefaultButton1 _
                 Or vbApplicationModal, "AddLineNumbers"
                Resume AddLineNumbersDone
            Case glrcFStateOpeningFile2
                MsgBox "Could not open 'c:\file2.txt'. The " & _
                 "file may be write protected or locked.", _
                 vbOKOnly Or vbExclamation Or vbDefaultButton1 _
                 Or vbApplicationModal, "AddLineNumbers"
                Resume AddLineNumbersCloseFile1
            Case Else
                Stop      'Should never reach here.
            End Select
        Case Else
            MsgBox "Unexpected error.", vbOKOnly Or _
             vbExclamation Or vbDefaultButton1 Or _
             vbApplicationModal, "Add Line Numbers"
        End Select
        Resume AddLineNumbersDone
End Sub
```

This listing shows a procedure that opens an ASCII file named C:\FILE1.TXT. It reads each line, adds a line number to the beginning of the line, and writes a new file, C:\FILE2.TXT, with the changes. There are two Open statements in the procedure that can fail, and you want to show the user two different error messages, depending on which one failed. Also, if an error occurs while the second file is being opened, you need to close the first file before exiting the procedure. The variable fState holds a flag indicating which open statement is being processed. When an error occurs, this variable is checked to determine which error message to display. Using the constants FSTATEOPENINGFILE1 and FSTATEOPENINGFILE2 instead of just the numbers 1 and 2 makes the meaning of the current value of fState more explicit.

Another technique for handling the state information uses line numbers. Yes, VBA still allows line numbers that were required in early versions of Basic, but you don't need them on every line. The Erl() function tells you which line number was most recently executed. For example, the preceding code could be rewritten as shown in Listing 16.6.

Listing 16.6

```
Sub AddLineNumbers2()
    ' Opens C:\FILE1.TXT and writes a new file C:\FILE2.TXT.
    ' Reports any errors opening the file
    '
    Dim strInput As String
    Dim lngLineNumber As Long

    On Error GoTo AddLineNumbers2Err

10  Open "c:\file1.txt" For Input As #1

20  Open "c:\file2.txt" For Output As #2

30  lngLineNumber = 1
    Do Until EOF(1)
        Input #1, strInput
        Print #2, lngLineNumber, strInput
        lngLineNumber = lngLineNumber + 1
    Loop
AddLineNumbers2CloseFile2:
    Close #2

AddLineNumbers2Done:
    Close #1

    Exit Sub
AddLineNumbers2Err:
    Const glrcErrPermissionDenied = 70
    Const glrcErrPathFileError = 75
    Select Case Err.Number
    Case glrcErrPermissionDenied, glrcErrPathFileError
        ' Permission denied or Path/File access error
        Select Case Erl
        Case 10
            MsgBox "Could not open 'c:\file1.txt'. " & _
            "Something probably has the file locked.", _
            vbOKOnly Or vbExclamation Or vbDefaultButton1 _
            Or vbApplicationModal, "AddLineNumbers"
            Resume AddLineNumbers2Done
        Case 20
            MsgBox "Could not open 'c:\file2.txt'. The " & _
            "file may be write protected or locked.", _
            vbOKOnly Or vbExclamation Or vbDefaultButton1 _
```

```
            Or vbApplicationModal, "AddLineNumbers"
          Resume AddLineNumbers2CloseFile2
      Case Else
          Stop     'Should never reach here.
      End Select
    Case Else
      MsgBox "Unexpected error.", vbOKOnly Or _
        vbExclamation Or vbDefaultButton1 Or _
        vbApplicationModal, "Add Line Numbers"
    End Select
    Resume AddLineNumbers2Done
End Sub
```

The Resume Statement

To return to the main part of the procedure from an error handler, you use the Resume statement. The Resume statement has three forms:

- Resume
- Resume Next
- Resume *Label*

They are described in the following sections.

Resume   Resume by itself returns control to the statement that caused the error. Use the Resume statement when the error handler fixes the problem that caused the error and you want to continue from the place where you encountered the problem. In the example shown in Listing 16.4, if the error handler ran a make-table query that created tblTable, you would use a Resume statement. Note, however, that if you didn't fix the problem that caused the error, an endless loop occurs when the original statement fails again. Use this form of Resume with extreme caution. In most cases you should provide a dialog where the user can choose to resume or exit the procedure.

Resume Next   Use the Resume Next statement inside an error handler when you want to ignore the statement that caused the error. Control returns to the statement following the one that caused the error, similar to the On Error Resume Next statement. Use Resume Next when you have fixed the problem that caused the error from within the error handler or when you can safely ignore the error.

Resume Label   Use the Resume *Label* statement when you want to return to a line other than the one causing the error or the line that follows it. Resume *Label* is similar to a GoTo statement, except you can use it only from inside an error handler. The example in Listing 16.4 shows this use of the Resume statement to jump to the label TypicalErrorHandlerSubDone.

Raising Errors

At times you may want to generate an error yourself rather than wait for one to occur. Other times you may want to cause the error to happen *again* inside an error handler. You do this by raising an error, using the Err.Raise method. Raise can take as arguments all the properties of the Err object. Thus you can raise a user-defined error by using this code:

```
Err.Raise Number:=65535, Description:="A user defined error"
```

This code causes Access to act as though an error with number 65535 occurred at this point in the code and defines the description as being the string "A user defined error". The normal handling of the error occurs, so if an On Error Goto statement is in effect, it then jumps to the error handler. The Err object's Number and String properties are set to the arguments of the Err.Raise method. If you don't specify an argument to the Raise method, Access uses the default arguments for the error number.

Inline Error Handling

If you have only one statement in a piece of code that can fail, you might not want to write a full error handler. The Err object with the On Error Resume Next statement can catch errors in your main code. This is called an *inline error handler*. To use it, lay out your code so it looks like the code in Listing 16.7.

Listing 16.7

```
Sub OnErrorResumeNextExample()
    ' Example showing the use of On Error Resume Next
    '
    Dim rst As Recordset
    Dim errSave As glrerrSaveType

    ' Some code that might generate a run-time error
```

```
' for example
On Error Resume Next

Set rst = CurrentDb.OpenRecordset("tblTable", dbOpenTable)
Call glrSaveErr(errSave)

On Error GoTo 0
Const glrcErrNoError = 0
Const glrcErrCantFindObject = 3011
Select Case errSave.Number
    Case glrcErrNoError        ' No Error
        ' Do nothing
    Case glrcErrCantFindObject   'Can't find object
        MsgBox "tblTable doesn't exist. Call the " & _
        "database administrator."
        GoTo SubNameDone
    Case Else
        ' Stop here with error message
        Call glrRaiseErr(errSave)
End Select

' Do some processing with rst

    rst.Close
SubNameDone:
End Sub
```

This code contains no error handler. Instead, an On Error Resume Next tells Access to ignore any errors. However, anytime a statement can generate an error, the contents of the Err object are overwritten. If no error occurred, the Err.Number property is 0. Otherwise, the Err object will contain values for the error that occurred.

Because the contents of the Err object are constantly being overwritten, you may want to save the current error to use later. Unfortunately, you cannot create your own objects of the same type as the Err object to save an error. Therefore, the procedure calls glrSaveErr(), which saves the error to a user-defined type. Listing 16.8 shows these procedures. You can find this code in the module basError in CH16.MDB.

Listing 16.8

```
Public Type glrerrSaveType
    Number As Long
    Source As String
```

```
        Description As String
        HelpFile As String
        HelpContext As Long
        LastDllError As String
    End Type

    Public Sub glrSaveErr(errSave As glrerrSaveType)
        With Err
            errSave.Number = .Number
            errSave.Source = .Source
            errSave.Description = .Description
            errSave.HelpFile = .HelpFile
            errSave.HelpContext = .HelpContext
            errSave.LastDllError = .LastDllError
        End With
    End Sub

    Public Sub glrRaiseErr(errSave As glrerrSaveType)
        With errSave
            Err.Raise Number:=.Number, Source:=.Source, _
            Description:=.Description, HelpFile:=.HelpFile, _
            HelpContext:=.HelpContext
        End With
    End Sub
```

Note that as soon as you have two different statements that can cause a run-time error, it is usually more efficient to write an error handler using the On Error GoTo *Label* syntax, since the overhead of constructing the error handler is encountered only once. If you use the Err object with On Error Resume Next, always use a Select Case statement with a Case Else clause to trap unexpected errors. Otherwise, error numbers without Case statements are ignored and may produce unexpected results.

Hierarchy of Error Handlers

Access error handling behaves somewhat unexpectedly when one procedure calls another. If the called procedure generates an error that isn't handled within the procedure, the calling procedure's error handler receives the error. Access acts as though the procedure call itself generated the error.

WARNING   If you have any calls to user-defined functions or subs in your code, you need to be very aware of this feature of Access's error handlers; it can cause control to unexpectedly jump into your calling procedure's error handler. For this reason, we strongly recommend that you include an error handler in every procedure in your application. This may seem like a lot of work, and it definitely increases the size of your code, but the alternative is worse. You don't want an error in one procedure causing control to unexpectedly jump into another procedure's error handler. This can easily result in bugs in your code. The best way around this problem is to always handle run-time errors locally in *every* procedure. It's worth noting, however, that this does not mean you can't make use of generic error handling/reporting routines. (See the section "Creating an Error-Reporting Subroutine" later in this chapter.)

To demonstrate the hierarchy of error handlers, FunctionA() calls SubB in Listing 16.9.

Listing 16.9

```
Function FunctionA()
    ' Sample function to show the hierarchy of
    ' error handlers.
    On Error GoTo FunctionAError

    Call SubB

    MsgBox "You might expect to get to here, but you don't."
FunctionADone:
Exit Function
FunctionAError:
    Select Case Err.Number
    Case 1
        MsgBox "You got here from SubB"
        Resume FunctionADone
    Case Else
        Error Err.Number
    End Select
```

```
Exit Function
End Function

Sub SubB( )
    ' Stub procedure. Generates an error, but doesn't
    ' handle it.

    ' Cause an error in this Sub. There is no error handler.
    Err.Raise Number:=1
End Sub
```

Access generates an error when it raises error 1 in SubB. Since SubB doesn't contain an error handler, control immediately passes back to FunctionA(). FunctionA() does contain an error handler, so it processes the error. If FunctionA() hadn't contained an error handler, control would have passed to the procedure (if any) that called FunctionA(). If Access gets to the top of the call stack without finding an error handler, it puts up an alert and stops executing the code.

Access acts as though the Call statement itself generates the error. The Resume Next in FunctionA() returns control to the statement following the Call statement; control doesn't return to SubB. If you use a Resume statement instead of a Resume Next in FunctionA(), the Resume statement returns control to the Call statement in FunctionA(). This calls SubB again, which in this case puts you into an endless loop as the error repeats.

The OnError Property and the Error Event

When you are using a form or report, under the covers Access is using Jet for all data access. Anytime Access has to populate the fields on a bound form or fill a list box, it is making calls to Jet. Any of these calls might fail for reasons such as the database being opened exclusively by someone else or a table having been deleted. The On Error statements described earlier in the chapter are in effect only while your code is being executed. But what can you do about errors that happen while Access is manipulating a form or report? Access gives you a way to trap those errors through the use of the OnError property. This property allows you to specify a routine to be executed when an error occurs. When you run the Code Builder (by pressing the "…" button for the property and then selecting Code Builder) on this property, you see a shell that looks like the following:

Sub Form_Error(*DataErr* As Integer, *Response* As Integer)

End Sub

DataErr is the value that would be returned by the Err.Number property had the error occurred in code. *Response* is a value you fill in before the procedure terminates. It tells Access whether or not it should report the error to the user. *DataErr* and *Response* are the variable names the Access Code Builder proposes, but you can rename them to any variable names. Listing 16.10 shows an example of a routine that handles the Error event.

Listing 16.10

```
Sub Form_Error(DataErr As Integer, Response As Integer)
    ' Reports errors for the form, attached to OnError property
    Const glrcErrNoError = 0
    Const glrcErrFieldNull = 3314
    Const glrcErrDuplicateKey = 3022
    Select Case DataErr
    Case glrcErrNoError        ' No error
    Case glrcErrFieldNull      ' Field '|' can't contain a
                               ' null value.
        MsgBox "You have left a required field blank"
    Case glrcErrDuplicateKey ' Duplicate value in index,
                               ' primary key, or relationship.
                               ' Changes were unsuccessful.
        MsgBox "This record is attempting to duplicate" _
        & "of another record. Try another value."
    Case Else
        Stop    'Unknown Error
    End Select
    Response = acDataErrContinue
End Sub
```

The variable Response can receive one of two values: acDataErrContinue or acDataErrDisplay. The value acDataErrDisplay causes Access to display the error message that would have appeared if you hadn't had an error handler attached to the form. acDataErrContinue causes this error message to be suppressed.

The function Error$(DataErr) returns the Jet error string associated with the error. (For more information on the Form and Report Error events, see Chapter 8.)

Using the Jet Errors Collection

Anytime Jet is processing data, it can generate run-time errors. Since Jet may report multiple run-time errors from a single operation your code performs, it maintains a collection of those errors. Usually, you are concerned only with determining that an error has occurred and reporting that fact to the end user. In some cases, though, you may want to detail exactly the errors Jet generated. For this you use the Jet Errors collection.

The collection is a property of the DBEngine object. When you handle an error in an error handler in your code, or an Error event handler, you can then browse the Jet Errors collection to determine specifically which Jet errors occurred while processing a statement. The code in Listing 16.11 shows how you do this.

Listing 16.11

```
Sub JetErrorsCollection()
    Dim db As Database

    On Error GoTo JetErrorsCollectionErr

    CurrentDb.Execute "qappJetErrorsCollection", dbFailOnError
JetErrorsCollectionDone:
    Exit Sub
JetErrorsCollectionErr:
    Dim errCur As Error
    For Each errCur In DBEngine.Errors
        Debug.Print errCur.Description
    Next
    Resume JetErrorsCollectionDone
End Sub
```

In this code, when Jet generates a set of errors, each of the error descriptions is printed to the Debug window. The Err object will reflect the top-most of the objects in the Errors collection. The Errors collection is cleared before the next Jet Engine operation is executed.

Creating an Error-Reporting Subroutine

Since any robust application will have dozens, if not hundreds, of error handlers in its code, you may want to create a generic way of reporting them. We have created a generic routine you can use to report errors to the user. The error dialog created looks like the one shown in Figure 16.1. Typically this routine is used in an error handler to report any unexpected run-time errors. Listing 16.12 shows the routine that is called to invoke the generic handler.

FIGURE 16.1:

Generic error dialog

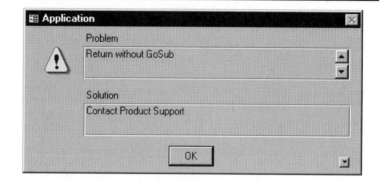

Listing 16.12

```
Public glrvarLogFile As Variant

Public Function glrHandleErr(errSave As glrerrSaveType, _
  Optional varNumber As Variant, _
  Optional varDescription As Variant, _
  Optional varSolution As Variant, _
  Optional varIcon As Variant, _
  Optional varButtonSet As Variant, _
  Optional varKeyMap As Variant, _
  Optional varExtendedInfo As Variant, _
  Optional varErrorTable As Variant, _
  Optional varTitle As Variant) As Integer

    'This routine reports a standard message dialog

    Dim varInfo As Variant
```

```
Static fInError As Boolean

'Check to see if we are recursively calling this routine.
If fInError Then
    'We are already processing an error. Don't repeat it
    MsgBox "We were already processing an error when " _
    & "another error occurred.", vbExclamation
    Stop
    Exit Function
End If

fInError = True

'If glrvarLogFile is not defined, define it
If IsEmpty(glrvarLogFile) Or IsNull(glrvarLogFile) Then
    glrvarLogFile = "c:\AccessAp.Log"
End If

'Build up a string to pass to the OpenArgs property of the
'dialog. This allows us to pass all of the information
'that needs to be retrieved by the dialog.
varInfo = ""
Call glrPutItem(varInfo, "esNumber", errSave.Number)
Call glrPutItem(varInfo, "esSource", errSave.Source)
Call glrPutItem(varInfo, "esDescription", _
 errSave.Description)
Call glrPutItem(varInfo, "esHelpFile", errSave.HelpFile)
Call glrPutItem(varInfo, "esHelpContext", _
 errSave.HelpContext)
Call glrPutItem(varInfo, "esLastDLLError", _
 errSave.LastDllError)
If Not IsMissing(varNumber) Then
    Call glrPutItem(varInfo, "varNumber", varNumber)
End If
If Not IsMissing(varDescription) Then
    Call glrPutItem(varInfo, "varDescription", _
     varDescription)
End If
If Not IsMissing(varSolution) Then
    Call glrPutItem(varInfo, "varSolution", varSolution)
End If
If Not IsMissing(varIcon) Then
    Call glrPutItem(varInfo, "varIcon", varIcon)
End If
If Not IsMissing(varIcon) Then
```

```
            Call glrPutItem(varInfo, "varIcon", varIcon)
        End If
        If Not IsMissing(varButtonSet) Then
            Call glrPutItem(varInfo, "varButtonSet", varButtonSet)
        End If
        If Not IsMissing(varKeyMap) Then
            Call glrPutItem(varInfo, "varKeyMap", varKeyMap)
        End If
        If Not IsMissing(varExtendedInfo) Then
            Call glrPutItem(varInfo, "varExtendedInfo", _
                varExtendedInfo)
        End If
        If Not IsMissing(varErrorTable) Then
            Call glrPutItem(varInfo, "varErrorTable", _
                varErrorTable)
        End If
        If Not IsMissing(varTitle) Then
            Call glrPutItem(varInfo, "varTitle", varTitle)
        End If

        'Open the dialog, passing in varInfo built above
        DoCmd.OpenForm FormName:="frmError", _
         View:=acNormal, _
         DataMode:=acReadOnly, _
         WindowMode:=acDialog, _
         OpenArgs:=varInfo

        'Get the ResumeStatus property set by the dialog
        glrHandleErr = Forms!frmError.ResumeStatus

        'The dialog is not hidden, but not closed. Set the
        'AllowClose property, then close the form.
        Forms!frmError.AllowClose = True
        DoCmd.Close ObjectType:=acForm, ObjectName:="frmError", _
         Save:=acSave

        fInError = False
End Function

Public Function glrKeyMap(ByVal bytKey1 As Byte, _
 ByVal bytKey2 As Byte, ByVal bytKey3 As Byte) As Long

        ' This routine builds a long from three byte values. The
        ' byte order in the long is 0 K3 K2 K1. All unused keys
        ' should be set to zero. Each byte represents one of the
```

```
' resume constants defined by glrRESUME*. The result of
' this routine is used in the varKeyMap argument to
' glrErrorHandler.

    Call glrAssert(bytKey1 >= 0)
    Call glrAssert(bytKey1 <= glrcResumeMax)
    Call glrAssert(bytKey2 >= 0)
    Call glrAssert(bytKey2 <= glrcResumeMax)
    Call glrAssert(bytKey3 >= 0)
    Call glrAssert(bytKey3 <= glrcResumeMax)
    glrKeyMap = bytKey1 Or bytKey2 * 2 ^ 8 Or bytKey3 * 2 ^ 16
End Function
```

The glrHandleErr() function takes the arguments listed in Table 16.2.

TABLE 16.2: Arguments for glrHandleErr()

Argument	Type	Description
errSave	Required	User-defined type filled in by the glrSaveErr procedure defined in Listing 16.7
varNumber	Optional	Overrides the error number in the errSave structure
varDescription	Optional	Overrides the description in the errSave structure
varSolution	Optional	Specifies a string to appear in the Solutions portion of the dialog box. If no solution is specified and the corresponding entry in the errors table is Null, no solution box appears
varIcon	Optional	Must be one of the following: vbExclamation, vbInformation, vbCritical, or vbQuestion. If no icon is specified here or in the errors table, an exclamation point icon is used
varButtonSet	Optional	Specifies which set of buttons appears in the dialog. Must be one of the following: vbOkOnly, vbOkCancel, vbYesNo, vbYesNoCancel, vbRetryCancel, or vbAbortRetryIgnore
varKeyMap	Optional	Maps the keys specified by varButtonSet to resume status value glrcExitSub, glrcResumeNext, or glrcResume. Must be built by the glrKeyMap() function
varExtendedInfo	Optional	True if the extended info button is to be available, False if it isn't
varErrorTable	Optional	Specifies a table of error statements from which the error number will be looked up
varTitle	Optional	Specifies the title that appears on the title bar of the message

The optional error table specified by the varTable argument has the columns indicated in Table 6.3.

TABLE 16.3: Column Names in Errors Table

Column	Description
Number	Number of the error message. This is the key value used to find the error in the table
Description	Description of the error
Solution	Solution for the error. If this is Null, no solution is displayed and the description box is expanded
Icon	Icon that should appear. Must be one of the following: vbInformation, vbExclamation, vbQuestion, or vbCritical
ButtonSet	Specifies which set of buttons appears in the dialog. Must be one of the following: vbOkOnly, vbOkCancel, vbYesNo, vbYesNoCancel, vbRetryCancel, or vbAbortRetryIgnore
KeyMap	Maps the keys specified by varButtonSet to resume status values glrEXITSUB, glrRESUMENEXT, or glrRESUME. Must be built by the glrKeyMap() function
varExtendedInfo	True if the extended info button is to be available, False if it isn't

When you call glrHandleErr(), it opens frmError and configures the dialog based on the information specified in the arguments. If you specify the varTable argument, glrHandleErr() looks up and displays any missing pieces that weren't specified by optional arguments for that error in the error table. You can use the table to create a generic set of text to display to the users. Based on which button is pressed, glrHandleErr() returns the resume status of glrcExitSub, glrcResume, or glrResumeNext. Your code should perform the appropriate action based on this value.

The code in glrHandleErr() builds a string using glrPutItem. This string contains all the arguments passed into glrHandleErr() and is used in the OpenArgs property of the OpenForm method. The form uses the information passed in to configure the dialog.

NOTE The glrAssert() function is described in the section "Using Assertions" later in this chapter.

You call the glrHandleErr() function using code similar to that found in Listing 16.13.

Listing 16.13

```
Public Sub ErrorExample()
    Call glrEnterProcedure("ErrorExample")
    On Error GoTo ErrorExampleErr
    Const glrcErrReturnWithoutGosub = 3
    Const glrcErrWeirdError = 4
    Const glrcErrInvalidProcedureCall = 5
    Const glrcErrOverflow = 6

    'One example
    Err.Raise Number:=glrcErrReturnWithoutGosub
    'Another example
    Err.Raise Number:=glrcErrWeirdError
    'A third example, overriding the description in the table
    Err.Raise Number:=glrcErrInvalidProcedureCall, _
     Description:="Not what you'd expect"
    'Another example, overriding everything
    Err.Raise Number:=glrcErrOverflow

ErrorExampleDone:
    Call glrExitProcedure("ErrorExample")
    Exit Sub
ErrorExampleErr:
    Dim errSave As glrerrSaveType
    Dim intResumeStatus As Integer
    Call glrSaveErr(errSave)
    Select Case errSave.Number
    Case glrcErrOverflow
        intResumeStatus = glrHandleErr(errSave, _
         varNumber:=27, _
         varDescription:="It didn't work!", _
         varSolution:="Fix it!", varIcon:=vbCritical, _
         varButtonSet:=vbOKOnly, varExtendedInfo:=True, _
         varErrorTable:="tblError", _
         varTitle:="Something Happened")
    Case Else
        intResumeStatus = glrHandleErr(errSave, _
         varErrorTable:="tblError")
    End Select
    Select Case intResumeStatus
```

```
        Case glrcResume
            Resume
        Case glrcResumeNext
            Resume Next
        Case glrcExitSub
            Resume ErrorExampleDone
        Case Else
            Call glrAssert(False)
        End Select
        Exit Sub
End Sub
```

This example uses Raise statements to force the invocation of certain errors. Normally you wouldn't include these types of statements in your code. You would, instead, just put in statements that can cause run-time errors.

If you then make the extended information available, a small button at the lower right of the dialog appears. Clicking this button "flops" the bottom half of the dialog open. The dialog then appears as shown in Figure 16.2.

FIGURE 16.2:

Generic error dialog with extended error information

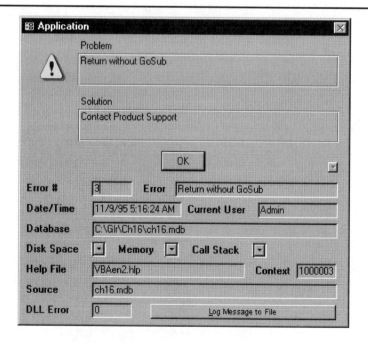

By using this error-reporting scheme, you can vastly reduce the complexity of your code at any given point, since you can handle all generic errors within the errors table. In addition, you can override any of the information in the table to provide information that is specific to any particular error. You can find this code in basError and frmError in CH16.MDB.

Implementing a Call Stack

When you are at any breakpoint, you can select View ➤ Calls to see which function caused the error. Unfortunately, Access doesn't provide any method for retrieving this information from your code. When you get an unexpected error, it's useful to log what code is being executed at that point and how it got there. Since Access provides no way to get at the information it keeps internally (that is, the name of the currently executing procedure), you must maintain the information yourself if you need it. The procedures shown in Listing 16.14 will help with this process.

Listing 16.14

```
Sub glrEnterProcedure(ByVal strProcName As String)
    ' Places the procedure name specified by strProcName
    ' on the stack, which is the glrastrProcNames()
    ' array.

    On Error GoTo glrEnterProcedureErr
    glriastrProcNames = glriastrProcNames + 1
    glrastrProcNames(glriastrProcNames) = strProcName
glrEnterProcedureDone:
    Exit Sub
glrEnterProcedureErr:
    Const glrcErrSubscriptOutOfRange = 9
    Select Case Err.Number
    Case glrcErrSubscriptOutOfRange  'Subscript out of range
        Static fInited As Boolean
        If fInited Then
            'Increase the size of the array by 10 elements and
            'try again. We never collapse the size.
            ReDim Preserve glrastrProcNames _
            (UBound(glrastrProcNames) + 10)
        Else
            'This is the first time, so give the array an
            'initial size, then set glriastrProcNames to
            'zero to make it point to the first element.
```

```
                    fInited = True
                    ReDim glrastrProcNames(9)
                    glriastrProcNames = 0
              End If
              Resume
        Case Else
              'Should not get any other error
              Stop
        End Select
        Resume glrEnterProcedureDone
  End Sub

  Sub glrExitProcedure(ByVal strProcName As String)
        ' Removes the procedure name specified by the strProcName
        ' variable from the procedure stack, glrastrProcNames.
        ' Checks to make sure that the procname passed in is the
        ' same as the top of the stack.

        ' Assert that the top of the stack is the same as the
        ' procedure name passed in. Usually this assertion fails
        ' if someone missed doing a glrEnterProcedure or
        ' glrExitProcedure in some other procedure.
        Call glrAssert(strProcName = _
         glrastrProcNames(glriastrProcNames))

        ' Do not underflow the stack
        Call glrAssert(glriastrProcNames >= 0)

        glrastrProcNames(glriastrProcNames) = ""
        glriastrProcNames = glriastrProcNames - 1
  End Sub
```

These procedures use a global array, glrastrProcNames, as a stack of procedure calls. Each time a glrEnterProcedure call is made, the current procedure is added to the array. When one procedure calls another, glriastrProcNames is incremented, and the next place in the stack is used to maintain the hierarchy. When a procedure is exited, the name is removed from the stack and glriastrProcNames is decremented.

To implement a call stack using these procedures in your own applications, import the code from basError in CH16.MDB, and then place a call to glrEnterProcedure at the entry point of every routine in your code. You must also put a call to glrExit-Procedure at the exit point of every routine.

To get any useful information from these functions, you must rigorously use the glrEnterProcedure and glrExitProcedure calls at the entry and exit points of every procedure. Listing 16.15 shows an example of how to use these functions. Because you have to call glrExitProcedure at the exit point, you will want to make sure you have only one exit point to your procedures.

Listing 16.15

```
Sub EnterAndExitExample()
    ' An example block of code showing how glrEnterProcedure
    ' and glrExitProcedure should be used.

    On Error GoTo EnterAndExitExampleErr
    Call glrEnterProcedure("EnterAndExitExample")

    ' Some code that might fail in an unexpected way

EnterAndExitExampleDone:
    Call glrExitProcedure("EnterAndExitExample")
    Exit Sub
EnterAndExitExampleErr:
    Dim errSave As glrerrSaveType
    Dim intResumeStatus As Integer
    Call glrSaveErr(errSave)
    intResumeStatus = glrHandleErr(errSave, _
     varErrorTable:="tblError")
    Select Case intResumeStatus
    Case glrcResume
        Resume
    Case glrcResumeNext
        Resume Next
    Case glrcExitSub
        Resume EnterAndExitExampleDone
    Case Else
        Call glrAssert(False)
    End Select
    Exit Sub
End Sub
```

The generic error handler described earlier in this chapter uses the call stack code to display the call stack in the extended information part of the dialog. Figure 16.3 shows the display of the call stack. Listing 16.16 shows the code that builds the RowSource property for the drop-down list box.

FIGURE 16.3:

Display of the call stack

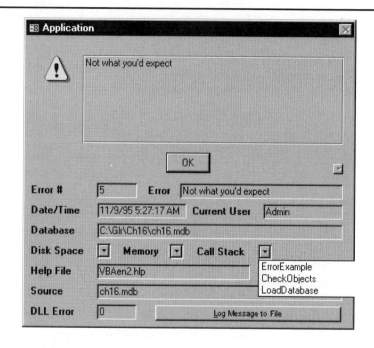

Listing 16.16

```
cboCallStack.RowSource = ""
For i = glriastrProcNames To 0 Step -1
    If i <> glriastrProcNames Then
        cboCallStack.RowSource = cboCallStack.RowSource _
         & ";" & glrastrProcNames(i)
    Else
        cboCallStack.RowSource = glrastrProcNames(i)
    End If
Next i
cboCallStack.Requery
```

The payoff for using this call stack code comes when you are trying to determine the current state when an error has occurred. Anytime users get a run-time error, they can press the Log button in the extended info part of the dialog, which writes the current state to the log file. The log file is named in the global variable glrstrLog-File and by default is "c:\accessap.log". You can then have your user send you the log file, and then you can determine exactly what was going on when the error occurred.

Another advantage of having glrEnterProcedure and glrExitProcedure statements surrounding each entry and exit point of your code is that you can add any global information you wish to those calls. For example, you might add information to keep track of how much time is spent in the procedure. This is called *profiling*. You can use the profiling information to help determine which routines need optimization work.

Dealing with Logic Errors, AKA Bugs!

As stated at the beginning of this chapter, there are three kinds of errors: compile-time errors, run-time errors, and logic errors. Access informs you of any compile-time errors when you use Run ➤ Compile Loaded Modules. Error handlers handle run-time errors. But what can you do about logic errors? If you were a perfect programmer, you'd never have any logic errors, because you'd never make mistakes, you'd always know exactly how Access works, and all your assumptions would always hold true. Professional programmers can't count on perfection, however. Logic errors, also known as bugs, are by far the most difficult type of error to find. In the remainder of this chapter, we share some strategies for reducing the number of bugs in your code.

Avoiding Bugs

It's close to impossible to write any substantial application without any bugs, but certain strategies can help you avoid inserting unnecessary bugs. You should develop the necessary discipline to use these strategies whenever you write code, even if you think you're writing a function to use only in testing or for your own internal application. Good habits are hard to develop but are also hard to lose once you develop them. The next few sections describe how you can avoid letting bugs slip into your code by following these rules:

- Fix bugs as they appear.
- Use comments.
- Organize your code.

- Modularize your code.

- Use Option Explicit.

- Avoid variants if at all possible.

- Use explicit conversion functions.

- Beware the simple Dim statement.

- Group your Dim statements.

- Use the tightest possible scoping.

- Watch out for "hidden" modules.

- Use consistent naming conventions.

- Use assertions.

Internalizing these suggestions will help you develop a good mind-set for avoiding bugs and for removing the ones that inevitably creep into your code.

As a single rule of thumb, the best bug-avoidance strategy is to take your time and to avoid the urge to make your code "cleverer" than necessary. At times you simply must use the newest, most complex features of any programming language, but in general, the simpler way is the better way. With this strategy in mind, there are some specific tactics that work well in Access coding to help avoid bugs.

Fixing Bugs As They Appear

It's critical that you fix bugs as they reveal themselves rather than wait until you have more features implemented; hurried cleanup at the end of a project will pressure you to apply Band-Aids instead of real fixes. If your application is failing when the invoice amount is exactly $33.00, don't just patch the procedure like this:

```
If curInvoiceAmt=33 Then
    MyFunction = curTheCorrectValue
Else...
```

Instead, you must figure out *why* the call is failing and fix its cause instead of the apparent symptom. This requires steady and systematic testing, which is something programmers tend to avoid. Would you rather write 500 lines of code or try 50 test cases on existing code? Most of us would choose the former, since writing code is fun and testing is boring. But if you keep in mind how little fun you'll have if your application doesn't work when it's shipped, you'll buckle down and do the boring testing work, too.

Using Comments

Old code is harder to debug than new code because it is less fresh in your mind. For most programmers, old code is any code that's more than two days old. One way to help keep your code from aging rapidly is to insert comments. There's an art to sensible commenting: it depends on adding just enough to tell you what's going on without going overboard and cluttering up your code.

The comment should state the intention of the code rather than tell how the code is implemented. This is an important point. Novice programmers have a tendency to write comments that describe how the code is implemented, as in this example:

```
' Make sure the numbers in the combo box and the text box add up
' to less than the acceptable total
If cboStartTime + CInt(txtSlots) > MAX_SLOTS Then
    ' If not, put up an error message...
    MsgBox "Not enough time in day", vbCritical, _
      "Schedule Error"
    ' ...and exit the application
    GoTo cmdSchedule_Click_Exit
End If
' Find the last slot that needs to be modified
intSlotLast = cboStartTime + CInt(txtSlots) - 1

' Set an object to the current database
Set dbCurrent = CurrentDb()
' Open a querydef object with the Prospective schedule query
' loaded
Set qdfSchedule = _
 dbCurrent.OpenQueryDef("qryScheduleProspective")
' Get the first query parameter from the Installer combo box
qdfSchedule.Parameters(0) = cboInstaller
' Get the second query parameter from the Date combo box
qdfSchedule.Parameters(1) = cboDate
```

Reading through code like this is like trying to understand a telephone conversation with a bad echo on the line. By trimming down the number of comments to a more sensible level, you can highlight the overall structure of the code and note any particularly tricky spots for future programmers, including yourself. Remember, if you've named your variables correctly, their names will act as mini-comments in the code itself. Notice that the comments in this version of the same example describe the intention of the code, not how it is implemented:

```
' Check to see that we have enough hours left in the day
If cboStartTime + CInt(txtSlots) > MAX_SLOTS Then
    MsgBox "Not enough time in day", vbCritical, _
     "Schedule Error"
    GoTo cmdSchedule_Click_Exit
End If
intSlotLast = cboStartTime + CInt(txtSlots) - 1

' Get a list of open timeslots to check
Set dbCurrent = CurrentDb()
Set qdfSchedule = _
 dbCurrent.OpenQueryDef("qryScheduleProspective")
qdfSchedule.Parameters(0) = cboInstaller
qdfSchedule.Parameters(1) = cboDate
```

A comment that is not maintained is worse than no comment at all. Have you ever read a comment and then stared at the code below it and discovered it didn't seem to do what the comment said it did? Now you have to figure out whether it is the comment or the code that is wrong. If your code change requires a comment change, make sure you do it now, because you probably won't get around to doing it later.

To Strip or Not to Strip

One reason for keeping the number of comments to a reasonable level is that comments do take up space in memory while your database is loaded. Some programmers go so far as to encourage comment stripping, the practice of removing all comments from production code. We don't recommend this, except under the most dire circumstances, since it requires you to maintain a commented version to work on and an uncommented version to ship, which increases the chance you will introduce errors by failing to keep the two versions in perfect synchronization. Since Access doesn't give you the ability to modify code programmatically, you can't just write a VBA procedure to remove comments, either.

Organizing Your Code

In addition to commenting your code, you should do whatever you can to keep it organized. This means you should use indentation to organize the flow of code. It also means you should split large procedures into smaller ones.

Indent your code so that statements that should "go together" are at the same indentation level and statements that are subordinate to others are indented one more tab stop. Although there is room for disagreement, most Access programmers lay out their code something like this:

```
' Initialize the array that governs visibility and
' set up records
For intI = 1 To intTotalTabs
    intShow(intI) = False
    rstLoggedData.AddNew
        rstLoggedData![State] = False
    rstLoggedDate.Update
Next intI
intShow(intTabNumber) = True
```

In VBA, many programmers use indentation both to match up traditional control structures (For...Next, If...Then...Else, Do...Loop, While...Wend, For Each) and to indicate levels of data access object activity (BeginTrans/CommitTrans, AddNew/Update, and so on).

Modularizing Your Code

Modularization is a fancy term for a simple idea: breaking up your code into a series of relatively small procedures rather than a few mammoth ones. There are several key benefits to writing code this way:

- You make it easier to understand each procedure. Code that is easier to understand is easier to maintain and to keep bug free.

- You can localize errors to a smaller section of the total code. If a variable is used only in one ten-line function, any error messages referring to that variable are most likely generated within that function.

- You can lessen the dangers of side effects caused by too-wide scoping of variables. If you use a variable at the top of a 500-line function and again at the bottom for a different loop, you may well forget to reinitialize it.

Using Option Explicit

In the Tools ➤ Options dialog, on the Module tab, you will find a check box labeled "Require Variable Declaration." Selecting this check box causes Access to insert the line "Option Explicit" at the top of any new module it creates. This statement forces you to declare all your variables before referring to them in your code. This may seem like a nuisance, but it will prevent some hard-to-find errors from cropping up in your code. Without Option Explicit, Access allows you to use any syntactically correct variable in your code, regardless of whether you declare it. This means that any variable you forget to declare will be initialized to a variant and given the value Empty at the point where you first use it. The hours you save in debugging time will make using this option well worth the effort.

Using Option Explicit is an easy way to avoid errors such as the one you'll find in the code in Listing 16.17. Errors like this are almost impossible to catch late in the development cycle, since they're buried in existing code. (Don't feel bad if you don't immediately see the error in the fragment; it's difficult to find.) That's why you'll want to use Option Explicit—to avoid just this sort of error.

Listing 16.17

```
Function UpdateLog(intSeverity As Integer, _
 strProcedure As String, strTracking As String) As Integer
    Dim dbCurrent As Database
    Dim rstUsageLog As Recordset
    Dim intFull As Integer
    Dim qryArchive As QueryDef

    Const glrcMinSeverity = 1
    ' Don't log activities that aren't severe enough to
    ' bother with
    If intSeverity < glrcMinSeverity Then
        Exit Function
    End If

    DoCmd.SetWarnings False

    ' Append a new record to the usage log
    Set dbCurrent = CurrentDb()
    Set rstUsageLog = dbCurrent.OpenRecordset _
     ("zstblUsageLog", dbOpenDynaset)
    rstUsageLog.AddNew
```

```
        rstUsageLog![Severity] = intSeverty
        If Err.Number Then
            rstUsageLog![ErrorCode] = Err.Number
            rstUsageLog![ErrorText] = Err.Description
        End If
        rstUsageLog![User] = CurrentUser()
        rstUsageLog![Date] = Now
'.
'. etc
'.
End Function
```

In case you missed it, the error occurred on this line of code:

```
rstUsageLog![Severity] = intSeverty
```

A small spelling error like this would cause only zeros to be stored in the Severity field and could cause you several hours of debugging time. Option Explicit lets you avoid these kinds of errors.

Avoid Variants If At All Possible

The Variant datatype is convenient, but it's not always the best choice. It's tempting to declare all your variables as variants so you don't have to worry about what's in them. The Access design team did not put in explicit types to make your life difficult; they put them in because they're useful. If you think something will always be an Integer, dimension it as an Integer. If you get an error message later because you've attempted to assign an invalid value to that variable, the error message will point straight to the problem area of your code and give you a good idea of what went wrong. Variants are also slower than explicitly dimensioned variables for the same operations, since they have the overhead of tracking which type of data they are holding at any given time. In addition, variants are larger than almost any other datatype and so take longer to move around in memory. These last two reasons alone should be enough to make you reconsider using variants whenever possible.

In some instances you have no choice about your datatypes. If you're assigning values to variables that might at some point need to contain a null value, you must use the Variant datatype. This is the only datatype that can contain a null value, and attempting to assign a null value to a nonvariant variable triggers a run-time error. The same goes for function return values. If a function might need to return a null value, the return value for that function must be a variant.

This same advice applies to choosing functions. If you know that a function can return only a string and never a null value, use the string version. For example, Left$() is often preferable to Left(), since the former returns a string and the latter returns a variant. Using the variant versions of the string functions also encourages you to be sloppy, since you don't have to think about whether or not you can use the string version. If you take the time to consider which is the better function for your situation, you're more likely to end up with code that works the first time.

Using Explicit Conversion Functions

There will be times in your applications when you need to convert variables from one datatype to another. VBA is forgiving about these conversions and most often does the work for you. For example, the following code fragment works without any intervention on your part:

```
Dim strState as String
Dim varState as Variant

varState = "CA"
strState = varState
```

As a matter of fact, you probably write code that does this sort of thing without even thinking about it. In fact, whenever you assign a value of one datatype to a variable of a different datatype, Access has to do some datatype conversion. You can avoid hard-to-find bugs by always using explicit conversion functions when converting datatypes.

For example, in the following code fragment, Access blithely copies the value from varY into intX, but in doing so it truncates the value of the number:

```
Dim intX As Integer
Dim varY As Variant

varY = 123.456
intX = varY
' Now intX = 123 and varY = 123.456
```

If your intent is to move the value from varY into an Integer variable, your code will be more explicit in its intent if you use the CInt() function. If your intent is to maintain the floating-point value, use the CSng() function. Reading this code, you know that something is wrong because you are assigning a Single to an Integer:

```
intX = CSng(varY)
```

You also need to be careful about passing information to routines that have parameters passed ByVal. Information passed in is coerced to the datatype of the parameter. Therefore, if you pass a variable with the Single datatype to a parameter of type Integer, Access truncates the fractional component of the Single when it creates the Integer.

Beware the Simple Dim Statement

Even the simple Dim statement can introduce subtle bugs into your code. Consider this statement:

```
Dim strFirst, strLast As String
```

The intent here is clearly to define two String variables on one line. However, this is not the way VBA works. The As clause applies only to the variable it immediately follows, not to all variables on the line. The result of the preceding declaration is that strLast is a String variable but strFirst is a Variant variable, with slightly different behavior. For example, strFirst will be initialized to Empty and strLast to a zero-length string. You must explicitly define the datatype of every single variable in VBA. The simplest way to ensure this is to get into the habit of declaring only one variable for each statement.

Grouping Your Dim Statements

You can declare your variables anywhere in your procedures, as long you declare them before they are actually used, and Access will understand and accept the declarations. For the sake of easier debugging, though, you should get into the habit of declaring variables at the top of your procedures. This makes it easy to see exactly what a particular procedure is referring to and to find the declarations when you are in the midst of debugging.

Using the Tightest Possible Scoping

Always use the tightest possible scoping for your variables. Some beginning programmers discover global variables and promptly declare all their variables as global to avoid the issue of scoping altogether. This is a sloppy practice that will backfire the first time you have two procedures, both of which change the same global variable's value. If a variable is used solely in a single procedure, declare it there. If it is used only by procedures in a single module, declare it with module scope. Save global scope for only those few variables you truly need to refer to from widely scattered parts of your code.

If you need a variable to be available globally but want to restrict the scope of procedures that can change that value, you might consider "hiding" it from the rest of your application. To do so, create the variable as a module global variable in a specific module. In that module, place any function that needs to modify the value of the variable. In addition, add one extra function that you'll use to retrieve the value from outside the module. If you want to be able to assign a new value to the variable from a different module, you can also include a procedure that will do that for you. In any case, no procedure in any other module will be able to modify the value of this variable. By hiding the variable in this manner, you can be assured that no other procedures in any other modules can modify your variable without going through your procedures. Listing 16.18 shows a simple case of this mechanism.

Listing 16.18

```
Private intCurrentValue As Integer
Sub SetCurrentValue(intNewValue As Integer)
    intCurrentValue = intNewValue
End Sub
```

```
Function GetCurrentValue()
    GetCurrentValue = intCurrentValue
End Function
```

Given the code in Listing 16.18, any procedure in any module can retrieve the value of intCurrentValue (by calling the GetCurrentValue() function) and can set the value (by calling SetCurrentValue). If you made SetCurrentValue private, however, no procedure outside the current module could change the value of intCurrent-Value. By protecting your *faux*-global variables in this manner, you can avoid errors that can easily occur in multiple-module applications, especially ones written by multiple programmers.

Using Consistent Naming Conventions

In addition to the conventions discussed here that help structure your code, consider adopting a consistent naming convention for objects and variables in your code. We (along with many other programmers) have standardized our naming conventions based on the RVBA naming conventions, which you'll find in Appendix A on the companion disk. A consistent naming standard can make it simple for you to find errors lurking in your programs, in addition to making them simpler for multiple programmers to maintain.

For example, say you need to add together two numeric values. You'd like their result to be stored with the appropriate precision. If you write code like this:

```
Dim number1 As Integer
Dim number2 As Double
.
.
.
number2 = 12.345
number1 = number2 + 23.456
```

Access assigns the sum to number1, but because number1 is declared to be an Integer, Access truncates the value. If you used the RVBA naming conventions, your code would look something like this:

```
Dim intNumber1 As Integer
Dim dblNumber2 As Double
.
```

```
.
.
dblNumber2 = 12.345
intNumber1 = dblNumber2 + 23.456
```

Given those names, it's clear that you're assigning the value from a double-precision number into an Integer and that some truncation is about to happen. With careful use of a naming convention, you can avoid just this sort of hidden bug. The tags on variables in an expression should all match. Tags that don't match should have conversion functions to convert their values into the datatype of the other variables.

Your Friend, the MsgBox() Function

As an alternative to setting breakpoints, you can use the MsgBox() function to indicate your program's state. With this strategy you decide what you would like to monitor and add calls to the MsgBox() function to return the particular information when you want to see it. You can enhance this technique by writing a wrapper for the MsgBox() function so that these messages are posted only when you have a conditional compilation constant set to indicate that you want to see debugging messages. This flag controls whether the glrDebugMessageBox() function should in fact interrupt execution of your code or whether it should just quietly return to the calling procedure. The glrDebugMessageBox function is shown in Listing 16.19. You'll find this function in basError in CH16.MDB. To use it in your own applications, import the module and call glrDebugMessageBox(), as described in the following paragraphs.

Listing 16.19

```
#Const glrcFDebug = True

Function glrDebugMessageBox(ByVal varMessage As Variant, _
  strCaller As String) As Integer
    glrDebugMessageBox = True
#If glrcFDebug Then
    glrDebugMessageBox = (MsgBox(CStr(varMessage), _
    vbOKCancel Or vbQuestion, "Debug: " & strCaller) _
    = vbOK)
#End If
End Function
```

You can sprinkle as many calls to glrDebugMessageBox() as you like into your code and make them all active or inactive at once by changing the value of the glrfDebug constant. Typically, you can use these message boxes to return news on the state of the program's execution. For example, here's a possible code fragment from your application's AutoExec() function (called from the AutoExec macro):

```
If Not glrDebugMessageBox("About to Start Logging", _
 "AutoExec") Then
    Stop
End If

varRet = StartLogging()

If Not glrDebugMessageBox("StartLogging returned " _
 & varRet, "AutoExec") Then
    Stop
End If
```

glrDebugMessageBox uses conditional compilation to include or exclude the body of the function. Conditional compilation tells the VBA compiler to include or exclude certain portions of code when it compiles the code. The #Const defines a conditional compilation constant. You can also define them in the Modules tab of the Options dialog. The #If and #End If define a block that is compiled only if the conditional compilation constant is true. Based on the value of the glrfDebug constant, the message box is displayed or not. If the constant is not set, it just returns True, and your code can continue. However, if you are in debug mode instead, the function displays whatever you pass to it, as shown in Figure 16.4.

If you click OK, the function returns a true value. If you click Cancel or press the Esc key, the function returns False, which in turn should halt your program execution back at the point where you called the glrDebugMessageBox() function. Using debugging message boxes is particularly useful when your code refers to the Screen

FIGURE 16.4:
glrDebugMessageBox() displays
anything you send it.

object and its ActiveForm, ActiveReport, ActiveControl, and ActiveDatasheet properties, because using the debugger causes these objects to lose the focus and thus their context.

The Access Debugging Tools

Once you've recognized that you have a logic error, you will need to track it down. Access provides a set of tools for debugging your application. These include

- The Debug window
- Breakpoints
- Set and Show Next Statement
- Viewing the call stack
- The instant watch
- Setting watches
- Step Over
- Step Into
- Step to Cursor

(See the section "Step Into versus Step Over" later in this chapter for a description of the last three items.)

The Debug Window

The Debug window, shown in Figure 16.5, gives you a place to investigate the effects of VBA code directly, without the intervention of macros, forms, or other methods of running the code. You open the Debug window by clicking the Debug Window button on the toolbar, selecting View ➤ Debug Window, or pressing Ctrl+G. Debug window contents are preserved as long as you are in a single session of Access, even if you close one database and open another.

The Debug window displays the last 200 lines of output at all times. As more output is appended to the end, older lines disappear from the top of the list. With the capability to scroll back the Debug window, you can position the cursor on an evaluation line and press ↵, and Access will recalculate the expression and display its value. If you want to remove the lines in the Debug window above your current

Debug window showing how to call a sub named ErrorExample

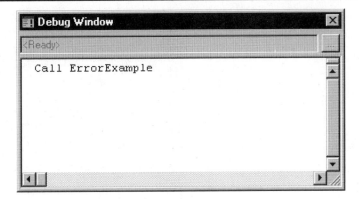

location, use Ctrl+Shift+Home to select then all, and then press Del. To remove lines below your current location, first select them with Ctrl+Shift+End.

Breakpoints

Breakpoints allow you to set locations in your code at which Access will temporarily halt its execution of your code. Figure 16.6 shows code halted at a breakpoint. Once Access stops at a breakpoint, you can use the Debug window to probe what's going on within VBA, checking the value of variables and confirming that your code is doing what you expect it to do. You can also use the Step Into and Step Over functionality (using the menu items, the toolbar buttons, or the F8/Shift+F8 key) to move through your code statement by statement so you can watch it execute in slow motion.

The Call Stack

Access has the ability to display the call stack when a function is paused at a breakpoint. The call stack lists each active function, with the current function at the top of the list, the one that called it next on the list, and so on. If the function was originally called from the Debug window, this is noted at the end of the list. If the function is called from elsewhere in Access (for example, directly from a Click event or from a RunCode macro action), there is no way to know from where it was called. Figure 16.7 shows the call stack as it might appear at a breakpoint in your code.

FIGURE 16.6:

Code halted at a breakpoint

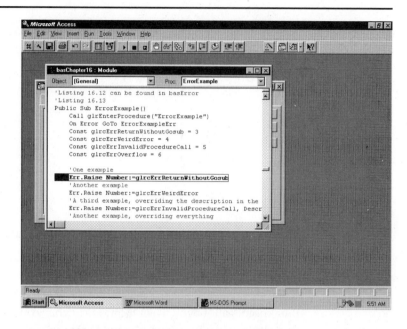

FIGURE 16.7:

Access call stack

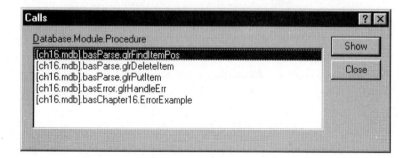

Watch Expressions

Access 95 has implemented a full set of watch functionality. Watches come in three varieties:

- Watch Expression
- Break When Expression Is True
- Break When Expression Has Changed

A watch expression is added to the top pane of the Debug window. Anytime you are debugging in break mode, all watch expressions are evaluated and shown. This is useful if you are single-stepping through code and want to watch the contents of a variable or an expression.

The Break When Expression Is True and Break When Expression Has Changed functionality allow you to specify some condition. When that condition is true or changes, Access immediately halts execution and puts you into break mode. These types of watches are useful for determining when and how a variable's value was changed. For example, say you know that somewhere in your code, a global variable named intValue is getting set to 0. You can set a Break When Expression Is True watch with the expression "intValue = 0". Then, as soon as intValue becomes equal to 0, Access puts you into break mode.

Instant Watches

The Instant Watch dialog is useful for quickly seeing the value of a variable. In previous versions of Access you had to print a value to the Debug window. Now you can just position the cursor anywhere within a variable name and press Shift+F9. The Instant Watch dialog, shown in Figure 16.8, then shows you the present contents of a variable. You can also select an expression, and Access will evaluate the expression. Clicking the Add button adds the expression as a regular Watch Expression.

FIGURE 16.8:

Instant Watch dialog

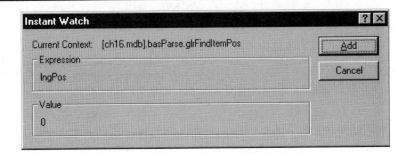

Debugging with the Debug Window

You can use the Debug window to test the results of any VBA code you write. Formally, the Debug window is named the Debug object from within Access. As an object it's rather limited, since its only method is the Print method. Using Debug.Print from VBA requests the Debug window to print the value that follows the command. From within the Debug window itself, you needn't specify the object, since it's the current object and just the Print command will do.

> **TIP**
>
> VBA provides a shortcut for the Print method, as have most previous versions of Basic. When in the Debug window, you can just use the ? symbol to replace the word *Print*. All our examples use this shortcut.

Running Code from the Debug Window

You can easily run any function or procedure that's in scope from the Debug window. For example, if you enter this expression:

```
? MyFunction()
```

in the Debug window, Access attempts to print out the return value from the function named MyFunction(), which it can do only by executing the function. To execute a subroutine, just call it directly from the Debug window:

```
Call MySub
```

At any time you can also check the value of a variable by entering

```
? intSomeVariable
```

in the Debug window.

Scoping rules apply as in normal code. That is, variables are available from the Debug window only if they're currently in scope. You can tell what the current scope is by looking at the top of the Debug window. It always reflects what it sees as the current scope. At any point, only variables and procedures that are available in the current scope are available to you in the Debug window.

Executing Code in the Debug Window

You can also execute code while in the Debug window. For example, you can set the value of the variable intMyVar by typing

```
intMyVar=5
```

in the Debug window and pressing ↵. Of course, the variable must already be dimensioned elsewhere in your code and must be in scope at the time. This prevents you from assigning a value to a local variable unless you are halted at a breakpoint in its home procedure. You cannot enter a Dim statement (or any of its cousins, including ReDim, Global, and Const) in the Debug window.

Any statement you enter for direct execution in the Debug window must fit on a single line. You cannot, for example, enter a multiline If…Then…Else for evaluation in the Debug window, although you can execute a single-line If…Then statement. To get around this limitation, you can use the colon (:) character to separate multiple VBA statements on the same line.

For example, the following code could run a loop for you, given that you had previously defined the variable intCount somewhere in your code and that it was currently in scope:

```
For intCount = 0 To 10:Debug.Print intCount:Next intCount
```

Using the Debug Window to Track Running Code

You can use the Debug window as a way of tracking a running procedure. As mentioned earlier in this chapter, you can use the Print method of the Debug object (the Debug window) to display any expression from within your running code. For example, running the function in Listing 16.20 (from basFibo in CH16.MDB) produces the output shown in Figure 16.9.

Listing 16.20

```
Function Fibo(intMembers As Integer)
    ' Print the requested number of elements of the
    ' standard Fibonacci series (s(n) = s(n-2) + s(n-1))
    ' to the Debug Window.

    Dim intI As Integer
    Dim intCurrent As Integer
```

```
        Dim intPrevious As Integer
        Dim intTwoPrevious As Integer

        intPrevious = 1
        intTwoPrevious = 1

        Debug.Print intPrevious
        Debug.Print intTwoPrevious

        For intI = 3 To intMembers
            intCurrent = intPrevious + intTwoPrevious
            Debug.Print intCurrent
            intTwoPrevious = intPrevious
            intPrevious = intCurrent
        Next intI

    End Function
```

FIGURE 16.9:

Output from running Fibo()

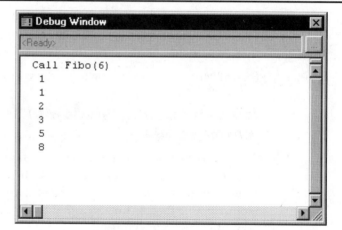

Handling Remnant Debug.Print Statements

You can safely leave Debug.Print lines in your shipping code if you wish. As long as the user does not for some reason have the Debug window displayed, these lines will have no visible effect and only a slight performance penalty. However, if you are concerned about the performance hit of these lines, you can surround your debug code with conditional compilation statements. For example:

```
#Const fDebug = True
    .
    .
    .
#If fDebug Then
    Debug.Print "Some output"
#End If
```

Using Breakpoints

Using a breakpoint is the equivalent of putting a roadblock in your code. When you set a breakpoint, you tell Access to stop executing your code in a particular spot but to keep the system state in memory. This means that all the variables the function was dealing with are available for your inspection in the Debug window. Access provides a toolbar, with appropriate breakpoint buttons, to aid in your debugging efforts. Here is the debugging toolbar, with each of the pertinent buttons labeled:

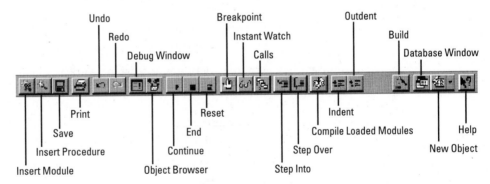

To set a breakpoint on a particular line of code, place your cursor anywhere on the line and do one of the following: click the Breakpoint button on the toolbar, choose Run ➤ Toggle Breakpoint, or press the F9 key. Access displays the chosen line in boldface type in the Module window. When you're executing code and you hit a breakpoint, the focus switches to the window with the breakpoint showing, and a dashed box surrounds the statement where execution is halted. Access suspends execution *before* it executes the particular statement. This way you can check or set the value of variables in your code before executing the chosen line of code.

Access does not save breakpoints with your code. If you close a database and re-open it, any breakpoints you have set in your code vanish. If you need to preserve your breakpoints across sessions, you can use the Stop statement, which acts as a permanent breakpoint and is saved with your module. Just as with a breakpoint, Access pauses the execution of your code as soon as it encounters the Stop statement. Of course, you'll need to remove Stop statements from your code (or surround them with conditional compilation statements) before you distribute your application, since they will stop the execution of your running code in any environment.

You can reset breakpoints manually with the Run ➤ Toggle Breakpoint command, the F9 key, or the Breakpoint button on the toolbar. You can also clear all break-points you have set with the Run ➤ Clear All Breakpoints item. This resets every breakpoint you have set, including those in global modules and those in CBF.

When Access halts your code at a breakpoint, you can choose where to continue execution. Placing the insertion point on any statement in the halted procedure and choosing Run ➤ Set Next Statement causes execution to begin at that statement when you continue the function. You cannot skip to another procedure in this fash-ion, though. If you are wading through several open code windows, the Run ➤ Show Next Statement item brings you back to the one where execution is paused.

When done with a particular debugging session, you can click the Reset button from the toolbar, press Shift+F5, or choose Run ➤ Reset. This halts the execution of all suspended procedures and reinitializes all variables. It clears the status of the currently running code so that there is no longer a current line of code, there is no current procedure, and all variables are reset.

Step Into versus Step Over

When a breakpoint has halted the execution of your function, you can continue to execute it in "slow motion" in two different ways:

- Choosing Run ➤ Step Into, pressing the F8 key, or clicking the Step Into tool-bar button causes your code to execute one statement at a time. If you're step-ping through your code in this fashion and the current line of code is a call to a user-defined procedure, Access opens that procedure's code on screen, and debugging proceeds there.

- Choosing Run ➤ Step Over, pressing Shift+F8, or clicking the Step Over toolbar button also executes code one line at a time, but only within the context of the current procedure. Calls to other procedures are considered atomic by the Step Over action; it executes the entire procedure at once. This is especially useful if your code calls code you've previously debugged. Rather than take the time to walk through the other procedures, which you're confident are in working order, you can use the Step Over functionality to execute them at full speed while you're debugging.

TIP

If you have more than one statement on a line, separated by colons, in your code, stepping through the code executes each of them in turn. The dashed box outline moves along each statement as it is executed.

NOTE

You can never step into code in a DLL. You *can* step into code in an Access code library; however, you cannot set a breakpoint in a code library. To debug a library, you must set a breakpoint in code in the current database and then single-step into the library code.

You can also use the Step to Cursor functionality to continue to a given line. In essence, it sets a temporary breakpoint at the current line, continues execution until the line is executed, and then reenters break mode.

Techniques and Strategies for Debugging

You can start developing a debugging strategy by understanding that bugs, despite the name, are not cute little things that scurry around in your code. Bugs are mistakes, pure and simple. And they're *your* mistakes; the program didn't put them there, and the end user didn't put them there. Removing these mistakes gives you an opportunity to become a better programmer.

Systematic Debugging

The first rule of debugging: You need a reproducible case to produce the error. If you cannot reproduce the error, you will have great difficulty tracking down the bug. You may get lucky and be in a situation where you can debug it when it happens, but if you can't reproduce it, your chances of fixing it are small. To reproduce the bug, you need as much information about the conditions that produced the bug as possible, but no more than that. If your users give you the hundred steps they performed that morning before the bug occurred, it makes your job difficult. Instead, if users limit the information to the essential three steps that actually cause the bug to occur, you can get somewhere. This isn't always that easy, though. Sometimes you can reproduce a bug only by following numerous steps or, for example, after the user has been using the application for four hours. As you can imagine, these types of bugs are much harder to find and fix.

The second rule of debugging: Debug data, not code. This means you should use the debugger and find out what the data is producing instead of staring at the code and speculating as to what it does. This seems a simple rule, but it is very effective at resolving bugs.

After you have found the bug but before you start fixing code, make sure you understand the nature of the problem. For example, a common error occurs when you declare variables to be of a specific simple datatype (Integer, Long, String, and so on) and, as part of your application, copy data from a table into these variables. In your own testing, everything works fine. At the client's site your client receives "Invalid Use of Null" messages.

There are two solutions to this problem, and each requires some understanding of the particular application. Clearly, you cannot place null values into Integer, Long, or String variables, so you might consider changing them all to variants. On the other hand, perhaps the solution is to disallow null entries into those particular fields in the table. Your decision on the solution needs to take into account the particular situation.

It seems obvious that you should change code only with a reason, but surprisingly, many programmers ignore this principle. "Experience" often masquerades as a reason when it is really a synonym for "wild guess." Don't just change your loop from

```
For intI = 0 To intCount - 1
```

to

```
For intI = 1 To intCount
```

until and unless you can point to your code and show exactly where and how the off-by-1 error is occurring. Take the time to thoroughly understand the bug before you try fixing it. Otherwise, you'll never know what you're fixing, and the bug will surely crop up somewhere else.

Finally, no matter how good you are and how sure you are of your work, make only one change to your code at a time, and then test it again. It's all too easy to fall into the trap of making multiple fixes without keeping records and then having to junk the current version and reload from a backup because you have no idea which things worked and which only made things worse. Take baby steps, and you'll get there faster.

There are two more bits of debugging strategy you might want to consider. Many programmers find "confessional debugging" to be one of the most useful techniques around. Confessional debugging works something like this: you grab your printouts and go into the next cubicle, interrupt the programmer working there, and say, "Hey, sorry to bother you, but I've got this function that keeps crashing. See, I pass in the name of a form here and then declare a form variable and then— oh, wait, that's not the form itself, but the form's name. Never mind; thanks for your help." When you get good at it, you can indulge in this sort of debugging with non-programmers as the audience or even (in times of desperation) by talking things through with your dog or a sympathetic (but bored) loved one.

Of course, there are times when confessing your code isn't enough. If you have the luxury of working with peers, use them. There's a good chance that other programmers can see the bug that you can't.

If all else fails, take a break. It's easy to get stuck in a mental loop in which you try the same things over and over, even though they didn't work the first time. Take a walk. Have lunch. Your mind's background processing can solve many bugs while the foreground processes are thinking about something else altogether. Many programmers have told stories of waking up in the middle of the night, having just dreamed about a bug they weren't even aware existed until then, along with its solution. Having written down the information during the night, they've gone into work, found the previously unspotted bug, and fixed it on the spot.

Debugging Difficulties

As you debug, you'll come across some particular problems you'll need to watch out for. Most of them equate to the software version of the Heisenberg Uncertainty Principle: Halting code to investigate it can change the state of your program, either introducing spurious bugs or (perhaps worse) hiding actual bugs. Unfortunately, there often isn't much you can do about these problems other than to know they exist. Try using Debug.Print statements to find the program's state when you run into these sorts of bugs.

Resetting the Stopped State

If you set up a function to present the user with a particular environment and then stop it midstream, the application often won't be in the proper environment for you to proceed with your debugging. For example, you may have left screen echo off, warnings off, or the hourglass cursor on. You may also be shipping code with the toolbars turned off and yet want them handy when you're debugging things. The simplest solution to this problem is to have a utility function available, either in your production database or loaded in a library, to reset the environment to a more hospitable state. Listing 16.21 shows a function (from basError in CH16.MDB) you could possibly attach to a keystroke, using an AutoKeys macro that will reset most of your environment. Once you've assigned this function to a keystroke, it's just a simple matter of pressing one key combination whenever you stop the code and can't quite see what you're doing.

Listing 16.21

```
Function glrCleanUp()
    ' Return the application to normal programming mode.
    ' Reinstate screen updating,
    ' reset the cursor to its normal state,
    ' and reset warnings.

    On Error GoTo glrCleanUpErr

    Application.Echo True
    DoCmd.Hourglass False
    DoCmd.SetWarnings True
    Application.SetOption "Built-In Toolbars Available", True

glrCleanUpDone:
```

```
    On Error GoTo 0
    Exit Function

glrCleanUpErr:
    MsgBox "Error " & Err.Number & ": " & Err.Description, _
      vbCritical, "glrCleanUp"
    Resume glrCleanUpDone
End Function
```

Avoid Screen.ActiveForm and Screen.ActiveControl

Code that refers to Screen.ActiveForm or Screen.ActiveControl won't work properly when called from the Debug window. When the Debug window has the focus, there is no active form or active control. Any attempt to access Screen.ActiveForm or Screen.ActiveControl from your code while debugging will result in an error. In event procedures, you can work around this limitation by using the Me object instead of Screen.ActiveForm.

Problems with Focus Events

If you are debugging forms that have event procedures tied to their GotFocus or LostFocus event, those events will be triggered as you move away from the form to the Debug window and back. If you are trying to debug such events, or other low-level events such as KeyDown or MouseMove, you can't use any of the standard debugging tools. Instead, think about sprinkling glrDebugMessageBox() calls into your code or even having the function dump status information continuously into a table or text file for later inspection.

Using Assertions

An *assertion* is a statement indicating that at a certain point the code should be in a certain state. If the code isn't in the expected state, an error message is reported.

Listing 16.12, presented earlier in this chapter, shows several examples of assertions. There is one function that has six consecutive assertions:

```
Public Function glrKeyMap(ByVal bytKey1 As Byte, _
  ByVal bytKey2 As Byte, ByVal bytKey3 As Byte) As Long
```

```
' This routine builds a long from three byte values. The
' byte order in the long is 0 K3 K2 K1. All unused keys
' should be set to zero. Each byte represents one of the
' resume constants defined by glrRESUME*. The result of
' this routine is used in the varKeyMap argument to
' glrErrorHandler.

    Call glrAssert(bytKey1 >= 0)
    Call glrAssert(bytKey1 <= glrRESUMEMAX)
    Call glrAssert(bytKey2 >= 0)
    Call glrAssert(bytKey2 <= glrRESUMEMAX)
    Call glrAssert(bytKey3 >= 0)
    Call glrAssert(bytKey3 <= glrRESUMEMAX)
    glrKeyMap = bytKey1 Or bytKey2 * 2 ^ 8 Or bytKey3 * 2 ^ 16
End Function
```

These assertions state that the values being passed in fall within a certain range. You use assertions to validate the normal functionality of the program. Listing 16.22 shows the procedure glrAssert.

Listing 16.22

```
#Const glrcFDebug = True
Public Sub glrAssert(f As Boolean)
#If glrcFDebug Then
    If f = False Then
        Stop
    End If
#End If
End Sub
```

The code in glrAssert simply indicates that if the value passed is False, the code should be stopped at that point. The value passed in is usually the evaluation of a comparison expression.

For another example of using assertions, suppose you have the routine shown in Listing 16.23.

Listing 16.23

```
Function BackupTape(ByVal lngMonth As Long) As String
    ' Part of a tape backup scheme. Reports a color of
    ' tape to use in rotation based on the month number
    ' passed in.
    '
```

```
' The constant glrcTapesPerYear indicates how many
' tapes are used in the rotation cycle.
'
' In:
'    lngMonth      A number between 1 and 12
'
' Out:
'    A string with the color tape to use in the backup
'
' Example:
'    MsgBox "Use the " & BackupTape(Month(Now)) & " backup
'    tape"
Dim strBackup As String
Const glrcTapesPerYear = 4

On Error GoTo BackupTapeErr
Call glrEnterProcedure("BackupTape")

' Assert that the month number is valid
Call glrAssert(lngMonth >= 1 And lngMonth <= 12)

' Select a backup tape based on the month
Select Case (lngMonth - 1) Mod glrcTapesPerYear
Case 0 ' January, May, September
    strBackup = "black"
Case 1 ' February, June, October
    strBackup = "red"
Case 2 ' March, July, November
    strBackup = "blue"
Case 3 ' April, August, December
    strBackup = "green"
Case Else
    ' We shouldn't ever reach here
    Call glrAssert(False)
End Select
BackupTape = strBackup
BackupTapeDone:
    Call glrExitProcedure("BackupTape")
Exit Function
BackupTapeErr:
    Dim errSave As glrerrSaveType
    Dim intResumeStatus As Integer
    Call glrSaveErr(errSave)
    intResumeStatus = glrHandleErr(errSave)
    Select Case intResumeStatus
```

```
        Case glrcResume
            Resume
        Case glrcResumeNext
            Resume Next
        Case glrcExitSub
            Resume BackupTapeDone
        Case Else
            Call glrAssert(False)
        End Select
Exit Function
End Function
```

The function BackupTape() determines a backup tape to use based on the month passed in, rotating among four colored tapes during the year. An assumption is made that the month number is between 1 and 12. Suppose the code that calls the function does something like this:

```
MsgBox "Use the " & BackupTape(Now) & "backup tape."
```

The Access function Now() returns a result that is the current date. Access will convert any date passed into a numeric datatype into the number of days since December 30th, 1899, with the part after the decimal indicating a fraction of 24 hours. When the result of Now() is passed into BackupTape(), the current date is converted into a number of days and the fractional part is dropped because we are passing into a Long. This is clearly not a number between 1 and 12. The assertion that the month number is to be between 1 and 12, using the line "Call glrAssert(lngMonth >= 1 And lngMonth <= 12)", means the code would stop immediately upon executing the statement. If the assertion were not there to catch it, the large number would be subjected to the Mod operator, forcing it within the range of 0 to 3. This converts the result of the Now() function into a valid month number. The code operates but does not give the result expected. This bug could be hard to track down if the assertion were not there.

Assertions put assumptions about your code into the code itself rather than relying on the programmer to always apply the assumption. Assertions are especially important when multiple programmers are working on a project, because the other programmers on the project probably won't know the assumptions the person writing the code has made unless they are explicit in the code. Assertions are like comments with the force of the compiler behind them.

In the Case Else statement of the previous example, the following code appeared:

```
' We shouldn't ever reach here
Call glrAssert(False)
```

Since an assertion of the value False always fails, this is a way of reporting an error about what should be unreachable code. It is useful to put in Case Else statements to trap for values that are unacceptable. As written, the code with this example will never be reached. But suppose someone changed the value of the constant TAPES_PER_YEAR from 4 to 6. Then the assertion would fail because there are no Case statements for the values 4 and 5 in the Select Case block.

Be sure to precede most assertions with a comment that describes why the assertion might fail: the month is out of range, the procedure name is not the same as the top of the stack, the code should never be reached, and so on. In some cases the comment might suggest how to fix the assertion. For example, it might suggest increasing the TAPES_PER_YEAR constant and adding more Case statements to the Case block.

Liberal use of assertions in your code will help in finding many logic errors. The trade-off is that they add slightly to the size and reduce the speed of your code.

Summary

As you develop code, you will run into each of the three types of errors. By using the techniques described in this chapter, you can make your life much simpler by producing robust and easily maintainable code. Follow these suggestions:

- Use a generic error-reporting procedure.
- Plan your code in advance.
- Don't get too "clever."
- Structure and comment your code.
- Use indentation and naming conventions.
- Modularize your code.
- Use Option Explicit.
- Minimize your use of variants.

- Use the tightest scoping possible.

- Use assertions.

When bug avoidance fails, make sure you use a systematic and structured approach to bug removal:

- Reproduce the bug.

- Debug data, not code.

- Confirm your diagnosis before you try to fix it.

- Change code only with a reason.

- Make only one change at a time.

The temptation is always present to attempt a quick-and-dirty fix rather than plod along with the systematic approach. Don't let yourself fall prey to this temptation. It usually wastes much more time than it saves, muddying the waters before it forces you back to the approach outlined in this chapter.

By using these techniques you can create code that will stand up to the beating your users will give it. If your code does fail, you can quickly locate the problem and resolve it with minimum effort.

CHAPTER
SEVENTEEN

Application Optimization

- Making your applications run more quickly

- Understanding and optimizing VBA's module loading

- Timing and comparing methods for solving a problem

As with any large Windows development environment, you can make choices when writing your own Access applications that will affect the performance of your application. How you create your queries, how you organize your tables, and how you write VBA code can all affect your application's speed. This chapter provides some suggestions about what you can do to make your Access applications work as well as possible.

Tuning Your Application's Performance

The faster your application and each of its components perform, the more usable it will be. No user (or developer) likes a slow application. But getting extra performance sometimes requires you to make trade-offs and may affect other aspects of the application's usability, stability, and maintainability. Thus, it's important to keep these other issues in mind as you tune your applications for speed.

Some of the many aspects of performance tuning are outlined here:

- Hardware and memory
- Access configuration
- Database design
- Query design
- Forms design
- Reports design
- Single-user versus multiuser, file-server versus client-server application design
- VBA coding

To create applications that perform well, you will have to address many, if not all, of these areas. Depending on the design of your application, some issues will be less important than others. For example, an application that has only one or two simple reports may not need much attention paid to this component. On the other hand, the same application may need a lot of attention in the areas of query and form tuning. This chapter addresses performance tuning, looking at each of the areas listed above.

Although we've provided some limited multiuser and client-server performance tips in this chapter, look in Chapters 12 and 14 for additional performance suggestions specific to those areas.

Speeding Up Access

Access is a complex piece of software made up of many components running on top of another complex piece of software—Windows. Hardware, of course, will also have a major impact on the speed of Windows.

Hardware and Windows Issues

Like most Windows-based programs, Access 95 runs more quickly on a faster machine. Microsoft recommends at a minimum a fast 386DX-based PC with at least 12MB of RAM on Windows 95 systems and 16MB of memory on Windows NT systems. This is really the *barest* of minimums, and you and your users will likely be dissatisfied with workstations of this nature. More realistically, the target machine should have

- At least a fast (33MHz or higher) 486-based processor
- 16MB or more of RAM (24MB when used on NT systems)

If you have to decide whether to get more RAM or a faster processor, we suggest you choose more RAM. For example, a 50MHz 486-based PC with 24MB of RAM will likely execute your applications more quickly than a 66MHz 486-based PC with 12MB of RAM.

For all installations you should also consider the following suggestions:

- Eliminate the loading of unused drivers and memory-resident utilities you rarely use.

- Remove screen savers, background pictures, and other unnecessary cycle-stealers.

- Eliminate disk-compression software, or at least consider placing your databases on noncompressed partitions. Access databases perform significantly more slowly on compressed partitions. Hard disk prices have fallen dramatically in the last few years; it may be time to buy an additional hard disk drive.

- Clean out your Windows 95 Recycle Bin regularly.

- Use a defrag utility regularly on your hard disks.

Configuring Access

You can adjust several global Access settings to improve application performance. Our recommendations include the following:

- Regularly compact your database. This arranges the data in the .MDB file so that it can be accessed most efficiently. Run a hard disk defrag utility before compacting. This ensures that your .MDB file is stored on disk in one contiguous file rather than a series of file fragments (which makes database operations less efficient).

- If an application is being used in single-user mode only, open it exclusively.

- If you've installed Microsoft Office 95, remove the Microsoft Office Fast Start and Microsoft Office Find Fast Indexer utilities from your startup group. These utilities run processes in the background that preload the OLE DLLs and make file searches faster, but they also use up valuable memory and processor time.

Speeding Up Queries and Recordsets

With Jet's sophisticated query optimizer, discussed in Chapter 4, you don't have to be concerned about the order of columns and tables in queries. The Jet query optimizer decides on the most efficient query strategy and reorders the query's tables and columns to best optimize the query. You can, however, help the optimizer by following these simple guidelines:

- Create indexes on all columns used in query joins, restrictions, and sorts.

- Use primary keys instead of unique indexes whenever possible. Primary key indexes disallow nulls, giving the Jet query optimizer additional join choices.

- Use unique indexes instead of non-unique indexes whenever possible. Jet can then better optimize queries because statistics on unique indexes are more accurate.

- Include as few columns as possible in the result set. The fewer columns returned, the faster the query, especially if you can completely eliminate columns from a table that is necessary only for restricting records.

- Refrain from using complex expressions, such as those involving the IIf() function, in queries. If you are using nested queries (queries based on the results of other queries), try to move up any expressions to the highest (last) query.

- Use Count(*) instead of Count([*column*]). Jet has built-in optimizations that make Count(*) much faster than column-based counts.

- Use the Between operator in restriction clauses rather than open-ended >, >=, <, and <= restrictions. This returns fewer rows. For example, use "Age Between 35 and 50" rather than "Age >= 35".

- When creating restrictions on join columns that are present in both tables in a one-to-many join, it is sometimes more efficient to place the restriction on the "one" side of the join. Other times it might be more efficient to place the restriction on the "many" side. You'll have to test which is more efficient for each query since the ratio of the sizes of the tables and the number and type of restrictions used determine which is more efficient.

- Normalize your tables, decomposing large non-normalized tables into smaller normalized ones. Since this reduces the size of tables (and therefore the number of pages required to hold tables), it causes join strategies that involve table scans to execute more quickly.

- In some instances, it might also help to *denormalize* databases to reduce the number of joins needed to run frequently used queries. (See Chapter 3 for additional design details.)

- When you have the option of constructing a query using either a join or a subquery, it's worth trying both options. In some cases you will find the solution that employs the join to be faster; in other cases the subquery-based solution will be faster.

- Avoid using outer joins if possible because they require a complete scan of the entire preserved table (the "left" table in a left outer join).

- For nontrivial queries, use saved queries instead of SQL because these queries will have already been optimized.

- Manually recompile queries when the size of tables or the presence or type of indexes has changed. (See "Forcing Jet to Recompile and Optimize a Query" in Chapter 4 for details.)

- When possible, use action queries instead of looping through recordsets in VBA to update or delete batches of data.

- When you need to use a snapshot recordset and you don't need to move backward in the recordset, use a forward-scrolling snapshot.

- When you only wish to add new rows to a recordset, open the recordset using the dbAppendOnly option.

When in doubt, experiment and benchmark various potential solutions. Don't assume one way to do it is faster just because it *should* be or because someone told you it was.

The Undocumented Show Plan Option

Jet 3.0 includes an undocumented option that allows you to turn on the logging of query optimization plan information to a text file. To enable this option, you must create the following Registry key using the RegEdit program:

HKEY_LOCAL_MACHINE\SOFTWARE\Microsoft\Jet\3.0\Engines\Debug

Add the "JETSHOWPLAN" string value to this key and set it equal to "ON".

Restart Access and open a database, and Jet begins to log query optimization plan information to the file SHOWPLAN.OUT.

A sampling of the showplan log is shown here:

```
--- qryCustomerItems ---

01) Inner Join table 'tblMenu' to table 'tblOrderDetails'
       using index 'tblOrderDetails!
       tblMenu1tblOrderDetails1'
       join expression "tblMenu.MenuId=
       tblOrderDetails.MenuId"
02) Inner Join result of '01)' to table 'tblOrder'
       using index 'tblOrder!PrimaryKey'
       join expression "tblOrderDetails.OrderId=
       tblOrder.OrderId"
03) Sort result of '02)'
04) Outer Join table 'tblCustomer' to result of '03)'
       using temporary index
       join expression "tblCustomer.CustomerId=
       qryItems.CustomerId"
05) Sort result of '04)'
```

You'll likely find the discussion of Jet query optimization helpful in interpreting the showplan results. Examining the showplan log for poorly performing queries should help you in determining how best to optimize these queries.

Showplan is completely undocumented and unsupported by Microsoft and should be treated like any other unsupported feature: with care. Here are some of the issues to consider when using it:

- If you close a database and open another database without exiting and restarting Access, the query plans for the new database will not be logged.

- The plans for some queries Access uses internally will appear in the log.

- The logging of plan information may adversely affect performance.

- The log file may get very large. You'll need to empty it out every so often.

- Showplan doesn't log the plan information for parameter queries and may log the information for other queries incorrectly.

To stop the logging of showplan information, set the JETSHOWPLAN Registry key to "OFF".

Speeding Up Forms

Most Access applications revolve around forms, so it goes without saying that any improvements to the performance of forms will realize large gains in the usability of your applications. The following sections detail several areas to consider when optimizing your forms.

Limiting a Form's RecordSource with Large Recordsets

It's tempting to create forms in Access that are based on a huge recordset of tens or hundreds of thousands of records. However, you will quickly discover a severe performance penalty when opening such forms or attempting to navigate to a different record using the FindFirst method. The problems are exacerbated when you attempt to use these types of forms in a networked environment, where forms will likely be retrieving remote data.

The solution is simple. Rather than giving users *all* the records and navigating around the form's dynaset, set up the form to serve up a single record (or some small subset of records) at a time. Then, instead of using the FindFirst method to move to a different record, change the form's RecordSource property. (Chapter 12 includes an example of this technique in the section "The Wire.")

Speeding Up Combo Boxes with Many Rows

Microsoft has improved the performance of combo boxes for Access 95, but you still need to be careful about creating combo boxes containing too many records. Unless users are running your application on very fast machines or have a lot of patience, you will find combo boxes inappropriate for row sources with more than several thousand rows.

Consider alternative ways of presenting the same data. For example, consider reworking the form so that the combo box is not grabbing so many rows. You might use other controls on the form to refine the search and reduce the number of rows in the combo box's row source. For example, have the user enter an employee's territory into a territory control to reduce the number of entries in an EmployeeId combo box.

Although the AutoExpand functionality Access provides for combo boxes is very popular with end users, it adds a large amount of overhead. Combo boxes will react to keystrokes more quickly if you turn off this property. (See Chapter 7 for more information.)

Other Form Speed-Up Tricks

Other things you can do to speed up your forms or reduce their memory usage include the following:

- Instead of opening and closing forms, load often-used forms hidden and make them visible and invisible. This uses up more memory and system resources, so you have to balance this technique against memory considerations.

- Reduce the complexity of forms. Break complex forms into multiple pages or multiple forms.

- Place controls containing memo and bound OLE objects on pages of a form other than the first or on ancillary forms that can be popped up using a command button. This allows users to browse quickly through records when they don't need to view these complex objects.

- If your form contains static pictures stored in Unbound Object Frame controls, convert them to use the new lightweight Image controls instead. To do this, right-click the control and select Change To ➤ Image.

TIP   You may find the Performance Analyzer Add-In (Tools ➤ Analyze ➤ Performance) helpful in locating and correcting performance bottlenecks in your application. Although its usefulness is somewhat limited, you may find it highlights problems you never thought of checking.

Speeding Up Reports

If you're creating complex reports, you may find they seemingly take hours to print. One reason for this is that Access creates a separate query for each section of the report. Many of the suggestions found in the section "Speeding Up Queries and Recordsets" earlier in this chapter also apply here since this is often more an issue of the underlying queries. In addition, you can try the following suggestions to improve report performance:

- Move query expressions onto the report.

- Avoid situations in which one query pulls the data from tables and a second query just filters the data. The more information you can pull together into one query, the better. One query uses less memory.

- Avoid including fields in the query that aren't used in the final output of the report.

- If you're using subreports, look at the queries on which they're based. Generally, subreports should not be based on the same query as the main report. If they are, try rethinking your design so you can work without the subreport.

- Add subreports to replace multiple expressions that call domain functions such as DLookup() or DSum(). By using a subreport, you can often get the same functionality you get with the slower domain functions, without using any expressions.

Optimizing VBA's Use of Modules and Compilation

Let's face it: when you first convert Access 2 applications to Access 95, they run more slowly. Jet is much faster in its 32-bit incarnation, but the Access user interface just isn't as perky as it used to be. Although specific portions are faster (combo boxes, especially), the whole package seems slower. Part of the slowdown can be attributed to the forms and reports engine, but a large portion may be due to the way Access and VBA interact. This section of the chapter explains some of the major issues involved in working with VBA, and the next, "Speeding Up VBA: Testing Hypotheses," suggests some specific ways you can speed up VBA code.

Understanding How VBA and Compilation Work

Instead of being a tokenized, interpreted language, as was Access Basic, VBA is a compiled language. Although this advancement promises a great deal of power in the future, it may be more of a drag in the present. This section, through a series of questions and answers, explains the issues involved with compilation of your VBA code and what you can do to control it.

How Does VBA Load Code?

In Access 2, when you loaded an application, Access loaded all the global modules into memory at startup. Form and report modules were loaded as necessary, but the global modules were always available, having been loaded when the application loaded. This meant that although application load time might be longer, form and report loading could, at worst, cause the form or report module to be loaded. Of course, loading a large module takes time; the code must be loaded from the disk and read into memory.

VBA loads code when it's needed. In Access 95, only modules called during the application's startup sequence are loaded as the application loads. That is, only modules that are needed by the startup form (or the macro called at startup) are loaded with the application. Then, as your application calls various procedures, VBA loads the appropriate modules, as well as modules containing any procedures or variables used by those procedures when they're needed. Certainly, for applications with large amounts of code, this "load on demand" feature allows faster load times. On the other hand, it will possibly contribute to slower form and report load times: as Access loads each object, it might also need to load global modules called by procedures in the form or report module.

VBA always loads an entire module if it needs any portion of the module. If it must use any procedure in a module, it loads the entire module. The same goes for a variable in a module: if your code attempts to set or retrieve the value of a variable in a module, VBA must load the entire module. This, too, can contribute to application slowdowns if you haven't planned accordingly.

Why Compile Code?

VBA must compile the code at some point before it can run the code. If the code hasn't been previously compiled, VBA must compile it on the fly, as needed. That is, as you open forms or reports with uncompiled code, VBA must compile the form/report module before Access can open the object. To make matters worse, it must also compile any code the form or report module calls, all the way down the call tree. You can certainly see that this would cause your forms or reports to open more slowly.

What Gets Stored When Your Code Is Compiled?

When VBA compiles your code, it stores both the original, tokenized text (it doesn't store it exactly as you type it but stores a tokenized version) and the compiled version. When Access prepares to run previously compiled code, it loads just the compiled version into memory and runs that compiled code. For uncompiled code, Access must load the original version into memory and then compile the code as needed.

When Should You Compile Loaded Modules?

When you choose the Run ➤ Compile Loaded Modules menu item, you're instructing VBA to compile only the modules that are currently loaded, including any form and report modules. Using this menu item is equivalent to choosing the Compile Loaded Modules toolbar icon. Because this action compiles only the loaded modules, it's possible that even if you've compiled all the loaded modules, some saved modules will not yet have been compiled. These uncompiled modules could contain syntax errors that won't show up until you actually run the code. Use this menu item (or toolbar icon) to check for syntax errors in the code you're working on; it's the fastest way to do so.

When Should You Compile All Modules?

The Run ➤ Compile All Modules menu item opens and compiles every module in your application, including the form and report modules. It performs a complete syntax check, as well. This is the only way to completely compile your application, and you must perform this action before distributing any application. If you continue to test your application using only Compile Loaded Modules, you may not be trying all the execution paths, which means that code you haven't worked on recently might contain a compile error.

You should consider the Compile All Modules action a waste of time, especially for large applications, until you're done writing code. When you're working on the application, you're guaranteed that the code will be in a decompiled state, and compiling all the modules in a large application can be quite time consuming. Use Compile Loaded Modules unless you're ready to distribute the application or when you want to check the performance of the application. (Because running uncompiled code is always slower than running compiled code, you can't judge the actual performance until you've compiled all the modules.) Be sure to use Compile All Modules when you first import an Access 2 application, to find code that requires modification for Access 95.

After you've used the Compile All Modules menu item, be sure to use File ➤ Save All Modules (see the section "What Does Save All Modules Do?" later in this chapter for more information) to save the compiled state.

How Does the Tools ➤ Options ➤ Module ➤ Compile On Demand Option Fit In?

When the Compile On Demand option is checked (and that's the default for the option; it comes this way, out of the box), VBA compiles only the code it must compile in order to run the current function and all its dependents. Although this does speed the development process somewhat (VBA isn't compiling code it doesn't need to compile for the current execution path), it's just delaying the inevitable. Sooner or later you must compile all your code. What's more, unless you understand the ramifications of this option, it can get you into trouble by leading you to believe your code is correct when, in fact, it's not.

To see the Compile On Demand option in action, follow these steps:

1. Use the Tools ➤ Options ➤ Module menu item to make sure the Compile On Demand option is turned on.

2. Create a new module, and enter the following code into it:

```
Function Test1()
    Test1 = Test2()
End Function
```

3. Create a second module, and enter the following code (which should cause a compilation error because the function Test4() doesn't exist):

```
Function Test2()
    Test2 = 1
End Function

Function Test3()
    Test3 = Test4()
End Function
```

4. In the Debug window, type the following, causing VBA to run Test1(). Note that this doesn't trigger a compilation error, even though the code is not correct, because you've turned on Compile On Demand and you didn't demand that Test3() be compiled.

```
? Test1()
```

5. Go back to the Tools ➤ Options ➤ Module dialog and turn off the Compile On Demand option.

6. In the Debug window, repeat step 4. Note that there's still no error, because you're running code that's already compiled.

7. Modify Test1() so it looks like the code below, and then run it in the Debug window, as in step 4. Now you'll trigger a compile error because you've turned off Compile On Demand and caused the code to be recompiled.

```
Function Test1()
    Test1 = Test2()
    Debug.Print 1
End Function
```

What Does Save All Modules Do?

The File ➤ Save All Modules menu item (available only when you're editing a module) saves the compiled state of all your modules. Access will now have saved both the original tokenized version and the compiled version. In addition, Access will track internally that all the modules are compiled and won't attempt to recompile anything before running your application. You should always choose this option after you use the Run ➤ Compile All Modules item. If you don't use this menu item, your modules' compiled state will be lost, and VBA will have to recompile before running the application. (If Run ➤ Compile All Modules had no effect because there had been no new changes to the code since it was last compiled, the Save All Modules menu item won't be available.)

What Causes Code to Be Decompiled?

Decompilation is the VBA programmer's curse. Compiling code can take time, and it happens when you least want it to occur—when you're trying to get your application started. To avoid decompilation of your code, you must know when it occurs and what causes it.

Access marks your VBA as being decompiled anytime you save a change to an object that might affect VBA code: forms, reports, controls, or modules. If you modify a form (or a report) or its controls, modify code in a global or CBF module, or delete or rename any of these objects, you'll cause Access to tell VBA that your code needs recompilation. If you make a change but don't save it, you'll preserve the compiled state.

VBA stores the project name (in Access' case, that's the name of the database file but not its path) as part of its compilation status. Therefore, if you change the name of a compiled application, Access sees it as being decompiled and forces VBA to re-compile the entire application next time it's loaded. (Remember, if you never save the compiled state using the File ➤ Save All Modules menu item, the application will be recompiled on the fly each time it's run.) This problem is exacerbated by the fact that most Access developers compact their databases into a new database, with a new name. If you do this you'll lose the compilation state of your modules. (You can solve this problem by renaming the compacted file back to its original name before reloading it.) Therefore, if you want to preserve the compiled state of your modules, you must also preserve the name of the database. The location doesn't matter—just the actual name of the database itself.

What Are the Effects of Compilation on Memory and Disk Usage?

Compiled applications require more disk space. As mentioned above, when you compile all the modules, VBA stores both the decompiled and the compiled code in your database. On the other hand, compiled applications require less memory because VBA loads only the compiled code when it runs the application. If you attempt to compile code on the fly, VBA must load the decompiled code and then compile it as it runs.

Are Modules Ever Removed from Memory?

No, modules are not removed from memory until you close the application. VBA loads modules into memory as it needs them. Once a module has been loaded, it's never removed from memory. That is, VBA supports dynamic loading of modules but doesn't support dynamic unloading. Don't forget that VBA will load a module if you reference either a procedure or a variable in that module.

During the development process, this dynamic loading of modules can cause memory usage to grow and free RAM to shrink. You may want to close and reopen the database occasionally to release the memory. Using the Run ➤ Compile All Modules menu item causes all the modules to be loaded into memory; make sure you close and reopen the database after compiling all the modules.

What You Can Do to Optimize the Use of Modules

Once you understand how VBA works with modules, you may want to take some extra steps to make your modules work as efficiently as possible. From VBA's point of view, there are two types of applications: static and dynamic. Static applications, the kind most developers write, do not allow end users to create new forms, reports, or modules or to modify controls. That is, these types of applications let users add, edit, and retrieve information but not modify the design of any user-interface objects. These types of applications can maintain their compiled state.

The second type, dynamic applications, allows users to modify the design of forms, reports, and modules and will most likely never manage to stay compiled. These applications will benefit from the suggestions for static applications but will need some extra effort, as well.

Static Applications

The following suggestions will help optimize either a static or dynamic application. Due to the overwhelming overhead of decompilation, however, they'll have a larger impact on static applications.

Create Streamlined Modules   Although it may sound obvious, try to minimize the amount of extraneous code in each module. Because VBA always loads a full module to reference any procedure in that module, the less code it must load, the more quickly your forms and reports will open. Try to move unnecessary procedures from your modules, and group procedures, if possible, by their use. Don't forget that referring to a variable in a module will also cause VBA to load that module. The goal is to load as little code as possible at any given moment.

Minimize the Number of Modules VBA Opens   When a form or report loads, VBA must load all the modules containing any procedures that form or report's module uses, all the way down the call tree. Each module, as it loads, forces VBA to load any modules containing procedures it calls. Your application will load more quickly if you simplify your call paths: try to group procedures so that VBA doesn't have to load as many modules when you load your forms or reports.

"Popular" global routines should be separated out into their own modules so that no "unpopular" code is loaded at the same time. The same goes for global variables since referencing their values will also cause their module to be loaded.

For example, imagine Module1, which contains four procedures, all of which call VeryUsefulFunction() in Module2. Module2 contains a number of other procedures, which also call VeryUsefulFunction(). When a form calls a procedure in Module1, VBA must also load Module2, which contains many procedures your form doesn't need. If you'd placed VeryUsefulFunction() into a new module, VBA would have to load only Module1 and the new module when you load your form, leaving the larger Module2 on disk until you need the procedures there.

Use Application.Run to Open Modules at Run Time   If you want finer control over the way VBA loads modules into memory, you can write your code in such a way that VBA loads code only when you request it. The trade-offs are significant, but you'll get your wish! Access supplies the Run method of its Application object, which allows you to run a procedure, given the name of the project and the routine to run. This way, the code for the procedure isn't loaded into memory until the moment it's first run instead of when Access loads the module that calls it.

For more information on using Application.Run and on using library databases in general, see the sections starting with "Creating Library Databases" in Chapter 23.

You can use the Eval( ) function, discussed later in this chapter, to achieve the same effect. Eval( ) can run only functions, not subroutines, but it can return a value from the function it called, which Application.Run cannot.

Using Application.Run does introduce some limitations, however, as follows:

- Although you can call functions using Application.Run, Access will always disregard the return value of the function.

- Application.Run cannot accept parameters that are user-defined types. If you must pass a user-defined type through Application.Run, you'll need to have it call a procedure with no parameters and pass the parameters in global variables.

- The project file containing the procedure you're calling must either be open already or be located in the path specified in the RefLibPath key in the Registry. (See Chapter 23 for more information.) Usually, this key will point to the directory in which Access has been installed (and if you change the Registry key, Access won't be able to find the Wizards unless you change their location to match the Registry key).

- If you modify the RefLibPath Registry key, the project must have .MDA as its file extension.

Dynamic Applications

In some applications you must allow users to create forms, reports, or modules. In these cases you cannot maintain the compiled state of your code, and it will normally remain decompiled. You can take some actions to improve the performance, however. The following sections make some suggestions on ways to make the best of this difficult situation.

Separate Dynamic (Decompiled) Code from Static (Compiled) Code

In applications that depend heavily on code in standard modules (as opposed to code in form/report modules), you may be able to achieve a happy medium that allows the bulk of your code to remain compiled, even though users make changes that would normally decompile the code. Consider separating your application into two (or more) databases. Place your compiled code into a database that's loaded as a library, and leave the user-interface objects in a database your users load. That way the code in the library database can remain compiled, yet users can make changes to the database as they need without affecting the compiled state. (For more information on creating a library database, see Chapter 23.)

The disadvantage of this compromise is that your users will need to create a reference to this library in order to use its code. As discussed in Chapter 23, you cannot create the database reference programmatically; it must be done manually. Because of the overhead of creating the library reference, you'll want to use this technique only when you have a large investment in standard module code that you want to keep compiled while users make compilation-unfriendly changes to the user interface.

Don't Bother Compiling   If your users will be making changes to the design of your application (adding forms or reports, for example), there's not much point in delivering a compiled version. As soon as a user makes a change, your code loses its compiled state. Removing the compiled code will save disk space when you distribute the application.

To remove all traces of the compiled code, follow these steps:

1. Create a new database.

2. Import all the objects from your original database into the new database.

3. Compact the new database.

One More Consideration: No Circular References in Libraries

Because of a design limitation of VBA, Access libraries do not support circular references. No matter how you try to obfuscate the path, no procedure can call another procedure that ends up calling a procedure in the original module. Even if you call procedures in other modules along the way, the procedure call will fail if it eventually calls a procedure in the original module. You will need to design your library database in such a way that you don't require circular references. One unfortunate solution is to place duplicate copies of procedures in multiple modules. (See Chapter 23 for more information on using library databases.)

What Else Can You Do?

There's no simple solution to maintaining the compiled state of your applications. You'll need to take special steps, and this will add extra overhead to your development process. The difference between running compiled code and decompiled code is quite obvious, even for moderate-sized applications, so it's worth taking the time to ensure that your applications are compiled when you need them to be.

Once you've tackled the major issues, you'll want to investigate ways to speed up the VBA code itself. The next portion of this chapter investigates some techniques you can use to improve the performance of the code. No such list could be exhaustive, and we've selected a series of ideas that we thought would make a difference in VBA code. The interesting part is that some things we *thought* would matter actually don't. In addition, some enhancements that made a small difference in Access 2 now make a very large difference in the speed of your VBA code.

Speeding Up VBA: Testing Hypotheses

As in any programming language, in VBA there are often many ways to accomplish the same task. Because you're dealing not only with a language but also with the interface and the underlying data, all tied together in the language, the choices are often even more complicated than with other, more standard languages. The following sections propose a series of random optimizations, some more potent than others, and some that are based on incorrect assumptions (that is, they *don't* help at all, and perhaps they hurt). Probably no single application will be able to use each of these, but you can add the ones that help to your "bag of tricks" as you program in Access. You'll also find a method for timing those optimizations so you can create your own test cases.

Creating a Stopwatch

Although you could use the VBA Timer() function to calculate the time a specific process requires, it's probably not the wisest choice. Because it measures time in seconds since midnight, it's not terribly accurate. Even though you'll most likely be timing intervals larger than a single second, you'll want a bit more accuracy than the Timer() function can provide. The Windows API provides the timeGetTime() function (aliased as glr_apiGetTime() in the sample code), which returns the number of milliseconds that have passed since Windows was started.

NOTE Not that it matters for testing purposes, but Timer() "rolls over" every 24 hours. timeGetTime() keeps on ticking for up to 49 days before it resets the returned tick count to 0. Most likely, if you're timing something that runs for 49 days, you're not terribly interested in milliseconds, but that's what you get.

To test each of the proposed optimizations, you need some mechanism for starting and stopping the clock. The subroutine glrStartTimer stores the current return value from glr_apiGetTime() into a global variable, lngStartTime. You must call this subroutine directly before any code you want to have timed. When you're done with the critical section of code, call the function glrEndTimer(), which returns the difference between the current time and the time when you called glrStartTimer, or the elapsed time. Listing 17.1 shows the declarations and code for the timer functions.

Listing 17.1

```
Private Declare Function glr_apiGetTime Lib "winmm.dll" _
 Alias "timeGetTime" () As Long
Dim lngStartTime As Long

Sub glrStartTimer()
    lngStartTime = glr_apiGetTime()
End Sub

Function glrEndTimer()
    glrEndTimer = glr_apiGetTime() - lngStartTime
End Function
```

> **NOTE**
>
> Most Windows programmers have used the GetTickCount( ) function in previous versions of Windows to perform their high-resolution timing. Although that function returned its result in milliseconds, it was never more accurate than the clock timer in your PC, which measures time in increments of $\frac{1}{18}$ second. The timeGetTime( ) function, introduced in Windows 3.0 as part of the multimedia extensions, uses a different hardware timer and can actually measure time with millisecond accuracy. Before Windows 95 and Windows NT, you couldn't have been sure your users had the correct multimedia DLLs on their system. With the new operating systems, you're assured that all users will have the necessary DLLs, and you can use timeGetTime( ) without worry.

Getting Reasonable Results

You will find that running any given test only once doesn't provide reliable results. There are just too many external forces in play when you're running under Windows. To get a reasonable idea of the benefit of a given optimization test, you need to run the test code many times within the given test case and then run the test case many times, averaging the results. For simplicity, each of the tests in this chapter takes as its only parameter a Long value indicating the number of times you want to run the test. Each function loops the specified number of times with the clock running and provides the elapsed time as the return value of the function.

If you want to add your own tests to this test mechanism, you must follow those constraints when planning your tests. In addition, for each test case, you need two versions: a "slow" version (labeled Test1a() in this example) and a "fast" version (labeled Test1b() in this example). Once you've provided the two functions, you can call the function glrRunTests(), which, in turn, calls both functions the specified number of times. glrRunTests() averages the elapsed times the functions return and reports on the comparative speed of the two functions. Listing 17.2 shows the glrRunTests() function. Notice that glrRunTests() takes four parameters, as shown in Table 17.1. glrRunTests() returns an Integer indicating the comparison between the first and second functions, measured as a percentage:

```
intAmount = Int((varResults1 - varResults2) / _
 varResults2 * 100)
```

TABLE 17.1: glrRunTest(s) Parameters

Parameter	Description	Datatype
strFunc1	Name of the "slow" function to test	String expression
strFunc2	Name of the "fast" function to test	String expression
varReptFunc	Number of times to repeat the function call	Variant
varReptOp	Number of times to repeat the operation in the function	Variant

In addition, glrRunTests() prints a string to the Debug window (so it's useful without an interface, for informal testing), like this:

```
Test1a vs. Test1b: 3.7       0.7            428%
```

This output shows the milliseconds elapsed while running each function, followed by the percentage improvement in the faster function.

For example, to call glrRunTests() to test functions Test1a() and Test1b(), running each function 10 times to average the results and having each function loop internally 10,000 times, call glrRunTests() like this:

```
strResult = glrRunTests("Test1a", "Test1b", 10, 10000)
```

Listing 17.2

```
Function glrRunTests(strFunc1 As String, strFunc2 As String, _
  varReptFunc As Variant, varReptOp As Variant) As Variant

    Dim varI As Variant
    Dim varResults1 As Variant
    Dim varResults2 As Variant
    Dim varDiff As Variant
    Dim intAmount As Integer
    Dim strResult As String
    Dim varTemp As Variant

    For varI = 0 To varReptFunc - 1
        varTemp = SysCmd(acSysCmdSetStatus, "Running " & _
          strFunc1 & "() Pass " & varI)
        varResults1 = varResults1 + Eval(strFunc1 & _
          "(" & varReptOp & ")")
    Next varI
```

```
    For varI = 0 To varReptFunc - 1
        varTemp = SysCmd(acSysCmdSetStatus, "Running " & _
         strFunc2 & "() Pass " & varI)
        varResults2 = varResults2 + Eval(strFunc2 _
         & "(" & varReptOp & ")")
    Next varI
    varResults1 = varResults1 / varReptFunc
    varResults2 = varResults2 / varReptFunc

    varDiff = varResults1 - varResults2
    If Abs(varDiff) < 0.005 Then varDiff = 0

    ' Better check for division by 0 and
    ' overflow, both of which can occur from
    ' a very small value in varResults1.
    On Error GoTo glrRunTestsError
    intAmount = Int((varResults1 - varResults2) / _
     varResults2 * 100)
    Debug.Print strFunc1 & " vs. " & strFunc2 & ":"; _
     varResults1, varResults2, intAmount & "%"
    glrRunTests = intAmount

glrRunTestsExit:
    ' Clear the status line.
    varTemp = SysCmd(acSysCmdClearStatus)
    Exit Function

glrRunTestsError:
    MsgBox Error, vbExclamation, "glrRunTests()"
    glrRunTests = 0
    Resume glrRunTestsExit
End Function
```

Using the Eval() Function

glrRunTests() uses the Eval() function to execute each of the two tests. (See Chapter 7 for more information on the Eval() function.) As a reminder, the Eval() function takes as a parameter a string containing code you want Access to execute. If you intend to use Eval() to execute functions, you should be aware of the various limitations involved in using this technique.

- Access performs no error checking on the string you send to Eval(). If it works, great. If not, you get, at best, a "User Defined Error" message. At worst, you crash (and lose data). You would be wise to check the string you're about to send to Eval() by using MsgBox or Debug.Print to display the string before its execution. This way you can verify that the string to be executed is, in fact, laid out exactly as you think it ought to be.

- Scoping rules are always an issue. Eval() cannot interpret any local variables, nor can it handle private functions. You can remember the rules this way: any object you want to send to Eval() must also work in macros. Just as VBA variables aren't available in macros, they aren't available once Eval() gets hold of the string to be executed. glrRunTests() uses local variables, but they become part of the string passed to Eval() and are passed as values, not as variable names.

- The string you pass to Eval() must represent a function that returns a value of some sort. That value will be the return value from the call to Eval(). Neither subroutines nor expressions are allowed.

> **NOTE**
>
> The effectiveness of each of the optimizations that follow depends on many factors, including the actual code in use at the time, the relative speed of your hard disk versus the processor in your computer, and other programs currently using Windows' memory and resources. Using Windows 95 or Windows NT and Access 95 makes the issues even more complex than they were when using Access 2. There might be a process running in the background that you're not aware of, and Access 95 and Jet both provide their own internal caching. The only sure way to provide accurate timings would be to remove all background processes and to reboot between each timing. That's not practical, so we'll mention again that the timing results presented here are for comparison only. You'll need to decide for yourself in some of the marginal cases whether the optimization will really help. Therefore, a word of warning: take any suggestions of optimizations with a grain of salt. Try them out in your own applications before swearing by them. As they say in the auto industry, "These numbers are for comparison only. Your mileage may vary."

Nineteen Possible Optimizations

In this section we present 19 optimizations, in no particular order. Some will actually make a difference in your applications; others are interesting ideas we thought might make a difference (and used to, in Access 2) but no longer actually do. We've left in the "losers," mostly to indicate that some perceived optimizations just don't help. To test each hypothesis, we've created two similar versions of a simple function. CH17.MDB includes the full source for both versions of each test so you can try them out yourself.

To simplify your experiments with the test cases we present here, you can use frmRunTests from CH17.MDB. Figure 17.1 shows this form in use. It includes a combo box from which you can choose the specific test case to run and spin buttons allowing you to specify how many loops to execute inside the routine, as well as how many times to call each routine. (See Chapter 7 for more information on creating your own spin buttons.) The View Slower and View Faster buttons pop up forms that pull the source code for the functions from memo fields in the underlying table, so you can look at the code as you test. Finally, the clock button starts the test, running the slow version as many times as you've requested and then running the faster version the same number of times.

Clearly, this method of testing is far from perfect. The order in which you run the tests might make a difference, and Access, Jet, and the operating system caches all make a difference, too. In our informal testing (and that's all this can be—measurements of relative differences), none of these factors made much difference. Reversing the order of the tests made almost no difference. Remember, the goal of these

FIGURE 17.1:

frmRunTests allows you to choose a specific test and run it, resulting in a comparison between the slow and fast versions.

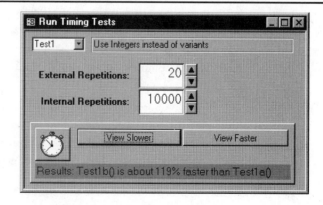

tests is to determine which of two methods is faster, not to gather exact timings. In each case we ran the tests on a Pentium 120 with 32MB of memory. (Some of the differences may disappear or reverse in low-memory situations as things are swapped back and forth from your Windows swap file.) The percentage differences we found depend totally on the specific tests we ran and the setup of our system, but we've tried to make them representative of the kinds of improvements you'd see, too.

The results of our performance tests are summarized in Table 17.2.

TABLE 17.2: Summary of the Results of the Access Basic Performance Tests

Test Number	Optimization	Approximate Effectiveness of Speedup
1	Integer variables instead of variants	around 100%
2	Integer division instead of real division	< 5%
3	Logical assignments instead of If…Then	10–30%
4	Len() for testing for zero-length strings	45–55%
5	"Not var" to toggle True/False	30–60%
6	timeGetTime() instead of Timer()	5000–7000% (no kidding!)
7	Use object variables	150–200%
8	Use implicit logical comparisons	Negligible
9	Refer to controls by number in loops	5–10%
10	IsCharAlphaNumeric instead of Asc()	500%
11	Transactions	Depends on your code and the amount of data affected
12	If…Then…Else instead of IIf()	Depends on your code
13	CreateQueryDef() instead of RunSQL	25–35%
14	For Each…Next instead of For…Next	30–40%
15	Remove comments from code	No improvement
16	Use bookmarks rather than FindFirst to find rows	> 300%
17	Drop default collection names in expressions	30–50%
18	Refresh collections only when necessary	1500–2000% (depends on the number of objects)
19	Use DBEngine(0)(0) instead of CurrentDb()	500–1000%

Some of the comparisons are more dependent than others on the assumptions made. For example, Test2, which evaluates the difference between using Integer and real division, couldn't be constructed in too many different ways. It's doubtful you'd get results differing much from those in Table 17.2 by rewriting the code. On the other hand, Test11, which compares making updates to a table with and without using transactions, will give widely differing results depending on the number of columns and rows updated within the transaction, the size of the data operated on, and any changes you've made to the default Jet settings in your Registry. Thus, it's important to be aware of the assumptions made for each test when interpreting the results.

We haven't duplicated the test code here. We've described the tests and the concepts involved, but you'll need to investigate CH17.MDB to see the exact details of the tests. In any case, you're very unlikely to use the specific code we've written in your own applications; it's the concepts that count. For each test case, the name of the procedure in basTests in CH17.MDB is TestNa (the presumed slow version) or TestNb (the supposedly faster version), where N is the test number. For example, the code corresponding to test case 5 is Test5a and Test5b.

Test 1: Use Integers Instead of Variants Whenever Possible?

Unless you specify otherwise, Access creates all variables using its default type, Variant. To hold data of any simple type, variants must be at least as big and complex as any of the types they can contain. "Big and complex" equates with "slower," so avoid variants if at all possible. Of course, there will be many times when you can't avoid them, but if you're just ill-informed or being lazy, your code will suffer.

NOTE This optimization makes sense only within VBA. If you're working with data from tables in your code, you *must* use variants. Because variants are the only datatype that can hold null data, and it's usually possible for data from tables to be null, you'll avoid problems by using variants. In addition, you may find that attempting to use specific datatypes when working with Jet ends up *slowing* your code. Because Jet uses variants when it communicates with Access, when you place Jet data into specific datatypes, you're asking VBA to make a datatype conversion, and that takes time.

Test 2: Use Integer Division Whenever Possible?

Access provides two division operators, the / (floating-point division) and \ (Integer division) operators. To perform floating-point division, Access must convert the operands to floating-point values. This takes time. If you don't care about the fractional portion of the result, you can save some time by using the Integer division operator instead.

The results of this test were decidedly mixed. Using Integer division made almost no difference (and it did make a difference in Access 2). In some other examples, working with forms, for instance, this has made a difference. It may be that VBA is smart enough to use Integer math internally if it can tell that that's what will work most quickly.

Test 3: Use Logical Assignments When Possible?

Like many other languages, Access handles logical values as integers. In addition, Access performs right-to-left expression evaluation. The combination of these two features allows you to make logical assignments directly as part of an expression. For example, many people write code like this:

```
If x = 5 Then
    y = True
Else
    y = False
End If
```

This code is wordier than it needs to be. The intent is to set the variable y to True if x is equal to 5 and False otherwise. The expression (x = 5) has a truth value of its own—that is, it's either True or False. You can assign that value directly to y in a single statement:

```
y = (x = 5)
```

Although it may look confusing, VBA will interpret it correctly. Starting from the right, Access will calculate the value of the expression x = 5 (either True or False) and assign that value to the variable y. Other languages, including C and Pascal, use distinct assignment and equality operators, making this expression a little clearer. In C, for example, the statement would read

```
y = (x == 5)
```

with the "=" performing the assignment and the "==" checking the equality.

Anyplace you use an expression like the If...Then...End If statement above, you should be able to replace it with a single assignment statement.

If you find these logical assignments hard to read, you may choose to skip using them, because the improvement in performance is slight. If, however, logical assignments seem natural to use and read, then by all means use them.

Test 4: Use Len() to Test for Zero-Length Strings?

There are several ways you can check to see whether the length of a particular string is 0. One method is to compare the string to "", and another is to compare the length of the string to 0. Comparing the results of the Len() function to 0 is measurably faster.

Test 5: Use "Var = Not Var" to Toggle True/False?

In many circumstances you need to toggle the state of a variable between True and False. You might be tempted to write code like this:

```
If x = True Then
    x = False
Else
    x = True
End If
```

You might think that either of the following solutions would be an improvement over the original:

```
If x Then
    x = False
Else
    x = True
End If
```

or

```
x = IIf(x, False, True)
```

Testing shows that neither is as good as the original expression (and the IIf() solution is much slower). But the best solution is to use the following expression:

```
x = Not x
```

That way, if x is currently True, it will become False. If it's False, it will become True.

Test 6: Use timeGetTime() Rather Than Timer()?

As mentioned earlier in this chapter, the Windows API function timeGetTime() (aliased as glr_apiGetTime() in the examples) returns the number of milliseconds that have elapsed since you started the current Windows session. The VBA Timer() function returns the number of seconds that have elapsed since midnight. If you're interested in measuring elapsed times, you're far better off using timeGetTime(), for three reasons:

- timeGetTime() is more accurate (milliseconds rather than seconds).
- timeGetTime() runs longer without "rolling over."
- Calling timeGetTime() is significantly faster.

Calling timeGetTime() is no more complex than calling Timer(), once you've included the proper API declaration for it. In the Declarations section of any standard module in your application, you'll need to include the statement

```
Private Declare Function glr_apiGetTime Lib "winmm.dll" _
  Alias "timeGetTime" () As Long
```

With that declaration in place, you can call it from any module in your application, just as though it were an internal Access function.

Test 7: Cache Object References?

In writing code you often need to retrieve or set properties of the various forms, reports, and controls in your application. Generally, you refer to these objects with statements like this:

```
strCaption = Forms!frmTest!cmdButton1.Caption
```

For a single reference to an object, there's not much you can to do speed up the reference. If, on the other hand, you're going to be referring to many of the properties of that object or using that object in a loop of some sort, you can achieve a substantial speed increase by pointing an object variable at that object and using that variable to reference the object.

For example, if you were going to reference all of a specific control's properties, you would be well served to use code like this rather than refer to the control with the full syntax each time:

```
Dim ctl as Control
Set ctl = Forms!YourForm!YourControl

Debug.Print ctl.ControlName
Debug.Print ctl.Width
' etc...
```

In addition, using VBA's new With...End With syntax would afford the same improvements. Your code may end up more readable using cached object references, but if you can use With...End With, it, too, can speed up your code.

Test 8: Don't Use Explicit Logical Comparisons?

When testing for the truth value of an expression in an IIf() expression or an If...Then...Else statement, there is no point in actually comparing the condition to the value True. That is, these two expressions are completely equivalent:

```
If x = True Then
```

and

```
If x Then
```

Leaving out the explicit comparison will make only a small difference in the speed of your code. You'd have to use this construct many, many times before this optimization made any measurable difference in the speed of your code, but every little bit helps.

Test 9: Refer to Controls by Number If Possible?

Access gives you several choices when you're referring to controls on a form. For example, given a form with 16 command buttons, you could refer to the first button (cmdButton1) in your code several ways (assuming that cmdButton1 was the first control to be placed on the form):

```
Dim ctl as Control
Set ctl = Forms!frmTest1!cmdButton1
Set ctl = Forms!frmTest1("cmdButton1")
Set ctl = Forms!frmTest1(0)
```

If you intend to loop through all the controls on the form, you have fewer choices. You can either build up a string expression that contains the name of the control or refer to the controls by number. The latter method is measurably faster, but you should use it only where you are looping through controls.

Test 10: Use IsCharAlphaNumeric()?

You may find yourself needing to find out whether a particular character is an alphanumeric character (that is, checking to see whether it falls in the range of characters from A–Z, a–z, or 0–9). One standard method for doing this in VBA is to compare the Asc(UCase(*character*)) to the ANSI values for the ranges. The Windows API provides a function specifically for this purpose, IsCharAlphaNumeric() (aliased as glr_apiIsCharAlphaNumeric() in the examples). In addition, you can use a similar API function, IsCharAlpha(), to check a character to see whether it's between A and Z. An added bonus of using the Windows API functions is that they're internationalized. Many characters outside the normal A–Z range are considered legal text characters in other countries. The brute-force comparison method would fail on such characters. To top it all off, using the API method is significantly faster than performing the comparisons yourself.

To use IsCharAlphaNumeric(), you need to include the following declaration in your application:

```
Private Declare Function glr_apiIsCharAlphaNumeric _
  Lib "User32" Alias "IsCharAlphaNumericA" (ByVal cChar As Byte)
```

Test 11: Wrap Table
Updates/Appends in Transactions?

Surrounding programmatic updates, appends, or deletes in a BeginTrans/CommitTrans pair can speed up the data operation. In general, transactions speed up database updates because Access stores all the updates within a transaction in an internal buffer (in memory, spilling over to disk) and writes them all to disk at once when the transaction is committed. As you might imagine, this can have a considerable impact on your application speed, especially if it is updating many records within a loop. In Access 95, however, Jet 3.0 performs this transaction buffering for you, and adding your own explicit transactions may or may not make a difference in the speed of your database operations. (See Chapter 12 for more information on Jet's use of internal buffering with implicit transactions.) Many factors affect how much of a performance boost you will realize when using transactions, including:

- The amount of free memory
- The size of the row being manipulated
- The number of columns in the row that are updated
- The number of rows being updated
- The Jet cache size and how it's being used
- The settings in the Registry that affect the time Jet waits before committing changes to disk

Any of these factors (or others) may affect this optimization, but you may find that a well-placed BeginTrans/CommitTrans pair can help in your applications.

NOTE You may also find that it *doesn't* help. Jet does a good job in this version of handling transactions itself, implicitly. You'll need to experiment with this one. Adding explicit transactions may help, or it may actually hurt. It's certain that this optimization will have less effect than it did in Access 2, because Jet 3 does a much better job of caching disk writes itself.

In our tests we found the use of transactions to be somewhat faster for our particular update scenario. These numbers are very data and situation dependent and are only indications that transactions *might* make a difference for you.

Test 12: Watch Out for Slow IIf() Components?

Shorter code isn't necessarily faster. Although this fact is documented in both the Access online help and the manuals, it's easy to miss: in the IIf(), Choose(), and Select() functions, VBA evaluates any and all expressions it finds, regardless of whether they actually need to be evaluated from a logical point of view. Given an expression like this:

```
varValue = IIf(fFlag, Function1(), Function2())
```

VBA will call both Function1() and Function2(). Not only can this lead to undesired side effects, it can just plain slow down your program. In a case like this you're better off using the standard If...Then...End If construct, which will execute only the portions of the statement that fall within the appropriate clause. Given the statement

```
If fFlag Then
    varValue = Function1()
Else
    varValue = Function2()
End If
```

you can be assured that only Function1() *or* Function2() will end up being called. The same concepts apply for the Choose() and Select() functions. If you plan on calling functions from any of these functions, you may be better served by using an If...Then...End If or a Select Case statement.

Beyond any optimization considerations, IIf() is very dangerous when dealing with numeric values and division. If this was your expression:

```
intNew = IIf(intY = 0, 0, intX/intY)
```

it would appear that you had appropriately covered your bases. Your code checks to make sure intY isn't 0 and returns an appropriate value if it is, rather than attempting to divide by 0. Unfortunately, if y is 0 this statement will still cause a run-time error. Because Access will evaluate both portions of the IIf() expression, the division by 0 will occur and will trigger an error. In this case you need to either trap for the error or use the If...Then...Else statement.

Test 13: Use Execute() instead of RunSQL?

When running an action query from your application, you have three choices: you can use the RunSQL macro action, you can use the Execute method of a database object to run SQL code, or you can create a QueryDef object and then use its Execute method. Using the Execute method of the database object or creating a temporary querydef and using its Execute method take about the same amount of time. On the other hand, using the Execute method of a database object requires one less line of code and seems like a simpler solution. Either solution is significantly faster than using DoCmd RunSQL.

The sample code shows two ways to accomplish the same goal: deleting all the rows from tblContacts. The slower method uses the RunSQL action to run the SQL string "DELETE * From tblContacts". The faster method uses the Execute method of the current database to execute the SQL string.

Using Temporary QueryDefs

Access provides a useful mechanism for creating temporary QueryDef objects: just don't provide a name! If you use a zero-length string for the name parameter of the CreateQueryDef() method, Access creates a temporary "in-memory" query. You no longer have to worry about the proliferation of querydefs and name collisions, and since Access doesn't write temporary querydefs to disk, they're a lot faster, too. Another plus: you don't have to delete temporary querydefs—they automatically disappear when the QueryDef object goes out of scope. For example, you can use code like this to create a temporary querydef:

```
Dim db As Database
Dim qdf As QueryDef
Set db = CurrentDb()
Set qdf = db.CreateQueryDef("", _
  "SELECT * FROM tblCustomers WHERE Age > 30;")
```

Test 14: Use For Each...Next Rather Than For...Next?

VBA adds the new For Each...Next construct, which allows you to loop through all the members of a collection or array without having to know the number of elements in the collection. "Is it faster?" we wondered. The tests proved that it's marginally faster, but it just doesn't matter; it's such a useful addition to the language that we'd suggest using it even if it were slower than the old method.

Test 15: Remove Comments from Loops?

In Access 2, removing comments from your code did make a difference in the execution speed. VBA is a compiled language, and comments ought not make a difference. As our tests show, this is true: removing comments will not affect the speed of code, all other things being equal. Be aware that excess comments consume memory, however, if you're using the decompiled version of the code (editing, for example), so they can adversely affect performance due to memory usage. This shouldn't concern you unless you have a massive number of comments, however. Their use far outweighs their detriments.

In repeated trials, removing comments never seemed to help, and if anything, it caused slightly worse performance more times than not. We give this technique an unqualified "don't bother." Unless you can prove to yourself that removing comments in your own environment makes any difference, leave them in.

Test 16: Use Bookmarks Rather Than FindFirst to Locate Rows?

If you're working with recordsets as part of your application, you may need to find a specific row, move to a different row, and then move back to the first. You can accomplish this in a number of ways, and some are faster than others. The fastest way is to use the Seek method of a table-type recordset. However, it's not always possible to use table-type recordsets. In those cases you might try using FindFirst to find the row, move to wherever you need to go, and then use FindFirst again to get back to the original row. Although this will work, there's a better method: use a bookmark to store your location before you move away. Then, when you want to move back to the selected row, the bookmark can get you there almost instantaneously. (See Chapter 6 for more information on bookmarks and recordsets.)

The example procedures first use the FindFirst method of a recordset to find a row. Then they move to the first row and back to the original row. The first version uses FindFirst for both record moves. The second one stores away a bookmark instead and uses that bookmark to move back to the original record.

Your performance on this test will vary, of course, depending on the number of rows in the recordset, whether you can use an index for the search, and how many times you execute the search.

Test 17: Drop Default Collection References?

When working with DAO and its objects and collections, you always have the option of writing complete object references or leaving out default collections in the references. (See Chapter 6 for more information on objects, references, and default collections.) Although leaving out the default collections in full references can help speed your code, it does make the code harder to read and its intent less obvious. The following examples compare using a full reference to the current database against using a shortened version:

```
Set db = DBEngine.Workspaces(0).Databases(0)
```

or

```
Set db = DBEngine(0)(0)
```

In our tests the shortened version was about 50 percent faster than the longer. Using different references might affect this acceleration, and you must always weigh the speed gains against readability losses.

Test 18: Refresh Collections Only When Necessary?

If you're using DAO and want to make sure the collections you're working with are completely up to date, you must first use the Refresh method of the collection. (See Chapter 6 for more information on refreshing collections.) On the other hand, refreshing collections is a very expensive operation in terms of time. The test case demonstrates just *how* expensive: in our sample case, with just two user-defined tables (and all the normal system tables), not refreshing the TableDefs collection before retrieving each tabledef's RecordCount property was 1300 percent faster than refreshing first. With more objects, this difference would be even more noticeable.

This is one of the few optimizations presented in this chapter that can make a visible difference in your applications, even if you weren't using Refresh often. For large applications, the speed difference can be very noticeable. Of course, if you're working in a multi-user environment and need to peruse the entire list of objects, you don't have much choice; you may well miss newly added objects unless you refresh the collection first.

Test 19: Use DBEngine(0)(0) If Speed Is the Only Concern?

If all you care about is raw speed, retrieving a reference to the current database with DBEngine(0)(0) is much faster than using CurrentDb(). When you retrieve a reference with DBEngine(0)(0):

```
Dim db As Database
Set db = DBEngine(0)(0)
```

Access returns a reference to an object that's already open. When you use CurrentDb(), however, Access creates a new internal data structure, which obviously takes a bit longer—actually, a lot longer. In our sample tests, using DBEngine(0)(0) was 500 to 1000 percent faster.

However, don't forget the trade-offs. (See Chapter 6 for more information on CurrentDB() versus DBEngine(0)(0).) When you retrieve a reference to CurrentDb(), you're guaranteed that its collections are refreshed at that time. If you use DBEngine(0)(0), you can make no such assumption, and you must refresh any collections you need to use. You'll have to make up your own mind, given the facts here and in Chapter 6.

Summary

This chapter has presented a variety of suggestions for improving the performance of your Access applications. We covered the following topics:

- How to optimize Access
- How to optimize queries
- How to speed up forms

- How to improve the performance of reports

- How VBA compiles and loads code and how you can best take advantage of this

- Suggestions for optimizing your VBA code

- How to test your own optimization ideas

Although we attempted to cover the major areas of optimization, this chapter is not meant to be comprehensive, but it makes for a good start.

At every point in designing any application, you're faced with choices. These choices affect how well your application will work, and you need to be informed about the trade-offs in order to best make these choices. This chapter focused on the major areas in which you can improve the performance of your applications.

PART VI

Interoperability

CHAPTER

EIGHTEEN

Accessing DLLs and the Windows API

- Calling DLLs and the Windows API from VBA

- Declaring DLL procedures

- Converting 16-bit Windows API calls to 32-bit API calls

This chapter discusses one of the most powerful features of VBA: the ability to call Dynamic Link Libraries (DLLs) from VBA procedures. DLLs are primarily written in C or C++, but you can also create them using Pascal and Delphi. Calling a DLL provides a method of performing tasks that standard VBA functions and statements do not permit. For example, VBA has no intrinsic ability to retrieve the amount of system resources available, but you can do it easily with the Window API.

Even if you are not proficient in C or C++, you can use DLLs someone else has written. The GLR32.DLL file on this book's companion disk, for example, allows you to perform tasks such as closing a program given its process identifier. Windows itself includes a number of DLLs with hundreds of useful functions. These functions are collectively called the *Windows API. API* is an acronym for "Application Programming Interface," and it is the set of functions Windows programs use to manipulate Windows.

Learning how to call the Windows API, and DLLs in general, allows you to vastly extend your ability to manipulate Windows. This chapter is divided into five main sections. The first section describes the basics of calling a DLL or Windows API call. The second section provides some examples of DLL calls. The third section, for more advanced users, shows how to construct a Declare statement to retrieve information from any arbitrary DLL. The fourth section takes a closer look at what goes on during DLL calls. The last section discusses how to convert 16-bit Windows API (from Windows 3.x) into 32-bit Windows API calls (Windows 95 and Windows NT).

Introducing Dynamic Link Libraries

In traditional DOS compiled languages, every application carries around every function it calls, and every application you create includes exactly the same shared code. For example, in standard C used from DOS, you call functions from the C runtime library to read a string from a file, get a character from the keyboard, or get the current time. These functions in the libraries are *statically linked* to the program, which means the code for the functions is included in the executable at the time the executable is created. The problem with this scheme is that if you have 200 programs that all write a string to the screen with the printf() function, the code for this function is reproduced 200 times on your disk.

Windows uses a different approach: libraries are usually *dynamically linked* to the program. This means that if you have 200 Windows programs that all write a string to a window, only one copy of the ExtTextOut() code resides on your hard disk. Each program includes only a very small amount of overhead to call this common code. These common routines reside in Dynamic Link Libraries, which normally have the extension .DLL and are stored in the Windows\System directory if more than one program uses them.

Programs that run under Windows call functions the operating system provides. These functions provide facilities to create a window, change its size, read and write Registry entries, manipulate a file, and so on. Windows stores most of these functions in three DLLs: USER32.DLL, GDI32.DLL, and KERNEL32.DLL.

To use a DLL you need to know the procedures in it and the arguments to each of those procedures. The Windows functions are well documented. To make a call to the Windows API, you just need to understand the documentation for the DLL call. For other DLLs you need to locate and understand the documentation for the DLL. Because traditionally DLLs have been designed to be called from C or C++, the documentation provided is usually stated in terms of calling functions from C or C++. For this reason you need to develop some skills in translating the terminology from the C perspective into the VBA perspective. This chapter provides most of the tools necessary and tells you where you can get the rest of the information you need.

NOTE
The Windows API includes more than 1000 functions. Describing them all is beyond the scope of this book (whole books have been written on the subject), but they are documented in several places. The Access Developer's Toolkit for Windows 95 contains a file named WIN32API.TXT. We have put a copy of this file on the CD-ROM that comes with this book. It has the Declare statements for most of the 32-bit Windows API calls, as well as the definition of most of the constants and structures used by the API calls. But to find out what the functions mean, you will need the Win32 documentation. You can find the complete documentation on the Microsoft Developer's Network (Level 1) CD-ROM. We highly recommend this tool as a source of information for developing Access applications.

Calling DLL Procedures from VBA

Calling procedures in DLLs is similar to calling procedures in standard VBA. The difference is that the body of the procedure resides in a DLL instead of inside a module. Before calling a function in a DLL, you need to tell VBA where to find it. There are really two kinds of DLLs, and you tell VBA how to call them in two ways:

- By specifying a type library
- By using a Declare statement

Using Type Libraries

The person who creates a DLL may do so in a special way, creating a file called a *type library,* which describes the procedures within the DLL. A type library usually has the extension .OLB or .TLB and is registered with the OLE component of Windows. The setup program that installs the DLL usually creates the proper entries with the Windows Registry to register the type library. If you select Tools ➤ References when an open module has the focus, the dialog shows all the type libraries that are available to Access. By placing a check next to the name of your type library, you tell Access that everything within the type library is available to VBA.

If you use a type library, there is no need to use Declare statements. The type library includes all the functionality of the Declare statement. In addition, type libraries avoid the difficulties of passing strings to DLLs. Type libraries use the OLE functions for the interaction with VBA, and OLE uses BSTRs for passing strings. (See the section "Passing Strings to DLLs: The Real Story" later in this chapter). The main drawback to all this is that the Windows API doesn't have a type library. You must use Declare statements to call the Windows API.

DAO in VBA is an example of a type library. The type library provides all the functionality of DAO to VBA; none of it is really intrinsic to VBA.

If you are calling a function specified with a type library, you can ignore the information in the rest of this chapter, which deals with calling DLLs through the use of Declare statements. You use functions specified with type libraries just as though they were an intrinsic part of VBA.

Using Declare Statements

A Declare statement is a definition you provide in the General Declarations section of a module that tells VBA where to find a function and how to call it. (You will find the details on the construction of a Declare statement in the section "How to Construct a Declare Statement" later in this chapter.) The important point here is that you need one to be able to call a DLL function that is not specified by a type library. Because there is no type library for the Windows API, you need to provide Declare statements for every Windows API call you make.

Because every Windows API function needs a Declare statement, someone has already constructed these statements for you. Access provides a file named WIN32API.TXT (you will also find it on the CD-ROM that comes with this book) that has all the Declare statements you need. You also need the definition of certain constants and user-defined type declarations. You can also find these definitions in WIN32API.TXT.

A tool named the API Text Viewer comes with the Access Developer's Toolkit. It also provides the Declare statements and other definitions you need. This tool simply searches the WIN32API.TXT and finds the proper entry. Unfortunately, the user interface on this tool makes it difficult to use; it is faster to use a text editor to find the Declare statement in the WIN32API.TXT file. Quite likely, shareware or freeware tools for providing Declare statements and other definitions will become available as the Win32 API increases in importance, so you may want to look for them on CompuServe or the Internet.

WARNING Do not include all of WIN32API.TXT in a module. This large file has at least a thousand declarations within it. The amount of resources it consumes will substantially reduce the performance of your application. Since you will probably use at most several dozen of the declarations in your application, just copy the ones you use into your module.

This is an example of a Declare statement:

```
Public Declare Function WinHelp Lib "User32" Alias "WinHelpA" _
 (ByVal hwnd As Long, ByVal lpszHelp As String, _
 ByVal uCommand As Integer, dwData As Any) As Long
```

As mentioned earlier, you place Declare statements in the General Declarations section of a module. After you specify the Declare statement, you can use the procedure that has been declared just as though it were an intrinsic part of VBA, with a number of important exceptions. The following sections describe these exceptions.

WARNING Because you *will* eventually make a mistake attempting to call a Windows API and cause a GP fault, it is important to save all objects that need to be saved before running any code that calls a DLL. Unfortunately, Access doesn't have the "Save before run" option that Visual Basic does, so you must remember to do it yourself. The first time you attempt to call any given DLL function, or when you make a change to a Declare statement, you must be extra careful, since that is when the GP fault will most likely occur. Either a bad declaration or a bug in the DLL can cause a GP fault and crash Access. There is even a slight possibility it will crash Windows 95, so be sure to save any objects in other programs running under Windows, too. (There should be no danger of crashing Windows NT.) Keep recent backups of your database, just to cover the slight possibility that it becomes corrupt when Access crashes. DLLs are powerful, but they don't provide the protection from your mistakes that VBA normally gives you.

Passing Arguments to DLLs

You pass arguments to DLLs exactly the same way you pass arguments to any built-in function, with two exceptions, described in the sections "Returning Strings from a DLL" and "Using the Any Datatype" later in this chapter. For example, to find out information about the system on which Windows is running, you call the Windows API function GetSystemMetrics(). You retrieve the Declare statement and some constants from WIN32API.TXT and place them in the General Declarations section of a module. The definitions look like this:

```
Declare Function GetSystemMetrics Lib "user32" _
 (ByVal nIndex As Long) As Long

' GetSystemMetrics() codes
Public Const SM_CXSCREEN = 0
Public Const SM_CYSCREEN = 1
Public Const SM_CXVSCROLL = 2
Public Const SM_CYHSCROLL = 3
Public Const SM_CYCAPTION = 4
' etc...  There are 75 of them.
```

After putting the Declare statement and constant declarations in the General Declarations section of the module, you can call the GetSystemMetrics() function just as though it were part of VBA. For example:

```
lngCyCaption = GetSystemMetrics(SM_CYCAPTION)
```

The form frmGetSystemMetrics is shown in Figure 18.1. The list box on the left shows each of the constants and is filled from tblGetSystemMetrics. You generate the return value by having your function call TestGetSystemMetrics(), a function we wrote that is defined in the module basGetSystemMetrics. TestGetSystemMetrics() does the call to GetSystemMetrics(). The function TestGetSystemMetrics() looks like this:

```
Public Function TestGetSystemMetrics _
 (ByVal lngIndex As Long) As Long
    TestGetSystemMetrics = GetSystemMetrics(lngIndex)
End Function
```

FIGURE 18.1:

The form frmGetSystemMetrics shows each of the GetSystemMetrics constants, its value, its meaning, and the return value from calling the Windows API function GetSystemMetrics().

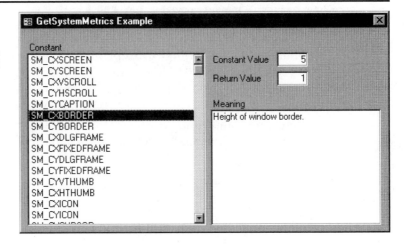

Returning Strings from a DLL

Windows has two ways of storing strings: BSTR and LPSTR. The section "Passing Strings to a DLL: The Real Story" later in this chapter describes the details of how these are stored. All the Windows API calls except those dealing with OLE use LPSTRs, not BSTRs. The problem is that a DLL cannot change the size of a LPSTR string. This causes difficulties when you need the DLL to return a value in a string.

Because a DLL that accepts an LPSTR cannot change the size of a string that is passed to it, the string needs to be big enough to accept the data to be returned before you pass it to the DLL. This means you need to fill the string with enough characters to create a buffer for the DLL to fill in. You normally accomplish this with the Space$() function. The DLL must not write past the end of the string, since that can result in a GP fault. DLL functions that return strings normally have you pass another argument that tells how much space has been allocated for the string.

The GetWindowText() function is an example of a Windows function that returns a string. You pass it a handle to a window, and it returns the text associated with the window into a buffer.

NOTE

A handle is a variable of type Long that uniquely identifies an object to Windows. The first argument to GetWindowText( ) is a handle to a window, also known as an *hwnd* or *hWnd*. Forms and some controls have an hwnd property that will return the handle to a window that can be passed into the GetWindowText( ) function. You should always retrieve the hwnd property at the time you're calling such a function, since Windows will assign a new hwnd to a form each time you reopen it.

The following is a Declare statement for GetWindowText():

```
Declare Function GetWindowText _
 Lib "user32" Alias "GetWindowTextA" _
 (ByVal hwnd As Long, ByVal lpString As String, _
 ByVal cch As Long) As Long
```

When you call GetWindowText(), control passes into the Windows USER32.DLL. The GetWindowText() function inside the DLL looks up the handle in Windows' internal data structures and fills in the lpString parameter with the text that is associated with the window. You call GetWindowText() like this:

```
Dim strReturnedString As String
Dim intRet As Integer

' Allocate enough space for the return value.
strReturnedString = Space$(255)

' Call the GetWindowsText function
intRet = GetWindowText(Me.hwnd, strReturnedString, _
 Len(strReturnedString) + 1)

' Truncate the string down to the proper size
strReturnedString = Left$(strReturnedString, intRet)
```

The Space$() function in this example returns a string of 255 spaces followed by a null character. A null character has the ANSI value 0 and is used in LPSTRs to terminate a string. This allows you to use window captions up to 255 characters. In memory, strReturnedString looks like this:

(See the section "Passing Strings to a DLL: The Real Story" later in this chapter for the details of how BSTRs and LPSTRs are stored in memory.)

The code then calls the GetWindowText() function. The call has two effects:

- It changes the contents of strReturnedString to be the caption of the window indicated by the hwnd argument, followed by a null character.

- It returns the length of the string placed into strReturnedString, not counting the terminating null character.

After the call, strReturnedString looks like this in memory:

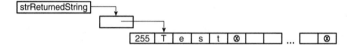

The length recorded in the header information of the VBA string hasn't changed, nor has any memory been deallocated—the string is still 255 characters long. Because the DLL cannot make the string shorter, before using strReturnedString you must truncate the string to just before the null character that GetWindowText() placed at the end of the string it returned. Fortunately, the return value of the Get-WindowText() function tells us exactly how many characters should appear in the final string. You then use the Left$() function to truncate the string. If you pass an invalid value for the hwnd argument, Windows returns a value indicating that the API call failed.

If you call a DLL function that doesn't return a value telling you how many characters are in the returned string, you can search for the null character to determine how long the string should be. The Instr() function combined with the Left$() function does the job:

```
strReturnedString = Left$(strReturnedString, _
  Instr(1, strReturnedString, Chr$(0)) - 1)
```

Obviously, the GetTextString() example shown above is frivolous: you can get the same information by just using the form's Caption property. However, GetTextString() works with *any* window in the entire operating system, not just windows that happen to be Access forms. We used the form's hwnd for this example because it was an easy hwnd to get. You can get the hwnd of other windows using other Windows API calls, such as FindWindowEx().

Using the vbNullString Constant

There are times when the documentation for a DLL function indicates that sometimes you need to pass a string and sometimes you need to pass a Null. A Null is a 4-byte zero placed directly on the stack. (For a full discussion of what this means, see the section "Understanding By Value and By Reference" later in this chapter.) The main thing you need to know is that to pass a Null, you can use vbNullString.

For example, a Windows API function named SetVolumeLabel() sets the volume label of a file system volume. The Declare statement for the function is

```
Declare Function SetVolumeLabel _
 Lib "kernel32" Alias "SetVolumeLabelA" _
 (ByVal lpRootPathName As String, _
 ByVal lpVolumeName As String) As Long
```

These are the two arguments to SetVolumeLabel:

Parameter	Meaning
lpRootPathName	Points to a null-terminated string specifying the root directory of a file system volume. This is the volume the function will label. If this parameter is Null, the root of the current directory is used
lpVolumeName	Points to a string specifying a name for the volume. If this parameter is Null, the function deletes the name of the specified volume

To set the volume label on the C drive to DRIVE_C, you execute the following code:

```
fRet = SetVolumeLabel("C:\", "DRIVE_C")
```

To delete the volume label using the method documented on the C drive, you need to pass a Null as the second argument. To do so, execute the following code:

```
fRet = SetVolumeLabel("C:\", vbNullString)
```

Passing a User-Defined Type to a DLL

Sometimes you need to pass a user-defined type to a DLL. For example, many of the Windows functions expect a RECT structure, which is a user-defined type, as opposed to one that is supported implicitly by the C or VBA language. To do so, you need to define an equivalent type in VBA. You can find the declaration in WIN32API.TXT. The structure in VBA is

```
Type RECT
    left As Long
    top As Long
    right As Long
    bottom As Long
End Type
```

You must pass a structure by reference. The declaration of a function that takes a RECT as an argument is

```
Declare Function GetWindowRect Lib "user32" _
 (ByVal hwnd As Long, lpRect As RECT) As Long
```

The form frmGetWindowRect from CH18.MDB uses this function to retrieve the location of the form on the screen (from the upper left-hand corner and measured in pixels). Figure 18.2 shows this form.

A call to GetWindowRect() looks like this:

```
Dim rectForm As RECT

If GetWindowRect(Me.hwnd, rectForm) Then
    txtLeft.Value = rectForm.left
    txtTop.Value = rectForm.top
```

FIGURE 18.2:
Using the GetWindowRect()
Windows API call to determine
the location of the window

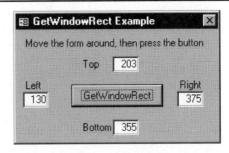

```
        txtRight.Value = rectForm.right
        txtBottom.Value = rectForm.bottom
End If
```

GetWindowRect() returns True if it succeeds in filling in the rectForm structure passed in. It then uses the values from the structure to fill in text boxes on the form.

Passing an Array

You can pass individual elements of an array just as you would use any other variable. For example:

```
Private Const COLOR_BTNHIGHLIGHT = 20
Private Const COLOR_BTNTEXT = 18
alngDisplayElementsSave(0) = COLOR_BTNHIGHLIGHT
alngDisplayElementsSave(1) = COLOR_BTNTEXT
lngColorSave = GetSysColor(alngDisplayElementsSave(1))
```

is the same as

```
Private Const COLOR_BTNHIGHLIGHT = 20
Private Const COLOR_BTNTEXT = 18
alngDisplayElementsSave(0) = COLOR_BTNHIGHLIGHT
alngDisplayElementsSave(1) = COLOR_BTNTEXT
lngColorSave = GetSysColor(COLOR_BTNTEXT)
```

Sometimes, though, you'll want to pass an entire array to a DLL. You may do this—but only for numeric arrays, not for strings or user-defined ones, unless the DLL understands a special type called a SAFEARRAY. To pass an array, you pass its first element. For example, the call to the SetSysColors() Windows API call is actually passed two different arrays:

```
Dim alngDisplayElements() As Long
Dim alngRGBValues() As Long
```

```
Dim lngCDisplayElements As Long

' Size the arrays for two elements
lngCDisplayElements = 2
ReDim alngDisplayElements(lngCDisplayElements - 1)
ReDim alngRGBValues(lngCDisplayElements - 1)

' Fill the arrays to set two system colors
alngDisplayElements(0) = COLOR_BTNHIGHLIGHT
alngRGBValues(0) = RGB(&HFF, 0, 0)
alngDisplayElements(1) = COLOR_BTNTEXT
alngRGBValues(1) = RGB(0, 0, &HFF)

Call SetSysColors(lngCDisplayElements, _
 alngDisplayElements(0), alngRGBValues(0))
```

This example is from code behind the form frmSetSysColors in CH18.MDB.

When passing an array to a DLL function, you must give the function some indication of the size of the array. You do this by passing another argument that gives the size of the array. Without this argument, the DLL cannot determine how large the array is and can go beyond the end of the array. If you pass in a size that is larger than the array that has been allocated, you are telling the DLL that more memory has been allocated than really has been. When the DLL tries to access the information past the end of the array, it will either get random bytes or a GP fault, depending on whether the memory it is trying to access actually exists. In other words, be very careful that you pass the correct size in that argument.

Examples Using the Windows API

What follows are two sets of examples using the Windows API. The first deals with the clipboard, the second with the Windows Registry. These examples show Declare statements and calls.

Using the Clipboard

Because, unlike Visual Basic, Access doesn't have a Clipboard object, this section demonstrates using Windows API calls to simulate the same functionality. The examples use the Windows API to produce two functions, glrClipboardSetText() and glrClipboardGetText(), that put text on the Windows clipboard and get the text from the Windows clipboard, respectively. The functions make use of 12 different Windows API calls and demonstrate most of the points mentioned in the chapter.

The function glrClipboardSetText() is shown in Listing 18.1. It works this way:

1. It uses the Windows GlobalAlloc() function to allocate some memory.

2. It moves the passed-in string into it.

3. It opens the clipboard.

4. It empties the current contents of the clipboard.

5. It writes the data onto the clipboard.

6. It closes the clipboard.

You can include these clipboard functions in your code by importing the module basClipboard from CH18.MDB.

Listing 18.1

```
Option Compare Database
Option Explicit

Private Declare Function glr_apiIsClipboardFormatAvailable _
 Lib "USER32" Alias "IsClipboardFormatAvailable" _
 (ByVal uFormat As Integer) As Integer
Private Declare Function glr_apiOpenClipboard _
 Lib "USER32" Alias "OpenClipboard" _
 (ByVal hwnd As Long) As Integer
Private Declare Function glr_apiGetClipboardData _
 Lib "USER32" Alias "GetClipboardData" _
 (ByVal uFormat As Integer) As Long
Private Declare Function glr_apiGlobalSize _
 Lib "KERNEL32" Alias "GlobalSize" _
 (ByVal hMem As Long) As Integer
Private Declare Function glr_apiGlobalLock _
 Lib "KERNEL32" Alias "GlobalLock" _
 (ByVal hMem As Long) As Long
Private Declare Sub glr_apiMoveMemory _
 Lib "KERNEL32" Alias "RtlMoveMemory" _
 (ByVal strDest As Any, _
 ByVal lpSource As Any, _
```

```
 ByVal Length As Long)
Private Declare Function glr_apiGlobalUnlock _
 Lib "KERNEL32" Alias "GlobalUnlock" _
 (ByVal hMem As Long) As Integer
Private Declare Function glr_apiCloseClipboard _
 Lib "USER32" Alias "CloseClipboard" () As Integer
Private Declare Function glr_apiGlobalAlloc _
 Lib "KERNEL32" Alias "GlobalAlloc" _
 (ByVal uFlags As Integer, ByVal dwBytes As Long) As Long
Private Declare Function glr_apiEmptyClipboard _
 Lib "USER32" Alias "EmptyClipboard" () As Integer
Private Declare Function glr_apiSetClipboardData _
 Lib "USER32" Alias "SetClipboardData" _
 (ByVal uFormat As Integer, ByVal hData As Long) As Long
Private Declare Function glr_apiGlobalFree _
 Lib "KERNEL32" Alias "GlobalFree" _
 (ByVal hMem As Long) As Long

Private Const GMEM_MOVABLE = &H2&
Private Const GMEM_DDESHARE = &H2000&
Private Const CF_TEXT = 1

'Error return codes from Clipboard2Text
Public Const glrCLIPBOARDFORMATNOTAVAILABLE = 1
Public Const glrCANNOTOPENCLIPBOARD = 2
Public Const glrCANNOTGETCLIPBOARDDATA = 3
Public Const glrCANNOTGLOBALLOCK = 4
Public Const glrCANNOTCLOSECLIPBOARD = 5
Public Const glrCANNOTGLOBALALLOC = 6
Public Const glrCANNOTEMPTYCLIPBOARD = 7
Public Const glrCANNOTSETCLIPBOARDDATA = 8
Public Const glrCANNOTGLOBALFREE = 9

Function glrClipboardSetText(strText As String) As Variant
    ' Puts some text on the Windows clipboard

   Dim varRet As Variant
   Dim fSetClipboardData As Boolean
   Dim hMemory As Long
   Dim lpMemory As Long
   Dim lngSize As Long

   varRet = False
   fSetClipboardData = False
```

```
' Get the length, including one extra for a CHR$(0)
' at the end.
lngSize = Len(strText) + 1
hMemory = glr_apiGlobalAlloc(GMEM_MOVABLE Or _
 GMEM_DDESHARE, lngSize)
If Not CBool(hMemory) Then
    varRet = CVErr(glrCANNOTGLOBALALLOC)
    GoTo glrClipboardSetTextDone
End If

' Lock the object into memory
lpMemory = glr_apiGlobalLock(hMemory)
If Not CBool(lpMemory) Then
    varRet = CVErr(glrCANNOTGLOBALLOCK)
    GoTo glrClipboardSetTextGlobalFree
End If

' Move the string into the memory we locked
Call glr_apiMoveMemory(lpMemory, strText, lngSize)

' Don't send clipboard locked memory.
Call glr_apiGlobalUnlock(hMemory)

' Open the clipboard
If Not CBool(glr_apiOpenClipboard(O&)) Then
    varRet = CVErr(glrCANNOTOPENCLIPBOARD)
    GoTo glrClipboardSetTextGlobalFree
End If

' Remove the current contents of the clipboard
If Not CBool(glr_apiEmptyClipboard()) Then
    varRet = CVErr(glrCANNOTEMPTYCLIPBOARD)
    GoTo glrClipboardSetTextCloseClipboard
End If

' Add our string to the clipboard as text
If Not CBool(glr_apiSetClipboardData(CF_TEXT, _
 hMemory)) Then
    varRet = CVErr(glrCANNOTSETCLIPBOARDDATA)
    GoTo glrClipboardSetTextCloseClipboard
Else
    fSetClipboardData = True
End If
```

```
glrClipboardSetTextCloseClipboard:
    ' Close the clipboard
    If Not CBool(glr_apiCloseClipboard()) Then
        varRet = CVErr(glrCANNOTCLOSECLIPBOARD)
    End If

glrClipboardSetTextGlobalFree:
    If Not fSetClipboardData Then
        'If we have set the clipboard data, we no longer own
        ' the object--Windows does, so don't free it.
        If CBool(glr_apiGlobalFree(hMemory)) Then
            varRet = CVErr(glrCANNOTGLOBALFREE)
        End If
    End If

glrClipboardSetTextDone:
    glrClipboardSetText = varRet
End Function
```

The function glrClipboardGetText() is shown in Listing 18.2. It works this way:

1. It sees whether there is some text on the clipboard that can be read.

2. If so, it opens the clipboard.

3. It gets the current contents of the clipboard.

4. It copies the contents into a string.

5. It truncates the string to the right size.

6. It closes the clipboard.

Listing 18.2

```
Public Function glrClipboardGetText() As Variant
    ' Gets some text on the Windows clipboard
    '

    Dim hMemory As Long
    Dim lpMemory As Long
    Dim strText As String
    Dim lngSize As Long
    Dim varRet As Variant

    varRet = ""
```

```
        ' Is there text on the clipboard? If not, error out.
        If Not CBool(glr_apiIsClipboardFormatAvailable _
            (CF_TEXT)) Then
            varRet = CVErr(glrCLIPBOARDFORMATNOTAVAILABLE)
            GoTo glrClipboardGetTextDone
        End If

        ' Open the clipboard
        If Not CBool(glr_apiOpenClipboard(0&)) Then
            varRet = CVErr(glrCANNOTOPENCLIPBOARD)
            GoTo glrClipboardGetTextDone
        End If

        ' Get the handle to the clipboard data
        hMemory = glr_apiGetClipboardData(CF_TEXT)
        If Not CBool(hMemory) Then
            varRet = CVErr(glrCANNOTGETCLIPBOARDDATA)
            GoTo glrClipboardGetTextCloseClipboard
        End If

        ' Find out how big it is and allocate enough space
        ' in a string
        lngSize = glr_apiGlobalSize(hMemory)
        strText = Space$(lngSize)

        ' Lock the handle so we can use it
        lpMemory = glr_apiGlobalLock(hMemory)
        If Not CBool(lpMemory) Then
            varRet = CVErr(glrCANNOTGLOBALLOCK)
            GoTo glrClipboardGetTextCloseClipboard
        End If

        ' Move the information from the clipboard memory
        ' into our string
        Call glr_apiMoveMemory(strText, lpMemory, lngSize)

        ' Truncate it at the first Null character because
        ' the value reported by lngSize is erroneously large
        strText = Left$(strText, Instr(1, strText, Chr$(0)) - 1)

        ' Free the lock
        Call glr_apiGlobalUnlock(hMemory)

glrClipboardGetTextCloseClipboard:
        ' Close the clipboard
```

```
    If Not CBool(glr_apiCloseClipboard()) Then
        varRet = CVErr(glrCANNOTCLOSECLIPBOARD)
    End If

glrClipboardGetTextDone:
    If Not IsError(varRet) Then
        glrClipboardGetText = strText
    Else
        glrClipboardGetText = varRet
    End If
End Function
```

The form frmClipboard in CH18.MDB, which is shown in Figure 18.3, demonstrates the functionality of the two functions. You select some text from the top text box, txtText. When you click the Copy button, the text box loses the focus. At this point the selected text is copied into the Tag property. The event handler for cmdCopy uses the Tag property to paste the information into the clipboard using glrClipboardSetText(). The Paste button just calls glrClipboardGetText() to paste the information into the bottom text box, txtPaste.

FIGURE 18.3:

frmClipboard demonstrates clipboard functionality.

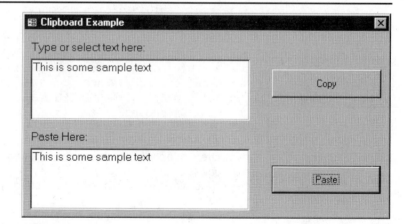

Registry Functionality

The System Registry is the cache for important data in Windows 95 and Windows NT. The Registry is organized as a hierarchical database of information. Data is indexed by a key and a value. The *key* indicates where within the database it can find the information. The *value* is the name given to a particular piece of information. You can store data of different datatypes in the Registry, including numbers, strings, and binary information.

You can look at the Registry by running REGEDIT.EXE (or REGEDT32.EXE on Windows NT). Figure 18.4 presents a picture of the Registry REGEDIT shows. The Registry is broken into a number of root entries, also known as *hives*:

HKEY_CLASSES_ROOT

HKEY_CURRENT_USER

HKEY_LOCAL_MACHINE

HKEY_USERS

HKEY_CURRENT_CONFIG

HKEY_DYN_DATA

Information about the current system is stored in the HKEY_LOCAL_MACHINE path. Information specific to the currently logged-in user is stored in the HKEY_CURRENT_USER path.

Although it is possible to store binary information within the Registry, you should never store executable code there. Also, there is still a place for .INI files: you

FIGURE 18.4:

RegEdit browsing the Registry

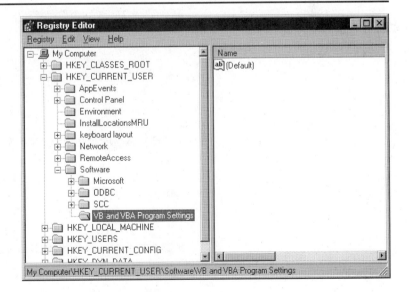

should use them when you need to store large amounts of data. The Microsoft Win32 Software Development Kit recommends that you store no more than 2K worth of information in the Registry for each application.

VBA provides some intrinsic functions that get and set some values within the Registry: GetSetting(), SaveSetting(), GetAllSettings(), and DeleteSetting(). While these functions are useful for setting and getting information about your program, they let you modify only a small part of the Registry database. Specifically, they let you modify only the \HKEY_CURRENT_USER\Software\VB and VBA Program Settings branch of the database. It is often useful to be able to browse and modify other portions of the Registry.

Browsing the Registry

Figure 18.5 shows frmKeys from CH18.MDB. This form allows you to browse the HKEY_CURRENT_USER branch of the database, including branches other than the Software branch. When you double-click a key in the left list box, the key traverses to its subkeys. Single-clicking a key displays the values assigned to that key in the right list box. Clicking a value displays the contents of that value. Clicking the Root button takes you back to the HKEY_CURRENT_USER key. This functionality demonstrates traversing the tree and getting values.

FIGURE 18.5:

A Registry browser that allows traversing the Registry tree

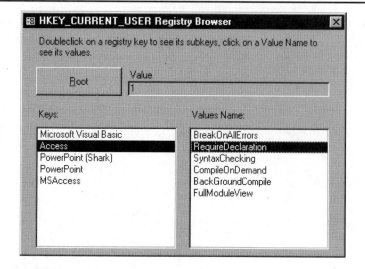

When you open the form, the form initializes the list boxes by calling the cmdRoot_Click event. This function calls glrGetRegistryKeys() from the basRegistry module in the same database. glrGetRegistryKeys() builds a semicolon-delimited string, which sets the RowSource property of the list box. The function glrGetRegistryKeys() is shown in Listing 18.3.

Listing 18.3

```
Public Function glrGetRegistryKeys(ByVal hKey As Long) As String
    ' Returns a semicolon-delimited list of all of
    ' the subkeys of this key

    Dim strRet As String
    Dim lngRet As Long
    Dim strClassName As String
    Dim cchClassName As Long
    Dim lngCSubKeys As Long
    Dim cchMaxSubKey As Long
    Dim cchMaxClass As Long
    Dim lngCValues As Long
    Dim cchMaxValueName As Long
    Dim cbMaxValueData As Long
    Dim cbSecurityDescriptor As Long
    Dim ftLastWrite As FILETIME
    Dim i As Long
    Dim strKey As String
    Dim cchKey As Long
    Dim strClass As String
    Dim cchClass As Long
    Dim retCode As Long

    strRet = ""
    strClassName = Space$(256)
    cchClassName = Len(strClassName)
    Call glr_apiRegQueryInfoKey(hKey, strClassName, _
     cchClassName, 0&, lngCSubKeys, cchMaxSubKey, _
     cchMaxClass, lngCValues, cchMaxValueName, _
     cbMaxValueData, cbSecurityDescriptor, ftLastWrite)
    For i = 0 To lngCSubKeys - 1
        strKey = Space$(cchMaxSubKey)
        cchKey = Len(strKey) + 1
        strClass = Space$(cchMaxClass)
        cchClass = Len(strClass) + 1
        retCode = glr_apiRegEnumKeyEx(hKey, i, strKey, _
```

```
        cchKey, 0&, strClass, cchClass, ftLastWrite)
        Select Case retCode And APPLICATION_ERROR_MASK
        Case ERROR_SEVERITY_SUCCESS
        Case Else
            Call glrAssert(False)    'Should never happen
            Exit For
        End Select
        strKey = left$(strKey, cchKey)
        strRet = strRet & strKey & ";"
    Next i

    glrGetRegistryKeys = strRet
End Function
```

Each location in the path is a key. The Registry function operates by using handles to these keys. A handle to a key, or hKey, is a long number that uniquely identifies a key. Various functions enumerate subkeys and values for keys.

The core functionality works like this:

1. The code retrieves a known handle to a key—in this case, HKEY_CURRENT_USER, stored in hKeyCurrent.

2. The code calls glrGetRegistryKeys() with this handle to a key.

3. glrGetRegistryKeys() calls RegQueryInfoKey() to find out the number of subkeys under this Registry entry and the maximum length of the keys.

4. For each key, a call is made to RegEnumKeyEx(). This gets the name of the key.

5. The code truncates the key down to the proper size, using the Left$() function.

6. The keys are concatenated together and placed in the RowSource property of the left-hand list box.

When you click an entry in the list box, the code shown in Listing 18.4 is called.

Listing 18.4

```
Private Sub lstKeys_Click()
    ' Fills the lstValues with a list of values based
    ' on the entry clicked on in lstKeys

    Dim hKeyNew As Long
    Dim lngRet As Long
```

```
    If hKeySelected Then
        Call glr_apiRegCloseKey(hKeySelected)
    End If
    lngRet = glr_apiRegOpenKeyEx(hKeyCurrent, lstKeys.Value, _
     O&, KEY_READ, hKeyNew)
    If lngRet = ERROR_SEVERITY_SUCCESS Then
        hKeySelected = hKeyNew
        lstValues.rowsource = glrGetRegistryValues(hKeySelected)
    End If
End Sub
```

> **NOTE**   ERROR_SEVERITY_SUCCESS is a constant representing the value 0. It is returned by Windows to indicate that the previous operation succeeded.

Whenever you select a key in a list box, the code opens the key and stores the hKey in hKeySelected. When you select another key, the code must close the first key, or Windows will continue to keep some memory allocated. The code then calls glrGetRegistryValues(). glrGetRegistryValues() is virtually the same as glrGetRegistryKeys(), except that it calls RegEnumValue() to retrieve the names of the values. The difference is that one returns a list of subkeys and the other returns the list of values associated with a key.

When you double-click a key, the code traverses to that subkey. This code is shown in Listing 18.5. It opens the subkey with RegOpenKeyEx(), closes the current key with RegCloseKey(), and then gets the new values to fill the list box by calling glrGetRegistryKeys() again. Finally, the code clears the right-hand list box and closes the currently selected key.

Listing 18.5

```
Private Sub lstKeys_DblClick(Cancel As Integer)
    ' Resets the list boxes to show the new key that
    ' was double-clicked

    Dim lngRet As Long
    Dim hKeyNew As Long

    lngRet = glr_apiRegOpenKeyEx(hKeyCurrent, lstKeys.Value, _
```

```
    0&, KEY_READ, hKeyNew)
  If lngRet = ERROR_SEVERITY_SUCCESS Then
      Call glr_apiRegCloseKey(hKeyCurrent)
      hKeyCurrent = hKeyNew
      lstKeys.rowsource = glrGetRegistryKeys(hKeyCurrent)
      If hKeySelected Then
          Call glr_apiRegCloseKey(hKeySelected)
      End If
      hKeySelected = 0
      lstValues.rowsource = ""
  End If
End Sub
```

Listing 18.6 shows the next piece of functionality, retrieving the key value when the value name is clicked in the right-hand list box. The code calls glrGetRegistry-Value() with the selected key and value and puts the value retrieved in the txtValue text box on the form.

Listing 18.6

```
Private Sub lstValues_Click()
    ' Shows the value that was clicked

    txtValue.Value = glrGetRegistryValue(hKeySelected, _
      lstValues.Value)
End Sub
```

Listing 18.7 shows the final piece of functionality: glrGetRegistryValue(). It calls RegQueryValueEx() twice. The first time it is called with the lpbData argument set to Null. This is to retrieve the datatype of the key into lngType. The second time it is called in different ways, depending on which type was retrieved. The return value of the function is set to the actual value retrieved.

Listing 18.7

```
Public Function glrGetRegistryValue(ByVal hKey As Long, ByVal _
  strValue As String) As Variant
    ' Returns a Registry value based on an hKey
    ' and a strValue

    Dim retCode As Long
    Dim lngType As Long
    Dim cbData As Long
    Dim strGetValue As String
    Dim lngValue As Long
```

```
glrGetRegistryValue = "<Binary Data>"

retCode = glr_apiRegQueryValueEx(hKey, strValue, O&, _
  lngType, ByVal O&, cbData)
Select Case retCode And APPLICATION_ERROR_MASK
Case ERROR_SEVERITY_SUCCESS
    Select Case lngType
    Case REG_NONE
        glrGetRegistryValue = CVErr(0)
    Case REG_SZ, REG_EXPAND_SZ
        strGetValue = Space$(cbData)
        retCode = glr_apiRegQueryValueEx(hKey, strValue, _
          O&, lngType, ByVal strGetValue, cbData)
        glrGetRegistryValue = strGetValue
    Case REG_BINARY
    Case REG_DWORD, REG_DWORD_LITTLE_ENDIAN
        retCode = glr_apiRegQueryValueEx(hKey, strValue, _
          O&, lngType, lngValue, cbData)
        glrGetRegistryValue = lngValue
    Case REG_DWORD_BIG_ENDIAN
    Case REG_LINK
    Case REG_MULTI_SZ
    Case REG_RESOURCE_LIST
    Case REG_FULL_RESOURCE_DESCRIPTOR
    Case REG_RESOURCE_REQUIREMENTS_LIST
    Case Else
        Call glrAssert(False)    'Should never happen
    End Select
Case Else
    Call glrAssert(False)    'Should never happen
End Select
End Function
```

Another Registry Example

The previous example showed how to walk through the Registry, but what can you use this technique for? It's very useful to be able to retrieve and set Registry entries, given the path through the Registry to a value. For example, you may want to retrieve the current value of \HKEY_CURRENT_USER\Control Panel\Desktop\ ScreenSaveActive. You do this by walking down through the various keys. We have provided a generic routine, glrGetRegistryValueFromPath(), that does the walking for you and returns the value of the key. The function is shown in Listing 18.8. You would call it with:

```
Dim strValue As String

strValue = glrGetRegistryValueFromPath _
 ("\HKEY_CURRENT_USER\Control Panel\Desktop\ScreenSaveActive")
```

> **NOTE**
>
> Chapter 19 provides another version of this code, which uses wrapper functions to call into MSAU7032.DLL. These functions perform similar functionality.

Listing 18.8

```
Public Function glrGetRegistryValueFromPath(strPath as String) _
 As Variant
    ' Returns the value from a registry path
    '

    Dim hKey As Long
    Dim strValue As String

    If Not IsError _
     (glrGetKeyAndValueFromPath(strPath, hKey, strValue)) Then
        glrGetRegistryValueFromPath = _
         glrGetRegistryValue(hKey, strValue)
        Call glr_apiRegCloseKey(hKey)
    End If
End Function

Public Function glrGetRegistryValueFromPath(strPath As String) _
 As Variant
    ' Returns the value from a registry path

    Dim hKey As Long
    Dim strValue As String

    If Not IsError _
     (glrGetKeyAndValueFromPath(strPath, hKey, strValue)) Then
```

```
            glrGetRegistryValueFromPath = _
             glrGetRegistryValue(hKey, strValue)
            Call glr_apiRegCloseKey(hKey)
        End If
End Function
```

glrGetRegistryValueFromPath() is calling the same functions we used for our Registry browser. It takes apart the path passed in, assuming the last entry is a value and the other entries are keys separated by backslashes. It traverses down through each key, using RegOpenKeyEx(), until it finds the last one. Then it calls glrGetRegistryValue() to retrieve the value.

NOTE Each Registry key has a default entry that has no value name. To retrieve the default entry for a key, follow the key name with a backslash when calling glrGetRegistryValueFromPath( ). For example, to retrieve the default value of the Desktop key mentioned previously in this chapter, you use \HKEY_CURRENT_USER\Control Panel\Desktop\.

Listing 18.9 shows the code for glrSetRegistryValueFromPath(), which sets a value based on a path. It executes virtually the same code as glrGetRegistryValueFromPath(), except that it looks at the result of the VarType() function on the strValue key passed in and calls RegSetValueEx() in the appropriate manner to write the value into the Registry. The only datatypes supported in this code are Strings and Longs. The other datatypes are stubbed out.

Listing 18.9

```
Public Function glrSetRegistryValueFromPath _
 (ByVal strPath As String, ByVal varValue As Variant) _
 As Variant
    ' Sets a value based on a registry path

    Dim hKey As Long
    Dim strValue As String
    Dim retCode As Long

    If Not IsError _
     (glrGetKeyAndValueFromPath(strPath, hKey, strValue)) Then
```

```
Select Case VarType(varValue.)
Case vbEmpty
    Call glrAssert(False)      'Stubbed out
Case vbNull
    Call glrAssert(False)      'Stubbed out
Case vbInteger
    Call glrAssert(False)      'Stubbed out
Case vbLong
    retCode = glr_apiRegSetValueEx(hKey, strValue, _
    0&, REG_DWORD, CLng(varValue), 4)
    Select Case retCode And APPLICATION_ERROR_MASK
    Case ERROR_SEVERITY_SUCCESS
    Case Else
        glrSetRegistryValueFromPath = CVErr(0)
    End Select
Case vbSingle
    Call glrAssert(False)      'Stubbed out
Case vbDouble
    Call glrAssert(False)      'Stubbed out
Case vbCurrency
    Call glrAssert(False)      'Stubbed out
Case vbDate
    Call glrAssert(False)      'Stubbed out
Case vbString
    retCode = glr_apiRegSetValueEx(hKey, strValue, _
    0&, REG_SZ, ByVal CStr(varValue), Len(varValue))
    Select Case retCode And APPLICATION_ERROR_MASK
    Case ERROR_SEVERITY_SUCCESS
    Case Else
        glrSetRegistryValueFromPath = CVErr(0)
    End Select
Case vbObject
    Call glrAssert(False)      'Stubbed out
Case vbError
    Call glrAssert(False)      'Stubbed out
Case vbBoolean
    Call glrAssert(False)      'Stubbed out
Case vbVariant
    Call glrAssert(False)      'Stubbed out
Case vbDataObject
    Call glrAssert(False)      'Stubbed out
Case vbByte
    Call glrAssert(False)      'Stubbed out
Case vbArray
    Call glrAssert(False)      'Stubbed out
```

```
        Case Else
            Call glrAssert(False)    'Should never happen
        End Select
        Call glr_apiRegCloseKey(hKey)
    End If
End Function
```

How to Construct a Declare Statement

When you first start calling the DLLs, you won't need to construct Declare statements. Instead, you will get them from some source, such as WIN32API.TXT. However, at some point you may call a DLL that doesn't have a Declare statement already prepared for it. In this case you need to construct a Declare statement from scratch. Also, the file WIN32API.TXT is not perfect. Some of the Declare statements don't allow you to call some of the Windows API calls with arguments of certain types. Also, we have found bugs in some of the Declare statements as we have worked with them. These may or may not be fixed in your copy of WIN32API.TXT, so understanding how to construct a Declare statement is a useful skill.

The Declare statement gives VBA six pieces of information about the procedure:

- The scope of the declaration
- The name of the procedure as you want to call it in your code
- The name and path of the containing DLL
- The name of the procedure as it exists in the DLL
- The number and datatypes of the arguments to the procedure
- If the procedure is a function, the datatype of the return value of the function

Given this information, VBA knows how to locate the function on the hard disk and how to arrange the arguments on the stack so they are acceptable to the DLL. The *stack* is a special segment of memory that programs use for storing temporary information. VBA pushes arguments onto the stack, the DLL function is called, and DLL manipulates the arguments. Then the return value is placed on the stack for VBA to return to your program.

The Declare statement defines the size of the arguments to a DLL function and what the arguments mean. It is *crucial* that the declaration be exactly what the DLL expects. Otherwise, you may be giving the DLL incorrect information, and that may cause the DLL to reference information in an invalid segment of memory. A General Protection (GP) fault is the result when a program tries to access memory it doesn't have the privilege to read or write. If you receive a GP fault, Access crashes without giving you a chance to save objects that need to be saved.

Defining the VBA Declare statement is similar to defining any other sub or function, except that there is no body to the procedure. The body of the procedure resides in the DLL. Once you have declared a DLL function, you can call it almost as though the code were part of VBA. Declare statements must appear at the module level. The Declare statement takes one of two forms, depending on whether the DLL function being called returns a value:

[Public | Private] Declare Sub *subname* Lib *"libname"*

[Alias *"aliasname"*] [([*argumentlist*])]

or

[Public | Private] Declare Function *functionname* Lib *"libname"*

[Alias *"aliasname"*] [([*argumentlist*])] [As *type*]

Here is an example of a Declare statement:

```
Private Declare Function FindWindow Lib "user32" _
 Alias "FindWindowA" _
 (ByVal lpClassName As String, _
 ByVal lpWindowName As String) As Long
```

If the function returns no value (that is, it is declared with the return type *void* in the C programming language), you use the Declare Sub format of the Declare statement. If the function returns a value (and almost all of them do), you use the Declare Function format.

Public versus Private

Just as any normal procedure declaration has a scope that determines what other procedures can call it, procedures defined by Declare statements also have a scope. You can call a DLL procedure from code only within the same form or module as the Declare statement if you prefix the Declare statement with the word *Private*. You can call a DLL function from any code if the Declare statement is prefixed with the word *Public*. Not using either Public or Private is the same as scoping the function with Public. A Declare statement in the General Declarations section of a form must have the Private scope. A Declare statement in a module can have either scope.

Specifying the Procedure Name

The function or sub name given in the Declare statement is the name that is used when you call it in your code. It must follow the same naming rules as for any VBA procedure name:

- It must begin with a letter.
- The other characters must be in the sets A–Z, a–z, 0–9, or an underscore character.
- It must be unique within the same scope.
- It must be no longer than 255 characters.
- It cannot be a VBA keyword.

If you don't supply an Alias clause, the name of the procedure must match the name of the function in the DLL. (See the section "Specifying the Alias" a little later in this chapter.)

Specifying the Lib

The Lib portion of the declaration tells VBA the DLL's name and also, potentially, its location on the disk. You must enclose the Lib name in quotes. It is not case sensitive. If the function you are declaring is in one of the main Windows DLLs, you can omit the .DLL extension. For example, you can use "User32", "GDI32", or "Kernel32". VBA appends the .DLL extension to these names. For other DLLs, you must include the DLL name.

If you do not include the path on the DLL name, Windows uses this order to search for the DLL:

1. The directory from which the application loaded (for Access, that's the directory from which Access is loaded, not the directory where your MDB is stored.)

2. The current directory

3. Windows NT only: the 32-bit Windows system directory (Windows\System32)

4. The Windows system directory (Windows\System)

5. The Windows directory (Windows)

6. The directories that are listed in the PATH environment variable

This order can cause some confusion. If you put a DLL in the Windows directory but there is an older version of the DLL in the Windows\System directory, the older version will get called. Furthermore, this order has changed from earlier versions of Windows.

Specifying the Alias

You may include an alias clause when you declare a procedure. The alias clause of the declaration is important because it allows you to change the name of the function from the way it was specified in the DLL to a different name in VBA. There are several reasons why you might use the alias:

- To change the procedure name in the DLL to one VBA allows

- To change the case of the DLL procedure call

- To set the procedure name to a DLL function that is only exposed by ordinal

- To have a unique procedure name in an Access library

- To leave off the "A" required by ANSI versions of Windows API calls

These reasons are explained in more detail in the following sections.

Changing the Procedure Name in the DLL to One VBA Allows

The names that programming languages such as C allow for functions are different from those VBA allows. VBA function names must consist of alphanumeric or underscore characters and begin with a letter. C function names often begin with an underscore. The function name you specify in the Declare statement must be a valid VBA procedure name. If the name in the DLL doesn't match the VBA naming rules, you must use an alias. The name in the DLL might also be a reserved word in VBA, or it might be the name of an existing global variable or function, and in these cases, too, you must use an alias.

For example, VBA does not allow function names with a leading underscore. If the name in the DLL is _lwrite, you might declare the function as

```
Declare Function lwrite Lib "Kernel32" Alias "_lwrite" _
 (ByVal hFile As Integer, ByVal lpBuffer As String, _
 ByVal intBytes As Integer) As Integer
```

This defines the function name lwrite() as the _lwrite() function in the Kernel32 Dynamic Link Library.

NOTE Although the _lwrite() function still exists in Win32, it is provided only for backward compatibility with 16-bit Windows. You should use the WriteFile() function in your code.

Changing the Case of the DLL Procedure Call

The name of the procedure given in the Declare statement is case sensitive. This means it must exactly match the case of the procedure name in the DLL. If you wish to have the procedure name in your code use a different capitalization than that given in the DLL, you must use an alias clause. This wasn't true in 16-bit Windows, so if you are converting Declare statements from old code, you need to be aware of this.

Setting the Procedure Name That Is Exposed by Ordinal

Every function in a DLL is assigned a number, called its *ordinal*. Every function in a DLL *may* expose its name but is not required to do so. The programmer writing a DLL chooses which procedures within the DLL can be called from code existing outside the DLL; these functions are *exposed*.

To call a function by ordinal, you must know the ordinal number for the function. You can find this information in the documentation for the DLL (if any) or in the .DEF file for the DLL. Tools are also available that can examine a DLL. Whichever way you derive the ordinal, you specify #*ordinalnumber* for the alias name—that is, a pound sign followed by the decimal number of the ordinal. For example, the same lwrite declaration presented earlier might be declared as

```
Declare Function lwrite Lib "Kernel32" Alias "#86" _
 (ByVal hFile As Integer, ByVal lpBuffer As String, _
 ByVal intBytes As Integer) As Integer
```

You may declare any VBA function to use the ordinal in the DLL, but if the name is exported, we recommend you use the name. This is especially important if you do not maintain the DLL. The DLL developer may assume that people will not call a function by ordinal if it is exported by name. Later versions of the DLL may not keep the same ordinal number for the functions in it but will most likely keep the same name.

Having a Unique Procedure Name in an Access Library

Each declared function at the same level of scope in VBA must have a unique name. Normally, this doesn't have huge implications, since you are not likely to give two different functions the same name or declare the same function twice in your own code. But if you are developing a library database that might be included on different systems and that library calls functions in a DLL (including Windows API calls), this issue becomes important.

Suppose your library calls the GetComputerName() Windows API call. If you declare the function in the library with Public scope but without an alias, VBA uses the name GetComputerName(). If users then decide to use GetComputerName() in their own code and declare it as Public, the name in their code conflicts with the name in your library. For this reason, public declarations in a library should always use an alias. Thus, you might declare GetComputerName() in a library as

```
Declare Function MYLB_GetComputerName _
 Lib "kernel32" Alias "GetComputerNameA" _
 (ByVal lpBuffer As String, nSize As Long) As Long
```

When you use the function in the library, you then use MYLB_GetComputer-Name() as the function name. By doing this, users avoid conflicts if they also define GetComputerName().

NOTE   All the public Windows API declarations in this book have been aliased using the prefix "glr_api".

Leaving Off the "A" Required by ANSI Windows API Calls

You can use the Alias clause to do any renaming of functions you wish. One common use is to rename ANSI Windows API calls that have a trailing "A" to the same name without the "A". The "A" is used in functions such as FindWindowA() to indicate that the arguments being passed in are ANSI strings. (You can find a further discussion of ANSI and Unicode functions in the section "Unicode to ANSI and Back" later in this chapter.)

Specifying the Arguments

You pass arguments to a DLL on the stack. The DLL expects those arguments to be placed in a particular order and to have a certain size on the stack. When VBA places arguments on the stack, it looks to the Declare statement for direction. Arguments placed on the stack appear as a series of bytes. The DLL groups and decodes those bytes to use them in the parameters for the DLL call. If the VBA Declare statement and the DLL don't agree on what those bytes mean, incorrect data appears in the parameters for the DLL call. When the DLL tries to use the parameters, it gets the wrong information. Worse, if your program doesn't place enough data on the stack, the DLL will read data left over from previous use of the stack.

Correctly declaring arguments is the trickiest part of using a DLL from VBA. This subject is discussed in the following section.

Converting C Parameters into VBA Declarations

Most DLLs are written in C. The documentation is usually in the form of a C header file (.h file) that provides the type and number of the arguments to the functions in the DLL. Based on the datatype required, you will need to convert it to an equivalent VBA datatype. Table 18.1 shows how to convert various C datatypes to VBA.

TABLE 18.1: Conversions between C Datatypes and Access Datatypes

C Datatype	Access Basic Datatype
ATOM	ByVal atom As Integer
BOOL	ByVal fValue As Integer
BYTE	ByVal bytValue As Byte
BYTE *	bytValue As Byte
CALLBACK	ByVal lngAddr As Long
char	ByVal bytValue As Byte
char _huge *	ByVal strValue As String
char FAR *	ByVal strValue As String
char NEAR *	ByVal strValue As String
DWORD	ByVal lngValue As Long
FARPROC	ByVal lngAddress As Long
HACCEL	ByVal hAccel As Long
HANDLE	ByVal h As Long
HBITMAP	ByVal hBitmap As Long
HBRUSH	ByVal hBrush As Long
HCURSOR	ByVal hCursor As Long
HDC	ByVal hDC As Long
HDRVR	ByVal hDrvr As Long
HDWP	ByVal hDWP As Long
HFILE	ByVal hFile As Integer
HFONT	ByVal hFont As Long
HGDIOBJ	ByVal hGDIObj As Long
HGLOBAL	ByVal hGlobal As Long
HICON	ByVal hIcon As Long
HINSTANCE	ByVal hInstance As Long
HLOCAL	ByVal hLocal As Long
HMENU	ByVal hMenu As Long
HMETAFILE	ByVal hMetafile As Long
HMODULE	ByVal hModule As Long
HPALETTE	ByVal hPalette As Long

TABLE 18.1: Conversions between C Datatypes and Access Datatypes (continued)

C Datatype	Access Basic Datatype
HPEN	ByVal hPen As Long
HRGN	ByVal hRgn As Long
HRSRC	ByVal hRsrc As Long
HTASK	ByVal hTask As Long
HWND	ByVal hWnd As Long
int	ByVal intValue As Integer
int FAR *	intValue As Integer
LONG	ByVal lngValue As Long
long	ByVal lngValue As Long
LPARAM	ByVal lngParam As Long
LPCSTR	ByVal strValue As String
LPSTR	ByVal strValue As String
LPVOID	varValue As Any
LRESULT	ByVal lngResult As Long
UINT	ByVal intValue As Integer
UINT FAR *	intValue As Integer
void _huge *	bytValue( ) As Byte
void FAR *	bytValue( ) As Byte
WORD	ByVal intValue As Integer
WPARAM	ByVal intValue As Integer

More Advanced Details of Calling DLLs

At this point this chapter has discussed most of the details of calling a DLL. Really understanding what is going on, though, requires a fuller understanding of what happens during a DLL call.

Understanding Passing By Value and By Reference

You can pass an argument on the stack to a DLL in one of two ways: by value or by reference. *By value* means that a copy of the actual value of what is being passed is pushed onto the stack. *By reference* means that the address of what is being passed is pushed onto the stack. Unless you tell it otherwise, VBA passes all arguments by reference. On the other hand, most DLLs are written in C, and unless you tell the C compiler otherwise (by passing an address), C passes all arguments by value. The VBA declaration *must* be set up correctly to pass arguments the way the DLL expects them to be passed.

The semantic difference between passing by value and by reference is this:

- When you pass by value, a copy of the value is placed on the stack. Any changes to the value inside the DLL have an effect only on the copy and do not change the value for the calling code.

- When you pass by reference, the address of the original value is placed on the stack. If the DLL makes changes to the value, the calling code will be able to see those changes.

To understand the difference, look at the declaration in C of the function GetFileSize():

```
DWORD GetFileSize
    (
    HANDLE hFile,              // handle of file to get size of
    LPDWORD lpFileSizeHigh,    // address of high-order word
                               // for file size
    );
```

The GetFileSize() function takes two arguments:

Parameter	Meaning
hFile	Specifies an open handle of the file whose size is being returned. The handle must have been created with either GENERIC_READ or GENERIC_WRITE access to the file

Parameter	Meaning
lpFileSizeHigh	Points to the variable where the high-order word of the file size is returned. This parameter can be Null if the application does not require the high-order word

The first, hFile, is a handle to a file by value. The second, lpFileSizeHigh, is a Long by reference. The function fills in the second argument. Suppose you call this function with the following code (from frmGetFileSize in CH18.MDB):

```
Dim hFile As Long
    Dim lngHigh As Long
    Dim curSize As Currency

    hFile = CreateFile(CStr(glrSTRDIR & lstFiles.Value), _
     GENERIC_READ, FILE_SHARE_READ, ByVal 0&, OPEN_EXISTING, _
     0&, 0&)
    If Not Err.LastDllError Then
        curSize = GetFileSize(hFile, lngHigh)
        If lngHigh > 0 Then
            curSize = curSize + 2 ^ 32 * lngHigh
        End If
        txtSize.Value = curSize
        Call CloseHandle(hFile)
    Else
        txtSize.Value = "#Error#"
    End If
```

At the point where GetFileSize() is called, a diagram of the stack looks like this:

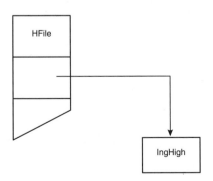

Notice that the value for hFile is directly on the stack (by value) and that a reference to lngHigh is placed on the stack (by reference).

> **NOTE**
>
> In computer science publications, stack diagrams traditionally grow downward on the page. We follow that tradition in these diagrams.

Passing Strings to a DLL: The Real Story

As mentioned earlier in this chapter, Windows has two ways of storing strings: LPSTR and BSTR. String parameters to DLL functions must specify which kind of string they accept. Internally, VBA uses BSTRs to store strings. If the function accepts an LPSTR as a parameter, the argument must be converted from a BSTR into an LPSTR before being passed in. The vast majority of DLLs that are passed strings expect to be passed LPSTRs, including all the Windows API calls (except OLE calls). This means you need some method of converting BSTRs to LPSTRs. To effect this, you should understand how BSTRs and LPSTRs are stored in memory.

An LPSTR is an address of a null-terminated string. A *null-terminated string* is a set of characters followed by a character with the ANSI value 0. An LPSTR is stored in memory like this:

A BSTR passed by reference, on the other hand, is the address of the address of a null-terminated string. It is stored in memory like this:

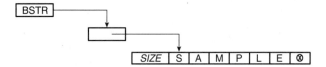

Since the stack is a small temporary storage area and a string can be up to two billion characters long, VBA cannot pass strings by value, storing a copy of the entire string on the stack, because they would overflow the stack. For this reason, VBA passes all strings by reference.

Here is an example: SetVolumeLabel accepts two strings. The Windows API definition states that those strings must be passed as LPSTRs. Passing an LPSTR by reference means you want to pass the address of the first character of the null-terminated string. Suppose you want to pass "C:\" as the drive name and "DRIVE_C" as the volume name when the function is called. This is how the function wants the stack to look at the time it is called:

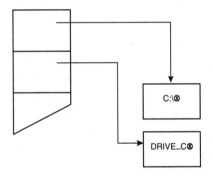

If you try to pass BSTRs by reference, you pass the address of the BSTR, which is diagrammed like this:

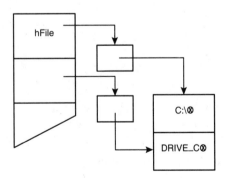

This obviously does not match the way the function wants the stack arranged. But if you pass the BSTR *by value*, you pass the address of the first character of the string, which is exactly what you want:

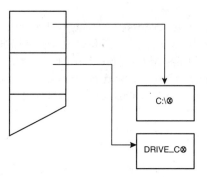

Notice that this is exactly the same as passing the LPSTR by reference. What it all boils down to is this: *passing a BSTR by value converts it from a BSTR to an LPSTR*. The way to perform the conversion is by specifying in the Declare statement that the string is to be passed ByVal. The Declare statement for SetVolumeLabel() looks like this:

```
Declare Function SetVolumeLabel _
  Lib "kernel32" Alias "SetVolumeLabelA" _
  (ByVal lpRootPathName As String, _
  ByVal lpVolumeName As String) As Long
```

The ByVal keywords in the Declare statement cause the arguments passed in to be converted from the VBA BSTRs to LPSTRs.

Using vbNullString—A Closer Look

As shown in the section "Using the vbNullString Constant" earlier in this chapter, you can also pass a Null as the second argument to delete the volume label (at least in Windows NT). How can you pass a null pointer? You cannot pass an empty string, because that would pass a pointer to the empty string. (Remember that strings are passed by reference.) Passing an empty string would result in a stack like this:

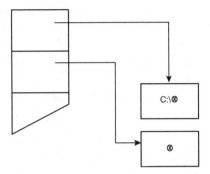

On the other hand, to pass a Null as the second argument, you want the stack to look like this:

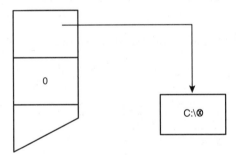

Notice that these two diagrams do not represent the same thing. The first stack passes a null pointer, and the second stack passes a pointer to a null character. So how do you pass a null pointer? You pass the vbNullString constant as the second argument. VBA treats the vbNullString constant in a special way. It is a 4-byte-long zero, but no type checking is done on it when it is passed as a string argument. Since the second string argument is declared as being ByVal, passing vbNullString causes a 4-byte-long zero to be placed on the stack. So to delete the volume label, you call SetVolumeLabel with:

```
Call SetVolumeLabel("C:\", vbNullString)
```

Unicode to ANSI and Back

The preceding discussion simplifies one more important subject about passing strings to DLL procedures: VBA stores strings internally as Unicode and converts those strings to ANSI at the time a DLL function call is made. *Unicode* is a character-encoding scheme that uses 2 bytes to represent each character, allowing representation of 65,536 different characters. The Unicode specification has assigned every character from every major language in the world to one of the Unicode values. ANSI uses only 1 byte per character and can represent only 256 different characters.

Internally, VBA represents every string in Unicode format. Whenever you make a function call, VBA intercepts the call if any argument is a string or a user-defined structure that contains a string. A temporary buffer is created, and then the strings are converted from Unicode, with the result placed in the temporary buffer. Then the pointers are fixed up to point to the converted strings. When the function returns, all strings are converted back from ANSI to Unicode before VBA returns control to you.

Here is a diagram of the string before calling the function GetWindowText():

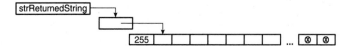

The string is internally stored as Unicode.

Then VBA makes the function call. In the process of making the call, VBA converts the string from Unicode to ANSI so it looks like this:

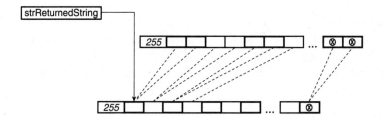

On returning, the string is again turned into Unicode.

This conversion from ANSI to Unicode has several implications:

- You must never try to represent binary information within strings. If the information is not human readable as ANSI characters, you must pass an array of bytes.

- You must call functions that expect ANSI strings. Any Win32 function that has strings as parameters comes in two versions. One ends in the letter "A" and accepts ANSI strings as arguments. The other ends in the letter "W" (for Wide) and accepts Unicode arguments. You must always call the function that ends in the letter "A". Typically, the Declare statement specifies an alias clause that defines the "A" version to be a generic name without either the "A" or "W". For example, GetWindowText() is aliased to be the function Get-WindowTextA() within the DLL. If you wish to pass Unicode to a DLL, you should use a type library.

- VBA not only translates string arguments passed directly, it translates strings defined in user-defined types.

Using the Any Datatype

Certain API calls require different types of arguments, depending on how they are called. For example, the WinHelp() function is defined in the C programming language like this:

```
BOOL WinHelp
    (
    HWND hwnd,          // handle of window requesting Help
    LPCTSTR lpszHelp,   // address of directory-path string
    UINT uCommand,      // type of Help
    DWORD dwData        // additional data
    );
```

The first two arguments are the hWnd of the parent window and the name of the Help file. The wCommand argument defines what you want Windows to do with the Help file. How the dwData argument is used is based on which constant is passed in for the wCommand argument. Two possible values for the wCommand argument are described in the following table.

CHAPTER 18

wCommand	dwData	Meaning
HELP_ CONTEXT	Unsigned Long Integer containing the context number for the topic	Displays the topic identified by a context number that has been defined in the [MAP] section of the Help project file
HELP_ PARTIALKEY	Long pointer to a string that contains a keyword for the requested topic	Displays the topic in the keyword list that matches the keyword passed in the dwData parameter, if there is one exact match. If there is more than one match, it displays the Search dialog box with the topics listed in the Go To box. If there is no match, it displays the Search dialog box
		If you just want to bring up the Search dialog box without passing a keyword (the third result), use a long pointer to an empty string

This presents a problem: HELP_CONTEXT wants a Long passed by value on the stack, whereas HELP_PARTIALKEY wants a string passed by reference; the way you call the function determines the datatype of the last argument. So how can you declare the function so it allows both choices? The answer is the Any datatype. The Any datatype tells VBA that at the time you declare the function, you don't know what the datatype is or how big it is. It defers supplying this information until you call the procedure. This removes compile-time type checking, so all the responsibility for passing reasonable arguments is in your court: you must make sure you actually pass reasonable data to the DLL call. The declaration for this function would be

```
Public Declare Function WinHelp _
 Lib "User32" Alias "WinHelpA" _
 (ByVal hwnd As Long, _
 ByVal lpszHelp As String, _
 ByVal uCommand As Integer, _
 dwData As Any) As Long
```

Notice that the datatype for the dwData argument is Any. At the time the function is called, you need to provide VBA with three pieces of information:

- The datatype of the argument
- Whether that datatype should be passed by value or by reference
- The contents of the argument

You can include ByVal or ByRef in both the Declare statement and the call. Whatever you use in the call overrides what is in the Declare statement.

You can call this function in two ways:

```
lngRet = WinHelp(me.hwnd, me.HelpFile, HELP_CONTEXT, ByVal 3&)
lngRet = WinHelp(me.hwnd, me.HelpFile, HELP_PARTIALKEY, _
 ByVal "FindThis")
```

The HELP_CONTEXT call to WinHelp() passes a "ByVal 3&" in the dwData argument. This provides VBA with the following information:

- The information is to be passed by value.
- Four bytes are to be placed onto the stack.
- The contents of the 4 bytes should be the value 3.

The ByVal indicates that the argument is passed by value. The ampersand (&) is an indication that the constant is a Long, not an Integer. Without the ampersand, only 2 bytes would be placed on the stack, whereas the function wants 4.

The HELP_PARTIALKEY call to the function provides it with the following information:

- The information is to be passed by reference.
- The information is a string.
- The string should be converted from a BSTR to an LPSTR.

All strings are passed by reference, and the datatype of the argument is a string constant. The ByVal here performs the conversion between the BSTR and the LPSTR. Because a ByVal wasn't included in the Declare statement for this argument, the ByVal is required in the call statement.

Using Err.LastDLLError

When you call a Windows API call from Visual Basic, the possibility usually exists that the call will fail. The function indicates this failure by returning some special value, such as 0 or False. When you are using the Windows API from C, you can then call a function named GetLastError() to find out why it failed. Unfortunately, calling GetLastError() from VBA doesn't report accurate results. The reason is that VBA itself is also doing Windows API calls. By the time you get a chance to call Get-LastError(), VBA has already messed up the result GetLastError() would have reported. To get around this problem, VBA implements the LastDLLError property of the Err object. This property is filled in with the error code of the last DLL call you made. You can use this property instead of calling GetLastError(). For example:

```
fRet = SetVolumeLabel("C:\", vbNullString)
If Not fRet Then
    If Err.LastDllError = ERROR_INVALID_PARAMETER then
        MsgBox "Due to a Windows '95 bug, the volume label" _
        & " won't delete"
    End If
End If
```

Using Callback Functions

A small percentage of the Windows functions require a callback function. A *callback* is a procedure *you* provide for *Windows* to call. Windows calls the callback multiple times, and with each call Windows passes arguments that reference an object in an internal data structure. For example, a call to the EnumWindows() function requires a callback. The callback function is called once for each top-level window currently open and is passed a handle to it until they have all been enumerated. In the C declaration, the argument in which you indicate the address of the callback has the datatype FARPROC or CALLBACK.

Because VBA cannot intrinsically handle callback functions, there are two ways to handle external functions that require callbacks. One is to write a DLL that contains a function that can be used for the callback. The other is to use a special OLE control that already has the callback function written. The OLE callback procedure generates an event when Windows calls it. At the time of this writing, no OLE control of this type exists, but VBX controls of this type have been available for Visual Basic for several years. (For example, Spyworks/VB from Desaware has one.) These controls should be available soon in OLE control versions.

User-Defined Types and DWORD Packing

When VBA passes a user-defined type to a DLL, it refuses to allow any particular declaration within the structure to cross a DWORD (4-byte) boundary. Instead, it pads out bytes so that the next definition starts on a DWORD boundary. This means that if you compile your own DLL, you must either provide that padding yourself or use the Struct Member Alignment option the C compiler provides. For example, if you have a structure that looks like this:

```
Type TESTSTRUCT
    intTest As Integer
    bytTest As Byte
    lngTest As Long
End Type
```

the structure in memory is represented like this:

```
intTest
bytTest
One byte of padding to make the lngTest align to a DWORD boundary
lngTest
```

so the structure takes up 8 bytes in memory. If, instead, the structure is arranged like this:

```
Type TESTSTRUCT
    bytTest As Byte
    lngTest As Long
    intTest As Integer
End Type
```

it is padded out to look like this in memory:

```
bytTest
Three bytes of padding
lngTest
intTest
Two bytes of padding
```

thus it takes up 12 bytes in memory.

If the DLL is compiled with the Struct Member Alignment option, the C compiler provides the appropriate padding to make the structure members line up with the way the structure is passed from VBA. On the other hand, you would be better off arranging the elements within the structure so they are DWORD aligned to begin with.

This implicit padding that VBA provides does not cause a problem with the Windows API, because the API structures have been DWORD aligned, but it can cause a problem if you use other DLLs. If the DLL is not compiled with the Struct Member Alignment option and has elements that cross DWORD boundaries, you cannot pass the bytes in the correct arrangement without doing a very tricky manipulation of the bytes within the structure.

Converting Windows API Calls from Access 2.0

If you are converting code from Access 2.0, you will need to revisit all your Windows API calls; many of them have changed. This is a significant amount of work.

Windows API calls come in four classes when ported to Win32:

- Calls that merely have to reference the Win32 libraries instead of the Win16 libraries
- Calls that now have additional functionality under Win32
- Calls that have a new extended version (For example, GetWindowExt has a new extended version, GetWindowExtEx.)
- Calls that are not supported under Win32

Use the following steps as a guideline to make the conversion:

1. Start by finding each of your Declare statements in existing code.
2. Look in the Win32 documentation to determine in which one of the four classes of conversions the call falls.
3. Replace the Declare statement with the new Declare statement (unless the call is no longer supported in Win32).
4. Examine every function call to your Windows API calls. Make sure the arguments match the datatype of the parameters in the Declare statement. A great

many of the arguments will need to be changed from Integers to Longs. Make sure these changes propagate throughout your code.

5. Save your database and make a backup copy.

6. Set a breakpoint on each of your API calls. Run your code. When you reach the breakpoint, verify that the arguments are both the correct value and the correct size. Then step through the call.

This is a lot of work, but it is absolutely necessary to get your code to work reliably under Win32.

Table 18.2 is not exhaustive, but it may help with some of the conversions:

TABLE 18.2: Some Windows 3.1 Calls That Need to Be Changed for Windows 95 or Windows NT

Win16 Call	Replace with
GetWindowWord	GetWindowLong
SetWindowWord	SetWindowLong
GetClassWord	GetClassLong
SetClassWord	SetClassLong
GetPrivateProfileString	(VBA built-in function GetSetting or GetAllSettings)
GetPrivateProfileInt	(VBA built-in function GetSetting)
WritePrivateProfileString	(VBA built-in statement SaveSetting)
MoveTo	MoveToEx
OffsetViewportOrg	OffsetViewportOrgEx
OffsetWindowOrg	OffsetWindowOrgEx
GetAspectRatioFilter	GetAspectRatioFilterEx
GetBitmapDimension	GetBitmapDimensionEx
GetBrushOrg	GetBrushOrgEx
GetCurrentPosition	GetCurrentPositionEx
GetTextExtent	GetTextExtentPoint
GetViewportExt	GetViewportExtEx
GetViewportOrg	GetViewportOrgEx
GetWindowExt	GetWindowExtEx
GetWindowOrg	GetWindowOrgEx

TABLE 18.2: Some Windows 3.1 Calls That Need to Be Changed for Windows 95 or Windows NT (continued)

Win16 Call	Replace with
ScaleViewportExt	ScaleViewportExtEx
ScaleWindowExt	ScaleWindowExtEx
SetBitmapDimension	SetBitmapDimensionEx
SetMetaFileBits	SetMetaFileBitsEx
SetViewportExt	SetViewportExtEx
SetViewportOrg	SetViewportOrgEx
SetWindowExt	SetWindowExtEx
SetWindowOrg	SetWindowdOrgEx
AccessResource	(No longer exists in Win32)
AllocDSToCSAlias	(No longer exists in Win32)
AllocResource	(No longer exists in Win32)
AllocSelector	(No longer exists in Win32)
Catch	(No longer exists in Win32)
ChangeSelector	(No longer exists in Win32)
FreeSelector	(No longer exists in Win32)
GetCodeHandle	(No longer exists in Win32)
GetCodeInfo	(No longer exists in Win32)
GetCurrentPDB	(No longer exists in Win32)
GetEnvironment	(No longer exists in Win32)
GetInstanceData	(No longer exists in Win32)
GetKBCodePage	(No longer exists in Win32)
GetModuleUsage	(No longer exists in Win32)
GlobalDOSAlloc	(No longer exists in Win32)
GlobalDOSFree	(No longer exists in Win32)
GlobalNotify	(No longer exists in Win32)
GlobalPageLock	(No longer exists in Win32)
LockData	(No longer exists in Win32)
NetBIOSCall	(No longer exists in Win32)
Throw	(No longer exists in Win32)
SetEnvironment	(No longer exists in Win32)

TABLE 18.2: Some Windows 3.1 Calls That Need to Be Changed for Windows 95 or Windows NT (continued)

Win16 Call	Replace with
SetResourceHandler	(No longer exists in Win32)
SwitchStackBack	(No longer exists in Win32)
SwitchStackTo	(No longer exists in Win32)
UnlockData	(No longer exists in Win32)
ValidateCodeSegments	(No longer exists in Win32)
ValidateFreeSpaces	(No longer exists in Win32)
Yield	(No longer exists in Win32)
IsGdiObject	(No longer exists in Win32)
IsTask	(No longer exists in Win32)
DefineHandleTable	(No longer exists in Win32)
MakeProcInstance	(No longer exists in Win32)
FreeProcInstance	(No longer exists in Win32)
GetFreeSpace	(No longer exists in Win32)
GlobalCompact	(No longer exists in Win32)
GlobalFix	(No longer exists in Win32)
GlobalUnfix	(No longer exists in Win32)
GlobalUnwire	(No longer exists in Win32)
LocalCompact	(No longer exists in Win32)
LocalShrink	(No longer exists in Win32)
LockSegment	(No longer exists in Win32)
UnlockSegment	(No longer exists in Win32)
SetSwapAreaSize	(No longer exists in Win32)

Summary

This chapter has covered the following topics:

- Declaring a DLL procedure from VBA
- Specifying the arguments

- Understanding passing by value and passing by reference
- Converting C parameters into VBA declarations
- Using callback functions
- Returning strings from a DLL
- Understanding the Unicode-to-ANSI issue
- Using the vbNullString constant
- Using the Any datatype
- Passing a user-defined type to a DLL
- User-defined types and DWORD packing
- Passing an array
- Using type libraries
- Using the Windows API
- Converting Windows API calls from Access 2.0
- Examples using the Windows API

DLLs are one of the three ways by which you can reach outside the bounds of Access into other Windows programs, the other two being DDE (see Chapter 20) and OLE (see Chapter 21). The DLL interface allows you to manipulate Windows directly through the Windows API, as well as to call your own DLLs. Combined with a C or C++ compiler and the appropriate knowledge, DLLs allow you to do virtually anything that is possible with Windows. But even without the use of C or C++, the ability to call the Windows API vastly extends the power of Access.

CHAPTER

NINETEEN

MSAU7032.DLL, the Undocumented Library

- File-handling functions

- Interfaces to Windows' common dialogs

- Font-handling functions

- Menu-handling functions

- Reading/writing values in the Registry

- DAO support

To make it possible for the Access Wizards to perform some of their wizardry, Access ships with a special DLL named MSAU7032.DLL. (This DLL replaces the similar library, MSAU200.DLL, that shipped as part of Access 2.) The functions that "live" in this library are meant to be called from VBA (because, of course, the Wizards are all written in VBA), and you can use them, too, in your own applications. The library includes a number of functions, of varying interest to you as an application developer, that break down into seven basic categories:

- **File-handling functions:** Check for file existence; split file name components; retrieve a full path given a relative path

- **Interfaces to Windows' common dialogs:** File Open/Close and Color Choosers

- **Menu-handling functions:** Clean a menu string; retrieve the text of a menu item; find the number of items in a menu; retrieve a handle to the Access menus or any specific menu; find the actual position of an item, given its condensed position; convert DoMenuItem numeric arguments into strings

- **Read and write Registry values:** Retrieve the number of subkeys and values for a given key; read and write keys and their values

- **Font-handling functions**: List available fonts and their sizes; retrieve the height and width of a given string in a specified font

- **Object-handling functions:** Retrieve a list of object names or a list of objects along with their types; sort an array of strings; sort an array of objects either by name or by type

- **Miscellaneous functions**: Check a file's national language; use Access' toolbar bitmaps; find the number of colors in a bitmap

This chapter discusses in detail each of the functions you can call from MSAU7032.DLL.

To use MSAU7032.DLL in your own applications, you need to ensure that the library exists in the current directory, the Access directory, the Windows directory, or the Windows\System directory. By default, Access places it in the directory that includes MSACCESS.EXE. If you're shipping an application using the Access runtime version and you need to use MSAU7032.DLL, be sure to place it somewhere where Windows will be able to find it. MSAU7032.DLL has been designated as distributable by Microsoft, so there are no licensing issues involved. You are free to distribute this file with any application, whether you use the retail version or the runtime version of Access.

WARNING Microsoft has documented none of the material in this chapter. That means that *any* of it can change (and some will definitely change) for the next version of Access. Because the current Access Wizards use everything in this chapter at one point or another, though, we feel strongly that you're safe in using the functions from MSAU7032.DLL in Access 95. Most of these functions will continue to work in future versions of Access (especially the functions that have nothing to do with Access, such as the Registry and Common Dialog wrappers), but we (and Microsoft) can make no guarantees.

WARNING The functions in MSAU7032.DLL were written for a specific purpose: to allow the Wizards to do their work. They were not written for general-purpose use, and may, at times, not do what you'd expect them to do. We've documented them here because they may be useful to your applications. They work fine in the examples we've tried, but they may or may not work in the situations to which you apply them. If these functions do not work as you might expect, do not curse at us or at Microsoft for providing shoddy software—the functions do work correctly, in the environment for which they were written.

Using MSAU7032.DLL

To use the functions in MSAU7032.DLL, you need to have the Declare statements for the functions available to your application. In addition, many of the functions require specific user-defined datatypes. As Access ships, the function declarations and datatype definitions are scattered throughout various Wizards and library databases. Although you needn't do anything special to use these functions and datatypes as they're declared in the Access Wizards, you'll find yourself doing extra work if you intend to ship your application with the Access run-time version. If you use the run-time version, you can't distribute the Wizard databases with your application. Therefore, you'll need some method of reproducing those declarations and datatypes in your own applications.

To make things as simple as possible, we've created a single module including all the function declarations and datatype definitions you'll need. Import bas-MSAU7032 (from CH19.MDB) into your application, and you'll be able to call any of the functions in MSAU7032.DLL. We've aliased each of the functions and datatypes so they won't conflict with the corresponding declarations in the Wizards and libraries if they're loaded.

NOTE
Many of the external procedure declarations in this chapter use numeric aliases. In Windows, when declaring the external procedure, you can refer to the item either by name or by ordinal number within the DLL. Using the number is actually a tiny bit faster, and it protects you in case the author changes the name of the procedure in a future revision. Mostly, we used numeric aliases because that's the way the Wizards have these functions declared.

File-Handling Functions

MSAU7032.DLL includes three file-handling functions, each of which performs one of the following activities:

- Checks for the existence of a file
- Splits a full path reference into its component pieces
- Gets the full path associated with a file

The following sections deal individually with each of these functions.

Checking for the Existence of a File

You can check for the existence of a file by calling the glr_msauFileExists() function. To call it, use syntax like this:

intRetval = glr_msauFileExists(*strFileName*)

This function returns 1 if the file exists or 0 otherwise.

For example, to check for the existence of C:\AUTOEXEC.BAT, you could use the following code:

```
If glr_msauFileExists("C:\AUTOEXEC.BAT") Then
    ' Do something
End If
```

TIP

To use any of the functions from MSAU7032.DLL, import basMSAU7032 (from CH19.MDB) into your own application. Many intricate dependencies exist between function declarations and user-defined data types, and it's just easier to import the entire module than to try to work out which pieces you need to copy.

NOTE

This function does its work by attempting to open the specified file with read privileges and deny write access. If another process has already exclusively opened the file, you may find that this function returns incorrect results.

Splitting a Full Path Reference into Components

As part of many applications, you'll need to take a full path reference, in the format

Drive:\Path\FileName.Ext

and retrieve any one of the single parts of the name (the drive, the path, the file name, or the extension) as a separate piece. The glrSplitPath subroutine (which calls the library function glr_msauSplitPath()) will do the work for you, filling in each of the various pieces.

For example, running the code in Listing 19.1 produces the output shown in Figure 19.1.

Listing 19.1

```
Sub TestSplitPath()
    Dim strDrive As String
    Dim strPath As String
    Dim strFileName As String
    Dim strExt As String

    glrSplitPath "C:\Windows\System\WIN.INI", strDrive, _
      strPath, strFileName, strExt
    Debug.Print "========================================"
    Debug.Print "Full : " & "C:\Windows\System\WIN.INI"
    Debug.Print "========================================"
    Debug.Print "Drive: " & strDrive
    Debug.Print "Path : " & strPath
    Debug.Print "File : " & strFileName
    Debug.Print "Ext  : " & strExt
    glrSplitPath "C:\", strDrive, strPath, _
      strFileName, strExt
    Debug.Print "========================================"
    Debug.Print "Full : " & "C:\"
    Debug.Print "========================================"
    Debug.Print "Drive: " & strDrive
    Debug.Print "Path : " & strPath
    Debug.Print "File : " & strFileName
    Debug.Print "Ext  : " & strExt
End Sub
```

Because the function in the DLL requires its parameter strings to be set up in a special fashion, you'll need to call this wrapper routine rather than the actual DLL function itself. The wrapper ends up calling glr_msauSplitPath(), but the calling conventions make it easier to call our wrapper instead.

FIGURE 19.1:

FIGURE 19.1:

The glrSplitPath procedure breaks a
full pathname into its components.

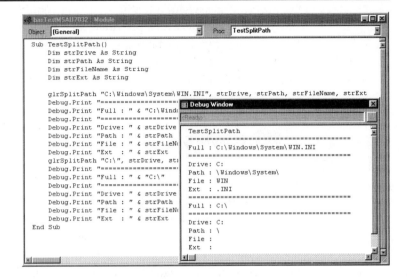

```
Sub TestSplitPath()
    Dim strDrive As String
    Dim strPath As String
    Dim strFileName As String
    Dim strExt As String

    glrSplitPath "C:\Windows\System\WIN.INI", strDrive, strPath, strFileName, strExt
    Debug.Print "===================
    Debug.Print "Full : " & "C:\Windo
    Debug.Print "===================
    Debug.Print "Drive: " & strDrive
    Debug.Print "Path : " & strPath
    Debug.Print "File : " & strFileNa
    Debug.Print "Ext  : " & strExt
    glrSplitPath "C:\", strDrive, st
    Debug.Print "===================
    Debug.Print "Full : " & "C:\"
    Debug.Print "===================
    Debug.Print "Drive: " & strDrive
    Debug.Print "Path : " & strPath
    Debug.Print "File : " & strFileNa
    Debug.Print "Ext  : " & strExt
End Sub
```

Debug Window output:
```
TestSplitPath
================================
Full : C:\Windows\System\WIN.INI
================================
Drive: C:
Path : \Windows\System\
File : WIN
Ext  : .INI
================================
Full : C:\
================================
Drive: C:
Path : \
File :
Ext  :
```

Getting the Full Path for a File

You can use the glrFullPath() function (which calls the glr_msauFullPath() routine
in MSAU7032.DLL) to retrieve the full path for a file, based on a relative path. For
example, if your current directory is the C:\Windows directory,

```
glrFullPath("..\OFFICE95\ACCESS\MSACCESS.EXE")
```

returns the value "C:\OFFICE95\ACCESS\MSACCESS.EXE", a fully qualified
pathname for the file. If you pass an invalid path to glrFullPath(), it returns a zero-
length string.

> **NOTE**
>
> This function can be confusing in its intent. It looks at the current
> directory and the relative pathname you've sent it and creates a
> complete pathname for the file based on that information. It does
> nothing more; it does not check for the existence of the file (you can
> pass it anything you wish for the file name), nor does it check to see
> whether the actual directories exist. Its purpose is to turn relative
> paths into absolute paths.

Because the glr_msauFullPath() function requires a small wrapper function to make it easy to call, we've provided the glrFullPath() function for you to call directly. To use it you must import the basMSAU7032 module from CH19.MDB into your own application. The glrFullPath() function ends up calling glr_msauFull-Path() in MSAU7032.DLL, but it's a lot simpler to call our wrapper function directly.

Using the Windows Common Dialogs

To standardize specific often-needed dialogs, Windows provides a series of common dialogs all applications can use. Access uses its own Print Setup dialog (one of the standard dialogs) but provides no mechanism for you to get to any of the others for your own applications. The code in MSAU7032.DLL provides a simple interface to the File Open/Save and Color Chooser dialogs. The following sections discuss how you can use the code in MSAU7032.DLL, along with the wrapper functions in basMSAU7032, to make it simple for you to use these common dialogs in your own applications.

NOTE The Access 2 version of this DLL, MSAU200.DLL, included an interface for the Font common dialog. This version, MSAU7032.DLL, does not. If you need to use the Font common dialog, you can either call the Windows API directly or use the Common Dialog OLE control that ships as part of the Access Developer's Toolkit and Visual Basic 4.

Using the File Open/File Save Common Dialog

You cannot have used Windows for long without noticing the standard File Open and File Save dialogs that most applications use. Windows provides them both, and MSAU7032.DLL makes it easy for you to use them yourself. The interface to the common dialogs requires you to send it some information, and Windows will do its job, pop up the dialog, and return information to you. Whether you are opening or saving a file, you must create a variable of the glr_msauGetFileNameInfo datatype. (We've defined this structure for you in basMSAU7032.) You fill out certain fields in the structure and then send it off to the glrGetFileName() function. This function either requests a file to open or a name under which to save (depending on the value in one of its parameters) and returns the structure to you, all filled out with the information the user chose from the dialog.

> **NOTE** Neither the File Open nor the File Save dialog actually *does* anything with the file. These dialogs just return a file name to your application, where you can decide what you wish to do with that file. It's up to you to actually open or save the file.

The designers of MSAU7032.DLL set the structure of the user-defined type, glr_msauGetFileNameInfo. If you were to call the common Windows dialog functions yourself, you'd use structures defined as part of the Windows SDK, which contain a few more fields and options. Because you're using MSAU7032.DLL to interface to the real library (COMDLG32.DLL), the available options are a bit limited. Table 19.1 lists all the fields in the structure, along with information on using those fields. Table 19.2 lists the possible values for the Flags field in this structure.

TABLE 19.1: Fields in the glr_msauGetFileNameInfo Structure

Field Name	Datatype	Description
hwndOwner	Long	Handle of the window that is to act as the parent of the dialog. You can use 0 if you don't want an owner, but this won't normally be the case. Use either the Access handle (if you want the dialog to be modal) or the handle of a form (if you don't). You can use a form's hWnd property to retrieve its handle or use Application.hWndAccessApp to use the Access handle
strFilter	String * 255	String listing the available file filters. Leave it blank if you don't wish to specify any. If you do specify values, use the standard format, Description1|FileSpec1|Description2|FileSpec2|, placing a vertical bar (|) after each item. The items must be in pairs (description, filespec). See TestGetFileName() in Listing 19.2 for an example
strCustomFilter	String * 255	Either an empty string or a list of two items as described in the strFilter item, above. This field allows you to specify a filter additional to the ones listed in the strFilter member

TABLE 19.1: Fields in the glr_msauGetFileNameInfo Structure (continued)

Field Name	Datatype	Description
lngFilterIndex	Long	Number of the file selection filter pair to use when the dialog first opens. The first pair is numbered 1. If you set this value to 0, Windows uses the selection pair listed in strCustomFilter instead
strFile	String * 255	File name to use when the dialog is first displayed. After you close the dialog, this field contains the full name of the file that was chosen (including its path)
strFileTitle	String * 255	On output, the file name that was selected, without the drive and path information
strInitialDir	String * 255	Initial directory that the dialog should use
strTitle	String * 255	Title for the File Open/Save dialog box
lngFlags	Long	Combination of 0 or more flags from Table 19.2 that control the operation of the dialog box. Combine them using the Or operator
lngFileOffset	Long	On output, the number of characters from the start of the string in strFile to the location where the file name actually starts. The previous characters will contain the drive/path information
lngFileExtension	Long	On output, the number of characters from the start of the string in strFile to the location where the file extension starts
strDefExt	String * 255	Default file extension to be appended to the file name if the user doesn't supply one. Don't include a period in the string

TABLE 19.2: Possible Values for the Flags Field in the glr_msauGetFileNameInfo Structure

Constant Name	Value	Description
glrcOFN_ALLOWMULTI-SELECT	&H200	Allows the user to select more than one file name. If more than one is selected, after the dialog returns the buffer, strFile will contain the chosen path followed by all the files within that path that were chosen, separated with spaces—for example, "C:\ File1.TXT File2.TXT". Choosing this flag forces Windows to use the old-style dialogs unless you also specify the glrcOFN_EXPLORER flag. In that case the pieces come back delimited with nulls (Chr$(0)) and quotes rather than with spaces
glrcOFN_CREATEPROMPT	&H2000	The dialog prompts users if the selected file doesn't already exist, allowing them to continue or make a different choice
glrcOFN_EXPLORER	&H80000	Creates an Open or Save As dialog box that uses user-interface features similar to the Windows Explorer. This is normally the default, unless you specify another flag that overrides it (such as glrcOFN_ALLOWMULTISELECT)

TABLE 19.2: Possible Values for the Flags Field in the glr_msauGetFileNameInfo Structure (continued)

Constant Name	Value	Description
glrcOFN_EXTENSION-DIFFERENT	&H400	Used on return only, this flag is set if the chosen file name has an extension different from that supplied in the strDefExt field. If strDefExt is null, Windows doesn't set this flag
glrcOFN_FILEMUSTEXIST	&H1000	Forces the user to supply only existing file names
glrcOFN_HIDEREADONLY	&H4	Hides the Read Only check box from the dialog box
glrcOFN_LONGNAMES	&H200000	Causes the dialog box to display long file names. If this flag is not specified, the dialog box displays file names in 8.3 format (eight characters for the file name, three for the extension). This value is ignored if glrcOFN_EXPLORER is set
glrcOFN_NOCHANGEDIR	&H8	Causes Windows to set the current directory back where it was before you loaded the dialog
glrcOFN_NODEREFER-ENCELINKS	&H100000	Returns the path and file name of the selected shortcut (.LNK) file. If you don't use this flag, the dialog box returns the path and file name of the file referenced by the shortcut
glrcOFN_NOLONGNAMES	&H40000	Specifies that long file names are not displayed in the File Name list box. This value is ignored if glrcOFN_EXPLORER is set
glrcOFN_NONETWORK-BUTTON	&H20000	Removes the Network button from the dialog
glrcOFN_NOREADONLY-RETURN	&H8000	On return, specifies that the returned file does not have the Read Only check box checked and is not in a write-protected directory
glrcOFN_NOTESTFILE-CREATE	&H10000	Normally, COMDLG32.DLL tests to make sure you'll be able to create the file when you choose a file name for saving. If this flag is set, it doesn't test, providing no protection against common disk errors
glrcOFN_NOVALIDATE	&H100	Disables file name validation. Normally, COMDLG32.DLL checks the chosen file name to make sure it's a valid name
glrcOFN_OVERWRITE-PROMPT	&H2	The dialog issues a warning message if the user selects an existing file for a File Save As operation
glrcOFN_PATHMUSTEXIST	&H800	Forces the user to supply only valid pathnames
glrcOFN_READONLY	&H1	If set before calling the dialog box, forces the Read Only check box to be checked. After the dialog is closed, this flag will be set if the user checked that check box
glrcOFN_SHAREAWARE	&H4000	Ignores sharing violations. Because Access cannot handle the errors that occur when sharing violations occur in this code, you should not set this flag
glrcOFN_SHOWHELP	&H10	Shows a Help button on the dialog. Although this option works, the button will not, so its use in Access is limited

When you specify the hWndOwner member of the calling structure, you're telling Windows which window to use as the parent for the dialog. The dialog itself will pop up in the upper-left corner of the window you specify. Choosing 0, Access' handle, a normal form's handle, or a popup form's handle all alter the location at which the dialog pops up. Table 19.3 details the possibilities.

TABLE 19.3: Results of Passing Various Window Handles to Common Dialogs

hWndOwner	Parent Windows	Application Modal?	Location
0	Windows	No	Upper-left corner of the screen
frm.hWnd (a normal form's hWnd)	Access	Yes	Upper-left corner of the Access MDI Client window
Application. hWndAccessApp	Access	Yes	Upper-left corner of the Access MDI Client window
frm.hWnd (a popup form's hWnd)	The popup form	Yes	Upper-left corner of the form itself. Use this technique to position the dialog where you'd like it

To call the function, you needn't supply values for all these fields. Listing 19.2 shows a simple case of using the common dialogs to retrieve a file name to open. Figure 19.2 shows the dialog box this function pops up.

Listing 19.2

```
Sub TestGetFileName()
    Dim gfni As glr_msauGetFileNameInfo

    gfni.strInitialDir = "C:\"
    gfni.strTitle = "Choose A File"
    gfni.hWndOwner = Application.hWndAccessApp
    ' Use filter 2 at startup.
    gfni.lngFilterIndex = 2
    gfni.lngFlags = glrcOFN_NONETWORKBUTTON
    gfni.strFilter = "Access files (*.mdb,*.mda)¦" & _
     "*.mdb;*.mda¦All Files (*.*)¦*.*¦"
    ' Add an additional filter, leaving the
    ' original string intact.
    gfni.strCustomFilter = "Text Files¦*.txt¦"
    If glrGetFileName(gfni, True) = 0 Then
```

FIGURE 19.2:

The code in Listing 21.2 causes this dialog to pop up.

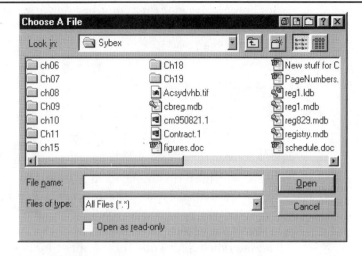

```
        MsgBox Trim(gfni.strFile)
        If gfni.lngFlags And glrcOFN_READONLY Then
            MsgBox "You opened the file read-only!"
        End If
    End If
End Sub
```

There are a few items to note about this function:

- Because all the strings in the datatype are fixed-length strings, you need to use the Trim() function to remove trailing spaces when you want to use the data that's in those strings.

- You can use several of the values in the Flags field to determine information about how the user opened the file (glrOF_READONLY, glrOF_EXTENSION-DIFFERENT, and so on). Check their state using the And operator, as shown in Listing 19.2.

- Most likely, you'll want to at least supply values for the fields used in Listing 19.2: strInitialDir, strTitle, and strFilter. You can, of course, supply other values, but those will be the most useful ones. Note that you must end each entry in the strFilter field with a vertical bar and that each entry must consist of two values: the text description of the filter item and the file specification that will select that group. In addition, if you want to use two different filespecs within a group (as we did in Listing 19.2), separate them with a semicolon (;) in the second portion of the group.

To choose a file name for saving, just set the second parameter to glrGetFileName() to False. That way, you've indicated to MSAU7032.DLL that you're trying to save a file rather than load it.

Selecting Colors

If you need to allow your users to choose colors within your application, your easiest solution is to use the Windows common dialog Color Chooser. Figure 19.3 shows the Color dialog in action.

Just as with the file name–choosing dialog, MSAU7032.DLL makes it simple for you to use this dialog. Because this function's data structure is far less complex, we've made the wrapper function's calling syntax a bit simpler: just pass to it up to four optional parameters, described in Table 19.4, and it will send the information to the common dialog for you. This wrapper function sets up the call to glr_msauGet-Color() and returns the user's color choice to the calling procedure.

Unlike the File Open/Save dialog, there are few options you can change when dealing with the Color dialog. Table 19.5 lists all the fields in the glr_msauGetColorInfo data structure. Table 19.6 lists all the options you can use in the Flags field of the structure.

FIGURE 19.3:

Windows color-choosing common dialog

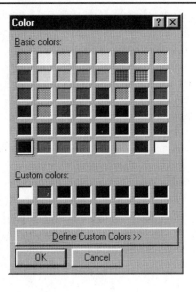

TABLE 19.4:   Optional Parameters for glrChooseColor

Parameter	Type	Default	Structure Member
SelectedColor	Long	0	lngResult
hWnd	Long	Application.hWndAccessApp	hWndOwner
Flags	Long	glrcCC_RGBINIT	lngFlags
UserColors	Array of Longs	All 0's	alngCustColors()

TABLE 19.5:   Fields in the glr_msauGetColorInfo Structure

Field Name	Datatype	Description
hWndOwner	Long	Handle of the window that is to act as the parent of the dialog. See Table 19.1 for more information
lngResult	Long	Contains the user's color selection after the user has dismissed the dialog. If the glrCC_RGBINIT flag is also set in the Flags field, you can place the initial color setting in this field, as well
lngFlags	Long	A combination of 0 or more flags from Table 19.6 that control the operation of the dialog box. Combine them using the Or operator
alngCustColors (0 To 15)	Long	Storage for up to 16 custom colors, as defined by the user

TABLE 19.6:   Possible Values for the Flags Field in the glr_msauGetColorInfo Structure

Constant Name	Value	Description
glrcCC_RGBINIT	&H1	Uses the color in the lngResult field to initialize the dialog box
glrcCC_FULLOPEN	&H2	Opens the full dialog box, including the custom color portion, when the dialog first appears
glrcCC_PREVENTFULLOPEN	&H4	Only the left side of the dialog will be available

To use glrPickNewColor() from your own applications, call glrPickNewColor(), passing to it values as described in Table 19.4. Listing 19.3 shows an example of glrPickNewColor() (from basTestMSAU7032), which loops until you choose the Cancel button on the dialog.

Listing 19.3

```
Function TestPickNewColor()
    ' A test case for glrPickNewColor()

    Dim lngColor As Long
    Dim varColors As Variant

    ' Set up an array to store the custom colors.
    varColors = Array(0, 0, 0, 0, 0, 0, 0, 0, 0, 0, _
     0, 0, 0, 0, 0)
    Do
        lngColor = glrChooseColor(SelectedColor:=lngColor, _
         Flags:=glrcCC_FULLOPEN Or glrcCC_RGBINIT, _
         UserColors:=varColors)
        Debug.Print "Color: " & lngColor
    Loop Until lngColor = -1
End Function
```

Working with the Access Menus

Although Chapter 11 covered in great detail the handling of menus using the Windows API, MSAU7032.DLL provides some wrappers around portions of the Windows functionality that you may find useful. To demonstrate the procedures available in the DLL, we've provided a DoMenuItem code builder (see Chapter 23 for more details on installing and using this add-in), in DMIBUILD.MDA. This example, shown in Figure 19.4, uses most of the menu-handling functions in MSAU7032.DLL.

FIGURE 19.4:

The DoMenuItem builder (DMIBUILD.MDA) inserts DoMenuItem statements directly into your code, along with appropriate comments.

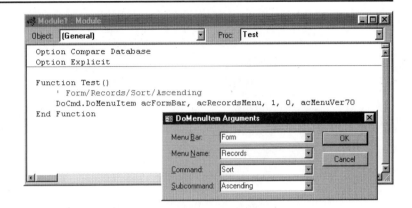

> **NOTE**　We must give credit where credit is due: most of the code in DMIBUILD.MDA is modified from code in the Access Wizards. The structure has been changed to meet the needs of this book, and variable names have been changed to follow our format, but we cannot take credit for all the code behind this useful builder.

Getting a Handle on the Access Menu Tree

As with most other resources in Windows, you'll need a handle to a menu to be able to work with it. MSAU7032 provides a function that will retrieve for you a handle to the Access menu tree. Once you have that, you can work your way down through the menu items, doing what you need.

To retrieve a handle to the Access menu tree, call the glr_msauLoadAccessMenu() function, passing to it a Long Integer indicating which menu bar you want loaded. In general, call glr_msauLoadAccessMenu() like this:

```
lngHandle = glr_msauLoadAccessMenu(lngMenuBar)
```

The input parameter, lngMenuBar, represents a menu bar ordinal value chosen from the following table, and the output value, lngHandle, is the handle to the selected menu, or, if the function call failed, 0.

Form	0
Database	1
Filter	2
Form Design	3
Startup	4
Visual Basic	5
Query	6
Report	7
Macro	8
Table Design	9
Form Datasheet	10
Table Datasheet	11
Query Datasheet	12
System Relationships	13
Filter By Form	14

To retrieve a handle to the Form menu bar, you could use a fragment like this (borrowed, more or less, from the module attached to frmDMIBuilder in DMIBUILD.MDA):

```
Dim hMenuBar as Long
Dim lngMenuBar as Long

' This line is not in the sample
lngMenuBar = acFormBar

hMenuBar = glr_msauLoadAccessMenu(lngMenubar)
If (hMenuBar = 0) Then
    GoTo RequeryMenuList_Exit
End If
```

If the function succeeds, it returns the menu handle. If it fails, it returns 0 (an invalid menu handle).

Retrieving the Item Count

Once you have the menu handle, one of the first things you'll want to know is how many items are on the menu. MSAU7032.DLL provides the glr_msauMenuItem-Count() function to retrieve this information for you. As you look at menus, however, you'll see that you can look at the items in two ways: you may want to know the actual number of items (including separators), or you may want to know how many menu options there are (excluding separators). The menu functions in MSAU7032 all provide the option for you to work in condensed mode or not (that is, to skip separators or not). Therefore, to find the number of menu items, call glr_msauMenuItemCount(), passing to it a menu handle and a flag indicating whether or not you want the answer in condensed mode:

```
lngCount = glr_msauMenuItemCount(hMenu, fCondensed)
```

Here, hMenu is the handle to a menu you've retrieved from a previous function call (you might have used glr_msauLoadAccessMenu(), or you might have used one of the menu functions from Chapter 11), and fCondensed is a Long Integer containing a Boolean value indicating whether or not to use condensed mode. The function returns the number of items on the given menu, including (fCondensed = False) or excluding (fCondensed = True) separator bars.

This fragment, from DMIBUILD.MDA, indicates that it wants the condensed number of items in the menu referred to by hMenuBar:

```
mintNames = glr_msauMenuItemCount(hMenuBar, _
  fCondensed:=True)
```

Retrieving Menu Text

Given a menu handle and the number of items on the menu, you might next want to walk through the menu and retrieve the menu text for each item. MSAU-7032.DLL provides a function, glr_msauGetMenuText(), that allows you to do this. It takes six parameters and returns the number of characters in the menu text. You call glr_msauGetMenuText() like this:

```
lngChars = glr_msauGetMenuText(hMenu, lngMenuItem, _
  fCondensed, fSimpleClean, strOut, lngMaxChars)
```

Table 19.7 describes the syntax for calling glr_msauGetMenuText().

TABLE 19.7: Syntax for Calling glr_msauGetMenuText()

Parameter	Type	Description	Comments
hMenu	Long	Previously opened menu handle	
lngMenuItem	Long	Index for the requested menu item (zero-based)	
fCondensed	Long	Boolean value (True or False) indicating whether or not to include separator bars in the count	If True, the function skips separator bars when locating menu items. If False, it includes the separators when counting
fSimpleClean	Long	Boolean value (True or False) indicating whether or not to perform a simple clean operation	For more information, see the section "Cleaning a Menu String" in this chapter, which describes the glr_msauCleanMenuString() function
strOut	String	Buffer to contain the output string	Must be large enough to contain the string before you call the function (Use the Space() function to "puff" it out, or use a fixed-length string.)
lngMaxChars	Long	Maximum characters in the output buffer	Initializes the output buffer with this much space before calling the function
Return Value	Long	Number of characters placed into strOut	

The following procedure (from basTestMSAU7032 in CH19.MDB) walks through all the items on the Form menu bar and displays the text for each item:

```
Sub ListItems()
    Const glrcMaxSize = 255
    Dim hMenuBar As Long
    Dim mintNames As Integer
    Dim strBuffer As String
    Dim intI As Integer
    Dim intChars As Integer

    hMenuBar = glr_msauLoadAccessMenu(acFormBar)
    mintNames = glr_msauMenuItemCount(hMenuBar, _
     fCondensed:=True)
    strBuffer = Space(glrcMaxSize)
    For intI = 0 To mintNames - 1
        intChars = glr_msauGetMenuText(hMenuBar, intI, _
         fCondensed:=True, fSimpleClean:=False, _
```

```
        strOut:=strBuffer, lngMaxChars:=glrcMaxSize)
      Debug.Print Left(strBuffer, intChars)
   Next intI
End Sub
```

> **WARNING**
>
> It's crucial, when passing string buffers to DLLs, that you "puff up" the buffer beforehand. The DLL cannot know whether or not space exists to write to, and it will always assume things are fine and just write to the address you've specified by passing the string buffer. If you haven't used the Space() or String() function (or a fixed-length string) to ensure that your string includes space for the text the DLL will place in the variable, you're very likely to cause Access to crash.

> **TIP**
>
> The function glr_msauGetMenuText() works with any menu bar, not just Access menus, and not just with menus you retrieved using glr_msauLoadAccessMenu(). This functionality is not connected with Access in any way, so you can use it for any product that uses normal Windows menus, once you've retrieved a handle to the menu structure. (That will normally happen by means of calling the Windows API, as described in Chapter 11.)

Retrieving a Handle for a Popup Menu

Of course, being able to retrieve only information about a menu bar isn't enough—you must be able to retrieve information about the popup menus hanging off the menu bar, as well. MSAU7032.DLL provides the glr_msauGetPopupMenu() function to retrieve a menu handle for any popup menu, no matter how deeply nested:

```
hsubmenu = glr_msauGetPopupMenu(hmenu, lngMenuCommand, _
 fCondensed)
```

Table 19.8 describes the syntax for calling glr_msauGetPopup(). See Listing 19.4 for an example of using glr_msauGetPopup() to display the items in a menu tree.

TABLE 19.8: Syntax for Calling glr_msauGetPopup()

Parameter	Type	Description	Comments
hMenu	Long	Previously opened menu handle	
lngMenu-Command	Long	Index for the requested menu item (zero-based)	
fCondensed	Long	Boolean value (True or False) indicating whether or not to include separator bars in the count	If True, the function skips separator bars when locating menu items. If False, it includes the separators when counting
Return Value	Long	Handle for the requested menu	

Cleaning a Menu String

If you want to display or use the text you retrieve from a menu structure (using glr_msauGetMenuText), you may also wish to remove the extra characters stored with the menu text. Most menu items include a hot key (an underlined character on screen that is stored internally with a leading ampersand [&] character), allowing you to access the menu from the keyboard. Menu strings may also include shortcut key names (such as Ctrl+N on the File ➤ New menu item) that you may wish to remove. Finally, you may wish to convert separators to one of two values: a single hyphen (-) or nothing at all (an empty string).

MSAU7032.DLL includes glr_msauCleanMenuString(), which cleans the extraneous characters from the text you retrieve from a menu. (Most of the other menu-handling functions in MSAU7032.DLL also call this function, internally.) To call the function, pass it the parameters shown here:

```
intChars = glr_msauCleanMenuString(strText, fSimpleClean, _
  strOutput, lngMaxChars)
```

Table 19.9 describes these parameters.

For example, the following fragment will return "This is a test" in strText and 14 as the return value of the function call:

```
Dim strText As String
Dim intChars As Integer
strText = Space(255)
intChars = glr_msauCleanMenuString("This &is a test", _
  False, strText, 255)
```

TABLE 19.9: Syntax for Calling glr_msauCleanMenuString()

Parameter	Type	Description	Comments
strText	String	The text to be cleaned	
fSimpleClean	Long	Perform simple clean (True) or more substantial clean (False)?	Either way, the function removes shortcut keys (stopping at the first tab character). If fSimpleClean is True, & characters remain untouched, and each separator is returned as a single hyphen. If fSimpleClean is False, the function removes & characters and returns an empty string for separators
strOutput	String	Buffer to contain the output string	Must be large enough to contain the string before you call the function (Use the Space() function to "puff" it out, or use a fixed-length string.)
lngMaxChars	Long	Maximum characters in the output buffer	Initialize the output buffer with this much space before calling the function
Return Value	Long	Length of the string placed into strOutput	

> **TIP**
>
> You're not limited to using glr_msauCleanMenuString() with menu text. If you have buttons on your forms that include hot keys but you'd like to display their names somewhere without the & characters, you can pass their names through glr_msauCleanMenuString() to remove the extra characters.

Finding the Actual Menu Index

On occasion you may need to convert a condensed menu index into an actual index. For example, if you're using functions from both MSAU7032.DLL and the Windows API, you'll need to work in terms Windows understands—that is, with actual positions on the menus, including the separators. To facilitate this conversion, MSAU7032.DLL includes the glr_msauActualMenuItem() function. Given a menu handle and a condensed index, it returns the actual position index corresponding to the condensed index you've passed in.

To call glr_msauActualMenuItem(), use code similar to the following:

```
lngActual = glr_msauActualMenuItem(hMenu, lngCondensed)
```

The first parameter, hMenu, is a handle to an open menu, and lngCondensed is the index for the item you care about, in condensed mode. The function returns the actual location of the menu item, including the separators.

To see this (and most of the other menu-handling functions) in action, try out Test-MenuItems (from basTestMSAU7032), shown in Listing 19.4. In the Debug window, run the procedure, and it will print out the contents of the Forms menu bar and the first level of menu items. It will also print out the actual and condensed index for each item.

Listing 19.4

```
Sub TestMenuItems()
    ' Walk through the 0th menu bar, printing out every item
    ' in the first level down, along with the
    ' condensed index and the actual index for the item.

    Const glrcMaxSize = 255

    Dim strBuffer As String
    Dim intChars As Integer

    Dim hMenuBar As Long
    Dim hMenu As Long
    Dim intI As Long
    Dim intJ As Long
    Dim intNames As Integer
    Dim intSubNames As Integer

    ' Load the Forms menu bar.
    hMenuBar = glr_msauLoadAccessMenu(acFormBar)
    ' Find out how many items there are on the
    ' menu (condensed).
    intNames = glr_msauMenuItemCount(hMenuBar, _
     fCondensed:=True)

    ' Now loop through all the top-level menu bar items.
    For intI = 0 To intNames - 1
        ' Retrieve the text for this item (File, Edit, etc.)
        ' and print it.
```

```
        strBuffer = Space(glrcMaxSize)
        intChars = glr_msauGetMenuText(hMenuBar, intI, _
         fCondensed:=True, fSimpleClean:=False, _
         strOut:=strBuffer, lngMaxChars:=glrcMaxSize)
        strBuffer = Left(strBuffer, intChars)
        Debug.Print strBuffer

        ' Now get the popup menu hanging off the top-level
        ' menu bar item.
        hMenu = glr_msauGetPopupMenu(hMenuBar, intI, _
         fCondensed:=True)

        ' How many items are on this popup menu?
        intSubNames = glr_msauMenuItemCount(hMenu, _
         fCondensed:=True)

        ' Loop through all the items, printing out the
        ' condensed index, the real index, and the text.
        For intJ = 0 To intSubNames - 1
            strBuffer = Space(glrcMaxSize)
            intChars = glr_msauGetMenuText(hMenu, intJ, _
             fCondensed:=True, fSimpleClean:=False, _
             strOut:=strBuffer, lngMaxChars:=glrcMaxSize)
            strBuffer = Left(strBuffer, intChars)
            Debug.Print , intJ, _
             glr_msauActualMenuItem(hMenu, intJ), strBuffer
        Next intJ
    Next intI
End Sub
```

Handling DoMenuItem Values

In all this discussion of the DoMenuItem builder, one issue has been neatly swept under the rug: how do you get a list of all the menu bar names? Sure, once you've specified a menu bar number, you can retrieve all the items on it directly from Access. But there's no way to ask Windows to retrieve a list of all the Access menu bars themselves.

To solve this particular problem, MSAU7032 includes the glr_msauMapDMI-ArgsDMIStrings() function. (*DMI* stands for DoMenuItem.) This functions allows you to retrieve the menu item text corresponding to any combination of menu bar, menu item, drop-down menu, and submenu item numbers. (Access' built-in menus are never more than two levels deep.) To retrieve the text, you pass the function four integers, representing the menu item you care about, and four string buffers the function will fill with your selected menu item text.

In this example, the InitializeFormBarList subroutine fills in the mastrMenuBars() array with a list of all the different menu bar names. This procedure doesn't care about any of the other strings (menu item, popup menu item, and submenu item), so it passes a dummy buffer for each. If your code requires all the strings, use a separate output buffer for each. Don't forget, as with any DLL call involving strings, to make sure your string buffers are long enough to contain data placed in them before you make the call.

```
Private Sub InitializeFormBarList()
    Dim intMenuBar As Integer
    Dim strTemp As String
    Dim strMenuBar As String

    ' All this code cares about is the top-level menu
    ' bar names, so pass in 0 for the commands and
    ' subcommands, and pass in a dummy address for all the
    ' text except the menu bar name.

    strMenuBar = Space(glrcMaxSize)
    strTemp = Space(glrcMaxSize)
    For intMenuBar = 0 To glrcMaxMenuBars - 1
        glr_msauMapDMIArgsDMIStrings intMenuBar, 0, 0, 0, _
         strMenuBar, strTemp, strTemp, strTemp
        mastrMenuBars(intMenuBar) = glrTrimNull(strMenuBar)
    Next intMenuBar
End Sub
```

WARNING In this procedure call, as opposed to most of the other procedure calls in MSAU7032.DLL, you cannot specify the size of your output buffers. It's imperative that your buffers contain enough space for at least 255 characters (no more are necessary, but the buffers must be at least that large), or the DLL call might try to write beyond the space provided in your buffer.

As you can see, this function provides an alternative for glr_msauGetMenuText but gives you very little flexibility. It always cleans the text for you (with the fSimple-Clean parameter set to False) and provides only condensed menu numbering. If you need to retrieve the text of a specific menu item without needing to retrieve a menu handle, however, this is a good way to do it.

Reading and Writing Registry Values

Although you can use the Windows API to read and write Registry values (see Chapter 18 for more information), there just *has* to be a simpler way. The functions provided in MSAU7032.DLL make it a little simpler, although they still require a bit of effort on your part. The following sections highlight the six functions included in the library that help you work with the System Registry.

> **TIP**
>
> If you simply intend to store your own application information in the Registry, you needn't fight with these functions. VBA supplies the GetSetting, SaveSetting, GetAllSettings, and DeleteSetting procedures, which allow you to get and set Registry values in a limited manner. See the section "Storing Information in the System Registry" in Chapter 8 for more information on using these functions.

To demonstrate many of the functions in this section, load and run frmStartupTips, shown in Figure 19.5. When you start Windows 95 you have the option of displaying a splash screen that contains a "tip of the day." Figure 19.6 shows the startup screen after the change indicated in Figure 19.5 has been made. Windows maintains, in the Registry, a flag that indicates whether or not to show the tips, as well as the next tip to be displayed. Figure 19.7 shows the Registry key and values containing this information, which is stored separately for each user profile on the system. In addition, Windows stores all the tips themselves in a corresponding key, global for the entire machine. Figure 19.8 shows the tips as they appear in REGEDIT.EXE.

FIGURE 19.5:

frmStartupTips allows you to edit existing startup tips or add new ones of your own.

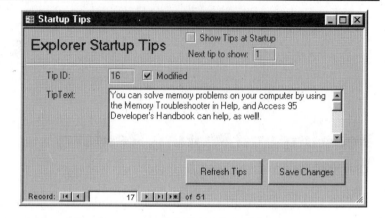

FIGURE 19.6:

You can control the tips in Explorer's startup by modifying the values in the Registry.

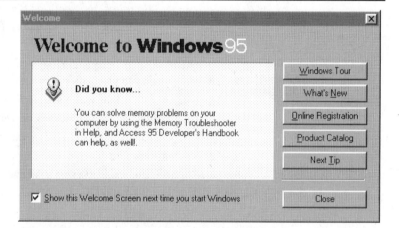

NOTE   This example will work correctly only in Windows 95. Although the functions provided in MSAU7032.DLL that work with the Registry will work equally well in both Windows NT and Windows 95, the startup tips this example manipulates just don't exist in Windows NT. If you need to discern which version of Windows you're running, take a look at the GetVersionEx() Windows API function. This function can tell you which version (Windows NT or Windows 95) you're running.

FIGURE 19.7:

Windows stores state information about the tips for each individual user.

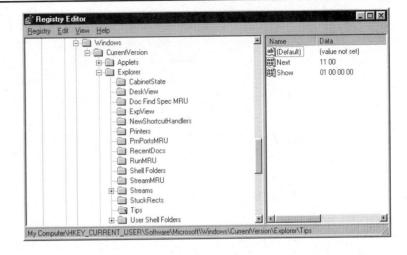

FIGURE 19.8:

You can modify all the startup tips, and you can add your own, as well.

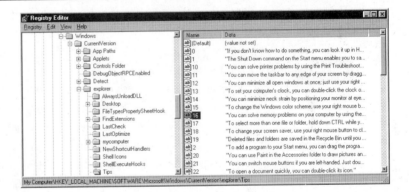

You'll find the code for the Explorer tips example in basTips, in CH19.MDB. The fragments of code in the next four sections are extracted from that module, as well.

WARNING Although these examples make heavy use of the Registry, this book does not intend to, nor can it, provide a reference or instructions on using the System Registry. Anytime you modify settings in the Registry, if you're not sure of what you're doing, you risk making your system unusable. Before you modify anything in the Registry, programmatically or manually, make sure you've backed up. (Export the whole thing to a text file.)

Retrieving Information about a Key

If you're interested in working your way through all the subkeys or values associated with a key in the Registry, you will need to know, before you start, how many of each exist. The glr_msauRegGetKeyInfo() function retrieves, for a given root key and path to a key, the number of subkeys and values associated with that key.

NOTE The terminology surrounding the Registry can get confusing. From our point of view, a *key* is a node within the Registry, at any level within the hierarchy. A *subkey* of that key is any key located at the next lower level in the hierarchy. A *value* is a named quantity, displayed in the right pane of the Registry Editor, and can be text, numeric, or binary. The Registry includes a number of root keys, as well, including HKEY_LOCAL_MACHINE and HKEY_CURRENT_USER.

In this example, you want to retrieve tips from the specific key:

```
HKEY_LOCAL_MACHINE
      Software
           Microsoft
                Windows
                     CurrentVersion
                          Explorer
                               Tips
```

as shown in Figure 19.8. The root key is HKEY_LOCAL_MACHINE and the key to check on is

```
Software\Microsoft\Windows\CurrentVersion\Explorer\Tips
```

You need to know, in this case, how many values (startup tips) are associated with this key. To do this, call glr_msauRegGetKeyInfo(), passing to it the preopened value for the handle to the root key, HKEY_LOCAL_MACHINE (defined as the constant glrcHKEY_LOCAL_MACHINE), a string containing the path to the key in question, and two Long Integer variables the function will fill in with the number of subkeys and values:

```
lngRetval = glr_msauRegGetKeyInfo(glrcHKEY_LOCAL_MACHINE, _
 glrcRegTips, lngSubKeys, lngValues)
```

MSAU7032.DLL will retrieve the information for you and pass it back in those final two variables. The syntax for calling glr_msauRegGetKeyInfo() is shown in Table 19.10.

TABLE 19.10: Syntax for Calling glr_msauRegGetKeyInfo()

Parameter	Type	Description	Comments
hkeyRoot	Long	Key to use as the root	Use one of the constants defined in basMSAU7032: glrcHKEY_LOCAL_MACHINE or glrcHKEY_CURRENT_USER, normally
strSubKey	String	Path to the key in question	Do not include the root key name or a leading backslash (\)
lngSubKeys	Long	Filled in by the function call with the number of subkeys underneath the specified key	Only subkeys located at the next lower level in the hierarchy are counted
lngValues	Long	Filled in by the function call with the number of values underneath the specified key	
Return Value	Long	Error code	glrcMSAUErrSuccess, glrcMSAUErrRegKeyNotFound, or glrcMSAUErrUnknown

For example, here's the code from glrFillTipTable() that retrieves the number of tips
to be had. (In this example, glrcRegTips is a constant containing the path to the key.)

```
' Get the number of subkeys and values under the key.
' It's the number of values you really care about here.
lngRetval = glr_msauRegGetKeyInfo(glrcHKEY_LOCAL_MACHINE, _
 glrcRegTips, lngSubKeys, lngValues)
For intI = 0 To lngValues - 1
    ' Retrieve the subkey information
Next intI
```

Retrieving a Value Name

To retrieve a value for a key, you must know the name of the value. (You can get
around this restriction using the Windows API directly, but this chapter attempts to
solve problems using MSAU7032.DLL with as few "raw" API calls as possible. For
more information on using the API to get to the Registry, see Chapter 18.) For example, the tips are all named with numeric text between "0" and "48" (possibly
more, if you've added some tips). The code in glrFillTipTable() loops through all the
values associated with the key, retrieves their names, and then, given the names, retrieves the values themselves.

To retrieve the name of a value, use the glr_msauRegGetValueName() function. As
in the previous function, you supply it with a root key and a path to the key in question. You must also give it the index for the value for which you want to retrieve
the name, a buffer in which to place the returned value, the size of that buffer, and
a Long Integer into which the DLL can place the type of value (Text, Numeric,
and so on) it retrieved. Table 19.11 shows the syntax for calling glr_msauReg-
GetValueName().

For example, once you've retrieved the number of values associated with the Tips
key, you can walk through them all, retrieving their names, with the following code
from glrFillTipTable():

```
For intI = 0 To lngValues - 1
    strValueName = Space(glrcMaxSize)
    ' Get the value name.
    lngRetval = _
     glr_msauRegGetValName(glrcHKEY_LOCAL_MACHINE, _
     glrcRegTips, intI, strValueName, glrcMaxSize, lngType)
    If lngRetval = glrcMSAUErrSuccess Then
        strValueName = glrTrimNull(strValueName)
```

TABLE 19.11: Syntax for Calling glr_msauRegGetValueName()

Parameter	Type	Description	Comments
hkeyRoot	Long	Key to use as the root	Use one of the constants defined in basMSAU7032: glrcHKEY_LOCAL_MACHINE or glrcHKEY_CURRENT_USER, normally
strSubKey	String	Path to the key in question	Do not include the root key name, nor a leading backslash (\)
lngValue	Long	Index of the value to retrieve	The index is zero-based
strValName	String	Buffer to contain the value name	Must be large enough to contain the string before you call the function (Use the Space() function to "puff" it out, or use a fixed-length string.)
lngMaxLen	Long	Maximum characters in the output buffer	Initialize the output buffer with this much space before calling the function
lngType	Long	On return from the function, filled in with the datatype of the value	For a list of possible types, see the constants starting with glrcREG_ in basMSAU7032. In general, the only datatypes you'll care about are glrcREG_SZ (null-terminated string) and glrcREG_DWORD (Long Integer)
Return Value	Long	Error code	glrcMSAUErrSuccess, glrcMSAUErrRegKeyNotFound, or glrcMSAUErrRegValueNotFound

```
      End If
       ' Do more stuff...
   Next intI
```

Retrieving a Value from the Registry

Given the name of a key's value, you can retrieve its actual value (yes, the terminology gets in the way here) using the glr_msauRegGetVal() function:

```
strValue = Space(glrcMaxSize)
lngRetval = glr_msauRegGetVal(glrcHKEY_LOCAL_MACHINE, _
 glrcRegTips, strValueName, ByVal strValue, glrcMaxSize)
```

This function, as do all the other MSAU7032 Registry functions, requires you to tell it the root key and the path to the specific key. You also specify the name of the value to be retrieved, a buffer in which to place the value, and the size of that buffer. MSAU7032.DLL places the value into the buffer and returns a status code. Table 19.12 explains the syntax for calling glr_msauRegGetVal().

TABLE 19.12: Syntax for Calling glr_msauRegGetVal()

Parameter	Type	Description	Comments
hkeyRoot	Long	Key to use as the root	Use one of the constants defined in basMSAU7032: glrcHKEY_LOCAL_MACHINE or glrcHKEY_CURRENT_USER, normally
strSubKey	String	Path to the key in question	Do not include the root key name or a leading backslash (\)
strValName	String	Name of the value to retrieve	
lpData	Any	Buffer to contain the returned data	lpData can be of any datatype, but if you're returning text data, you *must* precede this parameter with the keyword ByVal when you call the function. This tells Access to convert the buffer into a null-terminated string that the DLL can fill with text data
lngMaxLen	Long	Maximum characters in the output buffer	Initializes the output buffer with this much space before calling the function if you're retrieving text, or places the length of the buffer if you're retrieving a Numeric type (You can use the Len() function to find the length of the datatype.)
Return Value	Long	Error code	glrcMSAUErrSuccess, glrcMSAUErrRegKeyNotFound, glrcMSAUErrRegValueNotFound, or glrcMSAUErrBufferTooSmall

Writing a Value to the Registry

Once you've modified a startup tip, you'll need to write the new value back to the Registry. MSAU7032.DLL provides the glr_msauRegWriteVal() function to write data to a value associated with a given key. You tell it the (by now familiar) root key and path to the key, as well as the name of the value, the data, and the datatype.

This is the code fragment from glrSaveTipTable() that loops through the recordset of tips and writes the modified ones back to the Registry:

```
Do While Not rst.EOF
    lngRetval = glr_msauRegWriteVal(glrcHKEY_LOCAL_MACHINE, _
    glrcRegTips, (rst!TipID), ByVal CStr(rst!TipText), _
```

```
        glrcREG_SZ)
    If lngRetval <> glrcMSAUErrSuccess Then
        Err.Description = "Unable to save tip " & rst!TipID
        Err.Raise lngRetval
    Else
        intCount = intCount + 1
    End If
    rst.MoveNext
Loop
```

Table 19.13 describes the syntax for calling glr_msauRegWriteVal().

TABLE 19.13:   Syntax for Calling glr_msauRegWriteVal()

Parameter	Type	Description	Comments
hkeyRoot	Long	Key to use as the root	Use one of the constants defined in basMSAU7032: glrcHKEY_LOCAL_ MACHINE or glrcHKEY_CURRENT_USER, normally
strSubKey	String	Path to the key in question	Do not include the root key name or a leading backslash (\)
strValName	String	Name of the value to be written to	If the value does not exist, the function will create it
lpData	Any	Buffer containing the output data	LpData can be of any datatype, but if you're using text data, you *must* precede this parameter with the keyword ByVal when you call the function. This tells Access to convert the buffer into a null-terminated string that the DLL can fill with text data
lngType	Long	Datatype for the value in lpData. Must be either glrcREG_SZ (null-terminated string) or glrcREG_DWORD (Long Integer). Any other datatype will cause the function to return an error	This function's limitations, in terms of datatypes it will accept, makes it difficult to use in many situations. It can write only String or Long Integer data to the Registry
Return Value	Long	Error code	glrcMSAUErrSuccess, glrcMSAUErrRegTypeNotSupported, or glrcMSAUErrRegKeyNotFound, glrcMSAUErrRegCantSetValue

> **NOTE**
>
> There are two points of interest in the example: the parentheses surrounding rst!TipID and the CStr( ) function call surrounding rst!TipText. The parentheses around rst!TipID are necessary because of a strange interaction between Jet and VBA. It appears that anytime you're using VBA as a conduit to pass information directly from Jet to anywhere else (DLLs, OLE automation, and so on), you must have VBA convert the reference into an explicit value. You do this either by enclosing the reference in parentheses or by assigning the value to a variable of the appropriate type and then passing that variable on. The CStr( ) function coerces the field value into a string value. This conversion is necessary because of the special handling VBA gives to strings passed by value to a DLL.

As you can see in Table 19.13, glr_msauRegWriteVal() is limited in the types of data it can write to the Registry. If you need to write any values besides strings or Long Integers, you'll have to use the Windows API directly. Even in this example we've limited the functionality because of this: the values in the Registry that track the next tip to be shown and whether or not to show tips at all are stored as binary values. Although you can read the values with glr_msauRegGetVal(), you cannot write them out with glr_msaRegWriteVal(). (See Figure 19.7 for the exact Registry key and values. The glrGetTipInfo() procedure in basTips retrieves this information.) If you want to modify the example to allow you to save the values, you'll need to use the Windows API.

Retrieving the Name of a Registry Subkey

You may need, at times, to retrieve the name of a Registry subkey associated with a given key, given the subkey's index. For example, frmSoundList in CH19.MDB, shown in Figure 19.9, retrieves a list of all the default system events. Figure 19.10 shows those events as they appear in the Registry. (Look in basGetSoundList for more information.) To call glr_msauRegGetKey(), use the syntax shown in Table 19.14.

FIGURE 19.9:

frmSoundList retrieves a list of all the default system events and plays the associated sounds.

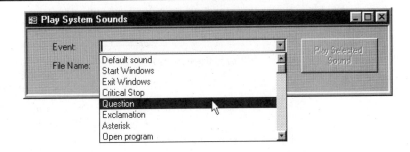

FIGURE 19.10:

Default system events in the Registry

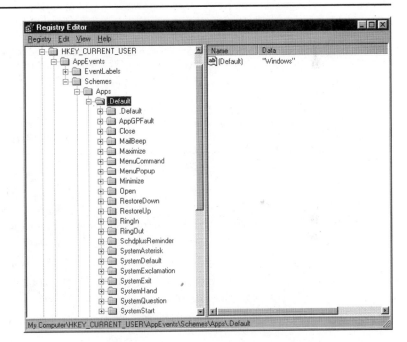

NOTE   If your computer does not support sound, you will not be able to test frmSoundList. If it can't find the requisite Registry keys, it will fail and display an alert.

TABLE 19.14: Syntax for Calling glr_msauRegGetKey()

Parameter	Type	Description	Comments
hkeyRoot	Long	Key to use as the root	Use one of the constants defined in basMSAU-7032: glrcHKEY_LOCAL_MACHINE or glrcHKEY_CURRENT_USER, normally
strSubKey	String	Path to the key in question	Do not include the root key name or a leading backslash (\)
lngSubKey	Long	Zero-based index of the subkey name to retrieve	
strName	String	Buffer to contain the subkey name	Must be large enough to contain the string before you call the function (Use the Space() function to "puff" it out, or use a fixed-length string.)
lngMaxLen	Long	Maximum characters in the output buffer	Initializes the output buffer with this much space before calling the function if you're retrieving text, or places the length of the buffer if you're retrieving a numeric type (You can use the Len() function to find the length of the datatype.)
Return Value	Long	Error code	glrcMSAUErrSuccess, glrcMSAUErrKeyNotFound, or glrcMSAUErrSubkeyNotFound

> **NOTE**
>
> The procedure that fills the combo box is actually a bit more complex than we've let on—it must do more than just retrieve the list of event names. Each event name has an associated "friendly" name, stored under a different key in the Registry. The example retrieves those friendly names and places them in the combo. You may find perusing the code useful as a learning tool.

The following code fragment shows the loop that retrieves all the default event subkeys. In this example glrcRegSoundList has been defined as

```
Const glrcRegSoundList = "AppEvents\Schemes\Apps\.Default"
```

and atypSounds() is an array of data structures. In those data structures, one of the elements is strUnfriendlyName, and it's that item this loop is attempting to fill.

```
For intI = 0 To lngSubKeys - 1
    With atypSounds(intI)
```

```
        ' Initialize the buffer.
        .strUnfriendlyName = Space(glrcMaxSize)

        ' Given an index (intI), get the particular key.
        lngRetval = glr_msauRegGetKey(glrcHKEY_CURRENT_USER, _
         glrcRegSoundList, intI, .strUnfriendlyName, _
         glrcMaxSize)
        If lngRetval <> glrcMSAUErrSuccess Then
            Err.Raise lngRetval
        End If
        ' Trim off extra junk at the end.
        .strUnfriendlyName = glrTrimNull(.strUnfriendlyName)

        ' Now go retrieve the friendly name. See
        ' basGetSoundList for the gory details.
    End With
Next intI
```

Creating a New Key

The final Registry-focused procedure in MSAU7032.DLL is also the simplest to use. It allows you to create a new key in the Registry. The glr_msauRegWriteKey() function is as user friendly as a function can be: it creates the key, and if the key is nested beneath other keys that need to be created, it creates those keys, as well. In addition, if the key already exists, the function just leaves it alone.

For example, to create this scenario:

```
HKEY_CURRENT_USER
    Software
        K2 Software
            Marketing
                Application 1
```

you could call glr_msauRegWriteKey() with the following parameters:

```
lngRetval = glr_msauRegWriteKey(glrcHKEY_CURRENT_USER, _
 "Software\K2 Software\Marketing\Application", "")
```

Windows will create the Application key, as well as any keys above it in the Registry that it must create in order to supply the path you've requested. Figure 19.11 shows the Registry after calling the code in the example. Table 19.15 shows the syntax for calling glr_msauRegWriteKey().

FIGURE 19.11:

Call glr_msauRegWriteKey() to create new Registry keys.

TABLE 19.15: Syntax for Calling glr_msauRegWriteKey()

Parameter	Type	Description	Comments
hkeyRoot	Long	Key to use as the root	Use one of the constants defined in basMSAU7032: glrcHKEY_LOCAL_MACHINE or glrcHKEY_CURRENT_USER, normally
strSubKey	String	Full path of the key you want to create	Do not include the root key name or a leading backslash (\). Windows will create any keys necessary to get to your new key if they don't already exist
strClass	String	Specifies the class (object type) of this key. Ignored if the key already exists. Normally unused	The Microsoft documentation (if you look up the RegCreateKeyEx() API function) for this parameter is cloudy, to say the least. Until you can find more information about what this parameter is really for, perhaps it's best to leave it as an empty string
Return Value	Long	Error code	Either glrcMSAUErrSuccess or glrcMSAUErrRegCantCreateKey

Font-Handling Functions

If you need to supply users with a list of available fonts and their sizes, MSAU7032.DLL can help you out. Performing this task from Access without an external DLL is difficult, if not impossible, because it requires a callback function, and that technique is not available from VBA. MSAU7032.DLL provides functions to retrieve the count of installed fonts; a list of those fonts; and for each raster (bitmapped) font, a count of the available sizes and a list of those sizes. The next few sections cover the use of these functions. In addition, we've provided a sample form (frmListFonts in CH19.MDB) that ties together all these techniques. Because these topics will be much clearer with a real example to discuss, you might want to take a moment to exercise frmListFonts before digging into this material. Figure 19.12 shows the form in use.

FIGURE 19.12:

frmListFonts allows you to view any font in any available point size.

Retrieving a List of Fonts

MSAU7032.DLL provides two functions you need in order to fill an array with a list of all the available fonts. The function glr_msauGetFontCount() returns the number of fonts, and glr_msauGetFontList() fills a passed array with the names of all those fonts. The code attached to frmListFonts' Open event calls both of these functions directly in order to fill the combo box on the form with a list of fonts. Listing 19.5 shows the portion of the code that handles this process.

Listing 19.5

```
Dim hDC As Long
hdc = glr_apiCreateIC("DISPLAY", "", "", O&)
If hdc <> 0 Then
    mlngCountFonts = glr_msauGetFontCount(hdc)
    If mlngCountFonts > 0 Then
        ReDim mafiFonts(0 To mlngCountFonts - 1)
        mlngCountFonts = glr_msauGetFontList(hdc, _
         mafiFonts())
        ' Get rid of the trailing null and spaces NOW.
        For intI = 0 To mlngCountFonts - 1
            mafiFonts(intI).strName = _
             glrTrimNull((mafiFonts(intI).strName))
        Next intI
    End If
End If
'
' the code continues...
'
Call glr_apiDeleteDC(hDC)
hDC = 0
```

As the first step when you work with fonts, you must retrieve information about the current display device. To do so, call the Windows API function CreateIC() (create information context) or CreateDC() (create device context). Either will do in this case because you're retrieving information only about the display device. Were you interested in modifying any of the device settings, you'd be forced to use CreateDC(), which requires a bit more overhead than CreateIC(). To get the handle you need, call CreateIC() (aliased as glr_apiCreateIC() in the example), sending to it the name of the device driver (DISPLAY, in this case), with all the other parameters set to empty strings or 0. This will retrieve a device handle referring to the current display device, as shown in the following code fragment:

```
Dim hDC As Long

hDC = glr_apiCreateIC("DISPLAY", "", "", O&)
```

Once you have a device context, you can request the number of installed fonts from MSAU7032.DLL. To call msau_GetFontCount(), just send it the device context as a parameter, and it will return the number of fonts installed for that device:

```
If hDC <> 0 Then
    intFonts = glr_msauGetFontCount(hDC)
```

Once you have the number of installed fonts, you can create an array to hold the list. That array will need to be made up of elements of the type glrFontInfo, as shown here:

```
Type glrFontInfo
    fRasterFont As Long
    strName As String * 32
End Type
```

where each element stores a True or False value, indicating whether or not the font is a raster font, as well as the name of the font. The code to resize the array looks like this:

```
ReDim afiFonts(0 To intFonts - 1)
```

To fill in the list of font information, call glr_msauGetFontList(), passing to it the device context and the array. The function returns the actual number of fonts it filled in and actually fills in the entire array:

```
intFonts = glr_msauGetFontList(hDC, afiFonts())
```

As the final step in this process, you need to deal with the extra characters the DLL call left in the array. Because the DLL treats the strings as though they were null-terminated and Access doesn't deal well with null-terminated strings, the function here includes a pass through all the elements of the array, truncating them at the first null character each contains:

```
' Get rid of the trailing null and spaces NOW.
For intI = 0 To mlngCountFonts - 1
    mafiFonts(intI).strName = _
     glrTrimNull((mafiFonts(intI).strName))
Next intI
```

You'll find the code for glrTrimNull() in basMSAU7032, so include that module in your application if you also want to use frmListFonts.

Last but not least, you must always release the device (or information) context handle when you're done with it. Windows maintains only a fixed number of these handles, so you must always conclude with code like this:

```
Call glr_apiDeleteDC(hDC)
hDC = 0
```

This code both releases the handle and resets its value back to 0 so subsequent code that checks the value of hDC knows it doesn't represent a device context anymore.

Retrieving a List of Sizes

For TrueType fonts, Windows generally presents you with a standardized list of font sizes:

8,9,10,11,12,14,16,18,20,22,24,26,28,36,48,72

The code attached to frmListFonts maintains an array, maintTTSizes(), that contains those standard sizes. For raster fonts, however, it is the font itself that determines the available sizes. Therefore, for raster fonts, the code needs to retrieve the list of specific sizes for the font. The procedure in Listing 19.6, FillFontSizes, fills the global array maintRasterSizes() with the available font sizes for the specified font.

Listing 19.6

```
Private Sub FillFontSizes(hdc As Long, _
 ByVal varFaceName As Variant)

    Dim strName As String

    If IsNull(varFaceName) Then
        ReDim maintRasterSizes(0)
        Exit Sub
    End If
    strName = CStr(varFaceName)
    mlngCountRasterSizes = glr_msauGetSizeCount(hdc, _
     strName)
    If mlngCountRasterSizes > 0 Then
        ReDim maintRasterSizes(0 To _
         mlngCountRasterSizes - 1)
        mlngCountRasterSizes = glr_msauGetSizeList(hdc, _
         strName, maintRasterSizes())
    End If
End Sub
```

To call FillFontSizes, you pass to it the device context you previously created and the name of the specific font. If the face name is null, of course, the procedure can't do its work and will need to empty out the array and just exit.

```
If IsNull(varFaceName) Then
    Erase maintRasterSizes
    Exit Sub
End If
```

Next, the procedure needs to determine how many sizes are available for the given font. To do this it can call the glr_msauGetSizeCount() function provided in MSAU7032.DLL. This function takes the device context and a font name and returns the number of available font sizes:

```
strName = CStr(varFaceName)
mlngCountRasterSizes = glr_msauGetSizeCount(hdc, strName)
```

Once you have the number of fonts, all you need to do is redimension the global array to be large enough to contain the list of font sizes and then retrieve them. To fill the array with the list of available font sizes, you can call the glr_msauGetSize-List() function in MSAU7032.DLL:

```
If mlngCountRasterSizes > 0 Then
    ReDim maintRasterSizes(0 To mlngCountRasterSizes - 1)
    mlngCountRasterSizes = glr_msauGetSizeList(hdc, _
    strName, maintRasterSizes())
End If
```

That's basically all there is to frmListFonts. When the user chooses a font from the list, the AfterUpdate event code requeries the list containing the available sizes for that font. In addition, it sets the properties of the text box that displays the same text to match the chosen values.

Finding the Screen Size for Text in a Given Font

At times you'll need to know the screen size for a piece of text, given a font name, its size, and its attributes. For example, you might want to set the size of a text box so that it just fits the text inside it, in which case you need to know how much space the text will take up. Imagine that you'd like to use different fonts, or different weights of the same font, in a row of text boxes on a form. The Access Developer's Toolkit (see Appendix C on the companion CD-ROM for more information) provides a Rich Text Format (RTF) OLE control that allows you to use mixed fonts, but you can "fake it" yourself for limited text. Access allows only one font for each text box, so you'll need to use a series of text boxes, each using a different font, one for each field. Figure 19.13 shows a sample form (frmTwipsFromFont) that calculates the width of the text for each field in the row, based on the font being used in each of the text boxes.

To call glr_msauGetTwipsFromFont, use the syntax shown in Table 19.16.

FIGURE 19.13:

Calculate the width and height of each text box as you change rows on the form.

TABLE 19.16: Syntax for Calling glr_msauGetTwipsFromFont()

Parameter	Type	Description	Comments
strFontName	String	Name of the font	Must match one of the installed font names, or Windows will make a substitution (that is, a guess)
lngSize	Long	Size, in points (as shown in the font size drop-down list in Access)	The point size must be between 1 and 127
lngWeight	Long	Weight of the font, chosen from the following list: 100 (Thin), 200 (Extra Light), 300 (Light), 400 (Normal), 500 (Medium), 600 (Semi-bold), 700 (Bold), 800 (Extra Bold), 900 (Heavy)	
fItalic	Long	Logical value indicating whether or not the text is italicized	
fUnderline	Long	Logical value indicating whether or not the text is underlined	
lngChars	Long	To use the average character width for the font in the calculations, specify the number of characters in this parameter	Fill in either strCaption or lngChars. If you fill in both, lngChars will take priority. This parameter interacts with the cchUseMaxWidth parameter: the DLL will use the maximum character width for the cchUseMaxWidth of the characters and use the average width for the rest, up to lngChars. Unless you fill in this parameter, the DLL disregards the value in cchUseMaxWidth

TABLE 19.16: Syntax for Calling glr_msauGetTwipsFromFont() (continued)

Parameter	Type	Description	Comments
strCaption	String	Text for which you wish to calculate the width and height. Either supply the text here (the DLL will calculate the actual width, based on your character string) or supply a length in the lngChars parameter (the DLL will use the average character width)	
cchUseMax-Width	Long	Number of characters for which you'd like to use the maximum character width for the font when making calculations	If you supply a value for lngChars, MSAU7032.DLL will use the average character width for the requested font when making its calculations. Supply a value in this parameter to specify for how many of those characters you'd like to use the maximum character width. This is useful if you want to display abbreviations, part numbers, and so on, that are short and must display all the characters, no matter what. The DLL will use the maximum character width for the first cchUseMaxChars characters and the average width for lngChars—cchUseMaxChars characters. This parameter is ignored if lngChars isn't greater than 0
lngWidth	Long	Filled in by the DLL with the width, in twips, of the text	This value seems always to be a bit short, based on experimentation in Access. We found that multiplying it by 1.1 (or perhaps a value even closer to 1.0) makes the value match reality a little more closely. You may need to experiment to get this value exactly right
lngHeight	Long	Filled in by the DLL with the height, in twips, of the text	
Return Value	Long	True if the function succeeded, False otherwise	

The sample form, frmTwipsFromFont, uses the following code in its Current event to set the size for each of the text boxes on the form. It loops through each control on the form, calling glr_msauGetTwipsFromFont() with the attributes of the text box's font, and sets the width of each text box to match the width of the text in the appropriate font.

```
For Each ctl In Me.Controls
    With ctl
        If .ControlType = acTextBox Then
            If IsNull(.Value) Then
                .Width = 0
            Else
                If glr_msauTwipsFromFont( _
                 .FontName, _
                 .FontSize, _
                 .FontWeight, _
                 .FontItalic, _
                 .FontUnderline, _
                 0, .Value, 0, lngWidth, lngHeight) Then
                    .Width = lngWidth * glrcAdjustforScreen
                End If
            End If
            .Left = lngLeft
            lngLeft = lngLeft + .Width
        End With
    End If
Next ctl
```

Object-Handling Functions

Many of the Access Wizards need to display lists of database objects. There are many factors to take into account when deciding which items you want to see on those lists: Are system objects visible? Are hidden objects visible? Exactly which types of queries do you want to see? Which kinds of tables (local, ISAM, ODBC) do you want to see?

You can make all these decisions using DAO (as shown in Chapter 6) to provide the list, but it's a lot of work and can be slow. To simplify this process, MSAU7032.DLL includes four functions to help you supply lists of objects. You can retrieve a list of names of objects and sort that list. You can retrieve a list of data structures that include names and object types, and you can sort that list. Each of the next sections details one of the four functions.

Retrieving a List of Object Names

If you need to provide a list of object names in your applications, you can certainly use DAO to create the list. (See Chapter 6 for more information.) On the other hand, MSAU7032.DLL makes it easy: you specify the object type and set some flags describing which subsets of that object you want, and the DLL fills in an array with a list of the items.

The sample form, frmDBC, in CH19.MDB (see Figure 19.14), is based on frmDBC from CH06.MDB. Instead of using DAO to fill its lists, however, it uses MSAU-7032.DLL, calling the glr_msauGetObjNames() function. Table 19.17 describes the syntax for calling glr_msauGetObjNames().

FIGURE 19.14:

frmDBC, using MSAU7032.DLL rather than DAO to fill itself

TABLE 19.17: Syntax for Calling glr_msauGetObjNames()

Parameter	Type	Description	Comments
varWrk	Variant	Reference to the workspace containing the database from which you want to retrieve object names	
varDB	Variant	Reference to the database from which you want to retrieve object names	

TABLE 19.17: Syntax for Calling glr_msauGetObjNames() (continued)

Parameter	Type	Description	Comments
intObjType	Integer	One of the standard object types: acTable, acQuery, acForm, acReport, acMacro, acModule	
lngFlags	Long	One or more values, combined with the Or operator, indicating which subset of objects you want to retrieve. For tables, use one or more of glrcBitTblLocal, glrcBitTblAttachedISAM, glrcBitTblAttachedODBC, and glrcBitTblAll. For queries, use the standard DAO Type constants (dbQSelect, dbQCrossTab, and so on), passed through the glrCvtQryTypeToBit() function, or use glrcBitQryAll to get all queries. For any type of object, use glrcBitObjSystem and glrcBitObjHidden to control the display of Hidden and System objects	
astrObjects()	String array	On return, filled in with the list of objects you requested	Before you call the function, you must dimension the array to hold as many elements as the maximum number of items to be returned. That is, if you're asking for a subset of the queries, make the array large enough to hold all the queries. On return, the intItemsFilled parameter will contain the number of items the function actually placed into the array, so you can dimension the array again at that point
intStart	Integer	Zero-based index, indicating where to start placing items into the array	Useful if you need to put more than one type of object into the array (if you want to list tables and queries at the same time, for instance)
intItemsFilled	Integer	Filled in, on return, with the number of items the function placed into the array	If this value ends up being more than you'd prepared the array to hold, you're pretty much guaranteed to crash. Make sure you dimension astrObjects() large enough to hold all possible items
Return Value	Long	glrcMSAUErrSuccess or glrcMSAUErrUnknown	

In frmDBC, look in the ListObjects list-filling function to find the interesting code. Listing 19.7 shows the initialization step of the function.

Listing 19.7

```
Dim db As Database
Static astrItems() As String
Static lngCount As Integer
Dim lngFlags As Long
Dim intSize As Integer

Select Case intCode
    Case acLBInitialize
        Set db = CurrentDb()

        ' Fill in astrItems() with the list of
        ' object names.
        lngCount = db.Containers(GetContainer( _
        Me!grpObjects)).Documents.Count
        If lngCount > 0 Then
            ' Set up the array.  It might be too
            ' many elements, but the code will resize
            ' the array at the end.
            ReDim astrItems(0 To lngCount - 1)

            ' Set up the flags, so you just open the
            ' items you want.  Assume you want all the
            ' tables (attached or otherwise), and then
            ' check on whether or not to show
            ' hidden/system objects.
            Select Case Me!grpObjects
                Case acTable
                    lngFlags = glrGetAppInfo(glrcBitTblAll)
                Case acQuery
                    lngFlags = glrGetAppInfo(glrcBitQryAll)
                Case Else
                    lngFlags = glrGetAppInfo(0)
            End Select
            ' Now ask MSAU7032.DLL to fill in the array with
            ' the selected items.
            Call glr_msauGetObjNames(DBEngine(0), db, _
            (Me!grpObjects), lngFlags, astrItems(), _
            0, lngCount)
            ' If it returned any items, resize the array to
```

```
                    ' just the right size.
                If lngCount > 0 Then
                    ReDim Preserve astrItems(0 To lngCount - 1)
                    Call glr_msauSortStringArray(astrItems)
                End If
' code continues...
```

This code works in a series of steps that you'll also need to follow when using
glr_msauGetObjNames() in your own applications:

1. **Dimension the array:** The array must be able to hold enough rows for all
   possible items. In this case, the code just retrieves the count of documents in
   the appropriate container. (The GetContainer() function simply converts container numbers into the appropriate names.) Of course, when it gets the
   count of documents in the Tables container, it's going to get tabledefs and
   querydefs, but that's not a problem. Once the code has executed, you'll resize
   the array to just the right size.

   ```
   Static astrItems() As String
   ' ...
   lngCount = db.Containers(GetContainer( _
    Me!grpObjects)).Documents.Count
   If lngCount > 0 Then
       ReDim astrItems(0 To lngCount - 1)
        ' code continues...
   ```

2. **Set the flags correctly:** In this example you want to see all items, honoring
   the system settings (Show System Objects/Show Hidden Objects). Therefore,
   call the glrGetAppInfo() function, which combines its incoming parameter
   with the appropriate flags (glrcBitObjHidden and glrcBitObjSystem) indicating whether or not to show system and hidden objects.

   ```
   ' From the list-filling function...
   Select Case Me!grpObjects
       Case acTable
           lngFlags = glrGetAppInfo(glrcBitTblAll)
       Case acQuery
           lngFlags = glrGetAppInfo(glrcBitQryAll)
       Case Else
           lngFlags = glrGetAppInfo(0)
   End Select
   ' the code continues...

   Function glrGetAppInfo(lngFlags As Long) As Long
   ```

```
      If Application.GetOption("Show Hidden Objects") Then
          lngFlags = lngFlags Or glrcBitObjHidden
      End If
      If Application.GetOption("Show System Objects") Then
          lngFlags = lngFlags Or glrcBitObjSystem
      End If
      glrGetAppInfo = lngFlags
End Function
```

MSAU7032.DLL does not use the built-in Jet constants (dbQSelect, dbQCrosstab, and so on) to specify the query types you want to see. Internally, the DLL uses a slightly different value to flag each query type. To convert from the normal query types to the flags the DLL expects to find, use the glrCvtQryTypeToBit() function, in basMSAU-7032. This function takes in Jet constants and returns the appropriate MSAU7032.DLL flag value.

3. **Call glr_msauGetObjNames():** Now that everything is all set up, call the function. This fills lngCount with the number of items the function actually placed into the array.

```
Call glr_msauGetObjNames(DBEngine(0), db, _
  (Me!grpObjects), lngFlags, astrItems(), _
  0, lngCount)
```

4. **Resize the array:** Once you've placed the data in the array, you must resize it so that it's just large enough to hold the items placed in it. If you're not going to sort it or you're going to add more elements, you can skip this step, but if you're sorting the array, this step is *crucial.* (See the next section for information on sorting the array.)

```
If lngCount > 0 Then
    ReDim Preserve astrItems(0 To lngCount - 1)
    Call glr_msauSortStringArray(astrItems())
End If
```

Sorting a String Array

To support the glr_msauGetObjNames() function, MSAU7032.DLL includes glr_msau-SortStringArray(). This function is useful in its own right: it can sort any array of strings you care to send it, not just object names.

Calling glr_msauSortStringArray() is simple: pass it an array filled with strings, and it will sort them in place. It returns glrcMSAUErrUnknown if anything goes wrong or glrcMSAUErrSuccess if it succeeds. You can use this function with any array of strings.

WARNING   If you pass an array to glr_msauSortStringArray( ) that has been dimensioned to contain more elements than it actually contains, the sort procedure will become confused and return your array with the empty elements sorted incorrectly. Make sure you redimension your array correctly before calling glr_msauSortStringArray( ).

Retrieving a List of Objects and Their Types

At times you'll need to retrieve lists of multiple object types, stored in the same array, and be able to discern between them (as when the Wizards provide a list of tables and queries in the same control). MSAU7032.DLL includes a function, glr_msauGetDbObjList(), that fills an array with data structures:

```
Type glrDBObj
    intObjType As Integer
    strName As String
    lngFlags As Long
End Type
```

Because this structure contains both the name and the type, you can tell the different object types apart once they're in your array.

NOTE   Although this structure contains a lngFlags field, MSAU7032.DLL disregards this field and always places a value of 0 into it. You can't remove it from the structure, or the DLL won't work, but you also shouldn't use the field.

The sample form, frmDBObjList, shown in Figure 19.15, allows you to experiment with all the options available for the lngFlags parameter to glr_msauGetDBObjList(). (The flags work just the same for glr_msauGetObjNames(), of course.) As you make choices, the form requeries the list box and shows the items in the array that has been filled by glr_msauGetDBObjList().

FIGURE 19.15:

Use frmDbObjList to test creating lists of objects

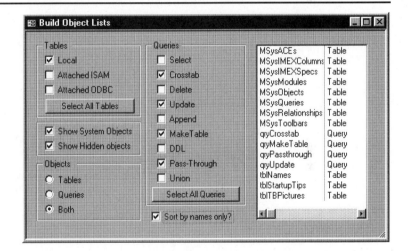

Table 19.18 shows the syntax you use to call glr_msauGetDBObjList(). You may find it interesting to dig in and see how frmDBObjList works, but in general, it follows the same set of steps outlined for working with glr_msauGetObjNames().

TABLE 19.18: Syntax for Calling glr_msauGetDBObjList()

Parameter	Type	Description	Comments
varWrk	Variant	Reference to the workspace containing the database from which you want to retrieve object names	
varDB	Variant	Reference to the database from which you want to retrieve object names	
intObjType	Integer	One of the standard object types: acTable, acQuery, acForm, acReport, acMacro, acModule	
lngFlags	Long	One or more values, combined with the Or operator, indicating which subset of objects you want to retrieve. For tables, use one or more of glrcBitTblLocal, glrcBit-TblAttachedISAM, glrcBitTbl-AttachedODBC, and glrcBitTblAll. For queries, use the standard DAO Type constants (dbQSelect, dbQCrossTab, and so on), passed through the glrCvtQryTypeToBit() function, or use glrcBitQryAll to get all queries. For any type of object, use glrcBitObjSystem and glrcBitObjHidden to control the display of Hidden and System objects	
atypObjects()	Array of glrDBObj data structures	On return, filled in with the list of objects you requested	You must dimension the array, before you call this function, to hold as many elements as the maximum number of items to be returned. That is, if you're asking for a subset of the queries, make the array large enough to hold all the queries. On return, the intItemsFilled parameter will contain the number of items the function actually placed into the array, so you can dimension the array again at that point

TABLE 19.18: Syntax for Calling glr_msauGetDBObjList() (continued)

Parameter	Type	Description	Comments
intStart	Integer	Zero-based index, indicating where to start placing items into the array	Useful if you need to put more than one type of object into the array (if you want to list tables and queries at the same time, for instance)
intItemsFilled	Integer	Filled in, on return, with the number of items the function placed into the array	If this value ends up being more than you'd prepared the array to hold, you're pretty much guaranteed to crash. Make sure you dimension atypObjects() large enough to hold all possible items
Return Value	Long	glrcMSAUErrSuccess or glrcMSAUErrUnknown	

Sorting the Array of DBObj Structures

To sort the array of structures, MSAU7032.DLL provides the glr_msauSortDBObj-Array() function. This function is simple to call: pass to it an array of glrDBObj structures all filled in and a Boolean flag, fNamesOnly, indicating whether you want to sort by object type and then names or just by names. For example:

```
fSuccess = glr_msauSortDBObjArray(atypNames(), True)
```

sorts atypNames() in order of names only, disregarding the object types. If you pass False for the fNamesOnly parameter, the function sorts the array first by object type and then by name. Try out this feature on frmDBObjList (check and uncheck the Sort by Names Only? check box) to get a feel for the differences. The function returns either glrcMSAUErrSuccess or glrcMSAUErrUnknown, indicating the success or failure of the function.

WARNING If you pass an array that is dimensioned to hold more elements than glr_msauGetDBObjList() actually placed into the array to glr_msauSort-DBObjArray(), MSAU7032.DLL may crash. Make sure you redimension your array to the correct size after the call to glr_msauGetDBObjList() to avoid this crash.

Miscellaneous Functions

To round out your whirlwind tour of MSAU7032.DLL, this final section includes three functions that didn't fit any of the other categories. These functions include retrieving an executable or library's national language, using toolbar bitmaps in your own applications, and finding out how many colors are used in a bitmap.

Retrieving National Language Info

Most Windows executables and DLLs contain information about the language and character set for which they were created, among other version-specific information. Table 19.19 lists some of the defined language code numbers, and Table 19.20 lists some of the character sets Windows currently supports. The combination of these two numbers makes up the language identifier for a version of a product.

TABLE 19.19: A Subset of Windows Language Codes

ID	Language
1046	Brazilian Portuguese
3084	Canadian French
1034	Castilian Spanish
1027	Catalan
1050	Croato-Serbian (Latin)
1029	Czech
1030	Danish
1043	Dutch
1035	Finnish
1036	French
1031	German
1032	Greek
1037	Hebrew
1038	Hungarian
1039	Icelandic
1040	Italian

TABLE 19.19:   A Subset of Windows Language Codes (continued)

ID	Language
1041	Japanese
1042	Korean
2058	Mexican Spanish
1045	Polish
2070	Portuguese
1048	Romanian
1049	Russian
2074	Serbo-Croatian (Cyrillic)
2052	Simplified Chinese
1051	Slovak
1053	Swedish
4108	Swiss French
2055	Swiss German
2064	Swiss Italian
1054	Thai
1028	Traditional Chinese
1055	Turkish
2057	U.K. English
1033	U.S. English
1056	Urdu

TABLE 19.20:   A Subset of Windows' Supported Character Sets

Character Set	Description
0	7-bit ASCII
932	Windows, Japan (Shift–JIS X-0208)
949	Windows, Korea (Shift–KSC 5601)
950	Windows, Taiwan (GB5)
1200	Unicode
1250	Windows, Latin-2 (Eastern European)

TABLE 19.20: A Subset of Windows' Supported Character Sets (continued)

Character Set	Description
1251	Windows, Cyrillic
1252	Windows, Multilingual
1253	Windows, Greek
1254	Windows, Turkish
1255	Windows, Hebrew
1256	Windows, Arabic

Although it's tricky to retrieve this information using API calls directly from Access, it is possible. To simplify the process, MSAU7032.DLL provides a single function call, glr_msauGetLanguage(), which tells you both values for any specified file or running module. To use glr_msauGetLanguage(), you must first declare it (or import basMSAU7032, of course):

```
Declare Function glr_msauGetLanguage Lib "MSAU7032.DLL" _
 Alias "MSAU_GetFileLanguage" _
 (ByVal strFileOrMod As String, ByVal fFileName As Long, _
 intLang As Integer, intCodePage As Integer) As Integer
```

The function takes four parameters, as described in Table 19.21. It returns one of four possible values, depending on the outcome of its efforts. Table 19.22 lists those values.

For example, to find the language version of the currently running copy of Microsoft Access, you could use code like the following, from basTestMSAU7032:

```
Function TestLanguage()
    Dim intRetval As Integer
    Dim intLang As Integer
    Dim intCharSet As Integer

    intRetval = glr_msauGetLanguage("MSAIN300", True, _
     intLang, intCharSet)
    If intRetval = glrcMSAUErrLangSuccess Then
        MsgBox "Language: " & intLang & ", Char Set: " & _
         intCharSet
    End If
End Function
```

TABLE 19.21: Parameters for glr_msauGetLanguage()

Parameter	Datatype	On Input	On Output
strFileOrMod	String	Name of a running module or disk file name	Not Used
fFileName	Long	Flag indicating whether strFileOrMod is a disk file or a running module (True for disk file, False for running module)	Not Used
intLang	Integer	Not Used	Language Code
intCodePage	Integer	Not Used	Character Set

TABLE 19.22: Possible Return Values for glr_msauGetLanguage()

Constant	Return Value	Description
glrcMSAUErrLangSuccess	0	No Error
glrcMSAUErrLangModuleNotLoaded	−1	The requested module isn't loaded
glrcMSAUErrLangOutOfMemory	−2	Out of memory
glrcMSAUErrLangCantRetrieve	−3	Unable to retrieve the requested information (Most likely, the file can't be found.)

Figure 19.16 shows the resulting message box for the U.S. English version of Access.

FIGURE 19.16:

Message box showing the current language and character set

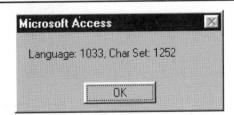

Retrieving Toolbar Bitmaps

As you've noticed if you've modified the button face of a toolbar button, Access provides a limited set of bitmaps from which to choose. Figure 19.17 shows the 86 that are available when you attempt to modify a toolbar's picture. More bitmaps are available for you to use on buttons, through the Button Wizard.

Access stores this collection of bitmaps as a single "slab" in MSAIN300.DLL. Figure 19.18 shows the bitmap as it's stored in the DLL. Storing the bitmaps this way saves on graphics resources, which are in short enough supply with major Windows applications running!

To do its work, the Button Builder required some method of retrieving a single bitmap from the "slab," and MSAU7032.DLL provides the code necessary to retrieve that bitmap. To make it possible to use the same bitmaps on all screen resolutions, the function returns a device-independent bitmap. To use the function, you need the following declaration:

```
Declare Function glr_msauGetTbDIB Lib "MSAU7032.DLL" _
  Alias "MSAU_GetTbDIB" (ByVal lngBmp As Long, _
  ByVal fLarge As Long, bytBuf() As Byte) As Long
```

FIGURE 19.17:

Palette of bitmaps available for toolbar buttons

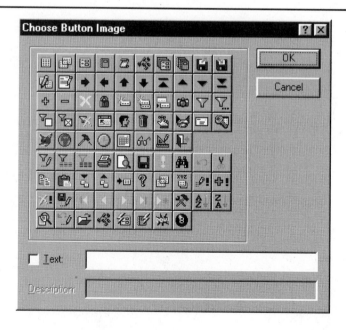

FIGURE 19.18:

The toolbar and button builder bitmaps are stored in a "slab" in MSAIN300.DLL.

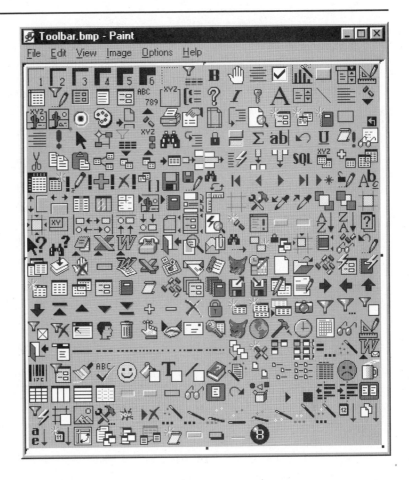

FIGURE 19.18:

The toolbar and button builder bitmaps are stored in a "slab" in MSAIN300.DLL.

The function returns 0 if it fails for any reason and a nonzero value if it succeeds.

In addition, you can't use this function without a table that lists all the pictures and their ID values (which indicate to the DLL where to start pulling data, inside the bitmap). In CH19.MDB you'll find tblTBPictures, which includes all the data you'll need. You must include this table in any application for which you'd like to supply this functionality.

WARNING   Because you're including this table in your application, you must be extremely careful to keep the table updated to match the current version of Access. The table we've supplied matches Access for Windows 95. Anytime the version of Access changes, you'll need to import bw_TblPictures from whichever library it's currently in. (In Access 95, it's in WZMAIN70.MDA.) Because Microsoft maintains complete control over both the table and the bitmap "slab," you have to make sure you have them synchronized. You could, of course, just link the table bw_TblPictures from WZMAIN70.MDA, rename the link to tblTBPictures, and use it externally. The problem with this solution is that you can't ship WZMAIN70.MDA with applications you distribute using the run-time application. If you import the table, you aren't fighting that restriction. We decided to import the table and not worry about the distribution problems.

Table 19.23 describes the three parameters for glr_msauGetTBDib().

TABLE 19.23:   Parameters for glr_msauGetTBDib()

Parameter	Datatype	Description
lngBMP	Long	Value from the TBBitmapID column in tblTBPictures, indicating which bitmap to retrieve
fLarge	Long	Flag: True to use large bitmaps, False to use small bitmaps
abytBuffer	Array of bytes	Buffer to hold the bitmap information

It's up to you to make sure strBuf is large enough to hold all the bitmap information before you call glr_msauGetTBDib(). We recommend you use the Space() function to ensure that it's initialized to the correct size. For large bitmaps you'll need 488 characters. For small bitmaps you'll need 296 characters. You might use code like the following to set this up:

```
Const glrcLargeBitmapSize = 488
Const glrcSmallBitmapSize = 296

' Arbitrarily use small pictures, this time.
```

```
fUseLargePictures = False

strPictureData = Space(IIf(fUseLargePictures, _
 glrcLargeBitmapSize, glrcSmallBitmapSize))
```

To retrieve a specific bitmap from the array of bitmaps in MSAIN300.DLL, you
need to find the correct row in tblTBPictures, retrieve the TBBitmapID value from
that row, and then call glr_msauGetTBDib(). Listing 19.8 shows code you could use
to retrieve a bitmap and use the bitmap to replace the picture on a specific button.

Listing 19.8

```
Private Sub RetrieveDIB(ctl As Control, _
 lngPictureID As Long)
    Dim fUseLargePictures As Integer
    Dim abytBuffer() As Byte
    Dim varRetval As Variant
    Dim db As Database
    Dim rst As Recordset

Const glrcLargeBitmapSize = 488
Const glrcSmallBitmapSize = 296

    ' Arbitrarily use large pictures.
    fUseLargePictures = True

    Set db = CurrentDb()
    Set rst = db.OpenRecordset("Select PictureData, " & _
     "TBBitmapID from tblTBPictures where PictureID = " & _
     (lngPictureID), dbOpenSnapShot)

    ' If there is a row with the selected ID, then
    ' load that picture.
    If Not rst.EOF Then
        If Not IsNull(rst!TBBitmapID) Then
            ReDim abytBuffer(0 To IIf(fUseLargePictures, _
             glrcLargeBitmapSize, glrcSmallBitmapSize) - 1)
            If glr_msauGetTbDIB(rst!TBBitmapID, _
             fUseLargePictures, abytBuffer()) Then
                ctl.PictureData = abytBuffer()
            End If
        Else
            ctl.PictureData = rst!PictureData
        End If
        rst.Close
```

```
    End If
End Sub
```

In the example code, you first need to find a particular row in tblTBPictures, given the primary key value for a row. The following code does that for you:

```
Set db = CurrentDb()
Set rst = db.OpenRecordset("Select PictureData, " & _
 "TBBitmapID from tblTBPictures where PictureID = " & _
 (lngPictureID), dbOpenSnapShot)
```

If you've found the row, you need to check the TBBitmapID column, because some of the rows don't pertain to data in the bitmap array but actually store their bitmap information in the PictureData column. For those rows you just copy the data directly out of the table instead of retrieving it from MSAIN300.DLL:

```
If Not rst.EOF Then
    If Not IsNull(rst!TBBitmapID) Then
        ReDim abytBuffer(0 To IIf(fUseLargePictures, _
         glrcLargeBitmapSize, glrcSmallBitmapSize) - 1)
        If glr_msauGetTbDIB(rst!TBBitmapID, _
         fUseLargePictures, abytBuffer()) Then
            ctl.PictureData = abytBuffer()
        End If
    Else
        ctl.PictureData = rst!PictureData
    End If
    rst.Close
End If
```

In either case, once the procedure has retrieved the data, it places it on the button's face by assigning it to the button's PictureData property.

Using glr_msauGetTBDib()

If you've used the Command Button Wizard, you know it supplies you with a list box full of pictures you can place on a button. Its main problem is that you can work with only a single button and its properties at a time. If you need to change the pictures for buttons you've already created, Access does provide a button picture builder, but going through the steps of using the builder for each button can be tedious. Figure 19.19 shows the Command Button Wizard in action.

We've created a small tool, frmButtonPix in CH19.MDB, that can take care of this task for you. Using the code shown in Listing 19.8, it can place any picture from

FIGURE 19.19:

The Command Button Wizard supplies you with a choice of bitmaps for your buttons.

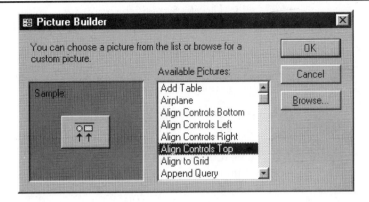

tblTBPictures onto any button on any form you have loaded. This can be a very useful design-time tool, and it works fine at run time, too. Figure 19.20 shows frmButtonPix running.

NOTE   If you wish to use frmButtonPix to change the picture on a button permanently, you need to open the form containing that button in Design view, use frmButtonPix to change the button face, and then save the changed form. Changes made to forms at run time are not saved with the form.

Because there's no simple way for frmButtonPix to know that you've loaded or closed forms around it, we've supplied the Refill Lists button on the form. This button

FIGURE 19.20:

frmButtonPix can change the picture on any button on any form.

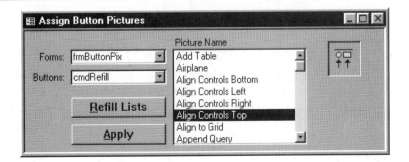

allows you to change which forms are currently loaded and then tell frmButtonPix about it.

Once you've selected a form and a button on that form, you can click the Apply button (or double-click the picture image on the form), and the code will apply the chosen image to the chosen button:

```
Private Sub cmdApply_Click()
    On Error Resume Next
    Forms(Me!lstForms)(Me!lstButtons).PictureData = _
     Me!cmdSample.PictureData
End Sub
```

To use frmButtonPix in your own applications, import both the form and the table (tblTBPictures), along with the module basMSAU7032.

How Many Colors in That Bitmap?

Although we can't imagine it will come up terribly often, you may need to know how many colors a particular bitmap requires. For example, the number of colors (also referred to as the *pixel depth*) is usually 2, 16, 256, or higher. You may, for example, want to limit the types of bitmaps users can store in an OLE object column in a table.

The sample form frmPixelDepth, in CH19.MDB, demonstrates the glr_msauGetPixelDepth() function. It's simple to use: you pass to it an array of bytes containing the bitmap, and it returns to you the number of colors in the bitmap. For example, frmPixelDepth uses this code to perform its calculations:

```
Private Sub Form_Open(Cancel As Integer)
    Dim abytTest() As Byte
    Dim intI As Integer

    For intI = 1 To 3
        abytTest = Me("imgTest" & intI).PictureData
        Me("txtPixelDepth" & intI) = _
         glr_msauGetPixelDepth(abytTest())
    Next intI
End Sub
```

As you can see, the code copies the image controls' PictureData properties directly into an array of bytes and then sends that array of bytes to the glr_msauGet-PixelDepth() function. If the function can decipher the array of bytes, it returns the pixel depth. If not, it returns 0.

NOTE This function works only with device-independent bitmaps (DIBs). It will always return 0 for any other type of image. Even for DIBs, the only possible return values are 2, 16, 256, 65536, 16777216, and 4294967296. In addition, the function does not verify that what you're sending it is actually a bitmap. It's up to you to make sure you're actually sending it data from a bitmap, not random bytes.

Summary

This chapter has introduced the undocumented library MSAU7032.DLL and demonstrated how to use most of its entry points. As with any other undocumented feature, the functions in MSAU7032.DLL and their use could change with any future release. Everything in this chapter was current as of the writing of this book, and because the Access Wizards use all the features described here, chances are they won't change much.

Specifically, the sections in this chapter demonstrated these areas:

File-Handling Functions:

- Check for the existence of a file.
- Split a full path reference into component pieces.
- Retrieve the full path name for a file.

Common Dialogs:

- Use the File Open/File Save dialogs.
- Use the Color Chooser dialog.

Work with Menus:

- Clean a menu string.
- Retrieve the text of a menu item.
- Find the number of items in a menu.
- Retrieve a handle to the Access menus.
- Find the actual menu position of an item, given its condensed position.
- Convert DoMenuItem arguments to strings.

Work with the Registry:

- Retrieve the number of subkeys and values for a given Registry key.
- Get a subkey name by its index.
- Get a key value.
- Get a value's name given its index.
- Create a Registry key.
- Write a key's value.

Work with Installed Fonts:

- Retrieve the count of available fonts.
- Retrieve the list of available fonts.
- Retrieve the count of available font sizes for a font.
- Retrieve the list of available font sizes for a font.

Work with DAO Objects:

- Retrieve a list of object names.
- Retrieve a list of objects and their types.
- Sort an array of strings.
- Sort an array of database objects, either by type or by name.

Miscellaneous:

- Retrieve information about a DLL or executable's national language.
- Retrieve a bitmap from the common button bitmaps.
- Find out the number of colors in a bitmap.

In addition, we've provided sample forms that demonstrate a number of these techniques. You can easily import these forms directly from CH19.MDB into your own applications.

CHAPTER

TWENTY

Using DDE

- Understanding DDE clients and servers

- Dynamics of a DDE conversation

- Topics and items

- Properties of the DDE commands

- Closing a DDE server

- Using Access as a DDE server

- Network DDE

Dynamic Data Exchange (DDE) is a Windows protocol and application programming interface (API) that allows one Windows program to exchange data with another or causes one program to trigger functionality in another. With DDE you can extract data from a spreadsheet in Excel, manipulate a Word for Windows document, or control your own Visual Basic program. By using DDE from other programs, you can extract data from an Access database, run a macro, or get a list of existing tables. DDE is a general language protocol for manipulating programs programmatically. This protocol is different from OLE automation, but there is some overlap of functionality. In the long run, DDE will be replaced entirely by OLE automation when all major applications support the new functionality. Until then, DDE is the method for controlling programs that don't support OLE automation. In addition, if you want to connect to programs on other computers on the network, OLE automation is not enough; you must use an extension to DDE known as NetDDE.

Clients and Servers

To be able to use DDE, a Windows program must support the DDE API. A Windows program can be either a DDE client or a DDE server. The *client* is the program doing the controlling; the *server* is the program being controlled. A Windows program can support neither, either, or both of these. Microsoft Access supports both. To establish a conversation between two programs using DDE, one program must be acting as a DDE client, the other as a server.

As a DDE client, Access can retrieve information from another program. For example, it can retrieve information from an Excel spreadsheet. When Access is a DDE server, another program can retrieve information from Access. For example, a C program can retrieve information from an Access query.

Dynamics of a DDE Conversation

Figure 20.1 shows an example of a DDE conversation. As you can see, a handshaking operation is going on between the two programs. The client requests something to be done on the server. When the server has completed the task, it indicates it has done so by sending either some data or an acknowledgment.

FIGURE 20.1:

Example DDE conversation

A DDE Conversation begins with the client initiating the conversation with the server

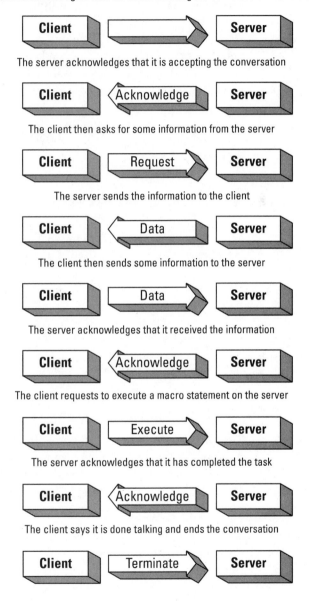

The server acknowledges that it is accepting the conversation

The client then asks for some information from the server

The server sends the information to the client

The client then sends some information to the server

The server acknowledges that it received the information

The client requests to execute a macro statement on the server

The server acknowledges that it has completed the task

The client says it is done talking and ends the conversation

If the data or acknowledgment is not received within a certain amount of time, VBA assumes the server is not responding and reports a run-time error. The amount of time VBA waits before reporting an error is controlled by the View ➤ Options ➤ Advanced ➤ OLE/DDE Timeout option. Because different hardware, software, and network configurations may take significantly different amounts of time to respond, you should permit the user to change this option. To do so, either let the user access the Tools ➤ Options dialog or present your own dialog and set this option through code with

Application.SetOption "OLE/DDE Timeout (sec)", *NumberOfSeconds*

Servers, Topics, and Items

When a DDE client wishes to retrieve some information from a running DDE server, it must know three pieces of information:

- A server name for the DDE server
- The topic
- The specific item of information to be retrieved

Each of these is described in the following sections.

DDE Server Names

The DDE server name is any name that the DDE server either registers with Windows when it starts or that it will answer to when you attempt to connect to it. Often a server will register more than one name. Access, for example, registers MSAccess, MSACCESS.EXE, MSAccess*InstanceNumber* (for example, MSAccess3246), and Microsoft Access. All the names are valid server names.

One important thing to note is that there is no version-specific name for DDE servers. If you are running two versions of the same application (such as Access 2.0 and Access 95), you will want to use the Shell() function discussed below to make sure you are connecting to the right program.

Topics

The client and server must agree on a topic when they establish a conversation. Each server has a list of topics it is prepared to discuss, and the client must select one of them. These topics vary in scope among different servers. For example, Access is prepared to discuss the following topics:

- Information about the state of Access—whether it is ready to accept DDE commands, which system items it can accept, which clipboard formats it supports, and which topics it can handle

- Information about an open database—which tables, queries, forms, reports, macros, and modules the database contains

- Information from any table in the database—the column names, datatypes, and number of columns in the table; and the data from the table

- Information from any query in the database—the column names, datatypes, and number of columns in the result set of the query; and the data from the query

- Information from any Access SQL statement—the column names, datatypes, and number of columns in the result set of the SQL statement; and the data the SQL statement returns

For each conversation you must choose one, and only one, topic. It is possible to have multiple DDE conversations with the same DDE server going on at once, each one discussing a separate topic. You can even have a DDE conversation with yourself, with the same session of Access acting as both client and server.

Items

Items are used once a conversation is established to transfer information about the topic. For example, if the server is Excel, the topic might be the spreadsheet Sheet1. The item might ask what information is contained in cell R1C1 on Sheet1. As another example, if Access is acting as the server and the topic is a SQL query, the item might ask for the next row in the rowset.

Interacting with Other Applications Using DDE Functions

With Access acting as a client, you can connect to any DDE server. To do so, you use the DDE functions in VBA. Other DDE clients provide more or less the same functionality as Access, but the syntax varies among the clients. DDE client operations are performed with the six low-level functions and statements and two high-level functions shown in Table 20.1.

TABLE 20.1: The DDE Functions and Statements

Function	Purpose	Level
DDEInitiate	Initiates a DDE conversation between Access and a DDE server	Low
DDETerminate	Ends a DDE conversation between Access and a DDE server	Low
DDEExecute	Executes an operation in the DDE server's macro language	Low
DDEPoke	Sends data to the DDE server	Low
DDERequest	Retrieves data from the DDE server	Low
DDETerminateAll	Ends conversations with all DDE servers	Low
DDE	Initiates a conversation, retrieves some data, and ends the conversation with a DDE server. Valid only on forms in the ControlSource property of text boxes, option groups, check boxes, and combo boxes	High
DDESend	Initiates a conversation, sends some data, and ends the conversation with a DDE server. Valid only on forms in the ControlSource property of text boxes, option groups, check boxes, and combo boxes	High

The DDE Channel

When the DDEInitiate() function succeeds in connecting a client to a server, Windows creates a channel between them. Conceptually, the channel is a pathway between the client and server through which all data between them flows.

Internally, Windows allocates a block of memory that contains the information about the channel. The number that references that block of memory is called a *channel number*. Each of the low-level DDE functions uses that channel number as one of the arguments to the function.

Because Windows has allocated memory, it is important that you always use a DDETerminate or DDETerminateAll statement when you finish the conversation with the DDE server; otherwise you will have lost some memory to Windows. For example, if you had a DDEInitiate executed every time you refreshed a form but did not execute a DDETerminate, eventually you would run out of memory. Access should implicitly execute a DDETerminateAll when it is closed, but in the meantime, each open conversation is eating memory. Due to some changes in the way Windows 95 and Windows NT handle DDE channels, you will probably not notice any change in free Windows resources, regardless of how many channels you open up. However, especially when dealing with older programs, it is possible to have some memory leaks, so you may lose some resources even when you terminate properly. You should test your code thoroughly, especially when connecting to older applications. Another problem is that many newer applications are using exactly the same DDE interface they used in previous versions, without taking into account other changes in the application. This can cause problems when you want to access some of the new features of an application through DDE. For example, Excel's DDE supports the Excel 4.0 XLM macro interface rather then VBA, and Access supports the running of macros and macro actions, but there is no direct way to run an Access or Excel VBA procedure.

DDE Functions and Statements

The following sections describe each of the DDE functions and statements. These statements start a conversation, read data, write data, execute macros, and terminate conversations with a server.

The DDEInitiate() Function

The DDEInitiate() function establishes the conversation between a client and a server. The syntax for the function in VBA is

varChannelNumber = DDEInitiate(*strServer*, *strTopic*)

The arguments to the DDEInitiate() function are the name of the application to which you wish to connect and the topic you wish to discuss. The return value of the DDEInitiate() function is a variant containing a Long value that identifies the conversation between the two programs. This value is used in the other low-level DDE functions. DDEInitiate() requires that the DDE server specified by the *strServer* argument already be running. The section "Starting a DDE Server" later in this chapter describes methods for ensuring that it is.

> **NOTE**
>
> In Access 2 and other 16-bit applications, DDE channels are represented by variables using the Integer datatype, but in Access 95 and other 32-bit applications, they are represented by variables using the Long datatype. If you are writing DDE code that you want to be able to use in both Access 2 and Access 95, you may wish to use a variable using the Variant datatype. You should also be careful to update the type of this variable if you are converting Access 2.0 code to Access 95.

The DDERequest() Function

The DDERequest() function requests information from the DDE server. The syntax for the DDERequest() function is

varRequestedInformation = DDERequest(*lngChannelNumber*, *strItem*)

The arguments to the DDERequest() function are the channel number returned by the DDEInitiate() function and the item you are requesting. For each topic a server understands, you can request certain items of information. You must read the server's documentation to find out which items a server supports for each topic; there is no general way to determine this information from the server itself. Unfortunately, it is often difficult to find the section on DDE within most documentation. You might try searching for *DDE* in the Help system for the application. The items are specific to each application; thus Microsoft Word uses document bookmarks for items, and Excel uses cells and ranges of cells.

For example, on an Excel spreadsheet using the topic Sheet1, the Excel documentation shows that an item you might request is the value of cell R2C4. This would be expressed as

```
varValue = DDERequest(varChannelNumber, "R2C4")
```

DDE Datatypes

DDEInitiate() returns a variable of type Variant, but DDERequest() expects a Long. VBA coerces the value of the variant into a Long before the call is made. If you wish, you can use

```
varValue = DDERequest(CLng(varChannelNumber), "R2C4")
```

Using the CLng() function to make the conversion is more explicit but is not required because Access will do the conversion for you.

The DDETerminate and DDETerminateAll Statements

When you have completed all DDE operations, you must call DDETerminate or DDETerminateAll to free the channel and release the memory Windows has allocated to keep information for the channel. The syntax for the DDETerminate statement in VBA is

DDETerminate *lngChannelNumber*

The argument is the channel number returned by the DDEInitiate() function.

The DDETerminateAll statement closes all open DDE channels. The syntax is

DDETerminateAll

Don't rely on Access or Windows to reclaim the memory it allocates with a DDEInitiate() until you exit Access unless you execute one of these two terminating functions. When you are debugging VBA code that deals with DDE, it is a good idea to sometimes execute a DDETerminateAll statement in the Debug window just to have Access clean up any open connections. Unless you take these steps, you should never assume a DDE channel will be closed if either you or the user closes the server application. This subject is discussed further in the section "Creating Robust DDE Code" later in this chapter.

The DDEExecute Statement

The DDEExecute statement allows you to execute an action in another program. The syntax for the DDEExecute statement is

DDEExecute *lngChannelNumber, strCommand*

What the DDEExecute statement can perform depends on what the server program allows. You must read the documentation for the server program to see the format of the *strCommand* argument. Normally the commands are enclosed in square brackets. You can execute multiple statements within one DDEExecute by enclosing each in square brackets.

The DDEPoke Statement

The DDEPoke statement inserts data into another application. The VBA syntax is

DDEPoke *lngChannelNumber, strItem, strData*

The strItem parameter is similar to the strItem used in the DDERequest() function (which means Microsoft Word will expect a bookmark and Microsoft Excel will expect a range or a cell). For example, to put information into a specific cell in an Excel spreadsheet, you would use

```
DDEPoke varChannelNumber, "R1C2", "1234.56"
```

The DDE() Function

The DDE() function is the high-level version of DDERequest(). You can use it only in the ControlSource property of text boxes, option groups, check boxes, and combo boxes. It performs the tasks of DDEInitiate(), DDERequest(), and DDETerminate rolled into one function. The syntax is

=DDE(*strApplication, strTopic, strItem*)

For example, if you create a text box on a form and insert the following line into the ControlSource property, the text box is loaded from R1C1 on the Excel spreadsheet Sheet1:

```
=DDE("Excel","Sheet1","R1C1")
```

The DDESend() Function

DDESend() is the high-level version of DDEPoke. It also can be used only in the ControlSource property of text boxes, option groups, check boxes, and combo boxes. It performs the tasks of DDEInitiate(), DDEPoke, and DDETerminate rolled into one function. The syntax is

=DDESend(*strApplication, strTopic, strItem, strItem*)

The return value from the DDESend() function is null if the DDESend() succeeds. If it fails, it returns an error. For example, you might create a text box on a form with this text in the ControlSource property:

```
=DDESend("Excel","Sheet1","R1C2",[txtData])
```

Then you could create another text box on the form with the name txtData. Anytime the data in the txtData control is changed and a requery is issued (using the F9 key), the R1C2 cell on the Excel spreadsheet Sheet1 is updated with the contents of txtData.

Starting a DDE Server

The DDE server must be running before a conversation can be established. You can make this happen in at least three ways:

- You can put up a message box asking the user to run the program.
- You can run the server application with the Shell() function.
- You can use Network DDE to automatically start the application when it is not already running. (Using NetDDE is discussed in the section "Network DDE" later in this chapter.)

Having the user ensure that the DDE server is running is the easiest way to deal with a nonrunning server. But why do this when you can have your application find and execute the server program? The Shell() function allows you to run another program. The format for the Shell() function is

lngProcessID = Shell(*strPathname*[, *intWindowstyle*])

The *strPathname* argument is the path to the executable to be run. If only a file name is specified, Windows searches for files in the following directories (in this order):

1. The directory from which the application (MSACCESS.EXE) loaded
2. The current directory
3. The Windows\System directory
4. The Windows directory
5. The directories listed in the PATH environment variable

The intWindowstyle argument specifies how the application is to be started. It can have the values listed in Table 20.2.

This leaves one problem: usually, the application is not in any of the locations Windows searches if you don't specify a full path. How can you get the full path to the executable? Normally you can find that information in the Windows Registry. For example, you can find the path to Excel version 7.0 in the default value of the Registry key \HKEY_LOCAL_MACHINE\SOFTWARE\Microsoft\Windows\CurrentVersion\App Paths\EXCEL.EXE\. By retrieving this Registry key, you can pass it

TABLE 20.2: Valid Values for the intWindowstyle Argument to the Shell() Function

Constant	Value	Meaning
vbHide	0	Window is hidden and focus is passed to the hidden window
vbNormalFocus	1	Window has focus and is restored to its original size and position
vbMinimizedFocus	2	Window is displayed as an icon with focus
vbMaximizedFocus	3	Window is maximized with focus
vbNormalNoFocus	4	Window is restored to its most recent size and position. The currently active window remains active
vbMinimizedNoFocus	6	Window is displayed as an icon. The currently active window remains active

into the Shell() function. You can retrieve this key using the glrGetRegistryValue-FromPath() function discussed in Chapter 18.

This brings us to one last point with a number of implications. Taking control of a running application may not be what the user had in mind. For example, if users start Excel, create a new spreadsheet, and then multitask running your program, they may not want you to mess up their instance of Excel. Often it is better to start a new instance of the application so you know it is in a clean state.

The problem is that several programs or instances of programs can answer to the same application name. If you have two instances of Excel running, each instance of Excel answers to the name Excel. This can happen if an instance of Excel was already running when you executed the Shell statement. When you execute a DDE-Initiate(), how can you tell whether you are communicating with the instance you just started with the Shell() function? The answer is that you can't if you use the DDE server name Excel. If you use a server name more than one server uses, Windows chooses an instance for the connection. Windows essentially takes whichever one answers first, and you have no control over which instance is chosen.

Fortunately, some servers answer to several names. One of the names many servers answer to is their server name, with a unique number of their instance appended to the end. The return value of the Shell() function gives this unique number. From this you could expect the following to work:

```
' Almost works
lngProcessId = Shell("c:\msoffice\access\msaccess.exe", _
 vbMinimizedNoFocus)
varChannelNumber = DDEInitiate("MSAccess" & CStr(lngProcessId), _
 "System")
```

However, the instance number Access registers is unsigned (in the range 0 to 2^{32}), but lngInstance is signed (in the range -2^{31} to 2^{31}). For numbers in the range 0 to 2^{32}, signed and unsigned numbers have the same internal representation. However, unsigned values appear as negative numbers for values greater than 2^{31}. More than half the time, the code works, because Windows usually assigns low numbers first. But eventually Windows starts a task with an instance number greater than 2^{31}, the highest signed Long Integer. When this happens, the DDEInitiate() function fails because the number stored in lngInstance is negative and the number in the topic registered by Access is positive. To convert the signed instance number returned by the Shell() function to a currency value that can store a larger number than a Long, you can use the VBA function shown in Listing 20.1.

Listing 20.1

```
Function glrUCurFromLng(lngSigned As Long) As Currency
    ' This routine takes a signed long and returns
    ' a currency that is the unsigned equivalent

    If lngSigned < 0 Then
        ' First convert it to a long
        ' Then mask off any high order bits
        glrUCurFromLng = CCur(lngSigned) - &H80000000 + _
        &H7FFFFFFF + 1
    Else
        glrUCurFromLng = CCur(lngSigned)
    End If
End Function
```

The function works by converting the number to a currency value. Because the Currency datatype has a wider range than the Long Integer type, it can store Long Integer values that have been converted. The rationale for the math performed on negative numbers involves the scheme computers use for representing negative numbers, called *twos complement notation*. The Long return value from this function is appended to the word *MSAccess* to form the proper server name:

```
' Works
lngProcessId = Shell("c:\office\access\msaccess.exe" _)
 vbMinimizedNoFocus)
varChannelNumber = DDEInitiate("MSAccess" & _
 CStr(glrUCurFromLng(lngProcessId)), "System")
```

To see the available DDE server names, you can use the DDESpy utility included with VC++ and various other Microsoft applications. However, be warned that this utility shows only servers that use the DDEML Windows library that makes DDE operations easier for C programmers. Servers that use a lower-level method of performing DDE through Windows messages (such as Word for Windows and Excel) are not shown by this utility.

Previous versions of some DDE servers, such as Excel and Word for Windows, would answer to a unique instance number the same way Access does in the above example. Although Microsoft has stated that no changes were made in the DDE interface of these applications, neither application will answer to the unique instance number, so there seems to be no reliable way to use a specific session of Excel or Word based on its Shell() instance number. Access 95 and other applications that use DDEML continue to support this functionality. If you wish to make sure you load the specific instance of Word or Excel that you start, your only option may be to use the Shell statement to also load a document or workbook, as in

```
strPathName = "C:\msoffice\excel\excel.exe sample.xls"
lngProcess = Shell(strPathName, vbMinimizedNoFocus)
```

and then use the workbook name as the topic. However, this option has a problem, too. The Shell() function succeeds if the program runs. You will not get an error if Excel runs but SAMPLE.XLS cannot be opened.

Creating Robust DDE Code

Someone once likened calling DDE functions to throwing messages over a fence and hoping for an answer someday. A DDE conversation requires the server to be running and to keep running (which can be likened to hoping the person on the other side of the fence will be there and stay there once the conversation has started). Because many things (such as running out of resources or a user's closing the application) can keep the server from being there, be prepared to handle the fact that any DDE statement can fail. Just because a DDEInitiate() succeeds doesn't mean you can count on the server's being there for any subsequent DDE functions. In addition, if you use NetDDE (which is discussed shortly), getting a valid DDE channel only means that you have connected to the NetDDE agent on another machine and that the Application ➤ Topic pair is one that has been registered with it; this does not necessarily mean that it has or will be able to connect to the application. What this means is that every routine that calls DDE functions should have an error handler to catch such events (see Chapter 16). The error handler can then clean up gracefully or try to reestablish the connection. Preparing to handle DDE failures requires many lines of error-handling code and also requires spending lots of time testing your code. Making an application that uses DDE robust (able to recover from errors) is a difficult and time-consuming task.

In Access 95, DDE error handling has been complicated by another factor. The vast majority of programs (including Access) are using a DDE interface that is virtually identical to the previous version. At the same time, error handling has changed under Access 95 to help keep track of the fact that an error can come from many different sources. (See Chapter 16 for more details.) The problem for DDE is that the same error codes that were returned in Access 2 are returned when an error occurs in Access 95, but the error messages for these codes no longer exist. This means you will have to supply error trapping that includes the necessary error messages for each error. The error messages for DDE from Access 2 are listed in Table 20.3.

TABLE 20.3: DDE Error Numbers and Messages

Error Number	Error Message
280	DDE channel not fully closed; awaiting response from the other application
281	No more DDE channels are available
282	Can't open DDE channel; Microsoft Access couldn't find the specified application and topic
283	Can't open DDE channel; more than one application responded
284	DDE channel is locked
285	The other application won't perform the DDE method or operation you attempted
286	Timeout while waiting for DDE response
287	Operation terminated because Esc key was pressed before completion
288	The other application is busy

TABLE 20.3: DDE Error Numbers and Messages (continued)

Error Number	Error Message
289	Data not provided when requested in DDE operation
290	Data supplied in a DDE conversation is in the wrong format
291	The other application quit
292	DDE conversation closed or changed
293	DDE method invoked with no channel open
294	Invalid link format; can't create link to the other application
295	Message queue filled; DDE message lost
296	PasteLink already performed on this control
297	Can't set LinkMode; invalid LinkTopic
298	The DDE transaction failed. Check to ensure you have the correct version of DDEML.DLL

NOTE
Of these errors, one of the more interesting ones is error 291, which occurs when the application to which you have connected has quit (either because you sent a Quit action or the user chose to close the program). Because this error is not caused by your code, it is not detected by its error-trapping routines. You can, however, trap the error in a form's Error event.

Closing a Shelled Program

The Shell() function is great for starting an instance of a DDE server, but how do you close that server when you are done with it? One way would be to use DDEExecute to execute a macro statement that closes the application you started. For example, with a connection to Word for Windows, you could use

```
DDEExecute lngChannelNumber, "[FileExit 1]"
```

to close the session of Word and save all unsaved files without prompting the user. It is important to be sure you have a form error event that will ignore the error 291 (the other application quit) that can occur. Some applications, however, don't implement DDEExecute. In those cases, closing the application can be more difficult. There is no VBA function or statement to do it, nor is there a simple Windows API call to close an application when all you have to identify the application is the return value of the Shell() function. We wrote a routine in C called GLR_glrCloseApp, included in GLR32.DLL on the companion CD-ROM for this book, that closes the application based on the return value from the Shell() function. Listing 20.2 shows the C source code that makes up the routine in the DLL. The GLR glrCloseApp() function simply enumerates all the top-level windows until it finds one with a process ID that matches the return value of the Shell() function. It then sends a WM_CLOSE message to the window. If the server is implemented correctly, it is closed after it prompts the user to save any objects that need to be saved. Because EnumWindows requires a callback function, you cannot implement this code within VBA.

The example in the next section shows this DLL in use.

Listing 20.2

```
/*=============================================================
GLR_glrWndEnumProc
=============================================================*/
BOOL FAR PASCAL GLR_glrWndEnumProc
(
HWND hwnd,
unsigned long lApp
)
    {
    unsigned long lInst;

    if (GetParent(hwnd) == hwndNil)
        {
        GetWindowThreadProcessId(hwnd, &lInst);
        if (lInst == lApp)
            {
            PostMessage(hwnd, WM_CLOSE, 0, OL);
            return 0;
            }
        }
    }
```

```
        return 1;
        }

/*================================================================
GLR_glrCloseApp
================================================================*/
BOOL FAR PASCAL GLR_glrCloseApp
(
unsigned long lApp
)
        {
        if (lApp > 31L)
            return EnumWindows((WNDENUMPROC) GLR_glrWndEnumProc,
                lApp);
        else
            return FALSE;
        }
```

Putting It Together

The subroutine shown in Listing 20.3 shows a complete example that performs the
following steps:

1. Starts an instance of Excel

2. Finds the name of the first sheet in the workbook by querying the system
   topic

3. Opens a conversation using the found sheet name

4. Provides some column headers on the sheet

5. Opens a snapshot on a table of financial information

6. Copies the financial information into the spreadsheet

7. Adds some totaling information

8. Closes Excel

Listing 20.3

```
Declare Function glrCloseApp Lib "glr32.dll" Alias _
  "GLR_glrCloseApp" (ByVal lApp As Long) As Integer
```

```
Function glrDDEExample()
    ' Demonstrates the use of DDE

    ' Example:
    '    In the Debug window type:
    '        glrDDEExample

    Dim lngChannelNumber As Long
    Dim strTopics As String
    Dim strSheet As String
    Dim rst As Recordset
    Dim lngRecord As Long
    Dim varPath As Variant
    Dim lngProcessId As Long

    On Error GoTo glrDDEExampleError

    'Set the DDE options
    Application.SetOption "OLE/DDE Timeout (sec)", 30
    Application.SetOption "Ignore DDE Requests", False
    Application.SetOption "Enable DDE Refresh", True
    Application.SetOption "Refresh Interval (sec)", 30

    varPath = _
     glrGetRegistryValueFromPath( _
      "\HKEY_LOCAL_MACHINE\SOFTWARE\Microsoft\Windows\" & _
      "CurrentVersion\App Paths\EXCEL.EXE\")
    If IsError(varPath) Then
        MsgBox "Unexpected error #" & Err.Number & " " & _
         Err.Description, vbOKOnly Or vbExclamation Or _
         vbDefaultButton1, "glrDDEExample"
        GoTo glrDDEExampleDone
    End If

    'Run Excel
    lngProcessId = Shell(varPath, vbNormalFocus)

    'Find name of first sheet in Excel
    lngChannelNumber = CLng(DDEInitiate("Excel", "System"))
    strTopics = DDERequest(lngChannel, "Topics")
    strSheet = Left$(strTopics, InStr(1, strTopics, _
     Chr$(9)) - 1)
    DDETerminate lngChannelNumber
```

```
'Open a recordset of sales data
Set rst = CurrentDb.OpenRecordset( _
 "select dtmQuarter, curAmount from " & _
 "tblSalesByQuarter order by dtmQuarter", _
 dbOpenSnapshot, dbForwardOnly)

'Now connect to the first sheet in Excel
lngChannelNumber = CLng(DDEInitiate("excel", strSheet))

'Plug in the column headers
DDEPoke lngChannelNumber, "R1C1", "Quarter"
DDEPoke lngChannelNumber, "R1C2", "Amount"

'Read the information out of the database and
'write it into the spreadsheet
lngRecord = 2
Do Until rst.EOF
    DDEPoke lngChannelNumber, "R" & CStr(lngRecord) & "C1", _
      Format$(rst("dtmQuarter"), "q, yyyy")
    DDEPoke lngChannelNumber, "R" & CStr(lngRecord) & _
      "C2", rst("curAmount")
    lngRecord = lngRecord + 1
    rst.MoveNext
Loop

'Insert Total
DDEPoke lngChannelNumber, "R" & CStr(lngRecord + 1) & _
 "C1", "Total"
DDEPoke lngChannelNumber, "R" & CStr(lngRecord + 1) & "C2", _
 "=SUM(R[-7]C:R[-2]C)"

'Format Column 2
DDEExecute lngChannelNumber, "[Select(""C2"")]"
DDEExecute lngChannelNumber, _
 "[Format.Number(""$###,###.00"")]"

'Size the columns to best fit
DDEExecute lngChannelNumber, "[Column.Width(, ""C1:C2"",, 3)]"

'Close Excel
Call glrCloseApp(lngProcessId)

'Close all open DDE connections
DDETerminateAll
```

```
    rst.Close
glrDDEExampleDone:
Exit Function
glrDDEExampleError:
    MsgBox "Unexpected error #" & Err.Number & " " & _
     Err.Description, vbOKOnly Or vbExclamation Or _
     vbDefaultButton1, "glrDDEExample"
    Resume glrDDEExampleDone
End Function
```

Using DDE Topics and Items

Each DDE server understands various DDE topics. You can identify the topics a server understands in several ways:

- Read the documentation for the server application.
- Execute a DDERequest() of the system topic of the server with the system topic.
- Experiment with using the name of open documents, workbooks, or databases (or whatever the main type of file for the application is).

Most DDE servers have a topic called *system*. Under the system topic is an item called *topics*. If the server you are connecting to supports this topic and item, the code shown in Listing 20.4 displays the list of topics available to the server named in the strServerName argument when you pass in MSAccess by typing

```
DDETopics "MSAccess"
```

in the Debug window.

Listing 20.4

```
Sub DDETopics(ByVal strServerName As String)
    Dim varChannelNumber As Variant

    varChannelNumber = DDEInitiate(strServerName, "System")
    Debug.Print DDERequest(varChannelNumber, "Topics")
    DDETerminate varChannelNumber
End Sub
```

The topics shown for Access are the system topic plus all the databases Access has open. Access doesn't qualify the types of the various databases. It also includes the workgroup or SYSTEM.MDW file. Interestingly, you cannot do anything with a DDE channel opened with the workgroup file as a topic. However, it is easy to use DDEInitiate() with a SYSTEM.MDW or a library name as a topic to see whether a particular workgroup file or library is being used.

Under the system topic are items that tell you information about the server. Replace the word *Topics* in Listing 20.4 with the word *SysItems* and you are shown the items the Access system topic supports. The Access system topic supports four items, as described in the following list. Most other DDE servers also support at least these four.

Item	Description
SysItems	List of items supported by the system topic in Microsoft Access
Format	List of the formats Access can copy onto the clipboard
Status	"Busy" or "Ready"
Topics	List of all topics Access DDE supports

Using Access as a DDE Server

Access has a fairly good set of server capabilities, allowing a DDE client to retrieve data in various ways and execute actions or macros. Only one major feature is missing: you cannot change the data directly using DDEPoke.

The Access system topics and system items were discussed in the preceding section of this chapter. But what can you do with the databases listed? You can

- Retrieve a list of the current tables, queries, forms, reports, macros, or modules
- Retrieve records from a table or select query
- Use a SQL query on any table or query in the database
- Run any macro in the current database (can be used with any topic)

- Use any valid macro action that can be used as a method of the DoCmd object (can be used with any topic)

To retrieve a list of objects, use the open database name as the DDE topic and TableList, QueryList, FormList, ReportList, MacroList, or ModuleList as the DDE item. The DDERequest() returns the names of all objects of the requested type separated by tabs (ANSI code 9).

To retrieve records from a table, select query, or SQL statement, you can construct the DDE topic in one of these forms:

dbName; TABLE *tblTablename*

dbName; QUERY *qryQueryname*

dbName; SQL *strSQLString*

dbName; SQL

If you use the last form, with just SQL, you can construct the SQL in pieces using the DDEPoke statement. In fact, you must do this if the SQL statement is greater than 256 characters. An example is shown in Listing 20.5.

Listing 20.5

```
Dim varChannelNumber As Variant
Dim strRequest As String

varChannelNumber = DDEInitiate("MSAccess", "CH20; SQL")
DDEPoke varChannelNumber, "SQLText", "SELECT *"
DDEPoke varChannelNumber, "SQLText", _
  "FROM tblSalesByQuarter"
DDEPoke varChannelNumber, "SQLText", _
  " WHERE [curAmount] > 500000;"
strRequest = DDERequest(varChannelNumber, "All")
Debug.Print strRequest
DDETerminate varChannelNumber
```

When your code retrieves information from a table, query, or SQL statement, the DDE item is one of the keywords shown in Table 20.4.

If you use the item "FieldNames;T", the second line is a list of numbers corresponding to the field names listed in the first line returned. (Lines are separated by an ANSI code 13.) The data numbers correspond to the datatypes shown in Table 20.5.

TABLE 20.4: Valid DDE Items for Access Acting as a DDE Server

Item	Description
All	All the data in the table, including field names
Data	All rows of data without field names
FieldNames	Single-row list of field names
FieldNames;T	Two-row list of field names (first row) and their datatypes (second row)
NextRow	Next row in the table or query. When you first open a channel, NextRow returns the first row. If the current row is the last record and you execute NextRow, the request fails
PrevRow	Previous row in the table or query. If PrevRow is the first request over a new channel, the last row of the table or query is returned. If the first record is the current row, the request fails
FirstRow	Data in the first row of the table or query
LastRow	Data in the last row of the table or query
FieldCount	Number of fields in the table or query
SQLText	SQL statement representing the table or query
SQLText;*n*	SQL statement, in *n*-character chunks, representing the table or query, where *n* is an integer up to 255

TABLE 20.5: Numbers Assigned to Jet Datatypes

Data Number	Datatype
0	Invalid
1	True/False (non-null)
2	Unsigned byte (Byte)
3	2-byte signed integer (Integer)
4	4-byte signed integer (Long)
5	8-byte signed integer (Currency)
6	4-byte single-precision floating-point (Single)
7	8-byte double-precision floating-point (Double)
8	Date/Time (Date)
9	Binary data, 255 bytes maximum
10	ANSI text, case insensitive, 255 bytes maximum (Text)
11	Long binary (OLE Object)
12	Long text (Memo)

> **NOTE**
>
> You cannot specify a field of type 9 through the Access Table Design view. Access sometimes creates a field of that type for you if you link a table to a database that uses that type. You can also create fields of that type directly through VBA using the CreateField method.

When you specify SQLText, the SQL equivalent of the table or query is returned. For a table, it is returned as "SELECT * FROM table;". For a query, it returns the appropriate SQL text. If you use the format SQLText;n, where n is a number between 1 and 255, Access returns the SQL SELECT statement broken into n character chunks, with a line break (ANSI code 13) every n characters.

The DDETest Application

We have written a Visual Basic program that allows you to request, poke, and execute commands on the DDE server to allow you to easily test a DDE server. This application is shown in Figure 20.2. To use it, type or select a server name from the

FIGURE 20.2:

DDETest application

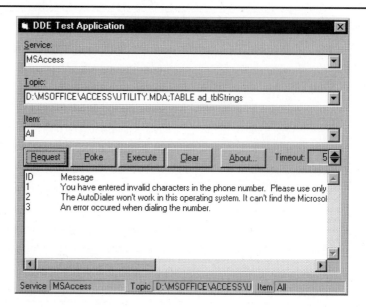

server combo box. Next, type or select a topic from the topics combo box and then type or select a valid item in the item combo box. At this point you can put information into the bottom text box to execute or poke to the server and click the Poke button. You can also click the Request button to ask for information from the server. The Clear button clears the bottom text box.

This application allows you to test your code, as well as to explore what a server is capable of.

The NextRow Trap

A common task in DDE is to retrieve the first row of a table with the FirstRow item and then use the NextRow item repeatedly to retrieve each row in the table. A problem arises, though: DDE can tell you only whether some task succeeded or failed. It cannot tell you *why* a task failed. This becomes important when you get an error from the NextRow command. The error may be telling you that you reached the end of the table, or it might be telling you that it received some other problem, such as someone's closing Access while the DDERequest() was being processed. If it is important to you to get the complete table, follow these steps when retrieving every record in a table:

1. Get the last row using the LastRow item. Store this in a string variable.
2. Get the first row using the FirstRow item.
3. Get each succeeding row with the NextRow item.
4. When you get an error from the DDERequest() with the NextRow item, compare the last row retrieved with the row stored away in step 1. If they match, assume you have retrieved the entire table. If they don't, you received an error.

Even this method cannot tell you whether you retrieved the entire table. The problem occurs when you are retrieving a table without a primary key. Tables without primary keys can have duplicate records—that is, every field in two different records can be the same. If the last record in the table or query has a duplicate, you may run into the problem. If you retrieve the duplicate record and the next record you request returns an error, you assume you retrieved the last record when you really didn't. Unfortunately, there is no solution to this problem.

Network DDE

With DDE, as with OLE automation, both the client and server must be on the same machine. However, on Windows for Workgroups, Windows 95, and Windows NT, there is an extension to DDE known as NetDDE. With NetDDE, the client and the server may reside on separate machines and have the conversation occur over the network. The server application thinks it is a local DDE request and will work in exactly the same way it would with conventional DDE. The main difference between DDE occurring locally and occurring across the network is the way in which you establish the conversation.

In its first incarnation under Windows for Workgroups, the NetDDE agent (which redirects the calls from the local PC to the remote one) was loaded by default, but under Windows 95 you must load it explicitly. Its name is NETDDE.EXE, and it is located in the Windows directory. You can load it by using the Shell() function:

```
lngProcessId = Shell("NETDDE.EXE")
```

The NetDDE agent is a Windows executable file that has no window, so you do not need to specify one of the windowstyle constants. You can also run NETDDE.EXE from the Start ➤ Run dialog, and you can even add the program to your startup group to load in when you start Windows 95.

Before executing any code, you must set up a NetDDE share for the DDE server on the network machine. This share, like the file and print shares of Windows 95, acts as an alias for a resource that another computer can use to refer to that resource. Although Windows 95 supplies a DLL called NDDEAPI.DLL to manage these shares, it is a 16-bit DLL, and you cannot use its functions directly from Access 95. If you want to create the shares directly from Access 95, you need to make some entries in the \HKEY_LOCAL_MACHINE\SOFTWARE\Microsoft\NetDDE\DDE Shares key of the Registry on the server. Because this method is not documented, the preferred way to create shares is to use one of the many available NetDDE share managers. These 16-bit applications will run under Windows 95 and can manage the NetDDE shares. These programs can also be used with Windows for Workgroups (and you can, in fact, use NetDDE to allow for easy communication across the 16-bit/32-bit barrier).

NetDDE shares under Windows NT are set up by a completely different method in order to fit into the NT security model, and you will have to use the 32-bit Windows NT share manager to create these shares and then "trust" them on Windows NT.

Included with the companion CD-ROM is a freeware share manager called DDESHR. This 16-bit Visual Basic application can help you create and manage Net-DDE shares. Other share managers are available, including some you can download from online services and one that is included in the Windows for Workgroups Resource Kit (which is also on the Microsoft Developer's Network CD-ROM). The interface of DDESHR is shown in Figure 20.3 and Figure 20.4.

TIP Under Windows 95, using the Registry functions in Chapter 18, you can add these shares directly to the Registry. (This is, in fact, the only way to manage shares directly from Access 95.) In addition, since the shares are located under the HKEY_LOCAL_MACHINE subkey of the Registry, you can use the RegConnectRegistry API call to create and delete shares on other people's machines, as well. This topic is a little beyond the scope of this chapter, but you may want to look into this idea further for network and application administration.

FIGURE 20.3:

The DDESHR program's main dialog

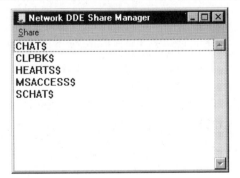

FIGURE 20.4:

The DDESHR program's new share dialog

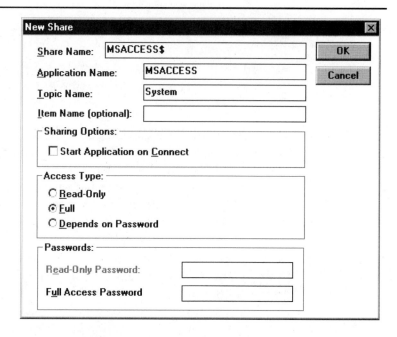

You use DDESHR to establish a special DDE share that is used in place of the Server-Name parameter in the DDEInitiate() function. In the most commonly documented syntax, the share, by convention, is a word followed by a dollar sign ($). The New Share dialog, shown in Figure 20.4, establishes a new DDE share. The following example uses Access as the DDE server and DDETest as the DDE client. In this example, the name of the machine on the network is Darkstar. The New Share dialog is filled in as shown in Table 20.6.

To connect to a DDE share, in DDEInitate() you replace the server name with the machine name, followed by the special share NDDE$. For example, to connect to the MSACCESS$ share on a PC named Darkstar, you would use

```
lngChannelNumber = DDEInitiate("\\Darkstar\NDDE$", _
  "MSACCESS$")
```

For the topic name, you specify the DDE share name you created—for example, MSACCESS$. The share you created specifies the topic to which this connection attaches. After you do this, all other DDE operations are the same.

This syntax can be awkward, and it does not mix well with existing DDE code that uses applications and topics rather than computer names and share names. A better

TABLE 20.6: The New Share Dialog's Fields

Field	Entry	Meaning
Share Name	MSACCESS$	The name of the DDE share. It is used in the DDEInitiate from the client
Application Name	MSACCESS	The application's valid DDE server name
Topic Name	System	The name of the DDE topic you want to access when this DDE share is used
Item Name	(blank)	Optional and not usually used. It allows you to hard-code the DDE item
Request (level 1 and 2)	(checked)	Decides whether or not DDERequest messages will be accepted by the server
Advise (level 1 and 2)	(checked)	Decides whether or not DDEAdvise messages will be accepted by the server
Poke (level 1 and 2)	(checked)	Decides whether or not DDEPoke messages will be accepted by the server
Execute (level 1 and 2)	(checked)	Decides whether or not DDEExecute messages will be accepted by the server
Start Application on Connect (level 1 and 2)	(checked)	Decides whether or not the NetDDE agent can start the application on the remote machine if it is not already running
Password (level 1 and 2)	PASSWORD	Sets the password that must be given to connect to the NetDDE share. (This password *must* be in all caps, or you will not be able to use the NetDDE share.)

method is to create a share with the following characteristics:

Field	Entry	Syntax
Share Name	MSACCESS | *	The application's valid DDE name, a vertical separator (|), and an asterisk (*)
Application Name	MSACCESS	The application's valid DDE server name
Topic Name	*	An asterisk or wildcard, to allow connection to all topics

The rest of the parameters can be set however you wish. When the NetDDE share uses this syntax, rather than using

$\backslash\backslash$ *ServerPC*$\backslash$NDDE\$ ➤ *ShareName*

for your Application | Topic pair, you can use

$\backslash\backslash$ *ServerPC*$\backslash$*ApplicationName* | *Topic*

By simply prepending $\backslash\backslash$ *ServerPC*$\backslash$ to the server name in your existing DDE code, you can now call any machine on the network.

> **NOTE**　Under Windows for Workgroups, you could not use your own PC name as a server name. However, both Windows 95 and Windows NT allow you to do so. You can therefore test NetDDE on your own machine and use it to take advantage of the "Start application on connect" abilities of NetDDE and avoid using the Shell() function entirely. The NetDDE agent actually uses the same Registry values to determine which program to run as we used with the Shell() function.

When using NetDDE with Access as the server in a secure Access application, you will want to keep some additional things in mind. The DDE/NetDDE security model does not really integrate with the Access 95 security model. This is because, when Access 95 is the DDE/NetDDE server, any instructions sent to it are done with the permissions of the currently logged-in user. (This is also true of OLE automation.) When you are communicating with Access on your own machine, this is trivial, but it may not be so when you are adding network awareness to your application with NetDDE. In addition, if you want to depend on the "start application on connect" abilities of NetDDE, you cannot directly do so with a secured application because you have no way to log on with a specific user and password and there is no way to use SendKeys to send keystrokes to another computer.

The most important uses for NetDDE are the same ones for which you may be using DDE in the first place, with one special advantage: because the server can be on another PC, you do not have to worry about the resources needed to load two applications on one server (which can be critical on low-memory machines).

However, there are many other uses for NetDDE that involve network and application administration. Most of them are beyond the scope of this chapter, but if you want to add this type of functionality to your application, you may want to think about some of the following uses of NetDDE:

- Creating Windows 95 shortcuts or Windows NT ProgMan items on other machines by connecting to the Windows shell
- Checking to see whether another user is using your application by using the *PCName*\MSAccess ➤ *DatabaseName* Application ➤ Topic pair for a NetDDE channel
- Using the [Quit] or [CloseDatabases] action to force the user to exit from the application
- Making use of a program without running it on your own PC. This is useful if you have a limited number of licenses for an application
- Emulating the functionality of RPCs (remote procedure calls) by instructing other computers to perform tasks rather than tying up your own PC

At present, NetDDE is the one extension to DDE that can provide functionality that OLE automation cannot. However, the next version of Windows NT is expected to have NetOLE automation functionality, so you may want to make all your NetDDE code modular. If you do this, in future versions it will be easier for you to substitute NetOLE automation code for your NetDDE code.

Summary

This chapter has covered the following topics:

- Clients and servers
- Dynamics of a DDE conversation
- Servers, topics, and items
- The DDE channel
- DDE functions and statements
- Starting a DDE server

- Creating robust DDE code
- Closing a shelled program
- Using Access as a DDE server
- The DDETest application
- The NextRow Trap
- Network DDE

This chapter has discussed the details of using Dynamic Data Exchange (DDE) from the standpoint of Access as a DDE client and as a server. DDE is one of the three ways of manipulating other Windows programs from Access. The other two are DLLs (see Chapter 18) and OLE (see Chapters 21 and 22).

By using DDE, you can combine Access with other applications. For example, you might have an application that constructs a Word for Windows document based on boilerplate text in a database and customer information. As another example, you might retrieve information from a spreadsheet that is created every month in an accounting department to be included in a sales database.

Anytime you use DDE, you should ask yourself, "Can I do this with OLE automation?" If the application supports OLE automation and you don't need the "network-aware" functionality of NetDDE, you should probably use OLE automation instead.

CHAPTER

TWENTY-ONE

Using Access
as an OLE Client

- Understanding how OLE automation works

- Writing simple OLE automation code

- Creating integrated solutions using Microsoft Office 95

- Using OLE automation to manipulate custom controls

OLE, a suite of Microsoft technologies that grew out of the original Object Linking and Embedding specification, has been maturing for several years. It comprises a number of documented interfaces application developers can use to share data and program components. One small part of the overall OLE specification (now in its second major version) is a process called *OLE automation.* OLE automation is a standard set of protocols for communicating with other applications and controlling them. You can use OLE automation to take advantage of existing software components as an alternative to creating your own from scratch. In this chapter we'll examine the basics of using OLE automation's power from Access 95 and show you how to create integrated solutions using programs such as those found in Microsoft Office 95. We'll also show you how you can use OLE automation to manipulate OLE custom controls, the new breed of software components that is quickly gaining popularity among developers. After reading this chapter, you should have an understanding of how the pieces of the OLE automation puzzle fit together and how you can use them to your advantage.

OLE Automation Basics

OLE automation is a complex technology that is relatively simple to implement. Its greatest strength is that it lets you work with objects from other applications using the same techniques you use now with Access objects. Before beginning to write integrated solutions using OLE automation, you should be familiar with the basics. In this section we'll explain the terminology we'll be using, where OLE information is stored, and how to examine an application's objects, properties, and methods.

What's Its Value?

If you've been working with Microsoft technology for any length of time, you must have heard the message "OLE is good." Ever since Excel 3.0 added the ability to embed documents, Microsoft has promoted OLE as a near-revolutionary technology. But what does it do for you? Specifically, what value is there in using OLE automation to control other applications?

OLE automation's biggest benefit is its capacity to let you use prebuilt, robust, and debugged software components in your applications. Just think how your development project would be affected if you had to build your own spreadsheet module instead of using Microsoft Excel. Clearly, for simple tasks you may decide to "roll your own," but as the complexity of a component increases, the benefits of using off-the-shelf software increase, as well. OLE automation takes component reuse one step further by allowing you to control objects using your own code, extending whatever built-in intelligence the objects may have. Finally, the architecture of OLE automation lets you do this unobtrusively. That is, you control objects using OLE automation the same way you control them in Access, using sets of properties, methods, and events. With a few extensions to your current understanding of Access and its objects, you can start controlling other applications' objects, such as those found in Microsoft Office (Excel, Word, PowerPoint, and Schedule Plus) and OLE custom controls.

Terminology

Before explaining how to use Access as an OLE automation client, we'll clarify some common terms we use in this chapter. Some of them have meanings that differ when taken outside the context of OLE automation.

OLE automation requires a client and a server. The *server* is the application or component that provides services to the client. It may have behaviors that it exhibits independently of the client, but for the most part it depends on the client's giving it commands to do things. The *client,* on the other hand, is the application that uses the services of an automation server. In a narrow context, a client application is one that implements a development language allowing you to write code that controls a server. Access is an obvious example of an OLE automation client. Other OLE automation clients include Excel, Microsoft Project, and Visual Basic. An OLE automation client need not be a development tool, but development tools such as Access are the ones of most interest to us.

In addition to clients and servers, you should be familiar with the difference between object types and objects. *Object types* are the classes of objects that an OLE automation server makes available for you to control. Object types have a defined set of properties, methods, and in some cases, events that dictate how instances of that object type look and act. When you write OLE automation code, you manipulate *objects*—particular instances of object types. You can think of objects and object types as being similar to variables and datatypes. VBA supports a fixed set of datatypes, but you can declare and use as many variables of a single type as you wish. In this chapter, when we discuss a server application's *object model*, we are talking about its set of object types. When we write VBA code, we're using instances of those types, which we call objects.

Object Classes

Before you can start controlling objects, you need to understand which objects are available to you. As you install applications and OLE custom controls, these components will make entries in the Registry that mark them to Windows as controllable. (Technically speaking, OLE automation servers are those applications that support the IDispatch interface of the OLE 2.0 specification.) Because each application may make more than one object available to OLE automation clients, you need to know not only the application name, but the object type, as well. This information is encapsulated in the class identifier, or class ID, for the particular object. Class IDs are expressed as follows:

ApplicationName.ObjectType

For example, Microsoft Excel exports a controllable Chart object that has an associated class ID of Excel.Chart. Furthermore, this convention lets you append a version number to the class ID to restrict manipulation of the object to a particular version of the software. Excel.Chart.5 refers to a Chart object that is manipulated by Excel version 5. Most applications register a pointer to the latest version installed on your computer, so leaving off the version number will force that version to be used.

While it is not always the case, most applications that feature a user interface (as opposed to "service only" servers, which operate transparently behind the scenes) register an Application object. Normally, this object represents the highest-level object in the application's object model, and from it you can derive most other object types. As we discuss the examples in this chapter, the use of class IDs should become clear.

Registry Entries

Applications use the Windows Registry to store their OLE automation settings. This allows Windows and other applications to determine easily which applications offer controllable objects. All OLE information is stored in the HKEY_CLASSES_ROOT hive (the Microsoft term for a branch of the Registry tree) of the

Registry. This branch is the replacement for the single Registry in Windows 3.1. If you installed Windows 95 or Windows NT over a Windows 3.1 version, the setup program will insert all existing settings into the HKEY_CLASSES_ROOT hive.

HKEY_CLASSES_ROOT stores information on file associations and OLE components. Figure 21.1 shows the Windows 95 Registry open to a set of entries within this hive. You can open the Registry by running REGEDIT.EXE from the Start menu.

You can see from Figure 21.1 that the Registry appears to list a number of entries that match the ApplicationName.ObjectType description we explained earlier in this chapter. For example, the figure shows one entry called Excel.Application. This is the entry for Microsoft Excel's Application object. However, you cannot directly control all objects using OLE automation. In fact, many of the ones listed are there to supply descriptive information for file types. To obtain a complete listing of the objects you can control, you'll need to examine the application's type library.

FIGURE 21.1:

Windows 95 Registry showing OLE
server entries

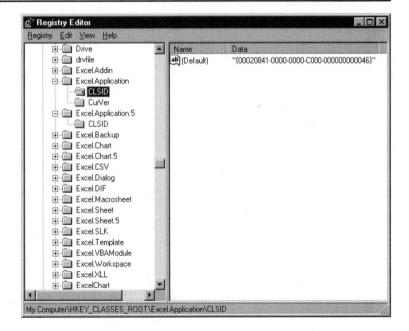

Type Libraries: The Key to Objects

Most large OLE server applications ship with a supplemental file called a type library. *Type libraries* are databases that list the objects, methods, properties, and events offered by a server application. OLE clients such as Access can use the information stored in a library to "learn" about another application. Type libraries offer a number of benefits:

- Access does not actually have to run the server application to interrogate its object model.

- The VBA editor and interpreter can use type libraries to perform syntax checking on your OLE automation code.

- You can obtain context-sensitive help for another application's keywords.

Most applications' type libraries have a .TLB or .OLB (for object library) file extension, and you use them in your project by adding them to the list of references in the References dialog. To do so, follow these steps:

1. Open a module.

2. Select Tools ➤ References. You should see a list of references similar to the ones shown in Figure 21.2.

FIGURE 21.2:

References dialog showing loaded and available references

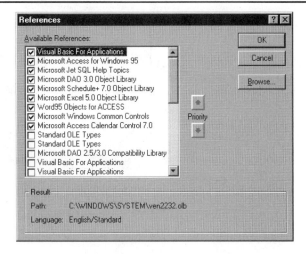

---

3. Check the box next to the reference you want to add.

4. If the reference is not listed, click the Browse button and locate the type library or executable file of the server you want to use.

Once you've loaded a type library, you can use the objects, properties, and methods in your VBA code. VBA will be able to correctly verify syntax, as well as provide context-sensitive help for the server application's keywords. One important issue is that the complete path to the type library is stored with your VBA project. If you move the type library or install your application on another computer, you will need to reestablish the link to the type library. (See the section "Custom Control References" later in this chapter for more information on resolving missing references.)

Browsing Objects with the Object Browser

Once you've added references to an OLE server's type library, you can use the VBA Object Browser to view a list of the application's objects, properties, and methods. To make the Object Browser available, press the F2 key in Module view, click the Object Browser toolbar button, or select the View ➤ Object Browser menu command. The Object Browser replaces the Procedures dialog in prior versions of Access. Figure 21.3 shows the Object Browser open to the Application object of Microsoft Excel's type library.

FIGURE 21.3:

Object Browser showing details on Excel's Application object

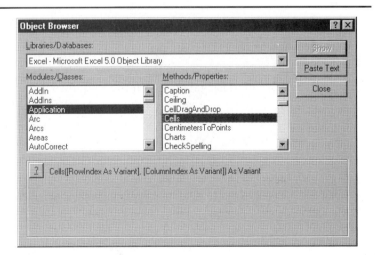

You can use the Libraries/Databases drop-down list to select another Access database or OLE type library. The Object Browser changes the contents of the Modules/Classes and Methods/Properties lists to reflect the change. The Modules/Classes list shows all the object types available from the server application. Selecting any one of them causes the Object Browser to display the methods and properties for that object in the right-hand list. Note that collections are also shown in the left-hand (object) list. When you select a collection, usually denoted by the plural form of the object type, the Object Browser displays the methods and properties for the collection, not the object.

Figure 21.3 also shows the Application object's Cells method highlighted in the right-hand list. Note the syntax example at the bottom of the dialog. The Object Browser shows you the calling syntax of the property or method, including any arguments. You can use the Paste Text button to paste this syntax into your modules at the current insertion point. Finally, if the type library being viewed supports a Windows Help file, pressing the Help button (the one with a question mark) will open that file to the proper page for the displayed property or method.

The Object Browser can be helpful, especially when you're using an OLE server for the first time. It gives you a "big picture" overview of the object model, allowing you to browse the individual objects and their properties and methods. As you become more familiar with a server application, you'll be able to write OLE automation code from memory, but until then, the Object Browser is a good place to start learning about what's available and how to use it.

Interrogating Your Objects: OLE2 Viewer

Although the Object Browser is a useful tool while you're editing code, another application is available with the Windows 95 Software Development Kit (SDK) that you can use independently of Access VBA and that can often reveal more in-depth information about an OLE server. The application is called OLE2 Viewer, and although it was designed to provide detailed information to programmers writing OLE client applications in C++, VBA developers can benefit from using it, as well.

Figure 21.4 shows OLE2 Viewer's main window. The left-hand pane shows the OLE-based applications installed on your computer. OLE2 Viewer gets this information from the Windows Registry. The right-hand panes show detailed information for the application selected in the left pane. You can see in Figure 21.4 that this

FIGURE 21.4:

OLE2 Viewer showing details on Microsoft Excel's type library

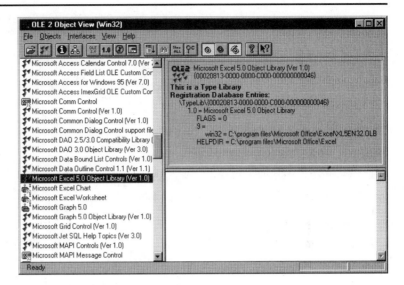

information includes the application name and object type, the unique class ID, and any Registry entries associated with the server.

You can get more information on OLE servers by double-clicking them in the left pane, although most of the additional information displayed is not directly related to the application's OLE server capabilities. If you wish to see a list of controllable objects, look for a type library listing. (They are denoted by icons that look like three red arrows.) Double-clicking a type library icon opens a secondary dialog, like the one shown in Figure 21.5, listing details on the objects available to OLE clients.

The drop-down list in the upper-left region of the dialog lists the distinct OLE Type-Info structures that define the objects exported by the application. These map to object types used in your OLE client code. Selecting an item from this list provides more information by filling the other controls on the dialog, as described here:

List Box	Description
Functions	Shows the functions that are implemented by the selected object. You know these as methods, in VBA's object-oriented nomenclature

FIGURE 21.5:

Detailed information contained in the Excel type library

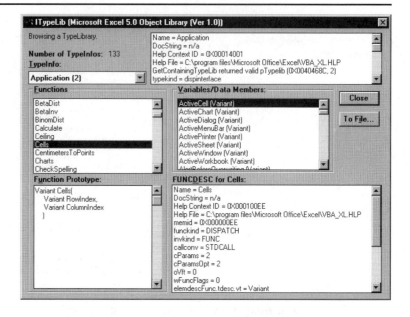

List Box	Description
Function Prototype	Shows the calling syntax for the selected function. Don't be confused by the syntax displayed. It's written in C++, which places the datatype *before* the variable name
Variables/Data Members	Shows the data members of the selected object. You know these better as properties
FUNCDESC for *method*	Shows additional OLE-related information on the selected method

Figure 21.5 shows detailed information on the Cells method of Excel's Application object. Compare the methods and calling syntax displayed with that shown by the Object Browser in Figure 21.4. You'll see they are almost identical, the only differences being that OLE2 Viewer displays C++ syntax and the Object Browser uses VBA syntax.

Creating Objects

All OLE automation sessions begin with the client application creating an object. By *creating* an object, we mean establishing a conversation with the server application and telling it which of its objects you wish to control. The result of this creation process is a pointer to an instance of the server's object stored in an object variable. Using this object variable, you can control the server application's object using the same techniques you use to control Access objects—by manipulating their methods and properties.

There are several ways to create an object in VBA. You can use the CreateObject() or GetObject() function, each of which returns an object pointer as a result. Alternatively, you can declare application-specific object types inside your code. The first time you use the object, VBA automatically creates an instance of it for you. Let's look at CreateObject() and GetObject() first, since they are the easiest to understand.

Using CreateObject

CreateObject() and GetObject() are VBA functions, and you can call them from your code just as you would any other function. Because they do nothing more than create an OLE automation object, you need to store the object pointer they return in an object variable. You can declare a variable using the generic Object datatype, or you can use a server-specific datatype if you have added a reference to the server's type library to your VBA project. While it is better to use specific types provided by the application's type library, you may encounter errors while compiling if you install your application on a computer that does not have a copy of the type library. Using generic Object variables eliminates this problem, but you lose the advantages of type libraries mentioned earlier.

CreateObject() accepts a single argument, a string containing the application name and object class, as described in the section "Object Classes" earlier in this chapter. When you call CreateObject(), VBA attempts to create an object of the type specified using the application specified. If it cannot create the object, perhaps because the application is not installed or does not support the object type, it fails with a run-time error.

If you have not written OLE automation code before, you might want to try a simple test that demonstrates the basics of OLE automation using CreateObject(). If you've used CreateObject() before, you may want to skip ahead. To try this test you'll need to have Microsoft Excel loaded on your computer. Then, follow these steps:

1. Enter the VBA code shown in Listing 21.1 into a new or existing module.

2. Set a breakpoint on the CreateObject statement.

3. Open the Debug window and execute Sub glrTestOLE. Access should halt execution at the breakpoint.

4. Step through the CreateObject statement. You should notice some disk activity before control returns to VBA. This disk activity is Excel being launched in the background. The object variable, objXL, now contains a pointer to an instance of Excel's Application object.

5. You'll notice that although Excel has started, it does not appear in the task list. Step through the next statement. At this point the Excel main window becomes visible and Excel appears in the task list. This behavior is representative of how Excel behaves as an OLE server. (See the section "Differences in Application Behavior" later in this chapter for more information.)

6. Execute the objXL.Quit statement. The Excel main window should disappear. At this point the object pointer stored in objXL is invalid because the object it pointed to no longer exists.

7. Execute the rest of the procedure. The final statement uses the Nothing constant to free up any memory the OLE automation session used.

Listing 21.1

```
Sub glrTestOLE()
    Dim objXL As Object

    Set objXL = CreateObject("Excel.Application")
    objXL.Visible = True
    objXL.Quit
    Set objXL = Nothing
End Sub
```

Using GetObject()

You can see from the previous example how you can call properties and methods of the OLE automation server object using the object pointer returned by Create-Object(). The GetObject() function is similar to CreateObject(), but instead of accepting a single argument, it allows for two optional arguments, a document name and an object class. The general form of a GetObject() statement is

Set *objectvariable* = GetObject([*docname*], [*objectclass*])

Note that both arguments are optional, but you must supply *at least* one of them. GetObject() is a more flexible function that you can use to create an object from an application's document (an Excel workbook file, for example) or from an existing instance of an application. The flexibility of GetObject() is revealed by the combination of arguments used. Table 21.1 explains the results of these combinations.

TABLE 21.1: Various Uses of the GetObject() Function

Combination	Example	Results
Document name only	Set objAny = GetObject ("C:\DATA\BOOK1.XLS")	The application associated with the document type is launched and used to open the specified document. If the application supports it, an existing instance will be used, and if the document is already open, the object pointer will refer to that instance
Object class only	Set objAny = GetObject (, "Excel.Application")	If the server application is running, an object pointer is created for the running instance; otherwise GetObject() returns a run-time error
Object class and empty document name	Set objAny = GetObject ("", "Excel.Application")	Same behavior as CreateObject(). Opens a new instance of the application
Both document name and object class	Set objAny = GetObject ("C:\DATA\BOOK1.XLS", "Excel.Application")	Redundant. Same behavior as passing only the document name, except that if the server does not support the document type, a run-time error occurs

As you can see, GetObject() is more complex than CreateObject(), although it does offer the benefit of using running instances of applications rather than launching new copies each time your OLE automation code runs. This is especially critical on low-memory computers.

Using Type Library References

In addition to using GetObject() and CreateObject() to create OLE automation objects, you can use type library references to integrate objects seamlessly into your VBA code. After adding a reference to an OLE automation server's type library (see the section "Type Libraries: The Key to Objects" earlier in this chapter), you can refer to OLE automation server objects directly in your code. The sample code shown here creates an instance of Microsoft Excel, displays the main window, and then terminates the application:

```
Sub glrTestOLE2()
    ' Use object without using a variable
    Excel.Application.Visible = True
    Excel.Application.Quit
End Sub
```

Using the New Keyword with OLE Automation

One feature of VBA that was not working correctly when this book was written is the ability to declare object variables using the New keyword. When you execute code using the object variable for the first time, VBA automatically creates a reference to the server application, launching an instance of it if necessary. You can use the New keyword either in the declaration or in a Set statement. For example, the two procedures shown here should both create new instances of Microsoft Excel, display the main window, and then terminate the application:

```
Sub glrTestOLE3()
    ' Use New in declaration
    Dim objXL As New Excel.Application

    objXL.Visible = True
    objXL.Quit
```

```
End Sub

Sub glrTestOLE4()
    Dim objXL As Excel.Application

    ' Use New in Set statement
    Set objXL = New Excel.Application
    objXL.Visible = True
    objXL.Quit
End Sub
```

Currently, trying to compile this code results in an "Invalid use of New keyword" error. What's even more curious is that the code shown below works once, correctly creating a reference to Excel's application object, but not twice. Running it again results in an OLE automation error. Resetting your code seems to correct the problem, but only for one time through.

```
Sub glrTestOLE5()
    ' Use object with a variable
    ' This works once but not twice
    Dim objXL As Object

    Set objXL = Excel.Application
    objXL.Visible = True
    objXL.Quit
End Sub
```

Because these features were not working correctly when we wrote this book, we have chosen to include this information in a sidebar rather than in the main text. Until such time as Microsoft can work out all the bugs, keep using GetObject() and CreateObject(). They seem to work all the time.

A Function for Creating Objects

Now that you've seen the theory behind the creation of OLE objects, we will describe a function you can use in your application that performs this task for you. The sample database for this chapter includes a function in basOLE called glrCreateOLEObject(), shown in Listing 21.2, that accepts three arguments, two of which are optional. The first argument is an Object variable that will store a pointer to the OLE object once it has been created. You can use the second and third arguments, varClass and varDoc, to pass either the class ID of an OLE automation server object, a registered document name, or both. GlrCreateOLEObject() uses a three-step process to create OLE automation objects:

1. It attempts to create an object using GetObject() and a document name, if one was supplied.

2. If this fails, it uses GetObject() with the class ID to create an object from a running instance of the server application.

3. If this fails, glrCreateOLEObject() tries again, using CreateObject().

We designed this three-step approach to minimize system resource requirements by using running instances of applications whenever possible. Although you may wish to have multiple copies of a particular program running simultaneously, you will need some hefty hardware to do so.

Listing 21.2

```
Public Const glrcOLECreateFailure = 0
Public Const glrcOLECreateRunning = 1
Public Const glrcOLECreateStarted = 2

Function glrCreateOLEObject(objAny As Object, _
 Optional ByVal varClass As Variant, _
 Optional ByVal varDoc As Variant) _
 As Integer

    On Error GoTo glrCreateOLEObject_Error

    ' Code for error creating object
    Const glrcErrNoObject = 429

    ' If a document name was passed try to
    ' create the object using GetObject...
    If Not IsMissing(varDoc) Then
        Set objAny = GetObject(varDoc)
        glrCreateOLEObject = glrcOLECreateRunning

    ' ...otherwise look for a Class ID
    ElseIf Not IsMissing(varClass) Then

        ' Temporarily disable error trapping
```

```
        On Error Resume Next
        Set objAny = GetObject(, varClass)

        ' If GetObject worked then return glrcOLECreateRunning
        If Err.Number = 0 Then
            glrCreateOLEObject = glrcOLECreateRunning
        ElseIf Err.Number = glrcErrNoObject Then
            ' If we got to here then GetObject
            ' must have failed, maybe because
            ' an instance of the server wasn't
            ' running--in that case try using
            ' CreateObject instead. If that fails
            ' then we're really out of luck
            Err.Number = 0
            On Error GoTo glrCreateOLEObject_Error
            Set objAny = CreateObject(varClass)
            glrCreateOLEObject = glrcOLECreateStarted
        Else
            GoTo glrCreateOLEObject_Error
        End If
    End If
glrCreateOLEObject_Exit:
    Exit Function
glrCreateOLEObject_Error:
    Select Case Err.Number
        Case glrcErrNoObject
            MsgBox "Unable to create OLE automation " & _
                "server object, perhaps because the Class " & _
                "ID is invalid or the server is incorrectly " & _
                "registered. Check the Class ID and try again.", _
                vbExclamation
        Case Else
            MsgBox Err.Description, vbExclamation, _
                "Error " & Err.Number
    End Select
    glrCreateOLEObject = glrcOLECreateFailure
    Resume glrCreateOLEObject_Exit
End Function
```

If glrCreateOLEObject() could not create the requested object, it returns 0, represented by the constant glrcOLECreateFailed. Otherwise it returns a value indicating how it created the object: 1 (glrcOLECreateRunning) if it used GetObject(), or 2 (glrcOLECreateStarted) if it used CreateObject(). You can use this information to decide how to treat the object after using it. For example, if you used glrCreate-OLEObject() to create a reference to Excel's Application object and the function returned 1 (indicating that the call to GetObject() succeeded), you would know that a copy of Excel was already running. A return value of 2, on the other hand, indicates that a new instance was started. You may then decide to terminate the application using its Quit method after you have finished using it. The examples in this chapter use glrCreateOLEObject() to instantiate OLE automation variables.

Controlling Other Applications

There are two primary uses for OLE automation: controlling other applications and controlling components such as OLE custom controls. Since controlling custom controls is so much like working with built-in Access controls, we will devote the bulk of this chapter to discussing how you can use OLE automation to control other applications.

Learning an Application's Object Model

The techniques involved in using another application's objects through OLE automation are the same as those for manipulating Access objects; the only difference is the set of objects themselves. Before beginning to write OLE automation client code, familiarize yourself with the server application's object model. Unfortunately, the availability and quality of documentation vary enormously, even among Microsoft products. As a general rule, those applications that have their own development language (such as VBA in Microsoft Excel and Project or WordBasic in Word) have better documentation than those that don't (for example, PowerPoint and Schedule Plus). Resources are available that you can use to learn another application's object model. Some of them are listed here:

- The *Microsoft Office 95 Developer's Kit* (ODK) contains information on creating integrated solutions with Microsoft Office, including object model descriptions.

- The *Microsoft Excel SDK* contains information for developers who wish to write Excel Add-ins.

- The *Microsoft Solutions Development Kit* is a resource for those developing integrated solutions using Microsoft Office and BackOffice products.

You can purchase all these kits from Microsoft.

Differences in Application Behavior

When creating OLE automation objects, be aware that server applications exhibit unique behavior when used as OLE automation servers, specifically when the application firsts start up and when you destroy the Object variable that references server objects. Differences in an application's behavior will dictate how you use it in your OLE client code. Table 21.2 lists differences in behavior of the Application object among the programs that make up Microsoft Office 95. As you use other OLE automation servers, you may want to note how they behave in respect to the list provided.

TABLE 21.2: Differences in Behavior among Microsoft Office 95 Applications

Application	Differences in Behavior
Microsoft Access	Launches as an icon with a Visible property of False. Changing the Visible property to True restores the main window; changing it to False minimizes the window. Additionally, destroying the object variable causes Access to terminate if it was launched via OLE automation
Microsoft Excel	Launches as a hidden window with a Visible property of False. Changing the Visible property to True "un-hides" the window. Destroying the object variable does not cause Excel to terminate
Microsoft PowerPoint	Launches as a hidden window. The application object does not have a Visible property. To make the application visible, you must set the Visible property of the AppWindow object to True. Destroying the object variable does not cause PowerPoint to terminate
Microsoft Schedule+	Launches as a hidden window. The Application object does not have a Visible property. To make the application visible, you must set the Visible property of a Schedule object to True. Destroying the object variable does not cause Schedule Plus to terminate
Microsoft Word	Launches as a hidden window. The application does not have a Visible property. To make the application visible, you must call the Application object's AppShow method. Calling the AppHide method hides the window. Destroying the object variable causes Word to terminate if it was launched via OLE automation

Multiple-Use versus Single-Use Servers

OLE automation servers fall into two broad categories: multiple-use servers and single-use servers. Multiple-use servers are those that require all OLE automation client processes to create objects from the *same instance* of the server. An example of a multiple-use server is Microsoft Schedule Plus. Only one instance of the Schedule Plus Application object can exist at any one time. Although you can view multiple schedules and, in fact, Schedule Plus opens each as if it were a separate instance of the application, only one instance of the executable file is actually running. Applications that are multiple-use servers are typically those that allow you to launch only one instance from the Windows 95 shell.

Single-use servers, on the other hand, are those that allow multiple *instances* of the application to exist simultaneously. Microsoft Excel is an example of a single-use server because you can have more than one copy of Excel running at the same time. This becomes important when choosing a VBA function for creating an instance of an Application object. Using multiple CreateObject statements with Schedule Plus always creates references to the same running instance of the program. Using multiple CreateObject statements with Excel, on the other hand, launches multiple copies of the program. On low-memory computers, you should use GetObject() with single-use servers to reuse an existing instance. This is why our glrCreateOLE-Object() function first tries GetObject() and then falls back to CreateObject() if GetObject() fails.

Memory and Resource Issues

One very important piece of information to keep in mind when creating integrated solutions using OLE automation is how controlling multiple applications at the same time will affect the overall performance of a user's system. Large server applications such as Excel and Word consume a lot of memory. While it is now more difficult to produce the dreaded "Out of System Resources" error, RAM is still an issue. Computers with fewer than 16 megabytes of RAM may perform poorly when many large applications are running, due to disk swapping. If low memory is a problem, you may want to consider closing each server after using it.

The other side of the coin is the time it takes to start and stop large applications. If you frequently use large applications as OLE automation servers, you may want to

Converting Access 2.0 OLE Automation Code

If you wrote OLE automation code that used Access reserved words in Access 2.0, you may experience problems when converting your applications to Access 95. In Access 2.0 you could not use methods or properties of other applications that conflicted with Access reserved words. To get around this, Access Basic let you use brackets to indicate that the method or property belonged to an OLE automation object. Unfortunately, the work-around for Access 2.0 causes problems when used in Access 95. A particularly insidious problem exists in code that calls Microsoft Excel's Quit method. In Access 2.0 you had to write code that looked like this:

```
objExcelApp.[Quit]
```

This forced the Access Basic compiler to ignore whatever was between the brackets. In Access 95 you can use any method or property without brackets. The problem is that when you convert code like that shown above, it compiles and executes but does not actually do anything. Excel appears to ignore the Quit statement until the brackets are removed. If you notice that some of your legacy OLE automation code isn't working correctly, check for brackets around method and property names and remove any you find.

leave them open despite the effect this will have on memory consumption. In other words, you will likely have to experiment to get the right mix of performance and memory utilization.

Creating OLE Automation Solutions with Microsoft Office 95

Statistically speaking, if you are reading this book you already own a copy of Microsoft Office 95. Since most copies of Access are sold as part of Office, if you're developing Access applications chances are your users own a copy of Office, as well. This gives you an opportunity to leverage the vast functionality in those applications by creating integrated solutions based on OLE automation. To get you started, we'll spend a large portion of this chapter demonstrating several sample applications that use Office components. You'll be able to see examples of how each can be controlled from Access. We'll also point out some of the minor differences and idiosyncrasies that still exist in this supposedly integrated suite of products.

Specifically, we'll show you three applications:

- A time-reporting system that pulls schedule information from Schedule Plus
- A mail-merge tool that inserts data from any form into a new Word document
- A data-analysis system that uses Excel to summarize data from Access tables

Each of these examples will highlight a slightly different aspect of using OLE automation. The Schedule Plus application demonstrates the basics of controlling a server application and shows how to work with Schedule Plus' odd collection scheme. The Word example focuses on translating WordBasic syntax into equivalent VBA code. Finally, the Excel example shows how to use existing documents as the target of OLE automation commands. As you read through the examples and test the sample code, keep in mind that the real message here is that OLE automation code is more *similar* to the code you're writing already than it is different.

Correcting OLE Automation Typelib References

Before delving into the sample applications we've created for this chapter, we need to say a few words regarding references to OLE server type libraries that are part of the sample database. These references allow VBA to examine the properties and methods of a given server and are explained in detail in the section titled, "Type Libraries: The Key to Objects" earlier in this chapter.

Type library references are hard coded. That is, the complete path to a type library is stored as part of a VBA project. Thus, moving or deleting a type library prevents VBA code that references it from compiling. Because the type libraries used in the samples are almost certainly stored in different locations on your computer than they are on ours, you will need to update the references before testing the samples. To do this, open any module in CH21.MDB and display the References dialog. For each reference marked as MISSING, click the Browse button and find the type library file on your computer.

If you cannot find the type library, perhaps because you don't have the particular product installed, uncheck its reference in the dialog and compile the VBA code. You will find several compile errors. To correct these errors, comment out the offending statements.

Example: Schedule Plus Time Reporting

To demonstrate the basics of OLE automation, we've created a sample application that uses Access to control Microsoft Schedule Plus and load schedule information into an Access database. The application is a simple time-reporting system that tracks the length of time spent on appointments and summarizes it by task and project. What makes this useful application possible is the relationship between Schedule Plus projects, tasks, and appointments. Tasks can be associated with a project, and appointments can be created that refer to tasks. In a sense, this application mimics the one-to-many relationships in a relational database.

To test this application, you'll need a copy of Schedule Plus 7.0 installed on your computer. To get the maximum benefit, you'll also need to create some related objects. You can associate a project with a task simply by selecting one from the drop-down list of projects on the Task form. To associate a task with an appointment, either drag a task from the task list to the appointment grid or right-click a task and select Appt. from Task from the shortcut menu.

CH21.MDB contains the application, which consists of two forms, frmOLESPlus and frmLoad; a report, rptTime; and some VBA code. The frmOLESPlus form can be seen in Figure 21.6. It features lists of projects, tasks, and appointments. You can click any project and see the tasks associated with it and do the same for tasks and appointments.

The form has two buttons; one initiates the loading of Schedule Plus information by opening frmLoad, and the other opens the rptTime report. The report, shown in Figure 21.7, summarizes appointments by task and project so you can see how much time was spent on each. You can imagine this application as the foundation for a more sophisticated time-reporting system for use by salespeople, consultants, or anyone who requires precise time tracking.

FIGURE 21.6:

frmOLESPlus form showing lists of projects, tasks, and appointments

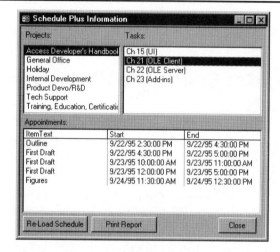

FIGURE 21.7:

rptTime report showing time summaries for appointments

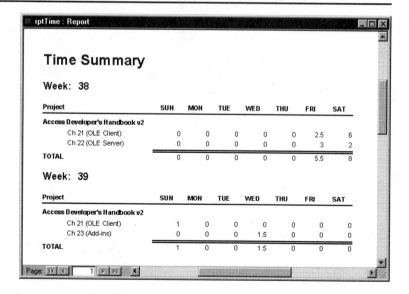

Schedule Plus Object Model

Figure 21.8 shows a hierarchical view of the Schedule Plus object model. Everything you can store in Schedule Plus using the user interface (and more) can be manipulated using OLE automation.

Note that the object model includes simple objects, such as the Application and Schedule objects, as well as collections of objects. The object model also includes metacollections. *Metacollections* are collections of objects of dissimilar types. Normally, collections are made-up objects of the same type, but the Appointments collection, for example, is made up of SimpleAppointment (nonrecurring) objects and RecurringAppointment objects. Although collections exist for each of these object types, you can create an object of either one using the Appointments collection. You cannot, however, refer to a SimpleAppointment using the RecurringAppointments collection, nor can you refer to a RecurringAppointment using SimpleAppointments.

FIGURE 21.8:

Schedule+ object model

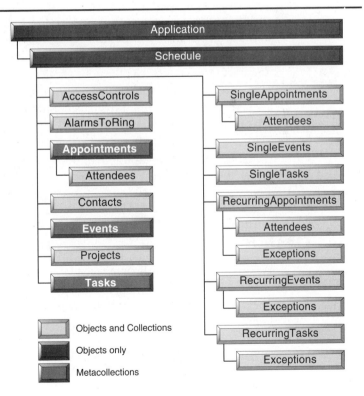

Schedule Plus Collections

As you can see in Figure 21.8, Schedule Plus implements, among other things, collections of Appointment, Task, and Project objects. The way in which Schedule Plus represents collections of objects, however, is a bit different from other applications and warrants a moment of examination. In other object-oriented applications, you can refer to individual items in a collection using either the object's name or its position in the collection. For example, the following two statements are theoretically valid ways of referring to a form in Access:

```
Set frm = Forms(0)
Set frm = Forms("frmAny")
```

Although you can refer to objects within a collection by name, the name Schedule Plus creates for objects is a unique, meaningless string of characters. It is unlikely you'll want to use these in your VBA code. This leaves the position of each object in the collection (also a semi-arbitrary value) as the only way to refer to an object. To remedy this situation, Schedule Plus provides a number of collection methods and properties (see Table 21.3) you can use to iterate through objects in the collection. If you examine the methods and properties closely, you should be reminded of DAO recordset manipulation methods and properties. In fact, the Schedule Plus documentation refers to collections as *tables*, and you can think of the contained objects as records in the table. Table 21.3 includes DAO methods and properties that act similarly to Schedule Plus collection methods and properties. Each Schedule Plus table has a "current record," accessed via the Item method, and you use the Skip and Reset methods to move the current record pointer to another object in the table. With this metaphor in mind, you should find manipulating Schedule Plus objects relatively easy.

Understanding the Database Design

We designed the sample database to model the relationships among Schedule Plus objects. Figure 21.9 shows the Relationships window from CH21.MDB. Foreign key fields in the tables correspond to properties of Schedule Plus objects that store the ItemID property of other objects.

TABLE 21.3: Methods and Properties of Schedule Plus Table Objects (Collections)

Schedule Plus Method/Property	Description	Similar DAO Method/Property
Item method	Returns a reference to the current object or a particular object (This is the default method for all collections.)	N/A
New method	Adds a new object to the collection	AddNew
DeleteItem method	Deletes an item from the collection	Delete
Skip method	Moves the current object pointer forward or backward a given number of rows	MoveNext, MovePrevious
Reset method	Moves the current object pointer to the beginning of the collection	MoveFirst
SetRange method	Restricts collection methods to a range of objects	N/A
IsEndOfTable property	Returns True when the last object in a collection is reached	EOF
Position property	Returns the current object's position in the collection	AbsolutePosition
Rows property	Returns the number of objects in a collection	RecordCount

FIGURE 21.9:

Relationships window from CH21.MDB showing fields and relations

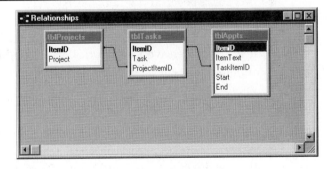

The code that actually populates the database uses OLE automation to examine each project, loading the information into the tblProjects table. It then does the same with Tasks and Appointments, loading data into the tblTasks and tblAppts tables, respectively. The order of events is important because of the foreign key relationships Access enforces.

Loading Appointment Information

One monolithic function, glrLoadSPlusObjects(), contained in basSPlus, manages loading appointment information from Schedule Plus into Access . It is called from the cmdLoad_Click procedure in frmOLESPlus. We could have just as easily put all the code in cmdLoad_Click, but storing it in a separate module makes it easier to import it into your applications. The module basSPlus, in CH21.MDB on the companion disk, shows the code that makes up glrLoadSPlusObjects(). We will explain key sections of it in the paragraphs that follow.

> **NOTE**
>
> basSPlus also contains a function called glrStripNull( ). GlrLoadSPlus-Objects( ) calls glrStripNull( ) to remove embedded null characters (ASCII code 0) in the Schedule Plus data.

Creating a Schedule Object

GlrLoadSPlusObjects() begins by creating a reference to the Schedule Plus Application object using our glrCreateOLEObject() function. We use the return value of glrCreateOLEObject() to determine whether Schedule Plus was running when the procedure began and set a Boolean variable, fNotRunning, to True if we forced VBA to launch Schedule Plus. We go to this much trouble because a user may already be running Schedule Plus, and we will later need to restore the application to the state it was in when we took control. Likewise, if the program was not running, we should be considerate computing citizens by shutting it down when we're done using it. Schedule Plus has a large resource footprint, and users would probably not like us leaving it hanging around.

Once we have a reference to the Application object (stored in objSPlusApp), we need to create a schedule object. If Schedule Plus was already running, we can use the schedule the user opened. If we are starting Schedule Plus for the first time, we must explicitly log on using the Application object's Logon method. Logon has a number of optional arguments, but calling it alone is usually sufficient to log on to Schedule Plus using the default user account. Table 21.4 shows the declarations of both the Logon and Logoff methods.

TABLE 21.4: Declarations for the Schedule Plus Application Object's Logon and Logoff Methods

Method	Arguments	Description
Logon	ProfileName (optional)	Name of the Microsoft Exchange profile to use when logging on
	ProfilePassword (optional)	Password used to log on to Exchange profile
	ShowDialog (optional)	True to display Exchange logon dialog
	ParentWindow (optional)	Window handle of owning process
Logoff	NotifyEveryone (optional)	True to log off Exchange completely and close all workgroup applications

We create a schedule object in the body of the procedure by setting an Object variable, objSched, to the result returned by the Application object's ScheduleLogged property. You need not use the currently loaded schedule if you don't want to. Table 21.5 lists several other methods and properties of the Application object used to create schedule objects.

TABLE 21.5: Schedule Plus Application Object Methods and Properties for Creating Schedule Objects

Method/Property	Arguments	Description
ScheduleLogged	None	Returns a pointer to the schedule for the logged-in user
ScheduleForFile	FileName	Name of a schedule file (.SCD) to open
ScheduleForUser	UserAddress	Mail system address of user account
ScheduleSelected	None	Returns a pointer to the active schedule when a user has more than one open

Matching Collections to Recordsets

The bulk of glrLoadSPlusObjects() involves loading data stored in Schedule Plus into Access tables using DAO Recordset objects. We've broken this into three sections within the procedure; they deal with Schedule Plus projects, tasks, and appointments, in that order. Each section is roughly the same, the only differences being the properties of the Schedule Plus objects and the fields in each table.

Each section begins by creating a Recordset object (rstObjects) based on one of the three tables in the database and another object (objObjects) that points to a Schedule Plus collection. GlrLoadSPlusObjects() creates the latter object by calling a method of the current schedule object. Here is the code that performs these steps for the Projects collection:

```
Set rstObjects = dbThis.OpenRecordset("tblProjects", _
  dbOpenDynaset)
Set objObjects = objSched.Projects
```

After creating these objects, glrLoadSPlusObjects() iterates through each Schedule Plus object in the current collection by using a Do Until...Loop structure. The Do Until statement examines the value of the current collection's IsEndOfTable property. If you've worked with Access DAO objects, this structure should look hauntingly familiar. Another Object variable, objObject, holds a reference to the current object in the collection. The collection's Item method creates the object reference. As we move through the collection, Item will return subsequent objects until we reach the end of the collection. Again, note the similarities between Schedule Plus objects and DAO.

Loading the Information

Once the procedure creates a reference to an individual object in the collection, it can load information about the object into an Access table. Because the unique identifier for each object is its ItemID property, glrLoadSPlusObjects() first tries to locate a record in the table with an ItemID value that matches the current object's, using the FindFirst method. If this fails (the recordset's NoMatch property is True), the function adds a new record to the table. Otherwise it uses the Edit method to update the existing information. After loading the information, glrLoadSPlusObjects() uses the Skip method of a Schedule Plus collection to move to the next object therein. Skip called without arguments moves one object forward in the collection. You can also supply the number of objects to move, forward or backward (using a negative number), by calling Skip with a numeric argument. Eventually, the Do Until loop will reach the end of the collection, IsEndOfTable will return True, and the procedure will move on to the next section. As each object is processed, we update a series of text boxes on frmLoad, the form from which glrLoadSPlusObjects() is called. Figure 21.10 shows frmLoad, which you can open by clicking the Re-load Schedule button on frmSPlus.

FIGURE 21.10:

The frmLoad form, which displays the load process' progress

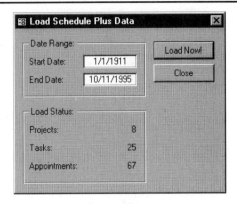

In addition to the mechanics of loading information into an Access table, two other elements of this procedure are worth pointing out. The first is how we use the var-StartDate and varEndDate arguments to glrLoadSPlusObjects(). You set these values by entering a range of dates in the text boxes on frmLoad. If you look at the section of code that loads appointment information, you'll notice that we call the SetRange method of the Appointments collection just prior to processing each appointment. SetRange restricts the collection to those appointments that fall within the given range. You may find this method useful as the number of appointments in your schedule file increases.

Second, after all the sections have processed and a message has been displayed to the user, glrLoadSPlusObjects() executes a number of statements to clean up after itself. You'll find these after the glrLoadSPlusObjects_Done label. First, we examine the fNotRunning flag and, if it returns True, call the Application object's Logoff method. You will recall we used fNotRunning to indicate that we forced an instance of Schedule Plus to be launched. If this is the case, we should shut it down when we're done. To do so, we call Logoff with a True argument. The next step is to close our DAO objects and free up any resources associated with our OLE automation activities by setting each of the Object variables we used to Nothing.

Example: Smart Mail Merge to Word

Our second sample application is an intelligent mail-merge tool you can use with any form in your database to copy data from the form to a Microsoft Word document. The tool is intelligent in the sense that it will try to match fields on your form with bookmark names in the document. Specifically, the tool must perform the following steps:

1. Launch Microsoft Word if it is not already running.

2. Load a copy of a preexisting Word template with one or more bookmarks defined.

3. Iterate through each control on the active form, trying to match control names with bookmark names.

4. Where a match is found, copy the data from the form to the Word document.

5. Give the user the option of printing the document after all data has been copied.

This example fulfills two goals. First, it demonstrates how to translate WordBasic commands into OLE automation methods, and second, it is actually a useful addition to most applications. Since it works with any form, you can add the code described below to any database and instantly give your users a simple export tool that integrates with their word processor.

Word as an OLE Automation Server

Microsoft Word is unique among Microsoft Office products in that it lacks an exposed object model. In fact, as an OLE automation server, it has only one object that you can create and control—the WordBasic object. By creating a reference to the WordBasic object (class ID Word.Basic), you can execute WordBasic commands on the instance of Microsoft Word you are controlling. Instead of using an object-oriented approach, in which you call methods and access properties of objects, WordBasic commands operate on the current selection. This could be a block of text, a table, or simply the current insertion point. When you write OLE automation client code to control Word, you will find that you use a great many commands to select the item on which you want to operate before actually issuing a command that affects it.

Microsoft Word does not have a type library. The best source of information on WordBasic commands is the Help file that ships with Word, WRDBASIC.HLP. Word-Basic commands do have an odd syntax, however, and must be translated into correct VBA syntax before you use them in your code. The next section, "Using WordBasic Commands," offers some guidelines for adapting WordBasic syntax. Perhaps the best way to create code for controlling Word is to use Word's macro recorder to record a set of actions and then cut, paste, and translate the resulting WordBasic statements.

Using WordBasic Commands

Despite Microsoft's goal of a common language shared among all its desktop products, Microsoft Word 95 still uses WordBasic as its macro language. Word-Basic's heritage is rooted in a time when individual product groups at Microsoft were responsible for their own languages, and thus its capabilities and syntax are quite different from VBA. Before you can use WordBasic commands, you'll need to translate them into VBA syntax. Fortunately, both WordBasic and VBA support named arguments, the only difference being how arguments are expressed. You can use positional arguments if you wish, but some WordBasic commands have a large number of mostly optional arguments, making the use of positional arguments confusing. Consider the code for WordBasic's EditBookmark statement taken from WRDBASIC.HLP:

```
EditBookmark .Name = text [, .SortBy = number] [, .Add] _
  [, .Delete] [, .Goto]
```

Note WordBasic's syntax for named arguments, which uses a dot before the argument name and a normal equal sign to denote the argument's value. This differs from VBA syntax, which uses the colon-equal sign combination (:=) to denote the value of an argument. The brackets indicate optional arguments. Each argument is listed with the datatype WordBasic expects. Those arguments without datatypes are used to take action, such as adding a bookmark. To convert these arguments to VBA, you must assign them a value of True. Therefore, assuming that objWord is an object variable holding a pointer to the WordBasic object, the following statement shows how you would execute EditBookmark from VBA to create a bookmark named MyMark at the current insertion point:

```
objWord.EditBookmark Name:="MyMark", Add:=True
```

In addition to commands that perform actions, WordBasic features a number of functions that return values. You can use these just as you do other functions in VBA or through OLE automation. The only difference with some WordBasic functions is that those that return string values have a dollar sign character at the end of their names. In earlier versions of Basic, you had to enclose these function names in brackets; otherwise the Basic interpreter would raise an error due to the odd naming convention. Because VBA supports function names with special characters, you don't need to do this in Access 95. In fact, you can leave off the dollar sign altogether if you wish. For example, WordBasic's AppInfo$() function returns information on Microsoft Word, such as its operating environment and version number, all as text. You pass AppInfo$() a numeric argument corresponding to the information you want returned. The following code snippet shows three equivalent methods for calling AppInfo$() from Access 95 VBA. (Passing the number 2 returns the version of Word being used.)

```
Debug.Print objWord.AppInfo(2)
Debug.Print objWord.AppInfo$(2)
Debug.Print objWord.[AppInfo$](2)
```

Using Word95 Objects for Access

Although Microsoft Word itself does not have a type library to support the use of WordBasic through OLE automation, Access 95 ships with a miniature version called the Word95 Objects for Access type library. This type library, WD95ACC.TLB, is installed in the Access directory and contains definitions for the WordBasic objects listed in Table 21.6. You must still use CreateObject() to obtain a reference to the WordBasic object, but the type library provides you with context-sensitive help from within VBA.

Creating the Word Template

The sample application included in CH21.MDB relies on the existence of a Microsoft Word template file with predefined bookmarks that correspond to fields on a form. We have included a sample template, which you can use to test the sample application, called Thanks for Comments.dot. Copy this to your Microsoft Office

TABLE 21.6: Methods Defined in the Word95 Objects for Access Type Library

Method	Description
AppActivate	Activates (brings to the front) the Word application window
AppRestore	Restores the Word application window
AppShow	Shows the Word application window (This is especially useful since, when a new instance of Word95 is created through OLE automation, the main window is initially hidden.)
DocMaximize	Maximizes the active document window
FileClose	Closes all windows associated with the active document
FileNewDefault	Creates a new document using the default characteristics
FileOpen	Opens an existing Word document
MailMergeDataSource	Returns information about the current mail-merge data source
MailMergeOpenDataSource	Opens a document or database and makes it the current mail-merge data source

Templates directory before running the application. Figure 21.11 shows the template open in Microsoft Word. The gray bars on the left side of the document are Word bookmarks.

FIGURE 21.11:

Sample template showing the location of bookmarks

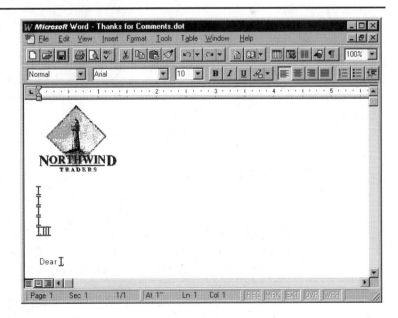

You define a bookmark by setting the insertion point at the spot in the document where you want to create the bookmark and then choosing the Edit ➤ Bookmark command. Figure 21.12 shows the dialog that appears. It lists any existing bookmarks, and you can click the Go To button to go to the point in the document marked by the bookmark. To create a new bookmark or redefine an existing one, enter the name of the bookmark in the text box and click the Add button.

You can see from Figure 21.12 that our sample template has a number of bookmarks already defined. These bookmarks are named after controls on a form that we will use to drive the data-merge process. A function (we'll describe it shortly) will look for each bookmark that matches a control name on the active form and copy the contents of the control to the document at the appropriate spot.

If you want to use our function with your own document templates, you will need to define bookmarks that correspond to control names on your forms. If you have a control that must be used more than once, you must append a sequence number, starting with 1, after the control name (such as the txtContactName and txtContactName1 fields in the sample template). Our function will look for additional bookmarks when it processes the form.

FIGURE 21.12:

Word's Bookmark dialog, showing bookmarks defined in the sample template

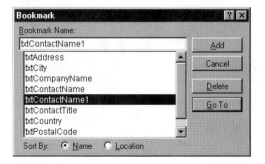

Launching the Merge Process

CH21.MDB contains an AutoKeys macro that defines Ctrl+L as a shortcut key that launches our initialization process using a function named glrInitMerge(), in basWord. The module basWord, in CH21.MDB on the companion disk, shows glrInitMerge(), which opens a form, frmOLEWord, that lets you select a Word template to use as the merge document. The procedure uses Screen.ActiveForm to capture the active form and then passes the name of this form to frmOLEWord in its OpenArgs property. frmOLEWord will use the active form to get the data for the merge process.

Figure 21.13 shows frmOLEWord, which features a list of Microsoft Word template files the user can choose from to use in the merge process. frmOLEWord also offers users the option of printing the finished document. The module Form: frmOLEWord, in CH21.MDB on the companion disk, shows the code contained in frmOLEWord's VBA module. It includes module-level declarations for several variables, including an Object variable to store the reference to WordBasic. VBA code in the form's Load event procedure calls glrCreateOLEObject() (Listing 21.2). If this function succeeds in creating an object reference, the Form_Load procedure uses it to fill the list of templates on the form. The procedure accomplishes this by first calling WordBasic's DefaultDir function with an argument value of 2. DefaultDir returns the root directory, where Microsoft Office templates are stored. The procedure then uses the Dir$() function to find all the Word template (.DOT) files in this directory. Once all the files have been found, Form_Load sets the list box's RowSource property.

FIGURE 21.13:

frmOLEWord showing a list of Microsoft Word templates

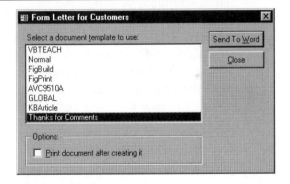

Copying Data to Word

After frmOLEWord presents the list of templates to the user, the user can select one from the list and click the Send button to copy the data on the active form to a new document created from the template. The module basWord, in CH21.MDB on the companion disk, shows the glrCreateFormLetter() function, which performs the task of copying data from the active form to the Word document. It accepts three arguments: a pointer to a WordBasic object (objWord), a pointer to a form from which to copy data (frmAny), and the path to a Word template file (strTemplate). Code in the

Click event for frmOLEWord's Send button calls glrCreateFormLetter() with:

- The module-level Object variable set during the form's Load event (mobjWord)
- A pointer to the active form when glrInitMerge() was invoked (created using the Forms collection and the form name stored in frmOLEWord's OpenArgs property)
- The selected template file, including the correct path and file extension

The first thing glrCreateFormLetter() does is create a new document based on the selected template by calling WordBasic's FileNew method. FileNew creates a new document and also makes it the active document. Subsequent WordBasic commands will then affect the new document. (Keep in mind that lacking a true object model, all WordBasic commands must operate on the active document, selection, and so on.)

After creating a new document, glrCreateFormLetter() uses a For Each...Next loop to iterate through each control on the active form. Using the name of each control, the procedure attempts to go to a matching bookmark in the active document, using WordBasic's EditGoto method. If there is no matching bookmark, an error occurs (which, oddly enough, is error 5, "Invalid procedure call"), and the procedure skips to the next control. If, on the other hand, a matching bookmark is found, Word places the insertion point at the location denoted by the bookmark. GlrCreateForm-Letter() then uses the Insert method to insert text at that spot.

You'll notice that rather than just inserting the value of the control, we use a function, glrValueFromControl(), to return a string to insert. We've done this so we can substitute meaningful strings for controls such as check boxes that hold numeric values. The module basWord, in CH21.MDB on the companion disk, shows the code behind glrValueFromControl(), as well as another function, glrFirstVisible-Column(), which returns the value of the first visible column of list and combo boxes.

Figure 21.14 shows a sample document created using our smart merge function. We used the frmCustomers form in CH21.MDB as the basis for this document.

FIGURE 21.14:

A completed merge document created using the sample Customers form

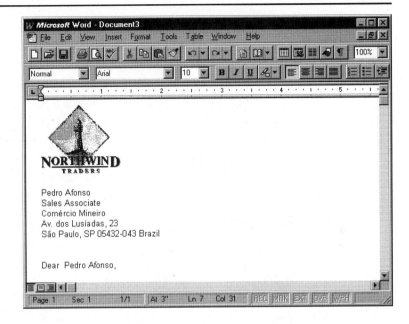

Example: Populating an Excel Worksheet

Microsoft Excel is probably one of the most satisfying OLE automation servers you can work with. It has a rich, well-documented object model that lets you control just about every element of an Excel worksheet, right down to individual character formatting within a cell (not to mention menus and toolbars, a capability sorely missed in Access). Excel is also an extremely functional program used by a great many people, making it an attractive candidate for the server in an integrated solution. In this section we'll show you how to update a simple worksheet and chart with data in an Access database. We've already discussed most of what you need to know about using OLE automation servers, so we'll keep this section brief.

> **NOTE**
>
> Microsoft Excel is an extremely complex application from a developer's perspective, encompassing roughly 140 different collections and object types. It is far beyond the scope of this chapter to discuss Excel's object model in depth. We've tried to pick an example that uses obvious and intuitive Excel elements, such as workbooks, worksheets, ranges, and charts. If you need more information to help you understand this example, consult the VBA Help file for Excel, VBA_XL.HLP.

Using an Existing File

One thing we haven't yet discussed is using an OLE automation server to manipulate an existing document. (Our Schedule Plus example gathers data from an existing schedule, but this does not fit the true document paradigm.) Manipulating existing documents is a technique that becomes critical when you need to retrieve data from a file that was edited by another process or even a human being. Since you don't have complete control over it, you must be careful when altering and saving it to make sure you don't inadvertently overwrite another person's changes. Using existing files is also a good compromise between completely manual and completely automated creation of documents. For example, the VBA code required to create a complex Excel chart can be quite long. It is often better to use an existing chart and modify only a few properties.

From a programming standpoint, you'll need to use the GetObject() function, as opposed to CreateObject(), when creating an OLE automation object that corresponds to an existing document. GetObject() lets you specify a document name and path instead of a class ID. As long as the file type is correctly registered, Windows will start the appropriate server (if it's not already running) and load the specified file. If you use our glrCreateOLEObject() function, you need only pass the path to a document file in the varDoc argument, and we'll try to use GetObject() automatically.

Our Scenario

The scenario for our sample Excel application involves a fictitious airline. CH21.MDB contains a table of airport codes (tblAirports) and a table filled with randomly generated lost-luggage rates for each North American airport for the month of January 1996. In our example we've also created an Excel workbook called STATREQ.XLS that allows users to request data on any given airport. You might think of it as a query form a user can fill out and send to someone else for processing. The workbook contains two worksheets. The Query worksheet, shown in Figure 21.15, lets the user fill in an airport code (the standard, three-character code assigned by the International Air Transport Association) in a cell. Our Access application will query the database and, based on the current date, return information on month-to-date lost-luggage rates. STATREQ.XLS also contains a second worksheet, called Results, with a table of data and a chart. In our example we'll show you how to perform the following steps using OLE automation to control Excel:

1. Open the workbook.

2. Retrieve the airport code from the Query worksheet.

3. Query the Access database.

4. Return the results to the worksheet.

5. Redefine the data range the chart uses to reflect new data.

FIGURE 21.15:

Query worksheet in STATREQ.XLS

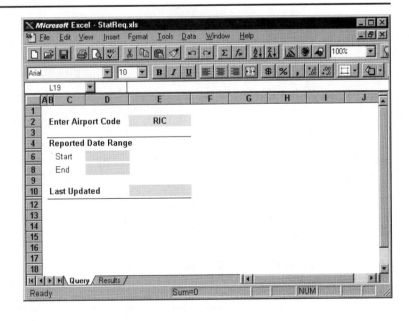

Creating an Object from an Existing Document

There is no user interface for our simple example function. Rather, we've created one procedure, called glrUpdateAirportStats, in basExcel, that handles all the processing. The module basExcel, in CH21.MDB on the companion disk, shows the subroutine. As you can see from the variable declarations, we use quite a few Object variables in the procedure, mostly to store references to objects rather than to repeat a complex VBA statement.

The first thing the procedure does is call glrCreateOLEObject(), passing it a local Object variable, objXLSheet, and the path to the STATREQ.XLS file. If glrCreateOLE-Object() returns glrcOLECreateRunning (value 2), then we know that objXLSheet has been initialized correctly using GetObject().

Now comes the interesting part. Since we use a document name with GetObject(), the object reference it returns will be of a class corresponding to the document type in the Windows Registry. In our case, .XLS files are associated with Excel.Worksheet object types, so objXLSheet will point to one of the *worksheets* in STATREQ.XLS. This differs from the other examples we've discussed so far, which used the Application object of each OLE automation server. Keep this in mind as you create object references to documents. The object you create will be somewhere in the middle of the object hierarchy, not at the top, as is the case with Application objects.

Because we will want to manipulate Excel's Application object in addition to a worksheet object, we need a way to create a reference to it. Fortunately, rather than using another call to GetObject() or CreateObject(), Excel objects have a Parent property that returns a reference to the object immediately above the current object in the object hierarchy. Using the Parent property, we can create references to both the Workbook object corresponding to STATREQ.XLS and the Application object using the following code:

```
Set objXLBook = objXLSheet.Parent
Set objXLApp = objXLBook.Parent
```

Working with Excel Objects

Once we have a few Object variables hanging around, pointing to some of the key objects in our Excel application, we can begin to manipulate the worksheets. Some aspects of controlling Excel objects are identical to Access VBA code. For example, to display the Excel main window and the STATREQ.XLS document window, we can set their Visible properties to True:

```
objXLApp.Visible = True
objXLBook.Windows(1).Visible = True
```

Other aspects, however, require that you write a bit more code. Excel, unlike Access, does not support the concept of default collections. For example, the following two lines of Access VBA code are identical because the Controls collection is the default collection for a Form object:

```
Forms("txtLastName").Enabled = True
Forms.Controls("txtLastName").Enabled = True
```

You must explicitly specify each collection when referring to objects in an Excel application. Therefore, the code that sets object references to the two worksheets in STATREQ.XLS, named Query and Results, looks like this:

```
Set objQuerySheet = objXLBook.Worksheets("Query")
Set objResultsSheet = objXLBook.Worksheets("Results")
```

Furthermore, Excel supports bang (!) syntax only for absolute range references on worksheets. You must use the syntax shown above, which utilizes the collection name and an object identifier (either a name or an index number) in parentheses, to refer to specific objects in a collection.

Updating the Worksheets and Chart

The bulk of the processing in glrUpdateAirportStats involves running a query against the tblLostCount table and poking the results into the Results worksheet in STATREQ.XLS. We do this by first creating a reference to a named range on the Results worksheet called rngResStart. (See the code snippet below.) This range corresponds to cell B4, the start of the range of values, shown in Figure 21.16. This figure also shows the Chart object, which we will update once all the data has been copied.

After creating a pointer to the range, we delete any existing data in the table by applying the CurrentRegion method to the Range object (which returns another range of nonblank cells surrounding the original range) and using the Clear method:

```
Set objXLRange = objResultsSheet.Range("rngResStart")
objXLRange.CurrentRegion.Clear
```

FIGURE 21.16:

Results worksheet showing data table and chart

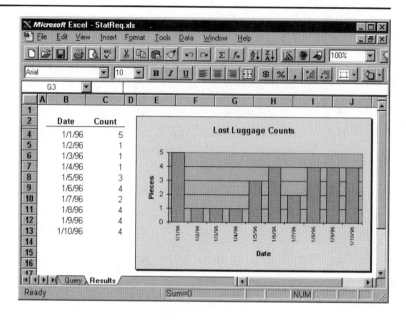

We can now copy the results of our query into the Excel worksheet by setting the Formula property of individual cells in the range beneath cell B4. To create a reference to the individual cells, we use the Offset method of our range object, objXLRange, with row and column offsets. A counter variable, intCount, helps us keep track of how many rows to offset from cell B4:

```
Do Until rstLost.EOF

    ' First the date...
    objXLRange.Offset(intCount, 0). _
     Formula = rstLost![DateLost]
    ' then the count
    objXLRange.Offset(intCount, 1). _
     Formula = rstLost![LostCount]

    intCount = intCount + 1
    rstLost.MoveNext
Loop
```

The last task remaining once the data is on the worksheet is to redefine the source for the chart to reflect the current amount of data. Once again, we can use the CurrentRegion method of objXLRange to return a pointer to all the data in the table. We use Excel's Union method (a method of the Application object) to combine the data range with cells B2 and C2, which contain the headings for the data and chart. Finally, we combine this with the ChartWizard method of the Chart object on the Results worksheet to set the new data source equal to the existing dataset:

```
objResultsSheet.ChartObjects(1). _
 Chart.ChartWizard Source:=objXLApp. _
 Union(objResultsSheet.Range("B2:C2"), _
 objXLRange.CurrentRegion)
```

To test glrUpdateAirportStats, you'll need to copy STATREQ.XLS to a directory on your hard disk and edit the glrcXLSPath constant accordingly. Then run glrUpdateAirportStats from the Access Debug window. GlrUpdateAirportStats should work regardless of whether Excel is currently running or STATREQ.XLS is currently loaded.

Using OLE Controls

Access 2.0 was the first application to support OLE custom controls. OLE custom controls, or *OCXs*, as they are sometimes called because of their file extension, are the successors to VBX controls, the modular components that helped make Visual Basic such a success. OLE controls encapsulate a certain degree of functionality that you can integrate into your application simply by placing one on your Access form. Access 95 integrates OLE controls much better than Access 2.0, but in most respects controls are used in the same way.

In addition to their being self-contained chunks of functionality, you can control OCXs the same way you control other applications using OLE automation. OLE custom controls implement their own objects, properties, and methods. In this section we'll show you how to control the calendar OCX that ships with Access 95. (We'll also briefly mention the TabStrip control that comes with the Access Developer's Toolkit in Chapter 15.)

Custom Control Registration and Licensing

Before you can use a custom control, you must make sure it is properly registered. By this we mean that the correct entries are made in the Windows Registry to enable the control's OLE functionality. If you purchase a development tool that includes OLE custom controls, such as Microsoft Visual Basic 4.0 or the Access 95 Developer's Toolkit, the installation program usually installs and registers the controls for you. If you acquire controls separately or are installing controls on your users' computers to support your application, you will have to register the controls yourself.

To register controls, you can use either the Custom Controls dialog in Microsoft Access or the REGSVR32.EXE program that ships with Visual Basic 4.0. Figure 21.17 shows the Access 95 Custom Controls dialog. You display the dialog by selecting Tools ➤ Custom Controls. As you can see, the dialog lists the controls that are currently registered and features buttons for registering and unregistering controls. The unregistering feature is useful for deleting Registry entries for controls you no longer plan to use.

FIGURE 21.17:

Access 95 Custom Controls dialog

To register a new control, click the Register button and select the control from the file dialog that appears. To unregister a control, simply select it from the list and click the Unregister button.

If you are distributing your application to others whom you do not want messing with the Custom Controls dialog, you can register controls using a small program, REGSVR32.EXE. The syntax of REGSVR32.EXE is shown here:

REGSVR32.EXE [/u] *filename*.ocx

You run REGSVR32.EXE using the path to the custom control you wish to register. The program uses information in the .OCX file to create the proper Registry entries. You can use the /u switch to unregister a control.

If you're using the ADT and its Setup Wizard, you can include any OLE custom controls your application uses as part of the installation file list. The installation program that installs your application will register the controls for you automatically.

If you plan to develop applications using OLE custom controls, you need to be aware of the new licensing scheme most OCX developers use. Unlike Visual Basic VBXs, which used a simple text file located in the VBX directory, OLE custom controls use Registry settings to control whether you can use a particular control in Design view. These Registry settings are normally created when the controls are installed, usually by some type of installation program. Creating these entries yourself on a computer for which you did not purchase a copy of the custom control is probably a violation of the vendor's license agreement.

Inserting OLE Custom Controls

You place OLE custom controls on forms by selecting Insert ➤ Custom Control while in Form Design view. This action displays the Insert OLE Custom Controls dialog, as shown in Figure 21.18.

The dialog's list box lists the controls that have been registered on your computer and are available to you. To insert the control, select the control name from the list and click the OK button. Access inserts the control on your form. You can then size it to meet your needs.

In addition to using the menu, you can create custom toolbar buttons for each custom control. To do this, open the Customize Toolbars dialog and select Custom Controls from the list of categories. You should see a dialog like the one in Figure 21.19, listing the available controls instead of displaying buttons. To create a

---

FIGURE 21.18:

Insert OLE Custom Control dialog
listing the available custom controls

FIGURE 21.19:

Creating a toolbar button for a
custom control using the Customize
Toolbars dialog

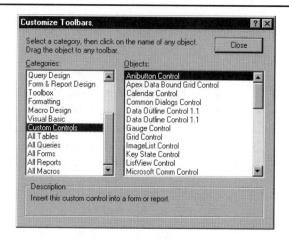

custom toolbar button, just select a custom control from the list and drag it onto a
toolbar. Access creates the button using the icon associated with the chosen control.

After creating a custom toolbar button, adding the control to a form becomes simply a matter of clicking the button and then dragging a region on the form, just as
for any of the built-in controls.

In addition to adding the control to your form, Access automatically adds a reference to the control's type library to your VBA project. You should see a reference
for the control listed in the References dialog after inserting it on a form. This allows
you to use the control's properties and methods in your VBA code.

Modifying Custom Control Properties

OLE custom controls have properties, just like built-in controls. Because OCXs are
hosted by an unbound object frame, when you select a custom control in Design
view, the Access property sheet displays properties associated with the object
frame. If you want to modify those properties specific to the control, you have two
choices. Your first choice is to select the Other (or All) tab from the control's property sheet. Here you will find most of the properties for the custom control. For example, Figure 21.20 shows the property sheet for a copy of the calendar control that
ships with Access 95.

FIGURE 21.20:

Custom properties for a calendar control

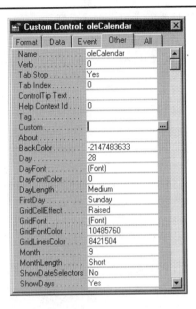

Your other option is to use the control's custom property dialog. Each OLE custom control implements a dialog that lets you modify its properties. Figure 21.21 shows the custom property dialog for the calendar control. You can display this dialog by clicking the Build button next to the Custom property on the Access property sheet (near the top of Figure 21.20) or by right-clicking the control and selecting Control Object ➤ Properties from the shortcut menu.

FIGURE 21.21:

Custom properties dialog for a calendar control

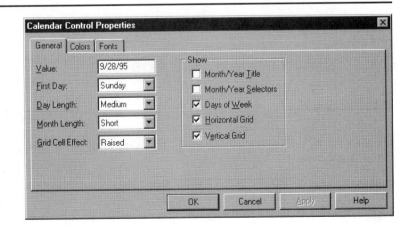

Using OLE Custom Control Events

OLE custom controls differ from Access controls in that they do not expose their events through the property sheet. Access controls have properties such as On-Click, which you can use to call a macro, VBA function, or code contained in the form's module. OLE custom control events are available only from the form's module. When you add a custom control to a form, Access adds event procedure stubs to the form's module that correspond to those supported by the control. To view these event points, you must open the module, select the control from the Object list, and then select the event from the Proc list. Figure 21.22 shows a module window open to the NewYear event of a calendar control. Note, however, that some of the events in this list belong to the unbound object frame, not to the control itself. These include the Enter, Exit, GotFocus, LostFocus, Click, DblClick, MouseDown, MouseMove, MouseUp, and Updated events.

FIGURE 21.22:

Event procedure for a calendar control's NewYear event

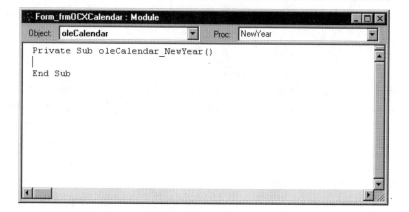

Using Bound OLE Custom Controls

A new feature of Access 95 is the support for bound OLE custom controls. For example, you can bind the calendar to a Date/Time field by setting the control's ControlSource property to the field name. There is no need to write any code; you simply choose the control source from the property sheet just as you would for an Access control. We've included a form, frmBoundCalendar, in CH21.MDB, that demonstrates this. This type of binding is called *simple binding* because the control is bound only to a single column. Some OLE custom controls also support *complex binding*—binding to an entire table, with the control managing individual fields. Some of the OLE custom controls that ship with Visual Basic 4.0 support complex binding. Unfortunately, Access, unlike VB 4.0, does not support complex binding from the client side, so you won't be able to use these controls with Access.

Calendar Control Example

To demonstrate the use of OLE custom controls, we have created a simple example using the calendar control that ships with Access 95. This control is an enhanced version of the one that came with the Access 2.0 Developer's Toolkit. Figure 21.23 shows our sample form, frmOCXCalendar. It's a rather rudimentary form containing only the calendar control, two text boxes, and four command buttons. We can use it, however, to demonstrate manipulating custom control events and properties.

You can use the buttons on the form to move from month to month and year to year. As the date changes, so do the month and year shown in the text boxes at the top of the form. You can use the mouse to click a day on the calendar, and that changes the date, as well. Double-clicking the calendar displays a message box containing the current date.

The module Form: frmOCXCalendar, in CH21.MDB on the companion disk, shows all the code contained in frmOCXCalendar's VBA module. It's not much code, a fact that testifies to the value of OLE custom controls.

FIGURE 21.23:

A sample form using the calendar OLE custom control

Manipulating OLE Controls

As mentioned previously, OLE custom controls are hosted inside an unbound object frame. The event code you see in Form: frmOCXCalendar refers to oleCalendar, the object frame control. To manipulate the control contained in the frame, you use its Object method, which returns a pointer to the embedded object. Using the Object method, you can then access the methods and properties of the control. For example, the calendar control has a GridCellEffect property that controls how the calendar's grid lines appear. To change this programmatically, you could use a statement like this:

```
Me![oleCalendar].Object.GridCellEffect = 2     ' Raised
```

Note the use of the Object method. This provides you with a direct reference to the control object without your having to use such functions as GetObject() and CreateObject(). If you've examined the sample code in Form: frmOCXCalendar, you should have noticed that we apparently haven't used the Object method. This is because Object is the *default* method for the object frame and is not explicitly required. Therefore, the following VBA code is equivalent to that shown above:

```
Me![oleCalendar].GridCellEffect = 2     ' Raised
```

In fact, the calendar control has a default Value property in addition to a default method. Value returns the current date displayed on the calendar. That's why we can use Me![oleCalendar] in the oleCalendar_DblClick procedure to refer to the date value in the control.

You also use the Object method (either explicitly or implicitly) to access the control's methods. Code behind the command buttons on the form calls methods of the calendar control to change the month and year. Thus, for the most part, you can manipulate OLE custom control objects in much the same way you do Access controls.

Custom Control References

One issue that arises when you use custom controls (or a type library from any OLE automation server) in your applications is that of type library references. When you insert a custom control on a form, Access automatically creates a reference to that control's type library (normally stored in the .OCX itself) in your VBA project. Access stores the full path to the control. This means that if you install your application in a different path on your user's computer, VBA will not be able to resolve the reference, and your custom control–specific VBA code will not compile. Because there is no way to change a reference using VBA code, your user must reestablish the reference manually by opening the References dialog, unchecking the references marked as missing, and then setting a reference to the custom controls in their new locations.

Access is somewhat intelligent about automatically resolving references for you. For instance, Access automatically reestablishes references if you create them for controls in the Windows\System directory or in the directory where Access itself is installed. If you plan to distribute OLE controls with your application, choose one of these locations as the destination for .OCX and type library files.

Using Custom Controls from Other Products

As the number of OLE custom controls increases, you will have a wider selection to choose from when building your applications. Beware, however, that not all custom controls work well with Access. Many of the controls that ship with Microsoft Visual Basic 4.0, for example, have features not available through Access. For example, Access does not support the ability to embed one OLE control in another, so you won't be able to create the same visual effect with some controls that you can with Visual Basic. As this technology matures, it will be easier to share components among development tools. Until then, treat new OLE controls with a degree of caution.

Summary

In this chapter we've explored the basic concepts behind OLE automation, including:

- The role of OLE automation clients and servers, the use of type libraries, and the creation of objects in another application
- The similarities between OLE automation code and the VBA code you write in Access
- How to manipulate other applications using objects, properties, and methods, just as you do Access objects

We used a sample application that demonstrated how to load data from a Schedule Plus schedule file into an Access database. We also showed how to manipulate OLE custom controls embedded on a form. In each example we stressed the similarities between OLE automation code and plain VBA code.

OLE automation can help you become more productive by giving you the tools to integrate other robust, feature-filled applications into a customized solution. In this chapter you've seen how you can use Access 95 to control other applications.

CHAPTER

TWENTY-TWO

Controlling Access as an OLE Server

- Deciding when to use Access as an OLE server

- Exploring the nuances of Access in the server role

- Creating a reporting system controlled from Microsoft Excel

- Learning to create OLE-friendly applications

With Access 95, Microsoft has added a capability long sought by developers looking for a way to integrate Access into solutions created with other tools. Access' new role as an OLE automation server opens up a number of interesting possibilities. You can now have one Access application that controls another. You can also create applications in Microsoft Visual Basic, Excel, and Project that use the services of Access to do such things as printing reports, creating tables and queries, and displaying forms. In this chapter we'll examine the reasons to use Access as an OLE server and demonstrate an example of its capabilities by implementing a system written in Microsoft Excel that uses Access to preview and print reports.

Looking at Access as an OLE Server

One paradox Access developers must face is that while it is now possible to use Access as an OLE server, the need to do so is probably smaller than ever. As companies such as Microsoft move toward a component-based approach built on OLE technology, huge chunks of a program's functionality become available without the need to actually run the program. A case in point is the Jet database engine, the component responsible for manipulating data and objects in an .MDB file. You can now use Jet objects and methods directly from any OLE client without going through Access. So, you ask, when does it make sense to use Access as an OLE server? Consider these situations:

- You need to do something that's possible only through Access, such as printing a report or creating a new form.

- You need to do something that requires launching a second copy of Access, such as compacting the current database.

- You need to create background processes that use information from an active Access session.

- You need to provide seamless integration between Access and another application.

Access 95 provides only one object that you can create using OLE automation: the Application object. Unlike other Office applications such as Word and Excel, Access does not feature document objects (for example, Excel.Sheet). As you might expect, the class ID for Access' Application object is Access.Application. Using this ID with the New keyword or either CreateObject() or GetObject() gives you an object pointer to Access' top-level object, from which all other objects can be referenced.

Using the Access Type Library

When developing OLE automation applications, you will find it helpful for several reasons to include Access 95's type library, MSACCESS.TLB, in the list of references for your project. First, it makes your code more readable by declaring object variables that map directly to the objects in Access. Second, VBA can use the type library to display context-sensitive help when you highlight an Access object name and press the F1 key. Third, if your development tool supports it, you can create an object reference using the New keyword rather than using CreateObject() or GetObject(). For example, the following code automatically creates a new reference to Access' Application object the first time the object is used:

```
' Create a new object of the proper class
Dim objAccess As New Access.Application

' Reference a property--Access will be started automatically
MsgBox objAccess.hWndAccessApp
```

Finally, if you use the New keyword with the syntax shown above, VBA can check your code for syntax using the list of objects, properties, and methods exported by Access. VBA would warn you, for example, if you misspelled the HwndAccessApp property or tried to use a property that did not exist.

Differences from Regular Access

Using Access as an OLE server is very much like developing applications the way you do now. The object model, methods, and properties are identical, regardless of whether you call them from a VBA module in an Access database or using OLE automation from an external application such as Excel or Visual Basic. Subtle differences do exist, however, in the way you use Access objects. First and foremost, all controllable objects descend from the Application object, to which you must create a pointer before using any other object, property, or method. When porting code from Access to another VBA-enabled application, make sure you qualify all "top-level" objects (those for which Access VBA can assume the context) with the object variable holding a pointer to the Access Application object. The following list identifies some of the common methods, descendant objects, and collections of the Access Application object that you must qualify when calling them from OLE automation code. For a complete list, use the Object Browser to interrogate the Application object for all its descendants.

AddAutoCorrect	Delete ReportControl
BuildCriteria	DoCmd
CodeContextObject	Domain aggregate functions (for example, DMax)
CodeDb	
CreateControl	Echo
CreateForm	Eval
CreateGroupLevel	Forms
CreateReport	GetOption
CreateReportControl	hWndAccessApp
CurrentDb	Nz
CurrentObjectName	Quit
CurrentObjectType	RefreshTitleBar
CurrentUser	Reports
DBEngine	Run
DDE functions (for example, DDEInitiate)	Screen
	SetOption
DefaultWorkspaceClone	ShortcutMenuBar
DelAutoCorrect	SysCmd
DeleteControl	

For example, the following code snippet executes perfectly well in an Access module:

```
Dim frmAny As Form

Set frmAny = Screen.ActiveForm
```

```
frmAny.Visible = False
If frmAny.Caption = Forms(0).Caption Then
    DoCmd.Close acForm, frmAny.Name
End If
```

To mimic the functionality of these statements using OLE automation in Visual Basic, on the other hand, you would need to declare and initialize an object variable and prefix the Screen, Forms, and DoCmd objects with it, as shown in this code fragment:

```
Dim objAccess As New Access.Application
Dim frmAny As Form

Set frmAny = objAccess.Screen.ActiveForm
frmAny.Visible = False
If frmAny.Caption = objAccess.Forms(0).Caption Then
    objAccess.DoCmd.Close acForm, frmAny.Name
End If
```

You must also keep in mind that since Access is operating behind the scenes when used as an OLE server, you must not initiate actions that require user intervention. For example, any message box displayed as the result of running a query or macro or opening a form or report will cause your OLE client code to halt while it waits for a response from the user. If Access is not in a state in which it can accept input (if the main window is hidden, for instance), there will be no way for the code to continue executing. In the section "Hiding the Access Main Window" later in this chapter, we will explain how to manage the user interface to display Access forms and dialogs when necessary.

Access OLE Server Behavior

You saw in Chapter 21 various ways to create a pointer to an OLE server, including a direct reference using the New keyword as well as the CreateObject() and GetObject() functions. Access as an OLE server behaves differently depending on how it is called. It also implements its Visible property differently from other Microsoft Office applications. The following paragraphs explain this behavior, beginning with the simplest scenario, using CreateObject() to obtain an object reference.

Access is by default a *single-use* OLE server. As with other single-use servers, using CreateObject() will always create a new instance of Access, the result of the function call being a pointer to that instance. When a new instance of Access opens in response to an OLE client request, it cannot be terminated simply by selecting File

➤ Exit or clicking the Close button. Instead of closing in response to these actions, it closes the current database and minimizes the main window. Access knows it was started via OLE automation and will not shut down until a Quit request is made or the object variable storing the Application object reference is destroyed.

When you call GetObject(), the counterpart to CreateObject(), Access behaves differently, depending on which arguments you supply. GetObject() accepts two optional arguments: a document name and an OLE class ID. If you pass an empty string as the first argument (the document name) and "Access.Application" as the second, a new instance of Access is created. Alternatively, you can cause Access to immediately open a database by passing a valid path and file name as the first argument. In this case the second argument is not really necessary, since Windows can infer which OLE server to use from the file extension. If you have given your database file an extension other than one of those registered by Access (.MDB, .MDA, and so on), you must supply both arguments. In addition, you can call GetObject(), omitting the first argument altogether and passing only the class ID as the second argument. If a copy of Access is already running, GetObject() will create a reference to the running instance; otherwise a new instance will be created.

Finally, you can create a reference to Access using the New keyword in VBA applications. Using the New keyword always launches a new instance of Access, which terminates when the object variable used is destroyed.

Running Access Reports Using OLE Automation

To demonstrate the general techniques required to use Access as an OLE server, we have chosen to implement a sample application that lets you browse and print reports stored in an Access database. We chose this example for a number of reasons. First, it allows us to demonstrate the very few additional techniques you need to master to use Access effectively as an OLE server. (After all, the rest of this book describes how to write an Access application *in Access*!) Second, printing reports is one thing Access does much better than most other development tools, including other databases, as well as applications such as Microsoft Word and Excel. Finally, printing Access reports from other applications, particularly those written in Visual Basic, is a capability a great number of developers who are disappointed with those applications' reporting capabilities have long sought. This section describes how we created the sample application, written using Microsoft Excel. The remainder of the chapter details a number of other techniques and guidelines to keep in mind when developing OLE applications with Access.

The Sample Application File

You will find the sample application contained in an Excel workbook named CH22.XLS. Figure 22.1 shows the application's main menu. Most of the code contained in the worksheet's sole module, basOLE, can be easily ported to other VBA applications, such as Microsoft Project or Visual Basic, with a few minor modifications.

The sample application was written in Microsoft Excel because that's one application you're likely to already own. Since a great number of copies of Access are sold as part of Microsoft Office Professional, we felt it would be a good choice. If you don't have a copy of Excel or wish to port the application to another development tool, we have included the VBA code from the project on the companion CD-ROM in a file called CH22VBA.TXT.

FIGURE 22.1:

Main switchboard for a sample OLE automation application written in Excel

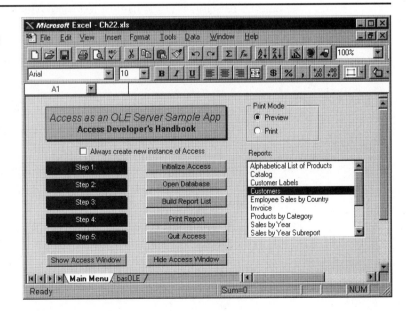

When porting the code, keep in mind that although VBA is a common language shared by a number of tools, the architecture and capabilities of the tools differ. For example, if you wanted to port the code to Microsoft Visual Basic 4.0, you would need to change the references to Excel objects (such as the main menu workbook) to Visual Basic objects.

Specifically, you need to do at least two things. First, you must change the Excel object references to object references appropriate to your development tool. Second, you must replace Excel-specific properties and methods with similar ones. The most obvious example of this is Excel's GetOpenFilename method. You should replace the code that uses this method with code that uses the common dialog OLE custom control, COMDLG32.OCX.

The Five-Part Process for Printing Reports Using OLE Automation

CH22.XLS contains a worksheet called Main Menu, which holds the application's interface, and a module sheet called basOLE, which contains all the VBA used in this example. The main menu worksheet features a list box and a number of buttons. Each of the buttons demonstrates one part of a five-part process for printing reports using OLE automation:

1. Initiating a connection to an instance of Access using OLE automation. A check box on the worksheet controls whether a new instance of Access is created or a running instance (if one exists) is used.

2. After a connection has been established, opening a database so a list of reports can be retrieved. The application first determines whether a database is currently open and if so, closes it.

3. Once a database has been opened, retrieving a list of reports and displaying it in the list box on the worksheet.

4. Printing or previewing the report, depending on the state of another check box on the worksheet.

5. Shutting down the instance of Access (if a new one was created) by destroying the object variable used to interact with it.

Each of these steps is explained in the paragraphs that follow, which also include the sample code used in the Excel application. You'll notice several things about the way we constructed the sample application:

- We use a module-level Object variable to store the reference to Access' Application object. Using a module-level variable allows several different procedures to operate on the same instance of Access.

- We often compare the object variable with the intrinsic constant Nothing to determine whether a valid OLE reference exists before using any of Access' properties or methods. Doing so prevents run-time errors if we inadvertently reinitialize the variable. This is particularly critical with Excel VBA applications because Excel reinitializes all module- and global-level variables whenever you make *any* change to *any* module in the workbook.

- After creating a new instance of Access, we hide the main Access window using a Win32 API function. This adds to the impression that the application is truly integrated and reduces the chance that the user will somehow mess things up by playing around with Access' user interface. You can choose to leave the Access window visible if you wish by commenting out the call to glrHideAccessWindow.

Initiating an OLE Session

The sample application uses a rather sophisticated procedure to initiate an OLE automation session with Access. Listing 22.1 shows this procedure, glrInitAccess, which first attempts to create a reference to a running instance of Access using GetObject(). If the call to GetObject() fails because no copy of Access is running, the error-handling code calls CreateObject() instead. Error 483 (represented by the constant glrcErrNoCreateObject) indicates that the object reference could not be created. You can override this behavior and always create a new instance of Access by checking a check box on the main menu worksheet. An If…Then statement checks the state of the check box and triggers error 483, thus forcing a call to CreateObject(), if it is checked.

Listing 22.1

```
Sub glrInitAccess()
    ' Set up error handling to trap the case
    ' where no instance of Access is running
    On Error GoTo glrInitAccess_Error

    ' Define constant for error generated when an
    ' object reference can't be created
    Const glrcErrNoCreateObject = 483

    ' Launch Access, initialize the object variable,
    ' and hide the Access main window
    If mobjAccess Is Nothing Then

        ' If the user wants to create a new instance of
        ' Access, force error 483 to trigger a call
        ' to CreateObject instead of GetObject
        If Worksheets("Main Menu").CheckBoxes _
          ("chkCreateNew") = xlOn Then
            Error glrcErrNoCreateObject
        Else
            Set mobjAccess = GetObject(, "Access.Application.7")
        End If

        ' Hide the Access main window
        Call glrHideAccessWindow
    End If
glrInitAccess_Exit:
    Exit Sub
glrInitAccess_Error:
    Select Case Err
        Case glrcErrNoCreateObject
            ' Unable to create reference or the
            ' user wants to create a new instance
            Set mobjAccess = CreateObject("Access.Application.7")
            Resume Next
        Case Else
            MsgBox Error(), vbExclamation, "Error " & Err
    End Select
    Resume glrInitAccess_Exit
End Sub
```

GlrInitAccess stores the reference to Access' Application object in a module-level variable, mobjAccess.

Opening a Database

Access provides two methods specifically designed to deal with opening and closing databases using OLE automation: OpenCurrentDatabase and CloseCurrentDatabase. While you can use CloseCurrentDatabase in Access applications, these two methods of the Application object are most useful in OLE automation code written in a tool such as Microsoft Excel or Visual Basic. Listing 22.2 shows glrLoadDatabase, a procedure that handles opening a database from the Excel application.

Listing 22.2

```
Sub glrLoadDatabase()
    Dim varFileName As Variant

    Const glrcFilter = "Access Databases,*.mdb;" _
     "*.mda,All files,*.*"
    Const glrcTitle = "Select Database To Open"

    ' Call the GetOpenFilename method of Excel's Application
    ' object to get the name of database to open--this
    ' method returns a string containing a full path to
    ' a file if the user clicked the OK button.
    varFileName = Application.GetOpenFilename( _
     FileFilter:=glrcFilter, _
     FilterIndex:=0, _
     Title:=glrcTitle, _
     MultiSelect:=False)

    ' Check to see if the user chose a database
    If VarType(varFileName) = vbString Then

        ' Check to see if a database is already open
        If mobjAccess.DBEngine.Workspaces(0)._
         Databases.Count > 0 Then

            ' If so, close it
            mobjAccess.CloseCurrentDatabase
        End If

        ' Open the selected database
        mobjAccess.OpenCurrentDatabase varFileName

        ' Hide the database container
        mobjAccess.DoCmd.DoMenuItem 0, 4, 3, , acMenuVer70
```

```
      ' Open the prevention form if it exists
      On Error Resume Next
      mobjAccess.DoCmd.OpenForm formname:="frmPrevent", _
        windowmode:=acHidden
    End If
End Sub
```

GlrLoadDatabase uses the GetOpenFilename method of Excel's Application object to display the common Open File dialog so the user can choose a database to open. If you decide to port the sample code to another development tool, you'll need to replace this method with another one that offers similar functionality (the common dialog OLE custom control in Visual Basic 4.0, for example). Provided the user chooses a file from the dialog, the procedure continues to try loading the selected database. It first checks to see whether a database is already open in the instance of Access pointed to by mobjAccess, by checking the number of databases open in the default workspace. If the count is greater than 0, the procedure calls CloseCurrent-Database to close whichever database is open.

WARNING Be careful when calling CloseCurrentDatabase to close a database you didn't open through OLE automation. If you try to close a user database with open, changed objects, the user will have to dismiss a series of confirmation dialogs before Access can close the database. This may cause the CloseCurrentDatabase to time-out and fail. Make sure your error handling is set up to cope with this possibility.

Opening the chosen database is a simple matter of calling OpenCurrentDatabase with the name of the database. OpenCurrentDatabase will accept any valid file name, including both full and partial path information. After opening the database, the procedure hides the Database window (an optional step) and then attempts to open a form called frmPrevent in the current database. This form helps prevent users from inadvertently closing a database while you are using it in your OLE automation code. (See the section "Preventing Users from Closing the Database" later in this chapter for more information on how this form works.)

NOTE

Unlike some applications, Access does not suppress startup code (the AutoExec macro and/or startup form) when a database is opened using OLE automation. Startup code that displays dialogs that require a user response such as clicking an OK button may cause your OLE automation to fail if the user does not respond quickly enough. See the section "The UserControl Property" later in this chapter for ways to make your application respond gracefully to being launched via OLE automation.

Getting a Report List

After opening a database, you can use the glrFillReportList subroutine (see Listing 22.3) to populate the Excel list box with the name of each report in the database. We accomplish this by using a For Each...Next loop to enumerate all the Document objects in the database's Reports container. If the list contains at least one report, the procedure selects the first item and enables the control.

Listing 22.3

```
Sub glrFillReportList()
    Dim objRptDoc As Document

    ' Make sure object reference is still valid
    If Not mobjAccess Is Nothing Then

        ' If so use a With...End With block to operate
        ' on the list box control on the main menu sheet
        With Worksheets("Main Menu").ListBoxes("lstReports")

            ' Clear the list
            .RemoveAllItems

            ' Use a For Each...Next loop to iterate through
            ' all the Document objects in the Reports
            ' container, adding them to the list box
            For Each objRptDoc In mobjAccess.CurrentDb. _
              Containers("Reports").Documents

                .AddItem objRptDoc.Name
```

```
        Next

        ' If there's at least one item in the list
        ' set the selection to the first item; otherwise
        ' disable the list box
        If .ListCount > 0 Then
            .ListIndex = 1
            .Enabled = True
        Else
            .Enabled = False
        End If
    End With
    End If
End Sub
```

There's really not much to say about glrFillReportList, because it uses the same technique to build a list of reports that you might use in an Access application. The only difference is the qualification of CurrentDB with the Object variable storing a reference to Access.

Previewing and Printing

Printing or previewing the report is where the fun starts in this sample application. Listing 22.4 shows the glrPrintReport procedure that manages this process. First, you must determine whether the report is currently open and if so, close it before opening it a second time. GlrPrintReport uses mobjAccess to call the Syscmd() function, which returns a value of acObjStateOpen if the report is open. You can see from this bit of code that including a reference to Access 95's type library makes coding easier by letting you use Access constants without your needing to redeclare them.

Listing 22.4

```
Private Declare Function glr_apiSetForegroundWindow _
 Lib "user32" Alias "SetForegroundWindow" ( _
 ByVal hwnd As Long) _
 As Long

Sub glrPrintReport()
    Dim strReport As String
    Dim intMode As Integer

    ' Get the report name from the selected item
```

```
        ' in the list box
        With Worksheets("Main Menu").ListBoxes("lstReports")
            strReport = .List(.ListIndex)
        End With

        ' Get the print mode from the option buttons
        If Worksheets("Main Menu").OptionButtons _
         ("optPreview") = xlOn Then
            intMode = acPreview     ' Preview
        Else
            intMode = acNormal      ' Print
        End If

        ' If report is already open, close it before
        ' trying to open it again
        If mobjAccess.SysCmd(acSysCmdGetObjectState, _
         acReport, strReport) = acObjStateOpen Then
            mobjAccess.DoCmd.Close acReport, strReport
        End If

        ' Open the report in Access
        mobjAccess.DoCmd.OpenReport strReport, acPreview

        ' Now if the report was opened in Preview view
        ' then we need to make sure the user can see it,
        ' right? So unhide the Access window and bring
        ' it to the front.
        If intMode = acPreview Then
            ' Show the Access window and switch to it
            mobjAccess.DoCmd.Maximize
            Call glrShowAccessWindow
            Call glr_apiSetForegroundWindow _
             (mobjAccess.hWndAccessApp)
        Else
            ' Hide the Access window
            Call glrHideAccessWindow
        End If
End Sub
```

Next, if a user decides to preview a report, we need to somehow put the Access main window in a position where the user can see it. We first maximize the report so it fills the Access window. (You'll notice that forms and reports opened via OLE automation are extremely small.) We then call a Win32 API function, SetForeground-Window(), to bring the Access window to the front. SetForegroundWindow() accepts a window handle as its sole argument and moves that window on top of all other open windows.

Quitting Access

The final step demonstrated in the sample application is quitting Access when you no longer need its services as an OLE server. GlrQuitAccess (see Listing 22.5) is a simple procedure that accomplishes this by setting the Object variable storing a reference to Access to the intrinsic constant Nothing. Not only does this free up resources used during the OLE automation session, it correctly terminates the connection to Access. By *correct* we mean that if we initiated the running instance, then that instance of Access will shut down. If, on the other hand, we did not initiate the instance (we used GetObject() to use an existing copy of Access), Access will continue running. The latter case assumes that the user had already launched a copy of Access and we should not automatically terminate it without warning.

Listing 22.5

```
Sub glrQuitAccess()
    If Not (mobjAccess Is Nothing) Then
        ' If a prevention form was opened, go
        ' ahead and close it from code
        If mobjAccess.SysCmd(acSysCmdGetObjectState, _
         acForm, "frmPrevent") = acObjStateOpen Then
            mobjAccess.Forms("frmPrevent").OKToClose = True
            mobjAccess.DoCmd.Close acForm, "frmPrevent"
        End If

        ' Destroy the contents of the object variable--
        ' if we launched Access this will shut it down,
        ' if Access was already running it won't
        Set mobjAccess = Nothing
    End If
End Sub
```

NOTE You can terminate a running instance of Access even if you used GetObject( ) to create the reference. Simply call the *Quit* method of Access' Application object before setting the Object variable to Nothing.

The sample procedure also includes code to close a form called frmPrevent in the open database if it exists and is open. This form prevents users from inadvertently closing the active database while you are controlling it using OLE automation. (See the section "Preventing Users from Closing the Database" later in this chapter for more information on this technique.)

While the sample application is simple, it does demonstrate a number of key techniques required to use Access as an OLE server, including creating an object reference, calling Access methods and properties, and terminating an OLE session. Given your knowledge of Access, as well as the techniques described in the rest of this book, you should be able to extend the examples given here into fully functional OLE automation applications. The remainder of this chapter discusses additional topics related to using Access as an OLE server, including calling user-defined functions using OLE automation and creating databases that work equally well whether run from the Access user interface or from OLE automation.

Calling User-Defined Functions from an OLE Client

In addition to using the properties and methods of Access objects, you can call user-defined subroutines and functions via OLE automation. By using this capability you can leverage functions already written, eliminating the need to rewrite them in the client application. You use two different methods to call procedures in an Access database, depending on whether they are declared in a global module or a form's CBF module.

Global Functions

Global functions are executed using the Run method of Access' Application object. In Access, Run executes functions or subroutines declared in a database that is not referenced by the current database, using the References dialog. (You can call functions in libraries or databases that are referenced without using Run.) You can see examples of this in Chapter 23. When controlling Access through OLE automation, you can use Run to call a procedure in the current database or any of the preloaded library databases, such as WZTOOL.MDA. Run accepts a variable number of arguments, up to 30, the first of which is the name of the function or subroutine you wish to execute. You use the remaining arguments of Run to pass any arguments the called procedure requires.

To demonstrate, CH22.MDB contains a function called glrListObjectsOLE(), which accepts a container name and an array (in the form of a Variant argument) as arguments and populates the array with the names of all documents in the chosen container. It also returns the number of documents as a result. You can call the function from an OLE client program by using Access' Run method. For example, the glrFillReportListOLE() function in CH22.XLS (see Listing 22.6) uses this approach to populate the sample application's list box with the names of reports from a database.

NOTE   The glrListObjectsOLE() and glrFillReportListOLE() functions are included only to demonstrate techniques for calling procedures and passing arguments to user-defined functions through OLE automation. The sample application does not call these functions. Since using glrFillReportListOLE() requires that glrListObjectsOLE() be declared in the selected database, the generic approach using the Reports container described above is used instead. If you want to test glrListObjectsOLE() and glrFillReportListOLE(), you'll need to replace calls to glrFillReportList() with glrFillReportListOLE() in CH22.XLS.

Listing 22.6

```
Function glrListObjectsOLE(strContainer As String, _
  varDocArray As Variant) As Integer
     ' Lists all the documents in a given DAO container
     ' and places the names into a passed array of
```

```
    ' Variants.

    Dim dbThis As Database
    Dim docAny As Document
    Dim intDoc As Integer

    ' Make sure argument is an array of variants
    If VarType(varDocArray) = vbVariant Or vbArray Then

        ' Clear existing values
        ReDim varDocArray(0) As Variant

        ' Get all document names in the container
        Set dbThis = CurrentDb
        For Each docAny In dbThis. _
         Containers(strContainer).Documents

            ' Increment the array and insert the name
            ReDim Preserve varDocArray(intDoc + 1)
            varDocArray(intDoc) = docAny.Name
            intDoc = intDoc + 1
        Next
    End If

    ' Set return value
    glrListObjectsOLE = intDoc
End Function

Sub glrFillReportListOLE()
    Dim varRpt As Variant
    Dim intRpt As Integer
    Dim intCRpt As Integer

    ' To pass an array to an Access function
    ' using OLE automation you must use a
    ' Variant variable and redimension it
    ' with one element (this forces VBA to
    ' treat the argument as an array)
    ReDim varRpt(1)

    ' Use the Reports list box control
    With Worksheets("Main Menu").ListBoxes("lstReports")

        ' Get rid of any existing values
        .Clear
```

```
        ' NOTE: to run this next line you must
        ' have a function called glrListObjectsOLE
        ' declared in CH22.MDB and that database
        ' must be the one open in Access. To use
        ' another database, copy the function to a
        ' module therein and change the reference
        ' to CH22 below to the name of that database
        intRpt = mobjAccess.Run("Ch22.glrListObjectsOLE", _
         "Reports", varRpt)

        ' intRpt will contain the number of
        ' reports in the loaded database--if
        ' there's at least one, add each name
        ' to the Reports list box
        If intRpt > 0 Then
            For intCRpt = 0 To intRpt - 1
                .AddItem varRpt(intCRpt)
            Next

            ' Highlight the first one in the list
            .ListIndex = 0
        End If
    End With
End Sub
```

By using the Run method you can pass literal values, as well as variables, as arguments to a procedure. If you pass a variable by reference, the called procedure can modify its value (as glrListObjectsOLE() does). When passing variables as arguments to called procedures via OLE automation, you must follow these guidelines:

- All passed variables must be declared as Variants in the calling procedure.

- Arguments can be declared as any scalar datatype in the called procedure.

- To pass an array, declare a Variant and redimension it with at least one element before passing it to the procedure.

The syntax of the Run method requires that you precede the name of the procedure with the name of the database (minus the file extension) it is declared in—CH22 in this case. If you want to use the glrListObjectsOLE() function in your applications, you must copy it either to a library database (and modify it to list the objects from the currently loaded user database) or to each individual database with which you want to use it. You must also edit the call to the Run method to reflect the name of the database in which glrListObjectsOLE() is declared. If this is a variable, you will need to parse the database name from the value returned from CurrentDB.Name or use another, similar method.

Form-Level Functions

Form-level functions, those declared in a form's module, are called differently from global functions. First of all, form-level functions must be explicitly declared as Public in order to be visible to calling programs. Once this is done, they become methods of the form and are called in the same way as any other methods that are using VBA. That is, you first obtain an object pointer to the form and then call one of its methods. The only difference with OLE automation is that you must qualify the Forms collection with a pointer to Access' Application object. Listing 22.7 shows a short procedure that calls a function named FClose(), declared in the frmCloseMe form from CH22.MDB. FClose() does nothing more than use the DoCmd.Close method to close the form, but it lets us express this as a built-in method of the form. (In the following example, assume that objAccess has already been set to Access' Application object.) Listing 22.8 shows the very small bit of code that makes up the FClose method, as well as an example of how you can call it from VBA code in Access. (We would have liked to call this function Close, but since that's an Access reserved word, we had to choose something else.)

Listing 22.7

```
Sub TestFormMethod
    Dim frm As Form

    If Not mobjAccess Is Nothing Then

        ' Open the form and set a pointer
        mobjAccess.DoCmd.OpenForm "frmCloseMe"
        Set frm = mobjAccess.Forms("frmCloseMe")

        ' Put some code in here that does something

        ' Close the form using its FClose method
        frm.FClose
    End If
End Sub
```

Listing 22.8

```
Public Function FClose()
    ' This public function acts as a new method
    ' of this form object. You can call it from
    ' VBA code in Access (see the cmdClose_Click
    ' procedure) or using OLE automation
    DoCmd.Close acForm, Me.Name
End Function

Private Sub cmdClose_Click()
    ' Calls the new FClose method of this form
    Me.FClose
End Sub
```

If you've created a method that returns a value, you can capture that in a variable in the OLE client's code, just as you would for other methods that return values. Just make sure you include parentheses (as well as any arguments) after the method name.

Writing OLE-Friendly Applications

As you begin to use the OLE server features of Access, you may discover it makes sense to use the same database both as a user application in Access and as the subject of OLE automation control from another program. The suggestions in this section are aimed at helping you create an application that can serve both purposes well. By keeping in mind that your user may not always be at the helm, you can greatly leverage your time investment.

The UserControl Property

Access exports a property of its Application object that is very useful when creating databases that will be used by both end users and OLE automation clients. Called UserControl, this read-only property returns True if Access was launched by an end user or False if it was started by a request from an OLE automation client. You should use this property in your own application whenever you need to know how Access was started. For example, you might use this in your error-handling code to suppress message boxes unless UserControl returns True. The section "Creating Your Own Error Stack" later in this chapter uses this technique.

Also check the UserControl property in your AutoExec() function or the Open event of your startup form and suppress actions that don't make sense for a database being opened by another application. For instance, it is unlikely you'll want to waste time displaying a splash screen during an OLE automation session. In cases like this, the UserControl property allows you to selectively display forms and messages that make sense for a human user.

Hiding the Access Main Window

One problem with using Access as an OLE server is that the default behavior of Access' main window is to remain visible, regardless of the value of the Application object's Visible property. Unlike other applications, such as Microsoft Excel, Access minimizes, rather than hides, its main window when the Visible property is set to False. If the window is visible, there is always a chance a user will activate it and do something that would confuse your OLE automation code (closing the active database, for instance). You saw in the section "The Five-Part Process for Printing Reports Using OLE Automation," which described the sample application, that we hid the Access main window immediately after creating an object reference using the CreateObject() function. This is the best way to prevent users from tampering with the application while your OLE automation code is running. Listing 22.9 shows two procedures, glrHideAccessWindow and glrShowAccessWindow, which hide and display the Access main window, respectively. It also lists the Windows API call ShowWindow, which is necessary to change the window's visibility.

Listing 22.9

```
Private Declare Function glr_apiShowWindow _
 Lib "user32" Alias "ShowWindow" ( _
 ByVal hwnd As Long, _
 ByVal nCmdShow As Long) _
 As Long
Private Const glrc_apiSW_HIDE = 0
Private Const glrc_apiSW_NORMAL = 1

Sub glrHideAccessWindow()
    ' Hide the Access main window using ShowWindow
    ' with the SW_HIDE constant
```

```
    If Not mobjAccess Is Nothing Then
        Call glr_apiShowWindow(mobjAccess.hWndAccessApp, _
            glrc_apiSW_HIDE)
    End If
End Sub

Sub glrShowAccessWindow()
    ' Show the Access main window using ShowWindow
    ' with the SW_NORMAL constant
    If Not mobjAccess Is Nothing Then
        Call glr_apiShowWindow(mobjAccess.hWndAccessApp, _
            glrc_apiSW_NORMAL)
    End If
End Sub
```

Both procedures use the HwndAccessApp property of the Application object, which returns the window handle of Access' main window. ShowWindow accepts the window handle and changes the state of the window based on a constant passed as the second argument.

NOTE We chose to create two procedures to handle hiding and displaying the Access window because you cannot call procedures with arguments from an Excel command button. You could combine these procedures into one that accepted the view mode, glrcSW_NORMAL or glrcSW_HIDE, as an argument.

Preventing Users from Closing the Database

If you don't want to hide the Access window when using Access as an OLE server (perhaps because you're using an instance of Access launched by the user), another approach to prevent tampering is to keep the database open until your OLE automation code no longer needs it. You can accomplish this by opening a form that cannot be closed until code is run from your OLE client application. CH22.MDB contains a form called frmPrevent, which uses a module-level variable to determine whether or not the form can be closed. Listing 22.10 shows the contents of the form's module.

Listing 22.10

```
Option Compare Database
Option Explicit

' Private variable to control whether form
' (and thus database) can be closed--set by
' public Property Let statement
Private mfCanClose As Boolean

Property Get CanClose() As Boolean
    ' Property Get for the CanClose property--
    ' returns the value of the form variable
    CanClose = mfCanClose
End Property

Property Let CanClose(fCanClose As Boolean)
    ' Property Let for the CanClose property--
    ' sets the value of the form variable and
    ' sets the state of the form's check box
    mfCanClose = fCanClose
    Me![chkCanClose] = fCanClose
End Property

Private Sub chkCanClose_AfterUpdate()
    ' Checking the check box lets the user
    ' close the form
    mfCanClose = Me![chkCanClose]
End Sub

Private Sub Form_Unload(Cancel As Integer)
    ' This code prevents the form from closing
    ' if the CanClose property is False--to
    ' close the form the user must click the
    ' check box or OLE automation code must
    ' set the value of CanClose to True
    If Not Me.CanClose Then

        ' If the form cannot be closed display
        ' a warning to the user if UserControl
        ' is True, otherwise just beep once
        If Application.UserControl Then
            MsgBox "Cannot close.", vbCritical
        Else
```

```
            Beep
        End If

        ' Cancel the close
        Cancel = True
    End If
End Sub
```

Code in the form's Unload event checks a user-defined property of the form called CanClose, which is initialized to False. If the property is still False during processing of the Unload event, the event procedure prevents the form from closing. Since Access will not unload the database if the form cannot be closed, preventing the form from closing prevents the database from being closed, as well. Code in glrLoadDatabase in the sample application attempts to load frmPrevent as hidden after opening a database. Code in both glrLoadDatabase and glrQuitAccess calls glrClosePreventForm (see Listing 22.11), which closes frmPrevent, thus allowing the database to be closed.

Listing 22.11

```
Private Const glrcPreventForm = "frmPrevent"

Sub glrClosePreventForm()
    ' If the prevention form was opened, set its
    ' CanClose property to True, allowing it to
    ' be closed, then close it
    If mobjAccess.SysCmd(acSysCmdGetObjectState, _
      acForm, glrcPreventForm) = acObjStateOpen Then

        mobjAccess.Forms(glrcPreventForm).CanClose = True
        mobjAccess.DoCmd.Close acForm, glrcPreventForm
    End If
End Sub
```

GlrClosePreventForm uses Access' SysCmd() function to determine whether frmPrevent is open in the loaded database. If so, the procedure sets the form's CanClose property to True and then closes the form. As explained in the previous paragraph, this will allow the database itself to close. If you want to use this technique in your applications, be sure to copy the frmPrevent form from CH22.MDB to your database files.

Being User-Input Aware

When designing your applications, keep in mind that any type of forced user input will interrupt the successful completion of actions initiated via OLE automation. A good example is the Employee Sales by Country report in Northwind.MDB. It's based on a parameter query that requires users to enter a range of dates before it can print. Launching this report from OLE automation (especially if the Access main window were hidden) would cause your client code to time-out and fail. If you need to use objects that require user input, you should at the very least display and activate the main Access window so users can take action while your OLE automation code is waiting. Ideally, however, you should not use objects that halt the processing of an object's method.

Creating Your Own Error Stack

If you want to call your own functions from an OLE client, one challenge you face is returning meaningful error information to your application. If a user-defined function called via OLE automation fails, your client application will receive an OLE automation error that may or may not be meaningful. One alternative is to maintain your own error stack in the server application, which the client can query to determine the status of any run-time errors. CH22.MDB contains code to do this in basErrorStack (see Listing 22.12). It works by opening a form containing an unbound list box and adding error information to the list. Since Access 95 forms can now expose methods and properties, you can retrieve error information from your OLE client application.

NOTE   If you write OLE automation server applications using Visual Basic 4.0, you can use the Raise method of VBA's Err object to return error information to an OLE automation client. VBA documentation states that not all host applications support using the Raise method in this fashion. Unfortunately, Access falls into this category. Using the Raise method in your code will produce a run-time error in your Access application, but this error will not be returned to any OLE client application.

Listing 22.12

```
Option Compare Database
Option Explicit

Const glrcErrForm = "frmErrorStack"

Sub glrInitErrs()
    ' If the error form is open call its ClearErrors
    ' method, otherwise just open the form (the
    ' error list starts out blank)
    If SysCmd(acSysCmdGetObjectState, acForm, _
     glrcErrForm) = acObjStateOpen Then

        Call Forms(glrcErrForm).ClearErrors
    Else
        DoCmd.OpenForm _
         formname:=glrcErrForm, _
         windowmode:=acHidden
    End If
End Sub

Sub glrPushError(ByVal lngError As Long, _
 ByVal strError As String, ByVal strProc As String)

    ' If the error form is open add the error
    ' information to the list
    If SysCmd(acSysCmdGetObjectState, acForm, _
     glrcErrForm) = acObjStateOpen Then

        Call Forms(glrcErrForm).AddError( _
         lngError, strError, strProc)
    End If
End Sub

Sub TestStack()
    ' Set up error handling
    On Error GoTo TestStack_Error

    ' Flush any existing errors
    Call glrInitErrs

    ' Fake an error
    Debug.Print 1 / 0
```

```
TestStack_Exit:
    Exit Sub
TestStack_Error:
    ' If Access was launched by the user display
    ' a dialog box, otherwise push the error
    ' information onto our homemade stack
    If UserControl Then
        MsgBox Err.Description, vbExclamation, _
         "Error " & Err.Number
    Else
        Call glrPushError(Err.Number, _
         Err.Description, "TestStack")
    End If
    Resume TestStack_Exit
End Sub
```

Listing 22.12 shows the contents of basErrorStack, which includes two procedures for managing the error information and one for testing purposes. The first procedure, glrInitErrs, opens the error stack form (frmErrorStack) and clears existing error information. Note that we open the form hidden so it is not obvious to users who may be working with Access. You should call glrInitErrs at the head of any procedure within which you want to trap errors.

After calling glrInitErrors, call glrPushError in your error-handling code to push error information onto the stack. GlrPushError requires three parameters—the error number, the error description, and the procedure name—and calls the AddError method of the error stack form (see Listing 22.13). TestStack demonstrates the use of the previous two procedures. You'll notice that it calls glrInitErrors immediately after establishing error handling with the On Error Goto statement. Further down in the procedure's error handling code, it calls glrPushError with the error information only if UserControl returns False. If the UserControl property returns True, the procedure displays a message box. This illustrates how an application could be used both interactively by a user and as the server for an OLE automation client.

Listing 22.13 shows the code contained in frmErrorStack's VBA module that manages the list of errors on the form. It includes public methods to clear the error list (ClearErrors) and add items to it (AddError). It also includes Property Get statements to return error information. You call each of the properties, ErrNo, ErrDesc, and ErrProc, by passing an index into the collection of errors, with 0 being the most recent error. Note the similarities between this technique and the DAO Errors collection. To determine how many errors exist on the stack, you can query the ErrCount property.

Listing 22.13

```
Option Compare Database
Option Explicit

Property Get ErrNo(ByVal intErr As Integer) As Variant
    ' Property Get statement to return a particular
    ' error number--works by changing the BoundColumn
    ' property and returning the data for a given row
    If intErr > Me![lstErrors].ListCount Then
        ErrNo = -1
    Else
        Me![lstErrors].BoundColumn = 1
        ErrNo = Me![lstErrors].ItemData(intErr)
    End If
End Property

Property Get ErrDesc(ByVal intErr As Integer) As Variant
    ' Property Get statement to return a particular
    ' error description--works by changing the BoundColumn
    ' property and returning the data for a given row
    If intErr > Me![lstErrors].ListCount Then
        ErrDesc = "#Error#"
    Else
        Me![lstErrors].BoundColumn = 2
        ErrDesc = Me![lstErrors].ItemData(intErr)
    End If
End Property

Property Get ErrProc(ByVal intErr As Integer) As Variant
    ' Property Get statement to return a particular
    ' error procedure--works by changing the BoundColumn
    ' property and returning the data for a given row
    If intErr > Me![lstErrors].ListCount Then
        ErrProc = "#Error#"
    Else
        Me![lstErrors].BoundColumn = 3
        ErrProc = Me![lstErrors].ItemData(intErr)
    End If
End Property

Property Get ErrCount() As Long
    ' Property Get statement to return the number of
    ' errors--works by returning the ListCount of the
    ' list box
```

```
    ErrCount = Me![lstErrors].ListCount
End Property

Public Sub ClearErrors()
    ' Public method to clear the error list
    Me![lstErrors].RowSource = ""
End Sub

Public Sub AddError(ByVal lngErrNo As Long, _
 ByVal strErrDesc As String, ByVal strProc As String)

    ' Public method to add an error to the list--
    ' works by adding text to the RowSource property
    Me![lstErrors].RowSource = lngErrNo & ";" & _
     strErrDesc & ";" & strProc & ";" _
     & Me![lstErrors].RowSource
End Sub
```

To demonstrate how this error stack works, we've included a test procedure in CH22.XLS called glrTestErrorStack (see Listing 22.14). It calls the TestStack() function in basErrorStack using the Application object's Run method. You can see from Listing 22.12 that we've intentionally forced a division-by-zero error in TestStack. Before you run glrTestErrorStack, be sure to edit the line containing the Open-CurrentDatabase statement to reflect the location of CH22.MDB on your computer. When you run the procedure, Excel uses CreateObject() to open a new instance of Access. This is necessary to create an instance in which the UserControl property is False. After opening CH22.MDB, the procedure then calls the TestStack() function, which contains the division-by-zero error. Since UserControl is False, this will place the error information on our custom stack rather than display an error message.

Listing 22.14

```
Sub glrTestErrorStack()
    Dim objAccess As Object
    Dim frmErrors As Form
    Dim intCErr As Integer

    ' Create Access Application object using
    ' CreateObject--this is necessary to create
    ' an instance where the UserControl
    ' property returns False
    Set objAccess = CreateObject(glrcClassID)
    If Not objAccess Is Nothing Then
```

```
' Open CH22.MDB--edit the line below
' to reflect the path to CH22.MDB on
' your computer
objAccess.OpenCurrentDatabase "CH22.MDB"

' Run the TestStack routine in CH22.MDB--
' this will generate an error and put it on
' the stack.
objAccess.Run "Ch22.TestStack"

' Get a pointer to the error stack form
Set frmErrors = objAccess.Forms("frmErrorStack")

' Check the error count--if it's greater than
' zero loop through each, displaying a message
If frmErrors.ErrCount > 0 Then

    For intCErr = 0 To frmErrors.ErrCount - 1

        ' Create an error message in this app
        ' by calling the ErrDesc, ErrNo, and
        ' ErrProc properties of the error form
        MsgBox frmErrors.ErrDesc(intCErr), _
            vbExclamation, "Error " & _
            frmErrors.ErrNo(intCErr) _
            & " in " & frmErrors.ErrProc(intCErr)
    Next

        ' Clear the error stack now that we're done
        frmErrors.ClearErrors
    End If
  End If
End Sub
```

After calling the test procedure, glrTestErrorStack gets a reference to the error stack form and stores it in the frmErrors object variable. It then uses this variable to examine the ErrCount property of the form. If there's at least one error (which there will be in this test case), glrTestErrorStack loops through each one, using the ErrDesc, ErrNo, and ErrProc properties to extract the relevant information and display it in an Excel message box. Finally, the procedure calls the ClearErrors method to flush the error stack. Figure 22.2 shows what your screen might look like if you ran glrTestErrorStack on your own computer. Figure 22.3, on the other hand, shows frmErrorStack after being made visible with the Window ➤ Unhide command. To

FIGURE 22.2:

Excel session showing error information returned from our custom stack

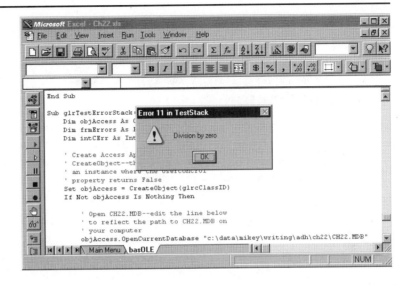

FIGURE 22.3:

Error stack form in Access showing a single error

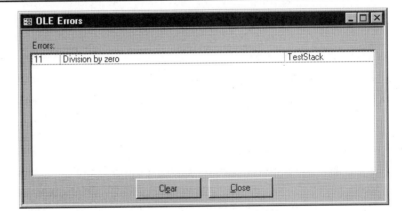

view this yourself, you'll have to pause execution before calling the ClearErrors method.

The downside to this approach is that you must manually query the stack's error count after each call to a user-defined function using OLE automation. This is because there will be no run-time error in your client application; from your application's perspective, everything will be fine. If you call a lot of user-defined functions with OLE automation, however, the additional information provided by our error stack may be well worth the effort.

Switching Back to the Client Application

In the sample application the user can print or preview a report. If the user chooses to preview the report, the code opens it in Preview view, displays the Access window, and moves it to the foreground. At this point it relinquishes control to the user, who can print the report, close it, or take any number of other actions. For users uncomfortable with the idea of switching between multiple applications, you can provide a way for them to return to your OLE client application from Access.

VBA offers an AppActivate method that accepts a window title as an argument. It activates the first application with a top-level window with a caption matching that title. If it can't find an exact match, it looks for a window with a caption that begins with the string passed as an argument. This is helpful for MDI applications (such as those in Microsoft Office) that include the caption of a child window in the title bar when the child window is maximized. For example, this statement would activate a running instance of Microsoft Excel, no matter which worksheet has the input focus:

```
AppActivate "Microsoft Excel"
```

If you expose the Access user interface to your users, as we do in the sample application, you can give them a way to switch back to your application by calling App-Activate in response to some event. Figure 22.4 shows a report from CH22.MDB in Print Preview view. If you look carefully at the toolbar, you'll see that we have added a custom toolbar button entitled "Return to Excel." This button calls the mcrReturnToExcel macro, which, in turn, calls glrReturnToApp(), a function declared in basReturn. This function accepts a window title and passes it to AppActivate. We used a wrapper function so we could call it from a toolbar button. Using this technique adds to the impression that Access is part of an integrated solution rather than an odd-ball component.

FIGURE 22.4:

A custom toolbar button activates Microsoft Excel.

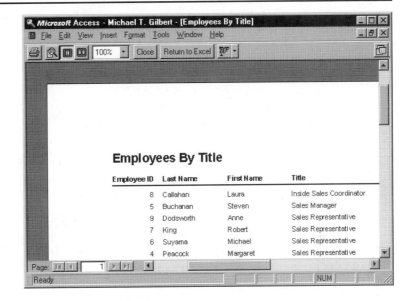

Summary

In this chapter we've introduced you to the few concepts you need to be familiar with in order to use Access as an OLE server. Since you can use all the same objects, properties, and methods you can when programming in Access alone, you should be able to write or port code that uses Access as an OLE server very quickly and easily. In summary:

- You create a reference to Access.Application using CreateObject(), GetObject(), or New.

- All Access properties and methods must be qualified with an object variable.

- You can use the Run method to call user-defined global functions.

- You can use UserControl and other properties to create OLE-friendly applications.

PART VII

Finishing Touches

CHAPTER
TWENTY-THREE

Building Add-Ins

- Understanding what Access add-ins are

- Creating library databases, including menu add-ins

- Developing property builders

- Designing and implementing custom Wizards

Access is a unique product in that it is aimed both at end users seeking an easy-to-use database and developers looking for a powerful development platform. Somewhere in between is a group of users who demand more than a simple list manager but don't have the level of expertise required to call themselves developers. For this group of people Microsoft has provided extensions to Access generally known as *add-ins*. Add-ins are designed to simplify complex tasks by walking the user through various steps using easy-to-understand dialogs. You can create your own add-ins to assist your users or make working with Access easier for yourself. If you're really ambitious, you can create add-ins that can be sold commercially. In this chapter we'll explain how to create a variety of add-ins and give a number of examples to get you started.

Libraries and Wizards and Builders, Oh My!

In this chapter we'll discuss several different categories of add-ins:

- *Libraries* are add-ins that contain functions users can call from VBA code in their database. Access documentation often refers to any type of add-in as a library database. In this book we'll use this term for library databases that contain nothing but VBA code called from user databases.

- *Builders* are add-ins that assist the user in setting a property of a database object, usually through some type of dialog. Access' property sheets feature Build buttons (the small buttons with an ellipsis [...] that appear next to property values) that launch a builder when clicked.

- *Wizards* are add-ins that create new objects in a user's database. You can build Wizards that create new tables, queries, forms, and reports. You can also build Wizards that create new form and report controls.

In the following sections we explain some of the common elements of Access add-ins. We follow this up with extensive discussions of each type of add-in, including how to create, install, and distribute them.

Unsecured Wizard Code

Unlike previous versions of Access, Access 95 Wizards are shipped in a secured state, so you cannot look at any of the source code they contain. The decision to secure the Wizards was made to keep the Wizard code in a compiled state for best performance and to protect a large investment by Microsoft in the Wizard technology, which is now almost as big a part of the base functionality as the program code itself. Microsoft has, however, made available unsecured versions of the Wizards with the proprietary code removed. They have also granted the right to distribute these libraries on the companion CD-ROM.

If you are serious about writing Wizards that look and act like those that come in the Access box, you might find a trip through the source code interesting. You won't find any comments, and the code is, at times, difficult to follow, but it offers numerous examples and tidbits of information that have proven invaluable to many Access developers.

Entry Points for Add-Ins

Access provides five ways for a user to launch an add-in. This chapter explains how to write add-ins to take advantage of these entry points, shown in Table 23.1.

TABLE 23.1: Entry Points for Access Add-Ins

Entry Point	Remarks
Menu add-in	To make menu add-ins available, select Tools ➤ Add-ins from Access' menus
Wizard	Table, Query, Form, and Report Wizards are available from the list of Wizards Access displays when a user creates a new object
Control Wizard	Users launch Control Wizards when they create a new control on a form or report. Users can disable Control Wizards by toggling the Control Wizard button in the toolbox
Builder	Builders help users set property values. Users initiate builders by clicking the Build button on an Access property sheet
Library functions	Users call library functions directly from their own VBA code

All add-ins, regardless of their purpose or entry point, are initiated by a function call. With the exception of library functions, Access calls all add-in functions directly in response to the events listed in Table 23.1, and the declaration of these functions is predetermined. The sections that follow detail the proper way to declare each type of function.

CurrentDB() versus CodeDB()

One important difference between writing DAO code in library databases versus normal databases is your use of the CurrentDB() function. In a normal database, CurrentDB() returns a pointer to the database in which the executing code is located. This is merely a coincidence, however, because CurrentDB() is actually designed to return a reference to the database that is loaded in Access' user interface. Using CurrentDB() in a library database can be problematic if you are trying to reference the library database, not the current user database.

To reference a library database, use the CodeDB() function instead. CodeDB() returns a pointer to the database that contains the executing code. When you are developing your library databases in Access' user interface, CodeDB() works just like CurrentDB(). When running in a library database, however, CodeDB() will reference it, not the user database. You'll see an example of using CodeDB() in the section "A Sample Form Wizard" later in this chapter.

Add-Ins and the Registry

Access 95 depends heavily on settings in the Windows Registry, and add-ins are no exception. Add-in information is stored in the Registry tree in several locations. Figure 23.1 shows the Registry open to the Access 95 branch (HKEY_LOCAL_MACHINE\Software\Microsoft\Access\7.0). Normally, Access stores add-in information directly under the 7.0 key. If you're using user profiles, however (see Appendix C on the companion disk for more information on user profiles), Access may also store add-in information on a user-by-user basis under the profile key for each user.

The following sections on libraries, builders, and Wizards explain how to create Registry entries for each type of add-in.

FIGURE 23.1:
Windows Registry settings showing keys for add-ins and Wizards

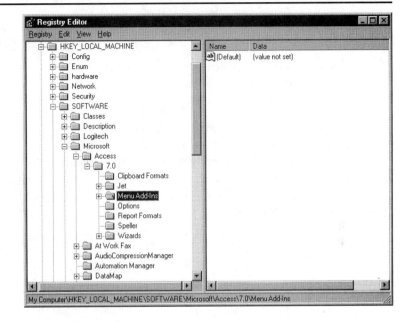

Creating Library Databases

Library databases are those that contain code modules with common functions shared by a number of applications. The benefit of creating a code library is that it relieves you from having to create and maintain a separate version of a function in each database where it is called. Creating library databases in Access 95 is relatively straightforward. The trick is making them available to other applications. (The concept of references, introduced in Chapter 21, comes into play here.) In this section we explain a number of issues related to creating library databases, including structuring library code modules, using library databases, and some of the reference issues involved.

Structuring Library Code Modules

What you put in an Access library database is really up to you. As you write more and more applications, you will find common functions on which you depend in each. These are all good candidates for library databases. How you structure your library databases, though, is important; it will dictate how well your applications perform and the amount of memory they require. Assuming that a "good" library database is one that loads quickly and consumes little memory, you can make decisions on how to structure library databases to meet these goals. To determine the best way to structure library databases, you need to understand how Access treats the VBA code they contain.

One improvement in Access 95 is *dynamic loading* of VBA code. In Access 2.0, all global modules (as opposed to form and report modules) were loaded into memory when a database was opened. This applied to library databases, as well as to user databases opened through the user interface. As a result, users paid a penalty of increased load time, especially of large applications, even if they never called a function in a global module. Access 95, on the other hand, does not load a VBA module until it is needed. Users still suffer slightly during the initial load process, but now this takes place incrementally rather than all at once. The important thing to understand about this process, from a developer's standpoint, is how Access determines when a module is needed.

Obviously, if your code calls a function in a particular VBA module, Access must load that module into memory. Access loads the entire module, even if you're going to call only a single function. The same holds true if you reference a global variable declared in a VBA module. Therefore, the first rule for creating library databases is to separate those functions that are called frequently from those that are called infrequently. By putting infrequently called procedures in separate modules, you will prevent Access from loading them until they are actually used. In fact, it is not too outrageous to suggest placing procedures that are called extremely infrequently in individual modules of their own. Alternatively, by centralizing frequently used functions in one module, you virtually ensure that the module will already be loaded into memory when you call a function it contains.

Beyond searching for simple references, Access examines the *potential call tree* dictated by a loaded module and loads any other modules that are dependent on the tree. A module's potential call tree is determined by the procedures in other modules that are referenced by procedures in the original module. Access preloads these other modules in anticipation of calls to procedures within them. This means that even if you break up your library database into several modules in an effort to reduce the amount of code loaded into memory, if you call procedures in one module from procedures in another, both modules will be loaded anyway. For this reason it sometimes makes sense to duplicate common procedures rather than maintain one copy in a single module.

Using a Library Database

In Chapter 21 we introduced the concept of code references as a way for you to write VBA code that called methods and used properties implemented by OLE automation servers. We also explained the consequences of moving, deleting, or otherwise altering a reference once you had created it. Access library databases are subject to the same reference requirements as OLE automation server type libraries. That is, before you can call a function in a library database, you must establish a reference to it.

We've included a sample library database called CH23LIB.MDA that contains two small but useful functions, glrMin() and glrMax(), which compute the minimum and maximum values, respectively, within a list of numbers. The module basLibraryFunctions, in CH23LIB.MDA on the companion disk, shows the definition of these two procedures. Note that both use a ParamArray argument to accept a variable number of parameters. (ParamArray arguments are explained in detail in Chapter 2.) We can use CH23LIB.MDA to demonstrate the process of setting a library reference and calling a library function.

To demonstrate the referencing process, you'll need to create a new database. Then, follow these steps:

1. Create a new module in the database.
2. Select Tools ➤ References to display the References dialog.
3. Click the Browse button on the References dialog.
4. Select "Databases (*.mdb; *.mda)" from the list of file types on the Add Reference dialog that appears.
5. Locate the CH23LIB.MDA file and click OK. You should now see CH23LIB.MDA in the Available References list box on the References dialog.
6. Click OK to close the References dialog.

You can now call glrMin() and glrMax() from the new database. To test this, enter the subroutine shown here (or something similar) in the new module and run it from the Debug window:

```
Sub TestFunctions()
    MsgBox "Minimum: " & glrMin(3, 7, 8.9, -3, 10)
    MsgBox "Maximum: " & glrMax(3, 7, 8.9, -3, 10)
End Sub
```

As long as you maintain the reference to CH23LIB.MDA, the test procedure will continue to compile and work. If you break the link, by either moving or renaming the library database, Access complains that the reference to CH23LIB.MDA cannot be found.

Library Database Reference Issues

In Chapter 21 we discussed what happens when your VBA project loses a reference to an OLE automation server's type library. Access issues an error stating that the "Project or library cannot be found" and then opens the References dialog to display the offending reference. Access exhibits the same behavior when it cannot find a library database reference by another VBA project (see Figures 23.2 and 23.3). When this happens, you have the same two options. You can either use the Browse button to find the missing database or uncheck the box next to the reference to remove it from the project. If you opt for the latter, you must remove or comment out all references to procedures or variables declared in the missing library.

FIGURE 23.2:

You see this warning message when compiling a module after moving or renaming a library database.

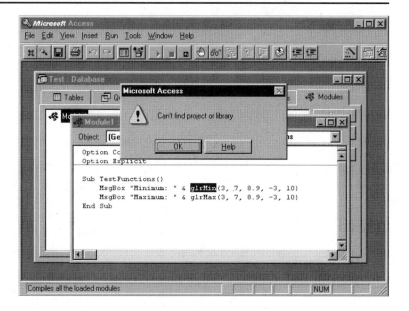

FIGURE 23.3:

References dialog showing that the reference to CH23LIB.MDA is missing

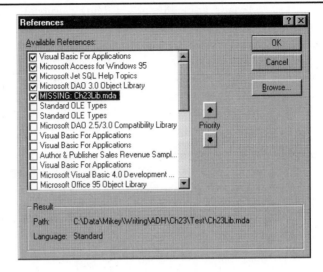

Lost references become an issue if you plan to distribute your library database to other users who might not install it in the same directory. Of course, you can insist that they install it to a particular directory, but most users don't take kindly to developers who insist on anything. Fortunately, there are several alternatives that will prevent references from becoming lost. First, if VBA is unable to locate a reference based on the *absolute path* that is saved with the project, it automatically tries to find the library using the same *relative path* as the database in which it is referenced. This means that Access will be able to find library databases if they are in the same directory as the database that uses them or in the same relative location. For example, if you create a database in C:\Test\Libs and reference it from a database in C:\Test\Apps, you can easily move them to C:\Prod\Libs and C:\Prod\Apps, respectively, with no problem.

If a relative path search proves unsuccessful, Access searches for the library database in the following places:

- The directory where Access is installed
- The Windows and Windows\System directories
- Any directory included in the environmental PATH variable

Finally, you can create a Registry entry that specifies another secondary location. This is a good idea if you plan to distribute several library databases, because it lets you choose one distinct location for installing all of them. To create these entries, add a Registry key called RefLibPaths under the HKEY_LOCAL_MACHINE\Software\Microsoft\Access\7.0 key. For each library, create a new string value with the name of the library database and a value indicating the path to that database. Figure 23.4 shows an example of this Registry setting.

FIGURE 23.4:

Registry key given an alternative location for library databases

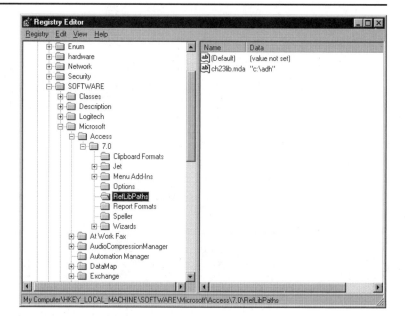

Circular References Are Not Allowed

Due to changes imposed by the integration of VBA into Access, you can no longer create circular references among libraries and database. This was never an issue in prior versions of Access because all public functions shared the same global name space. Procedures in any library could call procedures in any other. This is no longer the case. Any level of circularity is illegal. For example, Figure 23.5 shows two scenarios of call trees.

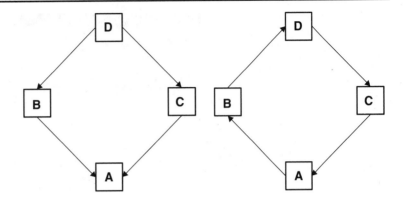

FIGURE 23.5:
Stacked, but not circular, references are allowed.

Given the first scenario in Figure 23.5, procedures in modules B and C can call procedures in module A. Procedures in module D, in turn, can call procedures in modules B and C. The second scenario is not allowed, however, because the call tree of A to B to C to D and back to A results in a circular reference.

Editing Loaded Library Code

Once you've created a library database, you should install it as described in the previous sections and test it by calling library functions from a user database. If you find problems in your code, you can easily make modifications without unloading the library and restarting Access. To do this, you first set a reference to your library and then open the Object Browser dialog and select your library from the list of libraries and databases (see Figure 23.6). You can then use the Object Browser to view both the modules in your library and the procedures they contain.

To view a procedure definition, select it from the list of procedures shown in the Methods/Properties list box and click the Show button. Access opens a module window and brings up the appropriate code. You can then make changes and continue to test your library.

Using Application.Run to Postpone Loading

In the section "Structuring Library Code Modules" earlier in this chapter, we explained that Access preloads VBA modules based on a given module's potential call

FIGURE 23.6:

Using the Object Browser to view
procedures in a loaded library
database

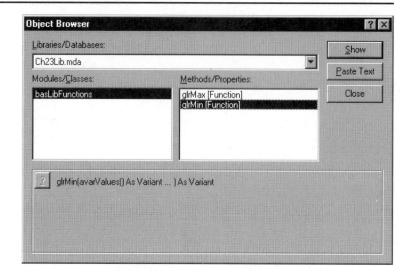

tree. This may result in excessive load times if a module has a particularly complex
call tree. You can delay load time until a procedure is actually called by using the
Run method of Access' Application object. You saw in Chapter 22 how you could
use Run to execute procedures in one Access database from another using OLE
automation. You can use the same technique to call procedures in library databases.
The advantage of this approach is that VBA does not try to resolve the reference until run time, preventing any preloading that might otherwise occur.

Run accepts the name of a procedure and up to 30 of the procedure's arguments.
You can use it to execute both subroutines and functions. For example, you could
modify the sample procedure listed above to use the Run method, thus forcing Access to delay loading CH23LIB.MDA until the Run method is executed. The sample
procedure shown below demonstrates this. (Note that the first argument to Run is
the name of the procedure.)

```
Sub TestFunctionsUsingRun()
    MsgBox "Minimum: " & Application.Run( _
    "glrMin", 3, 7, 8.9, -3, 10)
End Sub
```

Another benefit of using Run is that instead of loading all the modules referenced
by one module's call tree, Access loads only the module containing the procedure
passed to Run. You can also preface the procedure name with the name of a library

database (for example, "Ch23Lib.glrMin") to force Access to call the procedure in the given library. You might use this capability if two libraries declare different procedures with the same name. In fact, it is a good practice if you are writing lots of libraries because it prevents name collisions between your libraries and those developed by others.

Using the LoadOnStartup Key

If you don't want to maintain a reference to a library but still want to use Application.Run, you can force Access to look for procedures in other library databases using the LoadOnStartup Registry key. When you use the Run method and Access cannot find the specified procedure in any of the loaded or referenced libraries, it searches for it in any databases listed under this key. Figure 23.7 shows the key and two sample entries. You must add this key yourself (it is not created by default) and add string values for each of the libraries in which you want Access to look.

LoadOnStartup uses a format similar to the Libraries section of Access 2.0's initialization file, MSACC20.INI. Each string value contained in the key is named after a library database, including the complete path if it is *not* located in the Access 95

FIGURE 23.7:
LoadOnStartup Registry key showing additional libraries to search

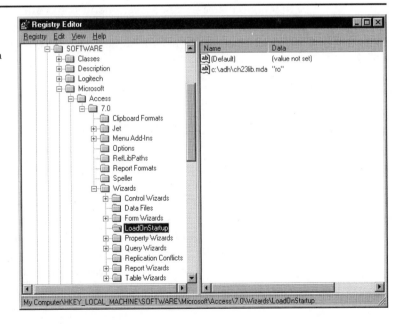

directory. The value must be "rw" for read/write. Unlike Access 2.0 libraries, however, databases listed under the LoadOnStartup key are not loaded into memory when Access 95 starts, as the key name implies. Instead, Access loads only the module and procedure lists. The modules themselves are not loaded until a procedure is executed using Application.Run.

Always Compile Your Libraries

One final topic regarding library databases relates to VBA code compilation. Because a library database contains nothing but code, you don't have to worry about the database becoming decompiled once you have compiled it. Therefore, since compiled VBA code loads and executes more quickly than uncompiled code, be sure to compile and save all modules prior to distributing it to users. A complete discussion of VBA compilation issues is provided in Appendix D on the companion disk.

Menu Add-Ins: The Simplest Add-Ins

Perhaps the simplest add-in you can create is a menu add-in. Menu add-ins are functions that are called by a menu command under Access' Tools ➤ Add-ins menu. You can call any function from a menu command by making a few entries in the Windows Registry. Figure 23.8 shows the Registry keys for the default add-ins, along with the Registry values for Access' Switchboard Manager add-in.

To create a menu add-in, you first add a new Registry key beneath the Menu Add-Ins key shown in Figure 23.8. Access will use the name of the key as the menu command on the Add-ins fly-out menu. You can see from Figure 23.8 that you can precede a character with an ampersand to make that character the access key for the menu command. After creating the key, you must create two String values, named Library and Expression.

Access uses the Library value to identify which database contains the add-in's main function. The Expression value contains the code fragment that Access must evaluate to invoke the add-in itself. In Figure 23.8, the value for Expression, =sbm_Entry(), is a function call, including the equal sign and parentheses. You can create your own menu add-ins very simply by calling a function in a library database.

FIGURE 23.8:

Registry entries for menu add-ins

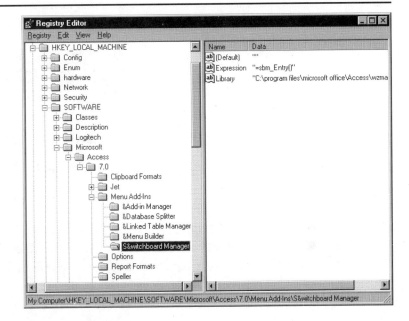

Building Your Own Builders

Builders (sometimes called Property Wizards) are subroutines in library databases that assist you in setting properties of objects in an Access database. When you select a property in Access' property sheet and the Build button appears—the tiny button with an ellipsis (...) on it—that's your cue that a builder is available for that property. Access ships with a number of builders. You can also write your own builders by following the few simple rules outlined in the following sections. We also describe two sample builders that are included with this book's sample files.

The Sample Builders

We've created two sample builders to demonstrate the basic requirements for creating your own builders. Both builders are implemented in CH23BLD.MDA.

You can use the System Color Builder to set Access color properties to Windows system colors by selecting them from a dialog that emulates Windows' Display Properties dialog (see Figure 23.9). Because there are three properties that relate to color, we'll need to install this builder to work with each one of them.

FIGURE 23.9:

Sample System Color Builder

Access 95 is much better than version 2.0 about using system colors. The default background color for new forms, for example, is the system color for 3D objects (like command buttons). When a user makes changes to these colors through the Control Panel, Access automatically updates each form. This was not the case in Access 2.0. You will find the System Color Builder useful when updating forms created in version 2 to make them compatible with Access 95 forms.

You can use the DoMenuItem Builder, shown in Figure 23.10, to create DoMenuItem statements in your VBA code. It manages the individual lists of menu entries and automatically creates DoMenuItem statements in any VBA module. If you use DoMenuItem statements a lot, you will appreciate this builder.

FIGURE 23.10:

Sample DoMenuItem Builder

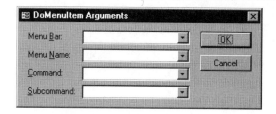

Writing a Builder Function

You create builders by writing VBA functions that Access uses to set property values. Access requires that builder functions follow a strict set of rules. These rules can be summarized as follows:

- Builder functions must be declared with a specific set of three arguments.
- Builder functions must return the new property value as a string.
- Any forms opened through code in the builder function must be opened in dialog mode.

The following table lists the required builder function arguments:

Argument	Datatype	Description
strObject	String	Name of the table, query, form, report, or module object on which the builder function is operating
strControl	String	Name of the control to which the property applies
strCurVal	String	Current property value

Note that the argument names are arbitrary. Only their position in the declaration is important. When you initiate a builder, Access calls the builder function, passing it values in the three arguments. This is similar in concept to the callback functions for filling list boxes (see Chapter 7).

In the body of your builder function, you can use the information provided by the arguments to decide how your builder function should continue. Once you've computed the new value for the property, you must return it as a String result of the builder function.

How you compute the new value is where writing builder functions gets interesting. You can do just about anything you wish inside the builder function: open dialogs, call other procedures, or query databases. The only restriction Access places on you is that you must open forms as dialogs. This ensures that code execution in your builder function will halt until the dialog form is closed or hidden. Access requires, when a builder function terminates, that the screen be left in the same state it was in when the function was called. Leaving nonmodal forms hanging around would violate this rule.

The structure of builder functions will become clear as we explain the two sample builders we've included with this book—a builder that lets you set object color values to Windows system colors and a builder to create DoMenuItem statements. First, however, we must explain how Access knows a builder has been installed. For that we'll need to take yet another trip into the Windows Registry.

Builder Registry Entries

The Registry settings for Access include a host of keys and values that relate to builder functions. Access maintains individual builder keys beneath HKEY_LOCAL_MACHINE\Software\Microsoft\Access\7.0\Wizards\Property Wizards. Each Registry key is named after the property to which it applies. When Access starts up, it reads the list of keys from the Registry and makes the Build button available for properties that have builders defined. Access does not attempt to execute a builder function, however, until a user actually clicks the Build button. Although only a small number of properties are assigned builders when you install Access, you can create builders for every built-in Access property. See the next section, "Creating New Builder Entries," for information on how to add Registry keys to do this.

Access allows more than one builder for each property. Each individual builder is denoted by separate Registry keys beneath the key that corresponds to a property. Figure 23.11 displays the Registry tree expanded to show the settings for Microsoft's default BackColor Builder. When Access finds two builders defined for the same property, it displays a dialog like the one shown in Figure 23.12 that allows the user to choose which builder to use.

The key name for each builder (MSBackColorBuilder in this example) is arbitrary and serves only to identify the builder to Access. Each separate key needs to be unique, however. When deciding on a name for your builders, be sure to keep that in mind. Each individual builder key must contain four values. You can see them in the right pane of the Registry Editor window in Figure 23.11. Each of these values is explained in Table 23.2.

FIGURE 23.11:

Registry settings for Microsoft's
BackColor Builder

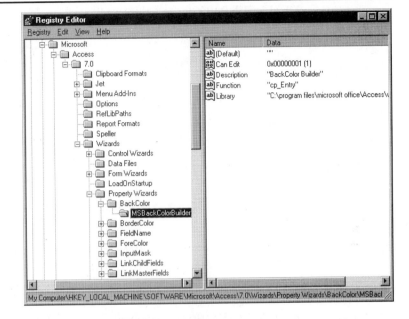

FIGURE 23.12:

Access dialog for selecting which
builder to use

TABLE 23.2: Registry Values for Property Builders

Value Name	Value Type	Remarks
Can Edit	DWORD	Set to 1 to allow a builder to operate on an existing value. It is hard to imagine an Access property with no existing value (even a null), but if you ever find one and don't want your builder to change it, make the Can Edit value 0
Description	String	Set to the description of your builder. Access will use this description in the builder dialog when more than one builder is defined for the same property

TABLE 23.2: Registry Values for Property Builders (continued)

Value Name	Value Type	Remarks
Function	String	Set to the name of your builder function with no arguments or parentheses. Remember that builder functions have a fixed set of arguments that Access will supply when the function is called
Library	String	Set to the path to the library database that contains the builder function. You can omit the path if your library database is located in the Access directory

Creating New Builder Entries

To add a new builder and have Access recognize it, you must create a new set of entries. In this section we show you how to make the entries to install the sample builders. Normally, though, you won't have to do this manually. The section "Distributing and Installing Add-Ins" later in this chapter discusses how to set up your library database so Access' Add-in Manager can automatically create the entries for you. Because Windows 95–compatible products such as Access depend so heavily on the Windows Registry, however, you should be comfortable with browsing and editing its contents. This example will serve as good practice.

To install our sample builders, you'll need to create a set of Registry entries for each. We'll start with the System Color Builder because it only involves adding keys to existing property entries. To install the System Color Builder, follow these steps:

1. Launch the Windows Registry editor by running REGEDIT.EXE.

2. Expand the HKEY_LOCAL_MACHINE hive to display the Property Wizard keys shown in Figure 23.11.

3. Locate and highlight the BackColor key and select Edit ➤ New ➤ Key. The Registry editor will add a new subkey beneath BackColor with the default name, New Key #1.

4. Overwrite the default name with a more descriptive name, such as GlrSystemColorBuilder. Your Registry should look like the one shown in Figure 23.13.

FIGURE 23.13:

Registry editor showing a new BackColor Builder key

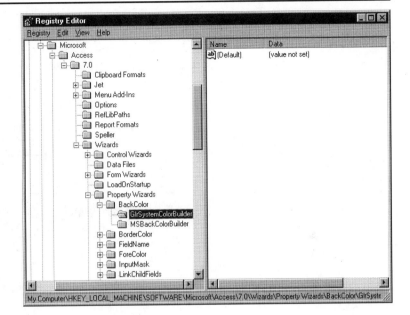

5. Select Edit ➤ New ➤ String Value to add a new String value to the GlrSystemColorBuilder key. The Registry editor assigns the name value the default name of New Value #1.

6. Overwrite the default name with "Description" and press Enter to save your changes.

7. Select Edit ➤ Modify or double-click the name value to change it. Enter "System Color Builder" and click the OK button.

8. Repeat steps 5 through 7 for each of the values listed in Table 23.3. Your Registry should now look like the one shown in Figure 23.14.

That's all it takes to install the System Color Builder to work with any BackColor property in Access. If you want to install the builder to use the other color properties, ForeColor and BorderColor, you will need to repeat the preceding steps to create new builder keys beneath each property key. If you find this too tedious, wait for the section "Using the Add-In Manager" later in this chapter. We'll explain how to use it to create these keys for you.

TABLE 23.3: Registry Values for the System Color Builder

Value Type	Value Name	Value
String	Description	System Color Builder
DWORD	Can Edit	1
String	Function	glrSysColorBuilder
String	Library	Set this to indicate the path to CH23BLD.MDA on your computer. For example: C:\ADH\CH23BLD.MDA

FIGURE 23.14:

Registry after creating settings for the System Color Builder

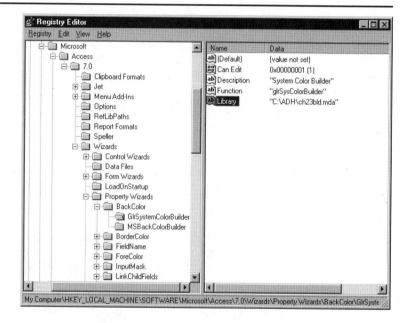

Installing the DoMenuItem builder requires basically the same steps we just described. The only twist is that the DoMenuItem Builder operates on a property for which there is no Registry key. You can install builders for properties that are not set up by Access by adding a new Registry key under Property Wizards, setting its name to the name of the property you want to manipulate. The DoMenuItem Builder, however, is a special builder (called a *code builder*) because it operates on VBA code, not an Access property. Therefore, to install it, you need to create a key called Module beneath Property Wizards. To install our sample code builder, follow these steps:

1. Highlight the Property Wizards key in the Registry and select Edit ➤ New ➤ Key.

2. Overwrite the default name with "Module" and press Enter.

3. Follow the steps described earlier to add a key beneath the new Module key called GlrDoMenuItemBuilder and the values shown in Table 23.4.

TABLE 23.4: Registry Values for the DoMenuItem Builder

Value Type	Value Name	Value
String	Description	DoMenuItem Builder
DWORD	Can Edit	1
String	Function	glrDMIBuilder
String	Library	Set this to indicate the path to CH23BLD.MDA on your computer. For example: C:\ADH\CH23BLD.MDA

If you do not follow this Registry structure exactly, Access issues an "Invalid add-in entry for *addinname*" message when you first launch it, where *addinname* is the name of the Registry key with invalid entries. Access does not provide any information in addition to the Registry key causing the problem, however. (For instance, it would be helpful to know the property key where the errant add-in was located.) If you see this error and can't find the problem, you can use the Registry editor's search capability to look for a key with the name of the errant add-in.

Now that the builders are installed, we can look at how they work.

The System Color Builder

How many times have you consulted the Access Help file to find the values for Windows system colors? While you can map constants to these values in VBA, you still need to enter the literal numbers in Access property sheets. The System Color Builder is a simple tool that sets these values using a dialog. Listing 23.1 shows the tool's builder function, glrSysColorBuilder(). (You can find this function in bas-Builders in CH23BLD.MDA.)

Listing 23.1

```
Function glrSysColorBuilder(strObjName As String, _
  strControl As String, strCurVal As String) As String

    On Error GoTo glrSysColorBuilder_Error

    ' Constant holds the name of builder form
    Const glrcFrmSysColBld = "frmSysColorBuilder"

    ' Open the builder form in dialog mode--this
    ' halts the code until the form is closed
    ' (by the Cancel button) or hidden (by the
    ' OK button)--note that we pass the current
    ' property value in the OpenArgs argument
    DoCmd.OpenForm FormName:=glrcFrmSysColBld, _
      WindowMode:=acDialog, _
      OpenArgs:=strCurVal

    ' Check to see if the form is still open--
    ' if so then the user clicked OK
    If SysCmd(acSysCmdGetObjectState, acForm, _
      glrcFrmSysColBld) = acObjStateOpen Then

        ' Set the return value to the value
        ' of the color combo box
        glrSysColorBuilder = CStr(Forms( _
          glrcFrmSysColBld)![cboColors])

        ' Close the builder form
        DoCmd.Close acForm, glrcFrmSysColBld
    Else
        glrSysColorBuilder = strCurVal
    End If

glrSysColorBuilder_Exit:
    Exit Function

glrSysColorBuilder_Error:
    MsgBox Err.description, vbExclamation, _
      "Error " & Err.Number
    Resume glrSysColorBuilder_Exit
End Function
```

GlrSysColorBuilder() simply opens the builder form, frmSysColorBuilder, in dialog mode and waits for the user to take some action. It passes the current property value (stored in the strCurVal argument) to the form in its OpenArgs property. Code in the form's Load event procedure sets the initial value of the system color combo box to this value. If the user clicks OK, VBA code in the form's module hides the form by setting its Visible property to False. Alternatively, if the user clicks the Cancel button, the form is closed. At this point glrSysColorBuilder() continues executing and SysCmd is called to determine whether the form is still open (but hidden).

If SysCmd returns acObjStateOpen, the builder assumes the user clicked OK. In this case glrSysColorBuilder() reads the value of the system color combo box and returns it to Access. It then closes the form. If, on the other hand, the user canceled the dialog, glrSysColorBuilder() returns the original property value. Note that you must return something as the result of a builder function; otherwise the property will be set to an empty string.

GlrSysColorBuilder() is an example of a basic procedure that demonstrates the minimum requirements for an Access builder function. It accepts the current value of a property, changes it in the body of the procedure (in this case, using a dialog form), and returns the changed value as a result.

NOTE   The System Color Builder form, which actually manages the process of accepting user input, contains a good deal of rather uninteresting code. Most of the VBA code is contained in Click and DblClick event procedures and is used to set the value of the combo box in response to mouse clicks. We have chosen not to include the actual code here.

The DoMenuItem Builder

We had a look at the DoMenuItem Builder in Chapter 19. It uses functions in the Access utilities library, MSAU700.DLL, to present the user with a list of menu commands. The builder creates a correctly structured DoCmd.DoMenuItem statement based on the user's selections. Figure 23.15 shows the DoMenuItem builder form.

FIGURE 23.15:

DoMenuItem builder form

Listing 23.2 shows the function that invokes the builder form, glrDMIBuilder().
Like glrSysColorBuilder(), this function is very small, serving only to open the
builder form, frmDMIBuilder, in dialog mode. Code in the form's VBA module
manages the lists of menu commands and the construction of a DoMenuItem statement. (For details on the menu-manipulation functions in MSAU700.DLL, see
Chapter 19.)

Listing 23.2

```
Function glrDMIBuilder(strObjName As String, _
 strControl As String, strCurVal As String) _
 As String

    ' Name of the DoMenuItem builder form
    Const glrcDMIForm = "frmDMIBuilder"

    ' Open form in dialog mode
    DoCmd.OpenForm glrcDMIForm, WindowMode:=acDialog

    ' If form is still open grab the value
    ' in the Result property
    If SysCmd(acSysCmdGetObjectState, acForm, _
     glrcDMIForm) = acObjStateOpen Then

        glrDMIBuilder = Forms(glrcDMIForm).Result
        DoCmd.Close acForm, glrcDMIForm
    End If
End Function
```

The important thing to point out is that glrDMIBuilder() returns a string containing the DoMenuItem statement (along with a helpful comment). Like all code
builders, the string is inserted into the active module at the current insertion point.

Figure 23.16 shows a module with the insertion point positioned just below the If...Then statement. If a code builder is invoked, either through the right-click shortcut menu or the Build button on the toolbar, any code generated will be inserted at this point. Figure 23.17 shows the dialog that appears when a code builder is invoked.

Code builders differ from other builders in that even when only one code builder is installed through the Registry, Access still displays the Choose Builder dialog shown in Figure 23.17. Normally, if only one builder is defined, Access invokes it automatically. There appears to be no way to circumvent the Choose Builder dialog.

Figure 23.18 shows the results of creating a DoMenuItem command that saves the current record. Note that Access inserts a line break before inserting the code generated by the builder. Additionally, all indentation must be part of the generated text.

FIGURE 23.16:

Module code prior to invoking a code builder

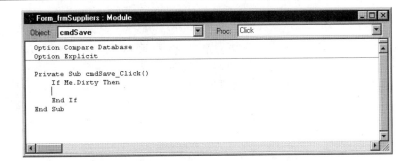

FIGURE 23.17:

Dialog that appears when a user invokes a code builder

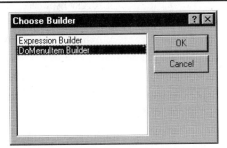

FIGURE 23.18:

Results of inserting
builder-generated code

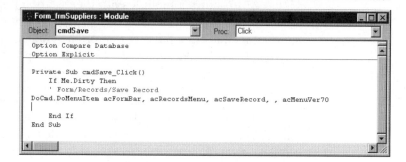

FIGURE 23.18:

Results of inserting
builder-generated code

> **NOTE**
>
> The DoMenuItem Builder generates a very small amount of VBA code. For code builders that create large blocks of code, it is often impractical to embed all of this code in the builder's module. In these cases you should use an Access table to store the generated code. Not only is this easier to manage, it makes updating the code easier, as well, because you can edit data in a table using much less effort than when editing multiple lines of VBA source code. The section "Using an Access Table to Store Code" later in this chapter explains how to do this.

Developing Custom Wizards

One of the most interesting areas of Access development is the creation of custom Wizards. Wizards let you extend the product in a way that is both unique and tightly integrated. In a sense, your Wizards become part of the product itself. In this section we show you how to create new Wizards using a framework that manages the mechanics of wizardry and lets you focus on defining the functionality of your Wizards. We demonstrate this framework using a sample Form Wizard that lets you create simple dialog boxes.

Access Wizard Functions

Before digging into creating custom Wizards, we must explain the built-in functions Access provides for creating new objects. Objects you can create with Wizards generally fall into two categories: data access objects (DAO) and user-interface objects. You create data access objects—tables and queries—using data access objects and methods. Chapter 6 provides a detailed discussion of DAO and how to use it to create and modify tables and queries. If you want to create Wizards that build data access objects, you'll need to integrate code from Chapter 6 into the Wizard framework we describe in the following section.

User-interface objects—forms and reports—are handled by a completely different set of functions. Access provides six functions that create and delete forms, reports, and controls. Table 23.5 lists each of these. In this section we provide a brief overview of each function. The section "Finishing the Process" later in this chapter gives examples of how to use them.

TABLE 23.5: Access Wizard Functions

Function	Description
CreateForm()	Creates a new form based on the current form template
CreateReport()	Creates a new report based on the current report template
CreateControl()	Creates a new control on a form
CreateReportControl()	Creates a new control on a report
DeleteControl()	Removes a control from a form
DeleteReportControl()	Removes a control from a report

CreateForm() and CreateReport() both take two optional String arguments that let you select a form or report template to use as the basis for the new object. The first argument is the path to a database containing the desired template, and the second argument is the name of the template. If you leave both arguments blank, the default template will be used (the form or report specified in the Forms/Reports tab of the Options dialog). Using templates lets you create new objects that already have a number of properties, such as size and color, predefined. Both functions return a pointer to the newly created object.

CreateControl() and CreateReportControl() take a relatively large number of arguments and create a form or report control as a result. Like the previously mentioned functions, both also return a pointer to the new control object. Table 23.6 lists the arguments for each. Note that only the first two, FormName/ReportName and ControlType, are required.

When you create a new control using either of these two functions, it is automatically endowed with the default properties for that control type. If you want to change any of these values, you can do so using the control object returned by the function. You will see, in the section "Finishing the Process" later in this chapter, that we do not use any of the optional arguments in our sample form Wizard. Instead we use the control object returned by the functions to set properties of the new control individually. We think using explicit property names makes code more readable.

DeleteControl and DeleteReportControl are subroutines that accept two mandatory String arguments, the first being the name of a form or report and the second being the name of a control. If successful, these procedures remove the specified

TABLE 23.6: CreateControl/CreateReportControl Arguments

Argument	Type	Remarks
FormName/ReportName	String	Specifies the name of the form or report on which Access should create the new control
ControlType	Integer	Specifies the type of control to create. It should be one of the control type constants listed in online help (for example, acTextbox)
Section	Integer	Number of the section where Access should create the control. It defaults to 0 (the Detail section) but can be any section (including report group levels) on the form or report
Parent	String	Specifies the parent of the next control. Controls that have parents, such as attached labels, move with them
ColumnName	String	Specifies the name of the field to which the control should be bound. For unbound controls, this should be an empty string (the default)
Left, Top, Height, Width	Integer	Sets the location and size of the control in twips. There are 1440 twips per inch. If you omit any of these arguments, the default property for the control type is used

control permanently. Finally, although it should be obvious, you can use these functions, as well as CreateControl and CreateReportControl, only in Design view.

One thing you should notice about these procedures is that they are not very object oriented. For instance, wouldn't it make more sense for CreateControl to be a method of form and report objects? Unfortunately, we are still bearing the burden of the original, undocumented (not to mention un–object oriented) Wizard functions from Access 1.0. As you read through the rest of this chapter, though, it should become clear how to use these procedures effectively in your own Wizards.

Defining a Wizard Framework

There are many ways to create Access Wizards or programs that use the Wizard functions. In this chapter we've chosen to develop a framework for writing Wizards that we think is both powerful and flexible. Our framework concentrates on the mechanics of a Wizard—eliciting user input and moving between pages on a dialog—freeing you to focus on writing code to make the Wizard do what you want.

Our Wizard framework is premised on the idea of using one main Wizard dialog to store information provided by the user and manage navigation using standard Next, Back, Cancel, and Finish buttons. Individual Wizard options are set by controls on one or more subforms that are dynamically loaded and unloaded in response to navigation commands. Each Wizard page corresponds to a different Wizard state. An Access table manages each state, including which subform object to load, as well as which buttons to enable or disable.

A Sample Form Wizard

To demonstrate both our framework and the Access Wizard functions, we've created a simple Form Wizard for creating input dialogs like the one shown in Figure 23.19. You can use this Wizard to create forms that ask simple questions or

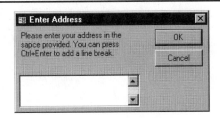

accept typed input. This example demonstrates a variety of Wizard techniques. Not only will you see how to create forms and controls, you will see how our Wizard framework lets us respond to choices the user makes.

Our Wizard has three distinct states, each of which is represented by options on a separate subform. The first Wizard state requires the user to choose a dialog type—either a simple prompt or an input box. Depending on the user's selection, the Wizard can then proceed directly to the last state, where final choices are made before creating the form, or to an intermediate state, where details for the input box are specified.

We will control the program flow by making entries in the state table and by adding decision logic to the VBA modules for each Wizard page. Figures 23.20, 23.21, and 23.22 show the sample Wizard's three states, each of which is implemented as a separate form.

How to Use the State Table

Each Wizard state can be represented by a set of values that control such things as which subform to display and which buttons to enable. Also crucial is the state to which a Wizard should move if the user clicks either the Next or Back button. We've chosen to store this information in an Access table (called tblWizState in

FIGURE 23.20:

The first Wizard state uses sbfWizDialog1 to set caption, message, and type information.

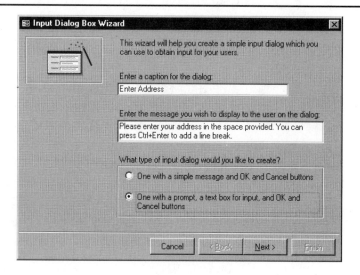

FIGURE 23.21:

The second Wizard state uses sbfWizDialog2 to set input box properties.

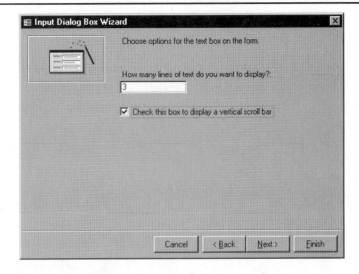

FIGURE 23.22:

The third Wizard state uses sbfWizDialog3 to save and display the completed form.

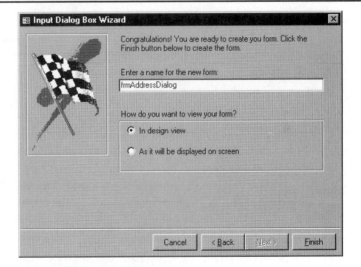

CH23BLD.MDA) because this makes it very easy to add new Wizards and states, as well as to modify existing state information. Table 23.7 lists the fields in tblWizState.

When adding your own Wizards to our framework, you'll need to create one record in the table that represents each Wizard state. To describe which values to enter, let's

TABLE 23.7: Field Definitions for tblWizState

Name	Type	Purpose
Wizard	Text	Wizard identifier
WizardState	Integer	State number
WizardForm	Text	Subform to load for this state
Comment	Text	Descriptive comments of the Wizard state
BackState	Integer	State reached by clicking the Back button
NextState	Integer	State reached by clicking the Next button
OptionalState	Text	State reached by clicking the optional button or the name of a function to call when the button is pressed
OptionalLabel	Text	Caption to display on the optional button
ShowOptional	Yes/No	Indicates whether the optional button should be displayed
EnableBack	Yes/No	Indicates whether the Back button should be enabled
EnableNext	Yes/No	Indicates whether the Next button should be enabled
EnableFinish	Yes/No	Indicates whether the Finish button should be enabled
ConfirmCancel	Yes/No	Prompts the user to confirm canceling the Wizard

look at the records in the table for our sample Form Wizard. Table 23.8 lists the most important field values.

Our Wizard uses three sequentially numbered states. The state numbers need not be sequential, but it is easier to follow the program logic if they are. The first state uses sbfWizDialog1 as the source object for the Wizard's subform control. From the first state the user can enter a caption for the dialog and a message to display on the form and can choose between a simple dialog or one with a text box for user input. You can see from the values in the state table that the only choice of movement

TABLE 23.8: State Table Values for Our Sample Form Wizard

Wizard-State	WizardForm	Back-State	Next-State	Enable-Back	Enable-Next	Enable-Finish
1	sbfWizDialog1	−1	2	No	Yes	No
2	sbfWizDialog2	1	3	Yes	Yes	Yes
3	sbfWizDialog3	2	−1	Yes	No	Yes

is forward. An EnableBack setting of No disables the Wizard form's Back button, and a BackState value of −1 ensures that even if the button were enabled, no state information would be found in the table.

By default, if the user clicks the Next button, the Wizard moves to state 2 (determined by the NextState value). Later on, in the section titled "Creating Wizard Pages," we'll show how to adjust this logic using VBA code to skip state 2. In this state, which uses sbfWizDialog2 to elicit input on how the input box should appear, the user can move either backward or forward. (EnableBack and EnableNext are both Yes.) Finally, in state 3 the Next button is disabled, preventing the user from overrunning the Wizard. Also notice that the Finish button is enabled only in states 2 and 3. This forces the user to enter information on the first Wizard page before building the form.

You should be able to see a pattern in how the Wizard state values are specified. When you create your own Wizards, you will need to map their logic to records in the state table.

Looking at the Wizard Host Form

Our Wizard framework uses one form that acts as the host for the subforms that make up individual Wizard states. Figure 23.23 shows the sample host form, frmWizardFrame, in Design view. The entire Detail section of the form is filled with a subform object. Our Wizard code will dynamically change the control's Source-Object property, depending on which state the Wizard is in.

Command buttons in the form's footer are used for Wizard navigation (Back, Next) and control (Cancel, Finish). You can use the button on the left, which has no caption, for an optional command. For example, it might make sense to include an Advanced or Options button in a particular form state. Our Wizard functions will dynamically update this control based on settings in the state table.

Code behind the Host Form

The module Form: frmWizardFrame, in CH23WIZ.MDA on the companion disk, shows the contents of the host form's VBA module. As you can see, it is a very small amount of code. Generic code in basWizards handles most of the navigation tasks. The code that resides in the form itself is mainly responsible for initializing the Wizard and maintaining its current state. Several module-level variables are defined in

FIGURE 23.23:

Sample Wizard host form in Design view

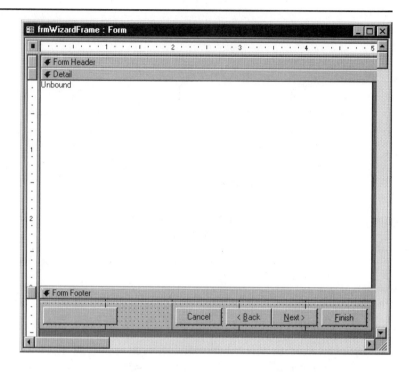

the Declarations section of the module. CurrentState is defined as a Public Integer, and we use it to store the Wizard's current state number. NextState is another Public Integer, which we use to store the state to which the Wizard moves when the user clicks the Back or Next button. We have declared these as Public so we can access them from other procedures. Similarly, mrstState is a Public Recordset variable, which we use as a pointer to records in tblWizState that apply to the current Wizard. We use a Private Boolean variable, mfCanceled, to denote whether a user has canceled the Wizard by clicking the Cancel button. We will use this variable later on when processing the form's Unload event. When creating your own Wizards using our host form as a template, you should not change or delete any of these variables. You should, however, change the value of the glrcWizID constant. This is the Wizard identifier specified by the Wizard field in tblWizState, and it should correspond to the value you use in that table to identify your Wizard.

Code in the form's Load event establishes the recordset used to retrieve state information. We use a SQL statement to query the tblWizState table based on the glrcWizID constant declared in the form. Once we have a pointer to the recordset, we can retrieve information about individual states and take some action, such as enabling or disabling buttons, and so on. If the SQL statement produces a valid recordset (that is, one containing records), we set the value of the form's CurrentState property to 1 and call the global function glrWizGotoState(), described in the section "Global Wizard Functions" later in this chapter.

Alternatively, code in the form's Unload event performs clean-up duties by closing the recordset object. It is also responsible for issuing a message box dialog if the user tries to cancel the form and the current Wizard state calls for a confirmation. Code in the Click event for the cmdCancel button sets mfCanceled to True and calls DoCmd.Close to close the form. If the recordset's ConfirmCancel field is set to True when the user cancels the Wizard and the user does not answer Yes to the prompt, the procedure cancels the Unload event and resets the mfCanceled flag.

As you can see in Form: frmWizardFrame, the code that responds to the Click events for the Back and Next buttons (cmdBack and cmdNext, respectively) calls a global function, glrWizGotoPage(). Each passes a reference to the Wizard form using the Me object, as well as a Boolean value. Which state to go to is determined by the value in the state table's BackState and NextState fields.

Finally, there is no code attached to the Finish button's Click event. This is where you place code that is specific to your Wizard. As we look at the sample form Wizard, it will become clear how to use this button's event.

An Example Wizard Form

The module frmWizardFrame showed the VBA code contained in our template host form. When you create your own Wizard forms, you will need to add code to the existing module that is specific to your Wizard. Listing 23.3 shows the additional code contained in our sample form Wizard. It is composed of nothing more than several form-level variables we will use to store values the user selected. The reason there isn't much code is that all the work of eliciting and validating user input is handled by the subforms that make up individual Wizard pages.

Listing 23.3

```
' **************************************************
' ** Add your own properties here              **
' **************************************************
' Change this constant to reflect your wizard id
' as set in the state table
```

```
Const glrcWizID = "SimpFormWiz"

' Public properties to store user selections
Public DialogType As Integer
Public DialogCaption As String
Public DialogMessage As String
Public LinesOfText As Integer
Public VerticalScrollbar As Boolean
Public OpenMode As Integer
Public NewFormName As Variant

Private Sub Form_Load()
    ' See frmWizardFrame for the rest of the code

    ' ***********************************
    ' ** Add your own startup code here **
    ' ***********************************
    ' This sets an initial value for LinesOfText
    Me.LinesOfText = 1
End Sub

Private Sub cmdFinish_Click()
    If Me.sbfWizard.Form.StateExit(True) Then

        ' ***********************************
        ' ** Add your own Finish code here **
        ' ***********************************
        If Application.Run("glrFormWizFinish", Me) Then
            DoCmd.Close acForm, Me.Name
        End If
    End If
End Sub
```

The most relevant code is in the Declarations section of the form's module. Here we've declared a number of Public variables we will use to store selections the user makes. These variables, described in Table 23.9, map directly to the user input controls on our Wizard pages. As the user leaves each page, values in the controls are saved in the Public variables. When the user clicks the Finish button, our Wizard uses these values to create a new form.

You'll also notice that code in the form's Load event sets an initial value for the LinesOfText property (1). A validation rule on the text box for this property restricts user input to values between 1 and 10. You'll want to initialize any variables your own Wizard uses in the Load event, as well.

TABLE 23.9: Sample Form Wizard Variables

Variable	Purpose
DialogType	Type of dialog to create—simple message (0) or text input (1)
DialogCaption	Caption for dialog box
DialogMessage	Text message to appear on the dialog
LinesOfText	For input dialogs, how many lines of text to allow
VerticalScrollbar	For input dialogs, whether the text box should have a vertical scroll bar
OpenMode	Whether the new form should be displayed in Design view (0) or Form view (1)
NewFormName	Name for the new form

Global Wizard Functions

While each Wizard you create requires a separate copy of the host form, all Wizards share a set of common functions in a global VBA module (basWizards). These functions handle the mechanics of Wizard navigation and control. The module basWizards, in CH23WIZ.MDA on the companion disk, shows the first of these functions, glrWizGotoState(). GlrWizGotoState() accepts three arguments: frmWiz, a pointer to a Wizard form; intState, the state to move to; and fForward, a flag indicating whether the user is moving forward or backward in the Wizard process.

GlrWizGotoState() is responsible for moving between Wizard states, a process comprising several steps. First, the procedure records data on the current Wizard state, including the position in the Wizard's recordset and the current subform Source-Object property. We may need to use this information later to return to the current state if an error occurs. After we've collected this information, the procedure executes the recordset's FindFirst method to jump to the row containing state settings for the given state. Once we have this information, we can update the Wizard's host form to reflect the new state by loading the appropriate subform.

Before doing that, however, we must make sure it is okay to do so. Why wouldn't it be okay? There are a number of situations in which you would not want a user to leave or enter a particular Wizard state until certain tasks had been completed or options selected. For example, suppose one Wizard state features a list of database objects from which the user must pick. Until the user actually makes a selection, we need a way to prevent the user from going forward. GlrWizGotoState() verifies that it is okay to leave the current state by calling a custom method of the currently loaded subform called StateExit (see the next section, "Creating Wizard Pages," for more information) using the following statement:

```
If frmWiz!sbfWizard.Form.StateExit(fForward) Then
```

We pass the fForward flag to StateExit so the method knows the direction in which the user is moving. If StateExit returns False, the procedure terminates; otherwise it loads the subform acting as the desired state's Wizard page into the host form by setting the SourceObject property to the value of the recordset's WizardForm field. Immediately after the form is loaded, we call a complementary method of the new subform object, StateEnter. Similar to StateExit, StateEnter determines whether it is okay to enter the desired state. If this method returns True, glrWizGotoState() calls glrSetWizardControls (described in a moment) and updates the host form's CurrentState property. If, on the other hand, the method returns False, the procedure restores the previous state's subform SourceObject setting and recordset position (by resetting its Bookmark property).

The module basWizards, in CH23WIZ.MDA on the companion disk, shows the glrSetWizardControls procedure mentioned in the previous paragraph and referenced in the source code for glrWizGotoState(). It is responsible for enabling or disabling certain controls on the host form based on values in the state table.

Most of the code should be obvious as to its purpose. Perhaps the only noteworthy item is the assignment statement for the recordset variable. Since we declared the Wizard host form's recordset variable Public, we need only preface the variable with a reference to the host form in order to assign it to a local variable in glrSetWizardControls.

Creating Wizard Pages

Now that we've explained the code behind the host form and the global Wizard functions module, we can discuss the creation of individual Wizard pages using Access forms. Creating a new Wizard page involves making a copy of the sbfWizardPage form in CH23WIZ.MDA. SbfWizardPage contains no controls, but it is the correct size to fit in the Detail section of the host form, and its VBA module also includes function stubs for the StateEnter and StateExit methods. After making a copy of this form, you should edit the form and its VBA module to add controls and code particular to your Wizard page. You will need to include the following bits of code:

- Code in the Form_Load event that reads current values from the host form into local variables.
- A Public function called StateEnter that returns True if state entry is allowed and False if it is not.
- A Public function called StateExit that returns True if state exit is allowed and False if it is not. If state exit is allowed, this function should transfer data from any local variables to the host form's variables.

Because the module in sbfWizardPage is only a shell for your own Wizard code, it is easier to describe the requirements of our framework if we look at the module of one of the sample Wizard pages. The module Form: sbfWizDialog1, in CH23WIZ.MDA on the companion disk, shows the code in sbfWizDialog1, the first page of our sample Form Wizard. The code listing contains the minimum amount of code you will need to provide as part of your own Wizard pages.

When the user moves to this page in our sample Form Wizard, we need to update the controls on the form with the current dialog properties. We do this in the Form_Load event procedure by examining the value using the subform's Parent property. Parent returns a pointer to the form in which the subform is embedded. Note that Form_Load will be executed when we set the SourceObject property of the subform object to sbfDialog1.

After the subform loads, the glrWizGotoState procedure calls its StateEnter method. Note that we have declared both StateEnter and StateExit as Public functions, thus making them accessible to procedures outside the form's VBA module. In our example we don't need to perform any validation before allowing entry to this particular state, so StateEnter simply returns True.

Our StateExit() function, on the other hand, is slightly more complex. Before moving to the next Wizard state, the user must enter a value for the dialog text. An If...Then statement examines the length of the text in txtMessage to determine whether it is greater than 0. If the user has not entered any text and is trying to move to the next state, the procedure issues a warning message, sets its return value to False, and terminates. This prevents glrWizGotoState from moving to a new state. If, on the other hand, all the conditions for leaving the current state are met (the user has entered a message), StateExit() returns True. This allows glrWizGotoState to load the next Wizard page.

Finally, another If...Then statement examines the value in the dialog type control (grpType) that determines whether the new form will be a simple message dialog or will accept user input. If the user selects a simple dialog, it does make sense to display the second Wizard page—the one that lets the user set properties for the input box control. In this case the procedure sets the NextState property to the final Wizard state number. This has the effect of bypassing the logic in the state table and jumping to a different state. You can use similar logic in your own Wizards to alter the user's path through your dialogs.

Finishing the Process

After working with various Wizard pages to make selections, users can click the Finish button to have the Wizard transform their choices into a beautiful new object. Depending on the complexity of your Wizard, this may require large amounts of VBA code. The code attached to the Finish button on our sample Form Wizard, shown in Listing 23.4, is extremely simple, however.

Listing 23.4

```
Private Sub cmdFinish_Click()
    If Me.sbfWizard.Form.StateExit(True) Then

        ' **********************************
        ' ** Add your own Finish code here **
        ' **********************************
        If Application.Run("glrFormWizFinish", Me) Then
            DoCmd.Close acForm, Me.Name
        End If
    End If
End Sub
```

You should notice two things about this code if you examine it in CH23WIZ.MDB. First, we are calling a separate function (glrFormWizFinish()) using Access' Run method to create the new form, and second, the function is located in a separate module in the database (basFormWizFinish). The reason for this was explained earlier in this chapter, in the section "Using Application.Run to Postpone Loading." Since the creation process could involve a large amount of VBA code, it would be nice if we could delay loading this into memory until the user actually clicks the Finish button. Using Application.Run to call glrFormWizFinish() breaks the dependency on basFormWizFinish and prevents Access from loading the module until the Run statement is executed. This technique provides better Wizard load time because Access does not need to load basFormWizFinish() along with the Wizard form itself. Of course, if the user cancels the Wizard process, we never waste time loading this Finish code at all.

Creating Forms and Controls

As we just mentioned, we use a separate function, glrFormWizFinish(), to create the dialog form defined by the user's selections in our Wizard. The module basForm-WizFinish, in CH23WIZ.MDA on the companion disk, shows glrFormWizFinish(), a procedure that uses Access' Wizard functions to create the dialog form and its controls. GlrFormWizFinish() accepts a single argument, frmWiz, that points to the Wizard form. Because we have defined the variables that hold Wizard settings as Public, frmWiz is all that's required to reference them from this global procedure.

Logically, the first thing glrFormWizFinish() does is create the form that will be used as our dialog box, using the CreateForm() function and no arguments. Access creates a new form in the current database based on the default form template and returns a pointer to it in the frmNew variable. We can now use frmNew to set several form properties appropriate for a dialog box. For example, we remove the record selector, navigation buttons, and scroll bars and change the form's size to 3 inches wide by 1 inch tall. As the following code fragment shows, we also change its grid settings and caption. We set the latter to the Wizard form's DialogCaption property:

```
' Build the form
Set frmNew = CreateForm()
frmNew.Width = 3 * glrcTwipsPerInch
frmNew.Section(0).Height = 1 * glrcTwipsPerInch
frmNew.Caption = frmWiz.DialogCaption
frmNew.GridX = 16
frmNew.GridY = 16
frmNew.AutoCenter = True
frmNew.AutoResize = True
frmNew.RecordSelectors = False
frmNew.ScrollBars = 0
frmNew.NavigationButtons = False
frmNew.MinMaxButtons = 0
```

After creating the form, the procedure goes on to create a label control and, if the user chose an input dialog, a text box. The following code fragment shows our use of the CreateControl() function, passing it the name of the form to create the control using our new form variable, frmNew, and the control type. The return value, a pointer to the newly created control, is stored in ctlNew:

```
Set ctlNew = CreateControl(frmNew.Name, acTextBox)
```

Although we could have passed additional arguments to indicate its control source, position, and size, we did not, opting instead to set these properties individually. Using specific property names makes the code easier to understand:

```
ctlNew.Height = frmWiz.LinesOfText * _
 glrcLineHeight * glrcTwipsPerInch
ctlNew.Width = 1.875 * glrcTwipsPerInch
ctlNew.Top = 0.75 * glrcTwipsPerInch
ctlNew.Left = 0.0625 * glrcTwipsPerInch
```

After the procedure creates the text box and adjusts the height of the form accordingly, it creates two command buttons—one labeled OK and the other Cancel. It places these on the right-hand side of the form. Once the command buttons have been created and their property values assigned, we must also insert some VBA code to make the controls work. We do this by calling a function, glrInsertCode(), which we describe in the next section. If the user chose to create an input dialog, we call glrInsertCode() to insert VBA code for the form's Load event to set an initial value of the control when the form is opened.

Finally, after the procedure creates the form and its controls and all the VBA code has been inserted, we can display and, optionally, save the form. The code that does this, shown below, first makes sure the new form is the active object by calling its SetFocus method. It then uses the Save method of the DoCmd object to save the active object (the new form) using the name provided by the Wizard form's NewFormName property. Finally, it calls the OpenForm method to display the new form in Form view if the user selected that option.

```
frmNew.SetFocus
If Not IsNull(frmWiz.NewFormName) Then
    DoCmd.Save , frmWiz.NewFormName
End If
DoCmd.Restore

If frmWiz.OpenMode <> 0 Then
    DoCmd.OpenForm frmNew.Name, acNormal
End If
```

Wizard code that you write is likely to be very different from the code in our sample Wizard because your code is specific to your Wizard's function. It should, however, have a similar structure—that is, a CreateForm statement followed by one or more CreateControl statements, and finishing with an action that saves and/or displays the completed object.

Using an Access Table to Store Code

Our sample Wizard must insert code into the newly created form's VBA module to enable the two command buttons. Rather than embed large amounts of code in the Wizard module, we store it in an Access table. This lets us modify it easily, without having to edit the Wizard code. The code table, tblWizCode, contains two fields, CodeID and CodeText. CodeID is a text field that acts as the unique identifier for each code fragment in the table. CodeText is a memo field containing the actual VBA code. Figure 23.24 shows tblWizCode open in Datasheet view. You can see that it contains VBA code fragments that we will use in our Form Wizard.

We've also created a function, glrInsertCode(), shown in basFormWizFinish in CH23WIZ.MDA, that inserts the code into a form's VBA module. GlrInsertCode() accepts five arguments and returns a Boolean value indicating success or failure. Table 23.10 lists each of these arguments and its purpose.

The bulk of the code that makes up glrInsertCode() handles the task of building a text string that will eventually be inserted into the form's module using the module's InsertText method. You will notice that glrInsertCode adds "Sub" and "End Sub" strings to the text it retrieves from tblWizCode. You should not, therefore, include an event procedure's declaration in tblWizCode.

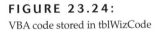

FIGURE 23.24:
VBA code stored in tblWizCode

CodeID	CodeText	CodeDesc
CloseMe	' Created by |1 on |2 ' Close the current form DoCmd.Close acForm, Me.Name	Closes the current form
HideMe	' Created by |1 on |2 ' Hide the current form Me.Visible = False	Hides the current form
LoadOpenArgs	' Created by |1 on |2 ' Set the default text box value Me![|3] = Me.OpenArgs	Sets the default value of a control on the form to the OpenArgs value

tblWizCode : Table

Record: 1 of 3

TABLE 23.10: Arguments to glrInsertCode()

Argument	Type	Remarks
strCodeID	String	Should be a value in the CodeID field of tblWizCode; finds the block of text to insert into the form's VBA module
frmAny	Form	Specifies the form containing the module into which we will insert code
ctlAny	Control	Specifies the control to which the event code applies. Note that this can be Nothing, indicating that the code applies to the form itself, not a control
strEvent	String	Specifies the name of the event to which the code applies (for example, "Click")
avarTokens	Variant	This ParamArray argument lets you pass substitution strings to the procedure that the procedure, in turn, will insert into the code

GlrInsertCode uses a For Each loop to iterate through any additional arguments passed to the procedure using the ParamArray argument, avarTokens. It calls glrReplace (not shown in basFormWizFinish) to replace all instances of a token (the pipe symbol, |, followed by a number) in the VBA code with an argument from the array.

NOTE

As it is written, glrInsertCode() works only with event procedures that do not require arguments. If you wish to use it with those that do (for example, BeforeUpdate), you will need to modify glrInsertCode() so that it appends the argument list to the procedure declaration instead of empty parentheses.

One important item to point out is the statement that sets the value of the form or control's event procedure property to the string "[Event Procedure]". It is not enough to simply insert a properly declared subroutine into the form's module. Access does not recognize that the code exists until you change the property value to "[Event Procedure]".

If you refer back to Listing basFormWizFinish in CH23WIZ.MDA, you'll see how we use glrInsertCode() in our sample Form Wizard. The statement that inserts code for the form's Load event is repeated here:

```
Call glrInsertCode("LoadOpenArgs", frmNew, _
  Nothing, "Load", CurrentUser, Now, strInputControl)
```

In this example the code fragment in tblWizCode is identified by the string "LoadOpenArgs". Once glrInsertCode() has retrieved it from the table, it is inserted into the form's module, and the form's OnLoad property is set to "[Event Procedure]". Passing the symbolic constant Nothing as the control argument forces glrInsertCode() to set the form's properties, as opposed to those of a specific control. Finally, three additional arguments are passed to the function. Tokens in the code stored in tblWizCode (you can see the tokens, |1, |2, and |3, in the code in Figure 23.24) will be replaced with these values.

Launching the Wizard

Like builders, Wizards are normally initiated by a function call from Access. While you can launch your Wizards any way you wish, if you want to integrate them into the list of standard Access Wizards, you must create a function with a specific declaration. There are two varieties of Access Wizard functions—one for tables and queries and one for forms and reports. Wizard functions for forms and reports must define at least one argument, regardless of whether you use it in your code. No arguments are required for Table and Query Wizards. Listing 23.5 shows the function used to initiate our sample Form Wizard, glrFrmWizEntry().

Listing 23.5

```
Function glrFrmWizEntry(strRecordSource _
 As String) As Variant

    ' Name of wizard form
    Const glrcFrmWizForm = "frmWizDialog"

    ' Open wizard form and let it do its stuff
    DoCmd.OpenForm FormName:=glrcFrmWizForm, _
     Windowmode:=acDialog

End Function
```

The argument to a Form or Report Wizard function such as glrFormWizEntry() must be a string, which Access will fill in with the name of a record source for the new object. This could be the name of either a table or a query. Access gets this value from the combo box on the initial Wizard dialog. Our sample Wizard creates an un-bound form, so we ignore this argument. If you are creating a bound form, how-ever, you would use this to examine the record source for field names and types. Access does not pass anything to Wizard functions that create new tables or queries.

You can define additional arguments to your Wizard functions if you plan on call-ing them from elsewhere in your application. For example, you might create a com-mon Wizard function that handles both forms and reports, depending on the value of a second argument. (In fact, this is how the Access Wizards work.) If you do this, however, you need to tell Access about the additional argument; otherwise the nor-mal Wizard functionality will be impaired. Informing Access of additional argu-ments requires making additional Registry entries, as explained in the next section.

WARNING You must adhere exactly to the rules for declaring Wizard functions. Any error in your Wizard function, including declaration, syntax, and compile errors, will result in Access issuing a "This feature is not in-stalled" error when you attempt to invoke your Wizard. As you can see, this is far from being the most descriptive Access error message ever written. If you receive this error, you will need to shut down Access before attempting to edit your code. This is because, once an Access database has been loaded as a library, it cannot be opened in the user interface.

The only task that remains is to tell Access about our Wizard so our users have the option of selecting it from the standard list of Form Wizards. To do that we'll need to make some more (you guessed it) Registry entries.

Wizard Registry Entries

Access separates Wizard entries into groups based on the type of object the Wizard creates. Figure 23.25 shows the Registry keys for the four types of object Wizards Access allows: Table Wizards, Query Wizards, Form Wizards, and Report Wizards. Figure 23.25 also shows the Form Wizard subkeys that define the individual Wiz-ards themselves. To add a new Wizard to Access' list of installed Wizards, you must add a new subkey beneath the appropriate Wizard type key. Access will use the

FIGURE 23.25:

Registry entries that define Access Wizards

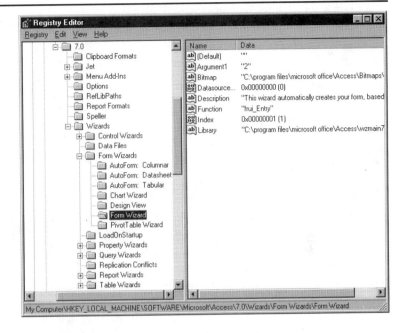

name you give to the subkey in the list of Wizards displayed to the user, so choose something short but descriptive. For example, to install our sample Form Wizard, create a new subkey called Dialog Form Wizard beneath the Form Wizards key.

In addition to the subkey, you'll need to create several Registry values. Table 23.11 lists the required value names for Table, Query, Form, and Report Wizards, along with the values for our sample Wizard. To complete the installation of our Wizard, you'll need to add these values to the Dialog Form Wizard Registry.

You will probably notice that these settings are similar to those for builders. The only setting that requires special attention is Index. Access gets hopelessly confused if this value is not set correctly. Unless you want your Wizard to appear at a specific position in the list, it is safer simply to omit this value and let Access place your Wizard at the end of the list.

If you have declared additional arguments to your Wizard function, you also need to create values for each one in the Wizard's Registry key. You can see in Figure 23.25 the values for Access' built-in Form Wizard and an additional String value named Argument1. In addition to the required String argument, Access' Wizard

TABLE 23.11: Object Wizard Registry Key Values

Value Name	Value Type	Sample Value	Remarks
Bitmap	String	Path to GLRWIZ.BMP	Defines the path to a bitmap (.BMP) file containing an image that Access displays in the new object dialog when the Wizard is selected
Datasource Required	DWORD	0	If set to 1, this value forces Access to require the user to select a data source for the object. A value of 0 means a data source is optional
Description	String	"Creates a simple dialog that displays a message or accepts input"	Lets you create a description of the Wizard that Access will display in the new object dialog
Function	String	glrFrmWizEntry	Defines the name of the Wizard function Access calls to initiate the Wizard
Index	DWORD	7	Defines the position of the Wizard in the list of Wizards. Must be between 0 (the first in the list) and 1 less than the number of installed Wizards. Must also be unique among other Wizards. If omitted, Access adds the Wizard at the end of the list
InternalID	DWORD	N/A	Marks the Wizard as one implemented by MSACCESS.EXE, not a library database, and indicates which internal Wizard function to use (You can't really use this setting; we've included it here for the sake of completeness.)
Library	String	Path to CH23WIZ.MDA	Defines the path to the library database containing the Wizard function. You can omit the path if the library is located in the Access directory

function, frui_Entry, declares an Integer argument denoting which type of object is being created. Since, by default, Access will pass the Wizard function only one argument (the record source), this Registry value forces Access to pass a second one (in this case, with the value 2). If your Wizard function accepts more than one argument, you must define additional Registry values named Argument1, Argument2, and so on, one for each additional argument. After creating the additional Registry entries, assign them the values you want Access to pass to the additional arguments when Access invokes your Wizard function. These must be hard coded as strings and cannot be evaluated at run time.

Figure 23.26 shows the Registry updated to reflect settings for our sample Form Wizard. To test the Wizard, open any Access database and click the New Form button on the toolbar or select the Insert ➤ Form menu command. Figure 23.27 shows the New Form dialog with the sample Wizard selected. Note the Wizard's name, description, and bitmap. These are all defined using the Registry entries described earlier in this chapter.

FIGURE 23.26:

Registry entries for the sample Form Wizard

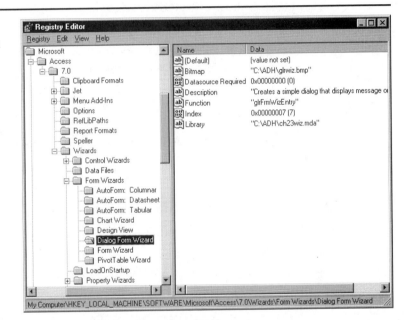

FIGURE 23.27:

New Form dialog showing details for the sample Form Wizard

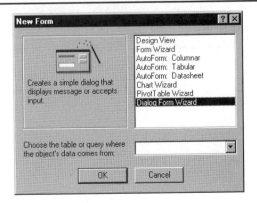

Our Framework in Summary

We have presented a great deal of information in this chapter describing how to create Access Wizards. The discussion included both the Access Wizard functions and our framework for creating Wizard dialogs. Try not to confuse the two. You can use the Access Wizard functions (CreateForm, CreateControl, and so on) in any VBA procedure to create new objects. We have included a description of our framework because we believe it is a powerful yet easy-to-implement way of creating Wizards that look and act like those that come with Access.

If you choose to use our framework, there are a number of things you need to do. We have described them in detail in this chapter. To summarize the steps for creating new Wizards using our framework:

1. Create a copy of frmWizardFrame. This will act as the host form for your Wizard.

2. Change the glrcWizID constant to the unique ID for your Wizards.

3. Add a Public variable to the host form's Declarations section to hold user choices.

4. Add code to the Load event of the host form to initialize the Wizard.

5. Add code to the cmdFinish_Click procedure that calls your object-creation code.

6. For each Wizard page, create a copy of sbfWizardPage.

7. Add code to the subform's Load event to initialize that page.

8. Add validation code to the StateEnter procedure to restrict entry to that state.

9. Add validation code to the StateExit procedure to prevent users from leaving that state.

10. Add code to the StateExit procedure to save values from the subform to the host form's Public variables.

11. Set the SourceObject property for the subform object on your host form to the name of the first Wizard page.

12. Add a record to tblWizState that defines the subform and options for that state.

13. Create a function that accepts a pointer to the host form and uses the form's custom properties to create a new object.

14. Create a Wizard function that opens the host form in dialog mode.

15. Register your Wizard so Access can display it to users and call its Wizard function.

Control Wizards: A Hybrid

In addition to object Wizards, such as our sample Form Wizard, Access supports Control Wizards that are invoked when a user creates a new control on a form or report. Access' Combo Box Wizard is an example of a Control Wizard. Additionally, you can create OLE custom control Wizards that are called when a user adds a new custom control to a form or report. We briefly describe how to create a Control Wizard in this section. You will find, however, that the overall process differs little from regular Wizards and builders.

To use a Control Wizard, the user must have enabled this option by clicking the Control Wizards toolbar button. We've created a simple Wizard that is invoked when a user creates a new text box. Figure 23.28 shows the Wizard's main form,

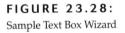

FIGURE 23.28:

Sample Text Box Wizard

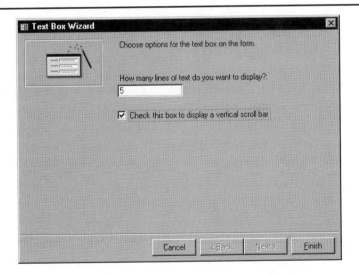

frmTBWiz. Our Control Wizard is extremely simple. In fact, we've reused the second page of our Form Wizard.

Control Wizard Functions

Like regular Wizards, Control Wizards must be invoked by a function. Access passes the name of the newly created control and its label (if it has one) as String arguments to the Wizard function. The module basTextBoxWizEntry in CH23WIZ.MDA shows the function for the Text Box Wizard that we've included with this book.

There are several things to note about this function. First, before any substantial processing begins, the procedure checks the return value of Access' CurrentObjectType method to ensure that the active object is a form. You can use this technique (as we have in this case) to take a different action if the active object is a report rather than a form. Next, this procedure sets a reference to the newly created control (stored in the ctlNew Control variable) using the control name Access passes to the function. You could use Screen.ActiveControl, but using the control's name is much safer and more intuitive. Once the reference is set, the procedure checks to make sure the control is, in fact, a text box and then opens the Wizard form.

Code attached to the cmdFinish button on the Wizard's host form simply hides the form and lets glrTextBoxWizEntry() continue. GlrTextBoxWizEntry() then sets the Height and ScrollBars properties of the newly created control.

Control Wizard Registry Entries

The Registry entries for Control Wizards are similar to those for builders. Figure 23.29 shows the entries for our sample Text Box Wizard. You can have more than one Wizard for each control, and these are grouped under the Control Wizards Registry key. There is a subkey for each control type (you can add ones that are not created by default), and each of these has subkeys for each Wizard that applies to the control. If you wanted to add a second text box builder, for example, you would create a new, unique subkey beneath the TextBox key shown in Figure 23.29.

The Registry values themselves (in the right-hand pane in Figure 23.29) are the same for builders and were listed in Table 23.2 earlier in this chapter. The only significant difference is in the use of the Can Edit value. In the case of builders, you almost always want this value to be 1, indicating that the builder can be invoked

FIGURE 23.29:

Registry entries for Control Wizards

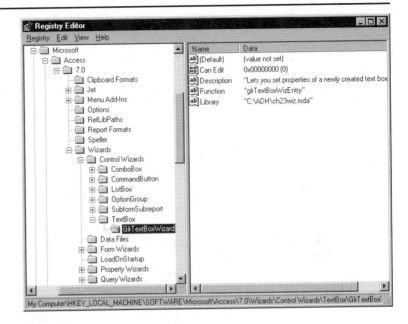

for an existing property value. Control Wizards, on the other hand, are normally used to create new objects. In this case it may not make sense to invoke the builder on an existing control. For this reason the Can Edit value should be 0. You can have reentrant Control Wizards, of course, but you may have to write extra code to account for this.

OLE Custom Control Wizards

We have one final word on Wizards. If you develop and distribute your own OLE custom controls, you can also install special Wizards to work with them. Access will recognize a Registry key for custom controls that follows the same rules as for normal Control Wizards, with a few exceptions.

First, before you install your Wizard you must create a new Registry key called OLE CONTROL WIZARDS (it must be uppercase) beneath the normal Access "Wizards" key. Then, instead of a control type, you must create a new subkey beneath the OLE CONTROL WIZARDS key using the class name of the custom control. For example, DBOutl.DataOutline is the class name for the data outline control.

From here the rules are the same as for regular Control Wizards. Create a new subkey beneath the control subkey with the values listed in Table 23.2.

Distributing and Installing Add-Ins

Once you've created a Wizard, you can easily distribute it to others by providing them with a copy of the library database. The only complication involves installing it on another person's computer and making the appropriate Registry entries. Fortunately, Access provides two mechanisms to ease this task: the Add-in Manager and the USysRegInfo table. In this section we describe each of these and how to use them to distribute your own custom add-ins.

Using the Add-In Manager

Using the Access Add-in Manager is usually the easiest way to install and uninstall Access Wizards, builders, and add-ins. The Add-in Manager uses a special table in the Wizard database called USysRegInfo to create or delete the Registry entries required for the add-in to operate. You invoke the Add-in Manager by selecting Tools ➤ Add-ins ➤ Add-in Manager from the Access menus. Figure 23.30 shows the Add-in Manager dialog.

FIGURE 23.30:

Access' Add-in Manager dialog

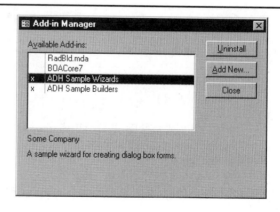

The list box displays all the add-ins the Add-in Manager knows about. Access builds this list by looking at all the library databases in the Access directory and examining their database properties. The Add-in Manager examines three properties for each library database in the Access directory: Title, Company, and Comments. Figure 23.31 shows the Summary tab of the Database Properties dialog for our sample Form Wizard database, CH23WIZ.MDA. You can see how values in these three properties are displayed in the Add-in Manager dialog in Figure 23.30.

FIGURE 23.31:

Document properties used by the Add-in Manager

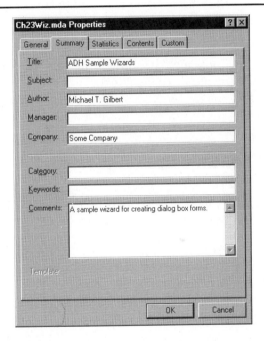

NOTE You must have Open/Run permission on a library database in order for the Add-in Manager to read its properties. If you do not have permission to open the database, the Add-in Manager displays a warning dialog and omits the add-in from the list.

A check box next to the add-in description in the Add-in Manager dialog tells you whether the add-in is currently installed. The Add-in Manager makes this determination by looking for values in the Registry that match those in the add-in's USysRegInfo table (which we describe in the next section). If the library database does not have a USysRegInfo table, the Add-in Manager cannot determine its installed state. You can toggle the installed state of an existing add-in by double-clicking the add-in on the list or by selecting it and clicking the Uninstall button. For add-ins that are not currently installed, the caption of this button changes to "Install," and clicking it installs the selected add-in.

You can also install new add-ins that aren't in the list by clicking the Add New button. This opens a browse dialog with which you can locate the library database containing the add-in. After you have found the add-in, the Add-in Manager automatically copies it to the Access directory and installs it. There is no way to prevent the Add-in Manager from copying the file. You can have add-ins in other directories, but your users will not be able to use the Add-in Manager to administer them.

Creating the USysRegInfo Table

The Add-in Manager depends on the existence of a table called USysRegInfo in your library database that contains your add-in's required Registry entries. USysRegInfo is composed of four fields. Table 23.12 lists each of these fields and its datatype.

The value in the Subkey field is the name of the Registry subkey you want the Add-in Manager to create when it installs your add-in. Previous sections of this chapter have described the keys that are necessary to install each of the various add-in types. Contrary to the Access documentation, you can have as many sets of entries

TABLE 23.12: Field Layout for the USysRegInfo Table

Field	Type	Remarks
Subkey	Text	Contains the name of the Registry subkey containing a specific Registry setting
Type	Number	Defines the type of entry to create: key (0), string (1), or DWORD (4)
ValName	Text	For Registry values, defines the name of the value
Value	Text	For Registry values, the actual value as text

in USysRegInfo as you wish. However, Registry entries that apply to a given add-in must all have the same value in the Subkey field.

When adding records to the USysRegInfo table for your own add-ins, the first record in each group should consist of the subkey name and the value 0 in the Type field. A Type of 0 instructs the Add-in Manager to create the subkey. You must do this prior to adding values to it. Once you have created the subkey, you add values to it by adding more records to USysRegInfo.

The format of the Subkey value is important. All values in this field must begin with either "HKEY_LOCAL_MACHINE" or "HKEY_CURRENT_ACCESS_PROFILE". These strings have an identical effect when installing your add-in, except when you are using User Profiles. In this case the latter string instructs the Add-in Manager to create Registry entries beneath the current profile instead of beneath Access' normal Registry structure. Normally you should use HKEY_CURRENT_ACCESS_ PROFILE unless you want to force the Add-in Manager to create entries under HKEY_LOCAL_MACHINE\Software\Microsoft\Access\7.0. The remainder of the Subkey value is the Registry key structure beginning with Access' 7.0 Registry key, including any preexisting keys.

Figure 23.32 shows the USysRegInfo table from our sample Form Wizard. Note the Subkey values that point to a new Registry key called Dialog Form Wizard. The first entry in the table creates the key (Type equals 0) and the rest add appropriate values

FIGURE 23.32:

USysRegInfo values for the sample Form Wizard

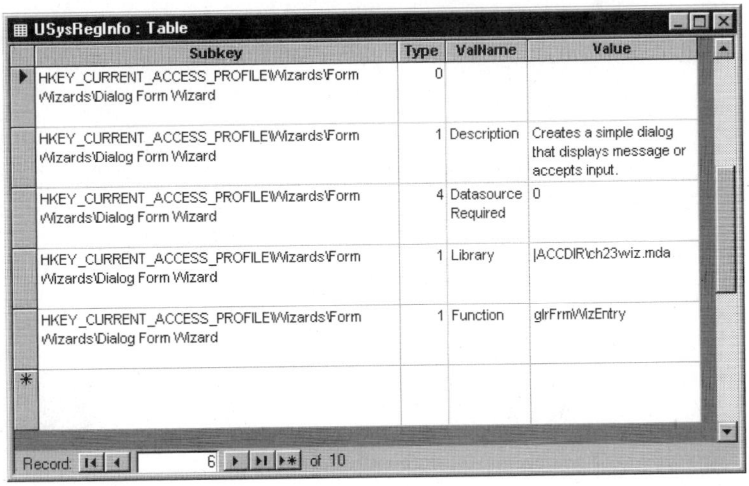

Subkey	Type	ValName	Value
HKEY_CURRENT_ACCESS_PROFILE\Wizards\Form Wizards\Dialog Form Wizard	0		
HKEY_CURRENT_ACCESS_PROFILE\Wizards\Form Wizards\Dialog Form Wizard	1	Description	Creates a simple dialog that displays message or accepts input.
HKEY_CURRENT_ACCESS_PROFILE\Wizards\Form Wizards\Dialog Form Wizard	4	Datasource Required	0
HKEY_CURRENT_ACCESS_PROFILE\Wizards\Form Wizards\Dialog Form Wizard	1	Library	\ACCDIR\ch23wiz.mda
HKEY_CURRENT_ACCESS_PROFILE\Wizards\Form Wizards\Dialog Form Wizard	1	Function	glrFrmWizEntry

Record: 6 of 10

for Library, Description, and so on. Note the string "|ACCDIR" in the Library entry's Value field. This is a token the Add-in Manager will replace with the full path to the Access directory when it installs the add-in.

Examine the USysRegInfo tables in the other sample add-ins to see how to create Registry entries for every type of Wizard, builder, and add-in.

Summary

In this chapter we've explored the very powerful capabilities of Access Wizards. Creating custom Wizards allows you to invest your users with specialized tools that appear as built-in features of Access. Specifically, we covered the following topics:

- Where Wizard Registry entries are stored
- How to launch a function from the Add-ins menu
- How to create a builder to help users change property settings
- How to design a custom Wizard using our Wizard framework
- How to make it easy for your users to install your add-in using the Add-in Manager

The information contained in this chapter should help you create your own custom Wizards easily and quickly.

CHAPTER

TWENTY-FOUR

Securing Your Application

- Making your databases secure

- Programmatically creating user and group accounts

- Programmatically checking and setting object permissions

- Listing all users with blank passwords

- Preventing users from creating new objects

In this chapter we cover Jet security in detail, outlining how and why it works the way it does and how to avoid common "gotchas." We also show you how to manipulate security programmatically using Access' security objects.

> **NOTE**
>
> Security in Access is a function of the database engine, Jet, not the Access User Interface (UI). (Chapter 4 discusses the Jet engine.) While the Access UI provides one means of managing security, Jet maintains security no matter what the client application—Access, Visual Basic, Excel, or other programs gaining access through the Access ODBC driver. Thus, in this chapter we use the term *Jet security* rather than *Access security*.

Security Basics

Jet 3.0 offers two overlapping security models:

- Workgroup-based security
- Database password security

Workgroup-Based Security

Since Access 1.0, the Jet engine has offered a sophisticated *workgroup-based* security model (it's also referred to as a user-based security model) rather than the more common database-based model most other desktop database management systems use. Under the simpler file-oriented model, security revolves around a database and is self contained within the confines of that database. Each database has its own security system that is independent of others. In contrast, in Jet's workgroup-based security model, every database used by members of a workgroup shares the same security system.

Database Passwords

For Jet 3.0, Microsoft has added a much simpler alternative: database passwords. This system allows you to set a single password for a database that all users must know to open the database. While much simpler to implement and use, this system is very easily compromised because all users use the same password. In addition, it doesn't let you track individual users' activity in a shared database. However, you can use both workgroup-based security and database passwords at the same time.

You set a database password by selecting Tools ➤ Security ➤ Set Database Password. Once this option is set, whenever you open the database you will be met with the Password Required dialog, as shown in Figure 24.1. You must have the database open exclusively to set the database password.

> **WARNING** Bug alert: Don't include spaces in database passwords; if you do and then compact the database, you won't be able to open it ever again!

To open a database that's been password protected programmatically, you must use the connect parameter of the OpenDatabase method. For example, the following code opens the Test24 database with a password of "dirt":

```
Dim wrk As Workspace
Dim dbTest As Database

Set wrk = DBEngine.Workspaces(0)
Set dbTest = wrk. _
 OpenDatabase("d:\bksybex2\paul\ch24\test24.mdb", _
 False, False, ";PWD=dirt")
```

FIGURE 24.1:

Entering a password for a database

The connect parameter is case sensitive. In addition, you must set the exclusive and read-only parameters (the second and third parameters) if you use the connect parameter.

> **TIP**
>
> If you're using workgroup-based security, you may wish to prevent a user from creating or removing a database password. To do so, remove the user's Administer permission for the database. You'll also need to remove this user from any groups that have this permission set. (See the section "Assigning Permissions" later in this chapter.)

The remainder of this chapter focuses on the more powerful workgroup-based security model.

> **NOTE**
>
> You can't replicate a database for which you have set a database password; you must first remove the password.

Jet Workgroup-Based Security

Jet's workgroup-based security is based on *users and their permissions*, not passwords. Most desktop databases employ password-based security if they implement any security features at all. (Jet 3.0 offers a limited password-based system too, now—see the previous section.) In these systems users enter a password that identifies them to the system as valid users. Every user who shares a given security level shares that same password, so the system is incapable of identifying individual users. In contrast, Jet's security model requires each user to have both a user name and a password. The password merely verifies that users are who they claim to be. Once verified, the password leaves the picture. With Jet, users manage their own individual passwords, which they can change at will without affecting other users. Passwords can be more secure since they're not shared by lots of users.

In a password-based system, each object has passwords associated with it that define its security. For example, the Orders table in Paradox might have a read-only password and a read/write password, so a user named Doug who knew both passwords would have read/write access to the table. With Jet, however, an object doesn't have any associated passwords or permissions. Instead, a user (or a group of users) has an associated set of permissions on a per-object basis. Thus, in Access/Jet, the user Doug or the PowerUsers group of which he is a member might have ReadData and UpdateData permissions for the Orders table.

Two Parts to Security

Jet security is made up of two parts:

- *User and group accounts and their passwords* are stored in the workgroup file. This file, usually kept centrally on a file server in a multiuser environment, is, by default, named SYSTEM.MDW.

- *Object permissions* are stored in each database.

For example, the security system for a small business, with three employees and four Access databases, might look like that shown in Figure 24.2. The workgroup for this company is defined by the company's workgroup file, BIZSYS.MDW, which contains the three user accounts and their passwords (Joe, Mary, and Sally) and the two group accounts (Managers and Programmers).

FIGURE 24.2:

Security system for a small business. The workgroup file, BIZSYS.MDW, contains the three user and two group accounts. Object permissions are stored in each of the four databases.

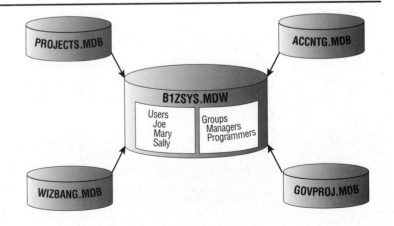

Each of the databases for this company—PROJECTS.MDB, ACCNTNG.MDB, WIZBANG.MDB, and GOVPROJ.MDB—would be tied to the BIZSYS.MDW workgroup file. Jet stores the access rights to each of the database objects in the individual databases. For example, the Managers group might have Administer rights on the table tblCustomers in ACCNTNG.MDB, while the Programmers group might have only ReadData and UpdateData rights for this table. The rights for this table and for all the other objects in ACCNTNG.MDB would be stored in this database, along with pointers to the account information stored in BIZSYS.MDW.

Enabling Security

Security in Jet is always on; it can't be turned off. The security system, however, remains invisible until you're ready to use it. This is possible because of the presence of several default user and group accounts.

Every workgroup file starts out with two predefined group accounts (Admins and Users) and one predefined user account (Admin). (Jet 3.0 has dispensed with the Guest and Guests accounts, although these accounts will still be present if you're using a version 2.0 workgroup file. See the section "Migrating Secured Databases to Access 95" later in this chapter for more information on converting secured version 2 systems to Access 95.)

Overriding Jet's Default Logon Attempt

Sometimes when you are developing an application, it would be nice if you could log on as a user, even when the Admin password is blank. You might want to do this, for example, to test out a user logging system. You can override Jet's attempt to log you on as Admin by using a startup option. For example, you can start Access as user Harpo with the password Marx using the following:

```
MSACCESS.EXE /User Harpo /Pwd Marx
```

Note, however, that this is useful only during testing. Your database will be anything but secure under this scenario.

When a user starts an Access session (or tries to connect to Jet using VB or another program), Jet always attempts to log on the user as *Admin* with a blank password. If this logon attempt fails, only then does Jet prompt the user for a user name and password using the Logon dialog. Thus, as long as you keep the Admin password blank (a zero-length string), security remains invisible. Well, almost. You can still create new users and groups and assign permissions to objects.

Managing Security

You have two ways to manage Jet security: the Access security menus and data access objects (DAO).

Security Menus

The Access menus provide a simple interface for managing security. They're outlined in the following table:

Menu Command	Use
Set Database Password	Sets or removes the database password (Once set, this menu changes to Unset Database Password.)
User and Group Permissions	Sets permissions for new and existing database objects for user and group accounts; changes the owner of database objects
User and Group Accounts	Creates or deletes user accounts; creates or deletes group accounts; clears account passwords; adds or removes users from groups; prints report of users and groups
User-Level Security Wizard	Runs the Access Security wizard
Encrypt/Decrypt Database	Encrypts or decrypts a database; available only when no database is open

Data Access Objects

Prior to version 2.0, Jet security was strictly a user interface affair. Fortunately, with the introduction of version 2.0, Microsoft added the ability to programmatically manipulate security. Using DAO, you can even do things that aren't possible using the Access menus. The DAO security model is discussed in detail in the section "Programming Security Using Data Access Objects" later in this chapter.

Workgroups

Security in Jet revolves around *workgroups*. At the interface level, a workgroup is defined as a group of users who work together. At the Jet level, a workgroup is defined as all users sharing the same workgroup file.

The workgroup file is a special encrypted database, by default called SYSTEM.MDW, that Access and Jet use to store a number of pieces of information having to do with users, including:

- User account names, their personal identifiers (PIDs), and passwords
- Group account names and their PIDs
- Information regarding which users belong to which groups
- Various user preference settings, including custom toolbar settings
- A list of the last four opened databases (for each user)

In a multiuser environment you can choose to place the workgroup file either on the file server or on each workstation. Usually, you'll want to place it on the file server, which makes the maintenance of user and group accounts much easier. On the other hand, if your security settings are fairly static, you could reduce network traffic by placing a copy of the workgroup file on each workstation.

Creating a New Workgroup

Microsoft includes a utility program called the Workgroup Administrator (WRKGADM.EXE) you can use to create a new workgroup (workgroup file) or to change to another workgroup. (The Access install program does not automatically add this program to the Start menu.) If you run this utility and choose to create a new workgroup, you are met with the Workgroup Owner Information dialog, as shown in Figure 24.3.

TIP   Since the workgroup file is such a vital part of security, we recommend regularly backing up this file and storing a copy of it safely off site. You should also consider storing a copy of the Name, Organization, and Workgroup ID fields in hard-copy form in a secure off-site location.

FIGURE 24.3:

The information entered into the Workgroup Owner Information dialog is used to uniquely identify a workgroup.

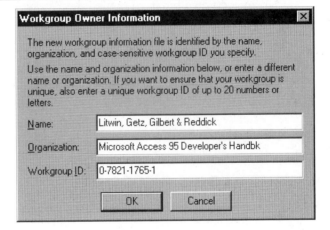

> **Workgroup Owner Information**
>
> The new workgroup information file is identified by the name, organization, and case-sensitive workgroup ID you specify.
>
> Use the name and organization information below, or enter a different name or organization. If you want to ensure that your workgroup is unique, also enter a unique workgroup ID of up to 20 numbers or letters.
>
> Name: Litwin, Getz, Gilbert & Reddick
>
> Organization: Microsoft Access 95 Developer's Handbk
>
> Workgroup ID: 0-7821-1765-1
>
> OK   Cancel

By default, Jet takes your user and organization name from the Access installation parameters, which you can view using the Help ➤ About Microsoft Access command. This is the information Jet displays when the Workgroup Administrator program is started. You can change this information to anything you'd like at this time (but not at any other time).

The third field in the Workgroup Owner Information dialog, Workgroup ID, is the most critical one. You can enter from 0 to 20 numbers or *case-sensitive* letters into this field. Take extra care to keep this entry secret but backed up somewhere off site. If you leave this field blank, you'll be warned, but you won't be prevented from proceeding. Once you commit your entries to these fields by clicking the OK button, you will have one more chance to change your mind, and then you will never be able to view or change them again. Thus, it's important to write down each of them.

> **WARNING** Access creates a default workgroup named SYSTEM.MDA when you install Access. To create this workgroup, it uses the name and company installation parameters and a blank Workgroup ID. *This makes the default workgroup file unsecure* because anyone who can get to the Help ➤ About Microsoft Access command with your copy of Access can break your security! When you need to secure a database, the first thing you should do is create a brand-new secured workgroup file.

Based on your entries in the Workgroup Owner Information dialog, Jet generates an encrypted binary ID called the Workgroup SID. Jet uses the Workgroup SID to uniquely identify the Admins group account—*not* the Admin user account—in the workgroup. The significance of this built-in account is discussed in the section "Special Status: Built-In Accounts" later in this chapter.

You can also use the Workgroup Administrator program to join a different workgroup. This allows you to participate in multiple workgroups, although only one can be active at a time.

User and Group Accounts

Jet uses user and group accounts to dole out security permissions. Only users and groups can have permissions. Both types of accounts share the same name space, so you need to ensure that all names are unique for a workgroup. Thus, you can't have a user and a group with the same name.

> **TIP** Microsoft uses the convention whereby user names are singular and group names are plural (for example, the Admin user and the Admins group). We've adopted (and recommend that you adopt) this same account-naming scheme.

In Access you use the Tools ➤ Security ➤ User and Group Accounts command to create and manage user and group accounts (see Figure 24.4).

FIGURE 24.4:

The user Geoff is a member of the Users, Employees, and Programmers groups.

Only members of the Admins group can add, delete, and change the membership for user and group accounts, but any user can view accounts (this is new for Access 95) and change his or her account password.

PIDs, SIDs, and Passwords

When you create a new user or group account in Jet, you must enter a non-blank, 4–20 character, case-sensitive *personal identifier* (*PID*). Jet combines the name of the account with the PID to create a *security identifier* (*SID*) for each user or group account. Once you've entered a PID, you can *never* view or change it.

TIP

We recommend that only a single database administrator create accounts and PIDs and that this individual keep a written off-site record. This will be useful if someone deletes an account that you need to re-create at a later date. This same person should keep a written off-site record of the user and organization names and the workgroup ID entered into the Workgroup Owner Information dialog, as well as a recent backup of the workgroup file.

After you create a new user account, you can add an optional 1–14-character, case-sensitive account password using the Change Logon Password tab of the User and Group Accounts dialog. (Unlike PIDs, passwords are optional.) Jet uses passwords only at logon time to verify the identity of a user.

Only users can change their own passwords, but members of the Admins group can clear another user's password. (This is a restriction of the Access UI—using DAO, an Admins member can change another user's password without knowing the old password.) You *can't* view an existing password using either the UI or DAO.

Both passwords and PIDs are stored in the workgroup file in an encrypted format.

Jet uses the internally generated account SIDs to uniquely identify user and group accounts across workgroups. Except for some of the special built-in accounts that are discussed in the section "Special Status: Built-In Accounts" later in this chapter, Jet treats accounts in different workgroups with the same name but different PIDs (and thus different SIDs) as distinct.

Groups Are More Than Collections of Users

A group account is more than simply a collection of users. In many situations you can use a group account in place of a user account. The following table contrasts the two types of accounts:

Attribute	User Accounts	Group Accounts
Has associated permissions for objects	Yes	Yes
Has a personal ID (PID)	Yes	Yes
May own objects	Yes	Yes
May log on	Yes	No
Has password	Yes	No
May own a database	Yes	No

Although you cannot log on as a group, you can do almost anything else with a group account, including owning objects. A group account may not own a database.

Special Status: Built-In Accounts

As mentioned earlier in this chapter, the Jet security system includes several built-in accounts that make it possible for security to remain invisible until it's needed. These built-in accounts include the Admin *user* and the Admins and Users *groups*. It's important that you understand how these "special status" accounts work; otherwise your database won't be secure. The following table describes the three built-in accounts:

Account Type	Account	Same SID for All Workgroups?	Comments
User	Admin	Yes	Default user account
Group	Admins	No	Members have special privileges
Group	Users	Yes	All user accounts are members of Users

None of the special accounts can ever be deleted from a workgroup. Each of these accounts is described in more detail in the next few sections.

Admin User

All new workgroups initially contain the Admin user account with a blank password. As mentioned previously, unless a command-line option is used to override this behavior, Jet always attempts to log you on as the Admin user with a blank password. Only if this logon attempt fails does Jet prompt you for a user name and password.

You cannot delete the Admin user, but you can remove it from the Admins group as long as Admins has at least one other member. This is one of the steps for making a database secure that are discussed in the section "Properly Securing a Database with the Access Security Wizard" later in this chapter. *The Admin user will always have the same SID for all workgroups.*

The Admin user is somewhat misnamed; even though it is initially a member of the Admins group, it has no special administrative powers of its own. It might have been more accurate for Microsoft to have named the Admin user account User or DefaultUser.

As long as the Admin user is not the current user when you create objects, it will not have any permissions on newly created objects.

Admins Group

The Admins group is uniquely identified across workgroups. (This differs from all other built-in accounts, which are not unique from one workgroup to another.) In fact, the Admins group draws its SID from the workgroup SID created by the Workgroup Administrator program. Jet requires that there always be at least one member of the Admins group. This requirement makes it impossible to have a workgroup with no administrator.

Members of the Admins group have special, irrevocable administrative rights. Their membership in Admins, however, *is* revocable by another Admins member. As long as they are members of Admins, they can grant themselves permissions to all database objects in the databases in their workgroup. (Access, but not the Jet engine, enforces this. It is possible, using DAO, to revoke Administer permission from the Admins group for an object. The object's owner will retain Administer permissions for the object.) In addition, members of Admins always have the ability to manage user and group accounts in their workgroup.

By default, when you create a new object, the Admins group gets full permissions to the new object.

Users Group

The Users group is the default group for all Access users. All built-in user accounts—as well as new user accounts created using the Access UI—will be members of the Users group. Access won't allow you to remove users from the Users group. (This is an Access limitation, however, not one that Jet enforces. Using DAO, you can remove user accounts from the Users group, but these users will no longer be able to log on to Access.)

Along with the Admin user account, it is the presence of the Users group account that allows Jet to keep security invisible until needed. This is possible because the Users group account has the same SID across all workgroups. Thus, if you wish to secure a workgroup, you must remove all object permissions from the Users group and refrain from using it to assign permissions. On the other hand, the easiest way to make a secure database unsecured is to assign full object permissions for each of its objects to the Users group.

By default, the Users group gets full permissions on newly created objects.

Assigning Permissions

Using the Access UI, you assign permissions to database objects with the Tools ➤ Security ➤ User and Group Permissions command (see Figure 24.5). Although you can change only one *type* of object at a time, you can select multiple objects (in contiguous or discontiguous groups) in the Permissions dialog.

FIGURE 24.5:

The Programmers group account has ReadDesign and ModifyDesign permissions for the basSecurityUtilities module.

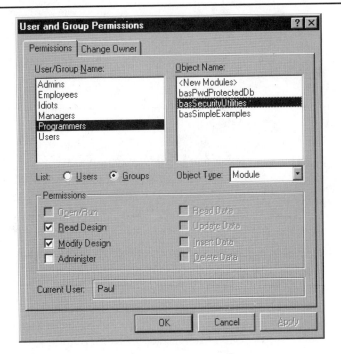

Which Objects Have Which Permissions?

Each database container object in Jet has a set of associated permissions you can set. Each type of object has a different set of settable permissions. For example, tables and queries don't have an Open/Run permission, but they have several permissions that control how data may be read or updated. On the other hand, forms, reports, and macros have no data permissions but do have an Open/Run permission. Table 24.1 lists each object and its permission set.

TABLE 24.1: Permission Sets for Each Type of Object

Object	Open/ Run	Read- Design	Modify- Design	Administer	Read- Data	Update Data	Insert- Data	Delete- Data	Open- Exclusive
Table		✓	✓	✓	✓	✓	✓	✓	
Query		✓	✓	✓	✓	✓	✓	✓	
Form	✓	✓	✓	✓					
Report	✓	✓	✓	✓					
Macro	✓	✓	✓	✓					
Module		✓	✓	✓					
Database	✓			✓					✓

Only the database itself and database container objects have permissions. This is paralleled in DAO, where only containers and documents have permissions. Controls, columns, parameters, toolbars, and other Jet and Access objects do not have permissions—which means they are not individually securable.

Access 95 has added a new permission for the database object: Administer. Although its name implies otherwise, this permission does *not* control the ability to administer permissions for the database. The database's Administer permission, however, does control access to:

- Converting the database into a replicated design master (This doesn't include creating additional replicas; a user needs only the Open/Run permission to create additional replicas.)

- Creating and removing the database password (The user must also have the OpenExclusive permission.)
- Saving changes to the database startup properties (This affects only Access applications.)

Permissions are not completely independent of each other; some permissions imply other permissions. For example, you can't have UpdateData permissions if you don't also have ReadDesign and ReadData permissions. Thus, UpdateData permission also implies these other permissions. Table 24.2 shows the interdependencies of permissions for table and query objects. If you have the permission in the first column, you also have the checked permissions to the right.

TABLE 24.2: Relationship between Permissions for Table and Query Objects

Permission	Read-Design	Modify-Design	Administer	Read-Data	Update-Data	Insert-Data	Delete-Data
ReadDesign	N/A						
ModifyDesign	✓	N/A		✓	✓		✓
Administer	✓	✓	N/A	✓	✓	✓	✓
ReadData	✓			N/A			
UpdateData	✓			✓	N/A		
InsertData	✓			✓		N/A	
DeleteData	✓			✓			N/A

Permissions for New Objects

In addition to setting permissions on existing objects, you can set permissions on new objects. You do this by choosing <New *objectname*> in the User and Group Permissions dialog (see Figure 24.5). This setting does *not* control the ability to create new objects; it controls only the permissions the account will receive for new objects. Although you can remove all permissions for new objects, this will *not* prevent users from creating new objects. In addition, since they will become the owner of any objects *they* create, they can always grant themselves Administer rights to these objects.

By using DAO, however, you *can* prevent users from creating new objects. We include a function in the sample database, glrSetPermissionDocCreate(), you can use for this purpose. (See the section "Programming Permissions" later in this chapter.)

Explicit versus Implicit Permissions

Users in the Jet security model have both implicit and explicit permissions. *Explicit permissions* are those permissions explicitly given to users and associated directly with a user account. *Implicit permissions* are those permissions users receive because of their membership in groups.

A user's set of permissions for an object will be based on the union of the user's explicit permissions and implicit permissions. A user's security level is always the *least restrictive* of the user's explicit permissions and the permissions of any and all groups to which the user belongs.

For example, say that user Joe has no permissions for the table tblCustomer. Joe also belongs to two groups: Managers and Programmers. The Managers group has Administer permissions (which implies all the other permissions for an object) for tblCustomer, and the Programmers group has only ReadDesign permissions for tblCustomer. Joe will have Administer permissions for tblCustomer because this is the least restrictive (or highest) permission for tblCustomer.

WARNING Don't make the mistake of removing a user's explicit permissions without bothering to check his or her implicit permissions.

Members of the Admins group (and those users having the Administer permission for a particular object) can directly view and set explicit permissions, but they can't directly view or set implicit permissions. Instead, you view implicit permissions by noting the group membership of a user and then looking at the permissions for each of these groups. To change implicit permissions, you must either modify the permissions for each of the groups to which a user belongs or add or remove the user from groups.

TIP Jet 3.0 includes a new property, AllPermissions, for the quick querying of a user's complete permission set. AllPermissions incorporates the union of a user's explicit and implicit permissions from DAO.

Who Can Change Permissions?

The following users can change object permissions:

- Members of the Admins group (for the workgroup in which the database was created) can always change permissions on any users. These rights can never be taken away using the Access UI (but they can be taken away using DAO).

- An object's owner—either the user who created the object or the user or group to which ownership of the object was transferred—can always modify the permissions for the object. This includes the ability of owners to give themselves Administer permissions for the object, even if someone else previously revoked these privileges. These rights can never be taken away.

- Any user with explicit or implicit Administer permissions to the object can administer permissions for that object. Another user with Administer rights can take away these rights.

- The database owner—the user who created the database—can always open a database and create new objects in it, even if the owner's rights to all the database's objects have been revoked. (The Access UI will allow members of the Admins group to *think* they have revoked the Open/Run permission from the database owner, but the owner will retain that right.) The only way to remove these rights is to import all of a database's objects and delete the original database.

What Happens to Permissions for Deleted Accounts?

When you delete a user or group account from a workgroup for an account that still has associated permissions, those permissions remain in the database. This can be a security concern; if someone can re-create the account and its PID, that person has a *backdoor pass* into your secured database. Thus, it's important that you remove all permissions (and transfer any objects the to-be-deleted account owns to a new owner) before deleting an account.

If someone re-creates an account with the same name but a *different* PID, Jet treats that account as a completely different account. It will not inherit any of the old account's permissions, because its SID is different from the SID of the old account.

> **TIP**
>
> The CurrentUser( ) function returns only the name of a user and therefore cannot be counted on to distinguish between users with the same name but different SIDs (either in the same workgroup at different points in time or across workgroups). This might be an issue when you are using the value of CurrentUser( ) to branch in your code or log activity to a file.

When you use the Change Owner tab of the User and Group Permissions dialog to list the owner of an object whose account has been deleted, Access lists the owner as "<Unknown>".

Ownership

In addition to the permissions that are granted to accounts, you need to be aware of ownership, because database owners and object owners have special privileges.

Who Owns a Database?

The user who creates a database is the database's owner. This user maintains special irrevocable rights to the database. As mentioned previously, this user will always be able to open the database. Only user accounts, not group accounts, can own databases.

Database ownership cannot be changed, but you can always create a new database using a different user account and import all the database's objects into another database. (This is how the Microsoft Security Wizard works.) If you then delete the original database and rename the new database to the name of the original, you have effectively transferred its ownership. The account used to transfer ownership must have ReadDesign and ReadData (where applicable) permissions to each of the database's objects.

You can use the Change Owner tab of the Tools ➤ Security ➤ User and Group Permissions command to view, but not change, the database owner.

Who Owns a Database's Objects?

Each database container object also has an owner. Initially, this is the user who created the object and may or may not be the same user account as the database owner. You can use the Change Owner tab of the Tools ➤ Security ➤ User and Group Permissions command to view and change object owners (see Figure 24.6).

The new owner for an object may be a group account. This is especially useful when you are managing OwnerAccess queries, which are discussed in the next section.

FIGURE 24.6:

Using the Change Owner dialog, Alicia is about to change the ownership for four tables from Kizzie to the Managers group.

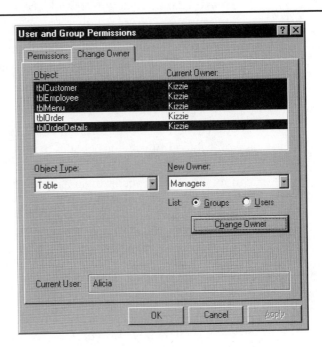

OwnerAccess Queries

Queries created in Access QBE have a property, RunPermissions, that governs whether Jet uses the query user's permissions or the owner's permissions when checking the security permissions for each of the source tables in a query. In Access SQL, setting this property to "Owner's" translates to the "WITH OWNERACCESS OPTION" clause.

This property allows you to present data to users who lack access rights to the underlying tables. Using this feature, you can effectively apply column-level and row-level security to a table.

For example, using an OwnerAccess query, you could let members of the Programmers group view and update all the columns in the tblEmployee table except for the Salary field. To do this, you would perform the following steps:

1. Remove all permissions to tblEmployee for the Programmers group.

2. Using an account that has ReadData and UpdateData permissions to tblEmployee, create a query, qryEmployee, that includes all the columns from tblEmployee except Salary.

3. Set the RunPermissions of qryEmployee to "Owner's" (or include the "WITH OWNERACCESS OPTION" clause in the SQL statement for the query).

One problem with OwnerAccess queries is that Jet allows only the query's owner to save changes to the query. Even other users with Administer rights to the query are prevented from saving changes to the query. This can present a problem if you are sharing the management of these queries among multiple users. In this case you may wish to transfer ownership of the query to a group account, but you'll have to temporarily change the RunPermissions property of the query back to "User's" before you can change the query's owner.

Encryption

As good as Jet security is, a very knowledgeable hacker equipped with a low-level disk editor might be able to directly open the .MDB file and break into your database. The only way to guard against such a hacker is to encrypt the database.

(Hacking your way into a database is far from a trivial task, but there are those who love such a challenge.)

Encrypting a database does not secure it. It is only one of a series of steps for properly securing a database. (These steps are discussed in the section "Properly Securing a Database with the Access Security Wizard" later in this chapter.)

Only the database owner or members of the Admins group can encrypt or decrypt a database. Jet uses an RSA- (Rivest, Shamir, and Adleman—the names of the inventors of the algorithm) based encryption algorithm with a key based on your workgroup ID to encrypt the database. Using Access, you can encrypt or decrypt a database using the Tools ➤ Security ➤ Encrypt/Decrypt Database command. The Access Security Wizard encrypts databases as its final step in securing a database.

It's important that you delete or safely archive all unencrypted versions of the encrypted databases to prevent security intrusions.

Encryption has two negative side effects. First, it reduces database performance (according to Microsoft estimates) by approximately 10 to 15 percent. Second, it makes the database uncompressible by programs such as PKZip, LHA, Stacker, and DriveSpace. (You won't be prevented from compressing the database, but the compression step won't significantly reduce the size.)

Programming Security Using Data Access Objects

So far in this chapter we have focused on defining the Jet security model and showing you how to manipulate it using the Access UI. You can also use Jet data access objects (DAO) to manipulate security. In fact, DAO lets you manipulate Jet security in ways the Access UI does not currently support. (For an introduction to DAO, see Chapter 6.)

In the sections that follow we introduce several reusable security functions, all of which can be found in the basSecurityUtilities module of the CH24.MDB database. Many of the functions are included in listings and described in detail; others are only briefly mentioned but are provided in basSecurityUtilities for your convenience. All the functions from basSecurityUtilities, however, are summarized in Table 24.3.

TABLE 24.3: Security Functions in basSecurityUtilities

Function	Purpose
glrAddGroupMember()	Adds a user to a group
glrCheckPermission()	Checks the particular bit or set of bits of a permission value for a document or container
glrCreateGroup()	Creates a new group account
glrCreateUser()	Creates a new user account
glrDeleteAccount()	Deletes a user or group account from the workgroup
glrGetAccount()	Checks for the existence of an account and returns the type (user or group) if found
glrGetObjectOwner()	Gets the account name of an object's owner
glrIsGroupMember()	Verifies whether a user is a member of a group
glrGetPermission()	Gets the entire permission value for a document or container
glrListUsersWithBlankPwd()	Prints all users with blank passwords to a text file
glrRemoveGroupMember()	Removes a user from a group
glrSetDbCreate()	Enables or disables an account from being able to create databases
glrSetDbPwd()	Sets the database password
glrSetOwner()	Changes the owner of a document or container
glrSetPermission()	Adds or subtracts a particular bit or set of bits, or replaces a permission value for a document or container
glrSetPermissionAdd()	Adds a particular permission bit or set of bits for a document or container. Wrapper function that calls glrSetPermission()
glrSetPermissionDocCreate()	Enables or disables the ability of an account to create documents of a particular type. Wrapper function that calls glrSetPermission()
glrSetPermissionReplace()	Replaces a permission value for a document or container. Wrapper function that calls glrSetPermission()
glrSetPermissionSubtract()	Subtracts a particular permission bit or set of bits for a document or container. Wrapper function that calls glrSetPermission()
glrSetPwd()	Sets the password for a user account

> **NOTE**
>
> The functions presented here often work on a single object and a single user, which are passed to the function as parameters. This helps make these functions generic. Unfortunately, it also makes them inefficient to use if you need to work on many objects or many users. In these cases you'd be better off modifying these functions to work on multiple objects.

Programming security with DAO revolves around two object hierarchies that correspond to the division in Jet security discussed in the section "Two Parts to Security" earlier in this chapter.

The User and Groups Hierarchy

You manipulate user and group accounts—the elements of security that are stored in the workgroup file—using the object hierarchy shown in Figure 24.7.

User and group objects are direct descendants of a workspace object; they are independent of any database objects. This is consistent with the physical location of the user and group account information—in the workgroup file.

FIGURE 24.7:

Data access objects hierarchy for users and groups

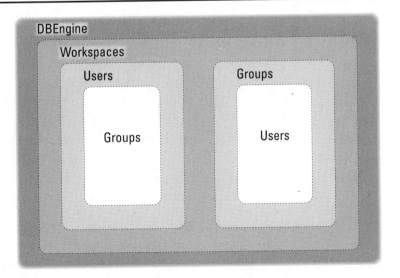

The user and group object hierarchies overlap. Each user object contains a *Groups* collection that contains the names of all the groups to which a user belongs. Similarly, each group object contains a *Users* collection that contains the names of all users belonging to that group.

The Collections and Documents Hierarchy

You manipulate object permissions—the elements of security that are stored in databases—using the object hierarchy shown in Figure 24.8.

Unlike user and group objects, permissions are manipulated using container and document objects that *are* descendants of the database object. Again, this is consistent with the physical location of these security elements.

FIGURE 24.8:

Data access objects hierarchy for containers and documents. You use these object collections to manage security permissions.

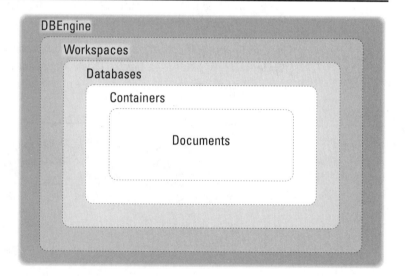

Managing Accounts

Using DAO, you can create, delete, and list user and group accounts. In addition, you can list the groups to which a user belongs and the users who are members of a group. Unlike prior versions of Jet, Jet 3.0 lets any user view user and group account information, although only Admins members can update account information.

Users Collections and User Objects

There are two types of collections of users: collections of a workspace and collections of a group account. The Users collection for a workspace contains all the user accounts for that workspace. The Users collection for a group account contains all the members of the group.

The Users collection has a single *property*, Count, and three *methods*, described in the following table:

Method	Purpose/Comments
Append	Adds a new user to a collection
Delete	Removes a user from a collection
Refresh	Refreshes the collection

The Users collection contains user objects. User objects have three *properties*:

Property	Purpose/Comment
Name	Name of the user. Read/write for new users not yet appended to the Users collection. Read-only otherwise
Password	Case-sensitive password for the user account. Write-only for new users not yet appended to the Users collection. Not available otherwise
PID	Case-sensitive personal identifier for the user account. Write-only for new users not yet appended to the Users collection. Not available otherwise

User objects also have two *methods*:

Method	Purpose/Comment
CreateGroup	Creates a new group object. When appended to the user object's Groups collection, this method adds the user to that group
NewPassword	Replaces an existing password with a new one

For example, you could use the following subroutine to enumerate the user accounts in the workgroup to the Debug window:

```
Sub ListUsers()

    Dim wrk As WorkSpace
    Dim usr As User

    Set wrk = DBEngine.Workspaces(0)

    Debug.Print "The Users collection has the following " & _
     wrk.Users.Count & " members:"
    For Each usr In wrk.Users
        Debug.Print usr.Name
    Next usr

End Sub
```

If you wished instead to list only user accounts that were members of the Managers group, you could use the following:

```
Sub ListManagers()

    Dim wrk As WorkSpace
    Dim grpManagers As Group
    Dim usr As User

    Set wrk = DBEngine.Workspaces(0)
    Set grpManagers = wrk.Groups!Managers

    For Each usr In grpManagers.Users
        Debug.Print usr.Name
    Next usr

End Sub
```

To create a new user account, you use the CreateUser method of a workspace object.

Groups Collections and Group Objects

There are two types of collections of groups: collections of a workspace and collections of a user account. The Groups collection for a workspace contains all the group accounts for that workspace. The Groups collection for a user account contains all the groups to which that user belongs.

The Groups collection has a single *property*, Count, and three *methods*, described in the following table:

Method	Purpose/Comments
Append	Adds a new group to a collection
Delete	Removes a group from a collection
Refresh	Refreshes the collection

The Groups collection contains group objects. Group objects have two *properties*:

Property	Purpose/Comment
Name	Name of the group. Read/write for new groups not yet appended to the Groups collection. Read-only otherwise
PID	Case-sensitive personal identifier for the group account. Write-only for new groups not yet appended to the Groups collection. Not available otherwise

Groups don't have passwords; you can't log on as a member of a group. Group objects have a single *method:*

Method	Purpose/Comment
CreateUser	Creates a new user object. When appended to the group object's Users collection, this method adds the user to the group

You might use the following code to enumerate the names of all the groups in the Groups collection of the default workspace:

```
Sub ListGroups()

    Dim wrk As WorkSpace
    Dim grp As Group

    Set wrk = DBEngine.Workspaces(0)

    Debug.Print "The Groups collection has the following " & _
      wrk.Groups.Count & " members:"
```

```
    For Each grp In wrk.Groups
        Debug.Print grp.Name
    Next grp

End Sub
```

To create a new group account, you use the CreateGroup method of a workspace object.

Creating New Accounts

You can use the glrCreateUser() function, located in the basSecurityUtilities module of CH24.MDB, to create a new user account. It takes as its parameters the name of the new user, the new user's PID, and the new user's password. It returns True if successful. This function, which requires the user running it to be a member of the Admins group, is shown in Listing 24.1.

Listing 24.1

```
Function glrCreateUser(ByVal strName As String, _
 ByVal strPID As String, ByVal strPW As String) As Boolean

    On Error GoTo glrCreateUserErr

    Dim wrk As Workspace
    Dim usrNew As User
    Dim strMsg As String

    Const glrcProcName = "glrCreateUser"

    glrCreateUser = False

    Set wrk = DBEngine.Workspaces(0)

    'Create new user account and append to Users collection
    Set usrNew = wrk.CreateUser(strName, strPID, strPW)
    wrk.Users.Append usrNew

    'Must also add user account to Users group
    usrNew.Groups.Append wrk.CreateGroup("Users")

    glrCreateUser = True

glrCreateUserDone:
```

```
    On Error GoTo 0
    Exit Function

glrCreateUserErr:
    Select Case Err
    Case glrcErrAccntAlreadyExists
        strMsg = "An account with the name '" & strName & _
            "' already exists."
    Case glrcErrBadPid
        strMsg = "You must enter a PID of between 4 " & _
            "and 20 characters."
    Case glrcErrNoPermission
        strMsg = "You don't have permission to perform " & _
            "this operation."
    Case Else
        strMsg = "Error " & Err.Number & ": " & Err.Description
    End Select
        MsgBox strMsg, vbCritical + vbOKOnly, "Procedure " & _
            glrcProcName
    Resume glrCreateUserDone

End Function
```

Creating a new user is much like creating any new object with DAO. glrCreateUser() works by creating a new user object using the CreateUser method of the default workspace. The new user is created when the user's object is appended to the workspace's Users collection. To be consistent with the Access UI— and more important, to make it so the new account will be able to open databases in the workgroup—glrCreateUser() finishes by appending the new account to the built-in Users group.

basSecurityUtilities also includes a similar function, glrCreateGroup(), for creating new group accounts.

Checking for the Existence and Type of an Account

You can use glrGetAccount() to check for the existence and type of account to which you pass the account name. It returns one of the following global constants that have been declared in the Declarations section of basSecurityUtilities:

```
Global Const glrcAccntUser = 1
Global Const glrcAccntGroup = 2
Global Const glrcAccntNone = 0
```

glrGetAccount() is shown in Listing 24.2.

Listing 24.2

```
Function glrGetAccount(ByVal strName As String) As Integer

    Dim wrk As Workspace
    Dim varAccntName As Variant

    Set wrk = DBEngine.Workspaces(0)

    'Turn off event handler and check line by line
    'to determine account membership
    On Error Resume Next

    varAccntName = wrk.Users(strName).Name
    If Err = glrcErrNameNotInCollection Then
        'Reset error variable
        Err = 0
        varAccntName = wrk.Groups(strName).Name
        If Err = glrcErrNameNotInCollection Then
            glrGetAccount = glrcAccntNone
        Else
            glrGetAccount = glrcAccntGroup
        End If
    Else
        glrGetAccount = glrcAccntUser
    End If

End Function
```

glrGetAccount() works by attempting to grab the name of a user account with the passed name. If error 3265 (glrcErrNameNotInCollection) occurs because the user account doesn't exist, glrGetAccount() resumes and attempts to grab the name of a group account with the same name. If both attempts fail, the function returns 0. This function *doesn't* require the user running it to be a member of the Admins group.

Checking for Group Membership

You can check whether a user is a member of a group using glrIsGroupMember(). This function takes as its input the name of the user and the group and returns True if the user is a member. glrIsGroupMember() is shown in Listing 24.3.

Listing 24.3

```
Function glrIsGroupMember(ByVal strGroup As String, _
 Optional ByVal varUser As Variant) As Boolean

    On Error GoTo glrIsGroupMemberErr

    Dim wrk As Workspace
    Dim usr As User
    Dim grp As Group
    Dim strMsg As String
    Dim intErrHndlrFlag As Integer
    Dim varGroupName As Variant

    Const glrcFlagSetUser = 1
    Const glrcFlagSetGroup = 2
    Const glrcFlagCheckMember = 4
    Const glrcFlagElse = 0

    Const glrcProcName = "glrIsGroupMember"

    glrIsGroupMember = False

    'Initialize flag for determining
    'context for error handler
    intErrHndlrFlag = glrcFlagElse

    Set wrk = DBEngine.Workspaces(0)

    'Refresh users and groups collections
    wrk.Users.Refresh
    wrk.Groups.Refresh

    If IsMissing(varUser) Then varUser = CurrentUser()

    intErrHndlrFlag = glrcFlagSetUser
    Set usr = wrk.Users(varUser)

    intErrHndlrFlag = glrcFlagSetGroup
    Set grp = wrk.Groups(strGroup)

    intErrHndlrFlag = glrcFlagCheckMember
    varGroupName = usr.Groups(strGroup).Name

    If Not IsEmpty(varGroupName) Then
```

```
            glrIsGroupMember = True
        End If

glrIsGroupMemberDone:
        On Error GoTo 0
        Exit Function

glrIsGroupMemberErr:
        Select Case Err
        Case glrcErrNameNotInCollection
            Select Case intErrHndlrFlag
            Case glrcFlagSetUser
                strMsg = "The user account '" & varUser & _
                    "' doesn't exist."
            Case glrcFlagSetGroup
                strMsg = "The group account '" & strGroup & _
                    "' doesn't exist."
            Case glrcFlagCheckMember
                Resume Next
            Case Else
                strMsg = "Error " & Err.Number & ": " & _
                    Err.Description
            End Select
        Case glrcErrNoPermission
            strMsg = "You don't have permission to perform " & _
             "this operation."
        Case Else
            strMsg = "Error " & Err.Number & ": " & Err.Description
        End Select
            MsgBox strMsg, vbCritical + vbOKOnly, "Procedure " & _
             glrcProcName
        Resume glrIsGroupMemberDone

End Function
```

This function checks for membership using the following statement:

```
varGroupName = usr.Groups(strGroup).Name
```

This statement attempts to set a variable to the Name property of the group object in the Groups collection of the user object. There's nothing special here about the Name property; any readable property of the group object would suffice. (With that said, however, you'll find that Name *is* the only readable property of a group or user object.) Because of the symmetry of the Users and Groups collections, glrIsGroupMember() could have also checked for the name of the user object in the

Users collection of the group object. The following alternate statement would yield the same result:

```
varUserName = grp.Users(strUser).Name
```

glrIsGroupMember() *doesn't* require the user running it to be a member of the Admins group.

Adding a User to a Group

Members of the Admins group can use glrAddGroupMember() to add a user to a group. This function takes as its input the name of the user to be added and the name of the group. It returns True if it succeeds. glrAddGroupMember() is shown in Listing 24.4.

Listing 24.4

```
Function glrAddGroupMember(ByVal strUser As String, _
 ByVal strGroup As String) As Boolean

    On Error GoTo glrAddGroupMemberErr

    Dim wrk As Workspace
    Dim usr As User
    Dim grp As Group
    Dim strMsg As String
    Dim intErrHndlrFlag As Integer

    Const glrcFlagSetUser = 1
    Const glrcFlagSetGroup = 2
    Const glrcFlagElse = 0

    Const glrcProcName = "glrAddGroupMember"

    glrAddGroupMember = False

    'Initialize flag for determining
    'context for error handler
    intErrHndlrFlag = glrcFlagElse

    Set wrk = DBEngine.Workspaces(0)

    'Refresh users and groups collections
    wrk.Users.Refresh
```

```
        wrk.Groups.Refresh

        intErrHndlrFlag = glrcFlagSetUser
        Set usr = wrk.Users(strUser)

        intErrHndlrFlag = glrcFlagSetGroup
        Set grp = wrk.Groups(strGroup)

        intErrHndlrFlag = glrcFlagElse

        'Report error if user already a member of this group
        If glrIsGroupMember(strUser, strGroup) Then
            strMsg = "The user account '" & strUser & _
              "' is already a member of the group " & strGroup & "."
            MsgBox strMsg, vbCritical + vbOKOnly, "Procedure " & _
             glrcProcName
            GoTo glrAddGroupMemberDone
        End If

        'Append user to group
        grp.Users.Append grp.CreateUser(strUser)

        glrAddGroupMember = True

glrAddGroupMemberDone:
    On Error GoTo 0
    Exit Function

glrAddGroupMemberErr:
    Select Case Err
    Case glrcErrNameNotInCollection
        Select Case intErrHndlrFlag
        Case glrcFlagSetUser
            strMsg = "The user account '" & strUser & _
              "' doesn't exist."
        Case glrcFlagSetGroup
            strMsg = "The group account '" & strGroup & _
              "' doesn't exist."
        Case Else
            strMsg = "Error " & Err.Number & ": " & _
             Err.Description
        End Select
    Case glrcErrCantPerformOperation
        strMsg = "The user account '" & strUser & _
          "' is already a member of the group " & strGroup & "."
```

```
Case glrcErrNoPermission
    strMsg = "You don't have permission to perform " & _
     "this operation."
Case Else
    strMsg = "Error " & Err.Number & ": " & Err.Description
End Select
    MsgBox strMsg, vbCritical + vbOKOnly, "Procedure " & _
     glrcProcName
Resume glrAddGroupMemberDone

End Function
```

This function, as well as several others in the basSecurityUtilities module, uses a flag, intErrHndlrFlag, to declare a state before executing a statement that may cause an error. The functions use this flag to give the user better feedback when an error occurs. glrAddGroupMember(), for example, uses this flag to replace a nonspecific missing account message for error 3265 (glrcErrNameNotInCollection) with a message that informs the user whether the nonexistent account is the passed user or group account.

glrAddGroupMember() refreshes the workspace's collections before checking for membership in case anyone has altered the group membership recently. (Otherwise, any recent changes made in the Access UI or by another user in the workgroup would not be included.) It then checks for the existence of the user and group accounts and whether the user is already a member of the group (using glrIsGroupMember()). If any of these checks turns up an error, glrAddGroupMember() displays a dialog and exits. Otherwise, the CreateUser method is used to append the user to the group.

Changing Passwords

You can use glrSetPwd() to change the password for either the current logged-in user or for another user's account. If you choose the latter, you must be a member of the Admins group. You pass glrSetPwd() the name of the account, the old password, and the new password. This function can be found in Listing 24.5.

Listing 24.5

```
Function glrSetPwd(ByVal strUser As String, _
 ByVal strOldPwd As String, ByVal strNewPwd As String) _
 As Boolean
```

```
    On Error GoTo glrSetPwdErr

    Dim wrk As Workspace
    Dim usr As User
    Dim strMsg As String

    Const glrcProcName = "glrSetPwd"

    glrSetPwd = False

    Set wrk = DBEngine.Workspaces(0)

    'Point to user object
    Set usr = wrk.Users(strUser)

    'Only Admins members can change other users' passwords
    'For Admins members, old pwd is ignored
    usr.NewPassword strOldPwd, strNewPwd

    glrSetPwd = True

glrSetPwdDone:
    On Error GoTo 0
    Exit Function

glrSetPwdErr:
    Select Case Err
    Case glrcErrNameNotInCollection
        strMsg = "The user account '" & strUser & _
        "' doesn't exist."
    Case glrcErrNoPermission
        strMsg = "You don't have permission to perform " & _
        "this operation or you have entered the wrong " & _
        "old password."
    Case Else
        strMsg = "Error " & Err.Number & ": " & Err.Description
    End Select
        MsgBox strMsg, vbCritical + vbOKOnly, "Procedure " & _
        glrcProcName
    Resume glrSetPwdDone

End Function
```

glrSetPwd() uses the NewPassword method of the user object. When you use this method, you are required to enter the correct old password if the account is the same as the value of CurrentUser(); otherwise you don't have to enter the old password—the string is ignored. This behavior is consistent with the Access UI, where you can clear someone else's password. The difference is that with DAO, you can both clear the password and set it to a new nonblank value in one step. (Of course, you have to be an Admins member to change the password of another user.)

The frmChangePwd form in CH24.MDB allows users to change passwords (see Figure 24.9). The event procedure attached to the Change Password command button calls glrSetPwd() after ensuring that the password was verified properly. This procedure is shown in Listing 24.6.

FIGURE 24.9:

frmChangePwd calls glrSetPwd to set a user's password.

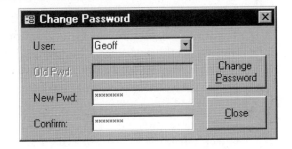

Listing 24.6

```
Private Sub cmdPwd_Click()

    Dim fOK As Boolean
    Dim ctlOldPwd As TextBox
    Dim ctlNewPwd As TextBox
    Dim ctlConfirmNewPwd As TextBox
    Dim strMsg As String

    Set ctlOldPwd = Me!txtOldPwd
    Set ctlNewPwd = Me!txtNewPwd
    Set ctlConfirmNewPwd = Me!txtConfirmNewPwd

    If Nz(ctlNewPwd) = Nz(ctlConfirmNewPwd) Then
        fOK = glrSetPwd(strUser:=cboUsers, _
        strOldPwd:=Nz(ctlOldPwd), _
        strNewPwd:=Nz(ctlNewPwd))
```

```
        If fOK Then
            strMsg = "Password changed!"
            ctlOldPwd = ""
            ctlNewPwd = ""
            ctlConfirmNewPwd = ""
        Else
            strMsg = "Password change failed!"
        End If
    Else
        strMsg = "New password entry does not match " & _
          "confirming password entry!"
    End If

    MsgBox strMsg, vbOKOnly + vbInformation, _
      "Change Password"

End Sub
```

The frmChangePwd form includes a combo box that allows Admins members to directly set the password for other users. The combo box is filled using a list-filling function. The list-filling function's initialization step, which fills an array with all users in the workgroup, is shown here:

```
sintUsrCnt = 0
swrk.Users.Refresh
ReDim sastrUsr(1 To swrk.Users.Count)
For Each usr In swrk.Users
    strName = usr.Name
    If strName <> "Engine" And strName <> "Creator" Then
        sintUsrCnt = sintUsrCnt + 1
        sastrUsr(sintUsrCnt) = strName
    End If
Next usr
ReDim Preserve sastrUsr(1 To sintUsrCnt)
```

Jet defines two built-in, but normally hidden, users—Creator and Engine—that have, or more likely just appear to have, blank passwords. (For those of you who are immediately thinking "security hole," hold your horses. Even though these Jet-defined users appear in the Users collection, you cannot use them to log on to Access.) In any case, the glrcboUsersFill() list-filling function skips over them. (See Chapter 7 for more details on list-filling functions.)

An event procedure attached to the form's Load event determines whether the current user is a member of Admins by calling glrIsGroupMember:

```
If Not glrIsGroupMember("Admins") Then
    With Me!cboUsers
        .Locked = True
        .Enabled = False
    End With
End If
```

This code ensures that the combo box is disabled if the user is not a member of Admins. Non-Admins members, however, can still use this form to change their own user password.

Listing All Users with Blank Passwords

A user account with blank passwords is the Achilles' heel of a supposedly secure workgroup. Using the Access UI, there's no way for a database administrator to quickly determine which users have left their passwords blank. Using DAO, however, you can accomplish this easily. We have written such a function, glrListUsers-WithBlankPwd(), which is included in the basSecurityUtilities module. The essence of the function is shown here:

```
For Each usr In wrkDefault.Users
    strUser = usr.Name

    'Skip if special engine-level users
    If strUser <> "Creator" And strUser <> "Engine" Then
        'Initialize flag that tracks blank Pwd
        fNonBlankPwd = False

        'Attempt to log on to new workspace with blank Pwd
        Set wrkNew = DBEngine. _
         CreateWorkspace("NewWorkspace", strUser, "")

        'If an error occurred on last statement, then
        'error handler will set flag to True.
        'Otherwise, able to log on, so Pwd must've been blank.
        If Not fNonBlankPwd Then
            Print #1, strUser
            fAnyBlankPwds = True
```

```
        End If
    End If
Next usr
```

glrUsersWithBlankPW() works by iterating through the Users collection in the default workspace and then attempting to log on to each account using a blank password. If it is able to log on to an account, it prints the user name to a file.

Other Account Maintenance Functions

There are two other account maintenance functions in basSecurityUtilities. You can use glrDeleteAccount() to delete a user or group account and glrRemoveGroup-Member() to remove a user from a group.

Programming Permissions

Permissions are properties of *documents* and their *containers.* Like other DAO collections, the Containers collection and Documents collection have a single property, Count, that indicates the number of objects in the collection. These two collections also have a single method, Refresh, that you can use to make sure the collections are current.

Documents and Containers

Container and document objects (which were introduced in Chapter 6) have several properties. They are listed in Table 24.4.

TABLE 24.4: Properties of Containers and Their Documents

Object	Property	Description
Container	Inherit	Determines whether any changes are inherited by new objects. If you set permissions on a container and set Inherit to True, Jet uses these permissions when creating new documents for the container
	Name	Read-only. The name of the container. For example, the Tables container contains a database's tables and queries
	Owner	Read/write. The user or group account that owns the object. By default, all object containers are owned by the engine user (This can be changed, however, using DAO.)

TABLE 24.4: Properties of Containers and Their Documents (continued)

Object	Property	Description
	Permissions	Read/write. A Long Integer that stores explicit permission information for the container. When you use this property with the Inherit property, you can set permissions for new documents of a container
	AllPermissions	Read-only. A Long Integer that stores the union of explicit and implicit permission information for the container
	UserName	Read/write. When you read or write permissions for a container, the permissions are account specific. By default, this property points to the current user. You use UserName to view or set permissions for different user and group accounts
Document	Container	Read-only. The container to which the document belongs
	DateCreated	Read-only. The date the document was created
	LastUpdated	Read-only. The date the document's schema was last changed
	Name	Read-only. The name of the document
	Owner	Read/write. The user or group account that owns the object. By default, the owner is the document's creator
	Permissions	Read/write. A Long Integer that stores explicit permission information for the document
	AllPermissions	Read-only. A Long Integer that stores the union of explicit and implicit permission information for the document
	UserName	Read/write. When you read or write permissions for a document, the permissions are account specific. By default, this property points to the current user. You can use UserName to view or set permissions for different user and group accounts

Permission Constants

Microsoft predefines several database security constants you can use to simplify the reading and writing of permissions. These constants are outlined in Table 24.5. They also can be viewed with the Object Browser. The use of these constants is discussed in the next few sections.

TABLE 24.5: Jet and Access Security Constants

Constant	Meaning
dbSecNoAccess	No access to the object
dbSecFullAccess	Full access to the object
dbSecDelete	Can delete the object
dbSecReadSec	Can read the object's security-related information
dbSecWriteSec	Can alter access permissions
dbSecWriteOwner	Can change the Owner property setting
dbSecCreate	Can create new documents; valid only with a Container object
dbSecReadDef	Can read the table definition, including column and index information
dbSecWriteDef	Can modify or delete the table definition, including column and index information
dbSecRetrieveData	Can retrieve data from the Document object
dbSecInsertData	Can add records
dbSecReplaceData	Can modify records
dbSecDeleteData	Can delete records
dbSecDBAdmin	Gives user permission to make a database replicable, change the database password, and set startup properties
dbSecDBCreate	Can create new databases; valid only on the Databases container object in the workgroup file (SYSTEM.MDW)
dbSecDBExclusive	Can open the database exclusively
dbSecDBOpen	Can open the database
acSecMacExecute	Can run the macro
acSecMacReadDef	Can read the definition of the macro
acSecMacWriteDef	Can modify the definition of the macro
acSecFrmRptExecute	Can open the form or report
acSecFrmRptReadDef	Can read the definition of the form or report and its module
acSecFrmRptWriteDef	Can modify the definition of the form or report and its module
acSecModReadDef	Can read the definition of the global module
acSecModWriteDef	Can modify the definition of the global module

Reading Permissions

You can read the permissions of an object simply by checking the value of the Permissions or AllPermissions property of the object. Permissions returns explicit permissions only, whereas AllPermissions returns the union of explicit and implicit permissions. They both return the Long Integer corresponding to the user's permissions for the object. For example, you could query the permission of the tblOrder table and store the value into the variable lngPermission with the following assignment statement (assuming you have previously set the db object variable to point to a database):

```
lngPermission = _
  db.Containers!Tables.Documents!tblOrder.Permissions
```

Often, you'll want to check whether a user has some minimum permissions to an object. You can do this using bitwise arithmetic (also referred to by programmers as *bit twiddling*). This works because Jet stores each individual permission as a different bit of the 4-byte Long Integer value. You check a permission value for a specific set of bits—some permissions are actually the result of setting several bits—by using the And operator to mask off the bits in which you are interested and comparing the result of the operation to these same bits. Using the predefined permission constants makes this easy:

```
fOk = ((doc.Permissions And dbSecConstant) = dbSecConstant)
```

fOk will be set to True if the document object has that permission—as defined by dbSecConstant—set to True, and False if the document object does not.

For example, you could use the following function to determine whether the user Kizzie has read permission for tblCustomer:

```
Function CanKizzieRead() As Boolean

    ' Checks explicit permissions only

    Dim db As Database
    Dim doc As Document

    Set db = CurrentDb()
    Set doc = db.Containers!Tables.Documents!tblCustomer

    doc.UserName = "Kizzie"

    CanKizzieRead = _
```

```
((doc.Permissions And dbSecRetrieveData) _
= dbSecRetrieveData)
```

```
End Function
```

If Kizzie has ReadData permission to tblCustomer, CanKizzieRead() returns True; otherwise it returns False. The trick in this example is to use the bitwise And operator to mask off the complete permissions with only the permission you are interested in—in this case, dbSecRetrieveData (ReadData permission).

CanKizzieRead() checks only for explicit permissions. We could have also checked Kizzie's implicit permissions by replacing the last part of the function with:

```
CanKizzieRead = _
 ((doc.AllPermissions And dbSecRetrieveData) _
 = dbSecRetrieveData)
```

There's another way to check a permission value against a constant that works *only* if one bit is set on in the constant:

```
fOk =  (doc.Permissions And dbSecConstant) <>0
```

This method, however, will *fail* with constants that have more than one bit set. Thus, because many of the security constants have multiple bits set, you shouldn't use it.

Writing Permissions

Writing permissions is similar to reading them. You have two choices when writing the permissions of an object:

- You can replace the existing permissions with a brand-new set of permissions.
- You can add or subtract a permission on top of the existing permissions.

To *replace* a set of permissions, you simply set the permissions to the new value. For example, you could change the permission for tblOrder to give the user Modify-Design permission using the following code:

```
Set doc = db.Containers!Tables.Documents!tblOrder
doc.Permissions = dbSecWriteDef
```

To *add* a permission on top of the existing permission set, you use the bitwise Or operator. For example, you could use the following code to add ModifyDesign permission to the existing set of permissions for tblOrder:

```
Set doc = db.Containers!Tables.Documents!tblOrder
doc.Permissions = doc.Permissions Or dbSecWriteDef
```

Using this method of assigning permissions is often preferable because it guards against inadvertently removing other permissions the user may have. For example, if the user also had ReadData permission to tblOrder, that permission would be preserved using this technique. This would not be true in the previous example.

To *subtract* a permission from a user while preserving all other permissions, you use the bitwise And Not operator. For example, to take away the same permission from a user, replace the second line in the preceding example with the following:

```
doc.Permissions = doc.Permissions And Not dbSecWriteDef
```

Checking for a Specific Permission

You can use glrCheckPermission() to check whether a user or group account has some permission bit (or multiple bits) set on. It takes these five parameters:

Parameter	Optional?	Purpose
lngPerm	No	Permission value of the object you wish to check
intObjType	No	One of the glrcObj constants (glrcObjDatabase, glrcObjForm, glrcObjModule, glrcObjReport, glrcObjScript, or glrcObjTable) defined in the Declarations section of basSecurityUtilities to indicate the type of object to check
varObjName	Yes	Name of the document object to check; leave Null to check the document container
varAccount	Yes	Name of the user or group account to check; leave Null to check permission for the current user

Parameter	Optional?	Purpose
fAllPerm	Yes	For user accounts, set to True (the default) to check both explicit and implicit permissions; set to False to check only explicit permissions; for group accounts, this parameter has no effect

glrCheckPermission() returns True if the account has the requested permission to the object. It's shown in Listing 24.7.

Listing 24.7

```
Function glrCheckPermission(ByVal lngPerm As Long, _
 ByVal intObjType As Integer, _
 Optional ByVal varObjName As Variant, _
 Optional ByVal varAccount As Variant, _
 Optional ByVal fAllPerm As Variant) As Boolean

    On Error GoTo glrCheckPermissionErr

    Dim wrk As Workspace
    Dim db As Database
    Dim cnt As Container
    Dim doc As Document
    Dim usr As User
    Dim strMsg As String
    Dim fPerm As Boolean
    Dim intErrHndlrFlag As Integer

    Const glrcFlagSetContainer = 5
    Const glrcFlagSetDocument = 6
    Const glrcFlagElse = 0

    Const glrcProcName = "glrCheckPermission"

    glrCheckPermission = False

    'Initialize flag for determining
    'context for error handler
    intErrHndlrFlag = glrcFlagElse

    'Optional parameters
```

```
If IsMissing(varAccount) Then varAccount = CurrentUser()
If IsMissing(fAllPerm) Then fAllPerm = True

Set wrk = DBEngine.Workspaces(0)
Set db = CurrentDb()

'If setting permissions for database, you
'actually need to use the MSysDB document
If intObjType = glrcObjDatabase Then
    varObjName = "MSysDB"
End If

'Point to the right container
intErrHndlrFlag = glrcFlagSetContainer
Set cnt = db.Containers(intObjType)
intErrHndlrFlag = glrcFlagElse

'Refresh the container's docs
cnt.Documents.Refresh

intErrHndlrFlag = glrcFlagElse

cnt.UserName = varAccount

'Only point to a document if the name is non-blank
If Len(varObjName) > 0 Then
    intErrHndlrFlag = glrcFlagSetDocument
    Set doc = cnt.Documents(varObjName)
    intErrHndlrFlag = glrcFlagElse
    doc.UserName = varAccount
End If

'Initialize permission flag
fPerm = False

If IsMissing(varObjName) Then
    If fAllPerm Then
        fPerm = ((cnt.AllPermissions And lngPerm) = lngPerm)
    Else
        fPerm = ((cnt.Permissions And lngPerm) = lngPerm)
    End If
Else
    If fAllPerm Then
        fPerm = ((doc.AllPermissions And lngPerm) = lngPerm)
    Else
```

```
                fPerm = ((doc.Permissions And lngPerm) = lngPerm)
            End If
        End If

        glrCheckPermission = fPerm

glrCheckPermissionDone:
        On Error GoTo 0
        Exit Function

glrCheckPermissionErr:
        Select Case Err
        Case glrcErrNoPermission
            strMsg = "You don't have permission to perform " & _
              "this operation."
        Case glrcErrNameNotInCollection
            Select Case intErrHndlrFlag
            Case glrcFlagSetContainer
                strMsg = "Invalid object type constant."
            Case glrcFlagSetDocument
                strMsg = "The object '" & varObjName & _
                  "' is not in the '" & intObjType & "' collection."
            Case Else
                strMsg = "Error " & Err.Number & ": " & _
                  Err.Description
            End Select
        Case Else
            strMsg = "Error " & Err.Number & ": " & Err.Description
        End Select
            MsgBox strMsg, vbCritical + vbOKOnly, "Procedure " & _
              glrcProcName
        Resume glrCheckPermissionDone

End Function
```

glrCheckPermission(), along with many other permission functions found in basSecurityUtilities, is flexible in that it allows you to query the permissions on a document object (for example, qryItems), a container (for example, Modules), or the database itself.

If you pass glrCheckPermission() a non-null value for varObjName, it determines the permissions for that document.

If, instead, you pass the function a null varObjName parameter and one of the object constants for the parameter intObjType, it determines the permissions for the container itself. This is equivalent to determining the permissions for any newly created objects.

If you pass the function a null varObjName parameter and the glrcObjDatabase constant for the intObjType parameter, glrCheckPermission() determines the permissions for the database itself. glrCheckPermission() accomplishes this by using a special document of the database container named MSysDB.

glrCheckPermission() then sets the UserName property for the container object to the account name passed to it or, if a null account name was passed, to the current user.

If glrCheckPermission() needs to check the permissions of a document, it sets the document object, doc, to point to the name of that object and also sets the UserName property for the document.

Finally, glrCheckPermission() uses the bitwise And operator to mask off the complete permissions with the value of the lngPerm parameter (the permission you wish to check). The following code accomplishes this for a document:

```
fPerm = ((doc.Permissions And lngPerm) = lngPerm)
```

Setting Permissions

You can add permissions to, subtract permissions from, or completely replace the permission value of an object for a user or group account using glrSetPermission(). This function takes five parameters:

Parameter	Optional?	Purpose
lngPerm	No	Permission value of the object you wish to set
intObjType	No	One of the glrcObj constants (glrcObjDatabase, glrcObjForm, glrcObjModule, glrcObjReport, glrcObjScript, or glrcObjTable) defined in the Declarations section of basSecurityUtilities to indicate the type of object to set

Parameter	Optional?	Purpose
intAction	No	One of the glrcPermission constants (glrcPermissionAdd, glrcPermissionSubtract, or glrcPermissionReplace) defined in the Declarations section of basSecurityUtilities to indicate the type of action to take
varObjName	Yes	Name of the document object to check; leave null to check the document container
varAccount	Yes	Name of the user or group account; leave null to set permission for the current user

glrSetPermission() returns True if it succeeds in changing the permission. It's shown in Listing 24.8.

Listing 24.8

```
Function glrSetPermission(ByVal lngPerm As Long, _
  ByVal intObjType As Integer, _
  ByVal intAction As Integer, _
  Optional ByVal varObjName As Variant, _
  Optional ByVal varAccount As Variant) As Boolean

    On Error GoTo glrSetPermissionErr

    Dim db As Database
    Dim cnt As Container
    Dim doc As Document
    Dim strMsg As String
    Dim intErrHndlrFlag As Integer

    Const glrcFlagSetContainer = 5
    Const glrcFlagSetDocument = 6
    Const glrcFlagElse = 0

    Const glrcProcName = "glrSetPermission"
```

```
glrSetPermission = False

'Initialize flag for determining
'context for error handler
intErrHndlrFlag = glrcFlagElse

'Optional parameters
If IsMissing(varAccount) Then varAccount = CurrentUser()

If intAction < glrcPermissionSubtract Or _
 intAction > glrcPermissionReplace Then
    strMsg = "Illegal intAction parameter."
    MsgBox strMsg, vbOKOnly + vbCritical, _
     "Procedure: " & glrcProcName
    GoTo glrSetPermissionDone
End If

Set db = CurrentDb()

'If setting permissions for database, you
'actually need to use the MSysDB document
If intObjType = glrcObjDatabase Then
    varObjName = "MSysDB"
End If

intErrHndlrFlag = glrcFlagSetContainer
Set cnt = db.Containers(intObjType)
intErrHndlrFlag = glrcFlagElse

'Refresh the container's docs
cnt.Documents.Refresh
'Set the container's inherit property so that
'any changes to it are inherited by new docs
cnt.Inherit = True
cnt.UserName = varAccount

'Only point to a document if the name is non-blank
If Not IsMissing(varObjName) Then
    intErrHndlrFlag = glrcFlagSetDocument
    Set doc = cnt.Documents(varObjName)
    intErrHndlrFlag = glrcFlagElse
    doc.UserName = varAccount
End If

'Overlay new permissions on top of the existing ones.
```

```
        'Use Or to add permission; And Not to subtract permission.
        If IsMissing(varObjName) Then
            If intAction = glrcPermissionAdd Then
                cnt.Permissions = cnt.Permissions Or lngPerm
            ElseIf intAction = glrcPermissionSubtract Then
                cnt.Permissions = cnt.Permissions And Not lngPerm
            Else
                cnt.Permissions = lngPerm
            End If
        Else
            If intAction = glrcPermissionAdd Then
                doc.Permissions = doc.Permissions Or lngPerm
            ElseIf intAction = glrcPermissionSubtract Then
                doc.Permissions = doc.Permissions And Not lngPerm
            Else
                doc.Permissions = lngPerm
            End If
        End If

        glrSetPermission = True

glrSetPermissionDone:
    On Error GoTo 0
    Exit Function

glrSetPermissionErr:
    Select Case Err
    Case glrcErrNoPermission
        glrSetPermission = False
        Resume glrSetPermissionDone
    Case glrcErrNameNotInCollection
        Select Case intErrHndlrFlag
        Case glrcFlagSetContainer
            strMsg = "Invalid object type constant."
        Case glrcFlagSetDocument
            strMsg = "The object '" & varObjName & _
                "' is not in the '" & intObjType & "' collection."
        Case Else
            strMsg = "Error " & Err.Number & ": " & _
                Err.Description
        End Select
    Case glrcErrBadAccntName
        strMsg = "The account '" & varAccount & _
            "' doesn't exist."
    Case Else
```

```
        strMsg = "Error " & Err.Number & ": " & Err.Description
    End Select
        MsgBox strMsg, vbCritical + vbOKOnly, "Procedure " & _
        glrcProcName
    Resume glrSetPermissionDone

End Function
```

glrSetPermission() works similarly to glrGetPermission(). The major difference is that instead of getting the existing permission value, it adds, subtracts, or replaces the permission value for the object using the following code (for document objects):

```
If intAction = glrcPermissionAdd Then
    doc.Permissions = doc.Permissions Or lngPerm
ElseIf intAction = glrcPermissionSubtract Then
    doc.Permissions = doc.Permissions And Not lngPerm
Else
    doc.Permissions = lngPerm
End If
```

Because we've overloaded glrSetPermission() with functionality, we've also provided for wrapper functions you can call instead, all of which do their work by calling glrSetPermission():

Function	Purpose
glrSetPermissionAdd()	Adds a particular permission
glrSetPermissionSubtract()	Subtracts a particular permission
glrSetPermissionReplace()	Replaces a permission value with another
glrSetPermissionDoc-Create()	Enables or disables the ability of an account to create documents of a particular type

The last function, glrSetPermissionDocCreate(), disables (or enables) the ability of a user to create a particular type of object by subtracting (or adding back) the dbSecCreate bit (&H1) of the permission property of the document's container. (If you use this function to remove the dbSecCreate permission of a user, you'll want to make sure the user doesn't have implicit dbSecCreate permission by virtue of group membership.)

Disabling the Creation of New Databases

Jet includes a permission, dbSecDBCreate, that is not exposed by the Access UI. However, you can set this permission of the Databases container of the workgroup file (typically, SYSTEM.MDW) using DAO. The function glrSetDbCreate() does just this. You pass it the name of the user or group account and a Boolean parameter that you set to False to disable database creation and True to reenable. Passing a False parameter will prevent the user or group account from being able to create new databases. (If you use this function to disable the dbSecDBCreate permission of a user, you'll want to make sure the user doesn't have implicit dbSecDBCreate permission.) glrSetDbCreate() is shown in Listing 24.9.

Listing 24.9

```
Function glrSetDbCreate(ByVal strAccount As String, _
 ByVal fEnable As Boolean) As Boolean

    On Error GoTo glrSetDbCreateErr

    Dim strSystemDB As String
    Dim dbSys As Database
    Dim cnt As Container
    Dim strMsg As String

    Const glrcProcName = "glrSetDbCreate"

    glrSetDbCreate = False

    strSystemDB = SysCmd(acSysCmdGetWorkgroupFile)

    Set dbSys = DBEngine.Workspaces(0).OpenDatabase(strSystemDB)
    Set cnt = dbSys.Containers!Databases
    cnt.UserName = strAccount

    'Turn on or off the permission to create new databases
    If fEnable Then
        cnt.Permissions = cnt.Permissions Or dbSecDBCreate
    Else
        cnt.Permissions = cnt.Permissions And Not dbSecDBCreate
    End If

    glrSetDbCreate = True
```

```
glrSetDbCreateDone:
    If Not dbSys Is Nothing Then dbSys.Close
    On Error GoTo 0
    Exit Function

glrSetDbCreateErr:
    Select Case Err
    Case glrcErrNoPermission
        glrSetDbCreate = False
        Resume glrSetDbCreateDone
    Case glrcErrNameNotInCollection
        strMsg = "The account '" & strAccount & _
        "' doesn't exist."
    Case Else
        strMsg = "Error " & Err.Number & ": " & Err.Description
    End Select
        MsgBox strMsg, vbCritical + vbOKOnly, "Procedure " & _
        glrcProcName
    Resume glrSetDbCreateDone

End Function
```

This function is analogous to glrSetPermission(), except that it works on the Databases container of the *workgroup* file. To determine the name of the workgroup file, glrSetDbCreate() uses the Access SysCmd() function, passing it the acSysCmdGet-WorkgroupFile constant.

Once the location of SystemDB has been determined, glrSetDbCreate() creates a database object to point to it with the following Set statement:

```
Set dbSys = DBEngine.Workspaces(0).OpenDatabase(strSystemDB)
```

The permission is then set using this If...Then...Else statement:

```
If fEnable Then
    cnt.Permissions = cnt.Permissions Or dbSecDBCreate
Else
    cnt.Permissions = cnt.Permissions And Not dbSecDBCreate
End If
```

Changing Object Ownership

You can use the glrSetOwner() function to change the name of the owner of an object. It takes as its parameters the object type, the name of the object, and the name of the new owner. It returns True if it succeeds.

glrSetOwner() requires the current user to be either the owner of the object or a member of the Admins group.

You won't be able to change the owner of any OwnerAccess queries in the database. You must temporarily change the queries to non-OwnerAccess queries before using this function. (See the section "OwnerAccess Queries" earlier in this chapter for more details.) glrSetOwner() is shown in Listing 24.10.

Listing 24.10

```
Function glrSetOwner(ByVal strNewOwner As String, _
 ByVal intObjType As Integer, Optional ByVal varObjName As _
 Variant) As Boolean

    On Error GoTo glrSetOwnerErr

    Dim db As Database
    Dim cnt As Container
    Dim doc As Document
    Dim strMsg As String
    Dim intErrHndlrFlag As Integer

    Const glrcFlagSetContainer = 5
    Const glrcFlagSetDocument = 6
    Const glrcFlagElse = 0

    Const glrcProcName = "glrSetOwner"

    glrSetOwner = False

    'Initialize flag for determining
    'context for error handler
    intErrHndlrFlag = glrcFlagElse

    Set db = CurrentDb()

    'Can't change owner of database
    If intObjType = glrcObjDatabase Then
```

```
            strMsg = "Can't change owner of database."
            MsgBox strMsg, vbOKOnly + vbCritical, _
              "Procedure: " & glrcProcName
            GoTo glrSetOwnerDone
        Else

        'Point to the right container
        intErrHndlrFlag = glrcFlagSetContainer
        Set cnt = db.Containers(intObjType)
        intErrHndlrFlag = glrcFlagElse

        'Refresh the container's docs
        cnt.Documents.Refresh

        'Set ownership on a document or a container
        If IsMissing(varObjName) Then
            cnt.Owner = strNewOwner
        Else
            intErrHndlrFlag = glrcFlagSetDocument
            Set doc = cnt.Documents(varObjName)
            intErrHndlrFlag = glrcFlagElse
            doc.Owner = strNewOwner
        End If

        glrSetOwner = True

        End If

glrSetOwnerDone:
    On Error GoTo 0
    Exit Function

glrSetOwnerErr:
    Select Case Err
    Case glrcErrNoPermission
        strMsg = "You don't have permission to perform " & _
          "this operation."
    Case glrcErrNameNotInCollection
        Select Case intErrHndlrFlag
        Case glrcFlagSetContainer
            strMsg = "Invalid object type constant."
        Case glrcFlagSetDocument
            strMsg = "The object '" & varObjName & _
              "' is not in the '" & intObjType & _
              "' collection."
```

```
        Case Else
            strMsg = "Error " & Err.Number & ": " & _
            Err.Description
        End Select
    Case glrcErrBadAccntName
        strMsg = "The account '" & strNewOwner & _
        "' doesn't exist."
    Case Else
        strMsg = "Error " & Err.Number & ": " & _
        Err.Description
    End Select
        MsgBox strMsg, vbCritical + vbOKOnly, _
        "Procedure " & glrcProcName
    Resume glrSetOwnerDone

End Function
```

glrSetOwner() works by manipulating the Owner property of the object, as shown here for a document object:

```
doc.Owner = strNewOwner
```

basSecurityUtilities also includes a function, glrGetObjectOwner(), you can use to get the name of an object's owner.

Properly Securing a Database with the Access Security Wizard

Follow these steps to properly secure a database:

1. Use the Workgroup Administrator program (WRKGADM.EXE) to create a new workgroup with a non-null Workgroup ID.

2. Start Access and create a password for the Admin account.

3. Create a new user account that will be the administrator of the account.

4. Add the new account to the Admins group.

5. Remove the Admin account from the Admins group.

6. Restart Access, logging on as the new administrator user, and create a password for this account.

7. Select Tools ➤ Security ➤ User-Level Security Wizard to run the Security Wizard.

8. Create the group accounts for your workgroup.

9. Create the user accounts for your workgroup, adding each user to the appropriate groups.

10. Set permissions on objects for the group accounts. If you wish to reduce permission maintenance, don't set any permissions for individual users.

11. (Optional) For the appropriate groups, set object permissions for the Database object and use the glrSetPermissionDocCreate() and glrSetDbCreate() functions to disable the ability to create objects and databases, respectively, as needed.

WARNING   Don't skip any steps—except the optional step 11—or you run the risk of thinking you have a secured database when you do not.

The Access 95 Security Wizard takes an unsecured database and creates a new secured database. Figure 24.10 shows the Wizard's opening screen. You must be a member of the Admins group to run the Wizard. The Security Wizard works by performing a number of steps, including the following:

1. It creates a new copy of the database that is owned by the user running the Wizard (who must be a member of the Admins group and cannot be the Admin user).

2. It exports all objects to the new database.

3. It rebuilds attached tables and relationships in the new database.

4. It removes all permissions on selected types of objects in the new database for the Users group and the Admin user.

5. It encrypts the database.

FIGURE 24.10:

Opening screen of the Access
Security Wizard

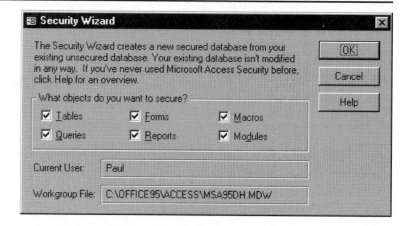

NOTE

In prior versions of Access the Security Wizard was available as a free add-in that you had to download from CompuServe or acquire through some other means. With the introduction of Access 95, the Security Wizard ships in the box along with Access.

Securing Code

To secure VBA modules or forms or reports containing event procedures, you first need to follow the steps for securing your database.

You secure module-based code so that users can't see it by removing all permissions to it. Using DAO, set the permissions of the modules to dbSecNoAccess. Users will always be able to run your functions, but you will have to provide objects the user *can* read that hook into the secured functions.

You secure forms and reports with event procedures by removing all permissions but the Open/Run permission. Using DAO, you set the permissions to acSecFrm-RptExecute. This also prevents users from modifying the form or report definitions.

If you will be installing your application at another site, make sure the owner of the objects you wish to secure and the owner of the database are secured users (not the Admin user or the Users group).

Grant permissions to the Users group for any objects to which you want users to have access.

Ship the database without the workgroup file with which you created it.

> **WARNING**
>
> Many Access developers have taken to creating functions that create a new workspace using code that employs the CreateWorkspace method to log on as an Admins-level user. This requires embedding the password of an Admins group member user in the code. The modules containing this code are then supposedly secured by removing all permissions to all accounts but the Admins group. We don't recommend this practice because Access stores module code in the system tables, and it's likely that a determined hacker could decode the OLE object that is used to store this code enough to discover the embedded password. (Fortunately, the main reason for doing this—the need to query group membership—is no longer necessary since all users can now read this information in Access 95/Jet 3.0.)

Securing Data

It's likely you'll want to grant database users at least ReadData security on some tables or queries; there's not much sense in your users using a database without access to any of its data. Thus, you need to selectively grant permissions to users.

Follow the steps for securing any database. Set necessary permissions on tables. Then, set the necessary permissions on queries and use OwnerAccess queries where needed for column-level or row-level security.

Grant permissions to the Users group for any application objects to which you want all users to have access.

Securing the Database Structure

In some situations you may want to secure your database schema. For example, you might be in a service industry that provides valuable data with a proprietary database structure. In this case the database schema is at least as valuable as the data you provide.

In this scenario users will be able to see the names of the secured tables but will be unable to see the relationships between the tables or the columns in the tables. This works best if the unsecured users need to have only read-only access to the tables.

You can secure your database schema by following these steps:

1. Create a secure workgroup file.

2. If you are concerned about users being able to see the names of your tables, rename them to nonsense names that have no connection to their content.

3. Split the database into a pair of "data" and "application" databases. (See Chapter 12 for more details.)

4. Remove all relationships in the data database if you don't want users to be able to see relationships.

5. Secure both databases using the Security Wizard.

6. Log on as a secure user and open the data database. (*Don't* remove Open/Run access to this database for unsecured users. If you do, unsecured users won't be able to read the data from linked tables.)

7. Grant yourself ReadData access for all tables in the data database. Make sure no unsecured user or group accounts have any access to these tables.

8. Using the same secure user account, open the application database and create OwnerAccess queries that use linked tables pointing to the data database.

9. Grant ReadData access to the Users group for the OwnerAccess queries.

10. Set the record source for all other objects in the database to the secured OwnerAccess queries, not the underlying tables.

If you follow these steps, unsecured users will be unable to view either the contents of any of your tables or the OwnerAccess queries. They will, however, still be able to see the names of the tables and open the data database.

Unsecuring a Secured Database

You can reverse the process of securing a database by following these steps:

1. Log on as a member of the Admins group.

2. Grant full permissions, including Administer permission, to the group Users for all objects in the database.

3. Clear the password for the Admin user.

4. Exit Access.

5. Restart Access and log on as Admin.

6. Create a new blank database and import all the secured database's objects using the File ➤ Get External Data ➤ Import command.

The trick to this technique is to give an unsecured group—Users —full permissions on all the objects and to then transfer ownership of the database and all its objects to an unsecured user—Admin.

Migrating Secured Databases to Access 95

You can move secured Access 2 databases to Access 95 by using one of the following strategies:

Strategy	Advantages	Disadvantages
Convert your secured database while joined to your existing Access 2 workgroup file; after conversion, continue to use the Access 2 workgroup file	Easy	You won't be able to take advantage of new security features, such as the ability of non-Admins members to view their group membership

Strategy	Advantages	Disadvantages
Convert your secured database; create a new Access 95 workgroup file with the same WID; create the same accounts with the same SIDs as the Access 2 workgroup	Takes full advantage of new security features	Requires you to have a written record of all accounts and PIDs
Document existing security system (account names, group membership, object permissions); unsecure database by assigning all permissions of all objects to the Users group; convert the unsecured database; rebuild security system from the ground up using different PIDs	Takes full advantage of new security features; can be used when you don't have a written record of the workgroup WID or account SIDs	Requires the most work

Security and Linked Tables

When you secure linked tables in an application database of a classic split database architecture (see Chapter 12), you are securing only the links, not the data in the tables. To properly secure the data, you must instead secure the tables in the data database. Don't bother securing the links; this security will be overlaid on top of the security of the data tables and doesn't really add anything because users will always be able to directly open the tables in the data database.

To link to (or refresh links to) tables in the data database, users must have Open/Run (dbSecDBOpen) permission to the data database *and* the ability to create tables—dbSecCreate permission to the TableDefs container—in the Application database.

Summary

In this chapter we have covered security in detail. You should now have a good understanding of the Access/Jet security model and how best to take advantage of it.

You have learned

- The basic structure of the Jet security model
- How to set database passwords
- How to use the more powerful workgroup-based security model
- That workgroup-based security in Access is made up of two components: user and group accounts stored in the workgroup file and object permissions stored in each database
- How to enable security
- How to use the Access security menus to manage security
- How to create a secure workgroup file
- How to manage user and group accounts
- How the special built-in user and group accounts work
- How to manage object permissions for users
- The difference between explicit and implicit permissions
- How object and database ownership works
- What OwnerAccess queries are and how to use them to get column-level and row-level security
- How encryption works and what it has to do with security
- The security object hierarchies
- How the security data access objects work
- What the permission constants are and how to use them to programmatically set permissions

- How to use DAO to manipulate accounts and permissions
- How to properly secure and unsecure databases
- How to migrate secured databases to Access 95

INDEX

Note to the Reader: Throughout this index **boldfaced** page numbers indicate primary discussions of a topic. *Italicized* page numbers indicate illustrations.

B

C

D

F

G

list boxes
  Access SQL with, 153
  BeforeUpdate and AfterUpdate events for, **371–372**
  BoundColumn property for, **361–362**
  callback functions for, **378–384**, *379*
  in client-server applications, 924
  Column property for, **362–363**
  ColumnCount property for, **360**
  ColumnHeads property for, **361**
  ColumnWidths property for, **360**, *361*
  vs. combo boxes, **355–356**
  for containers, 309
  ControlSource property for, **357**
  ControlType property value for, 331
  events for, 34
  filling, **376–386**
  for filling controls, **371–376**
  hiding data in, **363**, *364*
  multiple selections in, **364–367**, *365*, **390–397**, *391*
  Name property for, **357**
  RowSource property for, **358–359**, **376–378**, *376*
  RowSourceType property for, **357–358**
  using, 942
  values for, 326
ListContainers() function, 304
ListGroups() subroutine, 1429–1430
ListIndexFields() function, 292–293
ListItems() subroutine, 1162–1163
ListManagers() subroutine, 1428
ListNames() function, 275
ListObjects() function, 309, 320
ListProperties() function, 239–240
lists in SQL syntax, 154
ListUsers() subroutine, 1428
Load form events, 20
loaded forms, testing for, **451–452**
loading
  code, **1055**, 1346
  libraries, **1351–1354**
  Schedule Plus information, **1276–1279**

LoadOnStartup key, **1353–1354**, *1353*
local area networks (LANs), replication with, **809–812**, **816–817**, *816*, 876–877
local synchronization history log, 842
local tables in client-server applications, **913–915**
lock detection with Jet, 145
Locked property, 130, 375
locked record errors in replication, 850
LockEdits property, 756–757
locking
  in client-server applications, **754–758**, **912–913**
    alternative strategies for, **774–775**
    default optimistic behavior, **759–761**
    default pessimistic behavior, **767–768**, *768*
    optimistic locking with error handling, **761–767**, *766*
    pessimistic locking with error handling, **769–772**, *769*
    selecting strategies for, **758–759**
  in recordsets, 299
LockWindowUpdate() function, 724
Log Messages property, 217
logic errors, 984, **1013–1014**. *See also* debugging
logical assignments, **1073–1074**
logical comparisons, **1076**
logical operations
  for attributes, **315–316**
  with Jet expression evaluator, 134–135
  for permissions, 1445–1447
  in queries, 157
  with Rushmore query optimizations, 139
  with SELECT, 157
  for window styles, 442
.LoginTimeout setting, 905
Logoff() method, 1277
Logon() method, 1277
logs
  for events, 24–25, *25–26*
  for synchronization history, **842–844**, *842–843*
long datatype, 772, 1135, 1222–1223
lookup field properties, 120

M

O

Q

S

T

V

W

X

Y

Z

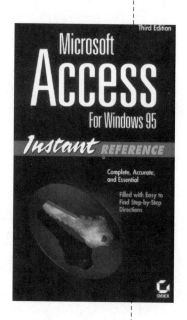

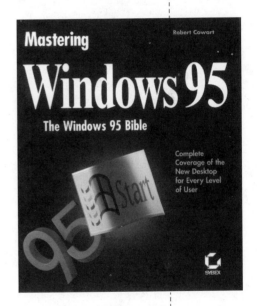

EXPERIENCE SUITE SUCCESS WITH OFFICE

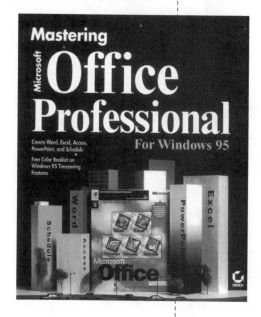

Learn how Windows 95, Word, Excel, PowerPoint, Access and Mail/Schedule+ can work together to solve real-world problems. Using a business process approach, the author focuses on accomplishing tasks, rather than individual program features. A practical book for savvy business people who want meaningful results, fast. Includes a pull-out color guide on Windows 95, revealing all the new time-saving features.

1,000 pages
ISBN: 1747-3

SYBEX

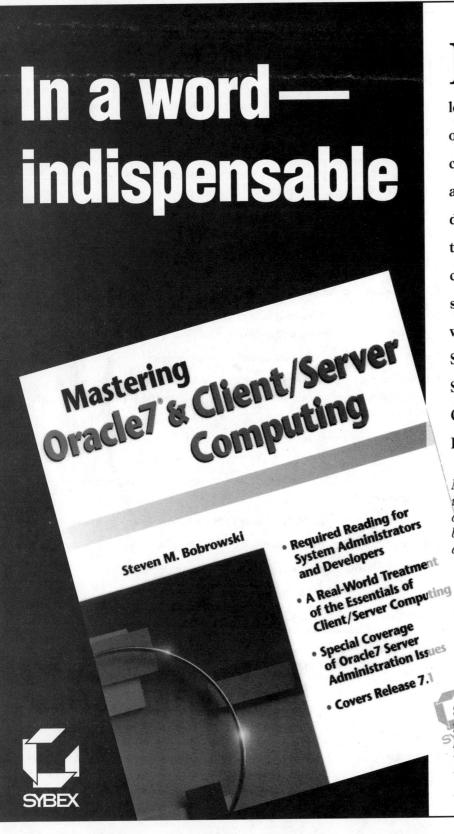

What's on the CD

This CD is a valuable companion to the book. It provides a wealth of information in a readily usable format to aid in your Access development efforts. We've included every significant example presented in the text, and not just the VBA code; we've also included all the tables, queries, forms, reports—*everything* to get you up and running instantly. The CD also contains the four appendixes to this book, lots of free and shareware utility programs, several demos of commercial products, and several Access add-ins to make application development even easier.

Here's just a sampling of what you'll find on the CD:

- Useful composite controls you can add to your forms, including a multiple-select list box and a spin-button control

- An Access add-in that helps you build DoMenuItem statements

- An Access add-in that serves as a scratchpad facility for entering SQL statements on the fly and viewing the output

- Two Access add-ins that help you optimize your queries

- A set of routines for creating screen-resolution–independent forms, so you can develop your forms in one resolution and deliver them to your users using a *different* resolution

- Ready-to-use popup calendar and calculator forms you can call from your code

- An OLE custom control that automatically creates tabbed dialog box forms to your specifications

- An OLE custom control for reading and writing values in the Registry

- Several free utility programs for working with Windows 95 Help files

- A shareware Windows program for zipping and unzipping files

- The unsecured Access 95 Wizards

- Demo versions of ClickBook, SPEED Ferret, and Transcender

For more information about the CD, including installation instructions, see the section "About the CD" in the introduction to this book and the README.TXT file in the root folder of the CD.